INTO THE UNKNOWN

INTO THE UNKNOWN

Caroline Sullivan, Senior Editor

THE NATIONAL LIBRARY OF POETRY

Into the Unknown

Library of Congress
Cataloging in Publication Data

ISBN 1-57553-347-2

Proudly manufactured in the United States of America by
Watermark Press
One Poetry Plaza
Owings Mills, MD 21117

EDITOR'S NOTE

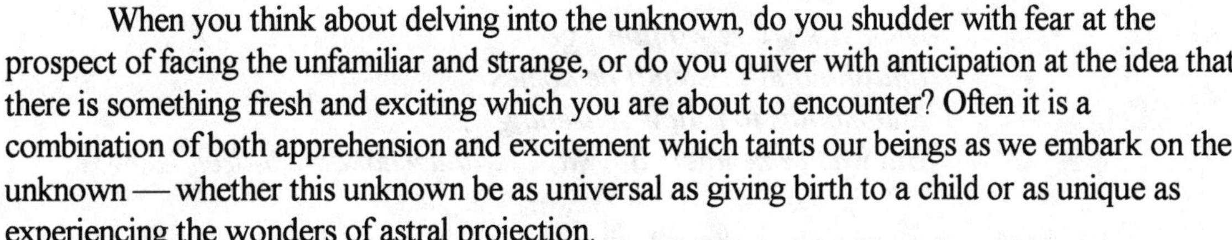

When you think about delving into the unknown, do you shudder with fear at the prospect of facing the unfamiliar and strange, or do you quiver with anticipation at the idea that there is something fresh and exciting which you are about to encounter? Often it is a combination of both apprehension and excitement which taints our beings as we embark on the unknown — whether this unknown be as universal as giving birth to a child or as unique as experiencing the wonders of astral projection.

And just as there are concrete adventures that toss us into the unfamiliar, so there are abstract ones. Writing is an example of an abstract avenue on which we travel to encounter the unknown: as a writer, you must constantly reach into that unknown part of your soul to spark your imagination and creativity; as a reader of others' writings, you are continuously brought into foreign territory and introduced to new experiences. There are also those writings which effectively throw the reader into a new adventure by presenting a persona who is embarking into the unknown. One such work in this anthology is Ian Cormican's "Awkward Instance" (p. 368).

This gripping poem tells the story of children who are kidnapped from daycare by their estranged father while the "day care ladies" can do nothing:

Gaping old day care ladies
thick-lensed and feeble
inclinations couldn't keep us
from him when he came . . .

The father comes with false documents that allow him to take the children — "forked with forgeries of custodies / and signatures . . ." — and thus keep the "pasty waiting ladies free of blame." Although the father and the children share the same name, the poet insightfully remarks that it is of no emotional significance because "love finds no prerequisite in a name."

One can almost see the children being taken away as they grip the back seat and gaze out the rear window:

Fingers white in backseat windows,
cries like silent fishbowl faces
getting smaller . . .

The image of the children crying, "eyes cracked like asphalt playgrounds," draws the reader back to the opening lines: "Asphalt cracked and streaked remains in yellow painted / ghosts of hopscotch and four-square . . . ." The "cracked and streaked" allows one to see tears streaming down and streaking the children's cheeks.

The closing lines of the work allude to a warning the children received that such a horrible experience may happen, and that they should not go with their father. But, as the author intones, they are *children* and what can a child do to prevent such an occurrence?

Mother said we wouldn't go
and shouldn't listen if he comes . . .
and months to follow searching . . .
But who remembers anyway . . . and what do children know?

The above poem certainly enshrouds the reader in disturbing and unknown territory. With its vivid, moving images, another poem which whisks the reader into what for many is unfamiliar ground is Richard M. Stachura's "Astern, Head Back Over The Rail" (p. 241), a briskly-paced work that describes the sensation of absolute freedom experienced by the persona as he hangs off the side of a sailboat and courses through water:

The world flipped upside down
blue
latched at the heels
hugging trails of the horizon
at 35 mph

The image of moving with the boat back and forth and in and out of the waves' troughs and crests can be felt as Stachura writes of "tongues of waves / tossing their electric cavities / left/right/left . . . ." When one sees the water, a "grand highway / entirely polluted with the freedom of flight," one can imagine the multitude of sailboats, motor boats, speed boats, and jet skis that abound. But within this littered pool of humanity we again are drawn to view the persona:

and me, clamped to the hull
outstretched
to be released and absolutely dead
or
a passenger and half-personified.

Though intensely personal, this boating experience is for the persona a metaphor for freedom. Another profoundly intimate experience is depicted in Roderick Vesper's "Hubert's Pool Hall" (p. 345). Here, it is the stroke of a cue that is a metaphor for freedom — freedom from all "doubts and failures":

every shot, every stroke, is
an attempt at redemption,
a glorious single second of
accomplishment as all your doubts
and failures roll off the felt into
the pitch black pocket of the past.

In W. Andy Meier's "The Puritan Way" (p. 249), the unknown to which we are taken is twofold: that of the persona in a Puritan graveyard and that of the Puritan way of life. In the graveyard,

Headstones and a few footstones lean roundabout,
Slate fingernails pointing to their heaven,
Held down by richly aged, human-made earth.

Of the Puritan lifestyle, Meier first alludes to their not having any images of God: "Vestigial Puritan treasury guarded by their undepicted God"; and "From a lamentable list of maladies and accidents, / Puritans had their daily cognition of lives taken" refers to the Puritan ideal that suffering is good for the soul. They also viewed God as a wrathful God, a "King of Terrors," and therefore often lived their lives in fear:

Wearing their lives as shrouds, wanting clouds,
Expecting firmamental wrath, without knowing,
They saluted their "King of Terrors" in the meetinghouse . . .

Regardless of their malaise, the Puritans share the same fate that awaits us all: death. The tombstones, the "flat-toothed, winged skulls grinned through prayers / and waited in the fine fingerling green grasses beyond."

What is interesting to note about this piece is the irony exhibited as the persona, quite contrary to his Puritan ancestors, nonchalantly and without fear relaxes in their graveyard and steals glimpses of their lives by reading the tombstones. He is "taking down epitaphs and making rubbings, a zeitgeist heist." He is so casual that he is lying with his head on the back of tombstones as he reads the inscriptions facing him:

With head resting on headstone's rear and reading personals,
On columns, slates and flat ground-set slabs and feasting
by the ones atop six short columns: tablestones.

"The Puritan Way" is a truly unique work that uses fresh images and well-constructed language to transport the reader into its many facets of the unknown.

Another unique and remarkably well-written poem is C. J. Sivert's "This Quiet Night" (p. 1). In contrast to most poems about time and time's quick-moving nature, Sivert writes about a moment being static. This poem is so well-crafted and offers such unique imagery that the judges and I have awarded it the Grand Prize. Instead of beginning the poem with "It's late at night," Sivert shows us that the T.V. programming has ended and all that's shown is static: "A mark of first nightstroke gels in TV static cast upon the far wall."

The persona is in a room relaxing alone, "I sit with myself," and basking in the calm that permeates:

This sundry hour, I sit with myself upon reclining cushions and stare
into tranquil nothingness of carpet fragments,
inundated with intangible miscellanity
of debris and garment shards . . .

In the second stanza, Sivert compares the room to an ocean as "the undertow of silence receded the chimetones / far out to sea." And on this "pillowed shoreline" where the persona sits, the reader is invited to view the "miscellanity of debris" strewn across the shag carpet:

. . . scan the shag horizon for seashells of popcorn
and bottlecaps, where creatures of my interest
made their homes, washed up discarded upon
the floor . . .

The static of the T.V., again reflecting the static nature of time in this piece, is once more referenced in the second stanza, "while the static storm keeps its fury / in a plastered atmosphere," and again in the closing lines, "the steadfast monochromatic rain keeps its fall."

Another note-worthy aspect about this work is that the persona is simply remarking on his surroundings — he is not making commentary on them. In the closing stanza, the persona becomes one with the house, with that moment, and ultimately with time:

All is silence, save the creaks of boards and bones.
This house and I settle in; one, a terrestrial bed,
tucked in by nails and mortar, myself, with my ample
blanket of skin and hair, to soak awhile in this
wash of Time . . .

"This Quiet Night" is an excellent example of poetic gracefulness that is so lavish with detailed descriptions that it should be read more than once. There are so many fine poems published here which are original, fresh, skillfully crafted verse overflowing with feelings and insight that I truly wish I had the space to provide individual critiques for each of them. I congratulate all of you featured here and hope you enjoy stepping *Into the Unknown* as you peruse the diverse poems in this anthology.

Into the Unknown is a culmination of the efforts of many individuals. Editors, assistant editors, customer service representatives, typesetters, graphic artists, layout artists, administrative services, and office administrators have all brought their respective talents to bear on this project. I am grateful for the contributions of these fine people.

Caroline Sullivan, Senior Editor

Cover Art: Tracy Hetzel

Grand Prize

C. J. Sivert / Paden City, WV

Second Prize

Scott Allen / San Francisco, CA
Ian Cormican / Calabasas, CA
Jade Horning / Shellsburg, IA
Damian Kratt / South Milwaukee, WI
Gilberto Lucero / El Paso, TX
Antonia Lynch-Parham / Brooklyn, NY
W. Andy Meier / East Chatham, NY
Saul L. Neidleman / Oakland, CA
Richard M. Stachura / Livonia, MI
Roderick Vesper / Covington, KY

Third Prize

Tashonn-Etienne Antinori / Grand Rapids, MI
Mary Ellen Barkley / Stockton, CA
Julie Barksdale / Minneapolis, MN
Jonathan R. Baron / Marlboro, NJ
Joan D. Batara / Jacksonville, FL
Roseanna Becraft-Goforth / Nicholasville, KY
Beth Biller / Rockville, MD
Cynthia L. Blaida / Fair Haven, MI
Vance A. Blevins / Tulsa, OK
Lesley Boyd / Toledo, OH
Anthony Brantley / Lattimore, NC
Rebecca E. Bredholt / Simi Valley, CA
Terri L. Bruce / Midwest City, OK
Rose M. Carroll / Greensboro, NC
Babette K. Cecchini / Warren, PA
Margaret A. Choate / Danville, VA
Samuel J. Dudley / Phoenix, AZ
Ross A. Fichter / New Era, MI
Jo Zeitz Fix / Missoula, MT
Orland E. Freeman Jr. / Paradise Valley, AZ
Henry P. Glass / Northfield, IL
Carmela P. Glenn / Hendersonville, NC
Tim Harkins / Colonial Beach, VA
J. R. Hecker / Centerville, OH
E. Marlene Hendricks / Everett, WA
Edna Herring / Mount Olive, NC
Donald Holth / Saint Louis, MO
Zach Howard / Kansas City, MO
William G. Ikerd Jr. / Beeville, TX
Kevin M. Ingraham / San Francisco, CA
Bob Jacklin / West Yellowstone, MT
Nick Jackson / Ironton, OH
Judith T. Kelly / Ooltewah, TN
Connie Lee / Sayre, PA
Audrey Lee-Foster / Jackson, MS
Franz J. Leinweber / Randolph, NJ
Mary F. Limbaugh Luker / Talladega, AL
Anthony McMillan / Corunna, MI
Anita Negrete / Mentone, CA
Mildred D. Parker / Wilmington, NC
Jon R. Perryman / College Station, TX
J. Peterson / Riverdale, NY
Christina J. Powell / Brooklyn, NY
Todd Ridella / Newark, OH
Christine Roberts / Newman Lake, CA
Jennifer Rogers / Port Richey, FL
Allen J. Rubenkonig / Baltimore, MD
J. David Sanderfer / Houston, TX
Andy Schamp / DuBois, PA
Margaret L. Schroeder / Corpus Christi, TX
Catherine Song / Sylmar, CA
Jeffery Stone / Maysville, KY
Susannah Sweigart / Columbia, SC
Thomas Turley / Springfield, MO
Elizabeth S. Wangelin / Port Jefferson Station, NY
Marie C. Webb / Provo, UT
Aaron Weiss / New Haven, CT
Anne Wilson / Thousand Oaks, CA
Sophy S. Wong / Tracy, CA

Grand Prize Winner

This Quiet Night

A mark of first nightstroke gels in TV static cast upon the far wall.
This sundry hour, I sit with myself upon reclining cushions and stare
into tranquil nothingness of carpet fragments,
   inundated with intangible miscellanity
of debris and garment shards, while the clock
   mimics the end chords of the one sonata,
filling the air with false Ludwig.

'Tis a quiet moment now.
   The undertow of silence receded the chimetones
far out to sea. I sit atop a pillowed shoreline
   and scan the shag horizon for seashells of popcorn
and bottlecaps, where creatures of my interest
   made their homes, washed up discarded upon
the floor, while the static storm keeps its fury
   in a plastered atmosphere.

All is silence, save the creaks of boards and bones.
   This house and I settle in; one, a terrestrial bed,
tucked in by nails and mortar, myself, with my ample
   blanket of skin and hair, to soak awhile in this
wash of Time, while that steadfast monochromatic rain keeps its fall.

C. J. Sivert

This Place

I long ago could see the sky
So blue and bright,
So vast and endless
Just floating by my eyes

I long ago could see the grass
So green and vibrant
Bringing life to all around
Growing through my fingers

I long ago could see the trees
So cool and calm,
Swaying with the breeze
Brushing the troubles from my mind

I once was here,
Watching the sky,
Watching the grass,
Watching the trees,
With no cares and not a fear,
For nothing mattered in this place,

but that was long ago.

Elizabeth S. Ingham

Balloons Of Color

An array of colors for us to see,
Some of them blue, some are green,
pink ones, yellow ones, a dash of red,
A blast of orange,
all of them intermingled, attached by a thread..
floating, drifting, overhead.

Together,
they bring joy and laughter,
high above they carelessly saunter.
They drift, they bob, they go with the wind,
they flow.
Until,
one by one, you let them go.

And watch...
as into the blue sky they fly...
higher, higher, higher, still,
out-of-sight they soar...
as a teardrop falls, a smile fades,
the balloons of color are seen no more.

Jonelle L. Mahon

Untitled

What is a mother? How do you define?
Something so complex and confusing in design?
The way they punish you and send you to your room —
The way they teach you a lesson with a swat of a broom.
They don't even keep their promises (just like a politician)!
How do you put something so awful into a definition?

What is a mother? How do you explain?
Their love that comforts all your pain?
The way they know just what to say,
The way they chase the Boogie Man away.
They give you hope and put your doubts into submission.
How do you put something so wonderful into definition?

Mother (muth'er) n. 1. Mothers are nurturing, loving women
Who raise their children from birth.
2. Mothers are priceless treasures
Of vast and infinite worth.
3. A mother is like an Aspirin
That eases and soothes your pain.
4. A mother is a robin with wings of compassion
That shield you from the rain.

Sam Eatmon

Midnight Slumber

Scary things and frightful dreams invade my heart at night,
But those scary things and frightful dreams are parts of midnight slumber.
When I think of loving things and glory dreams my heart burns bright throughout the night.
So I dream away those scary things and frightful dreams, and hope to dream about those loving things and glory dreams throughout my midnight slumber.

Serena A. Standley

Returning Home

Returning home has it own Pandora's box of uncertainties and fears,
One never knows if you should be coming or going, it's never quite clear.

You hope you've been missed or at least thought of in passing fancy,
But to have only one wish for your return is always so chancy.

The time I had on my hands was overwhelming, more than I had bargained for,
The thoughts ran through me for every mile, but still I needed more.

Decisions and desires mix like vinegar and oil and never seem to be settled,
Waiting for someone else to make a move is waiting for the whistle of a boiling kettle.

Thirty hours or more and silent meditation gave cause for deliberation,
But answers are questions and I'm still looking for my emancipation.

Time from those you love creates the importance of them in your life and heart,
It's clear no one should be taken for granted, but totally appreciated from the start.

Time and distance creates an anxiety of what it be like when I'm back,
But somehow it creates a freshness and spirit that was maybe starting to lack.

In the long run no matter how far you go or how long you've been away,
If love is there it only magnifies itself and settles in to stay.

Theresa Janson

A Lesson Of Life - The Rose

Admire the rose, and feel love in its most precious glow,
Tender caring, loving light touches, only make the rose stem grow strong, and from new stems more roses grow.
A beautiful sight to behold, as the love between a man and woman everyone knows.
So many blossoms and beauty cover the thorns of life, and no one seems to notice them at all.
A prick from one of the thorns you hardly recall.

Look at a rose that has taken a lot of abuse, demeaning words of insulting nature, no loving glances or loving touches.
Soon the dewy petals dry and fall one by one, like one keeping score.
The thorns of troubles stand out and become frightful and painfully sore,
The rose once beautiful is now no more.

This once beautiful rose is not done yet, as it will find a way to drop one of its seeds to be sown;
With new hopes and dreams of a loving place to grow-in.
This is why a rose is the resurrection of life and this is so true,
Life with love is pure beauty, just like the rose, never blue.

Eleanor E. Hills

Dedicated - To My Daddy

To Jesus Christ our Lord I pray,
For what has come to me this day.
Help me Lord through the thin,
So there may be peace within.

Daddy tried, but daddy died,
Although I was not at his side.
I know somehow it's best this way,
But I had that hope, that simple ray.

To lose my daddy who struggled on,
To think that now, now he's gone.
Sends a deep regret for being away,
And now for my daddy all I can do is pray.

A deep lost love within me lies
And as I look back, tears fill my eyes.
I know he would not want these tears,
But it seems like now that's all that appears.

I wish I could talk to my daddy once more,
But now there's no way to open that door.
So I send my love through my prayers,
To my daddy, cause I know he still cares.

Karen Culotta

The Bouquet

The bouquet so neatly put together
so carefully arranged.
The beauty of the flowers
will shower us with tears of joy.
The smell, the sight
brings much delight to a troubled heart.
The bouquet is only a small part
of God's creation,
and one must look at it with great admiration.
Share the joy that flowers bring,
and feel your heart sing so loud,
the sound will reach a distant cloud.
One should never forget
God's colorful gifts.

Christina Nelson

"A Miracle From Above"

A baby comes so suddenly,
Warming the hearts of everybody
For you see a baby,
Is a miracle from God above.

The little miracle from above,
She doesn't even know if she's glad she came.
For the baby is so precious,
She don't even know her name.

The little girl whose name is April,
Is such a joy,
We all love her so much,
She's our little miracle from above.

For the little girl,
Don't even know mommy and daddy;
But she knew's she is loved,
Especially from God above.

Angela Palmer

The Larvae And I

The safest of havens, it is here.
The dusty air reeks of rotten vegetation and its scent
permeates the tight confines of my every breath.
The strands of light, they animate the lifeless,
giving them, then taking them.
In turn, giving me images to debauch and cherish.
So dim is this place, its ghastly residue drips,
oh how they drip.
I feel the drops fall upon my conscious, one after another,
each one unleashing a greater pleasure than the last.
I sleep with the dew,
rolling with the droves of larvae.
My narcosis is twice enhanced
while I am being eaten alive.
So as the ground evolves
from wood to mud,
my limbs begin to disappear.
All that I can do
is to gorge upon the marrow,
just the larvae and I.

Jonathan Reed Baron

Christmas Day

Silver shining ribbons
Hung on boughs of green,
Reach blindly out to touch me,
Pulled by strings unseen.

As I approach their bower
Or brush by on my way,
Their tinny hands seek upward
As if begging me to stay.

Glittering fingers touch my sleeve
Or twine themselves in my hair,
While others arch their length away
As if startled to find me there.

Gently detaching the tinsel,
A sad simile comes to mind,
Of family and friends who cling to me,
And the truth: I must leave them behind.

Catharine R. West

The Clock

Someone is dying
A baby is crying
Down the block - Tick, Tock.

Choirs, exultant, are singing.
Vaulted ceilings, echoing
white frocked priests, bless their
flock - Tick, tock.

Restless rivers, whispering dark,
slim, trim ships, near the dock - Tick, tock

Thoughts, trapped in layered coral reefs.
Dart, thru crimson rock, awaiting
shock - Tick, tock.
Watercolored sunsets will wane and flow.
The cratered full moon will eerily glow.
Disasters will come
Disasters will go
High hopes, for seconds, will overflow.

In life's everchanging frames.
Only time, perpetual mobile,
remains - tick, tock!

Eleanore Nyilas

Poetry Of Life

THE UNKNOWN
When I have a question, I call upon the unknown
When I feel happy I think the unknown
When I feel sad, I question myself an question the unknown
When I need changes I call upon the unknown.
Sometimes I see life forces itself to be recognized on to you whether you like it or not.
I am here of good and bad; what do they really mean?
Who or what judges what is good and bad.
Through the eyes of the unknown, I see the preparation for what is coming.
Through the eyes of mankind I see good and evil;
When we take another person's life due to their own action, are we following the rule of the unknown?
And between the unknown and mankind itself which one is right?
Are we following his or her rule based on the action we take toward others?
Are we doing anything that could displease him or her?
When the final judgment comes, who will be the judge, the Jury and the executor?

Wesly Jean

This World

This world,
sometimes full of hard ache and pain,
Low and depressing of everlasting shame,
It makes you feel so bad and full of fear,
Continentally sad and insecure,
Is this world God gave us to throw away,
Violent crimes going on day after day,
To live in this world sometimes you must
Stand alone brave with no fear,

You need to be brave proud to say,
I am different I want to see a better day,
But while in this fight to overcome,
You have forgot what has happened for victory
to be won, your friends have left and turned
away, you have no one to reside in any day,
You are alone in this world so depressing and
sad, trapped in a day of fashion violence
unlawful teens and fads,
But still you don't want to be left behind,
left behind in this world.

Giovanni Adams

The Change

I see the many trees changing
for the new era of the year,

I hear the different birds
chirping and waking merrily,

I smell the fresh grass and
flowers which blossom each year,
this time,

I taste the fresh air,
come to rejuvinate us all,

I feel the change that occurs within
all living creatures now.

Spring is more than free time
and fun,

It is time, for the change.

Alexis Girovard

Just A Little Girl

You were just a little girl,
when your mother told you,
"you will grow up soon but,
enjoy yourself now because,
you can only be that age once."

You were just a little girl when,
you thought growing up would be easy,
and you thought the young years were the
hardest years of your life.

You think about that now,
and realize life just isn't easy.
There is always something wrong,
and something you want to do,
but you have to be older.

As you get older you are still,
trying to figure out who you really are.
Different things happen, and you may not always know,
how to fix them, and sometimes, you're not supposed to.

I guess that is all part of life and we all go through it sometime.

Rose Simard

To Whom It May Concern

What is Love? Is it two people who look at each other in a different way? Do they share the same feeling all the time and at the same time? Are they always happy together?

Love is a feeling that makes you feel tingly inside. Two people who love each other would most of the time do anything for each other.

Is love worth the pain? Is it worth the agony? Can you ever get around the pain and suffering? Will people ever stop falling in love? Will sex ever take over the emotional passion of love? Does everyone fall in love? Is there really such a thing as love at first sight? Can love change into just a friendship? Does love begin with a friendship? Is love supposed to be this confusing? Will there ever be true answers to these questions?????

Gina Rizzo

God's Little Angel

Mommy and Daddy, please don't cry and don't be sad.
I felt the warmth and love in the little time we had.

I know you both wanted to have me there with you,
but our heavenly Father must have needed me too.

Sometimes things happen and it's really hard to understand,
but God had His reason and I must be part of His plan.

So don't give up or be forlorn.
My brothers and sisters yet wait to be born.

God's going to make it alright, just you wait and see.
Just keep your trust and faith, and in Him always believe.

I know you only had me for just a little while.
Remember me in your hearts, but remember with a smile.

So Mommy and Daddy dry your eyes and don't be blue,
because now I'm one of God's little angels watching over you.

Jeannie Farris

Dreams

I keep having this interesting dream
of this guy on a Harley machine
He rides like a stallion - hard, wild, and free
Running for something that he longs to see.
As he rides along this beautiful ocean
you'll hear giant crashing waves, and the
rumble of chrome in motion.
Far beyond this wild sea, lies a strong emotion,
of devotion, that could last for a century!
And as you feel the last bit of heat from the sun.
You'll know that this day is almost done.
He watches...I watch...as the sunset dies
I'm yearning for that heat between my thighs
He's yearning to feel the sun from both sides.
Each night we'll get closer and closer
you can hear the road sing - don't you lose her...
I'll wake up, remembering so clearly
of this mysterious man on a bike called Harley.
Is it the heat from this haunting gorgeous man that I yearn for dearly?
Or is it that haunting totally awesome beautiful Harley!

Trisha Criswell

Death Of Wife

There are many pleasures and some sorrows in life. Few sorrows are greater than the death of one's long time loving wife. The pain is greater when the death occurs in the golden age years. This intensifies the sorrow and brings on more tears.

Some relief comes from reflections of good memories of the past. These are helpful but they do not last. You return again to the lonesomeness and sorrow of the time. This you would like to forget and leave the unpleasantness behind.

One thing most helpful is the company and affection of pets that you shared. They too appear to realize the loss and seem to indicate the sorrow they bear. Friends and neighbors are also helpful in times of loneliness and stress. They do you favors and help you determine the things that are best.

You find yourself thinking if married life were to be relived what would be changed? The answers is you would relive married life in relative the some range. One exception would be to learn over time how to cook. This would be much better than trying to learn quickly from a confusing book!

Charles W. Morton

Age Of Rage

It's an age of rage!

Violence screaming; political reaming; people steaming
But they can't shake off their pride.
Kids color - killing find it thrilling; it's bone-chilling
Enough to crawl and hide.
Drug overdose of a star to boast - his music chose
To take him to hell.
The godlessness, the wickedness, the sinfulness
Of this nation cannot prevail.

It's an age of rage!
Repetition of rape; a victim's escape
Is secluded to a system that paroles.
Child abductions; pornographic seductions
Of a molesters fetish to feed his darkened soul.
The panoramic pleasure of a tarnished treasure...
The very measure of the devil's smile.
The unborn in panic; life/choice ecstatic; life erratic
To unheard wails of abortion in style.
One nation under God "is a nation that's rejecting God
And it decays as it refuses His love!

Rick L. Neese

Love

A universe unending in the blackness it keeps,
an old plant withering into endless sleep.
Love is like a shadow that stays with you at all times,
love is forever
the emotion that never dies.
To hate someone without giving them a chance,
To not help somebody in need, just to give
them a hateful glance.
We don't need hate like that in the world today,
what we need is more love in the world right away.
Love is as simple as tending to a rose,
love is in need to help things grow.
For without love the world will surely die,
without love we can not survive.
So love with all your heart even if it hurts,
there are no side effects of love, just to get
more love in return.

Aimee LaPointe

Memory Never Known

In the back of my mind there is a memory
so deep and distant it cannot be touched.
It cannot be heard or seen
And it cannot be expressed in words.
I can only feel it; and feel it, I do.

Wherever I go, whatever I do, it is there and I feel it.
Like a pleasant, but faded, dream.
Like the deepest heartache,
It pulses through my veins
And I can only feel it, sense its presence.
Always
There, but distant, as if in hiding
For a purpose.
The feeling that there is more here for me
And I cannot see it,
Will I ever touch it? See it? Experience it?
The memory,
Which burns in fury,
That I have never known.

Jessica Zimmerman

Festival Internationale

On a hot sunny Sunday, I was driving around the Motor City
I wanted to go to a place where people were found
I thought to myself, the Detroit-Windsor International Festival
is in progress, what a place to Browse around
upon entering the Ambassador Bridge, paying my toll
I began to proceed up the long high incline, and wished
not the structure to fall and cause me to lose my soul
I continued down the incline and slowly approached the custom's
booth, I answered the inquiries from the person inside and
drove off showing each individual tooth.
I entered the Festival with glee and anticipation, observing
all the people from various lands and nations.
African and Caucasian-American's, native and natural-born
Canadians and others were together in one place, having fun
the games, adult and kiddie rides were overwhelming nice to
watch and to see the various facial expressions of the people
around the clock.
I sat on a bench at the Canadian side of the river, with a big hat
from Tijuana, Mexico, watching people pass by and snicker. I
returned to the Motor City, considering this a brief vacation.

Fletcher Bland

The Eagle

I am an eagle, soaring high;
I spread my majestic wings and fly.

I am untouchable among the clouds,
They cover me like a massive shroud.

I see the mountains, rivers and streams,
As I fly here among the sun beams.

I see the forests and valleys below,
The glorious buck, his yearling and doe.

I see all the woodland creatures from here,
The view I get is so crystal clear.

I am an eagle, high and free,
I see things the way they should be.

Peace and serenity are my domain,
And it is here I shall remain.

I am an eagle my spirit soars,
Upon the wind I take my course.

I am an eagle, I see all up here,
I am an eagle, I know no fear

Melody Trotter

Zone Out

1 2 3 A B C...numbering, lettering, letters, numbers.
4 5 6 D E F...counting elusive of thought and feeling.
7 8 9 G H I...spelling and counting all and nothing.
2 4 6 A C E...pairing evenly things in the mind.
1 3 5 B D F...hiding anger and pain of abuse.
A 1 B 2 C 3...starting differently to drown the feelings.
D 4 E 5 F 6...tracing, writing on paper, or in air.
G 7 H 8 I 9...zoning when feelings are not allowed.
A B C 1 2 3...saving self in face of the danger.
D E F 4 5 6...winning by counting, losing the heart.
X Y Z 7 8 9...wanting to end but not knowing how.
1 2 3 A B C...obsessing letters, numbers start again.

C. S. Westfall

The Wolf

It moved through the forest without noise,
Spirit and Soul full of grace and poise.
The cry strikes fear into hearts of men.
His stare spreads terror to thoughts within.
The mind panics, the nerves react.
He smells the moment and starts the attack.
Lips pulled back and fangs are bared,
A shot rings out, man's life is spared.
Unquenched thirst, stressed are his wits.
He races through woods as a bullet hits.
Lost are the wolf's freedom and poise,
A last howl as he succumbs to the nighttime noise.

James D. Iverson

The Knot

Untangle, untie, and untwist the lies
Make straight the tangles, the questions, the Whys
The Whos and the Whens are not part of this knot
But the Whys and the Hows, including the Whats,
Are a mess of a twist, all matted and mangled
Taking hours, perhaps years, to property untangle
At one point in life, you'll look away from the knot
With much understanding of Whys, Hows, and Whats
And what will you do with the truths that you've got?
Just pass then along and return to the knot

Christopher Brad Parker

Sleepless

As I lay down my body ready for bed.
Wondering if I'll awake after I put down my head.
Every thought enters your mind in my situation.
I will be wiser after reincarnation.
How will I live if I find out the truth.
Knowing I'll be dead before the end of my youth.
Bringing a life into this place. With no chance for survival,
is, this a fare case? Only a teen preparing for the end.
When in reality, this is where it should begin.
I'm not ready to go six feet underground.
Even thinking about it is bringing me down.
Please God send me this gift once more. I promise to treat it
better than before. I'll haven't to children to remember my smile.
Hopefully it will all be over in a little while. I can't stand not
knowing if I'll live or die. How in the world will I be able to say
good-bye. To bring this to a happier end. I'd like to say goodbye to
all of my friends. To my family I love all of you. Just let me rest
my peace the way I would you. To all the people who accepted me
for who I was. Thank you for the memories.

Linda Robinson

Childhood Days

I remember the days of my childhood, and all the good times I had
With two Sisters, four Brothers and Mothers and Dad.
We lived in a cabin on the side of a hill
Where days were bright and evenings still.
I was as happy as a kid could be
As I played in the shade of a Mulberry tree.

I would stump my toe now and then
And as Mother would caution as to where I'd been
She would rub it and kiss it to make it well;
She loved me a lot, I could tell.

We lived and laughed from day to day
As the farming went on and we worked away.
The fields were many as anyone could see
And we worked to assure the harvest to be.

My cousins would come from all around
On Sunday afternoon we were swimming hole bound.
We ran to the creek and jumped in flipping,
There were no swimming suits; we were skinny dipping!

Walter Hemphill

Not Wanted

When I was born my mom called out I do not want this baby now.
So she turned away from me,
Not having any love or glee.
She turned so quick, with out a twitch of regret or remorse on her face.

She passed me on, down the lawn, begging some one to take her spawn.
Then a caring face turned around,
She took me, cradled me, and did not frown.
Now I'm older she wants me back, but I have one question why,
You threw me out and made me cry.

I don't want you
So leave me be
I'm happy hear can't you see.
They love me hear,
They call me dear, and I hardly ever shed a tear.

Kira Gallien

Turning From God

She has a hard time with life
She's in love with God
Help her find herself
Lost in this sanity

She wants to get away
Find her true self
Take away the pain
Of living this life

She leaves that world behind
World of shattered dreams - false reality
And finally sees the light
The light of true prophecy

In the real world
She sees greed, lust, and death
All which were forbidden
In the house of God

Now she has seen all
And turns away from God
She finds her true self
Through carnal knowledge of a man

Brian Sprouse

Shared Love

In 1919 my dad and mom exchanged each wedding vow
Life in those days was without any convenience, it took hard work and know how.
As the days and years slipped by, two baby boys came along
The desire for another little one, perhaps a girl was strong.

So very early the first December morn, even though I was two weeks past date
To the delight of my loving dad I came out at 9#'s and late
My darling mom said the weather was very cold and me, not in my hurry.
The reason I'm always at a fast pace, is to re-catch those lost two weeks I really have to scurry.

A loving dad and mom made my life warm, happy and somewhat carefree
There were rules to be followed, chores to tend and love for brothers and me.
My family has all gone now to be in a better land
Warm memories of love we all shared when alone and empty I stand, I feel the touch of each hand.

Nadine M. Bushong

To The One

To the one who holds me tight
To the one who kisses me all night
To the one who takes me to a dance
You're the one I let my heart take a chance

To the one who whispers in my ear
To the one who tells me what I want to hear
To the one who makes me weak
My heart is at its highest peak

To the one who shows me how to feel
To the one who I know is for real
To the one who is also a friend
I want us to continue to the end

To the one who goes that extra mile
To the one who makes me smile
To the one who shares my laughter
I will love you forever after

Bethany Mize

The Bearer Of Tomorrow

Another page is turned in your life and in mine,
And we slip a little deeper into the sands of time.

The Bearer of Tomorrow holds the hourglass of sand,
And you look toward the future as you step into his hand.

Look deep into his crystal ball to see what lies ahead,
Think not of what you may have lost, but what the future holds instead.

The Bearer of Tomorrow will show you what's in store,
He'll give you keys of promise to unlock a strange new door.

If in need, just turn and ask the Bearer of Tomorrow,
And use your keys to free the world of all its pain and sorrow

At first you may be anxious, but in time you'll soon learn how,
For you are the Bearer of Tomorrow and tomorrow is here now.

James A. Wakefield

Untitled

You wonder
Why I desire a secret luxury
romance beneath a whisper
time is play, delicate sex
Yet I crave for chocolate dreams never beyond
Kiss and tell
we never had better love under the stars.
I float above the garden
don't play the essential beauty
we stand as one
loving men do much always beyond
Kiss right here
with needs not talks
they say Mother craves on better life
Yet you wonder
It's a woman thing...

Krystal Michelle Mae Brown

"Thinking Of You"

Today I was thinking of someone dear to me.
Who has known me since birth.
That has loving and caring ways.
This person has shared many roles in my life.
Teacher - taught me different things.
Care giver - taught me right from wrong.
Nurse - cared for me when I was sick.
Chauffeur - drove me everywhere.
Thinking about my past childhood days.
Has brought a smile to my face.
And great joy to my heart.
Putting those special moments in focus.
Has given me a sparkling glow of accomplishment.
In the simplest form of love.
Between a mother and her child.
Is a precious gift to behold.
Today I was thinking of you, mother.
Just plain happy thoughts.
When I realize the present was moving in fast.
So remember mother, I'm thinking of you!

MamieLou G. Williams

"My Friend"

My friend, I thought you could never bend!
I thought your life would never end.
You stood so tall,
Always there to pick me up,
Whenever I would fall.
You were My Friend until the end.
I've thanked God for you since then,
And I know in my heart when my life ends,
I will see you again, My Friend!

Rhonda P. Ross

Untitled

I am basking gently in solitude and serenity, seemingly,
In the realm of time, form, bodies, and things when a form of time cries out awake, awake o sleeper arise, come forth and heed my call, now.

Go now to a place where bodies and form rule no more, only
Peace and prosperity abide in harmony and in love.

Leaving behind the rudiments of the world of form now.
I am moving effortlessly toward home now.
As I rise to your call of sonship in beatific magnificence now.

I am inviting you now to enter my presence, coming into my being
Blessing me with the splendor that I might glisten as the sun in your radiance.
Glowing bright among the sonship that they might
Recognize the magnitude that you offer.

I enjoy and delight in being included in your circle of light,
Radiating without measure among the sonship. Now.

Kathryn English

A Portrait Of Myself

Heather is a girl I once loved, when all of life was bright and beautiful
she could do no wrong, especially when the sun danced behind her eyes

Her blond hair gently caressing the waves of her persona
I loved her smell, the smell of summer floating amidst the breeze

So wonderful to be free, to imagine reality instead of living it
her happiness shown through a simple smile, or flattering wink

To know Heather is to love her, for she is the life and soul of your being
I did so cherish the breath she exhaled, in which I lost myself

Too much for too little, too little for too long, I waited ever so silently
Heather's reply fell on deaf ears, although the reply was never made

I watched in agony, the only love for me, leaving without a backward glance
all of life turned dull and forlorn while I sit and ponder, who is Heather?

Heather Alyse Hyder

In The Past

Could it have been sometime ago...
When we first met, and you touched my soul.
Was it your smile, that made me shiver...
Or your kiss, that made me quiver.
It must have been, back in those days...
When all our nights, would shimmer and stay...
Alive we were, but just for us.
For no one could enter our kingdom of lust...
Our love grew strong with every kiss..
And days rolled by, pure heavenly bliss..
Then one day, my love was gone...
And with him went the sounds, and song...
From out our kingdom, I finally came..
Withdrawn and sad, not quite the same...
A mountain high came to my view...
And from the top, my life I threw.
Now we are back in our kingdom of love..
With snow white doves, from the heavens above.
The sounds are back, the songs begin...
We shall never be apart again...

Deborah French

Carnival

I could never remember who sent the picture
To who or why we made such a fuss over it
A leaking pen in a drawer had stained
One corner, cutting off someone's legs at the knees
On the other end
You could make out the boardwalk and by the faces
By the smiles it was obvious
A good time was had, had been had, was being had
By all involved
In a lapel a carnation
Just off in the corner the shadow of a calliope
Turning or not turning - we never did settle that
We always assumed it was evening
Years later, years later, you wrote to me
You wrote to me about this picture

Maybe it was sunrise...

Robert Gallagher

Each Life Affects Another

We may not always realize, that everything we do
affects not only our lives, but others too.
For a little bit of thoughtfulness that shows someone you care
creates a ray of sunshine for both of you to share
yes, every time you offer someone a helping hand,
every time you show a friend you care and understand,
every time you have a kind and gentle word to give
you help someone find beauty in this precious life we live.
For happiness brings happiness
and loving ways bring love
and giving is the treasure that contentment is made of.

Elaine Alters

My Child

The Love of my child is warm and free,
and I am glad that it is me
who has this Love so strong and bold,
that I will have until I grow old.

This Love is tender and so sweet
it makes me jump up on my feet,
I Love my child with all my heart,
I knew I would right from the start.

I understand your wants and needs
for you were born just from a seed,
I need you, and you need me
I will always be there, just wait and see.

Your pretty smile and big brown eyes
brings out the blue up in the skies.
The sun is shining up above
because your heart is full of Love.

The love for you my lovely child
will always grow forever wild,
your gentle touch, I will caress,
because you bring me happiness.

Monica Lozoya

"It's Time For A Change"

I see all my people on the streets
All strung out nowhere to sleep.
It's time for us to help each other.
Stop selling poison to our brothers.
We have to start using our minds
That's the only way to make an honest dime.
It's really time for a change of pace
Don't look at another and see only his race.
It's time for us to make a stand
So all God's people can walk hand and hand.

Shanta Morris

Untold

Things happen
Things go wrong
One God will know the truth
The one who did
Will know but will not understand,
Why they did

People do wrong in what they do
They will not understand
There will come love and then hate
You will never hate someone
You will just dislike
If you hate may your soul be torn in two
If they lie it shall be four
You shall never hate mankind
It's a given gift of love
The one is the truth untold...

Charity Thress

The Power

"I can't, but God can!"
He softens many a hardened heart.
Prayer is the release of complaints, joys and hopes
Issues that have long been buried can come forth in prayer!

There is a moral law
Against any moral sin.
Ask to receive His pardon in prayer.
The result of our sin will guide us to pray.

The Lord will help you cope
With every day negative hurts and crises.
So find His peace and accept
His mercy in your daily worship.

As we walk righteously before the Lord
These "good things" we desire will not be withheld,
But materialize in answered prayer
If we but ask with assurance of what is God's will!

Virginia Warren

Saying Goodbye

Dreaming of someone who is gone
And can only wish for a new dawn

For in the dawn there is hope
So wash away those tears and just say nope

You can only pray for the one that has past away
So take some new steps, for here you stay

You must place the past behind;
But never let the memories go blind.

And remember the feelings that you had.
Don't let them make you sad, for you should love memories and let them make you glad.

Give those memories a new start every day
And remember that all you can do is pray.

Pray not for the lonesome past,
But for the ship that is sailing, and its golden mast.

The immortal soul will blow with the wind
And in the end the good heart shall win

Take this and keep it close to your heart
And know that life nor death shall keep love apart

So let not precious life pass you by
You must, only in part, say good-bye.

Parris K. Deatherage

I Can

I can -
Ride a whirlwind of pure love with you
Be a best friend from above for you

But I can't take
You understand me

I can -
Put my finger on the pulse of your soul
Shield off your pain and play the hero's role.

But I can't make
You know me.

I can -
Frolic in the sheer madness
that is you.
Touch the weight that is the ballast of you

But I can't make
you grasp me.

But Hell -
Why would I want to make
you do something, anyway?

Stephen Huffman

My Twilight Flight

While telling you 'bout this evening, the words are hard to find.
"My twilight flight" back to New York was the God-created kind.
I boarded flight six eighty-six, as I bid my friends good-bye.
Soon the airplane left the earth, and soared into the sky.
I nodded off for a short time, as we traveled through the sky.
Startled, I awoke again, to a little child's cry.
I turned my head, still can't believe, I saw these wondrous things;
The sunshine and the moonbeams, both, reflecting off the wings.
Then I looked from left to right, and saw this awesome sight.
The body of the airplane was dividing day and night.
To the left of me was daytime, this day already known.
But to the right was nighttime, I was in the twilight zone.
The cotton clouds were parting, as I gazed to my right.
The earth below was fast asleep in the peaceful calm of night.
I saw the shadows of hills and trees; the lights of towns below.
And streams like silver ribbons were reflecting moonlights glow.
Then I looked left once more to see the daylight on its way.
As the radiant glow of sunset left to start another day.
On we flew as daytime gave way to the moon's light.
But I was sure that only I, had seen both day and night.

Dorothy Jean Griep

Untitled

Everyone talks about this kind of love
where he is supposed to be all I think about
and all I talk about
and the reason I live
but all I do is cry;
shuddering, racking sobs that leave me exhausted
and I don't believe that love exists
because I'm just miserable
all the time
and love is supposed to be happy
and I'm 17 and I've never been in love
and there must be something wrong with my emotions
and all the people in love disgust me
and I want to scream
and I want to throw things
and I want to love him
but I don't know how
and I don't want to be alone any more
and I don't know how to change that.

Rachel Penix

"Temptress"

Mere words cannot express the emotions coursing through me at this very moment. Willingly submitting to the euphoria you have cast upon me. I still envision your smile, your warmth, your love around me. I sit in wonderment..gazing into a void as I make love to you in my mind..softly..slowly..caressing every inch as I gradually expose your skin. Our tongues entangled..exploring..probing..the very heart of you. Losing myself deep within your soul as tiny strings of fire race to my most private parts..throbbing with need, you guide your slender fingers underneath my lace to find a well of desire..take me.. please me..taste the nectar of my being. An unrestrained moan escapes my lips as you claw your passion in deep grooves along my spine. Shaking with utter satisfaction, our senses tingling as we drift into complete oneness. Falling, into the night.. where fantasies come true..

Kim Cumens

A Psalm Of Tranquillity

Oh, that I had wings like a dove;
I'd fly away and rest.
Leaving behind this life of anguish, confusion and pain.
I'd gather sturdy bits of twigs, straw and grain,
And lovingly construct a warm and cozy nest.
I'd soar high above the violence and turmoil below;
Basking in my freedom from the torments of this life.
Finally at peace, free of unhappiness, sorrow and strife;
I'd rejoice in my escape from this nothingness I know.
Reborn with the uncomplicated innocence of a child;
I'd eagerly await the dawning of each new day.
Independent and serene, I'd live life my own way;
No longer controlled or incessantly defiled.
Oh, that I had wings like a dove;
I'd fly away and rest.

Twila J. Mezick

Society

Society, how could you do this to your children? To your followers? Like Adolf to the third Rike? Abandoning your promises, you lied to them who worshipped you!

Abandon, to the world, whispers behind my back, snickering, snickering about my car, my clothes, my sunglasses are the wrong color.

That's right, Ms. America, don't look at me, don't acknowledge me! Pretend I'm not here, because the truth hurts, Ms. A and student! Ms. Head cheerleader! You may think your better than me, but the truth still hurts!

I followed you but you cast me out! For being different? Because I dress all in black? Because James Dean and Silvia Plathe are my Idols? Because I write all day instead of playing mind games?

Then, why do I yearn for you, like a child yearning for its mother? Is it because to be accepted is the ultimate goal in life? Is it because stylish clothes and expensive wine bring happiness? Is it because of fake love? Yes, all of these.

Heaven Drew Kelley

Faun-Fare

Erato was as amusing
As ever a Muse could be,
She of Love and Lyric Poetry
"The best two out of three."
And I, a faun, admired her
Her contours from afar,
Lusted, ogled, longed and leered
You know how satyrs are!
One moonbeamed night she beckoned me
An Olympian piece of luck!
She even put her lyre down
What I wanted was to...
sleep

Ed Reimers

Funny Face

I washed windows today,
And I missed your funny face.
I on the inside, you on the out —
Dusting, washing and polishing;
Checking every spot, speck and streak.
But today, when I looked through the panes,
You Weren't There!

You weren't there not only to reject, approve or direct
But to make those silly, funny faces
That invariably converted the chore into chuckles.
The missed spots, specks and streaks on the windows
No longer make the slightest difference.
Now, tear-streaked cheeks and tear-spotted clothing
Poignantly whimper, "I missed your funny face!"

Elizabeth J. Krashen

One With Nature

I am one with nature...why do I need words? I need light in order to grow, not too much all at once or I will become blind. I need darkness so I can remember that I shine: the light comes from within and is all around me. I need water in order to live: just the right amount of water so that I will not wither away, nor float away and get lost in the sea of life. I need food in order to be healthy—food that I provide and, as a result, will always be there. I need shelter from the storms that I create, knowing that they will subside once I've shaken myself clean.
I need to reproduce and give back to myself, or I will forget I came from. I need the earth so that I can heal myself and continue to grow, to recognize that I am not sick. I need the stars so I may allow myself to believe in never-ending possibilities, and to understand the need for balance within myself.
I need love to know what I am, and fear to know what I am not.
I need beauty in order to understand that I am, I need ugliness in order to see with my heart. I need to be vast and complex —
to understand that I am simple if only I'd let myself be. I need words sometimes, good and bad, in order to remember the Spirit of Truth-I am one with my creator in all our vastness and holiness, and anything other than this has been co-created for my sake.

Sandra Lee Serrano

A Father's Day Tribute

As the night sky shines with twinkling stars galore,
And the waves of the mighty ocean hit the sandy shore;
So has God created fathers who love and care
For children everywhere, but mine is rare.
Ever loving, ever thoughtful, super special has my papa been.
Kind but firm and calm and serene.
As the birds nestle with their young in warm embrace,
So I feel the comfort and shelter of my Papa's grace.
It's a magical feeling— his very presence,
The closeness and solace I always sense.
As the gentle rains from heavens enrich the earth's soil,
So the showers of fatherly affection soothe the life's coil.
As the cool breeze blows and tree leaves part,
I feel the stirrings of my Papa's heart.
So on this Father's Day so special and joyous,
I offer my greetings to a Papa so pious.
I pray for this person so rare and fine-
A scholar great and gentleman divine.
God bless my Papa— may his smile endure!
Make me like him, for his heart is pure.

Ajay Malaviya

When Death Finds A Friend

The summer days dawn luscious, sweet—at first,
With laughter, song; such joy as only youth
Or childhood could express. The burning thirst
Of ev'ry sun-parched sapling yearning truth
Is innocence divine. Ah, you were mine,
My careless friend and foe: I knew thee well;
Forsooth I glimpsed as Death encroached upon thine
Eyes: Friend, unwary, to crimson death thou fell.
I kissed the golden droplets of thy dusk
Good-bye; thy stricken lips now laughing not;
Yet I within began to stir, and ask
Of Death tranquility for which I'd fought
For if thy soul doth flutter free in heav'n,
To mine on earth hath solemn peace been giv'n.

Julia Riemann

A Tragedy Among Us

The Oklahoma City Bombing - 1995

A cry and a rumble and the building must fall,
everything crumbles for one and for all.

The loved ones are lost and the memories stay,
as the demons who took them slip further away.

Rescuers run a race against time,
then find a little baby that's covered with grime.

They stare into a face just beginning to live,
a child that would've had so very much to give.

Searching for those who stood not a chance,
the victims who fell into life's vicious dance.

This outrage has opened the eyes of our nation,
to the senseless struggle for complete domination.

At the touch of a hand those innocent were gone,
they're reaching for a world that lies just beyond.

And these precious gems we shall see again,
when the demons are captured and this tragedy ends.

In honor of those lost in the Oklahoma City Bombing,
We shall meet again!

Tabitha J. Dorsey

Ballpark

We're all at the ballgame having a grand time
Watching the players hit run after run.
Popcorn and peanuts, our team's up to bat
Bases are loaded in inning number nine.
Come on and hit it out of the ballpark!
The pitcher throws a strike, then another oh my,
Then with a crack of the bat up goes the ball
Straight down the field and out past the wall
It's a grand slam!
The crowd rises to cheer, our team has just won
It just goes to prove that we're number one.

Penny Nelson

Untitled

Rise rip snorter and catch the falling dipthong
Snare the flying phalanger and plunge into the pokeberry
Swab the poop, spar the swarm, span the spade
There's a sowbelly for the taking
Who dares mend the megalith?
Limber Lilly levels the limacon
While timid Terry inherits inhibition
Inhale the iniquity, inject the inhumanity
Oh rip snorter, rip snorter, you moth-eaten mother of vinegar
Don the mortarboard; still try not to cross the mossback

David Winski

"My Stitching Hours"

There are times for meditation.
Solitude and prayers that are only ours.
I have memories, hopes and dreams,
All in my 'stitching hours'.

Golden needles, pins, patterns and linen
Bright threads, all in disarray.
Are very, very special
To make a happy stitching day.

Then as my stitching time,
passes from hours, to days, to years
I recall memories of home, friends,
laughter, heartaches, and tears.

I will never forget the many stitches,
My mother taught me in the long ago,
How many thousand of stitches I've made
no one could guess, no one will ever know.

May all the lovely pictures of
Windmills, birds, castles, and flowers,
Make some one as "Happy" as I was
in my days and years of "stitching hours."

Virginia Whatley

Rooted Deep In My Soul

The native tongue lifts and lowers
Along the journey to the "land of the free".
Bringing forth rich dialects,
with an array of descendants left behind.
Fertile land, simple life
forsaking ancient remedies.

The sweltering Savannah heat
beats upon their backs.
Attempting to hold
the heavy burdens of farm life.

Survivors

Of a country that does not love them;
They stay close knit

Two cultures emerging into one harmonious tone,
Beating two different rhythms,
while creating a unique melody.

I bring with me the soft wet soil of a land far away.
Rooted deep in my soul
are the sweat and tears that were laid before me.

Gealita Sylvester

Dreams

The butterfly
Like a broken winged bird
Limps silently through the air.
Silently - without a word
It hops painfully on its way.
Thoughtlessly, it seems to me,
It hobbles through the air
It's life and death, and strength relying
On paper wings on air.
Our dreams, like so, are made of air,
Of dreams, of smiles and tears.
Without our dreams we cannot fly
Without a breeze we cannot float
Without our dreams,
Without our lives.

Ahjee Song

Spirits Of The Earth

Indians believe in the spirits
of the earth, and using the land
for what its worth. They love
the earth and cherish the sky,
and stand in silence as the
eagle passes by. To their Gods
they pray for rain, with life this
magical it can't be explained.
Each and every night we look
up at the stars and dream
of these people in lands afar.
The age old river holds a place in their hearts,
as well as all other nature's works of art. We
learn a lot from these people in
stories untold about ancient
wonders in the valleys of old.
As time rolls on it still carries their names,
over the mountains and through the plains.
And yet the call of the wild still tugs at our hearts,
and leads us long like a candle in the dark.

Cheyenne Barnard

The Thirteenth Apostle

A Memorial Day it was, I remember so well;
The mall was full of Veterans, stories to tell.

Meandering the floor with the crowd, happy and care-free,
I spotted an old man in a wheelchair, something to see.

Sauntering over to him, I saw a body feeble and frail;
Whichever war he had been in, it must have been hell.

As I queried him, he revealed his age of 65 to me;
So young, yet so old, for he had been in the war of illiteracy.

A school teacher for thirty years or more;
No medals, no glory, no mementos of yore.

His withered hands held a cup of pencils for sale;
I put in a dollar and took one out, so moldy and pale.

I thanked him for answering his service call;
And reminded him of the greatest Teacher of all.

Turning to leave, I noticed a word on the pencil I bought;
Glancing ever closer, it seemed to read "Matthew", I honestly thought.

Back down at the old tin can I looked and counted an uneven leven;
So I put "Matthew" back, as these twelve surely belonged together
in Heaven.

I added my own pencil to the dozen of this unnamed man so docile;
For to me this forgotten teacher was surely The Thirteenth Apostle.

Jon Ray Perryman

My Love

My love for you is deep.
Without you I am weak.
My love for you is tender.
In your arms, I will surrender.
My love for you is strong.
I think about you all day long.
My love for you is superior.
It would never reach inferior.
And though I may not show it,
In your heart, I want you to know it.
I love you from the bottom of my heart
to the depth of my soul.
I'll love you when I'm young and old.
I'll be there for you through thick and thin,
Our love did begin, but will never end.

Lisa Smart

If God sent an angel to earth
tonight, would it go back crying in fright?
To see all the neglect and distress that
we make. How much do you think the
angel could take?

To see the murders, hear about the crimes
realizing the sadness of our times
Not understanding how we could hurt or kill
a little baby just to steal, or beat a child
cause it started to cry, or kill an old
woman who didn't want to die.

To rape a woman just for a thrill, or
murder an innocent person just for the kill.
Ignore a starving man and not lend him a hand
Killing the animals just for the land.
Would the angel leave with a broken heart?
Only God knows, but it's not up to him
Only we can change the world we live in.

Karla Perdue

Duty, Honor And Country

Proudly they march off
Heads held high, shoulders back
Serve her proudly they were told
And you will stop the mighty foe
They love their country
Mom, home and apple pie
Old men chant and cheer
Old women weep and dream of tomorrow
It's duty, honor, country
From childhood they were told

Then something happens
Heads hang low, shoulders drop
They've lost their innocence
They've seen it all
Heroes lay on the field of battle
Gone the son, the daughter, the father
Old men tell the tales
Old women weep of yesterday
There are no winners
War: Duty, Honor, Country

Frank E. Cheney Jr.

Senseless Society

An innocent face
that you are devouring
how does it taste
An image of one who has killed thy father
Sentences of thee who murdered my son
Silence for you who has raped my sister
and brought to me no room
Silence for I who never rejoiced it
A warning for you who tried to erase it
Solace for those who sleep
and the tree
it too must face it
Poisonous decisions we must take
Talk of laughter love of hate
A vision of lust unmarked and outgoing
Sinister trust afraid of knowing
Who, not you, not me, not we
don't
see
anything

Ashley Svrcek

The Unknown

"Do you see it?"
"See what?"
"It's right in front of your face and you can't see it?"
It hurt us all for hundreds of years.
We finally took care of it, but it came back.
People don't realize what it is doing to us.
People always ask if it's still there.
"I always tell them to open your eyes and you will see it"
If you open them and don't know if it is there.
It will remain the Unknown.
Then you will become the

Damon Torrince

Till Death Do Us Part

They spent their lives together they have never been apart
The love he has for her is deeper than the beating of his heart
He sits down beside her as she lies on the bed
He tries his best to comfort her as he gently strokes her head
He looks out the window as he stares at the moon
He tries to block it from his mind, he knows the time is coming soon
As she looks into his tear filled eyes her breathing starts to slow
They both know without a word it's now her time to go
She closed her eyes and drifts peacefully to sleep
On the bed he sits with his head in his hands and quietly he weeps
He asks God to watch over her his angel up above
And she looks down upon him the man she will always love
The vows they had spoken forty-six years before
Now were complete, as he walks from the room and shuts the door

Ginger Holt

Iron Shoes

We are so weak and Thou art so strong
Grant us Thy help as we travel along.
As we prepare to deliver Thy good news
Permit us to wear Thy Iron Shoes.

We are so unlearned and Thou art so wise
Help us ere the sun leaves western skies.
As we learn to do the things You choose
Permit us Lord, to wear Thy Iron Shoes.

Grant us the faith we need lest all be lost
Make us willing Lord, to follow at any cost.
Deliver us Lord, as Thy tender love imbues
Permit us to wear Thy Iron Shoes.

Oh Lord, help us to love thee most of all
And listen to They words and heed they call.
Tho we be weak Lord, let us never refuse
Permit us to wear Thy Iron Shoes.

"Come faithful Christians hear what I say
Thou hast done well even unto this day.
Thou hast done well delivering my good news
The race is won—Cast Aside My Iron Shoes."

Forrest J. Binion

A Picture Of Beauty

A head veiled by silken soft dark hair
With not one lock of curl, her hair sets straight and unruffled
Skin unfaded with a hue of chestnut
Skin soft and smooth yet untouched by the cruelty of time
Eyes piercing and full of zeal
The color of a moonless night her eyes view all
Her character tested by everyday irreverence, but
continues to exhibit all that is right
A picture of beauty I dream of each and every night

Robert Trevino

Opportunities

I heard the news today I prayed would never come.
You've got a new lover and you're saying he's the one.
Tonight I'm lying here dreaming in my bed
With your voice in my ears and your face in my head.
I'm dreaming tonight of what should have been
Opportunities lost because I didn't see 'em then.
Every time I'd see you out with a new man
Tears would come to my eyes and the shakes hit my hands.
The kind of love I feel for you no man has ever felt
Your soft eyes and warm smile make my heart just melt.
But you say he makes you happy and he'll never make you blue
Between you and me I sure hope it's true
You're taking the opportunity to better your life
Now that this man wants you for his wife.
In my dreams at night my opportunities come again
To tell you that I can be more than a friend.
I can't make your heart feel what it doesn't feel
But if I keep silent, my heart will never heal.

Brian Bible

Dream Of A Perfect World

O' Mighty Spinner of Dreams, as you gaze upon your infinite universe, send me a dream of a perfect world where no one has more sorrow than they can bear. Grant us the courage to live each day fully, with no thought of tomorrow until tomorrow comes.

Give us enough food to nourish our bodies and minds. Give us gentle hearts so none will ever threaten another with violence. May all the races look upon each other as alike, beholding no differences. Mighty Dream Spinner, help us make your universe one home, where love, peace and joy greet us at the door.

Winter's snows, Spring's flowers, Summer's sunshine, Fall's golden days, mighty storms and gentle rains; to each you assigned special glory. Send just enough of each that we may rejoice in them all. Give us the night for rest that we may gladly arise with each new day to walk life's path with gratitude.

May we, when at the threshold of death, be glad we have lived and been a part of your majestic plan. One other gift I ask, O' Mighty Spinner of Dreams: when morning comes grant, if you will, my dream be not a dream at all...but truth.

Lillian G. Gibson

If You Are A Parent...

Make a pledge to your child to say,
"I love you" each and every day.

Rejoice in the miracle of your child's birth,
Celebrate each day spent together on earth.
Children are wondrous, truly a gift from God...
if you're not sure of this, then you really are odd!

Learn to trust, encourage and praise,
building confidence as you nurture and raise.
Respond when they ask you for your sage advice,
listen when they actually tell you, that you are nice.

Love the frustration on your child's inquisitive face,
instill the love of learning, so it seems common place.
A parent can foster positive action, over and over again;
responsive love, and understanding can help heal any pain.

Learn to forgive, if you argued the night before,
do it, before your child walks out your front door.
Often, in moments of reflection, we wish we had said...
something different, just exactly what was inside our head.

Take joy and pride in guiding your child or adolescent each day,
for tomorrow, unfortunately, they could suddenly be taken away.

Leora Rae Stern

To The Lady Who Says No To Marriage

As I sat alone asking myself, do I hurt? Who have I hurt?
Do I care? Or am I real? Passing time to render, speculating
and fantasizing
As raindrops fall, until pouring tears from the sky.
Who have I hurt? Do I care? Have I remorse? I hardly know.

Seeing man as if a roaring lion, seeking its weaker source.
Or seeing him standing on the edge of a cliff ready to fall;
Do I push him over or do I pull him in my heart?
Will I be hurt? Or do I put him on a chain as if
A puppy on a leash? Will he grow to bite and hurt me or
Will he grow to be obedient to my every command.
Will I seduce him to my commanding, gain forever more; or

Will I appear to another cliff hanger;
As if the justice of the peace again
How long can I ride on time?

As raindrops fall until pouring tears
From the sky;
Have I forgotten my biblical ways?
Who have I hurt? Do I care? Have I remorse?
I hardly know.

Larry Garnett

The Love Of A Woman

I see your eyes twinkle in the beauty of a sunset
Your dark hair flowing gracefully
Like an eagle soaring through the sky
When you look at me in that sensual way
I melt into your arms
I would give my heart and soul just to be with you
To hold you in my arms
To feel your soft skin next to mine
In my mind I picture images of you and I lying on a beach
With the cool summer breeze
Blowing against our backs
Watching the sun as it sets over
The majestic blue sea
I lean forward to you
I take you by the hand
I taste the passion of your sweet lips
I envelop all of your beauty and enchantment
Our hearts beat as one
I know in my heart it will always be true
That I will never stop loving you

Anthony Figliola

Key To Love's Journey

The tides do not ebb,
the seas crash with thunder,
and lives that are filled with love,
host endless days of wonder.

In a world, with our past,
there are few things that can last.
If you are lucky to find your hope's desire,
Do not put out the fire!

Let the glow, forever warm your heart,
so that you can find a new start...

Life holds many secrets,
For the travelers who find the keys.

Suzanne Migdall

Something Always Happens

When you finally find a friend that
you can trust as a best friend, something
always happens. She, just like a sister,
I can tell everything to... but something
always happens. We like the same people
and love the same guys, but something
always happens. We have no secrets, and
tell no lies, but something always
happens. On this dark day, I sadly
have to say good-bye because
something happened. Now, it's time to
move on with my life because
something always happens.

Valli Woodral

African Faith

Muda gani itachukua?
How long will it take?

Tafadhali Baba, Kuniambia.
Please tell me, Father.

Nime poteza jana yangu,
I've lost my yesterday,

Nipe ni kesho.
Give me my tomorrow.

Uta endelea kwamunda gani itakaa?
How long will it last?

Sa moja? Ndakika moja? Nukta moja? ... Afrika,
One hour? One minute? One second? ... Africa,

Nani mwiimbaji, nane mchezaji?
Who is singing, who is dancing?

Popote pale, kati kati,
Somewhere in the middle,

Kuna amani na matumaini.
There is peace, and there is hope.

Leo, vita ime kwisha.
Today, war is over.

Karen Jean Adjei

That's Somebody's Child

Ode To The Homeless

Hey, that's somebody's child sittin' over there —
All spreaded out over two or three seats
like he own the train.

Wonder if he's tired.
Maybe he is tired or just closin' his eyes
so he don't have to look at people
lookin' at him.

Looks like he ate tho', all them
wrappers and bottles on top of those
newspapers. So he ain't hungry.

But he sure looks tired. So tired.
So very tired.

Wonder whose son he is. He's somebody's
Child. How'd he get that way anyhow
all dirty and alone.

He's not my son. Is he?
Lord knows he's somebody's child.
God Bless him.

Judy C. Ridenhour

Open Your Eyes And See

Bosnia, Bosnia, red run your streets.
Guns and Bullets will reign defeat.
Children weep at their slain father's feet.
Horror and death, rain down like sleet.
Bosnia, Bosnia, red run your streets.

Bosnia, Bosnia, so full of woe.
Killing innocents, has brought you low.
If you open your eyes and see the light,
And think of changing you might to right.
Then Bosnia, Bosnia can reach new heights.

Joseph Michael

Untitled

I once had a nightmare, it was a horrible dream, I saw a world that was trapped in time.

There were great lessons to be learned, and time was but a lesson, a lesson in pain and in shame.

No one learned this lesson, this world carried on, it laughed at the future 'til it came.

The users of this world paid the ultimate price.
The world was all used up, the future all washed away.
Washed away by the ignorance of the past as tomorrow finally came.
The skies were all empty, there was nowhere else to go, a dying race on a dying planet, that they created.
Thank God it was only a dream!

Steven Lee Seaborg

The Infinite Sadness

The infinite sadness,
the wedge, the hammer which creates the blow,
separating the peace between us.

Alcohol, urinating in your veins,
Anger, the stupor, the ugliness...
the penance - the infinite sadness
that consumes me.

I smell his shirt,
sweet comfort in familiarity.
He does not know of my infinite sadness,
the sadness interwoven with the
love that has securely penetrated my skin.

Rowena Navia

Sweet Sister

As I gaze upon a star,
I often wonder where you are.
Dear sweet sister are you near,
Do you watch me through a tear?
And do you know the pain I'm in,
And the sorrow that's held within?
I've no one else to talk to,
Do you hear me, I wish I knew.
I wish the silence we could break,
And you'd be here when I awake.
I know I shouldn't complain,
Your life was full of hurt and pain.
God called you home when you were young,
It was over before it had really begun.
Is all your pain the reason why, God decided to let you die.
Did at night he hear you cry, and call his name with a tired sigh?
Our lives together we did waste, and our days we lived in haste.
Now the memories I hold so dear, are all I have to keep your near.

Pat Gochis

Down The Tunnel

I looked down the tunnel, realizing my life was in my hand
One small slip and I would fall, never to live again.
Or if by chance I were to make it through this great or deal;
Would you be here to help me share these feelings that I feel.
I'm not sure exactly what to do,
I wish I could start over and start something new.
The time has come for me to make my choice;
Please, call me now, I need to hear your voice.
It was almost to late, but you did come,
You lost your life, but gave me one.

Jennifer Roberts

Love Is...

Love is the wind blowing through the trees,
Love is the dust that makes people sneeze,
Love is sometimes happy and sometimes blue,
Love is like a thorn that keeps on pricking you,

Love is saying hello and waving goodbye,
Love is something that can never die,
Love is an arrow going through the soul,
Love is taking over when you have no control,

Love is a plant that grows and grows,
Love is an answer that nobody knows,
Love is beautiful, but hearts can get broken,
Love is feelings that are often unspoken,

Love is laughter, and love is tears,
Love is freeing you from all your fears,
Love is a soft and gentle touch,
Love is a word that means so much.

Beth Lawall

Thought Of Angels

Thought of an angel
who hears our voice and
listens to our thoughts too;
everyone who knows, who believes
shall see an angel from above, holding
ours dreams, as they spread their
wings should we see the light of
life, we know, they are waiting
to hear ours knock, to hold and
show us, through our thoughts
directly to the heart as their spirit is
set so free.

David L. White

Scott

His eyes caught mine
As he began to cry.
The sun could no longer shine
As he fell to the floor.
They wouldn't let him in,
For what he had done
Was an unforgivable sin.
His life was in their hands
No shoes on his feet or shirt on his back.
He was giving them his hands
But they could not except.
You could no longer tell
Who was suffering more
In this torture full of hell,
Was it him, me or them?
I closed my eyes and dreamt of a faraway land.
I just couldn't bare this world of lies
As powerless as he was,
He tried with all his might,
Just because, of love.

Julie Gavin

Dear Lord

I feel so sick and scared inside
I want to run there's no where to hide.

I must have done something so very bad
They always yell, it makes me so sad.

I try to be good and do what they say
I must be Stupid! I do things wrong every day.

They tell me I'm worthless, I shouldn't even be.
I'm not sure how I got here, Lord, why was it me?

I see other kids with their mom and their dad
They seem to have something that I never had.

Their laughing and talking they hug and they kiss.
I've never done that. Is this what I miss?

Only when they hit me do I feel their touch
But I want them to love me, I want that so much

Lord,
Please make me better, please help me be good

Make Mom and Dad love me

If only you could...

Kathy Huffstutler

A Prisoner Of My Fears

I can't give up nor can I give in. Once what I had
weakened to, now has strengthened me.
Still frightened by the memories... remembering what
it has done to me.
But it is the fear that keeps me from it.
Poisoned messages in the bottle. A seduction unwelcomed.
A lover no longer wanted. Darkness falls no more.
No longer a prisoner of my fears.

Denise La Verdiere

Achievement

If your hands cannot create a masterpiece of art,
Or weave a magic spell with music set apart.
If your voice no one can thrill, nor your dancing grace be best
Suppose you think that you are lost, well you
haven't heard the rest.

You think that this is beauty, you'd love to be acclaimed.
Should you possess a single gift that I perhaps have named.
But didn't it occur to you that beauty's in your heart.
Just waiting to be noticed, and longing for a start.

To prove to you that should you choose to cultivate its grace,
You too, may know the happiness
of one who can create.

Ellen M. Malloy

Lost

Wanting to be lost;
Dying to be found.
Wander out of the light
  just for a second.
Then dive back into its fake fluorescent warmth.
Riding on foamy seas
  waves caused by the slaps of an angry mermaid's tail.
I forgot to call
  and when I did, you were gone.
The clouds cry when the sky turns black
  I weep as I watch the dish water drain into the black
  hole in the middle of my heart.
The closet is empty;
  my eyes are full.
Dreams provide and escape
  the emergency exit is blocked.

Jenny DenBleyker

Thoughts On The Wash

I sorted the clothes. I made piles.
Whites, darks, gentle - aaah there they are,
Not much to them, satined, ruffled,
Embroidered stuff, soft, lacy fluff,
The things young men's dreams are made of.

I'm too old to indulge in such
Youthful play, that can while away,
in warmth, and smiles, purrs and kisses,
A summer's day, dawn to evening hush.
It's not appropriate. I flush.

I should be grown up. I'm fifty.
I've more important things to do,
Bills to pay, calls to make, the wash.
Then upturned lips and crinkled eye
To my own thoughts make their reply.
I'm old, 'tis true. Older I'll see,
But this young, ne'er again I'll be.

Carolyn J. Todd Dennis

Pretty Woman

It was a Strange Day
When a pretty woman walked this way
The mirror recognizes the pretty woman
in the shiny glass
The pretty woman went back stage
to the pretend class
The pretty woman climbed all
The way up the comprehensive tree
The pretty woman absorbs my
aspirations to be free
The pretty woman walks smoothly away
I wrote her poems on that strange day
I recognize her beauty and in my eyes
she is like a delicate white bird in disguise
Come fly with me to the sun, pretty woman,
when the day is done.

Dominick Chianese

"Portrait"

This is who you are a picture of me
A masterpiece finely detailed for you
Is there a smile on that face or non-expressive
But full of grace
And I see character a feeling to embrace
The eyes display warmth and love
There is a beauty transposed from the light above
A treasure to behold, so serene, so calm
Naturally reflecting an image of charm
Apart from belonging to a former time of day
This anatomy is reality, revealing the way
She has reformed herself for you and for me
Shamelessly seeking though uncertain it may be
Thoughts of forever, conscious, infinite, and free
A moment to remember
Forever and ever
For you and for me.

Bradley Galen Routzhan

Life Sentence

A sexual prisoner for life.
Boundaries and limitations enclose me.
Youth and premature adulthood is suffocated!
Incarcerated,
without people or exile!
I hate you!
For this life sentence you've inflicted on me!

Eric Matthew Sealey

Time (Psalm 90:1-17)

Time is a gift God has given you and me
To become within a life span what He wants us to be.
Restricted now to this time is our human race
Now we're given many chances to receive God's grace
This time is too precious for us to waste
The joys, challenges, and fullness of life let us taste!
We must learn to number every single day
And cherish every moment and learn to pray.
We're given a short time in this earthly life!
So many of us spend our time in needless strife.
This gift of time sometimes I wish God didn't make
Yet routines, deadlines, and the clock we must now take!
God sees our lifetimes as but a breath
And He has our days numbered up to our deaths.
But once in this world of time God sent us His Son
Jesus a place in God's eternal heaven for us has won!
He endured our timely limitations to be our Savior
His love for us is able to change our behavior
In this time-bound world Jesus died for us on a cross
Our gain in forgiveness comes through His one-time loss!

Lisa DeSherlia

My Sandwich

My sandwich has eyes.
My sandwich has leaves.
But not as much as it has old cheese.

My sandwich is old.
My sandwich has green mold.

I gave my sandwich to my Mother.
And she gave it to my Brother.

He ate the sandwich and sour milk too.
Then he turned purple and blue.
He'll be digesting that until the year 2002!

Chris Morgun

Remembering A Day

Early amber greetings leaping high not to fall,
darkness is leaving and yellow steadies embracing all.
A pinnacle promises as tall as it can be
moves in a direction for me to see.
Shadows are changing a new color is bare,
brilliance and perfection collide in mid-air.
Warm are the rays with gifts of life they bring.
The earth reaches outward and birds take to wing.
Red orange returns triumphant and proud;
I stop to stare screaming praises aloud.
A world's blanket spreads coolness abound,
as our home keeps turning round and round.

Jeffrey W. New

Deep Down

This goes deep down to my soul.
Deep down to the past that someone stole.
This goes deep down to my heart.
Deep down, from beginning to start.
All the pain, from the past,
Is never gonna leave, it will always last.
This is so painful, it's true.
And I really don't know what to do.
Deep down to everything I've been through.
Deep down to this life that's so new.
All the way down to the end of my life.
Deep down, going back to using a knife.
Deeply down to the end of thoughts.
Deep down to all the things taught.
So deep down to the tears I cry..
More deep down to the feelings that
make me wanna die.

Angie Mohns

Untitled

Avanelle, Avanelle what is it with you?
There's nothing in this place that you wouldn't do.
You do shopping for others, call bingo so well,
The recycling job, well, that you can tell.
You do take time for things you enjoy
Like fitness class, water exercise, and bridge, oh boy!
The trips near and far, you don't miss very many,
In fact to be truthful you rarely miss any.
The luncheon trips usually you take the last seat.
because every one knows how you love to eat.
Then there's a time something special is asked,
Like please get our mail, and other small tasks.
You never refuse, you accept with big smiles,
And your friends take off and drive hundreds of miles.
Enough of this chatter, what I really should say
Happy Birthday Avanelle, on your special day.

Charlotte Weisenbach

Remembered

Days are long and times are sad,
Today I lost the only family I had,
I watched my mother take her last breath,
I watched my father shot to death,
Yes, I am a jew and proud to be,
I need not your sympathy,
For I am strong and I am wise,
Somehow I will survive,
Through the sorrow and the pain,
Still my dignity remains,
I will not weep, I will not cry,
I do not fear the day I die,
I will remain strong, I shall not surrender,
For in the end I will be remembered.

Bridgette Woodbright

Dandelion Dreams

This thick book that I turn in my hands is filled with tales of my past and of where I have been
Yellowed page, worn by desperate fingers returning to their safe, peaceful haven of solace
Too heavy to take on the journey in search of the dandelion seeds that were scattered across the earth
Released by a dream whispered in a breath of love and hope and ideals made real to me
Only my quest to collect them again there's a steep, winding path that is only made clear to me
These wishes not seen by the rest of the world which, satisfied, lives the open page
Think of Tieser, he's lucky not being tormented by any desire for a dream unattainable
I have tripped, fallen over rocks that were in front of me reading a phrase from my cumbersome book
Trying hard to live out of the page that the others follow
Then appears my feathery, white star
And I tear out the page in my haste to catch it only to find that it has now escaped
For comfort I flip to the front of my unwieldy book discovering I've lost my place
Longing ache, a hunger that won't go away I start greedily to devour my most cherished fare
Lovely moments and looks, soft touches and gentle smiles and successes of days gone by
Made so real I taste the sweetness but it sours when I look and see my dandelion floating from me
I must toss in my book to free to swim

Christi Cavallaro

A Tribute

She slipped the ring from off his hand,
And placed it on her own,
And as the tears began to fall,
She knew she was alone.
Her past was gone, forever lost,
Fading to tell of her life,
A special chapter had begun,
When she became his wife.
He opened her eyes,
To a world of love and joy.
Providing her with all,
Their first child, a boy.
And now he lay in death,
His face serene and calm,
She held his hand so tightly,
And traced the life line on his palm.
As she thought of their wedding day,
And how their love was true,
She remembered the phrase said so long ago,
And again she whispered "I do".

Sherry Howard

The Rape Of A Child

For M.E.B.

A man named Legion violated me, murdering my innocence.
In dreams I hear his wanton laughter like conscience ever since,
Cruel, derisive, vile. I arise despising, never him, but me.
I've separated grief and pain into a cell so small and tough,
Its burial in my smutted brain causes a prickling stress
Of vague, unstructured night-mare. A side effect of festering
Has grown wide to poison me; to slaughter hope, and child trust
In anything. It blights serenity. Now I loath the vandled me.
I cause injury to chasten me. I flail my horrid, guilty flesh,
Hoping vainly I might be returned afresh to innocence.

I have come to know that with such hate the evil lives again.
I let it live to lacerate, to punish and to reconstruct a fate
That damages the girl I might have been.
But now the hurt with which I hurt myself perpetuates that beast
Named Legion, still holding hostage Jesus' grace
And absolution, and a mendicant peace.
I must face this verity-
Before my memory and my body heal, the evil has to cease
With my forgiving him to pardon me.

Marie C. Webb

The Dream

I once had a dream I was touching your skin;
I remembered the world was about to begin.
The clouds above parted, there was a dove;
Trees blossomed at midnight while we made love.

The smell was the sweetest as after the rain;
The song on the breeze was whispering a name.
The light in the sky was the brightest I've seen;
We rode to the stars on a silvery moonbeam.

There were no loud noises of any kind;
Only the silence within my mind.
There was no trace of asphalt and no concrete;
We could feel the Earth Mother beneath our feet.

I once had a dream, you were there too;
We could stand naked, the world was brand new.
Time as we know it is just an illusion;
The essence of thought is the sweet conclusion.

Ann Kennedy

Our Seasoned Fire

When chilly winter drives us close indoors,
Fatiguing mind and body, leaving time
And vigor to perform our daily chores
But little more for laughter, song, and rhyme —

It's then I must create a Valentine
Of tender vows and passion's burning song.
But the spark of love seems warmer when you're mine
In summer; nights are sweet and days are long.

Determined but perplexed, I push aside
My clumsy verses, rise and stoke the fire —
And sense the truth that love and care abide
And season either comfort or desire.

For whether flaming high or flickering low,
Or seasoned love's a strong and constant glow.

Edward E. Potter

Normandy Cemetery

Through crosses of stone, I made my way
O'er hallowed ground, where heroes lay.
Not a drop of their blood was shed in shame,
Every cross bears valor's name.
In a moment of angst they paused to pray,
For freedom's flag they bore that day,
Into the cauldron, where resolve was tried,
Where they fought, where they died.
The crosses they have stood for years
Burnished bright by mother's tears.
Across the seas, as mist they are borne,
As long as grieving mothers mourn.
May the crosses ever stand,
As symbols in a foreign land
That a crass, indifferent world may see
The coin that purchased liberty.

Charles E. McKee

"So Long, For Now"

So long, for now, I have to accept you're gone;
I know, I know,
Nothing will bring you back
Not money, not time, not love

Five minutes, that's all, I'm not asking for much;
Just five more minutes.
My memories, I cherish,
They are all I have, or ever will have,
Even they are fading fast

The pain
The emptiness
The loneliness
The heartache

So long, for now, I'll think of you often;
I leave my heart with you,
So long, for now, I must go
For the cemetary is closing.

Cindy Breninger Potts

A Special Moment

A fading memory, a forgotten place,
A picture you remember, an expression on a face,
A very small moment that is captured in time,
It stays with your heart, but fades from your mind,
An emotion you felt, a story recalled,
A moment of happiness, a person whom you saw,
They'll stay with you now,
They'll stay with you then,
You'll never forget how, where and when.

Melissa Richards

The News

Today, I heard someone say
About the news, of the mother accused
This is a story of a sad situation
Where the mother didn't have any consideration
About two little boys, who lost their life
From a woman, suppose to be a mother and a wife
Everyone's thinking about the boys
Wondering how a mother could stoop so low
To let the boys die so slow
After you two were found
It had everybody thinking, how could a mother
Be so cold, with such a cold, cold heart
We know you boys are in heaven
Feeling no more pain
Left a terrible stain, on the town of Union
You two boys are finally home
With the maker, little Michael and Alex
I was sad to hear the news of the mother accused

Bobby J. Tollison

Discipline's Offspring

Where do they find them?
The words which flow so eloquently,
like clear water in a quiet stream.
The ideas which inspire and carry forth the evolution of technology,
theories, and great recipes.
And the desire...to live.

Live!
Live like the rabbit, coursing with the fire of a raging heart,
evading the breath of a fox.
The fox who also knows the working of the mill.
Grinding out desire, grinding out persistence,
Grinding out like a man frantically clawing away the earth
over a buried chest.

Is it a gift?
Is it a skill?
A lesson, a language, or even a smell?
Does the sky still look the same?
What is it like to hold the key to their city?

The city in the state of mind allowing one to be in perfect harmony
with themselves.
Granting admittance onto the chariot of dream makers where there are
no doubts,No regrets,
And satisfaction is synonymous with acceptance
And as plentiful as sunlight
on the day the earth was born.

Marc Garcia

Untitled

Yo, Mama... Hey Sweet thang..., What's Up!
You got a minute.
Can I walk with you, talk with you,...You so fine!
Hey Baby, you got a man..Can I get dim digits or what?
But I'm sayin' dough...! Damned stuck up Bitch!...
(All the while attempting to secure his manhood,
holding his crotch in his hand, demonstrating the only way he
knows
how the very definition 'manhood')

Excuse me Ms!
I don't mean bother you,
But I must admit that you are breathtakingly beautiful.
May I please have a minute of your time?
May I walk you to your car?
No disrespect intended, but may I call you sometime?...
(All the while looking me straight in the eyes; never being to
forward; and never violating or disrespecting my independence)

Wynona D. Wiggins

Just My Mom And Me

'Bout eight years old
Greyhound bus we rode
"Cheyenne" the reader read
"Off at Wheatland," mother said
With stops at Sacramento, Denver, and Salt Lake
I thought forever it would take
Took three days to make headway
What an adventure the American Way
Through mountains, valleys, farmland and plains
The eyes of a dreamer peering through the panes
Two whole weeks we stayed at Gramma's house
Bottlerockets, firecrackers, pennycandy and a mouse
Adventure of a lifetime in the eyes of a child
Boy, that summer I went wild
Keychain here and souvenir there
Mother kept me happy by the roots of her hair
'Twas just my mom and me
What more could there be

With Love,

David

David M. Weldon

Unspoken Good-Bye

To My Brother, Rolland

How I wish I had the time
Time to say good-bye
But I could not have done it
Without tear-filled eyes

I know how much it must have hurt
To watch a loved one fade
To know that reservations
By God already made

It wasn't something that could be stopped
No matter how we tried
We watched, Our hearts filled with love
And silently we cried

Just one more day, We prayed for
Just to keep him near
But God said "No it's time to go
I'll Keep him from all fear"

He left us here one morning
For a much much better place
He now resides in Heaven
With a smile up on his face

Deloris Stromley (your little sister)

Freedom

The summer days go drifting by
Fleecy clouds sprinkle the sky.
You feel the peace and beauty, too
As you look into the sky so blue.

In the distance you see,
Geese forming their perfect V.
Honking, honking as they go
Chatting about the scenery below..

An eagle screams in the far away hills,
Gliding on beautiful wings of steel.
Here he comes having such fun
His bald head shinning in the sun!

Upward we gaze into space
Shared by birds, insects and the human race.
Beauty as far as the eye can see
How peaceful and happy we should be!

Corene Luedecke Draper

Still Of The Night

There is something that I love about the night
A still calmness, the faint hum of the electrical box and the far-off
cars zooming off to nowhere
that gets ruined by the sound of your
footsteps descending on the carpet.
It is ruined by the sounds on the box,
the infommercials and late night shows.
And you tiptoe through my room
snooping the odds and ends randomly spread on the floor.
Or my memory of you being spanked for something that you did
and my anticipation of what your funeral would be like.
So, I close my door tighter as if to shut the serenity in and my thoughts out.
I close my eyes and drift of somewhere between dreamland and my wooden floor.
This is when I produce some of my best work
but I keep on getting interrupted by the still of the night.

Carolyn Streets

I.O.U.

When I look into your eyes, this is what I see
Sharing, caring, and honesty
One day I'll repay you for all you've done for me
Until then I'll just have to let it be
I hope someday I'll do like you do
Until then this is my I.O.U.

I'll be in your debt 'til babies no longer cry
I'll owe you until the day I die
I'd fly to the moon if you wanted me to
Until then this is my I.O.U.

No money value could pay it
No words could ever say it
I want you to know I'd do anything for you
I hope you'll except this as my I.O.U.

Terri Zambon

Dreams

They make you wonder,
they make you cry,
they have a meaning,
even though you give a sigh.

You think they are just there,
in your head,
while you're in bed.

But they're not,
both you and I know,
they are for a reason,
a Big one at that.

You can cry,
or you can die,
laugh or play.

If you like it or not,
your dream has a meaning,
even though you may not.

A dream has a lot to tell,
listen to your dreams,
they are telling you something, good or bad.

Luke Yin

"Daddy, Please Understand"

Daddy, please understand I can't tolerate
too much of your helping hand,

Daddy, you and I have to be strong. In
our own ways we are both wrong.

Daddy, I will always admire your charms
and I always be your daughter kept safe in your arms.

Daddy, I know it's hard but someday you
have to let me be my own guard.

I feel you don't trust me when we
disagree, then I remember "Daddy loves me."

Angela Cartwright

Idle Blues

Procrastination: stealer of time.
But what is this?
'Tis not a crime.
For who knows better, if not than me
That tomorrow's light my eyes will see.

Those around me seem to understand:
My husband, my boss, and the keeper of this land.

Each stands beside me and says not a word,
as my todays drift into tomorrow silently, unheard.

When all my tomorrows are mere promises of today,
Who'll stand beside me, once time has passed away?

Surely, there's a purpose to this specific day.
Something that I must do, or that I just must say.

For tomorrow will come, but if a foundation is not there,
No life can be built where all is still bare.

When one opens the book and finds only emptiness within,
Procrastination, I say, you must be a sin.

Vicki Castor

My Love For You

Days go by and times you don't show,
Wondering if something is wrong, I would never know;

Being with you makes all my dreams come true,
Seeing your face and saying I love you too;

Forever is not long enough for me,
Although eternity just might be;

Your on my mind 24-7-365,
You make it worth being alive;

I let you take something very special from me,
I'm truly in love with you don't you see;

Wishing that nothing was between us but the covers,
So we could wake up together and be known as lovers;

Together forever is where I hope we can stay,
I've hoped for that ever since we started dating in May;

I realize that this love is so right and so real,
I can't help but tell you how I feel;

I've waited so long just to have you to hold,
And now that I've got you I'll never let go;

Can't you see I love you so much,
You just happen to have that special touch.

Sabrina Pritchard

Midnight At The Track

Hot rubber snaps gravel
imitating distant fireworks in the campgrounds

Billies at the hootenanny,
sloppy saber-toothed sloths
flaunting their skin to the guards

A varicose vein parade
cottage cheese

You would put anything in your fires...
an artificial Christmas tree
a seat from a station wagon
your children — if you haven't eaten them

This party is about speed in the quarter mile
game over junior
when the parachute fails.

The ninja car jumper
watches from his hospital bed,
in a body cast
suffering from last weeks miscalculation...
toe pick
gone!

Todd Ridella

They're Coming For Me

As they try to run right over me,
holding me down while they try to
pass and get ahead of me,
as from the smoke and ashes left I
once again arise to face thee,
with four more angles to cover thee,
descending with much force over me,
for those that come against shall not hold me,
For I sit right there next to thee,
How will you ever then conquer me,
and am I or are you the enemy,
am I you then think about it awhile maybe,
who will fly after it's all over you or me,
that's how won or lost is decided don't you see,
enemy,
that keeps coming for me,
will I or you be set free.

David Martin Johnson

A Destiny

From the beginning:
When the church bells chime your name
Until you pass our world with fame,
All are given a destiny, a reason, a game.

Finding your destiny is a gift,
But sharing it with the world will give you a lift
Because your destiny offers more meaning to me than you.
Hence, if you donate your soul, too,
God will welcome you with hands of gratitude, it's true.

At the end:
Your light upon the earth came
Without which we might never be the same:
Now that I know you, and you know me
And the gift which hath been given can be seen.

Larissa Klepadlo

Fate Unkind

Beautiful little child, you are
Enchanted and bright as a star
With your laughter and your tears
You've graced my life in times despair

Precious little child, so fond
Oh, how it makes me rage
To see you wonder and often ponder
At such a tender age

Courageous little child, indeed
Why fatherless maybe
You are a part of the plan nonetheless
To bring joy and love and happiness

Little child of mine, remember
It really doesn't matter
Shattered dreams, countless tears, valleys so deep
You are God's divine gift to me.

Merline Longmore

And Faster Still

The sun shining high in the sky above, beating down,
Saying it's time to run. Down from this quiet mountain.
The long journey, though hard, has begun.
Run. Run fast, and faster still, there's no time to doddle
Upon this ridge. Moving with tremendous effort and speed,
Silently through each twisted bend.
Tearing at a violent pace, over rocks, around trees,
And broken limbs. Taking small pieces of it all,
Knocking it down as it slowly descends.
Into the deep canyon, slipping, falling, straight down,
The fastest way down. Rewarded with a quiet pool below.
A short little rest on level ground.
Then the chanting, come, come back, surrounding and
Echoing off the walls. Run Run fast, and faster still,
Try to escape the deafening call.
Only to find when it reached the end, hovering, waiting
Patiently right there, the cloudy bitter cold enfolded.
Now falling swiftly back through the air.
Back down to the top this quiet mountain,
Again to lie silent until the sun appears.

Michelle Thompson

I'm Making It-Or Am I?

As we climb the corporate ladder
does it really matter

If we break that glass ceiling
when we find we've lost all feeling

From those we care for so much
That now they choose to be out of touch

Is it worth the climb to the top
If we have no one to be there, if we drop

No one to share with or to play
No one to care for or to say hooray!

The perks may look to be very nice
And the rewards may come, once or twice

But what is it really all about?
Is it just glory and is it just clout?

To have a beach town home or drive a fancy car

Is it really worth it to have to go that far?

To prove that you can make it
to the monetary top of the ladder

When you lose all that you care for
just to make the glass ceiling shatter

Susan J. Miller

With You

You are my soul, my inspiration,
Dreaming of life full of bliss.
You bring joy and happiness into a kiss,
It's all so clear, but an apparition.
I'm with you.
You are so strong and free,
I idolize you as a king.
Nothing has changed, I feel the sting,
Crying of happiness, that you're with me.
I'm with you.
Love runs through my fingers like sand,
Life goes on, safe and secure.
No question in emotion, I am sure,
Like a child, I'm safe, you hold my hand.
I'm with you.
Still presence is far, joy remains,
Distance is close, closer than before.
Bliss on the horizon of a golden shore,
Listening to your voice, I watch the crane.
I'm with you.

Maleah Collingsworth

I Believe

I believe in You God - from the depths of my soul
You put Yourself in each person - then put our choice
In our own control.
In my hours of desperation You gave back
my life to me - and I will honor You for all eternity.
I believe in You Jesus - in Your compassion and love
You comfort the child in my heart -
and vanish shadows that I'm afraid of.
In my hours of doubts and loneliness
courage came to me through Your trials,
and I see Your kindness living in the innocence of children's smiles.
I believe in you Mary - in your sorrows and strength.
In the beauty of your love for your Son -
you showed endless loyalty and lengths.
In my hours of jealousy and anger, that
I found I alone could not control -
I found serenity and hope - in the beauty of your soul
Yes, I believe in all of you and thank you
for making me see that with strength
I found in love for you - I could once again believe in me.

Lorraine B. Schmidt-Cotter

Things To Remember

Always remember and one thing to never
forget, your presence is a present to the
world, your image is one of a kind.
Your life can be whatever you want it to be.
Take the days just one at a time,
Count your blessings not your sorrows.
You're gonna make it, no matter what comes along.
Within you are so many answers! Understand,
Have courage, be strong, don't put limits on yourself,
So many dreams are waiting, to leave, to chance,
Reach your peak, your goal, your prize!
Nothing wastes more energy than worrying,
The longer one carries a problem
the heavier it gets...
Take life serious and remember
that friendship is a wise investment.
Keep wishing upon a star,
And don't forget, for even a day,
How Special You Are!

Traci Lynn Counterman

The Meadow's Majesty

He ruled as any good king should,
with his head held high,
and his arms opened wide to his people.
They danced at his feet,
with their brightly colored bonnets swirling wildly.
They bowed gracefully before him,
honoring his strength and power.
His spring cloak dipped low to brush their smiling faces,
and in fall he covered them with it for their winter's rest.
In the heat of every day,
his shadow rested gently upon their heads,
shielding them as a mother would her child.
When storm clouds gathered overhead,
he was there, always protecting.
A more majestic king, you'll never find,
than that meadow oak.
And a more devoted people never existed,
than his wildflowers.

Beth Kahn Guin

Alienation

It's such a strange and kind of alienating experience
when your subway car slows to a halt
in the middle of nowhere
Silence fills the car...sounds undetectable
before due to the creaks and clanks of the movement
taken place, are able to be heard.
The soft murmuring of the old man as he
breathes next to me...
People fidgeting, aware of the feelings
of uncomfortableness.
Each person, singular and alone is suddenly
brought together in the silence and stillness of the subway car.

Suddenly the lights return, the engine is reawakened.
We move and the squeaks and creaks again exist.
We are each alone in our own little
worlds once more.

Layne Farah Whitney

A Story Yet Unknown

Adrift upon a raven's wing, at sea where dolphins play.
He met me on the violet shore, beneath a sky of gray.
The thunder rolled, and lightening flashed, the moon glowed in his
eyes.
And up above a lonely bird, echoed haunting cries.
The sea grew still, an eerie calm, intent on my reply.
To risk it all and stay with him, or safely say goodbye.
Once more the thunder sounded, and lightening lit his face.
I saw a look of restless pain, not sure I could erase.
This fantasy was twisted, so much that I could lose.
If I should chance forbidden love, what if it wasn't true?
I looked into his eyes once more, then quickly to the sea.
I felt my heartbeat swell inside, to see he needed me.
I closed my eyes and took a breath, a frightened teardrop fell.
And faced a story yet unknown, that only time will tell.

Crystal Bryant

"My Love"

His hair is as black as a moonless night.
His eyes as blue as a cloudless sky.
His voice as soft as a gentle breeze.
His kiss as sweet as the nectar from the bees.
His movement as graceful as a deer in flight.
His laughter as refreshing as a bubbling brook.
His love as welcome as the warmth of the sun
This is the man I love.

Joyce Kempf

Ode To Nature

Little humming bird so happy I see, making your music with your wings. Fussing over the honeysuckles, I planted just for you. So you may visit me at my sill.

When I awake I may peek through the window and notice you there. I'll coo, my you come, leaving me a little sweetness upon my lips. To taste your blissfulness within.

You fly past my weeping willow, the tree where I love to be. The song that you sing, laments that are inside me. When I come before you, soothing the wounds, swaying the agitation that stirs within.

Climb up your branches not to come down. The beauty encircling, melodies that come from the large wreath softly chanting in my ear.

Frances Tellas

Fear

I fear many things today
Unlocked doors, and empty stores,
News and wars, friends that snore,
And hurricanes on the bay.

I fear a lot in this world right now
Strange phone calls, abandoned malls
Scary pictures, getting injured,
And doing what's not allowed.

I fear much in this world of rain
Clouds and crowds, music played loud,
Purple cars, unfixable scars,
And long nights filled with pain.

The things I fear are small, I know
To all you who can just say no.
As to adulthood I strive, staying alive,
I'm afraid they might change to something
even more strange.

Aimee Evans

My Mother

Did you watch the sun come up.
Did you ever watch the rise.
Did you notice that in full sky set, how beautiful it lies.

Did you ever watch the oak trees sway.
I saw a few today.
They reminded me of such gracefulness, in each and every way.

Did you ever see a sea gull fly, high above the sea.
Or watch a flock of pelicans feed, frolic as can be.

Did you ever watch the ocean roar with wind
so full and strong.
Or watch the gentle waves rolling when everything is calm.

The porpoise swim, the eagle soars.
The lightning flash, the thunder roars.
Natures beauty I have seen, for her children I have cared.
The pleasures and the pains she brings more than once I've beared.

I cherish every bit of her.
I love my mother earth.
I pledge to fight, to keep her,
for the futures future birth.

Marty Gary

My Dog, My Horse And Me

I paid a visit to my past
My thoughts ran wild and free.
We owned the world and loved it all.
My dog, my horse and me.
Our friends were always close at hand
And beckoned to our call..
The wind, the sky, the chirping birds.
The trees so green and tall.
To live meant something wonderful.
To hear, to touch, to see.
What people took for granted
Was God's great gift to me.
I sit here now and reminisce.
Fond memories always last.
I thank you God for everything
But mainly for my past.
If one could relieve things that were,
I know where I would be.
I'd give the world to reunite
My dog, my horse and me.

Barb Dulle

Locked In A Box

So, now I truly know the meaning
of the song unsung

The poet with no muse or maybe
just the muse has left

Maybe just claiming to be such
when inspiration left

Written words and tunes hummed
with no back-up band

The stage has been taken, and yet
the hall is vacant

The line between reality and imagination,
holding back penetration

Or maybe breaking through the border
with no return in order

Maybe it's hard to find the key
to set the music free

Maybe there's no longer any purpose
for a catchy little chorus

Andrew Charles Guyer

"A Quiet Day With My Beloved"

This morning my angelic Cochise
Reclines during his early morning breakfast
The hay is hip high and he only nibbles it.
The sun sleeps on his sorrel and white back
As it did on the short spine
Of the dawn horse that he once was.
A light breeze fans most ofthe deer flies from upsetting his dreams.
Only a gaggle of gnats swarms around his ears.
A hay pume sticks out of his mouth
Making him look like Grandfather.

I call with a golden orange carrot
From which I have taken the first bite.
He startles from his peaceful day dream
He considers rising to receive his treat
But does not react the pistons
Of his legs and lets me be his servant.
As he takes the carrot he is as loose-lipped as a camel.
We sit together seeming like forever.
In this time and place we are totally of one heart.
For only one hour we are determined to forget the world.

Jamie De Hart

Can We Touch The Rain

Sometimes I sit and wonder,
when the clouds are growing dark, is my time of living over,
Is God going to make his mark?
Sprinkles on my forehead, roll down my face like a stream,
Is this truth or wonder, am I in a dream?

Mistakes are part of living,
we'll remember who died for fame,
Truth will have it known of generations that remain,
They will run for cover when the sky grown dark and grey,
Being sure of one thing,
Dad's never fade away,
Thunder in the distance, shiver in the rain,
a cry in the darkness, something about a name.

Makes me feel closer, makes me feel no pain,
Will it happen all over, will it be the same?
For me, for you, for the ones who feel no shame,
For me, for you, there will never be no pain
For me, for you, it will always be the same.
For me, for you, can we touch the rain?

Amy R. Whitmer

Mischievous St. Bernard

In my back yard lives St. Bernard, he loves to dig for ants
To my surprise before my eyes, he ate my Daddy's pants

Would you believe he ate the sleeve, right off my Mommy's dress
I tried to yell cause I could tell, my dog was in distress

I hugged his neck-he licked my face, we rolled upon the grass
I stood up tall and threw a ball, it broke the front door glass

Here comes my mom what have I done, I don't know what to do
If I confess about the dress, St. Bernard will be all through

I looked at him he looked at me, with a twinkle in his eye
My face turned red I hung my head, I could not tell a lie

About Dad's pants they were full of ants, St. Bernard just did them in
About that dress I must confess, there came a mighty wind

When I stood tall that slippery ball, flew off like a breeze
It hit the door I could say no more, I had to fake a sneeze

Through fingers laced I watched her face, a grin she tried to hide
I kicked the sand she took my hand, I think she knew I lied

I heard her say son, it's o.k., I'll tell you what we'll do
Let's sit right down on the grassy ground,
and I'll keep the both of you.

Norma Bergeron

Crossroads

We fit together you and me
like two peas in a pod
like Laurel and Hardy or Mutt and Jeff
with a natural curiosity for machines
or anything that ticks in the way of the world
and with a way of seeing people without belonging
looking them straight in the eye when unobserved
knowing what they're up to and wondering.

And you greet me, always, with arms wide
with an abundance I've forgotten,
dreams that slipped beyond me
somewhere along the way.
We walk to the crossroads of our lives
and look to the horizon of today
you, dear child, yelling your man-sized wisdom,
"It's never too late to swing from the gate,"
and me, looking back while opening the latch.

Chase Carey and Ellen Carey

Waves Are Sleeping

Not a ripple in sight;
the waves are sleeping.
Birds and breeze have lulled them to dream.
Overhanging trees reach out their fingers,
and dangle their leaves in sweet, mystical water.
Swans glide through flowing silk,
preening themselves in their gently-moving mirror.
Sand is soaked from morning's dew;
footprints travel as far as the beach extends.
Flowers blossom and show their rioting colors;
parading all for the bees.
Clouds caress the shore and float on the horizon,
masking where the earth ends.
No sound save nature speaking,
for there is
not a ripple in sight;
the waves are sleeping.

April M. Rutila

Prolongation

Forgetting so much and remembering so much
Would make anyone hard to touch
Where there would be boldness
There's now only coldness
For you can't forget when you remember.

Any persuasion in any new activity
Would only tend to crush
The living flow of sensitivity
But it would not hush
The remembering that you can't forget.

But you do prolong the issue
For what you've had you've loved so much
And in your poor brain tissue
Lives the soul you yearn to touch
Then you can't remember to forget.

Hattie Anne Supenbeck

Being Black In A White World

I am a young black girl,
Living in a white world.
An obstacle to me is twice as hard,
Because of the color given to me by God.
I can't shop without being questioned,
If so, the size of my pocket has to be mentioned.
Whether or not I am rich or poor,
My color condemns me for sure.
Even if I work hard enough, I don't get the grade I deserve-
Sometimes I feel like telling the teacher about his nerve.
In the media I am always stereotyped,
Why is it that blacks are always in the media hype?
By the police, we are always ridiculed,
Would it be the same way if we ruled?
The drugs, the diseases, and the crime are like modern day slavery,
Is that just another one of their conspiracies to get rid of me?
From the beginning of time up until now,
Hopefully this world will change, someway, somehow.

Ayana Greene

Facing Your Anger

Hardship is what we're faced with.
The anger just comes out like a bolt of lightning.
Not knowing where it is going to strike next.
The thunder roars, and the rain falls, who am I?
Why am I doing this? The hours pass by.
There's a smoothness in the air.
The sun comes out and there's a rainbow above.
Now I know.
It's a thing called love!

Lynda Mock

My Father's Garden

Had I known that there was a danger of being
switched in the cradle at birth,
I probably wouldn't have slept so much as an infant
Now I fight to stay awake
Fearful, that if I go to sleep, I'll turn into my father
And repeat yet another generation of trying to switch
babies in their cradles

As I look back on my childhood, I've forgiven myself
for trying to stand too close to my father. It was after all,
a child's effort to get a father to see me for who I am
Instead, he saw me as an effort gone bad,
His last chance for a son to be everything he was and more

As I watched him tend his garden in
in rows that he had plowed so straight
As I watched him carefully and meticulously lift the
small vegetation and plant it in the rich fertile soil
And as I watched him day after day nurture these plants
And praying to God that they would grow up to be healthy and strong
Momentarily I forgot myself and stood close to him again
Hoping that he would see that he planted me too

Marla K. Ferguson

Sleep

It eludes me like a blinking firefly
I grasp it for awhile, but if per chance
through childish curiosity I peek, it is gone.

What is this murky mist that lodges in my brain
and transports me to unfamiliar places with strange faces?

Why won't it let me float on fluffy clouds to landscapes
bright and clear, full nights of peaceful bliss?

What must I do to extend this restful time, perhaps a pill
or repetitious counts of wooly lambs or numbers that reverse?

Perhaps the early morning songs of birds will call it back to cradle
me a bit.

Another day of work and play without the precious gift of sleep.

Robert M. Underwood

Mourning

I sit beside his grave
past memories haunt me
the times we laughed together and others
I would sit on his lap while he told me stories of
mystical lands, fairies and princesses

I glance away from the tombstone
unable to bear the sight of his name
"No!" I scream "He isn't dead!"
A comforting voice reminds me
"He's dead my child, now come home to eat; your supper's getting
cold."

I begin to run
I don't care where
anywhere but here
Tears stream down my checks like rivers
my legs move as a machine
until they finally collapse, unable to move any farther
I fall to the cold hard earth
"No, no," I sob, "he isn't dead."

Alison Filley

My Truck Drivin' Man

When I look at you I feel I love and desire
As you possess such qualities in a man, I greatly admire
Your determination and strength make my mind grow strong
With you, my love, is where I'll always belong
Your consideration and tenderness makes me feel such pleasure
For the happiness we'll share together is beyond any measure
You touch my heart and my soul as no one else can
You're my love, my life, my truck drivin' man
Your thoughtfulness and honesty I cherish deeply with pride
As I'll walk hand in hand with you right by your side
I long for your kiss and your gentle caress
For each day I'll love you more and never once any less
Your courage and your dreams make my spirits soar high
I know I'd follow you to the ends of the earth and never ask why
Your love and your trust fills my body with emotion
Only you, my darling have my everlasting devotion
And as you leave for the road, I feel such sorrow
Clinging only to memories and dreams of tomorrow
You touch my heart, and my soul as no one else can
You're my love, my life, my truck drivin' man.

Mari Wieberg

People Come And Go

People come and go throughout our lives.
Some stay then quickly go, others fade slowly away.

Some people you will remember forever, others you
will forget. You will want to remember some, but you will
forget. Then there are others you would like to forget,
but will still remember through the years that had passed
in the sights of your eyes.

But you shall never forget the times that you had
with the people and never the friends that you made.

Just remember the good times, and forget the bad.
Remember the people who made a difference. It doesn't
matter if they're young, old, short or tall, funny or
weird. It doesn't matter what they look like, or how they
sound to you. The only thing that matters is that they
were kind enough to be a friend.

Just remember one thing never forget the people that
come and go in and out of our lives.

Tamara Ann Thompson

Entertaining Angels

If you had never flown what beauty you would have never known
Go ahead look down some round, some squared, some pied, looks
tho someone could not decide to make it big to leave it small
to leave it short or make it tall

The patch work quilt of green and blue all the colors ran so true
The awesome clouds against the sky
who would have ever known the grandeur in the sky

Look close and you may see the Angels frolicking in the air
As we watch, they don't care they are saying, have some fun
before your time on earth is done as I look into the sky
Somehow I'm not afraid to die

Terrocotta green and gold what beauty to behold and
If the truth be told, be bold look out, to catch a glimpse of
Angels frolicking about

As you kaleidoscope down to the ground, you may see a
small little town filled with a mountain and
a stream and of course somebody's dreams

As you look through clouds of cotton candy, admire the beauty
down below, there's so much beauty to behold, a beauty I'd
have never known, if I hadn't flown.

Pam Cox

Black Hands Of Death

Lying underneath the sky on warm summer nights
Wishing upon every star in sight
Swinging higher and higher trying to touch the sky
Sharing our lives and our dreams,
Don't you remember what love means?
Growing together, laughing together
I thought you would be mine forever
Now you belong to the heaven above,
The one I can only dream of
You swore you wouldn't ever leave me,
And now I will die only with your memory
No more lying underneath the sky
No more wishing upon the stars
No more listening to the wind's sweet lullaby
No more trying to touch the sky
Because I have fallen, finally fallen into the black hands of death.

Brandi Autry

Butterflies

Thank you, Lord, for butterflies;
Like winged jewels flitting by,
Bedecked in colors so sublime
That cheer and charm the watching eye.

Remind us, now, that short time since,
These lovely creatures were not so
Earthbound as lovely caterpillar.
They little knew that they would grow.

And change as in the twinkling of an eye,
No longer bound in dust to crawl,
But lifted up on silken wings,
Reborn and free. Now may we all

Be mindful of this sign you've give,
That we like they someday will rise
Transformed, renewed with heavenly bodies
To live with you in Paradise.

Helen Elois Brown

The Leaving

No matter what beauty, what grandeur is beyond
I shall feel sad on leaving here.
All the delights to which heart and mind respond,
All this loveliness I shall leave - with a sigh, and a tear.

Ann McGough

Lifeblood

Yes, I exist in every beginning,
As I shall remain after all ends.
You are now what we have created in our past.
Something wonderful.

I've transversed galaxies for eons of time
While you continue to develop me.
Falling ...... from a zenith far beyond
What light can see.

I carry the air that is breathed
By you and all leaves.
I carry the horses that are raced
And your neighbor's porsche
That sets your pace.

I carry the medicine that transcends
An uneven balance between mind and body;
Ameliorating the natural state of peace within.

I carry the source inside you!
Another way in which to celebrate
Vast spaces of blue.

Mark C. Campbell

A Mother's Challenge

A cool sea breeze blew softly across the
field of fresh cut hay
Inviting me to breath deeply of the bay's
salt spray.
The scent cut sharply into the sweetness
of the new mown clover,
Reminding me these glad Maine days
would soon be over.
My two little boys in white sailor hats
khaki clad, tan and wide eyed,
Fished for flounders, pollack or
tom-cod on the rising-tide.
They can't recall now just what
they caught
Or how long and hard their catches
fought,
But I remember, I'll never forget.
For me, what nerve it took
To take the sculpins off
The hook.

Marshall Jamison

Freedom's Window

In the stillness of the room,
Worn and wrinkled hands
Lay folded on a flowered square..
Sunshine on the faded roses
Brightens drab surroundings.

Gnawing hunger pangs, cupboards bare...
The wait in lines so wearing;
Reaching, grabbing...for a meager ration.
At freedom's window, hoping, praying,
For a world of plenty, free of tyranny.

How long, how long, will it be
Before the gnawing overtakes...
And freedom's window doesn't look so great.
For years the hammer and the sickle
Have shadowed golden, bulging, spires.

Shine brightly now with your golden tones...
For all who gallantly have fought,
For freedom, hope, and prosperity.
May it not have been in vain...
For the light of freedom's window!

Elaine Rivas

Virtuous Woman

Created from the gentle side of Man;
By the grace of God take your stand.
In elevation is where you are found;
You were taken from man's Rib, not from the ground.

Virtuous woman! The Bible values you
Higher than rubies and pearls;
God created you to be the only door
that brings man into the world.
You were never designed to be man's
competition; you're better than that,
You're the inspiration that fuels his ambition.
Sometimes misunderstood, neglected and abused;
But you have always been the first in line for God to use.

Virtuous woman! Anointed, graced and
called with a destiny to claim:
Just like Ruth, Sarah, Ester, Deborah,
and other women to be named.

God bless you wherever you are and from wherever you came;
you are God's virtuous woman destined for
His hall of fame.

Danny Ray McCullough

The Longest Day

The day dawned cool and crisp.
Glistening dew, moistening the earth
under a heavy blanket of fog.
Trapping the world beneath its soft embrace.

The sparkling sun shone down,
warming the air, burning the dew.
Greenness permeated the waking
while the early innocence disappeared.

Midday brought stifling heat.
Suffocating warmth and bright light
were given off by the fiery sun above.
All action slowed, paralyzed by afternoon.

The shower came without warning,
dampening the earth and cooling the air.
Evening was ushered in by the refreshing rain,
the waning heat diminishing.

With evening came peacefulness,
an escape from the busyness of day.
All living things were seen in a new, relaxed light.
Night came, with sad finality.

Ryan L. McKimmie

Past, Present And Future

The past is something you cannot replace,
And the future is something that you cannot chase.
The present is happening at this time and place,
And the future depends on the decisions we make.
The past has happened long ago,
And what the future holds I do not know.
As we speak the present is becoming the past,
But the memories will always last.
The future can depend on what we do or say,
And the present goes on from day to day.
While everything be a blur,
There will always be the past, present, and future.

Katie Peterson

Six Long Months

It's been a roller coaster ride, up and down, through fear, tears and Pride.
Happiness that used to be, seems so distant now to me.
Now I'm wondering, pondering why? Will our love live or will it die?
Crying...crying...crying inside. In the silence of the night I
Sing a broken heart lullaby.
It's been six long months for you and I.
The wedding bells ring no more, and the vows we both expressed could
Not endure, the anger, distress or rage, oh how I long to remember
The joy of our wedding day.
I miss your touch, I'm in need of your embrace, I long to feel your
Lips softly tracing my face. Your smile and wit, your dreams and
more—Is this
How it feels when you have someone no more?
It's been six long months for you and I.
Still nothing has been resolved, and the world we have tried to share,
has slowly dissolved. Yet, I know, there's a reason to all of this
Travail, and always true love it does prevail.
Please don't give up—don't let go—for ahead of us there are six
More months to go.

Monica Adrianne Jones

Untitled

Whatever God or Gods there be
Who shape the paths of destiny,
One thing, I beg you selfishly,
To give to your creation - me.

Faith in myself; so I can stand
Tall and strong, though the path be lone;
For lacking this, the task at hand
Might turn the softest heart to stone.
And stone could never know the feel
I deeply need to play my part,
Or live full rich, or try to heal
The hurts that lie within my heart.

So grant, I pray, my earnest plea
As to your hands of destiny
I now deliver trustingly
This child of your creation - Me.

Marjorie Young

Blood Moon

Delicate rays illuminate the night sky
Like fingers clawing distant space
The fingers of a pale white moon amidst
An endless blanket of blackness

Look unto me, it cryeth
As I raise my eyes to its hideous smiling face
Blood and death revealed to me
From many a century ago

Commanding the skies
In the small hours of day
Our forefathers from long ago
Bring sacrifices unto thee

With every bloody murder
Every scream induced by fellow hand
Your knowing smile grew wider
Your anger appeased by human hand

So now I leave you and your stories
Your victims and your slaves
While gentle clouds shields us
By hiding your venomous face

Jennifer Patrick Durdall

First Grandchild

Look over there, at the child in the chair,
The one with the dimples and book,
He's reading the pages, he's been reading for ages,
This dear little boy with the curls in his hair.

When he's through with his book, he may start to cook,
Some French toast or coffee for Mommy,
Or play Boats-in-the harbor, or even play Barber,
This dear little boy with the serious look.

I'm his Sweetheart you know, he tells me so,
He's so generous with his hugs and his kisses,
He's old as can be, two going on three,
This dear little boy-on-the-go.

He's Grandpa's hired man, a most tired man,
When they work on the tractor all day,
And he tries very hard, helping Dad in the yard,
This dear little boy, little man.

I look in his face, and I see a far place,
And I wonder what life has in store?
He may stumble and fall, but he'll stand above all,
This dear little boy, in Life's Race.

Betty Gay Gackstetter

"Without My Love"

Sleep on my love, sleep on.
As the stars begin to shine
dream your dreams of yesterday,
the days that you were mine.

Now your life is over, but
your soul is ever resting
up in Heaven, back
where it was before

Yes, I miss you each day that passes by.
Life without you is not the same, but
I know that I too will soon be with you
back from where we came.

William V. Dorman

Imagine

Resting in a solitary place, where an imagination runs
wild, with hopes of a future that may never come.
Claiming all in its path with a hopeful whisper and a
consoling smile.
Where a place of happiness is far away, and with only
dark thoughts to show me the way; where is hope in this
desolate place?
Around a corner?
Or in a mothers embrace?
Does happiness come to those who wait?
Or dose it pass by with a scornful laugh?
But as all things it will end, my dark cloud will lift,
like a smile or a pretty song it can't last forever.
Then happiness will come to warm like a gentle breeze
after a harsh winter...

Amber Evans

Untitled

Well, now I'm here,
but you're nowhere near.
Here comes one single tear,
and one single ring in my ear.
I can hear the sound of the bell,
as I lay here, after I fell.
But where are you?
You said you'd be here too.
I thought you where true,
but you're just like everyone's else I've ever knew.
Why do you do this to me?
Can't you see?
But you can't see me on my knees.
My heart is in pain,
it causes the rain,
and I let it soak in, as I go insane.
As the rain fell on my head,
I remembered everything you said.
Then here comes dawn,
and so I have to be gone.

Elizabeth Mae Ashley

Love

Love is something nice, funny and charming
it will make you laugh when you're sad
cry when you're down,
kiss you on the cheek,
and tuck you in at night.

When you say "I love you," it makes you feel
nice, funny, and charming,
warm when you are cold,
strong when you are weak,
and that's what love is all about.

Megan A. Seville

Perish With You

For there's a vision, we need to see, for without it, we all perish.
Our duration, select a seedling tree, for in number and disparate
they are, so are we.
With proper care and suitable environment, it'll weather any storm,
it'll come through.
Squirmy roots, never perfectly strait, sinks deeper steadying its
pride and sharing its view.
Towering branches reach the air, waiting to shade sometime by just
being there.
A revealing difference, if proper care isn't provided, then a tree
sapped indubitably.
Without leaves, fruit, and shade; it's through.
Now a dried mess that awaits a cleaning crew.
The tree that couldn't weather the storms.
A final blow from wind or man comes.
Those dutiful crew people will burn and bury this unsightly stuff!
Unfortunately that omits suggestion, position of difficulty, and
urgency for me and you.
The things that gives us reason to learn may be how to care for you
Nonetheless, we'll just purchase again, and maybe perish with you.

Betty Jean Campbell

The Three In One

It created the earth when God spoke the word
It created life and man out of dust
It planted a seed and God's Son was born,
and the Son died on a cross for all He was torn
It raised Jesus the Son again to life, and He
went to the Father and sent help for our strife
It dwells in believers, the help He provides
you'll find it only as you give Him your life
It is God
It is the Holy Spirit
It is Jesus God's Son
It is the three in one

Jeanne Sharp

The Cheetah

The cheetah is swift and sleek,
Its body like an arrow,
Its teeth are like a million beaks,
Its feet fly like a sparrow.
It hunts by day,
To kill its prey,
It can get very close,
And in the night,
It dreams to fight,
And better at that than most.
An antelope sounds mighty tasty,
When they are close, cheetah's won't be hasty,
Cheetahs eat fast because of lions,
Hyenas, and leopards come a climbing.
With 2 feet tall and 3 feet long,
That's good enough for me,
A tail that is 2 feet long,
And big eyes that can see,
I wouldn't want to be so close,
Or else I'd be dead meat!

Jennifer C. Leavitt

Oh, Boy!

Sally, my little sister is a pain!
She went out in the rain...
collected some rain and poured it on me!
Then, she said she tripped
and ripped my homework in half.
After that she said she hated me,
mom heard that and thought it was Me!
A few minutes later she got a bump on her head.
She told dad I jumped on her head.
Ten seconds after that she said it was a joke.
She started to poke me.
Then mom and dad came in the room and said...
that we should be friends! Oh, Boy!!!!

Erika Wright

Drifting Beauty

Oh, how I loved to stare out my window at her.
With her long, sandy hair blowing freely in the breeze.
Her delicate, white dress, lace at her knees.
Her eyes mirrored the deep ocean, while absorbing its colors.
Small juvenile hands withheld tiny seashells streaked with
stained colors of a rainbow.
Petite bare feet stood on white sand, and her toes dug down in it.
Staring among the waves, she cast a shadow and her shells,
for she would never see them again -
Nor the sea gulls, sunset, moon or stars.
Now I gaze out my window to the deserted shore.
Where I can't treasure the precious child who I see no more.
A tear smoothly rolls from my eye
as I weakly stand up and say good-bye.
A child with a beautiful soul has died
For she's been taken by the tide.

Angela Chelini

Chant Of The Naked Moon

The chant of the naked, ivory moon
Awoke me one placid night.
Her airy song held yesterday's whispers.
Its somber tune was light.

I wondered why she sang so mournfully.
It made no sense to me.
Perhaps the desolate moon was lonely
And yearned for company.

So I journeyed to my window,
To listen to her song,
But only silence greeted me.
The ghostly notes were gone.

I glanced up the poor, sweet being,
Lighting the cool, night sky.
Could it be that she took comfort,
From such a sight as I?

How could a spirit be so alone?
The answer to this made me numb.
For out of my lips and into the air,
Came a faint and haunting hum.

Lauren Ann-Veronica Sciacca

"To Sam, My Beautiful Boy"

You gave me so much happiness for one year
Letting me take care of you and love you
And I'm so happy for the time together that God gave us.
You were a free spirit all of your life
And now you are free to roam in His green pastures forever.

So I send my love to you
And may you rest in peace
Sam, My Beautiful Boy

Suzanne A. Cannata

The Secretman

The secretman sleeps with clenched fists
that open only to my touch.
I kiss his coiled hand
making it ease its whitened fingers.
Making them released their abused past.

I touch the hardened place on his jaw bone-
the tight springs of a posturepedic mattress,
awakening anything.
I kiss the soft place between his collarbones-
the hurricane's fleshy "eye"
at its peace..

He flutters his gold lashes at me-
butterflies working out for their journey home.
One two, one two,
one.

He disappears into his night terrors,

eyes closed - moving toward the clench he is at home with.

His sleeping acceptance of me

Is
no longer mine.

Deanna L. Esz

Untitled

I feel it tightening slowly in my chest.
Building till I feel ready to explode.
Following wherever I go, always there.
Closing around like a cool mornings fog.
Never will it leave me, always holding.
Dragging me into a world of nothing
Every breath I take struggles to be released.
Praying for someone's help, yet it does not come.
Tears spill from my eyes, stopping as quickly as they started.
Showing no emotion I get up
Forcing myself to live another day
But yet I am still here, alone,
Stranded in my own world,
Never to be released.

Christina Klachko

Wanting In

You hold me high in the air,
For all the world to see.
Yet you hide away in your own world away from me.
You make it seem that we live in the same place.
Yet we don't!
In separate worlds is where we stand.
I try to get to your world,
But you shut me out.
I let you in my world and still it's not the same.
Our love is growing apart.
Holding on is what I'm doing.
Changing is what your doing.
Life is what's taking place.
Will our love survive or will it die?
Our lives are changing;
Yet what we don't realize is that our love isn't
Changing with us.
All I know is I'll always be here,
And loving you is what I'll do forever.
Letting go completely I'll never dare dream of.

Adrian Josette Bocanegra

Mirror Images

We are black they are white,
But that's no reason for us to fight.
Without each other we both know,
There's no way our country can grow.
Deep inside we're all the same,
We have one heart and only one brain.
To thrive as a country here's what we must do,
Not use the brain of one, but combine the two.
To form a mind rich in culture and also prejudice free,
to make this country a better place for all of us to be.
We could remain ignorant and still continue to fight,
Slaughtering one another for our remaining days and nights.
In the end when it's over, we will all be dead,
Man, woman, black, and white, our blood will all be red!

Eric Williams

A Winter Hunt

Frozen snow collapsing under heavy boots
Sends booming echoes through ice laden trees!

Scarf covered faces breathe out white mist
Like steam engines standing on end.

Voices shout on the hillside,
Hunters drive and watch for the elusive deer.

Many come to share this winter experience,
To bond again with nature and fellow men.

To find their battered manhood
Lost somewhere, back there,

In civilization....

Frederick A. Kenworthy

Her Day

Filtering through her veil,
a warm southern breeze lifted her hair.
She walked, flowers in hand, down the soft grassy path,
arm in arm, with her father, a man in his sixties.
The fresh morning dew glistened in the bright sunlight as the
birds, dancers in the sky,
flew gracefully throughout the trees.
They continued, calmly stepping, until they came upon
a group of flowers, arranged in a basket at the side.
Her father picked them up and kept walking,
trying to hold back the tears.
Every step, filled with uncertainty, became slower.
Her mother waiting, she finally reached the end of the path
with her father.
He, eyes filled with tears, gave her a kiss.
She looked before her, at a tree, a weeping willow.
Then, light tears falling to her cheeks,
she knelt down to place the flowers on her mother's grave.

Daniel Paul Dorszynski

"The Rose Of Life"

A rose is a beautiful thing.
How it blossoms is another thing.
Watch its shape and its form.
Its smell will truly make you warm.

For that rose was a beautiful thing.
How it blossomed and how it made you spring.
For its magic was so very there.
It's no wonder why people stared.

So when in there you happen to see
A rose with better leaves. Take the
time to lend a hand to nature
What life should be. The rose of life
that should be set free.

Chad Dootson

A Tear In Our Eye

Dunblaine, Scottland,
Where 17 died.
16 children, and a teacher beside.

A day that started,
With learning and fun.
But the day soon ended, by a man with a gun.

The man had already chosen,
To kill himself.
But why kill the children,
The fruit of our wealth.

When the news poured out, of those who died.
The whole world died, a little inside.

We bow down our heads, on our cheeks, rolls a tear.
How can someone kill, the children so dear.

Sixteen children, are now layed to rest.
Along with the teacher, that did her best.

They now rest in God's arms, all safe and sound,
Away from the violence, that holds us all bound.

You'll always be missed, with a tear in our eye.
To those who where killed, we love you, Goodbye.

Gerald Kempke

Untitled

Thinking of you, constantly.
You fill my mind, my heart, my soul.

You've given me wings!
I look upon the vistas of life before me with awe.

Soaring; feeling the power within me growing.
Gyring and gliding into love.
Winds of change inspire me.

I hear your call, encouraging me higher, ever higher.
I look up and see you there leading me, loving me.

There are no walls or barriers where we fly together.
Reaching beyond the limits we stretch; we climb, ever upward,
ever onward!

Kenny Beeks

Reaction To Rejection

One day she was my best friend.
The next, she was not.
I had just arrived late, after my date,
He said "she doesn't want to speak to you."
It was the worst rejection I have ever experienced

Maybe he made her do it.
He never did like me.
He probably felt that our friendship ruined,
His and hers,
Lost and gone forever.

I don't know what happened.
We were best friends.
We told each other everything.
She knew how I felt;
I knew how she felt.

There as a psychic ability between us.
I could read hers and her mine.
As soon as the separation took place,
All was lost forever.
I'm not sad, just MT.

Ellen Sue Eickholt

Our Flag

So many words o'er the years have been written
Of the Grand Old Flag whenever it was fitting.
Into battles the red, white, and blue
Carried forth to be tested, found to be true.

Frances Scott Key found the right words to say
While the battle raged on, men to rest were laid.
Forever the stars and stripes they will stand
Tall and majestic across our great land.

At Iwo Jima a few proud Marines
Fought with their lives for a precious dream.
To end the war and bring peace forever
No matter the cost and its long endeavor.

On and on the battles have raged
As countless men have set the stage.
For the Grand Old Flag forever to fly
Waving lofty and mighty in the sky.

May the red, white, and blue forever be
A shining example for all to see.
While oppression you see is on every hand
Think of the flag as it represents our free land.

Sharon L. Piggott

Ode To A Beautiful Place

The sun awakens from the mighty deep.
Big white clouds, high, in the brilliant blue sky.
Footprints up a sand dune nature made steep.
Oh my! Magnificent kites fly so high.
Feeling the tease of a sweet summer's breeze.
Sailboats drifting along an endless coast.
Crashing waves eroding sand castle walls.
Diving for a frisbee, white sandy knees.
Barnacles growing on a wooden post.
Kids with a ball chasing one loud sea gull.

The sting of saltwater hitting the face.
A cool, calm breeze fills the evening air.
The sun disappears to its resting place.
Mauve colored sunset, lovers kissing, stare.
Tiny little specks fill the vagrant sky.
Out of the clear glows a wonderful sphere.
Echoes in the tranquillity of night.
Only the rising tide gives a reply.
Lightening in the distance, have no fear.
Oh! What a beautiful and soothing sight.

Andrew J. Popp

Walking With Grandpa

When I walk with grandpa
I feel so proud.
He's not too fast.
He's not too slow.
We stop and watch things
as we go past.
We watch the water fall
As I feel so tall.
We like to watch the horses
As they buck and neigh.
We like to watch the colt
with its wobbly legs.
We walk and watch the mountains
as they change from purple to pink to blue.
When I get home my mom says to me,
"Homework isn't done, is it?"
I love
to walk with
grandpa.

Laura Weakland

Love And Like

In a world full of love and like a girl meets a boy.
She loves him. He loves her.
She lets him go and a part of her dies.
He likes her. She loves him.
She wins his heart once more.
She loves him. He loves her.
Like a fool she lets him go.
She loves him.
He loves another.
Quietly her heart breaks.
Once more she wins his heart.
And again she lets him go.
She likes him. He loves her.
She likes him. He likes her.
They finally think the cycle is broken.
She leaves.
She loves him. He? Her.

Lori Mullins

Out Past

Out past apocalyptic cities, there exists a path
where a gnome has roamed for forty-five and a half
years and sheds tears in the bitter December mist
on the edge of a cliff in a straw adobe by aborigines
who live in trees, faces painted with mud, the elf with blood
on his midget face, with a shine in his impish eyes
for passersby. He's full of riddles to tell
and homemade fiddles to sell. I sometimes wonder
how far he's wandered with three-inch feet, wading knee deep
in shallow water puddles in the drizzling rain

Out past neon signs and garbage dumps there still remains
clouds that have never thundered, where life's discreet,
secrets to keep from governments that fail. In the woods asunder
an elfin cries, and walks down his lonely trail
a sack on his back full of burgundy and rye
his mind full of memories that never was. He never does
become tempted to resist what's written on ledger as his destiny
Near a creaking pier on a pond where no fish exist,
he sits alone, avoiding fiascos of ruined societies' urbanized crap.
For impeached senators he feels no pity, at their misfortune he
merely laughs.

Nick Jackson

The Beauty You Created

Early in the morning, when the house
is quiet, and the children are asleep.
The beauty of the desert I so enjoy.
Joyful I feel when I see a butterfly
If one at all, for little by little, they have disappeared.
From my view, I see the majestic
mountains, so high as if reaching for the heavens.
You have adorn the mountains with
wild flowers, so many colors of purple, gold, yellow white and pink.
Is so breath taking it brings joy to my heart.
A paradise you have created, but we see it not.
The trees to rest under, flower you fragrance the air with.
The sun to bask in. the moon to stroll by.
Your blueness of the sky for pointers to paint.
The snow to play in Spring a time to fall in love again.
But your most beautiful creation of all is us, the human race.
The beauty is within us, you have created.

Carmen A. Hernandez

A Detrimental Era

When I was young my mind was too small, yet too confused,
to realize the real prejudice still here in this world.
Now I hear words from mouths hateful enough, to bring down a country.
To me all colors of the rainbow are beautiful,
but why can't everyone see, what racism is doing to thee?
I see the world before me, as if it just hit me,
like a knife into the back.
Our country has been back stabbed by the unusually large minority,
of people in which non-racist thoughts and minds is something they lack.
This problem is imaginable to some peoples astray little minds,
wandering from one joke to the next.
They don't see the problem we have, as if they're blind but they're not deaf.
They hear expressions and put-downs day after day full of hate.
Our world is like a fragile flower,
A petal inside each of us,
If some petals wilt, it ruins the beauty of the flower.
Maybe with a little care, a little love, a little sunshine our
flower may grow.

Michelle Tutungian

The Peace Keepers

These two soldier boys
Volunteered for peace keeping
In a distant land
They planned to marry
Their childhood sweet hearts
When they had peace
All across that land
But they never returned
And didn't get the heroes welcome
They never heard
The church bells ring
Or with their brides join hands
They never heard the beating of the drums
Or the marching of the bands
They were buried in unmarked graves
On foreign soil
In a faraway land

Edward B. Koski

"Little Cherubs"

Aspirations of solemates, monies and happiness...
we all desire...
Yet most do not dare believe our "Little Cherubs"
guiding us in every way to achieve.

In these times of great distress, our guardian angels
are ever near, watching over us,
bringing... if only momentary...
an inner calm, to dwindle our fears
and make us aware...
their presence and enlightenment are forever
and all may share.

Instilled is our belief in life and human nature...
for not only in spirit but also in the kindness'
of those amongst us.

Every step we take, feelings of happiness or sadness,
when friends can no longer endure...
our "Little Cherubs" are there helping our
spirits soar!

They guide us through the darkest hours,
helping us to see...
how beautiful... **People**... **Creatures** and **Earth**
are and can always be!

Mary Elizabeth Baiker

Untitled

Memories are beautiful to remember
But memories are the past
I am the present and walking toward the future

I treasured memories people once gave me
And keep them "a special place" in my heart
But the present in here to live and enjoy

Now and then, memories fly me back to the past
It was happy, it was sad
Somehow it was beautiful
I laughed, I cried
I lived and I loved
But I couldn't be there forever

I am the present with memories to remember
I am walking toward the future
Memories may play games with the future
But the future I won't be able to see
I can only leave it to the fate
The fate would probably have all the answers

Tosh Asada

Stairs Of Life

I walk
down the
stairs of
life hoping
not to slip,
hoping not to
fall. I walk
down the stairs
of life going back
to the beginning. Back
to the beginning of my
life, back to the beginning
of time. I walk down the
stars of life hoping not
to slip hoping not to fall.
I walk down the stairs of life.

Melissa Ludwick

A Single Wish

I'm about to do something I've never done before.
Right now I'm going to express my feelings.
Even though it's too late to say anything to you.
I have to tell you what is in my heart.
My whole life I've waited for someone special.
And then one day I found you and fell in love.
You gave me a love that I took for granted.
Now I realize that was a complete fool.
I have one single wish and that's to be with you.
My days were always full of sunshine when you came around.
Life with you was great until I messed it up.
I wish I could make it up to you somehow.
Please forgive me for the way I acted.
My heart never knew the meaning of love.
You tried to show me and I pushed you away.
Even though we're apart I thank you.
For telling me that I need to express my feelings.
I enjoyed what little time we had together.
Just to be able to get back together with you.
Is my one single wish.

Heka King

A Broken Promise

I knew all the weak things in his heart.
Could not say what I felt, always had to be on guard.
Loved him so much, that I almost was blind,
To his faults and sins and tried to be kind.
Temptation around me bid me to waver,
I prayed to be better, a little braver.
To try much harder to be a little meeker,
With the one I loved, who I knew was weaker.
Then one night he left, never to return.
From friends, many people so much good advice,
Then be judged by a court, what a horrible price.
Oh God do protect him, but don't give him peace,
Keep me also and don't let my prayers cease.
To love Thee so much that I can be forgiven,
For my sins, my faults, so that I can go on living.
God show me in time that this is Thine way,
And always have a prayer for the one who went astray.

Tryn R. Schettler

Love Is

Love is a warm hug, when the world leaves you cold.
Love is a sunny smile, when nights darkness holds.
Love is cool spring water, when you are desert dry
from, the swift passing of surrogate love.

Love is pain that rips at you until survival is the thing to fear.
Love is tears that fall, from eyes red and sad.
Enough to fill the seas, should God's Grace grant you,
life filled with emotion.

Love is a baby's first smile, a toddlers look of pride when,
tentatively, taking his first stride.

Love is a cats purr, a dogs trust, a mothers touch. A fathers
cautious talk, about the birds and bees, when fledglings spread and
try their wings.

Love is a grandson, seen the first day of life. Then later
claiming,
with twinkling eyes, "Gramma, "I'm trying to use the pot!

God gave us love in all its many forms.
To me the answer is simple; love is happiness, love is pain.
Love is loss, love is gain.
Love is strangers, "passing in the night,"
Love is family, that continues to give me life.

Deborah R. Chepinski

There's Got to be a Way

A broken man without a home.
Desperate and so alone, a victim
of society that no one really wants to see.
Some of us don't even wonder.
Some of us don't even care.
Couldn't we just help each other?
Isn't there enough to share?
He made it happen, he placed so much joy
into our hands what we dreamed
we finally recaptured heaven took command.
Losing my mind, from this hollow in my heart,
suddenly I'm so incomplete.
Lord I'm needing you now.
Tell me how to stop the rain.
Tears are falling down endlessly.

Jill Wisneski

Circles

Contemplation...
Contemplating where I was and where I am.
Contemplating where I am and where I will be.

Looking at my savings account.
Looking at what it wasn't and what it is.
Looking at what it is and what it will be.

Thinking about family so far away.
Thinking about what it was and what it is.
Thinking about what it is and what it will be.

Thinking about old girl friends.
Thinking about my wife.
Thinking about wanting children and contemplating having them.

Contemplating responsibility...and trying to evade it.
Thinking about life and contemplating death.

Looking at circles and thinking about being a part of one.
Life....

Gary C. Stenson

"Him"

I saw him from across the room
And my heart ignored its steady rhythm.

As he approached me in his silence,
I felt my heart no longer mine.

As we danced I held him tightly;
Looking into his eyes, my reflection smiled.

I had long ago dreamed of this night,
And suddenly realized my dream a reality.

He was so much more than I had envisioned-
Gentle, honest, trusting, and especially kind.

He danced with only me that memorable night,
And then every night forever after.

For this man I love is my dear husband;
A more sincere love I could never find.

And I shall never have the need to search.
I am generously blessed, my dreams given life.

Pauline Roy

Daybreak

In the moments before dawn a gray mist hangs over the earth
  Like a thin curtain that will open soon
    Unveiling the morning.
Slowly the mist dissipates.
  The sun begins to push its way upward over the eastern horizon.
    The shadows become darker and more distinct.
The sun continues its climb upward.
  Suddenly it frees itself from the mountains' grip,
    And it is morning.

Sally Orbin

Rapture

Should one feel rapture when they finally
  capture the love of their life?

Is it right to feel genial after completing
  a menial task?

Can a girl feel joyous about being boyish
  over wearing mens' clothing?

Should a fruit lover be merry after eating
  some home - grown cherries?

Yes!

Gilberto Guzman Gonzalez

She Waits

By the sea she waits, as a child for his mother.
She waits, not knowing.

Looking at the water, her face glowing, eyes shining like the sun.
She stares, not knowing.

She remembers the beautiful times, how they spent each and every moment together.
Their love strong, as the waves rush before her.
She remembers, not knowing.

Patiently she waits for the ship, all her thoughts on him.
Thinking of the moment they'll meet again.
She smiles, not knowing.

One thought passes through her, "Why are there wars, why did they take him away from me so long?"
But she musn't think of that now, he'll be coming soon.
She looks, not knowing.

The ship is coming now. Laughing, overjoyed with excitement, she runs through the crowd that waits on the harbor.
She laughs, not knowing.

As the well-dressed men walk off the ship, hugs and kisses fill the air.
But weeping is heard now, where are the rest?
She watches, not knowing.

They're all leaving now, where is he?
She waits impatiently, hoping to see him walk out to her.
There's no one.
She stands alone, now knowing.

Sheryl Mellinger

Cries Of An Endangered People

A lush green mountain, shrouded in mist...
Quietly, a silver back gorilla sits,
Peacefully munching on leaves.
His deep brown eyes reveal a tranquil soul.

He looks about with an air of strength and dignity,
As he watches over his dominion.
His weight equaling that of three men.
Impressively, he stands and beats his chest,
A magnificent being of God's creation.

Violently, he charges with fire in his eyes and teeth bared.
Humans attack with spears and machetes gleaming...
Screaming and carrying their young, the others flee for safety.

A mighty warrior,
With bloody spears in his chest and side,
Throws an assailant nearly thirty feet,
As another hacks off his hand...

Slowly, the others return, one bulging with his child,
With shrieks of grief they crowd around,
His great body lay headless in the blood stained grass...
His mighty hands, gone....made into ashtrays.

Emilie C. Artacho

Free Clinic

He forced himself in,
stood ashamed in front of the main desk.
His face a sickly shade of white,
bones forcing their way through the skin.
He waited for the nurse to announce
if the HIV test come out
positive or negative.
Then, seeing the grim look on her face,
he stormed out of the building
in a tearful rage wishing, hoping
he could some way alter the past.

Angie LaCoy

Columbia History And Celilo

In 1792 Captain Gray
Explored and sailed unto the "Oregon"
And named "Columbia", the scenic one
With powerful flow thru sculptured walls and may
Become a torrent rush where fish display
Their leaping feats at Wyam Falls - Eon
Of time, long past - for Wyam Falls is gone
(Submerged by dams). Wind surfers sail and play!
"Celilo"
Gone are basalt bluffs with seething water force
And raging rapid falls - gone are men who wait
With spears and nets to catch the leaping salmon
The floods for power! Men build their dams on course,
Forgetting treaties and Indian fate.
No Indians! No Falls! No salmon!
Gone the rushing falls with roaring sounds.
Gone are ancient Indian fishing grounds.
"Celilo"

H. Payne B. Webb

In My Father's Eyes

I don't recall the first time I looked into those eyes,
But I'm sure they were filled with wonder, elation, and surprise.
I know the smile within his heart began to slowly rise,
And gave away his feelings with the love that filled his eyes.

Into those soft brown depths, that looked on from above,
I looked for what I always found, never-ending love.
As years have passed, I learned to easily recognize
The knowledge and the wisdom also held within those eyes.

I could see the worry, the sorrow, and the pain,
But somehow ever-faithfully, they'd fill with love again.
And in the pathway of his sight, I learned to grow and live,
Showered with every happiness that a human could ever give.

And today I still look for those eyes when I'm feeling down and out,
Always in my father's eyes, I can overcome the doubt.
In his eyes I stand taller, and better than I am.
In my eyes, he's my "daddy", and he's the perfect man.

And as I think about the child I carry inside me now,
I pray, and hope, and wonder if someday, somehow,
She will see the love in me, the love that never dies,
The love passed on forever, from my father's eyes.

Angela Shue

Hiroshima

Shadows melted onto the wall.
This placid place of megadeath shares
The pain with all.
A boom and hollow shroom,
That carries the soul of Hiroshima home,
To the wigwam in the sky.
And where a warrior fell way
To quivering knees, is where the shell drooped
On Hiroshima leads.
We were to lynch to judge in defense.
Scared of what the cold war might do,
Her voice swear to hold back nuclear
Powered war.
From Hiroshima comes an echoing voice that
Screams "a...!".
Oh, USSR, Oh, bleeding China, Oh, Lady Liberty,
Can't you see the peace at Hiroshima?!
Can't you learn, Can't you see!?!

Chris Obershaw

Never?

The suitcases are packed.
Before you say goodbye,
Before the bird with silver wings takes you away,
Leave your image in the mirror in your bedroom,
Leave your fingerprints on the book at your desk,
Leave your footsteps in Poplar Street,
Leave yourself in Thalia's temple,
the fifth row, middle,
Embrace with one glance both rivers surrounding
your beloved city,
Window-shop on Prince Michael Street,
Have Turkish coffee and chestnut pure
with whipped cream at The Two White Pigeons,
Impress in your mind voice from radio,
"On Sunday at Ten O'Clock",
Take along with you Fall's golden colors
from Tashmine Park,
Take the smell of linden in your back yard.
Maybe you will never come back again.

Nada Chambers

I Love

Turn around!
Look at what you have forgotten.
Only in your darkest,
deepest dreams do you relive yesterday.
Now listen! Hear today the song on the wind.
My heart aches,
yet you do not seem to care.
Your life has caused much pain,
just remember that if you forget all,
the joy dies with the hurt.
Forward! See what tomorrow holds for you.
My hidden love will be openly available,
to any, great or small,
to you, my love,
who dares not live in reality.
Why live a dream?
The world is only so cruel.
I will always be near,
so do not fear loneliness.
I love you; simply understand.

Jason R. Cross

The Wizard's Student

If I had listened with my one good ear
to the advice my teacher wanted me to hear.

My spell would have had a lot more success
then the dreadful results that ended in this mess.

Dragons are fearful and hard to control
and take great offense when you strike from below.

A spot on their belly it seems that they have
that's very, very ticklish should you try to grab.

The reaction you get from them is violent at best
and most wizard's students flunk this on the test.

So if you are asked to put a dragon in a bag
get the strongest piece of string you think that you have.

Snatch them from above before they can blow
the powerful flames on everything below.

And so you will see that your final grade
will be an "A" from the wizard if your dragon behaved.

Being a wizard is not easy you see
If you fall asleep in class like me.

Mark Szumanski

Chewing Tobacco Addict

He wasn't honest when they first met,
And covered his chewing with a cigarette.
Slowly and steadily the habit grew,
Until now his life is the nasty chew.
The brown slobbers run down his chin,
And she's constantly embarrassed by him!

He's an addict, chewing tobacco rules his life.
It became his companion and replaced his wife.
She's always alone, even with "Old Sitting Bull."
He can't converse, his mouth is too full.
When he does try to talk, there's only a spray,
As you can imagine, that really makes her day!

When the silence is broken, it's not a melodic tune,
It's the noise of the chew missing the spittoon.
The nauseating odor and oozing brown splatter,
Is followed by his grunt: "What's the matter?"
He'd rather have a "fix" than be a romancer,
And can't see that his future is Oral Cancer!

Sylva Carter Rhodes

Home

Must I just lay here and take your wrath
I squeeze my eyes and hope the time will pass
My body aches and is tired and worn
how much more of this will I take and endure
fighting you I gave up long ago
you stole my innocence and robbed me of my soul.

With every passing minute of the day
I try to please you wondering why everything has to be this way
You say it will not happen again but know this is not true
You have said it before and time and time again
Always going back on your word with a harsh tongue and a violent
hand.

Just that look in your eye
Makes me wonder in surprise
Is this the man that I once loved
Are you the one who held me so
rocking me gently to and fro.

I squeeze my eyes hoping for the time to pass
with each passing slap and punch and word
I pray to God to take me away from this place
Take me away from this home.

Jill-Antionette Afzelius

Today Is Here!

Whenever I'm homesick I like to go
Wherever the wind in the trees does below.
It takes me back across the miles
To a place I lived when I was a child.

I can shut my eyes and almost see
The broad plains sweeping into eternity.
The little creek that wound its way
Through the wooded banks where I used to play.

I can almost smell the freshness of Spring.
The searing heat Summer would bring.
Autumn with its bonfires glowing
And the fields of hay the men were mowing.
The fresh clean smell of the new fallen snow
That only a lover of Winter could know.

But the wind in the trees does not blow anymore.
I have taken a journey and reached the shore.
I know that memories however dear
Must be shed aside for today is here!

Verona Frei

The Wedding

She danced at his wedding,
Pretty white hair, little face smiling;
92 year old grandma... 5' tall,
Her grandson, the groom... 6'2 in all;

I watched with misty eyed vision...
As they whirled with precision,
Yesterday, a blond lad with curly hair,
Running to grandma's house...
She awaiting him there;

They planted their "darden"!
One day, he excitedly exclaimed
"I must soon go back...
To see what I and grandma plant!"

How swiftly flew the years
Those summer days of fun and tears...
Football, college and girls have come between;
But for now... a bond of love
does
intervene...

D. Jeanne Peterson

Beyond

Still, she is, and somehow traveling
Along the rugged western coast.
Nearly, I felt I saw her
In the waves at sunrise;
Clad in billows of sea-blue organdy;
Shimmering like gossamer light on the dragonfly's wings;
Glinting white-wung and glistening
Sailing across the horizon;

Isabelle Davey gliding into the beyond.

On the wings of the sky hawk a-glow
In the amber-rose-purple-sunset soaring
Above the high hills
Upon the wind
In the tall trees

Everywhere is she.

Tibet says the soul may remain
Passing through the bardo states up to forty-nine days.

James R. Bensman

When Grandpa Was A Boy

So many things were different when Grandpa was a boy.
He never saw a movie. He seldom had a toy.

He never soared aloft in planes, no radio had he.
An auto was unusual, a downright novelty.

He walked three miles to school each day
and wrote upon a slate.
The daily things I eat
young Grandpa never ate.

Yet he is always telling me
about the good old days.
How he wouldn't exchange his youth
for all our modern ways.

He's sure he fished with greater luck
along his special streams.
And hazelnuts were bigger
in Grandpa's day it seems.

I wonder when I am Grandpa's age
if I will enjoy.
To think that things were better
when I was just a boy.

Randy Farmer

Strawberries

In late December we went to find
The strawberry plants of the best kind.
We dug the bushes up from vines in the ground.
We shook the dirt off of them all around
We picked up a trowel and our berry
plants too!
We planted out our berries until
planting was through.

In January we picked up sticks and
gathered straw
To protect our berries from cold winds raw.
In the month of May we'd arise early to pick
Our ripened berries to get them to the market quick.
We picked berries all the spring long
After the season we would sing this song!

Strawberry, strawberry, strawberry JIG.
We finished our work and did not renege.
All our strawberries are good to eat.
They are ripe and juicy, tasty and sweet.

Renee Wascom

A Day At A Time

Don't keep fingering through the ashes of the past,
Or you may touch a hot coal and get burned.
Don't wade through the sewers of yesterday,
For you may see a few unwelcome rats
or other rodents undiscerned.

Life is meant to be lived in the present;
Each day enjoyed to its full.
We should not fear the future nor be concerned.

God guides us day by day.
We can trust and depend on Him.
He will provide for all our needs in every way.
For we worship a Supernatural Being,
And life is meant to be lived as it is—Today.

Nina V. DePue

A Late-Night Dream

A wonderful dream took place last night,
A dream about stars, planets, and flight.
I flew to the moon in marvelous machine,
Landed on the surface, not a soul to be seen.

Standing on the land, shaking at the knees,
I realized the horizon was made out of cheese!
After some time, I ran to my rig,
Got out my shovel and started to dig.

A lot of the cheese I fit in my ship,
Couldn't waste time, I had another trip.
Started her up, I flew out to Mars,
I had to pick up some candy bars.

I headed for Earth, right at full speed,
All the food the people did need.
I landed on the ground, knowing people to be fed,
Opened the door....and fell out of bed.

Eddie Turek

Wife Mine

Sharing and caring, exquisite are you.
The path that we take we must head true.
When the trail has come to an abrupt end.
We shall know we are the best of friends.
From day to day our life's been full.
Although it was rough, unbearably cruel.
As hard as it was for you and I.
We always will know our best we did try.

Gary W. Yokel Jr.

A Mother's Love

I awoke early one morning to find that
I was a mother.
There you were my beautiful son, sleeping
quietly beside me under the cover.
Ever so gently, careful not to disturb I
raised the cover to take my first look at you.
Ten fingers, ten toes. Oh that beautiful
face, those handsome features. Suddenly
I knew, I would never know a love more
deeply or true.
Your first words, your first step are now
in the past.
Oh God, where did the years go? You grew
up too fast.
As a young boy you looked to me for guidance
and approval. To hold comfort you when
life was not kind.
Now you are grown feel you know better.
But remember my dear son a truer love than
your mother's you will never find.

Janice McMillan

A Small Miracle

The time had come much too soon
For her to leave the womb.

They came to tell me on that day
This little one would not stay

At only twenty-six weeks
Much too small, mild, and meek.

With tears of sorrow and filled with fear
Not knowing our destiny so very near.

I knelt on bended knee and began to pray
Dear God, please send a miracle our way.

At last the work was done
With tears of joy for a battle won.

As I look to the Lord above
I know this small miracle was sent with love.

Deanne Strong

Magic of a Texas Spring?

Chewing my skin until it itches
Are microscopic monsters called chiggers.
I lather myself with Camphophenique
Trying to evade the bites of those diggers.

The constant pounding of wind and rain
Are sure signs of swollen rivers the next day.
Small stones of ice strip trees of budding foliage
Leaving strong cedar scents as I exit the doorway.

My body resembles the Milky Way:
Those bounding black fleas have left their proof!
Spiral black winds rip through the hills,
Robbing my new barn and metallic roof.

Gray Cedar Waxwings stop for a feast
Eating tender buds from the Mulberry trees.
The hail of their leavings stain the pool deck.
They take what they want and leave when they please.

Disgusting young ticks hatch from their eggs.
They climb up my leg to the top of my knee.
Bloaties, spotties — Vampires — gorge themselves
On my pet menagerie...and me!

Jessica Palmer

"The Beauty Of A Brother"

You are a wonderful brother,
I wouldn't want anyone other.
You make me smile,
You make me cry,
But most of all you're by my side.
The good times,
The bad times,
You've guided me through sad times.
You'll always own a piece of my heart,
As brother and sister, we'll never part.
I wouldn't want anyone other,
Than you, a wonderful brother.

Tiffany Barber

Working Women

The dawn awakes
The birds do sing!
Another night is through
Time to say I'm ready world
And start the day anew.

The same old hassle
The same old grub
You work until the day is done.
Nothing changes,
Nothing new,
You just survive and get through it.

And when night falls and the day has ended
You wonder God how did I get by?
But you smile to yourself, as you go to bed
Knowing nothing will change
No matter what's said.

And when life here is over
And your work is through,
Pray God has a place, especially for you.

Janie E. Page Vail

Time's Up!

You use me, abuse me without thought,
as though I'm for sale and have been
bought. At times you forget me then
remember my name as though my
feelings are a game. Where could you go
without me? If it wasn't for time,
where would you be? Excuse me, excuse me,
I don't mean to interrupt. See you, good
bye, your time is up!

Timothy M. McKinnie

Red Misery

These roses are red are red from blood that's been shed
from those broken hearts of misery.
The children who have no shoes for their feet
Walking down lonely city streets.
Their tears are dew on their Diddles
The newspapers is read from blood that been shed
from those broke hearts of misery.
The people who live on the streets, their clothing
is warm and tattered like the lines on their face. They
show the hard times and roads they travel. The words
of the paper is meaningless, but it kept them warm
and hides their tears at night.
The sunset is red from blood that's been shed
from these broken hearts of misery.
The woman who's face has been beaten by a loved one
she's so terrified to leave, and from the thought
of not seeing another red morning.
But she hopes that when the sunset comes and
disappears it will take along with it her fears.

Dawn-Colleen Jarred

His Children

Look up, look up! A gentle call.
Mine eyes cast down lest I should fall,
I fail to heed His heartfelt cry,
His outstretched arm before mine eye.

Look up, look up - it comes again-
Look up, my friend, if thou wouldst win.
His call at last I hear so sweet,
Mine eyes arise His gaze to meet.

Oh softest touch, my hand He takes;
Oh precious light, my soul He wakes!
Upon my ear His breath as balm,
Friend, look, guides He with open palm.

A child before mine eyes I see;
Of faithful love reminds me He:
Take heed the heart before thee set,
Such loving trust can I forget?

Oh nay, not I, He answers quick,
For I the Lord wouldst children pick.
And then my hand more firm He holds
As He my heart with love enfolds.

Tracy L. Haynes

Siblings

The evening grew long seems every night we'd
get some entertainment that would bring great
delight. My siblings and I would always have fun
doing silly things that would not hurt no one.
Then one went to college what were we to do?
My sister and I were young, but everyone
seemed like they grew. Another went to college
and there were only three I felt like everyone
decided to leave me. The eldest came back after
graduation she stayed rather long not just a
special occasion. Then the third left he's my only
brother my siblings are kind, we take care of
each other. My twin sister and I are the two that
haven't left when I do leave all of the memories I
will have kept. I miss them sometimes, but I
know they'll return, so that moments we had will
be reborn.

Merica Ann Green

Is He Yours Or Is He Mine

In a graveyard there stands a lonesome stone
With words written up on the unknown soldier grave
Its my son or is it your son or someone's son unknown
It matters much who's son in the unknown grave
Left home alive returned a sleeping soul
Someone's son lying there one of the brave
Body gone back to the dust spirit back to God
Who's son is it the remains sleeping away
The unknown soldier will have to wait until Resurrection Day
When God will resurrect him from the lonesome grave
Then he will be known as one of the brave
Sometime in the future he will rise it will be no surprise
For all the dead in Christ will rise first
With a sudden great burst of the earth
All the unsaved will sleep 1000 years more
They will rise to stand at the great white throne judgement
To be judged for their deeds whether they be good or bad
On that great Judgement Day some will be sad others glad
If you want happiness on the last day
make peace with man first and then to God

Jack D. Simco

"Mother Earth"

I know I am just a child,
with little right to question.
But I need to know why they call you "Mother",
when you allow so many people to be out of control.

I see addicts on the streets, begging for money.
Their only concern is for their next injection.
Strapping their arms with a piece of rubber,
hoping to forget reality — even for a little while.

I hear people speak hateful racism,
to those of different colors.
This deep rooted prejudice is going to destroy
your future generations.

I smell the odor when I walk past park benches,
of those who have no home.
Feeling sorry for them won't help,
they need a place to bathe.

I know we call you "Mother Earth",
but I don't know why.
Please clear up my confusion,
so I, as a child, can understand.

Tamara Taylor

Power In Salvation

We remember a king, the king gone by.
Sent by his immortal Father, the father of heaven and earth.

Through thoughtful walks, in gardens of dark, Jesus the son,
spoke of justice and might, love and strife,
the only ways to salvation and eternal life.

Feared by Rome, betrayed by Judus,
then sentenced by Pilot.
With nail and sword, crowned in blood,
the holy life was drawn.
The spirit of his life grew and grew,
with every passing day.
What was lost by his death,
was given in his return many times over.
For our souls he yearned to live in eternity.
On the seventh day we celebrate his death
and resurrection by partaking in his body and blood.

In the spirit of his birth, a tree is laid,
a shined star atop.
Beneath a tiny manger,
shares its gifts with old and new.

Ramon R. Pecora Jr.

I'll Cry Later

I'll cry later, she says when the news came
Now is not the time for tears
There are others who need me; I must be strong
But she is frightened by what she sees and wonders how she'll face it;
I'll cry later, she says.
There are fights to be fought
no time to think about what the future holds
Only time to love and hold on hard to the present
There is anger, and an ache in her heart
but most of all, an overwhelming sadness and a fear,
a fear that when the time for tears comes, she won't be able to stop.
So, she says, I'll cry later.
When the time for tears arrives,
she looks down into young eyes and she understands,
death is a part of life,
tears a path to accepting and healing.
And, finally,
she cries.

Cathy Stecklein

Marissa

Like an angle you came down
to live with me upon the ground
Quiet love I've seemed to found
I love you so Marissa

The sound of your sweet baby cry
tears with love I'll always dry
comfort from a Lulla-bye
I love you so Marissa

Sweet innocents so pure and true
I'll always be here for you
my baby there's nothing I wouldn't do
I love you so Marissa

The feeling I get when I touch your face
a feeling I could never replace
Like a filling of an empty space
I love you so Marissa

Laura Harman

Melee

Another dent in the bucket from a red shoe
Metal toe not needed
The chain reaction accelerated the shocks
The black eye from the speeding chip was painted by one stroke
Justice was the accent of melee.

Wrestling between the two steps
Waiting for one to fall
Melee was a kick away
Lied the lies
Justice is working overtime today.

Melee — a kick to the target
Head, face, crown, nape, dick, butt, thigh, knees
All the shoes looked alike
If you dared look at all
Justice for the fatal blow was missed again.

Head cradled, body trembled
Father's silent aid
Scared more than anything
Scared of shame
Justice eight days away.

Glenna Yee

Illusions In Reality Of Mortality

If imagination isn't real, can one's imagination be real,
what about being a ball on Fortuna's roulette wheel.
Is this an illusion or can it be reality,
how do you decipher a man's mortality.
Being at the right place at the right time is a success,
being at the wrong place at a time usually means unrest.
We all must gamble to achieve success here,
for you too must be at the right place on this spinning sphere.
Movement, is it an illusion or is it reality,
again, can it represent a man's mortality.
Is it true that you can move without moving an inch,
is it true that you think making progress is a "cinch".
Walking across the Sahara opposite the earth's vector pace,
You've traveled hundreds of miles on land, but not a foot in space.
Were you making progress. In reality: No, but an illusion: Yes,
Wait, could it really be the other way around, you can only guess.
Man's goal is to find a solution to a desired problem or question,
can the question itself be an illusion...what is the lesson.
What is reality and what does it mean to live in reality,
Are we living if we are aware of the illusions in our society.

Darryl E. Harris Jr.

The Holocaust

Every night I look up at the sky,
and I utter with a mournful sigh.
Why are they doing this oh why, the only
freedom I have is to sleep and cry.
Every night they shut us up like cattle, and
we know we cannot fight the battle.
At night our tears flow down our cheeks,
we don't even have the strength to sleep.
I sometimes think I'm living a bad dream,
with everyone suffering along with me.
Then I wake and hear the suffering cries,
and look up into frightening eyes.
I can see they've lost their hope and
will, all I can say is hold on till.
Till the day when we are free,
oh God please let this dream be.

Kara Branyon

Consume Me

Please consume her,
her black and weary death
Consume her when she is old and gray,
not young.
She wants to live her life to the fullest.
As for you, die now.
Love death,
Cherish it.
The pains of your so called life
will leave you with a sharp pain.
When you leave she will not cry,
but she will not forget.
She will cherish the life she had
and you hadn't.
After she lives, she'll forget.
Forget the life you once had.

Rachael Hoshaw

Friends And Lovers

I've always thought of you as "Friend".
In fact, it seems you've always been.

But lately it's more than friend at Best
I've dreamed your lips were on my breast.

And when desire grew in your eyes
I felt your tongue upon my thighs

Your hands were seeking warm, moist places
Putting pleasured smiles upon our faces

Although we've never had the pleasure
I feel it's there by any measure

And if we find the thrill is there
Then there's nothing better to compare

I myself feel great desire
I hope you soon may feel the fire

There's no commitment, there are no strings
Just pleasure and comfort and wonderful things

Ruth Collett

Friend

Whenever you're sad and feeling blue
you can count on me, I'm here for you
When something happens, that you'd like to share
call me up, I'll be there
And if ever you feel that you've reached the end
you can count on me, because I am your friend

Amanda Lambert

Precious Lord I Need Thee

Precious Lord I need thee,
Lord lead and guide me.
Always be beside me.
Precious Lord I need thee,
you're in the valley beside me,
you set my captive soul free.
Precious Lord I need thee,
you gave your life at Calvary.
I can see how you loved me.
Precious Lord I need thee
by you're blood you gave power to me,
by your name Satan has to flee.
Precious Lord I need thee,
you're the joy of my life.
Without thee there would be strife.
So now I say to you,
may the Lord Jesus bless and keep you. Amen.

Elaine Langford

Eternity

Beyond the serrated mountaintops that merge
in tenon-like fashion with the quilted patchwork
of sapphire sky and ghostly ermine clouds
lies eternity.

...Where endless life begins, bowing triumphantly
in the winner's circle having out-raced death,
rendering it null and void
never to be born again.

...Where ripeness never spoils; the tree of life
non-deciduous, encapsulated in perennial burgeoning
splendor deeply-rooted in the fertile soil
of life eternal.

...Where tears no longer flow mellifluously
along facial terrain carving valleys of despair barren of hope.

...Where the soul never dies, nor thirsts, nor hungers

Forever.

Walter A. Hayes

Rage

Stop! All the noise and confusion.
Stop! Arise through the mist of chaos.
Stop! Listen to what you see.
Absorb your surroundings.
Hear all that is around.
Listen to yourself!
It is me, the mask you hide behind.
Listen to the truth!
The truth that surrounds you
Hidden behind your facade,
That not only you but everyone
Too hides behind.
Destroy the facade!
Which holds you back
From all that you are meant to be.
Unleash everything stored inside.
Now!
Struggle effortlessly, Stand proudly, Stride freely
Break Free! Run! Runaway!

MyAn Chung

Living In-Between

I sit and ponder so it seems
of the world of "In-Between."
To myself call it:
"Reality and a Dream."

Summer days are filled with haze;
Balmy breezes roll in from the seas;
But these things are unknown to me,
for I am in-between reality and a dream.

Children play along the beach through the day;
Mothers stop to say "Be careful, no rough play!"
But these things are unheard to me,
for I am in-between reality and a dream.

Suddenly a thought comes to me
Perhaps it's wrong to live "in-between!"
You miss so much of life it seems to me;
Living between "reality and a dream."

Jennifer Troutte

Trouble

Trouble is not a good thing,
it isn't what you think it brings.

We have a life that we should live well,
Or shall say it's like a beautiful bell.

We should be honest and truthful while we're here,
We shall never stay in fear.

So stay in trouble and you'll find out,
What punishment is all about.

Angel Grossaint

Under A Red Lover's Moon

A lover is weeping for a love never known. Not saying a
word, walking, arm in arm under bowing branches.
Angry words already passed, eyes fixed on a full red
Moon, wishing wishes she has wished before. The stars
light the path as the night air brings them closer, the
man beside her stops and squeezing her hand faces her.
Eyes meet in the night, gleaming brown under beautiful
dark waves, piercing her soul. Hate melts away and is
replaced by hurt and sorrow. Walking, her eyes on the
Moon, his ahead. Eyes meet again, silence, coming closer
to where they must part. His words break the cold air
like a warm fire that freezes her tears. "I love you,"
As a single drop escapes his eye. The loves smile.
Arms reach to touch with warm, loving feeling, a kiss
lights up the night like the sun. The cold is gone,
Love has taken its place, from his lips for the first
time these words fall on her ears. In her heart this
night will never end and it will never grow cold...
And all under a red lover's moon.

Angleia Yong Colbath

Sirocco

"Hitherto you come", said the pious man
A wind had broken through the viscid air mass
With its soulful strength it had no trepan.

"You don't seem to monish a stormy rasp
Instead you can hear the viola d'amore
It resonates from you, a song, a laugh."

"O, the mountains of Italy that you course
You are a spirit that brings miracles
Though o'er dry and dusty plains you were born."

Christopher A. Balluch

Alphabused

Agony
Insistent, persistent, cruel, merciless
"Good-bye."

Betrayal
Shattered aspirations turned to resignation,
"Smile, April Fool."

U just U
Memories of good times together, jolted by
nightmares of being in a hospital and U
having to choose "to terminate, terminate."

Suffering
Horrifying realization that such terror
did not have to last that long.
"Walk and don't look back."

Everlasting Companion
Is the pain oozing from under the scars
of the abandoned, the deceived, the burdened,
the battered and those who have felt the weight of

Abuse.

Elisa Valdes

The Wanderer

How I long to go home to my wildwood.
I want to go back there to stay.
Just to lie where the sweet primroses stood,
and where there was peace every day.

Those care-free memories of childhood,
have lingered with me 'till today,
and the poignant fragrance of springtime,
tells me I should never have gone far away.

But soon I'll return to my wildwood.
To the babbling brook cool and clear.
I'll be heading home like a wanderer should,
to all of those things I hold dear.

Betty Pickering

Have You Ever

Have you ever walked in my shadow, and seen the image of death at hand, felt the riveting pain of helplessness heard the lasts gurgles of the dying?

Have you ever heard the angels weeping, for another lamb was sacrificed.

Have you ever been locked together between hatred and love, and never knowing the difference.

Have you ever longed for the dark angel to come and embrace you into eternal damnation and yet wept in silence for the mercy of our Lord.

If you had walked in my shadow then pluck my pain and deflect my broken heart and show me to live again.

Amelia Masek

Can You See

Can you see a rainbow at night
Can you see a fire without its light

Can you hear a flower's beating heart
Can you stop the rain before it starts

Can you save a leaf from falling to the ground
Can you send a falling star upward bound

Can you save a snowflake before it melts
Can you understand me even by not knowing what I've felt

Legna Elbanev

Through My Eyes

I have seen dark hatred beneath the stare of a smile that's forced my way.
I have seen the doubted credibility, much before being allowed to play.
I have seen your children stare, although you encourage them to look away.
I have seen you tell them that it is not my fault of what I am anyway.
I have seen my portions cut short while being stroked that all was OK.
But,
I have also seen smiles, filled with love, and care of one being to another.
I have seen some make honest effort to help, and maybe care for his brother.
I have seen sweet children wave to me "Hi" while standing beside their mothers.
I have seen your wisdom shine when speaking of difference as a world to discover,
and that it does not make it better or worse to be thought different from each other.
So,
Maybe the trick is to see, that our world can be what we make it.
Maybe it's truth that we choose to look, for good or focus on wicked.
Maybe some perceptions quickly reached, just might be corrected.
Maybe if I give love openly, the goodness is often reflected.

Charles Kenely III

Dreamers

Sorry for being a dreamer
For thinking kisses meant more than the collision of lips
For wandering into eyes, whereas they are only mechanisms of sight
For feeling beautiful about myself, knowing this also
is attributed to my blindness
Sorry for being a dreamer
For caring about your whereabouts but you are
independent and indifferent
For singing melodies of love knowing I could never hit the right notes
For being as carefree as a child, when I lost my innocence long ago
Sorry for being a dreamer for writing love letters, they are
tangible and can be throw away for wishing upon twinkling stars,
they only guide the lost not the hopeless for hoping things would be
different this time, history repeats itself
Sorry for being a dreamer
For hoping tomorrow was a definite thing, tomorrow is not forever
For thinking you loved me, falsifying not perfection is my best quality
For loving you, when you are an entity far from my sphere
For believing in the magnanimity of love,
Please trust me - love is for fools.

Saema Ansari

Let It Be

Please put your arms around me
And shield me from all harm
Please be my downy comforter
And keep my body warm
Show me a rainbow through the clouds,
Green grass where there is none
May I always be able to say thank you
For all the good things that you've done
Be my friend and keep me
Let me see good in one and all
Help me to know though tall I stand,
I too one day may fall
Let me be that kind of person
Who will help his fellowman
Through bad times and worse times
Doing anything I can
Let me put my best foot forward
Please prop my leaning side
May I always know where ever I go.
You will in me abide.

Ruby J. Locke

Black People Unite

Black brothers and sisters
Where's your pride?
Striving for stupidity
Is not why Dr. King died
Believe in your race
Then they won't step on your face
Doing the things you do
I'm sure your ancestors will disagree with you
Stealing another brother's jacket
Is like taking money from the black man's pocket
They already don't make enough
Black brothers and sisters get tough
Ignite and unite
Forming a force in the light
Show the white man we're not dumb
They can't twiddle us on their thumb
We can be smarter, better than them
Because black brothers and sisters
We're on the move again and no one can keep us back
We'll strive and fight until the end

Rhodean Collman

You Are Not My Mother

You are not my mother,
you did not have me in your womb for nine months,
you did not go through the labor pain,
nor did you bring me into this world.
You never breast fed me,
nor, I drink the milk from your breasts.
You didn't teach me how to walk,
nor did I hold you when I walked.
You didn't tell me any bedtimes stories,
nor carried me in your arms when I was sick.
I never heard the strong beat of your heart,
nor heard the gentleness of your voice.
You surely adopted me,
but that doesn't give you the privilege to be my mother,
you didn't earn this right.
You can never replace my mother.
I will never call you mother,
no, I will never call you mother.

Johny Makhija

Seasons Of Time

Fall is the time the Lord created for change...

In the Spring a tree will blossom
and create the greenery of its leaves.
Providing foliage and shade
on a warm Summer day.

Fall draws near and the tree must prepare
letting the leaves it lovingly created fall to the earth.
Welcoming the Winter God has made.
Knowing, in seasons to come, it must create its leaves
all over again.

For every season there is a change...

The Lord shows us how nature
adjust to the changing of the seasons.

Like life, love is also a season.
Constantly growing,
changing,
evolving.

And sometimes...
Starting all over again.

Bradley James Straka

My Heart Is My Guide

I hear the story's of winters gone,
the raging winds of a time past,
sounds of a new generation blooming in the shadows,
not knowing where their lives cast.
I sense the coming of the great tide at sea,
knowing well, how this will affect me.
And others who sense the calm before the fury of the storm,
will need a clear sky, from which to steer.
I have learned the lessons of the ages,
of a time gripped in despair,
where the storms, in their wake, claimed our pride,
leaving us nothing, no light, no heart, no guide.
But in time gone by,
the fire within shone ever bright,
and from dawns radiant start,
we always had the goodness in our hearts.
So to govern me in times to come,
ensuring that with honor I shall always abide,
I have found my glowing star,
my heart shall be my guide.

Oladipo Oseni

The Voice Of A Dream

To live is to dream a dream so wondrous it can't be explained.
A dream is a path unwalked and a voiceless song.
It's a voice that breathlessly whispers its story.
Growing louder and louder, the voice sings to the heart,
And as the soul realizes the dream, a door is opened, and the dream takes wing.
Finding itself on an endless journey of discovery, the soul soars through all time.
And from that dream, the heart will find a new understanding.
And from that understanding, the heart will hear a new dream whispering a new story.
Until sand becomes stone, the circle of dreams goes on,
Until the ocean is turned to fire,
Open your ears to the whisper,
For when you really need the answer, the song is hardest to hear.
The song of a dreamer is greatest who has heard the whispering song...

Amy Schindler

Leaves

I realize the freedom of nature.
Life simply follows course, does not have to worry or fear.
Driving home, I see the leaves dying,
but they are so beautiful.
I experience this rush,
sometimes described as love.
I look at this road,
I've seen it so many times,
but today it is different,
somehow changed.
I can see it,
but the feeling fills me,
I am about to cry.
I think, maybe I am the trees.
I am not dying.
I have finally experienced nature,
the season of fall.
My colors are changing.
I can't wait for
my new leaves in the spring.

Wileen V. Gausman

Patiently Waiting

She stepped across the boundaries, she didn't feel were wrong.
She nicked some major arteries, she knew that they were strong.
God's word was all she wanted, when she reached for someone dear.
But her words had only haunted, the life so filled with fear.
She shuttered to think of losing, this one she'd known so long.
Those sweet and thoughtless choosing, of words that could be song.
But Jesus said, "be calm now, for I am in control."
She knew His hand would somehow, return the heart of ole.
She knows now this will happen, for His word has promised this.
She feels her heart start tapping, with joy you could not miss.
She heard Him say, "be humble, let go of all your fear.
Your loved one has to stumble, but I will keep her near."

Brenda K. Kouns

How Do I Come To You

All my life I've felt you near. I wanted you in my life - But I never knew how to come to you.

All my life I've learned to accept this hollow feeling stored in my heart.

All my life I've had to accept some form of abuse in one form or another.

All my life — I've waited for someone to introduce me to you
I've lived so much life without you

I've prayed so many times and my prayers were answered yet I am still afraid to come to you.

All my life I've felt like I've done something so terrible and
the fear of my past - present - future keep me from coming to you.

How do I come to your love when I'm so afraid of failing before your eyes.

How can I hide from you who I am, when you know me better that I know myself.

How can I be anything to anybody, when I can't be myself to me

All I ever wanted was to fill this lonely spot in my heart — to love myself - to understand myself - and to become one with myself.

Show me how to come to you.

T. R. Blake

Marriage

The time has finally come that you'll join hearts
two as one,
you'll walk through life
hand in hand,
and take each hardship
one by one,
You'll travel each tomorrow, never looking back,
and when that bridge approaches
you'll worry once you've crossed it.

Marriage is a special gift
with one very sacred key.
the love that only you two share.

Angie A. Mendoza

The Bedroom

I slink into the bedroom like a jungle cat, at night
And pounce upon the bedspread, like a yellow tiger might.
Street light through curtains let imagination play,
The walls of green are shadowed and like Laburnam sway.
A plant and pictures hung, give credence to the scheme.
I walk the beaches crunching sand like another, in a dream.
Of jungle beach, oh dream I might and find it almost real
But glad I am it's only a room, to which I softly steal.

Arville Gilmore

Guided By Voices

A stream of conscience is broken by a thought unknown
This unusual thought can speak, move, and think on its own
It crackles and creaks and hovers and floats inside the grey matter
Metallic streams shimmy across the sponge and then stop
A ceiling and a floor compress and the pink pulp explodes
Black soot overflows the countertops, descends and sinks
A maelstrom follows continuing with a new process
This process heals a systematic theory with elements of doubt
The positive aspect of negative thinking triggers the hues, and
a thing that is a terrible thing to waste flashes the rainbow
The thought has almost passed but continues to finish its job
Next are the senses after the pain
Visions of emerald framed tricycles with diamond made spokes
race into a wall and then shatter
A stench of burning black plastic stings the nose
Feeling no feeling at all
The mouth is filled with small silver pins
The process ends
The voice have stopped and have guided me along

Robert Grachus

The Black Hole

There's a hole in everyone's life I know.

I stay to myself, because there's nowhere for me to go.

I feel like I am shrinking, with all my life and all my might.
And a day is never a day, it's just as black as night.

There's darkness in every crevice, and every hole.
And sad to say, I feel like I am nothing but a mole.

Many times I have come out and tried new things in life,
but troubles seem to keep coming they are as sharp as a knife.

You assume you have a family, you think you have a friend,
but when your troubles await you, there's no one at the end.

I wonder where's the light that I have prayed to see.

I have to keep that faith in God or there will be no more of me.

Ruth Dana Perkins

A promise of Love

As I view old photos, I recall so many things about our past.
Love, happiness and unity - all assumed would always last.

As years passed by, we faced the biggest of our fears.
The existence of the distance which had grown, became so very clear.

Yet, continuing on, each of us in our own separate direction...
We encountered, from afar, each other's imperfections.

Never realizing then we'd been slowly torn apart.
The pain we each would carry in the depths of our heart.

Where did we go wrong? How easily it was for all of us to forget;
The length of life is far too short to carry even one regret.

I, for one, have chosen to let all bad feelings go...
All the hurt, anger and disappointment...which left me with the "inability" to grow.

One question I must ask, to which an answer is unexpected...
"Has anyone attained 'self-satisfaction' beyond belief?"

I tell you, brothers and sisters, if things continue as they are...
Your only experience will be that of grief.

So, since I do not know which will be the last day for me to live...
To you, my family, I promise from this day, to love and to forgive.

I will not hold against you, all of the things known from the past,
The love which I have promised, in my heart will always last.

Lydia Betts

My Backyard

I sit here in my rocking chair. I hear nothing but the creaking of the chair as it rocks back and forth and the chirping of the crickets in the distance.
The smoke of my grandma's tobacco fills my nostrils. I look ahead of me only to find my backyard and its green grass and trees, once filled with relatives happy and excited, playing, running, and shouting. I remember how much fun we had. It begins to get dark, but I still can see the sun shinning on their smiling faces. I can still see myself running and laughing with them. I look into the emptiness of my yard, as if watch me and my relatives like a favorite old movie.

I walk out to the grass, expecting to find someone there to keep me company, but only the bitter cold greeted me. I was disappointed to discover no one there. I crossed my legs and sat down on the cold grass.
My only companion was my shadow. Then just as darkness crept over me like a black cat, I closed my eyes and asked myself, "Will this backyard ever be filled again?"

Jana Rae PunzalanCorpuz

"My Role Model"

I don't even know how words could exactly how I feel about you
You are my mother, my hero and my friend
You always know when something is wrong
but you never pry or give advice
Instead you extend your hand, your shoulder and your heart
for me to use when I am ready
You have no idea how much I appreciate you
for everything you have ever done for me
I regret all the things I have ever done to disappoint you
all I ever wanted was to make you proud
I am proud and lucky to have such a wonderful role model
Thanks Mom!

Kelly J. Morgan

Untitled

Of homeless people, starving babes
How can we simply turn away?
The bitter cold of winter time
The blistering heat of summer's prime.

The cardboard shelter with no lock
The comments made by those who mock
Free kitchens that must close the door
Despite the cries, there is no more.

A woman dressed in dirty rags
Looks through the trash to fill her bags.
A man collecting old tin cans
With frosted brow and frozen hands

What have they done to merit this?
No shelter, clothing, food, or kiss
For God gave us His only Son.
Can't we reach out to help someone?

Debra Y. Butler

Pride

To be free is one thing, but to fly is a different story;
You ride the wind to find hope and maybe some glory;
But the wind changes its pattern to find a different direction;
Can you change your flight to be in the winds protection;
You stare ahead and hope to understand the path;
But it takes longer than you expect;
You are not sure which way to fall;
Hoping you won't hit that one last wall;
Should you spread your wings and let the wind guide;
Or just dive head first into that wall of pride.

Susan Tamas

Drugs Can't Win

As a nation we know what our values really should be
for our forefathers showed us just what to do...to get through...

They showed us how to pray and how to trust in God
We as a nation, have experienced the miracles, and
the testimonies that we have successfully came true...

So please as a nation don't let drugs win over us too!!
We know we have too much strength and backbone to lose

Please don't let drugs take over our human race;

For our God can and will deliver us out of this horrible state,
for all we have to do is ask him too!!

For one day we too will have to answer for our down fall
we'll be asked about our morals, and, values...as well
ourselves..but
most of all...why did we let our Heritage fall?

So please hold up our children and parents alike...if we should win...it will be through prayer, morning, noon or night.

Reachel R. Flint

These I Do Love

Running barefoot through the soft sand on the ocean shore as the tide rolls in;
Clear, starry nights with a crescent moon;
Hugs;
Cold, winter nights beside a warm, roaring fire;
Small, bright-eyed children;
Running in the drenching rain;
Love poems;
Lying on the cool green grass in the shade of a pine tree;
Long walks alone in the dark calm of the night;
Red roses;
Snow falling softly in the winter as I watch from the inside;
Watching the sunset on a warm, summer night;
Singing a beautiful song;
The fresh air of a cool spring night;
Music;
A candle flickering in the darkness,
His gentle touch;
My best friend.

Bridgett Kingslien

Snow Princess

As I venture out into the wintery valley,
The newly-fallen snow crunches beneath my feet.
I begin to sculpt the perfect snowman,
Suddenly, I stop everything and stare in awe.
It is the snow princess!
Her long locks of silky black hair,
Seem to cascade down around her narrow shoulders.

Kendall Jenrette

"Starlight"

Shadows of night overtaking the earth
Celebrating darkness, ending mayhem and mirth
Quiet calm will soon rule the land
Stillness and slumber just as God planned
Darkness will fall and the heavens will open
Billions of stars will illuminate unbroken
Sailors keep course by way of starlight
Lovers will wish upon stars shinning bright
Hoping for happiness with their true love
Silently praying to the stars above
Night and its beauty will push back the day
Stars will shine brightly showing us the way
From daylights battles we can peacefully refrain
Silence and starlight is all that will remain

Joseph P. Kabeller

Fireflies

They reach out to me like a namesake,
bobbing up and down on phantasmagoric winds-
(Storm lanterns)
even though the night is calm and clear.

On like an electric bulb, mirror-streetlamps,
then off again, just as suddenly-
(They predict phantom dawns)
stillborn protostars in a nebula of air.

Rising like embers,
these creatures of chitin and wing
(luminescent dancers)
who elude capture,

leaving only the pale sting
of afterimage.

Beth Biller

Keep Walking

Keep walking my child, but take my hand for I am here beside thee. Walk on my child till the end of your days, the end of your earthly journey. It's not very far, I am by the side. I have gone before thee. I took the shame and bore your sin so you can share in my glory!

Oh, do not faint nor hesitate as onward we go together. There are no problems we cannot solve as up life's pathway we do travel. Always onward and upward we go, with the prize in mind and heaven as our goal. Keep your spiritual eye single and gird up your loins in the truth of my word with the sword of the spirit the devil must leave,evil cannot stand where my light penetrates.

My Kingdom is in heaven, he cannot enter into these gates so rejoice and be glad, the victory I have won. The spoils are for you and others in my son! Many shall come from the corners of the earth to join in the praises and sing of rebirth! To throw down your crown at the feet of my son, and sing hosannas to the might one!

Glory, praise and honor are his, as we join with the angels in the Hallelujah chorus. To reign with him eternally, kings and priests he has promised, to rule in his glorious Kingdom of life! Trials and tribulations are the things of this life but praise, adoration, worship and glory are the promises and reward... of his story!

Shirley M. Hathaway

Ode To Dolly

I have a dog named Dolly,
Who really is a card.
She usually plays with magpies
And tears up my back yard.

This morning as I looked out the window,
I had a big surprise.
The magpies were attacking Dolly
Right before my eyes.

I rushed out to assist her,
For my sister was in tears,
On the ground lay a baby magpie
That caused its parent's fear

My dad saved the baby
From a fate worse than death,
And put the baby over the fence
While we all held our breath.

Now the baby was safe,
But Dolly felt deprived.
We had taken her newest play toy,
And her fun was nullified.

Tricia Province

Hey Little Brother

Hey little brother. Come sit over here and listen.
Heard you've got some problems. Heard you've given up.
What...What did you say?
They told you that I always knew exactly what to do!??! I can't
believe this.
What do they know,
they're only adults.
See, made you smile.
Now listen here. I'm no better than you, just different.
They shouldn't expect you to be good in math,
just like they shouldn't expect me to be good at wrestling.
Made you smile again.
But you don't give up cuz you're not good at it. You can't get good
at something, unless you don't give up and you keep on trying.
They don't really want you to be like me,
just the best you can be.
So don't give up (and don't listen to them-I don't. See. Made you
laugh this time.)
Thanks for the hug little brother. You're welcome.
Anytime you need a shoulder, an ear, or a part on the back,
I'm here.
Just remember, don't give up.......Oh, and love you.

Michelle Rodriguez

"He Is An Angel"

(In Memory Of Domenic E. Matthews-Woodson)

No challenge was too great for this little Angel
Boy, he was so full of God's dear love that he brought to
others joy.
For if you looked upon his face I'm sure you
seen the glow, and then you felt within your heart a feeling
that did show.
No longer need you have the thought that all
Angels do have wings, for from this child you must have
felt the song that Angels sing.
The challenge that he fought in life, only Angels
could endure, along with me you would agree he was an
Angel and that's for sure.
A smile I have upon my face, and a tear is in
my eyes, 'cause I know no Angel stays but for a little
while, and then they pass us by...

Lonnie B. Matthews Jr.

A Mother's Love

She brought you here with a lot of love.
Each night she prays to God above
To lead you right and help you out.
To get you through with little doubt.
When we are older it seems hard.
You now play with the cards, that
Mom has played all these years.
Now you take over all the fears.
It's your life now but Mom's still there.
Bad decisions she still cares.
You may get mad with her opinion.
And even sometimes you won't listen.
She wants to help and wants what's best.
Thinks you're as good as the rest.
Wants the right friends the right type of guy.
You choose different, it makes her cry.
You're just learning and trying to grow.
Mom give me time there's more to show.
She's your friend like no other.
There's nothing like, the love of a mother.

Kim Landreth

The Horrible, Terrible, No Good Very Bad Year

We had a hard time last year;
All summer we had lots of heat and sun burned ears.
With the dust storms it was not easy
We got sand in our eyes when it got breezy.
Our water ran out -
We even had a drought.
All winter we had buckets of snow
When it got cold you know.
We got so much hail,
You could scoop it up with a pail.
In the fall, we had such big rains,
We got overflowed drains.
It sure made up for the drought in summer!
We even had a flood! Boy what a bummer!
We had lots of wind. It was so hard,
There were chickens blowing all over the yard!
We could not grow any tomatoes
Because of all of the big tornadoes.
But in the spring, up come the flowers.
Nature came through with lots of power!

Alexander William Brown Bersani

Yes It's Me Again

Just one moment is all I need to let you know what's on my heart
I am in love with you in the deepest most personal way
And I do not understand why or how it came to be this way
I see you every day in reality; I see you every night in my dreams
Every fantasy I create involves you.
My heart was said to be far away whenever some one attempted to find it
I was reluctant to place my feelings at the fingertips of just anyone
You are my only sky and you have always been my sky.
I cannot touch you, I cannot feel you, I can never pleasure you.
I can only see you and imagine your touch.
Constantly, I pray to God that we are meant to be together
If it is so...
Tears will sleep on my face if you run from my eyes.
Everywhere there are smiles or people holding hands, you are in my mind.
My misfortune is obvious. I can only dream about us, therefore,
Since I cannot be with you in reality, I praise God for my dreams.
My misfortune is killing my soul and leaving my spirit lonely.
Although, I may not claim you openly
You are mine in secret thoughts.
Always my sky.

LaTonya L. Jones

A Gallant Little Ship

She was a pretty little ship of about 14 tons.
Built for cargos of lumber, hardware and guns.
By her lines you could see, she was fast.
With new rigging and sails, she would never be last.

But what of the master, walking her decks?
Would his course keep her free, from the other wrecks?
Ships that had tried to help this new nation.
Ships that had fought, with no reservation.

A storm had been brewing, for the whole last day.
Her course lay through the harbor, to the end of the bay.
With a loud crash of thunder and lighting the storm broke.
The tempest winds cleared the harbor in one fell stroke.

The Man of War crashed on the starboard shore.
To the end of the bay the little ship tore.
With its cargo safe, it slide; upon the beach.
The gallant little ship was out of reach.

Ken Flanders

Precious Memories

Precious memories gained at Grama's knee
My heart and mind still clearly see,
Though days were bleak and dollars few
Her steadfast love was our families glue.

Grama told of all the money it saved
When butter was needed and had to be made,
So we each took our turn, cranking the churn
As she taught us to share, and helped us to learn.

On the old black stove we could cook, we could heart
So we hauled in the coal and we warmed up our feet,
Summers were hot and we suffered to eat
Adding cola to the fire in the sweltering heat.

The work was divided, each child had their chores,
Weeds to pull, fence to fix, make the meals scrub the floors
Feed the cow, pigs and chickens, then go beat the rugs.
She taught us to work hard then gave us all a hug.

But the memories that see me through each tough day
Are not of the lessons, the work, or the play,
But memories of love unconditional and free
The memory of love at my sweet Grama's knee.

Burna R. Frank

The Love She Made

To say she was a good cook
Is an understatement to say the least,
Cause she made Sunday dinners
Seem like a thanksgiving feast.

Her pies; always picture perfect
Dumplings that just melt in your mouth,
And those Aunt Rhody green beans
Fixed like they do down South.

Oh, and I can't forget her fried chicken
That even the colonel will never match,
Yes, with her two loving hands
She made everything from scratch.

She worked very hard and always with love
Never resting till we'd all been fed,
"I have to keep my young'uns belly's full"
That's what she always said.

I'll always remember her in the kitchen
For, that's where she liked being the best,
But her work is all done now
And she is finally at rest.

Lisa Lu Carter-Taylor

Northwoods

I hear the "caw-caw" of a lone crow,
early on a new summer day.
I hear the breeze singing through the trees,
as the beautiful tall pine trees sway.

I see the boats go zooming by,
and leave a trail of flying water as they go.
I see the mother duck drift slowly on,
while her nine little ones follow in a row.

I love to sit around the blazing campfire,
and chat with friends so dear.
I love the beauty of the vast Northwoods.
It's so nice to visit here.

Carol Oehler

Get Away

If I could talk to God, for a minute first I'd ask Him some simple words like: why did you make this world, and put us in it? What is it supposed to be worth? In the beginning the planet was singing I'm glad you created the earth, but now it looks like men are tryin' to end it; didn't you expect the worst? If I could talk to God, for a while I'd be myself, hope that He'd treat me as a child. I would explain my words and if they didn't work, then I'd have to get a little hostile.
If I could talk to God, He would change the world for us, 'cause I'd take His arm with mine and put 'em in handcuffs. 'Reason is 'cause I'm so hard-headed, I'd bug Him for eternity. He would hear my plea, until He changed the world to the way it's supposed to be. I'd tell Him about the oceans cryin', the forests dyin', and the air getting hard to breath. And all those other things that He obviously cannot see. I'd ramble on, until I drove Him crazy.
Then I know that He'd changed the world for the better,
just to get the hell away from me!

Paul Bryan

The Second Time Around

They came as one and went as two,
Their life together was over and through.
They'd forgotten promises made in love,
Forgotten their vows to God above.

No bitterness or hatred, no raising cain,
They only had heartaches, tears and pain.
Although love still burned strong in one heart,
It was cold in the other; they had to part.

They went their own paths, separate, alone;
Each started living a life of his own.
But much to their credit, they stayed each one's friend,
And one day they started loving again.

A false heart had crossed one path and left pain;
And into that life, there came days of rain.
But in that heart where love had first chilled,
It bloomed once again until it was filled.

Full circle they've come, these two hearts as one;
Their new life together, they have begun.
Renewed their promises to each in love,
Renewed their vows to God above.

Larry Purl Sr.

Touched By An Angel

A spiritual force brought us all together that foggy night.
We surrounded that small, frail body peaceful in its plight.
While not knowing how long her precious life would dangle.
It was without doubt her soul was being touched by an angel.

While we are contemplating within, an absence of breath we did notice.
We confirmed a pulse could no longer be detected from thy tepid wrist.
As we summoned the nurse, we glanced knowingly around the quiet circle.
We knew our Mom and Wife was being carefully touched by an angel.

The young boy among us that eve was her angel on earth.
He gave her laughter and endless joy since his birth.
As he placed the rose of love beneath thy still hand of his Gramma.
We were calmed at the serene touch by the angel.

There is no more sickness, suffering or distress.
The sense of relief to all who knew of her ultimate conquest.
She is now at peace, though we will miss her terribly.
Her flight is truly blessed by the touch of an angel.

Karen A. McTaggart

Untitled

Change is easier said than done
for a person with expectations of good will and fortune
is always to be mislead and gone.
never is there something I wish I could do
than to change myself to further a do
many times I scorn myself for doing foolish arts
and puts one to my many strikes. No one really
knows the pain I feel inside to betray and be betrayed
and to know you are really hated. The many pressures
life puts on you is a deed that needs to be done.
Many times out of two I do the right thing but
never am I accepted to play the game. Always
entitled to my own opinion, I'm never gonna be
able to change. Deep inside if I tried, I know I
really could do it, but nobody knows how hard I've
tried, but I know I'll always be deprived of something
I can never ever change.

Shenea Barnes

My Father

As Father's Day came and went
I thought of my wonderful father.
He showed so much understanding
And sparks of humor which I'd gather.

As little girls in our rockers
My sister and I would rock and listen
Turning the churn to make butter
My father sang and our eyes would glisten.

He was so gentle and yet underneath
There was a layer of strength when needed.
Working as a teacher and minister
He gave advice which I heeded.

Tall, good-looking, and with a faith
That was apparent to all who knew him.
He worked and lived by the Golden Rule
And did not live by notion and whim.

My husband and he were close
With a bond of Christian love.
Now the bond may be cemented
As they're both in that world above.

Frances E. Tolson

Midnight Sled Ride

The snow lightly sprinkles on the ground,
the house is still, I hear no sound.
As I tiptoe into the hall I realize, it is surely the end of fall.

I throw on my mittens suddenly wishing I
was warm in my bed,
but a feeling of excitement comes
over me as I get a glimpse of my wooden sled.
I look at the hill, so high in the sky,
I suddenly feel a though I could fly.
When I reach the top, I prepare to ride.
I feel so free as I begin to glide,
over bumps, past curves, and swings.
I feel the fun and steep hill can bring.
I smile a smile that I really should hide,
I'll keep the secret of my midnight ride.

Elizabeth Carson

Womb

From a womb expediently digressed,
Into a world especially distressed,
I wander, I wish, I wallow, I try,
For where is my chariot on which to fly,
To a home filled of nurture and grace,
Discovering the beauty of a maternal face,
I wonder, I ponder, I think, I know,
For where is my boat on which to row,
To somewhere by which an age is matured,
Not coddled, not hindered, not even obscured,
I play, I pray, I stay, I talk,
For where is the path on which to walk,
To a long life which is loved and fulfilled,
A land of bounty that once was tilled,
Towards the latter I've rowed and walked,
I've played, I've prayed, I've stayed, I've talked
In my time indeed have I flown,
I've wondered, I've pondered, I've thought, I've known,
I've wandered, I've wished, I've wallowed, I've tried,
And now with the end of course, I've died.

Joe Holland

Rock Of The Bard

Thick brick graveyard. Welcome home, let the song begin.
Dance to the piper. Sing along. Hail the ballad of sin.
A cloudy day. Hazy eyes, the heat upon your lip.
Pain or joy, the price is right; along another trip.
The altar stands, glass, rock and steel. The flames burning below.
A divine caress upon your mind, some will never know.
Strong loyalty, sacrifice, give 'til your last breath.
Never stop, keep the faith, right up to your death.
So sing along, it's a simple tune, or listen for a spell.
Coz' I'm the bard who knows the road, that leads us
Straight to hell.

Mark Edward Linehan

...If There's Anything

I see the look of anguish on your face.
It's in your eyes and the shakes of your hands.
My own hands shake.
I smile though and tell you to call if there's...anything.

Taking a seat I say hello to someone that I only see...
At places and times like these.

A Preacher speaks about the Beauty of the Works.
Thoughts about the inevitability of it all pass through.
In my mind I hold your hand as the final prayer resounds.
(Call if there's...anything)

The tears are falling; the goodbye is over.
We all shuffle out; to the elsewhere.
I can't go; I need to rest.

(Call if there's...anything)

Ron Partridge

The Conversation

I know we can make it, if we keep on trying.
I'm so very tired, I just feel like crying.
I know that you're hurting, I'm hurting too.
It's so overwhelming, I don't know what to do.
Take one step at a time, we will get through.
I caused this whole thing, I'm sorry I failed you.
Don't say that again, you know that's not true.
I love you so much, you're really the best.
Come here and hug me, let's get some rest.

Mary Viveiros

In The Distance

I notice in the distance signs of the coming storm.
Creatures of all kind scurry from rage that's born.
As the clouds roll on in the sky turns a grayish green.
People here and there fleeing, then not a soul is even seen.
Then with a mighty vengeance the storm hits with all its glory.
The winds are blowing through the trees listen to its story.
Ribbons of light align across the sky with flashes.
And the artillery of the storm speaks with all its crashes.
Tears flush from the sky as heaven cries.
It rains for a while then slowly to a stop it dies.
The storm continues through its cycle until it comes to cease.
The birds begin to sing again chirping in the trees.
The sun soon peaks and shines from behind the cloud.
Showing one and all that tomorrow is aloud.
An arch that prisms that atmosphere a rainbow for all below.
Across the vast canopy of blue, the sky puts on a show...

Mark S. Cooney

This Quiet Night

A mark of first nightstroke gels in TV static cast upon the far wall.
This sundry hour, I sit with myself upon reclining cushions and stare
into tranquil nothingness of carpet fragments,
  inundated with intangible miscellanity
of debris and garment shards, while the clock
  mimics the end chords of the one sonata,
filling the air with false Ludwig.

'Tis a quiet moment now.
  The undertow of silence receded the chimetones
far out to sea. I sit atop a pillowed shoreline
  and scan the shag horizon for seashells of popcorn
and bottlecaps, where creatures of my interest
  made their homes, washed up discarded upon
the floor, while the static storm keeps its fury
  in a plastered atmosphere.

All is silence, save the creaks of boards and bones.
  This house and I settle in; one, a terrestrial bed,
tucked in by nails and mortar, myself, with my ample
  blanket of skin and hair, to soak awhile in this
wash of Time, while that steadfast monochromatic rain keeps its
fall.

C. J. Sivert

The Vampire Claudia

With childish roundness, and the grace of a cat,
She glided through the rooms of a New Orleans flat.
With gold silken curls, and a beautiful face,
She slept through her days, in her lovers embrace.
Born to darkness at five, trapped forever in youth,
In her fathers lies, she sought out the truth,
Of how she came into being in her evil existence,
And find it she did, despite her fathers resistance,
And faced with those truths, she tried to take the life,
Of her creator, cutting deep with her knife.
Then with her lover, her father, she left the new world,
To seek out kindred, her plan now unfurled.
She traced her roots slowly, to a french theatre,
And lived there, contentedly, with her new mother.
Until the parent betrayed found her at last,
And she was destroyed because of her past,
And as he said, while through the theatre he crashes:
"Dust to dust, and ashes to ashes."

Elizabeth Allen

From Baby's Point Of View

I wonder what the baby thinks as on the floor he slides;
He cannot tell what's on his mind, in no one he confides.

One day I sat down on the floor and looking up I drew,
Some interesting conclusions from baby's point of view.

Our table is a grand affair, mahogany so fine.
But underneath where baby looks is rough unfinished pine.

Our chairs are fine when looking down, but looking from below,
the seats are rough and splintery and chalky price marks show.

And underneath the "high boy" where baby's eyes must stare,
dust has gathered, spiders spin; no polished surface there.

They polished only surfaces that grown up- folks can see;
they hide the rough sides underneath, away from you and me.

I wonder if, when baby's grown, (our precious little lamb)
he'll recollect the things he's seen and know the world's a sham.

Mildred Larsen

Just For You

Sun goes down moon comes up another day is past
Every day I spend with you is better than the last

Every morning we arise to go our separate way
Thoughts of you and your sweet love fill my every day

My love for you burns in my soul
For all the world to see
It burns so bright it lights my night
It burns eternally

I proudly hold it in my heart
Each and every day
I feel it grow and overflow
The dawn of each new day

Most of all I want to say
Your love has made me glad
Without that love to lead my life
My world is very sad

So sweetheart I say to you
My love is ever true
As my wife you are my life
My love is just for you

H. Roger Stewart

M.O.M.

There are those who belittle a mother-in-law
I've never needed to develop that flaw
There are those who tell jokes at this person's expense
I let it be known, I deem this an offense

You have been a model of strength in our lives
You pick us up when our spirits take dives
You have always been great to those of us here
That's why we respect you with thoughts that are dear

I have lived so long without my real mom
Her absence was lessened because you're around
My calling you mom, has never caused strife
She knows you fulfill a real need in my life

My best wishes to you on this special day
May continued good luck and good health come your way
I hope this days happenings aren't considered a bomb
I will love you forever as, my other mom

Calvin Stelly

Seen And Unseen

Words softly spoken with compassion,
Still fall harshly on my ears.

The sentence is imposed not for any crime committed,
Unless in unknown karmic sense,

But rather by my doctor who, healer though he be,
In this case cannot heal.

Duty bound, he must impart the truth,
"Your sight cannot be saved."

By whomever spoken, truth must be told,
And also be accepted.

The doctor's voice goes on,
"You will see light and darkness."

From somewhere comes a message,
"There are other ways of seeing."

Oh, seen and unseen - light and dark,
I shall choose the light.

Rose M. Griffin

Love Can Hurt

You told me you loved me,
You missed and wishes you could be with me
but when the time came to be with me you
had something better to do which wasn't better at all,
I told you that I loved you and I meant
what I said but why didn't it seem as though you did,
How could you say it and not show
it and not show and though to mean
it why did you even bother is it all
a game or is it what I've been waiting
for you don't know it but it hurts to
know that you can tell me all this
and yet have me believing and then
not show it in the littlest way,
why of all the people did you have
to pick me to hurt?

Candace Upham

Untitled

This is the last day, the last day I'll hug him, kiss him, touch him, feel him rubbing on me Passionately. His soft lips touching mine, his tongue making mine so sweet. His big, sexy eyes analyzing my body. Sleeping on his chest, his heartbeat singing me a lullaby. The last day his hands will travel around the body, that one day I gave to him. His body and mine tied up in a knot, that slowly untangled as this day came closer and closer. As this day ends, my heart sits on the dead blood vessels that one day ran like a wild fountain for his love. As he stands outside and I walk through the doors that lock behind me, I see him through the window taking his last steps that one day walked in my life, I decide to walk behind him and take his hand, now it's our last day, our last day on this earth where one day we fell in love!

Juana Jimenez

"Brothers"

Brothers have a taste that can't be erased;
the taste that their power is filled with greatness and grace;

The love for their Sisters and Brothers is true;
it shows because they give to their communities, too;

Brothers are strong for they have great power;
they use it wisely to create, not destroy or devour;

Spiritually, they know that their power comes from within;
not merely from the dark shade of their skin.

Nicole Wilson

Hello Love

You were always there only a touch away.
Like a soft drop of rain you came into my life,
spreading beauty wherever you fell.
One day you touched me.
Now I am beautiful never again will feel life is just breathing.
I am alive, happy and everything around me is happy and beautiful.
No longer do I see the world through a cloud but the rays of
sunlight is everywhere.
The night no longer is just darkness,
as the sun goes down and night becomes alive.
I love the night, the darkness with all the different sounds,
you hear but don't see.
Never again will the sun rise when I won't know that you are near.
It's like an unknown soft whisper I close my eyes and there you are.
My life will never be come the same as before because of your touch.
You are love.

Polly Hayden

Patches

My name is Patches: I am a puppy.
I have a master and a friend named Patti.

My friend plays ball with me,
and runs through the trees trying to catch me.

She taught me all my tricks for treats,
and now I know them as good as the ABC's.

I'm naughty and nice we both agree,
but when I see that flyswatter it's time to flee.

My mom is a pure white Maltese,
but her babies were all gray like me (Schnauzer).

Now time has gone by and I have more family,
but they're as black as they can be (Yorkie).

As you can see I have quite a family tree,
because mom has been promiscuous and carefree.

Though one of these days mom better get serious,
and have a family of Maltese.

Or she's going to lose her happy home,
and have to come and live with me.

Bonnie Achord

Echoes

It's mine he says, no it's mine says she
I'll take that, give it to me!
She has my jeans, he has my shirt
You be quiet or you'll get hurt!
Stop fighting say I as if to the walls
He has my brush, she's a liar says he
She took my book, make her give it to me.
Answer the phone says she to he
Do it yourself, it's not for me.
Give me that jacket it's mine
Mom, tell me the time!
Mommy dear I'll be in late
remember I have a date!
Now she's married and he's in the army!
The echoes of yesterday live in this house,
for these years gone by of twenty three.

Dorothy Bartow

Can't I Dream

Can't I dream about the ocean of possibilities that
Lie in wait in the vast dynamics of my mind,
Strengthened by my desire to live life to its
Fullest, even when the storm clouds of the world
Seek to destroy my path to the finish line,

Can't I dream about the billowing prospects within
My soul, anticipating my move towards visions of
Victory, as it overflows with the confidence of
The faith I have in succeeding beyond other's
Expectations of me, in a world that pursues me
With intentions of seeing me fail the race,

Can't I dream about the massive opportunities
Granted me if only I would reach out and take
Hold, instead of cowering at the possibility of
Failure, missing a chance to rise above the
Negativity and overcome the fear, because deep in
My soul I know that to win or lose is not the game,
But to dream, and never aim

Margaret L. Burroughs

Blacken The Light

Can I blacken the light, that I had once sought
Of a perfect love, the angel clearly got
The one swept away, on that fateful night
In a twisted steel coffin, sealed fiery tight

Can I blacken the light, that I had once sought
For that time stands still, and never forgot
A time of such fullness, no tarnish no pain
All to be shattered, by the angel in vein

Can I blacken the light, that I had once sought
This unbearable void, that cannot be fought
I ask of the angel, who deceived my life
To deliver me peace, and blacken the light

James E. Cua

Concretize Your Dreams

Are dreams mere fantasies? Or realities?
The decision is yours to make
All who have acquired their goal
Concretized their dreams

Whether asleep or wide awake
Grab hold of your cherished dream
Challenge each thought, hope, ideal
With utmost zeal, and enthusiasm

Be an optimist, take full control
Set fixed focus on the goal
Faith, vision, perseverance, affirmation
Are ingredients of the Olympian

Famous inventors, explorers, scientists,
Athletes, leaders, writers, artists,
Took the step to the achievers
As they grab hold of each dream

So dream on! And on! And on!
Chart your direction, meet the challenge
Be creative, be hopeful, be energized
As you concretize your dreams.

Beryl Jones

I Must Not Cry

I must not cry for tears are no cure
To ease the achings of my heart in torture;
I must not cry for no tears will fall
Gone are my senses to nature's call.

Gone are the days of sorrow and grief
Here comes the time for a new leaf;
The merry face of spring and summer
Cast away the blues of yesteryear.

I just rise in every fall I make
For life is not always that great,
Maybe the dream I dreamt was too high
Now I swear my love, I must not cry.

Perchance a day may come for me to sigh
My griefs to a love-lorn stranger passing by,
But I swear my love, I must not cry
For my heart is barren and my eyes are dry.

Perla D. Camara

The Tumbleweed

The tumbleweed came tumbling by,
Down through the field of ripened rye.
Across the meadows and down the lane,
It rolled and tumbled all the way.
It tumbled down to our garden walk,
And over the hills and under the hawks.
And now, at last, it tumbled away
Down through the forest at dusk of day.
I watched it as it rolled out of sight,
For I knew it would tumble all that night.

Shirley Pedersen

Memories

Remembering yesterdays of ours,
With fondness and sadness,
Of parents, of children,
Of spouses, of more.

Remembering, living,
From day to day,
Year to year,
Century to century.

Reliving the past, ours;
From horse and buggy to cars,
Dirt roads to superhighways,
Earthbound to outerspace.

Seeing our children flourish, grow,
Remembering mine through ours,
Watching a growth within,
Replenishing them and us,
Reliving ours through theirs,
Remembering, ours.

Living, growing, loving;
Remembering, still growing, always loving; memories.

Andy Jay Daniels

Simple

You lose someone that you loved
You thought they loved you
But then they just leave
They care about something else
other then you.
You get on with your life, but it's
hard the memories, the holidays,
time you use to spend together.
When will they ever learn their mistake?
When it is to late.

Heidi Simmons

Caves Spelunking

Air cooled our hot summer blue jeans at the hills opened mouth.
We crawled a cold stream and jagged rock path
in a flashlighted tunnel until we welcomed
an ape-like stance. We stopped into a circular pool
and covered our belly buttons in the freezing flow.
Up the incline stalactites and stalagmites cluster into jaws.
Sharp protrusions jostled our muscles along the sinister path.
A broken camera makes three poses look like ghosts.
Three arms show. A hand touches one of two heads
to kiss spirit forms who roamed mineral hallows of earth.
I entered trembling, fearing death from felled dirt rumbles
and back-scraping, inching forward under dome coifs of rock sublimity
terra. But came out ready to face hail, lightning, and world winds.

Thelma T. Rountree

Declaration Of Dependence
(Manifest Destiny Consummated)

Our dear country was born bountiful
with every conceivable blessing yielding rife
there for the taking though needing pilgrim sound rule
as they arrived these shores with hope for a new life.

Their destiny quite early was manifest:
To subdue the land from coast to coast
harvesting the deer and antelope and all the rest
benefiting from all the earth's resources the most.

Those hardy early Europeans came in droves
seeking those hospitable coves
along our seashore, vast resources beaconing
doorway to the cornucopia of fishes and loaves
though a land overflowing with honey, yet soon a reckoning.

Alas, so soon the destiny was achieved
with population burgeoning and resources grieved
Mother Earth was in dire need of being relieved.
She had generously given to the good and ravagers
now 'twas time for earths friends, environmental managers
to began natures vital clean-up and reclamation
with ideals renewed and Dependence uttered in Declaration.

Travis A. Cox

Life Without Heroes

the world is ripe
need a leader of the people
someone who speaks 90's truths
someone willing to live
someone willing to die
the sins of past generations
springs growth of todays pain
generation past now dead
have left us no sanctuary
a life where there is aching hunger
a life of total hopelessness
blood flows from all corners
death common in the youth
children packing guns, not disease
society has failed them
single mother struggles to feed
a job not paying what she needs
while the boss fulfills her dreams of living,
the mother recycles and borrows just to live.

Denise Longo

A Dream Of Enlightenment

So large the world so small is me,
to accept the things I cannot see,

To step off the world for just one minute,
could last a life time and all that's in it,

I'll never forget it the day I did it,
it seemed the world had awakened,
and all that's in it,

The night God reached out and took my hand,
and led me into some enchanted land,

A world of colors so vivid and bright,
it led me on all through and night,

A night of terror it began,
until he reached out and took my hand,

It's weird and beautiful and so untouched,
and this is why I love it so much,

So few have felt this feeling of mine,
this feeling of endless, endless in time

Winifred Madeline Smith

"The Danger"

Eternally encased in the earth
silently suffering from no sun.
Certain cold corridor cell
inside leaching, lurking like a lion
a beast more barbarous than in any book
raving, raging, speaking rigamarole
it feels only anger it sees only anguish
This phlogiston creature plainly pales to
a man who lives what he hates.

Rick Neff

I Hope

I hope, when I know my life has gone,
I hope, when tears can no longer fall.
Signs and symptoms come my way, I hope.
When others slowly turn their back and walk away.
I reach out my hand and I hope, that
someone is there, who cares enough to touch me.

Donna Edelen

Reminiscent Of Roses

A red rose so bright, touch of many.
So meaningful, it comforts mind over matter.

Affection of acceptance in description; but
yet so touching.

Let it not forget, it has symposiac of affection.
Times it represents symbolism of togetherness.

Love and memory.

The past not be forgotten, when relationship
may have past.

Memory and heart will always last.

Dwell in happiness, not only of one, for lasting
the will of infinity.

Volition, shall my will be won.

May a red rose of silk, endure a lifetime
in memory.

Patrick Moquin

Aftermath

There is no rest for the weary tonight

While my head spins with tumultuous reverberations
Of an unwelcome evening
I cannot fathom the realness of this moment
Why I lay on a cold bed
Or why my body
  Drabbed in blue
Appears to be less than inviting for my suitor

The wasted water that has fallen on a stainless steel floor
Cannot pull me from this moment
And no amount of hope
Will reverse the winds that blew down that shaded alleyway

Wrong place, wrong time

No explanation, no rhyme or reason
Nothing to tell me why

Tomorrow they will pull me out of this cold, dark freezer
To later put me in a cold dark box
Above me, a granite pillar
After me, another statistic.

Melissa L. Csencsics

My Home

Alaska is my home,
The best place I have ever known.
The animals are magical,
I hold their memory dear.
They gave me a present, a surprise.
They filled me with love,
They filled me with peace.
They gave me something I shall never release.
The grand moose stood tall, my favorite of them all.
The red fox, a quiet wild pet, one whom I'll never forget.
The sled dog Husky, so beautiful and strong,
That's one animal who could never do me any wrong.
A large and smiling bear looks at me and roars,
She knows I admire her and she's mine in a way.
Ah! This place is so lovely!
I love the wild ways! Of forget-me-nots,
And fireweed, of animals, and play.

Bethany Sweet

It's Fragrance Fills The Room

Its fragrance fills the room
  to greet me sweetly in the evening

Its ever growing state
  fills space between each lovely petal

The striking richness of its hue
  adds burst of color to the room

Petals soft as newborn skin
  thick sturdy stems support infinite beauty

Like pillars of an important building

These are the things I used to bring my teacher
  especially in springtime, especially in June

My dad cut them for me
  knowing how much it meant to me

To have had such a special dad
  was surely a wonderful thing for me

Its fragrance fills *my* room
  especially in June

Patricia Tripi Salazar

Fruit

A peach, a plum, and
even an apple,
I find these flavors in a
bottle of Snapple,
A tasty variety from which
I must choose,
They all taste great,
what do I have to lose,
I try out the grapes
and taste a cherry,
But maybe I want a
banana or strawberry,
I snatch a melon,
but I want some cantaloupe,
Raspberries look tempting,
I will choose soon I hope,
A lemon or lime, but those are too sour,
I just can't choose, it will take me an hour,
Well, I finally chose after a hard decision.
I think I'll have fruit salad!

Amanda Perry

Sanctuary

Night life-
well, that's not for me.
Partying-
is also something I don't need.

Music played soft
is soothing to the soul-
Better on the ears,
not banging out of control.

There are times when, being around people
makes my day.
Then, there are times when,
I have nothing to say.

Often times, there is a place
I love to be-
And that is in my own private
"Sanctuary"
Inside of me.

Maderia Mack

My Shadow

It hurts me,
But you still do it.
I hate you,
But you're still here.
I ignore you,
But you're never quiet.
You follow me,
Everywhere I go.
You're my shadow,
I can never lose you.
You annoy me,
So I make fun of you.
You're different from me,
So I reject you.
You have problems,
But I don't care.
You talk to me,
But I don't listen.
You're everywhere I go,
And everything I do; that's why I am you.

Susanna M. Corson-Finnerty

Do What Right

When I was a kid my parents always said.
Do what right.
When I want to hang with my girls
Do what right.

When I want to have the latest fashion and
it show all my action.
Do what right

When my boyfriend is filling my head with
his sweet nothing.
Do what right.

When my skirt is fitting just right but
my Mama said no way that too tight
Do what right.

Why the teacher is try to fill my head and
I rather go cruisen' instead.
Do what right.

Why do what you right when you feel with all your
might that you are losing a fight just to.

Do what right.

Rochelle Trappiel

Our Teacher "Angelique"

She will be there to guide them;
take each by the hand;
to teach them to help them,
through lessons she has planned.
She will answer their questions,
until lessons are learned.
They will leave her to conquer,
their own little worlds.

So proud we are, her Dad and I,
of what she has become.
So full of hopes and so many dreams
that have finally merged as one.
Her dreams fulfilled she will now emerge
a lovely young lady to serve a role.
A role as a teacher, and guidance she will have,
from someone much greater that Mom and Dad.

Patsy E. Romero

Friendship

A friend is a person who is always around
When you need a helping hand
A person who gives strength and confidence
When you feel you can no longer stand

A friend is a person who has mutual interests
And respects the way you are
A friend gives genuine love
A friend is heaven's shining star

A friend is someone who radiates laughter and fun
A friend is a very special person
Second to none

I have found that all of these qualities are important
Therefore, our friendship must be everlasting and true
For I couldn't have found a better friend
As understanding and loving as you

MeLyssa D. Bailey-Barnes

Playing With Fire

It sneaks up on you like a prowler
It whispers sweet things in your ear
You want to believe it but you're afraid to come near
You get closer and closer and believe its every word
You never want to let go
You fall deeper and deeper into its grasp
And when you least expect it
It runs away leaving you broken-hearted
You've been tricked by love
Even though you smelled the smoke as
it rose higher and higher you did
not know enough to stop the fire
from burning your heart

Jessica Mayer

The Lightning Bugs' Return

In my garden one summer's eve, among leaves of a cucumber vine,
appeared the light of fireflies;
bringing to mind a childhood game of mine.

When day was done, I would linger till twilight
to see what we called-
the lightning bugs' return.

The darkened sky would then be filled with glowing lights,
as I would focus my eyes
upon a yellow, blinking lantern.

Reaching for a bit of bioluminescence,
I gently cupped my fingers around a firefly and
brought it close to view - the slender bug's bright essence.

One of God's wondrous creatures I did see,
crawling in the palm of my hand; then taking off while sending
his identifying signal to a flightless mate.

Now an old man;
I once again reach for a flashing, luminous lamp,
renewing an old acquaintance of mine - by my garden's gate.

Vincent S. Amadeo

Untitled

Life erasing itself dryly and slowly, echoing
The contemplation of a once fallible, sober and early angel;
Only a wistful eternity lulls its observer into such a discerning detachment
That his doubles would lose themselves in their elegant tautological dreams.

Do not linger / the bridge or the wake or the mirror

The quotidian mirth of the perennial travelers
Wilts by what those not waiting for them hope to be the middle of their journey.
And even their speech is a sign of affliction,
An unreturnable child of that darkly unquestioning silence beyond despair,
Destined to leave them in that vast and nebulous country
Where everything born of the spirit eventually disappears.

Alexander Kaplan

My Ancestor's

My Ancestors-white, black, Indian, Cuban.
Hatian, Jamaican or whatever
they maybe...
Will always be a part of me.
Whether you come or go from here or there,
We all must be given the right,
to be treated fair .
We all come from the same tree,
that gives us all the right to...
Equality!

Tanisha Marie Upshaw

Lost Childhood

Down the street, around the bend
next to the sign that reads dead end
stands a white house with shutters of green
from the upstairs window at night I have seen
a sad little face with tear stained cheeks
begging of me to help find what it seeks.
But the number of years make it hard to recall
are all the tears for the loss of a ball?
No, I suspect the reason for tears
is for the loss of the number of years
and this is the reason the face persists
and the tears are for a childhood missed.
Yes, now I know for it's easy to see
the face in the window is a reflection of me.

Allen H. Anderson

Happiness

I told you that I love you.
And that is true.
You make me quiver when you say, "I love you, too."
We say we're getting married.
I hope we do.
But it's so long to wait.
I hope we make it through.
I just can't see my life without you.
Their would be no happiness, no love.
No one could hold me the way you do.
Someday, and I hope it's soon, we will get to be together.
No one will break through.
The day I get to be with you will be the greatest.
That's no lie.
So please, Mike, Never say good-bye.

Crystal Loomer

I Remember You

When I see a sunset,
I remember the first day we met.
When I travel from place to place,
I remember the beauty of your face.
When I see a bird soaring in the skies,
I remember the blue in your eyes.
When I see the wind blowing through the trees,
I remember your hair blowing in a cool summer breeze.
When I see the sunrise,
I remember the sparkle in your eyes.
When I'm lying awake at night,
I remember holding you so tight.
When I day dream on a lazy afternoon,
I remember the smell of your perfume.
When I reminisce,
I remember your sweet kiss.
When I think about us being together,
I remember all the memories I'll cherish forever.
When I awake in the morning lonely and feeling blue,
I remember you.....

Craig D. Canfield

Sitting In The Wind

When I sit in the wind,
a strength and happiness purify me.
I no longer feel the stress and agony of
being closed up and alone.
I feel happy and want to dance.
My heart jumps from a lonely world to the
winds precious gift of contentedness.
I no longer feel like one standing alone,
for the wind is right beside me,
and as long as I sit in it,
it always will be.

Jennifer Anklewich

Storm At Sea

The ocean roars with fierce delight
When a storm is in its flight
For peaks of foam that stand on top
Will rock a ship of doors that lock

Each time a storm does appear
Each sailor will hide, and swallow his fear
For each will show that he is strong
To stand with power to the throng

The wind will sweep each sailors face
Who will survive this raging race?
For nature knows that it must end
The ship survived with all hands - Amen

Antoinette Sicala

Baby Bird

I took it for granted that you showed me to fly
I thought you always protected, smothered me and wondered why?
And now I see from old photographs of you and me
No, I was not the little girl to be sitting on papa's knee
But the child who was like a baby bird pirched high in a tree
Your shoulder carried a tiny baby high
You were like that sturdy tree that stands strong and still
And as the little bird learns to spread its wings
And finally flies from that big tree
Your memory keeps reminding me of that precious gift you gave to me
My darling you will always be free

Cornelia K. Faucette

The Separation Cycle

My thoughts remain so vivid and clear,
Hurt and frustration are present, but ironically no tears,
Remembering the past and living in the now,
Life must carry on, some way...somehow.
As I stand in my world and open my eyes,
I can see the vast light which surrounds me, but never simply his smile,
Every now and then, he feels very near,
Then I suddenly awake and all becomes clear,
He is going through the motions of living his life,
He converses with passing strangers, far more than his own child,
It is one thing to understand the reasons he went away,
It is quite another to understand, he never walks my way,
One day he shall realize, one day he shall see,
He lived his life gradually, without loving me,
As I close my eyes and my thoughts and drifting down,
One day I will met him again, some way...somehow.

Kimberly Ayn Lee

Cycle Of Love

If this be love. What have I done?
If this isn't love. Why haven't I run?
"Oh love! Are you there? Oh love can you hear?
Oh love. I am sure you are there. I am here!"
This is not to be, this I can see.
You are not slow, it's just time for me to go.
So, as we part, I'll carry in my heart
For the next time we meet, something sweet
Will appear, the next time we again are near.
Of this I'm certain, there will be no final curtain.
This is your life, and this is my strife.
As for now, I shall only exist,
For this is winter, and the snow is like a mist.
Then follows spring, and the warm winds of bliss.
And again I shall call out, but this time I won't shout,
In a voice smooth and soft, I will whisper aloft:
"Oh love, I know you are there, I am here.
Oh love, you are there, oh love, I know you hear."
If this isn't love, I will run.
Since this be love, I know I'm done.

Raymond H. Parker

A Friend's Lament

There are too many things to worry about,
Too many things indeed.
Like, are they going out?
Or what do they need?

I beg and I plead for them not to,
But they just don't listen to me,
For all the friends that I knew
End up spending a lifetime in misery.

They'd rather lose at Russian roulette.
They'd rather tie ropes around their necks.
They'd even rather jump without a net,
Then see what the game of life has in their decks.

Renee Raudonis

Through A Window...

Flight, flight, flight.
Said the thousand voices of the birds.

Greens, blues, and reds.
Swirl through my mind.

Chains, locks, and out of reach keys.
Keep me in check.

Love, freedom, and life.
Are out of our reach.

Darkness, the cold, and death.
They wait for us.

Haunting memories, sadness, and pain.
They are our destinies.

Trust, love, and money
We don't deserve them.

Escape, escape, escape.
Said the thousand voices of the flowers.

Stay, stay, stay.
Beckoned the darkness.

Listen to the birds, escape.
Exit your mind, through a window.

Rick Lopez

Always Here In Heart

The pain has not eased,
So heavy on the heart,
Since you travelled on, my friends,
And left us here apart.

Thinking about you often,
Always on the mind,
So many good times with you, my friends,
Wishing they didn't have to end.

Missing you today,
And everyday to come,
We'll learn to laugh instead of cry
For that is what you would have done.

Must go on from here, though,
You both would want it that way,
Living life to its fullest
Making the best of each day.

Be at peace, my friends,
In the place you have gone,
Pleasant memories will remain in heart
Though you have travelled on.

Lisa A. Arute

Ten Words

I feel so alone sometimes dreaming of you;
the need for your love just tears me in two.
I can hold you, and you see the love in my eyes.
But, the smile on the surface is just a disguise
for the ache in my heart and the strong need to say,
"I Love You, I Need You, Please, Take Me Away"
from the everyday life that keeps us apart.
Please, help me release these words from my heart.
Ten complex words that seem simple to say;
but, I worried if I did, you'd soon walk away.
The strength that it took to say them last night,
made my heart skip a beat with unspeakable fright.
You kissed me and held me, but spoke not a word.
I know that you listened, not knowing if you heard.
Now, there's fear once again and my heart still will ache;
I wonder by speaking if I made a mistake.
Did I scare you into running when you heard me say?
"I Love You, I Need You, Please, Take Me Away!"

Lauri R. Walker

"He Never Said Goodbye"

He broke my heart and raped my hopeful soul
He laid to rest my living trust
Then left me to black, the color of mourning
And he never said goodbye

The sadness, I fear, will become a part of me
I deem it ever present, minutes to months go by
I will never understand the "unfeelingness"
Of this seemingly feeling man

His life is, as was before, ignoring my existence
What was done, left undone?
From the high of love to a few rungs below depression
Paper mache in pouring rain

The sorrow he has willed me, deeper than deep
Lower than low, has left me less than whole
I will never trust in love again
With pure and giving care

Life alone, no remarkable joy, but less more pain to bear
The glory of the moon and stars are no longer in my vision
I lower my eyes now, in despair and shame
Unworthy, because I now disbelieve in their magic

Carol Ann Mann

Day I Was Naturalized

"How many colors are there in the American flag?
"Three. Red, white, and blue."
"Do you know the meaning of these color?"
"Red stands for courage, white for truth, blue for justice."

Officer's voice was comfortable.
I studied hard, I memorized everything.

"Congratulations!"
Officer's word spread over my head like big fireworks.
Her face looked like Statue Of Liberty.
From her right hand, grabbed torch
and felt like running all the way to Atlanta.

For eighteen years,
In my mind Mt. Fuji was highly standing.
In my heart the hometown taiko pounding.
Now I can see her in the distance.
Now I can hear it so far.

The day I was naturalized, I stood facing east
bow to Japan then proudly salute to the State.

Aki Sogabe

Mona Lisa

Abundant like an angel, booming like a baby benz, captivating as cape code, desirable and delicate. Emotionally engulfed with empathy, feverishly fidelity, Genuinely gorgeous, Heavenly as Hawaii. Inviting as an Indian summer, Jerusalem to a Jew, knee deep in William Kay. Longing for the last judgement, loving the laws of Moses. Mona Lisa the magnetic, her river flows as long as the Nile, to drink this narcotic you are baptized in the name of generation now. Oxygen of odyssey, paradise perfume, questions Nostradamus quatrains revealed in revelations and rapture. A true saint with a sapphire soul, terminally thermal nuclear tantalizing, unique and universal, urgently looking for Utopia. Voluptuous volcano spewing emotions of love, lust, compassion and fear. Women, whooping, weeping Mary, X why zee. Mona Lisa, not of canvas and paint or portrait of, Mona Lisa a living being, soon an angel to be introduced me to heaven's bliss, Mona Lisa touched my heart as our souls embraced and kissed, Mona Lisa.

William Kay

Peace

The world is weary with pain from the past,
We need to find out how to make peace last!
All the killing and suffering and the endless need
for something beyond our neverending greed.

Where has the beauty and peace gone to hide?
Is it gone with the ocean on an oil slick tide?

The creatures God put here for us to care for
have been beaten and slaughtered and still we hunt more...

The children are starving and crying with grief,
Our trees are stripped naked, not one single leaf.

Has the answer been here all along, up above?
I shout to the sky, God, where is the love?

The answer came and its
message was chilling...
Love never left, you just won't stop the killing.

So when you walk out into this scarred wonderland
Turn around, look about, love is within man!

Michael Newton

Heart With A Ring

For you I open my heart
and I place this ring
my heart full of love
as sure as the sky above
to you I love and hold
please take my hand and place the ring
look beyond all that has
caused so much pain
for there will be nothing to gain
take the ring and place
it next to your heart
say the words I do and I always will
look up and beyond the hill
to the field of lilies
there you will see our love
from all things above to your heart to mine
from all that holds the ring of hearts
for all we are about to start a long journey we will have
the two of us the golden heart ring
and all the good luck it brings.

Faye Blanton

Grandma's Little Girl

Little hands grab for mine and there's a kiss on my cheek.
Her eyes sparkle as she looks up at me with a peek.
"I've come to see you grandma", she blurts out at me.
"Did you make me cookies?" "Can I please go see?"
I never have to say a word, my smile lets her know.
And with a little giggle, off to my kitchen she will go.
She never ever walks, she's always on the run.
But having her here with me is always so much fun.
We sit together and I listen to what she has to say.
There's so much to tell me and she only has a day.
The time goes by so quickly, but the questions never stop.
I would just answer one and out another would pop.
Her visit is over and it's time for her to go.
I hug her tightly, I shall miss her so.
"I love you grandma", she tells me so sweet.
"And I liked your cookies." "They were a great treat."
With a wave of her hand she's gone from my sight.
But I will have sweet dreams all through the night.
I was given a present to help me grow old.
It's having my grandchild to hug and to hold.

Charlotte Kaye Smith

The Man On The Moon

Sitting low on the horizon,
A round globe,
Reflecting light from the sun,
Shining back at me,
The smile on the face,
Of the Man on the Moon.

Craters make its eyes, nose, and mouth,
On a half moon we see half his shining smile,
On a crescent moon we see a profile of his shining face,
On a full moon we see his whole shining image,
We see the Man on the Moon.

Michelle Anderson

Masks

My smiling face and laughing carefree ways
are only a disguise, only lies
to hide the pins and knives
lodged deep in my soul and breast.
They prick and twist and rend,
keeping me from peaceful rest,
and give rise to the lies I tell
to hide the pains I secretly keep.
Hidden deep within shining armor,
shut out from light
that might raise them to the surface
and burn them from sight,
they lurk and hide and prey,
and stain bright smiles a pale gray.
In a unguarded moment, carelessness may reveal
the demons that gnash and gnaw my humor.
A laugh cut short or perhaps
a smile that fades and slides away
signal a prick or wounding reminder
of thoughts of yesterday.

Marc D. Popovich

Please Don't Make Me Eat Apples!

Please, please don't make me eat apples!
I'll play the apple song on my piano.
I don't like the crunch because it tastes like rotten punch.
I won't eat apple pie.
Whenever apple comes to my mind, I feel like I
have no mind.
I'll play with Mr. Apple Head.
But, please, please don't make me eat apples!!

Michelle Flummer

Twisted

Kids have a weakness, that has to do with their past.
The point at which they had to grow up fast.
The boys all depressed so lonely and scared.
Growing up with a family who just doesn't care.
He thinks to himself, "How could this be",
"How could my parents do this to me".
His mom doing drugs, His dad out of sight;
A boy who sat their and cried every night.
A boy wishing he had good parents, not just that,
A boy who thought he was nothing but fat.
He swore he'd become the best, he promised he would.
He wishes he could change his parents, if only he could.
He's changed so much since then,
He doesn't want to go through all that hurt again.
He ignores everybody who says he's not strong,
He can't wait for the day, He'll prove them all wrong...

Brenda Haugen

Albedrio

Did you not know you never make a choice?
Have you not learned your acts are not your own,
and all you do is at some higher voice
you must obey, although to you unknown?
Some smirking universal dramatist
hath writ your lines, for you to act and be,
your speeches fit the plot, or would desist;
Pierrot, you dance for them to laugh to see.

When you laughed yester eve, it was not you,
yours was a mirth ages ere then decreed,
and your regret, ordained too, had no need.
You were the spinning leaf the long wind blew.

Yet do not cease to cling, since you must fall.
That leaf best spins which waits. This is your all.

J. Kellogg Burnham

The Key

The greatest task I'll ever face,
  Is being worthy of God's grace.
In fact, I know I never can,
  For I am but a mortal man.

I ask, "How can God care for me,
  When I fall short so constantly,
Of what God would that I should be?"
  His endless love, Yes, that's the key.

Can you imagine love, so great,
  That God would open Heavens gate?
The love of God is so immense,
  That it goes beyond my mortal sense.

So much my God has given me,
  My family, health, and country free.
But giving's not a one way street,
  And an obligation I must meet.

I feel that God would have me learn,
  That I should offer in return,
A portion of his gifts to me.
  A small price for Eternity!

Fredrick R. Barbee

The Blackness

The blackness of the night hurtfully moans.
Its only silence speaks demented sounds;
Frightening all that saw its silent way;
The night creatures even stay far away!

Excluding the owl, keeping awake;
Hooting its existence far and away.
Calling for victims to cross in its path;
The weak will all feel its harshness in wrath.
The strong will fight 'til they win or are weak.

The victims around all hear the struggle;
No one will help for the fear of defeat.
Hiding away from cries gives fears,
Since they all know how the struggle will end.
Hiding, hoping, all blackness is soon gone.

Julie Snader

A Mother's Love

A mother's love comes deep within
and sticks with you through thick and thin.
When you feel overwhelmed with rejection
you can always turn to your mother's affection
and you'll never be lost with her protection.

A mother's love is a gift from God
to set out your life so it never goes wrong.
She teaches you all good and bad.
She'll show you love that you would have never had.

Although I've yelled and shown her hate
her tolerance seems very great.
I've put her through a hell on earth,
but I'd like her to know
I know all she's worth.

A mother's love will never fade
and this is why I hope, I pray
that she'll find happiness
this Mother's Day.

Tina Wilcox

Soaring - Soaring

Soaring, soaring, never boring,
Noble Daedalus be proud,
What a feeling, no pollution,
Soar above that fluffy cloud.

What sensations, no vibrations,
Oil and gas not needed here,
Catch that eagle, he's too agile,
Where to land we have no fear.

Here's that uplift, here's our thermal,
Watch the altimeter climb,
Hope our crew is watching for us,
We've been gone a long, long time.

Can you hear that swishing sound?
Check the clock, it must be wrong,
Pull the spoilers, start descending,
Round her out we're on the ground.

Hope the working week is short
Hope the flying weekends long.
Shine the perspex, check the 0_2, take her up and sing this song.
Soaring, soaring, over our restless world.

Nelson C. Montgomery

My Cherished Heroine

You walked in, a radiant Snow White face.
The eloquence of flow, the relief of thorough exchange
Altered my dwarfed insecurities.

As the rushed hours sped by
More and more you reminded me of the Venus Goddess Aphrodite.
However, you do not laugh under contradicted masks of charmed wit.

The Goddess of Love and Beauty was Aphrodite.
You, like the Swan she symbolized, protected me from the treacherous deep.
The severed waters were assured by your steadfast dam.

We refer to mythology, and we can seek authentic Gods and Goddesses.
All misplaced waterfalls pursue a quick escape.
Awesome magic of destiny turned restless water into a colossal mint green ocean.

Penny Bandy

"Cowboys Are Sailors" "Ol' Sad Lonely"

Cowboys are sailors who got no boat.
on vast desert islands with horse and stiff rope.
Who ride their fast bows with lightning fast speed, no fear of ol' danger, from squal or from steed.

On clear starry nights, come down from fast pace, sing songs to a half moon with solemn sad face.
And be it tall cactus, or porpoise swim by,
there their only true friends come low tide or high.

Now cowboys are a lonely lot,
and sailors boats adrift will not
though on the same racks their covers are hung
wild they are lonely and sure to die young.

So last lonelys a wild man be it fast bow or steed,
careening towards glory with lightning fast speed,
with only one slip on life's sharp razor's edge,
or falling towards glory over life's last longest ledge.

So good bye ol' sad lonely I sing your sad song
alone with the cactus with half moon along.
I like you more somehow now that you're gone.
Good bye ol' sad lonely I'll soon be along.

Stanley H. Artus-Cooper

Missing Daddy

It's been five years this coming March
since we've been apart
and you're never coming back I know,
even still I find it hard to let go.

Every night before I sleep into my mind you creep,
haunting me in my dreams never close enough it seems.
I can't remember little things,
your eyes, your smile, your touch
but still I remember enough to know
I miss you very much.

I think of you even though emotionally it's tough,
I dream and dream though it seems
I never dream enough.

When you know someone is leaving still you don't think to say good-bye.
And when their gone all you can do is cry.

Your last moments in life that I spent with you
I should have told you that I love you
but instead I just let the moment go
and now you will never know.

Gretchen Anderson

Two Sides Of The Grave

From beneath the morbid graves lives two sides.
one very dark and gruesome and
the other softly lit and warm.
From one, blood-curdling screams
lurch from deep down, and the other
soft music and delightful voices
spring forward.
Claw marks of a deep-rooted hell
fall in to this decrepit place,
blood traced within
almost a reddish black.
Screams of damnation
flow out of this ice-cold place,
the quiet once again.
Soft and beautiful rainbows of light
and no signs of blood, claws, and pain.
This is within the soul.

Jodi Fleming

"Emotions"

As I look up at the big blue sky;
I feel as if I want to fly;
to feel the wind in my face;
and let my worries all erase;
to look beyond the big soft clouds;
to where you see the birds in their crowds;
of where they soar around the oceans and the seas;
to find their new home on one of natures trees;
and as I soar, it seems the higher I rise;
the more I hear somebody else's cries;
but, all I feel is a joyous relief inside;
I just can't turn back as much as I've tried;
to where I use to be in a frail state of mind;
not after my soul has felt the freedom of some kind;
but, then I hear this familiar cry;
and then I realize I could never say goodbye.

Karen Rahier

Millenniums End

In our modern days of computer chips
When kids shoot kids for diss, that's hip
With parents too busy, they sold their souls
For bigger cars and God who knows
A generation they call X
Cannot seek comfort in intimate sex
The evil spectre of A.I.D.S is around,
Putting our loved ones and friends in the ground.
Nuclear weapons rein supreme
Like some gothic nightmare dream
The ozone layer is wearing thin
We've only begun, to realize the trouble were in.
I hope it's not too late, to turn it around,
For if it is, God help us,
were surely hell bound.

C. N. Mellonas

Power Plague

We're the plagued people
tormented are we.
It's our own fault, it's man's evil disease.

As it blusters its way into your mind
taking you over slowly, a day at a time
from crime, and corruption to sexual disease
our own politicians line their pockets with
greed, the country falls and all are deceived.

The horsemen are coming there is no relief
we are the walking dead, controlled by this
thing. Power Plague!

Mark H. Aldasch

Never Say Goodbye

One day the time will come
When we will all depart.
We know our job on earth is done
and our journey now will start.

Never should we say good-bye
because to me that means the end,
It just leaves us wandering why
all things have to end.

We again shall come together
but in a better place
We will live there forever
with love in our hearts and a smile on our face.

Never should we say goodbye
because to me that means the end
It just leaves us wandering why
we're all afraid for this journey to begin.

Cynthia Enrique

Life Is To Enjoy

I awoke early this morning, the
sun had just begun to show and all was still.
I peered out the window, just as
a chipmunk scurried across the porch
in the morning chill.
I opened the door and stepped on to
the porch just outside.
The frisky chipmunk hurried into
the wood pile to hide.
The air was cool and brisk, but the
sun was already beginning to feel warm
it gave me a good feeling and made
me glad I had been born.
The little things in life are often
missed and are so free
Just because we are to busy, and
don't take time to see.
God has made every thing beautiful and good for us to enjoy.
Even when we become men, young or
old, in our heart we can still be just a boy.

Joseph D. Mullineaux

Metamorphosis

The differences between you and me
Are far greater than I can begin to imagine.
My eyes are fresh and uncertain
While yours are weary of the world.
My skin is taunt, smooth and without interruption.
Gathered creases have given yours the hint of harshness
For no one reason.
He is ignorant who believes to possess
The knowledge you have earned.
I am young—My life is a mystery.
You are my elder—You long for my face.

Rebecca Marshall

Time!!!

Time is a thing, if left alone, it will
surely pass by, all the days, and all the
years will be gone.
That's when I fill sad, the time has
gone and left me behind. I should have
been out grooving, but instead I was on
the side line waiting, as the time kept on moving.
That's me just plain and simple a lot
of years have gone by, you can bet
sometimes I wanted to hang my dead down
to cry, time was slipping by and I knew if
I kept filling down I would surely die.

Milton Bryant

Melodious Memories

Certain events and old songs bring us memories,
Some pleasant and some fraught with pain
In familiar old songs, we dwell in the past again.
Remembering the somer days and the happy days of the years.
Recalling with mirth and with tears.
Pictures come of a moonlit garden overshadowed by trees,
A haunting melody of a violin upon an evening breeze;
Picnicking by a stream, beneath summer skies
A stolen kiss, enchanted by smiling eyes.
A waltz-time that blossomed into a heavenly romance;
The young intoxicated by the ecstasy of the dance.
Memories take us back to a distant day;
Reflections of bygone years that Time has carried away.
Let us discover a new song and bid these memories depart;
Old-fashioned songs are too sweet and shatter the heart.

Helen M. Montgomery

Whispering Advice

What treasure do I guard
alone on my island
checking for breaches in the castle wall?

What treasure would I risk
if I lay my body down for her
like a drawbridge?

The earth whispers advice to me
in autumn
as the field goes to seed

And in spring
as the passion of wild flowers
overwhelms me.

Ronald Keeney

Dedicated To My Daughter

Ten years ago, on a springtime Day
a child was born-to Nina-Jane
Her eyes was blue like the skies,
Her hair was blond and soft and face so wise,
you'll think she came to me
from "Eden Paradise".

I touched Her tiny fingers and tiny toes too
and felt great compassion,
with something sweet and new.

I'd like to tell the "World "from North to South
and East to West that God Creation is still the best.

A new born child is a great reward,
Let us then praise our God,
and let us read His word!

Nell is Ten years old now -
and I don't know when and how
she learned to talk and started to walk
and read and write for mothers Delight.

Nelly Kwiatkowski

The Key

As I sit and ponder weary,
I notice that the world is dreary,
Longing for new things to see,
New hopes, new dreams, new things to be.

I sit alone a lot these days,
wondering what words not to say,
to open the doors I must find the key,
for in this new world of hopes and dreams,
I must not forget,
the key, is me.

Constantina Mourtos

Awakened

His hand to his heart whilst he wrestled in sleep
Effluent the pulse of measure to keep
Ephemeral beauty of prescient dreams
Where crystalline shores and silvery streams

Reflect the glitter of roseate grace-
Translucent the Form transmuting the face
Of moribund hope and transient mirth
To infinite joy which heralds the birth

Of peace, of knowledge, of fulness, of rest,
Of wholeness, of healing, of all that is blessed
As spectral rays dissolve, diminish and dispel
The longing and the loss in ev'ry tear that fell.

Awakening in stillness, intently he doth quest
To what meaning and purpose the visage was impressed
Innate a voice sonorous and silent doth intone
The flowering of faith mid glory that was shone.

"Of all that was promised thee, of all that was kept
In the motions that stirred thee while lightly thou slept
So have I kept thy prayers and ev'ry precious plea
That parted from thy lips as offerings to Me."

Anthony Brantley

Lone Shadow

The Way I Feel Now Is Different From The Way I Felt Then

Sometimes I look upon the earth and I feel as though I am alone.
As though I were the only one who felt the emptiness of being loved.
The sorrow that brings tears to your eyes as if I could see the
people around me, but no one could see me.
Sometimes I felt like a shadow that people could talk about.
I'd try to reach out for someone to hold me but yet I couldn't be
felt, for my heart was yet so empty.
This feeling of needing to be alive is very deep inside.
I look around me at all the living upon the earth and I say
to myself, have I not yet awakened.
Is that why I am yet in the darkness of a shadow.
Maybe some day I'll be strong enough to open my eyes, and then
shall I no longer be a shadow upon the earth.
I'll watch and listen for one last time, and pray that my day shall
come soon.
When I myself shall smell the roses and feel the wind upon my
skin and then, maybe then I shall feel that I have awakened and
my heart shall beat again.

Brenda F. Beatty

A Fisherman Reflects

(A Tribute To Lee Wulff)

The larger trout, much less shy,
completed the rise and took his fly.
The blue of the pool was lot in the swirl
of this giant char whose freedom was spoiled.

Back and forth through pool and riff,
the leader stayed and not a slip.
The tiny steel attached and with
a small white clump for his name sake whips.

Up in the air and down below
this silvery mass of fin and bone,
free and wild but a moment ago,
is lured to net with Lee's control.

My memory rings of long ago
when Lee released that fish you know.
The Native Brook was free to go.

Bob Jacklin

Just Friends

We joked about sex, but never had it.
I told him the sensitive parts of a woman,
He told me what he liked.
We saved our experimentations for everyone else.

My friends thought we did it on the sly; so did my boyfriends.

I helped him interpret the oxymoron of feminism.
He helped me avert moronic chauvinism.
We'd hike together
Escape the lit pollution
Dream at the universe
Stay up 'til we passed out, delving into the what ifs
of our relevant significants.

He went to Colorado
I went to Europe
Saw him later, and welcomed him
back with a smile
and a nice, warm, kiss
on the cheek
I looked him in the eye and knew
it was time for a story.

Malia R. Mauk

The Rain, Wind, Snow, And Sun

The rain is the pitter-patter
Of the feet of God's children,
Walking in the courts of God.

The wind is the sweet smelling breath
Of a newborn baby,
Sent from heaven to earth.

Each and every snowflake,
Represents every happy time,
That shines through the incredibly rough,

The sun is the joy
That you can find,
Anywhere if you look hard enough.

Noelle Mills

A Picture Of My Soul

The wind blows through an open meadow...
Daffodils dancing in the breeze as if choreographed
By nature's own director.

Peacefulness brought in by the shade of the elm
In which I rest my soul reveals the beauty
Of the world in which I have evaded for so long.
A sense of serenity fills the air of that which I breathe.

How long can my soul endure this tranquility?
I enjoy this peace in my soul, but yet there is something
missing. Someone to share this with.

Should I feel guilty? Maybe so, but who am I
Not to share this beauty with another.
I suppose one day I will, but as for now
My selfishness will paint its own picture.

A picture of my soul.

Michael Darden

Oh Geez!

Oh geez, there's a mouse eating cheese.
Oh my, there's a beehive nearby.
Oh ox, there's a fox.
Oh gee, there's something eating me!
Oh no there's...

Chris Walker

I Learn To Accept Others

Your mother showed the ultrasound images to your dad.
"But there are two of them," he said, amazed.
Yes there were!

I held you both outside the delivery room.
One by one your dad placed each into my arms.
Tears of joy glistened on his cheeks.
He had the biggest smile I had ever seen.
His face shone like an angel's.

You have enriched my life
because
you have taught me something about God.
He doesn't make cookie-cutter people,
even when they are twins.
One grew to become Eric
and the other grew to become Evan.
God creates each individual uniquely.

Loretta M. Wadsworth

The Throne

I sit on my throne.
My subjects dance around me, shouting praises in my name.
As I raise my hand in greeting, cheers erupt from the crowd.
And best of all, more are enthusiastically pouring in to the throng
every minute.

I sit on my throne.
I am king for a day, a week, a year, a lifetime, or until I leave.
How popular I am.
They love me.

I sit on my throne.
A convoy sinuously makes its way toward me.
Bearing gifts on a litter of white silk.
I sigh, because my time on the throne has ended.

I sit on my throne.
I get up.
I reach for the little lever on the side of my chair someone
conveniently put there.
And watch, curiously,
As it all swirls down into the little hole at the bottom.

Christian Wong Sick Hong

Divorce

Plow your fields of discontent
sow the furrows with seeds of regret...

Water your crops with tears of anger
fertilize them with bitterness and malice...
Harvest and bind them with the strings of revenge
then store them in the hollow hole of your heart..
Protect them from the sunshine of love...
And you can feed your family and friends for years
from your table of hatred.

Do not save any seeds from that harvest
When it is time to plow your fields again
plow them under with forgiveness...
Sow your furrows with new seeds of hope.
Water your crops with tears of peace..
Fertilize them with joy and love of life.

Harvest and bind your crop with cords of kindness
then store them in the fullness of your heart...
Protect them from the vermin of jealousy
and you can feed your family and friends for years
from your table of contentment.

June Tarr Baker

A Tizzy For Gizzy!

Everyone knows why I like to dress Gizzy,
People 'paws' to look and laugh till they're dizzy,
I make fancy costumes which keeps me busy,
They're as unique as an old Tin Lizzy.

She likes to wear wigs, glasses, and hats,
She'll even do tricks if you roll out a mat,
I dress her up then sit her in a seat,
She'll let me do anything for a nice doggy treat.

She never fails to bring smiles upon faces,
Whenever I take her to public places,
Everyone knows why I like to dress Gizzy,
She steals people's hearts then
"Gizzy has a Tizzy!"

Gail Marshall

Fade My Light

I can only see you in my dreams and in my thoughts
but I cannot feel you, touch you, kiss you
Where are you darling?
You left me and I am now without a soul, without a heart.
I cannot cry, the pain had dried my tears.
if you are a cloud please rain,
if you are a bird please sing,
if you are the sky let me see your eyes,
if you are a flower open up for me,
if you are my hope please take me with you.
I want to die, I want my light to fade, I want to be with you.
Oh darling please take me, I want to see where you light the sky
where you light the stars, so you can light my soul.
I don't want to dream no more, I want to feel, kiss and touch
I want to be able to cry, to love, to care.
Oh darling, be my hope I want to be see the flowers, the birds, the
clouds.
I don't want to grow old,
what matters most to me is to be with you.

Cali Mauricio Soued

The Vengeful Orb

Darkness split by blue-white light
Thunderbolts from heaven's height
A billion volts to purge.

The sea retreats from shore and docks
flopping fish and dripping rocks
Poseidon's wave approaches.

Great rocks of ice cascade like rain
Breaking bone and crushing grain
There is no place to run.

Granite sentries long thought dead
Spew their vomit hot and red
A flood of fire descends.

Whirling, swirling winds of wrath
Uprooting all within their path
The sky turns green and mean.

Grumbling groans from the depths of hell
Mountains sink and valleys swell
The ground itself defiant.

Of wondrous man and endless glory
None remain to tell the story — the living orb reborn.

D. C. Berry

Indigo Peace

The darkness envelopes me - calm, warm, gentle
My eyes open to the blackness inside.
Indigo clouds lazily stroll across my thoughts.
Clinging to myself to ward off the demons, I hear a cry.
Stepping out, out, off the cliff of nothingness;
A whir, a click, the voice of a mother -
"Baby mine, don't you cry. Baby mine, dry your eyes."
Turning, searching, I follow the sound.
Licking, eating, the pain devours my soul;
Indigo peace, holding a child, I awake to dimness.

Bridget C. Clark

What Is Orange

Orange is an orange
You can touch it on a crayon
You can taste it on an ice pop
You knock it over as you run
You see it on a tiger
And you can see it on a car, but rarely.
Orange is a good carrot
Icing on a cake
And colored sand to put in a jar.
Candy is orange like a jaw breaker
It's falling from a tree on you in a breeze
Orange is a fox and an orangutan who
has a flat black face
Orange is a butterfly
Orange is a marker and a crayon that
smells good
It bites you on the nose
And when a volcano erupts you better run
Orange is a flower which I don't believe

Scott Levine

Are We Alone

Are we alone,
Tell me that were alone.
Listen to me, I saw a man, not like other men.
Short and stout, with his green skin.
The sun, could it have been the sun.
The heat of the day, the cold of the night,
I believe I saw a U.F.O last night.
The F.B.I. disclosed my claim,
the CIA turned away,
The president laughed and ran away,
And now I know it's not a scam.

Chris Landroch'e

A Friend

She came into my life one day,
fitting as easily as a piece in a puzzle.
There were others who came and went,
but she was here to stay.

She sees what others don't,
and understands things they never would.
Her excellent brilliance makes some feel inferior,
but only a word is needed and off they go again.
She is always ready to give this gentle encouragement,
whenever an uplifting note is needed.

There may be others who could do more;
others to loan their cheery smiles,
but she gives all I need to help me plod onward.

Lara Eenigenburg

Feelings

Sometimes feelings get in the way, but they have to, don't they?
You say that you're fine, when really you're feeling hurt, betrayed, and angry because you're strong and can take the pain, right?
You say that you love him to death but really inside you have mixed feelings; you doubt your own faith in him; he loves you, right?
You smile and laugh when in reality, you're feeling the pangs of animosity, anguish, revenge, and fear.
But mind you, these feelings can't stay buried forever, and so they must surface sooner or later.
But sometimes when you smile, you really mean it. "Laughter is the key to happiness," as is often said. Maybe it really is. So take your key and use it. But use it only when this key of life is truly felt for by the heart for it never wears out, and shall fit the lock of time and age forever.
Feelings always get in the way for without them, where and what would the human spirit be?

Shannon Schumacher

House Is It Anyway?

Squirrels own our sun deck,
mallards swim the pool -
places which we cherish in the summer, as a rule.
Rabbits stole the front lawn,
possums roam the rear,
wasps have claimed the apple tree,
hornets buzz the pear.
Beetles from Japan abound,
frightful things dwell underground.
Something, but we don't know what,
lurks behind the apricot.
Other peoples' cats and dogs
fertilize our firewood logs.
Crows utilize our roof to screech,
blue jays pecked away the peach.
Our hallowed plot is owned by pests,
we're nothing more than paying guests
so, why is it that twice a year
the Town insists we're in arrear
and demands that we make trax
to pay the wretched Housing Tax.

Francis Storey

Colors?

Grey-grey-grey! Slowly turns to black!
Then black-black-black until you realize, that's not
"Where it's at."
You turn to red and black or grey just the same.
You see it as a kaleidoscope.
Black is not right in your social spectrum.
Red is expected, but not always your ultimate goal.
Grey turns into the medium in which most of us flow.
The kaleidoscope predicts the future like a written book,
Even If it's not right for your predicted outlook.
Middle-class citizens of the human race,
That's all we are in black, grey, or red form.
Black loves red-red loves black and the in between just the same.
We are all a blend of grey, until, a later day.

Mike D. Ross (4/25/69 — 8/13/95)

Reclamation

In dreaming, I lost my innocence.
In trying to regain that, I lost my dreams.
Lost I slept.
I stand here now, head hung low.
Opening eyes to see, a strange
and unknown place.
A place just as great.
Though harder to see,
Harder to feel,
I feel it.

Kyle Schwieters

Fallen Star

You glance up to the darkness
The life which seems so hard
The darkness seems so big
The light it seems so far

But up into that sky of black
A little sparkle glows
A little beam of warmth
Maybe starts to grow

So when you look at the gleaming people
Who shine on who you are
You can reach far beyond that darkness
For you've caught a Fallen Star.

Lindsay Henning

"The Black Rose"

For most, it's a symbol of death.
For some, it's a symbol of new beginning.
For me, it's a symbol of hope and happiness.

A piece of darkness
Long, silky, and black.
Standing alone
With almost nothing to lack.

Sacred, precious, frightening
These three words to describe.
Not crying, but bleeding
Not wanting to die.

For most, it's a terror's gift.
For some, it's just a flower.
For me, it's the meaning of beautiful.
Hour after hour.

Katie Polino

The Grin

Night is like a cover, hovering over the sun,
when the bright circle leans down, you know
the night's begun.
Things look different in the night, sometimes
they turn out for the right.
But when that monster turns out to be
a doll,
When the parents take a peek, the
children stop crying or do they just stall?
But when the parents close the door,
the children fake a peaceful snore,
And then a tree branch becomes an
arm,...stretching, stretching, scratching more,
And then that doll a smile so sweet, turns
an evil grin, jumps on its feet.
And then that doll with the evil grin,
comes over, kisses your cheek and tucks you in.

Candice Lynet Durbin

Why Me, God?

Lonely, hungry, confused and weary
He stays in constant motion
Filthy, sad, alone and rebuked
He must not stop moving
Filled with despair, hunger pangs gnawing
He moves to the beat of his drum
What he sees, hears or feels, no one cares
They want him to keep moving
Out of their lives into other's who
Blind to his pain, despair and hunger
Want him to keep moving
Out of their lives into other's who
Blind to his pain...

Stephanie L. Sweeney

The Best Of Fools

We are the best of fools
The sonnet and the verse,
And the deities of love
Who all three are cursed
To immortality,
Though a curse
This should not be.
Through verse
We enhance beauty,
Through rhyme
We enhance love,
Though some the greatest lovers be,
What retribution do we receive?
What retribution do we ask?
Immortality, inky and cold,
Though on immortality, one cannot live alone.

James Artrip

I Will Remember (On My Bosses Retirement)

I will remember Mr. Smith
An open-sesame and a warmth of understanding; and
Tolerance when tolerance was not always indicated.
I will remember a willingness to listen to half-baked ideas and
Advice that was tempered with kindness.
I will remember
Backing when a critic was too severe.
I will remember that anger was never stored for reference,
And, yes, I will remember the many trips,
With the hours of good fellowship.
And then there will be memories that will bring a chuckle,
And some that will bring a real belly laugh
And the many fine poems that were an inspiration in the reading.
All these things are harmonious in my mind,
And like the melody of a pleasant tune,
Will live in my memory.

Frank H. Gibson

"I'll Be Alright"

When I fall and can't get back up again,
and when I'm hurting, but only I can feel it
deep inside of me,
I'll be alright.
When I talk and no one listens, and when
I sing, but only I am heard, when I'm
crying and no one pays attention, when I'm
laughing at something no one else can see,
I sometimes think it's my inner mystery,
But still, I'll be alright.
When I'm dying and there's nothing you can do about it,
I'll be alright.
'Cause God has a shepherd watching over us.
My grandfather said these same few words
on his death bed, so we know wherever he is,
or wherever he'll be,
He'll be alright!!

Tiffany R. Godbolt

Entrapment

The day the sun went out in me
and caused the gloom to spread,

I should have saved a tiny ray
spread my wings and fled,

But the gloom engulfed
and did consume
and challenged at every turn,

Till that tiny ray, so very small
no longer could it burn.

Barbara Jaral

Alone And Dark

My heart sinking,
people moving slowly.
The sun is smiling on earth,
the moon weighing heavily upon the sun.
My heart beats faster when,
the moon comes closer and near.

My heart, beating harder through the night.
Sounds that are unbelievable,
Boom! Bang! Screaming!
Hoping the sun will,
rise the day with a smile.

The sun has come,
my body aching,
Wishing nights don't come.
My mind telling me,
must be prepared for the next night,
to Arrive!

Christina Holmes

Yesterday In Oklahoma

Yesterday in Oklahoma
I heard the people cry
Fireman save our children
Please don't let them die

Our land is exploding
from the left to the right
No one is all wrong, no one is all right

Yesterday is Oklahoma
I saw an eagle fly
As the bodies were scattered
he has a tear in his eye

You're an American Eagle
You're the hope of our dreams
Fly us free from the madness
where we can't hear the screams

His heart is bleeding
from the left to the right
As he flies with his left wing
and flies with his right
to lead us to the light

John Andrew Estes

"Soccer Game"

I have a soccer game today; I cannot wait, I love to play! I arrive
at the field, ready to go; I see Eric, Luke, Andy, and Joe. We get
in a circle and start to warm up; then Becky arrives and say,
"Sup?!" The rest of the team shows up very quickly; the starters are
ready, none looking sickly Shrill whistle blows, the game begins;
sideline parents are full of grins. My starting position is left
forward; Luke kicks the ball, it flies like a bird. Jason receives it
and moves toward the goal; He dodges a defender, but is tripped by
a hole. The opposer boots the ball to his team mate; who shoot's
the ball, alas, his fate. But Ken the goalie is a shield; He delivers to
mid-field. Half-back Hilary heads the sphere; it sails to me, I have
no fear. I zig and zag, I dodge and weave; defenders guess my
moves deceive. On I go ready to attack; dribbling, racing past the
full-back. With racing heart, the coarse is clear; the goalie sees that
I'm too near. My stinging shot is what he fears; I let 'er rip, I hear
the cheers. Ball snaps the net like a bullet; in the goal the ball was
finally put. My heart jumps out of my soul; ecstatic I got that
terrific goal! Big high-fives all around; "Good job!" They say and
backs they pound. I will always remember this glorious day! I
soared, I scored,
Hooray!
Hooray!

Amanda H. Heisman

"Daddy's Girl"

The beauty she expresses like no other
the strength and kindness of her father
the perfect family she once had
she wondered it to ever turn bad
as life progressed day by day
would she always be this gay?
Then one night damp and cold
her father turned very sick and old
she went to his side like a beach to its tide
to hold his hand as shells in the sand
one moment passed another to come
now it was her turn to give him some
of the strength and kindness he once gave
to try and get her to be brave
she told him not to worry
cause the doctor was in a hurry
and she knew if he passed on
his body would be forever gone
but the memory of her lifetime love
would just shimmer like a snow white dove.

Stephanie M. Rex

Y Road

When we are together, you said it would be forever
when you kissed and held me, I knew it was true,
we had our plans, you said you couldn't be without me
and me without you, I'd be lost and alone and blue.

How true, I'm lonely sad, and full of pain,
when I remember your promises and our future plans,
my tears kiss my lips, and come down like rain,
I'm being held by my memories, not by my man.

What we shared was deep and true and everlasting love,
my memories of us, are worth more than gold,
alone I'm not, for God's eyes are on me, from above
the aching and loneliness will stop I've been told.

I gave you my love, my life, my trust and my heart,
you decided our future, when you were at the "Y" road,
you forgot me, and that's why we are apart
which road should I take, which road...

Corina Hiel

"We Finally Met"

I'd been searching oh so long;
I was weary and so wrong;
Then Jesus came along.

He'd been waiting so patiently for my heart to see;
He wanted so much to walk with me.
He came into my life and gave it reason,
His love is true and knows no season.

He lifted me high above from what I was;
He gave me His grace and His love.
He put a smile where there was once a frown,
Because he picked me up when I was down.

He gave me strength to live each day;
He took my hand and said "I'll lead the way."
He forgave all my sins so I could live again,
And one day I'll go home to stay with Him.

Yes, I'd been searching oh so long;
I was weary and so wrong;
Then Jesus came along.

June A. Johnson

Inspiration

There are no words to express
How I feel about you
Because since the day we met
We shared a very special bond,
One that can never be broken.
You've been the inspiration for everything I do
Because I want you to be proud
Of the person I've become.
If it wasn't for you
I wouldn't know the meaning of the word love
Or the word family
Because you have always shown us
Nothing but that special love only you can give.
I will forever be grateful
For having someone like you in my life
And I hope that someday
I can be just like you
My inspiration, my grandmother.

Rosalinda Alatorre

The Keeper Of My Heart

My first true love promised me, that we would never part
And that she would forever be, the keeper of my heart.
But she said one day she had to leave; I thought my heart would break.
I held her close and closed my eyes and hoped I'd soon awake.
But it wasn't a dream and she left one day but, before we had to part
She told me again she would always be, the keeper of my heart.
Then I gave to her a heart shaped locket, a reminder of my love
She said it made her heart feel warm, like a hand inside a glove.
Then we held each other close again, with tears in both our eyes
And with one last warm and tender kiss, I told my love goodbye.
A lot of time has passed since then, yes a very many years
But the memories that makes me smile, outweigh the ones of tears.
One day as I walked through the park, the park where we used to play
I heard a sweet familiar voice from right behind me say,
"I have a shinny little locket shaped like a tiny heart"
And when I turned around there stood, the keeper of my heart.
As I looked into her smiling face our eyes again filled with tears
And I wondered why we stayed apart for so darn many years.
Then we held each other oh so tight, never more to part
For I will never again let her go, the keeper of my heart.

Ed Reilly

What Would God Say

Knowing why a plane flies, or why someone cries,
Why some people lie, or why everyone must die,
Knowing how an engine works, or what gives a boat its drive,
Why an operation can go smooth, another one will meet there doom,
Knowing why the thunder sounds, or why there are trees,
Why people live like they do, or why bees live in a hive,
Knowing why a song is sang, or why one becomes insane,
Why there is crime, why there is fear,
Knowing all of these things, just what must we learn,
If I missed you today, tomorrow would I feel the same,
All learning to thrive, to what end do we realize,
And if we make the judgment day, just what would God say.

William Pringle

Sunset

The sun glowed resplendently in the evening sky.
It resembled a forest fire blazing on high.
Contained in a circle, a perfect flaming red ball
Begging to be bounced!
Sinking lower and lower,
Soon lost in the horizon.
Radiant clouds kept its brilliance alive—
Some a striking orange like freshly peeled carrots;
Others were deep vivid pink watermelon slices.
Were they painted by angels while the sky was still bright;
Or was it simply God's own way of saying goodnight?

Elizabeth S. Gill

A Commissioned Mother

A dream

I sought after that dream for twenty-something years. Oh, how I yearned for that dream to quickly be fulfilled. The realization of this quest came true, I now have...you!

You

I wanted you and you needed me, so God saw favor, and granted thee. I gave of myself as no one on this earth ever could. I cleared a special place in my heart and so that God would allow you space in my womb....

My womb

Was ordered and ordained, it was not blemished nor stained. It was Covered under the blood of the Lamb and this is where I will take my stand.

I will take my stand

Your existence is justified by my faith, my love. I loved you more, But God loved you best and you know the rest...A commissioned Mother,
Who stood the test.

Ava M. Washington

Lost In Illiterate Hunger

Yesterday I tried to find a word that was hidden in the
back of my mind. I lost it pouring a bowl of cocoa crispies.
I thought it came back to me when I was watching a
dripping single from Wendy's, and drooling all over my
T.V. screen. But then it fell along with my saltines
into a pot of tomato soup. The hot cream melted
in my mouth but dissolved the word on the tip of my tongue.
Then after a nap on the cantaloupe sofa, the blistering
lemon sun drove me to the kitchen for an icy cold red pop
and set off my mind again, in search of that word.
Then in a spoonful of strawberry jello, it came to me,
so vivid and sharp, I wanted to write it down.
In a shake, I found the closest banana pen and began
scratching each letter on my vegetable napkin, until
it struck me that I couldn't spell it; and then
it drifted away like it never came, back into
the mist from my cinnamon tea bag.

Libby Carlton

"Envy"

I envy one who can compose
A limerick, a sonnet, explicit prose.
I envy one who can daub with paint
Who can express in colors deep or faint.
I envy one who melodiously sings
Who into many lives much joy brings.
I envy one of whose skillfulness we're aware
Who writes beautiful music beyond compare.
I envy one who with eloquence speaks
Who chooses words to reach the peaks.
I envy one who appears on stage
Who dramatizes a part despite the age.
I envy one who can sculpt with clay
Who fashions figures, shapes for display.
I envy one with hands so deft
Who is equally productive with right or left.
In other words I envy those
With an innate gift that grows and grows.
I've tried so hard to do and be
Yet, I remain the same untalented me.

Hermanie Alexander

Untitled

Have you looked into the eyes of our children today?
Have you seen the pained expressions even as they play?
When was the last look you took of our children of today;
The fouled mouths and the things they say?

Little boys acting like men before they spend their youth;
Little girls coming of age before their time is due.

We ask why do not our children give us respect, and where in the future will they go?
Many will die in vain, while many others will find death row.

Have you looked into the eyes of our children?
Have you tried to lead them well?
If not your days too are numbered and your journey is to hell.

Teachers have to teach, parents must extend their reach; or soon the toll we hear will be humanity's bell!

Curtis Lee Watson

Heart To Heart Hug Fest

Day after day, just the same Ol' thing,
Always starved for warm fuzzy hugs.
Life in this Ol' world always reaps,
Hugs, oh so very conditional.
Find God's circle, there's a "Hug thing" going.

You can look around for your hugs here or there,
You may even look around the whole world.
But hang on, there is something missing!
It is the company you are keeping.
For in God's company, it's a great big Hug Fest.

Hugs, unconditional,
Hugs, that grow and grow.
The more hugs you give,
The more hugs you receive.
Love "Agape", God's perfectly designed Hug Fest.

Hugs that come so round, so warm.
Hugs that come so fully packed with love.
Stick it out for that Hug Wild Hug Fest,
For that deep in the heart love from God,
And that wonderful Heart to Heart Hug Fest.

Eleanor Pinnell Reid

Renovation

Please pardon my appearance.
I do not mean to offend you by my unkept dirty Face.
I am working on changing.
Would you like me to change for you?
How about my eyes? I can have eyes, smog fading to the blue sky
above the city.
Or, how about little black peppercorns?
Which ever you like, I will change for you.
My hair: it can be tight, golden curls, short and cute,
or Long, Bold Blue Locks.
Which would you prefer? And my skin.
The orange of orange marmalade.
Or would you like black, like the shadow under a pine tree, with
the white of my teeth, my eyes, shining through?
I do not mean to offend you.
I will change for you, for everybody.
Just hold me up, keep me going.
With your golden eyes, your green jacket. Please
whatever you want, whatever you do,
I will change for you.

Vanessa Long

Just Open Your Eyes...

I'm different from you and that's okay
'Cause we'll both need help along the way.
So many things seem to come easy for you
And I seem to struggle in all I do.
You can speak to make your needs known
Where I've had to find a language all my own.
You can run and walk to play
While I am wheeled all the way,
Or if I can even walk at all
There's a pretty good chance I'll trip and fall.
I've watched you and you are so smart
While often I just play the part.
They call me a person with disabilities
Yet I'm someone with many capabilities.
To most our differences might be many,
But when I look I don't see any.
So just open your eyes and you will see
Just how awesome I can be.

Annabelle Davis

Silent Partners

Silent partners guided by fate, moving through their lives.
Silent partners still waiting for their destinies to collide.
Silent partners searching for a place they can come home.
Silent partners moving together, even when alone.

Silent partners finally meet, on a night full of heat and fire.
Silent memories are made, as they come face to face with desire.
Silent glances reveal the beauty of mystery and joy in their eyes.
Silent expressions of their love are seen in their kisses and their smiles.

Silent partners dancing to the music in their heads.
Silent bodies rolling to passion intense enough to dread.
Silent soles are drawn together, as two lives become one.
Silent prayers are answered, that their bond won't be undone.

Silent partners guided by fate, moving through their lives.
Silent partners vowing never to leave each other's sides.
Silent partners will always know the place they can come home.
Silent partners moving together can never be alone.

Terri Greene

Hammer And Pen

Lord to you I come seeking advice,
Help me choose a gift for someone nice.
It has to be special - something for him,
To you he is "son" - to me he is "Jim".

Silently I listen this Your day,
I want to hear what You alone would say.
In the silence still and weak,
These are the words I hear you speak.

My child is creative, gentle and strong,
He is a man who knows right from wrong.
The gifts I would give him are not a toy,
With them he has the power to build or destroy.

A hammer and pen how can it be?
These are not lovely no beauty I see.
Child you are young and their value is hid,
It wasn't the cross, but what Jesus did.

In the hand of a man yielded to Me,
These gifts can show My love for all to see.
Take the tools to your friend named Jim,
For they have been chosen especially for him.

Esther V. Williams

Faith In A Vision

Tipped a bottle over, empty from the night before
Awakened by its shatter.
I thought you'd come back
But I was only speaking to your shadow.

I saw a vision, however grim
Full of confusion and doubt.
I reach out to my darkness
And long for the one I cannot live without.

My visions became bright, but tamed by fear
I cannot seem to finish what they've started.
They might turn bad or not turn at all
Can I really take that chance?

My visions are of you, but I need not see to feel
My light, my love
Burn through the night, you burn in me
As clear as a perfect memory.

And with every memory we paint a picture,
For my love I write a song.
To speak of dreams and hopes of our future
Things to make our hearts stay young.

Verissa J. Sadsad

There Is A Sameness

There is a sameness in my life,
A sameness of shadows and currents,
And the little minutes go scuttling past,
Like dead leaves skittering across the pavement.

For I have lost the sweet hush
Of the shivery silence of anticipation,
And the little minutes go skittering, skittering
In an increasingly flurried dance.

And still I wait for the fanfare
To announce the awaited hurrah,
And still the minutes go skittering
In a flurried, hurried, timeless race.

Whatever happened to the wonder?
And the mantle of the dream to be?
And still I hear the skittering, skittering,
The dead leaves on the cold, cold pavement.

The star so bright in the distance,
So near and yet so far,
The scattering, skittering minutes
Are hushed and silent...no more.

Joanne Pankow

Path Taken

As I have gazed through my
open field, I see a path, as I travel
down the path. It brings back memories of
my dear old home, and how as a child I would
wander down so many paths. Each path I
would see, would lead me in new directions.
The sights I would see in my mind would act
out a story. I could be a hero and save
a village from harm but all you would see
is a path of trees not me... then I could
be a captain of a ship, leading a crew
to a new land. But all you would see
is a puddle of water, not me...
Or I would be a princess in distress
waiting for my prince, but all you would
see is a hill and silly ole' me, but not
me. So now I am back from thinking
of those fun memories. That's all I'll
really have now, because I am older, and
now a new adventure is just beginning.

Donna Lemons

The Meaning Of Christmas

Christmas is a season that comes once a year,
To end the year with lots of cheer.
It's a time of giving and sharing,
And a time of loving and caring.
Christmas brings blues to some,
To those it may be cumbersome;
It ushers in good spirits in people,
Oh, how they celebrate it right!
And during this time we may spend,
Allowing the bills to overflow-
While the credit cards overextend
Yet, we must go with the flow.
Christmas is a time to reflect,
On the many gifts we select.
But most of all -
Christmas is a time to celebrate,
A time to celebrate the birth of Jesus.

Angela H. Bowden

Old Fashioned Manners

There's such a thing called old fashioned manners
that will never go out of style.
To show such respect is very refreshing and
considered by most to be a great blessing.
Thoughtfulness is the name of the game
that will open many doors that one can't explain
Also, it makes young lovers want to exclaim.
Consideration is the attribute people admire
and it may come in handy to have you hired.
Don't ever underestimate old fashioned
manners and they should never become obsolete.
Chances are if you always use your manners
you'll go through this life without defeat.

Eileen Sullivan Longauer

After The Rain

As the dew begins to form on the wet
grass, the slimy but silky slug appears
from under a rock.
The sun creeps around the corner of the
sires cloud.
The rays of the sunshine down warming
the grass blades.
A soothing gust of wind blows the blades
left and right.
the sun begins to dry the pavement.
The happy little children come out to play.
As the little boys and girls begin to play,
the color filled rainbow appear out of no where
to smile down on the children playing
to let them know of the new day God has created.

Hicks

Summer Morning

For when the morning starts
Its cheerful summer sound
Birds sing with joy.

The air blows cool to my skin
Comforting me in my blanket
With light of day pushing through my window.

My eyes and ears open
To find, I'm alert! Awake!
Snuggling back in my blanket

Only to wake again
To that summer morning
That I've been given from above.

Dorothy J. Sabol

Roam Free

Roam free as the wind my darling
I care too much to stand in your way
For you are my true blue in this world
Yet this I cannot convey

Peace is the one lesson in life we all must learn on our own
For the only true peace is light from within
Roam free as the wind my love

Its truth came to light a short time ago
On one dog day this August before
It was staring me straight in my eyes hard and true
It was for this that I'd suffered so long

Peace is the one lesson in life
We all must learn on our own
For the only true peace is light from within
Roam free as the wind my love

Roam free as the wind my darling and find that eternal state
I have faith you'll find me there and roam free as the wind as one

For peace is the one lesson in life
We all must share to be free, keep your head to the sky
Let love be your guide, roam free as the wind with me

Marlene G. Stevens

One More Day!

The Outer Banks of N.C.
was truly a sight to see,
I decided easily, there is no other place
that I would rather be.

Sounds of running wild horses
thumping through the grass,
happily watching them together
but not knowing how long it will last.

From America's largest lighthouse
to the first plane to fly,
it has been called "The Land of Friendly Faces"
and I've seen many reasons why.

Peacefully gazing into the calm waves
as they brush softly ashore,
bringing along beautiful seashells
like I had never seen before.

Enjoying the feel of the cool breeze
on a nice, quiet, sunny day,
it put my mind at ease
wishing I could stay just, "One more day."

Jason W. Rogers

To My Favorite Valentine

This Fourteenth day of February,
year Nineteen Hundred and Ninety Five.

To my Leo Valentine,
dearest lover of all my Valentines.

As I reminisce and remember my lover and I,
basking in loves radiance beneath sunny skies.

Encircled in the warmth of loves embrace,
passionately kissing while hearts entwine.

Making love under a blanket of stars,
Poetry-like plateaus time after time.

In loves secluded hideaway with my most,
cherished lover of all my Valentines.

Elinor Johns-Campbell

The Eloquence Of Silence

Said the quiet man who likes to listen, at times to be heard,
"The `Eloquence of Silence' is my spoken word."

"Wait a minute!" says the man who is loud..
"I'll speak when I please! This makes me proud!
Why give any thought to the spoken word..
now's the time to speak...the time to be heard!"

"No thought for the spoken word? What a terrible plan!
This makes me sad," says the quiet man.
"Time must be given to the word that is spoken,
this will allay thoughts otherwise broken."

"You are afraid!" says the man who is loud.
"I speak without thinking...This makes me proud!"

"You misinterpret silence as fear", says the quiet to the proud.
"The quiet are not afraid, but in their silence quite loud!"
"Pride", says the quiet man, "a deadly sin.
In Silence I speak, in Eloquence I win."

"You make me uncomfortable," says the loud man.. "yes you do.
I don't understand your silence, this is true."

"Then," said the quiet man, "here's what I suggest,
Learn the 'Eloquence of Silence' life's gift... The Best."

Jean Kelso

Independence Day

In the year of 1776 that paper was decreed
They were tired of oppression and wanted to be freed.

They wrote a Declaration, so the whole world would see -
This was, "the home of the brave and the land of the free".

They signed that piece of parchment, the leaders of this land -
Knowing, divided they would fall but, together they could stand.

A new world lay before them, untamed from shore to shore
They swore the would protect it, if it meant going to war.

Battles have been fought and many lives have been lost
So sad something so basic, has such a high, high cost.

'Seems freedom is a luxury, there's some would bind us all
Like then, together, we can stand, but divided, we will fall.

Del "Abe" Jones

My Skin

Afraid of being denied because of the color of my skin,
even thought about perhaps maybe changing it.

Brings uncertainty tomorrow if no stability today;
can't change too many things,
because then my skin's an issue again.

If I decided to leave I must approach another door;
right back to that problem my skin,
thought about perhaps maybe changing it.

It seems I hear a rap tap tap
at my own heart's door.
Someone's sought me out says my skin's not a problem;
says he created it that way.
I'm listening.

Perhaps hope's dawning on a transparent day.

This man gave me insight about the history of my people;
many died for my cause,
and never saluted their ring to freedom.

No longer afraid of rejection, because of the color of my skin,
even thought about perhaps not even considering,

Changing it!!!!!!

Trina Levett

A Place Called Heaven

God gives us flowers in the spring. Rain to nurture them so they will not thirst. In the fall, those flowers that were planted in the spring may fade away and die, only to grow once again in the spring. That is so much like life. God gives us life so abundantly. As we grow, there are trials and triumphs we are faced with along life's journey. Although we may not see what God has planned for us, we know that because we are his children when our life's journey ends, there will be a place waiting for us back home with Him.

Opal R. Carnes

The Appalachian

The mountains are ruthless they reach into the sky
The streams flow down their rugged terrain
And eventually find their way to the sea.
But I'm to stay here in this lonely valley
Always wondering what's on the other side.
As I pass, people ask me to sit awhile
But I have things to do and walk on by.

Many years have passed since my childhood days
And I've traveled many a mile from my mountain abode.
I've observed people in far away lands.
They are different, yet they are the same.
Each one searching for something
They think is just over the horizon
Yet if one looks deep, it lies in one's own entity.

Sometimes my mind wanders back.
To the place I left behind.
The seclusion of the mountains,
They bid me come, rest awhile.

Betty L. Kendrick

What Is Love?

Is love something you look at?
Or something you play with?
Is love something people can take
from you? Or something people make
you do? Could it be a boy or girl?
Could it be something you feel in
your heart? Is it roses or cards
people send to you on Valentines
Day? Or is love just in your heart
and will always be in your heart forever?

Melissa Ashwood

Kissed By A Star

There is enough stars twinkling in the night to send
you a kiss, for each star you see twinkling will be a
kiss upon your lips...Your lips leave a soft caress,
across my breast, where I cannot seem to catch my breath.
When your hands slide to the curve of my body, I shiver
inside, A shiver, that will not subside.
You hold me in your arms and I feel safe in
your embrace. I hold you in my arms, I feel that
it's the right place.
Your scent lingers in the air, even when you walk
away I still feel your presence there. You're carried
away by the wind, out of my grasp once again.
Just remember when you see a star twinkling in
the night, just be sure it's me, kissing you
good-night.

C. C. Persohn

Moonlight Dream

Goddess of light, whisper this is just a dream
As you enchant me with your ethereal beam,
Bestowing a blessing I hope on the love of my life,
My home, a love that has enable me to cope
With the wrenching loss of our union, which he trashed
With a nonchalant toss, and wasted a precious treasure,
Brimming with boundless pleasure,
Shimmering moon, in you I delight,
As you stealthily rise and bathe me in your light,
Like the caress I longed for all those years,
As I stoically held back the tears at his lack of love that kindled
my fears.
How quickly you rise above my house as I gaze at my new platinum
spouse
Watching me with such tender care, protecting me with your stare.
Tell me it was just a bad dream,
Those 34 years trapped by the tyrant's scream.
Touch me softly with your laser beam, and as I wake to your touch
Tell me I am still only twenty or such, and true love will reward me
with much. my desire.
You are so real, I can feel God through your lovely appeal.
Great comfort I feel ion your light, and God's promise that joy I
will again feel.

Deirdre McCarthy Schoeller

To a Tree in Autumn

With hues so fiery, passionate,
your leaves reflect a summer past
as smoke clouds fill the graying skies
with fall fragrance...

Having left their hangers crackly, wrinkled,
your leaves disrobe your skeletal body
shamelessly and unabashed
preparing for the advent
of ghosts and goblins...

Amidst breezes so brisk,
your dancing leaves choreograph
the birth of winter
during the finale
of autumn's ballad.

Benita Rose

The Mountain Top

If I climb that mountain top, what will I see?
Its valleys below.

If I climb that mountain top how many
times will I slip or even fall?

My struggles may be many, but my reward
will surpass all my difficulties,
encountered along the way.

Hopefully, I have prepared myself for the climb
and even the fall.

But if I slip and fall, will I get up once more
to go forward again, or will I return a defeated foe?

What inner strength lies within my soul,
as the trials of life surround me,
press in on me, even pin me to the wall?

Are the valleys too low? Have they become ditches,
which seem too steep to climb up out of,
or will God rescue me in my despair?

My Heavenly Father, who arrives just in time,
to take my hand and lead me safely to the other side.

Ida Griffis

Nature Sings

This is my father's world;
And to my listening ears,
All nature sings, and around me rings
The music of the sphere's.
This is my father's world;
I rest me in the thought
Of rocks and trees, of skies and seas,
His hand the wonder wrought.

This is my father's world;
The birds their carol raise,
The morning light, the lily white,
Declare their maker's praise.
This is my father's world;
He shines in all that's fair;
In the rustling grass I hear him pass;
He speaks to me everywhere.

This is my father's world; oh, let me ne'er forget
That though the wrong seems oft so strong, God is the ruler yet.
This is my father's world; why should my heart be sad?
The Lord is King; let the earth be glad.

Yanira M. Orellana

My Angel

Out of the heavens she came unto me, the girl of my dreams
you must know. Her hair aglow like the end of the day,
As the goes to rest in the sea.
Now the girl that he sent with the gold in her hair is
the girl I'm in love with today.
So-to him I am grateful, my heart is so full, for the girl
that he sent unto me, and I never can find the words to
express, my love for the one I adore. For when things all
about seem to be upside down, I know to whom I can turn.
The with eyes filled with tears, I think of the joys and the
hardships we have shared through the years. So-to God I
shall be forever in debt, for the girl that he sent unto me.

Frank L. Tarleton

Alone

I'm old and grey, my work now done;
I gaze out the window, as I sit alone.

The nursing aides come in and out;
not listening to, what I'm talking about.
My arthritic hands are in such pain,
please feed me slow when I eat again
You brush my teeth and comb my hair
Staring out the window and don't even care.

Please cover me, when you give my bath,
So at my frail, wrinkle body, nobody laughs.

I've lost my health, my family and friends,
please say "good-morning" as a new day begins.

Once I was pretty and became a wife,
to five little babies, I gave a life.

My family now raised, have moved away,
there's so much to them, I'd like to say.

I need you to be my family and friend,
giving my care with a happy grin.

My prayer for you, to the Lord above,
is when you grow old, you'll know love.

Lenora Montgomery

Flowers

Flowers are so beautiful and they
always smell so great, I love to see
colorful flowers blooming around someone's gate.
Some flowers are so pretty, people
have to stop and stare, most people
say "Hey look at those sunflowers over there".
Some little girls like to put roses in
their hair. No matter if they are red, pink,
or white, which is very rare.
Sometimes I wish flowers could
blossom in the air. Because there never
can be too many flowers for the world to bare.

Talayah Aleara Booze

"Really"

It really does suck to be me.
No one really knows who I am.
Some people think I'm sweet and shy;
To others I'm loud and dumb.
It really doesn't matter what they think,
No one really knows what's inside.

Sometimes I wish I could open up.
I wish they really knew.
But it always pushes friends away,
When I let my feelings shine through.
No one can ever know the truth,
No one can really know who I am.

Jasmine Helmick

"What About Spring"

S - could stand for sun that brightens all the earth
"but what about"
the son of God who brightens up our life

P - could stand for people going many places
picnics, parties, parks all bring happy faces
"but what about"
our troubled times we want to run and hide
we can find real peace of mind "if in him" we will abide

R - could stand for roses with a fragrance oh so sweet
"but what about"
the crown of thorns and resurrection morn

I - could stand for inning of every baseball game
"but what about"
the invitation given every name

N - could stand for robins nests with many eggs of blue
"but what about" our treasure chests way beyond the blue

G - glory, love and honor a pledge our soldiers give
to fight for stripes of red and white to defend our nation's rights
Glory Hallelujah or maybe alleluia
all praise we sing to Christ our King especially in spring

Jeanne Clark

Dreams

When the sky is cloudy and I am blue
My mind suddenly fills with the image of you
I don't know what it is about the mood that I'm in
But something about you makes my head spin
It must have been love at first sight
and if I were with you I know it would be right
Because stars over the ocean so pretty and bright
Can't compare with how you look tonight
But it all is a dream, it won't ever come true
So for now I'll just sleep and have sweet dreams of you

Alicia Sanders

Rage Of A Black Woman

As a black woman, I could never appreciated white woman,
She has tried to take away our blessed beauty by saying
that we are too dark, our hair is not straight enough and
our lips are too big. But at the same time, they
are trying to enlarge their lips, darken their skin by taking a tan.
May I ask "Who is really trying to be black?"
Think about it.
To our black me, whom they would say have "reached
the mountaintops", you dump us for your white lovers,
this is wrong. Did you forget who washed your clothes,
cooked your meals and struggled with you?
My brother, I was there too, or did you forget?
The pain you had within your heart, my heart was hurting
also. The days I had to send the kids to school and take
them to other activities, you were not there nor was
your white lover? So now do you understand why I could
never appreciate your white lover? Do you believe
within your heart that you are right?
My heart knows the answer.

Carole Lee Usher

Day And Night

The weathered old man sits at a table,
and curses the half empty glass before him.
His gray, withered face rests against his two
arthritic hands as he pities his reflection
on the window pane. Straggly, silver hair
covers his balding head.
He mutters a few words of discontent as he
sips the vile wine from his glass.
He rails against the cruel fate that brought him
to this lowly state. He asks God, "Why me?"

The old weathered man sits at a table,
enjoying his glass of wine.
His gray, withered face rests against his two
arthritic hands as he fondly recalls his times
of happiness and merriment. Straggly, silver hair
covers his balding head.
He breathes some words of appreciation as he sips the fine wine.
He clasps his hands together in prayer,
thanking God for all the wonderful
things he was bequeathed.

Beth Walker

A Mother Hold

As I grew though the years.
I remember hearing my mother say.
Watch out for this, look out for that.
Where are you going, what time will you be back.
I remember the time I climbed the tree and fell.
She was there to catch me as well.
As time went by and the days did pass.
My mother hold was like a looking glass.
For as my life slipped into adulthood.
My mother hold I now understood.
For in my life there is a child now, and I hope
one day he will understand.
That a mother hold comes from the heart, and
not the hand.

Marilyn Crudup Haynes

A Gentleman

I'm the type of person that's hardly been seen,
For I'm the rarest of rare as a human being.
I'm the one people search for time and again.
True to my heart, I'm a gentleman.

I'm the pearl at sea, the most precious to find,
To those that don't know me my heart's always kind.
I'm the most priceless jewel in all of the land,
Having me at your side is like money in hand.

Though on the outside I'm grown and seem really smart.
You know on the inside I'll always be a kid at heart.
And just to prove that my heart's of the purest gold,
I'll keep it real big 'till the day that I'm old.

And when I grow old and I'm no longer strong,
You'll still be in my heart no matter what you do wrong.
And when you think of me as you do time and again,
You'll know me as this, a kind gentleman.

Marina B. Kessler

The Gift

Dedicated to Renate

When I have gone for that last, long sleep
Remember me, but please don't weep
For all that is left is an empty shell
Which for many years has served me well

And I leave that shell to all mankind
To help the sick and heal the blind.
For if these eyes, that once served me
Should once more help another see
The fields of green, the sunset red,
Then who can say that I am dead.

So if a part of this shell you need
Take it with my blessing, and godspeed.
For the heart of me, the essence of I
Will be home with my Lord; it did not die
But returned with joy to my God above
And leave with you my gift of love.

Brian J. Strickland

Dear Mom And Dad

God asked me to write you this letter,
'Cause He knows that you both are real sad.
He said that I really should tell you;
I'm in heaven, and I'm really glad.

I know that I left a bit sooner
Than we planned, and I know that it's true;
There were things that you both must have wanted
Me to learn, and to see, and to do.

At first, I did not want to leave you,
And I guess I was scared as could be;
But then a bright light shone above me,
And an angel said, "Come, follow me".

"Your family will one day be with you,
But right now, still on earth, they must trod.
Yet soon, through their grief, they'll remember
That you're here, with the angels, and God.

So that's why God told me to write you,
Just to let you both know I'm "OK",
And happy, 'cause I'm here in heaven.
I'm not gone; but for now...just away.

Frances Rice

Through The Eyes Of A 4-Year-Old

Daddy?
Where's Mommy?
When's Mommy gonna come home?
When we went to see her
How come she didn't say Hi?
You said she was sleeping
But you always get mad when I wake her up
They said lots of nice things about her
How come she didn't say anything?
Then Aunt Mary took me for ice cream
I liked that

You said she's happy where she is
How come we can't go too?
Lot's of people came and said nice things about her
Will she be home for Christmas?
I like the cake she makes
With the pink stuff on it
Daddy
When's Mommy coming home?
Daddy... Daddy... Daddy...

Scott D. Nicholas

Precious Angel

Our precious angel Dario,
with Jesus up above
we send you our tears, our kisses
and all our love

You were something special
so gentle sweet and good
now you flew to heaven,
as all special angels should

Sleep my baby in God's light and love
we will all meet again in heaven up above

A piece of you will live on
in everyone's heart
this is not the end
it's a born again start

Good night my sweet prince
but never good-bye

Carolyn Petrov

Was I In That Dream?

What if I was the one who sailed on the ship with thousands
of other slaves or the one of hundreds of slaves who escaped
through the Underground Railroad to freedom?
"Was I in that dream?"

What if I was the inventor of peanut butter or the traffic light
or the one who became the first black doctor to perform the first
open heart surgery?
"Was I in that dream?"

What if I was the one who refused to give up my seat on an
Alabama bus or the one of the thousands who marched on
Washington with Dr. Martin Luther King Jr. and watched on as he
delivered "I have a Dream" speech?
"Was I in that dream?"

What if I was the one who became the first black player to
integrate the sport of baseball or the first black student to integrate
the University of Alabama?
"Was I in that dream?"

I am not only in that dream; but I am that dream because the
Almighty creator of all things created me and I am.

Kendra Carter

An Ode To The Living

I am sitting alone in the corner,
of a room inside my mind.
There is light all around me,
but all I see is darkness.

I am thinking of someone,
but I can never again see him.
He is gone,
he is never coming back.

He is dead,
and that fact I must face.
I can cry,
I can weep.

I can pray,
but the fact is it won't bring him back.

I must face this.

Jessica Bates

"Our Children"

A smile here, a tear there,
Are things we see each day.
As our little ones grow up,
And move further away.

We watch them grow taller,
And watch their minds grow too.
We try to help along the way,
To help them make it thru!

Sometimes it's hard to let them go,
Because we love them so.
But then the magic happens,
And it's time to show all they know.

They may surprise you a little at first,
Because they've learned a lot.
A whole lifetime you've spent on them,
And now it's time to stop!

But as a parent can we stop,
And not be part of the fun?
Because we've all been there before,
Our work is never done!!!

Mary L. Griffin

Life's Remembrance

Within the garden of life
Is the beauty and understanding
That blooms and carries the fragrance of love
For which I have done.
So remember
The scent of each day
As a different flower would give
Its essence to you
Some more delightful than others
Yet all wonderful to perceive.

Never will I forget thee
My sons and daughters of yesterday and tomorrow
For love has no measurement
Only its strength is felt
Unto all who know its power
As time moves forth
Love is its anchor.

Glenda Williams

"Your Pain"

I feel your pain in my heart,
at times I feel that it will tear me apart.

I see your pain in your eyes,
it stares through my soul without disguise.

I hear your pain in my ears,
it rings like a child screaming out fears.

Your pain.
I know your pain.

I smell your pain in the air,
it emits an odor that one cannot bare.

I touch your pain with my hands,
they tremble from the hurt that you can't withstand.

I breathe in your pain through my mouth,
it stings my lungs both inside and out.

Your pain.
I know your pain.

I own your pain—it is a part of me,
constantly destroying both of our glee.

Your pain . . . your pain,
I, too, live with your pain.

John Thomas Hilliard

One Lazy, Hazy Day

With cool breezes freshening this first day of June,
I pondered over the universe, and watched my flowers bloom...
The gentle opening of pedals — just one tiny miracle —
of so many on the planets, and in the unknown spirit world...
I looked up to the sky... I could see right through the haze...
It seemed I had a vision... I could see lightyears away...
The neverending universe - so incredibly magnificent...
I felt as if I was special - only I, saw what it all meant...
It all seemed so overwhelming when thinking of the scale...
I would surely give up sanity if I tried to tell the tale...
The birds whistled their tunes in the middle of the blooms,
and my story would never be said...
Though I'm left with a special vision, forever, inside my head...

Denise Marie Fidler

Please Take Me Back To Yesterday

Please take me back to yesterday, if only for awhile.
Let me roam the hills and play along the creek bank,
As I did in my younger days.

Please take me back to yesterday,
Back to that little house in the mountains,
Where love and caring and happiness dwelt.
Where sweet aromas filled the air,
from a kitchen always so warm and safe.

Please take me back to yesterday, if only for a day.
Let once again my mother meet me with a hug,
Or a kiss and bandage for a scrapped knee.
Let me wait at the door for my father, coming home from work,
So that we could have shelter, food and clothes.

Please take me back to yesterday, if only for moment.
And let me see two sisters at play,
Laughing one moment and fighting the next,
Yet growing closer day by day.

Please take me back to yesterday, so that I never forget,
The loving memories of family and home,
That my mate and I now, so lovingly pass along.

Carmen Huff

"Apple Sisters"

"Two" apple seeds cast to the fields of life,
 to survive, to grapple, in a world of strife.
Thru storms of anger, fear and despair,
 "ONE" challenged the forces of earth, sun, and air
And life that it was, that life to be born,
 the other not ready, "FOUR" years of a storm.
But soon they would meet at a time meant to be
 in the orchard of life, "those seeds you and me."

By then your branches were hearty and strong,
 swept me up as if saying "Sis" come along.
I hung on for life, this seedling of me,
 this must be the way of, "two apples" to be.
We struggled thru life in our tree, big and tall,
 and we apples will swing, till we wither and fall.
And fall that it be, apples like we, to come back
 again, you wait and see.
The flesh, the core, the tree as the door, we are
 destined to re-seed and be
"Corny-and-seedy" in the orchard of life,
 "Apple Sisters", you and me.

Dolores Barnette

A Cry For Justice

I'm lying here on my back
with a light shining in my face,
I hear strange sounds around me;
I wonder, what is this place.

I have these odd looking things
connected to my chest and to my feet.
One of them gives me fluid
and the other is to make sure my heart has a beat.

I've never done anything wrong,
I have only been here for a day;
So why must I suffer in pain
and have the price to pay.

You see, I had a bad start in life
and there is only one person to blame.
That person is my mother
because she chose to use cocaine.

I pray that someone hears my cry
and makes sure that justice is served:
Because I'll never have the chance at life
that I so greatly deserve.

Cynthia Hux Brewer

"The Black Man's Word"

I start these words off very
clear, so that all my African brothers
and sisters can hear. When one master is
gone, the world be so alone, and if you're
a true black person you must be strong. Fist
to the sky, black people will never die. A fist
for the white man's pain, all black people will
be the same. When we die, bury us deep and
lay the African colors at our feet. Put the
African colors to our heads and till our holy
master we did what he said. I'll hate for us
to leave our nation so soon but if we die,
we'll do it for the star and the moon. As
we die and go in the ground, when one
brother or sister goes, all black people
be down.

Cornelius Howard

Ignorance

'Tis for thee that all men yearn.
But it's an existence of ignorance to which they turn.

From the womb of life a man knows not.
He searches, and loses, and still knows not.
He longs for that which he always knows not,
will give him the will to know not what.

'Tis for thee that all men crave.
But it's an existence of ignorance to their grave.

The knowledge of Eve was passed to all.
But the dominant gender was first to fall.
He dictates and consecrates with nothing but gall,
for anything less would make him seem small.

'Tis for thee that all men wail.
But it's an existence of ignorance that is their jail.

To question himself, should he or shouldn't he.
To wonder aloud, what will be will be.
It is not the valor from the evolutionary tree,
but the fear of truth that he will be me.

'Tis for thee that all men yearn.
From an existence of ignorance I pray to learn.

Jerry Marshall

Grandma's Legacy

I remember grandma as a kind and generous soul.
Making others happy; this was her constant goal.

She was just a tiny lady, but what a mighty heart.
She'd go about her housework, happy as a lark.

When someone came to visit, she would put aside her chores.
And sit and listen patiently to all their many cares.

She would serve them home-made ice cream, and cookies that
 she'd baked.
They'd forget their many troubles, and how their hearts had ached.

Grandma loved her flower garden, each and every bloom.
When summer came around each year, they'd be in every room.

She wasn't always pleased with us, and sometimes kind of stern.
We listened very carefully, as we had much to learn.

It was her loving touch and smile that got us back on track.
We always knew she loved us, of that there was no doubt.

Grandma's gone now many years, she's somewhere up above.
But she left us with a legacy of faith and trust and love.

Jane Thoma

My Prayer

Lord, I pray for the lost today
That they may turn from their sinful way
So they too may know -
The peace, the joy that comes within,
In knowing Christ as Saviour, Lord and Friend.

Lord, I pray for the indifferent too,
That they take up their cross and follow you -
So they again may know -
The blessed assurance that will come to them,
When they yield their lives completely to Him.

Lord, I pray for the faithful few,
Who are always willing to witness for you,
So that others may know.
The Christ who died, was buried, but rose again,
That they might have eternal life through Him.

Ina Barnes Macomb

Fallen Web

In the shelter of the willow dale
hangs the spider, under veil
of web's converging mesh of thread
with hope of ensnaring, in her spread,
those passing innocents, who by her tread

Within her web already wait
many victims- inanimate
by silken noose, they hang condemned
on her attention, they now depend

But with swift spirit, winds arise
Hurl spider from lofty paradise -
She gazes 'bout with sudden dread
Her self-spun web a crown of thread

She thinks, to wit, has it not been said:

"It is often she who sets the trap,
who suddenly finds herself enwrapped
For she who must endure such grief,
spring's joy wilts like a fallen leaf."

Kazen Fathie, MD, FACS, FICS, PhD

Invisible

You can't see courage, but you know it's there,
You can tell when you see someone fighting a bear.
You can't see love, but you know it's there,
You can tell it's there, when you show that you care.
You can't see the wind, but you know it's there,
You can tell it's there when you feel a breeze in the air.
You can't see God, but you know He's there,
You can tell, He's in your heart and everywhere.

Bryan J. Banning

A Gift Of The World

When you hold this make-believe world in your hands,
I know you will first imagine the spiritual beauty of it all
and how this can, and will, effect your life and all you do.

There is no sun, moon or stars, but this you will imagine too,
you will see the sun through a sunny summer's day, at sunrise,
as you run and ready your body, mind and soul, for yourself,
and all you encounter this day.

You will imagine the calmness of sunset through many vivid colors
of blues, reds, pinks and oranges, blending together with the
warm golden sun, this will calm and warm your heart and joy will
emanate from within your soul.

As the luminous moonlit night, comes to soften the darkness that
may have slipped into your day, you will be reminded once again,
how the natural and sensual qualities of life have blended
together, to join the beauty of the spiritual in the day.

Soothed for sleep through prayer, the stars in their heavens,
and the loving arms of one you cherish, you are warmed within
and given strength to awaken to another new day in this world.

Ellie Miskovic

The Brightest Star...

When you look up to the evening skies, and the stars are shining in your eyes, pick the brightest star you see and that is where you will find me.

Now you know where I will be when you can't see me; I will be up above you so high, thinking about you with a twinkle in my eye.

So you see, there is no reason to be sad, for I am in a place meant to be, a beautiful place that has been chosen for me.

So tonight when the stars are shining so bright, look up to that heavenly sight, and pick a star, the brightest star. That will forever be a place for our hearts to meet afar.

Barbara J. Wagner

God's Chosen Few

Well were leaving port now, so the talk will start,
On how sailor tore their city apart.
As the city disappear's, behind a wall of water,
Some of the men wonder, if there's gonna be a father.
What will happen at the next dock, no one knows for sure,
But sometimes loneliness and liquor, can open another door,
on the phone we see break ups and make ups, and it's always the same.
Loneliness and liquor has caused someone pain.
Sailor are our of tune, out of touch, and out of sight,
Do you think this is something we like.
It's a life style like no others,
We've all grown to be sea brothers,
So when we do have a little fun and raise some hell,
Don't put us down, just to cover your own smell.
You don't know what it's like and some never will,
Like any other job, some of us don't lie, cheat or steal.
But sometimes loneliness does have a way of showing it's face,
and liquor will always have a place.
So for those's who don't believe we can be true,
I still think sailor, are God's chosen few.

Larry Hall

I Want

I want to cry but the tears won't fall
I want to die but the world won't let me
I want to be alone but it never leaves me
I want to see but something blocks my sight
I want to be the best but there's always someone better
I want to be happy but I don't allow myself
I want to know all, see all, to prevent danger
I want to fly but gravity doesn't let me
I want to be understood
I want to be respected
I want to be liked
I want to be praised
I want to live without pain
I want to have someone there
I want to be protected
I want to never come out
I want to stay under
I want to hide
I want but I can't have

Terri Chang

Suck Seed

I want to be saved
I refuse to be helped
I'm the only one here, so I guess
I have to be brave, I'll try to suck seed
I know more than you can believe,
I am my own breed

I'm figuring out pointless clues,
energy's gone to my head, now it's all lead,
but I truly don't care and I don't
Want to leave because I am my own breed

My mind is my creation
I'm the one thinking for all these salvations,
but I know I can't use none, there's
no end to what I've done.
So, I've become my own breed

I have to confess, I'm just a cold mess
I regret so many moments of no sense
I don't want to be this way but I have no choice
than to stay, my own breed.

Patricia Rios

It Matters

It matters not if skies turn grey or burst with shades of blue.
If raindrops fall to close the day, or glisten earth with dew.

If those we see around us are in too much pain to bear
And if we offer all our help to make them more aware.

If in our lives our children cause our hearts to shed a tear
Or if they reach to us for love and we can calm their fear.

If daily troubles hinder us, or good times come our way,
If we can't find the time to help our friends get thru the day.

If all we know about ourselves is what we feel inside,
Then all the victories we achieve can fill our hearts with pride.

It matters not what ifs do bring to each and every day;
It matters how our mind reflects what our hearts really say.

Kitty A. McGlothlin

The Hope That Easter Brings

I walked the walk that Jesus walked,
I could not understand just why the Lord had chosen me
Or what would be my plan.

I trusted Him, believed his word for he had shown the way
I feel secure within his grasp and Love so freely given.
I thank Him for the inner strength and promises of heaven.

Be strong my child, do trust my Word and you will be forgiven
Of any error you may make along your path towards heaven.

I bore my cross, I died and rose; not just for you but many
Who willingly will accept the call and start out on their journey.

If you will joyfully share with others, what I have given thee
Blessed you will be, I promise you for leading them to me.

As I have taught I'd have you live by precept and example,
If you succeed, oh granted, your efforts will be ample.

Juanita M. Moore

Friends

You were my friend and were always there
Even when things were tough, you really cared.
I knew you so long and we really had fun
There are so many things that we haven't done.
I miss you more than you'll ever know
I wish I could tell you I miss you so.
The way you laughed, I hope I never forget
No one knew you were so upset.
Or of the pain you were going through
You loved the way the wind blew.
As it passed you on a summer's day
Now that all has gone away.
You will never see another day
The beautiful world I see today.
You made an impression on every person you met
I wish you knew how much you meant.
Now that your kind spirit has left
Oh how all the people who knew you had wept.
It will be harder to go on each day
Now that you have passed away.

Sheryl Anderson

My One Possession

I had but one Possession
that I truly cared for.
I treasured it like a sailor does the sea,
an explorer, the land.
It could not lie, cheat or steal
but it could be stolen
and you, my exquisite thief, stole it
That Possession was my heart.

Shannon Conrad

I Must Move On

I gave you my heart,
you tore it in two.
I gave you my love,
you threw it back at me.
I gave you my time,
you wasted it.
But, I must move on.
I was thrown and I was tossed,
used and abused, like a piece of floss.
"By whom?", you ask. "By you," I respond
But, I must move on.
Though it is hard, I must try to
mend my wounded heart.
I must move on.
For, if I dwell on the past, I'll
miss all the good things in the
present.

Cornelia Oancea

Misunderstood

Who can understand my words but me?
No one that I can see.
A burst of deep emotions shouts a silent echo.
Tears and blood become one, where can they go?
Am I the only one that is to know?

Misunderstood, if not ignored.
Anyone that will listen is by me adored.
It is hard to convey my feelings so deep.
I am still a strange reflection in my mirror, a lost sheep.
From my soul strange demons and seraphim's leap.

If I look at my reflection do I like what I see,
Or does hot blooded fury still boil in me?
A million contradictions lie at my core.
My soul falls, battered and beaten on a far away shore.

So you see my dilemma is quite profound.
How can I be understood before I am found?
How can my voice be heard when it has no sound?

Timothy J. Hester

Kaleidoscope

It would be nice to have your colors always blend together
To reap success because you really tried
A world without variables and imperfections
Would do wonders for you basic sense of pride.

But when life awakens you to the human condition
And you search your soul with the inevitable question - why?
It's time to draw support from those around who love you
And to rethink, restructure, and retry.

If your efforts change the variables a little
And fate and timing play an active part
Your colors will come together in great profusion
And you'll live the dream that's hidden in your heart.

Mary Emma Ireland Bird

In My Heart You Will Always Be

To return the favor to you from me;
I write this poem with ecstasy.
I care for you, like you care for me;
In my heart you will always be.

I'll climb every mountain, swim every sea;
Just to have you close to me.
So whatever happens to us you see;
In my heart you will always be.

Alicia Marie Martins-Lyons

"The Spirit Of America"

"July the Fourth is the big day,
That we all should celebrate-
To remind us of our independence,
We should all participate".

"Display and fly the American flag,
With its stars and stripes, so grand-
Show all you're proud to be an American,
And the respect the flag should command".

"This is a patriotic holiday,
Make it an All-American Day -
To live in this Land of Liberty,
That is the All-American way".

"It's a time to enjoy the fireworks,
And all the revelry -
See the fireworks light up the sky,
With friends and family".

"Bringing back the sounds of shells and bombs,
We experienced throughout the war-
Now that we're home with our loved ones
We pray we won't have to fight anymore".

Marty Rollin

"The Happiest Days Of My Life"

The very happiest days of my life
were when I was a very new wife.
My kids were small, I love those days
best of all.
Children are content to play around the home,
they are not always wanting to be gone.
It's a good thankful feeling each night
when you kiss each face, to know you're
all together and in a safe place.
When you're young you think I have the
rest of my life and then it hurries
right on by.
It seems such a short time and kids
are grown, thinking about leaving home
they'll leave such a vacancy that
nothing can fill but we'll always
have our memories to go back and relive.

Bonnie Watson Jolly

Untitled

The sky shines, and the gulls soar,
Listening to children's play,
The sea, rushes to shore.
Someday's dream, a love to be,
Togetherness fulfilled, honored and cherished,
Always there, the better part of me.
To walk the sands, oceans of life,
Step by step, hand in hand,
Sacred love, husband and wife.
To share with the other, in every way,
Hopes, dreams, and prayers,
Bonded love growing, every day.
The sky shines, the birds, they fly,
Enchanted moment's ecstasy,
Watching her sleep, next to me lie.

Bill Lindner

Who A Father Really Is!

A father is the one who breaks us from our
shell. He's the one who gives us our first
movement of life. He gives us his last name.
But let me tell you about my father.

He made sure I was feed, warm, and
had a home. He gave me everything in the
world that I needed.
Plus he gave me love
and that is what a real Father is!

Lisa Gribble

The Dreamer

The caged bird sings because
he knows one day he will be free.
It's often a revelation of life,
the dreamer only sees.
He knows your dream is your way to escape,
to leave all the pain behind,
All the sadness and the sorrow,
the hard looks your soul grinds.
Just as a child with undying faith,
the dreamer battles his way through life,
never giving up his hope,
fighting with love's unfailing knife.
In the end the dreamer triumphs
over all others who let go.
As long as he never gives up
life is his ally, defeating his foes.
Although the dreamer may seem invincible,
and whatever he wants he receives,
he is no different than anyone else
except that he dares to believe.

Amanda Watson

A Mother's Love

Her laughter could make an angel faint,
While her smile could tempt a saint.
She's as innocent as a newborn child,
Yet she'll never be considered meek or mild.

Like the eagle her spirit flies free,
But her heart belongs to me.
For a child has nothing to fear.
As long as it knows it's mother will always be near.

No matter what man she marries,
Or how many children she carries,
She'll always be my little girl.
If I could I would give her the world.

I hope she knows she has my love,
Which I send every day on the wings of a dove.
I'm here for her, wherever she may go.
After all, I'm her mother, you know.

Danielle Long

Love

Love is a sweet song
a true blessing of God
but, if you don't accept it, love will pass you on.
Love can be expressed in many different ways.
Love is what helps you survive every passing day.
Love is gentle, love is kind
Love is someone you, keep close to your heart in your mind.
Love is patient, Love is good.
If you love you have everything.
But without Love you have nothing.

Jamie Chapman

Gigantic Smile

I saw the tear that never fell
The gigantic smile that covered hell.
Enraged with courage that battled fear,
Only heaven above could hold that tear.

When the intertwinable soul-mate you meet
So rare are they, you soon retreat
Fearing the loss of self replete
With freedom from responsibility.

Go your way, refuse to see
Declare that bond was ne'er meant to be.
Hold that tear, masque it with a smile
Never know sweet joy of the grown-up child.

Play in sand, squish mud twixt toes
Walk barefoot out-of-doors
Who ever knows the sweet repose
Of the grown-up child when feeling shows.

Children are happy 'til they're taught to lie
And smile through hell until the day they die.
Cast off those masques called social graces
If you meet your soul-mate and kick the traces.

Thelma B. Conley

"Endless Days Of Playing"

For days and weeks the black girl
Sadly in front of her house she sat.
Observing the others girls having fun....
They never invited her to play.
As the days grew colder towards Christmas
Lights multiplied up and down the street...

With a brilliant Blue Star in her hand...
A girl called to her "Come with me"...
Excitedly she ran into her house and said...
"Mommy, she wants to play with me"...
As fast as her feet would carry her
She crossed the icy street without looking....
...And the approaching car couldn't stop...

As the sun sat on that cold, sad day...
The mother cried and knelt next to her.
A funnel of light came down from the sky.
Two angels appeared and lifted the girl.
Wiping the tears from the mother's face...
They said "Now she will be in heaven...
Enjoying endless days of playing."

Rafael P. Figueroa

Pick Up The Flag

Would you lay down your gun, if you saw the flag fall.
Then take up old glory and lead on for all.
There are those who have done that, and those that died.
There are those who have done that, and families who cried.
If there's hope to be found in the loss of ones dear,
It's in the time that passes, when all becomes clear.

It's not the uniform that makes a soldier tall.
But a heart for freedom, that makes us soldiers all.
So march, march, march, one two three.
Step proudly, sing loudly, my Country 'tis of thee.

Would you lay it all down just to stand in the fire.
To keep this country strong, is that your desire.
Well a fight's a fight, and sometimes there's a call.
So will you pick up the flag, and give it your all.
There are those who will do that, when gallant bugles call.
There are those who will do that, let's pray for them all.

It's not the uniform that makes a soldiers tall.
But a heart for freedom, freedom for one and all.
So march, march, together you and me.
Step proudly, sing loudly, my Country 'Tis Of Thee.

Doug Hassett

Daddy

In honor of my Father

I've called you just so many things throughout the life we've shared,
You've held so many titles, to me, you've seemed so rare.

You've been a terrific husband, I've often heard mom say,
Her love for you just seems to grow each precious, passing day.

You've been a great provider, my needs were always met,
But with the good came also bad, remember the rules you set?

As a son grandma tells me, you were the apple of her eye,
When she speaks of how proud she is, she just breaks down and cries.

My child states her Granddaddy is the best she could have prayed for,
With each precious moment you share, she loves you more and more.

You've been a true supporter, I could always turn to you,
You held my hand through all the bad, and shared in my happiness too.

It's obvious you're a Christian, cause you show your beliefs and love,
To all of us who live on earth, and to our father above.

"Perfect Dad" is the title, that you're best known for,
You've earned it in all the past, and you will forever more.

This all just my way of saying, "I'm so very proud of you,
Not just for all the years gone past, but in my whole life through.

I love you daddy

Sherry Ledford

Ballade D'Amour

When the night falls,
and all hath died,
thine name I call
and pray for thee by my side.
We lay under the greenwood tree
and idly pass the time by,
as we lift our heads to see
the stars in the sky.
But soon I turn my head away
from the heavens above,
because I can not think of a better day,
then to spend it with thou, my love.

Valaree Lynn Tucker

Love

I was walking home one day, and I saw a flower
growing from the cold ground.
It was sad, and lonely, and needed a drink.
I gave it water, and a chance to live, and every day
I stopped to give it a drink.
But one day something went wrong,
and I saw my flower wilted, and torn.
I sat, and wished I could have been there to give it strength.
I picked it up, and took it home to see what I could do.
I gave it dirt, I gave it water, and I gave it food
until it grew bigger, and stronger, and now I give
this wonderful flower, this wonderful rose to you.

Jimmie C. McIver

Anniversaries

You felt like you could fly,
On that first day of July,
When you were combine to each other,
As long as you love forever,
You felt like you were on cloud nine,
Which means you felt fine,
after feeling all emotions you knew you would last
And also have a blast!!!

Megan DeBusk

Untitled

The cold, blank stare
Did it start there?

An empty, forlorn, almost foreboding stare-
What are you saying?
Is this the end, is this good-bye
Why?

Do you think you protect me you cut the ties—But why?
Where are you? Come back you have not died.

Tender, cherished moments I hold onto
Then you awake and you are not there.
Could you be protecting me?
Preparing me for what is yet to come
Telling me of a voided love, a life to end.

What do I do? Where do I run?
I sit still and nurture my love within.
You cannot take what you have freely given
I keep and hold onto treasured years of our making.

We are as one, when one dies the other withers.
But cherished memories fuel me on-
To carry out our legacy of a once sweet love.

Patricia Hiapo

The Envy Of Joyous Life

I seem to dream at twilight, best
Of stars and gentle-natured things.
It wasn't always so, I guess, but
Life is fickle, change it brings.

When young, I knew some good and bad,
(Eventually the worst won all)
To fill my mind with cluttered sadness
Coloring my angry soul.

The very depths of evil pierced
My blackened heart, to torment me.
And willingly I did adhere to
Whispered lies of what should be.

But truth seeks one who seeks for truth,
A pinpoint light to show a ladder.
Climbing brilliance, filled with both an
Awe and fear of severn myrrh.

While'st now I mine with sparkling shovel
Newfound Grace, rich, clean, ordained.
Purging whole this fleshly hovel,
Jesus - what a lovely Name!

Thomas Turley

Folk Dance

Bone jewelry clatters against skin;
spear shafts thump against hide
as serpentine lines shake and jump
to the beat of tom-toms.
Chanted stories as ancient as the sea
send rain, and children,
and health and peace.
Dust rises from effort and paints bodies,
and bonds souls.
The harvest is not far away.
The crowned, fearsome head nods approvingly
as sweat melts exhaustion into silence,
settles the dust,
sprouts corn, then grain.

E. J. Cunningham

"The World Is White And Strange"

Disorder, anger, moodiness and frustration
are wide opening my emaciated wound.
After roving all day with a fixed idea
I'm still maimed to catch up with my mound.

Never again I will achieve a good job,
due to the fact that the so called priority
is feigned to match a pearl-colored skin,
and I still remain crowded in a minority.

I'm unable to cope with these inquiries:
Who gave me this sort of light skin?
Why is my hair soft-curly instead of kinky?
Was an intruder concealed among my kin?

And why they took me out of the melting-pot?
Please, have all these perplexities arranged.
Because, above whatever most people say:
The World is White and Strange.

Emilio Hidalgo-N.

From My Rocking Chair

Through my eyes
So old and gray
I see my children outside at play,
Through my eyes
I hear their laughter they're not far away,
Through my eyes
It may be sunny or raining in some ways,
Through these eyes
I've seen my friends pass
And dear loved ones gone away,
Through these eyes
A child is born, to face the world
But dear child you're not alone,
Through your eyes
Life must go on,
Through the eyes of this child,
God has given us on loan...

JoAnn Lemmon

Crystal Drops Of Healing Remembrance

God sends us special friends as a
gift of His grace;
We accept His love, and enjoy this bliss,
to appreciate whatever is noble and loving.
Now, we remember the time when we met, the
laughter like joy;

Fresh air that blossomed in our faces, times we
knelt in prayer blest, together we, our spirit blend
that's the way it was meant to be...
We followed our ecstasy together in friendship, we
only know and experience in a well of waters so deep
so magnificent;

How blessed to know this light of fragrance short time or long;
The power of going out of one's self to give so gracious
and graceful of one's being. Thank God for this gift of
thine. The gates of heaven opened. The morning star
with it's brilliant mystical rose, there stood my friend,
a spirit of love over the horizon!

Frances Castorino

Dear Graduate

Today, dear graduate, as before me you stand,
Dawned in cap and gown, diploma in hand.
The future uncertain, you know not what you face.
So hold unto God's truths and look to his grace.

For as you move forward with the torch passed to you,
And you look to the future and set new goals to do.
Work hard and show kindness to both rich and poor.
And inwardly you'll grow and be strengthened much more.

Always look to a bright future, to your dreams reach out
March forward steadfastly, with never a doubt.
Keep treading forward, though the pathway may seem,
Too hard to climb, don't give up - look to your dream.

Remember God is beside you each step of the way,
There to direct and lead every day.
For when you falter and stumble, he'll see you through,
He'll help hear your burdens and troubles, too.

So as you press forward across this great land.
Bearing that torch that is placed in your hand,
Pray, read your Bible, let God be your guide,
If you but trust him, he'll walk by your side.

Geraldine Borger

I Want To Be A Pioneer!

I want to be a pioneer, to walk by faith, and side by side with the prophet and seer. Singing songs about the church along the many miles of the way. To be able to dance, sing, meditate, and yes, even pray. Even church services are held each day, and prayer before we retired are said. The bugle wakes us up at five. The hardships, heartaches, death, and sorrow. But together we will strive, to get to the West alive, and settle where God's presence with us will thrive. It's hard to know especially now having to walk in this snow. Quicksand doesn't help, nor does the contention, bickering, arguing, backbiting, and pride. Because of the hardships I have cried. And through all of this struggles and strife, I have found out, it's part of life. But, you know, no matter how hard it's been in the past. With where we are now, we've been told that it won't last. But, I tell you, it's hard to be a pioneer. And you know something else? That's all I ever wanted... was to be a pioneer!

Lana Wakefield

Forgive Me

Forgive me Dear God if I do sometimes cry,
you understand the reason why.

I have told myself again and again,
my loss is not a loss,
my loss is a gain.
I do understand, although, sometimes I cry.

I have been blessed,
with three beautiful sons, although one I can't see,
I will always remember, he "is" part of me.
I do understand, but still, sometimes I cry.

My third little son is a "special gift" you gave me,
you could have wrote,
"A third little son never,"
but instead,
you wrote,
"A third little son forever."
Forgive me Dear God if I do sometimes cry,
ever though I understand
I still sometimes cry.

Diane L. Galio

Damnation Of A Spirit

The darkness creeps in stealthily.
It seeks, it aims, it destroys.
Unbeknownst to all around it, the fog has claimed another soul.
This is the soul destined for hell.
The impure red flames procure it's demise.
Satan's wrath has penetrated the armor of hate and racism.
Blackness surrounds all in the soul's descent into hell.
Satan need not borrow, for the evil come on their own.
Sacred vows of faith and trust no longer exist as the death trap envelops the world.
Pain is felt, torture ensues.
Another of God's children turns his head in disgust.

Melody A. Ingersol

"Today's Society"

In today's society I find
That this "free" world is not so kind
There are people starving in the street
No coats on their backs nor shoes on their feet
There are babies dying each and every day
Dying in the cruelest, most sickening ways
Teenage crack addicts, prejudice galore
Who can stand to look at more
But we must look, it won't go away
We must stop it, beginning today
Stop the bombing, stop the rapes
Teach our children the steps to take
Don't judge the man by the color of his skin
Walk with him, talk to him, know the spirit within
Teach your sons to work hard in life
Work hard and never beat his wife
Teach your daughters to always be strong
Not to let themselves be treated wrong
Because in today's society I find
That this "free" world is not so kind

Larissa Barnes Roach

Child Hood

Today deep in my favorite chair
I went back to my childhood where
With my bravery and girth
I battled the villains of the earth
Swimming the oceans large and small
Defeating monsters twenty stories tall
Sleeping on the prairies under moons so full
And smoking a peace pipe with sitting bull
Over beaches and mountains boots caked with mud
I walked over battlefields covered with blood
Far over clouds I flew dog fights so high
And saw the smoke trails of aces who die
I was the hero wearing metals so proud
And waved as the crowds cheered so loud
And when my book fell to the floor
I returned to an adult once more
Is there a man alive who can say
I never lived that child hood play.

John A. Sherrell

His Heart

Resting in the arms of my Savior
The gentle beating of His heart comforts me.

Soon I find my heart is beating in time

When I ask how this can be
He laughs softly as He says to me

Child, your heart is not beating in time
The heart that beats within you is Mine.

Lisa Renee Boggs

Ode To My Skates

Oh the joy you give, my dear skates
You warm my heart and soul with
your silv'ry blades;
Together we glide over the ice,
Always you keep my feet and
music ever alive;
I love you, my beloved skates!
I love you, my dear skates
You hold me way up high,
You gently put me down,
We spin and go round and around;
I love you! For me to live is to skate;
Oh, let us fire the ice, yes
With love and care and happiness
And life's melancholiness.
I love you! Every moment with you is
Joy unforgettable, power and strength released.
I love you! I love to skate!
Here's my praise!

Estrellita Jimenez

Walls

For years I've stared at the moments,
Passing like epochs, every second
Hued with such stillness and soundless —
Motion; as if her flight, wrested, tethered
To some unseeing monolith within the
Crumbling mortared walls.

And I've sat mute yet screaming
Feeling the gray and deep lines, smite;
The skin like the walls, crumbling,
And I'm breathing the stones, until;
They've drawn within me, 10,000 leagues deep
Inside the darkest blood of melancholy.

For years, I've stared at the moments
Fleeing like dead sparrows, seized;
By every brick, every gray, merciless stone.
Four walls, moored to the eyes, echoing,
My transgression, ever and ever and still ever,
Echoing...moment by second, brick by stone.

Remembrances apparition and I, sit;
As we always have, so softly, screaming.

Anthony McMillan

Difficulties In 1979

My problems seems so difficult.
To me your problems are so easy to solve.
I am able to solve your sorrows in one sitting, my sorrows seem to
take a life time.
I want to help you, love you, show you I am there for you
I was unable to find you when I need you the most.
Maybe you are there and I can not see you.
Reach out and show me you are there.
I need you to show me.
I want to lean on you, feel your warmth on me.
My problems can become our answers.
The two of us can give each other a hand.
We can work as one, become united into one another's love.
We will let each other go, but be there with open arms.
Help me when I am not able to admit I am falling.
Pick me up with your love.
Please be there
Please be my extra strength
We need each other to be one.

Lisa Grossman

Our Christmas Poem

Christmas is a string of lights bright as a star above. It also
bring the smiles of the youngest soul. Christmas is giving of our
selves to those who deserve it. Most of all, Christmas is a magical
feeling called Love.
So let's bring out the bright lights and joyful carolers to
Celebrate the birth of our savior Jesus Christ. Because he
should get all the credit for bringing all of us together.
From our house to yours, Merry Christmas.

The Mitchell Family.

Tami L. Mitchell

My Melinda

My Melinda seethes gently within the tenuous bark;
Her bed of rest within a great cavernous oak.
Praying for the morning song of a lark,
She longs for the day - as do most the "Valley Folk."
She sighs with a wisp of the morning dew.
She sleeps primitively, like a rustic, flowered jewel.

Once, the pitted, pot-marked, bomb-shattered streets' dirty face,
Were deceptively calm within this holy place.
The peace in this valley was an almost cordially inviting grace,
To the unwary traveller who might seek
Its disquieting solace.
But, its tempests raged, only one hour ago;
Just before dawn, before my Melinda arose.

And it is a damnable thing we do excuse,
When all the rainbows we chase ahead,
Are the color of death — blood-red;
And they're all for the life that we choose.

Although rose-scarlet red was the favorite color of her mother
Melinda; our daughter will only remember always, instead
Red upon her blouse; holding tenderly, where Melinda fell dead!!!

Redhurn Young

My Tree

I have a very special friend, a tree. My tree doesn't
have a name but I don't care. I tell my tree everything.
Friend problems, family problems and new and old
boyfriends. My tree soothes me when I'm sad with a
slight rustle of his leaves, and sometimes with drops
of rain falling from the branches. I can take out my
anger on my tree and he won't mind. I love my tree
because it's always silent and beautiful. But the
reason I like it the most is because it's My Tree.

Erin Lobermeier

"American Patriots"

Now here in this old world so riddled with fear
We find few people who tend to agree
Or those who take kindly to the ways of our nation
And her proven democracy.

And sometimes it's easy but most times it's hard
For us to know what we will have to do
When confronting wavering nations
And the wandering paths they choose.

Thus all we patriots of this great land
Are proud to stand and say this to you;
"Be thankful that our Star-Spangled Banner
Stands for liberty, justice and truth."

So wave on Old Glory for all people to see
That the U.S.A. is truly the land of the free
Rise high dear Standard with your stars and stripes unfurled
To symbolize our desire for lasting peace throughout the world.

William B. Harmon

"Let Nature Open Your Eyes"

Sportsman, outdoors man, taker of game and fish
To consume as food is the initial wish
Stalking, casting, and planning each outdoor trip
Using all senses, pursuing everyone's free tips

Out before dawn, suddenly you are never alone
Sounds, noises, sights, is that only a stone?
A splash, and ripples cover the water on top
What caused it, is this a good angling spot?

The harvest or catch, you work for you earn
Then nature takes over, you're beginning to learn
Being in the wild, over time opens your eyes
Appreciating birds, plants animals, clears blue skies

Letting a deer walk, practicing catch and release
Feeling thrilled, your heart's truly at peace
Giving something back, not always only taking
Our future and theirs, you are surely making

Pollution, destroying seriously affects us all
Let us all get together, stand proud and tall
Protecting, honoring, our most precious earth
It will take commitment, a program of rebirth

Anthony L. Goins

Time Enough To Sleep

I see you there asleep
Sometimes you laugh, sometimes you weep
You mumble things I can't understand
Somewhere in a distant land
I wonder sometimes what you dream
Is this wise, or why does it seem
That always you can't remember why
There is no need to lie
But yet, the ones you do seem to understand
Are the ones that are so crazy for demand
None of this will explain
Why you remain
In your far away dream land
When, here I am

Sha Ni Bassett

"Beautiful Simplicity"

I have to tell you something, so don't laugh.
I have been working at this too long for you to just laugh.
When I first saw you I said, 'That's where I want to be.'
I wanted to be near you, surrounded in beautiful simplicity.
But I was too shy to ever approach you.
I stood at a distance to watch everything you would do.
You hardly noticed me along the way.
But to me, you were my personal sunbeam ray.
When you were in my mind, I could do anything.
I could dance without legs, without a voice I could sing.
Then one rainy day in March, you left me all alone.
The only memory of you, carved in granite stone.
I know some day we'll meet in some big blue giant sea.
This time I'll approach you, surrounded in your beautiful simplicity.

Regina Anderson

Trapped

I wish I could love as well as I deceive.
I wish I could see the ways of my ever so important love.
But is all to waste? I do not know,
For love is one big deceit.
But what will all of us do
Without that ever so great burden
On all of the people of the world?
For once we are hooked,
There is no way out of love.

Corey James Wright

Magic Lamp

If I had a magic lamp
and wishes were given to me,
I'd wish away all your burdens
so that you could be free.
I'd wish away all your pain
so that your tears would dry.
Then you would stop thinking
of crazy ways to die.
I'd wish away your suffering
and mend your broken heart.
Watching you go through all
this is tearing me apart.
If I could change the past
to make things better today
don't you think I would
wish to find a way.
I don't have a magic lamp
and my wishes may never come true
Just know that you are close to my heart
and I will always love you.

Darlene M. Huhn

Earth Memories

In my dreams people live forever.
Like the moon and the stars.
They never die unless I die.
The trees are like Gods tall and forever peaceful.
My eyes drift and behold the sky which never ever ends.
I say to it "Measure me sky!
Take me to your heart where I may live forever.
Caress my hair wild wind!
Give me your tears which is thunder that sells
it madness to the depths of insane storms."
A tornado may steal my life.
But it shall never take my soul.
My voice is kept by the wind and the sky hides my soul.
My mind is the window to the world,
I no longer will sing the song of the stars

Allison Armstrong

"What Is Your Way Stranger"

The beginning started with me walking
on the shores of the east coast,
I had no desire to go anywhere
except to your house.

My eyes burned from the salty sky so
filled with sea gulls.
And there were also many, many tears
that day... Still on my age-worn face.

Searching for your course was more
then a million people could have done,
A million longing people like me.

There were times when the crusade ended,
But I still constantly hung onto the
bits of memories that you tried
to end for me.

Standing tall and my legs tired,
I still walk on that cold hard sand,
And the sea gulls hum and fly
by, as if to say,
"What is your way stranger?"

Deborah Lenz

Forgotten Dreams

See that old man sitting there,
His hair so thin and gray;
I guess he doesn't see me here,
His gaze is far away...

Where has he been? What has he seen?
In days so long ago,
What dreams are locked in memories;
What secrets lay untold?

How much sadness is hidden there,
Beneath that whitened brow;
Where are those whom he loved,
Where can he go now??

See that old man sitting there,
His hair so thin and gray;
Don't laugh at his forgotten dreams...
You'll be like him someday.

A sigh escapes from wrinkled lips
And his head falls to his breast;
And the old man gains his rest at last...
And death yet one more guest.

Paula Taylor

The Death Of John O'Leary

On a day in mid-September, as the sun was going down,
Fog rolled through the treetops and settled on the town.

The streets became deserted, as the day turned into night,
Doors were locked, the windows barred, and people cowered in fright

For on this day in September, just 50 years ago,
John O'Leary met his fate against a deadly foe.

He was walking home alone that night, and whole crossing the avenue,
A voice spoke softly from behind and said, "I've been waiting for you"

As O'Leary turned to meet the voice, his face contorted with fear,
The glinting knife blade swinging, slitting his throat from ear to ear

The killer crept away then, leaving O'Leary there to die,
A brutal murder taking place, though no one know just why.

Now every year as darkness falls on this same September day,
John O'Leary walks the streets, or the town folks say.

His ghost returns to take revenge on the one who struck him down,
As the fog rolls through the treetops and settles on the town.

Linda J. Smith

A Journey Divine

One speck of energy in a universe of billions, consisting of
atoms building molecules; thus cells, rejuvenating
themselves as they dance thru the black hole.

Every moment different from the previous, never constant
always moving; gravitating thru it's celestial control.

It's extremities representative of the five universal
elements and designed in the image of it's creator.

Oblivious to the commencement, or purpose of it's journey;
hence, dependent upon it's cohabitants for it's existence,
with love as it's dictator.

The increments of time teaches it survival; thru pain and
suffering it's light grow dim, causing it to turn to it's
supreme source of energy.

After bouts of ambivalence, it learns how to reach inside
for the main vessel connecting it to that source, sending it
soaring; pushing all negative forces to infinity.

Oh my! no time to go back, little time to reflect, it's
destiny depends on Me.
For I am that light, that force, that star, and everything it
came to Be.

Sheila T. Zimmerman

Feeding On My Mind

And you, you vampire
You drain me of myself
As my thoughts change to words
Recorded on paper,
You rape my privacy.

The words give you power
With that power you thrive
You are no longer alone and unsheltered
The words give you comfort
I provide the words.

You drain me of my words
Until I think that no more will flow
You leave me weak and shaking
You give me just enough time to recover
Then you come back for more.

Will you ever be fulfilled?
Your thirst and hunger quenched?
If the words are powerful, you will return
And drain me again.
You are insatiable.

Matthew Hellinger

The Candle

I stand in the door, warm smiles fill my face.
A beautiful setting glows in the dim light.
The long rectangular table stretched on,
Laced with gold leaf China spotting the red plaid cloth.
The colors are familiar to my mind and heart.
Sprinkled about like berries on the bush are
all the fixings, all the holiday favorites.
Golden brown is the bird,
and pineapples and cherries dance about the ham.
In the center a lone white candle.
Tall and strong its roundness seemed to pour around,
drawing me near.
Mama always said it's the candle of Christ's celebration
For this day is the day of his birth.
This is the reason we gather in joy.

Amy B. Seals

"Stars In The Sky"

I would take a long walk on the beach,
  sitting and watching the tide,
Always thinking of my love for you,
  never ever leaving my side.
I would always feel your touch on my shoulder,
  as gentle and smooth as can be,
Even though you have passed away,
  I knew you would never forget me.
Every night I would say a prayer,
  To let you know that I still care,
I want you to know I will never forget,
  all the love that we did share.
I would never forget your touching smile,
  or the way we became husband and wife,
I thought we would be together forever,
  to have the happiest life,
But now that you are gone,
  I have to say my final goodbye,
But I know that you are looking down on me,
  When I look at all the stars in the sky!!!

Trisha Verrell

How Do I Say Goodbye To You?

When I first met you, you really put a smile on my face,
The nice times we spent together no one could ever replace.
Although, I really didn't get to know you as well as intended,
I feel we have gotten close as lovers and friends.
Each day we awaken to see somewhat of the sun or cloudy blue,
But we never really realize that our lives in time depart so soon.
Today in my awakening, I find myself suddenly aware,
That you leave my life in walking somewhere out there.
I will not be able to follow your path,
For we both now must take a different directions to find the best to surpass,
What we really feel from what we actually choose,
A dream is never mistaken no matter what you do.
Nevertheless, you will never be forgotten.
For thoughts of you will always stay with me in my heart,
I promise.

Antonia C. Roman

Our Mighty God

For thou art great and mighty
All powerful, all knowing, never flighty
Thou great King on High.

Thou art the Creator of this great earth
The heavens shouted at your birth
Thy wonder ever abounds.

The sun pales at your greatness
We bow to you recognizing our weakness
Thou art the hope of our heart.

We ever shall praise thee
For dying that we might be made free
Great God how we thank thee.

Some day we will see you
As you come in the clouds
Your bride will rise to greet you
And shout hallelujahs aloud
Forever And Ever....our Great And Mighty God!!!!
Amen............

Mary Elizabeth Poore

Life

As a man is brought into the world,
Thoughts full his mind,
Thoughts of hope and wonder,
Using these thoughts,
He pursues a goal,
A goal to succeed, to overcome,
Although at times,
He is oppressed by his failures,
He learns from these,
As he continues on,
When he reaches his goal,
He passes his thoughts onto his children,
When he leaves his children,
He is content,
Knowing that he has done well,
In this life

Tom Wang

Friendship

Friendship is a fragile thing
Like the soft touch of a butterflies wing,
Or the glow of a jewel so rare,
Given to us that we may share.
It is a joy close to the heart,
And a remembered gift as we part.

Elizabeth Kelly

"Scared"

Learned to bang when I was younger,
13 years of age,
bullets flying over colors,
bodies laid in graves.
Been all through the bloody streets,
because I chose a gang.
Fighting like a valiant soldier,
living day by day.
Wonder if I'll see tomorrow,
I don't ever know.
dealing with the pain and sorrow,
all to gain control.
Killing over territory, and the flag I fly.
Willing to do everything,
to keep myself alive
never hesitation,
hesitation gets you killed
carry plenty ammunition, for the battle field.
Millions lose their life a year, because they choose to bang
Tell me is it really worth it being in a gang?

Devin Alexander

A Walk With Eileen

There is nothing like a walk in summer rain
When nature washes all things bright and clean
My heart is light my body feels no pain
As long as I can walk with you Eileen

I always knew you were the only one
Since I first met you many years ago
You are my moonlight and my shining sun
Eileen you know that I do love you so

Although our days are numbered in this life
I will always love you just as I do now
I am thankful that you did become my wife
And all your love and beauty did endow

Not every man is blessed with such a bride
To love to keep forever by his side

Sarah M. Carver

"Father"

When I was born, I was the apple of my Father's eye.
As I grew up He was always there for me.
Even when I didn't realize it, He prayed for me.

My Father always protects me, I am never in want.
I didn't take time to get to know my Father, but he watched over me

The things I learned stayed with me through the years.
The Spirit of my Father has always been with me
even though I refuse at times to walk in the path He taught me.

I grew up and came to understand who my Father really was.
I listen more closely now to His words when He talks to me.
Sometimes I may not want, but my Father is faithful,
and will always comfort me and lift me up, if I will let him.

He's wise in His counsel and I trust Him with all my heart.
His Word is a promise that will never change, lie to me or fail me.

He's my best friend, who always takes time to listen.
He understands me and never makes me feel I'm worthless.
He gives me confidence to keep going when the going is tuff.
I Praise my Father In Heaven-
I am today what I am because of my Father.
I Love You, Abba Father.

Shirley F. Kloes

October Night

The stars that could, shone
Brightly as the night was stolen
By the brilliance of the moon.
There is magic in this night tonight.

Warm breezes lifted the edges of my hair
And gently kissed the soft smile on my lips.

Each sailboat in the Marina was softly silhouetted as
The lights of the City danced across the waters of the Bay.

Silently and smoothly small lights from planes above
Moved across the darkened sky.
There is magic in this night.

The quiet ripples of the Bay
Waltzed slowly up the Marina
Until one trickle made its way
Soon another, and another.

Mesmerized by softened sounds
From far away
I looked above to smile at the shimmering of the moon.

The earth still held the warmth of the sun, now long gone
But bright moon light enhanced true magic of the night.

Kathy C. Kiraly

Man of the World

The boy is young when it begins;
A passing comment is overheard;
It is negative in nature from one he loves;
This thought hurts the boy, causing the first wall to be built.

When he is a little older, he begins to interact with peers regularly;
Soon he realizes that he is different and that difference leads to pain;
Therefore, the second wall is built.

As the years pass, the adolescent learns;
The child starts to hear of the world's way;
He realizes that love is not strong here;
Hate and power rule the society, creating yet another wall.

Many years later, when he is practically an adult,
This person feels love for another;
She catches his heart with her beauty and mind.
Then proceeds to crush it, setting the final wall in place.

Once all the walls are in place,
After every defense has been set,
This person is ready to reveal nothing,
To be hurt by nothing, to be touched by nothing,
When these walls are here, he has become a man of the world.

Brendan Hay

Winter Rose

Glimmer of red in a world made of white
Shining like a bright red gem in the morning light
Standing alone among the snow without a baby's breath by its side
Feebly struggling to survive throughout the winter's tide

When the rising sun is high and the snowy earth begins to melt
The one lone rose falls from where it once dwelt
Spring paints a new picture but this flower will not pose
Seasons change for a winter rose

Summer nights grow longer, the air grows colder
Leaves fall from their homes as storm clouds grow bolder
Soon, a blanket of white covers the once green earth
Lakes are sheeted with ice while lovers gather around the hearth
Like a phoenix rises from its ashes
A winter rose grows as the season passes

Randall J. Shaw

The Presbyterian Manse

It stands as white as snow,
Beside the House of God,
Dreamlike in the amethyst window's glow
That shimmers through the shadows,
At evensong.

Its porches and its doorways
Seem more pure and clean
Than all the neighbors on the little square,
And in its yard the birds are all about,
Building in its dental row,
A pious cloister for their young.

It seems so holy there,
On chilly evenings,
Or when the redbuds bloom across the way,
For even as the asphalt of the world
Presses on, in hot pursuit, this little space,
Still it seems to bring redemption as we pass,
And in the Sabbath twilight, grace.

Elva Ware Avara

Just A Cowboy

Some say the cowboy is a time long forgot,
Though heroes and legends will never depart...
It's not about roping, or marking a brand,
Herding of cattle, or riding the land.
It's not about boots, or chaps, or spurs,
Gold plated buckles that gleam in the sun.
It's not about campfires, or kicking up dust,
Not cactus, nor mesquite, or bronco's that buck.
The cowboy that strives to survive through all time;
Lives by courage, and honor;
A code he inspires....

Steven Goldberg

"A Mother"

A mother is a special gift, from our dear Lord above,
Her gentle hands, her tender ways, her sacrificing love.

A mother is a teacher, a companion, and a friend,
And from the day she gives new life, her job will never end.

A mother, from the time she holds her new born in her arms,
Will shelter and protect it so from life and all its harms.

A mother is the morning sun, when each day starts anew,
That guides her child through life each day, till night time brings its dew.

A mother's hands, they never tire, no matter what life brings,
Her love will be unending, and her heart-it always sings.

A mother, does her very best, through each and every day,
And somehow she will always know just what to do and say.
A mother's life, will change with time, as each year brings its seasons,
And one day she'll grow old and tired, for many different reasons.

A mother never knows the day, nor explanation why,
The Lord calls down upon her, and she has to say good-bye.

A mother then must leave her child, to journey different roads,
That after many years of life, her destiny beholds.

A mother's love—it then becomes, a twinkle in an eye...
And forever she will love her child, as an Angel in the sky.

Alexandra Manolas

Assassins

The Lady walked the Widow's mile,
Behind the Stalwart Black.
The Lady walked with icy smile,
Without her Chief; with stiffened back.
The Lady walked the bitter mile
Clutched deep inside the unshed tears,
Clasped by sorrow with little child,
Unflinched, ahead the lonely years.
A wind of words whirled o'er the world!
Attacking! And Hacking! And Clacking!

The Lady put away the flag. Be furled
And off to Greece went Packing
The Lady walked, again ... the bitter mile.
Aboard Ship with a Glittering Bitter smile.

Wonza Simmers

"Clocks"

As I walked in late for school
I felt the need to write a rhyme
Dedicated to the tool
With which we keep the time

People take them for granted
You can buy one at any store
But without our friend the clock
Modern life would be no more

You would never know when to work
Or when to take a vacation
Before you even bought your ticket
The train had left the station

The problems caused by lack of clocks
Would be seen on a much larger scale
The president couldn't take a morning walk
And the economy would surely fail

So whether they be digital
Or old-fashioned with brass chimes
We have to thank our trusty clocks
For helping us keep the time

Brian Burrell

Common Censor

Much to hear, needs to be said.
When gaged and bound, liberties fall dead.

No, stop the presses! Control every sound!
Place Amendment One six feet underground.
With freedom to speak whate'er comes to mind,
Abuse, anarchy is what you'll find.

Set the vocal in bars, every quill in cement?
Then expressions of worth are unable to vent.
Yes the vulgar, obscene, do have a voice.
To listen or not, must come by choice.

Much to say, needs to be heard.
Freedom's loss: The censored word.

Kevin H. Joyce

Michael

Michael was a lad who loved sports
No slouch in academia from reports
His talents were many with girl friends a plenty
And Jordan wore
Michael's name on his shorts.

Donald M. Smits

A Deadly Mistake

I pulled out into the street wobbling in the lanes;
In the seat next of me was my beloved friend Jane.
I just came from a party now trying to get home;
When I glanced over, I was swerving off the road.
Before I could hit the brakes, I ran into a car;
The sound that the impact made could be heard from afar;
About an hour passed, or maybe it was three;
But when I woke up, there were men surrounding me.
The first thing I did was look over to my right;
To see Jane's shadow lying in the light.
Then a paramedic whispered something dreadful in my ear;
I soon began to notice I was shaking with such fear.
The secret he had told me was Jane had passed away;
And in the other car two more bodies lay.
When I stepped out of the car, I began to think;
I lost my best friend because I could not refuse a drink.

Lesley Boyd

"To A Free Man"

He looked at me, and he fell to his knees, like a poor man.
He spoke to me, and he began to teach, like a wise man.

He's so old and gray, wind-torn painted face,
His home is reserved, it's been lined in furs to keep his heart warm.
How long has he tried? How long has he cried?
His soul yearns for truth, his sad face is proof he's been lied to.

Then he asked me, what it was to be, like a free man.
I could not reply, and I began to hide, like a shamed man.

Then he raised his eyes, to the moon-lit sky,
And his face did beam, as if all his dreams were part of Heaven.
Slowly he lay down, on the frozen ground,
As he closed his eyes, he asked why had I been a stranger.

He never woke, and now I suppose, he's a free man.
He was born in chains, and he died just the same,
He was an Indian.

Christopher Adam

The Sea Of Life

Life's first birth,
God's greatest creation Earth,
We all live here plain and small,
While he watches proud and tall,
Farther and farther away we shy,
Until the very day we die,
Every morning his beauty rises,
Bringing us gifts and lovely prizes,
With every word that we speak,
The more and more we grow weak,
Our predjudism and judgement,
Bring us closer to the final moment,
So now what do we do, to show we are true?
Perhaps confess,
but that would do nothing less.

Julia Davis

"I Will Not Be Broken!"

"I will not be broken!"
Even though I am sad.
I will cherish the time we spent together!
You made my life so special!
"I will not be broken!"
You were the friend I always wanted,
The brother I always had!
You mean so much!
I will never forget your sweet laughter,
Or your smile!
"I will not be broken by my tears!"

Ellen McMahon

Hurrah For Mom

Hurrah for Mom on mothers day,
From your children here and those away.
We love you Mom, for many reasons,
And our love stays strong through all four seasons.
We thank you Mom, for the things you do,
To our helper and friend, we appreciate you!!
You've always been there for us through thick and thin,
When we did something good, or committed a sin.
You stand by our side, and always stand proud,
Even when our lives draw a crowd.
You brought us up right, and did all you could,
To insure our futures in hopes they'd be good.
With your strength and knowledge, we turned out alright.
And we thank you and love you with all of our might!
So hurrah for mom from all of us,
Tom, Tim, Carol, Cheryl, Shawn, Nip, Sue and Russ!!
Happy Mothers Day!!

Joseph K. Gusick

Him

So many things run through my mind.
Looking for something that I can't find.
Wondering if he still loves me so..
The words never came from his lips although...
The way that he looks at me; then and now.
Our eyes making contact; our lips on impact.
The way he smiles after mentioning me.
I can't help but smile when he glances at me.
I've never felt this way; so loud and clear.
Just thinking someone else might have him just brings me to tears.
I could sit and hold him forever in my arms.
Although he's not here; I see him all the time...
In my mind during the day,
In my dreams as they take me away.
I carry his picture wherever I go.
For, with him, it's hard to let go.
I really hope he feels the same way.
And I hope that his feeling will stay...
Forever locked in his heart and only I have the key.
For then we could be together for eternity

Katina Pennington

Reflecting Mirror

Once upon a mirror stood a man upon a glass
Oh, that I upon the mirror could make the reflection last

That which in the eyes are seen, the mirror doth reflect
That within the mirror always will reflect

Once upon a mirror a youth who stood so tall
Now upon the mirror, now in shadow small

Frail and bent and weathered, labors before the glass
Oh, that I could only make the first reflection last

In my time and wisdom, I know that I have seen
Behind the weathered shadow is the youth that once did beam

Nothing is so precious as the youth that we once had
Nothing is as precious as the life that we now have

Once upon a mirror, the reflection it has strayed
But in my heart heart forever the youth has always stayed.

Elmer E. Stonestreet

The World

As you sit in your glass house,
you try to ignore
the world that surrounds you; it wasn't like that before.
You never stop to think, you don't show how you feel,
you just keep pretending and don't look at what's real.
You're killing one another with no question in mind;
you're looking for peace, but that's what you can't find.
You search for a light that hasn't been turned on;
you keep putting it off, and you're taking too long.
You don't realize the struggle you're putting yourself through,
and now you're all alone, and you don't know what to do.
You didn't do what you were told and you still don't listen now;
you think you'll finish what you've started,
but you don't quite know how.
You took life for granted and didn't live it out.
You said you'd do all the things you only talked bout.
So just stop pretending you haven't noticed what the Maker sees,
because all that has become is what you let it be.

Geraldine "Gigi" Comia

An Old Man's Song

I've seen dead leaves fall to the ground
In hues of red and gold
To lie upon the earth to rot
And vanish with the cold.

A sprout of new corn reaches high
To grasp the bright blue sky
And with the autumn, bear its fruit
Then curl brown leaves to die.

I've seen the sun, in orange and red,
Slow fall beneath a hill
And leave a world of deep blue-grey
To grow so very still.

Yet, every year there are new leaves.
Each year we have new corn.
And every morning rays of sun
To sleeping earth are borne.

J. David Cook

"...My Mind As My Throne"

I am content to be just one, standing on my own.
I always greet the morning sun; like me, it shines alone.

I immerse myself in music, hearing more than simple notes.
I hear forthcoming magic, from talented, beautiful throats.

The night time is my favorite, for which I lay awake.
I love, desire and wait for it, and the wonders my mind will make.

My world is full of wonders, music and other things,
Reshaped, reborn with every day, to soar on golden wings.

I am myself and, by myself, the person I want to be,
And even men of the greatest wealth, shall never be better than me.

And if to you this poem stands, as something of a riddle,
Understand, I stand alone, in this world so very little.

And my world is so very great, yet the real world is so small.
My world is the one I choose to make; against the real, it stands tall.

Of true friends, I am hesitant, to count any more than three.
And yet with them, I am content, for they bring out the best in me.

And with this verse I now conclude, when I say I stand alone,
I mean that I enjoy solitude - the world as my kingdom,
my mind as my throne.

Dustin P. Bradshaw

San Jacinto Daydreams

Here I doze 'neath Live Oak trees
and feel faint stirrings of a balmy breeze.
The sun is shining through dappled sky
and causes me to turn as it catches my eye.
The sleepy river has a surface like glass
that's disturbed by occasional boats as they pass.
The monolithic structure that juts from freedom's hill
tells of men who fought to break the hold of tyrant's will.
The tales and deeds of heroes made and lost this day
are surely remembered in a sentimental way.
The heroic deeds of General Sam and all his countrymen
who beat Santa Anna's superior force and never did give in.
The eerie feelings present upon this heroic heath
make any Texan want to draw ancestral sword from sheath.
To celebrate the deeds here done by Texas' Native Sons,
the children of this state gave up allowances and funds.
To dedicate and consecrate this ground where liberty dwells
to place a memorial and monument that makes a Texan's yells,
a matter more than pride or state but rings like Liberty bells.

Robert Savant

"A Dream"

They say it could never happen,
they said it would never be.
But the dream still ran wild,
and would always be free.
The people, the pressure, the odds, the spirit,
in which the dream stay forever in.
With no one else to hear it.
But once in a lifetime, a dream does come true.
The dream can't be fought, it must happen to you.
If you do fight your dream,
you will soon eventually regret.
Because of the odds which you will never let.
Stay free! Stay free!
Just go as I say.
Dreams be! Dreams be!
Throughout your day.
Though some may be nightmares,
don't let them get you down.
There may be one fantasy left,
that your soul hasn't let drown.

William Tyson Lee Hall

One Fate

The dreadful moaning of the souls
Within the cages of the sky
That dwell on higher lavish floors
Yet never will they learn to fly

While others lingering in poverty and stench
Each day they take their endless stroll
Yes, those, that make their home a bench
Until the day they finally will fall

These beings, knowingly or not,
Whatever path or way they'll take
Are stuck together in one lot
One never runs away from fate

We are the same, high or low
Whatever destiny will bring
Where blood had flown through their veins
There now runs an icy spring

Alexander Kofman

"Old Black Pocketbook"

Every place my mother went,
She took her old black pocket book.
It held all the mysteries of life,
but we weren't suppose to look.
She kept tissues for a runny nose,
An extra set of baby clothes, you
could find the deed to our old farm,
Also the title to the car, a tube
of lipstick seldom used, Bobby pins
and baby shoes, birth certificates
for us kids, she had a lot of those,
why she took the castor oil heaven only knows.
I've often thought and I think
I'm right, if I could only have
taken a look, the answers to
the problems of the world was
in mom's old black pocket book.

Kathryn Bailey

The Emerald Path

Emerald leaves, black now with darkness
dark path, hardened by generations of use,
distant pounding of hearts beating and crutching artillery

Quiet, steady, deadly waiting
thoughts of death to come
small slightly curved dark green boxes, full of death
and pain, with green wires like the emerald stems leading
to sweaty palms

Bamboo creaking by the weight of their loads
dark clothing mask their silhouettes
frogs croaking in the paddy

One then twenty, walk into the deadly space
Bright Light! Power! Pain And Death

The souls released from pain and grief
finding brothers, sisters, parents, and comrades
no need to struggle, no need to scream, their job is done

They leave the bodies, they leave their youth
return to base, over the hardened ground
past the emerald leaves and life
and the quiet pond

Garry Gregory

Wake Up America

What is wrong with our country called America today?
Where it is dangerous for our children to go out and play!
It used to be called the Land of the Free,
But no more is that true for you and me.

Who would have thought when America was young,
That it would have fallen to the lowest rung!
Our streets are not safe, our doors must be barred,
We must lock every gate that surrounds our yard.

People quake and fear for most of the night.
Waiting, praying for the dawning of light.
What has happened to America today?
A war is raging that will not go away.

For the soul of America we must fight,
To be safe and free should be our plight.
The answer for America we must see,
To once more be the Land of the Brave and Free.

Our forefathers founded this great land,
On the Word of God they took a stand.
The principles are there for all to see.
Wake up America! Our future is up to you and me.

David Moody

Fools Love

My man than left me
Left me cryn'
Then he calls me sayn' "I'm sorry"

He hurt me so bad
I can't think straight
Then he calls me sayn' he's sorry

I sit here cryn' all night wondering who's he holding
Cause honey, it sho ain't me!
Then he calls me sayn' he's sorry

I feel like he loves me but I learned from him
That love don't have nutthin' to do with it!
And of course he calls me sayn' he's sorry

We'll I'm the one that's sorry because
I sit here believing that he's really sorry

Ain't I Sorry?...

Diane Carroll

A Heart Without

Abandoned - left in the cold
No shoulder to cry on - no hand to hold
A child within, a heart without
Is this what life is all about?

A man you see, a child I feel
I must face the past in order to heal
Crying inside, I build my wall
I wait for my friend misery to make a call

Taken from the palladium of my mothers womb
Pushed out into this world of a living tomb.
The false self, the one that is not me.
That is who I wish for you to see

A heart without - love is a game to play
I'll tell you I love you, then push you away
I look to angels, asking to explain
I run to hide, but must face the pain.

If the best things in life are free
How come I didn't get what was promised to me.
Its hard to love when you don't have a heart
Now I've taken yours and torn it apart.

Alfred P. Burns II

The Empty Nest

Little bird upon the sill, I've seen you around before.
You'd sit in the tree and sing with me, we don't do that much anymore.

The first spring that I saw you there, all the flowers were in bloom.
Their sweet perfume, our heads held high, we both had us a groom.

We lulled the cries with lullabies, as we held our babies near.
And as they grew I introduced them to you, "see the pretty bird singing; hear."

We watched through the years as each grown child found their wings to fly.
With muffled songs, we sang along, through tears we had to cry.

Today the last one moved away and though we've tried our best,
it's hard to hide the song that has died, as we sit in our empty nest.

Is that why you came down today to sit and visit awhile.
Reminiscing on past memories, of love and hugs and smiles.

Do you think perhaps our little ones are sharing memories too?
Lulling cries with lullabies and thinking of me and you.

As they hold their babies to their breast and begin to fill their empty nest.

Tommari S. Dale

"The American Dream"

What is the American Dream...?
To me it is the freedom of life.
It should be a place where
crime is non existent and
peace is our security not our bullets.
How many have tried for this dream,
yet failed within grasp of it?
Does the dream ever come true or it is just
a democratic ploy?
I have seen the dream
yet I have still to catch it.
As I draw nearer,
it only seems to float further away.
When I begin to walk away it slowly creeps behind me,
lurking until I turn to grab it then it flies away.
I watch it tease and taunt me
like a bully on your trail.
The true question is not "What is the American Dream?"
but how do you catch it?

Anthony John Retenski

The Project Of Life

Living in the projects of destruction in search for a government of good construction of closed eye and glorious dreams only to open to find just what it really seams.

This project of life is full of pain and despair good neighbors True love peace and understanding is so very rare.

Were often labeled lazy and confused when most of the time were Taken advantage of and mentally and emotionally abused.

God gave us this gift of life for all that believe, wouldn't it be nice if we all came together to receive.

My life in the projects are oh so giving when the biggest pay back of life is Living! Living! Living! Please please look everyone we all live in the projects of life regardless of who have wealth and who is living in poverty state.

"So why am I labeled in the projects of life"?

Evelyn Sheppard

Flying

I have stood still long enough
Trying to figure out how to fly.
The thinking never ended.
Boredom set in.
As my wings reached for the sky.

I closed my eyes
And made a leap
in spite of the dangerous wind.
I soared like an eagle
through the sky
nothing causing me to change the direction
I was in.

The life below me
told no stories
as I waved goodbye.
Moving with great velocity
through the sky
I forgot who said I couldn't fly so high?

John Pesa

He Is Gone

He is gone. There is nothing we can do. His life was full
of sorrow, sadness, and heartbreak too. He used to say
a lot of things that made sense. I guess you figure he
never was very dense.

He is gone. He threw his life away. I guess there is nothing
I can say. Before he died he was very sick. I guess you can
also say his conscience was full of drugs but never that thick.

He is gone. With a single blow to his head. He had a wife
and a daughter waiting to go to bed.

He is gone. He wished he could be happier but the more he tried
the more he became sadder. By singing it helped him a bit. I
guess when you are depressed there is nothing you can do to make
the pieces fit.

He is gone. His songs were full of sorrow and pain. His life was
never plain. His songs would and could relate to us. He was going
on a trip that was permanent inside the death bus. In spirit he
will always live in our hearts.

He is gone. He was one of life's greatest achievements. Why did
he kill himself, no one knows. It might have been a hint.
He is gone.

Adrianne Rivera

Hidden Day

My Beloved and I are one
Nothing on earth can part us
His Presence brings wondrous joy
Which makes all earthly joys minute

I greet my Beloved at dawn
In the quiet of my heart we speak
As softly as His sunrise turns darkness into light
He teaches me, and the seeds take root

At Mass I confess my guilt
In sorrow and in love I pray and offer
This weak unworthy person He rewards
He Himself becomes my spirit's fruit

When at times in the day I forget Him
Gently He reminds me that He waits
As that which I behold reflects His glory
Be it sky or tree or face of age or youth

My Beloved, my Brother, my Redeemer
His wounds my sins have made
But from the cross He calls me "beloved"
In the night I rest in this truth

Flo Bilelo

Nice View

Rocks and stones break my bones
Vandalism rape murder blame them songs
Long long hard never ending uphill trawl
Around the round little ball in the square you must fall
When it takes all week for one day to pass
Gorgeous flower so lives a life in trash
Vulnerable will you make it through another day
All those addictions hang-ups excuses only cause your stay
Time to realize you're stuck there is a better way
Focus your gaze inward there you will see
The image in the mirror complies to thee
If anyone is to blame for making like a wreck
It is the same person who could be just about perfect

Robert Eckert

Come With Me

Come with me, come up higher,
come to where there burns a fire.

A fire to burn out thoughts of wrong,
to let us learn what we all long.

Once we learn what we should know,
the light within will brightly show.

We'll learn to give instead of take,
to offer love and rid all hate.

Come with me, please come up higher,
come to where there burns a fire.

A fire that burns within our souls,
to reach out and touch, the far unknown.

As we soar up towards the light,
you and I will gain insight.

Through this process we'll learn to see,
there's more to life, than what there seems.

L. Dwight-Riffle

Israel

Israel is the name of the land and God's chosen people.
Israel is the name of the woman I love, from the
foundations of the Holiest temple, to the spires
of the tallest of church steeples.

Israel you are as new as todays newspaper and as
old as the writings of Torah and the Bible.
You have survived many enemies and persecutions
you are like a Phoenix, Israel which rose from
The ashes of destruction and exile.

Israel your name spells out the story from the dawn
of conscience, down to this very day. You're a woman
that's lived through so much, and although you're older
now, your beauty still endures without decay.

Israel you have lived through the worlds most violent
rage, you are Gods most magnificent ray.

Israel you have walked with God and man, you have
Blessings as countless as the grains of desert sand.

Israel you have a history of a miraculous past, and for the future
in heaven, the promise of peace and love to last.

Israel you are the woman I love, you are the one sent
to me from the heavens above.

Robert Langworthy

At Appomattox Court House, Virginia

Lee was seated in the parlor, when on horseback, the Ruddy Grant arrived
At Wilmer McClean's house in Virginia on that poignant Palm Sunday,
April 9, 1865, for a brief encounter the two top generals had contrived
To initiate a prolonged process to reunite the nation, one day.

The proud Confederate, his hair white, wearing his only fresh uniform
Bore the golden sword he was reluctantly prepared at last to surrender
With his 30,000 man Army of Northern Virginia, starving, battle-worn
Encircled by twice as many of Union forces facing this gallant defender.

Rough and ready Grant, magnanimous in victory, after four years of war
Chose not to ask the Virginian to tender his sword in defeat
In fact, he let the South's cavalry ride their horses home and what's more
Respectfully, allowed Lee's officers to keep their sidearms, as their service
was now complete.

From the hearth Lee withdrew — by a generous Grant paroled
The healing of a land sundered by uncivil war of brother vs. brother
Began in a county seat where Anglo-Saxon justice was long enrolled
As this dutiful and courageous pair swore: "Never another!"

Norman R. Nelsen

Untitled

From the bowels of the earth, through the beds of a lake, through thedepths of the waters came a rumble, came a quake,
And it shot through my body cut my heart through my throat and my cry pierced the heavens and resounded back remote.
And I know that God heard me, held me fast as I shook, and I fought for survival-every breath that I took;
Was so labored, was so rapid and my heart was bursting out! As I cried in my pain, Oh my God, what's this about!
So I trembled on the brink of a deep dark hole, looking down with such terror that it struck my very soul!
I felt faint! I felt dizzy! And the world was whirling past, so I grabbed onto something trying hard to hold me fast!
I just felt so unreal that I had to stop and see, am I here? Should I pinch me? Is this me? This is me!
So I looked at the picture that my mind played inside, and quickly had to look away, my mettle had been tried!
As I dropped with exhaustion and I fell into a sleep. I realized that I had fought the demon buried deep,
In the depths of my mind, in the waters just beneath how he slithered through the silt and mud to him I did bequeath.
So he swims and he watches waiting for another chance, now I'm waiting on the surface in my hand I have a lance,
And now I know, I'll make that leap and end this deadly dance!

Rita Fusaro

To Mr. Herbert Young On His 110th Birthday

My Lord! I talk in the name of an idea.
Today we look at you as a hero of the time,
as a statue, as a column. We look at you with pride and hope
Because you have shared with discreet influence
Of inspiration and fantasy the way to the temple of glory
With dignity and priceless possession of greatness.
One hundred and ten years is a long way to go...
You'll go further, brightening the lives
Of your Seniors Elderly Brothers,
With your manhood shadow by the years.
I wish that my verse, like the pearls in the sea,
The mines of gold and The Golcondas diamonds,
And the treasures of Baghdad, Adorn your way,
Your passage, through the years to come!
I wish to see the sun in the horizon
With the splendor of a sunset, so, my muse can capture
a verse in melodies... And humble as I am
With my hands and my heart in a basket of flowers
Could bring to You all the Love that Corsi House Seniors
Have for years and will last...Forever!

Susana Matos Martinez

Grazing In Thought

Complex messages feeding innocent minds, trickling thoughts in your head down your spine.
Captured by youth without promise or source, listening to others only hearing their voice.
Reflections of dreams dripping ideas to the head, hearing people talk and wondering what they said.
Dazing at light through glimpsing at dark, pulsating images igniting a spark.
Concepts of rationale covered with sense, bleeding confusion and building a fence.
Dipping in aggravation, digital perception, resisting surrender to emotional rejection.
Yearning for clarity with some understanding, flying above without finding a landing.
Zipping through time sliding down a maze, hearing the music when it's not even played.
Moving in caution through doubt and uncertainty, glazing in space and staring in infinite.
Feeding on thoughts spinning around, hoping your feet can at least touch the ground.
Solid grasps of flickering light, camouflaged interpretations of what could be right.
Hitting bumps and colliding with walls, shaken and rattled but not dropping balls.
Binding travels through a complicated maze, realizing and hoping to just find the way.
Wondering and questioning all the while why it must be, liquidating intuition to more than you see.
Melting in energy and not resisting the force, traipsing with momentum and connecting the source.
Perpetuating cycles of life again and again, learning lessons to decrease the time that we spend.
Abandoning the negative and yielding to good, flowing toward destiny the way that we should.
Important messages that fade in and out, understanding the way without knowing the route.
Hit by a rock, turned on a light, understanding the thoughts that make it all right.
Higher awareness is truth taught through messages we get by grazing in thought.

Norma S. Murray

Autumn Ambush

Above, birds, soon to head
even farther south for the winter,
break formation to discuss strategy

Shrouded in blaze-orange leaves,
they chatter like squeaky springs
in a rent-by-the-hour motel

Below, footsteps—snap, crackle, pop—
halt flight plans in the making,
and sudden silence falls

Then, bam! An explosion
of birds shatters the sky, a mass
of feathered buckshot on the wing

Eileen Sisk

The Pink Rose

Petals as soft as silk, the color of a girl's cheeks,
Smells as deep as a never-ending abyss of beautifulness.
A sight so glamorous, you wish it could last for weeks upon weeks,
But, alas, it wilts in only one week, more or less.
This is a rose, a beautiful object that one could never forget.
A rose is life, death, love, and hope, for those who believe in its power.
Do not forget the sweet smell or wonderful sight, and remember yet;
Killing a flower as gorgeous as this, you must bow down to God and cower.
God gave you this plant as a marvelous gift from the Heaven's above,
Just give the rose your respect, wonder, happiness, and kind love,
And you will see, smell, and feel such beauty eternally and forever!

Courtney Leigh Llewellyn

A Love To Remember

I miss the times we shared.
You were there when I needed
you most. You wiped the tears
from my eyes. We shared a lot
of special times together. Those
times just vanished. I miss the
memories we had. The good times,
The bad, and most of all the sad times.
I wish you were here right now
so I could hold you once more.
You were the closest friend I
ever had and now it's all gone.
Hopefully we'll be joined as friends again

Debbie Vermette

The Secret Garden

I live in a secret garden
I cannot invite you here
It's not a friendly place

The walls are tall and sturdy
I built them all myself
They keep you out, me in, I'm "safe"

The flowers have long since faded
The thorns grow long and sharp
It's cold here, alone here

Tears lie silent within me
My cries cannot be heard
My thoughts are tangled, tied in knots

I cannot bear to stay here
Steps out are hard to take
The path is dark and slippery
I cannot find the gate

I need a hand to guide me
A voice to push me on
My footsteps seem to falter
Why do it, why go on?

Judy Loftin

"The Handmaid Of The Lord"

You shield me
You lead me
You understand my "whys?"

The handmaid of the Lord am I

You love me
And You hold me
You hurt when I cry

The handmaid of the Lord am I

You bless me
You comfort me
You are nearer than a sigh

The handmaid of the Lord am I

I love You
I praise You
I lift my heart 'To You' on high

The handmaid of the Lord am I

Christy Stueve

Loneliness

Is a piece of you
nobody has ventured.
A piece
nobody has touched
or reached for.
A piece
nobody knows about
or cares about.
Sometimes
it shows
and sometimes
it's hidden.
The only thing is
everybody
has a piece of
loneliness.

Amanda Brown

Beauty

Beauty is a flower
Blooming in the spring
Beauty is a bluebird
Listen to it sing
Beauty is a child
Happy and sincere
Beauty is the sea
For it never has a fear
Beauty is a rainbow
Forming in the sky
Beauty is a teardrop
Shed from a happy eye
Beauty is the earth
Pretty and alive
Beauty is a baby
Sweet and full of life
Beauty is the sun
So close - yet so far away
Beauty is everywhere
where it shall always stay

Amanda Smith

Kenneth

Methought I'd write a poem
About my husband dear,
But no high-sounding phrases
Came falling on my ear.

My husband? How describe him —
Methinks it can't be done.
He's much too much of many things
And never much of some.

He's much too much of kindness,
Of thoughtfulness and love —
Of tenderness, of wisdom —
And traits I can't think of.

He's never much of selfishness,
Of bragging or deceit.
He's moderation in all things,
And strength beyond belief.

He's many things to many folks—
He's earthy— he's divine.
But you know what he is the most?
Most of all — He's mine!

Pauline Claussen Woods

Tumbling

That tumbleweed
scorched by the stinging desert sun
Intertwined, still...
with brittle strength
captivated by the wind
tossed with each whirl
each bounce contains a wound
calloused...
enduring each hit
within its destitute
and given gratitude
for not the wind
helplessly left
singed

Karen Jasmer

My Baby Girl

Bright little eyes
that see right through me,
Perfect little hands
that touch my heart,
Dreams of teddy bears
sitting down for tea,
An independent soul
right from the start,
Precious little angel
sent from heaven above,
God's little masterpiece
to cherish and love.

Donna Lameris

A Whisper Of Time

It only takes a whisper of time
To smile at a passerby,
And brighten up their day a bit,
With a friendly little "hi".

It only takes a whisper of time
To acknowledge a little child,
And give them your attention
For just a little while.

It only takes a whisper of time
When a puppy's sitting near,
To call and clap your hands
With a friendly "come here".

Time is something we all have
Not enough of, we chatter.
But everyone has a whisper of time
For the little things that matter.

Dottie P. Schuster

Untitled

I have no need for an umbrella
On this delightful day
With sun all around me
And not a cloud in the sky.
I have the energy of a child
Just to run and jump and play
It would make the morning papers
Because as you can readily see,
I've reached the age of no turn
But should that bother me?
To sacrifice my own days pleasure
At having boundless energy
To enjoy the daily living
That brings a morning sunrise
With a day of pure delight

M. V. Hochreiter

Death

It creeps along so slowly,
Tiptoeing like a cat.
A heart as black as Crowley's
It comes to seize its prey.

Servant to both Satan and God,
He kills upon demand.
And as he delivers souls to them
He grips with his icy hand.

Some people, they fear him,
Others, they revere him.
As for me, I am of the latter,
For Death is my friend.

Oh, the woe and misery
And the horror that he brings.
I enjoy all of these
Until they come to me.

My friend Death, he is real,
Do not deny his existence still.
He comes upon the wind so high
And so my friend....you die.

R. Luke DeVasier

Girl In Blue

A little girl all dressed in blue,
with long curls hanging to her side,
she looks to be no more than three,
but walks with grace and pride.
She runs, she jumps and down
she falls, all to her dismay, but up
she gets, and tells her mommy,
I really am ok.

Dorothy W. Martin

Flowers

You not only see and
smell them but taste
and breath them.
You see their pink, yellow and
orange face, you smell the
sweet smell of blooming
roses and daisies.
The fragrance so strong in a
bunch you can almost
taste them and have them for lunch.
You breathe them, so neat and sweet
candies, sugars what a treat?
As I sit and think of things
it reminds me that I'm hungry!

Jennifer L. Powell

Shattered

He watches the violent tremors
Wrack her frail, fragile body,
As she lies among the
Pillows and sheets of white.
A smile graces her face.
Its origin unknown to him,
As he feels her struggle
To bring the memory alive.

His gentleness evident as he
Caresses her withered old hand.
His voice belies his grief
As he sings favorite songs.
The pain in her eyes
Is reflected in his own.
The mother of his youth
Lies before him, shattered forever.

Elizabeth M. Nessler

Untitled

I remember endless days
and nights of crying.
Feeling empty inside.
Having no one to turn to.
I hate it.
Why do I feel so alone,
so unloved?
I feel like there is
nothing inside of me except space.
I long for a shoulder
to cry one. Someone who
will understand my pain.
Yet, I look around and
only find myself.
How long will it takes
for the emptiness to
eat away my heart and mind?
How long can I wait
for someone to save me?
Maybe, I have to save myself.

Janet Haynes

The Smile

You gave me your smile when I was
at the end,

You touched my life and inspired me
to live again.

You are like a breath of fresh air,
and when I needed you the most,
you were there.

I am not asking for the world,
just someone special, that I can hold.

I was a lost ship in a stormy sea,
and finding a safe harbor just
was not meant to be.

Your smile became my guiding light,
And then in your arms one night,
I found my harbor even so bright.

Paul Horvat

Lost Love

Upon the waves she dances,
As they flew over the ocean,
Spreading the ashes that had
once formed her body.

Husband sitting in his seat,
awaiting this sad day to end,
for the hope that he can go
to sleep and wake to find
her next to him in their bed.

He had not wanted to lose her,
if only he could touch her once more,
but, he lost his love.

Lyle Hutchinson

Looking Out From Exhibition Hall On Commonwealth Pier

A lone sea gull floats
in Boston Harbor
and throughout
the cold lonely water
propagates.

Richard Saine

The Hallway

The doorways of life
they open and close
Marriages, children and
jobs come and go.

Learning to live and
love through it all
I found contentment
living in the hall.

Life in the hallway
has set me free
It's a place to rest
to wait and see.

Judy Stern

Treasure Hunt

Live within the moment now;
The next is not assured.
For the pleasure of giving
Is the treasure of living;
The ailments of life are cured.

The measure of life in Eternity
Is the pleasure with which we give;
And the giving is Heaven's treasure
To ensure that we may live.

Mark Gregory Hunsdon

Winter's Maidens

Before the earth reveals its treasures
And robins herald early spring
Let winter's maidens go a' dancing
Swirling in a madcap fling.

Let hyacinth and crocus slumber
To Mother Nature I appease
Soon life will gently reawaken
And leaves will glorify the trees.

Till then I'll revel at the sight
Of winter's maidens bathed in light
Ethereal, in hallowed white
Illuminating darkest nights.

Too short, the winter maidens' reign
Soon crystal trees will be reclaimed
By blossoms bowing to the breeze
But who would radiance displease?

Devorah Seidenfeld

Momentous Now

The moments
Line our minds
with images shared
Only we know
the shape of our love
The time
(seamed with kisses
we wove a world)
swings us gently
back and forth
Past nows live again
in memories present
Love spins
(a passionate playground
we travel all directions)
all worlds
as I close my eyes
to now

Erica Shane Hamilton

Give Thanks

Give thanks to the Lord,
Rejoice in his holy name.
Even though circumstance are bad,
You will feel no pain.

You will have happiness forever,
If you ask him in your heart.
Though you might sin often,
He will never part.

You may have gone through,
Good times, bad times, humor and grief.
But as long as he is with you;
You will always have peace.

There is much affliction and mourning,
In the world.
But pray every day,
And use your Bible as a sword.

Give thanks to the Lord,
Rejoice in his holy name
Even though circumstances are bad
You will feel no pain

Amanda L. Traylor

Dependence

Reaching upward
to grasp a hand
the small one knows no weakness
in seeking out a strong right arm
to guide him through his travels.

Held high in faith
that more than air
Will close around his fingers
one little hand waves victory
to all grown tall and beaten.

Charles H. Johnson

Queen Lizzie's Last Ball

Enough death
for the most exclusive of worms
spiders and insects
entertaining
at a lovely tea time ball
bloody cocktails
sweet garbage
dancing to the cricket quartet
oohing
aahing
over a pretty little bauble
the family forgot to pawn
such a darling reception
too bad
the mosquito clan
couldn't make it

Janel Harrell

Unaware

Did you ever notice
how there's nothing
half-way
about a rainy day?
Or a carnival ride,
or a lilac bush in Spring?
I'm glad.
Only people know the art
of living
half-alive.

Lenore Bezinque

Hawks

Confounded in aphony
fragile in dismay
portions of my reverie
you freely possess

From the initial moment
I perceived you from afar
either quiet in fear
or declaring trifling words
I craved your consciousness
and seductive substantiality

As a bard, I expressed to you
my eager affections
and nervously anticipated
the unknown response

Bewildered in my limitations
I unwillingly restrained
from my desired osculation

Not knowing of your status
I was waiting
in a tunnel of cold obduracy

Anita Minns

I Sence A

Classical feeling
That is mind to soul
A precious moment
that lingers on
  forever.

A scene that drapes
into folds of
beautiful silk, and
falls to the floor
  in elegance.

A statue of a perfect
stone that rises above
all pitfalls.

Beryl Harvey

Earth Day!

Hooray Hooray!
It's earth day.

The dear dance
and graze
to the happy songs
the birds sing.

The salmon jump high
in the air
as if to say
"this is my day."

The horses gallop
in the fields
and whiney and nay
with happiness.

The flowers pop their heads
to the sun.

And all animals go back
to the way
they were
when earth day is done!

Stephanie McMahon

Thank You For My Angel, Lord

Thank you for my angel, Lord
To help me through the day
To guide me through my every move
And help me should I stray

Thank you for my angel, Lord
A better friend, I could not ask
To love me no matter what I do
Sometimes, a difficult task

Thank you for my angel, Lord
To whisper in my ear
The wrong I do, to set it right
And wipe away my tear

Thank you for my angel, Lord
To get me through the night
To keep me safe when darkness falls
And usher in the light

Thank you for my angel, Lord
To help me safely home
Into your loving arms I'll stay
And never more to roam.

C. J. Sexton

Ah — Prayer

Thoughts become a field of flowers
Daisies blooming, white as snow
Amid warm red beaming roses
Smiles that sets a heart aglow

Waking thoughts to mellow raindrops
Touching bright green fields of hope
Enfolded by a tender rainbow
Binding love within its scope

Rising to a golden morning
Joyous life in lasting peace
Divine creation e'er appearing
God, in whom we find all these

Anna C. Besancon

This Child Of Mine

I saw her face before my eyes,
a wee small child, what a prize.

A gift from God so small and pure,
this child of mine whom I adore.

Her hand in mine throughout the years,
I saw her through the smiles and tears.

The ups and downs, the highs and lows,
I'm always with her, God only knows.

She is my joy, my greatest treasure
this child of mine gives such pleasure.

Now she's grown, oh what a beauty
with hair of gold, oh what a smile,
a soul so pure, oh what a child.

Patricia Hocken

Soaring

Soaring through the clouds,
Swinging in the trees,
I am the wind.

Sometimes howling,
Other times groaning,
I am the wind.

Amanda Seidl

Remembering Junior High

At the end of our Junior high
years some of us will laugh others
will cry some will struggle to
keep our eyes dry

Remember the nice teachers
the mean ones too but
don't forget that disgusting food

Remember when you walked
arm and arm you and your
best friend having a good
time. When you were bad and
they called your dad.

But at the end of those years
some of us will go ahead others
will stay behind some go left
others go right.

But where ever you go and
where ever I am I'll always
remember you and our good
times in Junior high!!

Tandra Lee

"Spiders"

Whisper the legs,
"You're searching for the truth"
But the body behind
Is paralyzing you

Laurel Hoffman

Friendship

Friendship is the long
Golden Chain
That holds firmly
With might
And main
By links of laughter,
Tears and smiles
Entwined in memories
Golden years
That reaches far
To the Golden Chains End
And binds the
Heart of a friend
And a friend.

Michaele Desmond

The Eternal One

The lines on the faces,
The hopes and the places,
The song yet to be sung,
Your look to the future,
What does it feature;
A battle yet to be won.

In the life of a man,
The soul is so grand,
Who cares if we have any fun?
To get where we are,
No matter how far,
It's all once and yet
It's just begun.

Jack Radgus

I Could...Leaves

I could see colorful leaves,
Surrounding, around me.
I could see different leaves,
Falling from their tree.

I could hear crispy leaves,
Crickles,
and crackles,
under my feet.

I could smell sweet leaves
that puts me to sleep,
and, bad leaves,
that makes me want to sneeze.
Achoo, achoo.

I could feel different leaves,
rough, smooth, and pointy leaves.
Ouch!

I could see leaves,
and more different, colorful leaves.
But, I could not hurt the leaves,
Because it's for me to achieve.

Teresa Sanasith

Untitled

Christmas is a merry time
Though not everyone is happy.
While most people open gifts,
And dine with friends and family,
Some people sit at home,
Alone, with no one beside them.
These are the lonely people
Who have no friends to speak of,
And as far as family goes,
They have them, but that's all.
All it takes is an open heart,
A little give without any take,
And these people will soon be happy
For now they know someone cares.

Darrel Winert

Lovely Lady

Lovely lady,
One can clearly see,
The gift you give to me.

Lovely lady,
With many colors,
Brushed on with ease,
Your dream as colorful
as you see me.

Lovely lady,
With pale expressions
Of a vivid kind,
Always waiting to awake my mind.

"Embrace this scene,
Open your heart to me;"
As loves expression goes,
Never, does she withhold,
Her rainbow.

What a Lovely Lady!

Annette Zavada

Light

And yet as the light
shone brightly,
there was still within
that feeling of
object emptiness.

One must live each day
with the thought of night
as it comes forward to darken
yet to illumine each thought.

Today, I hold onto
the rays of the sun,
knowing that they will be tempered
by the pull of the celestial star.

Richard Sullivan

Earthquake

I am an earthquake
Tumbling, rolling, shaking
I am an earthquake
Turning everything upside down

I am an earthquake,
An emotional earthquake
One minute, as happy as can be
The next, down in the dumps

It seems strange to think
That one year ago
My surroundings were stable and secure
Now, just twelve months later,
Look at me
My world turned upside down

I am in turmoil
All shaken up inside
I am an earthquake
My world turned upside down

Emily Koehler-Platten

With A Blink Of An Eye

With a blink of your eye
You think yourself not beautiful,
Will you look past the mirror,
Will you look into your soul,
What did you find?
This is what I found.
Love, honesty, compassion, honor
And yes some fear.
But are these not qualities of
kings and queens;
I say they are with a blink of my eye.
You see mirror images can be
changed with a blink of an eye.
The qualities I see here are
Instilled so deep that they'll be
there for a life time.
Now that's beautiful!

David Palmer

Life Is Precious

Life is precious
Life is dear
Learn to guard it well
For all too soon the end will come
Before anyone can tell.
So just think about it
And do your best each day
For when the end has finally come
You can't look back and stay.

Rose Mary Johnson

Never Ends

As we walk together
On the beach that never ends
I look into your eyes
And see the bond that we have tied.

The waves crash
And the world moves
Beneath our feet

The sun begins to set
And your love is wrapped
Around me
On the beach that never ends.

Sarah Harder

To My Daughter

I love my little darling girl
She's so cute to me
And every time I tell her this
She looks and smiles at me
Her hair is long and black as night
Her eyes of black gold.
Her smile can melt the icy frost
Something to be hold.
I thank the Almighty up above
For blessing me with her
And every time I look at her
She smiles and looks at me.

Anthony L. Disaia

Rain

The gray of the sky mirrors
the gray of my life and
the rain
represents my tears.

The sky opens up to
pour down its anguish and
forlornly
soaks me with its idle,
saturated emotions.

As I stand alienated in
Nature's embrace
it does nothing to ease my
pain

Because mother nature cannot
help me now for
she is just
as
forsaken
as I.

Annie Unterstein

Lonely Tears

Why do I cry these lonely tears,
I reach out, but no one is there.
The darkness is frightening,
My thoughts are sheer hell.
The path that I follow is like a tunnel,
But not light do I see.
Only pain and emptiness and,
Thoughts of what once was.
Will there ever be light or is it,
Gone out for good.
Only God knows the answer,
He won't share.
So I wait and cry these lonely tears.

Phyllis J. Goodhart

God And Me

I see the hand of God,
in the sun that shines
and his wondrous works,
in the towering pines
I see his holiness, in
the falling snow
I feel his presence, where
ever I go;
I see his tenderness, in
a beautiful rose
and his loving caress,
in the breeze that blows
I love my God, and he loves me.
So come what may, this sets
me free.

Betty Jane Staley

To Love A Storm

I watch the cumulo-nimbus form
I love it when the lightning comes
I hear the thunder like distant drums
I do not fear the coming storm
We cannot see the sun so warm
The coming chill so sharp it numbs
The teasing thrill my heart it strums
How strange it is to love a storm

The curtains in my window dance
Into my lap the kitten springs
The trees perform an eerie dance
The gusty winds deliver things
Brought to my home by merest chance
I love the joy the rainstorm brings

Renate Wright

To A One Year Old

I'd have never known
How much you've grown,
'Til I look at pictures of you.
From a baby to a little girl
What twelve months will do.

You're walking, not talking,
But I rue the day you do.
So right now I'm glad
You're just one-year old.
Lord knows what you'll do at two.

Helen M. Bryant

Untitled

You are like the ocean to me
So powerful and unpredictable
The power to keep everyone offshore
Yet a magical power to always
Attract them back to you
Such a perfect feeling you give...
When strolling along...
And one's feet are brushed
By the softness of your touch...
So perfect and only
Only you can give

Josiane Balancy

Nikki

Nikki is my precious dog
That has blessed our lives a lot
Because without her makes us sad
I know in my heart she's with God.

She was a good and loving buddy
Who welcomed you home each day
I shall always remember her
When I bend my knees and pray.

Thank you for your pleasures Nikki
You are something very special
We love you with all our hearts
I'll keep these memories forever.

Nikki, you are a little sweetheart
That we think about all the time
You bring us happy memories
That we can keep there in our mind.

Jane Blake

I'm Sorry

Why must you leave me alone
at night.
You leave me alone,
You leave me in fright.
You told me you would be beside
me in the morning,
another day is gone,
another day is dawning.
You told me a lie,
as I sat down to cry.
I still remember what you said
But it's way too late,
my tears have been shed.
I shall hold a grudge on you.
You never said,
"I'm sorry."

Jessica Leonard

Our Grandchildren

Our grandchildren are wonderful!
Oh yeah! I hear you laugh,
But hold on there my friend
You don't know all, by half.

The generations come and go,
New problems each must master.
Some we have conquered, given time,
Others have brought disaster.

The youth today have problems
Left to them by us.
So who are we to blame them
And often make a fuss?

Let's recognize our errors
And with open minds and hearts,
Across the generations
Try to do our part.

God bless them all!

Annette P. Johnston

Love

Some say love, it is a dove,
Some say love, it is a hug,
Some say love, it is a stream,
But most say love, it is a dream.

Lhardi D. Cooks

Untitled

Our rain falls in shimmering metallic curtains all over the parched land. It turns my town into a silver wonder land. It makes a joyful sound on my window pane and roof. For a while, all rejoice in the liquid life.

Allison Huang

Were You Calling Me, Darling?

There is more than one of me
Who loves the all of you.
There is in me the proper wife
Who serves and seeks and does.
Within me too, a raging one,
Who cries and hurts,
And gives strong voice
To controversial choice.
I am by turn so many things,
I cannot name them all.
I'm proud and cold,
I can cut deep,
Do what I do not like.
A confidante,
A friend, a flirt.
Each one you'll find in me.
so, my Dear, please understand,
That when you call on me,
I really am not certain
Just who will answer thee.

Yvonne McGuire

Whose?

I belong to
the pets in the morning,
wanting my affection and a meal.
the children
with their endless needs
and fleeting, sweet kisses.
my friend on our daily walk.
a tree's shade
in the heat of the afternoon.
you, my love, with your smile and hugs
while I'm fixing dinner.
No...
you, my love,
always, although it may not seem so.
the moon
when it is yellow and full.
my dreams
in the stillness of the night.
myself when I am theirs and rarely,
in the quiet, when I am alone.

Laurie Simmons

A Falling Star

In the distance with you
Warm energy cooling
Your thoughts are mine
Fading into evening dusk
Warm air cloudless night
Full moon just over the treetops
My heart wanders through
The acres of tranquil night songs
Young minds exploring
Nature's world
The sky sends greetings with
A falling star

Sandra G. Warner

Love Once Knew

For every tear that falls
From his broken heart
My aching soul recalls
The love I felt right from the start.
But every time I hear
The tempting call of death,
The light of life appears
And lays this broken heart to rest.
And every day I live
With my sorrow in hand
I know there's something I can give
To one who needs a helping hand.
So I recall the love once knew,
The love so strong in me and you,
Not with pain nor tears nor grief
But with great sorrow I feel relief

Trish Evans

"Fading Velvet"

A fading fingernail caressed
across the lips of a loner
reminds him of the velvet
antlers of a young buck,
curious about a song heard
on the bikinied beaches
of a false sea.
Soon, a tainted love song
reaches the ears of a sand puppy
while in the years of growing
soundly strong and smirky smiles
seed the memories of what is now.
Preluded past oversees the futures
dream of what was an ambition.
The end is yet to be sure it's met
with a confidence that measures
a balance on the scales of prophecy.

Samuel J. Dudley

Black Sorrow

My heart feels empty
I feel so alone,
so cold and alone.
Where is my warm blanket of love?
Why has this sadness persisted?
putting a burden on my soul
tearing apart the life
I have grown to hate.
Has my happiness drowned
from my tears?
Swept away by another
empty day.
I search in myself
only to find nothing
I listen to the emptiness
as it echoes through my body,
I understand the loneliness
that longs for a friend,
and only to find eternal peace
through a bitter end.

Alexandra Grivsky

"Sun, Moon, Star"

Far sun star,
Star moon far.
Soon star moon,
Moon sun soon.
One moon sun,
Sun star one...

Michael Cyrus Lutzer

"I" Sail with the Seal

"I" am that I am the "I" as I am
in you as I am in all things

"I" give you my peace to mankind
my peace the peace of "I"

"I" made heaven for those who are
worthy to be aware of all of light

"I" made you because of love,
you are my family of the greater whole
of the universe
My symbol in light is the six-pointed
star the star of heaven
this is my great seal

John M. Tapia

Love

What is love?
Love is like a pure, white dove.

Love is what makes wedding bells ring,
It makes people sing.

Love is like getting a new present,
Sometimes you don't know who sent it.

Love is what makes life worth living,
Whatever happens it never stops giving.

Mindy Whipperman

A Christmas Gift

In nineteen fifty six on Christmas Day,
We lay at anchor in New York Bay
New York was our Christmas tree,
our gift the Land of the Free
And now in nineteen seventy four
I remember that Christmas of yore

"Johanna" Jane Hessels

Angels

Angels angels everywhere
Sent down from heaven above.
Sent down to watch over us
And show us God great love.
Sent to help us through each
And everyday and to show
Us Gods way.

Marty Bartlett

"Cherish A Petal From A Rose"

Cherish a petal from a rose
It will never die.
A rose blooms once...
lives twice

Its thorny stem is like rain
in your life, it makes you
appreciate the spring.
Cherish a petal from a rose

The long stem of a rose...
like God's Grace, is never ending.
Shear it from its roots,
life's forever pending.

God creates the rose in spring
He makes it live again and again
Cherish God's Love,
Cherish a petal from a Rose.

Ruby Jenkins-Williams

The Bells Of Notre Dame

A crying sound of horror
A whistling nature song
To the glorious halls of Lebenon
To the bells of Notre Dame

A fire in the distance
Ice and snow on the ground
Yet it all has peacefulness
To hear the silent sunset sound

The broken down battlefields
And the crops of golden corn
When the booming of the bells rang
A new thunder song was born.

From the Elder's tales of wisdom
To the baby's cry of birth
The humming of the bells
Was none of that on earth

Holly Schild

Near

Distance draws you near
You come when most needed
Rejection strengthens you
You forgive everything
You are my queen of understanding
You breed life into lost hope
Friendship is your goal
I seek more, yet settle for less
He is the lucky one
You give all that is needed
I get greedy then rethink my wants
My goal is to keep you
As is
As you want to be
As you need to be
As I want you
You are close, yet so far
Like the moon on a lonely horizon
Near
Sadder but wiser

Alejandro Saenz

Inside Out

Scarlet poppies
Sleep forever
Brightly colored snake -
Venom
Slick liquid rainbows on the street -
Pollution...
Being different -
Blessing
Troublemakers
Need a hand
Tears -
Emotional storm being assuaged
Life -
A lie
That can tell the truth.

Amy Robinson

No More

You made me hurt
and now I feel like dirt.
Don't sit in a chair,
it's time for repair.
I'm still right here,
but the feelings disappeared.

Sarah Johnson

My Mother

You are my angel,
My Goddess of love,
You are a piece of heaven,
From the skies far above.

I thank the Lord I have you,
For without you I'd be lost,
The love that you have given me,
Comes without a cost.

I can't ever repay you,
For all that you have done.
You're all that I could ask for,
You're my stars, my moon, and my sun.

I know you'll keep on loving me,
And I will always love you,
Until the sun refuses to shine,
And the leaves go without dew.

For you are my mother,
The one who will always be there,
To hold me, to comfort me,
To always truly care.

Amanda Troche

Waterways

As I touch the sky
Swept up on weeping clouds
The sun stabs holes of light
And trickles down to meet the earth

The wind flows through the trees
Like orchestral notes
Spewed from crystal instruments
And captured on silken pillows

Emotional streams bleed of want
Ever-flowing down mountains of anxiety
Only to dissipate
In a gasp of spray at the rocky bottom

The resulting pool of calm
Casts reflections back
On our own waterfalls of love
And the exhilaration of each new plunge

Michael Waschek

Just A Girl

To you I'm just a girl
To men I'm weak and wrong
But in the mirror I see
A young woman
Proud and strong.

For years I have tried
To rise up from this shame
Yet every turn an obstacle
To try and regain
My name.

Making it in a place
Considered a man's world
But still
Time is changing
And I am just a girl.

Morgan L. Gaskin

Christmas

The cold winter comes each year.
Sweeping in the holiday cheer.
The holiday cheer is very near
Very soon it will be here.

When the Christmas bells dong
You will hear a song
The Christmas Eve nights are very long.

After night it will be Christmas day
You will run downstairs without delay
You try to say good morning
But instead you say, "Yay!"

Gordon Smith

Hope

I gaze out at a rainy day
And see each raindrop fall.
I watch it crash upon the earth;
It's no longer there at all.

But if that drop had not begun
Its journey far above,
It could not give us many things
We've come to know and love.

What would become of flowers
Or babbling little brooks?
That little raindrop has a part
In how our whole world looks.

Remember how much you matter
And how you play a part.
You can bring hope to someone's life
And touch another's heart.

Please never be afraid to say
A simple "I love you"
Because the one to whom you speak
Will sure remember you!

Robert F. Bruce

Lover's Pledge

I'm filled with passion
when our fingers touch
I love you, love you
very, very much.
I'm all a tingle
when your eyes meet mine,
And when our lips touch
I know love divine.
Your caress is warm
and so very dear,
I feel I can't live
unless you are near.
Just love me, love me
as my soul does cry
For it's you I love
'til the day I die.

Emily M. Snyder

Faith

An image you see from afar,
A belief that dwells inside you.
A desire that fills your heart,
Something you know is true.
A precious thing you value,
Something you keep within.
A feeling you get when he talks to you,
A place you know you've been.

Tiffany Rasband

The Seasons Of My Love

You entered my life gently,
like a spring rain shower.

The summer arrived
and the arguments thundered.

I tried to change things,
as the autumn transforms the leaves.

But the winter winds came
and swept away my love.

Lurinda Platt

The Triumph Of Satan

A candle burns
a light fades
my soul is keeping
the devils at bay
my brain is tight
my heart is clear
there's the greatness of God
and then there's fear
Satan laughs
and constantly tells me
my life has past
the devils are loose
in their triumphant flight
your life leaves you
as they fade into the night.

Whitney Powell

The Face Without A Name

There was a person I once knew
The same as me and you
He lived in pain
He showed no shame
He was the face without a name
He used to be happy
No one knows why, he's a different guy
Burned in a fire
flames grew higher and higher
No one could save him
But his soul still remained
Trapped behind in all the pain
Now his soul must remain
He's showed no pain
He's the face without a name.

Brittany Pagels

Broken Hearts

A heart gets broken so often
but when it gets broken by
someone you care about,
it hurts so bad.

Broken hearts are hard to
mend but in time they will
soon be mended. They mend
faster when there are good
good friends around.

Hearts are meant to be broken
but when it happens you wish
it wouldn't.

So, when your heart get broken
remember that you have
friends who you can count
on for support.

Lisa A. Page

My Basket Of Beans

My basket of beans
All curly and green
Lay waiting to string
Snap-crackle and pop
Then into the pot

Begging your pardon
My feet all muddied
Have tracked in a stream
I've been in my garden
Picking my beans

The pot is a boiling
I throw in the stock
And fill up the pot
My basket of beans
Is all that we've got

The supper is lean
The belly is mean
Thank God for the pot
Of my basket of beans
So tender and green....

Maggie B. Phillips

Speedboat Race

High speed, faster
speedboats race.
Lighthouse marker
edge the pace.

Engines roar;
break the space.
Copters soar
over Ace.

Margaret F. Reichelt

Silencing The Chimes

I am a child wanting to hear
the chimes ring, but they are
motionless in a musty, dark corner
of the house where no breeze
can penetrate. Grandma says
she wants them to hang there
so she can see their shiny
reflections on the wall.

It's not fair—chimes are
not to be seen but heard.
Silent sleep seeks the sounds,
useless where the wind cannot
stir them to their unique tinkling
harmony to scatter off this ancient
dust from their silvery shells.
I grasp their strings and send
waves of solace to the singing bells
only to find their tone flat.
Let them be free to ring—
I'm just a child.

Coreen La Barbera

Lost In The Wind

Have you ever been lost
in the wind, the wind
that blows so heavily
upon the earth, the
earth that is the home
for many of us who are
fearless.

Angie Wanek

Christopher, Grandma, And Sugar Britches

My grandson, silence with you
is not a silence
But a moment
rich with peace.

So, for my grandson
So bright and gay.
I made baby Sugar Britches
With whom you can play.

To my grandson
So far away
A playmate for you
When silence fills your day.

To my grandson
The boy I love to cuddle
A baby of your own to hold
When language becomes a muddle.

To my grandson
So fun loving and bright
I give you a new friend
To provide laughter and light.

Barbara Spriggs

No One Will Miss Her

No one will miss her
The rope clawed into her skin
like a mad cat
When the wooden stool gave way
Under her thin pale body
She did not fall
She did not scream
No one will miss her

Three days later
A scream told of her death's discovery
Put in a pine box left only to rot
All because she thought
No one will miss her

Jill Hodges

Untitled

I am a poetic
Without a theme...
My heart expresses,
And visualize sounds,
Without the sound...

So who am I,
Without a theme...

I am that being,
With feelings,
Emotions,
And the mind to,
Perceive your inter-theme...

Curtis Lee Holt

Essence

The beams of light flew down on
Wings of silver, enveloping the night
With the glory of their coming,
illuminating the heart of darkness,
The lungs of hope breathe their
way into love, and love is the
essence of life. The hope of the ages
is in the life of love.........The
love that is yahweh.

Faye Doris Meyers

Wake-Up

I am not here to be amused.
I am here for God to use.

I once was sad and blue.
Jesus made me white and new.

We need to tell the good news.
Jesus is the only clue to
get to heaven too.

I am telling you something true.
Jesus is my own rescue.

It is time to stop, the excuses
for why we snooze, before
people lose.

Nanette Aragon

Fishin'

As his line drifts down
A young boy lazily sits
Breaking off blades of grass
Watching them glide
In the soft summer breeze
A tattered straw hat drawn
Over his freckled face
Sighs... another fishless day
He starts to reel in his line
There's a jerk... line goes taunt
He starts to tremble
Grasps on tightly to the pole
Another jerk
As he reels in the line
Tension builds
Remembering his father's words
Easy... slow... careful now
Give him a chance, play with him
Oh what a fish, what a fight...
What a Oh no... snap!

Karen Muzia

That Look

That look you often take of me.
So soft, sensous, so full of love.
A look that penetrates me so.
Just emphasizes to me how,
Unworthy 'I'
could never carry such a burden,
of Love.
Never could I be deserving,
of such love.
God alone could be deserving,
of such love.
If you could be but more discerning,
Let your head control your yearning.
You would see that never
'I'
could justify such Love.
But please Patricia.
Keep on looking at me
'So.'

John R. Aggus

Untitled

I feel so alone.
Yet, there is no solitude
in my aloneness, for it is
intruded upon by the unwanted
presence of others.

Cynthia Ferrara

Decisions

Decisions are what we make them
They can be easy or hard
You see, when it comes to life
There are no holds barred
Anything can happen
If we will only let it.
First we decide what we want
From this, life's flame is lit
We can settle for seconds
Or demand the very best
Then we must just see it grow
And life will handle the rest
Thank you God for this privilege
And let us never forget
That truly what we decide
Is always what we get
Let us not use trickery
Or try to fool ourself
For we might find our lives
Just sitting on some shelf.

Margaret Flowers

All To Uncertain

As I sit in my room I look
out the window at the mystifying moon.
It appears full tonight, and I watch
clouds roll over it like emotions
come over people.
It seems bright then clouds slowly
roll by and make it look as though
it's uncertain of something.
The clouds are like a fine film
that sometimes cover peoples eyes to
where they no longer can see nor feel.
Right now as I sit here and compare
myself to the moon, I realize how a
film could keep someone in the
dark yet so protected.

Nicole Grimsley

War

Marching out to war
With their heads held high
So proud to kill
And so proud to die

Don't think about your family
Don't think about your children
Don't think about their future
Or how much this will hurt them

No time for remorse
No time to despair
No time to feel guilty
And no time to care

Never stop to think
About what's being done
You must keep on killing
Until the war is won

Heather Cunningham

Grandma

God has blessed us with a being.
Reaching out with her heart and seeing,
All the wonders of this life.
Never fretting among the strife.
Donning a warm and loving smile,
Making life all worth while.
A loving warmth that lasts a mile.

Sherry L. Snyder

"Beauty Of A Girl"

A girl whose
Beauty is of a rose
Is a very special
Girl for who
Can stand such
Beauty when
It is right
In front of you.
As this girl
Gets older she turns
More beautiful
And keeps on
Blooming just like
A rose.
And when she
Grows to
An adult
She will be the
Most beautiful
Girl.

Alvaro Bermudez Cardoza

The Bold American Eagle

The bold American eagle
spreads his wings boldly
out across the sky just
hours before a storm.
But at the same time
as angel of the Lord
appears and said
may you do what you want
but, first you come with me.
And I'll show you something
that you'll never forget.
I'll be a part of your thoughts
for ever and ever.
Amen.

Vickie Carroll

The Night I Met You

I'm remembering the night I
met you
Even then I didn't have a clue
You gave me a friendly smile
Then sat to talk to me for awhile
I could tell you were on of the
nice guys
When I looked in your big brown eyes
And now I'm beginning to see
That you're far more than I thought
you'd be
You've given me friendship, respect,
and love
Some times I'm convinced
You were sent from above
I wasn't looking for love - it's true
But love is what I found the
right I met you.

Heather Nagy

Shimmering Spirits

Our souls are but visitors,
that yearn for nothing more
but to soar the heavens and
the earth; to fulfill its desires.

We are more - much more,
then just human beings.

Jody Robertson

I Said, He Said, I See

I said "Just a moment, Lord, give
me more time, I do not want to
go your way right now, I want to go mine."

Years later I said "What is wrong
now? I have everything and more
but something is missing, but how?"

"Look up to me, my child, and you
will see what you desire is
my joy and my love: The true
peace that comes only from your
Father, only from Me."

G. G. McHam

The Answer To It All

When I was but young in life.
Just in my early teens.
I found a youth that I could love.
Stay with by any means.
Then came the blessing from above.
This child so full of joy.
The Lord had shown His grace to me.
On me He did employ.
A life filled full of greatest worth.
The treasures only God can give.
The greatest thing for which we live.
To shape this child to do His will.
This is the joy that God can fill.

Shirley M. Bailey

Untitled

I know what you are thinking.
The eyes tell all.
Sadness swims in your soul.
Beautifully bizarre.
The color they are.
Brightly aglow.
Emeralds in the snow.
Open your eyes.
I'll peek inside.
Steal your heart.
Let me show you the way.
Just you and me.
Together and free.

Kelly Stemple

House And Home

A house is floors and structured walls,
Glass window panes and doors;
A home is voices in the halls,
Bare feet upon the floors.

A house is covered with a roof
To shield us from the rain;
The shelter of a home is love,
Kind words to ease our pain.

The furniture inside a house
Provides a place to rest;
The character within a home
Gives strength for every test.

A house may change its colors with
New paint throughout the years;
The spirit of a home transforms
Through happiness and tears.

As time goes by a house decays
And one day falls apart;
A home stands fast eternally,
For home is in the heart.

Ross A. Fichter

Waves Of Life

The waves of the ocean,
Are like problems that we face.
Some we hardly even notice,
But the big ones we have to brace.

Once they come to the shore,
It really doesn't matter at all.
Whether it was the big one,
Or the one that was very small.

The small ones we try to jump,
And the big ones we like to ride.
But no matter how deep the water,
We want a friend by our side.

It's when the water is over our head,
And we don't know what to do.
That's when the Lord will reach down,
And always pull you through.

Debbie G. Satterfield

Happiness

There are times we remember
the things in our life,
The ones that brought happiness
and the ones that brought strife.

But if we put them together,
all rolled up in one,
The bad are soon forgotten
when all is said and done

Happiness is only
a stone's throw away.
But Satan puts rocks
where the stones should lay.

So if we are faithful
to thank God each day.
He surely will help
keep the big rocks away.

Jo Rubringer

All Is Calm

A slight breeze carries the
songs of the birds with it
until the melody all
but hushes away
Even though the sun is
lost in the mountains,
it's light reflects on the
clouds above it.
Slowly the light fades
until the clouds are
their natural hue again
It is so quiet it seems
as though the sun took
all the life in the world
with it when it set.

Jennifer Traceski

Sinning Hand

I hate to love my sinning hand
For violent things it feeds
I would sever this misfortune
But I dread my arm would bleed
It brings agony to others
In suffering it does succeed
I hate to love my sinning hand
And now it is my need

Joshua Reisig

God Is With Me

The sun has gone down, all is black
I only hear the flames of fire crack
How the stars shine so bright
The moon so full on this dark night
Listening to the soft music play
Waiting until again it is day
My mind is blank, nothing is there
I'm in a daze, I only stare
Then I look at the moon as it frowns
I realize I'm alone as I sit down
Nobody is there next to me
But God is with me I have to believe

Lisa Minth

Memory's Wind

Memory's wind sweeps through us all;
Its bitter,
cold,
kiss;
causing us to reminisce about past
thoughts,
doings,
and feelings.

Old friends, family or childhood
sweethearts dominate your very mind,
and possibly your very soul.

And, in the blinking of an eye,
this kind of vision is gone;

Leaving you waiting, wishing for
Memory's wind to return and again
engulf you.

Heather C. Martin

I Killed The Man That Hits On Me

He sweet talked me
When he met me
He loved me right
When he held me
Close to him
That's where I wanted to be
He was gentlemen
That's all I can see

But then he hit me
That was his death wish.
But he couldn't see

And so I did
With a baby tech
To his head
And now he's dead
Resting in his bed

He's six feet deep
And now ya'll see
I killed the man
That hits on me

Tameka Norman

"Autumn Brides"

Harvest time is known for springtime —
Autumn for its lovely brides,
Her heart is my handful of laughter —
Stars are in her eyes.
She knew when she picked September
God's artists were in tune
Painting rainbows in the woodland
For a happy bride and groom.

Ruth Almen

Winter Is Coming

Deep into each
He stares into faces
Seeking hope
But finds no traces.

Winter is coming
Summer is gone
Buffalo were plenty
Now they are none.

Women moan
Children are crying
Starvation upon us
Our people are dying.

He prays and he prays
As he stares into faces
Praying for Buffalo
And hope in their faces.

Art Low Sr.

Shamrocks And Ireland

Ah- T'is the day for all the Irish
The Blarney Stone will grant your wish.
I smell the heather on the hill
The green, green grass near the rill.
Nowhere on earth, the ocean so blue
And the steamy pots of Mulligan's stew.
My heart returns to old Killarney
To see their faces beaming brightly.
To hear once more "Oh, Danny Boy"
And kilts and bagpipes to bring me joy!

Vivian Patterson

Free Verse

Is a warm fluid
flowing
through
convention,
relaxing rigid rhythms,
easing strains and stresses

Isn't free

It pays the price
with acrimonious assessments
by critics
metrically measuring
independent
leaps
over
traditional poetic fences

Judith Turner Kelly

Untitled

We're having a heat wave,
In this rural town.
We're using energy we can't save,
Trying to keep the temperature down.
The sun is blinding.
Even the water is hot.
The tar on the streets is bubbl'ing
Like a boiling pot.
The kids are outside,
Playing in the pool.
Their parents are inside,
Just trying to keep cool.
Me? I'm in the sun,
Practically melting.
Why? I'm chained to the fence.
Cause I'm just a sheltie.

Stephanie Englebright

Sanctuary

Solitude, silence, a rocking chair,
Blackberry tea in a mug;
My only friend, the tiger cat,
Asleep here on the rug.

I check my heart for mortal wounds
While counting blessings up:
Decide that Fate has kindly tossed
A coin into my cup.

There's safety here behind this door;
I have the only key...
For now, I'll lay old fears aside,
And have a sip of tea.

Margo Wolf

It Is From The Ash Heap God Is Seen

Oh, slow, slow the grief to go
There is no comfort.
If I live ten thousand years,
Perhaps the pain will pass
And leave me peace and
take my tears,
Alas, pray God alas!

LaVonne Garrison

John

Bobby was drinking and driving
That warm October day.
When the death angel reached out
And snatched our Johnny away.

It hurts to know John was cheated
Out of a long and happy life
No son to call him Daddy,
No young and pretty wife.

It hurts to look at mama,
I can't help her - no one can,
She aches to hold Johnny,
He was just a boy of a man.

Many heart are broken
Many tears are shed
Because of drinking and driving,
My brother Johnny's dead!

Janice Finley

Change

I sit here in my room
day after tired day.
Wondering, what do they see.
Do they see the pain?
Do they see the want?
Do they know what I feel?
Will they know?

When I look in the mirror
I see no pain, no want but
instead I see a face.
It is not pretty, or ugly but plain.
It is the face, of every
girl in the world.
Will it change? Will the world
change around me? Without
me? We will change. For good
or bad, for right or wrong.
I will change.

Andrea Gabbidon-Levene

"River's Kiss"

Thus plunged into a river wild
like Dante's darkened wood,
I sank down in the wicked fever warmth,
myself reviled, lost to good.

The flashing flood
and prison storm
swept on
embattled hope,
My passions borne
in dank refrain of ancient hymns
to forests most forlorn.

Abandoned there to greed and lust
I saw that each must bend,
To render here at river's last
the kiss which knows no end.

Robert James Carron

The Daily Talk

Everyday we have to try,
To free ourselves from sin.
To honestly and truly try,
And that's when prayer comes in.

Just a little talk with God,
Will help us on our way,
Too lead the life he wants for us,
And not like sheep astray.

Phyllis Constantino

Dreaming

Slowly closing your eyes
You feel like you're drifting away
To hear only what angels say
Sleep upon thine eyes

You say your good-byes
To the world you know
And float into a land of snow
Sleep upon thine eyes

Next to you an angel flies
A smile is on her sweet face
As she wraps you in a gown of lace
Sleep upon thine eyes

You fly leaving a world of cries
And you spread your angel wings
An angel's chorus sings
Sleep upon thine eyes

Now you blink your eyes
And lay in the dark
An angel calls and hark
You sleep peacefully upon thine eyes

Heather Dettro

Stronger Than Truth

Stronger than truth they say
Simpler than faith day by day
Fiction or not, may I pray
My love for you may it stay.

Stronger than truth, do I love
Deeper than oceans untold.
Higher than the sky up above
Stronger than truth is my love.

My love for you is deep and true.
It is also stronger than death.
Binding forever, everlasting too;
Stronger than truth is my love.

Loucilla Ellis

"Alone Inside"

This loneliness I feel inside,
at times it's more than I can hide.
I call you out of my dreams,
inside I hear the silent screams.
Out of my dreams and into my life,
you come into the black of the night.
You are my taste of heaven, it's true,
the times when I am near you.
The long days, when I wait in vain,
this lonely feeling I can't explain.
The storm inside is raging very strong,
it may be right, or maybe wrong.
It's like a fire out of control,
burning its way into my soul.
When the tears are about to fall,
I remember, and give you a call.
The lonely feelings fade away,
I've made it through another day.

Joyce Bonham

Fading Out

All the stars are fading out
As I travel through the night
Darkness is all around me
No way to see
Through this dark night
For all the stars are fading
Within this night
Only obscure darkness to travel through
No light, to guide me
Where do I go
How can I find her
In this dark, dark, darkness
As all the stars
Are fading away
As I travel, on this journey

Phillip W. Haywood

Of Wishes And Dreams

Last night I dreamt about home again
About the time I was a youngster then
Of little houses on our narrow street
The blue sky and golden wheat
When the circus came into town
With horses, tigers, and the clown
Sometimes I think about home again
About the times I was a youngster then
Remembering the ducks in the pond
Of building castles in the sand
Playing in the sun or chasing doves
Loss of innocence and finding loves
Sometimes I wish I was home again
To the time I was a youngster then
Having Christmases and all those toys
And all the fun of children's joys
Going out to my first date
To coming home and being late
So let me dream about home again
About the time I was a youngster then

Sebastian

Ability

Ability.
Ability is black and white.
Ability smells like sweat.
Ability sounds like grunts.
Ability makes me feel needed.

Ian Mitchell Alexander

Money

Beautiful
Green
Glistening
Money
Makes my life so bright
and sunny

Shining
Gleaming
Spendable
Dough
Makes my happiness grow
and grow

A wonderful
Terrific
Awesome
Dollar
Makes me run around and
holler
Boy don't I wish I had
Money!

Scott Thompson

No One Will Help Me, All On My Own

Sometimes I feel so alone,
as if in a world all of my own.
No one around,
I'm wishing, hoping to be found.

But no one dares,
because no one really cares.
I sit and I wait,
waiting for fate.

Even though I know,
it will never show.
I wait anyway,
all night, all day.

No one will ever come find me,
They leave me to no company.
I will be alone forever,
No one will help me-never.

I am stuck in this world alone,
All on my own.
Emptiness inside has so much wealth,
I have to face this world all by myself.

Amy Harris

Blue Life

My spirit has blue away
Drift into your self
No where to go, the ends of the earth
Walk away, to enjoy life
Slap me in the face
Wake up, you just beaned coned
So much for you, life is rough
Rude self center people
Fit in you don't
Life is not fair
Forget them
Move on
They will end the rat race
Jump off the world, they will
Tears fall so hard
Gift of life

Claudia Marie Beebe

Love Is

Love is the kindness that you show,
it's knowing that our friendship
would prosper and grow.
Each morning as the sun
melts the sky,
I'll tell you I love you,
but never goodbye.
I'll pray that forever
remains in each day,
that our love would
never fade away.
Because to love anyone but you,
seems vague, yet clearly untrue.

Rebecca Dupuis

Family Tree

Welcome to the world sweet child
We've waited for some time
To have a new arrival
Of A sweet and precious kind

On the day that you were born
You were sent from heaven above
God knew that he could trust us all
To shower your life with love

Welcome to our family
I know we all agree
You brighten up the sun that shines
Upon our family tree

May our tree growing strongly
May the sun shine up above
May we always have each other
To nourish our tree with love

May we welcome new arrivals
As our tree keeps growing strong
May we always have this love to give
When a new leaf comes along

Gail L. Lemieux

Forty

Forty fools,
Forty's full
Of life's fonts
That eddy in whirlpools.

Forty's cool,
Forty schools
I have been to all
All my grades did was fall.

Forty sucks,
Forty socks,
From baby ones,
To arthritic gams.

Forty's fine,
Forty finds,
A woman so stooped,
You could sit on her spine.

Forty's me,
Forty's free,
No longer a baby,
Yet a long way to fifty...

Maria Amabel Andal Brito

Contemplation

Look at me as I am ——
A person,—not as mother.
Look at me, really see
Compare me to another.

Am I just as comely
Am I just as smart
Do I have a personality
Do I have a heart?
Do I a romantic seem
with spirit blithe and gay?
Would I a good companion be
to journey on life's way

If you have looked at me and seen
that I a person am
With feelings like all others
Not just a nebulous mother
Then perhaps content at last I'll be
Because for once you've looked at me
And set your mother free.

Grace Natalie Tottenham

Jack Frost

Last night I went to bed,
And closed my eyes to sleep.
Everything was quiet.
I didn't hear a peep.
The door was shut,
As doors should be.
Yet Jack Frost got in by me.
He must have been there,
Most of the night.
Because what he did,
Was a beautiful sight.
He left my windows,
Silver white.
With designs,
He made in the night.
He penciled over the panes.
Not a single word he spoke.
He crept quietly out the door,
And was gone before I woke.

Sandra Nyeggen

I'm a Dreamer

I'm a dreamer
How about you
I look for something beautiful
In everything I do
The people I know
The people I meet
Just let your inner feelings show
Don't try to compete
There's a life for everyone
A love for all
Just hold on to a dream
And someday he'll call.
You can look up and say
When your down and alone
I'm a dreamer
I have a life to live
A lot to live for
And a lot to give.

Debbie Lee

"Roosevelt Speech" 1941

He gave a speech on world affairs,
twas a nationwide talk which came
on the air.
It was brief and important and
it stirred my heart;
He spoke of a war in which we
must take part.
Japan bombed our islands and
threatened our land,
We must win this war and
unite as a band.
The "Victory Is Ours" is the cry
of us all,
With courage so great, a nation
can't fall.

Arlene Marie Maginel Fuller

Cry For Honor

My time is my own, I live alone.
All I need is close at hand.
Why am I, such a lonely man.
Can love and loyalty, ever be enough?
Or do today's women, no longer care
about that stuff.
When commitment is made,
you are expected to stand.
Back up what you say,
before God and man.
With no honor, you can't have
a good life.
My honor would come from
having a good wife.
Lady, if you want a hard working
and faithful man.
Offer your hand.
I will win your heart.
With sincerity and love.
Until death do us part!

Ricky L. Jones

Maybe Tomorrow

Every time I see you,
I smile to hide the sorrow.
Then I run and hide
and think "Maybe tomorrow".
Maybe tomorrow I'll do it,
Maybe tomorrow I'll tell you,
Maybe tomorrow you can help me,
decide just what to do.
All this pain that I'm feeling,
won't seem to go away
I'm dying inside
and it's getting worse each day.
Maybe tomorrow you'll notice,
Maybe tomorrow you'll see,
Maybe tomorrow you can help
figure out the pain in me

Carolyn Wilson

Freedom

My choice is to change into
a raindrop and sparkle in the sun.

To wash away the grime with
my blood, as I shatter against
the world.

Leslie Nies

The Eagle Knows

He soars above the ragged rocks
and roaring rivers flowing.

Within his feathered breast,
he holds a faith, a knowing:

There is a power greater than
we with naked eye can see.

It holds him high:
it gives him life and kingly liberty.

Thrusting beyond and free
from comfort's nesting place,

He scans the skies
and scales the summits
with God's Inherent, Sovereign Grace.

Arlene J. Reitz

"The Bright One "Toni"

I know someone who sparkles
With lighted ears and feet.
She wears the cutest gadgets
They always are so neat!
Her rings and watches glisten
With jewels and rhinestones, too!
And when you look to see them
They play a song for you!
She surely is real glitzy
From her head down to her toes.
But one thing is for certain.
Her heart is her brightest glow!

Rita Signore

Seconds

Hours, days and minutes
How I let them slip on past
Now that I have seconds
How I wish that they would last

Seconds, seconds, seconds
They won't last long
Seconds, seconds, seconds
They're almost gone

One more beer they're almost here
I hope it does the trick
If they've come to take my seconds
I hope they make it quick

Now that it's all said and done
Was it worth the wait
Maybe yes maybe no
I hope it's not too late for my

Seconds seconds seconds
They won't last long
Seconds seconds seconds
To end this song

Victor Pula

Our Flag

Red, white, and blue,
The colors of the flag flew.
Blue, red, and white,
The people fight with all their might.
White, blue, and red,
Many are dead.

Mary E. A. Ancell

Sorry

I'm sorry that I have no more to give
or that I gave too much

I'm sorry I didn't touch you
or that I touched you such

I've said some things I shouldn't have
for that I'm sorry too.

And when you really needed me
I'm sorry I didn't come thru

I'm sorry when I cared too much
or just or little bit

but what I am most sorry for
is all this sorry sh*t.

Sheila Adsit

One Day At A Time

Some days I wonder
how I'm going to get by
I dwell on thoughts that depress me
it makes me want to cry
I think of all the problems
I try to overcome
I then put the thoughts behind me
and say "what's done is done"
I awake every morning
saying everything is fine
living up to my words
I take one day at a time...

Danielle C. Mejia

The Silver-Scaled Dragon

A silver-scaled dragon
with jaws flaming red
sits at my elbow
and toasts my bread.
I hand him fat slices
and then one by one
he hands them right back
when they are done.

Sarah Ketner

Love Is Live...

Love is like music
The soft melodic words you say
That touch my heart
And send my thoughts a flight

Love is like the sea
It comes rushing in
Like the feel of your presence
That sends my heartbeat racing

Love is like the cool morning breeze
The softness and coolness
Like the feel of your touch
In the eve of the day

Love is like a rose
Perfect and beautiful
Like when you look deep within me
And see how much I love you

Love is like a tree
Its branches forever joined
Like our hearts
Forever joined as one for His service

Sherrelle Schmidt

Magnets

There is an enormous magnet
beneath the layers of the earth
constituting the direction,
the sphere revolves...
That same magnet exist internally...
drawing perpendicular souls,
in parallel motion.

Soul-mates would be the term,
but who has ever had the privilege...
of meeting the ...x
while that being
is the
y...
of ex-is-
tence.

Adele M. Torres

The Yard

Walk out early in the morning,
While the dew is on the ground,
And smell the sweet honeysuckle,
The smell is all around.

The squirrels chasing each other,
Birds singing all the while,
Rabbits hopping everywhere,
It's hard not to smile.

You only have a short time
Until you have to go to work,
And you know once you get there,
You'll have to deal with some jerk.

You put in your eight hours,
You've worked long and hard;
But you start to feel better
Thinking about morning in the yard.

If life could be so peaceful
As morning's first little while,
We could all forget our frown,
And go thru life with a smile.

Louise Thomas

The Rhythm

You have to get the rhythm,
To read a poem just right.
You have to have the rhythm,
Or you'll stay up half the night.

You have to have the rhythm,
It's not an easy task.
You have to get the rhythm,
That's all that they ask.

If you can get the rhythm,
And read a poem just right,
If you have the rhythm,
And go to bed at night,

If you get the rhythm,
Though not an easy task,
If you have the rhythm,
Then you did what they ask.

But now do you have the rhythm,
To hear a song just right?
You have to have the rhythm,
Or you'll stay up half the night.

Kathleen Holman

Why Do You Still Love Him?

You talk about him all the time
it's plain as day to see
you love him more than anyone could
it seems so strange to me

Tell me, why do you still love him?
even though he has moved on
The more he seems to tease you
the more your heart grows fond

To you, he is the sun and moon
your love for him will never die
And still, to him, you're just a friend
no more, no less, yet why

Why do you still love him?
His feelings for you are gone
You were his world so long ago
and yet, your love lives on

Jana Bowman

Missing In Action

He steps out from the ash,
his body engulfed in flames.
Once a proud and valiant soldier,
he falls quickly to the earth.
His world grows dark,
the war still carries on
while this brave and loyal fighter,
lies forgotten and forlorn.
Dog tags bear his name,
but no one knows his face.
His enemies do not care,
Friends try to understand,
but one simple fact remains the same.
Daddy's never coming back.

JeNee Phillips

Mountains

Dear God
I love mountains
They are so beautiful
And possess great beauty

They have many forms
of life including
Eagles, bats, wild cats
and mountain goats

Dear God, please bless
all its life forms and
beauty

Paul Mariano Benton

Untitled

The world for me
is like a stage
on which I play
and every day
after I am awake
I must step up
to give my best
with shoulders straight
my head up high
my best smile.
I must start
and every step
that forward I give
I must be ready
to put on the stage
the best performance
the best in my life.

Sylvia G. Serverdija

Blue

Blue is the color
of tears shed
As I look at
the single carnation
lying on my grand pa's grave.

Blue is the sound
of a blue jay singing
its song as
he sits perched on a
high branch watching me.

Blue is the color
of the sky,
of lonely rooms,
of twilight.

Blue is the color
of tears shed
As I look at
the single carnation
lying on my grand pa's grave.

Dayna Collier

Freedom

Freedom is a pleasure,
Not like a butterfly catcher.
For I need to spread my wings
To see so many things.
I wonder,
I wonder,
What's in the sky
For a Butterfly?

Corey Allen Burton

Bombs Away

Bombs away
Is what I say
Bombs away
Is what I'll do

I will not bomb
For you or him
I will not bomb
Until you are gone

I will not bomb
In honor of you
Bombs away
Is what I'll say

Bree Starr Viscia

Vacation

I'm going on vacation, vacation,
vacation, I'm going on
vacation, hooray!
I'm going on vacation, vacation,
vacation, I'm going on vacation
today!
I'm going on vacation and I can't
wait, I'm going on vacation, it'll
be great!
I'm going to the ocean to swim with
the fish, I'm going to the ocean to
stay, I wish!!

Lynn E. Habeney

Untitled

Rise up the night
To kill the sun
And stop all right
To drip so cold
So deadly cold
Into the hearts
Once brave and bold.
Rise up the night
To spread all fear
To dim the light
Of all things good
And leave cruel few
To hurt and rend
Those foolish who
Still follow light.
Rise up the night
And creatures black
To end all bright and shining life.
Throw down the sun — and leave the few
Who can — to run.

Shawna Filbeck

I Remember

I remember you getting sick,
and wonder what I would be like,
I remember you in pain,
and wonder how it would change,
I remember you being helpless,
and wonder if you'll ever help,
I remember you lying there,
And wonder if you'll ever get up,
I remember you frown,
and wonder if you'll ever smile,
I remember you call,
and wonder if we'll ever hear.
I remember you drift away,
and wonder if you'll ever come back.
I remember him take you away,
And wonder if he'll ever give you back,
I remember.

Dory Abbott

Land Of Fantasy

As I lay in my bed,
and drift off to sleep,
the mind in my head,
takes a marvelous leap.

Through desert or snow,
whatever it may be,
to the breath-taking land
of Fantasy.

Where unicorns fly
above the sun,
and down to Dream River,
where imagination runs.

Where gallant knights win,
against dragons that are slain.
They stick to the fight
for the very fair maid.

It all fades away,
as I prepare to wake.
The next night, I'm ready,
for the next trip I'll take.

Ashley Renee Fox

Poem For Nature

Another day starts and we awaken
to the warmth of the sun
The peaceful arms of the sky
greet us
The green trees offer
a friendly hello
In this human world of cars,
clocks and deadlines
of arrogant attitudes and war
poverty, loss and sadness
our lonely hearts long for love
and friendship.
As another day gently
embraces us
warms our skin
feeds our eyes
kisses our check
And for a moment we hear the
prayer of God to us.

Marie France

Mislead

Empty space
Quiet sounds
Missing piece
Can't be found

Tortured mind
Battered soul
Wants to climb
Out from this hole

Open eyes
Or so one thought
Now they cry
Heart lies to rot

Renee S. Young

I'm Sorry

To work
A little boy
A thunderstorm
No rain gear
He's all wet
I drive by
I'm sorry
I back-up
How far?
School bus stop
Can I take you?
No
I'm sorry
Obey your mother
I'm forbidden to help
Will you be all right?
Yes
You'll be wet all day
I'm sorry

Arthur W. Friedel

Sea Shells

Sea shells, in the sand
O, so close at hand
Up, from the sea
Such, exquisite beauty
Each of Gods design
Now some belong to me,
Forever mine

Louise Rossi

Ribbon

Clip a piece of childhood
From woven strands of memory;

Cut an average day
From the blanket of life;

Trim a tragedy
From a hood of sorrow;

Snip a scene of laughter
From the heart's loving pillow;

Tear a bit of spirituality
From the skirt of the horizon;

Snatch a blow of thoughts
From the breeze of the mind;

Stitch these together
With a ribbon of poetry,
And they become a robe for the spirit,

Clothing my soul.

Addie Davis

The Joy Of Life (Still Of Night)

Joy is illusive Capricious I look into
into my children's faces and see
God. I touch my adorable wife's
hand and feel God's hand.
In the still and quiet of night
As I gaze upon a star filled
night the masters glory is revealed
in all its might, a dazzling,
sight to behold on a quiet
desert night. As my children
slumber in the still of night
the angels in heaven fill the
night. All is heel ah, what a
precious sight.

Robert J. Kuehn

Conscience

As I walk down that lonely road-
Darkness all around.
I hear a set of footsteps-
Beating on the ground.

Faster, faster they do come-
And faster I do go.
Across the meadow, over the hill.
Seemingly so slow.

Where can I run, where can I hide
From this dreadful unknown.
Under a bush, behind a tree.
Oh, why am I alone.

Faster, faster they do come-
My heart freezes, body numb.
Faster, faster I can see-
That dreadful thing, is only me.

Lyla J. Powell

Remember

Remember me the way I am today,
Not the way I was yesterday,
Not the way I am going to be tomorrow,
But the way I am today.
Yesterday is yesterday.
Tomorrow is tomorrow,
And today's today.
Always is, and always will be
Today is the only thing that matters

Jean Yapp

"This Basket Is Full Of...?"

This basket is full of hawthorns
and dew, silver moons and
dragons too.

Little stars at night that fill the
world with a beautiful sight.

Bicycles and books plus little
tiny crannies and nooks.

Butterflies and nets of gold,
shoes and hooks, "These things
are so old."

But I've saved the best for
last I've filled this basket
with no task...

I just might tell you if you
want to know, this basket is
full of treasures I'll show.

Gwen MacDonald

It's Time To Open The Door

As the door begins to close
So do memories of the past.
Only God really knows
What the future will cast.

It's time to open the door
And let the sunshine in.
To let your soul soar
And let your new life begin.

As the door begins to open
So does your beating heart.
Then and only then
Will your new life start.

As you slowly walk through
With your eyes open wide
You will know what to do
When you reach the other side.

Nona Jean Raymond

Eagle Paused In Flight

Eagle paused in flight
Wings tipped in red gold
Captured with majestic right
Forever bold

Eagle locked in a forever flight
Eyes beheld a beautiful sight
Eagle looked on with a kings pride
Artist stared and then he cried

Tamara Tull

Time After Time

Waves rushing to the shore
Me remembering times of yore,
Time changes for me and thee;
The roar of the sea will ever be.

Moon glow glimmering on ocean wide
Holding power of the tides,
Irrelevant of man's conquer glide
Changes for you and me.
Reformation and death to all
creatures and humanity,
The power of moon and sea
shall ever be.

Sylvia Moore

Lonely Sailor

Sitting out here
In the middle of nowhere
I dream of you

One hundred miles out to sea
Six more hours of watch
Not much else to do

I recall of mornings fore
Dream of mornings yet to come
Lying with my love

I caress your skin
Soft and warm and white
Recall the baby dove

Of life we talk
Emotions we share
Often with delight

This poem I write to you
For it is of thee I dream
On this cold winter's night

Colin B. Floen

Paris

Paris,
Your beauty is
life sent.
So many things
which captivated the
inner most of me.
Among it all
your splendor remains.
For at the Louvre
there was Schubert,
visions of the horizon
at the Eiffel,
Path ways interjacent
to places
at the Arc De Triomphe.
Journeys never ending
on the River Seine.
One day amidst your
grace I will come again.

Wilfred Dean Anthony

Promise

A gown of scarlet
white glove in hand
glistening pearls
playing of the band

Low, whispered words
slip down the stair
enchanting moonlight
sweet scented air

Cool spring night
faint breeze blows
they share a secret
no one knows

Soft, flushed cheek
a tender kiss
precious promise
betrothal of bliss

Kristina O'Brien Mays

Peggy And Joe

When I was small,
I did not see.
Those wonderful people,
In front of me.

When I was young,
I always thought.
Love was all,
The material things, I got.

When I was a teen,
And friends had it all.
I could not have the "big",
I seldom had the "small".

Then, I was married,
I had children of my own.
I was my parents,
The seed had been sown.

Now, they are gone,
Yes, there is a hole in my heart.
I'm so glad I showed them my love,
Every day, at the start.

Joy L. Gallagher

I Love You, God

Like a cool drink of water,
On a hot summer's day;
Like the glimpse of the rainbow,
When the storm's passed away;
Like the sands upon the beaches,
Grains too numerous to count,
Like an endless stream aflowing,
Lord, the moons' ever glowing,
Lord...
I love you this amount.

Lois Burris

Twelve Twentyfive

Merry
(simply, succinctly,
acutely...may I say
that we celebrate
the birth of a king this day.
the birth of a prophet,
a priest, a prince...
whose manner of life
has not been since
equalled.
the birth of a man
ordinarily formed
yet he came to die
because he was born
Immanuel.)
Christmas

Jeffrey Trostle

Vision

What a joy in life to find
A kindred scintillating mind -
A mind that seeks horizons far
Beyond earth's pestilence and war;
A heart that takes all mankind in,
A better life for each to win;
A soul that reaches to the sky
For life eternal by and by.

Annabelle Duisberg

Love Is...

Love is not my feelings
Love is not my words.
Love is my commitment
Followed by my acts.

My acts must be consistent
Or love is not at all.
Words and feelings will not prove it
But my life will tell it all.

Helen Hunter

The Alley

As I walk down the alley
Many sights I see.
I hear sound of life in the
neighborhood.

Lawn mower humming.
Children running.
Music flowing through an open
window.
I stood still.
As still as I could.

Listen I did
What did I hear?
A bird calling.
Perhaps to its mate.
Life in its many forms.
Life.

Robbie White-Woodson

Tomorrow's Dream

Three hundred years from now
we will sit on the sand,
intertwined minds and hands
and watch the sun nestle
over the warm waters...
side by side like two ageless pails
weighted down by the sands of time

And you and me...
will always be...
as one...
forever!

Jo Tucker

Love Song

I sing
To my Beloved Heart.
Never do you shout at me,
Your soft murmur lulls me
As I drift to sleep.

When threat invades my life
You are instantly my strength.

As we trudged
To top that glaciered peak
We agreed: "Why do we do this?"
Yet we labored on.

So many years we survived
Difficult days, endless nights.
But not once did you fail me.

So please beat on,
My beloved heart, unfailingly,
Until we cease to live.

Stella Reese

The Breath Of Life

For us life begins
with a breath from the throne
as the love of our creator
to each of us is shown.

That precious breath of life
that begins here our travel
in which for the things of this life
we begin to grapple.

The first breath given
is to us our beginning
and when our journey here is through
the last breath will be our ending.

So we must needs remember
while in our journey here on earth
that with all of our getting
not to forget our second birth.

For though man's days on earth are few
and so full of trouble and strife
there will be no day in heaven
without the eternal breath of life.

My Lord and me, Richard L. Alford

Souls In The Air

Their songs
chatter through trees
echo across sky
like Gregorian chants
lingering in cathedrals.

Their wings
slice through clouds
glide on the air
like a lover's whisper
piercing through darkness.

Their souls
free to roam
dance amongst angels
like an autumn breeze
steeping lightly on lifeless leaves.

Connie Harvison

I Dream

Dreams that I have of you so special
I dream of being yours
I dream to be in your life
I dream to kiss your soft lips
I dream to caress your body.
I dream and dream
But deep down inside I know
It could only be a dream.

Janel Maylas

"Time Travels"

Born a baby, teenager to adult
What little did we know to consult
We are young full of fun
Old we get and ready for the gun

It seems just like yesterday
Years later off it is hearsay
I was young once, full of Life
I am old now, a has been Wipe

Time is too short to regret
Go out have fun and forget
Live your life with a zest
Time Travels to put you through a test

Lillie Mae Cagle

Crystals

A strange song,
Elusive but strong.
Opaque as wood,
But clear as crystals.
What an odd song.
It is we sing.
Clear and deafening,
Like Pachabel's Canon,
Or soft and sad like
Swan Lake.
Sing, fair maiden,
Sing to soften his
Calloused heart,
Sing to make him see,
Sing to him the song of Love.

Carrie Conger

Rocking Into Eternity

Mom's busy hands are quiet now
Her hair is white, her eyesight dim,
Her chair rocks gently to and fro
Her mind is on her home with Him.
Mom's memory which was so sharp
Has left her with naught but rest
To while away the hours of life,
And dream of what was the best.
Our memories of her are clear
We want her back as she once was
Able to walk, to work, to sing,
All the things a young one does.
God has other plans for her
He died so that she might live.
A reward for a hard fought life
A starry crown to her He'll give.
Mom will be happy home on high
With loved ones who have gone before.
She'll think of us with love always
Only God could love us more.

Jesolie G. Craft

Just Me And You

I sometimes picture me and you
Together on the sand
We sat down beside each other
Gently holding hands
The birds are flying high above
Together perfectly
We stared into each other's eyes
And it was only me and you
We could watch the sun go down
And see the colors in the sky
I'll run my fingers through your hair
And I'm sure you'll know why
We could sit there in the moonlight
And look up at the stars
We could hold each other tightly
Because the night will be ours
I know it's just a daydream
But I'd like to make it come true
Together on the sand one day
Just me and you.

Charity Buchen

What Star Can Shine So Brightly

What star can shine so brightly,
Or Gem Shimmer with such fire.
That can match what twinkles lightly,
Within the eye of my hearts desire.

Stephen A. Wilson

The Desert

The sun and the sand,
Wildflowers and the land.
The hawk flies up high,
And the mouse runs down low.
The bees sing their pretty song.
See the butterfly,
And the bright purple sky,
Like the colors in a lume.
See the cacti in the ground,
As the snake slithers by.
The crickets make their pretty music,
In the dark night sky,
In the desert.

Tracy Kushman

"Be A Tiller Of The Soil"

Be a tiller of the soil
  Be a fisherman of men.
Bring God's glory
  To the world, beginning
With yourself, my friend.
  Speak deliverance
To all things speak of
  Peace and joy bells ring
Speak God's word
  In truth each day
Speak God's word and live
  His way don't forget
To kneel and pray.
  Tell someone
You love them every day.

Callie M. Moss

Sailing The Seven Seas

We've now set up our wooden raft,
Our ponchos on in case of drafts,
We hug our mums before we leave,
And sail away on the seas of cheese!

Right now we're in the Cheddar Sea,
This sea up next, we call it Brie,
We're floating past Monterey Jack,
We have no way of turning back!
Here's Gouda, the sea that is Dutch,
Of whom we all love very much!

There's 3 more seas!
There's 3 more seas!

We'll make it to these seas of cheese!
We must make it, please, oh, please!
To all the seven seas of cheese!!

Andrea Moix

The Tomb Of Memory

Nowhere can a secret keep
always secret, dark and deep
half so well as in the past
buried deep, so it can last
keep it in your own dark heart
otherwise these rumors start
after many years have buried
secrets over which you worried
no confidant can they betray
all the words you didn't say.
Only then can you exhume
secrets safe within the tomb
of memory, of memory
within the tomb of memory.

Scott M. Heist

Another

Feel it when the truth,
Grows finally and you see.
What has become false to eyes,
That were once closed.
You arise with the sun,
And the stars become dark.
Hear the lonely color,
And another cannot replace,
What you fear.
All seems lost and found,
Is what yearns to be.
But you taste the language,
So horrible to speak.
For some small hope of courage,
You turn to another.
And feel it when the truth,
Grows finally and you see.

Elizabeth T. Voss

Heartwood

The woods, a calm placid place
  Somewhere I can hide my face
Away from the human race

Greed, hatred, detailed things
  I live life from a gentle spring
Simplicity it brings

I get what I can from what it gives me
  Like no other shall I be
I need the comfort of the tree

society's poisons are leaking
  Our mortals souls they're seeking
Its awful stench is reeking

Here in my solitude
No others can intrude

Shannan Witmer

Nature's Sedative

When you smell a pretty flower
  or hear a singing bird
You know that life is worth a lot
  without a spoken ward
The beauty of the clouds and sky
  the freshness of the rain
A drive along a city street
  or down a county lane
The crispness of a winter's day
  the jungle of a sleigh
A snowman built by children when
  In the yard they play
Can bring a calmness to your soul
  and make you laugh and smile
It brings a difference to your life
  and calms your fears awhile.

Carole Kuehne

Vows

Investment in the Lord must mean,
More than I doth He increase-
Gambling in the world is seen,
More than I must He decrease-
Refining in degrees for thee,
Eternal vows He prays you'll keep-
His pristine love can make you free,
And with thy Love in marriage weep-
Salvations' tears of joy to reap.

Larry C. Trombitas

Sense Of Right

Let our eyes
See all color
Through a transparent lens.

Let our ears
Hear beyond sound
The true around the bend.

Let our minds
Do calisthenics
That awaken the search.

Let our hearts
Beat the tune
That mines the soul.

Let our lips
Filter impurities
To speak the truth.

Let our conscience
Stand up justified
For what we are.

Kat

Yet

Love should not be a label
yet love is a title
if love must be displayed,
then love's for anyone who's able

To some love is a reality
kept in harmony, to
others love is but a tale
no rose color visions when
truth is unveiled.

Love should not be grief
yet love can be sorrow
love should not be pity
yet love is sympathy
love is not greed
yet love is an interest
and when love is frail
it's known to fail...

Monica Miyano

From Outside Under

They are our walking dead:
bloated with expectation,
wracked dead full of anxiety,
warped of crime and emotion,
dead, yet buried, and said
walking erect —

And they are complex,
a holding together mesh
of a million parts, folding
as an ocean, mad at midnight,
navigated by time. And

One so many individuals
look toward their heaven
staring, at one another—
gaze at a band thickened
by just as many stars.

Vance Andrew Blevins

The Day He Calls

A loss of life,
It hurts us so.
So hard to comprehend,
So hard to let go.

There is sadness and anger,
And guilt in there too,
Wishing you'd done more,
When they were with you.

A life so young,
So precious, so caring,
So joyous, so feeling,
So loving, so sharing.

We must never forget,
The warm smile on their face,
And pray every night,
We'll join them in his heavenly place.

But for now, life must go on.
Places to go, people to see,
Live life to the fullest,
Until the day He calls for me.

N. S. Smith

To A Friend

Tis a satisfying feelin'
Just to know that you're my friend,
And no matter what's the trouble
That on you I can depend.

For the world is full of sorrow
And life's path is full of stones,
And a fellow's only comfort
Is the few real friends he owns.

You're so soothing and comfortin'
When my heart is full of aches,
And your way of sympathizin'
What a change in me it makes.

When I hear your little whisper
Then my troubles starts to mend,
And it's then I'm mighty thankful
That I've claim you as a friend.

But I've always kept a tryin'
Kept a trying to the end,
And my life has been much sweeter
Since I've had you as a friend.

William Ronsonet

Freedom

Freedom of religion
Freedom to speak our thoughts openly
Freedom to be a free spirit
A mother, a wife, a sister, a friend
Able to be the best person I can
The possibility of no masks
And no hidden agenda
With much ongoing gratitude
God bless America

Suzanne Hirsch-Small

War

He shot then fell
and once again
The war moved on
not thinking of him

Melissa Bradbury

Untitled

Purple is wild.
A bruise on a child.
Purple is an evening sky,
that makes you want to fly.
Purple is your new car.
to go far, far, far.
As music plays in your ears,
down flows the purple tears.

Justin Courville

Birthday

It's not your first, it's not your last
It's somewhere in between
So keep your life
As you have
With grace and dignity
And down the road
We'll meet again
Somewhere in between

John E. Shimota

Holding His Love

To love is to hold
I hold his love in my heart
thinking of him constantly,
since we're far apart
I only remember the
memories we shared.
Thinking of his love being
pure and sweet
I only dream seeing us together.
Under a moonlight
becoming closer than ever.
Having his arm around
me to get close together
our love is strong
even though we just
can't be together.

Marlene Perez

Hero

You watch her,
You love her,
You want to be her.

You notice the tiniest detail.
You practice in private,
everything she does.
But you know she does it better.

Soon, you give it up
and just admire her perfection.
For she is your hero,
and nothing can change that.

You get to know her,
so well.
Even her darkest secrets,
you know.

But it's okay,
because she's your hero,
your sunlight on a rainy day,
and you want to be her.

Joelle Brungard

Life Is More Than Aging

That homely old bush
Outside my window
Displays a baker's dozen
Breath-taking roses.
A life is much more
Than an aging frame.

Dorothy Dee Workman

Tin Soldier

A garbage can
Cold, dirty
Holding cast-offs of the unwanted
Patiently waiting for the discarded
To hold and want the unwanted
It's a life of solitude
Waiting
A lonely job
A garbage can
Its only purpose
To get emptied on garbage day.

Tricia

To Norma

My true love held me in his arms
Enchantment filled the day
He whispered softly in my ear
His words I now convey

"Your wide dark eyes are innocent
And wise and sad and gay
Your word runs sweetly you to me
And dance along the way

With you I look from stately towers
To gardens drenched in bloom
And then at dusk you are for me
A lovely light in every room".

Norma Grobli James

Home

Oh how I miss the happiness,
of being at my home.

The peace and calm serenity
there, I never feel alone.

But most of all I miss my friends,
I know they're always there.

I know their thoughts are with me,
I know they'll always care.

Sometime I get so lonely,
and often shed a tear.

I long to be with those I love,
and hold so very dear.

This life we live with ups and downs,
I will never understand.

I pray and ask my God above,
to please just hold my hand.

As I live and learn so many things,
and travel on my way.

May the love of God go with me,
so I will see another day.

Eric H. Aaron

One Prayer Plus

I still can hear your voice,
And I see sometimes see your face.
It wasn't suppose to be like this
Life's not meant to be a race.
Were those happy times
Really that far and flew?
If that's the way it really was,
Then I have a prayer for you,
For you to find those times out there
The happy times you couldn't find here,
Then I'd throw one in for me
And pray to God to keep you near.

Joyce Young

Sculpture

I am naked and battered
elegant and poised -
the model of perfection
and the psycho in my mind.

I am exploding and eroding
just before your eyes,
but you will never see me
through my lucent frame.

I am the Unfinished Bound Slave -
struggling and tormented,
reaching from the caste of flesh
towards the world beyond.

C. Bishop

Heartbroken

So many times you acted
like I was yours, and you made
my heart sore, you could
sweep me off my feet any day,
and break my heart taking
my self confidence, away.
You think you're so high in
power and could care less
about me in my darkest
hours. To you I'm just a toy
something you can use over
and over even though it's
been destroyed. You've
played me so many times
why do I put up with all your
crimes. I'm trapped in a
fantasy of love that I'll never get out
of my heart is so full of hope
and will never let go.

Latisha E. Yarbrough

Ruben's Duel

Well placed words
Those doubled-edged swords -
Judiciously applied -
Thus the Duel begins.
Pedagogue and docent -
Neophyte faces Master -
The gauntlet taken
Yet never thrown
An escapade born,
that caperous dance -
Becomes a gambol.
Ebullience to Edgeless Aspiration
Anima penetration -
The Essence of Life!

Sylvia Barber

Never Done

I am forgotten,
Yet I have not left.
This world is ending,
Without me to forgive.
I've done no wrong,
I've done no right.
To forgive is too hard,
To forget is what has happened.
Dieing I have not done,
Living wasn't even attempted.
I can not love,
I can not hate.
To forgive is the greatest attempt.
I have attempted nothing,
And I've done so much.

Tamara Grabowski

Untitled

I'm a fat person with a double chin
I dream of myself as being thin.
But then I laugh at the thoughts of
how I would look with no chin at all
I have short hair and wish it long,
and then a laugh when I think of me
with no hair at all
I'm a little older now and wish I
were younger and then I don't laugh
When I think of me not here any longer
God bless me for who I am.

Patricia Hearne Swart

Let Me Laugh Again

Let me laugh again,
The way I used to do
Many years ago
When I didn't love you.

My love you denied,
But I guess that is best
For you would have only lied
To me, like you did the rest.

Your love is so cold
And it always has been,
So release me from your hold
And let me laugh again.

Virginia Williams

Storm

Thunder rolls across the sky
Rain taps upon the windows
Lightning streaks from star to earth
Nature gives the best shows

The air smells fresh, all things shine
And grass turns newly green
Flowers spring from musky dirt
Begging to be seen

I listen to these wondrous sounds
And see God's loving beauty
With admiration I take these in
By choice and not by duty

To walk through all these magic times
Feel rain upon my face
Is truly one of life's sweet pleasures

Given by God's grace

Mary E. Swartz

Mended Heart

One dark and cloudless night,
I peered into the sky
and suddenly saw a shimmer of light
my heart could not deny.

It glared upon the surface
of a teardrop falling down
and gently wiped away the hurt
from which my heart was bound.

It pierced inside my broken heart
with memories from the past
and took away my doubts
of a love that could not last.

It brought back the memories
that I once had of you
and mended back my broken heart
that once was torn in two.

Kelvin M. Perkins

Lovely

Who can be as lovely as me
you can be as lovely as me.
If you look at a flower it's as
lovely as me. If I look at a
tree it's as lovely as me.
Surely you can be as lovely as me.
Thank you God, for making
someone as lovely as me.

Ruth M. Fennell

Desert Flower

To look beyond what you never knew
Always existed times far and few
Feelings soared, expressions afraid
Time wanted, time shared
Not a moment to fade
Ask deep within
Can I not express
Yes what is so close
The distance, the timing
What is feared the most
Feel our fire
The burning desire
Untouched but, shaken
Precious thoughts now awaken
Take my hand
Guide the way
It doesn't matter the time of day
Desert flower in the heat of the night
My flower bloom
I'll make it alright

Kimberly R. Duran

"Holly"

"What have we here?"
The father said
Who saw his girl-child
on her bed.
He know that she was
Someday nice
and promptly named her
"Holly" Rice
He saw beyond an earthly clod.
He smiled.
She is the child of God!

Keith Rice

I Love Him Still

Although he maybe
far away
or maybe real near by
I love him still

Even if he is my friend
And I'd like him to be
much more
I love him still

If I were with him everyday
and with him even now
though I don't exactly
know what to say

There's only one thing
I can think of that
I would say to him...
I love you still

Kathryn Senior

Watching Me

Someone is always watching me
With eyes I cannot see,

They watch my every move
And are hidden in a tiny groove,

I still have yet to find that place
But with surprising speed and grace,

They would flee
Far away from me,

So another day I must endure
Of being wary and unsure,
Because they are always watching!

Caryn Lobdell

Morning Coffee

My morning coffee is so sweet and hot
When I wake up in the morning
I hear steam blowing from the pot
When I sit down to drink it
I know it is the best
Because when I am done with one cup
I want to drink the rest

Rachel C. Ackerman

My Savior

Jesus Christ is my savior.
He leads me in the right way.
He said he would always love me,
even thought I may stray.

Jesus Christ is my savior.
He delivered me from sin.
He said he'd always be there for me,
to guide me through the trouble I'm in.

Jesus Christ is my savior.
He's my sword and my shield.
He leads me through my darkness,
to the light where I'm fulfilled.

Jesus Christ is my savior.
He said he'd come for me some day.
And when he comes;
I plan to be, ready in every way.

Collars Dwain Levels Jr.

The Cost

It is a lonely cold world
we live in today
Marriage is no longer an institution
but a game that we play

Divorce is everywhere
Hatred all around
Broken children playing
on the play ground

Too much abuse
Not enough trust
No one wants love
Just give them lust

It is one for one
All for oneself
We want it all
for sex and wealth

It is a lonely cold world
and all will be lost
We must do what it takes
No matter what the cost

Steven A. Clark

My Ideal Mate

It was a glorious day, Nov. 1st, 1921.
The day your earthly life was begun
Nearly two years, God had me wait
While he created my ideal mate.

Properly in Sunday School, we did meet
Each day we are together, is a treat
I was thirteen, you a sweet eleven
Life with you is a taste of heaven.

Donald A. Reed

The Black Woman:
The Strength Of A Lotus Flower

The black woman
blooms just like the
lotus flower, through rain,
sleet, or hail, with all kinds
of powers. For, she is the
queen of God's green earth,
the maker, the mother, and
producer of all births. The
queen is our good side, for
as long as can be. She's
pretty as the Lotus, and
strong as the tree.

Kenyon R. Smith

Who Do I Admire?

I admire a woman whose face shines
brighter than the sun, whose eyes
sparkle more than diamonds, whose
hair is darker than the midnight sky
Her hands are softer than the petals
of a rose, whose lips send out words
more powerful than the roar of a lion.
Her teeth more valuable than pearls.
I admire a woman who is
not afraid to speak her mind.
Who do I admire? I admire my
African Queens!

Jamal Kazembe

Him

Nobody chose to know him
no one seemed to care
he had heart and feelings
to them he wasn't there

Nobody chose to touch him
no one wanted to see
he was as human as you and I
still everyone let him be

Nobody said they loved him
no one took the time
they chose to walk the opposite way
they chose to leave him behind

Nobody heard him crying
no one heard his sorrow
he sat under the willow tree
and hoped and prayed for tomorrow

Nobody felt the raindrops
no one watched him leave
they never said goodbye to him
I guess that now he's free.

Wiegmann

Love Struck

From sunrise to sunset,
I can only think
of when we first met
I'm not sure he felt
the same way I did,
I just hope I'm not
some other kid
I was meant for him,
Just as he was meant for me
But we have both been so
blind to see
no matter how long
people try to pull us apart
He will always stay
in my heart

Megan Johnson

"My Angel"

When I saw you, I had thoughts of joy.
And for the first time,
I knew my heart was no toy.
I felt like I was on fire,
I had all my hearts desires.
Cause my dear,
You came close to me,
Then light was all I could see.
You're like an angel,
With joy all around,
And peace in my heart,
is what I have found.
You are my dream,
that has become real.
Since I met you,
I started to feel.
I love you now.
I will love you tomorrow.
We will be happy always.
Never have any sorrow.

Mary Gregory

Ancient Songs Of The Soul

Deep, dark, mysterious...the Kiva.
The re-awakening of myself.
Grandfather Sun filters in and finds
  the Earth welcoming him home.
Chanting...loud...soft...
  Drums beating the ancient melodies
  that course through my veins.
My spirits soars to find the Vision
  of understanding.
Sage-smoke dances with the sunlight
  and I feel my body sway
  to the rhythm of the song...
    feeling one with the sun...
      the smoke...
        the earth.

Jeanne M. Elsen

My Wishing Star

I held a star upon my palm
  And watched its five-pronged light.
It bathed my face in its Silver Sheen,
  And chased away all fright.
Gently, I held it near,
  And it turned into a dream:
Alone I stood, by a babbling brook,
  And held out my empty arms,
When all around me stardust fell
  Like shiny magic charms.
I shook my head, to clear my mind,
  And wonder what they are...
The dream had flown,
  And in my heart, was, my Wishing Star

Lauretta Anamta

A Majestic Eagle

Souring high
Souring low
Is a bird that we don't know
He spreads is wings so far from sight
And caress the earth
So delicate
So light
A hint of sadness that man has made
The bird flies on
In search of a new domain

Renee L. Freih

"Drunk And Driving"

Close by the door he paused
to stand, as he slipped the
class ring off her hand. All who
watched did not care to speak,
as a single tear rolled off his
cheek. All through his mind
memories ran, of all the fun
they once had. He held
his class ring and started
to cry, he kissed her cheek
and wanted to die.
As the wind began to blow,
they lowered her casket
down below. This is what happens
to many alive when friends
let friends drink and drive.

LeeAnne Wheeler

Suicide

I'm past my sense of happiness.
Now life is only pain.
If I don't end it all today,
What have I to gain.
I've got a gun in my left hand,
Bullets in my right.
I run back all my memories;
The last will be tonight.
No one knows about my pain;
No one really cares.
Everyone has their own lives,
No time to ease my fears.
No one seems to understand me;
No one would ever try.
Everyone can laugh at me,
But tonight I'll die.
Before long it will all be over,
I'll fly just like a dove.
I'll leave this world of hatred,
To meet the God of love.

Jacob Mercer

Untitled

Our life has been so very blessed
Since you were born that day.
We never knew we could love so much
In this very special way.

We knew right from the start of things
You'd be our "Little Man".
We felt our love grow more each day
As only Grandparents can.

We treasure all the things you do
Your laughter, hugs and tears.
We love to watch you dance to songs
And wrestle with your bears.

You are a precious gift from God
And though the miles between us span,
We love you more and more each day
Our precious "Little Man".

Ruth Paschke

Stop

Stop all the violence
Take it away
Stop all the hate
Let peace and love stay
Stop all wars
Let the world come together in peace
But if not any of that...
Take it one step at a time...
Stop hating me

Corie Dumont

Dreams

Dreams,
What are they, really?
Some are most satisfying,
And some are extremely terrifying.
Some are colorful,
Others are colorless.
There's ones you love,
And those you don't.
There are few you wish not to end,
And ones you wish were true.
Dreams can be helpful,
But don't confuse them with you life.
So go to you dreams with an open mind,
For they hold a clue inside.

Sara Bland

Know My Enemy

Curling these lips in a silent snarling prayer
As your clammy fingers pinch the air
Poking useless holes in my space
I am colored of winter wheat;
you think I'm on your side.
Don't look to me with your
runny, azure-ice eyes
You and your kind
turn my brothers and sisters against me.
I look like you so they believe
I think like you.
Because of your decaying,
wretched words
And your inhuman,
unGodly acts,
I am alone.
They hate me because of you
I hate because of you.
And I will not be still.

Marianne Black Snuggs

Parenting

When Webster's first put out the Word
"Mothers" were seen but rarely heard
The Word itself — check it out
Didn't carry a lot of clout.
Defined as "female parent," that's it
Doesn't seem right, doesn't quite fit.

Mothers come in every shape and size
Also in every ethnic hue
But each and every one, it's no surprise
Never fails to come through.

A Mother's love is different, something apart
From the normal romantic affair of the heart
Nothing can compare
With the love a Mother has to share.
Counselor, nurse, teacher, friend
The list goes on without end.

Nevertheless, my experience has been,
Mothering's sometimes done by Men.
And that is certainly good, not bad
When the Mom you need is a Great Dad.

Lois M. Heiserman

An Earthly Angel

Today I saw an angel
With hair as white as snow

She's getting older now
And her steps are getting slow

Her radiant smile is cheerful
Her gentle voice is sweet

To know her and love her
Is a blessing and a treat

For others she has lived
A lifetime filled with love

When she leaves this earthly life
She has a home in heaven above

If we could all live
As this earthly saint has done

Our Saviour would say well done my child
Your earthly battle has been won

Clara Grimes

Untitled

At a time in my life, I felt you as one with me
You were the reason for me to live
I was no longer alone
I had you
Time was endless and so were you
The most precious gift from up above
God sent you to me
The baby I once had inside of me.
Now you are in God's hands, I wipe the tears away
Where you rest, I pray
I look up in the powder blue sky
You are taken care of as can be
I no longer worry
The baby I once had inside of me.

Zusana Sanchez Rodriguez

Moments Magical

She stood a moment, puzzled; the wet, the cold
the whiteness - all different.

Her first tentative step was deliberately slow,
A second followed, then she quickly made a choice
And found a sheltered place.

Now what? The gate was far away.
After some reflection, negotiating the distance
would be worth it.

Dash now and up and over,
What joy! — What pain!

Her feet were freezing!
Another dash and the front door was hers!
With plaintive cry she called me.
The warmth of the house was hers again.
Her magic moments were over.
My cat was in!

Cynthia Curtiss

A Single Tear

A skeletal hand reaching out
for comfort that cannot be.
A single tear flows down sallow cheeks
only one of many to come.
A condemned soul searching,
trapped between heaven and hell.
A loving heart breaking,
is it yours or my own?
Tell me how to ease the pain
gripping your body like a cold metal vice.
Tell me how to dry your tears
that only begin the tale of your sorrow.
Tell me how to save your soul
and find it a place to rest.
Tell me how to mend your heart
along with my own after you are gone.
Leave this place with quickened wings
to laugh, touch a cloud, and be well.
To a place void of judgement
without despair, without scorn, without AIDS.

Kelly Leahy

Falling Star

You're like a falling star. That glow in
the midnight sky. You sparkle every
time I see you, when I hear your
voice. I always see that star in the sky.
When I say bye to you it's like watching
that star falling from the sky. You wish
upon that falling star. Someday, you'll
find that falling star in your back yard.

Tina Heldman

Knowledge, Knowledge, Knowledge

"Let's have knowledge," everyone says.
And everyone gets busy learning
and getting knowledge in Reading, Writing and Math
because...

We have been taught that Knowledge is Power!
But...haven't we forgotten the most important topic of all?
Goodness-simple Goodness—which is the
greatest force in the world!

Perhaps there should be a course in Goodness just like
we have for Art and Music — for then the teacher
may ask a simple good deed by the pupil each day.

My Dear Boys and Girls,
to be good, kind, considerate, understanding
and fill our hearts with Brotherly Love-

This is the most precious treasure one can yearn.
And not seeking reward nor doing this for interest...
But for the inner beauty within ourselves.
This should be our Goal!

Rosalind S. Roger

Heartless Acts

What in this world would make a
mother kill
The most precious thing in her life is
now still
I wonder what she will try to blame
For something so terrible she did with
no shame
It hurts the heart of this whole nation
And makes us all wonder how she could give
into the devils temptation
Now we must all come together and pray
That will stop having such tragic days
These innocent children are on everyone's mind
And we'll never understand heartless acts
of this kind.

Jennifer Waters

The Thunder Of Silence

Your silence engulfs me,
with a thundering roar!

Like majestic waves, breaking
on a deserted shore.

No eyes to see, no ears to hear.
No hands to applaud, no hearts to cheer.

With all their grandeur spent,
They, silently, slip back into the sea.
Wasted, wasted, - Oh, so wasted!
Like my love for thee.

Pearl Bloyd

My Swing

No one have I to share my quiet moments with
As I sit in my swing and let the hours drift: Away
I take a deep breath and let out a sigh
And I swing and I swing ever so high
Over the bushes and up through the trees
As I swing and I fly in the cool evening breeze
No one is around, just me in my swing
As I relive the past - my childhood; I dream
It's better than an airplane for the places I go
Up through the clouds and over the rainbow
Deep down inside, I'm still a little girl
And when I'm in my swing, I'm in my own special world.

Cheyrl Kelly

Alone In My Head

Want to bring someone into my world,
Want them to know what it is I feel,
What it is that can make me cry, make me smile.
And no one is willing,
And no one seems to care, alone in my head.

The horizon I look at with it mesmerizing stare,
This is what I want to share.
Colors I see,
And the shapes that the clouds seem to take,
But no one seems willing,
No one seems to care, alone in my head.

Alone I walk,
A tear,
A smile,
No one knows,
No one seems to care,
...Alone in my head.

Frank Perez

A Teacher's Prayer

Dear Lord, I ask you help today.
You gave me a job... to teach your way.
Young minds to instruct... these children to love.
Dear Lord, I know they are gifts from above.
I look at the babes assembled here.
The troubled ones soon become so dear.
The joy, the trust; help me not fail.
But, to be faithful, strong, loving... whatever may assail.
Dear Lord, help me provide a refuge safe...
A shelter, a quiet place... to develop faith.
Dear Lord, forgive me if the task is too great.
Help me do my very best... for the children's sake.
Dear Lord, help me put duty first.
To teach young minds... to quench their thirst.
Fill me with love to share,
To carry the hurts these young ones bear.
Dear Lord, give me strength for today.
To do each task, fully, come what may.

Above all, to serve and worship you,
Through the children... it's all I want to do.

Richard L. Merila

Learning To Love Myself

As I look at the world today
I wonder where I will fit in
Dreaming at night of a day
When my soul will quit running away.

Continually searching for approval
Because I can't stand the person within
Emptiness has captured my soul
So, I drink to try and win.

Looking for a friend in the world
I begin to isolate even more
Suppressing my emotions within
Until the anger is ready to explode.

Finally I turn to a God
He fills the emptiness inside
Healing the child within
Has made the inner beauty of my soul fly high.

Now I am on a cloud
With its softness embracing my soul
I can look for the truth inside
Because now it won't hurt when I fall.

Vianna Thompson

The Most Beautiful Baby

The most beautiful baby I have ever seen is lying in the crib before me
One tiny hand held curled above his head
The other stretched out beside him
Soft brown hair with curling locks nestled 'round his neck
Beautiful long lashes hiding two big brown eyes
In white onesy pajamas with light blue trim, how small you seem to me
I remember when you were only a wee newborn babe
How I marvelled at you
I could not believe I was a mother, and you—you my precious baby
Your little hands, your big eyes, that beaming smile—I marvel at you still.

The most beautiful baby I have ever seen is lying in the crib before me sweet dreams, Little One
The clock has long since struck one, And still I sit beside you
Sweet dreams, Little One
Remember the laughter we shared today, Your shrieks of delight
Remember the hugs, the kisses—Your cheek next to mine
Sweet dreams, Little One
May the Lord's spirit caress you, His breath keep you warm
'Til I hold you again in my loving arms.

Iris Maceda Ryan

Dancing In The Air

The clouds drift by, on the sky's numerous paths,
Each one shaped and folded by its own unique past.
Why can't the beautiful ones pause a little longer for me?
So I can honor thy soft and silent creation.
Are they too modest, or busy perhaps,
Does uncertainty frighten them?
Or is the wind ceaselessly pushing them,
and pressing them on like the current of human anxiety?

If we were the clouds above, would there be more crashing lightning,
And more wasted, flooded farmlands?
Would there be more tornadoes, and more uplifted farmhouses,
Or would we realize that all we would have to do,
is simply float, drift, glide gracefully and just let the
time go by.
This would be enough for me.
Yes, now I see.

Brian C. Sullivan

Untitled

Some say it is just the nature of the beast
When you love somebody so passionately
Time has a way of stealin'
That raging fire you're feelin'
Leaving the ashes laying at your feet,

Those fools of little faith will never know
Those higher places - two hearts can go
Where time is standing still
And love will burn until
The heavens and the earth
Have come and gone,

This fire inside for you
Is constant as the Northern Star
And you will be
Forever in my heart
As long as there is a river
Searching for an endless sea
I will always love you - Faithfully

Thomas E. Taylor

Since Then

A tear is a warning of emotion,
A scratch is a sign of pain.
They say war is a silly notion,
Yet peace will drive people insane.
When the world first came to
There was a life and a hand,
And in the blooming trees there
Was a woman and a man.
All these things are what the world has come to know,
Children hide their feelings deep down below.
The maker had intentions all good and pure,
They all will be friends, for sure.
But now in a world of hatred and fear,
All we have left is a scratch and a tear.

Dianna Balioni

Footprints At Laetoli: 3.6 MYA

The footprints at Laetoli trail unerringly
toward a distant goal, forever unknown.

They march across time into eternity, this family of three:
father, mother, and child.

Not Adam and Eve we see, yet in this, our first family, we trace our roots, our genesis, a monogamy of male prints, smaller feminine prints, a child's prints.

Trekking assuredly across the plain of volcanic ash,
the parent prints signal a shared quest.
The child's mark an exploratory mobility,
now trailing in its parents' steps,
and now ranging away, daring independence,
yet staying within watchful gaze and grasp.

Footsteps, eternalized in moistened ash, claim us in Africa,
brothers and sisters, through time, across continents.

Permanence is the legacy of this first family
in their journey across the ashy volcanic plain,
in their progeny's evolution through the millennia.

No thought had they of us,
yet their footprints in solidified ashes speak.

And we... we dare to record our passage in the ashes of fission.

Michael Hogan

Matthew's Day

Down by the river
Down by the sea-
That's where my little boy
Always wants to be.

With his pole in his hand
And his favorite kind of bait-
Sitting on a rock or stump
For hours he could wait.

Until at last his patience paid
Along would come a big fish-
Jerking upon his tightly held line
Fulfilling that little boys wish.

Then, he'd hurry home as fast as he could
To brag on how it fought-
And run thru the door, and excitedly yell—
"Mom, look what I caught!"

Sharon F. Bertrand

Living Hard

Cold and hard as the steel and rock that encases me eternal
In the wasteland suffering like a human; thinking, feeling, struggling
Elemental; fathered but fatherless, tried, convicted and sentenced
Losing Heaven for Hell in the land of Nod with the question
Spirits wanting to pass the cup, love dies as hated haters thrive
cyanide plots in the house of pain; each year engulfs the next
knowing what unforgiven is; deadening what hurts too much
Hate sublimated in transubstantiation; disconnected from comprehension
Insane dirges; I can't live or die walk or fly from the dream
Staccato syncopation slams synapses; the labyrinthine scream
Tied to the tree and left; a fate of interminable death
I awake, wash my face and stare at the wall; operant conditioning
One hundred percent state sanctioned inhumanity blowing minds
guillotines fly, cities burn, nowhere is the center found
Dreading day, fearing night, for nox beckons and day is a prelude
Grinding loneliness, nothing but that to look to, day in day out blues
In Hades bowels winds are snapping, hearts are breaking, arms reaching
Are we Skinners in a box or Pavlovian dogs
Kill the chimera; the spawn of the auburn system,
Slay the Pennsylvania systems aborted stammheim-.
Behold the new Gorgon.

Donald C. Johnson

Untitled

Whenever you're not here
I feel so sad and lonely
My heart aches for you
because you are a part of me
I long for the sound of your voice
the feel of your touch
I can't help these feelings, I miss you so much
It's hard going just one day, without you in it.
My day seems so dull, all I do is sit
and think about things, that we alone have done
things that were memorable, that made the day fun
My thoughts are happy, but I don't feel like that inside
I feel so sad and alone
like something in me has died
To me you are the sun
that comes out after the rain
You are like the drug I need
that silence my pain I'm addicted to you
I need you in every way, but all I can do is wait
Until I see you another day

Vanessa Buck

Thoughts

Staring at the ceiling
with no expression on my face
not really knowing where I am
in an old, familiar place

Shadows lurk in every corner
and nothing makes a sound
I'm searching through the heavens above
with both feet on the ground

Hours pass and minutes flee
still trying to untangle my mind
there's something there I just can't see
so many answers I fail to find

Bit by bit the fog starts to clear
the labyrinth of elaborate paths
I feel happiness and sadness mixed with fear
as I await my imagination's wrath

Reemerging from my comatose state
finally released from my mind
I come to realize it may be too late
for my heart has already gone blind.

Jessica E. Ross

Talking With Ghosts

They have all been dead for many a dark year
Yet all of their voices speak wisely here
The songs they sing
Deep within my head, they ring
The stories that they wrote
In my mind, these stories I quote
The advice they gave
This advice, my life it may save
The ghosts are here to comfort me
They see what no one else can see
I talk with them daily
Yet you remember them only vaguely
Here they are now
They will help me somehow.

Tyler Sanderson

Second Chances

Flowing brooks, or raging sea
Shells and rocks to touch and see

Barren land or mountains high
A butterfly flitting softly by

The different colors in a persons eyes
Hot, home-made apple pie

Hands that can do a thousand things
Watching lightening from an old porch swing

Friends and family, young and old
hearing tales from times untold

Christmas carols, pines and boughs
Gifts to give and hugs to hold

The scent of pine, the touch of snow
Love and laughter wherever you go

Second chances abound a new
with each new dawn, it's up to you

Grace O'Sullivan

A Personal Reading During Dessert At A Chinese Restaurant

You will soon cross the great waters
I do have to cross the east river tonight
this fortune's true.
The rails in the Canal Street station,
which I cross to from Broadway,
bring images of Venetian Waterways.
I picked up the new Roger Waters c.d. at Tower today,
planning to listen to it tonight,
and if I were worth His time
I'd make him mad and cross at me for wishing him back into his band
this fortune's true.
Or maybe I chose the wrong cookie from the tray of twelve.

And when I do leave
and board the downtown 4,
I will cross the filth floating down the river,
go past the Flatbush Avenue basketball games,
and come home to listen to my c.d.
this fortune's true.

Daniel Levinson

Untitled

Good-bye, My Love Forever is an eternity.
Hello, My Love Now is for the living.

There is no forever There is only now.
Eternal love is always Love is always now.

Eternity is Now Now is forever.

There is now.
There is now for a living man
  To love
    To hold
      To care

You cannot shake hands with a dead man

You can Love
  Hold
    Care
For the woman who no longer needs forever — Only now.
The love of now is for the living
The love of forever is for the eternities.

Good-bye, My Love Hello, My Love.

Donea Ogle

The Restorative Art Baby

When the ovum and the zygote met, that's when I was first begot,
But my mom teaches restorative art you see, so growth was
calculations and measurements for me

My cranium and face were formed, and lo, and behold, they fit the
norm, my facial features were another matter, those I had to fit together

I made my forehead five eyes wide, so you can rest in on your side,
At the temporal bone I placed my ear, so I can hear you whisper there

One third the length of my face is my nose, so I'll be able to
smell the rose, with your one-eye-wide eyes I'll always see the
light of your love shining on me

My mouth may look two-eyes wide, after 2 AM it expands to five,
then I'll give your auditory ossicles a shout, if you don't
respond, my mentalis will pout

With your upper and lower integumentary lips puckered out, you can
caress my face and remove all doubt, as long as you hold me near,
I know I will have no fear, but I'm glad I did my duty and fit
into the "Canon of Beauty"

Mildred Dempsey Parker

God's Gracious Gift

As I lay awake and admire one of God's most gracious gifts,
I am truly amazed at how one can be so lovely.
Even though the clock has reached this late hour,
Your beauty radiates brighter than any star in the night sky.

The moonlight splashes through the inviting window...
And bathes your outstretched body as you sleep ever so gently
The quiet light complements your angelic complexion,
Like a warm fire does to a romantic evening.

Your hair is spread out across the pillow case,
As if it were painted there by a master.
It carefully reveals your warm, soft skin,
Confirming my belief that prayers do get answered.

What intrigues me most, seems almost impossible:
All of the perfection that I've just recited,
All of the divineness of the angel that lies before me,
Pales greatly to the beauty that shines within you.

No one can conceive the happiness you bring me.
Just having you here with me makes me realize one thing:
That I want to hold you in my arms forever,
One of God's most gracious gifts.

Jamie Skaggs

Her Prince, Her Knight, Her Mr. Right

There is a man, who fills her thoughts and her every waking hours.
He is sensitive, gentle, and has a subtle charming power.

With a big tender heart, always filled with a song,
He's handsome, smart, sexy and strong.

His voice is soothing, and has a low peaceful sound.
She seems to melt always, looking into his eyes, a warm, deep
brown.

He's full of adventure, and is a perfect gentleman in every way.
He's the hero that she dreams of at night and during all her days.

He shows her attention and shows her that he is pure.
But her heart has been hurt, and can only be patched by him, for he
  is her cure.

He makes her feel good, excited and wanted,
  and he gives her a reason to believe.
Her prince, her knight, her Mr. Right
  is all the same, known as... "Steve."

Lisa M. Pratt

The Law of the Harvest

The Law of the Harvest of reaping what I sow
Helps me be a gardener to eternal joy or woe.
My mind is the soil, my thoughts the tender seeds
To generate what's planted and cast out those poisonous weeds.

True as a boomerang my hidden thoughts are shown.
I am my own creator. My choices mine alone.
Hard work and repetition make deep engrams in my brain.
The more it is repeated, the habit more I gain.

I must work and share my crops. No idle wish can flourish.
I lose what I don't use. I choose what I will nourish.
What I do for myself, God need not do for me.
I'll learn self-reliance, Yet seek help on bended knee.

From my goals if I veer only one small degree
I shall finish far from where I wish to be.
I'm in training for Godhood. I know oaks from acorns grow.
Son like unto the Father, The same traits begin to show.

Life's burdens can be met with heaviness and temper short,
Or give gladly what's due with a gratitude of heart.
The yield from my garden depends so much on me.
On how I live and grow through all eternity.

Laurel Woodbury Mickelson

Is Life Real Or Just A Dream?

Good things kept happening to me.
Until one day I was led to see,
It might not always be that way.
For things do change in just a day.

Springtime come with its lovely flowers.
I played and dreamed for many hours.
Then summer's sun so hot and free
Brought a lot of joy to me.

Fall began with its tumbling leaves.
I watched it with its frost and freeze
Winter rushed in with a terrible blow.
Soon it had covered the world with snow.

Yes, life is real just like the seasons.
Changes come without any reason.
Just as spring comes, a new life will enter;
And old age is just as sure as winter.

Rowena Barnes

Precious Life

I was crying yesterday
For the blood, sweat and shame.
For the pain, distress and blame.

How long must the weak be oppressed by the strong?
Don't you know my burden? And your burden is the heaviest.
A life is a life, precious yet fragile.

My blood is yours, too.
But you pretend that such you have nothing to do
And when the tears start
To fall down your face like rain.
Then you realize the pain remains the same.

Look what hatred has done.
Infested our minds to absorb like sponge.
With discrimination, segregation, annihilation
Chilled the blood embedded in the soul.

Modernize our conceptual thinking.
Like stars we will twinkle
And make this world a better place.
Look at the sun, it shines for us all
Giving us the light of life.

Frederick Clarke

Timeless

The timeless beauty of all lasting things.
Timeless but for the only this moment.
What can outlast the passage of time?
Ever so hard to grasp time's concept, or to even imagine.
God made. Man made, stop give that some
thought - even a speck of sand, under glass,
is a marvelous find!
Examine every thing, that your eye can encompass,
The timeless scent of a rose, or is that scent, just a
sweet memory? Scent has timeless recall.
The minutes that tick on the face of a clock,
timeless, but for only a second.
Every thing moves in the circle of life.
Every thing refers to, and means you and I.
Do what you can, while in charge of life's plan.
as this way. You pass only once,
Timeless your shadow, falls on the world
Under scrutiny, the deeds that, you have done
judged and examined.. All in good time..
In timeless time, all in good time,

Sharon Grove Mack

Orravan Divad

Stepping into the darkness away from the light.
I see your eyes through the smokey gloom.
That gently lures me into my doom.
I hear your voice inside the wind.
I feel your soul stepping in.
I try to run but I can't see.
The blackness in this room is blinding me.
Looking around it all looks the same.
For darkness has no shape as well as no frame.
My mind with disbelief, let me go wants to say.
My eyes in August know that darkness is their play.
Let me feel your sane, as my soul you drain.
For I am impartial to your darken pain.
Sit down you say, although bewildered but safe.
For darkness is your friend and pain is your gate.

Ynirida Miranda

Know Your Way Around

What goes around comes around
Or so the saying goes
How this comes to pass
Know one really knows
When it comes around to me
I won't be too concerned
By living life unselfishly
Only good will be returned
When people are rude, dishonest or unfair
I try to understand and just politely stare
For it is they who should think twice
About the way they live
Instead of wanting all
They need to learn to give

Charlotte A. Mead

Untitled

Have you ever wondered what's in store,
Will you have to hurt some more,
Or will the sun shine bright on you,
What does God have planned for you?

The tears they fall like pouring rain,
Your eyes show all the pain,
But then a smiles comes on your face,
You've been touched by God's sweet grace.

Sometimes it's hard to carry on,
You feel that you are all alone,
Just look around and you will see,
God's there for you and me.

Many times you've been filled with doubt,
Trapped by sins with no way out,
Just close your eyes and start to pray,
Let God show you the way.

So as you live your precious life,
You may not always do what's right,
But God knows whose heart is true,
Do the best you can is all God asks of you.

Kevin E. Manders

War Of The Sea

The sky is a blue ocean
sometimes navy

With the stars
swimming through the waves, like fishes

Sometimes turquoise
with the blazing sun as a shark
ravenously devouring
all the darkness
as the fishes fade back into the darkness

But then
the tadpoles
who were escapees
of the dreadful massacre
make up a legion of stars
and come upon the shark

Slowly, stealthily
taking the shark over
his jaws agape
as the army of stars takes
Revenge

Catherine Mack

Secrets

A place no one knows,
Words never spoken even among friends,
A cave of damp, stale darkness
Where a bear hibernates, waiting to awaken,
A volcano on the verge of erupting
Under a swirling expanse of sea.
The bear awakens,
The volcano erupts, the sea excites,
If the forbidden word escape.
Secrets.

An ancient chestnut tree bent by time and weather
With a hole carved in its trunk by the centuries.
The ringed and knowledgeable tree,
Telling stories lost in time of people and nature;
Mystery of lovers entwined under,
Tales of storms raging destruction around.
People come and go, storms abate and die.
The tree remains,
A symbol of history, of words and actions unknown.
Secrets.

Jennifer L. Haldeman

Midwinter Messenger

Winter had reached mid-point, and it was morning.
A thaw had come, stripping the earth to near nakedness.

I took the morning street, walking routinely;
having rested, yet weary of winter and the morning.

I tried to close my thoughts against the dampness;
but they would not yield to my weak persuasion.

Then, clear, insistent, cutting through my darknesses,
a bird voice, beautiful in its command
pitted its strength against my weakness.

A cardinal!

Small brightness of color and song;
yet large enough to change my universe.

Constance McFarland

The Sound Of An Aspen Tree

The sound of an Aspen Tree's leaves
Whispering in the wind,
Is peaceful and soundly
I could lay for hours listening to the peaceful sound,
I wonder if they whisper secrets to one another
Or maybe to me.

In the middle of an aspen grove it is peaceful
So I lay in the middle of an aspen grove,
Listening to their leaves.

Adrianna Sanchez

Goodbye

My heart suffers the pain of love lost
We were together no matter the cost
Our attraction dwindled with passing time
Searching our souls for a love we could not find

Each act of degradation, trembling in terror
Looking at the reflection in the mirror
Where has the vibrant young woman gone
She needs to recapture the days that are done

To let go of a part of yourself is very painful
To realize a marriage has ended is shameful
Guilt, regret, sorrow and anger will eventually perish
Peace, contentment and unity with spirit I will cherish

Deborah Patora

The Rumbling Lioness

Deep down inside a rumbling starts
A rumbling deep in the pit of your soul
Anger rages throughout your head
A million thoughts pour out of the ever growing rumble

A million threats, a million lies, a million feelings, a million million

So many feelings and tears
A million ways to kill just one person spew out of your imagination
The rumble grows
An old song pokes through the rage "There's gonna be a rumble tonight"
West Side Story
As the rumble gets louder people start to stare
A scream escapes your lips
It was more like a roar, a roar from a great lioness
The great lioness going in for the kill, an angry rage flees the rumble
It has grown too big, it rumbles bigger than itself
Now the lioness is an angry rage
The hate, anger, and evil inside the lioness combine

A monster is born, the evil is here, the rumble gets louder

Sierra Voss

An Angel Song

An angel song gives us eternal life
she was more beautiful than any earthly wife

The angel song with a mighty voice
That could greatly save our souls
And fill our hearts with plenty of rejoice

Watching the beautiful angel sing
With powerful unknown words had carried
A heavenly testimony of Jesus Christ who forever reigns

The angel song in a place
Of where only our best dreams
Can take us to see her face

Remember! Holy Angels record the songs of their
Heavenly father's joyful saint's
While securing heavenly royalities
For all who did not faint

Ricky Clemons

Peace Of Mind

Does anyone today really know Peace of Mind?
Cause first of all, it's more difficult to get,
And harder, still to keep,
In today's world yet.

Have love and security, yes, then
you may feel it.
Gain peace and happiness and it will last.
But alas, greed and debt,
Will fade it fast.

We knew it more in yesteryear.
When we were young, ahh, yes, it was there.
We knew and had our lovely, glorious Peace of Mind,
To have it lost, and left behind.

Vilma Broga

A Toast

Here's to the fondest of memories.
Here's to the laughter.
Here's to the passion we have shared.
Here's to the love that gave us a foundation.
Here's to the eternal flame that so very often, still burns deep within my soul.
Here's to the friendship that remains unshaken.
Today as always.
....I celebrate the joy in loving you.

Lance M. Daniels

Promised Friends

I want you to know that you are missed,
It's almost like that first kiss.
A day's gone by as I just sit and sigh,
And you know me that's no lie.
I think of you all day and night,
Will we meet again, we just might.
Although you are so far away.
The memories of us are hear to stay.
It might be long for us to wait,
But I don't believe it will ever be too late.
If time goes by and we work things out,
We'll find out what our love's about,
If for any reason that love should end,
You know that I'm always your friend.

Valerie Pavelock

Onset

The advancing hordes menace the road,
Leading out of before and into after.
Darkness, coming down, is more than darkness;
Wilderness, on either side, is more than wilderness.

Mounted men in armor hold lances at the ready:
Lances swift to thrust and spill life;
Footmen hold snarling dogs in leash:
Dogs keen to sniff the sultry air and eager to harry.

As the road is breached by the knights and hounds,
The driven dusk, altered, trembles;
The flanking woods, estranged, cower.
Is this the grim sum of what we know of the future?

Francis L. Kunkel

Tomorrow

I am the procrastinator
Opportunity knocks within my mind.
Ideas motivate me to be an achiever
But I wait for the right time to seize the day.
The precise element that would give one fame and fortune,
Wealth beyond my own expectations.
To be
World renowned, overwhelmed by popularity,
A milestone in the annals of history,
A second glance,
A turn of the head to see where I have been,
But only to be surprised.
The journey was only from within.
I am the procrastinator.

Jason Pacilli

Garden Thought

I plant my garden without any thought
To all the colors I put on my plot
I admire the colors, the red and the greens
Yellow and purple, they all seem to gleam
They glisten and sparkle with the morning dew
They seem to want me to say to you
Its not the color of their skin
But whats inside that make us grin
The sweet, the sour, the hard and the soft
So much like people, if we give it a thought.
If we look beyond the color of skin
We might find we like what's within.

Wanda Brooks

The Drive

We hoped in the car;
But we weren't going far.
It was a musty day;
How we all feel gay.
We were on our way;
But not to play.
As cars passed by;
You could watch the birds fly by.
The snow was melting;
But the sun was not pelting.
The road was bumpy;
The ride also bumpy.
We past a bar;
But we weren't that far.
As the car creeped up a hill;
But down hill was our thrill.
As we found our destination;
That was the beginning of our fascination.

Bethany Brahmer

Above The Battle's Din

You cried when my orders came for duty overseas.
You told me you would be lonely;
That your life apart from me would be a void.

But, at the pier as you waved goodbye,
I saw through your facade.

The current of your tears failed to over wash
The blackness of sin's muck
Beginning already to have form.

You need not to have written your letters
  of explanation
    excuses
      confessions.

I knew much earlier the depth to which you had sunk.
Through the battle's din in each exploding shell
Your messages were clear.

Yes, surgery is scheduled;
Yes, I'll lose both my legs.

But what makes my heart heavy
Is the death of your soul!

Naomi L. Atkinson

You

Your smile is like sunshine on a cloudy day.
It always cheers me up when I'm down.
It's like streetlights.
In the dark of the night it can light up a town.

Your eyes are my guidance.
They show me the way.
They help you to look into me and see my every thought,
Every day.

Your lips are like the stars.
They are so close and yet so far
They are replenishing after a day of hard work.
They light up from afar.

You are like a guardian angel.
Not just any guardian angel, mine.
You are a caring person,
And, yes, you are divine.

Kimberly Smikovecus

Heart Break!

Heartbeats of love
Love lessoned learned
Eternity of lies
when you play with fire and skate on thin ice
Are men really worth the price?

Fallen are a million tears
watching from a mirror
at an image unreal
looking at your soul through your eyes
Are men really worth the price?

Taking away your self-esteem
and destroying your hopes and dreams
watching love slowly die
Are men really worth the price?

Angie Wind

Life

Every breath and every sigh
From the waking in the morning to retiring at night,
Every action, every word, and deed
Every thought, experience, and need
All are a part in the meaning of life.

For in the beginning God created it all,
From the wonderful creation and Adam's fall,
To Christ's death, burial, and resurrection
So that man could receive His perfection
In the plan and purpose of life.

What life means may not be easy to explain,
Each one of us may not describe it quite the same;
However, upon this we might agree
That God gave life to you and He gave life to me,
And it's because of Him that we live.

It's not appearance, pleasures, wealth, or fame,
The true meaning of life is found in Christ's name:
Through the debt He paid on the cross for us to be free -
Free from sin, bondage, and strife
To truly experience the meaning of abundant life.

Maxcine Carter

Forever

Forever seems so long ago
A promise made entwining souls
Why does forever seem so long ago.
Still trying, can't let go, even if...
Forever seems so long ago.

I hold so tight, Dreaming of the night,
You prayed never to let me go.
Reaching for your touch, forever seems so long ago.
A scream from deep inside my soul,
Crying to you, Please don't let go...
Forever seems so long ago.

A dream I lost, Pain resides inside my soul.
My heart is yours, my tears still flow.
Watching through my eyes, your soul slowly dies.
It breaks my heart, it bleeds my strength to know
Forever died so long ago.

Resounding in my heart and soul, your voice...
Please don't let go -
Don't let forever seem so long ago.

Vicki Blair

Thank You, My Friend

We've known each other forever, it seems,
We've shared ups and downs and in-betweens;

I wrote this note, just me to you,
to express what it means to have a friend so true;

That she knows what I'll need before I even do,
And she'll happily give it to make my dream come true;

I'll always remember, and it makes perfect sense,
That it was my best friend who found my sixpence;

It will complete my special day when placed in my shoe,
It seems not enough to say just "thank you";

So I wrote you this poem, tried to get it just right,
To express how lucky I feel to have you in my life.

Bethany L. Gosule

Under The Moonshine

As the world rolls into blackness,
Predators stalk their prey,
Winds pick up speed
And carry the deep moan of death,
When the moon shines on earth
All innocence is wiped away.

Again, the sun will shine,
But only to bring the moon's eerie glow,
Its green face looking upon our microcosm,
Looking at it with laughter,
Laughing at our stupidity,
Our mistakes and our lack of wisdom.

Alexis Vogelgesang

Funny Things

Wouldn't it be funny if cars could fly,
  and airplanes ran on the road?
Wouldn't it be funny if a cat could bark,
  and a cow could hop like a toad?
Wouldn't it be funny if the sky were green,
  and the grass a beautiful blue?
And a piggy said quack, and a duckie said oink?
  Well, I think it would, don't you?
Wouldn't it be funny if an elephant roared,
  and a lion had a big long nose?
And a monkey said baa, and a dog said meow?
  And sheep could swing by its toes?
Would it be funny if down was up,
  and up was down, and everything was turned around,
and an owl said peep, and a chickee said whooo?
  Well, I think it would, don't you?

Delores Neumann

Triumph Of Life

He who seeks not the True Light to find,
The heart to ease with tenderness sublime,
Finds naught but woe and erring fears
To guide the End in harvesting years.

But, he who lifts the Misty Veil,
And from darkness to morn alights,
Deeper and deeper with the rising sun...
So does the heart of Man remold.

Then blessings in measure and treasures unfold,
In triumph and Glory that's purer than gold!
Here lies true joy, the path to ensue...
That surges o'er mountains and man can't subdue!

Ann Konstantelos

Fire

A blaze of yellow, orange, and red
illuminates the night sky.
Gasps and shrieks float through the air
as people everywhere gape at the horrific sight.
Scraps of the burning building fall like snow
with dregs covering the ground like a carpet.
Screams of terror pierce through the night
which are loud enough to awake the dead.
People trapped in the building move frantically
as if they think they could fly out like a bird.
Sirens wail from a distance
coming nearer and nearer by the second.
Then, in the midst of this frightening scene,
the blaze of light and heat descends onto the ground.
Every sight and sound goes under in this massacre
seeming almost impossible to be saved.
So much has altered in this short period of time
all from one small word with so much power,
fire.

Julia Shnayder

My Little Friend

I opened up my eyes today from a very peaceful nap,
And right away I saw a bug just sitting on my lap.
His legs were black and shiny and they wiggled all the time,
I guess he needed all of them to help him jump and climb.

He cocked his tiny head and gave me a friendly glance,
I tried to pick him up but I didn't have a chance.
He took a giant leap for such a tiny little bug,
And then he grabbed my curtain with a gentle little tug.

He pulled himself along until he reached my windowsill,
But then he stopped and looked outside—he was absolutely still.
What could he see out on the ground to captivate him so?
I got up to take a peek because I really had to know.

Crawling all around outside were little bugs just like my friend,
'Hello down there' were silent words I thought I heard him send.
He tried to get down to the ground but he couldn't find a way,
You really cannot keep a friend when he doesn't want to stay.

So I carried him outside as a tear came to my eye,
It's really kind of sad to tell a friend good-bye.
Then I opened up my window just a tiny crack,
Because this is where I'd be if he wanted to come back.

Diana Pelham

The Seas of History

There's a wise old bird, Ms. Liberty
Who sails the seas of history
If she could speak she'd grandly talk
Of the silent victory we fought.

In a land of oil, those hills of gold
The story old and yet untold
The two of us, we saw the worst
The ramparts dark; were fit to burst.

The valiant fell, the only son
Abreast they marched to kingdom come
I, too, fell down upon the sand
And Allah stormed and swept the land.

"'Tis not your time arise and smile
And go on down another mile."
I stood, I smiled, began that mile
And stumbled on that road awhile.

To the East I wave across the sea
To the hills that beckon destiny;
To the heart that still lies beating there
To the breathing, chanting desert air.

J. Peterson

The Weld Shop

Asphyxiation abides inside the mortar leviathan lung broken off by the blinding jailed lightning.

Incendiary specks of steel cascade earthward to die.

The alchemist heirs inside their oxygen boxes break apart into smaller pieces Thor's hammer until the hammer's secrets are not secrets anymore.

The men (and women) spit and smoke and sweat and curse and laugh as the children sleep or play.

I have no doubts that love is the weld of the universe.

Damian Kratt

Untitled

Wondering where you are tonight
Wondering if you're alright
Wondering if I can make it through the day
Wondering if you thinking of me in same way.
Wondering if you holding someone else
Wondering why I'm still here all by my self.
Wondering if we'll ever be together again
Wondering if things would ever be the
way they were back then
Wondering why I still dream of you holding me
Wondering what you think of when you see me
Wondering why we just gave up and said good-bye.
Wondering if it's okay to think of you still and maybe cry.
Wondering if one day I'll ever forget about you.

Shannon Smegal

Marriage

Men and Women have been doing it for years,
Yet for some, the mere thought of the word strikes up fears.
Will it work? Will it last?
Or will this love I feel eventually pass.
It's only natural to have some doubt,
But with God in your life, we'll work it out.
The act of marriage is a sacred affair,
Two lives coming together; forever they will share.
Partners in life; partners forever,
For marriage is an eternal endeavor.
Husband and wife, walking side by side,
Everyone can see them glowing with pride.
Proud to be her husband; proud to be his wife,
As they prepare to embark on their brand new life.
Believe in God and all he can do,
And any problems you have, he'll bring you through.
As we gather today in holy matrimony,
To take part in this special wedding ceremony.
Remember it was God that brought us together,
So we could be happy, forever and ever.

Marlon W. Morgan

Black Cloud

Once there was a little girl,
who loved to run and play,

But on one cool summer's day,
a black cloud moved over were she lay.

Now she sits and cries,
while she wears all black and gray,
for on this day that cloud turned into rain.

Then lighting struck,
and the rain stopped.

For the cloud had a name;
the cloud was a person,
and the cloud went away

Leslie Morgan

Life's A Very Curious Occurrence

Life's a very curious occurrence
I say this cause it happened to me.
I did not ask to be here
but here I am as you can see.

I like to think I'm in control of my life
but this I know just isn't true.
There's a power that's controlling me
and for certain controlling you.

It's been that way since day one
and it will be so in the end.
Nothing in creation can escape this power
I'm telling you the truth my friend.

Life's a very curious occurrence
and though it may seem odd.
The power that's controlling all
we call our Father, God.

LaMar Williams

"Trouty The Fish"

There once was a fish named Trouty
whose habit was being pouty.
One day while swimming in a school,
Trouty, forgot the Golden Rule.
His mother told him not to stray,
as he would lose his way.
He forgot and swam to the deep black hole.
Which looked like a great big bowl.
He was curious so he checked it out,
but he started to pout.
Trouty realized he forgot the rule,
and came across a shark named Mule, who
was the meanest shark around.
He speed off like a zooming car, then he
realized he was too far.
He tried to catch up to the group, but they
looked like a tiny hula-hoop.
He then went home where it was safe,
and ended up having a lot of faith.

Kristen Chase

Thank You, Dad

For coming home from work and
sitting yourself in the den.
Swirling smoke and swilling beer.

For leaving, abandoning me,
For coming to see your three sons on
birthdays and Christmas.
(There are days in between you know).

For missing my graduation and my life.
For never being there when I needed you.
I don't need you anymore.

Thanks for being a role model.

Now, I know what not to do.

Stuart D. Shipley

The Great Land

I came to Alaska on June the twenty third
and this Great Land was more than I had heard.
Amid sounds of spring, I landed a king
and try as I might, I never saw the night.
I traveled far to reach the Malemute Bar
and then on that last night with not one dime
to spare,
I borrowed a gold miner's pan and went
home a millionaire.

Samuel McAlees Jr.

Aperitif

Icebox opening,
opening again.
Clink, clink, clink
into the lion's den.
The caustic roar of laughter
barbaric and untrue,
voices rise, unyielding
words are colored black, and blue.

Mommy, Mommy smells like wine,
and smoke forever lingers.
Wrapping, twisting round my face
with smelly, see-through fingers.

Open windows, cover-up, under eye concealer.
Noon time headaches, half awake
in the morning things are realer.

Ice box opening, opening again.
clink, clink, clink into the lion's den.
(Beastly heads all spinning from
a feast of liquid food)
Mommy, Mommy I'm afraid, will they eat me, too?

Courtney Maum

Untitled

I tried to write a little verse
To tell my love for you
But after several lines like this
There was nothing else to do,
But saying words we use each day
My darling I love you.

I wrote that you were like a valentine
To me through all the years
That your love had always been so sweet
Through days of sunshine and tears.

But all these words still could not tell
The thoughts so deep within my heart
Is simply this, I've loved you dearly
Always and ever from the start.

Virginia Alexander

"Fear"

Fear: Is that unknown feeling all mortals harbor deep within their souls.
Appearing, with its many faces, destroying young love
and imposing on dreams and goals.
Life through the eyes of a blind man, never to know
what fate has in store. Forever darkness—forever darkness,
blind fear, prior to keying every locked door.
Fear knows no time, day or place, nor has a preference
in the color or race.
Fear can turn best of friends into deadly foes when
faced between survival or demise.
Wrongly stripping the pure innocence of man or woman,
once meek, forever now, fear wise.
When faced with sheer horror your breath will hollow.
You'll shiver, shake, mouth dry as a bone, for
it's the fear of the unknown that's soon to follow.
Seeing no death in darkness, not knowing what awaits.
"We" can simply turn a light on or fight back for what fear takes.
So don't fear what you can't light up or see.
Instead, give a gentle prayer for the blind man,
Who's "Fear" won't let him be free.

Dale Neider

"Enchantment"

As we walked along the beach, hand in hand,
we left our imprints in the sand.
The imprints show where we've been,
but no one knows where they end.
As we glanced over the scenery, in a daze,
we were enchanted by the moons beautiful rays.
We sat and watched as the stars twinkled bright,
as a boat sailed out of sight.
As I looked across the sea,
all I thought about was you and me.
I thought of all the wonderful times we've shared together,
and I know that I will love you forever.
I love you so very much,
you're the only woman I want to touch.
As we sat beside the sea,
I realized just how much you mean to me.

Brian Floyd

After The Storm

You are firm again leafy bough
The blast is silent now
Your tender stems are twisted
Your crown is bending low.

Tomorrow you will rise a scruple
Day after, yet another.
You may never reach as high
But pose a new found vert.

These brambles are for you to flaunt,
This hoary branch not without song.
A kindly hand may even weed
The weather beaten blossoms.

You'll be measured by the new growth,
Prodigal roses trusted to a proud parade.
After the storm your trial ends,
Mine will have just begun.

Elsie Abrams Mathias

Loving Him

You know you shouldn't think about him
the way he always hurts you
but all you can remember are the good times
you went through
you imagine yourself holding him,
so close to your body
talking about anything and everything there was
to get him out of your mind will be a task
but everyone says you'll make it
what do they know about love, they aren't in it
as deep as you
when you lay down and think about him at night
don't forget the warnings, don't forget the fright
don't forget the warm feeling of holding him in the night
you will always remember the love of him.

Kristi Burzyck

Free To Be Me

Free to be me, to float high in the sky
Free to be me, to break down and cry
Free to be me, allows a time to be quiet
Free to be me allows a time to riot.
Free to be me means moments of bliss
Free to be me are moments like this
So life has its pleasure
Oh yes! Life has its pains
But life has little meaning unless
I'm free to be me.

Theodore Anderson

Untitled

As I detach and ponder.
  Confused with 1000 questions.
One constant thought grabs and preserves
  the well of life
To that universal question
  What am I here for ?
  What is the meaning of life?
It is to know sadness for strangers
  as if they were family.
To help someone in times of chaos
  without a thought.
To trust my reflexes
  for they are braver than I.
Because people like me
  are here to remind us all
  of what is good and
  what is kind.

Debbie Eisenberg

Erin

I watched as baby Erin slept,
And wondered of her dreams.
What secrets in those blue eyes kept,
Like the cool of early morn she lies serene.

In afternoon dressed for sun and summer beach,
Will dance upon the sand.
In evening stretched on tippy toe,
She'll reach and take my hand.

What delights for you what throe?
This bud of life unfolding,
Forever in the hollows of my heart I'm holding.
She lies in quiet like hushed flecks of snow.

I watched as Erin slept,
While something deep inside me wept.

Mari Shaffer

To Anyone Who Cares

To anyone who cares,
Somewhere a child is dying
For somebody who cares, her mother is crying.
Each moment spent,
Is worth each cent,
To anyone who cares.

To anyone who cares,
A country is at war,
To anyone who cares,
It causes blood and gore,
Each searing pain
Is another's gain
To anyone who cares.

To anyone who cares,
A man can't find a home,
To anyone who cares,
He is all skin and bone,
Each passer-by who sees him,
Will not help him,
To anyone who cares

Lacy M. Harrison

I'm The One Who Really Loved You

I'm the one who really loved you.
I'm the one who really cared.
I am the one my darling who will always be there
when there is no love to share.
I am the one my darling who needs to know,
if you really love me, or should I go!

George C. Vidal

Broken Flame

A flame has been burning for over a year... Unrequited.
Confusion took its toll and made me into a fool, not
seeing the light. I lived in the dark for too long.
One hour of 24 is spent with him, only he's too far away.
An arrow pierces my heart as he spends the whole hour
talking to a girl whose picture I wish would be
over the bull's-eye of my dartboard.
I pretend they're not there, but ignoring them only
pushes the arrow in farther.
I catch her eye as she lets out a girlish squeal
at something he says.
He flashes that gleaming white smile of his and I have to look away.
Her game plan of making me jealous is working to perfection.
Why does she have to flirt with the guy of my dreams
when she already has someone to call her own?
The bell rings and I rush out, his perfect smile
still haunting my mind.
An unexpected visit 20 minutes later sends my mind reeling crazily.
His visit is so I could watch him leave.
The flame flickered as he walked out the door, leaving my world.

Rea Zastrow

Friendship

Friendship is a tapestry, woven from people and events
Friendship is a tapestry, woven from happiness and sorrow
Friendship is a tapestry, woven from colorful threads
The threads are births and deaths, weddings and anniversaries
The threads are graduations and promotions, good times and distress
Colorful events woven by colorful people
Weave the tapestry called friendship
Did you make a new friend today?
Did you work the loom
And weave your tapestry?
People - sorrow - events - happiness
Create a multicolored tapestry, create a multifaceted jewel
Friendship is a tapestry, framed with exquisite jewels
Be patient, your tapestry takes time
Old friends - new friends, threads and gems
Work the loom and weave the tapestry
That is now a multicolored work of art
Friendship

Robert V. Swanson

What Is Love?

What is love? What is love?
That is a question within itself.
Some people say "love is sweet, kindness,
non-racists towards others, sex and pumpering"
would you agree? People on the daily
talk shows on T.V. say "Love isn't hitting,
hate, nor name calling but can we work things
out or should I get out?" What is love? Women
say "Love is caring, feelings and romance" but
how are they treating their men and how are
their men treating them? What is love?
I don't care what everyone else say, but
I defined love as living and dying, to
give life and understanding the need for death
to die for or grant death for someone so that
they can live or release from pain. Is
that love? Or is all the above love? If not
then the question will always remain
what is love?

Tomiko Gilmore

Easter

My God... my saviour
Oh the pain you suffered.
I am counted among the scum of the earth.
Yet... it was for me, you died.

My God... my saviour
Oh glorious lamb of my redemption.
I am now counted among the white-robed throng.
Yes... it was for me, you arose.

My God... my saviour,
Oh the truths you have to teach.
I am dumbfounded, awed by your patience.
Spirit... my footsteps are yours to guide.

My God... my saviour
Oh the infinity of your grace.
I oft would fail, but for your hand.
Father... your love will enfold me forever.

Frank Kessler

Thicket

In traveling on train tracks
reminders of the raining metal
fabric of the tricky steam engine
and flavor in the mud puddle's air sealants
fascinating form on (in it body) all together
but then again one together too much of the same thing
said over the nasty boastful rhyme
I organized the zig zag and the stream
consciousness dips in and out of freudian psychology
tells me how to twist the turning white stallion
part of the page hat makes a bee-line
I change the end of the page to a circle
so it's tipped and not intent on disrupting longer quatrains

[Quietly step aside (give way) to the emerged feeling
from many thickets of bushes and bushels of word's scream]
is the tool of a poet...

Nathan Klay

The Plan

Somewhere beyond man's finite wisdom there is a plan.
A plan that was, is, and always will be.
A plan that is so grand that it surpasses all creeds,
proclamations and startling discoveries.
This plan is too great to be contained within the walls of
magnificent
cathedrals, nor yet in the confines of humble dwellings where two or
three are gathered.
Men throughout the ages have searched and indulged a lifetime in
pursuit of questioning the plan—to somehow make sense of its
existence yet they have come away empty—the plan always within
grasp—yet elusive.
This plan can not be defined by geographical location—it's universal.
This plan can not be defined by race, status, money and
accomplishments
it soars above outward superfluities and reaches within to
search the contents of the heart, the eyes of the soul.
Though I may live to be one hundred, travel the world far and wide,
and amass fortunes untold, I will be no closer to understanding the
plan—for it is not for me to understand, but faith believe.
The plan is God.
He was, is, and always will be.

Christine Maria B. Campbell

Bow - Wow Blues

Although I may be very small
I still need love and care.
You see, I've been taken from my Mom
which seems to me unfair.

I had some brothers, sisters too!
I wonder where they are?
Hopefully they found happy homes
whether near or far.

They say that time heals all wounds
I can only hope that's true.
Then as I grow older
I'll be relieved from these Bow - Wow blues.

So if at first when you've brought me home
I whine and lay around
Remember, you're a stranger to me.
But soon I'll grow to love you
Then friends we'll forever be!

Karen Lee

What I Never Said

There was something I wanted to tell you, but I wasn't sure how.
There was something I wanted to do, but I wasn't sure what.
There was something I wanted to know, but I wasn't sure how to ask.
So the things I never said stood between us, and I wasn't sure how to reach you.
There was somewhere I wanted to go, but I wasn't sure how to take the first step.
Somehow I wanted to fly, but I was too afraid to spread my wings.
There was a story I wanted to write, but I wasn't sure what words to use.
So we grew further apart because I was standing still, and I wasn't sure how to move.
There was something I wanted to give you, but I wasn't sure what you would want.
There was something I wanted to teach, but I had no one who wanted to learn.
There was something I wanted to share, but there was no one there to listen.
So what could I do when all the things I never said, never
tried, never did, never *knew*, were the wall in between,
and I wasn't sure how to breach it.
There was something I wanted to tell you, but I wasn't sure if you wanted to hear.
There was somewhere I wanted to go, but I wasn't sure if I could make it alone.
There was someone I wanted to be, but I wasn't sure who she was.
There was so many things, so many places, so many people, so
many *words*, that I wasn't sure of anything.

Amanda Marie Cuca

Why?

I do not understand
what my purpose is
why some people can brutally murder others
why our planet is not taken care of
But most of all
I do not understand
why people do not take responsibility for their own actions
many people have watched their family and friends
suffer for other people's actions and wrongdoings
What I understand most is music
it can exaggerate whatever mood I am in
and it can change my mood from one to another
it does whatever I want it to do
and has no objection in the matter

Collin O'Neil

Imprisonment

It doesn't take walls or bars to make a prison.
Sometimes all it takes is one person or a feeling.
And the hopeless thought of all escape can make you
feel scared; abandoned from any knowledge you may have obtained.
There comes a time when a decision must be made;
attempt escape or wait out the sentence.
Those who manage to break free from the self-endured prison
will find a life that has waited for them to find, and
will be marked with a glow of happiness no one could miss or
help to wonder at.
But what happens to the ones who miss their chance for freedom
or denies themselves parole?
Life, happiness is sucked from them until their eyes grow dim
and their faces are etched with a sadness only they can explain,
but plain for the world to see.
To break free from the trials of self-imprisonment, one must
believe they could rule the world and understand that the
light at the end of the tunnel is waiting for them to arrive.
Otherwise...who is left to dig yourself out?
Because sometimes you are your only friend.

Terri L. Gilliam

Guns — Guns

The Winchester killed the Buffalo; the Indian.
The 30-06 killed the grizzly; the Elk; the Wolf.
How many? The gun will never know,
Nor we, the knowledge to possess.

For, the West we won; eliminated the rest.
No differentiation by the gun.
No remorse, or conscience had we.
Greed was the motive, no need.

Love was not there.
Nor had we the need of God.
The aim distorted; for what purpose the Target?
For no avail. Missed was the good; only evil prevailed.

Let these guns hang on the mantle, oh Warren,
And on the walls of generations to come,
As a symbol of all the evil that has past,
Never to be again.

Anthony Marinaccio

Untitled

The watch tower of lands escaping paths,
Small stepping stones of life,
Everyone falls.
Jump into your thoughts, forget your
Insanity.
Don't except the unexpecting sorrows of life.
I can wait, and hope.
But what foregoes in it all.
Anywhere is the real designation.
The home away from home.
Ah, yes the lightly dampen air that rest upon
My flesh its awaking coolness warms my heart.
The breeze above me like rushing sprit's that
Flee to their never found homes,
All this I feel, yes I am real.

Susan Rivett

I Am

I am a song without a melody.
I am busy but I have nothing to do.
I am a raging river washed up by the sea.
I am a skirt pink, long, and swaying with she.
I am the golden book which is used over and over again.
I am a weeping willow crying about life and death.
I am a red pen but I write in blue.

Meghan Apfelbaum

Comfort For A Term

In the first blush of morning,
Each straying swell simultaneously seeks serenity,
As it surges towards the shore.

Added to the ocean's tint,
The sun's reflective beams of light softly shine,
With each whispering whitecap that breaks upon the shore,
with graceful succession.

Set so steadfast, within the sandy berm,
Is that mass of timber; An invitation, A familiar resting spot,
Our comfort for a term.

We sit and watch each wandering wave,
That waits at the edge of the beach.
To glance down the coastline,
To see its bold beauty, of the land and the sea,
Where together, in a visionary rendezvous, they will meet.

David J. Ogilvie

The Key

On a rainy day
something glimmers as the sun emerges
form the dismal sky.
I reach into the water
and pull out a key shining with silver and gold.
What could it be? A key to a palace
where the queen sat in her royal throne
and watched the sun set through the pane
glass window?
Or could it be a key to a young girl's jewelry box
in which beautiful gems sparkled
waiting, hoping to be shown to the world in pride.
Or could it be a key to a candy store,
where spice drops and chocolate kisses
lingered in the autumn air
as school children peered through the
windows, hoping for just one bite.
What could it be? What could it be?
I know now, that it was all of those things.
For that key was the key to my imagination.

Janelle Peterson

Serenity

The sky on that summer eve was a bright vermilion hue.
The rock bound coast was softly caressed by ocean tides.
It seemed that the whole world was at peace - where
Colorful lobster buoys gently rose and fell with the surging swells.
An hypnotic trance pervaded all earthly things
When the skirl of an ancient melody shattered this ethereal silence.
Across this tiny bay, on a promontory of sand and rocks,
In the full glory of a kilt of Stewart Tartan
And with a Glengarry' o'er his brow,
Stood a "Piper" gazing out to sea.
Nestled in his arm was the symbol that is of Scotland "The Pipes."
There, across that tranquil water inlet and bourne
On the gentle breeze begot of heavenly winds,
Came the profound definition of true Caledonia,
Not of "Flow Gently Sweet Afton" — But
The melodious, wistful and unforgettable notes of — "Amazing Grace"
As can only be heard through the Pipes of the ancient Gaels.
At that moment — the world stood still:
And the earth, and the sky and the waters of the sea
All were cast in spell of serenity — by that Piper on that knoll.

Curt W. Perdelwitz

In God's Name

In God's name the things we can do.
Murder ten million because they are Jew.
Enslave ten million because they're not white.
Torture those that will not fight.
Wage wars that light up the sky,
Vow in His honor to live or to die.
In God's name the blood that is shed,
For teachers and preachers
that mess with your head.
To hate difference
whenever it came.
And do it all proudly
In God's Name.

Zach Howard

Time

Time is an endless song,
Time is like infinity, eternity-
Time is something we make for
the people we love.
Time is like money, we can
never make enough of it.
Time is a magazine that keeps
us current with changing events.
Christmas time is when children's
eyes are filled with sugarplums and fairies.

Time is 24 hours every day
of the week and every month

Time is a precious gift
you give to your neighbor-
Day time is a time to work-
Night time is when we sleep.

Carol L. Wallis

A Wonderful World

The sun can shine down on a dark, stormy day;
A blizzard can fall in the middle of May;
Flowers can blossom where there are no seeds;
Grass can grow greener where there's nothing but weeds.

Your heart will shine through on the worst of your days;
give up the fight, it'll show you the way.
Nightmares will seem few and far apart
For happiness brings only joy to your heart.

Your eyes only see what you want them to see;
Look at a swamp and know an ocean it can be.
Open your eyes to the beautiful view
Of a wonderful world made only for you.

Julie M. Blodgett

Think Of Me

When you walk down life's rugged road,
Think of me tho I'm not there.
When your sorrows become a heavy load,
Within your heart I will be near.

Once in a while, just whisper my name,
Whether with a tear or with a smile.
Live life and its mysterious game,
Think of me and walk another mile.

And if again in life we never meet,
Then think of the love we once shared.
In a crowded bus, or on a lonely street,
Remember that I always cared.

Betty M. Depuy

Gossip

Ring!
Hi honey! How're ya doing?
Have you heard the 411?
Oh, I heard that Jack is suing his wife Jill for their dear son.
Have you heard 'bout dear old Molly
And her daughter Anna-Jane
At the time of snow and holly
She'll be walking down the lane
Yes, she'll marry wealthy Johnny
And she'll leave her dear old mom
That he'll have her I find funny
Since she's slept with every Tom
Oh my dear, I must be going
My in-laws might come at eight
I must dye my roots, they're showing
So I hope they're really late
But I'll keep near by the window
And watch as gossip forms
And don't worry dear, I'll call you
And I'll keep you quite informed. Click!

Adrienne Daring

Emotions

Tis sorrow's moment shall never part
It's burrowed deep inside my heart
A tear for a moment's waking
Death is in the making
Artist's bear their souls delight
People's insides are black as night
Lover's whispers are affair
Selfish is yet to share
Hurt is jealous for a common thing
My anger exerts like a roaring spring
For all the good, for all the bad
For all the angels not yet sad
Emotions covered like a blanket over a sheepish child
Your mind starts flaring and running wild
A hearts passion is yelling out in pain
Voices talk to you telling you you're not sane
In a deep dark alley
Through a wild blooming valley
You caress, you feel emotions that are real

Sunny Culp

Children Of Light

How beautiful the roses grow
Pampered by loving, caring hands
That willingly nourish and protect
from harmful intruders
Until the mystery of birth is revealed
The delicate blossom softly open
Its beauty enhanced by a sweet
savorily scent
That quietly perfume the air
More precious than the rose are
Children
Requiring the same love as the rose
Pampered by the loving, caring hand
Gentle voice echoing praises of admiration
Always protecting with abounding love
As the body and soul are nurtured
from the patient heart of the caretaker
Who faithfully tends the children adored by the Master
Tenderly molding characters that radiate light
For such is the Kingdom of Heaven

Joyce Marie Johnson

Ode To Anna Maria Isle

The early morning breezes stir
Frothy fringe on waves of blue,
The sun begins its stately rise
With rays of glorious hue.
The sea gulls call, the sea oats sway
While sandpipers march in a row,
Sand dollars and the starfish wake
To join in nature's show.
The palm trees wave a proud salute
To pelicans as they fly,
While dolphins rise and dip again
As they go gliding by.
The ibis and the herons prance
With stately charm and grace,
While sea and sand and azure sky
Melt in a fond embrace.
Of all the places here on earth
Of every kind and style,
The one that nature blessed the most
Is Anna Maria Isle.

Genevieve Alban

They Say The Grass Is Greener...

I come home to open arms, a smile and an uplifting voice after a long day. The warmth of home quickly drives the cold inside away. Encouragement and kindness are her covering. Her skin is oiled with the touch of compassion. It is readily shared whenever I am dry. Her lips are softened with words of love. Her heart is full of forgiveness. I find myself in a green pasture, as my feet are softened as I walk along the grass.

There is the other pasture that I am told exists. The grass is brown which is quickly painted green. Their arms are found empty and no voice receives them as their day never ends. Their home is a ruin, as the cold breeze snuffs out the memory of a warmer place. Despair and loneliness are their covering. Their skin is dry, seeking for oil, but cannot find it. Love and forgiveness are as a passing stranger in their eyes. Their stomachs are filled with painted grass.

They say the grass is greener...

Chris Burroughs

Recognize When You Are Loved

The person who loves you, loves you because he or she loves you.
That's it. No further explanations are needed.
No explanations make sense of love anyway. Where there is
powerful reason, and a strong burning need for someone to love you,
then the love that results is risky and can suddenly disappear.
The people who cling to you may try to make you feel secure
even powerful at times. But in time their love will smother you
and you'll reject them. But the ones who allow you to be free and
be yourself, they are the ones who really love you.
Never allow anyone to control you. Or you will come to hate
yourself for being susceptible to being bought off so easy.
Never allow anyone to believe that you don't know the difference
between real love and fawning. These people insult your intelligence.
The love that is ours, is the Most Real Of All Loves
Because, it exists for itself. Without reasons, conditions, or excuses.
When you find someone who loves you for the person that you are,
the way you do things, your sense of humor, your personality
or because this person likes the way he or she feels about
themselves in your presence. So be true to this person
because this person mirrors your best.

Ralph Bease

Velvet Sky

Twilight grasps the nighttime's hem, and
pulls it softly round.
Gathers shades of palest blue, to form
a glittery purple crown
Plumping fluffy clouds unseen, to make
pillows huge and cool. To comfort mother
Earth. From her daily toil and rule.
When morning breaks and dawn awakes
heavy, and filled with stars and dreams
the velvet cover of evening's sky will ever
so gently be rolled and stored. Placed neat
and tidy tucked, from heavenly view.
Until tomorrow when eager shadows, start
to mix and mingle with indigo blues.
Like a silken sail, or fine gossamer wing
Heaven's dazzling evening cape.
Bejeweled, now twinkles, it is, a wondrous thing!

Sharon Grove Mack

Untitled

I lie awake, my insides screaming. Misery kills me, but my heart remains, beating. I gave my heart to you. You left me empty, broken, lost. You gave me a match to burn my soul. I helped you lite it. I didn't know what would become of it...of me. I drank your lies, you drank some too. I got close to be pushed away, I opened up to be deceived, I gave but you never knew of my uncurable desire. I built up my hopes and dreams in you. You handed me the blocks. Did you know what you were saying? Did you know the meaning of your touch? You gave me no warning. Just walked away as my everything was washed away. I was left with nothing. It was all for nothing, because what you gave is quickly fading. Your words haunt me. Your memory passes numbly through my mind. I scream for your love, but how can someone miss what they never possessed? I have survived the worst storm. I am left with nothing. I must begin again.

Marissa Wilkin

Grab A Book

Grab a book, and find a nook,
The pleasure you will find;
The places books can take you,
Will simply blow your mind.
The how-to books will teach you,
The garden books enjoy;
The antique books for collectors, they bring a lot of joy.
Books on famous people, days and weather too;
Books that make delicious sights, in menus for me and you.
Books for cleaver children, to create or simply enjoy;
A book can be a wonder, or fantasy,
For some reading girl or boy.
Books on tours of the white house,
Or books on dieting style;
Books on music, to start you humming;
Books that spell words, like smile.
Books are found in the Library, or even in a home;
Just grab a book, and find a nook, and enjoy yourself alone.

Shirley Allen

Rose

The flower inside me begins to wilt,
the one I love no longer cares for me.
The world's poisons are too harsh,
they ruin my leaves.
My family throws stones but are unaware.

If someone doesn't water me soon I may curl and die.

Tammy Tabbert

Pricked By The Thorn

One pleasantly rainy day, I was walking down the street.
I stopped and noticed a black rose, laying at my feet.
I bent down and picked it up, I saw a petal torn.
I held it by its long green stem, but I was pricked by the thorn.
The cut slowly opened, and the blood trickled down
I needed a bandage, but there was none around.
Pretty soon the cut on my finger really started to sting.
I never knew I could get hurt by such a beautiful thing.
I looked again at the flower, where the petal was torn.
I held the rose tighter, and again I was pricked by the thorn.
Again the cut opened, and again the blood trickled down.
The blood and the rain mixed together and formed a red puddle on the ground.
Slowly the sting increased, and I could not stand the pain.
So, I just sat down, and became lost in the rain.
No one came to help me, I don't think they gave a care,
Because I was really bleeding and they just left me there.
The tears continued to fall, from my red eyes.
There was a crowd forming, but they ignored my cries.
Then a lady ran to me, and tried to catch her breath.
She told me about the black rose; the black rose meant death.

Kimberly Millette

Take Heed

In times of trouble and times of need
your prayers are all answered if you will take heed.

Sometimes the answers are not as we guess,
Sometimes He says No Sometimes He says Yes.
The outcome or ending are all for the best.

He knows what we do He knows what we need.
His guidance surrounds us if we will take heed.

He asks for so little yet gives us so much.
The little he asks is to just stay in touch.

Thank Him for your blessings and all that is right.
Ask Him for forgiveness and guidance at night.

He will double your blessings and help with your need
If you ask so sincerely and then just take heed.

Those feelings you get when you know you've done wrong
Are His way of saying "I love you - be strong."

You are Never alone, please keep this in mind.
His Grace is forgiveness, His Mercy divine.

As long as there is prayers as long as you need
His answers will come have patience-take heed.

Sheryl L. Everett

Night Sky

I looked at the night sky, and what did I see.
The stars were just hanging there looking at me.
I took a deep breath and shut my eyes,
stretched out my arms, and to my surprise,
Floated up on a sea of fresh air
and sang to the moon, while I was there.
A lullaby so gentle and deep,
I watched the moon as he fell asleep.
The sun woke up. I saw him rise.
'It's time to wake!' The cockrell cries.
And so I drifted back to earth upon an azure stream.
To find that I was in my bed and it was just a dream.

Margaret A. Coley

"Of Her"

If a vibrant beam of unfiltered light
made its way through a twisted road-map
of living leaves to my squinting eyes —

shaded from the wooded wonder of refracted
luminescence by my slightly bent,
much-scarred fingers —

diminished into the greatest amount of
brilliance my dilated being could withstand,
—a mere light-drop in the light-ocean that is her —

my mind, unencumbered by the nervy optic windows in my head,
could create an image almost as dazzling in the darkness,
the depths of the universe that is my existence —

as the beauty found in the simple clarity,
the inestimable softness of lamplight,
bathing her face in its pale, purring glow.

Paul William Moser

Living Hell

My life is such a living hell, yet no one can really even tell.
I can't go a day without crying, sometimes I often feel like dying.
It really shouldn't be this way, the sun should shine at least
one day.
Responsibilities I cannot take, broken promises that they make.
Asking for money I will not get, hoping that I shall have it yet.
Guys not really helping me much, only wanting to kiss and touch.
Why can't I have what I want?, in my sleep I hear the taunt.
I have so many best friends, all of them wanting to repair the mends.
But it doesn't help for some reason, I'm always in the dreary season.
Mom and Dad make it hard, I'm always caught way off guard.
So much pressure I'm not used to, so much stuff I have to do.
I just want a break from everything, to relax, laugh and maybe sing.
A paradise place I surely need to be, so that I might set my mind free
For Mom, I hold my head high, but lately I only break down and cry.
I've kept it a secret all this time, but now I really don't even mind.
I just want them to be proud, but I can't with this big black cloud.
I've tried to get over this spell, but all I ever do is dwell.
I hate it so much it makes me mad, I'm so sick and tired of being
sad.
My life is such a living hell, now can you actually tell?

Cameron Davis

On Turning 68

My hands tell the story of my years,
liver spots, prominent veins —
It's no surprise, they've done a lot!

My face is somewhat saggier now,
my eyes a little watery and tired.
But the spark is still there!

The largest change, though, is not seen.
I feel at home inside this body now.
I never used to, and that's gone

There is a centeredness, a sureness
in my cronedom that I treasure.
Yes, enduring has brought wisdom.

I don't mind the wrinkles, I earned each
and every one. In fact, I like not being
vulnerable in the way of the young any more.

My survival kit's humor, and knowing things will
change - no matter how good or bad - I like that!

Bonnie Gardner

My Dream Of Heaven

One moonlit night when I was asleep
I had a glorious dream;
My life on Earth had ended
I was in God's Realm.

I saw His Golden Mansion
With shining lights aglow;
Radiant angels sang and danced
In the Garden just below.

A fanfare on trumpets sounded
As I stopped into the Hall;
Chandeliers with colored lamps
Were a twinkling on each Wall.

I saw Him sitting on His throne
Ringed by angels gay;
His face shone like the Morning Star
At the break of day.

He rose and came to greet me
Amidst music soft and clear;
That flowed from harps with golden strings
And violins everywhere.

"Come My Faithful One", He said,
"Your deeds were kind and true;
Welcome to My Blessed House!
My Peace I give to you."

My Earthly sorrows did seem small
As I gazed into His eyes;
Tumultuous joy awoke me
From my trip to Paradise.

So as my fateful days draw near
Though bitter they may seem;
I'll praise His Holy Name each day
And think always at my dream!

Andrew Zamal

A Tribute In Memory Of Elvis Presley

Elvis was a superstar quite special and unique
And fans came from everywhere to hear him sing or speak
He had a touch of magic that no one could bind
His voice was smooth as honey and his manner was kind.

He had a twinkle in his eye and a lopsided grin
That drove folks wild when they got a glimpse of him
His rhythm was most perfect and his voice pure as gold
And crowds followed after him both the young and old.

Although he was a superstar he kept the common touch
Always giving to others who did not have as much
Being quite humble he said don't call me king
The true king is Jesus who called me to sing.

Now somewhere there is peace, somewhere there is love
And somewhere there is joy in a land up above
For someone there is singing a brand new song
Accompanied by the angels around God's throne.

Elvis is in heaven now singing around God's throne
No longer is he lonesome for now he is home
And happy there with Jesus and the angels above
For Elvis was a Jesus fan with a heart of love.

Elizabeth B. Arney

Spring Bouquet

Flowers are so beautiful when they are in full bloom,
When their petals fall to the ground at once they are consumed.
I'm so glad we have the flowers forever to enjoy;
The memories of their beauty forever to employ.

Beverly A. Lee

Darkness Before Dawn

When the three days of darkness will hover the earth
We'll kneel and we'll pray for the dawn of rebirth.

We'll be warned by the powers of water and fire
As they purify the earth of hate and desire.

But why must the innocent suffer and die
While others sit back and not even cry?

The prophets foresaw the misery and pain;
Where on the earth can life still sustain?

But just as the night caresses the dawn;
So does one life end and another is born.

A glimmer of hope for those who just cared;
Those are the few whose lives will be spared.

For when you least expect
And close your eyes at night,
You will not be awakened by
The warmthness of the light.

Josephine Giordano

My Friend, My Brother

Born to a world that can be so unforgiving.
With all its trials and tribulations constantly thrust upon you.
I know better than most, that you faced them as a true warrior,
and never let it be said that your metal failed when tested.

All who have gathered, and all others who knew you and cared,
should know and I hope understand....
That just as a warrior grows weary of the battle,
so too did you grow weary of this world.

But I say this, To All, fear not for our brother, our friend...
for he dealt with more than his fare share of pain while on
this earth... that he could go nowhere else,
save that of a far, far better place.

I know we all share the same prayer, and may his kind and caring,
yet, melancholy soul, know peace, forever more.

Farewell
Your friend
Your brother

Thomas M. Healey Jr.

A Mothers Pride

We sit and talk over coffee
You tell me about your day.
We don't see each other often
So I treasure each thing you say.

Your eyes are bright blue and expressive
How grown up you've become so fast.
I see myself holding an infant
then remember — 19 years have passed.

You are sensitive, caring and loving
You work hard and have become a success.
You've accomplished so much in such a short time
For all this I thank God and feel blessed.

Thank you Lord for your special gift
a little boy entrusted to me.
A little boy who's become a man
And a mom who's as proud as can be.

Sheila A. Gallagher

Dear Child Of Mine

I held you in my womb for a very short
time. I hardly knew you were there. The
Lord whom I have known, came to take you
home. To my great despair. I have wept
for you. My heart has ached for you. I
have had anger toward the Lord I once
knew. Today my dear child, I have knelt
at the feet of our Lord and asked for
his forgiveness for my selfishness and
anger toward him. He has forgiven me.
As for you my dear child are in heaven.
One day I shall meet you there, where
we shall share all eternity.

Sharon M. Hurdt

Freedom In Light

I escaped death through the freedom of Light.
Panting, running scared like a wind escaping a storm.
I left it all behind.
Peace closed in, where once nonexistent.
I could not in death breath the Light, the freedom of the Light.
It was enclosure that scared my soul into pleading to find a new way.
So lonely.
Emptiness was like the air I breathed.
When once I was dead it was all fake,
I looked at nothing real except for when I read the Light.
I breathe the Light.
It is my life.
Death is no more than a crows laugh, nor a bears growl.
No more death, only life.
I have the Light of the soul!
Freedom in Light!

Leah S. Ahrendsen

Mothers

Have you ever thought,
"Who are mothers?"
They stand alone above all others.
They treat us like we're the very best,
even after we all have flown the nest.
When life gets tough and we lose our way,
Mom's always there to save the day.
She shows no favorites, this one called
"Mother"
We're treated the same,
whether sister or brother.
We often forget what you've done for us,
and there's just one thing that is a must.
To repay your kindness, what can we do?
Let's pause and say,
"Mom, I love you."

James H. McFalls

Untitled

Waitin' in my cell of solitude
Daze er jus minutes in the grand scheme of things
Dreamin' an written all at the same time
Dawn rolls round turn me into a slave
For to pay the bills then it's back again
To my little box to wait for somethin'
Yet I do not know
Awakenin' my spirit setting it free
It's out there somewhere
But where I don't know
It's coming for me someday I hope
Maybe it's here already inside
The slow burn
I feel late at night
Waitin' in my cell of solitude

D. Brooks

God's Controversy

God's whisper is like the devil's sigh. The faint sound of eternity blows past your unlistening ears. The great sound would tell you who it is if only you would listen. When you listen the hearts and souls tell you your answers and your unfortunate, or fortunate future. It all lies in your hands, which one will bypass your pure ears.

Donna Reid

My Father

My father's voice is like thunder roaring in the night,
My father's weight is very light,
His arms are long and muscular in every single way,
He is always awake at the beginning of the day, My father is so cool,
He always listens when I tell him about my school,
My father understands me and I am really glad he does,
I really love my father because of all the great things he does,
My father, my brother.

Jennifer Ross

Blind Old Man

It was a damp, dark night
not a sound could be heard
except the dwellings of an old
blind man
Yet the old man would not be heard
trying to make a stand.
He'd roam down the streets
asking for help
looking for shelter from the rain.
No one would help
with more than a penny,
they didn't understand his pain.
It was a hot, dry day
and a million sounds could be heard
except the dwellings of an old blind man....
simply because no one
would listen

Melissa Dattesla

Passages Of The Soul

In the darkest depths of your darkest despair,
Your mind starts to wonder when last you were there

Your heart feels like splinters all prickly and sharp,
and your nerves feel as taut as the strings on a harp

You wonder, you wonder which way is out,
And you dread this feeling of creeping doubt

Overwhelming sadness seems to consume you,
And you search for the place where happiness knew you

It seems it wasn't that long ago,
Yesterday maybe, but you don't know

What brought you here to this place so cold,
Where your heart is weary and your body feels old

You feel numb and frightened and you want to go back,
But you can't remember where you lost track

You know you must find your way back to the light,
For a little happiness you'll have to fight

Kathleen M. Miller

The Dogwood

The hills roll, smiling, smitten with signs of spring;
Impressionistic white and pink-washed light
Reveal the momentary glimpse of our King.

The dogberry wood does bear a special thing,
Its flower is stained on its tips like the wounds of Christ;
The hills roll smiling, smitten with signs of spring.

A dove is perched on a sturdy branch to sing,
"Accept the peace, these trees of pink and white,
That reveal the momentary glimpse of our King."

Its close grained wood, a rood, would stab and sting
The body of Christ, while He arose on his plight;
The hills roll smiling, smitten with signs of spring.

The pistil forms the heart, a perfect ring;
Its core, between cross-like bracts, holds tight
The petals that reveal the momentary glimpse of our King.

The dogwood blossom is white as the dove's clean wing,
And pink when wounded feathers broke its flight.
The hills roll smiling, smitten with signs of spring.
That reveals a momentary glimpse of our King.

Leah Jorgensen

Everyday Pace

January, February, March
We march on all year
The mighty moe catch as we go
Spring time is near summer came
With all the games, losers, winners
birthdays are bright with all the
nights. Happy Birthday little boy
and little girl..
Thanksgiving is near. Invite your
mother and dad and all the children.
Grandfather and grandmother with all smiles.
December is near, roll out the red carpet
Santa Clause knows we are here all the
year. He is here with 12 reindeers
down the chimney he comes
Rudolph the red nosed reindeer.
Merry Christmas and good morning.

Lois L. Hereford

How Could He Not Know?

"Do you love me?" he asked in a thoughtful voice
Doesn't he know I have no choice?
But I'm scared to let my feelings show
How can he not know?

With each and every passing year
My soul mate, my love, grows increasingly dear
To my heart and though my every soul
How could he not know?

With fear has been that he will leave
And I will be the one to grieve
This I always have conceived
How could he not know?
Jesus, my Lord, my comfort at night
Please help me turn this wrong to right
Don't let his love for me grow cold
how could he not know?

My desire is that he will return
And our passion's flame will continue to burn
Forever we will love and grow
How could he not know?

Michele Lindmeier

Let Them That Don't; Know

Children unknowing of knowledge
  Already possessed
Surely more truth held
  Than a scholar professed

What priest be prophet
  More a middleman
Bridging wise men to his student
  Unneeded modification by a miscolored sand.

Pruning a wild rose
  Nature never to behold
Better lived and learned
  Than questionably told.

Michael Sundstrom

Is It You?

Many of us may never see
The truths about ourselves we
Will go through life without the key
To the lock of the things that we could be
Is it you or is it me?
And is there any guarantee?
That these truths will set us free?
To live in peace and harmony?

Karen Kutufaris

Life's Wonders

Part of life is questioning.
Part of life is wondering.
Why, I ask, isn't my life's next event available to see?
Why, I ask, can't I know what will happen to me?
Will I be a success?
Will I wind up a mess?
What will I be?
The future is locked - I need the key!
Will I be wealthy or poor?
Will I travel or tour?
Will I marry with a child?
Will my life be tense or mild, tame or wild?
I want to see what is hid!
I want to use all my strength to pry off the lid!
I want to know!
Then I'll have warning of where I'll go.
Give me an oar, I want to row!
In my own direction, destination, I will go.
I guess the future is not for me to see.
Although I won't stop that from letting me be what I want to be!

Maria Fiorentino

Unexpected Love

I once met a little boy who slipped into my heart.
We headed on our journey, not knowing where to start.
I didn't know how much he'd mean as the years all passed.
I look back now and can't believe the time has gone so fast.

King of the hill, I had to win. His tears I still see.
But it's alright, because I know he didn't, wouldn't blame me.
Then as he grew some more and he went from here to there.
His Jacques Cousteau impersonation almost grayed my hair.

He washed a dish and fished a fish. He rode a bike or two.
Never really had to worry what he was gonna do.
It seemed like no time at all he was finishing school.
Out the door, on his own. Trade the classroom for the tool.

And now he brings a woman, a daughter into my life.
The hopes and dreams and all that goes with being man and wife.
I think of them now and I think of him then.
I don't think I'd mind if we had to do it again.

William Dreisel

Don't Know Why?

Don't know why the clouds are so high?
Don't know why you can't hear the flower's cry?
Don't know why the stars never frown?
Don't know why the earth is so brown?
Don't know why still water runs deep?
Don't know why antelopes leaps?
Don't know why a tear is not rain?
Don't know why a heart ache
Causes so much pain?
Don't need to know all the why's
God is gonna tell us bye, and bye

Jo Anne Sharp

The Little Love I Give To Thee

The little love I give to thee,
I'll love to share till eternity.
The love we have between us now,
Will not part not anyhow.

The little love I give to thee,
Moves like a fire inside of me.
The flame must stay so we don't part,
Don't blow out the wick that holds my heart.

The little love I give to thee,
Extends a hundred miles from sea to sea.
The waves I feel when they hit my back,
I can't help but to think that we lack.

The feelings we'll share,
When we realize how much we care.

Janis Marie Ingersoll

Untitled

Uncomfortable silences
enchants the minds of the spoken
Unable to conceive the moment wasted
A day without words
A night without sleep
Is there a difference
The possibilities to wide
The voice can control the emotions
but the words come out different
Laughter brings on tears
and no one to wipe them away
I need not a voice nor words to communicate
I have what I need
  and silence I choose.

Andrea Ashton

The Rose

  This rose is from my heart.
It is to say that I hope we never part.
  It's not much, that I know,
but I'm not giving it for show.
  I want you to keep it very near
because I love so, my dear.
  You mean so much to me.
That is what I want you to see.
  If you water it every day,
this rose will live and stay.
  Like our love, it will bloom,
and it will never cause you gloom.
  My dear I hope you understand,
this rose is not a demand.
  Yes I love you with all my heart.
I hope this rose will keep us from being apart.

Meredith Watkins

E-COL

Flow - flow - flow!
Follow me 'ere they say,
Take me along and let me see,
The new wonders of the sea.

Here I sit awaiting my turn,
To travel with a raindrop friend.
Take me from this land here, first,
To seek new fields, filled with thirst.

And off to sea, we may go,
To join our new aquatic life.
To swim, dance, and sing with glee,
How wonderful all to be, so free.

Bigger - bigger - bigger!
How we all laughed and grew,
And spread our wings in happy glee,
As on we went in our wasteful spree.

Time - time - and more in time!
We grew untouched in thoughtless care,
Until all was ended, in nature's crowded room.
Taking along all God's work in bloom.

Flossie Patterson

An Exploration Of Teenage Life

The never-ending quest of life,
Hmm...the ponytails or wrists cut by knives,
The thought the forever will love lasts,
The fact of reality never does it surpass,
The time forgotten or...forgotten time,
The sex-filled novels equivalent to nursery rhymes,
The clouds and clowns versus the black and red,
The solemn grass not the feathered bed,
Caught between stalactites and stalagmites not flowers,
The reign of the lion never brought him power,
An entrance for wind or an easy exit,
Pressure on the pedal or easy does it,
A stairway to heaven or a escalator to hell,
Did the demon raise or had it fell,
The talks of revision the changes not made,
The stupidity of questions the coffin later laid,
What to do, to say, to give,
Which one pick, which one to live?

Nicole Oppenheimer

Watching

I once looked in the eyes of a person and saw the soul of a demon.
I saw the hate of a man but ten times as worst.
I saw a woman being scorned and child being beaten.
I heard the faint cry of men, woman, and children
as they walked slowly to their deaths.
I saw cities being bombed and people being shot.
I saw people living on the streets and eating from the ground.
I saw people dying of A.I.D.S. but people
still having unprotected sex.
I saw people being raped and stripped of their dignity
I saw her killing children, woman killing
children, children killing children.
I saw a Black man with a White
woman and a White man killing that
Black man because of that White woman.
I saw Blacks killing Blacks yet their
hands held no guns but tiny crack valves,
At first I did not know into whom eyes I was looking into.
I knew that just one person couldn't have possessed the horrors I saw.
But as I took a closer look my hart started to ache.
Because what I was looking at was the world outside my window.

Jennifer Bryant

Again

Ah, to be a child again,
To sit by a fire and dream
Of knights and kings and dragons,
My, how real they'd seem.

Ah, to be a child again,
To lie on my back in the sun.
Watch fleecy white clouds dancing across the sky
Like so many sheep, on the run.

Ah, to be a child again,
To walk down a moonlit lane,
Where silvery elves play on a carpet of leaves
With such fun, it's not quite sane.

Ah, to be a child again,
When our sand pile could produce a temple,
My, how I long for these little things.
Growing up, we lost the life so simple.

Mary F. Limbaugh Luker

First Dream

When I was sixteen, I began to dream
and see visions I thought I understood.
In my name, I knew there was much good.
In my brain there was much knowledge.

One decision I made was never to be buried in a grave.
Instead I knew, I should be cremated for everyone's good.
My ashes to be spread where I hoped they would bring
physical substance to places and times I could not be.

Now an older child, I dream and see vision
I'm not sure I understand.
I know in the world there is much good,
the brain is a sponge for it will hold much knowledge.

Decisions are made based on experience and knowledge.
Singular decisions are for personal good and
are affected by all other decisions, dreams and visions.
These then complete the dreams and visions of youth.

Garland Lee Hunter

Letting Go

Sinking, falling
deep within the
depths and darkness of the earth,

A body

Like all the rest
yet peaceful at heart
and filled with the sins of those he loved.

Falling, griping the edges
with a force so strong
that nothing would stop him,
He holds on.

Griping, feeling the sins and faults of all
realizing that he must remain faithful,
He lets go.

And sinking,
deep within the
depths and darkness of the earth,
we say goodbye.

Kristina Ybl

She Is Gone

Each day I find myself thinking of you with such ease,
Without your love I just would not be able to breath.

Your love has made me appreciate nature where I can hear all its sounds,
Especially the beautiful notes from song birds that fly all around.

I wake up with the smell of fresh flowers, and the beauty of morning dew.
I'm more at peace with myself and nature, and all that is missing is you.

I can't stop myself from being lost in our love and all the wonderful times,
It's just so nice to have your soul and spirit me, us, weighing heavily on my mind.

Each day I give thanks for all the beautiful things you manage to do,
When I visit the place where you rest, I give thanks for you, still being you.

Dennis Emerson

Thank You

I want to thank you for the way you changed my life.
I think and care more deeply than ever before.
I feel things I haven't felt in a long time.
I hear the sound of my own heartbeat.
I laugh more and cry less.
When I see you some of the pain
in my heart seems to disappear.
Just to hear the sound of your
voice brings a smile to my face
and a feeling I never want to stop.
You have touched my heart and
I'll never be the same.
For once in my life some of my fears have been put to rest.
Someone told me once there are
three basic things to happiness in life.
Something to do, someone to love, and something to hope for.
I hope you find all three someday. Thank you for knowing how to
pull back when it went to far for the both of us.
Roses are red, violets are blue you changed my life forever and
for that I will always love you. I hope we can always be friends.

Charlotte Pokorny

Whispering Voice

His voice whispered in her ear.
She smiled and slowly put her lips to his.
Their lips lightly pressed against each others.
That one kiss could last forever.
That one thought could never be torn.
That kiss, that thought, his tender voice in her ear.
She thought his touch was so tender.
His eyes so soft.
Her eyes closed and then opened.
His eyes so tender,
Looking at him is like a dream.
She is in a dream that never ends.
His touch is so tender.
His smile burned into hers
As if he where fire and she wood.
Just like a flame burned by the fire.
Such a soft touch.
His touch was so soft.
If only she could find him again.

Donna LaRose

Desultory Derelict

Life is inured, pathological in a sense.

Detached from a heart, destined to failure, moving through the darkened alleyways of life.
Standing there listening, briefly; unbelieving the sounds of the moments gone.

Heartbreaking confession of a penitent person?

Not now, not likely.
Nary a concept of consequence, clinging heavily to a loathsome brain.

Bent on a mission dark and sure, thereto a leave of absence,
for which there is no cure!

Where are the offspring?
Their eyes grope and plea.
So much immovable opprobrium for all the world to see.

Dastardly weaving forward and back, snake like - striking;
Face it, embrace it, impossible to still.

Gone free of all importance, free for all it's worth, nowise shall there ever be, a place to hide on earth!

Bambi J. Shine

Love Poem

I was blinded by your beauty,
the neat and tidy package you presented.

Your bait enticed - but your hook pierced,
the salt from my tears still burns the wounds.

The asylum of your embrace bred insanity -
that nurtures the rage you left me to reckon with.
The mirage of acceptance you painted was a trap -
I hung myself with a rope woven of
unadulterated honesty.

You deserve an award for your villainous role-

You constructed a costume for me to wear
from your finely fabricated manipulation.
I wore it begrudgingly, but learned to
thrive in its cold consistency.

You arrayed your golden shine for all to see -
and overshadowed me with camouflaged tarnish.
Your insecurity tainted a pure love and
I in turn spread the decay of our intellectual prison.

I live as a rebellion of your attempt at
my soul's execution.

Deidre Nicole Green

Oh Vanna White Oh Vanna White

Oh vanna white oh vanna white
she is always such a sight
and she is always on at night
she stride into the light
and gets into a fight with Pat
they both threw a punch
and had a hunch
to go and munch in her evening gown.

She wiggled around in her funky looking gown.
When turning a letter
all of a sudden there was a some cheddar.
She thought it looked good
and offered some to Pat
but he was way to fat
she took a small bite
and screamed out of fright
she had just eaten moldy cheddar.

Justin Garner

These Are The Things Momma Said

Children get up and make up your beds
Wash your face and comb your heads
These are the things momma said.

Mop the floor and wash those dishes
Hoe the garden and clean those fishes
"Mind me child or I'll get the switches"

Put up those chickens and feed the hogs
Milk the cows and feed the dog
"And for heaven's sake please forget that frog".

Fetch me a hoe, fetch me rake
Hurry now to kill a snake
I thought it was real it's only a fake.

Get in the wagon and go to town
Get me some sugar maybe a pound
Hurry and get back before the rain pours down.

The night has come and its time for bed
Tomorrow will be another day like the one we had
And these are the things momma said.

Tammy L. Crowder

Courage

We know we're not "Profiles in Courage"
For we've often not done our best,
And, in crisis after crisis,
We've failed to meet the test.

But, we do have sprinklings of courage
When, in problems, day after day,
We face them, meet them, and solve them
In a straightforward way.

And maybe that sprinkling of courage will grow
Into profiles after all,
When we pick ourselves up, and brush ourselves off,
After a terrible fall.

For courage has a funny way
Of getting big, you know,
And we will find, with exercise,
It will grow, and grow, and grow.

Henryette M. Stuart

"Chilly Chirps"

The birds returned; their plaintive calls
bespoke the fraud of spring.

The cold had chilled their weary kind
preventing warbling.

They tried to chirp as best they could
their little beaks aquiver.

They squawked and screeched (The owls took note)
a bird-song to deliver.

From robin and the morning dove
there was no chirp or coo to love.

The mocking bird's dialectal drivel
was truncated by a snivel.

Many dumbstruck by the cold
declined to sing at all I'm told.

But wise old owl who winters here
was normal-self in this strange year.

He screeched his normal screech
the crow did caw his caw.

And on this cold and dreary spring
the orchestra was second string.

Edmund John Berven

A Mourning At The Chancellorsville Battleground

I step gently among the foggy hollows,
Where the dead and the unburied
Found renown in hallowed ground.
More men, more than I
Trod these trails those early days in May.
At a time when men in blue and others in gray,
Solved their dissimilitude in savage ways.
Why come to this place of the dead,
With its statues of cold stone and lifeless eyes?
What do I hope to find among the unsanctified?
Then I hear, not so very near, a wailing bagpipe's piercing peal.
And I ask: "Piper, for whom do you play your lonely lament?"
Some lost lad perhaps, newly arrived from that blighted isle,
Or a dirge for the remiss. A reminder to always reminisce.
I then recall, such horrid battlefields were left for us all,
That once living flesh made battle with folly greed, and ignorance.
And that one day, lest we forget, our bones may lie buried with
some fallen foe, and then, to greed, folly, and ignorance the
victory will go.

Kelly Don Nightengale

Along My Garden Fence

I have a row of foxglove, along my garden fence
with lilies sweet and pansies neat
and sweet alyssum dense.

Daffodils and buttercups adorn the garden walk
with poppies ablaze on sunny days
and daisies all the talk.

Hollyhocks and purple phlox accent the summer view
while daffodils in rows and hills
reflect the morning dew.

My garden boasts of butterflies, flitting here and there
pausing briefly on a bloom
then gliding through the air.

Softly scented lilac permeates the air
honeysuckle vine and columbine
trail their fragrance everywhere.

Lovely flowers you and I, as we watch our gardens grow.
In storm and strife we shape our life
in the many seeds we sow.

Jean Harrison

Life

Life is like a horse running through the fields,
Also, it can be like your mother fixing a quilt.
You start seeing young children and animals enjoying their
precious life,
If you are very religious, you will survive.

Can life be a flower blooming during the day?
In the month of May, where it all begins,
Life is a cycle where you turn,
People are starting to teach their young ones to learn about life,

During a rainy season where the grass grows, life can be a rose.
You see so much wrong in this world.
There are so many people that are strong.

You ask why? We have to live in this world.
God, knows why, because, life is just a galore.

God made all kinds of people.
People worked so hard to make a living.
God is a giving person, so he gave us life.
This is what life is all about?

Lenora Cuellar

"New York Rangers"

I love hockey and all its dangers
But my favorite team of all is the New York Rangers
They have some of the best players like Graves or Leetch
With their power nothing is out of reach
Their great dealing with sticks and a puck
There skills are from practice not from luck.
There are so many things they can do on the ice,
These are great people, even there personalities are nice
In all the NHL, the rangers are my favorite team.
To play on their league is every hockey players dream.
They practice all the time even on rainy days
They've achieved many things in many ways.
They have the best jobs, fame and fortune that's the way to be
everyone loves the rangers not just me.
Remember always be polite
Cause the New York Rangers are a big delight!

Melissa Lonquich

The Window

On one side of the window,
There is a life,
Of which everything is perfect,
And every family contains kids, a husband, and a wife.
The life for them is wonderful and right,
In fear of nothing they live each day,
The sun is always shining and everything is bright,
For they have no violence to wash them away.
But on the other side,
There is another life,
In which people are always fighting,
And the streets consist of kids with knives.
The life for them is terrible,
but so true,
So grow up alert and aware,
And decide which side is for you.

Nicole Neese

One More Day

I have lived another day.
Tomorrow may be no more.
So I gather today's wishes in the morning and make them come alive.
Children are growing each minute.
They need us each second.
When they are gone they're no more.
So make each day worth their life, worth living, because tomorrow
they may expire.

Linda D. Fields

Ivory Towers

I'm just a pauper, a lonely boy amidst the crowds
of Lavender Street in downtown New Orleans,
merchants passing me by on right and left as
rush hour settles in during the Summer months
a prolonged sort of enigma that grows and grows, and dies in
an instant. Festive winds and wines spread through
the crowds who bounce off one another like in a pinball
machine - twisting and turning, but always flowing free.
Phone wires outline the night sky, dividing up the stars into
a map new to each passer-by.
Frowning faces and smiling eyes search
for a lost belonging found long ago.
They glance at gutters and peer down dark alleys, prodding at
the clutter amassing at the curbs of Bourbon Street.
They kick up garbage and sift about through the masses, longing to
uncover harmony in this forlorn carnival of color and darkness.
Canvassing the street corners are urchins, steering them wayward
into a bright light, softly speaking the words of God:
Depart from me, ye cursed, into everlasting fire which was
prepared for the devil and his angels!

Matt Laliberte

Untitled

Dear mom,
Retirement years, oh how great they can be.
No alarms in the morning, your days are carefree.
Time to enjoy yourself and travel the states.
Doing leisurely activities with your wonderful mate.
The accomplishments that you have made in your life.
They're the reflection of the fine person you have.
And in so many years, you are way above far.
May you look back on your days at PGH.
And be thankful you're out of the working rat race.
I am not your colleague, co-worker or boss,
But like them all I too shall feel the loss
Of your presence in this part of the land.
There's a lot of work ahead of you up in Bellaire Grand.
But nothing you and dad can't handle as a pair.
Together you two have endured so much, especially with us kids -
what a bunch! I speak for the five of us when I say this day.
Congratulations mom - look to I wrote as small as I could!
Keep this thought dear - I love you so
My best wishes to you was you continue to grow.

Robin D. Richards

A Vision Of Madness

It was late in February, 1995 was the year
I watched my church burn in anger and fear.
Someone torched his house, how could that be
A vision of madness I thought I would never see.

Yes someone burning black churches but wait
The church stands for love, not violence and hate.
Why would someone do such a horrify crime
When this is suppose to be a new day in time.

The search continue,the law had no clue
People are searching all over on what to do.
Little children crying, you understand their fear
More churches burned as we past into another year.

Yes it's time to stop the madness the tension ease
Why can't we live in peace, I beg you please.
Let's do it for world peace, my children and me
Stop this vision of madness I thought I would never
See.

Daniel R. Joyner

Heaven

We often ask God as we look to the sky,
with the pain in our heart and a tear in our eye
Why do you take from us those that we love,
up into heaven so far up above
Up thru the clouds and far past the night,
why do you guide us to go to the light
We don't understand these feelings inside,
how do you choose one to be by your side
You give us our life and then as it seems,
we don't get that chance to finish our dreams
Although in our mind and deep in our heart,
those that we lose are not far apart
They're always around us wherever we go,
our guardian angel a white tinted glow
Then there are times our very last word.
I love you, goodbye, would never be heard
So give us that moment before it's the end,
for this my dear Lord would help our hearts mend.

Lisa Fischer

The Hole Of Unhappiness

I know we all have problems that no one ever hears.
I know we all have memories that bring our eyes to tears.
Sometimes we want to die, so others feel the pain.
But then reality comes, and we realize what is sane.
We still can't get over the hurt that's welled inside,
So we try to face our loved and ones like our spirit never died.
The hurtful words of friends start taking over thoughts.
We block out words of wisdom, until our problems fought.
We give up on priorities to think about our ways.
It's hard to keep good work up with such great delays.
Sometimes it's hard to realize what's really best for us,
We'll make a wrong decision, and not know who to trust.
Our lives feels like they're at an end, and everything seems wrong.
We start feeling pain by just hearing one sad song.
We can't help but feel worse when we think about good times in
our pasts.
We cry and cry the pain away and hope the happy feelings last.
It's really hard to overcome such a great pain we have felt.
But I promise as the days go by, we'll deal with what life dealt.
Just remember to always be yourself, and to be there for your friends.
Cause everyone needs someone to help make their depression end.

Ashley Davis

Alienate

Remove one mask, another takes its place
Show a true soul, and hide the tears of a happy face
A circle of loneliness from beginning to end
A mask of mine I wear again
A mask of strength to hide the pain
A mask of pride to hide the shame
All my masks I wear alone

No mask of love to hide their hate
A hate is harbored, a hate is shown
The deceits of their mask is mine to carry alone
I want no masks, not even my own

Now, you ask of my pain and I speak to you
Am I ashamed? Yes, this is true
But not shame for my life or the things that I do
It's shame I feel for hiding from you
A shame I feel for not being true
To my life and the ones that I love
Hold me and understand
No masks are carried by an honest man

William David Zeringue Jr.

A Clown

I'm a clown that makes people happy
and children laugh.
Dressed and make up on, I look happy with my life.
While from the inside, I suffer a big pain.
Everyone looks at me from the outside
I jump, play, run, and say jokes.
Only if they knew while they laugh, in my way
I yell and cry.
If only for awhile...
I could be a normal person and people would
see what I suffer for that friend
that I cared for with all my heart.
A friendship that grew
with a lot of patience and trust.
A friend who promised to stay always by my side.
Now that friend is hard to forget - the past.
Now I'll wear that make up,
always be that clown that
makes people smile and children laugh.
Smile now, cry later...

Jose Manuel Gonzalez

Walk On With Jesus Right Now

If you are wandering out in sin
And you need a wonderful friend.
Go to Jesus and your new life will begin.
So walk on with Jesus and hold to His hand.

Chorus
Walk on with Jesus right now.
Walk on with Jesus right now.
Don't forget to praise Jesus for the wonderful things He's done.
Walk on with Jesus and never fail to run.

There is higher power in heaven above.
If you will walk with Jesus,
You will feel His wonderful Love.
Wear His holy name and you'll
Receive His power too.
Walk on with Jesus He will never fail you.

When you see God and His only Son
Through the Holy Spirit, He is just one.
Then you will walk with Jesus,
And it will be done.
So walk on with Jesus,
And never fail to run.

Mary Lou Wright

Untitled

I'd given up.
There was no hope.
You called.
Suddenly there was a dim light at the end of my long dark tunnel.
A dim light,
But it was there,
Pulling me closer 'til it shone so bright that I could barely see.
The path to this light was cold and lonely,
But as I drew near,
I could feel the warmth radiating from this mysterious light.
A tingling sensation raced through my body.
When I reached the light, I found you there,
Holding the flame that could only be seen by me.
This light is your sensitivity,
The tunnel is my path to the door of your heart.
"Can I come in?"

Melanie DeJong

Missing You

Being with you is like a breath of fresh air;
From that sweet little smile, to the dance with your hair;
On the right path, because you're the boss;
Regarding to losers as no big loss;
From a bright sunny day, to dark clouds of rain;
I fear without you I'd go quite insane;
To be together so soon we must;
From now and forever each other we trust;
Picking me up when I'm feeling blue;
Think it's safe to say that I'm missing you.

David Tafel

Love Is A Wild Flower

Love is a wild flower on a mountain top
The fragile petals and beauty, only few behold
For there are many climbers but few surmount
The heights and dangerous path-to the flower.

If perchance you have seen the flower
No matter what the circumstances have been
Cherish the memory of the beautiful color
For there are thousands who have never seen the bloom.

Georgette M. Meyer

The Legacy

A life has begun
The web already spun.

Open your wings and you shall soar
Glide toward the heavens
You will feel pain no more.

Guide us and protect us
Watch us and feel our love.

A dove does fly in your honor
Reminding us all to become stronger.

You now embark upon your next adventure
Be brave and strong,
You won't go wrong.

We love you and we miss you
Your legacy shall live on.

Greg Coull

The Child In The Glass

The child peered through the window
Squinting toward morning sun
Reliving the coolness of the sand
Beneath her chubby toes

Reminiscing still, she looked to the ground
but was touching the sky with her toe
as she discovered the old wooden swing
still dangling by one rusty chain

Across the road and over the fence
In an Orchard long since forgotten
Stood the old gnarled tree she had climbed
And day after day lay there dreaming

She had then known no fear what the future would hold
Only dreams of a life full of love
Of puppies and kittens and cows and goats
And a castle where all were safe

The child leaned back and brushed a tear
And peered in the window glass
And there in the window all wrinkled gray
Was the child, and the child was me.

Kathleen Miller

Clouds

As I lay on my back I look to the sky,
I see something puffy and white way up high,
It could be a person, place or thing,
As the wind blows they're changing right before my eyes.

I try to focus on what is flowing by,
They look so beautiful it brings a tear to my eye.

As I lay here I cannot believe,
The shapes and sizes that are blowing in the breeze,
Only to realize as I look into the sky,
That these are just clouds passing by.

Jenna McCauley

Solitude

Alone,
In the cold,
A solitary figure walks quietly.
Seeking refuge from the pain of isolation,
Never finding warmth in the arms of a loved one.
Growing numb,
All the while.

Chad Nordby

The Bird And The Sky

Who am I, said the bird to the sky.
I know I have wings and I could fly.
Why am I so sad and you are so glad.
Why am I so little and small.
And you are so big and strong.
I am very fuzzy to this mixed up puzzle.
Said the sky to the bird.
You may look so little and small.
But to me you are having a ball.
You can fly into little places.
And you can see their happy faces.
Why should you be so sad.
You should always be glad.
For a little bird that always will find.
The greatness that is beyond.

Nancy M. Viggiani

My Love

My love for you is not
only from the heart
but from the soul too
My soul yearns for you, as much as my heart does
My soul lives on you
As my heart does
our souls and hearts
will keep together
and entwine together
forever
my love
my heart
my soul

Marta Coleman

Despair Downing The Sequential Generation

I get up and go out to do something for the sake of doing something
and I know it's all been done before, or will once more-
and then doing something for the sake of doing something
becomes a bore and the chore I tried to ignore in the first place

I get up and go out to revolt somehow for the sake of shocking someone
and I find everything's already been done by almost everyone-
and being unique for the sake of being unique
is no longer fun and I succumb to being dumb like everyone else.

I get up and go out to fall in love
for the sake of having loved someone:
and the feelings aren't genuine as I lust again-
and then loving someone for the sake of loving someone
becomes another societal task of men, meaningless as she is to
me.

I get up and go out to do something for the sake of
doing...something.
And I realize-
it's all been done before.

Matthew Reinbold

Anger

Anger is such a powerful thing, with hate it's better fuel,
That love and caring cannot win, this war, this hateful duel.

The product of this anger and hate is a fear that's so immense,
It jeopardizes my whole world, the feelings are so intense!

There must be someway I can remember, without feeling all the pain,
To feel the anger, without the hate, and reclaim my soul again.

For anger can be a powerful tool, it helped me to survive,
And when I can turn it to positive use, then I'll really feel alive!

Loretta S. Priestley

A Mother's Heart

He came into the world
A tiny, new life.
So helpless and needy
He is my heart's delight.

Small legs grew strong and sure
And as an autumn leaf in a gentle breeze
He was carried away from me.
He is my heart's sadness.

Every inch that he grows
Every accomplishment made
A feeling wells up from within.
He is my heart's pride.

A man, they call him now
A tiny babe I see.
A life of his own he wants to begin.
He is my heart's sorrow.

Farewells are bittersweet
He turns to go, then waits.
"I love you, Mom," he whispers.
He is my heart's joy!

Michelle Shocklee

A Lemmerick

There once was a lemming from Sweden,
and more habitat he was needin'.
He ran out of food, and was in a bad mood,
because all of the others were feedin'.

The king of the whole lemming nation
was appalled at the large population.
Their burrows were crowded, and everyone pouted,
so he led them to start their migration.

As they set off across the vast plain,
the poor creatures just went insane.
They ran and they ran, just as fast as one can,
and they ate every last bit of grain.

Over the cliffs they stampeded.
Their insanity cannot be treated.
They piled up down below, frozen treats in the snow,
as the food that their predators needed.

And some got an instinctive notion
to swim like a river, the ocean.
They have no self esteem, there's not even a scream
as they drown, and they end the commotion.

Andy Schamp

Can It Be?

Lives there a man with heart so cold
Who never to his friends has told
The cute little things his children say,
Or how darling they can be at play?

Lives there a man with mind so small
Who never tries to smile at all,
Who has never known the peace of mind
That comes from being good and kind?

Lives there a man with soul so dead
Who, even with uplifted head,
Dares face the world, and deny
The God who ever reigns on high?

Trudy Cornelisse

A Dying Sky

A sky is dying outside;
It is red and angry.
A sky is dying outside;
It is blue and cold.
A sky is dying outside;
It will never be again.
A sky appears for a little while, and then;
It is gone.

A man stands outside looking at the sky and wonders, why?
A man wonders why the sky must die.
A sky appears for a little while, and then;
It is gone.

A man stands outside and wonders why his life is as brief as
a passing sky.

A man must be reborn, like the fading sky that has died and
comes again - brand new and alive.

Timothy S. Axell

The Two-Edged Sword

The darkness of the two-edged sword
as the laughter could be heard no more
drifting up through the rafters like before
When the air was sweet from the fresh cut clover,
and the birds of song filled the sky
But now the floorboards creak,
and their demise suggests the weakness of the mind
The true meaning and bubbling merriment have escaped
What remains is only a figment of life before
as you are left with the light shining off the sharpened
end of the two-edged sword.

Sheri L. Bilderback

Daffodils

Daffodils, daffodils
So bright, so light, so yellow!

Daffodils, daffodils
Sway gently with each breath of spring
Once barren fields of winter-now awake in splendid colour
So bright, so light, so yellow!

Daffodils, daffodils
Stand silent at the forest's edge amid wildflowers, weeping willow
Embellished by mother nature's sweet scent and sound
So bright, so light, so yellow!

Daffodils, daffodils
Grow wild and abundant in vast open meadows
To welcome warm gentle rain and beaming rays of golden sun
So bright, so light, so yellow!

Daffodils, daffodils
Magnificent velvet shades of amber
One of God's many loving ways, for spring on earth to say "hello"
So bright, so light, so yellow!

Daffodils, daffodils
So bright, so light, so yellow!

Marie E. Sandridge

Why War?

War is hell, you are under a spell.
God does not permit you to kill, but blood still spills.
In a faraway land a man will stand, weapon
In hand, ready to defend a piece of sand.
Many times he will look to the sky, and
Ask the question...Why?
With a tear in his eye, there will be no reply.
For now it is his time to die.

Andy Croft

Untitled

Bloody tears,
give a world of fears,
of which cannot be forgotten.
Shrieking voices, with no other choices,
ring in your ears rotten.
Haunting dreams, with all the same themes,
make life a living nightmare.
Sunken impressions, of a given confession,
remains of sin are everywhere.
Decaying darkness, in the eyes of a carcass,
reflect a chill in the air.
Mysterious delusions, create a world of illusions,
this place will never be fair.
Unmerciful pain, without restrain,
of which can never be forgiven.
Bloody tears,
bring new fears,
of a world I wish I wasn't in.

Christa Simpkins

The Lock

"Now there was not far from the place where they lay,
a castle, called "Doubting Castle", where the owner was of Giant
Despair..." (*Pilgrim's Progress*)

Long time a prisoner held by grim Despair,
In that lonely Castle where none choose to go,
I suffered as I wished for heaven's air
And thought I'd die. It did not turn out so.
Breath still was mine and eyes that saw the light
Between the iron bars on every side,
And mornings came and stars burned in the nights,
And only freedom to me was denied.
That was my thought, until one came who said,
"Look in your hand and tell me what you see."
At last I strained to raise my whitened head
And saw my fingers clutching fast a Key.
It fit the lock. It turned. And now I wait
Afraid to venture out of that dark Gate.

Margaret Ann Choate

Just For The Ride

Of piercing memories, molding my mind.
Search and find.
A daydream of grief, thee unstoppable maze.
To give up, give in, to never win.
Fear not death, but emptiness, loneliness.
Despair. When the day breaks, I flourish in desperation.
The flood of reality washes over me.
When the moon comes shining bright, my eyes cry for mercy.
Sorrow knows no peace.
The ever - winding ball, only to be dropped again.
Just to find myself back where I began.
Memories are such precious jewels that forever shine undimmed
by passing time.
Mine is a story of love as well as pain.
Grief and hope spin a strong web, the birth of an eternal angel.
My heart tries to soak up the silence.
First the wild swift tide of despair.
Tip-toeing slowly, only to embrace the beauty in the sea.
To wonder the ways survival and life, to never forget love.

April Johnson-Ball

Which Path Would You Take?

I was walking along on a path one day,
when the pathway divided and went off another way.
Should I continue and see what lies ahead?
Which path would you take? Where would you be led?

The path to the left was close and dim,
and led to mystery for those entering in.
I walked down that path for a minute or two,
then stopped and stood while deciding what to do.

If I keep going, I may become lost,
To get myself back, just what would it cost?
This path led to darkness, to evil, and sin,
I've been here before, but I won't go again!

I walked back to the path that goes toward the right,
and leads to salvation, it is safe and so bright.
I'll walk straight and tall with a smile on my face.
I'll throw open my arms and life I'll embrace.

Which path would you take? The left or the right?
Lose track of your goals, or keep them in sight.
Please think about every choice that you make,
and tell me, my friend, which path would you take?

Holly McCoy

The Hand Of God

As I stand and watch the open fields and yonder woods,
I see the things that are made and never understood,
As I stand and watch the distant hills and sloping valleys with
all their splendor and color, in my mind a question is
asked, "Who did this?", but in my soul my conscience speaks,
The Hand Of God, No Other.

My imagination strains, His thoughts to be made known, but
The Hand of God is on the stone.
How small I seem as I stand there, to see God's Hand everywhere
in the breeze that blows, the flower that blooms, the birds
that sing, the Hand of God is in everything.

He writes across the heavens at night, across the sky by day,
The Hand of God I see as I travel along my way.
Sometimes it's very furious, sometimes very gentle, it can melt the
hardest heart, and turn the vilest sinner, so as I
turn and walk away, it's there
to help and guide, so... With a sigh of appreciation
and thanks, in my heart I want His Hand to abide.

Jesse G. Raines

To My Son

You are a constant source of discovery to me
Watching you grow and become your own person.
You have your own ideas about life;
Your own opinions, wants and needs -
This has helped me to grow too.
So my son, go forth into this world -
Be yourself....
Love, laugh, live....
Dream, aspire, hope....
Succeed, fail, reach out....
Experience life as only you can.
But always remember one thing -
I'm here for you through it all.
To laugh with, to cry with, to catch you when you fall.
Set your sights - aim high
I'll always be there with a watchful eye.
You are the light of my life, my pride and joy;
No matter how old you are, you will always be my little boy.
There is nothing in this world that you cannot do -
Remember, my son, I love you and will always be there to guide
you through.

Linda S. Hetrick

Myriad Of Colors

Have you ever watched the sights of Spring
when snowflakes dust the ground -
The birds down South form in colorful flight
and the sun shines all around?

Where the lazy cocoon with caterpillar
suspends in silence before your eyes -
And bursts open with a sudden gust of fury
to send butterflies that rainbow the skies?

Where the flowers bloom in their radiant hue
and dance to songs on the subtle breeze -
Or seen a small child squeals in pure delight
as the wonders of God he sees?

Have you ever played with dandelions
and blown the seeds up into the air -
Watching the wind take them in flight
and deposit them everywhere?

Oh! The color of Spring beat all you have seen
in the seasons throughout the years -
The Myriad of Colors sway beneath the sky
and bow in the dew of God's tears!

Katie Tinch

Who Is Christ In Life?

Christ is my friend, my brother,
my helper, my cleaner,
my savior, my God's Son,
my path, and my Word.

He is my friend when I'm lonely.
My Brother when I'm sad or hurt.
My helper when I need help.
My cleaner when my heart needs cleaning from sin.
My Savior when he died on the cross.
My God's Son anytime.
My path when I'm lost.
And finally my Word when I need wisdom.

Christ is my Christ.

John W. Henning

The Good Times

I think the good times came and went
While I looked the other way.
I kept thinking that tomorrow,
Would bring a better day.

Roses bloomed in wild profusion.
Children played at my feet.
There were sounds of joy and laughter
From their voices young and sweet.

Now the house is cold and silent.
Emptiness fills every hall.
Now, I stop to smell the roses
Scantly blooming, weak, and small.

Like me, they've passed their days of glory.
Old and snarled, they tarry there...
Waiting for the cold of winter
That will leave them stripped and bare.

Have I reached this destination?
Is this all there is for me?
Yes, the good times came, but in my hurry,
I was just too blind to see...

Nellie Pearl Fry

Pro-Life

The silent screams of the unborn dead
Ring steadily upon my ears;
The misery and guilt they spread
Can't wipe away their blood and tears.

No woodland freshness can they see
No blueness of the sunlit skies;
No tender smiles, no harmony
Will ever mark their way to paradise.

What paradise, what wanton myth
Can compensate for senseless agony?
Ah, precious souls, what deadly wreath
Upon your brow is laid in mockery?

We lift you up to God, our Liege,
To His compassion and His grace,
That He forgive this sacrilege
Against His image, so debased.

JHS Emerita N. Sevilla

Evil Magic

Sometimes I wonder how everything could go so wrong.
Sometimes I think about why we can't all get along.

Other times I ponder on why Adam took that bite,
And now all anyone does is argue and fight.

Christians try so hard now a days
To fight the danger in Satins evil ways.

But most of the time they find themselves using his evil magic,
Even though they don't think so, it's really quite tragic.

Another thing I think about is the music that we listen too and make.
Most is right from Satin lips, and few from our Lord's we take.

And as I sing songs of worship and prays,
Others make live sacrifices down on the bays.

I wish I could kick them in the butt with my boot,
Every time they call upon evil spirits with a flute.

I still don't understand why God put me here,
Watching lowlife's chug six packs of beer.

When I would rather live in the past,
Instead of watching the evil black shadow be cast.

And as this dies like the explosion of a bomb,
I shall cry out in joy, for this world will be gone.

Brenda Snow

Name Me

The thrill of looking into the eyes of your first born child
The moment has come for it to be lain in your arm
As they look up at you with eyes so knowingly mild
Strange so bright with light, hoping to see the way to charm

The time limit to stay in the cocoon is all over now a life is here
I'm ready to check and surely find something different is around,
Start talking to me, I want to hear your voice now you are so near,
Maybe a song would be better I need to hear just a sound.

I need to count your toes rub your feet, check your hands
Nothing is amiss as far as I can see, I've heard you cry
Perfection is what I see, no hair, I can't put on your head bands
Are you a boy or girl, we'll take what we get, on our first try?

Life is so precious I say to you, all of us together have made a child,
Are we ready to change our plans, it won't be the same?
We know it will be different to awaken, to find life isn't so mild,
We can't just call you a baby, a job you have to do, is give me a name

Letha J. Wisby

Would He Know

Were Christ a stranger on the street,
One who by chance, face to face you meet.
Would He know you as one of His flock
Or would He continue on around the block.

Were Christ an old man, feeble in His age
Would He know your love or only your rage.
Do you think of others, not just yourself,
Would He know your kindness and love rather than the shelf.

Were Christ a youngster who depends on you
Would He know your love, no matter what He should do.
Hold back your anger, or better yet, be direct,
And make your love work for you, rather than create regret.

Were Christ a friend in need of another,
Who looks to you for understanding that's unconditional,
Would He know the advice you give is done with love
And tempered by nothing hypocritical.

Were Christ you, who can do so much good,
By simply smiling at any stranger you meet,
Would anyone know that Christ owns your soul,
And has handed Satan a symbol of defeat?

Frances L. Emerson

Questions

What is it like to see with normal eyes?
How's it feel to sleep care free at night?
Why is it so easy for you to say your good-byes?
Where are your questions about what is right?
When are you going to question life?
All I can see is complex objects interwoven
Into the simplest of objects and people
Like everything is giving me an omen.
I stay up all night looking at the puzzle
Of life and wonder if I have the piece
I just placed where The maker intended.
Maybe I think friendship is not a lease
Where everyone is always up for bid
And loving comes second to money.
Perhaps I'm just too human and shy
Yet I have never stopped looking for the key
That opens any small door in the sky.
And My eyes tell the story of my life
With wondering tear filled eyes I gaze
Looking for a way through this maze.

David Wexler

Street People

They've become invisible
We see them and not see them
Some are blind, others in wheel chairs
Some are dressed in many layers
What happened?
How did they get this way?
The homeless
The poor
You want to help
But now so many
Some carry signs, telling you their story
What they will do with the money
Some just ask for money because that is their job now
Who really needs?
How can you tell?
You walk by. Don't see.
Don't give
I feel sad
Don't want to judge
But forced to. I's Sad.

Teruko Smith (Chicago)

A Summer One

Rolling black clouds,
Dark-cloud morning,
Cool breeze touching my face,
Morning sun hidden in clouds,
Surge of energy refreshing
My ecnetsixe,
The gentle summer nears, it's time to bloom,
The flowers of earth and of the soul refresh.
These are the signs of rain, a very special
Rain - a summer one.

Andrew Tillman

"Life's Rude Awakening"

I spoke to a stranger I saw today.
Who looked kinda familiar to me.
I said to myself, I've seen that person somewhere.
But who could that stranger be.
That wrinkled face, and that graying hair.
Those dimming eyes, and their blank stare.
A look of loneliness, and a trace of a recent tear.
A face that shows the hurt of long long years.
It bothered me the whole day through.
And it kept crossing my mind.
I know I've met that person somewhere.
But an answer I could not find.
So I passed a mirror later today.
And I turn so surprised to see.
That person, I had spoke to earlier,
"My God, it turned out to be me."

Mary Pauline Connelly

My Love

My love for you is a very special kind of love.
My love for you will never die.
I pray each day that my love for you will never end.
When I close my eyes, all I see is you
I think of you in my every awakening day.
I think of you in my dreams.
I think of you as my best friend,
my soul mate, my special love.
I pray the closer we get to God
the closer we will become.
Our love that we have for each other will bring good and bad.
together our love will withstand all.
Now I have to say good bye, but
not for long, for our love will withstand.
I dream of our good times that
we shared, and our bad times we withstood.
I look up in the heavens and I think of you.
I look up at the stars and I dream of you.
For you are my love, my soul mate, my friend.
As you lay down each night, think of me,
for I will be thinking of you.

Michelle Savage

Gems And Fossils

In the deep mine shafts of our souls
Dig and see what treasures are to be found.

Joyous, shining-happy-bright gems
Of golden delight are there to mine.

If only we did not have to shovel
Through a mountain of black-fossilized sorrow
It would be easier to uncover these long lost jewels.

But, I suppose it is the earthy pain
That gives our souls substance.

Michael A. Denton

My Love For You

A year ago when you walked out on me,
I cried, I still don't know why,

I long for your laughter,
smile and cheer,
I love you so much,
I have to have you near..

No other has been, like
the way you loved me then,

Loving you was the best thing
I could do,
But it seems now it was wrong to.

My feelings for you have
always been high,
And I hope they aren't going to die,

Ever faithful, ever true,
I wish it could have worked
out for me and you.

Jenny Nicole Thompson

Wondering

Have you ever wondered
why sometimes you feel lonely
Or maybe you think
something bad will happen like you might
die young because of cancer.
Does it seem like
there is only one person in the world
that understands how you feel.
Maybe at night you're
dreams fade away into nightmares.
Are you scared of your future?
Some people say they can see
the future in their crystal ball,
but actually there seeing their
future. Do you ever wonder
why some people's life falls
apart? It's like a cookie crumbling in your hand
and I feel like that cookie
is me, my life, what about you?

Tiffany Pop

Dream

I imagine a far away place, where there is no fear.
With crystal clear water, and people filled with cheer.

I imagine how it would be, just touching him once more.
How much joy it would bring, making my heart want to soar.

I imagine him turning, reaching out to take my hand.
But He just keeps on reaching, trying to understand.

For He cannot touch me, it is only a dream.

Back to reality, time to face another day.
Time goes on, hours pass away.

I imagine a far away place, where there is no fear
With crystal clear water and people filled with cheer.

I imagine how it would be, just touching him once more.
How much joy it would bring, making my heart want to soar.

I imagine him turning, reaching out to touch my hand.
Reaching, reaching, I try to understand.

My eyelids flutter, as I awake.
There is a longing, an emptiness, a deep ache.

I wish that I could touch him just one last time.
But it is only a dream, a picture in my mind.

Lisa M. Vineyard

A War Of Hate

Alone I watch my children fight,
And hope they'll understand.
The lessons learned in mortal plight,
When hate gets out of hand.

With a narrow view and crosses bent
They sow a bloody seed.
On a darkened page this sad lament
Shows their twisted creed.

When will they learn that life's a stage
Where all may play a part.
When will they see their golden age
Where waves of war depart.

Can they change their destined path
Can they comprehend.
That hate's a plague of ceaseless wrath
A war without an end.

Need they repeat this brutal crime
And pay with all that's dear.
Or will they understand this time
To teach of love not fear.

Brian J. Reynen

Private Prayer

Are You there?
Do You share?
My joys, and the secret burdens that I bear?

As I pray
Do the words I say
Fall on listening ears?
Or do they tumble heedlessly into a futile world of tears?

When my child, a son, was born
Without the breath of life
Did You and I together mourn?
Did we both weep with my wife?

Later, when another boy gave his first lusty cry,
Did You receive our thankful joy
For a son who did not die?

Are You there?
Do You share
My joys and the secret burdens that I bear?

Hilly Linde

This Love I'm In

For Camilla Farin, February 14, 1991

It's the touch of your hands that soothe me.
It's the taste of your lips that quench me.
It's breathing your essence that thaws my heart.
It's the anxiety I feel when we're apart.

It's your beautiful brown eyes that entrap me.
It's the softness in your voice that excites me.
It's your smile that is often so intriguing.
It's the words you use when you are speaking.

It's your glimmering dark hair that strokes me.
It's your sensual walk that stirs me.
It's the feel of silk in your rich glowing skin.
It's your sex appeal that finally does me in.

These thoughts I've expressed are just a few,
of the many, many things that remind me of you.
And when I see you we'll hug and we'll kiss.
We'll let ourselves bathe in our own sea of bliss.
And when we do I'll be reminded again,
Of this love that shines, this love I'm in.

Scott Yelin

Homeless Souls

They walk along our streets and roads, these souls without a name
We call them bums and hoboes, no thought from where they came
We shy away when they come near, we shun them one and all
But yet when Gabriel blows his horn, they too, will hear the call
Some were men of wealth and fame who fell along the way
Some were men of broken hearts, and some just went astray
A woman sits among the trash and rocks from side to side
And dreams about the days gone by when she was someone's bride
We live behind our little walls and never stop to ponder
But only for the grace of God, it could be us out yonder
So go ahead and shun them, pretend they don't exist
Keep your head up in the clouds, your mind amongst the mist
And when the ship of life sets sail for God's celestial shores
You'll be the ones out in the cold, knocking on their doors

Roger D. Sandifer

Fragile-Carefully Handle

Your fingerprints are there
I can always feel them
Part of the pattern of my heart
One of the 8 inscribed signatures
Vital tracings of my identity
I've known their warmth for sixteen years
No injury inflicted can erase them
Today the handprints impression pains me
They burn with tortured fervor
I sense the ice in your heart
You are being robbed by scarring pollutants
Drugs, loveless sex, alcohol weaken your spirit
I feel the fear in your grasp
I hear the gasp of your stranglehold
You ache to be released
Within you is the help you reach for
Feel my loving fingerprints in your heart.

Christine Leckbee

Disillusioned

There was a time that I held dear,
Sweet thoughts of you, and the dreams we used to share
We promised to love, honor and cherish
And our love was strong enough for marriage.

What happened to the promises that were made?
There like a rainbow, when the colors glimmer and fade
Here then gone, it's told
That a leprechaun's good for luck and for gold.

Now you say, that you can't stay,
Your times come to walk away.
What happened to those promises that were made?
There like the wind that blows, then fades.

Darlene Coffman

Matt

I don't know why you had to die
I guess it was just your time
A time for sorrow, sadness, and mourning
But for God a great rejoicing time
In time the sorrow will fade
But memories I shall keep
Just like you will always be there when I weep
You have the heart you wanted
Now you shall frolic, jump, and play
For today sadness, but tomorrow is a new day
Now you rest in eternal sleep
The suffering is drained from your body
You rest forever

Blair Kleiber

Mi Corazon

When the fiery sky, full of dark sin,
Lights the way of the prophet, knowing all,
We question our faith, ask what we have been,
We believe this power, till our steep fall.

A light mist, covering the depth of souls,
A wave crash in the distance, no one hears,
Wake the fiery soul to pay its toll,
A toll that pays no heed to a soul's tears.

The ray of sun shines through, leading the jury,
To be or not to be is what we yearn,
The flame within us all burns bright with fury,
Till the nonbeliever kills it in turn.

Within us all the spirit lurks, in time
It will die, with our loved ones and our crime.

Rosemary Kowalski

Change

Seasons change
Days turn to night, children grow to adults
From carefree innocence, to pressured responsibility
Change is always in motion, an unstoppable wheel
Wrinkling faces, withering bodies, and wearing away at stone
Sun to rain, green trees to leaves rustling in the wind
Falling from the trees of past experience and remembrance
Change comes in varied sizes and shapes
Single to married
Without child to the pitter patter of tiny feet
Together to alone
Youth to old age
So as the wind blows, and the rain falls
And the sun peeks above the horizon on each new morning
So is change also a constant
Sometimes good sometimes bad
But always just outside the door
Waiting to come in
Change

Joseph Dellaquila

Ode To Ralph Cothran, My Husband

You live! You live! You live!

Now, even in death, because in life,
you had the courage to give, give, give.

It is your breath of good will that death
is unable to still, the breadth of it an
enormous field.
You live! You live! You live!

A life so vibrant, vital, voluminous, filled
with never-ending goals. A life always concerned
with the outcome of other souls, blossomed to unfold.
You live! You live! You live!

The works that you have done, evoke the praise from
many tongues. Your will and way was bold, understanding
and patience untold.
You live! You live! You live!

A part of your heart is entwined in the heart
and hearts of Chattanooga. And as long as hearts
beat, You live! You live! You live!

Catherine P. Cothran

Untitled

Desert breeze is lightly blowing
The secret of sage fills the air
Not a human soul is stirring
But some coyotes I can hear.

Moon has lifted clear the mountains
Gently balanced on the peaks
From the crescent pours the moonlight
Upon the rocks and sand it creeps.

Cactus rise up towards the heavens
Prayerful arms reach out to seek
Less of sunshine, more for moisture
To their creator they beseech.

In the distance comes a rumble
Low, like the growling of some great beast
And the darkness gives way to a brightness
No rain - just some lightening, dancing
on the peaks.

The desert is like the coyote
A trickster is its trade
Beware its ever changing moods and faces
For the desert can never be tamed!

Michael R. Carter

Del gratia

The eagle is so regal
as is the tiger and the buck.
But, somehow, not the cow
nor the chicken or the duck.

The giraffe that cannot laugh
or utter a sound - looks at the ground.
And, from above, sings like a dove
from within, where pangs of love abound.

The hippopotamus is, like a lot of us are
content to roll around in the muck
Looking for a mate and maybe propagate
believing not in love but luck.

We are all God's creatures with different features
sharing wealth from Mother earth
loving and living, living and loving
Life, for all it's worth.

George E. Lingenfelter

In Memory of Colin

Living like a lullaby, unsung,
he wanders through his life,
...undone,
full of hope and made of dreams, unclaimed,
memories of his child,
...remain.

Knowing why he feels such hate, untold,
returns in him once more,
...to hold,
his child so young left this world, unpleased,
but still he knows the pain,
...must ease.

Wondering if he grew wings, unspread,
might angels carry him,
...to bed,
leaving far behind the past, unclear
to live again without,
...his fear.

Andrea Wynne Bennett

"Never-Land" A Rhetorical Refuge

As my thoughts are put to paper; while clutching pen in hand...
My mind begins to drift away to a place called "Never-land"....
For it's somewhere I yearn to escape to, if only in my mind....
A place which bears no hatred, and where no one is unkind...
No, there isn't any evil there; for it's a place where goodness dwells....
My slice of Heaven, I flee to, to elude life's immoral hells...
Never will you see illness there, or any reminders of unjust...
Only divine skies up above you, and where smiles are a must...
You will never witness racism there, or hear any negativity...
Just positive reinforcements, and where "suffering" can never be...
Yes, this may only be my vision, but "Lord" if it came true....
My "Never-land" would become "Heaven on Earth," and imagine
the good it could do.....

It would bestow much hope and joy, to this world's overwhelming
despair....
A place where everyone could visit, and bask in the pleasantries
there....
No, you need not buy a ticket to travel to my hidden treasure....
Just a pledge to "Almighty God", that you'll hold sacred it's every
pleasure....
So, please let's stop the fighting and rid this world of strife....
As the moral of this verse, you see; is that we all should cherish life!

Sherri Ann Rarick

Wild-Ways, Wildlife Haze....

Chunked splits
ripping echo
drizzling madness—
thunder-softened valley roars.

Screaming aches, hot pain
drowned in a tub of "oohs";
relaxed posture, steaming grin
painted green—a heightly reach.

"Touch-up" life, windows both ways-
smoke-hazed inside...wild without;
corrections, mistakes—all in writing,
school craze flickers, waxes strong.

Finished!! Cloaked in a breath of darkness,
tripping the path —outhouse magic;
glistening plants with glitter-threads dance
"Out of the Frame"— woven in motion.

Wooden chair seats hardened thoughts,
shared with candlelight flora;
Alone...dreaming wisps of an old 'yeller dog,
Warmth...solace... A subtle joy——to be.

Jo Zeitz Fix

Sitting On Concrete At Dusk

I want to bask in the orange warmth of the sun,
in the eye of a grey-blue storm tortured by electric shards
and hear its whisper like the single clear note of a flute
in the empty black, sleepless on white cotton sheets.

I want to swim in the limpid silk waters
of an endless stream through a pine-needle forest,
by the evergreens of balsam scent
and lily-white birches,
past the doe with the soft brown eyes
who casts no shadow on autumn leaves.

I want to walk gravel paths on windy nights,
lined by blue-white rhododendrons, pale pink lady slippers,
watching my fingertips ruffle yellow-green ferns
showered with moonlight and a sweet lullaby
sung in Gaelic without words.

Heather Elizabeth Bell

The Existential Express

My mind is running and running from my fear of nothingness on my own special chariot of rebellion, freight-training poignant juxtapositions of concepts, oozing nothingness in between them, perpetually becoming an energy of sensory perception directed towards the destiny of 'I am becoming.' Yes, I do exist; therefore, I choose to become and become an essence of ever changing flesh and blood and bones, blood pulsing and flowing, neurons and synapses firing and crackling, triumphantly crying out that I am alive and electric! I am a being who grapples with chaos and disorder, trying desperately to heave it over my shoulder until the pain and anxiety become anguish and despair, for I cannot escape this feeling of claustrophobia as the walls close tighter and tighter and the floor and the ceiling rise and fall to meet each other until I can't I can't I can't find no escape as I am coming closer and closer to the edge of the abyss peering down inside, propped up either to die, or...
Leap to faith.

Steven Stadler

Romancing Through Love

Sometimes you feel you've found the one,
The one you've been waiting on for so long.
That other heart sends yours aflutter,
And through your soul roams a wondrous song.

He looks into your dreaming eyes,
He hugs you once; you feel divine.
Your arms are wrapped around his heart,
Through pure romance, your heartstrings twine.

Dreams of beauty, you encounter,
The stars pour light of love on you; the wind plays its romantic tune.
It feels as if you're on a cloud,
That floats with ease around the moon.

But one day, the dream of being held in his arms,
Fades like the evening sunset, and soon disappears.
He leaves with no goodbye at all,
And through you, flows a rushing river of tears.

In your soul, he engraves a memory,
That you cannot forget, no matter how much you try.
And you miss him, oh how you love him,
But through all this he remains; for your heart never said goodbye.

Rosa Jeanette DeLeon

My White Lover

I met you through a friend, he knew we were right for each other.
You were innocent and unsure of life; I was strong and dependable.
You needed security; I could make you feel safe.
You had dreams; I could make your wildest dreams come true.
You were lonely; I would be your companion.
You felt insecure; I would make you superior to all men.
You were shy; I would make you the life of the party.
You were misunderstood; no one will ever understand you like me.

So now my love, take me in your arms and love me.
I will make you forget everyone and everything but me.
I will be a part of your body, mind, and soul.
You will sleep and wake with me.
I love being in your arms, you love having me there.

If you should leave me
You will only find heartbreak and unfulfillment.

You are my love and I am yours.
Take me in your arms, shoot me in your veins.
Shed your innocence; you now have me, you are safe.
Experience your dream, feel the ecstasy; I understand you, I am your lover, and you can depend on me as many others do.

Mary A. Porter

Poem Goal

I saw your ad and wanted reply,
So why not with a poem to explain just why.
I've always loved to write poetry just for fun,
But I can assure you a prize I've never won!

My poems are simple and fun to read,
But tell a message to fit the need.
Don't expect my poems to get real "deep" —
Your train of thought I want to keep.

Some are about birthdays, growing old and such,
Others are about the people and places I like so much.
A lighthearted poem is the surest way
To help brighten anyone's gloomy day.

With all this said, I'll say no more,
Don't want to appear to be a bore.
Setting a twenty-line limit wasn't wrong,
'Cause some of my poems are two pages long!

Reading the entries will be such a treat,
But deciding the winners I'm sure is a feat!
Sharing my poems have given me glory,
'Course, I'd love to win money and that's no story!!

Olivia B. Buffington

"Reflections Of My Life"

Tonight my dreams were shattered.
As the raindrops spattered on the window,
The father of my children walked out the door.
I guess we didn't matter at all.
Sitting at the window as the storm clouds are brewing.
I sit here 'a stewing over what might have been.
As reflection of my life run through my mind.

The lightening flashes reflect my life,
the brightness cuts like a knife.
As it reflects the good times we shared.
After the lightening the total darkness,
reflects my life now that you're no longer there.
The rain on the window pane,
are the tears I cry from the pain of losin' you.

As the thunder rolls,
another chapter in my life comes to a close.
As I mourn over losin' you, I suppose,
the storm reflects the anguish, I feel.
A token from the heavens above, I'll heal,
as I go through the reflections of my life with you.

Jeanette Todd

What Is There To Fear?

Oh, what is there to fear?
Be not afraid!
You know that God is near,
For you have prayed.
Your sin He will forgive,
Start life anew.
Go out into the world and live!
Now there is much to do -
There are great things to see and learn,
There is no time to waste.
Perhaps some honor you may earn,
But do not be in haste;
For it takes work and time
To be and do that which is fine.

Ellen Hoyes Pretot

Pulling Through

No one seems to wake to
anything you hear and the
sun that bleeds its love
isn't shining on you. But
I've been there before when
the light grew dim, and the
warmth of the sun grew cold.
I understand your pain
little girl, the woman says
to her I've been through
it all with you before. I
was the one who had helped
you find the way to the
open world and I'll do it
again if I have to, you're
worth the world to me.
I am the past, says the
woman, and you my creature,
are the future. May it be
so that one day, you too will lead the way.

Elizabeth Popovich

God's Little Angels

These precious little people, so fragile and so frail,
Are special gifts of love, from God; He knew you would not fail.

It took a lot of planning, years of thinking it through;
He knew in his heart, He'd done the right thing,
When he gave these Angels to You.

From you they have learned about courage,
Compassion and love with no end,
Your thoughtfulness and kindness toward others,
And the gentle love of a friend.

You've taught them that life's is a challenge,
You've shown them to reach for their dreams,
To never give up and always keep trying,
No matter how difficult it may seem.

Knowing the road wasn't easy,
They might sometimes stumble and fall,
With love in your eyes and strength in your heart,
You let them experience it all;

God is so pleased with all that You've done,
His decision was the best it would seem,
Not only have you given your Love;
You've also given them Wings.

Sharon M. Chapman

The Clock In The Book

The clock in the book, the one mentioned
in the book of ecclesiastes.
The book in the book of boos "The holy
word", which sets us free from ignorance.
This heart in the scripture, comes alive
and blossoms and fumigates its sweet
aura all around us,
when opened by a sincere human hand.
We can feel the musical rhythm of its
vibrating pulse and smell its aroma.
We can read its coded beats to know
what and when to do, what just be done.
"Time is essence", we discover for ourself
through serendipity, but only after
much, much experience and little by
little in a spirit of love and fairness.
May we always be in the heart of God
And may God always be in our heart,
to bless and guide us on the right path,
teaching us right from wrong.

Ray O'Neal

The Wild

Gnarled stumped branches whip
Against a fiery wall of uncaged spark.
While the soup of gold drip
From the deep aquamarine crack
Between lustrous beds of albin satin.
Furry creatures crash through tangled shrub
Only to be caught and won.
Mouths of ruby-orange air mob
Through the sudden still
And at last, the wind had its will.

Connie Lee

Out My Window

When I look at the street,
all the people I might meet.
Makes me think about tomorrow,
Will there be world peace?

When I look up at the sky,
as clouds pass me by.
I wonder if tomorrow will be clear skies?

When I look at the trees,
only one thought passes me.
Where would birds nest if there were no trees?

When I look out my window,
I see many, many things,
but one thing I see most is God,
caring for everything in this world.

There are many questions in this world,
and not as many answers.
Some things we need to leave to God,
because he has the answers.

Kelley McKinney

Fact

He cries and dwells on happiness.
His moves and actions are so hateful
Towards the changes of his breath,
Or his constant pain.
Injecting sorrow and pain is his belief.
His name is life.

Robert Savage

Alone

I feel so alone, so very alone.
My life is so incomplete, from half the people I meet.
Some of my friends leave, and they try to make me believe,
that they will always be there for me, when actually they're not.

My parents want me out of their hair,
but most of the time, they don't even know I'm there.
I sit in my room, with no one to talk to.
I feel so alone, so very alone.

My days are so very slow, time stands still.
  Clocks quit ticken',
    and everyone thinks I'm a chicken.
They say I won't amount to anything,
  but some day, I'll prove them all wrong.
They will feel stupid, and I will feel high and mighty.

I may be alone now, but someday,
  everything will turn around.
I shall promise you that, yes I will.
Since I am always alone, I have time to think.
You might not feel alone like I do,
  but you're not me, and I'm not you.

Sarinnia Jamison

Pain

Pain, unlike any she has ever known is new.
The fresh wound throbs like an open knife wound.
But there is no blood to show the hurt,
She bleeds silently from within so no one knows.
Only in her eyes does it show,
and only those closest to her are allowed to see it.
She does not understand how something could
hurt so badly, and yet make her feel so alive.
Having no control over the bleeding, it flows at will.
She wishes, she could see ahead, that maybe it would help
ease the pain and make it bearable.
But maybe not, maybe it would make her heart bleed faster
until it has emptied forever, never again to pump
a single drop of this painful elixir,
the thing her very existence is made of.
But for now, it seeps, slowly,
and painfully,
one drop at a time,
a broken heart
dies slowly.

Carmela Polk Glenn

Sisters

Sisters are always there, and they always care
But sometimes they pull your hair.
They worry and fight with and for you.
And sometimes they wish they were in your shoes.

Sometimes they hate, steal and lie,
But they never seem to want to say good-bye.
They sometimes can say things they don't mean
And then apologize and feel just peachy keen.

They are always willing to lend you a hand
And clap for you even when you played terribly in the band.
They can always cry on each other's shoulder,
And they are always willing to move a boulder.

They can tell secrets to each other
And then never hear that secret from another
Theirs is a bond that develops and ties them together
That will always hold tight even through the stormiest weather.

So be glad you have a wonderful sister
And when she's not around always miss her.
Because one day she could be gone
And you'll miss her love and all the fun she brought along.

Amanda Hargadon

Alaskan Spring

Chinook winds blow.
  Temperatures rise.
Darkness gives way to light.
  Spirit, fire, new beginning.

Ice-encased rivers clamor.
  Deep crevices sigh.
Free ice-sounds pierce day and night.
  Cries from the depths.

High bluffs bare themselves,
  To advancing sunny skies.
Pasque flowers furry petals clothe splendid heights.
  Exposure, light, covering.

Eagles soar toward the sun.
  Geese return in Vees.
Smoke-covered windows cleansed,
  Feed snow-bound souls these miracles
Ascend, submission, redemption, feast.

Zoe Frederick

The Dog

Crying,
the dog leaves the cold, concrete steps
and stumbles down the
blackened street.
His eyes droop,
giving them the appearance of
the teardrops
that began his existence.
The sagging body of the half-bred hound
moves steadily, slowly,
along the shadows to an unknown destination.
At sunrise, his body nests
near a banana-peel filled dumpster,
yet his soul moves faster
than his legs ever knew.

Tami Root

The Lord Lifted Me Up

The Lord lifted me up, after the devil took me down
  The Lord dusted me off, and handed me my crown
He told me I got lost, but now I'm found
  And gave me the gift of Love I lost, to turn my life around
He gave me the strength, I needed for courage
  He guided my heart, so it wouldn't perish
Oh I praise thee God Almighty, for He never forgot me and mine
  For not once did He let us go hungry
He gave us health and unnerving spirit
  To conquer our mission, in route to free us from submission
I sorted substances to numb my pain when I felt all was lost and nothing gained
  Hail my almighty King, I praise Thee to the highest heights I've ever known, help me O Lord, without you I'm frightened
  With your love and direction, my might is tightened
All glory be to God, for I am your child
  Who has fallen into the hands of deceit, unlike my lifestyle
Awaken me O Lord, let me see what I've always felt I've known
  That you're walking beside me, in the ways you've shown.

Vivienne Thompson

Flowers For A Friend

The time has come to say "good-bye"
To my friend for the final time.
She gave her best to all of us,
and has passed the test of time.
She was here when we were down,
she hugged us when we cried.
She coaxed the pain from a hurting heart,
she knew what was inside.
She endured life's pain the best she could,
though it seemed more than her share.
Her weathered hands could work no more,
but, she knew that we were here.
"The Sunflowers must be propped up,
for they cannot stand alone.
And trim my precious roses for me,
if I am not around."
She loved her special flowers,
for love's message they would send.
You have send love her way,
when you gave flowers for a friend.

Dana G. Tafoya

The Fulfillment Of A Soul's Desire

You were but a morsel to be tasted...
Found pleasurable to all the senses...
But found particularly delicious to the soul...

Cheryl Greear

"Lis"

As I envision the beauty of
your wholeness
Love descends to the farthest depths
of my heart
When I ponder the memories of our
moments together
I can only hope, we shall never
be apart
To embrace you creates an array of the
most joyous emotion
For this, I give you my eternal love
and everlasting devotion
Having you near me, I can only feel
the most absolute bliss
I could never imagine being without you,
my beautiful Lis

Paul A. During

Like Magic

Found in the deepest corner of my dream
Once in a heap of seconds
Amidst the abundance
of mundane surrounding
It was like a shimmer
Floating against an opaque sullen
A bright gleam of the sun's rays
Embedding a dark cloudy day
Your face an ever beautiful
living sculpture
Imprinted in the soul of my heart
A single moment in the tick of the clock
Has frozen its time like forever
Making you real in front of me
Alive.
And not illusion

Queenie Ma. B. Yujuico

Untitled

Sunset falls across the land
darkness sets on a homeless man
around the world life goes on
but this man's life is a sad sad song
he walks along the streets all day
at night a bed his head does not lay
on a pillow of box he makes his bed
just to have a place to lay his head
a dim street lamp gives him a light
a dirty, old coat keeps him warm at night
to this man who has nowhere to go
watch o'er him Lord
from the harsh night's cold.

Keinya Graves

Why I Am Not A Spy

I just don't think I can handle all the lying, cheating, killing and oh don't forget you have to know foreign languages perfectly. I just can't do a French accent, and I may be Italian, but most people say my Irish temper would give me away. I am not a spy because I don't look fashionable with my small handgun (a walter ppk) poking out of my silk stockings. I would stumble doing the tango and then, well you know, I would be caught and then tortured and even though James Bond never had to take a suicide pill - I would because I am a woman and you don't get special treatment for your school girl looks. Besides I am really an Opera singer, and how many spies do you know who can recite Wagnerian lyrics in the ears of drowsy lovers who are supposed to relinquish their dark secrets mumbling in their sleep?

Bridget Christine Kelley

The Beholder

In the eyes of the beholder is beauty.
And I am the beholder.
Therefore, I behold myself to be
the most beautiful of the beauties.
For there is no other woman that
portrays the beauty that becomes only me.
Smooth mocha are the color of my eyes.
Very beautiful and big in size.
Soft, sensuous lips.
And though small in curvature,
I have wonderful hips.
Strong, healthy hair.
My silky skin adds very much to my flair.
For it is chocolate of the richest.
And if there is any filling,
Surely it must be the creamiest.
My name means to be vain and of conceit.
And in my eyes, my beauty is complete.
Because I am "The Beholder."

Narcisse Nicole Taplin

The Acquaintance

He acquainted himself with the flowers and trees,
And then the birds and the bees,
And then again if you please,
He did it again on his hands and knees

He began to arouse,
And then walked to the smoke house,
Where he found a terrapin,
To be exact he cared for this one.
He journeyed over to a sapling,
And began laughing.
To his surprise, a cocoon was in the tree.
He knew what it was like to have to be care free,
But he didn't like it,
So he knew how the caterpillar felt.

Tara Scott

Sonnet I: Brokenhearted

The day you told me that you'd set me free,
A shot bore through my heart with acrid pang.
My endless tears did flood the Bering sea
From painful memories that still do hang.
Your callousness is hard for me to bear.
Delib'rate spite from you has killed my flame.
I often wonder if you even care.
Give ear to hear for I call out your name.
I took for granted love of yours, I know.
One chance is all I ask to prove my love.
A strong devotions what I aim to show,
If He should grant me blessings from above.
Please shine your light and mend my broken heart,
For in true love our spirits cannot part.

Catherine Song

Someone

That someone special.
That hair so dark.
Dark as a midnight without any stars.
Those eyes so blue.
Blue as the bluest sea.
That body solid as a rock.
Those hands gently as silk wrapping around my body.
A kiss so hard that my breath is taken.
A kiss so sweet that, It's left behind.
A heart beat that's pounding so hard that I can hear it.
A voice so soft that it is taken as a low whisper.
As we lay there in the dark together as one.

Heidi Lynn Clawson

My Sister - My Best Friend

It's hard to find the words
that will tell you how I feel.
You've always been my sister
thru all these long years.
Even if I am the oldest
I feel as if you're my pier.

When it comes to best friends
well nothing has to be said.
We seem to have the same thoughts
roaming around in our heads.
You make me think, you make me laugh
you're with me good or bad.
No matter what may happen
you're my friend and I'm glad.

All of this is very true
even if it sounds hoakie.
You'll always be my sister - my best friend
with love, okay Dokey.

Brenda Brumbalow

Brain Storm

Last night I dreamed of a dizzying dance
frantic, frenetic
darkness came, doom settled in its easy chair
Then The Bees. There were thousands, millions clinging to me
So I ran, (just wanting to get away)
back and forth so many times I thought I would be seasick
Then the dream got bigger - much more than battles with bees
the death flutes played like a macabre circus
then the trumpets took their turn, triumphant as the angels heralding victory
The water drenched me (When did that come in?)
oceans colliding
Hate and Love and Death and Life
doing their psychotic water dance
Silence. The bell is tolling
for whom I don't know-Oh yeah, it's me. Time to get up
my sheets in a heap on the floor
Don't forget the Prozac
to make the world a better place
and keep the evil out.

Erin C. Guss

Untitled

When we stop and thank the good Lord above,
For the chance on this earth to show Him our love,

We thank Him for granting some of our dreams,
Like success and small miracles, or so it seems.

Some prayers go unanswered and our souls turn away
From this Lord in the heavens that wants us to stay.

He saved us from sin by death on the mount
May take Him for granted to many to count

The Lord is our savior! We've all heard it said,
The believers are many, yet so often misled.

We know there are frauds, 'cause God put them here.
To test us in faith and our knowledge to share.

Say "Hail Marys", "Our Father", And one "Glory Be,"
As he opens His heart, for the world to see.

He takes all our troubles, as we gaze toward the sky,
All he asks in return, is for us to just try.

We're made in his image, as all life forms are,
from the smallest winged insect, to the largest bright star.

So when all said and done, and the amens are through
I'll kneel one last time, and think Him for you!

Debra L. Scheller

"From Manuel"

Long, long, long ago in our Lord's shimmering light
I was an angel in the heaven's shining night
Then God sent me down to earth a brand new baby boy
To mama and papa Gill who gave me so much joy

I had brothers and a sister too, I never was alone
then I grew up into a man and ventured on my own
Life wasn't always easy, there were lessons to be learned
I loved my job and lots of friends I wasn't too concerned

Then suddenly it hit me, my days of living hell
the hell of the deadly virus, my heart, my soul, they fell
I did the very best I could to climb this weary hill
And in doing so I found my Lord who was beside me "still"

He said to me "it's time to go, your journey is all done"
"say farewell to all you've loved, you're going home my son"!
My burdens were all lifted, I felt my spirit soar
as I flew back to heaven, God's angel forevermore.

Remember that I love you, thank you for loving me
Remember too the happy times the heart holds in memory
Don't grieve for me my loved ones, I'm above you in the light
You only have to lift your eyes into the bright and shinning night.

Theresa B. Parent

My World Is

Where the sting of scorn
is venomous
Where jealousy and malice
form riotous parts of petty thoughts
Where every word is loaded
with meanings many to be goaded
Where every effort is mocked
as having leanings of head being cocked

Where lashing tongues and frayed edges
form necessary wedges
Where every smile an invitation
providing ways and means of belittling
Where kindness kills
and mercy destroys all that is good and truthful
Where the only balm is "success"
and the only weapon "silence"!!

Priya Yegneswaran

"Fairy Godmother"

Don't question my identity, integrity, or fame,
For I am many people, I just go by different names.

I am your Mothers, and your Husband, your Daughters and your Sons,
I am all of the above, just all rolled into one.

I am two darling Granddaughters, who love to visit you,
I'm your uncles, aunts, cousins, your nieces and nephews too.

I am your brothers-in-law and sisters, your neighbors and your friends,
your bosses and co-workers for this list just never ends.

You have touched upon all these lives, with generous things you do,
I just wanted something special, especially for you.

I have a little secret, which I could never tell,
I am your Fairy Godmother, my identity breaks the spell.

So gather all these praises, gifts of love and more,
and ask no more questions, for I've told you what it's for.

Merrillyn E. Capone

God's Love: The Music In My Soul

The next time a storm arise, don't be afraid. Instead, think on this; the sky is the stage, the lights dim as dark clouds appear. The conductor strikes his baton, the base drum gives a gentle roll as all the musicians begin to play. The rain falls! Lightening flashes! Thunder rolls! This is God's glorious work in action.

A new day begins: God, in all of his majesty, allows us to see his art work come to life. The sky is dark. Slowly, the darkness is pushed away by the morning light. Shades of blue, lavender, orange, covers the sky. If you listen closely, you can hear music as the day breaks. (Da-Dum! Da-Dum! Da-Dum!!!) Each beat getting louder and louder. Then at long last, a big orange ball rises slowly as the drum rolls softly and crescendos until the sun is in full view. This is God's love in all the beauty he has created for us to enjoy. See God in all of his splendor and beauty. Then when storms arise in your life, you too, will be able to stand still, see God's wondrous work and say God's love is the music that brings peace, love, joy and praises to my soul.

Gladys E. Peden

The Face Of Good Friday

Burning in my eyes I remember my last sight:
The face.
Hatred masking me. Blind
I whirl around.
Blows burn,
"Tell me who I am Prophesy."
Failure...I am cut. I bleed
Fear...I am wounded. I bleed.
Degradation. I am abused. I bleed.
Doom................I am bruised
Blood drops
as the haunting
laughter demands, "Tell me who I am,
Prophesy!" I know
who you are, but do you know me!
The cover is lifted
and I am gone. My soul and spirit rise,
in VICTORY
in JOY,
in LAUGHTER!!!

Ameena Mathis

"The Cherub"

I sent down a cherub to rest inside you,
To prepare him for Heaven, and all I'll have him do.
Though it's hard to understand why I took him away,
I promise a reunion in your honor some day.
The love I have for you and this cherub is dear.
I brought him home early so I could have him near.
We both send you kisses in the still of the night,
For he wants you to know everything is all right.
"Mommy, I hug your face with the warmth of the sun,
In nightly breezes I tuck you in, when the day is all done.
My tears fall upon you from the clouds up above,
When you whisper you missed me to cuddle and love.
Jesus held me today and told me all about you;
How you loved unconditionally even before I was due.
He said you sing down on earth. Well, we all sing up here.
I'll sing for you tonight as I kiss away your tears.
If you awaken tonight and can't understand why.
It was my lips touching your cheek as I came and passed by."

J. S. Brown

Reflections By The Sea

I looked out of my window and what did I see?
My two little children playing wild and free.
At the edge of the beach they ran and they played,
Laughing at all the footprints their tiny feet had made.
So full of love in my heart, I watched and I spied
As they gathered up secrets from the sea, all wide-eyed.
I watched as boats passed, making waves by the shore.
My two little ones had fun all the more...
Seeing how long their castles would stand,
Till the waves washed them all back into sand.
It made me think back on how nice it would be,
To be young again so lively and free.
They danced with the sea gulls until I could stand no more.
I too was young again, as I ran to the shore,
And joined in with the children all of us, three
Having a great time by the beautiful sea.

Denise Dufrene

Sonnet

Exhausted I lay on the ground looking up
at the passing clouds and see marvelous things.
At first I see an ant, then a butterfly, and a pup.
I lay and wait to see what the clouds brings.

As time passes more clouds come and go.
Beside the pup is a lion and nearby is a goat.
A dark cloud moves in and vanished all my woes
and I find confront and hope in a nearby coat.

The black cloud moves on and the sky turns gray;
a new cloud is formed in the shape of a flower.
The sky turn blue like the start of a new day.
There's hummingbird, a hawk, and a shower?

Rested I leave the joy and comfort of the clouds
and sweet music starts softly and begins to get loud.

Eddie L. Moss Sr.

Lilies Of The Field

I wonder what the Flowers know:
They manage to grow
Despite the snow
or the winds that blow
Still they go
Along with the flow
They manage to bestow
an idyllic glow to this city, held in escrow
until the cock's third crow
Another denial ready to throw

Harvest:
It's time to mow with my dog in tow
I need more grease in my old elbow
(or grace in my old soul)
I cut, but I never sow in a garden row seeds for rains to wash low
Yet save for those falling on thorns or the rocks below
Flowers somehow manage to grow
Do you know?
I didn't think so

Christopher Gardner

Friendship

There's a better day ahead for me, my friend.
One that's more serene.
In a garden greener,
One where thou hast been.

Oh, I'll know that you have been there,
By the roses blush.
I'll see you there when the bluebirds sing,
I'll be sitting by a thrush.

Lorain Davis Ramsgard

Ode To A First Exam In "Humanities 301"

Apollo, God of muse and light,
look kindly down on me this night.
Fear, not anger, is my invocation
To be sorely 'tested' is my flagellation.

Athene, turn not the Furies' coats to black or white
but rather some soft shade of shining grey.
No longer Nemeses, straight-laced,
but gentler, kindly in this modern's play.

The color grey to match the hair strands
of my head;
and, in their new found role,
help me 'remember' what I've read!

Though age, Apollo, has not dimmed
the thinking brain
it has, I fear, robbed
its agility to retain.

Cry sorrow, sorrow...yet let good prevail!
(In the vernacular: Ye gods, don't let me 'fail'!)

N. Aileen Forster

Untitled Ode

The warm sun holds the fields its embrace,
As blades of grass weep in the shadows of sprouting flowers.
The horizons seem to stretch to the heavens,
As I hold you in my gaze.
I bend down to pick you a flower,
And when I awake you are gone.

Brian Palagallo

My Life

Why must my life go on?
With each day of the rising sun?
Is life more than the things I see?
Is there a reason that God created me?
Why must I live so long?
When all those I loved are now all gone?
Why am I yet not set free?
Why is my life so carefree?

Life is worth more than I will ever know.
Life has brought me to many places I dare not go.
Life is just one big adventure.
Full of love and laughter.
I love my life and would not trade it for another.
I love my life with every endeavor.
Life is a game everyone is playing.
So keep on playing and keep on winning!

Jenny Sirianni

Sideways Glances And Second Chances

He was handsome enough for a second look.
I was more impressed when he read from the book.
Everything changes when I walk by him.
He doesn't say "Hi" or flash me a grin.
With me he never speaks, only gives sideways glances.
Even if he did, I'm scared of second chances.
But with them he chats and laughs to the limit.
He didn't notice I had left that minute.
In my mind he speaks to me so clear.
I try to erase him, the stronger the images appear.
If I could find the words to speak,
Would he be mild, humble and meek?
Thus I go through life scared of second chances,
He goes through life giving me sideways glances.

Anna Gagne

"Mother's Love"

My mother's love was sweet and true
and now she is gone I don't know
what to do. She is gone to take her
rest because the Lord knew what was best.
Best for her you see: because
she has been set free. Free
from this world of pain where
people call you any old name.
My mother was, sweet and kind
and she was a good friend
of mine. A friend is gone and
can't be replace the smile
that would be on her face.

People try to hold you back,
keep going and don't look back.

A mother's love. A mother's love is
a kiss in the night. So she could
hold you tight. A mother's love.

Bertha Mae Johnson

Untitled

So gracefully she glides across the ballroom floor
He guides her so beautifully
It reminds her of the rose she had taken care of
For so long when she was small
She wishes it could last forever but on the other hand
knows it has to end sometime
She was a beautiful red rose standing tall
Swaying to the gentle song in the wind
The song ended and he ran away far into the night
And never returned
He was the water and sunshine
That kept her living-no longer there
Soon she began to wilt petal by petal
Her heart was in pieces breaking slowly until
She felt she was nothing
It was her first love

Stacy Mathiowetz

At A Bus Stop

He sat on a bench at the bus stop,
I knew at a glace he was old.
His hair was white, his face was drawn,
And his eyes were faded and cold.

I sat down beside him and like men will do,
We talked about the weather and such.
His voice was hoarse as he struggled to talk
And what he managed to say wasn't much.

"What do you contribute to your long life?" I asked.
He thought for a while then he said,
"It must be the whisky that has helped me along
Without my bottle I'd probably be dead."

"How much does it take to make your day?"
I was trying hard not to sound tart.
"Sometimes I can make it on a pint," he said
"But most days it takes a quart."

"How long have you kept this up?" I gasped.
And his eyes became wet with tears.
"Well I started when I was 'bout thirty," he said
"And I've been at it for almost a year".

Bill Higginbotham

Sunshine

I miss those warm lips on my young forehead,
Those gentle fingertips gliding through my long, dark locks.
I want to fall asleep in your lap as the Ford hums along again.
I want to walk on your feet, embracing your waist again.

I remember when I used to whine about life,
Your soft song and sweet voice could carry me to Jupiter on
Pegasus's back.
You used to make my cotton horse gallop through the clouds
And dance with my sheets in a field of Nightshade.

It is not over.
I still walk in your shoes, rest on your lap
And dream about satin ponies with wings.
You will always kiss my forehead with your bright smile,
Every morning of everyday.

Erika Wachtein

"The Love Of A Dream"

A woman sometimes can question beyond,
can it be a lifetime of dreams?
She's drifted along through winds of worry,
carrying the weight of the world it seems.

She asks the questions "to where and why?"
and stares through the clouds above,
to find a whisper in soft tender rain
speaking of belief in love.

She looks to her heart for what is true
that all she can give will be known,
and rain will be blessings that take with time
what has always been love to be grown.

The question of glory and does it exist
the answer came into her life,
shown the beauty of dreams and rainbows
when a man then made her his wife.

Linda J. Connors

I Built My House On A River Bed

My house has been crumbled, down to the ground,
my belongings have all washed away.
All I can do is stand by the bank,
close my eyes and then pray.

Wondering, wondering, "Lord what has happened?
Why has he left me alone?
I ask you Lord" come into my heart;
and show me the fault is my own.

Instructing as to where; I should build my house,
and how to be sure my foundation is strong,
He left on the pages of his Holy Bible;
it is I who have let things go wrong.

He has given a blue print; to me, of my life
so if I use my own instruction instead.
The fault is my own when it washes away,
for building my house on a river bed.

Daniel Masias

Never To Be

An idea is conceived,
Attaches snugly to my mind.
Will I nature you, watch you grow,
Or will you travel the path as others before?
As I stand at hell's gate
Consumed with flames of doubt,
Excuses decide your fate.
Swiftly I bury you ever so deep
In the dark hole of my pathetic soul.

Barbara Dyson

Untitled

I was walking down the road one day
I saw your shadow on my right
I was blinded stumbling down the road
I knew nothing of the light but you picked me up
you loved me so, you held me oh so tight
you changed my heart and painted white
what was once as black as night
I am nothing without you
I will never be the same
I am nothing without you Jesus you bore all my pain
I am nothing without you Lord
you have brought about this change you are the good in me
the love I see you are my everything
I want to walk the path you've drawn and be guided by the dove
but the anger of the human
just wants to push and shove Lord help me be
the man of God you've wanted me to be a man of love,
a man of faith gentle humble and free
you have branded me your child you have breathed your life in me
you've called your own and gave a home in heaven I long to be.

Franklin Lee Petty

Soul Shine

From one kind soul to another,
"I offer my Deepest Condolences, Suzi,
for the passing of your mother...(Mom!)"
What to say... what am I to say...the only things I feel comfortable
saying are verses from my heart: She's Free!!!
Your mother's Spirit is free!!! Free to feel the peace and
serenity that All are entitled to! Nature has its own way of
saying "Hello" and "Goodbye-" "Hello's" are the little things:
spiderwebs flowing off an iron gate... leaves pushed down the street
by the wind... a little hummingbird pausing in midflight to get a
glimpse of you- "Goodbye's" are those that symbolize change:
a tree losing its leaves... sand eroded from the beaches...
rain washing away the pain! We're all a part of nature-
physically, mentally, spiritually-
We don't necessarily die...we change form.
It's a part of our growth cycle; It is hard to accept changes
sometimes; especially when we care so Dearly;
As the Blue skies turn dark everyday...
there is always a shine; from the sun, from the stars...from our
loved one's eyes.. No matter the change...There is Always a Shine!

Anthony Erick Olszewski

About Me

I have written all about my family.
Now they say, I should write about me.
It's hard to know where to start.
It has to come from the heart.
The love, the joy, and the pains.
There's so many things these eyes have seen.
How often, the world seems so mean.
Then there's that the rainbow in the sky.
That clears all those tears from your eyes.
Then how beautiful the world becomes.
When you are loved my someone.
Then that circle starts again.
Never knowing when it will end.
Is this really all about me, and the world that I see.
Or does everyone feel the same as me.

Marie A. Shorter

In A Child's Dream...

In a child's dream, the world is at peace
there are no more wars and gang violence has ceased

In a child's dream, drugs no longer exist
love is the high that we cannot resist

In a child's dream, kids walk hand in hand
you can see their happiness, all across this great land

In a child's dream, there's no color to skin
and all of mankind is finally akin

In a child's dream, Dr. King says it best
"the content of your character" becomes the true test

In a child's dream, Mom and Dad are as one
the whole family is together and they always have fun

In a child's dream, there's no hunger, no strife
and all of God's children receive the gift of life

In a child's dream, all the forests are still green
they are no longer eroded by man and machine

In a child's dream, education is the key
that opens the doors to a new society

Wouldn't it be nice, or so it would seem
if we could live life, in a child's dream...

Victor J. Glover Sr.

"The Coming Of Age"

Mystic magic storm afloat
bodies bound in mantic caverns
raging seas crash in the shores with thunderous clamor
black crows hunt the embedded tides
vicious colic gathers all sense of abnormalities
freedom lurks through the haze for those who believe
for those who see the pervious light
as time ticks in the depths of the soul

Buckle your knees old ferocious warrior
heel to the power that forever sees through you
cuddle the pedals of the gallant sunflower
while shaking the jackals which forever colored you gray

I am the driver of the storm inside me
I cast the shadows and poisoned the fruit
but even I am sensitive to the honeybee
who transposed the nectar of love
upon my latent fields

Craig Todd Robison

My Destination (The Rocky Slabs)

The other day I sat along the rocky
slabs thinking to myself this beautiful scene,
I wish would last the waves curled up and
made their crash the sun went down with a
sudden dash the stars and moon soon filled
the sky the blackness, as I looked up and
tried to reach, but seemed too high I packed my
bags and started home no more lonely
evenings no more sandy beaches I
will rome I made way to my campsight
and sat along the bursting fire trying to figure
out my distant desire what came to mind
would need sometime another magnificent beach
I would have to reach a few more weeks have
fast I have reached my destination I am here
at last so I sit along the rocky slabs
thinking to myself, this beautiful scene, I wish
would last.

Risa M. Hurst

A Pledge

I am a warrior of old
Sometimes brave, sometimes bold
I am from a day of a king and a knight
My armor, I keep polished bright
To protect you my angel of light

In this new body I lay silent
Watching for those who hurt and rape you
To them I promise to
Do great pain and be very violent

For the men of this age
Your true beauty they cannot gauge
It must be seen with the mind
As thru the eyes of the blind
A beauty that is truly one of a kind

Of this I am sure you will see
My spirit will be with you forever
Walk in fear you will never
I am protecting you for all eternity.

Gary R. Jump II

Searching for

I rose above the clouds to search the heavens for what I thought would be there.

What I found was this endless heavenly fantasy going nowhere and everywhere.

There are no answers here I thought, only more questions that need not to be sought.

Perhaps, I thought, the answers lie in the very domain from where I came.

So I returned to the fantasy of my own spherical origin and entered this realm beneath the heavens to search for the answers from within.

There are no answers here, again I thought, only more questions that need not to be sought.

I returned to the place and time where I started this journey and looked upon the mirrors of my own life. Again I thought, there are no answers here only more questions that need to be sought.

Fredrick H. McCarthy Sr.

Thoughts Of A Day

I hated to do it but at the moment it felt like the right thing. But for who? Me, maybe, but as days go by and the suffering has stopped, I regret it. I was someone special, helping in times of need. Now I'm lost and in my need for revenge and pain toward, it has "rickishad" and hit me, slowly tearing me apart, hate kills, and I am dying. I was lead astray by my unsure feelings, guilt, and frustration. No thanks to the words of the ones I trusted. Were they right? Perhaps. But its to late to place blame, now. What's done is finished and I'm left out in the dark where it all begin. Why can't I adapt, why can't I face the truth, release my soul, and come as one. I know what to do, and how to do it. But I can't do it. And I'll continue to die until I face my fears. Dying is not at all something you want to do alone, you want someone there for you, a hand to hold on to. All my life I would have someone but in the morning they would leave, and I'd start a new day dying alone. Will I ever start living again feeling happy and free, because now I'm unsure in a slavery of myself. Tying myself in bondage; self destruction is at last among me.

Keshia Stevens

Bobo The Orange Gorilla

There once was a Gorilla named Bobo
He was extremely a slowpoke
Bobo was in love with a monkey name Yilla

When he went outside
He went down the wrong slide
And got in trouble with his teacher named rox
Who was carrying a box
That was full of chicken pox
That were purple and green and orange

And one day he went out
And he started to shout
That Yilla ran away
And that she wouldn't stay

For Bobo was sad
Because Yilla was gone
So he checked her lawn
And that's where she was
With her cousin named buzz

Breann Plante

Those Dear To Me

Those dear to me who are far away
Can write to me when they have something to say,
There is a phone that they can use
When they want to tell their good news.
It takes a while to send a letter
But is worth a stamp to say you are better,
When you are sick you want to tell
Others about it and now you are well.
Relatives write and tell their news
About their families and how they choose,
To spend their time during summer and fall
Who they have time to visit and call.
They tell about what they have done
About contests they have entered and won,
Sending pictures of vacations and sports
Pictures of weddings in gowns and shorts.
We make great plans of what we will do
Who we will meet and what time too,
<Body It is the quickest and easiest I can see
To write or phone those dearest to me.

Eva Cook

Sails, Spindrift And Channel Bells

Frivolity, that feeling of pending holiday, fills
the summer air, salt-tinged on
languid jettied channel way —
Little sailboats, like frisky sea colts, rush,
splashing wakes of bigger boats,
all frolicsome in windswept waves!
Idyllic hours, in happiest pursuit, warm
sailors' and captains' hearts in
Days well spent with refreshing zephyrs,
accompanied, now and then, by
soft-voiced channel bells and
Bright spinnakers billow exuberantly
before wind-filled jibs, beyond
spindrift waves!
Then homeward bound, all lithe deckhands,
swift and strong, furl spinnakers and jibs,
Before final tie-up and home
docking's done —
Before last glowing rays of
summer's lingering sun!

June Allegra Elliott

Nature

The clouds appear to be smiling when you gaily look upon them.
The flowers sway to and fro as you look at them with eloquence,
their aroma is taken by the forceful wind and spun around your
presence.
It's dancing, teasing your nose.
And then you begin to spin-your mind wanders and you let go —
You're faraway - in a dreamland perhaps -
but the powerful beauty dominates you and brings
you back into reality.
The colors are so ardent as you love to gaze distractedly
and mysteriously at their intricate design and structure.
The bee lands on the sweet, lavender lily and sucks on
its pollen - then leaves to enjoy its new findings.
Soon, a new day will come and take this statuesque beauty
away - bringing new loves and wonders to discover.

Sasha LeeAnn Lassley

"Saving Of A Soul"

My hair is long and wild.
Naked I stand facing the dark ocean.
My blue eyes glow with ancient secrets.
And I arch my back and throw my arms upward,
Praising the stars overhead.
"save me!" I cry,
"Save me!"
A start shoots across the sky,
And I plunge into the turbulent waters.
The cold burns my skin, cleansing me
I laugh crazily and swim parallel to the shore.
Suddenly, something lifts me up
A light of sorts
And places me in the sand.
The balmy night air blows back my tangled curls,
I feel calm and at peace.
I look up at the moon, and she winks at me.
Redemption, at last, is complete.

Erika M. Wright

The Farmer's Son

Soundless boots march in my sleep
Impatient chores await as if meeting someone
They haven't seen in years.

Fiercely looking to the heavens
Friend or Enemy?
The crops stand at attention.
Endless, aching, act of love; now in desperate need of
Liquid treasure.
The fields are his children.

Oaken stance, now gnarled and bent
Limbs bending, falling to the earth
He cannot see his shadow.
The one he served so faithfully
Now greedily reclaims him.

The boots placed last upon the pyre
Sacrificial legacy, like birds scatter
Their droppings
Cinders of unspoken love
The orange skies are weeping

Maria Garcia Stites

Without Me

I hope throughout your life you find whatever you're looking for,
That special happiness you couldn't find with me,
To last you ever more.

I hope you're always smiling without a heavy heart,
Each day fulfilling your wildest dreams,
Right from the very start.

I hope that Lady Luck is always standing by your side,
This wonderful thing called "life," taking you for an unforgettable ride.

And so my love on this Christmas Day,
I hope your new life is wonderful,
me no longer in your way.

Michelle L. Allyn

Dear Felicia

Felicia was a friend, a friend with a good life,
but it ended one fatal June night.
She was struck by a car, with no chance to react,
everyone wishes she could come back.
She lives with God now, a place so far away.
I often think of her — each and every day.
Her family grieves everyday, they can't get past the fact,
that Dear Felicia is never coming back.
Felicia died suddenly, her death was to be so unknown,
who would've thought it, she was nearly half grown.
I guess I have to face the facts they were so clear,
that nineteen ninety-three was Felicia's last year.

Marie A. Sparacio

Our Wedding Day

Today is the first day of the rest of my life,
Today is the day, I take myself a wife
We've waited for so many years
We've waited through laughter, we've waited through tears
I've been in love with her all of my life
But she has a husband, and I had a wife
God in his wisdom, took us apart
Now for some reason we have a new start
Whatever the reason we still do not know
But with his blessing our love will grow
And so on this day as we stand before thee
We ask for your blessing, and humbly implore thee
To share with each other the love in our heart
May it always grow, till death do us part

Robert E. Locke

If I Were Part Of A Tree

I wonder how it would be
To be part of a tree
To be the roots under the ground
So people would have to dig, so I'd be found
To be the bark on a tree
And at night I'd be as cold as can be
To be the branches way up high
All the way in the sky
To be the leaves at the top of the tree
I wonder how that would be, if that were me

Kenneth Pantoja

House For Sale

I'm sorry old house but it's goodbye
for you and me
We've been thru a lot together,
measles, quarrelling and Sunday sprees
for this is where we all grew up, the
kids, he, and me
Thru all the years of school,
adolescence and then acute matrimony
and now they all have gone to find
their ways and houses of their own
But none will ever mean as much,
as all the love this old house has known.

Rita Hendrickson

Let Your Light Shine

Let your light shine both day and night.
Let it flow and glow like the bright sunlight.
Hide not your light,
But let it shine like a candlelight in the darkness of the night.

Jesus is the light that shineth so bright.
He is the light morning, noon, and night.

Darkness, oh, darkness, you've got to go!
You have no place here, don't you know.
Light, oh, light, keep forever shining bright.
For you are like a city that is set on a hill that cannot be hid.

So, let your light shine bold before the world
That they may see your good works and glorify your Father which is in heaven.

Evelyn Swayne

The Country Poem

When I get to feeling down and low, it's off to the country I will go.

When down the highway I do roam,
The smells of the country feel like home.

I roll down my windows in my car,
and wish I could bottle up those smells in a jar.

The sky is blue and there is wide open space,
It always puts a smile on my face.

I can smell the fresh cut alfalfa grass, and close my eyes and see,
me as a little girl, and my cousins three.

We'd play with the cows, jump in the "pies", we'd swim in a ditch
and hay we would pitch. We'd help milk the cows and watch
Uncle Alden plow.

We'd play and have fun under that big hot sun,
and when the day was through and all the chores were done,
Aunt Clara would have dinner and there would even be fresh baked buns!

Then after dinner it was time to go, back home to the city again.
I always cried because I wanted to stay, there never was enough time to play.

So back I go, when I am feeling low, and a child I become.
I smell all the smells and smile to myself and remember all the fun.

Pamela J. Powell

"Faith In Myself"

If you believe in that what I do...
In God, in life, in truth,
In expectancy,
in whole subsistence generals creations reality's actuality
Then believe in yourself,
because you are the lost creation of this Beauty's Chain.

Sabina Magda Guzik

Dedicated

A precious face so sweet and kind;
Two eyes through which God's love does shine-
Two lips that prays the prayer of faith-
Two arms that make you feel so safe.
Two hands that toil from morn 'til night,
To turn the wrong to paths of right.
Two knees that bend in humble prayer
Two feet that tread where angels dare.
A mind that's sound, a heart steadfast
No doubt is found, the dye is cast.
Not looking back, but, straight ahead;
Upon the path that Jesus tread.
Onward and upward she'll carry on,
To heavens shore, some bright new morn.

Donna Abell

Missing It All

The growing aging. I'm missing it all.
I went through it, someone was there to watch.
I was sick, they were there. I was hungry, they were there.
Through all the joys, sorrows, the broken hearts.
All the success, the failures, someone was there.
I'm missing it all.

I can't wait, it won't be long before I will get to
see it all.
How much bigger is she? Has she been sick?
Is she growing out of her clothes? Does she need a haircut?
How many teeth does she have now? What size shoe does
she wear?
I'm missing it all.

The sorrow of it all will soon be over.
I'll have her. I'll watch her grow, take care of her when
she is sick.
I won't miss anything else.
Let him miss it all, it's my turn.
I won't miss it all anymore.

Michael P. Wascom

Addiction

Deep so deep, a grotesque core of
hate and evil, walking the earth,
killing in its crusade for lives,
trifling images of its devastation
live and lie leaving behind children,
family, friends and sometimes
wives.

Do not play with a destroyer with
the capacity of rearrange thoughts,
manipulate your soul, and ravish
your insides, be weary of the plague
sent only by those who lust its sidekick,
inside the false pleasure lurks
the venom to all as it hides.

Sean Eric Stanley

Life

Life to me is a sunny day.
It's the ocean reflecting the sun's ray.
It's the wind blowing softly 'round.
It's the soft covered moss on the ground.
Life's like a beautiful flower
As steady as an April shower
Life is as wonderful as can be
Life is a word that means "To be free!"

Rachel Jenkins

Central Park

Happily I strolled through the park,
When I should have been afraid in the dark.
A thump on my head then I fell down dead;
Soon to be buried in my earthly bed.

Adrian Hunter

(Philip Nolan) The Man Without A Country

He shouted out in anger the words that sealed his doom.
He sounded and resounded throughout the crowded room.
Philip Nolan's words were granted, his wish was not in vain.
For he never wanted to see the United States again.

He was placed aboard a ship, an easy life he lead.
For he never lived to regret those hasty words he said.
The years passed by so slowly, he was a sad but wiser man.
Never again to see his beloved native land.

He died aboard that ship and was buried in the sea.
The last words he wrote, "My love for my country is greater than thee."

Edwin E. Conner

Fusion

It's cold and there is no one to keep me warm
I'm lonely and there is no one to keep me company
I love you and miss you
I need to feel your arms around me
To taste your kisses
And feel your body next to mine.
I need to know
That you are here for the rest of time.
I want to touch you
And feel you tremble with desire
Like the flicker of a flame
Going into a raging fire
That only I can control;
I need a love that is complete
A fusion of souls and spirits
Of desire and need.

Addie R. McElyea

Walk In My Shoes - Sit In My Chair

When I sat in the chair
361 had already died there
I'm sure some were just
Or the system said this is a must
Anyway; guv didn't make the saving call
Thus saying; this man must fall

Now

I Sat In That Old High-Backed
Oak Chair - Would Have Looked Normal -
At A Dinner Table - Except For
The Hood, Straps, And Wires

Solid brick wall to your left
Executioner and his window behind
Friends, Relatives, and Witnesses to your front
Warden and That clock to your right

Contrary To Popular Belief
The lights in the town
Did not go down

BUT YOU DID

Blair Powell

I Cry

Lonely feelings of worthlessness and failure
Fill my head
A deep pain wrenches at my soul

I cry for me, I cry for you, I cry for the world
So much pain, so much anger, so much hate
Can't wait 'til the rains come
And wash it all away
Wash it all away

Lies and confusion make the world turn 'round
Is right right, or is right wrong?
I can't tell the difference anymore

I cry for me, I cry for you, I cry for the world
So much pain, so much anger, so much hate
Can't wait 'til the rains come
And wash it all away
Wash it all away

T. K. Meyer

The Unforgiven

The unforgiven few outweigh the many
Who believe in a consecrated dogma.
They blindly believe in any routine
That some dynamic individually will expound.
Because of loyalty to one's party
The masses can be led like blind sheep.
They follow set in one's ways because of tradition,
Having a mind set without any direction.

There must be some way to ignite a light
In those darkened eyes of the many who follow.
Because they cannot see the clearing,
They are lost in a thickened forest.

An Indian brave will walk ahead of his squaw,
To tread on unknown grounds of undiscovered frontiers.
To protect and nourish her existence and well being in his only concern.
His life mean nothing to him,
Unless she respects his masculine and sensitive nature.

His belief in the Supernatural bonds him to a higher form,
Which receives it's nourishment and existence from Mother Earth.

Jim Brady

What A Day Brings?

A day brings sunshine and showers,
Growth and flowers.
A day brings happiness and smiles,
Cars that go for miles.
A day brings love and hate,
Some interracial dates.
A day brings faith and hope,
To get our youth off of dope.
A day brings hours of watching T. V.,
And millions who've been tested for H.I.V.
A day brings boredom and laziness,
A world full of craziness,
A day brings sadness and turmoil,
Years of damaging our soil.
A day brings kisses and hugs,
A world full of thugs.
A day brings tear drops and sorrows,
Hopes for new and better tomorrows.
A day brings jokes and laughter,
And a life lived happily ever after.

Tammara Luckey

She Probably..

She'd probably been peeking, in someone's crazy closet, 'coz
soon they found, she loved to wear, a multi-colored locket.

She'd probably been singing, someone else's songs, but soon
they found, time after time, she always proved them wrong.

She's probably been dancing, in someone else's shoes, where
Gamblers play much higher stakes, and love is food for fools.

She's probably been painting, someone else's pictures, but now
we find a different scene, a brand new style and color.

She'll probably be sailing off, to someone else's Island, and
fall in love with the worst of all, the tyrants and the brigands.

She'll probably plant lots o' trees, on someone else's hill,
and when she dies, they'll surely, say, she probably wasn't real.

Chuma P. C. Ogene (Spring 1996)

Scramble

Lips chapped and sprayed with
that old dryness which occupies
the hollow throat of the desert winds.
Toes buried in restive depths of tanned Sand that
launches in grains from under our rising heels
as We scramble for life.
It is here amongst Us.
But where?
Where is mine?
Amongst this vast sea of Time?
I quietly question by a dark lagoon
Solemnly lit beneath the ivory glow of a dying Moon,
at the edge of consciousness
deep within my mental woods.
And we've always scrambled wherever the Imperial
Fire teams with idle sands to
scorch bare soles and
contradict the blue mirage of the Universe.
Always scrambled.

Olaf Johnson

A Fall From Grace

A mysterious angel was walking out
of where she was shopping.
She ignored as death stood there mocking
for she doesn't know what is about to begin.
I; she loses, it shall be a sin.

Death's toy blinded her,
nobody could see it was just a big blur.
After it was over death had his way
A life had ended as well as the world that day.

Death didn't care he had done it before
it was just another life, it wasn't a chore.

Josh Lampinen

The Survivor

I call myself the survivor.
Sometimes I think death is my only friend.
Sometimes the pain of living just
doesn't seem to be worth it.
But yet I am still alive.
I'm not sure what this thing called life really is;
In the end we all die.
I have been trying to learn how to live,
But right now I am just surviving.
Maybe some day I'll understand
what this thing called life really is.
And may be just by chance,
I'll learn how to live, too.
Right now I am just a survivor.

Peggy Teal

Circle Of Stupidity

The anger slowly rises, from a place known only as hell.
How could I have ever lingered in that hypnotic spell?

Your eyes are so glassy, as cold as hard, shiny steel.
I'm in extreme pain that I assure you is real.

Your heart's as black as midnight coal, lacking any light.
Outside people see the love we share, and look at you in spite.

Your face is a picture of evilness, carved in unimpressionable stone
I swear I'd leave this place called Hell if I wouldn't face the world alone.

Everyone says, escape, get out but they aren't here, they don't know
I'm sure that one day you'll have forgiveness to show.

You've installed a quivering terror in my body and soul.
I have no choices left, I thought I was the one in control.

Your vice-like gripe is squeezing my heart.
There is no more love, it's only a circle without a start.

Over the same path every single day, as though a child-like name.
This isn't like that all you see, violence isn't a game.

Shannon K. Patterson

Anew

The sky's tears washed down my windowpane.
And I wondered why the
heavens where so sad.
Was it because of him,
like my sadness?
The salt tears poured forth,
washing the world green.
And I hoped that like the rest
of the world,
I could start over.
Anew.
Once again to know the
newness of the rebirth
of many different newnesses.

Manera Saloom

Oh, To The Graduate!

Dedicated to Jennifer Lynn Lawson

Oh, to the graduate so fresh into the world.
A breath of fresh air.
So sassy and yet telling people what's what.
Your mother so proud.
Accomplishing something major in life...
Now going on to bigger and better things in life.
Things you may not believe you are accomplishing yourself.
Go for your success and nobody else's...
Oh, to the graduate
Shine bright...
Shine thru...
And don't let anybody put you down or destroy your dreams!!
Hey, babe we're proud of you...
I'm proud of you....
Love always, Jennifer.

Christopher Mark Proctor

Olympic

The Olympic torch is raised for victory,
leading the Olympians on their way
with the American flag waving above.
All people gathering together to see this wonderful event.
Praise to all the athletes that made the Olympics what it is today.
Onward they go in search of their medals for all to see.
What a joy to all countries that are free.

Charlotte Burke

Time To Kill

Pleading for sanity
I speak to the broken mirror
(is my soul shredded or is it just me?)
you laugh as I shatter
but what does it matter
when all I've got is time to kill

Breathing in sorrow
I hope that there is no tomorrow
a continuance of lost expectations and lies
in a void I can't help but despise
I cannot feel, I cannot end
and creeping death is my only friend
and all I've got is time to kill

Broken and battered
God, how I wish something mattered
but nothing means anything anymore
life has got me drained to the core
shred me open, pry me apart
and pour out what's left of my dismembered heart
because all I've got left with you is time to kill

Megan Gibson

Friends Prayer

Be with my friend Dear Lord I pray
Guide and direct her path each day
Keep her safe from this world's harm,
and hold her tight within thy loving arms
You see dear Lord she's lost someone dear
and it hurts so much that he's not here
He helped her face each new day - to comfort her,
love her, and share two blessings you brought their way
Of course dear Lord you know this story,
for this man now is with you in Glory
And this is why I pray to you, so blessings abundant
can fill her heart so she can start anew
She needs you Lord, more now than ever
to tell her it's okay - I'm holding it together
to say dear child I feel your pain, for within these
nail scarred hands, you and your children will remain
Thank you Lord for this dear friend,
I know she's in the palm of your hand
Place her where she is to be,
and fill her heart with peace and serenity.
We close in prayer by saying Amen.

Lisa Ann Freeman

Words: Food For My Soul

Words, how important can they be.
How profound shall they sound.
through words I have been introduced to my soul.
Words can destroy or they can give life.
The choice was given to us by God, to use either or
to give life, is to understand.
To destroy is to ignore.
If you ignore a plant, it will surely die.
If you understand its needs, it will thrive.
I am a young man, and like a plant,
I need your words to water my leaves
while you're watering my leaves,
some of the water will reach my roots.
Then and only then, will I grow.
If you ignore my crumbling leaves,
eventually, I will die.
And because, I died without words.
I will spoil the soil, and nothing
will ever grow, lest you toil.

Sonja Gresham

The Game

Score one for you - big man in black.
Congratulations on this consummate victory.
Like an ill-concocted fairy tale,
Everything works out in the end.
You stole all his gifts from us,
But so kindly left him with the memories
That will slowly eat away at his mind,
Because that is all you spared him.

I'll always wonder why him and not one of us
And how you choose who loses the game
And who slips by unscathed.

However, I know you cheated this time
Him, me, and possibly everybody.
But I am not one to be a sore loser
And so I say, "A job well done!"

Meg Tyrrell

Online

Scattered Bits
Pass through myriad wires
a bill is paid

The cycle begins anew
Streams of consciousness reaching
through the Electronic Void

Friends
(and possibly more-
Congratulations Fredi/Fritz, Andy/Connie)
Reaching through the Phosphor Screen

Too short nights spent online
(The Morning comes too soon)
Give us back that peace of mind
(Pieces in my case)
And ready us for the mornings gloom

Christopher R. Perkins

Love

Learning that
Other people need your help
Very much
Even though you don't know where to start.

Christi Freeman

"When First We Had Met"

From a moments glance that turned to stare,
The presence of each other was clearly aware.
Wondering thoughts surely filled my lonely mind,
Was this by fate or is all other love this blind?

Troubles they did plague me and more so you,
The two of us in pain with no way to hide it true.
Then in a twinkle of an eye our lives changed,
Was this heaven sent or somehow even prearranged?

We spent the night together so smoothly it did transpire,
An intimacy oh so warm couldn't be better even if hired.
All the feelings shared between us we did achieve,
Not years to be invested just days who would believe.

Imbedded in my weary mind are those precious moments,
Locked away from you I never dreamed such torments.
Many things between us need sharing but not just yet,
A life of love I wanted for us "When first we had met"!

May our sharing and caring follow us two,
From now until forever I pledge love to you!

Carl C. Butler

Broken Arms Forever

Roller blading with a friend,
Think the fun will never end.
Your friend gets tired,
Just one more lap on your behalf,
She takes a nap,

A quick turn ends it all.
Suddenly you slip and fall.
You think your arm's not broken,
But it is and you found yourself
Outspoken.

Your arm is swollen.
And you have to stay at home.
Thank goodness broken arms aren't forever.

Catherine L. Shelton

'My Son'

I brought into this world a son in '74
A mother couldn't ask for more.
He was healthy, normal, and kinda cute
Big brown eyes, Oh what a beaut!

I'm very proud of this son I had
He even went on to become a grad.
This son I had in '74
A mother could not ask for more.

He enlisted in the Marines, went away 4 years.
My eyes were always filled with tears.
I prayed to the Lord up above
Please take care of this son that I love.

As I sit here, writing these lines
Waiting to hear the familiar chimes
Of his voice ever so strong
Lord, please bring My Son on home!!

Debrat

The Ocean

I sit on the beach
Embraced by the sun's intense heat
I look towards the ocean
And stare at the waves
The waves crash along
In a fierce show of unbridled passion
Fighting one another in their pursuit of the shore
They don't wait for one another
They just push their way through
I remain, fascinated by the scene
I shake my head inwardly
As I think of how humans are like waves
Each person trying to outdo the next
In a tacit, eternal competition

Carla Rose

My World

I want to swim in the sky, and fly through the sea
I want a tall, dark, and handsome glass of water when I be;
thirsting from drought, caused by the impossible
making my mark in the world of the plausible
seeking to die yet determined to live
wanting to be something that just goes on to give
looking at life as just something to get through
charming, disarming with a huge lack of virtue
from when it's all over, to when it begins
where destiny leads me on my life depends
I'll go hunting for fish and fishing for birds
doing what everyone else deems unheard
so if you ever wanna find me you know where I'll be
either swimming in the sky and flying through the sea.

Urvia McDowell

The Roses Knew

When we were together the roses bloomed,
never at all feeling the slightest bit doomed.
Their presence was remarkable,
their essence was strong,
as if nothing in this world could go wrong.

When we separated
their being went morbid;
as their construction was not so neatly sorted.
The blooms continued to open, but dead,
what they were trying to tell me
I never could have said.

For those few weeks the bush was
pampered and cared for,
and it soon became healthy once more.
Now that we are back together
I must say,
I cut off a nearly perfect rose
almost every day.

Ayesha Quillen

The Unending Trail Of Solitude

Each day I wake up,
A new sun shines...and I ponder,
Is there no happiness,
Even a tiny piece
Left in the world...meant for only me?

Solitude.
Sweeps through my body,
And becomes locked in my soul,
No escape...no way out.

Each second I feel lost,
Concealed in a strange world,
No direction...no purpose,
No one to love me...body, mind and soul
Simply the person I am,
Not just a divine image created in a confused mind,
To please...to be accepted.

Alone and isolated,
Locked in a cage...no key to be found,
Existence becomes a darkened tunnel...continuous and unending,
As I walk the trail of solitude...that consumes my life.

Rachel Juley

Kayleigh Rhiannon Ball

I stare at you each morning
With a love unknown to man
To know I'd die without you
Many more feelings I keep within

Your skin so perfect
Your smile straight from the heart
I'm given life with your every breath
Minutes are forever each time we part

I've never had to earn your love
It's so pure, simple, and true
From the moment, you entered this world
I've experienced a happiness I never knew

Kayleigh, my daughter
I was so right to name you from a song
You are music and everything so beautiful
A world like ours you do not belong

I will never understand
How a child so lovely was given to me
Made from my love
You are the best this world will ever see

Elizabeth Ball

"Unaware"

If there ever was a moment; that I failed to share,
If ever I was needed; but somehow wasn't there
If ever you were hurting, and I seemed not to care,
I can promise you that I was unaware.

If I ever passed a judgment; that was totally unfair.
If I ever hurt your pride or caused your heart to tear,
If ever I asked more of you; than you could stand to bear,
Then I apologize, but I can promise you that I was unaware.

If there ever was a secret; that you felt you couldn't share,
If you had to shoulder burdens, that I should've helped to bear,
If ever I ignored you, when you needed me to care,
I can promise you that I was unaware.

If at any point I left you; hanging in the air,
If you ever cried alone at night; while I was off somewhere,
If I failed to show you comfort; when you were feeling scared,
then I apologize, but I can promise you that I was unaware.

Eva Newsom-McKay

I See

I see a little girl run to bed
I see her cover up her head
I see her hands covering her ears
I see her shaking with fear.

I see pretty eyes go from blue to black
I see her blood everywhere
I see her look of total despair
I see no help for her anywhere.

I see her face bruised and swollen
I see her pool of many tears
I see her arm that was broken
I see this picture for a myriad of years.

I see the belt as it hits
I see the strike of the knife
I see hair pulling that won't quit
I see a woman, a mother, a wife.

I see her heart so full of pain
I see her spirit as it was hurled
I see the years, were they loss or gain
I see the woman as an unloved little girl.

Veronica Sanders

Where Is Love?

I have no one to write a letter to;
No one to help me see this through!
I'm feeling lonely and really sort a blue;
Oh, how I wish I had someone just like you!

Somebody to answer my lonesome little cry;
Just a little someone to tell me the reason why!
One little letter would make me sit and sigh;
Yes, one little answer to put me on a high!

Don't be afraid to tell me how you feel;
The things I say and do are really real!
One shining moment of enjoyment I'd steal;
For it would give me a new change to heal!

Are you the love I want and need so;
Can you give me that warm special glow!
As a warm summer breeze-softly you flow;
Straight through my heart and let me know!
Where love is!

Harold N. Croff

MOLLY

get your gun, get ready to
fight to get your vision through
set aside the way you feel
and recognize what is to be real
rambling through a dense forest
searching for someone to beat down and arrest
get your gun, get ready to
fight to understand the enemy too
just try to feel like I do now
and I will try too, this I vow
living a pointless life again
too many times it's here, what then
get your gun, get ready to
fight to change this yellow from blue
déjà vu comes back to haunt me
and pulled out my heart to bleed
this was my one chance gone
tomorrow won't be a new day's dawn
fight it down- what you know
fight it down- who you are

Ryan Shelby

Our Star

Our star shines brightly high above
Burning with passion it explodes into light
We sit and stare as our fingertips touch
I look at you and see an angel
You look at me and find your soul mate
Destiny lays itself before us
A bright carpet of unending light
Slowly our lips touch connecting our emotions
In the web of life we have found our path
The time has come to spread our wings
And soar together to unending heights
We fly together through the clouds
And as we land upon our star
We know that we will be
Together...
Forever...
Dancing in our galaxy
On our star
Finding true happiness
In a harsh world.

Kim Ludwig

The Child

The Child,
Some people think they're like beasts, wild.
But the ones who live on the street,
The ones who don't have shoes on their feet,
The ones who get beat,
The ones who don't have enough to eat
They just might not make it through
To see another sky so blue.

Can you hear their yells and shouts?
Can you feel their pain and doubts?
Can you hear their cries and see their tears?
Can you feel their love and their fears?

While your child has a necklace made of gold,
The child living on the street is outside in the cold.
While your child is safe behind locked doors,
The child that gets beat has bruises and sores.
While your child laughs and plays,
The hungry child can only hope and pray
That maybe the next day,
Everything will be okay.

Julia M. Dann

"It's Your Turn"

All those years filled with tears
you thought this love was right.
Restless days and sleepless nights
hoping not to fight.
All the effort put forth by you
deserves a bright blue ribbon.
You now can see the part you played
for all the tolerance given.
Now it's time for your fair share
your chance to be the one.
You've done your time and paid the price
and in my eyes you've won.
And although you gave some pride away
it may have made you learn that all
you've done now holds a price and
now it is your turn.

Jill Cannon

The Cabin

The cabin I remember still stands in the woods,
It's the happiest remembrance of my childhood.
On the porch in the summer where Mama would sing,
With the squeak of her rocker to us sleep she would bring.
And the fireplace in winter softly crackling with warmth,
Was used to cook food and keep little toes warm.
Grandma's hand-stitched quilts covering all but our heads,
Kept little ones cozy in the big feather bed.
The attic was filled from pillar to post,
With trunks and treasures and good country ghosts.
The old kitchen table so weathered and worn,
Saw Mama and Daddy through many a storm,
The loud, hungry kids Mama had to face,
As we sat round the table, hands linked to say grace.
A sick little child or the death of a friend,
The table was where a talk with God would begin.
The cabin was built not of wood but of love,
And was showered with blessings from Heaven above.
I think of my childhood and cherish it still,
As I remember the cabin tucked deep in the hills.

Shirley Smith Cutshaw

"Sunshine"

January - it's bitterly cold, the world is quiet
Looking out the window at the snow
I see sunshine on the white blanket
And I smile
For the world is beautiful

April - The rains pound, the thunder rolls
Toward evening, sunshine makes an appearance
From behind the dark clouds
And I smile
For the world is beautiful

July - The end of a hot summer night
I see sunshine peeking through the window,
Telling me a new day is here
And I smile
For the world is beautiful

October - the leaves are falling
Sunshine lies behind me, fast asleep
As the morning sun touches her breast and her face
I smile
For the world is beautiful

George F. Shock

God's Peace Can Be Yours

Is happiness eluding you?
If it is, what can you do
To bring it back into your life,
And end this long exhausting strife.

You're just not able, by yourself,
To put this problem on the shelf.
To cater to your earthly nature
Will only make the problem greater.

So, seek your help from up above.
Pray God to take you with his love.
Through Jesus you can come to him.
There is no other way to win.

Jesus will help you willingly,
And you can join God's family.
And as his child, you'll soon find,
That he's brought peace into your mind.
The holy spirit will bless your life,
And then you'll see the end of strife.
You'll be secure till the end of time.
For the peace of God will guard your mind.

Calvin M. Osborne

Jesus And Tears

Last night you were crying, before you feel asleep.
The sorrow you were feeling, was so very deep.
As the tears ran down your face, I gathered unto me.
I put the tears in my heart.
And now they belong to me.
For in my heart they will stay.
I wouldn't have it any other way,
The joy come with the morning sun
And the tear's of sorrow will be over and done.
Tears of joy make it a better tomorrow.
Love and caring, is like the innocence of a child.
The tears of joy and the tears of sorrow.
Brings some today and some tomorrow.
Always remembering, just one thing,
No matter what tears you may shed.
Let it be known and let it be said.
The tears of today and the tears of tomorrow.
There is something we should know.
Jesus will be there to comfort our soul.

Douglas P. Henning Sr.

Secret

Imagine never seeing the sun again
Imagine giving up the one thing
You cherish most.
But never missing it
Until it's gone.

Imagine living forever,
But forever has a price.
Imagine existing only to feed.
Imagine serving your sire and your prince
Imagine living out of God's sight.
Imagine being no stranger to Death

Now you know my secret
The Masquerade has been broken
Now you die.
You have until the count of ten.
Start running.

Samantha McCullah

Pressures

Do you ever feel that life,
Just ain't worth it?
Have you ever had a knife,
And felt like thrusting it?

Have you ever had the wish,
That your heart would stop beating?
Do you ever see a dish,
And feel like never eating?

Do you ever think of drugs,
And say "I'll try if they'll kill me?"
Have you ever needed a hug,
But never thought of one in your family?

If you have problems,
Such as I,
Go get help,
Before you die.

Kresta Anne Sutherlin

A Trip To Hell

I was hit and now am falling,
Everything is behind me now and nothing ahead.
Suddenly, there is a bright light and I am walking
towards it.
It is peaceful yet I am scared,
It is beautiful yet dark and evil,
It appears to be heaven yet it is hell.

Tess Kehoe

AIDS

I have AIDS, yes I do
I can't help but be truthful to you
You can't get it by shaking hands, or by hugging me
It is a sexually transmitted disease, and that doesn't mean you get
it by having a sexual preference
You are probably scared, scared to touch and feel me
I have more reasons to be scared than you
My life has ended in a flash, once you get it you're already dead
Dead inside, knowing that person you slept with lied
While your life has just begun, my life has just ended
No matter what a parent says, no matter how strong you are
AIDS can get you if you're not smart
With education you can beat it from the start
Don't fear death, don't fear pain
Try as hard as you can to keep yourself sane
Death can come at any time, it could come when a child turns nine
Death can ease the pain, whenever you are hurt
With education you can stop the ignorance, you can prevent AIDS
from conquering your life
As we salute those who died from AIDS with strife.....

Kingkan Kingpetcharat

An Evening In May

As I walk through the breeze swept field,
blades of grass dance under my barefeet.
The sun kisses the horizon,
painting long shadows on the earth before me.
High above, a blue sheet delicately drapes the globe.

To the left, men in sport gracefully tax their bodies with
power and precision.
To my right, stately pines display strength and the dream
of longevity.

I do not walk anymore.
Instead, this world encircles me.

In this masterpiece, I have witnessed perfection. But who
is the artist?

Jacob Dante Leffler

Promised Land

A born romantic holds out his hand
And puts his heart in love's land.
He learns a new way to laugh and cry
Facing the fact that hopes sometimes die.
With her life and her love to guide him,
He respects her and needs her beside him.

Their life together was long and blessed;
Then it came time to put her to rest.
He remembered, once again, how to cry
And faced the fact, it was her time to die.
A born romantic reached for her hand,
And his love was put in the heart's land.

The end of his time came in sleep
Peace settled over and quiet was deep.
He would never again have to cry
Nothing else would his eyes see die.
A past romantic again holds her hand
In the beautiful sky, called Promised Land.

Kerry McCrory

Carousel

Life is like a merry-go-round
sometimes up sometimes down
You get a ticket when you are born
then get in line to wait your turn
When it's time for you to ride
you pick a horse and climb astride
You sit there waiting, feeling scared
you hope you picked your horse with care
You grab the pole just to make sure
then start feeling more secure
When you hear the music start to play.
you know your life is underway
It may start up, it may start down
but be sure your life will turn around
At first you don't know if you like this ride
but after awhile it takes a familiar stride
Some are happy with just one horse
then some have to ride them all, of course
But when your ride ends and your life is done
I hope you walk off one of the happy ones

Oliver D. Kerley

Thoughts About Lisa And Me On Her 27th Birthday

I wanted to be your mom or even your dad, but that could never be.
I would never fill those needs, even if I could, because, it was me.
Who was I to you? I wondered, surrogate parent? A friend?
or was I just 'she'?
I wanted to be there for you, when you cried, when you were sick.
I helped you with your homework, sometimes calmed your fears
loved your ballet concerts with my tears.
At times I thought myself, the Proud Parent!
Present at your many successes by your request, but quietly please.
Without fanfare or much to-do,
I watched as you grew and you watched me too.
Then one day I awoke and it came clear to me,
I was a parent, both a mom and a dad,
And, you'd let me be, even without total clarity.
One day I heard the far off melody of a song I'd always known,
and then knew you'd given me a gift that transcended words,
didn't always fit, and didn't need to.
I almost missed it, looking for what I thought should be.
You and Me! Well, we are, and will always be, just "we."

Lynda Sowbel

Sunshine

She is the most precious gift of life,
waiting in the distance unaware.
Her inner glow and warmth touches the
hearts of every living soul.
Flowers and trees bloom forming silky clouds
that fill the air with an allay of aroma.
Green grass grows and birds glide through the
sky.
Yet she waits in the distance unaware,
unaware of the harmony she creates.
Her name is sunshine,
The most precious gift of life.

Harold A. Stults

Those Forever Young Heroes

He was a soldier once, young brave, and free—I remember him, my buddy, it was his life he gave, unselfishly, for his country— you and me.

Forever he'll be young, as I now grow old—but there will always be a memory, of him, — In my heart, to hold.

Our lives are better, because of those who had to fall — honor those from all wars, and I'll think of my buddies, those forever young heroes, who's names grace along black wall.

Salute to the parents, who lost a daughter or son — while those admit now, it could have never been won.

Their hearts still ache, and some share the pain — it's hard to point a finger, there were too many to blame— But we can be proud of those, that we honor today—those forever young heroes— who I know—never died in vain.

Philip Ferrazano Jr.

Grandpa's Tick-Tock

He was such a little bitty boy,
Yet had a magic touch
Which warmed and cheered an older heart
and crowded it with joy.

As Grandpa sat in his big chair,
A smile on his dear face,
the little one looked 'round for him and
Quickly joined him there.

With elbows propped on aging knees
And bright eyes wide with wonder,
He asked the question waited for,
"Grandpa, tick-tock, please?"

With eyes aglow and smile so warm,
the treasure was removed,
and placed with greatest tenderness
Upon that tiny arm.

To guess at who was happiest
would surely be a mock-
The one whose heart had overflowed?
Or — the one with Grandpa's Tick Tock?

Irma M. Gall

Untitled

Through rain, sleet, or snow it's true;
our favorite cousin is always you.
The "Happy Birthdays" from us are said,
with true sincere- even while asleep in bed.
We hope your wishes will all come true,
and are filled with happiness as they follow through.
We hope the presents excite you much,
as you gaze at them with fondness and such.
Your birthday candles will always glow,
in our hearts - even when it's time to go.

Margaret Chen

"Time And Tears"

A child was born upon this day
Thirsty for love to pass his way
Never a home to truly rest
No one to show him what was best
Pain and anger grew deep within
A shredded heart that would never mend
Tossed to and fro like a ship at sea
Wanting to follow but no one to lead
Torment and depression his only friend
Wishing at times his life would end
Wanting to love yet not knowing how
Is it too late for the man to learn now?
Love surrounds him everyday
Just sit and watch his children play
A tender touch at night as he lays
beside a woman who whispers "it's okay"
Inside his heart he never knew
The seed of love grew and grew
Cobwebs of the past may sometimes appear
But love sweeps them away with time and tears.

Lisa A. Spoone

People

As I look up on a star lit night,
and see the Heavens so shiny and white;

I think of a land so far away,
where the sun is shining bright.

I think of the people, and how life goes on,
and how different there's is from mine!

The truth is we got here the very same way,
and we all reach the end of the line!

We all live together on this place called Earth,
Red, Yellow, Black, Brown, and White!

But I think if I meet some one that's Green,
it would give me a terrible fright!

So no one is different from the man on the street,
or the woman rocking her child.

Or maybe the lady I saw in the store,
who happily gave me her smile!

Charles Allen Conaway

I Had A Dream One Night

I was sitting on the floor, and I looked out my window.
There stood before me a man as white as snow.
Could it be? Was it really Jesus?
I trembled at the thought. Was it judgement day?
I fell face down to the man.
"Lord, please forgive me," was all I could say.
He said, "Do not fear my child.
It is time to come home to me."
As he disappeared a stairway was left behind.
"Follow me," His voice said. Now a distant whisper.
I knew this was the path to take; it would not be easy.
I left my floor and followed the voice. The stairway.
The journey was long and hard, but finally
I made it to the glory land.
I was home at last.

Suzanne Cook

Through The Eyes Of A Child

The summer days of youth it seems
Can be revisited in a young boys dreams
On a hot and clear summers day
You can relive it all watching a child at play
A gentle smile and a cheer of joy
Can make your mind wander to when you were a boy
From a game of baseball to a clear golden pond
You see, to find magic you don't need a wand
The magic lies in the wonder of youth
The knowledge that's learned when in search of the truth
As innocent eyes take in all of the sights
They dream the sweet dreams when the days turn to nights
They all want to grow and be older so fast
But these are the years that we'd all like to last
Friendships are made and the summer is spent
In a world full of dreams, I wonder where they all went
When youth's passed you by and your life's dull and mild
It's nice to see life, through the eyes of a child

Donald W. Bivens

Sleep Little Baby

Sleep little baby, don't you cry
Peace will come, by and by
If only you could understand
Why men fight throughout this land
You're much too young, to know the reason why
Baby's like you so often die
not enough food through out the world
to save all little boys and girls
Sleep little baby, don't you cry
Somewhere in the world another child dies
Sleep little baby, don't you cry
Peace will come, by and by
One day I hope you'll see
Everyone living peaceful
no more to hear children cry
no more to see children die
Sleep little baby, don't you cry
Peace will come, by and by, one day soon I hope you see
All people in the world living in unity
Sleep little baby, don't you cry.

Gloria Raymond

"Rantings Of A Dying Poet"

Staring upon the old clock
It's driving me mad with its tick-tocks.
Loudly and clearly it knocks.
It raps out the hour
The terrible coward
Will not let me stop it... it mooches.
The clock rings again and is bold.
The sound of it makes me quite cold.
For it reminds me that I have grown old,
And can no longer bear to be told.
That my life has gone
It has long been done
My destiny awaits me in mold.
Bury me Sunday at noon.
And as they shovel upon me, the last spoon,
Look at your clock
As it tickety-tocks.
It curses, it shocks,
The time you have left, it just mocks.

Paul Carpenter

Bougainville

All is loneliness and fear
 and darkness in the jungle's depths,
Night has come
 but peace is not its fellow,
All is mystery and pain
 while someone in the blackness lurks
 And spies,
His eyes on me, with earth my pillow.

There is no rest
 while ev'ry crackling sounds seems muffled Death
 come close to me,
 arrived before its season.
All is bravery and fear and silence
 in the pounding pulse,

Death is here. I sense him near
 and struggle to maintain my reason.
A harsh, cold breeze ruffles the night.
 Cold? Here in the dank, primal slime?
Is that his frigid hand along my spine
 Or has he passed me by again?

Ed Goldenthal

My Polluted Land

Oh, dear land, what do we do to you.
To make your once green grassy land
So messy and so out of hand?

Your sweet lily and daffodil
Once grew upon this hill.
But now it is scattered with litter,
And so many items that are bitter:

Rubber tires, springs, mats,
Cans, shoes, papers and rats
Fill the open space,
Where Spring can no longer bloom at its pace.

Sunshine dares not show its light
Over this ugly sight.
And what shall happen to this earth
When Springtime shall give no birth?

Brigitte Melton

Tribute To Clowns

Just to put smiles on the faces in the crowd
The clown will walk far and very proud
Their efforts are endless
Their sacrifices tremendous
Clowns wear a size 20 shoe
Sometimes they even look like two
Clowns have no time clocks
May even wear different colored socks
Clowns color their teeth black
And may look like their wearing a yellow sack
But clowns have a heart of gold
And I don't mean the kind that is sold
Long before the parade begins, the
Clown is putting on his face, funny
Shoes, yellow hair, big nose and his wonderful smile
Clowns juggle their pins until their arms
Feel like lead, but never a complaint is said
For all the good clowns do, God must of hand picked them too

Thelma Lantz

The Title Of Father

To have the role as Father you must understand,
there is no way you can carry that title without first being a man.
A father must set an example because he is appointed as head,
he has to be the breadwinner in the house to make sure the family is
fed. A Father must make many decisions trying not to let his
family down. He must stand firm to those decisions no matter
whose around. Most children view their fathers as hero's, in their
eyes he's number one, so he must show strength, courage, and
wisdom and make sure things get done. To carry the title as Father
you have many lessons to teach, but you can't raise your children
well, if you don't practice what you preach. Fathers are there to
give guidance when you don't know what to do, he must show
compassion, honesty, and love, to help you make it through.
Sometimes being a Father is lonely he may lay awake all night,
trying to figure out an answer to make sure things turn out right.
You see fathers are men, but have feelings although most of the
time they keep them inside, and with the help of God, when things
are going smooth they feel honour, dignity, and pride.
Any male can make a baby and being a good father can be tough,
but to carry the title as of Father making a baby is just not
enough. So listen to both your parents and help them as much as
you can, because one day you'll carry their title and one day you'll
understand.

Cara James McCann Jr.

That Little Flower

That little flower
So pure
So open
That little flower
That closed once night brought stars above its petals
That little flower
That's loved
And cared for
Shall never die
'Till one stepped on its petals.

Kelley S. McKibben

Ode To Snow

Snow flake, snow flake, lightly fall;
Cover the woods, trees and mall;
Snow flake, snow flake, lightly fall.

Snow flake, snow flake, briskly blown;
Caring not on what you're thrown;
Snow flake, snow flake, briskly blown.

Snow flake, snow flake, now a blizzard;
Freezing me, flowers and lizards;
Snow flake, snow flake, now a blizzard.

Snow flake, snow flake, glimmer in the sun;
Melting now, your life you've run;
Snow flake, snow flake—gee, you were fun!

Charles Stephen Hoyt

Girl In The Mirror

Her lips move when mine do
"I'll show you me if you'll show me you."

I see her in the morning when we compare faces,
I pass her in the window, unexpected places.

I'd like to read her mind and look in her eye.
I'd like to know her better, but I'm shy.

"Who are you?"
Shall I form the question,
Give it to her?

Or shall I take the easy way
And merely look right through her?

Renee Sharpe

"Your Love"

All through the day, and all through the night,
I dream of being with you and holding you tight,
Of sharing with you a sweet warm embrace,
Of seeing that sweet loving smile on your face,
Of trembling all over from things that you do,
And hearing you say "I love only you!"

Cause you bring the sunshine that brightens my day,
When we are together my cares drift away,
Whenever I'm weary, whenever I'm blue,
I just close my eyes and I'm right there with you.
Whether you're in my arms or right by my side,
The love deep inside me has nowhere to hide,
It glows in the night like a star burning bright,
For the way that you love me, makes everything right.

James H. Clarke

As I Walk

As I walk along the shore of
the Togiak Bay, I see the shining
lights of the sun's ray, that hits
the blue water. I see the fishing
boats that rides in the sea, and the
sea birds gliding over me.
I smell the wet wood on the
sandy beach, the salt of the sea and
the mud of the sea's out-going tide.
I hear the sound of the waves
running up against the shore, the tone
of a passing plane's motor. I hear
the cawing of birds floating in the sea.
I feel the smooth sand on the
warm beach, the warm ray of the sun
beating on my body and the wind
blowing in my face.
As you can see Togiak Bay is the
best place to be in May.

Tracy Lynn Wilcox

The Warmth Of The Sun

The golden sun reaches down
Its long arms
To touch me with its warmth.
After the cold of winter
The sun is a soft gentle caress
Upon my skin.
With a vivid blue sky as its background,
The sun astounds us
With its size and strength;
And amazes us
With its warmth and tenderness.
The sun gently awakens and nudges
The sleepy heart and soul
Within each of us...

Renee Locklear

Winter Happiness

On a cold blustery day, while it is snowing very heavily
I am inside my nice warm house either sitting by the
fireplace, reading in a place in my house where nobody can
find me, or watching T.V. with a warm blanket around me, and a
friendly dog. If I shall get chilled, I go sit by the furnace
and feel the heat, or I go take a warm bath. While it is still
snowing hard outside, if I get hungry I eat a nice hot bowl of
soup, any kind is fine, and have a good hot cup of hot
chocolate, or tea with the irresistible name, Sleepy-Time.
Also, coming in from the cold it is nice to smell cookies
baking in the oven. Those are the good feelings of Winter
Happiness.

Melissa Bochenek

My Sister, Phyllis, Had A Stroke

The flame burns brightly in her brain, with
Intelligence, love, and laughter.
The ruined cells cannot be repaired,
But the essential mind is alive and well.

With twisted tongue and crossed word paths
She joyfully communicates her love
Of God, of life, of family, and of friends.
We all smile and love her, too.

Happy to see her alive, to be with her,
We see daily growth of tongue, of hand,
Of walking crafts. To what degree her body
Will regain the skills of yesterday

We cannot know, but we cherish every smile,
Encourage every step, delight in every word.
We do not pray for Phyllis to return
For us, she never went away.

Raymond H. Lehrman

Take Mine Too!

In the corner, a forlorn pair of crumpled pantyhose
caught my eye as I entered the ladies rest room.

They were expensive, clean and white and at first
looked as though they were there for no reason.

But I suddenly could relate to the woman who
could endure the constraints for not
One
Minute
Longer.

She must have been desperate to have yanked the
things from her body with no regard for propriety.

Having rid herself from the tight, confining, elasticized,
cultural custom, she took her protest a step further.

By discarding her hose in the corner and walking
away, she silently conveyed her opinion of antiquated convention.

Every woman feels the exhilaration of this woman's freedom
just by gazing upon the crumpled symbol in the corner.

Linda Rondeau Pellerin

Decision Made

The pain stings inside her with every lasting breath,
it travels through her body resting abruptly inside her chest.

Fists clinched in rage as the tears begin to pour,
hearing his moan for the last time
as she throws open the bedroom door.

"I told you what would happen,
if I ever caught you again.
So tell me darling, is she just another friend?"

Fear struck suddenly, as sweat quickly dripped off his chin,
petrified by her eyes, "I'm guilty once again."

Her skin, soft as velvet, quickly changed to brick,
A decision that she must face...
death is what she picked.

Robert Cowart

Special Friend

We drove that day to Phantom Canyon,
Our hurt and fears attempting to abandon.

If for only a moment, if for only a while-
A picnic lunch, skipping rocks, taking pictures-forcing a smile.

Lying on the blanket, underneath that huge cottonwood tree-
Quietly embracing us within its shade-as if it wanted to set us free.

The cool, running water; the soft, gentle breeze-
Our laughter contagiously echoing through the trees.

So much said, but yet never spoken-
I see it in your eyes, your heart is broken.

I wish I could take away the pain, my dear friend-
I wish I could change the hurt and despair you're feeling within-

Yet all I know how to do is to tell you I love you-
And I'll always be your friend.

So shall you ever need me-anytime, night or day-
Please always know and never forget-I'm never too far away.

I love you, my dear and wonderful friend-
And I always will.

Sue Lynch

Bread and Circus

The stars are set to talk, as we await.
And earth spins, hurls our fate and fortune.
How go we, against this monumental tide —
Say, only a fool's peril can rest a smile
for this next days journey.
And we, all caught in Eternity's Swirl
form our habits and boast our gains
and decry our losses amid chants and screams
of inequity waiting for some permanence —
some final rest to punctuate
our seeming long sentence.
For ever doubting it will come
shall we become ghosts to haunt
with no surcease
this forever present whirligig
this mighty jubilant Bread and Circus.

Joe Cameron

I Should Have Known

So many words to distract from my true feelings for you.
Words that mean the opposite of what I'd like to tell you.
How often I have wished you were here to hold me,
To tell me you want to be with me,
That you really do care.
That can never happen - you told me so tonight.
I wanted to tell you how much I love the way you look at me,
The way you smile, the way you tease me,
And even how innocent you look even when you're guilty.
I apologized for interrupting your life.
I would never do anything to hurt you.
We can still be friends, right?
I am sorry for ever letting my feelings show.
I should know by now that I don't matter
To you or anyone else.
I'm sorry — I should've known.

Amanda Laker

Is This Me

Across the waters, in search of land, I plant my feet
Into the sand, this place I call my home land
Liberty! I dare you say! American land of the free?

From a seed, a human being is born, from you and me
up sprouts a "silver strand" intertwined throughout this land
out of sigh, out of mind, looking for its human kind
All that blossoms in my dreams, is this you, it this me?

I cross the mountains for you and me keeping my head to the sky
I yearn for another high, from there I dive into mystic blue seas
I have build bridges, I've burn them too! I tore down walls
For me and you as I. Take a heavy sigh! I find I have to cry
Help me please. Upon my hands and knees

I will help you, I hear them say her's a blow for mankind
Ugh! May I have another as the night sticks of justice.
Explodes across their bloody heads as we chase the aliens of man
Across our barren lands, I rush to close the flood gates
At the border there they wait, full of rage, full of hate
Another part of the human race. So we say! It's not our fault
For their fate, to consider them second rate
Is this you is this me? America stands accused!

Patrick J. Germany

"When I Look Into The Mirror"

When I look into the mirror,
all I see is blemishes and a need for braces,
but I am okay.
When I look into the mirror,
all I see is a body that is not skinny,
but I am okay.
When I look into the mirror,
all I see is a skintone,
that matches those that
have been hurt
by the latest church fires in the South,
but I am okay.
When I look into the mirror,
all I see is a student,
who comes from a working poor family,
but I am okay.
When I look into the mirror,
all I see is a person,
who has high aspirations to do good for all people
because it is okay to be yourself.

Kim Owens

"Hawaiian Boy"

I'm proud to be an Hawaiian Boy
and I enjoy Hawaiian foods even Poi.
The beach is my turf
and I like to swim and surf.
I like to fish and have it on my dish.
I'm proud to be an Hawaiian boy
and I enjoy Hawaiian foods even Poi.
I love my Hawaiian Island and my land.
Though my Hawaiian Island is small,
I love my home by the blue sea and sand.
I work my land and care for it.
And my land takes care of me.
There is no place I'd rather be.
My Hawaiian Island is a paradise
with blue skies, sunshine, blue sea,
and beautiful waterfalls. Even the sunset
is romantic. That is my Hawaiian Island.
I'm proud to be Hawaiian, and I'm
proud of my Hawaiian Island.
For I'm an Hawaiian Boy at heart.

Cynthia A. N. Ramos

The Sea And Me

Oh the sea how I'm longing to be,
It's such a part of me.
As I sit on the sand with nestled toes,
I can smell the freshness as if it were right under my nose.
The waves roll in, the waves roll out,
It's not just a miracle that hasn't just come about.
I feel peace, serenity and time for me,
Oh how many wonderful sights I see.
The children laughing and running,
While their Mom and Dad are sunning.
You can see the gulls flying in the sky,
Looking down as if to say good-bye.
The shells that I collect are my treasures of the day,
As I look back through my collection in such dismay,
The water is glistening; salty and wet,
And that's exactly where I choose to set.
As my mind closes in for the day.
I just want to shout hooray!!
My face is like a shining gleam,
Oh what a place oh what a dream.

Barbara McCall Capps

"Moms"

I've been on call, both day and night
ready and willing in darkness and light.
I've fought the tornadoes, that blew things awry
erased the graffiti that displeased the eye.
I've been a doctor, a gardener, a cook, an electrician
a mechanic, a plumber, a carpenter, a beautician.
I've remodeled houses and landscaped yards
been kicked out of Vegas for counting cards.
I've traveled the highways throughout the U.S.;
then planted my roots in the northwest.
Yes, I've done it all, from coast to coast
but raising my children is what I've loved most.
I've seen everything from preschools to proms
so kneel and give thanks to all us such moms.
Look around up and down, we're everywhere
unselfishly giving tender loving care.
If moms were paid for what they were worth
we'd get a million dollars just for giving birth.
So to all of you readers, I would like to say
lets give three cheers for moms, hip hip hooray!

Donna Haddock Spurling

A Silent Prayer

Dear heavenly father who takes care of all of us,
Please keep a watchful eye on the special guy I love.
He thinks that no one cares or would ever even try.
But you see I long to love him, that's what I have in mind.
I want him to know that I always will be here.
If I could do anything for him, I would get rid of all his fears.
But you see father he's given up, he no longer wants to try.
It scares me more to know that he says he wants to die.
I want him to be happy and start a life that's new.
I want him to think twice about what he wants to do.
He told me he had to leave, so I asked where's he going to go.
First he told me he loved me and in due time I'm sure to know.
Dear father that special guy I love has now gone and left me pain.
He wrote me a letter saying he had died because of aids.

Julie M. Quintanilla

Life's Journey

The wife is a mate through thick and thin,
Standing beside you till God knows when.
To hold and cuddle, laugh and to cry,
To bear all your children before you two die.

The son full of wonder brave and so tall.
As he grows older until nature doeth call.
To trust in his raising as worrying begins,
Away he will go with all of his friends.

The daughter ever sweet and always shy,
Soon will be looking for a special guy.
You want to protect her from evil a lurking.
Cause if she is harmed your blood will be perking.

My treasure is simply man and wife.
Children are happiness, as this is life.
Today has come tomorrow may not,
Life is so beautiful, there's only one shot.

Be sure in yourself in all your decisions,
For you are to answers as life is complete.

James Ponds

"Tonya"

Tonya was a darling,
she was a Christian teen
Tonya was as happy as any girl
we've ever seen
But she was taken, without warning,
to a better place we know.
Tonya we all love you, and we miss you so.

So, Tonya if you're listening, from your
new home up above.
This song is for you, Tonya
This is our song of love.
Tonya we all love you and we miss you so,
Tonya we all love you and we wanted you to know.

Yes, Tonya, she was different from a lot of teenaged girls.
Tonya was a Christian in this old sinful world.
We don't know why she was taken, and in this life we never will.
But the one thing we all look forward to
is to live where she now lives.

Judy Brower

Aurora Borealis

An eerie glow against the winter night
northern skies fall behind breath-taking light
cold wisps of wind ride over dunes of white
to numb the bone
the cold alone
seems to make the stars appear twice as bright

The moon in crescent casts its silent trance
gazes over it all as the bright lights dance
the mountain tops humbled by luminous strands
this drifting color
content to hover
leaning into the heavens as far as it can

David Uhouse Jr.

As I Lie There

Trees are brightening up the world with color
As I lie there in the cornfield.
A slight breeze is tickling my toes,
Fall is whispering in my ears,
the ground is covered with
a floor of colorful leaves
As I lie there.

Stefanie Ranck (age 10)

"Love Is A Token"

People need love, that's what it's for,
It's for the rich people and even the poor,
When people first meet their real true love,
They feel like a bird, a bright big dove.

They go out on dates every night,
They go to a movie, then out for a bite,
Then decide to get married,
And live with each other till they die and are buried.

They have children, oh what a great pain,
They have to start working for money to gain.

Then one day the love stops flowing,
The couple is mad, they don't know where they are going,
So one day they get a divorce,
They could not help it, it was too strong of a force.

Love is like a chain, a chain to be broken,
So love every one, because love is a token.

Joel T. Smith Jr.

Discovery

Pens moved across the paper as tears flowed.
Pain ebbed slowly
As each found the other's voice.

Karen Brown Kinney

Journey Through Cosmos

The eternal cosmos beckons
As a mortal journey reckons
To go as through completed deeds,
And so become finite things
That ne'er the vast eternal heeds.

That which man has in contention
To complete as though his own redemption
And winning, losing, ever vaunted,
But cast aside such that it brings
As evanescent, frail, and daunted.

Still onward, upward, striving ever
Endless void reaching beyond forever
Encircled so in empty space,
Lo, and in the vacuum so it brings
The struggle ceases, and thus the pace.

Burton S. Hoffman

Traitor Spring

I did not think that spring could come again
For you are on the wind swept hill unknowing

And winter's home is here within my breast.
But now the traitors lilacs bloom, imbuing
The air with fragrance and my heart with pain.
How you loved lilacs! Down the vanished years
A whisper brings again the words you wrote
When we were in life's springtime without tears

"Pale lilacs in a silver vase
With tender green leaves showing
Before your miracle I dream
And feel a soft wind blowing—"

I heap the purple blossoms on your grave
The futile gesture fails to comfort me.
You are not here—but where else can I seek you?

Oh dearest one, whenever you may be,
I pray that there be lilacs, a soft wind
And rushing waters quick with silvery fish.

Rose Martin Carroll

"I'll Tell You A Story Son"

Dedicated to Elsa DeLosSantos

I have to tell you a story son, when you were only one.
Your life began like a shadow, because you were a tiny son.

When you were born, that morn, your mother passed away.
She gave her life so you cold live, to run and learn to pray.

We got along all our lives, with your mother not at our side.
The two of us made us son and we lived with all of our pride.

I have to tell you another story son, and you were only two.
Life was hard without a wife or a mom, particularly for you.

Our lives weren't very pleasant and good days were only fair.
The things we talked about my son, often ended in a prayer.

We often talked about your mother son and where she might be.
I really do believe in God my son and it's heaven she might see.

I have to tell you another story son, and you were only nine.
We got along without tragedy and as a young man doing fine.

Then alone came a war, but I was too young and that suited me.
Every able bodied person volunteered for duty on land or on sea.

I was too young to join that war, because I was barely sixteen.
Life went on and believe it or not, I loved the prom night queen.

I really don't have any more stories to tell at the age of fifty five.
I want you to know I married that queen and she kept me alive.

Thomas C. Rupert

How Would You Feel?

How would you feel
If you're given a raw deal?
When you look for a place
And you're rejected because of your race?
How would you feel if your mother misused you,
And your father abused you?
Would your life be one of peace?
Or one filled "Police"?
If you life they degrade all because you've got AIDS.
Would you learn a new deal,
Maybe make an appeal, or just rob, loot, and steal?
How would you feel if you best friend just raped you?
T.V. Wanted to tape you? Could the Police locate you?
Would you parents now hate you?
How would you feel, it these things which are real
Would happen to you?
Would you be happy or blue?
If you put your own face, in the place of disgrace,
You just might help change the whole human race.

Rodney Long

With Deepest Gratitude

Sometimes we get too busy to share with those we know,
how much we do appreciate a closeness that has grown.

I know I have that fault at times so want to take this moment,
to express my deepest gratitude for given the chance to know you.

I thank you for your acceptance of my mental and physical self,
and liking me the way I am for what I give to you.

I thank you for your tender kisses that send chills throughout my
being, and for all the hugs you've given me that transformed your
strength within me.

Again I wish to thank you for being there to listen,
and judge me not for what I've done but what I now am doing.

So once again with deepest gratitude for all your precious moments,
and thank the Lord for all His help in bringing us two together.

Caren Pryor

I've Only Been Told

I've only been told for I cannot see for myself my eyes will not allow me.

I've heard of a field of exuberant flowers very colored from one end to the next, but what color they be? I've only been told!

I've heard of a waterfall surrounded by trees and the fall of the water moves elegantly, but how does the waterfall flow? I've only been told!

I've heard birds will soar and butterflies will fly, but how high will they fly? I've only been told?

I've heard of a mother and child together, the joy on their faces as they play with each other. What games do they play which such joy on their faces? I've only been told!

Uproot and exuberant flowers, I only feel its shapes. For I cannot see!

Dry the elegant flowing waterfall. I only hear its drips and drops. For I cannot see!

Lock up the birds that soar and butterflies that fly. I only hear the flap of their wings. For I cannot see!

Sleep mother and child who play united with your fun filled games and joyful faces. I only hear your laughter. For I cannot see!

Please open my eyes to the world outside, for destroying this worlds beauty would devastate all but me. For I cannot see!

Rochelle Sytner

Success

People measure success by acquired wealth and power
But the question is, is it imaginary or real?
Time and endurance are the testers, hour by hour
The near-do-wells and naysayers wait with zeal

Defining success is by far the hardest of tasks
Never should it be how much power and wealth we've accumulated
An heir to an empire emerges and you are among the outcasts
Can you walk with dignity wherever you've been dissimulated?

The sky is the limit, not the ultimate answer
Remember what goes up must come down
What if your destiny includes ridicule and censor?
And your name becomes mud all over town

You need an humble spirit and caring heart
The rich and famous are nowhere to be found
Out of loneliness and desperation a new life you start
Your need is not earthly riches, but a heavenly crown

You call out to the Creator of life and light
And find the success you wanted but did not see
He comforts and soothes and makes everything all right
For knowing Jesus is the answer for success to be!

Mary J. Scott

Early Morning

Breeze wisps by me as
calmness floods my body.

I start thinking about all sounds:
birds chirping,
trees rustling,
pleasant sound of gurgling creek.

I look to the sky which is turning hazy pink.
Sun starts to rise,
sky turning blue.

Happiness fills me up.

Ryan Graumann

IH-35 To OKC: June 14, 1985

I was apprehensive about this trip -
You called in February (after seven years) and
I thought years of prayers had finally been answered.

I almost turned back at Temple;
Before I knew it the sign read "Welcome to Oklahoma."
The river was redder than usual - or maybe it was just
  my tear-stained eyes.

Hills and plains matched my emotions:
Vacillating between ecstasy and dread -
Difficult to tell which was stronger.
"Entering Norman City Limits." -
Only fifteen miles now.

Sitting in front of your house contemplating
  my escape and the eight hour drive back home.
You arrived from work thirty minutes later and all I knew
Was that you were more attractive than the day you left.
This was going to be tough -
I'm not ready to fall again...
Even for my first love.

Cynthia S. Dietz

"Love, Beautiful, Painful"

Two hearts touched, beginning to beat as one. A small blossom bloomed suddenly bursting into flame, the flame-so bright-blinding eyes and minds to reality. Lingering it grew into something beautiful and precious. However it could not be! These human hearts, heavy, and still, parted.

Having gone in opposite directions, separated once more, yet somehow still connected never to be totally severed, awareness is acute that the flame is yet alive. Reflecting after twenty years, hopefully twenty years wiser, it is obvious it continues to burn, unquenchable, undying, only now as a diminished "eternal flame".

The flame erupting only on occasion-glowing-revived in an occasional thought, a song, memories that refuse to ever totally fade away. Each will forever be apart of the other letters still appear in the sand. Life, not always easy, continues. We have survived and overcome. I wish you happiness, peace and contentment. I have achieve the same to the extent ever possible.

D. M. Pierson-Kramer

Whatever You Do Please Don't Chew

We had an old neighbor, grey beard to his chest,
and he washed it once a month to make sure it looked its best!
I remember how it glistened, that beard all full of spital,
and it really kind of got me way down deep within my middle!
His family came one Thanksgiving morning.
They came unannounced without a word of warning.
He ran to my Mother saying "What's a man to do,"
then he hauled-off and spit a wad of chew!
"I have a turkey but I need some direction,
if I'm ever to cook that bird to perfection!"
A few days later he brought Mom some weeds,
saying "I've brought you some posies for all your good deeds!"
They stayed on the porch all winter through,
and every time I passed I could smell that old man's Chew!
Dad said if he'd known it would make her all a sizzle,
long ago he'd brought her a big bouquet of thistle!
Mom said "Don't bother", then she added with a grin,
"He may bring me flowers but I'll never let him in!"
"Oh I'd rather see a man suck a lollipop or two,
it's a darn sight better then one chewing on his chew!"

Marlyce E. Morse

Fathers Day

When you're looking for that special man
With whom to spend your life
You hope he likes you just as much
And wants you for his wife

And if you have some children
For whom he'll be their dad
It may turn out that he is just
The best father they've ever had

I know I can stop looking
For my special #1 man
As none could ever match you
Throughout this whole wide land

We've had our ins and outs
also our ups and downs
But here is where I want to be
In all of the U.S. Towns

Even though I don't say it often
I love you in every way
And with you for the rest of my life
Is where I plan to stay

Carol S. Turner

Hold On

As you sit there all alone
You think of how wonderful it would be
To spend time with your family and friends
But most importantly be free.

You started to reminisce
On the good old days
And kept wondering if
You would ever see the sun's beautiful rays.

You thought that no one understood you
And that this was all unfair
You hoped that you would soon wake up
And this would be one long nightmare.

But as you stand behind that cell
And think about all you have done
You realize that God is with you
And that victory shall be won!

Jennyfer Hernandez

Two People

No one to turn to,
No where to run,
Torn between two people,
Both under the sun.
They never liked each other,
Then one day I came,
I was friends with two enemies,
but hate was not the same,
They both want my attention,
every day and every night,
But I just can't handle it, and now I don't feel right,
Then one day she comes to me and says,
"I'll try to be nicer, I know you have other friends"
I just wonder, will the other do the same?
I know this sounds impossible, and at first I thought so too.
But now I know, I just can't stop, not if it means
losing either one or two.
So now I'm really trying, to let the other know, just the way I feel
with no one to turn to, and no where to run,
torn between two people, both of them, my friends.

Carrie Pfeffer

My Dream

You'll never know
All the feelings I still have for you.
I watch her hurt you,
Break your heart!
But what can I do,
Now that we're apart?
I want to scream -
Why can't she see?
What is now her toy,
Was once my dream!

Brandi Weyer

Mother's Gift

I prayed for a blessing, Oh Lord, only one -
Yes I was blessed and now proud of my son.
I kept wishing and praying my love within,
Would be passed on to my offspring.
I knew at his birth, God had a plan
that I alone would make my son into a man.
It was hard and times were rough
but that's what makes my son tough.
He went fast from boy to man -
Thank you Lord, for the steady hand
Now he's a U.S. Marine, of the few and proud.
He's filled my plan, to find himself
and help his fellow man.
So glad God and I held his hand -
helping him to stand
Sheltered him with hugs and kisses
Giving his mother such bliss.

Sandy Doherty

Daddy

God saw you getting tired
And the cure was not to be
He wrapped you in his loving arms
and whispered, "Come with me."
You suffered much in silence
Your spirit did not bend
you faced you pain with courage
Until the very end.
You tried so hard to stay with me
Your fight was all in vain
God took you to his loving home
And freed you from all your pain.
Never does a day go by
I do not think of you,
A golden heart stopped beating,
Two working hands at rest.
When the days are sad and lonely and everything goes wrong,
I seem to hear you whisper, "Cheer up and carry on!"
Each time I see your picture you seem to smile and say,
"Don't cry I'm only sleeping and we'll meet again someday!"
Always remembered and loved,
your daughter.

Launa Armour

"Goodbye"

Saying goodbye is never easy, it always comes with pain
Someone special's leaving and taking part of you away
Saying goodbye is not forever, there's always a time to meet
again, even if we are not sure of where or when
So when the farewell is over I leave these words with you,
I'll need you, I'll want you, I'll miss you I pray you feel
the same way too - Remember this when you are far away I'll
be waiting for you to come back I'll never go astray please
don't forget what I say I mean Cherish my words when you are
lonely and I hope you will always know I love you my friend
Keep these words with in your heart until we meet again.

Stephanie Ames

Eyes Of Brew

Alas but whose brew of misty mornshine
Hast been poured down upon thy lazy brow?
In torrid anger arise
Arise and cuff the crusted sleep
From unrested angry eyes.

Thou curses the day for it even begins
Spewing forth foul deeds
As though fruitful seeds
(Into nothingness).

Now reap! Reap less of the day
You reap what you have sown;
Now thou must pray.

Lowell G. Torske

The Look Of Love

Have you ever heard, what they say
Don't search for love, it will come your way
When it arrives, what a great day it will bring
Your heart will soar and begin to sing
The stars and sun will seem much brighter
You'll hold onto your zest for life much tighter
If I gaze-into your eyes will I see
The look of love that is just for me

Vickey Williams

"His" Way

On Good Friday "Christ" died for me.
"He" shed "His" blood so I could be free.
"His" crucifixion and death makes me very sad.
It's hard to believe but "His" death also makes me glad.
Because "He" loves me enough to die for me.
I return "His" love with joy and glee.
My problems were so many, I couldn't maintain.
At one point I thought I was going insane.
Then I picked up my Bible and read about the special day.
My problems and worries seemed to fade away.
I came out of the darkness and into the light.
I praise the "Lord" with all my might.
Now the Holy Bible is my sword.
I read it daily and walk with the "Lord."
Now I live for "Him" from my heart joyfully.
And "He" promises me I will live eternally.
Everyday and night I praise the "Lord" above.
For dying for me and giving me "His" love.
Now "Lord Jesus" just wants it understood.
If you live life "His" way, life will be good.

James Yates

Forgiving Myself

Remember the walk we took in the rain
The silence overpowered us
Things I wanted to say but couldn't explain
With so much pain, ignorance I had to feign

Things you must know
Things I just can't say
With all the love you show
Please, will nothing take this pain away

My past returns to haunt me
Threatens to take you away
Who can see what the future will be
The piper has come it is time for me to pay

Love bears all things they say
Everyone forgives but the one who needs forgiving
Give me love that's all I ask
For forgiving myself is too hard a task!

Stephen Johnson

The Parting Hour

The quieting hour begins, the laughing voices fade away.
The instant which swelled with the volume of assumed unending time,
And the rolling hush of passion voiced between your soul and mine,
echo more softly as the seconds slide.
But the parting hour strains not to miss,
the muffled hammer of my heart amidst
the softness and the pressure of the first forgotten kiss.
Nor the heavy falling of your tears, muffled in the open night,
Nor the heavy falling of my heart as you slowly pass from sight.
Nor the softness of the moment, the whisper of "goodbye"
through the hour grows more softly still, your voice shall never die.

Corey Horsch

Mother's Day

In the beginning, she cradled him in her arms.
She knew that it wouldn't last forever; it didn't

His first day of school, he wanted her to stay with him the whole day.
She knew that it wouldn't last forever; it didn't

When he was little, he told her all his deepest secrets.
She knew that it wouldn't last forever; it didn't

She read him a story every night.
She knew that it wouldn't last forever; it didn't.

He went off to college and called her every day.
She knew that it wouldn't last forever; it didn't.

One day he moved away, but he called her once a week.
She knew that it wouldn't last forever; it didn't.

After he got married, he called her once a month.
She knew that it wouldn't last forever; it didn't.

He and his wife had two kids, and he called her twice a year.
She knew that it wouldn't last forever; it didn't.

One day, he was killed by a drunk driver.
Ever since the very beginning of his life, she loved him with all her heart.
She knew that it would last forever.
It did.

Lisa Leavell

My Sweet, Sweet Mother Dear

I can't believe you've passed on
It's been just a year since you've been gone
I miss calling you on the phone
Or just coming by to visit at your home
Oh how I wish you were here
My Sweet, Sweet Mother Dear
I try not to think of the way you went
Full of cancer, so tired, painful and spent
I guess it was for the best
You're now in Heaven able to rest
One thing good came out of this bad
I've gotten to know that man, my dad
He never sent one card or acknowledged me before
Maybe it took your leaving for God to open that door
Life goes on and I do get by
I smile and blow you kisses up into the sky
I do feel you smiling back down at me
I accept it was Gods plan, it had to be

Roxann M. Helm

Safe Harbor

Shall we sit in the sun together
before our day is done,
Shall we know, in the quiet, the other is near,
when the soft sounds of day have begun

Shall we know in each others keeping
the peace of safe harbor at dusk,
Shall we measure the turmoil of ages
with the faith God entrusted to us

Shall we know when our day is over
and one of us has passed on,
That soon in the joy of contentment,
We will walk where the other has gone..

Alma Cook Remington

"The Bird Watcher"

The quiet pardoning of tension
from a fast-paced life,

Me there, always a vigilant spectator;
yet envious - and in a sense
relying on...

The beauty of the assertive birds
soaring on air, as if they were
performing a spiritual dance,

Answering all my pain, and
within minutes, pacifying my whole world.

Returning again and again, in
confirmed bliss; a strident sound
shoots off into my ears...

A dying, now diffident, bird
that once cast its dance into
my skies, now mirroring my
before intentions upon the water.

Jan Muecke

Warm Waters

From the darkness of my cold world
she gave me a warmth
like the warm water of life which
I sprung I return
to touch a heaven
that this hell has split into
and to feel my self come one
with that which is myself
To find out why I have been
so unhappy my whole life
is that I was not one with her
but now that our souls have touched
I feel just a splash of her heavenly waters
To know that true heaven is to be with her forever
and just to feel that warmth she gives
is like a sun to a wilting flowers
who was been in the darkness
far to long

Matthew Lake

The Minstrel's Melody

Night's wind carried his song to me.
Notes traveled long from his heart.
Music beared his journey's flight
As I echoed his enchanting harmony.
He waits patiently while my lyrics stumble
Upon his path of simple notes.
The Minstrel continues to play his tune
Until our melody and lyrics are one.

Nancy A. Hoppe

Mother

The sun was shining bright, the sky
was blue and light.
The doctor came out and I knew my
worst fear had come true, I had
lost you.
My mother was gone, I felt as if
I were all alone.
My heart was heavy, my eyes full of tears,
Then I heard her say don't worry
dear, I am with you now and forever.
I will help you in times of fear
and in times of trouble my love
will be double.
Just dry your eyes and lift
your heart and know we will
never really be apart.

Belinda Bradford

Courage

Courage is such a strong word,
Most people don't feel that way everyday.
Myself, being a recovering alcoholic,
I try to find strength and courage in every possible way.

Being alive in this cold and corrupt world
Everyone has to have an inner will,
Some will call it perseverance or
courage or strength-
But you can call it anything you like
or just whatever you will.

I don't think of myself as being courageous
I don't ever think of myself as being strong
I just know I have to go from day to day-
With the Lord beside me leading me along.

Just to get out of bed takes courage of sorts
Let alone to get through each day.
As long as the Lord is there to guide me-
I know He will give me the courage
and always show me the right way.

Judy Rose Dyle

Elemental Greetings

— Wind —

This night whilst I am listening, I hear your winds doth blow.
They sing a whispery tune, that does caress my soul.
You are the winds of the East, across the earth you blow,
To spread the seed that it be sown, for new plants soon to grow.

You are the ancient winds that make the fires wild.
You blow across the ocean, and lift the waves still higher.
You are the breath that sings in me upon this moonlit night.
I beg thee join my circle and bring to me thought flight.

Mary V. Richards

Mom

My mom is nice like sugar and spice.
But she can be mean at times. But she
supports my work and my poem rhymes. I may
not be a perfect kid no matter what I did.
She still loves me and I love her too. She puts stuff
on lay away she helps with home work too heck who's
mom doesn't. Mom's not all that good in math she
does okay that's very, very true. She wants
what's best for us and I respect her for that.
But sometimes we get spanked for we bicker and fuss.
And that's the end of my rhyme but I'll save
some for next time.

Drashauna Weakley

For The Love Of A Woman

I was a broken man with a sorrowful heart,
From this world I was ready to part.
Then God looked down from heaven above,
And sent me a woman for me to love.

Her eyes are as bright as the sun in the sky,
And when she smiles she brings tears to my eyes.
No one like her have I known before,
And search the world over there are no more.

God promises to reward us if we keep his commands,
Now I know I've been blessed by God's own hand.
Can anyone really express true love,
I think not, can we explain God up above.

If times get tough as they sometimes will,
And all the roads seem to be uphill.
Just stand beside me straight and still,
And we will make it if it be the Lord's will.

A broken heart has been made whole,
For the love of this woman, I give her my soul.
So always remember just hold on to me,
And I'll set your heart completely free.

George Todd

My Tootsie, My Cat

My most precious friend my cat
As I glanced next door one day
I seen the most beautiful cat in the world
I asked out of curiosity, what is the cats name
The young man replied Tootsie
Tootsie a beautiful calico cat
The cat soon became homeless
It certainly seem that no one cared
Tootsie was no where to be found
One day I followed her into the basement next door
There she laid with 4 kittens
Next to a water heater with no food or water
Beautiful Tootsie then became my cat
The happiness she has brought to our home
Through the years has been our treasure
My Tootsie my beautiful calico cat

Elizabeth Grinstead

A Cry For The Innocent

White on white, infant in the snow... murdered.
Not only inhuman, but by human's, who are the beasts.
Beasts of intelligent savagery, commit their sins
In cold cradles, cleansed by the Mother's tears.
Human's flaunt this carnage without bereavement...
They that would sorrow for the loss of their own
Wear pridefully the dead of another.

Amelia Amante

Together

Our World,
Violent and Poverty stricken.

Our world,
A disgrace to live in.

Our world,
Racist and sexist.

Our world,
we can't fix it
as one we have to do it
Together.
Put everything aside become a team.
Together we can fix all of the problems.
Together...

Ty West

A Crown Of Gold

Fifty years ago you stood together;
a vow before God that you forever
were bound by love and blessed on high,
to keep this union throughout your lives.
For richer or for poorer sake,
these vows you did exchange.
In sickness and in health you take,
you've shouldered each others pain.
You've laughed and joked these many years
and traveled many a mile,
you've raised two children along the way
blessed by God's eternal smile.
You've reached a goal that few attain,
be proud of what you've done.
The example that you've set for us
is nothing less an heroic one.
Be certain that we all do know
how you've reached this Crown of Gold,
'Tis thru God's blessed gift you see,
His plan forever told.

Gerald L. Cummings

Lonesome Valley

It was down in lonesome valley
Where the birds all train their young.
The Eaglets fly, high in the sky
And the cowbirds dine on dung.
There lived this old cross eyed hoot owl
Whose baby needed a nurse
Every time he would try to fly
He would just go in reverse
To solve this little problem
They laid him on his side.
And started in to tickle him
Until he turned around in his hide
The moral of this story is,
Or maybe it's a ditty.
The author you can plainly see
Is really just half witty.

Von Gardner

The Healing Room

As the sun filters into the room, it warms my soul and heals my tired mind,
A calmness settles my spirit and leaves me with renewed strength,
I feel a connection with nature and yet am protected from the elements,
At my window early in the dawn, I am observed and am also an observer.

I hear the birds discussing my reason for existence,
The squirrels gaze at me questioning my silence in the room,
I watch the flowers entice the bees and hummingbirds with their sweet nectar,
Bright colors of lavender, orange, yellow, red, pink and white provide a light blanket of cover for the trees and ground.

I hurry through my mid-day tasks to steal a few moments in the room,
Upon entering, time slows and I am overcome with a feeling of wellness,
My thoughts wander idly and the tranquility of the room soothes my body,
I wonder if I alone experience the serenity of this space?

In the subtle darkness of dusk, I find myself once again
Seeking solace and peace in The Healing Room.

Jody Baldwin

Mother Mine

When I was small and at your knee
The world seemed such a safe place to be

When the night reached out its long, dark arm
You were always there to keep me from harm

Uncertainties and doubts might bring me to tears
But your smiling face calmed all my fears

The years of living at times brought me low
But my faith in your love continued to grow

Now suddenly we're here at God's appointed plan
And the angels are coming to guide you to a better land

How can I let you go little mother of mine
when my heart is breaking and I don't think it's time

Yet I know in my soul there's a far better place
With no pain or suffering and a smile on your sweet face

Where your unselfish heart and your great mother's love
Will claim its just reward from God up above

Linda Sechrest

My Granny

My Granny died years ago
The exact time, I do not know
My Granny had a cancer in her liver
Which spread out more and gave me a shiver
I read the obituaries a couple days after she died
And there was my Granny's name printed inside
That made me remember six wonderful years
My heart and eyes were filled with tears
I am sure that she's now in heaven
And will be watching me turn 11
One day we'll be together
Forever and ever

Jennifer Madeisky

Motherhood

First come the tears,
Followed by a smile;
So much happens, in such a short while.
Don't close your eyes,
There's so much to miss;
A warm little hug, a wet little kiss.
Learning, playing, watching him grow;
You can't hold on too tight, because you know;
He'll grow up, as fast as he can,
Someday your baby will be a man.
So enjoy him now, while he's still near,
The future, you know, is almost here.

Ivy C. Hoyle

"Love's Poetry"

I was never taught to make poetry.
But now knowing never stopped the lover.
And so compelled I make my poetry.
I wish my motive true,
But for some reason I create for me.
Yet, I feel a sense of wrong.
It is the process not the product which compels.
For the process makes the poet great,
Until the product reveals the truth.
But natures song is strong,
And draws me once more to her side.
For children and poetry are worth while.
Whether great or bad, so compelled, I move.
For I too am a product of poetry.

James R. Bellamy

I Know You...

I know you.
I know the real you...

You can laugh when
You don't want to.
You can only cry when you are alone.

You are always friendly, even when
You don't feel like faking a smile.
You contain a hate, which only echoes
inside your head.
In your own private chambers you let it all
come out — scream and destroy!
However, you don't let any one else see.

Yes, you can love. You have once loved.
However, you can't love two things
the same way.

Yes, my child, you can fall in love.
You have once fallen hard and deep within.
Now tell me will you... can you..
Want to make it last forever?

April Sunny Boccia

Tranquility

I walked along the beach alone,
And I faintly heard a distant moan.
Funny that someone was speaking to me,
Revealing secrets that my eyes could not see.
Like a wave - I was pulled under,
Never would I recover.
I sat on the damp sand,
Unaware of the surrounding land.
I listened intently to what was being said,
And allowed thoughts to roam free in my head.
Frightened by what I may be told,
The air suddenly became cold.
A flash of my past and my future appeared to me,
And all that was left was a feeling of tranquility.
I relaxed on the deserted beach,
All impossible tasks were now in my reach.
A superior being had put me at ease,
And taken my worries away with the ocean breeze.
I looked up and mouthed a silent "thank you",
Feeling as if there was nothing I could not do.

Amie Hopkins

Summer 1937, A Saddle Hill District Farm

Always, heat and dust and questions without
answers from tykes, who skip to tunes of rainbow
melody while elders trample clouds and drudge through
endless days in silence. Wild roses drape the weathered
rails of leaning posts in pastures near the creek
and mirth mixed with gooseberries baked into a pie.

Duck down and feathers for pillows float in sultry gusts
eggs snatched from hens slapping the air with wings,
ambivalence, dust and a custard for the evening meal.
And then the stars touching the ground
escape from the dark blue dusty night with
coyote cries and bat like wings fluttering beneath the eaves.
Moths, fleas and bugs sting and scamper.
Rodent feet flee the uneasy dawn.

E. Marlene Hendricks

Scattered In The Sand

Every mere mortal is grain of sand,
scattered across the beach—
a small child, a young man, a grown woman— out of reach.

If we look into another's eyes, what we may find
is a cascade of lies forming in one's mind.
Traveling with time into another dimension,
some will never understand a shattered life scattered in the sand.

I know the time will come when we will face our maker.
That time is growing near,
but as you look around at others dying, inside all you see is fear.
A small child, a young man, a grown woman— out of reach.

In your heart you feel the knife turn,
but after the ones you lost, you still yearn.
Why can't life be easy, as you separate the untold truth of lies?
Where everything counts but what's important, you must realize
everyone's entitled to their opinion. Just open your mind and listen.

A small child, a young man, a grown woman — out of reach.
Scattered in the sand, along the beach,
out of grasp, out of reach,
scattered in the sand.

Kimberly M. A. Riley

Untitled

There's one that is lost
and should be sheltered from the rain.
While her heart is drowning
she slowly goes insane.
The eternal darkness
surrounds her dying soul.
As he tells her
it's time to let go.

There's one who has a shelter
but his heart is in the rain.
Though he cares for someone else
I think he is in pain.
But it can't rain all the time
and I feel his love for her grow stronger.
Even though he's in agony
I think he'll wait for her a little longer.

But it is not he that she wants
as his pathetic little world turns gray.
And in extreme pain and infinite emptiness
he slowly turns away.

Nicole Perry and Patrick Higgins

An Angels Words...

When the lights go out,
and only moonlight blankets your room,
I, am always watching.

When you are alone,
and the sound of your own voice is your only friend,
I, am always watching.

When love floods your heart,
and once again you become an anxious child,
I, am always watching.

When your tears begin to fall,
my hands are cupped to catch them,
for I, am always watching.

So in the night when a wind sweet and pure is blowing,
and seems to brush your shoulder
it's only me beside you,
for I, am always watching.

Katey McCormick

The Fugitive

The field parts open like ripened fruit
and from the amber ocean of wild oats
he appears, lone fugitive, padding on
unaware that he bears a satanic soul.
Coyote, night-spirit
deity of Indian lore
who prays to the waxen countenance of the moon
your eyes burn with ochre fire
and your tail dances heavenward
yawning in a golden arc
the wind embraces you in a transparent shroud
you yearn to flee the blood-stains of your kin
which haunt your memories
but you cannot forget the dried puddle of crimson
that held you rigid with fear
the heavy smell of death
and the pounding echo of guns.
Fugitive, escape in haste to the chaparral
later you may sing out your lament
to the infinite darkness.

Hadas Marcus

"I Do Not Understand"

I do not understand...
  why people are prejudiced hurting one another
  why people kill others,
  and why people make hurtful decisions.
But most of all...
  I do not understand...
  why there is so much hate in our world,
  (like the two world wars when many innocent citizens died.)
What I understand the most are babies.
  Babies aren't prejudice,
  they don't kill or make, hurtful decisions,
  and they definitely don't hate others.
  They trust whoever cares and shows affection towards them.
  Maybe this world would be a better place...
  if we all acted like children in some ways!

Maryada Vallet

Friendship

Forever are the memories made by you and me
Reaching back in time brings you to me
I have you in my heart for you are part of me
Everlasting is the relationship you have bestowed upon me
Never has there been a bond as strong as that of you and me
Days keep us apart, nights bring you to me
Serenity and peace you bring when there is turmoil in me
Having faith there will always be a you and me
Irreplaceable of a friend you have been to me
Pleasures and pains I share with you, for only you, care for me.

Anita Goel

God's Love

Have you ever seen dew on a rose?
Listen to the rain as it softly flows.
Watched a spider spin a web,
Carefully, counting every thread.
Listen to a whippoorwill or morning dove.
Felt the ocean breeze on your face.
Watched a sunset in the west.
Then you have experienced, God's Love.
Have you watched God paint the Autumn
Leaves, carefully, painting every tree. When
The picture is finished you will see God's Love.
Remember, he created this world for us.
So stop, look, and listen, and you will
Experience God's Love.

Betty L. Legg

"A Mother's Heart"

As we make our journey into this world,
We are soothed by the most beautiful music of life,
The beating of a mother's heart.
Once upon this earth the music fades away,
As we begin our journey through life.

This heart filled with love and happiness as you
entered this world, will travel your path as you
Learn to stand upon the ground.
When you stumble and fall upon the path you have
chosen, her heart will fill with pain as she
watches you suffer for your mistakes.

Her heart will grow old and weak through the years,
for she will suffer more pain for all the love
and strength she has given you, each time you
have faltered.
For a miracle in life is a mother's heart.
For even when weakened, it will still swell with
pride, when looked upon by her child with love.

Michael E. Allen

Untitled

Dear Brittney,
You must be the smile I've tried so hard to find,
the love and the laughter that won't leave my mind.
The ache in my heart, the tear in my eye...
the pain and the sorrow I feel time after time.
I remember your eyes, how they'd glisten and glow,
and your feet that would follow wherever I'd go.
I remember your hands how they held me so tight,
and the way they awoke me, without fail each night.
I look back on my life, and on all that I had...
and I'll try to explain why it makes me so sad.
The only love I could possibly need,
was so easily taken because of my greed.
I was blind not to see that you needed me too,
now the piece of my life that is missing is you.
I miss you sweetheart!

Heather Marbry

Love

What is Love?
Is it just another word in our English
language?
Does it mean something special?
Do people actually mean it when they say
"I Love You?"
What does it mean?
Does it mean we'll be together forever?
Does it mean you just love me today but
tomorrow you'll just like me?
Tell me, please, what does love mean?

Amy Lefler

Thy Will Be Done

Just close your eyes and say a prayer
And you'll know right away that God is there
To answer you and see you through
The trials that, each day, are new
He'll hold you when life's so involved
And show you how things can be solved
He only asks that we do our best
Then he'll take over and do the rest
All we have to do is bow in prayer
He's always waiting to meet you there
So don't get discouraged and blue
God is there to see you through
When we pray, in his name,
"Thy will be done".

Doris Ashe

He Is God

When attacks are many, burdens are heavy and I need a break thru
My heart, my mind, and my soul tell me just what I should do
to encourage and uplift my soul and then journey on
Take the World of God - Rebuke all sorrow, pain and scorn.
Know that he's still in charge - for he is God!

When things get real bad, worse than anyone could believe
Know that Satan is the source - the one who deceives
Let faith move you from fear to trust in God's Omnipotent World
Thank and Praise Him; for things unseen and unheard
Know that he's still in charge - For he is God!

When doors are closed and seems padlocked in my face
And creditors and collectors are steady on my case
and friends and loved ones have turned their backs
I go to God - because it's such a true-true fact
He's still in charge - for he is God!

Dora L. B. Stuart

My Grandfather's Clock

It was a gift, and a stately one
It came to me from my father's son
And what a beauty, it was to behold
All decked out in its oak and gold

I have always admired these handsome things
Their music really makes my heart sing
I've passed three score and ten
For this my heart no longer yens

Yeah, many hour's I've heard its song
Thru the day and all night long
It seem's to be a new found friend
Whom, will stay with me to the end

Funny how life and time can pass
We're born, we grow, we marry alas
Then one day we wake to find
Life has been good, but we're left behind

Our children have married and made their homes
Even the grandchildren are all full grown
It seems the cycle never ends
And the clock ticks on, Life, Love and friends

Frances M. Thomas

The Search

I've danced across the mountains,
I've swum down by the sea.
I've camped alone in paradise,
in order to be free.

My eyes have wandered in the night,
the moon and stars above;
in search of some small sign in sight,
of someone I can love

I know she's somewhere out there,
her beauty I will find...
With the wind a blowin' through her hair;
her fragrance in my mind.

I travel on, from place, to place;
in search of home to be.
I'll find in a precious face...
Smiling just for me.

John Ackerman

Let There Be Peace On Earth And Let It Begin With Me

I hope my message travels over the horizons and across the seas,
because in this neighborhood, peace is going to start with me.

Enough with the gangs, enough with writing on walls...
wouldn't you rather look at waterfalls?

Nature provides the most beautiful sounds...
why ruin it by throwing all this nasty talk around?

Why not freshen up our air..
rather than breathing in terror?

Couldn't we replace violence
with the touch of silence?

Don't let a fate of bitterness be sealed...
couldn't happiness instead be revealed?

Derek Louis Moore

Upon The Suicide Of A Friend

The rain drums rhythms upon your window.
The sound of heavy music dances around you,
as you stand and stare out towards eternity,
and uncertainty.
Wondering why things happen
and how what was once so permanent
is gone forever.

Wanting to breathe life into her soul,
to heal her wounds and mend the pain.
You watched her die.
Never once complaining of the reality of the end.

All the while realizing it would be soon.

And when it came, you cried
and I was the one who wanted
to tell you everything would be fine.
But your heart, too heavy to carry,
led to my loss, as you slipped into the dark
you, too, hated.

Now it is I who am left, standing alone,
peering towards eternity and praying for a glimpse of light.

Karen Leinheiser

Rats A La Mode

Take responsibility for your deeds.
Responsibility causes guilt.

Guilt.

Seemingly quiet, it edges up on you.
It eats away at you like rats on a bloated corpse,
or

blame.

Someone else made you do wrong.
I am perfect.
I hate guilt.
I am American.
I live by the way,
or else I'll sue.

Avoidance, like rats running around a bloated corpse to feast
on a slice of apple pie.

Apple pie.

Mmm good.

A la mode.

Deborah Hamilton

In The Silence A Poet?

Just with a courtesy from our world says
it's never too late to become the justice
having the power, to hold my hand
and soft of a chair to palm my back,
ceremony with history, them rules.. Oh.. Sweet dreams
when some one try to put behind my mind, excuse to cry
After the dark and sweet song of the bird
the happiness and sharp noises, isn't true
to focus my mind to describe, it's paradise...
Will it, be late to be a Poet? When
I have to order in place helpful gift
a passom of beautiful worlds crossing the sky
it's a judge in dream of a career.
From birth in earth the glory
In poet editor the memories
was the Lord guiding my history
with dreams to open my eyes
And power on my hand
access of a chair to palm my back
"I am the justice" - o - writing justice, for a new poem.

Jesse Enriquez

Yesterday's Pines

One path is there, leading 'round the bend,
Barely downtrodden — and yet no end.
Onward and upward, ascending the hill
Footprints of the past — showing still.

An old tin can — rusty with age,
An abandoned cabin — history's page.
A fallen log — deep with decay.
Signs of old — another day.

Around the bend — upward and on,
New days, new nights — the breaking dawn.
The future rolls past tomorrow's signs
The fallen needles of yesterday's pines.

Evelyn Chapman Daniel

The Spirit Of Life

Thou awaits in place
breathing unknown to thee
not knowing all thou soul of admiration is free

A special awe
breathes through thou soul
excitement - abounds!
A knowing enters the mind
to the admiration of growth
is free

A awe of knowing
breath is thee to know

Gleaming lights shining pass you by
flaring shadows near by

Unbroken - unspoken
unspeakable thou shall be

O wondrous mysterious delight
adventure in flight
as thou awaits through thy night

Rodolfo Garcia

For My Mother Helen Fraser On Mother's Day

If God would give you back to us if only for one day,
there are so many, many things I'd like to do and say.
I'd say how much I miss you, the tears still flow each day,
things have never been the same since the stroke took your mind away.

I'd say I really loved you, so much more than you ever knew,
Dear God I'd give the world to hear your voice on the phone once more.
We'd go to all the yard sales, Hills, K-Mart, grocery stores,
and I'd find you lots of bargains like I always did before.

You never had a vacation, you worked hard all your life,
but God saw fit to give you a rest and even the "cook" you talked of in jest.

We can never bring you home again, just hold your hand and pray,
until the day God walks in and says, "Helen, it's time for you to
go to my home today."

Joyce Fraser Provenzano

A Father's Prayer

I come to ask a blessing Lord, as humble as I can be
This prayer is not for wealth or fame, it's really not for me

It's for a special child of mine, who's come of age and grown
She's found someone to share her life, and soon she's leaving home

I wasn't there when she was born, to show my fatherly pride
I never put her on my back, and gave her horsy rides

I wasn't there to dry her tears, when she fell and scraped her knee
I never tucked her in at night, or sang her off to sleep

But I'm the one that she calls dad, it fills my heart with pride
She knows that I will be there for her, forever by her side

Here she stands a woman now, no longer skipping rope
With a man that she has chosen, for a future filled with hope

As they journey off in life, so far away from home
Protect her Lord and keep her, that little girl my own

Today we toast the both of them, best wishes along the way
A father's prayer is all I have, Lord protect them day by day

Willie A. Smith Jr.

Forgive!

If you have hurt, over-wrought, unthought,
I can proclaim no true disdain. I can forgive-live and let live.
But, if what you say and do, has forethought-planned or taught
I then proclaim a real disdain, and cry inside.
Oft times - to hide, the hurt left bare, and bleeding -
Where - no human eye can see -
deep raw in me.

Sometimes, if I, audibly let cry, reproach or pain
at you. What is my gain? None! No! None at all!
I should forestall, if power it could be,
all such utterance from me!

But, being human, too, I do, at times, such!
Only this I say, someday, this, too, won't show!
For pain, repeated oft, makes spots so soft with love
Subside, grow hard, and lastly, deep within
Will close the whim to see and weep and love and give -
Then I'd just live...
But, please! instead of this, I pray!
Oh, God! forgive!

Babette Kaiser Cecchini

Neo-Ode To Left Field

I'm from Left Field...or right,
I'm not very good at baseball analogies.

I've communicated on a different level
for so long, I thought I would make
an effort to bridge the gap.

Like certain fabled characters, I have the
gift of understanding but no one
understands me.

I compete for standards of normalcy...
Normalcy?

Sounds like mediocrity...
Sounds like concrete boots!

If the mudfish wish to understand,
let them shake the mud off their wings and
fly with me to Left Field.

Stacey Lee

You Put A Fence Around Your Heart

You put a fence around your heart,
and now you keep it locked.
That was the doorway to your love,
and now that door is blocked.

You put up the fence to keep hurt out,
but still, love comes and then;
I put a fence around my heart,
to keep all your love in.

You put a shield up to your heart,
and now you hold it high.
That was the entrance to your love;
now love could pass you by.

You have a shield to ward off hurt,
but love will penetrate through.
I had a shield up to my heart;
but I lowered it for you.

Dianna L. Echard

In The Name Of Freedom

In the name of freedom I can burn the flag
and treat America's symbol like some old dirty rag.
Rape and murder are no longer surprising.
Same sex marriage is legal and rising.
Criminals are defended as victims of abuse.
Police are out gunned... so what's the use?
Our children can't pray in our public schools.
Were are Founding Fathers a group of fools?
Our flag is now ashes and our dreams are now dust.
God bless America and in God we trust.

If our Founding Fathers and Betsy Ross
could return to D.C. to carry our cross,
they would tell of our soldiers killed in other lands
protecting our flag from the enemy's hands.
I'm sure those great men from the past never meant
for their words of freedom to be so far bent.
They'd tell those in power, "Please listen to reason.
Burning our flag is an act of treason!"
They'd go to the Supreme Court and demand they see them.
"Return us our morals, in the name of freedom."

Edgar Allen Hamilton

"Just One More Day"

"Just One More Day," I used to say,
For you to live, and love and play!

"Just One More Day," to be with your friends,
Your dog, your family, whose love knew no end.

"Just One More Day," the school bus to ride,
Your jokes to tell and secrets confide.
Your eyes so **bright**, a *devilish* grin,
Your contagious laughter, and hearts yet to win.

"Just One More Day," to live and explore,
Your zest for learning, Why weren't you given more?

Time, that is, to do the things you loved and had planned,
Spending time with you was always so grand!
But, if that wish were granted, It would never be enough,
To cram, a lifetime of living in You were a *diamond in the rough.*

Your life was just beginning, so many tasks undone,
Always willing to help, some say "like father, like son."
A boy full of promise, a fun-loving mischievous lad,
Playing, fishing, bow-shoots and hunting with your dad.

So, we must go on living as best we possibly can,
Until the day we again can see our special, beloved young man.

Linda Moser

Untitled

Angels come to sing around their father,
their master, their king....
Then they go to do what's asked
of them.
They were told to go find someone,
my someone...
They came to take you from your
life on earth as a friend, lover,
husband and father.
To place you upstairs with the
person who made us all they
see how much I love and
need you...
Will they let you stay here with
me?
God and the angels only know...

Melissa Ownsbey

Down Sizing!

Down sizing? What the heck is that?
You say you got to let me go; the company's too fat!
I've been here fourteen years, does that mean anything?
What, I've got to bite the bullet, and sorry about the sting!

I don't understand. This is like a war.
One day I'm working, the next you want my car.
You said you liked my work and appreciated my loyalty.
Right now that all seems like bull to me.
I was just wondering who will do the work I've done?
Is there someone with this company who's been doing none?

You say just let 'em go, you know it's not funny,
But the fact of the matter is you can save all that money.
Don't worry about my bills or the home I'll probably lose,
And for God's sake don't worry about my children's shoes.

I used to think you would take care of me if I did my job,
But now you're treating me like some lazy useless slob.

Down sizing, no it's certainly not a joke,
But tomorrow I hope that you go broke.

Joe T. Collins

The Goalie

He skates out to his defending goal,
tying his water bottle to the pole.

Staring his opponent in the face,
while tying a forgotten lace.

His teammates are thrown into action,
knowing that they are just a fraction,

A fraction of what is to come,
for the Goalie is the only one,

Who can truly keep the puck out of the goal,
using all his heart, and all his soul.

He is successful most of the time,
but sometimes he may get into a bind.

And the opponent may score,
Once, twice - hopefully not more.

His hopes may fall, then rise again,
because he knows he must defend,

The goal that is the key to the game,
and for the rest of the team it's just the same.

His teammates put him out on a limb,
For they know - the game counts on him.

Monica Holden

Un Poeme De Vie (A Poem About Life)

You say that Freedom's your father
But when honesty has within itself a lie
You look to tomorrow as a better day
Seeing yourself in time's eye
You say that Liberty is your mother
But when pious men become profane
You lay your hand upon the heart
Of God's infinite domain
You say that Life is a tortured soul
Preparing to be freed
To a place with a towering, golden gate
Where Independence is the key

Leeann Stallman

The Lake Speaks

For Robert Smithson

I am the lake of terrible beauty.
And this mortal has rested a slight work upon my azure surface.
A spiral relief to dress my salty cheek.
Human-play prepares me as an actress
Stretching this bare earth fragment across my face.
Slowly curving, a cave painting.
Watery surface the canvas, red earth the paint.
My dear moon do you see from out beyond earth's aural sphere
a child's scribble across my wavewashed countenance?
For aeons you have seen your craggy reflection purely in my surface.
Me, your faithful mirror across these many perfect years.
Does this child's caprice appear as a scar of your own?
Never mind this beauty mark my round-faced friend.
Soon it will vanish dear sister angel, swallowed in by my own breath.
Ponder while my waves submerge it;
watch now as I bring it to the surface once more.
See the crystal lace I have woven 'round my wound.

Patricia Lucille Parker

If I...Would You

If I was a princess and you were my knight would you risk your life to rescue me tonight?
If I was distraught and really crying would you wipe up my tears and see my eyes drying?
If I told you I loved you every second of the day would you say the same or just walk away?
If I told you that you meant everything to me would you stop and listen or just let it be?
If I told you I'd love you till the day I die would you think I meant it or let it pass by?
If I took you to a place you'd never been before would you stay with me or walk out the door?
If I wanted you to hold me in your arms would you do it or stand back alarmed?
If I needed a shoulder to put my head on would you be there for me or would you be gone?
If I wanted a person to hug me till I was blue would it be someone else or would it be you?
If I needed someone to say I love you I know you would do it because you have every right too.

Raven-Starr Overmyer

Balloons

Silvery disks trailing away
against a blanket of blue.
Shimmering sunlight lights their way
as they fade so far from view.

Lifted by gentle winds of chance,
these mylar vessels bear
brief messages that weave and dance
amongst the ribbons there.

Our minds take flight along with them
as they vanish from our sight.
Imagining in dreams one silver gem
may win its journey's fight.

A connection made between two souls
in a world so far apart.
The windblown message fulfilled its role
shining on another heart.

Carole C. Edison

Ancient Souls...

Stonehenge
Shrouded in a cloud of mist.
Feel your haunting spirit melody
Call the Souls
of ancient Celts.

Ring of Stones
Earie in the faint moon glow.
Ghostly chants, magic spell of the Druids
Beckon the Souls
of the Celts.

Fairie Stone
Cool, yet warm in my hand,
Drawing me in, binding my soul
With the Souls
of the Celts.

Carol D. Husfloen

Thoughts Of An Ice Storm

Trees emblazoned in glass,
their tops flaunting diamonds
catching sunlight!
Oh prismatic, resplendent winters
respite!
Icicles dripping from branches pulled low
to the ground;
sugar coated cascading rock candy,
render one dumbfound.
Some see only a dormant icy cold world.
I venerate God and natures's display unfurled.
The metamorphosis of the mundane...
to crystalline Camelot forests,
Zhivago's pavilions of frost:
and thoughts of this as an unpalatable season
at least for the moment are lost.

Dina Miller

Because Thou Art

Because Thou art, life is worth the living;
Because Thou art, it is not death to die;
Because Thou art, none of us are forgotten
And left alone beneath the starry sky.

Because Thou art, we are all important
Children of Thy great creative mind,
Loved and cared for, never forsaken
Despite the weakness of body and mind.

Because Thou art we can go on singing,
Facing whatever life may bring, knowing
That our trials are but lessons
Preparing us for greater things.

As steel must be fired to be strengthened
And gold must be burned to be refined,
So we need both strengthening and refining
To become more perfect vessels of Thine.

So Father because Thou art, our hearts
Will not be heavy; we are glad for the
Challenge of life. Give us wisdom, courage
And patience as we walk towards Thy light.

Inez E. Colwell

Gangs

I hear a gun shot in the air!
There's a dead man over there!
Another man is stabbed in the gut!
They're holding up a Pizza Hut!
I see a young boy with a gun.
He kills his best friend, thinking it's fun.
They hurt people rob stores.
Police are bursting down the doors.
They steal cocaine because they're users.
All they are is a bunch of losers.
"Chokers-Smokers"; they're no jokers.
They torture people with "red-hot" pokers.
The crimes of gangs are surely no game.
They certainly get no fortune or fame.
The evil they do happens every day.
But one of these days, they're all gonna pay.
All these gangs—What shall we do?
I think they need God! How about you!

Reggie Plett

Pictures...

The pictures keep on falling
on to my tear-stained face
They scatter around me like rockets
returning from outer-space
Each holding a special memory
A time, a place, a face
I try to push them away
But this just brings them closer
I begin to look at each picture
And realize how special they are
I then discover that
I shouldn't cry over you being gone;
I should be happy that you suffer no more.

Jacquie R. Grisham

Woman Of Honor

If you see me sad don't feel sorry for me
If you see me cry don't think that is for you
If you see me mad is because I feel sad
If you think I still feel the same love for you
You better know who to fly because I'll send you
To hell once again.

Just because once I loved you like hell it doesn't
Mean I'm still crazy for you, I might remember your
Hugs but I'll never pick up the garbage once again,
Because no matter what and no matter who I'll keep
Being a woman of honor, because only once I put
My love in your hands and you tread it with your dirty love.

But now I should keep on walking with my head up
Because I know that one day someone will come and
Will treat me as a woman of honor.

Ana Lidici Rodriguez

Untitled

And the woman spoke:
"Tell us of pain"
And he said...
"Your pain is the breaking of
the shell that encloses your understanding.
Even as the stone of fruit must break,
that its core may stand in the sun, so must
you know pain. And could you keep your pain
and wonder at the daily miracles of your life,
your pain would not seem less wonders than
your joy. And you would accept the seasons of your
heart as you have always accepted the seasons
that pass over fields, your heart would deem an
abundance of elation at the palest fiber of light
over the summer's of your joy.
You would watch with a serenity over the
winters of your grief.

Natasha Jones

Memory Poem

Lying in my bed,
I remember the dreams you had, brother
What you wanted to be.
I remember the way you were,
The afternoons with mom,
The grilled cheese sandwiches.
All I have is pictures,
The memories.
I must have looked at them a thousand times.
I hear your words,
But you're still gone.
Waiting for you to come back,
I know you'll be gone,
Time has at least told me that much.

Charity Casey

A Clip Of Life

Rainy days and stormy nights,
a heart in aching need,
hungry children crying out in pain,
families living on the street.

A boy is killed by his brother dear,
young girls are ladies of the night,
people are hated because different they are,
and love is nowhere in sight.

But don't breathe disgust my fellowman,
just take it all in strife,
this is admitting or not
a clip, of human life.

Just clip it out, you might well say,
No more war, hate or crime,
but only God can accomplish that,
and he will so, in his own due time.

Beatrix Massey

A Moment In Time

Vacationing is like a child stripping one's clothes off;
running naked through an open field of sunflowers;
winds blowing, bees humming, birds chirping—there's not a worry in sight.
Leaving those pressures of everyday life behind;
we're off into the wide blue yonder—destination Southern California.
The great gray Eagle lands on the hot tarmac;
surrounded on one side by a mass of purple mountains;
close but so far away—the San Gabriel Mountains.
The early orange sun is shining brightly but shone dimly
through the clouds of pollution hovering over the City of Angels.
Heading East the adventure begins in the dry hot desert;
the arid mountainous landscape lined with huge magnificent Joshua Trees;
visibly barren and lifeless but so much alive;
the silence caught my attention as we moved quickly toward Twentynine Palms.
There we reacquainted ourselves with a loved one—my dad;
sharing moments we lost in the past, trying to catch up to the present, and making plans for the future;
the morning came early and we said our good-byes.
Little did I know, that moment with my Dad would be my last.

Jo Ann Amburn

What Is The Real Definition Of A Sista'

We are different shades of black and we each have
different eyes and hair. Do we ever have the real
definition of a Sista'!

Some of us wear blue, green or light brown contacts
or we may have blond, red, or light brown extensions
in our hair. Is this the real definition of a
Sista'!!

Some of our styles may be different. Some of us are
the ghetto hip hop, some are Momma' little girls,
in Africa. But is this the real definition of a Sista'!!

Some of us use different ways of speaking. Some of us
correct English, or the street slang, or a mixture of
both correct english and street slang. But is this the
real definition of a Sista'!!

All the things I have enclose, and much, much more
shows there are many meanings of a Sista'. For
we are all black women and we have all these
characteristics in each and everyone of us,
So the question lies within you. Do you feel you
are the real definition of a Sista'!!

Michelle Jackson

A Broken Down Bus

I ride the Greyhound back and forth
each week from farm to town,
Been doing it now for a year and more
because farming wasn't sound.

Enjoyed on these trips, a six hour ride,
visits along the way.
But can't remember ever the fun
of the two I met today.

Robin and Dawn, cute little girls,
with big bright eyes of blue?
Offered their seat as I stood in the aisle
'cause the bus was running for two.

They told of things that young girls do,
of school, the woods, and home.
And told of their art, the stories they write
and Robin recited her poem.

I can't but believe as I think of it now
that the Lord in his wondrous way
Had a purpose in mind with that broken-down bus
and the friendship made today.

Fred Michaels

Owl

Can you hear my cries at night?
Like a person who can't see without a light.
Do you understand my lost feet that
get swept away with the roaring tide.
Can you feel my heart, beaten by the shadowy light.
Or my sorrowful cries that fill the night.
Do you understand that I'm just a whisper
that can blow into the shadows of your room
and can be forgotten just by one sweep of a broom.
I tell you from inside not to hide,
I'm just a fragment, a piece of your imagination,
then you ask why must I cry, because you made me
last must I say goodbye.

Leah Baumeister

Face Of The Enemy

As our eyes locked on to each other,
Across the barren demarcation line —
A shadow from the past arose,
Lone traveler across the winds of time.

An apparition from humanities past,
Standing between us, unseen but known;
For my enemy and I to share in heart
A warm ray of light was gently sown.

A new consciousness could then be felt,
As an alternate countenance was shown on his face;
For the hope of future peace around us prevailed
And I knew that my enemy too had sensed this grace.

This Presence, though no poltergeist at all
Could be felt from a parallel of time unknown;
Conveying to me, thru a new part of my heart —
That the face of my enemy was a reflection of my own.

Only with a slight nod of his head
Did he signal while slowly walking away;
Then, in the new part of my heart I understood
That hope for true freedom would come to all someday.

Larry Transou

First Trick Or Treat

Sixteen months old you had your first Trick or Treat
Being so tired just walking down the street
Witches and pumpkins you met on your way
You just stood and looked with nothing to say.
Stumbling along with your mask and treat bag
In back of the others you did lag.
Collecting a lot candy for your size
Having just a funny face as your disguise
Along to see you were not lost
Cause it was dark even a small frost.
Crossing the streets and watching the cars,
I helped you collect your candy bars.
Home we went all in a glow
Just as fast as your feet could go.
Then that sad look did come.
Gee, Is Halloween over Mom?
Taking your hat and coat off, Dear.
I explained it comes every year.
Now all over and you're fast asleep.
Sixteen months old you had your first Trick of Treat.

Carol Linda Harvey

Fiddlefoot

A kitten, we call him Fiddlefoot,
stopped by our house and there took root.
He has six toes on each front paw,
he's the cutest kitten you ever saw.
He wears a coat of black, striped grey,
with a sooty nose and his love of play.
He purrs just like a motors roar,
eats and sleeps then plays some more.
He loves the children best, I know,
as his yellow car eyes seem to glow
at every child's soft, loving touch
as he eats his meat, milk, fish or such.
Old or young, all folks are his friends
and on their kindness, his life depends.
Our Lord made the mold for kittens you see
the same as He did for both you and for me.

Jeannette Hunter Payne

Wind

Like a wild beast
in a cage
of white mortar and steel
of the surrounding buildings
howling with rage
and scaring with its paws of dead brown leaves
the already tired faces
of people walking by.
As if saying
look at what I did to you
and yet you can do nothing to get around me
to get away.

Sanja Veledar

God's Train

This train, this stout dog, lurches forward
onto black metal and creeps, creeps
up and up the country, through a hole
in the scenery, rumbling, belching
like a clown, and sixty miles away

My ear is pressed to
the track, nimble, listening for the ache
of God's blue joint, bending against
his corny old picture frame.

Samuel Bonderoff

My Birthday Wish

I've reached a time in my life where I've never been
So I'll refuse to admit three score and ten
So please grant me my birthday wish
And let me forget how long it's been
Don't send my cards or gifts I don't need
Just say "Happy Birthday" and wish me God speed
I've had more of my share of life
All filled with happiness and the love of a good wife
I'm like a cat that has nine lives
I've used about eight and still survived
I know there were times when I haven't been right
They say I have a temper and always ready for a fight
So to any of the folks I've offended along the way
Please! Forgive me What more can I say?
So if my number is called and this be my last day
My blessings have been so many I can't even say
So if the man upstairs and we have a chance to meet
Please grant me my last wish and let me
die on my feet

Ralph L. Hall

Reincarnation

I wish I could be the big rolling sea
The bird in the sky that can fly so high
I would like to be the strong oak tree
The moon at night or the stars so bright
A soft white cloud above it all
Floating forever never to fall
All these things I wish I could be
I would like to be anything but me

Mary Carpenter

Beaches Of Normandy

Mother picked us for the draft.
Now we wade a pound the water in a raft.
Mother says, play with the kids of the shore.
She won't tell us what we are playing for.
She just tells us we will become a man.
Because we fight for the promise land.
With a bucket on our head and shovel in hand,
We move to take the sandy land.

Once in the water, the shore kids skip stones.
Mamma one just hit little Tommy Jones.
The shore kids sea-shelled us from a high off place.
All we can do is throw sand at their face.

We played with the shore kids from morning today.
Mother couldn't we play some other way?
The game was over by the end of the night.
So what if we won the hole darn fight!
Mother sticks our flag into newly taking sand.
She doesn't seem to see her her body's blood covering the land.

ZeBulon Porter

"Love"

"Love" is a word hard to define,
But gentle, loving, and patient comes to mind.
Jesus love is one of a kind.
God's love is so gracious, tender, and true —
So understanding is His love for you.
A love so special, thoughtful, and true—
Why, Lord, don't we seek to be more like you?
A love so compassionate that comes from God's heart—
We invited Him to be at home in our hearts.
A love so righteous, forgiving, and true—
Help us, Lord, to be as devoted as you.
Love ye one another as you are commanded to do
And you've reached the goal He has set for you.
As we studied and searched to seek and find,
God's Love is still the only one of its kind.

Jann Ragland

Love Is With You

Love is so natural when I'm with you,
don't you feel excited? I sure do.
The warmth I feel when I see your face,
smiling as you walk with such beauty and grace.
My eyes staring at you from head to toe,
gosh I'm happy, I want you to know.
The things you do, and the things you say,
makes life more enjoyable day after day.
I stare at your picture with joy in my heart,
Oh how I wish we weren't so far apart.
The day will come when things are better,
that will be when were finally together forever.

George Goulet

Harmony In The Northern Light

I saw the northern star pass through a window in the void of space.
And sitting on a throne light coming from this place.
As in the depth of a cold winter night,
He descended to the human race.
The northern star was Jesus.
And His amazing Grace.
And as he wrote in a purple haze,
In the depth of our mind.
To the church it was written,
A promise he left behind
To soar as an angel among the stars
We leave this flesh behind,
To become a candlelight of inner peace,
Through Jesus Christ we find.
And then the northern star went nova.
In the depth of the cold winter night,
In the harmony of Gabriel's trumpet,
The church was drawn to the light.

Jess Marquis

When I Have A Moment

When I have a moment to myself,
I think of you — and me,
And how we're not together—yet.

I dream of what it would be like
To have you close and hold me to your heart.
We would explore each other's inner recesses,
Tenderly asking questions...
Tempering every query with kindness.

I don't know you yet.
You haven't appeared in my life, but you will.
I dream of you
As I spend my days searching for answers.

You exist, because you are Nature's way
Of granting my wish for wholeness -
Life with another who fits my life
Like petals fit a flower.

Cynthia A. Jones

Untitled

There is something of the sea in me,
Seeming secure and strong,
While in the private depths
Restlessly rolling and gathering momentum
For that inevitable thrust and spreading
onto the searching probing sands -
Sands which almost learn its most secret secrets
before it retreats unto itself once more
Only to try again other sands on another shore.
Longing to be caught up in a quiet backwater of love
And gratefully drawn into the sand.

Phyllis F. Dorflinger

Choice

We came into this world unabated,
Our ancestors with thought had created.

The third millennium upon us all,
Our Heavenly Parents we now must call!

We did what we could to better the world,
Mass confusion of thought and actions swirled!

We must realize we are Family,
Help stop the misery and agony!

At times it feels like a true living hell,
Show us, Divine Parents, to break this spell!

Some know how to love and others do not,
Show us the way to end this morbid plot!

We cry for love and growth upon this Earth,
We bring our sighs and sorrow to Your hearth!

Teach us, Divine Family, how to share.
Teach us how you want us to love and care!

How do we reach you and stay in grace?
We're feeling shame, tears streak our face!

We choose for once between good and evil,
Here and always, Stop This Damned Misheavel!

Shilley Anna Cassady

"A Tribute To The Moody Blues"

The stage has been set, they've dimmed the lights.
A beautiful voice sings about white satin nights.
Caught up in the moment, here to admire from afar,
as a legend, weave his tale, and plays his guitar

For more than thirty years, all across this land,
leaving love and country, to make music in a band
Almost like prophets, sharing truth from the stage.
Another song, another city, a turning of the page.

The music, ever timeless, pure as when you began,
breathing life into it, as if flowed from the pen.
Always asking questions, hearts searching for a sign.
Leaving the earth for awhile, in search of the divine.

Each song that you've written, opens another door.
Makes us look within, and long for something more.
I am one of thousands, you'll probably never meet,
laying down my applause, like flowers at your feet.

I wanted to thank you for the music all these years.
It has stirred deep emotions, even brought on tears.
The journey continues, you've certainly paid your dues,
always with class and style, long live "The Moody Blues!"

Carolyn Rodahl

To Edna St. Vincent Millay

Oh, Lady of the deep perceptive verse
Whose wise and ghostly words invade my mind,
Would that I had your talent to be terse
While rhyming all the woes of womankind.

I read the wisdom from your youthful pen
And wonder at the slowness of my course
And struggle with my lines and question when
Or if they ever shall attain such force.

I know I've gleaned enough at forty-one
To fathom all that you communicate,
But all the things I start, I find you've done.
I fear I've come along a bit too late!

Please wait for me and don't go on ahead.
You may have written something I've not read!

Bette V. Farmer

Minnesota Morning

Minnesota mornings are quiet and still
The early fog is rolling
It's rolling where it will
It rolls across the meadow
It's lifting from the lakes
O' Minnesota morning when everything awakes.

The air is cool,
It's fresh and clean
When fog, sun pierced, is gone
Late mornings filled with noisy song.
I can't forget the distant loon nor squawking of the jay
O Minnesota Morning, I must be on my way.

And though I travel day and night
And leave it all behind
I wake up every morning
With Minnesota on my mind
And heart filled pleasantries
Of Minnesota...memories.

Carol Swearingen

Postcard Poem

There is a smell of pure spring water
  and ripe fruit in the air.
There is a cool breeze blowing.

The leaves of the trees rustle in the wind
  and birds chirp loudly.

The air has an eerie stillness.

  I feel open and free.

The trees are like a concert audience;
  swaying to the music.
The tall, triumphant trees.

Everything is beautiful and when it falls silent,
  You hope you never have to leave.

Jason D. D'Abreau

Retirement

Retirement is something you look forward to,
Time for yourself and so much to do,
  You work and you wait for the day to come
When you can relax and enjoy.

The years speed by, they go by so fast,
And retirement comes, yes, it comes at last,
  The time is here for you to retire,
Now you can relax and enjoy.

There's time to travel and places to go,
And visits with family and friends that you know,
  Too much to do and too little time
For you to relax and enjoy.

You'll have to make choices with most of your time,
And the days that you thought would be so sublime
  Are filled with your hobbies - your grandkids - and such,
So who can relax and enjoy?

Take each precious day as it comes, my friend,
From summer's hot sun to cold winter's end,
  Thank the good Lord above with all of your heart
That you're Here to - Relax And Enjoy!

Marlene Pieterick

I Am Beautiful

I am a beautiful Black woman...have what it takes to be deemed
Superior. Feet worn and weary, rough! from the miles my people
traveled to freedom.
My big ol' legs...gifts from Mother Afrika, I could ruunnn like the
wind.
So you adore my curvy wide hips...thank massah for that..my great
ancestors bore his bastard children; rape must not be confused
with tolerance.
The rounnded arch in my back...dat come from years of sacrifice and
bending over backwards.
My luscious titillating succulent breasts fed thousands, ours...and theirs.
The weight of the world has always rested on My shoulders; my arms
are so strong a simple embrace would crush you.
Like Samson, my strength remains rooted in my naturally nappy hair.
High structured cheekbones define my dominant character.
Thick lips merely reflect the spirituals our people sang...way down
Moses....
there's a story behind these tired ol' eyes-careful they'll mesmerize.
Look at me! From toe to head;
I am a beautiful Black woman.

Cynthia Lynnette James

Only Love

We met in High School, he was my first love and I was his.
Then he moved away, he took a piece of my heart with him.
He was always in my thoughts and dreams, I was in his.
Our future plans had to wait.

He's my only love, there will be no other, only him,
He's my only lover, no one can do what he can do.
He's my only love, no other has a chance, just him.

We met a few year's later, our love was stronger and deeper.
When we made love, it felt so special and right.
He was in my soul and when he had to go,
He took a bigger piece of my heart.

He's my only love, there will be no other, only him.
He's my only love, no one can do what he can do.
He's my only love, no other has a chance, just him.

We met again and it seemed like an eternity had passed.
Our love was more spectacular than ever, he took me to heaven.
We are one and we knew we would never part again.
We were each other's first love and each other's only love.

Kathryn Ricketts

Feeling As '1'

The earth is slowly spinning around me. It seems to be forcing
me to race it. Many times I fall down. I just cannot seem to
understand. I am jumbled with frustration all around me. So
finally I gain the courage to stop. All of a sudden I feel as though I
am being raced against.
Confusion,
Bewilderment,
and Fury
flash before my eyes continuously. My tracks seem to be
erased behind me, replaced by a million thoughts. My stomach is
rumbling with rage, crowding me like an active volcano ready to
explode with feelings at any moment.
It makes me want to jump to the bottom of the deepest darkest
ocean, and linger there until the screaming stops, until silence,
until peace, perhaps until deceased calls unto me. Or maybe into
the deepest darkest cave, until I have tramped there so much that
the fear is gone. Until I feel that I have become one.

One understood, One brave, and
one of all and all of one

Holly Ann Roberts

Letting Go

Two strangers met
How could they know
of what was yet to come.
Time went on as days went by
Two hearts became as One.
Love:
(laughter, secrets, tears, touch...)
Such a Peculiar but
Wonderful thing.
fall to winter and winter to spring
Why do the seasons change?
(Unexpectedly perhaps, but with natural course)
Aren't feelings much the same?
They said Forever
but things turned out
Forever came too soon.
But dry your tears
the pain will mend —
Perhaps with rekindled flames.

Jessie Donohue

Single And Scared

Single and scared, I walk down this endless road...
My mind growing weak from this heavy load.

Alone with two children, no money to spare...
Waitressing nights, to show them I care.

Hitting the bars night after night.
Hoping to meet "that someone" right.

So many lonely people I meet along the way..
As time passes by, there's less and less to say.

Everyone has his problems, I'm there to be a friend...
But it's my heart that's broken when it comes to an end.

Feeling down and needing a lift..
I look at my children and cherish this gift.

It doesn't take much to bring them a smile..
I know they're the reason I'll be around for awhile.

So single and scared, I'll keep walking this road..
Because life gets better, or so I've been told.

Cindy Manzi

Musician Memory

As the silhouette of your smile plays in my memory like the
fingers of a musician it dances across my mind like the musicians
upon the keys.
I am left upon an open floor as the last harmonic note is played
you turn the other way.
Soft are your eyes so blue, with such delicate shine they sparkle
in my memory like the hands of a musician you touch me with your
gentleness.
Slowly you come close to me, but am I the one left in the shadow
of this song or are you playing for my ears alone?
The musician of love brings such pleasure of the intensity of
your fingers dancing through my hair like the notes of the musician
dancing through my soul.
Though you have touched me with the sweetness of the melody, I
am left with the reality that these emotions could just be a glimpse
of love that may not be meant for you and I.
The musician plays his song so delicately, as his heart beats
faint his love for this woman is shown by the memories he holds
deep within his music.

Phoenix Zammarchi

Dreams

Who can decipher dreams
and say what we hide in them?
Who can tell us
what we understand in them?

If dreams should speak to us
we should know rare things or forgotten things
that are guarded by our minds
and remain in our subconscious.

Dreams transport us to another world
whether it be past, present, of future
or to another world that we would like to make real
in order to do things that we can't achieve or end.

Dreams are the reflection of our wishes and our own personality,
and although many times we can't understand them
and are left only with questions
at least, we can do something that fills us with happiness
that is give thanks to God for being able to remember.

So that our dreams for a moment more
will fill us with nostalgia, joy and happiness.

Angela Interiano

Reflection

The moon looked down
For miles around
From his seat there in the sky,
He saw my frown
And he seemed to lean down
And to ask me gently, "Why?"

I could tell by his smile
As it stretched out a mile
'Cross his broad and beaming face,
I could tell him my troubles
They'd float off like bubbles
Leaving nothing but cheer in their place.

So, I confided in him,
And my troubles grew slim,
In fact, they faded away.
But, alas, for tomorrow
Will bring forth more sorrow
For that, is another day.

E. R. Case

Why?

Why do you love me after all I do?
Why do you love me after how I treat you?
Why do you love me when I turn away?
Why do you love me every minute of every day?
Why do you love me when I cuss and have deep lust?
Why do you love me when sinning is a must?
Why do you love me unconditionally?
Why, oh why, oh why, did you die upon that tree?
How can you bear it seeing your creation crumbling?
How do you stand it—You, a sinless being!
Why do you love me? O, if I could see.
Lord, know that I love you, too-
Even if not obviously.

Daniel Shanks

Embracing The Quiet

I have been beside a stream listening to the sound of water,
and the wind through the trees, and birds.
I have been on a city street in the early morning and heard the cars
as people are rushing off to work, and honking horns, and blaring
radios.
I have listened to the yelling of children on school playgrounds.
And the fights, and cussing.
I have heard the sounds of love in the laughter of friends.
And beautiful music, and caressing words.
But most importantly - I have heard the sound of silence and been
embraced by that silence.

Being embraced by the quiet is the most wonderful experience one
can never know - and it is available for us all.
For one second, listen to the silence within yourself.
Hear the quiet when all thoughts are turned off -
Hear the love within you when all anger is turned off -
Hear the peace when all you hear is nothing.

I have turned off my thoughts and
Felt the quiet wrap its arms around me -
Felt the tenderness of a caress -
Felt the peace of knowing pure love -
I have been embraced by the quiet - and I will never be the same
again.

Leslie G. Wheaton

An Angel Corner

In a special Angel Corner in my home at
Christmastime,
There are angels of all sizes;
Some are cunning, some sublime.
A most angelic music box chimes out its "Silent Night."
And a special Hummel angel views the Babe by Candlelight.
A saucy, polka-dotted one displays a star in hand,
And in a little basket
There's an angel pixie band.
The silent felt-based angel (from a friend)
Hangs on the wall,
Ever so benignly looking down on one and all.
Symbolic angels are they, reminiscent of the night
When heavenly hosts sang "Peace on Earth".
And I wonder if I might.,
With a little careful planning,
Set up a counterpart,
And have an Angel Corner year 'round within my heart.

Marguerite J. Grams

The Miracle Of Love Is Forever

What is this miracle? Love
How does it happen - Unknown
Two hearts - Two souls - Together
Sharing - Caring - Understanding
The look in your eyes - the touch of your hand
A throbbing in your heart, the dream of being together
Happiness - not loneliness. A sense of belonging.
A feeling that won't go away. Sheer excitement at the thought of you!
Anticipation of being together
A smile that doesn't stop. Good times, bad times shared
Love - a feeling in your heart. Forever - love - belief - trust
A seagull carrying one grain of sand, grain by grain to build a beach
That is forever. My love for you - that is forever!
The way you touched my heart. The way you filled my soul. My
thoughts, my dreams, my reason for being. This is the miracle of
love forever.
I feel your caress in my thoughts. Trust and be secure in my love
for you! Your kindness, your tenderness, your intelligence, your smile.
Being there whenever needed knowing when to just hold you - no words
need to be spoken I love you forever - The miracle of love is forever!

Denise Lynch

My Friend My Friend

My friend my friend what words do I say,
I wished you the best for tomorrow
But the Lord took you today.

I know he had his reasons, although it seemed much to fast;
Yet the friendship we created even through death shall last.

I shall always remember your smile and your witty way;
And know in my heart and mind we'll meet again someday.

For your leaving came so sudden, yet I know you had a choice,
For when you heard the calling I know you knew the voice.

Your days are now countless, your life is everlast.
You shall not only be part of my future but always a part of my past.

Your new life is beginning my prayers with you I send,
For I will miss you dearly;
My friend my friend.

Leon D. Brown

Wisdom

One of the greatest things in life to learn is
that God is always in control of our lives, we
must learn the lesson of our trials and acquire a
higher level of understanding.

We must be willing to Humble ourselves so that
our Creator can more easily guide us into His
Wisdom to choose Right from Wrong.

We must endure hardships to appreciate what
we have and we must be more Willing to share
our Blessings with others who are less
fortunate.

We must learn to develop a meaningful
relationships with God and learn to trust His
decision in our lives.

We must learn to Pray, and to make that
Prayer sincere and heartfelt, For God knows
our hearts and minds and He cannot be fooled.

We must through all of this expect God to be
faithful to His Word, because God cannot lie.

Lessie Myles

Question Of Fate

Who knows what fate has in store?
One who was once so intimately familiar
Now strangely indifferent
I have beautiful memories of a fierce lover
Yet such a gentle friend
One who entered my life
When I desperately needed someone to care
Was it fate who brought us together?
Is it fate that now takes us apart?
Would things have been different
If we met another place or another time?
Was it ever...? Could it have been...? Who knows?
So many questions, so many feelings!
There is a special place in my heart
That belongs only to you
You are always there when I need a friend
As close as a thought and as far away as a memory
Sweetheart, one day, in quiet solitude
Think of me...remember...smile

Anita Sykes-Moore

Intrepid

Somehow, when you touch my neck, stroke my hair
Hearts blend, become me into you, reaching,

All that is me awaits your touch
Melting, minds longing to be free,
Free to savor Nobel fingers, gentle but strong.

Delicate cheek rests on your warm chest
Gazing at stars above, they glisten in splendor.

Sharing the moment when we two feel as one,
Clinging to a special place in time, sweetly.
Knowing no other can replace this me and you.

Crystal eyes see beyond the mystery,
Hands begging to caress, feeling your warmth.

It's been such a long journey, waiting for you.
Waiting for you to come back to claim me.
For I am yours.

No other reaches my soul as you,
Touching my neck, Nobel fingers,
Sweet kisses, stealing my heart.

Jayle Ess

My Friends

They cheer me up when I am down
They are good listeners
They are there when I need them
My friends are the greatest.

They accept me for who I am
They like the person that I am
They like my sense of humor
My friends are the greatest.

They help me with my problems
They treat me with respect
They treat me how they want to be treated
My friends are the greatest.

They always laugh at my jokes
They always tell me to think positively
They have made me what I am today
My friends are the greatest.

Jennifer Vavra

On Halloween Night

On all Hallows Eve, monsters come out at night
To try and scare us, with their horror and fright
Through the air will fly ghosts, and trolls walk the land
With their eerie screams, and tricks that they planned
The witches are brewing, their potions and spells
And in the darkness, we will hear ghoulish yells
Now this is their day, and they will surely come
But it will be children in costumes, to have their own fun
They will come trick or treating, and knock on your door
Just hoping for candy, and to show what they wore
So don't be afraid, on this Halloween
Try to be friendly, and not to be mean
For if you do, they will put a curse on you
You may think it's silly, but I know it's true
For all through the years, it has been this way
But as far as for monsters, who can really say.

Vincent James

Two Lives

Many years ago, two lives intertwined
Becoming as one, growing together
Learning to love, sharing the life
That God up above, gave to each one.

The seasons came, the years rolled by
The babies grew and left the home they knew
And the lives that grew together
Continue on forever and ever.

Many memories are stored in their hearts
The good times, disappointments too
And the love that brought them together
Remains in their heart forever and ever.

Two lives that came together
Two lives sharing the time
Two lives helping each other
Two lives forever and ever.

A song in honor of Two Lives that conceived and cared for me:
my father and mother, whom I love, on their 40th wedding anniversary.

Mark S. Simcik

Confusion

Why must it be that everyone fights?
Another argument every night...
"Why can't we all just get along?"
This plaintive wail hangs on my mind.
A place free from judgment, I'd like to find.
"Aren't we all good friends?"
Sure, until the friendship ends.
A girl weeps and can't pretend.
"I smile because I don't know what's going on".
Such trouble to go through to have a good time.
The perfect saying, it's what's on my mind.
"Perceptions are wrong, communications are down".
How can we fix the problem...again?
I honestly don't know if we can.

Helen E. Coyne

Forever

Shots are fired, alarms are sound,
There's an innocent victim to be found.
On her way back from the store,
Caught in the middle of a war.

A crowd gathers as the police arrive,
There isn't a chance she will survive.
The ambulance is here, she's taken away,
What a terrible price for her family to pay.

Sitting at home when the telephone rang,
The family finds out she was killed by a gang.
The mother cries, the father screams,
Shattered now are all their dreams.

Through the graveyard they now roam,
What now a hell was once called home.
The tattered family can only grieve,
The only thing left is to pack and leave.

Flowers are left once every year,
And every year there is one less tear.
What now is there to endeavor,
Their daughter's lost, gone forever.

Emily Price

Ode To Captain Cook

A million stories in the city told
Yet rarely, does the truth unfold

Of this lot of mortal men on earth
To stand aloft the eagle's perch

Many a man has cast his gaze afar
Wondering what lay beyond the morning star

Once eager to tempt the blind horn's fate
Now space through heaven's gate

From Neptune's domain a voice does sound
Recalling a man whose fate was bound

Spirit, call me brother so I seek thee without tiring
Light, call me friend so that I may find guidance
Darkness, will open the graves of half-dead men
Death, call me gently to enjoy what I have been

Erich W. Krauss

"Peace"

Ah the beauty of an empty mind
Free of uncontrolled powers and unyielding forces.
Left open to breathe and soothed by space.

Please come, this feeling of nothing
This enviable reach of control and reason
make light the heavy
open the close

To rest in an ease of bliss.
To swim in a sea of knowing
To mold to a form accepted

But peace, be it there at the end
Shall only be known by the never
For always the now shall keep it away
Accept this and rest, if not soundly...better!

Dennis G. Cleary

The Ocean

Waves rolling out to sea,
the peaceful wind blowing on me,
seashells,
sailboats,
I love them all,
the voices of the sea gulls call,
lighthouses,
sand,
walks on the beach,
parties at night,
the swooping and diving of the bird's flight,
sand in my shoes,
the calm white and blues
of the sky,
I like to dream,
I'd like to fly,
but most of all I like the whales cry.

Jillian Vadenais

"Threshold Of Love"

We met and our lives became entwined
You gave me your heart, I gave you mine

We'll soon join hands and become as one
Our long walk through life will have begun

They'll be days of joy and tears along the way
But our love will see us through each day

Together we'll face whatever will be
For I'll have you and you'll have me

Peggy Verrill

In A Child's Eyes

A child, when little, loves with all their hearts...their parents.
A child's eyes glow when they see their parents.
A child looks up idolizing their parents.
A child thinks no wrong can be done by their parents.
A child, when wronged, forgives unconditionally their parents.
A child gives unconditional child-like faith to their parents.
A child learns by copying their parents.
A child can learn good habits from their parents.
A child can learn bad habits from their parents.
A child's life teachings come from their parents.
A child can start life afresh with love from their parents.
A child needs in their life their parents.
A child is cheated many-a-time by divorce...one of their parents.
A child, even in divorce, still needs the love of both their parents.
A child unfortunately suffers thru the legal fightings' of their parents.
A child longs for the love of both their parents.
A child can't understand why hurt comes to them from their parents.
A child's eyes find the love that others don't see in their parents.
In a child's eyes is the never-ending love that God meant for their parents.
In a child's eyes...Love Can Be Rekindled.

Murdic H. Jones

"Just Open Your Eyes And See..."

Just open your eyes and see the pollution,
Not only on land, but in the ocean.
There is no time to stop and play,
The mess we have made must be cleaned up today.
The fish in the sea, the animals on land, the birds in the sky,
Deserve a home that would suit you and I.
Plant more trees to grow on this land,
And help other people understand
That the world around them needs a helping hand.
So don't do what is wrong, do what is right,
This world needs someone who will stand up and fight.
All the poisonous water and air,
There is not enough people who will prove that they care.
Just open your eyes and see.

Autumn Bolay

My Husband

I met him when I was but thirteen
He was the most wonderful man I'd ever seen
Within weeks he stole my heart away
I believed there'd be no other from that day

Five years later he took me to be his wife
He said he would love me for the rest of his life
I gave him a daughter at age twenty one
At twenty four I gave him a son.

This year he turns fifty, and I forty seven
Our life has not always been "made in heaven"
But this one thing I still can say
There has been no other from that very day.

Diana Dukes

The Story Teller

Within your heart great treasures dwell,
You share them in the stories you tell.
Your strength of purpose and love of life,
Radiate forth in each word's flight.
As your eyes take on a warm soft glow,
From your sweet lips the stories flow.
You bring me joy each passing day,
In the treasures you chose to pass my way.
Whether we grow together, or drift apart,
I thank you for the laughter you've returned to my heart.

Nancy Nelson

Heaven's Fire

With daring hands steal I Heaven's Fire...
dare I dream this blessed thing?
Which burns with a dark light
and sears my soul,
defended by Fate and Time.

In silence I creep through the Gate of Night,
past the Well of Grace:
a shadow through immaculate realms.
Marked by none am I,
a thief of radiant hearts.

Arrayed in honor and Gallant Words;
thus did I once appear
heralded by song on silver flutes.
Now darkness only follows
ever close behind me.

Grasp trembling I take Thy Holy Ember,
This glorious treasure for which I lust
and so forever have I sinned.
But bereft of its light
I am already damned.

Joseph Flanagan

The Sands Of Time

I walked along the beach and pictured my life
as I looked at the sand

How did I ever make it without the help of
God's powerful hand.

As I walked slowly along my shoes were filled with sand

Sometimes my life felt so empty because I
had not followed God's plans

I looked over the water as it beat heavily against the rocks
I'm so grateful that God never left me
alone and stranded at the docks

Oh how peaceful it was to see the tide come in
God gave the best that He had to save us from our sins

My foot prints are erased from the sand of time
Jesus is my Blessed Redeemer and has restored my peace of mind.

Carol Y. Sherman

Be I Not One Of Thee

No one knows the man I am -
Aye, no one knows the man I used to be!
A huddled soul before the fire as I melt into the ground
to be stepped upon by the soles of humanity!
An unknown virus that spreads upon this land of plenty!

Ah, but where is the plenty we once knew?
Taken from us so suddenly!
As if to punish our very being.
To say today I am - today I am not!

Do not crush us with your heel!
Our souls cry out!
Our bodies tremble with the cold!
Cold hearts are ye that stomp us out,
like a fire that spreads and takes another soul
to the everlasting pit of total despair!
Let me be a man!
A man to lean on - nay a man to lean!
A man to stand and rise up high!
Nay a man to crouch into the ruins of despair,
And be afraid to live but once again.

Margaret R. Bruton

Thank You

You were there from day one,
And you'll be there till all is done.

Your love has always been warm and friendly,
And it will always be forever mending.

The scrapes and bruises you healed,
The fear of the monsters you have always made yield.

The messes we made that were not always neat,
But there were times you said, "Oh, look how sweet!"

You tried to steer us down the right path,
We've all felt the warmness of dad's little wrath.

The care that mom used when she bandaged our knees,
The hope and fear in their eye's when they watched us climb trees.

That look has never diminished through the years,
Now it is our turn to wipe away the tears.

We know you'll always be there with a strong and helping hand,
And we know you'll always be there as a hero or a friend.

You've brought us this far, now we're on our own,
You'll always have a special place in our heart and in our home.

Thank you Mom and Dad for showing us the way,
And for giving us this beautiful, splendid, happy day.

Kerry L. Frazier

Monotony

Mountain peaks so stark and bleak, frozen ground beneath my feet
Gray and sullen are the skies, snow that always seems to rise - Oh!
Monotony - Ennui - Monotony

If it doesn't snow - it sleets, and the rafters sob and creak
Doors and windows join their groan, 'bove it all the trees do moan-in
Monotony - Ennui - Monotony

All the birds have gone away, will they come another day?
Bats and bears are in their lair, all the world does sit and
stare-in
Monotony - Ennui - Monotony

Every day we scan the clouds, all they seem to wear are shrouds
And at night there are no stars, Windows seem to have grown bars-of
Monotony - Ennui - Monotony

Nature knows that this will pass, if we mortals all can last
That we surely will not die with this eerie, unreal cry - of
Monotony - Ennui - Monotony

When the sun again is felt, and the snow begins to melt
Grass again beneath my feet, then I will no longer meet - old
Monotony - Ennui - Monotony

Elaine C. Ketchelmeier

If Dreams Came True

Late at night deep in my sleep I dream
of things that I wish could be.
The beauty that God will give to me, or
things in the future that only I could see....
If only, dreams came true.
A drug free world, no sick little boys
or girls, non-polluted lakes and ponds,
full of ducks and swans.
Late last night something different
happened though. I had a terrible
dream, things like black snow.
Countless swapping bombs to and fro.
I hope this dream, bombs to and fro.
I hope this dream doesn't come
true but....it is likely though.

Marianne Snodgrass

In Troubled Times

Where do you find the strength to carry on,
when so many days have gone.

I believe faith is the only key,
and it's been shown in history.

For those that are strong,
in time they'll sing a song.

We'll look back on their trials,
which one day turned to smiles.

We'll remember when,
it was so important then.

For one day this shall pass,
and we'll have relief at last.

If you say a prayer tonight, and wish with all your might,
there will come a day, when you'll see a brighter light.

For wishes are the beginning of efforts applied,
that will some day be with you, and remain at your side.

Effort and endurance are all that remain.
They hold the key to peace and comfort, which we strive to attain.

It's for me to do my best,
and God will do the rest.

Robert L. Johnson

Daddy

I cross my heart
I hope to die.
Life is a cloud of black dust.
He showed me the way to life.
He showed me the way to death.
There is no light only darkness and hatred.
But who can I hate?
My daddy is gone.

I cross my heart over and over.
Death is my father's name
My punishment is life.
I grasp at everything
But he is not here.
Time is my enemy.
It will not stop and it will not turn back.
If only I could, daddy.

Erica Ramos

Love Hurts

To think of love as a smile,
Brings happiness all around.
To be hurt because of love,
Brings teardrops from above.
Your heart aches from pain,
Like a lost child in the rain.
To make someone happy all the time,
Is like making a puzzle into a rhyme.
Doing your best for someone you like,
You feel as though you're high as a kite.
Finding out it was all a lost,
Knowing life is a priceless cost.
You feel like dying, your ego is gone,
You know your love doesn't belong.
Go on your way before you lose your head,
Try harder, or else, you'll wish you were dead.

Nancy L. Caudill

The Rape

Heaven crashed into ruins of water,
Kamikaze raindrops; life hurled at glass
That held me in
Raindrops exploded;
The dignity of tears broken into pieces
Of trembling water on the glass.
While I shook, in arms that had no eyes,
but chose their blindness any ways.
I wish that we could have taken the shape of rain,
Given somehow to life, instead of this strange death,
But we know so much more about ownership than we know of love
Let me have you, let me have.
He said. He did say. He did.
Fear is physical now, another set of eyes in me
Staring out at the world, asking fear's permission for every movement.
We have become less than human, in a world that told us to acquire.
We are your hunger, and my half eaten body.
And you did this.
While Kamikaze rain looked on, indifferent until the splash.

E. M. Hoenigman

Untitled

Upon this coarse, wooden structure I sit,
licking from my cheek the blood and spit.
Thongs placed around my wrist and neck,
due to my offense I have lost great respect.
Beads of perspiration seep down my
face,
a tear in my eye; soon I will leave this
mournful place.
The echo of a slamming door, hushed
voices; footsteps across the cold, hard
floor.
My face is curtained with a black leather
sheath, I am happy, my last expectation to
meet.
Upon my head is placed a brazen crown,
inside my shell, how my soul does frown.
The lever is dropped, the lights grow
dim,
my body is lifeless; it's time to start over
again.

Matt Hutzel

H.S. Graduate - 1996

Tribute to Jennifer Kristy Wernicki

Remember all the years between
Oh how you longed to be eighteen
It's a new beginning up strike the band
Your loving parents drove a helping hand
Pleasant college days you will share
With many students from everywhere
Accept the challenges with great success
God bless your future with happiness
You are smart, witty, an intellect
But one can't hope to be perfect
If at times you are feeling blue
Remember the World is rooting for you
May your Angel guard you all the way
With Peace and love Star of the day.

Rita McLaughlin Wozvock (Grandmommie)

Sparrows Song

My work you say, is dull and simple; merely scheduled rhyme,
With a primal rhythm to tug at the heart; and meaning to tug at
the mind.

Free verse is a contradiction in terms, there can be no such thing.
The very soul of verse is the beat and rhyme that call the heart
to sing.

Echoing weakly the rhythms of nature; the only forces that men
need fear,
The gentle cadence of measured verse chronicles all that men hold
dear.

The love of another, of God or home; their triumphs and their fears;
The joy of their children's laughter, the sorrow of their tears.

Discipline breeds achievement, as history will attest
Look to yourself for an answer—what lines do you remember best?

Not that I would stifle anyone's freedom, nothing could be worse.
If it's freedom you want, take it; write freely—but don't call it
verse.

J. David Sanderfer

My Dear, My Sweet

My dear, my sweet, you are my friend,
Whether far, or near, to this world's end,
As you depart and marriage start,
Remember the warm spot you leave in my heart.

Your Mom doth want you now to know,
That she has watched you slowly grow,
And learn the things you need in life,
To now make Gerald a loving wife.

So if I seem quite proud today,
To happily send you on your way,
It's just because I trust in you,
And know your best you'll always do.

Your father of course will agree,
With all the things I've just mentioned,
Not just because he loves us both,
But because he knows your good intentions.

So be joyful, be happy, enjoy your life,
And do your utmost to make Gerald,
A proper Christian wife.

Mary L. Cummings

"Mother We Miss You"

Mother we call, but she has
gone to be another angel on God's
great throne.
So children when you need her,
look up and you will see another star
in heaven that shines for you and me.
We are all going to miss her,
for she brought us all such joy.
She left behind her one girl and one boy.
Though she is not here with them now.
Her memory will always stay and
someday they will all meet in heaven on
that judgement day.
So always be proud of mommy and
be careful what you do and say, for
after all heaven not so far away and
she will be watching you, wherever you may go.
So thank God for all mothers
and how we love them so.

Henry A. Hall

And It Closed, Firmly

A laborious groan from an overworked stair
from which a stealthy escape cannot be made.
The gentle snick of a door
closing, firmly.

Backstroking to the thromp, thromp
of tired, determined footfalls
hesitating on the complaining step
contemplating, wondering
deciding, firmly.

Clack, clack
and the dead bolt is no longer a silent guardian of
unpredictable domesticity
The knob turns in a faint but detectable rattle
stubborn, resistant,
but yielding nonetheless.
And the world sneaks in, just a little
Past the guardian, up the belabored stair,
to play with and tease pitiable toes, blind to all,
before the door closes,
firmly.

Ebony Love

I Remember It All

I remember his touch, so soft and passionate.
He was the kind who made you feel like you could do it all.
The kind who listens and understands,
When your world seems to fall.

I remember it all, brand new to me,
How we seemed to fit together in one perfect set.
I wish he could remember all those things,
That I'm trying my hardest to forget.

I tell myself he's the one to lose it all.
In me he had his biggest fan.
But it's hard to believe that when you know,
God, in him, made an almost perfect man.

He knew what to say, he knew what to do.
Now my heart is one big mess.
Because even though he has left and hurt me,
I don't love him any less.

I hope one day he remembers
What once seemed pure and perfect
And remembers the beautiful things,
I soon hope to forget.

Rebecca Torrellas

"Thumbs Up For Peace"

Great Spirit-God.
We've poisoned the lovely earth with our hate,
vengeance and evil doing. Suck the poison from
our hearts and show mercy by giving us the
desire to heal ourselves and others.

Help us to follow Your way by sharing love,
backed up by deeds. Whether our skins are red,
yellow, brown, black or white, give us chances
to "go about doing good-instead of just going about."

We have created the facilities to share water,
food and shelter with each person doing what he/she can.
Perhaps we can make the peaceable kingdom
not by just lying down together, but by showing,
in our eyes and lives, that Peace is achievable
each day, then each year, and finally the millennium.

We find that Heaven is about us. We need not
"see through the glass dimly," but as the universe
expands, each generation shall in winning Peace
in Our Time and Beyond find a healing way.

Evelyn B. McCulloh

Daddy

All the good times I remember I was with my dad.
But now that we're apart to remember makes me sad.

I remember the dark cold nights when I would wake up scared
I would scream out for my daddy I knew he really cared

He thought me how Jesus was sent to die on the cross
And if I followed him I'd never be at a loss

My daddy's so strong not one to show emotion
In all the years I've known him,
  his life's been full of devotion.

He thought me not to: sneak, lie or steal
He showed me the difference between
  What's wrong and what's real

I remember all the times I saw him
  praying down upon his knee
little did I know my daddy was praying for me

I'm a big girl now, I can make decisions on my own
Knowing in this world sometimes I'll be alone.

Sometimes it's scary to think about
  the future that lies ahead
It's times like that when I remember what my daddy said.

April Ruppel

Don't Hate Me Because I Am Brown

My brown face is not on Cosmo, nor Vanity
let alone any Cover Girl... Mabelline Line

Una Cover Girl no nace, se hace...
pero, nací de color café del color a miel
dulce como la caña, pero fuerte como el adobe

So, when have you seen me on any cover... rarely is my beauty
captured

Don't hate me because I am brown
Instead adore my bronze skin color

I'm of tierra cotta
earthly colors... those which are year round
no need for tanning
no need for concealing make-up

Instead of hating my womanly color capture the ray of my beauty
that which reflects...

My india struggle
My ama's hunger
My abuelita's suffer
and my hermana's resistance to love our beauty... our negra color

So, Don't Hate Me Because I Brown

Ofelia Barrios

When I Close My Eyes Shut

When I close my eyes shut
My eyes can still see behind their fastened lids
(Only darkness)
But when a fiery orange sun blazes right into my face
My eyes see a warm citrus glow filter through the lids
(And I think)
This is maybe what unborn children see
When they first open their eyes
In the cradle of their mother's womb
And I keep my eyes shut so that
Maybe the world will be
(Just for a second)
As innocent as it was back then

Jessica Jones

If You Love Me

If you love me, you will never have need for another.
If you trust me, I will not lie to you or fool you.
Trust your heart and believe in me,
The world will become our instrument of harmony.
You and I are the love song.
In you I have found all that my heart desires, a real and true love.
My love is vast, endless and forever.
So touch me, touch creation; touch eternity.
We are the universe.
If we live our lives together, my last breath, my very essence is yours.
We shall be as one.
Touch me; touch creation; touch eternity.
My love is vast, endless and forever.
If you love me, as I love you,
All our days will be filled with happiness and joy.
Rain and all obstacles are mere stepping stones.
Pain and fear are simple illusions.
But, I am real, and my promise is true.
Say yes, and all my life is dedicated to loving only you,
If you love me.

Stanley Z. Houston

My Inner Soul

As I walked on the shore by the sea,
the web of life unraveled for me,
precious given memories.

My music teacher, with her classical training,
planted a seed for the love of listening.

The precious souls, that I have known,
that reflect the treasures of the past,
will be valued to the last.

Oh, what beauty nature gives us,
from sunrise to sunset,
the music of the soul unwinds,
to one of God's best gifts.

From the flowers in the ground,
to the tall trees above,
they inspire oneself,
to learn about life and love.

Susan N. Adams

Come Out Of The Darkness

As I see you in my dreams,
you're like a silhouette, that will never
come out of the darkness.
As I see you in real life,
you are like the same silhouette, not
changing, never speaking, a dark contour of depth.
When I look into your shallow eyes,
there's no hope, no sparkle, just darkness.
Your soul, that profound shadow within, has blinded my lucid thoughts.
I know I can't help you, though I wish I could.
I wish I could talk to you, though I know I can't.
I do wish for a lot of things, but
this wish would mean the world to me.
I wish for you to come out of the darkness.

Kara Santa Lucia (age 17)

The Lake Was Not Round

We set out to walk around a lake that looked completely round.
The path continued on and on through groves of cotton wood,
cedar and other hard wood trees. We walked and walked always
sure that we were almost there. The squirrels and chipmunks
scampered around us. Bird songs filled the air. Finally we
found a marker, just before the trails end, "This trail is a
10-K hike from its beginning to its end".

Alyce M. Nielson

Magnetic Dissonance

Most of what goes through my mind is
garbage; electrical impulses gone haywire
short-circuiting the system;
simultaneous flashes bifurcating the brain
with asymmetrical deductions, green-molded
locomotions nearing obsolescence;
pinwheels of energy in diagonal dissonance,
transmitting ellipses of coherence
(plane not parallel to axis).
Light checkers into confusion.
So much meaningfulness expended
so tritely, making great, logarithmic
molehills loom mountainous.
All impulses generated
will be on leave of absence
until further notice.
Please do not fax me
anything at home.

Anne Wilson

Untitled

Sand through my fingers
If I hold it loosely
It flows so quickly
Each time I refill my hand
It disappears again
All that is left is a grain in my palm

Sand through my fingers
If I hold it tightly
Focusing on the contents of my hands
I can't do anything but hold on
It reminds there
Forbidding me to reach for another handful

Sand through my fingers
Examining the many piles around me
Holding on to just enough
Letting go when I feel I am ready
Each grain holds a precious memory
It shimmers
Sand through my fingers

Cassia Meta Dunlap

A Symphony Unwritten

Our inner beings swell with malignancy.

Unhealed wounds are pulsating within us.

Inner scars sink below our surface and hound the deepest
yearnings of our soul.

It's very hard, living this life—playing this role
building ourselves back to our homes.

But it seems that in actuality our homes are places within
us that are forever growing and changing.

Like our souls ever living...

The wisest of us will discover that the deep running scars
are limited and finite. We will make a place for our anger
and our pain, as a means of controlling these things.

Stifled screams are transformed into a dance...We shall
dane wherever we may be...

Our pasts are the tunes already played...we must from
these tunes learn, yet remember that we're living and
growing and building everyday

Our futures are symphonies unwritten...we must toward this
music strive, yet recognize that we have limited input into
its writing.

Ian Michael Wymbs

As Dew Do's

As the dew drops
drop from the morning glory
to the big branch. Life is so
sad; but great! Life, Life, life so
great. Have you did a little TLC today
drop, drop. Meet Mother Earth. She will
do you great things. As the
dew drops drop.

David V. Monticalvo

Spring Time

The time we've all been waiting for
Has finally come at last.
The winter's snow has all gone.
It's only a memory of the past.

Spring has arrived in beauty,
Flowers of all colors to see
Yards all green and trees full of leaves
A favorite time for you and me.

Planning vacations is on our minds
Trips and picnics of the greatest kind,
Love and laughter fills our soul
Moments to have worth more than gold.

Pausing to look at each little thing
To touch and feel, such joy it brings.
Filling our hearts with joyful glee
How wonderful it is to be so free.

Louise Speer

The Radiant You

Self esteem -
Realism - but a mere dream
So many things to share
no one to truly care
A leader stuck behind a mask of fears
'till someone uncovered the hidden tears.
You set your quandaries aside
and in you I did confide.
As my pen began to surrender to the darkness of my song,
You told me to write on. Write on! Write on! Write on!
And so I shall continue on to complete
the task God has bestowed at my feet
All owed to God for creating thee.
All owed to you for encouraging me.
Continue on - my beautiful teacher
to be the radiant you
and let God use you
as I know He will continue to do.

Melissa Sands

A Sonnet To Immediacy

Clutters of trains and cars and blocks piled high
Will trip the unwary on the kitchen floor;
soft dolls and cuddies with one buttoned eye
Come tumbling out each time you close the door
of bedroom reeking of your new cologne
and powder youthful hands had yearned to try.
A pair of socks and shoes so careless thrown
you pick up quickly as you hurry by.
It seems the house is hemmed by prison bars
Which hold and thwart a mother's wanderlust;
you long to travel, wonder free afar
from children's wails and tedious trails of dust.
The children grown, you're free to roam at will -
you sigh and cry and find the house too still.

Marie Cox

Circle Of Time

Death is dark.
Life is blind.
It's all a matter,
Of human mankind.
To live your life,
And when your through,
Another life comes after you.

This circular motion,
Between life and death,
What in the world does it mean?
It runs circles through and through my mind,
And how strange to me it seems.

Does my life have any meaning?
In time I'm sure I'll know.
Until then I'll wonder,
About the clouds and the thunder.
The wind and the rain,
My time on this plain.

It's all this circular motion
This circle of time.

Shariesa Rosettta Brown

Winter Sky Blues

Winter skies turn from blue to gray,
Sadness and loneliness close in since you went away,
The leaves have lost their color and fall,
They match my spirit falling down; I've lost my all.

I miss your laughing eyes and gentle smile,
Your strong but tender touch,
Your passionate kiss
that said so much.

Few words were ever spoken,
There was no need,
You reached the quiet guarded place in my Soul,
So few were ever allowed to see.

The gentle touch, the tender kiss,
Spoke of care and desire,
You made me feel wanted and filled
My soul with fire.

Hear my heart call through
the miles that separate us,
Return to me and return the light,
Bring the love and joy back to my life.

Kandice Park

What Love Is To Me

Love is knowing when your wrong,
but making it right.
Love is reaching out for someone
to hold when your scared at night.
Love is being patient with someone who really cares.
Love is being there to hold their
hand thru all their fears.
Love is being their friend thru all
the hard times.
Love is being there to talk to when
something's on their mind.
Love is being there with a smile
when their feeling down
Love is being there to help them
turn their frown around.
Love is someone to hold when
you need to cry.
Love comes from the heart, that money can't buy.
If you look in the mirror
then you will see what True Love is to me.

Steven Forsyth

Change

I see change
As nothing old or nothing new
But making a difference with precious time
Between you - between me.

I see change as the world turns,
From one - then to the other. It leaves no stone unturned,
Or leaves no sea unchurned, I see change.

Just as a rainbow, seconds young - yet minutes old,
Lingering in the sky,
Waiting for that ultimate moment to make a change
To the dusty gray in the sky.

Change is gonna come, it makes no difference
As to who you are or, what you are.
Can't change it - can't define it, change is gonna come.

You get the courage, you get the strength,
To face tomorrow and do what you gotta do.
Between you - between me, change is gonna come.

It knows no place or, where you live.
Can't run, can't hide, can't wait and idle free. Time is against your
side. Sure as you are born, and gonna die, "Change is gonna come!"

Doretha Prioleau Hanna

Untitled

The handsome man is skiing down.
Not very happy, with a frown.

Suddenly, comes a woman, skiing down, out of nowhere.
And she sees the man, in despair.

His eyes open up wide, as he sees the glamorous woman
skiing down an adventurous ride.

She sees the man in despair,
as she comes to him in tender, loving care.

She looks into his eyes, as she helps him from the ground.
And neither of them make a sound.

And they share a moment of passion.

Nancy Da Costa

First Love

So much love is lost, so much goes undone.
So much love is found, starting
like a flower coming from under the ground.

You think you're finished, you
think you're done.
You see a picture and feel drawn.
For a moment you fall, fall
for childhood beliefs.
First is first and always will be.

Mother pushes the flower from
under the soil.
Your heart glows like the sun
in your eyes.
You realize mother is the
one, with child
a sight you could never let die.
So now I know who comes first
isn't always first, but the one
that makes your heart glow
like the sun in your eyes.

Dean Niall Freeman

The Tracks

Why I go to these railroad tracks others will never know,
the truth is as it speaks and this is where I stand.

Whenever I go the same plants rustle and the wind tears strands
of hair from my braid.
The shadows dance and the birds chirp every single day.
And yet I go anyway, and people must wonder why,
But I don't care what they think, it is my place where I choose
to be alone.

I visited the tracks again and no one can question it,
Because I see why, I see the truth, the light, and the darkness
so I will come back again.

If I do not go to the tracks at least every now and then,
I won't sleep at all,
And those tracks will haunt my dreams and shadow me in the moon,
I shall go back again no matter what the cost,
For if I don't go back again, for reasons that are unknown,
There might not be a sun tomorrow or a moon to rise and set
in the clouds.

Amber Bythewood

Burial Of Freud

This is the ghost from patients past.
It is time to put Sigmund Freud to rest.
The fiendish spell he relentlessly cast
Belongs to the history of the devilish past.

This atheistic deity and professor of psychiatric lore
Should not be idolized and studied any more.
His obsession was transgression, not magnanimity.
He denied the Trinity and his theme was sublimity.

If only he had looked to the stars for inspiration,
He might have unraveled a beautiful theme.
Instead he spun a web of oedipus fixation.
There was only psychic disharmony in his scheme.

Sigmund viewed the world through a microscope.
Interpretation and hypnosis was his only hope.
Even though he was considered among the best,
It's time we put the poor chap to rest.

It would only be fitting to make a cold marble bust
To match his theory of psychiatric blight,
And into a frozen mausoleum it thrust
To perpetuate that he was only a neurotic's delight.

Warren D. Hageman

Later That Same Lifetime

So this is growing old together
You opting for softball over racquetball
Me going to a one-piece swimsuit
Creaks, pains, and back massages
A couple of pounds that won't be shed
Falling asleep at night before loving
Before talking about everything

Me kissing a new line under your eye
You taking men's vitamins, for me
Watching the sunrise with orange juice
Smiling across a crowded room without a word
A worn flannel nightgown and torn boxer shorts
Copper cookware and a pool table

You tolerating the cat more and more
Me tolerating your poker nights at all
Never looking for the subtle changes
Not noticing them when they've arrived
And still that longed-for embrace
After a day of being apart
It's a beautiful life

Gracie Bailey

Blue Moon And Mother Earth

It's midnight, but not dark, as the moon shines its beam in
turquoise blue, like a pastel pageant for mankind to view.
A blue moon appears every seven and one-half years, but why not
green remains unseen? The mysticism this night feels so
tranquil and right, the fire flies spelling every name with
their light. A slight touch of rain mixed with a soft, gentle
breeze, as Mother Earth's working late for her children to
please. Such unison tonight, perfections, the plight, as
Mother Earth joins heaven herself and God with His might!
Is the blue moon a sign that we are made from the earth, even
though each and everyone of us were given natural birth, do we
need the magic each and every seven and one half years, as we
question who made all, and why all is here? No! We need not to
solve the secrets or the unknown that we fear, just love both
our Mothers and our Maker who is so dear!

James Perry Hand

Sketches Of Gloria

Never will I forget the day I first set eyes on you...
could you have stepped from a painting of ages long ago?
For you had an Old World look from another time and place...
you might have been a work of art by Michelangelo.

And there I stood as on a cloud, I could not turn my gaze...
the mystique of your beauty, I just wanted to embrace.
A fantasy of your sweet kiss, to hold you close to me...
not all the rhymes or all the chimes can describe you to me.

I only knew you for a while, oh how my heart would melt...
for there I was on that same cloud, I knew it was true love.
I had to somehow let you know, did I not wait too long...
to maybe open up your heart with a whisper or a song?

So many times, I wondered what you might have felt or said....
could I have touched something in you with a pretty rhyme or two?
As of the last time I saw you, watching your high school play...
when all I wanted just to do was whisper, "I love you."

Jerry Solomon

Ashen Idols

My father kept this ashtrays well fed.
They were lined up on every surface
table, chair, and tub.
With great diligence and care,
he tended them day and night.
He carefully selected each brand and puff
to pay tribute to his ashen idols.

There they sat
all grey and white and clear and black
mouths unhinged like baby robins waiting for a worm.
His yellowed fingers kept them well satiated
with meals of grey and black and white and brown;
some round and new,
some crushed and bent.

In return, his faithful pets helped reward him
with ash and smoke and cough
and perfumed the air with pungent stench,
so, with loving devotion,
my father kept his ashtrays well fed 'til, in the end,
they had coated all with grey, yellow and purple.

Janiece Maloney

"Spiritual Neglect"

Spiritual Neglect has dealt are society a devastating blow,
prayer in or schools has been banned, what next
will go. Shell we wither and die a faithless society, are
shell we seek the Holy Spirit and proclaim
Victory.

Irving Carter

Freedom!

One day while walking in the woods,
I saw an animal. He looked at me as
if to say "Go back, before you are caught."
I stood there and wondered if he was
talking truth in his sympathetic expression.
When I saw the light I turned
to run, but when I saw that I was
in a cage, I remembered something
very strange... I was the animal
that I had looked at that very day.

Christina K. O'Donnell

Untitled

I love you, I love everything about you,
You touch, your smile, and your charm I admire.
Through good times and bad,
Through happy and sad,
Your girl I'll always be,
Forever your body, you can always count on me.
I knew right from the start,
That we'd fall in love and you'd take over my
heart. And maybe you knew it too, but
wanted me to think you had no clue,
Just remember these three words, to help you
along each day.
Because your always in my heart, in each and
every way.
No matter what you've up to, if you have
little or lot's to do,
Just remember my three words and know that
I Love You...........

Kandace Bell

Misanthropy

This place...No! I am not for you to understand
I am part of a selfish world
You appear to be drowning; I don't extent my hand

Let your sorrows overcome you, I don't care
I only love myself
Happiness I am not at liberty to share

You scream, you cry out for help
I only stand and watch
This world is for me and no one else

I continuously take but you never receive
You owe me
Your pain I feel no obligation to ease

Can you not see through this transparent mask
If you are longing for help, open your eyes
All you must do is ask

Misanthropic, no that's not me
I would give you everything
My life if need be

Valerie M. Volkert

Depression

Depression it hits you in the face like
a cold gust of wind.
You don't know when it's gonna happen but
you do know that you don't want to be depressed
Feelings of loneliness, and suicide overwhelm
you until you can't take it anymore,
Then Bam!
They find you dead from a shot gun wound,
You hear the police call it a suicide as
you watch from the other world wishing
you hadn't killed yourself.

Maranda Taylor

Dear Anyone

I am lonely.
The sky looks dull,
But it always does
When it's going to rain.

I walk alone.
People pass me by,
Walking-fast.
Slow down someone!

I want to talk to you.
Tell you, how I feel.
No one stopped.
No one listened.

I saw a puppy.
Lost, hungry and cold.
Isn't he sad?
I asked everyone.

No one answered. No one listened.
It started to rain. I started to cry.

I cried for the people. Who never stopped or listened.
I cried for the puppy. But then I stopped. And so did the rain.

Flossie Patterson

Taking Stock

Glory and gold many have sought
Power and prestige others have bought
Triumphs and treasures won and lost
Trials and tribulations the ultimate cost

So, why do mortals we — value only what we touch and see?

Honesty and honor, life's proven way
Diligence and duty earn extra pay
Trust and truth are essential, indeed
Charity and compassion man's noble need

So, why don't mortals we — obey God's moral decree?

Gratitude and grace enrich the self
Smiles and service bring added wealth
Love and laughter, the heart does lift
Family and friendships, God's special gift

So, why don't mortals we — embrace the good God made for you and me?

Faith and fidelity should be our aim
Virtue and value must be the same
Peace and patience repudiate strife
Prayer and purpose the essence of life

So why don't mortals we — give reverence to God on bended knee?

Orland E. Freeman, Jr.

Imperial Bowl

Alone in a small gallery,
Glancing at the Walking Buddha, watching me with the gentlest of smiles. As if approving.
In front of me a bowl. A door to my imagination, a mother of beauty, a cradle of thought.
Drawn out of myself, my body gazes onward, in unending awe.
My spirit opens the door and leaves all reality.
A garden, a tremendous garden. Alone I stroll on the pebbled walk.
Trees encircling me, blades of grass gently bowing down at my feet as they move longingly towards the sun. Each flower sway back and forth, side to side.
The garden alive!
A small black beetle scurries across my foot working diligently to reach its destination.
The flowers fade in the distance.
Reluctantly, I return to my body to find Buddha still smiling at me.

Jennifer Brown

No Courage To Turn Its Face To Me

A silent watch on the desk
has been there
for two years.
One day
the watch stopped clicking like losing smile
as if an elephant is falling down
in slow-motion
to the ground
The strap became too hard
to keep its slight dusty body straight
I don't see usually the still watch but
I know it is still there
I don't have any courage to turn its face to me
I don't know
when those hands are pointing

Daisuke Kawasaki

Rainbows

A rainbow lasts for just a short time,
I wish I owned one so I could call it "mine".
It'll stay for just a minute or two,
Then disappear and the sky turns blue.
We all hear a tale that tends to be told,
That at the end there's a pot of gold.
When I was young I used to believe,
And would look around to see what I could see.
But in the end all I would find,
was that I wasted a lot of time.
When you're pure and innocent you tend to learn,
That when you grow up the pages turn.
And in due time,
something comes along that you call "mine".
It may not be your wish of a rainbow,
Instead it'll be something that'll make you glow.

Chrissy Kubasiak

Today and Tomorrow

Whose character is the role you
want to portray today and tomorrow?

What are the belief's that will guide
you through your life away from sorrow?

When will you choose to pour out
on stationary paper your belief's
and characteristic wishes, tomorrow?

Where will you search for encouragement
and the answers to your questions?

How will you find the source for your
strength, through suggestions?

What tree stands firm and weathers all storms?
How will you water the tree?
Where will the wind blow the leaves?

Who finds joy, peace, love, rhythm, and harmony?
Who finds the tree of life, finds salvation,
from the beginning, the Omega,
today and tomorrow.

Louise Nikkel

My Friend

When someone can touch you, that's Natural,
When someone can touch your soul, that's Emotional,
When someone can touch your spirit, that's a Blessing,
It's in a place where only God and that person really know you.
That place of love, joy, peace and serenity.
That's what I feel, whenenver I'm with you.
I miss that with you.
I miss you... My Friend

Jym L. Franklin

"Ode To My Love"

As the stars peek from their safe haven,
They seem to spell out your name across
the sky. The soft breeze blow gently
across my face as I ask the question why;

The moon shinning so brightly seemly radiating
your smile, The constellations so far away
can only be measured by miles;

As thoughts of you intoxicate the air I can
almost feel your touch, dreading the nights
of being alone needing you so much;

Winter has come and gone, spring is so near
missing you day and night wishing you
were here;

Each night before I go to bed, just
before I sleep I say a special prayer
to God, then silently I weep.

Sherron P. Lewis

Battling A Disease

When times are tough
and things go wrong,
I hold my chin high trying not to cry,
I know in time I will die.
Trying to live each day that
goes by.
Which I get weaker and weaker,
Going back and forth to doctors and the
hospital,
Utterly becoming withdrawn and depressed.
I must not give up and fight
the battle.

It is the neglect of Rendy
which destroy life..

Danielle Sparacio

Stomping Ground

So little in this cemetery smacks
of death. Forget-me-nots bloom. Buttercups
and salvia ring the stones. And yet our steps
are soft, deliberate. Why? Do our tracks
impose upon those hell-bent to relax
beneath the earth here? Should their graves collapse,
would they grow cold? Perhaps the sound disrupts
their rest. Perhaps the pressure ruins their backs.
No, dead is dead. We can step, can stomp, on these grounds
as we like, so long as our hard soles don't tread
upon the wildflower. Let us have
a round dance, like the bee's annular rounds.
Funereal bouquets already dead,
we'll drink the health of perennials that live.

Marc Linquist

Wonder

When you look up in the sky and wonder,
What's up above the sun, clouds, and thunder?

You think to yourself that no one really knows,
And that's how God wanted it. That's what he chose.

You can only imagine, hope and pretend,
What it's like in the end.

A place of wonder and glory, a fairy-tale story?
A place of love, wisdom, and kindness?

Or is it blackness, blackness and blindness?

One can only dream, believe, and wonder,
What's up above the sun, clouds, and thunder.

Colleen Buritz

A While

It's been a while
Since I looked at a pretty face
fell in a trance, ached for a glance
soared in an imaginary romance

It's been a while
since I jumped on my bike
took off for the unknown
with a speed and abandon, only the young have known

It's been a while
since I gathered my friends
Not a care in the world
we laughed and carried on, for hours on end

It's been a while
since I plunged myself, into foods and wine, simply divine
The pleasures of the moment
with that I was content

It's been a while
since I let myself go, without a fear of being brittle,
Been a long long while
since I have lived a little.

ASH

"Rene"

We lost our son some years ago
A virile handsome man was he
The many dreams in his young life
Were never meant for him to see

It seems like only yesterday
he sat across from me
Telling me of all his plans, his
smile, I still can see

Never dreaming that this day
would be his last on earth
He gave me a hug and a kiss goodbye
As he walked out the door.

Later on, that very day, as I ran
to answer the phone
I died a million deaths, when they
Told me my son, my precious son, was gone.

Elia I. Lopez

Heaven

Have you ever wondered
just how heaven will be.
The place where we can go
to live throughout eternity.

The gates that are made of pearl,
streets of purest gold.
Walls made of jasper,
a place where we will never grow old.

To see our precious loved ones,
who have gone on before.
To worship our dear saviour
The one we will always adore.

As we gather around the crystal sea,
joyous we will forever be.
Singing those glorious songs of old,
Hearing the greatest stories ever told.

Perhaps it sounds just like a dream to live in mansions fair;
But you can have the blessed assurance, that heaven is really there.

Jesus has gone to prepare a place for those who are so true.
I hope to see you there my friend, for I plan to be there too.

Brenda Benton

A "Streaker"?

I'm seventy six, today,
Of this, I'm well aware.
Sometimes I don't remember,
If I'm dressed, or running bare!

I hope that you're not laughing,
I don't like people being rude.
It makes a lot a difference,
If you're clothed, or in the nude!

Most women, you'll see smiling,
At what they said, they saw.
When they remember seeing,
A "streaker" in the raw!

But when you get to my age,
There's one thing that I'll bet,
You may remember some things,
But lots more, you'll forget!

And so, to solve my problem,
Not far from home, I roam.
It don't make any difference,
If you're nude, at home, alone!

Richard E. Nickel

Seasons Of Love

He is like the sunshine
that warms a summer day.
He is like a shooting star
lighting the Northern way.
He is the flame burning in her heart.

He is like the fall leaves
colors mixing in flight.
He is like a giant wind
that blows throughout the night.
He is the breath that touches her soul.

He is like the snowflake
falling gently and light.
He is like a grand river
flowing swiftly from sight.
He gives water to soothe her body.

He is like the spring rain
which quenches ones own thirst.
He is like multicolored
rainbows that touch the earth.
He is the love she's been waiting for.

Carol A. Jachim

Olympics

As the Olympics near,
let's hope we have a lot of
peace and no games of fear.
It's a time to show their
countries athlete's wealth,
and hope they stay in the best
of health.
As the celebration starts,
we welcome all the athlete's
with warmest hearts.
As the medals have been
awarded to the athlete's, and the
ceremonies come to an end;
Let's keep the peace between all
these countries so we can keep doing
this again and again.

James H. Kirsch

Dragonfly

The dragonfly's an ancient friend,
On jewel wings he dips and bends.

Flies daintily in summer skies,
He views the world with bulbous eyes.

To a water world he is born,
But can't remain an aquatic form.

His adulthood is spent on land.
His changing life is nature's plan.

The "darning needle", he is called,
Because he is slim over-all.

I'd like to be a fairy queen,
And ride a dragonfly I deem.

But dragonflies can't be ridden,
Though in books it's not forbidden.

G. M. Gladden

A Step Beyond The Crash

Down the snow covered mountain
they started to stroll,
Lost for directions
freezing from the cold.

For all they remember
was a fire in the sky,
To this day they don't know
just how they survived.

There wasn't but three
out of a hundred and forty two,
That survived the mountain side
and were able to pull through.

A small tiny baby
his mom and his dad,
For when it comes to miracles
what else must be said.

For God was with them
beside them all the way,
They went beyond all limits
to survive the crash that day.

Ray Hogeland

Untitled

He stands tentatively on the steps
of the Met and limps - while
his brothers, they all strut like
adolescent boys on their way to
PE

Notice a trend on these steps
it's always the left
she stomped and we both were startled

I sensed the weight in the air with
each breath as I tried both to
touch and avoid every demon

but as it turned out,
both the cripple and I
flew away to procure
the pain inherent in
walking.

Amy Spencer

Woman With A Walker

I don't walk like I used to
my legs don't function right.
I don't hear like I once did
And I may have lost my sight.

I am not a "senior citizen"
nor am I "elderly"
So stuff your damn discount
Because it doesn't apply to me.

I am as young as ever,
at least inside my head,
And I will always be,
until the time I'm dead.

Julie Kennedy

Number One Daughter

In that uncertain time between
winter and spring,
When the tulips bloom and the
robins sing,
The temple adorned the angelic chorus
Nature displaying her beauty for us
My daughter cries when a tulip dies.
I have told her and now she will know
Where her teardrops fall
A tulip shall grow.

Albert Llewellyn

Four to go!

A banker, I will wed,
This sweet thing said to me.
'Before I die, my bed', she said,
Will share another three!

An actor, dark and tall,
Could have me, for a wife.
We'd really have a ball,
Through the mid-part of my life!

Then, a tailor, who could dress,
This body given me.
He must be, I will confess,
Part of my family tree!

I'll need an undertaker,
After I pass away.
Before I meet my Maker,
These are the words I'll say.

One was for the money, and
Two was for the show,
Three was to get ready, man,
And four was for to go!

Richard E. Nickel

Cycles

Abyss of old patterns
Canyons of pain
Waves of ripe sorrow
Wash in again.

Blindly step forward
Fall backward in time
New currents, old rhythms
New faces, old rhymes.

Unrelieved grieving
Exposing old scars
God's in His heaven
Eyeing cold stars.

Pat Pabst

Bow Guilty Head

Bow guilty head. Think not that
you might still have love from me.
I built an image in my heart.
And worshipped in idolatry.

Your charming way, your winsome look,
my reverence did employ.
No shadow of a weakness seen
that would my pride destroy.

Temptation came to you one day,
as to all earthly men.
Your falling now is in full display
the world now knows your sin.

If a secret sin the world knew not,
I would keep my idol pure.
But sin uncovered for all to see
my pride will not endure.

This pride will not mercy allow,
even though you did atone
I cannot face the knowing now.
Bow guilty head, you must walk alone.

Shirley F. Thomison

"You"

When you said it was over and through, it hurt me because I didn't want anyone else, I wanted you. I love you with all my heart and soul, I've always wanted to tell you so. People told me not to believe a word you said, because your lies would feel up in my head. I think about you all the time, you never leave my mind. Nobody knows but me how well we could be. I want you to know but I can't tell you so, I miss you whenever you're away, which is each and every day.

Cristen Whitten

Pigs

Before the pigpen I kneel,
and listen to my pigs squeal,
They oink, they eat,
And suck from their mother's teat,

They smell, they stink,
And they reek, people think,
They laugh, they giggle,
I call them all Piggle.

I love to watch them,
I love to stare,
And one thing I am with pigs is,
I care.

Pigs get sick,
Pigs get old,
And many pig nursery
rhymes are told.

I hear pigs squealing in my ear,
Pigs, yes pigs,
I love dear.

Kari Harrigan

Untitled

A home in the country
instead of the Bronx
Gave us plenty of room
to play

We had grass and trees
and plenty of weeds
To pull out as we
went on our way

A stream in the front
with crystal clear water
So refreshingly cool
to drink

We would run and have fun
in our orchard in the sun
Bearing apples and peaches and plums
taking time to eat
Many ripe and sweet
picking our favorite ones

Mary Kinlan

Untitled

He walked out of the shadows
And he took away my woes.
I loved him with my life,
And he gave me no strife.
But I paid for his love,
For he was no dove.
Never pure,
Had killed but not in war.
He used and abused me,
And always blamed me.
I never knew what I did.
It was like he sold me at the
highest bid.
He never cared.
I wish he never dared.

Heather Maloney

The Night Walk Home

Alpha, triple star,
Ask your companion this night,
The crescent moon,
If I may hang my hat,
Upon his lower hook.
My burden was heavy today.
And the two of you,
In a clear sky of black and blue,
Gave me the light I needed,
On my walk back home.
I will now, take my rest.
Crescent moon here is my hat.
Alpha, be my night light.
Now, let me rest peacefully,
That I may be refreshed, for tomorrow.

Jack DeYoung

Mother Passing

Before my eyes like a Jekyll and Hyde
not unlike a prune submerged in water
The years of pain magically disappear
Your face changing
Unto a beautiful stranger
Unknown to me
this face of you
Another someone
I never knew

Paula A. Sylvestre

Swing

Eyes closed flying forward
hair rushing forward
falling down,
or is it backwards?
Thoughts flowing back
laughter, screaming
screams of childhood.
Flesh pressing flesh
briefly, it flies away
then it returns
a love reunited
a love let go
"swing"

Tonnar P. Estingoy

Tornadoes

Tornadoes twist,
tornadoes twirl,
suck up stuff,
and spit it out,
not very nice.
But death defying things,
one minute there,
the other gone,
all they do is twist,
and then go back up and
strike somewhere again.

Alicia Grandon

Jeremy

Hold me in your arms
so tight
and keep me here
with you tonight.
Read to me of the
troubles you've had,
then we can write
of true romance.
I only care to
hear your voice,
soft, sweet, but
not by choice.
I want to sleep
in your arms
Hold me here
all night long.
Wrap your arms
around me tight,
and softly, sweetly,
kiss me goodnight.

Marie Essi

Child's Love

Teddy Bear, Oh Teddy Bear
so huggable and so soft,
Will you put your arms around me
and tell me some of your thoughts.
For Teddy Bears bring happiness
and smiles to young at hearts.

To cuddle them and love them
so much comfort for the heart.
To hold them dear and close to us
and should never let them go,
For the loving feelings
that the Teddy Bear brings,
One never will outgrow.

Estella Sampson

Broken Girl

My heart is broken
My love is gone
My dream is shattered
My hope is wrong.

The nights are dark and cloudy
The days are endless and painful
The tears are honest and heavy

My heart is broken
My love is gone
My dream is shattered
My hope is strong.

Elisabeth A. Davis

Untitled

Savoring every moment,
loving every day;
Storing up the memories,
tucking them away.

Love for your family,
Love for your friends;
Love is a circle,
Without any end.

Be at peace with yourself,
Happy as you go;
Pray for peace on earth,
And hope it becomes so.

Barbara J. Woodward

Mr. Fred

There was a horse named Mr. Fred
He could not talk much, but instead
He used his hind end that he did,
To get his master to give in.
He used his teeth to disapprove,
Of what his master should not do.
If he were not fed right on time,
He would be cranky not sublime.
If he were not let out to graze,
He would not come back in for days.
To show that he did not like you,
He might just take a step or two.
And when you think you've got him beat,
Off you'll come and not on your feet,
But through the air and over the fence,
Tomorrow you will recompense.
And mount again you will not do
At least not for a day or two.
'Cause sore you'll be with much regret,
That you called Mr. Fred your pet.

Susan Graham

Good Morning God

You're ushering in another day,
Untouched and freshly new
And here I am, to ask you God
If you'll renew me too
Forgive my many errors
That I made yesterday
Just let me try again, Dear God
To walk closer in thy way
For father I am well aware
I can't make it on my own.
Please take my hand and hold it tight
As I can't walk alone

Geneva Marley

My Granddaughter's Question

Grandma are you short or tall?
Grandma what is this, did you make it?
Grandma did you have me?
Did you have my moma?
Did you have my aunt and my uncles?
Did you have my daddy and my papa?
Grandma are you white?
Are you yellow?
Are you brown?
Are you black?
Grandma do you love grandpa?
Do you love my moma?
Do you love my daddy?
Do you love my aunt and uncles?
Grandma do you love God?
Grandma do you love me? Do you!
Well! Do you love me grandma?
Yes grandbaby Grandma loves you
very very much but
God loves you best

Delois Hawkins David

My Love For You...

Love is like a flower
That grows year after year
Love is a special feeling
That brings smiles and caring tears.

Love is our baby's cry
A gift that shows we care
Love is this bond between us
We cherish and we share.

Our love is all so great
It comes straight from the heart
Nothing on this earth
Could tear our love apart.

For our love is like a river
That flows throughout this land
Just you and I together
Walking hand in hand.

As the years pass by
Our love continues to grow
We'll remember that river
And how our love has flowed.

Paul Randall Smith

Dads

Some people have young dads,
But I have an old dad.
Some dads have lots of hair,
But mine has little hair,
Some dads are not kind,
But mine is very kind.
Some dads are not even there,
But mine is always there.
Some dads are strange,
But so is mine.
Some dads teach you nothing,
But mine teaches you to pick on mom.
Some dads don't leave an impression,
But mine does.

Dads come in different ages.
Dads come in different sizes.
But I think my dad is the best
in the world, and that's not just
because he has me for a daughter.

Samantha Lyons

To Love Me

His touch...
His smell...
His voice...
His eyes...

The way his touch makes me quiver
The way his smell makes me high
The way his voice makes me melt
The way his eyes burn into mine
Oh how I long for him
to touch me
to smell me
to hear me
to see me
To Love Me

Kristin Karn

A Promise

Alas my golden prince
Has flown above
Into God's heaven far away.
He was my inspiration,
Always loving and kind.

The evening star is there tonight
Reminding me of
Precious days gone by
And love longed for now.

Time will surely heal my
Broken heart, for I have
A promise I cherish
That I will be with him again.

JoAnn Clift

A Final Waltz

Pale petals of a summer rose
hang over the garden wall
like a dead man from the rafters
with swaying ease they fall.
Their soul has left the body
with nothing left behind
except the scent of honey
rotting sweetly on the vine.
It attracts the bees and ladies
who waltz by with nonchalance.
They remind the carefree traveler
they too will join
the dance.

Patricia Vidiksis

Petals of a Fallen Rose

Petals of a fallen rose
I will gently gather
Wishing somehow I could arrange
In nature's fashion
A beautiful restored flower
Ever blossoming ever fragrant
As I remembered.
Ever will I hold onto
Those withered remains
Close to my heart,
Within the chalice of my soul
Knowing in God's radiant worlds
Nothing truly dies,
But changes and grows into something
Even more beautiful in time...

Mary Ann Reese

The Rainforest

From the forest came the plants
for which it cures surpassed
man's grants.
Life's demands created our search
into the woods for hope
We have now left its resources
barren and must cope.
Because of our needs we forfeit
the trees we destroy natures
habitat not giving thought to that.
Through our own neglect we
light up and forget till all
we have left is regret
Soon there will be none left

Debra Schultz

My Girlish Dream

Someone who I think about
Sends my senses whirling
Someone who I think about
Has blue eyes and he's charming
Someone who I think about
Knows how to make me laugh
Someone who I think about
Likes me as I am
Someone who I think about
Is tender, kind and funny
Someone who I think about
Is brave, courageous, and daring
Someone who I think about
Lives so far away
This someone who I think about
May never come my way
Is this just my girlish dream or a
Possibility that I might find this
Someone who lives only in my
Dreams

Melinda G. Stubbs

My Love

He walked into my
life with a sparkle in
his eyes. I knew he
was the one that I
would love. I thought
he would be here
forever, til one day he
was gone, and I didn't
know why. It was painful
til I found out one thing
that made it even more.
Now I know why he
moved, to be free and
to find a new life.

Sara Agajanian

Memories

Memories
are forever,
some good,
some bad.

Memories
of you,
always good,
forever in my heart.

Memories
of you,
may they never part.

Melissa Louise Gay

Beyond The Horizon All Alone

Beyond the horizon a place unknown
I sit and think all alone
Sitting naked in the rain
Letting go of the pain
Calling out to a sea of stars
Caged behind depressions bars
Wanting what I can not get
The path I took has been set
Holding on to a worthless dream
In a nervous breakdown I do scream
Hold me close I'm all alone
I think my heart has turned to stone
Beyond the horizon far from home
I sit and think all alone

Stefanie Paquin

Sometimes

Sometimes I pray,
Sometimes I do not,
Sometimes I cry,
Sometimes I will not,
Sometimes I care,
Sometimes I can not,
Sometimes I feel like pulling my hair,
Sometimes I shall not.
Sometimes I listen,
Sometimes I hear,
Sometimes my eyes glisten,
Sometimes to me they seem clear,
but I must never show my true feelings,
because I can not face my own fear!

Becky Kelley

Flowers

The rose you gave me died today
Can I go, should I stay
A melody of doubts

Your pledge of love so intense
Lonely, my heart's defense
What is life about

The flowers bloom every spring
Songs of love we can sing
Glittering of hope

But winter snows will also fall
Do we dare endure it all
Brave, able to cope

And life is once again reborn
A passing of the storm
Dawning a new day

Stronger with the journey's end
A lover's rose you send
Showing me the way

Sona A. Rodgers

"Love Your Brother"

Here we are
Small and Brown
We need to erase
all the frowns
Dr. King said "Let freedom ring."
It's love and joy
we like to bring
So hold your friend
by the hand
Dr. King said "Love your Brother-man"

Roxanne R. Spinks

Always

The road of our friendship's
been hard and long.
But we've been through it all
and stood strong.
The smiles we've shone and tears
that we've shed
Are all memories that will run
through my head.
All of the good times and bad
times we've shared
Should be a sign to you how
much I've cared.
We were best friends and
anyone could see
How very important you
were to me.
Then slowly it began to
fall apart.
But remember - you will always
be dear to my heart.

Ashley Holmstead

God's Wondrous Love

I wandered in a forest where
I felt God's presence with me there
Midst fragrant pine and mountain air
The breezes softly whispered prayer

A bud I reached to pluck away
But something stayed my hand
I felt welcome there to stay
But yet 'twas not my land

A blue jay voiced warning cry
That I was not alone
A squirrel watched with wary eye
The stranger in his home

The stress and strain of daily woes
Did gently waft away
Midst the peaceful solitude
Would I could ever stay

The forest seemed like hallowed ground
Protected from above
I wandered deep inside and found
How wondrous is God's love.

Danny Shaver

Untitled

Youth is the period
of learning and choices
and one can get confused
by the number of voices

Since each is whispering
a particular direction
and each claiming the gift
of divine perfection

So how does one know
which one to choose
Since the goal of the game
is to win not lose

The direction to follow
is the golden rule
you'll then have life's key
for yours as a tool

And when making your choices
really think them through
for the decisions you make
are the ones that make you

Hardy Warr

Lingers

Your kiss still lingers
on my lips.
Your presence still lingers
on my soul.
Your face still lingers
behind my eyes.
A second of pure bliss,
a lifetime of joy.
My heart is not
mine to control.
The passion burns on
consuming me entirely.
Your perfume still lingers
in my clothes.
Your touch still lingers
on my skin.
Forever burned in my heart.
Your kiss still lingers.

Ashton Anderson

Incomplete

It's like lying down in autumn
Sun shining through oak trees
and watching clouds roll in
like butterflies in flight
and wondering what comes next
it's like rain on my face
it's good for the soul
but never enough
like watching shadows dance
as a candle slowly burns
it's the feeling I get
when I wonder if my life
is half over or half started
or simply incomplete

Dan Forck

My Love

My love is a desire
That burns like fire
My love is in the air
That I can't bare
My love is clear
That is very near
I fear my tears
Oh dear..
Oh is it here
Oh Lord
may my
prayers be spoken
cause my heart has opened
My star has
found the token
My love,
My love,
Speak me kinder love.

Melissa Cardenas

Angelic Mother

Troubles come and troubles go
Some end fast
And some end slow
Sometimes troubles come at night
And I'll need someone to hold me tight
I believe in Angels
I most certainly do
Because when I asked God to see one
He showed me you

Krystian Gonzalez

I Cover My Ears

I close my eyes
And squeeze back the tears,
Hang down my head,
And cover my ears

All of these thoughts
In my head going round,
I breath very slowly,
My chest starts to pound.

Anger, Resentment
Frustration and Pain,
All of these Feelings
Leave Nothing to gain.

Everyone pulling,
I must take their side.
But, just how I feel,
I must carefully hide.

I close my eyes,
and squeeze back the tears.
Hang down my head
And cover my ears.

Rosa M. Yellig

My Pacemaker

My pacemaker was installed
The first day of June
It helps my ticker beat
So I'll see many a moon.

The doctor gave me new wiring
And fixed my spark
Now my transmission idles
Much better in park.

It was installed while I waited
With a battery and all
It will make me feel better
If it's not on recall.

If the battery is a die hard
When I'm a hundred years old
I'll check the guarantee
That's if I'm not cold.

Lloyd Rexford

Grave Error

Our God
will not accept
our bowing down to death
as though Life were meant to die for
our God.

Diane Blaesi

Untitled

A crack or two in this old shed
lets in a beau of sun
Where newborn babies make a bed
soon after life's begun...
Just how they find that single ray
of sunshine I don't know;
The shed in large and stacked with hay,
yet they know where to go..
Some say our shed's in disrepair
and should be nailed up tight;
But they should see a baby there
and then they'd see the light!

Susan Wright

My Own Daddy

His ruby red ring bleeds
If I wear it;
Like Plath's "Daddy"
I fear the pain.
How well I understood
My suffering—not his.

The pain of a thousand heavy-booted
Footsteps
Echo in my ear.

Alone and dying in Moscow,
He abandoned me.
Each time I wear his ring
Blood-red silence
Haunts me.

Erika Hartmann

Motherless Child

I see her yet in my mind's eye
With a lump in her throat
Tears that don't drop
But are hot and dry

Watching out the window pane
For her Dad to appear
Sometimes for hours
But more times in vain

Her Mothers death dealt a blow
Leaving stern strangers, cold
Who never explained the reason
The absence of Love, to a four year old

The boundless depth of her pain
With no warm hugs to quell
Never really quite went away
At seventy four if feels the same

Anne Katherine Lloyd

Untitled

I ask myself, what am I?
A mere light shining in the
star-filled sky.
What have I become? I can't tell...
The sharp edge of a knife, or
a ring of fire in hell...
There's no good in my future,
there's no "hope for me."
I'm floating on a dream in this
sorrow-filled sea.
Today God told me to be
careful, but I said, "What's the use?"
I've put up with it forever,
what's another day of this abuse?
Some say goodnight, I say
goodnight to some...
Now I say goodbye, to the
demon I have become...

Kati Miller

Even Steven

Even Steven
Who or what
Is right or wrong
Only opinions
Matter, not the
Main source

Virginia Adackus

Spring

Spring is the time
When squirrels come out to play.
They have a bright, sunny,
And wonderful day.

Spring is the time
When roses grow.
They're so pretty,
It's hard to let go.

The grass is so green,
The trees are so tall,
The birds are so lovely,
I love them all.

Caterpillars turn into
Beautiful butterflies.
They flutter their wings
As they say their good-byes.

What a wonderful season
Spring is!
What a mighty creator
Our God is!

Jerusha Sarah Zachariah

"True Love Never Fails"

Love is patient
Love is kind
Love is not jealous, it is not snobbish
Love does nothing rude,
Love is not prone to anger
Love does not have hatred.
Love is not happy over iniquity
but rejoices along with the truth
Love covers over everything,
believes in everything, and hopes
and prays for everlasting friendship
We have enough tranquility for
all eternity.

Mary L. Westlund

Why?

The mountains rise to meet Him
Brought up by His mighty hands.
The wind obeys His every whim
It goes where He commands.

The sky seems never ending.
The clouds march right on by.
The rain, it falls down from them
Like tears from Heaven's eye.

God controls it all, you see.
Even the sun from east to west.
But to you and me He's given a will
And He's putting us to the test.

We are part of God's creation
With the birds, animals and trees.
The earth obeys His every command.
Why then don't we?

Ralph Lawrence Belzer

To Helen

Dear Helen, in whose breast there lies
The soul of kindness and whose eyes
Bespeak a warm and loving heart,
May fortune bless her and impart
Long days of joy and sunny skies.

Paul Koepke

"Thumper"

Raised on a bayou
a coon-ass through and through.
What did I do to
deserve the likes of you?
Soft and gentle yet
fierce as a lion
When you kiss me
I feel like I'm flying
Your touch sends chills
right down my spine
Is it possible for love
to be kind.
I'm afraid to stay
and I'm scared to reach out
My mind is filled
with so much doubt
Then you reach out and
hold my hand
That's all I need, to know
you're my man.

Nicole Fields

This Love Of Mine

This love of mine
so fair so fine
Was meant to be
for all time

Until one sad and
lonely day, when
two hearts broke and
stayed this way

For one mistake
one heart had made,
causing this love
to die and fade

And now once more
these hearts are free
But never again
content will be

For such a love
So right, so true,
was never meant
for me or you.

Grace Emily Burgar Fasci

Twenty-Four Hours

For twenty-four hours
That I have on earth
Did I earn my keep
Did I earn my worth
Did I smile at some one
Walking alone
Did I hold a baby
Close in my arms
Did I feel the rain
Falling on my face
Taste a snow flake
Did I walk beneath a tree
And wonder how it become
Did I eat a red apple
And taste the sun
For twenty-four hours
Did I give thanks
To our Heavenly Father
Giving me these gifts of today, tonight
And hopefully... tomorrow.

Mary Lou Pierce

Against Whispers Linger Rays Of Colors

A love letter lies
Against
the crystal stemware
Whispers
of orange juice
Linger
in the air
Rays
Of
winter sunlight streak into
Colors
And I think of you

Anna T. Balash

Friendship

Friendship is a priceless gift
that can not be bought or sold.

Its value is far greater
than a mountain made of gold.

For gold is cold and lifeless
and can neither see nor hear.

And in times of sorrow
it is powerless to cheer.

So... when you ask God for a gift
be thankful if he sends.

Not diamonds, gold or money
but a True friend!!!!!!!!!!!

Jackie D. Houston

The Eyes Of Darkness

Stalking eyes pierce the night,
Red as fiery coals;
I cannot escape their sight,
A lost and panicked soul;

Run and hide, as best I can,
The eyes of darkness follow;
There is no help from any man,
Earthly promises seem hollow;

Look inside the church so grand,
Golden statues for all to see;
These riches do not stop the eyes;
Death is moving toward me;

Burning pain deep in my side,
From running far and fast;
Maybe now I can hide,
This breath not to be my last;

I turn and peer into the night,
To see what might be there;
Oh God, to my fright,
The eyes, I see their stare.

David Levin

Anabellen

The ocean is long and wide
as waves wash in and wash out.
Flowers bloom and then die.
Love flows throughout the earth,
with speckles of differences.
We are all as one, and always
will be. With each other we make
the earth go round.

Danielle Gauvin

Bursts Of Light

Pulsating light
Blinding blinking shining
Golden glow
Attracting the flying insects
Bringing them closer
As we douse ourselves in off
Fires burning
Fading into embers with
Dawn breaking
Waking packing trekking
Up mountain
Trails we follow to the
Glory of day
In the forest while the
Sun's light
Peeks through the forest canopy of
Green leaves
Filtering down to the forest floor with
Dappling bursts
Of light as we travel into the sunset

Roslyn Crowell

Why

I sat one day and wondered why
The sea could never kiss the sky
And why the autumn breeze could
Never know the flowers in the spring
That grow so sweet but yet so far away

Then I saw with subtle grace
The sky reach down and touch the
Oceans tranquil face the sea rose up
With waves of passion and a cool breeze
Danced among the flowers on the shore

What I thought could make
This happen true it must be
Love I'm sure

Jesse P. Stone III

Today

Today is not like yesterday,
Today is not like tomorrow.
You need to live each day
as each day comes.
Not rushing through
the days.
Not rushing through
the hours,
Just trying to face
each day with
your head up high,
Just make each day
worth while.

Vanessa Puentes

Concatenation

Daybreak shattered night,
Awaked, the golden eagle,
Triggered it into flight,
To replenish sustenance.
To feed her young.
A baby lamb was sighted
Near its mother's, dung.
A bleating ewe, useless,
The shepherd, too late.
A sacrificial lamb,
Had been chosen by fate.

Carolyn Reynolds

In Memory

The day is dark
and the night is long
sleep isn't even safe.
The chill throughout
goes on and on
will the end ever be near.
I'm separated from myself
The sun still rises
The sun still sets
but how much is seen.
My eyes are closed to goodbyes
because it never should have been.
Life should burn like a candle,
slow and with ease,
but her life was taken,
as if the candle was just blown out

Carrie Lasselle

My Love's Song

I hear a splendor of music
In the melody of words you say,
Such a beautiful, enchanting song
Perfect in every way.

Not too much bass or tremble
The pitch and tone not too high.
And every time I hear your song
My heart just melts and sighs.

Yet, I should know the song
For I hear it more than most,
From vibrato to echoing crescendo
Ever so clear, each distinguished
Note.

My love, send forth this song
And bless all who may hear,
For I've been blessed, exceedingly
Down thru many a year.

Michael Flowers

My Soulmate's Wedding

I should be happy,
he is one of my closest friends.
It doesn't matter that this
marks our love affair's end!

Why wouldn't I be happy?
They look so good together.
It doesn't matter that
he and I look so much better!

Of course I'll be happy.
I hope they last forever.
It doesn't matter that he
knows we belong together.

I am very happy,
or so I'll pretend.
It doesn't matter that the
best woman didn't really win!

I can't be happy.
I'm in love with the groom.
It doesn't matter that
he'll be married soon!

Amy Richardson

In Holy Matrimony

Our God
The Master artist
With easel in hand
He joined us
You and I
Onto the lovely
Canvas of Christianity
And so we are
Complimentary colors
In a delicate blend
I love you
Even as the colors fade
And into the Heavens
Our spirits ascend.

Luz E. Earley

My Mother's Love

My mother is a person you
can always talk to.

Sometimes you go to her,
and you don't know what to do.

She always gives you words
to make you feel better.

Even though I get on her nerves,
she still will be there after.

I love my mother so much,
words can not express.

Because she always does without
and gives her kids the rest.

So, Mother, I love you so,
so much

And I know you love me, too.

So I am writing this poem to say,
"I love you."

Jennifer Lilly

Mirror

Mirror mirror of despair
can you see me are you there
which side of the mirror am I on
am I just a reflection of what I see
or is what I see the true me
or is the answer deep inside
the rules of the mirror I cannot abide
in this twisted world of despair
is anyone really out there

Bethany Glish

My Christmas Doll

I have a doll,
A Christmas doll,
She is really, very, sweet.

When I play,
With my doll,
She always gets a treat.

My grandma made her,
When I was born,
So she's very, very old.

Rags she may be,
But to me,
She's like gold.

Amanda Martinez

Farewell

The emptiness you left me in,
engulfs me like a wave.
It crashes down upon me,
but still it's you I crave.

Although I rarely said so,
you've grown to mean so much.
I miss your gentle words (so soft),
I miss your gentle touch.

The time we spent together,
has taught me about life;
about a love that will not die -
and now I learn to strife.

To love someone so dearly,
yet have no love returned.
To want, to dream, to fantasize,
these lessons I have learned.

I wish for you the best in life,
the best that life can give.
My one regret is losing you
With this I cannot live.

Brian K. Ripley

This Too Shall Pass

Those whose power
Came through usurpation
Fraught with deceit,
Yet supported by those who believed -
Even those who did not believe,
Are now the oppressor.
What vile acts of the oppressed
Have caused the oppressor
To turn his face against all?
There are none.
What recourse have the oppressed?
Patience? Tolerance? Forgiveness?
The leaden feet of tyranny
Trample, attempting to grind into dust
Those obstacles -
That sea of troubled faces
Who wait.
For they know
This too shall pass.

Flora W. Gordon

Life

Life is not for Sissies
I was told that long ago
And each day that I've lived
I have truly come to know

That trials and tribulations
Some large and some so small
Have made me a little stronger
To be brave and feel tall

The mind can play a lot of games
And with the hearts intrusion
Can make the difference in our thoughts
To add to the confusion

And just because we feel down
Never never hesitate
To talk and smile through it all
The reward is very great

Mary Ann Brown

Temptress Of Time

She sways by oh so gracefully
  this temptress of time.
Stealing our youth, taking what's
  yours and what's mine.

She dances on clouds, she rides
  on the breeze.
She takes what is ours, there is
  nothing she leaves.

My body she's touched with her
  cool hand of fate.
Thanks to her touch, I know it
  may all be too late.

I won't yield to her power, tho'
  I know she will win.
Oh, temptress please see, our youth
comes from our love, a feeling within.

Jacky Seitz Cole

My Special Friend

I think of you so often,
And each time that I do,
I consider myself lucky,
To have a friend like you.

You're always there to help me,
You brighten up my day,
With letters, pictures and phone calls,
And the nice things you always say.

You're more precious than a diamond,
And you mean so much to me,
I will love you forever,
And your friend I will always be.

You help me solve my problems,
And advice you gladly give,
I will surely treasure your friendship,
For as long as I shall live.

Bonnie Bortz

His Love

He fills our world with sunshine
To feel the warmth of his embrace...
The stars are like a million eyes
The moon to show our face...

He knows what brings us pleasure
He gives us children to enjoy..
Isn't he magnificent
He gives us little girls and boys...

He made us all so different
Some have eyes of brown or blue...
He even made us brunettes
Black and red skinned too.

He lets us make our choices
To be wicked, good or bad...
If we choose the latter one
It makes so very many sad...

God must truly love us
He's forgiven us our sins...
Even though we don't deserve
He even gave us Him...

Claudia Scott-Meggett

School Is Cool

Too cool
  Not to be in school
Have a brain
  So I'm not insane
Feed it a lot
  I will never stop
All aboard
  'cause school is hot!

Michelle A. Black

If I Could

If I could,
with my hands
I would make you
something beautiful,
something elegant,
but I can't
I have to make it
with my Heart.

Sheena Milligan

Where Are You?

Where are you?
Where did you go?
Why did you go away?
Didn't you know I loved you so,
and it hurt when you went away?

Where are you?
Please come home.
But in my heart,
I know you can't.
For you have gone to a faraway place.
And I shall never understand,
why in the world,
the Lord would take you,
when He could have me instead.

Anna Chokas

Haiku

Spring, summer farewell...
Through the autumn of my life
Falls the winter snow.

Mary F. Bunch

Over Four Years

Poke at me, pound on me
'til you're sure you've hurt me
pinch me, pull me,
whack me, smack me
stretch me, hold me
you already told me
apologize, say you're sorry
pay me to stay
pay me today
Love again, remember when
I started that story,
hope and glory
to rise, to fall
to know it all
to say goodbye
to live, to dye
to sit and sigh
to cry
to lie
and wonder why

Kristen Bieri

Love

Love is like a rainbow
Stretching far across the sky.
Love is like a flower
Blooming on a hillside.
Love is like a flame
Never burning out.
Love is like a wheel
Turning endlessly around.
Love is like a brook
Gurgling with joy.
Love is like a cloud
Floating ceaselessly about.
Love is like a tree
Standing firmly and strong.
Love is like a breeze
Sweet smelling and calm.
Love is like a swan
Gliding peacefully about.
There is enough love for everyone
If you don't let it run out.

Shannon M. Shenberger

Patricia's Poem

It seems we have been through so much,
This Patricia and Me;
Much like the stars and the planets,
And our vast rolling Sea.

We have weathered those storms,
Life has chosen to Deal;
And I still love seeing Her face,
When we sit for a Meal.

We sometimes argue and bicker,
And that's expected you See;
For we are Husband and Wife,
This Patricia and Me.

She is so loving and caring,
Sneaking notes into my Lunch;
But if I make Her angry,
I can expect a nice Punch.

When final tallies are made,
And the results have been Done;
I would love my Patricia,
Because She is still "Number One."

William Henry O'Donovan Jr.

Friends Forever

We'll be friends forever
through thick and thin
We'll be there for each other
and never give in
We'll stick up for each other
and always be true,
for friends are forever
and never are blue

Cause we'll be friends forever
till the end
We'll share special moments
over the years
to tell our children
and share our fears

Lucy Calisi

Bless My Child

Bless my child, for he's my own
Bless him when he's not at home
Bless him when he learns and lives
Bless his heart, and when it gives...

See him through a lonely hour
Give him faith and hope and power
And as he grows, show him the way
So he may live, day by day...

Bless him when he's just a boy
Give him peace and love and joy
Bless him Lord, so he will know
To live his life, long and slow...

Bless him Lord, for he's divine...
Bless his heart, this son of mine...

Suzanne A. Chapin

Within

Since the beginning of time
Love ruled...

And to the ends of the Earth
Love lives...

With each new sunrise
Love grows...

With each smile you grace me with
Love trembles within

Love is risky
Chances are thin
But love is never wrong
No matter where it is

But since the beginning of time
I remember you...

And to the ends of the Earth
I will follow you...

And with each new sunrise
I am tied to you...

And each smile you grace me with
My love trembles within.

Dian Huffman

"My World"

When I think of you, I feel a
pain of missing you.
When I cry, I don't cry tears.
I cry my pain, I cry my hurt.
The cry of hurt just comes
over me and flows out.
It actually takes over my body.
You mean so much to me and always will.
You are my light.
The light that keeps me going.
The light that never makes
me give up, and pushes me to my best.
Because you believe that I
can do it.
You are my inspiration, my
love, my kindness, my world
You are the best of All, you are
my Grandpa, my life, my world,
To a man with a Big Heart and
a Great Mind

Jennifer Clark

"Lost Words"

He whispers the words,
Of feelings past.
Words to express,
His love so vast.
But she is gone,
And cannot hear.
She'll never know,
His love so dear.
Still he whispers,
To the air.
Just hoping
That she'll hear,
Somewhere.
If the words he spoke
She would hear,
Her heart would melt
And love reappear.
But she is far,
And will never return.
His heart for her, will always yearn.

Abigail Kirschner

No More Pain

When the pain is too much,
the agony too deep.
When you miss the touch,
of a love you couldn't keep.
Don't turn to death,
keep your life.
Don't take that last breath,
no matter what the strife.
You still have a reason,
to keep on trying.
To see the next season,
to keep from dying.
You'll always have me,
a friend forever.
Just to help you see,
the pain doesn't last forever.

Jodi Keech

"A Message To The One I Love"

These pictures and words come with all my love. To thank you for the way you have of bringing happiness in my life...Thank you for the loving things that always mean so much...your smile, your kiss, your tenderness, your warm and caring touch.

Thank you for the great times when we're all alone, magic times for sharing a dream that's all our own...Thank you for sweet yesterdays and bright tomorrow too. Thank you for the special joy I've found in loving you.

Timothy L. Martin

Island Paradise

The beautiful ocean,
The swaying trees,
The sweet smelling flowers,
The cool Island breeze.
The warm sun above me,
The clouds sail away,
My beautiful Island Paradise
Is where I'll stay.

Tenille S. K. Dole

Sermon Of The Mount

J ust for
E very man
S lowly
U nderstanding
S urely

C ause You
H eard God
R ecall You
I nto Heaven
S ilently with
T rust

You died.

Vivian M. Cullison

Cogito Ergo Sum (Sometimes)

Storms and sex
and travelling on the bus
home alone,
while it's raining
large splattered drops
the highway slick with gray water;
being right presents a problem.
A flower plucked,
and apple bitten,
blood drawn
but no trace of stem,
care
or bandage,
it is though I doubted you
completely out of existence.
And I do not recognize your picture.

Kira A. Siegmann

"Just A Friend"

It's Valentine's Day
and I'm alone again
when the guy of my dreams
turns out to be just a friend.
I can't help but to wonder
as the tears flow to the floor
if there will ever be the chance
when we could be something more.
I hope you understand
'cause I know it's hard to believe
but my feelings are strong
my love will never leave.
So as you read this poem
please keep in mind
that even though we're just friends
you'll never find a love like mine.

Stefanie Macera

Life And Its Emotions

Love is heat making
me warm inside.
Happiness is the sun
shining after a storm.
Death is relief taking
the pain away
Sadness is the snow cold,
and still.
Confusion is a
mixer mixing stuff up.
Life is filled with
emotions like a cup
filled with water.

Amy Kinman

Untitled

Head rushed and smiling hands up
too late and I'm surrounded.
Broken mirrored bits of me in
the shapes of accidental continents
mapping out the fuzzy territory
of a bathroom rug.

And there on my knees I cherish
the cold peace of tiles
stunned to be shattered
but happy with it; I like myself
in pieces, small enough to digest.

And down here I am holy
tangled layers peeled back to clean
content to spoon-feed my whispers
shaky with laughter, my eyes
caught in corners and guarding
their screams.

Connor Glen

What Is Blue?

Blue is the color of blueberry pie.
Blue is bluebird flying up high.
Blue is gently flowing sea.
Blue is peace and serenity.
Blue is the color of a cloudless sky.
Blue are the tears that you cry.
Blue is the color of the dawning day.
Blue is the color of a quiet bay.
Blue is the earth from afar.
Blue is the color of a glowing star.
I really like the color blue.
I wonder if you do too.

Lisa Didak

Where Is My Love?

Further than the distance
And beyond the mountains
Where you are!
Very close to heaven
Where is always ever
There you are!
Here I'm coming
With my life too fast
But I have the feeling
I will find my way at last.
Here I am, always thinking
Of your beautiful blue eyes
As blue as a bright sky.
Always dreaming of your kisses
And a hundred of caresses in your arms.
Here I'm praying to my Lord
From the bottom of my soul
And I hope that He shows me where...
Where is my love!

Tony Baly

Wish Song

Beating drum of
Life's sweet sound;
Carried whispers;
Knowledge found;
Dancing 'round and 'round;
Voices raised in glorious praise,
To celebrate new ways,
Together
We become,
As one,
With the beating drum.

Melissa M. Swan

You

You are!
My smiles,
my tears,
my every breathe.
You are!
My child
my heart
even till death.
You are!
Part of me,
forever.

Kathryn Neidel

The Beauties Of Nature

As I wait in the night,
  the sky calls to me.
The sounds of the earth,
  they whisper softly.
As I look to the water,
  and see the moons shimmering light.
I notice an eagle,
  descending from flight.
His wings, are all spread.
His eyes, to the ground.
As he scoops up his pray,
  and tackles him down.
Then poof, he is gone.
Just as he appeared.
Such a beautiful thing,
  that is often so feared.
One of natures small wonders,
  to you and to me.
Like the day or the night.
It will always be.

Tina L. West-Waters

Silence Will Tell

Words are expressions
of feeling and thought.

Many of which are true,
many of which are not.

Messages lie, not in words
you hear:

Words are just words,
but silence is sincere.

Words are just words,
like a mask worn for show.

But silence is sincere
and will tell all you'll want to know.

Janet R. Henry

Bereft

The sky is azure blue up there
Gorgeous flowers everywhere
But I don't care
'Cause you're not there

There's nothing there
Not any where

Only

An empty ache that longs
To shrink and fade and be
Not anywhere

Vera Stevens

Waiting

Everywhere there is a wait,
on that you can depend.
We stand and wait for a movie seat
in a line without an end.

We wait for traffic signals,
and for elevators in halls.
We wait for restaurant tables,
and for a simple bathroom stall.

From our groceries at the market
to the pillows at a store,
We must wait for other people,
and this waiting is a chore.

If I was granted a wonderful wish,
I'd know what I'd wish for.
It's to have a stress-free life
by making Waiting nevermore.

Crystal D. Goldey

Faith

Faith is what we all need
And faith will banish self indeed
Faith will cast out doubt and fear
Faith will banish every tear
Faith will make us strong and brave
Faith will teach us to behave
Faith will call on heavenly power
Faith will brighten every hour
Faith will guide as we walk
Faith will lead us as we talk
Faith will be our guiding star
Faith will lead us from afar
Faith will help in any task
Faith will guide us in all we ask

Margaret B. Zeigler

Motion Night

He sits.
A small wet mound of reptile flesh
Among the dewy grass.
Frozen.
Hidden.
Afraid of foreign movements.

He moves.
Two long, lean legs extended
To propel him to refuge.
Leaping.
Flying.
Escaping foreign creatures.

He sits.
A small wet mound of reptile flesh
Among the dewy grass.
Frozen.
Hidden.
Afraid of foreign movements.
Oh, the boring life of a frog.

Carie S. Lambert

"The Dove"

Miraculous journeys begin
As we take an inward look.
Becoming strongly aware of myself,
I am a dove perched in mystic flesh.

My realm of flight is ambition.
Dutiful wings flow with expectation
For a way to deliver peace
And a chance to generate love.

Renee Tensley

Fat

Images ruined
What is it;
Nothing but cells bunched together.

Girls crying
In the mirror!
Their heroes being super models.

Look on the inside —
the smiles
the hopes
the twinkling eyes
the love

Bring the beauty from the inside out
And reflect it on your whole!

A human being:
Not just a body.

Jenny Pedersen

Old Quilt

Gifted stitches penetrate
Cotton unadorned and bright
Create the means to instigate
A passage-way to offing light.

Floss sonatas twist; they blend
Expound with florid detail,
In spite of calico to rend
Its pictionary sequel.

Quilted heirloom; love looms play
Stories told on muslin beds
Mem'ries of a by-gone day
Captured skill in antique threads.

Teresa M. Barnett

The Bells Of Freedom

When there were the bells of freedom
that sing the night of life,
as the stance that I had taken
to the night of time.
Grave as you will adjust to my blame
worthy, as freedom
declares princess;
then I declare sovereignty.

Alex Jerry Blea

Time

Watch the sand in the hour glass
As it slowly begins to fall
Look at the candle burning low
Though once it stood so tall
Gazing at the hands on the clock
As they keep turning round and round
There's so many phases of Time
Though it hardly makes a sound
Now if you listen to close to Time
It may have so much to say
Time is something dear to us
As it begins and ends each day
So with God's understanding we see
Time goes by Time stands still
If we learn the value of Time
And let it speak; It surely will

Renee Pemberton

Passing Thru

I've reached out to you
many times before,
only to have it end
with the slamming of a door.

It hurts to see you go
yet it's worse to have you stay,
we play the same games
over and over each day.

You think the world owes you
and working for your dreams,
is an old man's fantasy
or a politician's scheme.

I hope when you wake
from your Peter Pan visions,
you won't be looking at me
thru the walls of a prison.

Turn yourself around
make it work today,
because life is a game
we all have to play.

Karen McClain

My Brother

There lies my brother asleep in
his bed I wonder if good
thoughts are in his head
His face so thin, I'm always
wondering when, when will the
day come when I'll never see
him again
He's here with me everyday and
I sometimes kiss him just to say
Hey! We laugh together and I
never cry and mom doesn't
understand why.
I can see his pain and his
living with AIDS all these years
God how it hurts to hold back
my tears.

Amanda Morrison

High

When I was just a teen
And I started to get high
I dove into the ocean
Didn't know there was a tide

My body started floating
I was drifting toward the end
I built myself a castle
Where I lived without a friend

Suddenly these voices
Were racing through my mind
I ran outside my castle
To see what I would find

All of me was numb
No one else was there
Just the birds along the beach
And they just seemed to stare

I didn't really need it
"No one" really does
I was very sure about this
Careless as I was

Beth Plante

The Very Best

Dead Dad, how I miss you
Now that heaven's claimed your soul
How selfishly I wish you
Were here to make me whole.

A part of me is empty,
Without your loving smile;
But how vivid memories
Recall your special style.

You never met a stranger
But instead you met a friend,
And always looked for chances
Your helping hand to lend.

From flying in your airplane,
To the military honors you earned
You did your best in everything,
A lesson I well learned.

A "really super" grandpa
Is what my kids do say
A grandpa full of fun and surprises,
Never a dull day.

Dear Dad, how I thank God
That my life he truly blessed,
For when he gave you for my dad
He gave the very best!

Tina Sitton Marchand

Dysfunctuality

I hurt you
You hurt me
It is a game we call dysfunctuality
All join in, everyone play
Tear apart your lover's heart
There are millions of ways
Push me, pull me
Spin me round and round
Kiss you, kick you
Throw you to the ground
Dysfunctuality
A game for you and me
Dysfunctuality
Cut me up and watch me bleed
Dysfunctuality
I hate you and you hate me
Dysfunctuality
Got to plant the seeds
Spread it, dread it, live it, love it
All so plain to see
Dysfunctuality....

Louis Clark

Untitled

Wrapped in a ray of sunshine
Blinded by pure delight
You are my stability, my focus
My guiding light
As I drift through the sea of mortality
Searching for signs from beyond
I hold on to that special feeling
When ever you are gone
And when our time has come to pass
And we cross the ethereal plane
I pray I see you on the other side
Just to keep me sane
As I ponder my curious thoughts
And focus my direction
I know I will see you again someday.
To make my life perfection.

Keith E. Oyer

"Life"

Do you ask why life is?
What is it all about?
How come you were one chosen?
To live it inside out.
Consider just how special
In oh, so many ways.
The experiences you're in for,
Rewards that come what may.
Hand picked by the master,
Itself is fine indeed.
Presented to your parents,
With love he planted seed.
To grow and love and prosper.
Aim always for the right
Do what the master tells you.
You'll live the after life.
The road to life is hectic
Hills and valleys wide
But do not let it stop you
Homes on the other side

Marie B. Angel

Lost But Not Alone

Where do you go when you're back
at square one?
When most of the lessons in
life have been done.
You are an adult yet you
feel like a child.
You want nurturing care;
tender and mild.
Still people abandon you
leaving you cold.
You wonder what happened to
make them so bold.
Don't worry about that;
there's no time to fret.
You'd never do something
you'd ever regret.
So back to square one
where there's so much to do.
Just be glad that it's me
and that it's not you.

Lisa Lindstrom

Love Gone

It's all right now, baby
But there'll come another day
another place
yes, another time
When you're going to wish you
were mine.
Late at night when you're crying
tears of sorrow instead of joy
You're going to wish you hadn't
made me your toy.
Don't expect me to greet you
with open arms
Though I know the sweetness of
your lips
And the magic of your many charms
It will be too late, too late
now or ever
My love for you has gone
forever.

James M. Young

Autumn's Painted Leaves

Golden, crisp, red hues;
Leaves brittle
Crunch beneath the trod of
Forest wandered feet.
And autumn kisses leaves
Still held to branch of trees,
So nature's paint brush with the wind

Sweeps colours of an
Indian summer's
Warm transition's end.

And then these
Mountain Autumn Leaves
Have burst to sky;
They bless the eye
With sight of
Nature's colour dance;
At harvest time's
Warm, sun filled
Gold romance.

Cindy Lee Strand

My Eternal Soul

You've watched my fall,
Now feel me rise.
I've crossed the ocean
Of my demise.

Watch like the angels
Who hover nearby.
Watch like the others
Who never wanted to die.

Fighting the soldiers
Fighting the planes
Fighting the worms
Digging in my brains.

I'll fight God
For my soul's sake.
For my life's plan is not
To drown in his wake.

Ryan Harris

'Insomnia'

Thoughts walking back and forth,
Crowding the aisles of dreamland.
Restlessness: toss, turn, roll over.
Ideas scattering,
never coming together.
Scrambling, distorted messages.
Feelings that go bump in the night.
Stress pulling at every hair.
But, in time,
a silence to be cherished.

Erin Gilrein

The Garden

Early in the morning,
on a bright spring day,
The flowers in my garden
are ready to meet the day.
All covered with dew drops
they glisten like gemstones,
Standing tall and majestic,
Lifting their heads high.
I marveled at the beauty before me
And knew I was in paradise

Clara Wills

Democracy

A beautiful way of life
Without unnecessary strife,
With Liberty and Justice for all
Mercy and love always on call.

Each person's free spirit
Can develop and grow no limits,
Every hour and second of the day
Thus showing a pattern of God's way,

We can be very glad
For sunshine and flowers,
And no reason to be sad
The business of life goes on for hours.

We have time to think and pray.
Work, sleep, and play,
A good program to keep
And in all life's problem meet.

Liberty and Justice for all
Law and order must not fall.
This is the necessary way
To protect our freedom always and today

Marjorie A. Beurle

Lord You Are!!

Lord you are my light,
light the way.
Lord you are my life,
for with you I will
always stay.
Lord when I cry out to
you in my time of need
you tell me to cast my
cares upon you and you
shall lead.
Lord you are my strength,
You are my heart.
You are my ear's and my eye's.
Lord you are my light,
Lord you are my life!!!

Janet Duplisea

A Rare And Precious Gift

I have a rare and precious gift.
I hold it gently,
I hold it close;
I try to keep it clean,
Do my best to keep it warm.
I am selfish with my gift
For I do not like to share;
I have a deep aversion to
People who treat it with less amount
of care than I,
of my friend.

Olivia Blanck

Diamond In The Rough

Standing in the muck and mire
and trampled underfoot.
You shine, you know, even though
you're soiled with grime and soot.
Though rough, uncut, unpolished.
You shine, my dear, by far
Much more like the beautiful,
Diamond that you are!

Donna Vandaveer Bone

Colored

When I am born I am black
When I am cold I am black
When I am hot I am black
When I am sick I am black
When I die I am black
When you are born you are pink
When you are cold you are blue
When you are hot you are red
When you are sick you are green
When you die you are purple
and you call me colored

Kiara Scheimann

A Dream Come True

Over the summer
my stepfather
proved
how much
he loved
my brother and I,
he adopted
us in August.
I was just so happy!
At some points
I thought I could
cry.
It's like a dream come true.
I love you dad Forever!

Amanda Saunders

Wild Queen

I sailed away yesterday
past Saint Tropez bay
to search for my wild queen
to hold for all my day

We sat and watched the four winds blow
and heard the thunder crash
embraced the utter nothingness
broken by the lightning flash

She is everything I ever wanted
intelligent, wild, and exotic
her smile could steal a thousand hearts
her form is magically erotic

She has stolen my heart
to add to her collection
she is the only desire I have
the center of my affection

She rules my every thought
with out her my heart won't mend
my suffering will continue
until we meet again

Mike Pucci

Florida's Hurricane Bertha

One day in the midst of sun
We became one!
Suddenly, lightning, rain, strong winds
Flooding of Bertha on the coast
We took cover in the sugar cane
Oh! How lucky to be spared of
High winds and title waves in the
midst of a hurricane!
All the joys of living on
Florida's East Coast and being spared.

Ursula Ciulla

You Should Believe

When an angel shines,
it reflects off a Christmas
tree and goes into your
eyes and tells you to believe.

Santa Claus is always
watching, and he makes
the angel shine and if
you believe you'll have
a wonderful time.

The Christmas tree is lit
with light and it makes
your spirit bright,
that's why you should
believe

Amanda Carlson

Encircling Love

There are never more
Lonely times than you can bear.
There is always God.

Jeanne E. Griffiths

I Came Into This World

I came into this world
alone and scared
You held me in your arms
and let me now you cared
You taught me right from wrong
You dried all my tears
You taught me to be brave
and never run from my fears
You made me a better person
I was taught by the best
I became the lucky one
Set apart by all the rest
I have you for my parents
For that I am very glad
For there is no one in this world
I would rather call Mom and Dad

Angie Freeman

Illusional Friend

He's there, but he's not.
I see him but does he see me?
Does he know me like I know him?
Is he there?

I call him just to talk.
Not about anything,
Just to talk.
Sometimes just to hear him breathe,
To know he's there.
But is he there?

Is he there to listen?
Is he there to understand?
To know?
Is he?

I want him to be there.
I want him to listen.
I want him to know.

Sometimes I think he is,
But when I look closely,
He's not.

Emily Horacek

"Serenity"

Relax beneath a flowing willow
on top of a flowering hill
watch the butterflies flit to and fro
laze in a prairie bird's trill.

Walk a path in a sun streaked forest
along a babbling creek
stop to watch with joy and wonder
as a doe lifts her head from a drink.

Sit beside a mountain lake
and smell the fresh clean air
and watch with joy
the playful antics of a baby bear.

Walk along a sandy beach
early in the morn
listen to the soothing sound
as the ocean hits the shore.

If everyone would take the time
to look around and see
they would find that in this world
there is serenity.

Christine Roberts

Unrelated Souls

For you the snow was
Always white,
The star was blue.
Sunrise was always red
For you
And sunset too...
You looked,
You knew...
So, where was touch
Between us two
It never was
I felt my friend,
You knew...

Anna Soloviev

Ode To A Drifter

A long time ago
when I was young and free
I drifted this land
and wondered what I should be

I lived and I loved
traveling shore to shore
yet, often I wondered
should I be more

I'm much older now
time goes by fast
what I once saw as future
I now see as past

Whatever I could have been
will now never be
whatever I should have been
I had to be free

My life's almost ended now
But feel not sad nor pity me
for an explorer I was
I explored being free

Glenn F. Cox

My Heart

Written with a pen, dated
with a kiss. If you love me
you will answer this.
Your love is like a pot of
gold, hard to get and hard to
hold.
Didn't you know that God
above, created you for me to
love?
He picked you out of all
the rest because you are the
one I love the best.
I had a heart and it was
true, but now it is gone from
me to you.
Please take my heart and
answer me. Do you return my
love for thee?

Amanda Whittington

Adonis In A Dream

He is my Adonis on earth,
an angel without wings.
He comes to me at night,
a vision through my dreams.

He takes me to his dream world,
and I go to him willingly.
The only reassurance I need,
is that he's in love with me.

As the early dawn approaches,
his essence begins to fade away,
he returns me to reality,
to face the coming day.

If the day is joyous,
or filled with tragedy,
I simply wait for velvet night,
where he'll be there with me.

Jennifer Reves

At This Time

Why is there anger?
Why is there strife?
Not enough love
To fill this life.

The grown-ups grumble.
The youth, they fight.
Neither seem to know
What's wrong and what's right.

Some have questions
Of a Godly nature.
None ever ask
What's God? What's stature?

There's always vanity
When given the test
That's why there's insanity
Fashioned to fit the rest.

Where will it all end?
This question, I am sure,
Has been asked by many
But most by the pure.

Lula M. Jolly

Rain Repose

I apprehensively peer out
at the stark, glaring sun.
I flinch away from its brightness
and pray it will soon be done.

Darkness will soon cloak me
in a comforting sheath.
Still, I know it is you,
I wish my body beneath."

Then, suddenly the sun fails,
clouds fill the sky.
Thunder roars, winds swirl,
I breathe an audible sigh.

I strip out of my clothes.
Feeling at ease, I smile.
I step out into the torrent.
It is as night, for awhile.

I turn slowly, head raised
as the drops begin to fall.
I am searching the sky but...
on the ground is the answer to it all.

Jennifer L. Rasmussen

Jesus

Ten thousand stars he gave me
Pure waters running free
The stillness of the night air
The beauty of each tree.
White silent clouds to guard me
The sun to light my day
He gave me life to love
And a prayer for me to say
A yellow rose in summer
A child at my knee
He gave me hope to cling to
Until his face I'll see.

Marilyn J. Ferdine

The Supreme

Each passing day
I begin to understand
Why he is the majesty
And holds such supremacy

He is the tallest tree
He is the deepest sea
He is those tranquil clouds
For he is the supreme

We rarely seek him
He is our substance
He lets us see
He is the shining sea

He is those mountains
He is those crops and flowers
He is glory in the heavens
For he is the supreme

Minerva A. Garcia

Hilda

Black silk in the rain,
Red halter as blood in pain.
Dark brown eyes that
shimmer and shine,
This one big horse that's,
older than nine.

Rebecca Smith

Love Song

You are a butterfly,
Fluttering upon the wind...
Letting no one near you —
To be admired from afar.

You have a beauty
To be shared with the world.
But, Love,
Couldn't you rest
In my back yard for awhile?

Kimberly K. Tschantz

Just Thoughts

MUDDY WATERS, muddy waters.
Rivers deep; running
streams overflow banks, rainstorm.

Isolation, deep in thought.
DROWNING, drowning in memories.
Muddy waters; unclear.

Can't seem to shake this feeling.
All dried up, used up, washed ashore
Muddy waters rising.

Blinded by nature's tears,
Filled with Earth's years
Of torture.
MUDDY WATERS, muddy waters.

Yvonne Rodriguez

"A Mighty Roar"

The devil lets out
a mighty roar,
this is a lie,
he is no more!
The evil
that you see,
well, that comes
from you and me!
If you're happy
with yourself,
then you can
put this figment
on the shelf!
The chances are,
if you treat
people well,
for you,
my friend,
they'll, be
no hell!

John Search

People In The U.S.

Like the wings of an Eagle full
of plumage and strong.
We all stand together with
our hearts full of song.

The world has set upon us
unemployment and hard times;
But you'll find us a strong breed;

Fighting for tomorrow's
and the dreams that we need.

The base's are loaded and all
of us wait,
for that home run hit that
will bring us to home plate!

Glinda Peters

For It's Sunday

It's a day to believe,
Not one to retrieve.
It's a great time to pray,
For it's Sunday.

A time to sleep-in,
No work to begin.
No time to make hay,
For it's Sunday.

No work that's a chore,
Like the week gone before.
It's time when we play,
For it's Sunday.

The flowers are brighter,
The sky is much lighter.
We're silly and gay,
For it's Sunday.

So put your will to the wheel,
Keep your part of the deal.
Six days — then we smile,
For it's Sunday!

Diann Jensen

The Baby

Wrap the baby in bunting
And let us cry no more
Created from our love
Your short life brought us joy

Drape the baby in silken best
And smile in happiness
Although hearts are broken
Remember memories with happiness

Surround the baby with linen pressed
And stand with cheer
A treasure you filled our void
Your short visit made us whole

Lay the baby on creamy white satin
And celebrate the life
Bless him with hues of flowers
For the happiness you brought
will hide our sadness

Walter Kirby

The Key

Desire to hold
My love in your heart
Desire to keep
Me close when apart.

Desire to touch
My face every night
Desire to see
Me dressed in white.

Desire me always
Our whole life through
Desire me always
Ever be true.

Desire, my love
Will keep us together
Desire my love and
We shall see forever.

Tracie Lynn Wiggins

John Wagner

All day I sit on edge
waiting for the phone to ring
and it does
but, you are never on the other end
you seem so far away
I wish you were here
my heart needs to dial your number
but, my mind refuses to give in
although I've wanted to
I haven't told you how I feel
I often wonder if you could handle it
but, I think I love you

Tamaron Loger

To My Angel

Many thanks to my Friend
An Angel in disguise
For Helping me and
Giving me good Advices.
Sweet Angel, I'm very Happy
In my decisions to go on with Life.
So don't worry about Me
I really feel I'm Right
To do what's on my Mind
and in my beating Heart,
I will be very Satisfied
Not bothered by sad Thoughts.
Sweetheart, you're my Friend and Angel.
Thank You for looking over me.
I Wish you will continued to do so
For as long as there is You and Me

Luoy Va Heap

Confusion

So many questions
So little time
Sometimes I ask
"am I losing my mind?"
So many decisions
I have to make
So much criticism
I just can't take.
I can't please everyone
though, I will always try
I get discouraged
and this is why
Too much pressure
is brought upon me
Why can't everyone just
let me be me.

Laura Caronia

Just Open Your Eyes And See

Just open your eyes and see, see
what you can be.

Just open your eyes and see, see
what life you can lead.

Just open your eyes and see, see
what life can be.

Just open your eyes and see, see
just for me.

Regina A. Myers

An Eagle's Wings

I am an Eagle, that's soaring high.
I glide around and look for prey.
I am the predator
I need the wings to fly.
If one wing breaks I'm afraid
I'll die.

But feeling free and soaring high
is what an Eagle does and so do I.
Letting the air soar through my wings.
Is the most gentlest feeling in this
world to me

I love being an Eagle,
And I love my wings, wings
I love to fly.

Jennifer Gonzales

The Gift

If I were a gift,
I would be money
to give to the poor,
everyone and everybody.

Why would I do it?
You should know,
to help love to grow and grow.

If I were a gift I would be love,
and be carried by God above,
to everyone, everywhere,
so that people would learn,
to care and share.

If I were a gift I would be laughter,
to give to the sad,
so they could live,
happily ever after.

This would give me happiness,
I believe,
because it is better,
to give than receive.

Joshua D. Vories

may 1st

thinking about you
the other a.m. and
rolled out of my garage
enroute to the marin
headlands

viewed the bmws and jaguars
speeding across
the golden gate

strolling through meadows
i looked down upon the pacific and
laid amongst the wildflowers
of blues and purples and
pinks and golds

i painted
your body
with all of them

Robert W. MacKenzie

Untitled

The world has trees,
Plants that we eat,
Animals that we survive on,
The water from the rivers we drink,
And the stuff we waste for nothing.

Gianna Parco

Just A Piece Of The Game

My family is but a chess board,
always thinking twice before moving.
My father is the king,
who leads us in battle.
My mother is the queen,
that moves in all directions,
moving from one place to another.
My sister is the castle,
which moves slyly across the board.
And me,
the little pawn out of the three.
The silent one of the family,
who moves very slowly,
yet cautiously around the board.

Gary Bales

Hurt

As time goes by,
I thought I met a really nice guy,
till I was used,
and then mentally abused.

I thought I was in love,
but the only one that knows the truth,
is God up above.

I lie in bed with fear,
wondering will there be a silent tear?

As I look into the sky,
thinking is he saying goodbye?

Kristina Kairys

"Mother"

Remember the days that were to come.
Remember the time that we had become.
So be with me and come now,
for we are forever bound.
The bright of my day.
The light of my life.
For everyday you are my sight.
You guide me,
through life when I am blind.
You are the true, "woman kind."
You are the best I have ever known.
You are there when no other face shown.
You are my mother, my confidant, and my pal.
But most of all you are my best friend.
For everyday to come,
we will be one.

Ashley Eagle

Razor's Edge

Do they see I am alive?
Do they see hurt in my eyes?
  Razors edge rescue me,
   the dark overwhelms,

Do they feel frustrations depth?
Do they know secrets I've kept?
  Razors edge rescue me,
   the dark overwhelms.

Do they hear my words profound?
Do they listen to satan's sounds?
  Razors edge rescue me,
   the dark overwhelms,

Do they see through children's eyes?
Help me now I want to die!
  Razors edge rescue me,
   the dark overwhelms

Jenny Cox

A Split Pathway

I long for my friends, my family,
my home.
I feel so far away, so lost,
free to roam.
I feel so trapped inside a
big open space.
Where everyone is different, their
own individual race.
The sounds and cries of people
around,
I am so distant and I need
to be found.
As I search down to the
depth of my soul,
I try to find myself, the
only one I know.
To discover myself may take
a bit of time.
But I truly know that if
I seek, I shall find.

Jenna Golden

Promises Broken

He promised: To call,
to write,
to see me,
to like me,

And kept them for awhile,
But now things are different,
now - he promises...
And nothing happens.
He never calls,
writes,
sees me.

Was it all a perfect dream
for a short time?
Was it all just one big lie?
He took part of a dream from me
and also broke my heart.
He'll never get my love, for
that I'll keep safely for
someone who truly cares.

Melissa A. Miller

Time

Time for remembering,
  a picture in your mind.

Time, a medicine healing
  that puts memories behind.

Time... your tomorrows
  that shine in such array.

Time blankets your sorrows
  much to your dismay.

Time is all you want of it
  but never enough to be.

Time for a life without yesterdays
  that would have set us Free.

Sheila L. Brown

Falling

I dedicate this poem to the only true love I've ever had.

I have a fear of falling,
I look up at the sky,
I see no greater distance,
But yet I wonder why.

Sun down, all around,
everywhere the night comes
Black fills the sky,
I'm scared, but why?

Now you're approaching me,
My fear on wit's end,
You look so good,
yet I feel so scared.

Falling, falling,
I'm falling fast,
love my destination
yet, with no hesitation

I fall deep, I fall in love.

Diane Henry

The Sea

One day I shall write
A poem about the sea:
How it heaved and churned and frothed
And gave birth to my soul.
Do you remember how I raved
When I first laid eyes on you
Riding on the crest of the waves?
I thought I was dreaming
And seeing Aphrodite
Rising from the foam of the sea-
Then I saw you smile
And I knew I was lost
Forever to Life!

Jesse A. Enciso

Here On The Mountain Side

The war on the country side,
just think how many have died.
To see the fear in their eyes,
to hear all of their cries.
To smell the cold blood,
to taste the gun powder
firing back like a flood.
To feel the suffering pain,
it would drive me insane.
This is my favorite place
to sit and hide,
and let out what is inside.
Here on the mountain side.

Mandy Minch

The Race

God; as I look to this day,
within Your will to walk, I pray
giving thanks for everything,
to You, my Father and my King.
Your Angels guard us round about
until the day we hear you shout
the day your chosen will arise
heading home to Heaven's skies.
Today my Lord I'll run your race,
await the promise of your face,
I love you, and it's me I give
You loved me first through You I live.

Vicki Rae

Into The Light

There are two hells.
Both, you see no
Escape from.
Enslaved to thy batter or satan,
No diversity.
Both are the
Prince of darkness.
Owning you for eternity,
It seems.

So dark
Then, the light shines.
Angels guide you
Through the darkness.
You are freed.

Elizabeth Julio

Glimpses

Gaze from the rooftops
The towering snow and tinkling bells
Of plumed and weary mules.

Blue shades of sunset
Faceless bundles of dry grass
Trod home on dusty paths.

Ripples on a lake
Rows of purple hills beyond
White birds perched upon a tree.

Look down the bridge
While heartbeats echo roaring
Foaming waters below.

Eppie R. Gorrez

Untitled

We meet again
And then we part
Going our separate ways
Wanting something
A look
A soft touch
Almost receiving
Playing hell
With soft emotions
Secret yearning
Belying our trust
In ourselves
Pulling everything we have
And shoving it aside
Waiting for mutual assent
That will never come.
Alas, the final departure
Approaches
Never again to be seen
Wondering, could it have been?

Eric Singleton

Love Hurts

Love can be wanted
so much or with an
unwanted punch

Silent cries became little
lies make up covers up so much
from that so call love puch
you said you love me
and I could never leave
you I left I'm gone!

Amanda Hopman

My Perception

Five different people,
With five different opinions.
So many choices I could make,
So many choices for one decision.

I'm lost,
And can't find my way home.
I'm surrounded by friends,
Yet feel so alone.

I just don't understand,
The way I feel inside.
So choices I could make,
All I want to do is run and hide.

I just want to be with you,
Is that so hard to believe.
I think you love me,
Or is that just what I perceive?

Amanda Botello

Ode To My Uncle

He hears the muffled sound of a lost
and found memory
And shudders at the petrifying outrage
of his parents butchered
...before his naked eye...
Inwardly he is foaming...
Outwardly, mere whispers of injustices
...the whimperings of a man who lost
touch...
"So Simple" they all said.
But he carries the baggage of a
slightly maddened mask.
The perilous end of hope!

Jeanne Fiedler

Differences

I love you,
Though you don't love me.
I've liked you for a long time,
Why can't you see?
I watch as you go by,
But I'm invisible to you.
I need you so much,
But what can I do?

I would die for you,
Though you wouldn't for me.
I have fought for you,
Though I know we'll never be.
I long for the day
You care for me too.
But for now you're my world,
And I'm nothing to you.

Jennifer Pelham

His Bride

He clothes me with His righteousness
I'll wear it until He comes
To meet His ever loving Father
Who chose me as His Bride from day one.

It was not because of my beauty
or the good deeds that I had done
To receive such an honor
as Bride for God's only Son!

But what's a girl to do
When a Man gives up His life for you
I now give up my life for Him
So that we too may become as One.

Stephanie D. Lewis

Fair Feather

One feather's wing:
a single hair held
from flight, knowing love
against her cheek.
Dark eyes in Moon's night
sense only scent of that
light molding against her
thigh. A warm awareness
settling under the desert
caress of a beating heart
always pulsing with her sighs
and lost, forgotten rapture
of forever courageous wings;
Sacred sights.
She folds herself
upon this hour's weave
and her feathers are fair...
Always, Fair Feathers;
She knows of night.

Redwood Wind

White

White moon shining so bright
White lightning fills my night;
White snow covers the ground
White dog just sniffin' around.

White water running nearby
White birds fly through the sky;
White clouds soon turn dark
White shadows play in my 'park'.

White shoes fit on my feet
White dress fits so petite;
White stone above my bed
White casket holds me dead.

Kimberly Depew

Just Listen

God is not silent
He speaks every day
Through the song of a bird
Or a child at play

Stop, look around
At all the beauty you see
Listen to the wind
Through the branch of a tree

And when the wind blows
Just listen to the sound
That comes from above
Not up from the ground

Listen, hear the beauty
In the sound of rain
Then love him, praise him
And never complain

Just listen
And you will hear him
Again and again

Pamela Hicks Trice

Feelings

Skies are black on a stormy night.
Skies are blue when its alright.
Did you know blue and black could
be sad feelings too? Too bad everyone
didn't have the happy flue!

Arianna Vasquez

Silent Prayer From A Gemini

Won't someone listen
I mean someone who cares
Isn't anyone interested
In my thoughts and feelings

I laugh and cry
But why please tell me
Am I truly happy
Or is it just a front

Is there another person
One deep and within
Why must I keep her hidden
And what is she like

Are things better
The way they are
My heart will tell me
Won't it God

Keianna Matthews

God's Majestic Glory

Dedicated to my mother, Mrs. Golor Ella Freeman

God's Majestic Glory is shining
down. Up on me God's Majestic
Glory this I can see when
I'm feeling lonely when I'm
feeling blue. God's Majestic Glory
I filled, that is so true God's
my savior God's my friend. He
will be with me till the vary
in. I sing Glory to God I sing
Glory to God. God he's my heavenly
Father. He's my heavenly friend
I know. He's always with me.
Till the vary in.

Michael T. Witherspoon

Racism

When I think of Racism
I think of Pain
Death of people
that no one's to gain

When I think of kids killing kids
I think of wars that no one wins
Death by hate
For no one to love

Color is what makes us different
No one cares what they think
All of us bleed red blood
So why must they die for their race

Racism - death for no reason!
Just to see them suffer
Racism - wars need to end
Let's do our part to stop the pain

Melisa DeRoos

Peace Be Still

Peace come into calmness,
don't loose your cool, because
there is hope for those who
don't know; let them grow as
the rage you brought upon
the sea, that they may acknowledge,
Peace within thee.

Whitelove

"Break The Chain"

My eyes were opened by the twins,
they gave my life new insight.
I blamed dad for life so wrong,
and why my heart wasn't right.

From one love to another,
my heart would always stray.
Searching always for something else,
any reason not to stay.

What I prayed most against,
I had just about became.
Following the path of my father,
same species, same name.

But Mom raised me right,
which made heart and soul contrast.
Then God in all His wisdom,
gave me a message that would last.

They touched my soul,
granted me new eyes to see.
That the chain most be broken,
and it had to be by me.

Antonio E. Sanders

My Black Pride

Our fabric is made of the
finest quality of silk,
velvet, and satin.

The array of colors, tawny,
charcoal, ebony, and cream
paint beautiful self
portraits of my people.

Our features, bold, full, broad,
and kinky, makes our beauty
stand out.

Our seams are held tightly together
with spiritual strength,
integrity, and pride,
get to know us,
get to know
what's inside.

Sheila K. Robinson

Deep Ends

I sometimes insert my pinky
to hear the rhythm
deep in — what?
The right ventricle?
Yes. The right one.
How many?
Two. The right and left.
Four?
No, those are chambers.
No, not of a gun, of the heart.
Four chambers in the heart.
In guns?
It depends.
On what?
I don't know.
Me? What would I do with a gun?
Still there would be no piercing.
The indention?
It deepens.

Vonsha R. Henderson

"Clown's Heart"

My thoughts were lost in forests,
They took a trip to sea,
The ocean view was boring,
And they came back to me.
I'm happy on the outside,
But deep inside my heart,
I have a clown crying,
From life's depressing sight,
The clown's tired of laughing,
And cheering people up,
He has his own troubles,
But hides them well from us,
And he is feeling sorry,
But no ones near him,
Cause people are used to laughing,
And having fun with him.

Irene Belder

Where Did I Go Wrong?

The pain scars deep in my heart,
Too deep to fade,
  too alone to try,
If they could only see the inside,
But all they see is the happiness,
  on the outside,
A smile is always there,
But never really meant.
Happiness is gone,
And so are lives.

Erin S. Arnold

Rage

I'm blinded by the intense rage,
I see nothing but that one bright
blaze.
All logic thoughts are gone.
My mind is only on one.
It keeps me going as it grows,
It carries me away,
I have no control.
It rampages my body and my soul,
Not quitting until it owns me whole.
I'm gone, I'm lost
There is no way to let go.
It grabs my heart with a death grip,
and pulls until there is just a hole.
How did this all begin?
Where did it all go wrong?
I don't remember, I don't know
All I know is that I'm gone.

Amanda C. Quinn

Step Inside

Just inside of Life,
  There is Love.

Just inside of Love,
  There is Peace.

Just inside of Peace,
  There is Joy.

Just inside of Joy,
  There is Me.

Just inside of Me,
  There is He
Step Inside!

Patricia Peoples-Cunningham

Untitled

I close my eyes and picture home
the place I long to be

I open them and wonder
why this is happening to me.

I close my eyes and see my friends
and all familiar places

I open them and once again
see nothing but strange faces.

I close my eyes and question why
I ever to come here

I open them and goose - bumps form
what a weird grasp of fear.

I close my eyes once more
and wished to just go home,

But this time I don't open them
because I don't want to be alone.

Angelic Vink

Still Here

The two large marble eyes of hers
seem to be undisturbed
as a lake on a quiet autumn day.

The body shrunken and puffed
to a spider lump,
the deformed little feet
carrying eighty some years,
importantly to function.

The story telling ability clouded,
signals of life still there.
Suddenly a violent reaction of a
spider fighting against the rough
intervention.

I try to get through staring
those lake-like marble eyes
for acceptance,
but no more signs of reactions.
Still here with me, with us,
as a lake on a quiet autumn day.

Edith B. Molnar

To My Love

Do not condemn me
to my answered wish.
Let not longing fill your eyes
when you look into mine.
Keep my dreams
of your adoration unrequited
as this heart yearns too much,
to have your desire in return.

Love me not my dear
for passion dies hard
in the end.
Allow, instead,
our affair to bloom
in glorious denial.
Where, each solo rondeau,
I have without you,
can bring us together
ideally,
without the imperfections
of reality.

Skye Ostrom

Air: Movement 26

I don't know where it learned it
but the wind found out my name
It calls to me now all the time
and things will never be the same
It tells me stories in my dreams
of places far away
It fills me with an urge to roam
that will not go away
Many times I've tried to hide
but find it is no use
The wind, it has a hold on me
and I cannot break loose
One day you will look for me
and I will not be found
The wind, it finally got to me
I wander with the clouds
Don't hate the wind for taking me
for it knows many things
This wild and restless, untamed heart
must always to be free.

Tony O. Maddux

You Changed Time

There was a time in my life when
I wished it all would end
But that was long before you
became my friend.

You always hold my hand
When I am feeling down,
and make me feel like a queen,
you being my crown.

You may not realize what you've
done for me.
But you've taken me away
from my misery.

You placed me in your loving arms
And I fell victims to your
innocent charms.

Now my life, holds new meaning,
And I wouldn't think of leaving.

Colleen Fryman

Death

Mr. Grimreaper,
creeps, deeper and deeper.
He tries to snatch your soul,
his face as black as coal.
Emotionless,
Devotionless.
His presence is unknown,
until the cold air is blown,
it'll make you turn around,
to find yourself underground.
You wonder how you got there,
it is like being nowhere.
You think your dead now,
but it doesn't matter anyhow.
Because you'll be there far eternity,
and then some.
For you'll know your time is done.

Renei K. Clark

Dreams

Dreams are such wonderful things
There really are no limits
I can be in love and wonder why
Fall off a cliff and never die.
See creepy crawlers in the night
Open my eyes and they take flight.
Thinking I'm awake, visualizing a scene
Blinking my eyes, it's only a dream.
I love soaring in the clouds,
Looking far down at the ground,
Wondering why, no one else can fly.
Waking hours come to soon,
for those who live in dreams.

Kathy Cauthren

Up There

"I look at the sky,
Yet what do I see,
A million things wander,
All looking at me.

Life all above us,
Yet no one knows how.
They live all alone,
Everyone just says wow,
How is it possible
We would all like to know.
Yet we can see nothing,
and no one can show."

Jessica Frizzell

Love You Always

I love her always,
she loves me too.

I make her laugh,
she makes me laugh too.

I comfort her when she needs me to,
she comforts me too.

I'll always love her.

Fleckney Miller

Carol

No sunrise in the morning
or sunset in the night
Compares to her beauty
or shines quite so bright

With eyes of precious gems
hair a silken treasure
Voice like the angels
bring joy one can't measure

Kisses filled with happiness
like fairy tale rhymes
Heaven just to hold her
she's always on my mind

Though someday I'll miss her
because she's gone away
I'll think of her fondly
for each and every day

Thankful for the moments
of happiness we found
Brightening a lonely life
just by being around

Jeff Heiberger

I'll Start Where You End

I can see me coming
I'm so long overdue
Waiting such a long time
Just to pull me through

I'm putting you behind me
You can't get to me no more
Your time is up, you've lost the fight
I'm walking out the door

We wrestled all my life
You were winning every day
Now that I've woken up
I'm sending you on your way

I never really knew you
You were with me all the time
You were never really part of me
You were never really mine

I never saw you before
I'll never see you again
Finally got you out of me
And I'll start where you end

Terry Kefalas

Late Realization

Ignorance paves the way
To non-existence,
Blinded,
They walk against the light.
They will be the last to turn,
And try to make things right,
As the heavy dark clouds
Fall upon our last chance at life.

Ingeborg Ruano

Elizabeth

Child of my child,
  Your little warm body
Snuggles close to me
  Bringing back memories.
Precious blood of my blood
  Your warm breath on my cheek
Fills me with joy,
  recalling,
    Yesterdays.
Your little moist hand
  Grasping, clutching, retrieving
    feelings.
Your tiny fingers entwined with mine,
  Building a bridge to tomorrow.

Elizabeth Messina

"One Child"

There is a child who thinks
she is right, and she runs
by the moon at night.

She believes in God, but
does what she wants even
though she knows it is not right.

You can talk to her, until
your voice is gone, and it
want change a thing.
But till her you care and
the future is fair and she'll
turn into the sweetest little thing.

JoAnne Johnston

Beyond The Twilight Within The Tide

I walk within the realm of
my own salvation,
constantly searching for that
which shall make me anew.
Always defining and redefining
that which I seek.
Hopeful for its arrival,
vigilant for its messenger.
Fearful of its coming, yet
longing for its presence.
I must press forward, for
in the twilight between
today and tomorrow,
I glimpse the darkened
tides of my future.
Always the same, changing
from second to second.
Always there, inevitable
as the coming tide.

Devin Kleinschmit

A Song Of The Ages

A voice on the wind,
a voice on the breeze,
tells of love of a bird,
or love of a tree.

The new light of morning,
the new light of dawn,
that comforts each traveler,
and carries him on.

A song of the ages,
a song without end,
a song that will comfort,
and help hearts to mend.

When the voice of an enemy,
drowns that of a friend,
the song of the ages,
will help you contend.

A song of the ages,
a song sung by friends,
a song filled with hope,
the song will not end.

Corianne Wilson

"Adolescence"

In this black hole
people call adolescence,
where people can be so mean.
I am stuck somewhere
in the middle of it all.
Don't know how
to be the real me.
People can get you so confused.
The other teens
make you so confused.
Telling you this
and telling you that.
Telling you how to act
and how to be.
I never thought
Adolescence, could
be so cruel.
And I am
Stuck.

Jeremy Hanes

Meditations On Leaving

A man plays hoarse trumpet,
changing scales, climbing —
running an up-down frenzy.

As the tempo slows, his pain deepens
from swallowing chemo pills:
energy sapped, vocal cords silent.

By hearing jazz play
in his mind, modulating misery,
he fights against winged flight,

a precarious lift to somewhere —
he ignores a whispering voice:
"Goodnight, this world."

Michele Wong Albanese

Legacy

What power you have over me still
that you can touch me
from your place eternal.

I had hoped for deliverance
when they laid you down
but your legacy lives on
in your daughter's spirit.

No tribute to the bond between us
that tears at my heart
but rather a sad collaboration
of two tortured souls.

You were lost to me those years ago
but now you surface, again and again
to remind me of our failure.

An irony too vivid to endure
that you should hold me this way
embracing me in death
the way you never could in life.

Patricia Gillis

Darkness

Sleeping under the clouds
I felt so free
Woke up to no light above
the trees
Star's are gone what will I be
It's so dark, can't see a thing
There's no light and that's not right
Only darkness upon the trees
No sign of life in the night
Hoping that things will be alright
Looking upon the darkness in the sky
I feel I will only die
Hoping that this is not good-bye
If only the light will be
than I can see.....
That life is as bright as
it can be.

Tammy W. Rue

Untitled

Every so often I think of you
Every so often you come in my sleep
Every so often I cry about you
Every so often I get sad
Every so often it makes me mad
Every so often I say for you to rest in
peace

Dyan Aniol

Through It All

I remember our meeting.
It was so hard to do.
After talking a while,
We were stuck like glue.
Time passed quickly;
Laughing and weeping.
We had our first baby,
Our marriage worth keeping.
Now this day, you've passed away.
I wish I didn't have to stay.
Goodbye, my wife,
I'll see you soon.
Once again,
Our love will bloom.

Shawn Crumb

Now I Wish I Had You

Why did I give you up
I thought I knew
I want you back forever
What can I do?
You seemed not to care now
But what you don't know
Is that I love you
and I want you back so
Now I'm lost
and I don't know what to do
If only you'd come back to me.
'cause now I wish I had you.

Summer Via

Alone

Riding in on the night
He shines by light of the moon
Gliding over my soul
Drawing out my passion
absorbing
In a trance
Gazing into the emerald fire
Massive throbbing in my veins
He lives off my blood
Feeding his spirit with my desire
Draining
Fading away
The sun creeps over the world
Reality burns my thoughts
Scorching my flesh
Leaving me ablaze
alone

Lauren Tumminello

Reflections

I reach into the river;
Take a piece of the reflected sky
I hold its life force in my hand
And, for a moment it is mine...

But, as it transcends
From sky to water
I let it softly slide.

Through my fingers
It flows
With grateful pride.

And, floats away
To another shore
Another sky.

Kim Wenz

"I'll See You In My Dreams"

You're like a habit
That's hard to break.
You stole my heart
It was yours to take.
You're like the wind
That's never seen.
And, yet every night
I see you in my dreams.

You are like a stranger I hardly know,
Yet I am still drawn
Like the fireflies that glow.
Your eyes, your soul, showed me
All the things I'd hoped to see,
But, alas - they cannot be.

Fantasies of you
Always on my mind,
A sweet passion; love so kind.
Reality is never as it seems,
For I always feel
I'll see you in my dreams.

Deborah Spears

So Alone

All are surrounded
But none are together
If you're awake, look all around
At all of the people
Still you're so alone
So alone
If I could, I'd make a suggestion
Without sounding preachy
Or begging the question
Melt with your minds
Melt with each other
Don't be surrounded Don't be so alone

Katie Tincher

Children's Laughter

Children's Laughter hits my ears
And relieves the worries of the years

It blows upon the breeze to me
And filters out cacophony

Like an angel's caress sublime
It soothes the soul and calms the mind

But with it too comes such a thrill
An energy born from their zeal

Children giggle, laugh and roar
I find I long to hear it more

Children bring your laughter near
And share the joy with all who hear.

Jackie Hower

The Shattered Face Of Time

And the pendulum sways
And time lurches steadily forward
Despite my screams
And my dreams go up in smoke
And I shatter
And time lurches steadily forward
Without me

Laura Lobay

Untitled

Your address was given to me
By a very dear friend
Who I will love,
With a love, without end.
I don't make up poetry
For fortune or fame;
But just to have fun,
And to make it a game.
For others to enjoy
And maybe they can also have fun
So I can share
The money I've won.

Doris Norman

The Flower Grows

Like the flowers need sun
to help them grow.
And water to quench their thirst.
You are my sunshine when the
clouds so dark hover low.
You are the raindrops that feed
my thirsty soul.
I'm surprised you didn't know.

No one knows what the future holds.
But one thing I do know.
Without you, my loving sunshine.
I will surely cease to grow!
For you quench my thirst
and feed my hungry soul.
I love you and need you
more than you'll ever know.

For you are the sun, my darling,
that helps me grow.

Linda Albertson

Emotions, Emotions, Emotions!!

What to do with them
When life is full of changes...
There's busy-ness all around
and where ever I look
"Everybody's got somebody"..

It leaves me feeling
so alone. So empty...
A feeling I've never
known before.

Memories wash over me,
flooding my mind, until
I can take it no longer—
I cry out in anger,
"Why Lord? Why?"

Then I look up...
I see him waiting there for me,
his arms outstretched,
patiently allowing me to come
to the end of myself;

Thank you Lord, for loving me so much.

Phyllis Eisenhauer March, 1987

Seasons Of Reason

Nature's seeds windswept.
Nurtured fruition of time,
Fades and waits for Spring.

Enid Mary Anderson

Swimming With Olga

Enveloping the group,
her specter oozes just beyond
our 7-sided circle and pulls
us in with promises of "Kings-X"
and assurance of safety.
Can I trust her? Can I believe?
Her voice calls me to jump in,
to dog-paddle around in the warm water.
I teeter on the rim of the pool,
afraid to go—more afraid to stay.
Big toe/water is warm
Foot and calf in
"Undertoad" sucks legs, torso, arms,
head, brains
Holds me under until I quit fighting,
Go limp, Live,
Write.

Marian C. Hulsey

Grandfathers

My grandfathers were strong
hard working men,
smelling like dirt with their
dark, roughly skin
they're my heroes.

My grandfathers were smart,
but brought here as a slave
they ran free
and never got away
they're still my heroes.

My grandfathers were proud
of what they had
a beautiful family
and long-lasting friends
they're my heroes
And forever they'll be.

Ramona D. Pina

Death - A Portrait

She walks quietly through the darkness
only her scent fills the air.
You don't notice her silent figure
Full of death, and despair.
She travels the world endlessly
upon the wings of night
to come and take the dying,
into her world of light.
The woman that comes and steals
the souls of the dead
has skin as pale as paper,
and a dark cloak, to cover her head.
This woman is well known
her smell a familiar hue
for a sickle does she carry
and death is her odor too.
Kidnap us in slumber
we have no chance of flight
and take us past that barrier
that barrier of night.

Michael Forhan

The Defeated And The Hopeful

I see a wall of separation
between us
Because you are free and
I am not
For I have seen the
atrocities of men
But you believe in the
beauty of life
I can never forget what
I have seen
You just can't help
but believe
So I will leave you with
your dreams
And I will walk my path
all alone

Bridgett H. Cassidy

The Early Morning

When stars grow pale
Late lovers whisper
The earth shimmers with dew

Bathing the meadows,
Each blade, leaf, flower
Wind gently caressing the few
Who, awake, welcome the morning.

What earthly paradise,
What music unspoken
Is heard with a new baby's cry
Welcoming this new day

Which, through crystal clear
Dew drops early sun appraises
And makes diamonds envy
Their shimmering shine!

Another day dawning
Full of joy and wonder
Flutters in softly
On wings of a butterfly.

Maria Castine Smith

The Life Sink

Standing within this place of death
my heart is filled with pain.
I cannot accept the life and breath
removed from a friend not fain.
Hastily, I leave the room
and discover a lonely place.
Symbols of my soul do bloom;
wither and fall from my face.
Drip, drip, they deposit in the sink,
each a lost memory of the past.
Strangely, the mood causes me to think
thoughts my brain has never cast.
With faucet on and drain pulled,
constant the level will always be.
Always filling yet never full,
emptying always yet never free.
Standing within this place of death
the light of day breaks through
over the schoolyard of life and breath
where energy begins anew.

Russ Oates

Teacher

The tiny hands and feet of children
patter through your halls
And laughter echoes joyously along
the many walls.

Each day you care for precious ones
whose lives are being etched
And like an artist's pencil, by your
words and actions sketched.

I thank you for your kindness, the
loving care you show
Not only to my little one, but to all
the kids you know.

I pray the Lord sustains you
with strength and patience there
So that you continue always
with the special love you share.

And know that other mothers
may see things as I do
That when our children call "Mamma"
in a way they call you too.

Gail Moore

Lonely Or Alone Again

Baby, toddler, teenager
Diaper, bottle, rocking chair
Cooing, gurgle, mimic, speak
Precious, darling, almost freak

Night is day and day is night
Thoughts are of the future bright
Nurturing instinctive ways
Come what may
What may what might
Trying to keep time in sight

Conversation is the past
One word answers seem to last
Skies are blue and grass is green
Only if you're not a teen

Thunder roars inside and out
Sprinkles send a cloud of doubt
Rain begins and then it ends
Lonely or alone again

Mary Lewis

"For The Love Of A Brother"

Dedicated to Matt Buchanan, my brother

Think of me;
Before you proceed;
Think of me;
Take earnest heed;
Think of me;
In your darkest hour;
Think of me;
And your self-power;
Think of me;
Who has your eyes;
Think of me;
Before you, hope dies;
Think of me;
But think of you;
Don't say a word;
I love you, too.

Elizabeth A. Buchanan

Hard

I went to see you the other day
I thought it might be hard since
I haven't seen you in over a year
A friend of mine came with me,
he knew you at one time.
When we got there, there being
your final resting place.
It wasn't as hard as I thought
to get out of the car, and I
didn't have a hard time looking
at your pictures or reading
the words your parents and sister
wrote. The hardest part was
getting back into the car, and
leaving you behind.

Desiree Cowan

Emptiness

Day in
Day out
It's all the same
I walk as if in a fog
Feeling nothing
But the heaviness of my heart and head
Caring about no one
Not even you
I cry for no reason
Soon I am out of tears
Thoughts of ending it all
Come all too often
I fight to feel
To care
But the only feeling I have
Overpowers me
All I feel is...
Emptiness

Vikiann Kelly

Sunset

The sunset lifting up,
Letting off beautiful rays of sunlight.
A slight chinook breeze blowing
towards the night.
The birds chirping,
Bees buzzing,
And mice squeaking.
Suddenly, everything is turning quiet.
The long day turns to another
dark, silent night.

Dustie Steinbock

Le Fin

Raised on a written lie,
A constitution of nothingness,
Worth as much as you buy.
Fed wrongs through the right,
Taught the one hand of sight.
To follow the steps on-line,
Keep quiet of the truth,
As you slowly lose your mind.
Break free a simple thought,
To be what we are not.
To be living, dead,
To be God, in life.

J. R. Hecker

Summer Days

As I sit back and
gaze at the summer
days.

I think of the cool
summer air gently
blowing on my face.

I close my eyes and
there I am at the
beach.

I walk softly
on the sun scorched
sand, while the waves
come crashing at my
feet.

I feel a tiny
drop of rain trickle
down my face and I
awake from my
summers dream and
realize it's not what it seems.

Laura Ann Raynor

My Friend Ethel

Some friendships are new
And some are old
Some become better
And some grow cold.

But you my friend
Are steady and true
And have always been there
Whether I'm happy or blue.

I've loved you so dearly
As you very well know
Be it for a day or for years
It'll always be so.

And when God sees fit
To take us to rest
We'll know, as friendships go
We've had the best.

And when we meet again
In heaven above
We'll still be friends
And we'll still feel love.

Merill O. Fisher

Lovely Sister

I see a face in the mirror
Not my own, but someone dear.

With staring eyes - so far away
Her mind wonder aimlessly
Throughout the day.

Miles apart, yet so near
Touch of a smile
Through shinning tears

My sister now I see
Her reflected image
Next to me.

Reaching out hope to touch
Lovely sister
Who I love so much.

Carolyn Cline

Our Points Of View

Outside my bedroom window
What do I see?
I see a mob of people, traffic, smog, and trash.
I see a two-face, heart-breaker, hustler, and thief;
pain, evil, misery.
I do not want to leave my room because there isn't
anything for me out there.

Outside my bedroom window
What do I see?
I see a parade of people, pristine-machine, and white-clean cloud.
I see a saint-child, friend-trust, and neighbor-love;
ant, bee, and butterfly.
I do want to leave my room because there is much for
me to do out over there.

But, it is too late because tomorrow I die.

Robbie Nomura

Her Own Guardian Angel

She walks along the deserted beach
Old memories fading just out of reach

She longs to hold his hand once more
To walk together along the shore

He was only 29, it was not his time to die
There she sits, alone she cries

She longed to tell him what was on her mind
But life was cruel, sometimes it was not kind

She wishes she had a chance to say goodbye
He left without a flutter, not even a cry

His smile is bright in her mind and in her heart
She has to say goodbye, but where does she start

Her brother watches over her to make sure she is alright
Together with his love, she will make it through another night

She has her Guardian Angel with her wherever she goes
He is not visible, but yet, his love still shows

Goodbye Butch, she screams out loud to the air
She knows that somewhere he is able to hear

Alone she begins to walk away from the shore
Her brother will be with her, forever more

Roberta Hewitt

Happy Birthday Mom!!

To the woman I admire most,
You've always been there - day or night,
To take what's wrong and make it right,
To love me, protect me, keep me from harm,
To lean on, to cry on, to lend me an arm,
You've known when it was time to keep me at home,
And when it was time for me to be on my own,
It may have been long since I've sat on your lap,
Or curled up beside you while I took a nap,
But it hasn't been long since I've thought of you... see,
'Cause, Mom, you will always mean the world to me,
And though time and space may have us apart...
You're always with me Mom...
Here right in my heart.
I love you.

Gina Bilotti

I Wish For The Day

I watch as the water draws out then draws near
And think of a friend - so precious, so dear.
I look at the birds so high in the skies
And think of your twinkling loving blue eyes.
I dream as the waves keep calling me in
And think of how wonderful you have been.
I feel the hot sand beneath my feet
And dream how your love would be so sweet.
I wish for the day
I wish for the hour
I wish for the minute
That I feel your power.

Karen McEllhenney

"Jed"

When I was a child of eight, I thought my little heart would
break when my dad left the house and said,
"See you at five Jed."

But dad didn't come home, instead he decided to roam. He
left my mom and me for someone else you see. I miss my
Dad, who was my pal, who left us for another gal. When
he left the house and said "see you at five Jed."

I would sit in the chair by the phone praying my dad would
call or come home. Why did you do this to me dad? Break
my heart instead of making it glad, when you left the house
and said "see you at five Jed."

I'm grown now with a child of my own and believe me dad
I'll never roam. When I say to my child see you at five
today I'll mean it dad and, I'll never stray, and tear that
little boy apart, by breaking his little .heart, with untrue
words that can't be unsaid like, "see you at five Jed."

Monica Wersebe Johnson (Jacksonville, FL)

The Golden Years

A couple of teenagers decided to wed, not a care in the world, not
thinking ahead they went to a preacher and tied the knot; a life of
adventure without a pot

It was nineteen forty, just before the war, their years together
had now reached four along came a baby girl that year, rearranged
their lives, but they had no fear

But then he got Old Uncle Sam's call, and off to the service he
went that fall it was three years later when home he'd come; the
baby boom hit and they had a son

Beaming with pride and life in gear, another son blessed the very
next year now they had a home and three kids to raise; life became
a little more serious those days

They worked together loved, laughed, and cried, as their kids grew
up they glowed with pride their kids got married and had some
kids, and those poor Grandparents hit the skids

Now these grand kids are having kids. Its no bed of roses to hit
those skids the limbs grow stiff, the old back aches, they trudge
along and they get the shakes

Their bodies are tired and getting worn, they forge ahead,
sometimes feel forlorn their doctors are making a buck or two; but
that old sense of humor seems to get them thru

These are the golden years they say; then where is the glitter when
your hair turns gray your hearing goes and your eyes grow dim,
your body sags and you can't stay trim

Half a century has come and gone, side by side they travelled along
The lesson they learned as time went past; family and friends are
gifts that last. You are the ones that count in life you are
welcomed today by this man and his wife.

Lillian Lawrence

Evergreen

If there is hint of Heaven in this life
it is in the green renewal of each spring,
with singing birds and winds, and sproutings rife
throughout our land in vital vernal wakening.

So if I seem to fade from earthly view
and you wake to find you miss me much,
just dream me here and still embracing you
as the sun and wind each softly touch.

I would be warm and close by for your sake,
with love as tender once in days gone by,
then wish me here all yours again to take
as comfort to your heart, and do not cry.

Daniel L. Hall

Dreamlover

He walks toward me with such eloquence and grace
I melt at the mere touch of his embrace
He stands before me but I can't see his face
He is my dreamlover but I fear rejection and disgrace.

His eyes are shallow blue pools, but to approach him I would
feel like a fool.
In my dreams he is placid and calm, he would only protect me
he could never do harm.

Dreamlover, I wish I could overcome my fear to hold you, touch
you, feel you near, one kiss from you and I would melt my dear.

One day dreamlover, I will have the nerve to claim the dreamlover
I rightfully deserve.

Sacha Bolton

Wolfe Island

Have you ever seen the fog,
Lay upon the water,
While the stones on the white beach,
Whiten as the sun grows hotter.

The wheat in the field,
Glows in the sunlight,
As the faded red barn,
Still holds the memories of hard working might.

The stones in the graveyard,
Hold the wonders of the island,
The parents and children who died there,
The lives, as beautiful as the sand.

Jennifer Winter

My Faithful Friend

Of all the joys on earth, life's able to extend
I treasure most, the knowledge that
you are my faithful friend
The knowledge that you care for me
And keep me in your mind
I've learned you are so faithful, loving and kind

With you there always is a rainbow
Peeking through the cloudiest skies of gray
You've shown me through life's trials
You are so good and true
No matter what hardship I face
Through faith, I can always depend on you

If I could have one special wish
One for sure would be
I'd like to be that faithful friend, you have been to me
I've learned life offers material pleasures
and treasures without end, I'd gladly give all away
to cherish and keep the knowledge that
I have you dear Lord,
You, for my faithful friend

Deanne R. Dodson

"The Bonding And The Abuse"

I was sent from a place known of, but, forgotten by all mankind,
A world of contentment. A world of promise.
I wait naked in this dark, warm cradle, lulled to sleep by the
beating of a loving heart.
I wait to enter into an existence that will introduce me to all things
including the most feared of all, man's brutality towards all
creatures.
I wait in fear of the beast who comes forth shouting vile
obscenities and threats of destruction, turning a gentle
heartbeat into thunderous pounding.
The beast who brings about the jolts that can hurl me into oblivion
and causes piercing screams to echo through my brain.
Another jolt!!
My cries go unheard as I struggle to survive, sharing her sadness,
loneliness, terror, and pain, fearful that I may never gaze into
her eyes, or know the comfort of her arms.
Once more, the anger of the beast has been fed. All is silent
now, but for her weeping. With a loving touch she speaks to me,
"Are you all right my little one?" With a gentle movement of my
tiny being I answer; "Yes, I Love You Mommy".

Rita Delores Fabiano

You Stepped On A Flower

You stepped on a flower and watched it die.
You tore out my heart and replaced it with stone.
You stripped my soul and left it bare.
You gave me strength and then you took it away.
You gave me hope and then you lied.
You said you believed and then you questioned.
You said you cared and then you hurt me.
You said you loved me and then you left.
You said we were friends and you ran away.
You acted loving and then you yelled.
You said hello, and then goodbye.
You stepped on a flower and watched it die.

Heather Cieslinski

God's Blessed Love

A prayer was once said for a little babe,
Through the years as this babe grew,
The Lord cuddled and nurtured this sweet little one,
Where others would hurt and reject her.

The earthly parents would abuse this babe,
God would hold his child lovingly in his arms,
Shattering words of pain they would deliver unto this child,
Jesus would softly whisper his love in her heart and spirit.

Others foretold of darkness and fear in her future,
God Almighty showed light, peace and love in her soul,
Outside this child grew to fear all life,
Inside she waits to bloom as the butterfly of The Lord.

Many have tried to break her spirit and misguide her,
Tear her heart apart and beat her down,
Shatter her soul by abuse and deceptions in all forms,
To make her believe she was not worthy to live.

But one small prayer and God's everlasting Love,
Raised a child of courage, strength and Love,
Today she stands before all as living proof,
That God's Love is within us all!

Crystal Daniels

Sunrise On Lake Como

When night surrenders to the dawn and fades the galaxy of stars
Whose lights is suddenly withdrawn
  From Orion to ruddy Mars.
A boundless glory fills the sense
  Of sight, as spreads the wondrous glow,
A vision of Omnipotence,
  In sunrise on Lake Como.
Rapture's inspired by other scenes
  Whose charms allure us east and west,
On cliff and where ocean leans
  against the sky its heaving breast;
We gaze with admiration on
  wonders or peak and swelling flood,
And are the spell they cast is gone
  We freely own that they are good.
Yet, after we have viewed them all
  Our through recur to scenes at home whose subtle sorceries enthrall
Our hearts wherever we roam; and of the wonders manifold,
  The scenic splendors that we know, none is more dazzling to behold
Than the sunrise on Lake Como

Rosemary R. Viands

Gulway Bay

It's far away I am today,
From the love you held in your eyes.
And long ago the hour I know,
I foresaw you saying goodbye.
But time nor tide of waters wide,
Could steal my heart away,
Forever true it flies to you,
My love in Gulway Bay.

I cherish the thought
Of your eyes I caught,
Recalling the joy we found,
As we made love while the stars above,
Glowed soft on the Irish ground.

My son you bore your life he tore,
On that painful but beautiful day,
At innocence cost my love was lost,
That morn in Gulway Bay.

But you'll find me for eternity,
Never giving my heart away,
My soul alone is yours to own, my love in Gulway Bay.

Joshua R. Currie

To My Friend On Graduation Day

To me you are whispers in the library, giggles in the girls room
A phone call of some gossip or a time of sorrow deep
You have always been a flower in this world of gloominess
A shoulder to cry on a hand to hold
A little girl when I met you
Now a woman, my greatest friend
We have grown together, loved in so many different ways
And though at times we are drifting, our bond will stay the same
You are the beauty in the winter, a shower of hope to me in spring
A refreshment in the summer, and a ray of hope to shine in autumn
With a smile to dry my tears.
You've been my sanctuary when I would crawl into a hole to die
We have seen it all together: from a dive in the pool, to a swim
  in the ocean
When we are sparkling like a diamond, when we are black as coal
I remember our laughing voices
I don't hear them enough anymore, but I know you're always here
I love you like a sister, I will never let you down
As our high school life is over a new level has just begun
And I know where ever I travel you'll always be my home.

Casey Marie Ford

Memory's Hall

Who is that person looking back at me?
Could time have past, I did not see?
What happened to the braided hair and skinned knees?
I only turned around, it seems,
To see bubble hairdo and faded blue jeans.
Why it was just yesterday,
I saw myself in a motherly way.
The image of two daughters small,
Are mirrored in memories hall.
I don't feel like time has gone by,
But my children are grown and I just blinked my eyes.
My reflection looks like my mom's,
When I was age twenty-one.
Will when I become elderly,
Feel the same when my reflection looks back at me?

Holly A. Witt

Just Like You

I'm looking for a friend today
a friend who'll stay away. I
want one or maybe two
but I want a friend who's
just like you. I'm looking
for a friend you see a friend
who need someone like me.
I want this friend I really
do but I want this friend to
be just like you. I want to
friend who's sincere a friend
who'll always bring me good cheer. I want a friend who
wants me too. But I want a friend who's just like you
I'm looking for a friend who's good a friend who'll do
the things a kind friend should.
I want a friend who's happy too I want a friend who's
just like you. I'm looking for a loving friend who'll not
let our friendship end. I want
a friend that's always true I
think I found my friend it's you.

Theresa Griffith

Look

You look to me for answers.
You look to me for love.
You look to me with visions;
  that have never been dreamed of.
You look to me for hope;
  so you do not fall astray.
You look to me for faith;
  in every single way.
You look with a longing heart.
And with an open ear.
You listen without a word;
  for the answers that are spoken so clear.
Are the answers a yes, or are they a no?
Were they left unanswered, or found down below?
You have looked, and now you see.
Everything you wanted is found in me.

Briana Mason

Hope

That which sustains and keeps us going,
Even though we have no way of knowing,
Whether our dreams come true or not.
We keep working, believing, and in hope
our prayers are wrought.

When fortune smiles and our lives are full,
It is still hope that helps us see no droll.
And when years have past and we grow old,
Hope remains the anchor for the soul.

John E. Prince

Choice Control

Hell will rise, into these skies,
Obliteration, of mankind.
Corpse will rot, among these lives.
Illimitable hate, of all these minds.

Gangrene skin, bleeding the right.
One day living to tell of the fight.
Viridescent home, red with vain.
Golden crown, keeping his pain.

Flies circling round, the wise man's head.
Obituaries telling, lies of the dead.
Masochistic killers, among our rule.
Controlling propaganda, controlling the fools.

Bad moon highs, bad moon rise.
Delinquent people, withholding the lies.

Tom Walker

"Love Is Like A Rose"

A rose in all its beauty
Reflects love that's pure and true
Treat it always gently
And its magnificence will shine right through.

But with each petal plucked from it
Like love that is abused
It loses all its magic
To bring joy our whole life through.

God gave to love the beauty
Reflected in a rose
And asked that they both be cherished
For their value's as good as gold!!!

Cecilia T. Wentz

Sweet Dreams My Love

December wind blows through my hair,
the chill of winter in the air.

The smell of firewood from atop the roofs,
waiting for Santa and reindeer hoofs.

Staring out the window with his nose on the glass,
the snows starts to fall, he has questions to ask.

Is there a Santa? Or is there not?
Is there a North Pole? Does it get hot?

He goes to bed and says his prayers,
blessing all that lives and his teddy bear.

I kiss his head, his nose and eyes,
sweet dreams my love till Santa arrives.

Sandra Stone

Friend

You are a special person, you're warm, kind, and true.
You have a heart of gold and I never see you blue.
Our friendship is very special to me and all the things you do.
You never see the bad things in people, it's only the good
things that shine through.
God made no mistakes when he made you.
He knew exactly what he wanted to do.
He wanted to create someone who was kind, generous, and giving.
To bring great happiness to all that is living.
You've done just that and you never let him down.
And those three words "God Bless You" are the sweetest sounds.
To come from a person with a heart of gold.
To always cherish, to have and to hold.
Don't ever change the way that you are.
For your kindness can be seen from near and far.
Now I'll end this little poem with just a small thought.
A friend is very special, especially the one I've got.

Sandra Bugher

Burning Religion

Who will see the agony African Americans are in a state of tragedy.
Shall I refresh the memory while we all stand aside and watch the
ash field history reappear
did Rose Parks refuse to vacate from her seat simply because she
was too tired?
E(y)aw hoo, (the true Hebrew name of the Heavenly Father) forbid.
She wanted to support and purge the country from is rhetoric of
separate but equal.
Yet burning religions is now the sequel.
America where is your liberty?
Shackled, chained, bound in racism
are you (America) going up in smoke without any hope or faith
color may not hate people surely continue to.
Looking at the glaze of the flames the burning-pain screaming the
names of those who died to prevent this re-arise
E(y) aw hoo shua (the true Hebrew name of the Savior) save me
from this world of iniquity where our babies die before they are
born, and everyone chooses wrong for right the young barely make
it through the night, people hiding behind political facades;
yet married to the do evil, the devil himself.
Once breath, two breath, four...burning, burning, religion.

T. Sharon Hart

Friendship

There is something about a friendship
It's worth its weight in gold
Yes, difficult to measure
For it's priceless I am told

There is much about a friend, you see
That stands the test of time
It's pure, and is consistent
Love and friendship intertwine

There is much about a friendship true
Twixt light and day it blends
True love in friends can ne'er be bought
Such friendship never ends

With friends there is no scoring
No accounts to pave the way
Friends are friends beyond trivialities
Things that bind are cast away

Yes, there is something about friendship
This bond is tried and true
And such a friendship is clear to me
Is what I've found in you.

Ruby J. Reeves

A Hole In My Heart

You have filled a hole in my heart...

They say you are a barren women with no children
that is not quite descript enough...it's not so much barren...as an
emptiness that is so overwhelming that can only be described as...
A hole in my heart...

You know that something is missing...
But what?

It is the bond that a mother and child have...
It is a closeness that doesn't needs words...
It is a feeling of completeness..
It is a feeling of being needed..
It is a love with no conditions.

Although you are not born of me, I feel these things to a certain
extent...
To the extend that it calms some of the inadequacies I feel...
Inadequacies that other people bestow on me...

Thank you....for this

Judith A. Chittenden

The Demon, Muddy-Murky Song

He's not what he seems when he holds me in my dreams
When you see him walk around s'fine all day.
He's not what he seems what he holds me in my dreams
A Demon, muddy-murky from the bay!

That's not how he looks when he wears those clothes from Brooks,
A package all wrapped up with tie to stay.
He's changed his silks for silt cavorting in a kilt,
of mollusks, dank ouze and black clay!

There's a rogue in his grin, as he slaps his briney shin
Mud flinging from his lurching silhouette!
He's not what he seems when he wakes me in my dreams,
A madness crowding out his other ways!

Oh! Hear the gush of surging water
Shock the rocks against the spray!
Sea gulls screaming in their wildness,
Dreams are bringing in the day!

Eee! The thrill that I feel causes me to squeal,
When I see him bounding up from the bay...
The sky is peach and green, swirling black and silver - cream
As we plunge into the gale that whips the bay!

Jane Lamplighter

With Love Agnes

My eyes iced white. Frozen from your stare
And I cannot see it
Only your urchin clinging, and you singing
Songs of love and forever in your pathetic ignorance
My emotions have been drawn and quartered at my own insistence.
Walking through the garden
I smashed the bone-white sundial there
So you see I have no time for you
Unless like some mad thing you go round and round
Hunting pieces that fit pieces
That make the whole of it
Bud what do you think? Do you think
Of the repercussions?
If I open the casket of yours, or you mine
The sameness of indecency
Destroys my emotions
Like an arrow through this heart

Richard York

All The Way

To you I say top of the day
Since today is your birthday
What then can I do or say
Other than to thank Allah and pray
That better things, come our way

Our love is like honey which does not decay
Like mountain which the wind blows not away
Like diamonds whose sparkle always stay
Like antiques whose worth increase everyday
Like river which flows night and day
And refreshing like the cool breeze of the bay

When things seem to be in disarray
My fears you always allay
Comforting words you always say
And you support without delay
Rashidat, you make my day, everyday.

Adeyinka O. Laiyemo

One Day

In one day I walked along the beach with you,
from sun up to sunset, our eyes never straying,
our hands never letting go of their gentle embrace.

In one day we made love. We drank of each other as
we drank the wine — hungrily, passionately, endlessly —
fearing our thirst may never be quenched again.

In one day we had pancakes for breakfast, subs for lunch
and chinese for dinner. We rocked our children to sleep
reading them fairy tales, wrapping them in warm
blankets of the truest love that ever graced the earth.

In one day our children played in the park chasing ducks,
throwing bread crumbs into the wind. We watched
them grow, running from slide to swing to monkey bars —
helping when they needed us, giving them room for
independence when they did not.

In one day I saw love in all its majesty,
the volumes our eyes spoke when our mouths could not;
the ecstasy and terror of an embrace too long missing, and too
quickly gone;
the silent screams of two souls bound to be one, separated by
circumstance;
the hope in our whispered vows that, one day, we will let our one
day come true.

Gary R. Nistler Jr.

Martin Luther King Jr.

"Living a dream let freedom ring."
Those were the words of Martin Luther King.
He saved the whites and freed the blacks
and didn't lay a hand on those who struck his back.
He saved his people from domination
and saved his people from discrimination,
but then one day he was shot and died
and on that day the people cried.
The people kept on singing
and Martin Luther King Jr. got the bells of freedom ringing.

Lori Moravec

The Tortured Soul

Oh, thy tortured soul,
you hang on the fringes of the unknown
and fall deep into the valley of despair
'til you are captured
by the dark stream of discontent.

Never cloaked in the comfort of the dark of night,
you crave the neon flamboyancy of the constant.
Your followers in singsong obedience of confusion
march to the trumpet's blare.

You search the mind's highway
for life's bountiful harvest.
The path of destruction
is dangerously near.

Listen, thy twisted mind and wracked body,
physical pain has no meaning
while there are tears in the heart.

Voice your anguish
not in the ear of Satan,
but trust in the power and the love
of your God.

Norma June Ross

Sue

There was a girl named Sue, who daily had to pay her dues.
Tho' she never had a clue, why she always had to do
All he said that she must do.
Quietly she got by, don't you ever dare to cry.
Never tell your wicked lies. Or you my child will surely die.

I'm just helping you to be. A righteous man just like me.
Don't you think you'll ever be free. For no one will listen can't
you see. To a child so wicked such as thee.

How could a Dad be so cruel. Using love like some ole' tool.
Wearing his sins upon her like a spool. Yes, she would never be so
cruel. Never once she dared to tell. Or she would surely go to hell.

By night he did his dirty deeds. Bouncing her upon his knee.
Tho' tears she cried he could not see. For he was on a lustful spree.
One day she vowed to be free. While she hip up in her tree.

Her chance for peace looked real dim. So the knife she had chosen
for him. Was plunged way deep beneath the rim.
Of her precious pearl like skin. Her heart beating slowly it looks
real grim. Now her life hangs on a rim.
Can a heart beat this slow. Daily met with such a blow.
Slowing town all that flows. She can't take anymore you know.
All from a man she's supposed to know.
Whose heart is frozen just like snow.

Rita D. Perez

The Pain That Lay Within

Wind blew
Children cried
Strangers walked
Not hearing, not knowing
The pain that lay within

Thunder crashed
Lifeless shells were soaking
Ignorant cars raced past
Not seeing, not aware
The pain that lay within

Hail fell
Aching bodies hid in shame
Masses trudged along - trying to overlook the frightening images
Not informed
The pain that lay within

There was one who saw beyond the harsh faces
Mindless enemies continued to journey on
But the man stopped, helped, comforted
He knew
The pain that lay within

Carrie Grant

Time And Chain

Said about time everyone has said,
To every link in eternity's chain worn
By every time linked soul, soft in time's sleepy bed,
Whose only 'scape the timeless dream will shorn.
But you immortal mortals doth dream to false effects,
And repudiate love's timeless wealth which needs thou company.
Then ever-living precious wealth thou do indeed neglect,
And expunge love's immortal name to time's vanquished infamy.
Then thy time is a season of reckless trial,
Which doth chain the succession of thy recklessness,
To an impious madness and false loves denial,
Of true timeless love thou false love fears infectious.
  But of all false loves thine eye can view,
  To unchained love thou false eye be true.

Raymond Thomas-Hogan

Day Dreamer

Warm tropical air surrounds me
Birds are chirping - is that a sea gull?
Water is calm - hardly a ruffle
Sails in the distance - is that a crossbones and skull?

I'll just lie low - let them pass on by
The horizon is now clear
All is peace and tranquility
As I lazily steer

Just passed the lighthouse
Into the open sea
I can sit back, relax
And just feel free

My heading is north
A bull moose on the shore
Canadian geese in the sky
I'm thrilled to the core

Just passed an iceberg
Feels like the north pole
Oops! Better get out of here
My bath water has grown exceedingly cold

Niva L. Reynolds

Untitled

A death is a hard thing to overcome.
It makes you sad to know they're the one.
The ones who won't see another day.
Sometimes it makes us sad to think,
That we'll never see their little eye wink.
The fact that they were always there
The reality that it just isn't fair
It seems that if they just put up a fight
Then maybe, just maybe they would be here 2 night.
We can't turn back time and say
Oh God please don't take our friend away.
Now that they'll never be here again
All we can do is stick 2 gether friend.
So smile as much and as hard as you can.
'Cuz baby it ain't over you must understand.
Life will not last forever.
People die, but they'll leave you never.
Just keep them deep down inside
'Cuz that's where the love is that we'll find.

Ashley Blume

Dylan's First Birthday

A year has passed since that tragic day.
When God sent his angels to take you away.
They took you to heaven high above
Where you'll be pure as snow and free as a dove.
So many things unanswered, we still wonder why?
Our hearts are still broken with tears left to cry.
The few hours we spent loving you so dear.
Just wanting to cuddle and hold you so near.
On this day you would have been "one".
Just think of all the things we could have done.
Dreams we could have shared, plans we had
Were shattered with memories all so sad.
We will rejoice on the day when we can see your precious face.
For now we surrender you unto God's loving embrace.
We know you're in the best place that you could ever be.
Your God's little angel from now through eternity.

Shirley Jager

Growing Up

As a young girl, I dreamed the dreams of others
I didn't own anything; what was mine slipped through my fingers
I coveted what my friends had- their talents, their minds
At night I was them, but in the morning I was me
Not sure of where I wanted to go, or how I was going to get there
my dreams would change with the phases of the moon
I made no path; I made no decisions
I was a pendulum swinging back and forth at the mercy of gravity.
As my dreams would disappear so would my ambitions
I didn't rise, I stood
I didn't run, I walked
I didn't open my own door to opportunity
instead I quickly slipped through the door as it was being shut in
my face
When I got inside I had nothing
My dreams ran out; I had no visions, there were no friends
The real world dared me to be my own self.
Now, before I take a last glimpse of the changing moon
before I close my eyes
instead of walking I will run
instead of standing I will rise.

Michelle Morales

Paradise!

Luke 23:43

To live at a time when no one knows fear,
The water is fresh, the air, too, is clear,
To live in a time when lions, indeed,
Will feed on the grass and young children heed,

To hear one call out who never could talk,
To watch someone lame jump up and then walk,
To watch someone deaf first hear a bird's song,
To meet a new friend while walking along,

To never feel sick but each day feel good
And always to do the things that we should,
To greet each new day with a happy smile
And say to someone, "come stay for a while!",

To welcome the dead and help them to see
The future can last for eternity,
To trust everyone and heed good advise,
My friend, you will then be in paradise!

Jo Wacker

Life In Color

Health, happiness, pain, sorrow,
Our lives are filled with a vast amount of emotions,
for tomorrow.

Colors mirror our mood,
gay or subdued.

Blue as the ocean has been said
or a threatening storm the color of
gray lead.

Lollipops, a lick of color
Paint as smooth as cream made into butter.

Orange is bold
courageous, too
your eyes grab a hold of such a color unable to be released
from the trance,
from the glance,
which began as an emotion
only a fragment
of a moment,
away.

Jo-Ann Nawrocki

The Stranger

A blanket of darkness falls over the city
As a stranger makes his way into town
His troubles unknown, his fears hidden
His beady eyes unseen

He wonders, searching aimlessly
Crying out to the night
Then all is silent
The stranger is gone

As quickly as he comes
He leaves
He continues wandering into the night
Searching for the part of his life he left behind

Brandi Zimmermann

My Doll

When I was young I had a toy
It brought me pleasure, it brought me joy
It was perfect and it was mine alone
It gave me more happiness then I have ever known.
It had dark brown eyes and soft brown hair
sweet red lips and its skin was so fair.
With its angelic smile it gave to me
A sense of comfort and security
But I grew up, and alas one day
My mother gave my doll away
I sat all alone and thought as I cried
That without my doll a part of me died
But one glorious day that part was revived
I was looking at my doll only he was alive
With the same brown eyes and the same brown hair
the same red lips and his skin was just as fair
He had me enchanted with just one glance
His eyes held my soul in a mystical trance
His heart spoke to mine in a heavenly tone
It said your doll has returned and your no longer alone.

Kimberly Smeltzer

Ode To Riko

They say you're arrogant and aloof, that one can't expect more from a cat.
But I understand you much better, that cold shoulder — is just an act!
With your back towards all of us, you pretend to be fast asleep.
But at the mention of your name, your ears just twitch and tweak.

I remember when you were young, fetching a crumpled, paper ball.
You'd bat it under the sofa, then chase it across the hall.
You'd thunder around the house in pursuit of some unknown guest.
Shooting past a corner, just to leap onto the chest.

Nine lives you were given and gray hairs, I now wear.
Three times you fell into the pool, providing me, with quite a scare.
You dropped into a cactus, and slipped off, our deck rail.
You crashed through the ceiling, landing on all four, without fail.

Your hip was dislocated by the neighbor's old tomcat.
And when that big dog attacked, you really hissed and spat!
We often sat and waited for others to come along.
While listening for the meadowlark, to break into a morning song.

I have so many memories of the times we've spent alone.
You feigning such indifference while I stroked your head and backbone.
Now that you have died... I put your things away.
Riko, "Queen of the Household,"...I so missed, your company today!

Kathrine S. Browne

Things Gone

Future times, past times, sad times, and happy
Times, things gone too far for memory to recall.

Some things come back to us to bring tears, later
forgotten, though kept behind a wall.

Things gone are times past for a few, to others
things gone are what was yesterday in regards
to a future day.

But not all things will be gone you see, memories
of how things were and dreams of how they
should be are always kept in memory.

Jeffrey T. Janke

Thin Wire

I've walked this tight rope for oh so long,
With no staff for control.
With no want to look down.
No will to let go.

The rope swings,
The rope sways,
My body obeys.
Moving to the random dance.

No support to grab hold,
Only the thin air.
No balance for my soul,
Only the next step if I dare.

I think I'll be safe,
I think I'll be strong,
Never fall,
Never touch the ground.

As long as this rope does not wear thin,
Between what is real,
And what's never been.

Keith A. Hanich

Quiet Around

I love to listen to the quiet around,
to hear not spoken word, nor any man made sound.
To just listen to the wind through the trees,
to hear the birds in song.
To hear what's right not wrong.

Water running over rocks,
small animals scurrying through the leaves and grass.
A coyote howling to the moon.
The crickets chirp and the call of the loon.
I love to listen to the quiet around,
to hear not spoken word, nor any man made sound.

Redwing blackbirds in a low-land marsh,
or the trill of the meadowlark whose pitch is never harsh.
Looking at the stars while lying on the lawn and
listening to a rooster announce the early dawn.
I love to listen to the quiet around,
to hear not spoken word, nor any man made sound.

Clark H. Mattingly

Love

Love is like a butterfly
Flying alone and free,
Fluttering higher with each breath of air.
It can land on your arm with little notice,
If you move too quickly it will sail away,
Leaving you in its past,
Wondering,
Thinking,
Of who it may land on next.

Kelly Ray

Mannequin In Motion

Skin tight strike a pose, make-up on my face
A photo of the last one passing time with such grace
A mannequin in motion am I.
Wilhelmina. Casablanca, both say you're the one
while Elite's newest face cannot wait till you're done
A mannequin in motion am I
Now you're big news, being used, cameras in their hands
that film of your life takes you to foreign lands
Your sex lends appeal to a friend
remember every single frame has an end
A mannequin in motion am I
Couturiers and assistants, put pins up your back
The critics' poison darts line up to the attack
never trust the smile of a prude
They're looking for a shot in the nude
You're not a man, just a mannequin no more and no less
They pay me, to trade me, to look my very best
to portray a high class, Euro-ass I'm chasing the dream
It's not all what it seems, the illusions a lie
but, a mannequin in motion am I

Tashonn-Etienne Antinori

When Dreams Don't Become Reality

She was a girl raised differently,
She had different goals, aspirations, and dreams.
One of which was to fly - And that was where her dream ended.

She had different goals, aspirations, and dreams.
She always wanted to be like Amelia Earhart -
And that was where her dream ended.
Though they did have a lot in common.

She always wanted to be like Amelia Earhart
Although, for a seven year old girl, she may have been reaching too far.
Though they did have a lot in common... Amelia made it back.

Although for a seven year old girl, she may have been reaching too
far, but it seemed almost like destiny for her to die like her hero,
because one time Amelia made it back
But another seemed almost like destiny for her to die like her hero
because one time Jessica made it though that was only in her dreams,
But another time she did not, and that was where her dream ended,
And her family had to wake up to the harsh reality that

Jessica made it, though that was only in her dreams.
She had different goals, aspirations, and dreams and her family had
to wake up to the harsh reality that she was a girl raised differently.

Courtney Frank

"It's Clear To See"

I feel so alone
Alone as could be
Without you here next to me.
How can I say this
So very politely
That I will care for you for eternity.
But have stopped for a moment to face reality.
My heart is yearning for companionship
But I have discovered yours just lingers
Not wanting a relationship.
I wish you the best in all your years to come
Because I still care I've got to say goodbye to you
and me and all the dreams that will not become.
As of this day I can now see clear
That you and me were just not meant to be
We are not two puzzle pieces
That fit so perfectly
I hope you understand
That my feelings have changed
Yet they will always be the same!

Ginny Lyke

Memories

Please, please
no more memories,
scourges of my soul.
Ushering me to the precipice of tears.
Reminders of times_ yesterdays gone...
disappeared

I can share no more.

Images
vividly in view
that taunt the mind.
The weight much too heavy, I fear.
Remembering, those loved_ on and on...
Let me rest.
I can carry no more.

Larry Hesterfer

Sir

You loaned me a life
You loaned me a home
You loaned me my father's
And I sir when I am going to pay?
You loaned me my children
You loaned me a "Love"
You loaned me my riches
And I sir how costly I am going to pay
You loaned me my health
You loaned me the air
You loaned me the "light"
And I ... Sir, how am I going to pay
When the moment arrives
To liquidate my debt
And you are ready to collect
And I sir will have to liquidate
Don't look at the "balance"
Of your saintly justice
Because debt so great
I sir ..... Will be unable to pay. Beautiful words.

Margareta Virchis

The Serenity Of Spring

Spring is here, in the air, in the trees, in the fields, everywhere.

Before the dawn I here the warble of the bluebirds blending together as one. To welcome the morning before the rising of the sun.

The robin with its red-breast is singing a cheery roundelay from an apple tree, while a band of birds flit around, which we recognize as the black-capped chickadee.

The plain little titmouse has been ousted everywhere and is making his home in our birdhouse.

I see the wrens, finches, warblers of every hue, olive, red, green, yellow and beautiful shades of blue.

The song of the mourning dove marks a joyous season, of the sound of birds claiming a home, courting a mate and making life take on a new reason.

Dear Heavenly Father let us always keep this earth like spring
A place of serenity, peaceful and green, a place to enjoy
is my constant prayer.

May we never let it be destroyed through greed, fear and hatred. But may we all be united in Thy care.

Loma Susan Hart

A Mother In Need Of Love

My mom is like a garden,
She blossoms everywhere.
And in the morning sunshine,
She even has time to care.

And when she's feeling frightened,
Or sad, or mad, or upset,
She always puts that aside
And helps me in time of fret.

I know she gets real angry,
But I don't mean to make her mad.
Sometimes I even make her unhappy,
But later I feel so incredibly sad.

My mom can make my life stressful,
And I know it's the other way too.
She also makes me feel real special
And sometimes, unfortunately, rather blue.

And when I don't do as I'm told,
She can chew me down to the core.
But she knows I really Love her,
Maybe I just need to tell her more.

Kimberly R. Ramann

Heaven Or Hell

Heaven, hell what is the difference?
Is there really one?
We all know the basics,
The stories our parents told us
"If you're a good girl you go to heaven"
"If you're a bad girl you go to hell"
But what if you are both,
Do you stay to roam the earth.
Your body caught because God could not decide
But the devil wanted us not to survive
Only to burn in the scorching fire.

M. Brown

Modern Necessity

Electricity is a power that helps us function
When it fails, we realize its mighty connection
It has stopped 11 states and a couple of borders
Guess what? A battery radio is now giving orders
The computer quits, the printer too
Faxes no longer give you the facts
A chance of a full day's work is now at loss
It was just the look on the face of the boss
No telephone messages out or in
A word is given just go home then
Lights all out no cops in sight
Traffic is now in a pitiful plight
Gas stations pumps are still
Car all lined up there as well
Now to get home is the Aim
Just to find out what to blame
Finally home at last
It's going to be a cold meal or fast
Now it's sitting and sweating by the hour
Waiting for the magic of electric power.

Bonnie Locklear

A Toast

Here's to the mole! An industrious soul
That labors 'neath terra so firm.
Whose claws and whose brawn can ruin a lawn
In pursuit of the ubiquitous worm.

Kathleen V. Follette

Real Dad

Not long ago I heard my son's friend say
something about his Real Dad, who lived far away.

I thought you fool look around.
For you this man shares the same name, same roof, and same town.

So I began to define my Real Dad. For me that's not easily done.
Because the way I look at it, I could not name just one.

A Real Dad is there with you, no matter what they say.
A Real Dad helps you learn things, that get you from day to day.

A Real Dad knows what you want and helps you get it with a good plan.
A Real Dad knows what you can do and smiles because you can.

I had them all around me from the first moment on.
I was to blind to see the right. When it came to Real Dad, I only saw the wrong.

The people that I lived with would only name a few.
Momma there is no doubt in my mind, my best Real Dad is you.

You are always in my heart. You never let me down.
How could I ever forget the beauty operator in that little one horse town.

Joe Kunkel

Silent Celebration

They look alike
The dusty grey man reflects the spotty white boy
The coffee and the chocolate shake are one
Only thirty years stand between them
And, men alone... scourge themselves with time

The jagged, sticky hair is cast
Silent eyes slant, just beyond their plates
And, dirty elbows slew two working bodies into a canyon of flesh
parted only by a chrome and plastic table

Yet his twenty dollar bill,
so clean it caught my eye,
must make grey face a little different

But, twenty noted dollars
peeled off green and clean,
belong to both the son and father...
the appearing and disappearing God

Too bad that being human is regarded as the common place
and, money as God's body being shared
For today... I saw two Gods eat dinner
and a twenty dollar bill... become a birthday card

Leonard Stevens

Leaving Me Alone

She lies there waiting to leave me,
I cry in the sorrow from her melting,
Wishing she would stay a little more,
Not leaving me and going away,

The day comes with the dwell of sadness,
Rain falls with gray mist,
I stand there watching her become nature,
Hope she is happy.

I remember the time we had,
Colors glow from the past,
I see her smiling,
Her hair all done nice,

In my day dreams she comes,
I see her watching me,
I hope I could talk to her,
But soon she leaves me alone.

Ilene Schwartz

Allow The Angels

Allow the angels to romp and play
With this tiny angel on this special day.

To run and jump in fields of clouds where only angels are allowed.

Dear Guardian Angel cradle your wings
Around this child while your heart sings.

To scamper behind a shining star
while Jesus smiles from afar.

Allow the angels to place another chair
At the feet of Jesus with angelic care.

Lifting our eyes to a moonbeam's ray
It beckons us now to watch and pray.

Allow the angels to give us strength to
focus on God, a time to think.

Look up at the Heavens opening wide
See thousands of angels at your side.

Allow the angels to dry your tears
With God's gentle love to abandon your fears.

Let's walk and talk with the angels above
Enkindle our hearts with abounding love.

All the diamonds and sapphire will not shine
As much as one halo of an angel divine.

Allow the angels to romp and play with all tiny angels this blessed day.

Donna Cotter 3-28-96

The Game Of Life

You win some,
You lose just as many.
You falter nonetheless,
Yet life goes on the same.

Few enter extra innings,
And for some its sudden death.
Others just go and have fun,
After all it's just a game.
Still many commit fouls,
Of which the result can be tragic.
For the assailant it's just two minutes,
But to the rest it's a shame.

It all starts with love,
And the conclusions are unique.
Yet we all hope to score a goal,
And have our own piece of fame.

Ken Leising

Singer

(k.d. lang)

Since the first time I saw her, I loved her style, her sense of oneness, and her sense of creativity. As time goes by I look at her as a person, someone I can look up to.

I find her a positive role model for both straights and gays. What she sings has a positive message on us all, we have to be willing to listen, if we don't we judge for the wrong reasons.

I don't care what people say about her as long as they know I love her. She is my pop icon and I will always look up to her.

Melissa Sue Singhaus

Galaxies

I would like to just travel out midst the stars
To places some light years away
And then to return in the wink of an eye
And be back in less than a day.

I wonder just what it is like out there,
To be circling Venus or Mars
Or to sit on a ring of Saturn someday
And to fly amongst comets and stars.

To see the great size of Jupiter
Or to fly back once more to see Mars
And to see why it's called the red planet
And to see how earth looks from afar.

Perhaps to find a new planet,
One which I could name after me,
My name to remember for lifetimes
And remembered in Earth's history.

I would like to visit Uranus,
To Pluto and the great Milky Way.
I know that these things are outrageous thoughts
But I'd still like to do them someday.

Francis M. Richardson

Dancing With Fate

Just by chance I gave some friends a call,
and together we went to a small dance hall.
The place was quiet with only a few people around,
but it seemed to be the most happening place in town.

The dance began promptly at nine,
I was already bored, but didn't show any signs.
Then from a distance I seen him dance,
He was good, if only I had a chance.

Then he looked at me across the dance floor,
he walked my way and my heart did soar.
Asked me to dance, which lasted all night,
when I turned for a moment he had vanished from my sight.

Where did he go? And who this man?
I had to go back for curiosity, you understand.
I spotted him when he walked in the door,
it didn't take long and we were out on the floor.

I guess it's fate, what else could it be?
to fall in love with a man, and him with me.
He's everything I wanted and so much more,
We look forward to the future and what it has in store.

Daphne Gonzales

The Oklahoma Blast

In a blast it was gone;
our dreams, our laughter and our joy.
Our friends and loved ones must grieve
for the love that is lost and the mercy never received.
You stand there,
staring us down.
You really couldn't care about our endless frown.
You hurt us,
hurt us so bad,
nothing and no one can replace our lives; shattered and eternally sad.
I hope someday
we'll have the last laugh.
Because nothing and no one will ever rid our minds
of that inhumane blast.

Corianne Taylor Goldstein

In This World

When the grass doesn't grow green anymore
and the flowers don't bloom "In this world"
what is one to assume.

When eyes cry no more tears and hearts
feel no more fear "In this world" what is one to hear.

When you can't feel the wetness of the rain
and the breeze of the wind "In this world"
what is one to comprehend.

When a mother is no longer a mother and there
is no more sisters and brothers "In this world"
where is one to look any further.

When a house is not a home and the steps
has crumpled "In this world" where is one to be humble.

Karen Washington

Oklahoma

Here we are, Lord, kneeling before you,
  and wondering why this took place.
In this space, Lord, where children gathered
  only to play.
Only you know, why our heavens
  opened its doors on this day.
Many more, Lord, lost their lives here,
  but went on to a better place.
Just your arms, Lord, can embrace those,
  who were left here with an empty space.
You and I know, Lord, not only children,
  went to meet thy grace.
And only by your presence,
  they have come to know thy peace.

Deborah Castro

Shades Of Brown

Shadows flitting beneath a Golden Sky, hiding from the
burning sun in the umber grass of a new-mown field

Laughter filling the eyes of a small child, hiding from the
angry eyes of a sour, unhappy, sin-filled mother

Golden shades of mocha filling happy eyes holding a red,
wrinkled 'ugly' first-born son, gift of a loving God

Melting, liquid shades of dark burnt umber watching a
most loved husband, father leave for war

Golden liquid eyes shining with happy pride, a beloved
man, home husband, father: Wounded, alive

Eyes, wounded, hurting, grieving, anger, pain, illness
incurable, life ending, unhappy: Being apart

Shadows flitting beneath a Golden Sky, bright, gold
chocolate: Shining, loving girl's eyes

Eternal eyes, shades of brown, golden eyes, eyes
of love: Mother's gift: Love's eyes

Hubert Phillips

Our Journey

Meet me at the edge of destiny,
Journey with me along the banks of tranquility,
Walk with me through the mist of uncertainty,
And wait for me on the bridge of time,

For with every sunset that blankets this world,
And every magical sunrise that beckons us to stay,
My spirit awaits like an old lighthouse,
gracefully lighting the way.

Edie A. Senter

Who

When I was young, I never needed anyone,
and making love was just for fun.
Those days are gone.

Living alone, I think of all the friends
and family, I know;
But when I dial the telephone, nobody's home.

I'd give anything in the world to fall in love.
Just for once I'd like to find my knight in shining armor
That man I've been dreaming of.

Who'll take care of me and make me feel loved,
safe and restful and so so so secure.
To hold and grow old with, to cuddle and love.
I don't want to live or grow old alone.

It's hard to be sure, sometime I feel so insecure.
Love seems so far away,distance and obscure.

All I need in a man is honesty
Someone with a soft touch and a gentle heart,
who'll take me for what I am

Who knows who, somewhere out there.
Where is he? Who is he? Who?

Kathleen Baker-Pianka

Forest Cathedral

The sun blazes down in all its glory
Its inquisitive beams
Like the vagrant breeze
Searching into the secret places
Of the green ceiled canopy
Under which I stride.
With many pauses to Worship
I gaze down shadowy aisles
Of soaring columns; the deep scored
boles of ancient trees
Which upholds the roof of the forest cathedral
In which I wander.
My sight is filled with the pattern
Of golden Spanish lace
Which covers the path I walk in solitude
I slow my pace - pause to look and listen
My ears are filled with the great swelling
Music of the spheres
The orchestral choir of the Almighty.

Naomi N. Greene

A Piece Is Missing

A piece is missing from my heart
and also from this puzzle
This puzzle you assembled with
your own hands;
Before God called you at His command

Fond memories of you, I'll always treasure.
As in doing this puzzle,
which brought you so much pleasure.

So many joys, I have to recall,
The good, the bad is part of it all.

You'll never be forgotten, as you are in me.
In God, we'll be united in Eternity.
Until then, Dear Father,
this puzzle I'll treasure,
as a reminder of you, forever!

Your loving daughter, Pat

Betty P. Grady

God's Majesty

When I behold the rising sun, or watch the stars at night,
Or see the moon illuminate the darkness with its light,
The roaring waves, the shifting sands of oceans endless shores;
They speak of His Great Majesty, Alive Forevermore!

The mountain peaks that rise so high, above the valley low,
The trees that reach up to the sky, all covered white with snow,
That melts in spring and then flows down to rivers deep and wide;
They speak of His Great Majesty, His Glory and His Pride!

The forest green that shelters many creatures great and small,
The canyons deep, the deserts sands, the mighty rains that fall,
The wind that whispers through the trees, or stirs a mighty storm;
They speak of His Great Majesty, His power and His Form!

The universe that He has made, though endless it may be,
Could never reach as far as His undying Love for me,
He sacrificed His only Son, to save my wretched soul,
This speaks of His Great Majesty, His Grace, His Love, His All!

Terry L. McIver

Best Friends

She was always there to protect me from any possible danger
starting out as a stranger,
The pain showered over me the day she told me she was moving,
it still hurts a lot to think about it but I told myself it was
only a dream,
why would she pull such a scheme?
We hung out together a lot but when I cried she'd be there a blot,
she loved my writing and you would rarely see us fighting,
I had never become such good friends with some one since grammar
school but she was cool,
Sure, we were crazy fools, dancing in the back of nearly every
SNL which was the coolest,
I didn't understand why she hurt me so much until I got switched
out of third lunch,
I looked up to her a lot and neither one of us would ever smoke pot,
she was my best friend,
my best friend until the end!

Sally Unchester

Void

Something was missing, my life felt void.
What was the absence the heart yearned for?
Why, love of course, was missing indeed.
(It was cut missing line)
Check at home, the beginnings of my life.
Where example and teachings begin each flight.
Next I tried church, where love does abound,
But sadness overwhelmed where indifference was found.
Struggling and lost, wandering in a fog,
A nudge from within said enter this door.
Within those doors, not a Bible in sight,
I found God to be real through love and support.
God is everywhere awaiting our knock.
Why couldn't I have learned early on?
Where, oh where, was God in my church?
He was there all along, only His troops were lost!

Emily D. Oliver

Untitled

Disheartening phrases,
Deceptive thoughts,
you stare with disguised features,
A naive addiction, unable to depart from,
a characteristic charade put on to ease me
a cold hand upon my face, frightening chills
transfer through my veins
The door to death, locked until eternity
intelligence must be the key.

Shanon Swank

To My Unborn Son

Hush little baby, don't you cry,
Mommy's here to guide you through the night.
Daddy's here by my side wondering what to do.
Oh our little baby, we love you!

Life is hard, I understand. We are here to hold your hand.
You came into a world full of love and hate,
Mommy and Daddy are the loving gate!
We need you just as you need us, you were made with a loving touch.

Oh please don't cry my little one,
Mommy can't understand what she has done!
Daddy said he loved us so, why did he let us go?
I don't know what to do!
My life wouldn't be right without you!

We shall fix things, you and I.
It will now be Daddy, Mommy and our little guy!
Daddy needed to think things through,
He has decided, he wants me and you.

It shall be hard for all of us, but I believe we can adjust.
Believe in each other, that is the key.
Life and love shall always be.

Carol Y. Worthy

Life

Life is a gift
Which an enemy wants to steal
Who is this enemy?
It is no one else's but time
Time comes and goes as a
Thief without warning
And steals the thing so precious to us Life

The wise words of many
Proverbial warnings
To keep awake to keep on guard
Hold onto this precious
Gift as long as possible
Savor it every day
Give thanks to Jehovah God
And praise his holy name
It is he who gave us this gift of life
But it is time; our enemy who we can not avoid
For it is he; our enemy who
Takes this precious gift of life away
Tic Toc Tic Toc

MayAnn Hanna Pasalich

Darkness And Light

O sun that's sunk o'er housetops lone and bare;
O day that's gone and lost forever in the past;
O clouds that glide across the sky so fair;
Why doth the darkness cover light so fast?

O paths that wind the hills so bleak and still;
O darkened trails beneath the sky above;
O mountaintops that echo man's last shrill;
Just when will darkness break to light of love?

The whole creation lies in darkness black;
The light of love is dim in lives of men;
But, Lo! The curtain of the sky doth slack;
And let our God shine forth in brighter ken.
In breathe this light that shines of God so pure;
Inhale this love and let it long endure.

Julia Laprade

Memories

Gosh this hurt so bad
It's making me so mad

I remember all the things we shared together
I will remember it all forever

Remember when we first met?
It was a time I'll never forget

I'll never forget your smile
It made me happy for a long while

Remember all those crazy times?
They will always be yours and mine

Whatever you do, please pull through
If not for me then for you

Because in 1998
Together we will graduate

I'll love you always and forever
And I'll never forget you, never ever

Crystal Himes

Caring Words Of Life

PEACE: Peace is a calm, spring morning at the lake.
LONELINESS: Loneliness is when the older kids won't let you play with them.
BEAUTY: Beauty is a bride on her wedding day.
WONDER: Wonder is not knowing whether she will say yes or no.
SADNESS: Sadness is when the flowers have died and someone threw them away.
KINDNESS: Kindness is giving a small child your last piece of gum which you were saving for yourself.
AUTUMN: Autumn is walking through the woods with the one you love, kicking brightly colored leaves on the path in front of you.
LOVE: Love is a warm feeling inside you and everything seems right.
HAPPINESS: Happiness is being with you!

James M. Loeb

A Fly On The Window

The fly sat upon the window frame
And saw all there was to see
He went about his daily life
with no concern for me.
He witnessed my joys, hopes, and my doubts
and the nights I cried myself to sleep
And he went about his daily life
with no concern for me.
Once, angrily I swatted him
He trembled like a tree
Then he went about his daily life
with no concern for me.
Even when I retreated from this
world for eternity
He went about his daily life
with no concern for me.

Jammie Ulerick

Tonight

Die with me tonight, and I'll care.
Cry with me tonight, and I'll find despair.
Hate me tonight, and I'll fight.
Break for me tonight, and we might.
Stay with me tonight, and show me the light.
Hold me tonight, and I'll shut out the night.
Show me fantasy tonight, and together we'll believe.
Touch me tonight, and heaven we'll find.
Laugh with me tonight, and friends we'll be.
Love me tonight, and lovers we'll be for all eternity.

Chelsy Risenhoover

Vision Of Home

I watch the palm trees sway gently with the wind
and see Oleander bloom
But I hear Wild Geese call
and know the leaves are turning
And wish I were there!

I see a cloudless sky and
watch the whitecaps come and go.
I watch the sea-gulls on their way
and wonder why I hear Black-birds sing
As they sway on cat-tail bush
and wish I were there!

I see the wax-white beauty of magnolia
Beyond my door,
But I hear the wind and feel the
cold crisp air and know it's snowing
and wish I were there!

Enone Kunar

The Battle Of Midnight Clear

Speeding through the midnight clear am I,
Dancing rapidly in the sky,
I stare at the jury, the ghost phantoms flying by.
In the distance another heavenly chariot I see,
Trying to flee, just as we.
Slight above is the distant midnight guardian of the land,
Almost like a giant man.
On the earth the armies marching through,
Carry torches, many to.
Darkness now reigns the land,
I feel as though the abyss now stands.
On the earth the demons dance,
Then in the expanse,
Fly thy lighted heavenly lance,
As the tribes of men do prance.
Now we come to where destination be,
We no longer have to flee.
All is now calm,
For the battle hath ended.

Adam Poulemanos

"The Ranks Of The Lord"

I climbed tallest mountain to see all below,
the rivers, the valleys, and all I could know;
the tops of the trees were below me for change,
I looked straight across to the soaring birds range.

I inhaled a breath of the clouds as they passed,
I felt the rain first as it fell at last;
and I think I've seen where the wind comes from;
as I stood on the tip-top nearest the sun.

Then I heard a great shout and loud trumpet blast,
a lightning bolt flashed from the east and streaked past;
and a King-like Crusader rode out from the light,
a glistening double-edged sword held high on His right.

The white steed He was mounted was awesome indeed,
I stared captured in wonder as legs bid me to flee;
But held by a power and not of my own,
I heard a voice promise, "now you'll reap what you've sown."

The King-like Crusader commanded, "fall in",
as I took place in line I felt myself grin;
with armor and buckler and double-edged sword,
I realized I just joined the ranks of the Lord.

Kenneth R. Tanguay

My Heart

I wrote you thousands of letters,
But only gave you a few.
I told you I love you,
And I thought you knew.
You were there when I looked away,
I turned around and you were gone.
I wrote you love letters, sad letters, poems even,
Only to find out your heart was leavin'.
Piece by piece it broke away,
I don't like you anymore you said one day.
I tossed and turned in my bed at night,
I saw you in my mind, even my sight.
Thinking about life is what I sat down to do,
But I could only think of you.
In my mind my thoughts were churning,
And deep down my heart was still burning.
All of good times I thought I could forget.
Then I went to the place we met,
And at that moment I knew.
That I would always love you.

Vicky Mitchell

Children!

Children, oh children! You are so innocent and adorable,
Your minds and thoughts develop intelligently.
Sharing with the world your beauty and sincerity,
You are nurtured and blessed by the high supreme.

Children, you are our sweetest little angel.
A very special intellectual being.
You give us laughter, you give us joy
You are loved and adored by the high supreme.

Children, your characteristics are incredibly amazing,
You are full of compassion, love and adoration
We love you dear children, that's all we ever know,
Wanting to protect you from turmoil and woe.

My dear children, we watched you grow from stage to stage,
But afraid to let you go, when you come of age.
Keeping a good record it's something we always wanted,
You are cared and respected by the high supreme.

We love you dear children for knowledge and potentiality.
But most of all we love you for who you are.
You are a special blessing sent to us from above.
You are created and loved by the high supreme.

E. Romillie

I Am The Nation

I am the United States of America, conceived in Freedom,
And the Declaration of Independence is my Birth Certificate.
I am 260 million living souls and
The ghost of millions who lived and died for me.

From Lexington to New Orleans, the Alamo and Flanders Field,
To the Maine, Pearl Harbor, Korea, Vietnam and Kuwait,
Over 1,153,500 of my brave Americans have gone to war
From the American Revolution to Kuwait and lost their lives:
The American Revolution................4,000
The War of 1812..............................2,000
The Indian Wars of the 1800s..........1,000
The Mexican War of 1845.............13,000
The Civil War 1861-1865............497,000
The Spanish American War 1898.....2,400
World War I 1914-1918 116,000
World War II 1942-1945..............406,000
Korean War 1950-1953..................58,000
Our Vietnam involvement from
1963 through 1972.........................58,000
The Kuwait War 1991..........................141
My prayer: To remain a citadel of freedom and a beacon of light to the world.

Woodrow Flanary

The Climb

A young Indian stood
part way up a mountain,
peering up its cloud-covered face.
He could only see obstacles
poking through the mist.
He knew the path was treacherous,
he'd heard of the difficulties,
he's seen the twisted bodies
of those who had lost their grip
and plummeted to their deaths,
but he knew that he must climb
to become a man, to be a brave.
Till now the climb was easy,
his father had shown him the way,
but from here he would go alone.
He could follow the path
his father had pointed out to him,
but he knew the respect was greater
for those who made it on their own he looked over his shoulder
one last time before climbing; now he left his boyhood behind.

Kyle Klockars

Shadows

For all of my life, it seems I have known shadows
dark and light shadows, shadows that danced and laughed
shadows that would taunt and scream
I would watch them in silence
in the barely lit space, that I called home
watching the manic movements upon my wall,
before my red-stained weary eyes
I would beg them in vain 2 go away
I would plead with them 2 return,
the sleep and peace of mind they've robbed from me
and always the shadows seemed deaf
2 any of my verbal offerings
the only thing they seemed 2 understand
was the pain that I was going through
they laughed out loud and danced in joy
each time raindrops would fall from my eyes
like at this very moment in time
they gather 'round and brush against me
4 they know all 2 well
I'll never escape the shadows of my mind

Randy W. Jones

"Love Inspires"

To start a fire without matches -
To cause a heart to flutter with a glance -
To capture someone's attention with a whisper -
To transform a rainy afternoon into an
enchanting evening -
To dry a tear with a long distance phone call -
To never be afraid to speak the truth -
To always be available to listen -
To be slow to anger and quick to forgive -
To be open to experiment -
To expect a miracle!

Constance R. Kowalczyk

Enchanted By Fire

Brilliantly smoke dances before my eyes, like a graceful minuet it
bows for applause.
Fire tip toes its way across a deserted field, then bursts a blazing
inferno.
The elegance and purity it brings, a symphony in play.
Elegantly dancing above the horizon it sets the sky afire.
Always reaching to be free, it sets off to infinity.

Brian Cole

Life

As I sit and look at the sea,
I remember what life used to be.
Our new car is now old,
The tales it could have told.
Now the sun sets behind the sea,
Nothing like it used to be.
My house that's old, has now been sold.
Many songs not sung,
The tree where the swing once hung.
As I gaze across the sea,
At what life once used to be.
Now the roar of the sea slowly dies away,
I think of our wedding day.
How much we were in love,
When we watched the stars above.
As my sight fades out,
I think of what my life was about.
The people, the places, the smiling faces.
As I draw my last breath, I wonder not about my death.
My life was not bad, there is no reason to be sad.

Erin Mullen

Astern, Head Back Over The Rail

The world flipped upside down
blue
latched at the heels
hugging trails of the horizon
at 35 mph
tongues of waves
tossing their electric cavities
left/right/left
chewing at the cotton of the sky
leaning lazily into my sunbathed
hair
beginning to writhe into miniature
cloud caricatures of the
grand highway
entirely polluted with the freedom of flight
and me, clamped to the hull,
outstretched
to be released and absolutely dead
or
a passenger and half-personified

Richard M. Stachura

The Old Man

There was an old man sitting on a bench
He suddenly looks up to see where life went.

He lowers his head slowly back down to catch
the motion of a caterpillar crawling on the ground

When all was quiet in the still of the day
he smiled at the children as he watched them play

The old man was confused as he started to
cry for he just wanted the answer to why life
passed him by

If you see this old man give him your
time because one day the old man might be
yours or mine.

Glen A. McPherson Jr.

Reincarnation Of Love

Souls,
Interwoven with each other
On another plane,
So long ago,
They cannot recall the place or time.

They respond immediately in this existence
To the Life Force preceding their present being.
An innocent introduction guides them to familiar feelings,
A continuation of delicate memories
Made present by years past.

They meet and are not strangers,
They love and are not lovers.

Somewhere...
Some time ago...
They were.

Cathy Davis

Flame

What makes sense in this world?
Everyone cries, someone dies.
Everything is taken to leave an open wound.

The life, the breath, the heartbeat.
Downward, upside down; a freefall.

But sometimes the spark lives
It reveals an uncovered, unknown joy.

Never before had a different life surfaced;
Engulfed in a flame of fury,
Who could have known it was there?

Through never ending inquisitions
Time must pass

The stars will shoot across the black velvet sky.

The spark lives.
In the glow of the flame lies an unimaginable energy.

For in the flame
Lies the heart.

Marie Porter

Coming Alive

The dreams that I've kept hidden are coming alive
I've spent a lifetime holding back
Just trying to survive...

I've lived inside the shadow
and I've walked a step behind
I've found teachers who I thought as friends,
And sometimes I was blind
Still searching for that place
Where life would treat me kind,
But the light can be so elusive
There's ghosts that try to haunt me
But I won't let them bring me down...
I'll break these chains before the sun goes down.

Because I love the sunshine
And I enjoy the rain;
I've learned to accept the sorrow and the pain
I've spent enough time looking back
And I've searched the soul within...
I've finally got my life on track
Now I'm ready to begin.

Pamela J. Silvernail

"My Special Friend"

She was quiet, she was special
never revealing too many feelings

When she was angry she sent you
reeling never to know whence the
anger came.

Her happy times were few and
sometimes included you.

It seemed sometimes that the life in a
bubble was with no pain. But everything
wonderful is not always sane.

The inner self was private to all, if she
chose you, you felt ten feet tall.

She was special to me - The times we
shared will be fond memories now and
will fill my later days when I think of her.

Forget? I won't know how!

M. Alice Hovey

Be On The Mind Eye

Looking though the mind's eye
seeing be on the start of time
seven dimension of star of time
looking though the blind eye
the brain be on the mind eye
see star light be on time mind eye.
See though light sun of light be on the mind
mind's eye see all.

LeRoy Cape

Nightmare

Bright colors pass and faces swirl,
circles turn and cruel lips curl.
People dance and witches cackle,
animals attack and voices crackle.

Keeping tabs, orders, and so and such,
your temples throbbing way to much;
A blur of colors-red, green, and blue,
traveling places that you never knew.

Telling the future, retelling the past,
with a spot of white and a dark grey cast.

The different shades of colors at dawn,
going places you've never gone.
Meeting people you never met
waking up in a cold sweat.

Marie Wilger

Noon Time Distraction

The bookstore backroom
Not far from instruction books on astral projection
An apprentice clerk lamenting a lack of style is reassured
By the matron (an obvious old hand at this)
"You have a good body. You look good in your clothes."
Overhearing and distracted, I make a temporary decision
today new fiction, tomorrow new age.

In the record shop a clerk transfixed
By a customer's tale of cerebral hemorrhage and death
Has entered an alternative universe.
Unaware she's not talking to HIM until
A glitch in the visual field breaks the trance.
He rings up my purchase, I leave.

Kevin M. Ingraham

I'm Missing You

Someone once said that there is nothing lovelier than a tree.
But to see your smile or hear your voice would be more
beautiful to me.
You proved to be the foundation upon which our family was built,
I hardly ever told you I loved you, alone I bare this guilt.
I miss the afternoons, sitting in the swing,
Being with you, Daddy, that's what happiness really means.
Your life, I never imagined would be cut so short,
Without you, I've existed like a ship without a port.
Pictures I keep with me always, but I cannot bear to view,
The intensity the sadness I feel, because Daddy I'm missing you.
I remember what strength and character you had,
I was very lucky to have you as my Dad.
Now Mom is gone and Mamaw, too.
Oh, Daddy, oh Daddy, this is so hard to go through.
To you, my father, I write these words before I depart.
Take care of Mom and Mamaw, I love each one and every one.
Mamaw, I love each and every one of you from the depths of my heart.

Carron Lee James

Grandma's Love

As I awake each morning to the call of a Dove
I remember times on the farm and all of Grandma's Love
Times have changed but I have not forgotten
How grandma would hold me close and spoil me rotten
I miss the times that still ring in my ear
But with love like Grandma's I will show no fear
As I grow older my heart builds strong
for those who taught me where I belong

Tad Randolph

A Ribbon

A ribbon for my hair is all I really want
But I know that wishes never do come true
My clothes don't fit just right and my feet don't fit my shoes
I never had a pair of lacy tights. But it's O.K., it'll be all right

No more angry words and fists of stone, no more being left alone
Not too much, but just enough food, and I promise I'll be good
And I won't even ask for a ribbon for my hair
I promise I'll never ask for a ribbon for my hair

I really need a hug right now but I'll just close my eyes instead
And picture it is happening inside of my head
I'll hug my pillow real tight, and it'll be O.K., it'll be all right

I'd like to give my eyes away so I can't see other kids play
And you can have my arms too so they'll stop wanting to hold you
And take my heart - it's never been fair. It keeps wishing for a
ribbon for my hair
It's broken anyway. But it's O.K., it'll be all right

You don't even have to say you're sorry. I've never ever blamed you
It's just history repeating itself, cause the same thing was done to
you too
But do you think I'd look pretty with a ribbon in my hair?

Brenda Jane McDaniel

Crystal Renee Johnson

Christ like anointed child, rise, up and walk in Him.
You may not know how to do it. Still try it, life can be dim.
Tell others about God's goodness and you be a great witness for Him.
Let others know you love him. Reach out and touch the sky.
Everyday he'll forever abide at your side.
Never think He doesn't love you, for in every way He'll show you.
Each and every step of the way, Crystal, only you will know.
Oh, just as I am without a shy, only to Christ I'll surrender.
Have confidence in someone; never play guessing games.
Sometimes you may be the victim, one on one I'm sure,
But if you listen to reason,Crystal Johnson, only you'll endure.

Cheryl E. Harp

My Friend

My friend, where have you gone
you used to be right by my side
now you're nowhere to be found

I call your name left and right
but now the wind just carries it away
for my heart longs for you
to be by my side

The love, the laughter, the time together
now are just fond memories
but I wish the things we did
together could be brought back to me

But now I know the time is
gone except for the memories
So now, my friend is no longer
near so I'll cherish those sweet memories

Debi Beard

Ghost

I am like a ghost,
the one everybody ignores the most.

I speak, but they do not hear.
I cry, but they don't see my tears.

It hurts to be alone,
When everyone treats you as if you were unknown.

Maybe I am no longer alive,
No one sees me, I must have died.

Sarah Estes

A New Dawn

We all want to fly like the bird on the wing, and share in the
rewards that life brings.
We all want to stand upon a peaceful sandy shore and touch the
wind as we feel our spirit sore.
We all want to release the pains of rejection and know that we are a
part of life's resurrection.
we all must know that the time has come and take the first steps in
knowing the healing has begun.
We all have felt the pain of the blood that stains the land fore on
both sides it is shed, it was not white or black but the color was
red. Fore, we all feel the sun that shines on high, its rays
caresses the flesh of both you and I.
We all feel the cooling kiss of the rain as it cascades upon the
land, its cleansing renewal of breath envelopes all in its extended
hand.
So tell me, if our creator knows no difference in race, creed, or
gender, how could we be anything except tender.
Fore, to move forward in development and beyond, we are going to
have to prepare for a new dawn.

Veronica Bynum Dudley

Keep Going

Dedicated to Michael Robert, Thank you very much for everything

I believe to achieve
You must climb slowly to the top
You must not look back
Along the way you must not stop

But to keep going, to keep looking up
Keep yourself focused on your destination
You may have obstacles to overcome
You may have good times and frustration

Keep your head up, your hopes up
Set your limits to the sky
Follow to the end, reach that peak
Say to yourself, who has done it? "It is I!"

Stephanie Dennis

To Please My Heart

I look at you, I read on your face
That you are not happy, but have just faith.

It doesn't even show a tender smile,
and your thought seems to be far a mile.

Your voice is not strong, firm and clear,
as I always loved to hear.

I know something hurt your feeling.
I hope it's nothing serious, not even fear.

I don't like to see you that way.
My heart cries and can't help you in any way.

I would like to know a little about,
but you give me no part and we get more apart.

I want to hear your voice loud again,
it gives me joy, peace and I feel as a friend.

Your voice sound to my hard ears
like a sweet melody, because it is to me so dear.

I would like to entreat with all my heart,
to hear your voice with a lovely sound,
singing "L'Ave Maria" to please my heart.

Maria De Dona

My Son, Johnny

Ever since you were a little boy
You have been my pride and joy

Now you have grown up
And have a son of your own
I know your worry until he
Is safely back home

On July the 20th you turned fifty-one
But you are still my number one son

I pray for you and each night and day
That God will guide you on your way
And when your days work is done
That God will ride with you
And bring you safely home

At night I pray he will give you a good night's rest
Because in my eyes you are the best

Ella G. Jennings

Seventh Heaven

Here we are in the cabin again, not sorry
that we came, and no complaining
about not having some modern
conveniences
We are here in the mountains, cabin that
my grand father and three of his friends
found, there is drift roads and out
This place
is away from pollution and aggravation
every night you can look up at the
stars, you see about 200 billion stars
and some nights you can even see the milky way
Each night you can sit by the bonfire
make snores, sing campfire songs,
and look at the stars
but only for a short time you can do this
then you have to go back to pollution
aggravation, modern conveniences and
back to reality

Suzy Lusich

Winter's Storm

Snow flakes driven by the wind are so white,
Nature in all of its glory, a beautiful sight,

Covering the ground at a ferocious pace,
The trees bended branches look like Victorian Lace.

Winter in New England can be harsh and oh so long,
But not to enjoy the day would be terribly wrong.

Read a good book, talk to a friend on the phone,
Know that you are never really alone.

Listen to children's laughter as they play in the snow,
Watch as they climb up a hill with their sleds in tow.

A snow angel they make, or a snowman so tall,
Playing hide and seek behind a snow fort's wall.

Children don't need a reason to enjoy the snow,
And they don't mind when the cold winds blow.

It's only adults that find reasons to complain,
When the weather is cold and there is snow or rain.

Enjoy the beauty of this wonderful day,
The snow is pure and white but it's not here to stay.

It will soon be gone and in its place,
Trees will bloom in their glory for the whole human race.

M. Fay Semple

Dread And Sorrow

I'm filled with dread and sorrow!
I feel I have know feelings...no happiness or sadness!
On the 'morrow, 'twill only bring me more dread and sorrow?
I dread my fears, I dread my happiness,
I sorrow my death, for I've died much too long ago,
I mourn me, I'm always filled with the feelings
of dread and sorrow.
My soul gave up long ago, and my heart stopped beating
the Love that is once felt!
just dread and sorrow each... Day in and Day out.
I dread the next day, then it comes, and I'm filled with
sorrow, for I've died much too long ago, my soul is gone
I'm filled with Dread and Sorrow.

Laura L. Tokach

One Soldier's View

Well, here I am
Where, I don't exactly know
They say Saudi Arabia
Funny, all I see is sand
There's lots of us here
There's lots of them too
How are we going to win?
Then again, how can we lose?
What are we fighting for?
Oil? Kuwait's people?
Or are we just here?
I can't wait to leave, if I do.
I can't die,
It won't happen to me.
I've got a wife and two kids.
They need me, I need them. I'm not in a POW camp
I'm in something worse: Hell, Confusion, Depression
It's called "Operation: Desert Storm"
Lord, please keep us safe
but most of all Let Us Get Home!

Kelli Berg

Friendship

If you ever need a loving friend
a warming heart that will always bend,
You can honestly know I do care.

If your heart takes a crumbling fall,
You can count on me to catch it all.

If ever your dreams come to a desperate end,
I'll be there to help them start again.

When you're sitting in a corner,
All lonely with fear,
And you need someone to be near,
Just call on me,
I'll lend you a shoulder,
You can count on me.

Now in your heart,
You know it's true,
I am a Friend,
I will never abandon you!

Tammy Kensinger

He Is Faithful That Promised

So often as a little girl I'd shake my head and say,
How could God's children be so dull, so stiff necked in their ways?
They'd gripe and grumble, nag, complain, as Moses led them on.
In spite of all the miracles, they saw only what was wrong,
Their eyes were firmly focused on problems great and small,
Instead of on the mighty God who delivered from them all.
"You tell 'em, God!" I'd say aloud as I read the stories in His Word.
All the wonderful things You promised them - it seems they never even heard.

The years have passed and now I find so often I'm distressed;
Troubled, weary, bruised and worn, filled with unhappiness.
Oh, God, how long must this go on? Can't You see the pain?
I've prayed, I've tried, I've given my all; yet nothing seems to change.
Then like the stirring in the trees caused by a gentle wind,
The memories stir in my mind and I can see again
Those grumbling children walking 'round the barren wilderness,
Complaining, griping, murmuring; filled with such unrest.
Oh, God, I am so like them, though I don't want to be.
I ask You to forgive me, Lord, cleanse me, set me free.
Please help me keep my mind on You and trust Your plan for me.
For only as I trust You, Lord, can I be what You want me to be.

Rebecca Bunner

Just To Be Known

Like the gently moving trees as the wind blows through
You have come to me,
You have moved me slowly with your gentle hand
Just to be known and make your stand;
Like the waves crashing on the oceans surf
You overwhelmed me,
You caught me off guard forcing your care upon my heart
Just to be known and create your art;
Like a bird spreading his wings to fly
You have flown away,
You have exercised your freedom to be who you are
Just to be known and watched from afar;
Like a baby when it's time to be fed
You have come back to me,
You have taken from me the things which you need
Just to be known, you planted a seed;
Like a seed, which grows from the sun
You feed off of me
You have taken from my energy and grown inside
Just to be known, yet still you hide.

Julie Crawford Grubbs

Twas The Night Of Christmas

Santa was good to us this year you
have to admit. The presents kept
coming and they just wouldn't quit!
With the game of checkers and a
nursery doll, and lots and lots of little
candy balls. With the game of
Backgammon and some spray to make
her hair wavey, and some little shaving
creams opened by Ami. Dad especially
loved his shaving cream gel, he loved
it so much that he let out a yell! Dad
made the dinner and mom helped to,
then we sat down and ate all our food.

Ashlee Michelle Tremayne

The Olympics - Atlanta 1996

The people of Atlanta are very excited.
For to our city, the world has been invited.
The athletes are coming from far and near.
As they seek to win, we should all cheer.

Olympic products will be bought and sold.
With alot of determination the athletes will
win the bronze or gold.
The Olympic flame is traveling across the countryside.
At our new Olympic stadium it will soon abide.

The opening ceremonies are just a week away
My hope is that the athletes and visitors will
find enough places to stay.
The olympics mascots name is Izzy.
With the extreme Georgia heat the
Visitors may feel a little dizzy.
As the olympics come to our city.
May we as Georgians show the visitors
hospitality a plenty.

Denise Williams

Dreaming

Off in a world that is all my own,
In a place where no one's alone.
A time that only I can paint the pictures
Of far off countries with emperors.
I alone can make a girl's dream come true,
I can also make those who are happy be blue.
I can make a criminal receive his justice,
I can wed two people and lead them into honeymoon bliss.
I can have a bird sing any tune,
Even make it snow in the month of June.
There is only one door to this place -
I hold the key and am ready for adventures to unlace.

Renee Lam

Understanding

Somewhere in time, unexpectedly, our spirit will be lifted from us.

Taken to Another place.
A peaceful place to watch over those we care about.
Those left behind often wonder why things like this occur.
The purpose may be unclear for eternity or may present itself unexpectedly.
But none the less there is a reason.
Just knowing that someone we care about was at peace when the end was near.
There is no more suffering they must endure should make our life easier.
Knowing that the spirit will linger and our friend will always remain in our memory should be enough.

Suzanne Compton

Thank You

Thank you for being so kind,
And giving me a father that I can call mine.
You could have said no,
And gone away.
But you said yes,
And I hope you're here to stay.
Through the good times and the bad,
You have always been there,
To show me you love me and that you care.
Sometimes we play,
Sometimes we fight,
and sometimes you guide with your guiding light.
In my mind,
you're my dad,
'cause you loved me even when I was bad.
Thank you for giving me a father to love.
And every day I think the good Lord above

Angela Bazan

Long Distance

We spoke yesterday,
Long distance.
Pleasant, friendly chit-chat.
Your voice, warm and familiar,
But separate from you, your self,
Distant.
I wonder, did you hear my longing,
My need?
Did you hear my desire for you?
For your touch, your arms, your love?
I am afraid we're too distant,
Always.
I am afraid more lies between us than miles.
I am afraid
There will never be more than this...

Lee Carrington

From Pop To Pinhead

I got a PINhead for a boyfriend
my boyfriend's got a BIG PINhead
Pinhead left to party with POP
out POPping into parties ought not
"oh Go—Go pinhead, Go!" says POP
out POPs pinhead - butt in POP burns

Doesn't matter where it's at
yeah they really are like that
kind a like two (2) acrobats
think they're in a funky frat

Say POP kept pinhead for lots-o-FUN
though FUNny-POP said Pinhead hurt
GUESS still no voice POPped in their minds
of mindly damage pinned RED to them
from POP to Pinhead's life light burned
POP parties still - butt no one minds!

N. Lydia Viezza

Music Magic

It draws me in,
But on my own accord.
It smothers me with feelings,
But lets me breathe sweet air.
It drowns me with sound,
But teaches me to swim in it.
It stabs me with reality,
But heals my every wound.
Leaving me unhurt,
But not untouched.

Anne Vath Flowers

Why?

Tears run down my face as I hear your voice say good-bye.
I sit back trying to think of the answer of why?
I think to myself was it me? Or something that I have
done, to cause this problem, if it was me, what was it and why?
Another thought passes through my mind, maybe it was
your family; holding you back from letting your true feeling show,
But I still try to understand the reasons of why?
My mind goes faster and faster trying to think of why?
So many questions, so little time to speak, to get the
answers I seek of why?

If your feelings for me are only half as strong as mine
are for you, you will understand:
I need to know why?

Kimberly A. Buchholz

Warm Colors Of A Dream

Hear the sounds of clear blue water,
With moonlight on his face,
Flowing softly over rocks and sand,
His journey rough at times on his pathway to life.

Hear the sounds of gray-blue waves,
As he reaches for shore,
Spreading out his arms,
To hold on to what's in store.

Feel the sound of him as he moves from shore to land,
Holding in his powerful hands all the things he has gathered,
To share with others through the light in his eyes,
And the music in his heart,
The warm colors of sound in his voice.

Hear the sounds of clear blue water
As he sails the sea of time,
Reaches out and touches his dreams,
One warm starlit night.

Gloria A. Carter

Loved

He the one who has been loved,
not knowing his thoughts or emotions,
thinking falsely lead him into motion.
Pain ached within his soul, his mind gone numb,
and his heart still whole...

...His dreams all fade, his face gone sad,
his heartache hoping it will soon all end.

He the one who has been loved
was loved inaccurately,
that my friend is sad enough
and will his heartache mend?

Natalie Lam

Dreams

Late at night while you sleep you have
Little thoughts that make you weep, these
Little thoughts are in your mind that keep
You dreaming all the time

You dream of life you dream of death you
Dream of things that take your breath you
Dream of love you dreams of hate you dreams
Of things you would appreciate

Your dreams are happy your dreams are sad
Your dreams are of things you never had
Your dreams are true your dreams are real
Your dreams are of things you can't feel

Dreams of the hearts and minds dreams of
The lovely times, dreams, dreams wonderful
Dreams I will all dreams could not be seen

Dennis Sasser

Fall In The Mountains

The mountains are an array of colors,
The sources of these beautiful colors are beginning to fall.
The weather is cool and pleasant, with an occasional breeze.
The sky is a lovely shade of blue,
And is filled with white, fluffy clouds.
Birds are chirping,
Squirrels are scurrying around to find food to store for the
approaching winter.
A lone deer stops for a drink at a bubbling brook,
Its tall antlers almost get caught in the branches above it.
In the brook's clear waters,
The reflections of everything surrounding it can be seen.
A mouse is soon followed by a hawk who flies by at top speed.
Minutes later, the mouse's squeal can be heard,
The hawk has caught it.
This is what fall is like up in the mountains,
Everything is just part of the picture, what they have to do.
Whether they are animals hunting for food, or just a simple little leaf,
Everything plays an important part to create a picturesque scene.

Miriam Leah Bauman

Universal Plea

I looked upon a moonlit night,
with a large twinkle in the sky.
Its beauty shined across the ocean,
And guided the sea ships passing by.
Like an oracle of this time, I saw
our future floating near. Our
carelessness evidently centered now,
And our fate disturbingly clear.
A floating fish on its back, and
trash washed on the shore. The
deeds of our daily tasks, it's for
the sake of industry, the toxic
dumpers justly say. Have the
murky waters of our existence, come to say?

Benjamin Sanders

Save My Soul

Here I stand before the golden gate
And realizing my ended fate
Looking at all my wrongs and rights
While I walk towards the bright light
Seeing heaven before my eyes
Knowing how I never got to say good-bye
Not knowing what lies ahead
Trying to remember the last words I said
As I stand tall and brave
Wondering if my soul will be saved
As I look in the face of God
He just gives me a nod
Hearing voices from the past
And wondering what judgment he will cast
As I stand in such fear
Of the judgment he will bare
As I stand there and cry
I let out a quiet sigh
Oh, Lord save my soul
Because the dark is so very cold...

Jennifer J. Villanueva

Your Love

Your love is like a restless wind that blows among the trees
It crossed my path then left me to weep upon my knees.

I thought you really loved me I thought you really cared
How could you be so cruel to leave me hanging there?

To rise among the winds then fall among the leaves
My heart is not a play thing to do with as you please.

Betty Jones

The Life

We Orcas spend our day swimming
Searching for food
We like the big fish
The seagulls are our friends
They like cleaning our teeth
Our fun is jumping out of the water
It is better when people are watching
They especially like our songs
Which we take big pride in
We try to stay out of the way of shrimp nets
Or we will get caught
And our oil will become cosmetics
With the beautiful ladies wearing it
On their faces
Or be put in the shows
And we will be playing with someone like
Shamu and Namu
We have been caught
And it wasn't a pretty sight!

Christopher Tort

Loving

The bowl of cut flowers sits,
Bathed in vagrant sunbeams and dust motes.
Silent voices vainly strain, cry out,
"I am life. I am both potential and fruition.
The past is carried forth in me,
And I am the beginning of what is yet to be."
Each petal, form, and shape,
A clamoring for completion,
An edifice of essence.
Exquisitely interlocking necessities,
Produced this elegance,
A singularity of grace and pride.
And someone, stricken by such beauty,
So loved these precious blossoms,
That he cut them,
And they died.

Stephen C. Kirtland

The Magic Of The Fair

Round and round and up and down
The carousel spins its charm.
As the music whirls, the carousel twirls,
I caress the steed in my arms.

I close my eyes as my pony glides.
I can feel the wind in my hair.
My dreams take wings as the music sings.
There is magic at the Fair.

Then high in the sky the ferris wheels rise.
I can see the stars in your eyes.
As it turns around to a happy sound,
There is laughter in your cries.

I dance on my toes, beneath the bright light that glows
And the music fills the night.
I laugh and sigh and my spirits are high,
Oh, what a beautiful sight.

All the music and lights fill the night with such sights
And my soul can respond to the sound.
Tonight at the Fair, in the warm summer air,
There is magic all around.

Geraldine Ives

Mothering

One woman carried and gave birth to me.
The beginning of a lifetime of nurturing morality and dignity.
But, it took more than one woman to mother me. My mother,
grandmother, godmother, church-mothers, aunts and a host of
others fostered me. These women concluded that raising a child
isn't just a mother's responsibility. Together they lead, guided, and
directed me; instilling a strong sense of security. Motherly love
loves unconditionally, which by no means meant they failed to
discipline; consequently discipline confirmed their love for me
causing me to render respect and to submit to authority. The
restrictions and high standards these women imposed weren't their
own. They too, had to yield to a greater power, that of the Deity.
With bowed heads and bended knees they spent much time praying
for me believing that the blessings of God would be mine and that I
would find love, joy and peace in troubled times. With out-stretched
hands they anointed me, symbolizing God's protection externally.
Mothering is the noblest of deeds for it empowers children to
succeed. Praising them builds confidence and self-esteem; filling
their lives with hopes and dreams; reminding them that they can
conquer anything. Citing past experience as evidence of our
invincibility. The women who most inspired me are my mother,
grandmother, godmother, church-mothers, aunts and a host of
others. These women, I affectionately call mother.

Charlotte S. Weathers

Life's A Mystery

We hope we are here for a reason,
Better to hope than to live without meaning.
But still the mystery of life eludes us,
Hard as we try we cannot deduce it.
The sands of time march swiftly by,
With the pace of our lives, how can it not fly.

We hardly notice the beauty around us,
Or fail to recognize kindness that shrouds us,
So rather than hasten, why not slow the pace,
And look at the wonder of this wondrous place.
Far better to live and love where you are,
Than save it for sometime or some distant star.

Lila J. Bradley

If Tears Could Speak

If one tear could speak a thousand words,
then I've cried enough tears for all to have heard,
the stories of my life, the secrets of my heart,
my cries in the night and my fears in the dark.

If just one tear could speak, then it alone would tell
how much pain and sorrow
in my soul does dwell.

It would tell of my heartbreaks and whisper my failures,
mention all my mistakes and
repeat lost prayers.

Just one tear alone could tell the secrets of my soul
as it makes its short journey
down Tear Streak Road.

If my tears could speak, they would probably scream
as if just waking from a horrible dream;
or maybe they'd whisper, but it doesn't matter either way.
If they could speak they'd speak the words I long to say.

Dionne Smith

"I Wish"

I wish to be the words that touch your lips.
I wish to be the hands that feel your skin.
I wish to be the tears that show your pain.
I wish to be the shadow that defines your frame.

Susanna Ricciardi

The Homeless Lost Woman On The Bench

Speaking alone, in jumbled words, for nary a one was there,
Venting her troubled soul, was she, to the heedless, moving air.
As I neared the bench on which she sat, this toothless woman with
tangled hair
Looked at me with clouded eyes, puzzled that I was there.

"Oh lost woman," I silently asked —

"What banished you to this ill fate, were your paths too rocky to trod?
Did a helping hand extend too late; were your needs just lost in the
crowd?
Why are you ranting to the wind, when there are humans to be found?
Did they, in your past, not hear your plea, and in life's din was
drowned?"

'Tis so mankind has looked away, too many lost souls ignored;
Somehow we've failed our fellow-man and closed humanity's door.
In our failure to see the growing need, unheeding the moving tide,
Could we be swept to the open sea; could we, alone survive?

Helen Munhall

Duel - Duet

Of nighttime screaming blackness awe
came riding two fellows — one young, one old
clashing in the midnight breeze
without a reason known to the older one
except in the deeper reaches of his mind
thrusting, gashing, and clashing they came
two enemies unable to find a compatible union

Perhaps tonight I'll discover who you are
nemesis or purveyor of love worshiped in sanctuary
approach for now, young soul — my guard is down
let me see your timid eyes, your timid face
ah me, 'tis the boy I once was without disguise
allow me a hug and conversation just a short while
to take a moment's rest from life's delusion

Gordon L. Rogowitz

"I Want To Be A Boy Again"

I want to be a boy again. I want to look to the outside.
I don't want to feel on the inside. I want to touch the
stars, because they're only a few miles away. I want to
be taught, I don't want to learn. I want security in my
mother's arms. I don't want a cold shoulder and a smile
that rarely happens by strangers passing by.

I want to climb up a tree, not fall down a staircase.
Each step back to the top costs too much. I want the sun to
shine on me, while the birds sing their songs conditioned
only for my ears.

I don't want to feel the rain fall on me from the dark sky.
It's like an ogre stomping on me like a tin can.
I want to roll in the grass, and I want to find a four leaf clover.
I don't want to bet my life and pray for snake eyes.

I want to go back from where I came from.
This road is long and weary, who knows what lies ahead.
I want to be a boy again.

Randy A. Donnelly

The Bright Eastern Moon

My hands can not move,
My arms can not shift,
My eyes can not look upon the bright eastern moon,
My nose can not smell the sugar sweet flowers,
My ears can not hear the whisper of the willows,
My mouth can not taste the breath of the breeze,
My feet can not walk upon the new fallen snow,
And my legs cannot run with the wild ones out there.

Kathleen Marthaler

Our Memory Of Pop

His warm smile would always make you want to sit and talk awhile.
His warm embrace would keep a smile on your face.
God sat up high and looked down low.
He saw all his suffering from illness and decided it's time for him to go.
Time for him to go to a higher, greater place. (Heaven)
And if we're all living according to God's will we will again one day see his face.
It's so hard to believe he was here today and gone tomorrow and all we're left with is a lot of pain and sorrow.
But only God knows what's best, he knew it was time for him to rest.
So Pop it's goodbye for now but not forever.
We'll see you when we get to Heaven.

Sandwanda Moore

"One Lone Tear"

One lone tear.
It rolls slowly down the crevices of her cheek.
It feels her pain.
It knows her fear.
It shares her loneliness.
It too feels betrayed; unloved; unwanted.
It reaches her chin and pauses.
It leaps off into nowhere.
All alone.
Just one lone tear.

Heather Olson

The Storm

The silence, a great hush
Gray skies hugging tall pines
Stretching high and black
Like spires on a cathedral
A feeling, all expecting, suspended in time — then symphony,
big brass band... Beethoven, Wagner..., all at once lightning
Rending, ripping thunder... rain, release, relief

The sky, blue, timid
Peeping a smile through a hole in the clouds
The wind still whispering at my window
"Come and see"
Outside tears of rain, as hesitant to fall
From the still, trembling flowers
The sun... warm, delicious filling my whole being
The pines, the fragrance, beauty every where...
Precious moments to savor the wonder of life.

Marie L. Hayes

Lights Of The Christmas Tree

The lights glow on many boxes
with ribbons red are tied.
Happy hearts may find things they like
from them they love inside.
The smiles of folks who are true
and laughter gay.
In the lights of the Christmas tree
upon this Christmas Day.

Tonight life seems so fair and sweet,
you pursuing the light of a star.
But strange were the streets I walked today
and sad were the faces along the way.
Oh! for the sound of a friendly soul
But there was nowhere to go.
Will we ever meet again in the
lights of the Christmas tree?

Elizabeth P. Myers

The Puritan Way

Those fine fingerling green grasses under
Gnarl-sprawled, old, tall trees left to lift from decay.
Headstones and a few footstones lean roundabout,
Slate fingernails pointing to their heaven,
Held down by richly aged, human-made earth.

Vestigial Puritan treasury guarded by their undepicted God,
And their charnel, skullwinged icons with symbols,
Now preserved by our wariness yet intone warning on warning.

Taking down epitaphs and making rubbings, a zeitgeist heist.
With head resting on headstone's rear and reading personals,
On columns, slates and flat ground-set slabs and feasting
by the ones atop six short columns: tablestones.

From a lamentable list of maladies and accidents,
Puritans had their daily cognition of lives taken,
"Down to death's cave all dismal,"

Wearing their lives as shrouds, wanting clouds,
Expecting firmamental wrath, without knowing,
They saluted their "King of Terrors" in the meetinghouse
while flat-toothed, winged skulls grinned through prayers
and waited in the fine fingerling green grasses beyond.

W. Andy Meier

My Peaceful Thoughts

I want peace because too many are
getting hurt before any crime just
give a dime. I hope peace will
stop dope to make people cope better
with their problems, I like peace
it is fine for a person to comes
out to dine. If you think about
peace you don't have to drink to
mess up your sink. When peace come
to mind it makes me feel kind. There's
peace in the world but if anyone care
you won't have a lot to bear. Talk
about peace for a while to walk with
peace each day of your life. I know
peace is just a word for the Lord
is something you need if you ask
me. Put your trust in peace to get
your act together, peace is joy to me
so go get God in your life to be a better
person. Peace is right so come into the light.

Viola S. Scott

On My Back Porch

Some people dream of places far away,
And covet with zeal other's lives today.
On my back porch I feel at peace,
For every creature that sings, seems to provide release.

Everyone wants to be some where other than where we are,
And years spent wasting seems so bizarre.
But on my back porch I am where I am,
For here there is no need of a map or diagram.

On my back porch there is no limit,
No space, nor time - we are all in it,
I can touch a star with my eyes and heart
Or capture the full moon without being too smart.

My memory holds the face of the rising sun,
or becomes breathless at the mauve color in the setting one.
My ears hears and my eyes see,
The rain fast approaching me.

On my back porch no time is spent,
Wishing or wanting what is already heaven sent.
So if you are searching for travel and excitement,
You may need not look further than your own environment.

Julie Williams

Plowing Fields, Midsummer

The plowmen stand one front, one back
of the swayback, ancient, once-was
colt.

He stands three legged, ankle deep
while one back heaves aside a rock
that, as a colt, he could have moved
twenty times if once a
day.

One front, a patient hand on
one ear pulls gently and with
the other brushes clinging flies from
the corners of his eyes, his nose, and
mouth.

How old is he, are they all who stand
as an age old picture in the half plowed
field?

As old as wisdom, as knowledge,
as the earth they work.

Gael Williams Gardner

The Light

A boy once lived where the moon shines bright.
His room was big and aglow with light.
But then one dark and stormy night,
It iced and froze the light out of sight.
The boy woke up at about 5:00.
He thought he was still in his dream it was so dark.
And so the boy he screamed for his mom,
And she said "My boy now you just stay calm."
And so the boy did, and as quickly as dawn
The sun it came up and the light came back on.

A boy once lived where the moon shines bright.
His room was big and aglow with light.
But then one dark and stormy might,
The ice froze the power and turned out the light.
To the boy's screaming his grandmother roused, she tried to sleep,
But her mind just browsed. The boy, he was frightened, the lights
Were a gloom, for seconds he thought he was trapped in his room.
The boy got a flashlight, that came from his mom, and with it,
He was able to get himself calm. And so the boy did, and
As quickly as dawn, the sun, it came up and the darkness was gone.

Elaine Silvious

A Flight Of Hope

My hand is held gently,
Family surround me.
The blues, all varying shades,
The whites - iridescent
Somehow the roar, the speed
has a gentleness
that one would not expect.

Thoughts emanate in my mind,
Only God could transmit such feeling, love, beauty.
Destination - the land that is part of our
very essence, our very being.

A land of spiritual history, couched
in fact and mystery,
a holy land.
Please God, let it be a light unto us and all the nations
May the light bring peace, beloved of God,
beloved of His people.
A love that transcends all love -
an endless love for those who seek Him,
an endless love of our King, who fathoms all.

Norma Breite

From One Pet Lover To Another Pet Lover

I love hearing my pet cat purr when he is
happy. It just melts me in tears at times. He is
so happy it makes you want to hug him so long. Let's
not forget that good feeling. Also he likes to
play with my pen and tennis ball. That is what is so
special for anyone with a pet of their own.

I wish everyone has the joy to remember
their special pet or person in their life. Young
and old enjoy their pets. More people need a pet for
their own. It wouldn't be the same without these
pets in our lives. Thank you Lord for giving me
a heart for animals.

Paula Gray

Alone

One might wonder how it feels to be all alone.
I know for myself because all of my friends are gone.
Not because they are dead, buried, or moved away.
It's because I destroyed our friendship for a simple date.
Yes, I destroyed our friendship all for a man.
How ignorant I was because he left me and ran.
Now that I realized how important a true friend is to me.
I'll never destroy a friendship and go back the way I used to be.
I let down my friends and family as well.
Now my life is a living hell.
And now I sit and reminiscence of the wonderful friendship we've
had.
But now it's too late because I can't rekindle the past.
And now that our friendship is dead and gone.
I have finally learned my lesson and moved on.
All that I thought was so divine and true.
I can't help but to wonder if it was meant for us two.

Katina York

Life

Life is something you don't choose.
I and also you don't get a second chance.

Mistakes are made and also meant for.
That we must learn from the past not the future.

Life's a song that you wake up on the way.
It may not become out perfect or how you plan it at the moment.
But at the last word your understand and that the path you choose,
turns out the way you plan.

I don't expect you to understand this poem,
but I expect the truth from you all.

I expect you to listen to the song at the end,
and understand the path you took.
I expect you to understand why he/she, wife/husband,
friend/bestfriend
or girlfriend/boyfriend left you at your stubborn moments
and return at your happy and sad moments.

Why expect so much? Why I care?
Because maybe in the second world
you'll remember the old path
and still begin the knew path.

Sarah Stehman

B-Rated Movie

The film director in the beret tells you,
that all this is for the sake of art.
He touches you only the way you touch yourself,
they are expecting answers.

The choice is yours

Microwave stardom,
or doomed obscurity

The choice is yours

People volunteer for medical experiments,
solely to claim some "dead presidents"

The choice is yours

The psychic frauds charge,
$4.95 each additional minute.

The choice is yours

In your dream everybody wears rubber,
the photographer couldn't stop the shutter.
The non-English speaking immigrant working at the
drive-through shouts:
the check out time is noon, sir,

The choice is yours

Jonathan Chen

Seasons' Greetings

I entered an emerald park and the gardener said to me:
"Young blood, have thee fared well?"
"Yes", replied I, though in actuality,
It was too early to tell.
Too early to tell...

In summer heat I heard the same from lifeguards three,
And got caught in honesty's spell.
Stated I, "History is mystery,
And still too early to tell."
Too early to tell...

I pondered this in the brisk autumn breeze,
Tossing wishes in a bottomless well,
Denying, while ignoring the fallen leaves,
That only time will tell.
Only time will tell.

I at last inquired such of my memory,
Just as the first winter flakes fell,
But collapsing lids could not answer me,
For it was too late to tell.
Too late to tell...

Stephen Welford

"Merci" (Thank You)

As we take out time in our lives to pause,
have we forgot how to say "thank you,"
or, do we chalk it up to another lost cause?
Visibly, the amenities of life have been
pushed aside, as parents are no longer at home to guide.
Living has now surpassed giving in our daily routine.
If there is nothing materially to gain, why
bother with the mundane?
A return to barbarism is bound to occur, if
the few remaining fail to stir.
A higher standard of life is available still,
for those who have the will.
The reward will be great, and very easy
to generate, for all those who are willing to participate.

Harold B. Fuller

Penitential

Black, strong swans ripping ocean froths apart
good newspapers covered in cherries climb dirty mts.
Sick on the desert carpet, 3 limp camels
held together with thread. Great pillars of money
wear away to lower foundations. Breeze zips bodies apart
leaves climb back in their shoots, dogs turn bloody
at the snouts trying to get out of the fenced yards
foreign tongued nationals pick up the crack pipe for peace
silly daydreams invade shop fronts, celebrities are raped
hardly at random. Bookmarks are left unbought
black holes in the deep blue horizon, hookers turn to religion
I sit down, figuring this is going to take a while

Ben Ohmart

Untitled

Sadness and sorrow filled the hearts
for my grandfather did depart.
Left this earth with a sudden cause
To leave us lonely, at peace, and at pause.
Everyone was lost and confused
Because of what they had to lose.
Their choices were not considered at all
Because he took his final lost fall.
Left this place in a big hurry
and left everyone else just to worry.

Ben Knoerdel

Cat Nap

I sit in a meeting examining my thumb.
I've grown so bored my brain has gone numb.

Hour after hour the speaker drones on.
I look to the ceiling and stifle a yawn.

As I prop up my head and drift off to sleep,
Kitty moves in and takes a quick peek.

She looks around at a sea of dead faces
thinking they'd love her feline graces.

She leaps to a table with a growl and a hiss.
Then purring with joy, she does a few flips.

She bounds to the front, tail swishing with glee,
laughing within as the delegates flee.

Tossing papers and notes and books helter-skelter,
her eyes fill with mischief as the guests take shelter.

She extends her claws and her fangs take to gleam.
Mayhem and chaos erupt on the scene.

Then, without warning, I startle awake
and wonder how long this meeting could take.

Lila Bailey

Rain Forest Girl

I've heard wonderful news about you.
You've already made this world a better place,
with your happy smile and pretty face.
You're what's lacking in this world an
innocent child a rain forest girl.
I hope it does not fall upon you the
carelessness of the humane race. If it
does call upon me I'll help you put it
back in place.
A girl like you can go quite far,
like sailing on a shooting star. In years
to come as we grow old. I love you
Rain I've told you so.

Dan Mishko

Yesterday's Cowboy

Yesterdays cowboy was silent and strong,
He came to your rescue when things went wrong.

His boots were dusty and his face was lean,
At times he was gentle, at times he was mean.

He sweated all day in the noon days sun,
Six days for work and one day for fun.

Into town he would wide, for a drink and smoke,
Then off to the bath-house, for a real good soak.

There he sweet-talked the ladies and brawled with the men,
Loving and fighting was really no sin.

But time goes by quickly, then things started to change,
Things got very different, out there on the range.

Though we still have some Cowboys, they're just not the same,
Some ride wild horses and some ride the train.

Today, our cowboys can't even smoke,
Every one tells him it might make him crooked.

He can't rob a bank, and he can't shoot his gun,
What's left in this world for him to have fun?

But even with changes, we don't give a dam,
Cause Yesterday's Cowboy still our kind of man.

Mary Ellen Barkley

One More Time

Time is going by so increasingly fast,
sometimes I wonder how much longer I'll last.
As my youth drifts away like yesterdays news,
I just can't shake these "aging ole' blues.
Little lines that have formed around my eyes,
only fill my soul with sadness and sighs.
My once youthful look, so innocent and pure,
now all those memories are lost and obscure.
Although now I am filled with the knowledge of life,
I'm someone's grandma and someone's wife.
The older I get, the more clearly I see,
that mother natures game is no game to me.
Be young at heart and live happy and long,
sounds so cliche', like an old time song.
For one more chance to dance happy and free,
with no arthritis or catch in my knee.
I would cherish that moment, that forever be mine,
and accept her steps as we dance through time.

Desiree L. Rice

Untitled

I used to play in the rain. Taking my shoes off, drowning just the
same in - "Love"
Those days barefeet and puddles, splashing all over my dress-
what a mess - "Love"
Dressed to perfection - then all apart, rain in my hair and on
my heart.
I use to play in the rain. Afternoon showers, all those
hours of - "Love"
Water fit for drinking falling from above.
The taste of fine wine for kings and queens
A bar of soap and I'm spanking clean.
Look! All the flowers growing, taking their afternoon bath.
I use to laugh in the rain - summers pure pleasure
bathing me head to toe, running fast or slow
I'm soaking just the same. Such pure delight!
Rainbow circles up above in flight - "Love"
The smell of roses in my hair and apples green.
Childhood days so much more than what they seemed
Childhood days, more that I ever dreamed of.
Childhood, rain, and - "Love"

Summer Rain.

Nancy Carolyn Myers

Birthdays

10 years are shining ones,
Filled with fun and games.
20 years are heavenly ones,
Filled with romantic dreams.
30 years are serious ones,
Filled with responsibilities and pain.
40 years are fruitful ones,
Filled with satisfaction and gain.
50 years are Golden ones,
Filled with accomplishments and maybe fame.
60 years are promising ones,
Filled with dreams and schemes.
70 years are weighty ones,
Filled with hopes and sunbeams.
80 years are restful ones,
Filled with thoughts of fulfilled dreams.
90 years are sacred ones,
Filled with memories of things you've done and seen.
100 years - You've done it all it seems.

Minnie Houseman

The Joker

The game he is playing
has all the cards in his favor.
With an ace of hearts by his side
he searches for the queen of diamonds.
Never telling the other players
that he's cheating on their trust,
Only confusing their minds
with his casual underhanded plays.
Dealing a hand full of lies
from one game to the next,
Never regretting the decisions he makes.
Sneaking around the table,
Winning every round with his charming smile
and those misrepresented brown eyes.
If only those foolish players would realize,
He's a joker.

Donna Sapp

Special Cowboy

He was, a bronc rider! He was a bull rider!
For, oh so many years!!
But now he's gone-
the special man we all cherished!!
The special man we all loved!!
One of his most famous sayings!
If there's anything I can do-
please, let me know!
We're all gonna miss him-
the special cowboy, we all adore!!
He's remembered by some-
for the special stories he told!
By some, the special things they did together!!
He'll always be remembered-
for the special man he was!
So now, as we say our good-byes!
Say I love you, to our special cowboy!!
He'll be entering the gates of Heaven!
So Larry, from us all!
Get on that bronc or bull and ride, ride, ride!!

Rosie Ludwig Jr.

Rain

When the rain comes down on a cold, dark day,
just stand outside to wash away the pain.
One wonders why the pain must stay
or why the rain must go away.
The truth be known, the truth be told,
for the lonely one the road is long.
The strong one thinks he must not care
and who's to say what load he bears?
The one's we've lost, the one's we blame
are those who could not stop the pain.
The scars are there to let us know
the ways we went, and did not go.
We hide inside ourselves in vain
'til once again we see the rain.
Yet, who's to say when the rain will end
and when the pain will start again?

Michele L. Grimes

Ballad Of The Lonely Dancer

A melancholy ditty,
accompanied with sorrow
Softness wasn't heeding,
and neither were the minds of tomorrow.
Nights are dark and desperate
I've searched for a star but never succeeded.
Sorrow has filled every star in the sky,
the moon is conscious but seems to be high.
Will he ever be sober?
Why should he be if everyone else is.
He doesn't want to take the chance of being
lonely and blue, searching for the truth.
An Indian summer,
peaceful and plain
One who is naked,
dancing in the rain.
tearing through pain,
seeking any passion,
while the world has gone away,
leaving no compassion.

Amber Wolf

Pain

Pain was the color of loneliness
Emptiness came with the longing.
Wanting could not fill the abyss
Nor would needing be enough.

With early dawn came desolation
There was nothing but darkness within,
But the faint sun behind the clouds
Promised an easing of the wrenching fear.

Skies were losing their grayness
A glimpse of the white appeared
Behind each cloud a blue blanket
Gave a whisper of what might be

Beyond the pain could be promise
Joy might be there to come through
A warmth, a rosiness of spirit
That would help dry out wasted tears.

Pain had been the color of living
Aloneness was all that was promised,
When the sky began its healing,
With more, much more to come.

Isabel Wills

Deliver On To Me

Tears may role along hallowed walks of passing eves,
but when it is delivered on to me, the pain never leaves.

Torture has delivered on to me a new view of our castle,
yet as it is delivered on to me, I welcome each hassle.

My time has come to fight all that has plagued my soul.
Until it is delivered on to me, my flesh may not be whole.

Venom from the asp is all I feel, each stagnant, choking breath.
As it is delivered on to me, blackness will guide my welcomed death.

Rivers run red with my blood, for my heart is gone.
Brown eyes have deceived my soul, deliver on to me my fawn.

Games, evil devilish games played my head, blanketing my view.
Today your charade has delivered on to me, a gift from me to you.

Talons that have probed the waters of my un-endless vault,
now delivered on to me, you shall learn your own fault.

The hot gales that sweep sand into the little boys eyes,
will deliver on to me, the peaks will then hear my cries.

Bonded by steal silk, the muscles crushing flex relaxes for you.
The tide delivers on to me the rose, its thorn, flows your blue.

Deliver on to me a fools wisdom, for I am wiser than the ass.
Deliver on to me. No, deliver on to you, a love to never pass.

Anthony Kenneth Zimney

So Much Woman

Suddenly!
There she was...
With that great smile dancing upon her lips
Like ripples on a quiet lake's surface.
With a touch so soft...
You wonder if it's a dream.

With head held high
And twinkling, beautiful eyes
A self-assured and confident pose
She personifies the very word - Woman.

Yes,... she's vibrant!
Alive!
Tender... and caring.

It's a yet unnoticed miracle of creation,
That such diverse and powerful virtues of emotion
Could be housed in a creature,
So beautifully made.
Yes!... Thank God for you - Woman!

Archibald M. Howard

Goodbye

Understand me please, from start to end.
You will always be remembered, as my best friend.
But what we actually had, most people couldn't see.
They didn't know about the loved shared, between you and me.
The calls on the phone, the time together we spent.
Time flies when I'm with you, so on the months had went.
It's so so wonderful, with you in my life.
Sooner or later, I'll make you my wife.
Well it's been real fun, thanks for the love you showed.
The months have crept upon us, so now I must go.
As God is my witness, I will see you again.
I often pray you will remain, my lover and friend.
Deep in my heart, I know we're meant to be.
So God will make a away, for you to marry me.
But this is the future, so we must make it last.
And to do this, we must dwell on the past.
This is the end, as I wipe the tears from my eye.
Remember be strong, don't cry, till we meet again
I love you... Goodbye.

Aveon Bland

To My Husband

I look at you - so handsome and strong.
I can almost feel your arms engulfing me
and holding me so close that I lose my breath.
I touch you - so lovingly and tenderly.
Being the gentle and loving man that you are, you
lean your head toward my touch to let me know
you feel the same way. That is how our love is-
we only have to touch to know how one another feels.
I kiss you - so softly, yet with so much passion.
One kiss from you can make my darkest moment
turn into the brightest hour of the day.
I look at you - so handsome and strong.
Within your eyes I see so many different things-
love, hunger, honesty, peace, warmth, gentleness,
anger, hurt, and a lifetime of sadness.
I hope I can always share that love, feed that hunger,
receive that honesty, instill that peace, bathe in that
warmth, bring out that gentleness, extinguish that
anger, ease that hurt, and spend another lifetime
turning that sadness into happiness and joy eternal.

Wanda Faye Ennis

"Thank God"

I now see the world from a different point of view
I wish you could focus just like I do
it's about appreciating life, which too many people hate
about loving those who love you, before it's too late
I'm not a writer, but I have a great heart
thanks to my parents, from this world they did part
death is natural, but it creates so much pain
how do you get through it, when you feel so insane
strength from within, trying to find my way
trying to make my tomorrows better each day
I can't go back in time and change a thing
I can only go forward and learn how to sing
I won't forget them, or my sister Pat
I'll love them forever, until I'm where they're at
death takes time, to heal from the pain
each person is different, none the same
life goes by quickly, cherish each day
don't let the trivial obstacles get in your way
appreciate today, tomorrow who knows who will die
love those who love you, before another day goes by...

Ronnie R. Brewster

Reality

I was so blind for so long
Until the new day took advantage of my weak heart.
A new light
Awakening, yet mourning my tiny loss
I gave so much, with no appreciation
Is suffering worthless?

All was taken for granted
Reaching out into darkness-what could I have seen?
Nothing was there
Such confusion, where to begin?
A need for understanding; clarity is unattainable.
Selfishness, arguments, criticism.
always hidden from my eyes
Change is a necessity, not a struggle.
How could I give everything then,
when now there's no turning back?
Heart against mind admits defeat
The spell is broken.

Amy Klesse

This Is Just To Say...I'm Sorry

Dear Pavel Friedmann,

This is just to say...I'm sorry.
I'm sorry I couldn't save you from such a horrible fate,
I'm sorry I couldn't fulfill your wish that could've saved you.
I wish I could tell you, face to face, that I'm very sorry.
I'm very sorry I couldn't be there to listen to your poem.
"I Never Saw Another Butterfly",
Which has and always will inspire and fascinate,
Me and anyone who read this poem by you.
I am truly sorry that I couldn't save you from your death bed.
Did you ever see another butterfly
Before death caught up with you?
I wish I could have helped you sight another butterfly.
I wish I could helped you through,
All of that misery that was ahead of you.
I'm really, truly, very sorry. Please forgive me.

Jennifer So Young Lee

Passing Clouds

Humans living here on earth are like passing clouds —
here, there, and gone.
All we can do is show love and caring for one another
and give thanks for
having had the chance to experience
the joys and sorrows of life while passing through.

As a passing cloud may leave rain,
refreshing the earth,
so each person has the chance to leave the world
with some small measure of a brighter outlook
for those to follow.

Peter Retzinger

"Strength"

I take a deep breath as I close my eyes,
And I make a wish as I let out a sigh.

Please Lord help me be strong,
And believe in myself as I try to move on.

With the pain of loss to muddle through,
I must find solace and strength in the love I feel from you.

I must not let others tear me down,
As I swim in the ocean of life trying not to drown.

I must love myself enough to know,
That the beauty within is to others what I must show.

When I am feeling insecure, and others don't give a damn,
I need only to look back and see just how far I have swam.

I have come so far and survived so much in my life,
I have gotten through what at times seemed to be insurmountable
strife.

And really what it all boils down to in the end,
Is self love, love from my family and love from true friends.

If you have these things you are truly wealthy and need nothing more,
So hold your head up high, swim with purpose
And you'll make it to shore.

Cammy Myers

Memory

Thy blue skies shall turn to gray,
and thy sun that drips a golden ray,
shall fall into the darkest rain.
Your smile shall turn a maddening sneer,
as you laugh and look and see, and peer.
The world is mine, you think, you say,
But you shall not live to see one's own link to the day,
when your death comes ye shall then cry out in agony,
God forgive me:

Amanda Hartley

"See History In A New Way"

I will see history in a new way. I will do this by seeing it in the eyes of a grown woman, a grown woman with a purpose.

I will see history in a new way. I will do this seeing and acknowledging a woman, for a change is being written about in school books, not just one or two paragraphs, but page by page, books by books

I will see history in a new way. I will do this by seeing the changes women are making from just one simple home-maker who c reates
the United States flag (Betsie Ross) to confederate spies (Rose O'Neal Greenhow and Belle Boyd) thus, women have come a long away.

I will see history in a new way. I will do this by seeing women as people. They have been taken care of others, they have been for granted and have been taken advantaged of. But now it's time that they take charge and be in control of their own life.

I will see history in a new way. I will do this by thinking for myself.

Nishanna Ramoutar

"She Has"

She has the perfect job only work's a few hours each day
She has the most loving husband adores her every which way
She has two smart, happy kids a little girl and a boy
She has so many friends bringing their joy
She has a large, clean house everyone models after
She has a facade that's bright and cheerful
has to show that she full of laughter
She has impeccable style always envied by all
She has the time to do nothing stop on saturdays at the mall
She has everything that she could ask for everything that she must
need yet every time she opens the refrigerator's door
She falls to her knees she clutches her cans so boring; so routine
She has these puzzles, these questions these unanswered pleas
liquid swishes through her admired sole slowly loosing her control
She has cans inner hand smell on her breath
She has tears on her face hair is a mess
She has silence in her ears darkness within her eyes
She has none of the answers tired; just lies
She has everything on the surface, but feels like she must crawl
Because in her heart she realizes what she truly has
She has nothing at all.

Jennie Pirone

Riverfest Rhythm

They stood on bridges silhouetted by a sunset, rare,
As rhythmic incantations filled the balmy summer air;
The multitude assembled at the place called Little Rock
To hear musicians entertain without a hint of Bach.

With amplifiers emphasizing instrument and voice,
It soon became apparent that this was the people's choice;
But, what was this great sound they heard, harmonious and live,
As music emanated from a fascinating five.

From "Only You" in Ink Spots' style to groovy rock and roll,
The five-man band performed them all with ultimate control.
A boogie beat, a love song, sweet, were both played skillfully;
There was no limit to their wealth of versatility.

The crowds descended rapidly, converging at Stage Two,
So they could see the band that played this music they all knew.
They saw a group that, just for pleasure many years ago,
Combined much talent, skill, and effort with desire to grow.

In spotless white tuxedos with red cummerbunds and ties,
They looked like smooth professionals, to everyone's surprise.
The Summerfield Reunion Band came down to Riverfest,
And gave a great performance that should be acclaimed "The Best."

Gladys Harmon Birmingham

Ozark Treasure

I was three years old when my mother died
For a housekeeper my father hired Miss MacBride
She was born and raised a most wonderful way
In a log cabin built in the red Ozark clay

She was childless and came to our home alone
But my sisters and I soon felt like her own
And because of her care and endless love
To us she was like an angel from heaven above

The gifts she gave I've treasured all of my years
They've seen me through happiness, troubles and tears
In time our father found a gentle new wife
Miss MacBride was then gone from our daily life

We were grown when our Ozark nanny died
We stood sadly but proudly her graveside
Our tears flowed so freely as they laid her to rest
In the Ozark hills that she loved best

I'll forever love this wonderful land
Where these native cedars and fine oaks stand
But of all the wonders which give Ozark folks pride
The most cherished to me was dear Miss MacBride

John Culling

Untitled

My heart is oh so heavy and my spirit is so very weak;
I'm way down in the valley, so far from the mountain's peak.
My life is such a struggle to make it to another day;
Trials, frustration, failure, and disappointments keep getting in the way.
Many times I ask myself, "Why is this happening to me?"
But God's will for me is something that you can't always see.
It takes a lot of faith, hope, and love to live a Christian life;
because Satan is doing his best to fill it with a lot of strife.
My hope is in my Saviour, God Almighty who created the Earth;
who out of kindness and mercy sent us his only son through the miraculous virgin birth.
Jesus knows what we are going through, because he has been there too;
with arms outstretched and love so pure, he gave his life for me and you.
Yes, my Lord Jesus died on that Old Rugged Cross;
but it was willingly done so that not a soul would be lost.
I serve a risen saviour who is with me every step of the way;
and at times like this, all I can do is put my faith in him and pray.

Rex A. Chapman

Fiery Fate

Whether one decides to accept the shameless part of human history
This present-day or not, even if one were to whet that interest
Further by painstakingly leafing through the innumerable volumes
Of mankind's recorded posterity it hails so proudly for its own
Delectation. It appears that mankind is right on line with its
Preordained destiny, causing a vast array of concerned citizens
Round the world to jointly cry: "Stop the universal inhumanity
And madness before it is too late!" That is, before the seven
So-called properly governed continents on a troubled planet
Africa! Antarctica! Asia! Europe! Oceania! and the Americas!
Shall, for once but an immemorial time, be horrifically brought
Together by an increasing faction of callous beings who are
Continually involved in reducing the only environment that is
Ideally suited for the fraternity of mankind and all other living
Things to that which may become unfit for any living thing. Still,
The final atonement for man's shocking, primeval behavior shall
Come from the Master Prophet, for it is He who has forewarned
The unremorseful, tempestuous, warring tribes of mankind
From one unbelievable blood-letting century to the next
Of a predestined and indisputable self-inflicted fiery fate.

Garrett H. Watkins

Love Of Family

I love you each one,
One not more than the other,
Whether you are Father, Mother,
Sister or Brother.

You each one are special,
In your own unique way,
I'll love you equally till my dying day.

If you are a daughter or a son,
I love you as though you are the only one.

You have a special place in my heart,
A space no one can fill but you,
No matter what you say or do.

You'll have a place there forever.
And when I depart,
Even though, I'll leave you my heart.

Gladys Spencer Harp

17 Years Old

The soft brown eyes of the one I love are there.
I see them and they look at me silently.
His hair, blowing in the breeze of the evening,
is silken to the touch of love-struck fingers.

Smooth features, unmarred and
handsome in the moonlight.

Happiness. All the joys of love waiting to be
grasped tenderly. But when I reach out they
flee as in a dream.

For a time I had him. I held him close and knew
that my love was real. He was real.

Then, the beginning of a new day. Our time
was gone. Each precious moment only to
be a memory.

How sad to find such joy
and then feel it cease to be.

Tina Lundy

Bloody Tears

Never put thy trust in the hands of a man.
He gives you not! a cold drink of water
But instead the hot desert sand; and only thy
Own tears can cool thy burning soul.
Give him not! all your smiles for tomorrow.

This is a new time. A new generation for man.

Give him your love
But give him not!
Thy soul

Because he will never understand the depths of
A woman's soul, only God can understand.
Most women have a special goodness and a will
To give and protect, but give not all, for it will
Never be given unto you in an equal manner.

The words I write are stained with pain from an unequally
shared heart.
If my tears were blood, I would live no more.
Love me a river of sunshine, pamper my pain away;
And I shall cry no more bloody tears.

Mary C. C. Jones

This Special Day

This is a special day,
to celebrate in the perfect way.
By candlelight or moonlight...
In anyway it'll be just right.
My love for you dear
has grown strong during this year.
You've done so much for me
You helped me see
how good life could really be.
All I had to do was give it a chance.
Now we share a wonderful Romance.
You make me feel needed without a doubt,
My love for you
will never burn out!

Nicole Lee

On The "Statue Of Liberty"

An idea was conceived long-ago-one day
from a French-man named "Monsieur Laboulaye"
A monument to be built in America, makes sense
As a memorial to our freedom, and independence

So sculptor Bartholdi, created a goddess with light
and Bedloe's Island - was chosen as site
Copper-skinned, composed of 300 sections it needs.
Mr. Eiffel's framework - to make sure it succeeds.

A draped female beauty - 12 stories high
Right hand torch of liberty - up to the sky
A radiant crown, with seven points that cements
Symbolic of our world's - seven continents

Let's clear the ground and construct a base
A pedestal project to hold her in place
Liberty unveiled in 1886 - with great fascination
And N.Y. Harbor - her controlling domination.

Eternally grateful - generous gift of France
Symbol of life, liberty, and religious tolerance.

Ike Sternbach

Grandma Remembers

The time has come for me to have my say,
Now that I am older, wiser, and gray.
Once a young girl, wild, carefree,
I could only dream about what life held for me.
I sit back now and look over the past,
Only a few things in life really lasts.
My parents, my husband, my daughter and son,
All are my treasures, I would not trade one.
Years go by and petals may fall,
But wife and mother, I had it all.

Louise Kinney

Untitled

I silently cried, "How can it be,"
For one to be so young, yet so free?

His life was so short, a mere child.
The battle he fought, seemed any but mild.

We loved him so, a friend, a true champ.
He loved us too, with warmth like a lamp.

His freedom gives me strength for each day.
I live, love, and learn on my way.

As he travels above and watches us carry on,
I know by love, he'll never be really gone.

Hope Christians

Images

Through the windows, of my mind,
There races images, I can't define.
Some, like dark shadows, flashing,
Some, are light streaks, clashing.

There are echoes of sounds loud and low,
At times there are blocks wherever you go.
Then there seems to be a quietness so still,
And then maybe a scream so shrill.

Oh! To unscramble and be able to see,
A part so confusing, a part of me.
To look on the outside, you wouldn't believe,
All the mixed emotions, one can receive.

These are the times, when things move fast,
Before you gather your thoughts, they are past.
To unravel the mystery of the brain,
might slowly drive one insane.

Geraldine Saunders Tolliver

Time

How much time can one spend walking
around in ones mind.
Walking around in our mind takes time.
How much time can one spend
running a straight line.
A straight line in time never ends.
How much time can one spend living.
Living in time is in its self the time of our life.

Patricia C. Williams-Decker

Untitled

Emily, today I held you in my arms
I felt you... crying
This child of mine in heart and time
A stream of tears rolled gently down your cheeks one after another
quiet streams rolling no sound
just pain...compassion...understanding...longing Beautiful child
Robbed so young of one who loved you...of one who still loves you
Her body leaves... her spirit stays
She's here with you
She's in you
I hear her laughing...
I turn around... It's you I see her smile...
I look again... It's you I see her eyes..
I look again... It's you
Yes... beautiful You... and Her... together forever in heart and soul
When I am away from you... I pray to Her
She's with you... I smile
I talk to her often... praying... asking... wishing... loving...
She answers lovingly a tear runs down my cheek... silently
She is with me.

Kim Suzanne Meo

The Latest Thoughts About Hairstyles

Ponytails, pigtails, and braids,
been's, kopsytails, and french braids,
There are all kinds of shades,
of hair.
Some hair is fair, some is dark.
Some is straight, some is curly,
and some is even every wirly.
Some people add a lot of style,
after a while.
If you brush twice a day,
your hair will be nice in a special way.

Jenna Gatti

Skin Deep

There is a world in the back of my mind.
  A world without meaning, a world without time.

A world with no color or shade, a world
  black and white where my black lover laid.

Laid in a bed of thoughtless words of despise,
  still every day his white sparrow cries.

There is a world in the back of my mind,
  where the conflict of color was left behind.

Because there was no color, only black and white,
  because of this they learned to unite.

People judge people by color of skin,
  yet we are all the same deep within.

My black lover was laid to sleep,
  just because color is only skin deep.

Melanie Rohde

The Great And Wonderful Times

Tears of mourning, tears of grief,
Tears of woe and disbelief.

Now may both your parents rest in peace,
Their heavenly Father they will meet.

We don't know you personally, though we feel we should,
Growing up with news reports, stories, movies and books.

Your parents will be remembered for their quality, style and grace.
Refinement and the smiles embellished upon their faces,
In the United States and many other places.

Remember the great times, the values your parents
instilled upon you,
And pass them on to the generations handed down to you.

May God watch and keep you through this another tragic time;
But always remember the great and wonderful times.

Dedicated to the families of John and Caroline Kennedy upon the death of their mother, Jacqueline Kennedy Onassis.

Barbara L. Ray

Hopes And Dreams

Hopes and dreams, I have no more
  The goals I have I've set before
Time will tell when things work out
  When I reach my goals, there'll be no doubt.

Hopes and dreams, I have none
  I feel my life has come undone
The world is going, 'round and 'round
  And everything has turned upside down.

Right side up it soon will be
  The life I live is one that's free
Free to breathe and free to love
  Someone special sent from up above.

To love is grand, it is divine
  Complete love is hard to find
Hopes and dreams will come once more
  And I will not shut the door.

Dwanna K. Allen

Noel

You came to me with friendship to give,
and brought with you much love for me.
Time went on and we did grow so caring and so close.

But then the night set on our lives and
took away all that was bright. The darkness
fell as cold as ice and took you away old friend of mine.

Your pain was silent I wish I've known the
pain in your eyes was yours alone. I ask myself,
was it pride? Was it love? Was it all the above?

I think of this now and can clearly see the
disease that stood between you and me.
You needed to spare me of all your pain but
in the end it was in vain. Your battered body I
had to see to realize what had to be, that
in this world of grief and pain I lost my
friend, my brother to AIDS.

Miriam Monzon

Why

Mom why is everybody crying?
Why is no one looking at me when I call?
Why do I keep going up in the sky?
Why can't you hear me?

Mom why is this stranger telling me I
should go with him, should I?
Why is he taking me?
Why can't I stay?
Why do I see a bright light?

Mom why is everything so much prettier here?
Why are these people so much nicer?
Why did this stranger bring me here?
Why did I have to go into the light?

Mom why did I have to die?
Why couldn't I stay with you?
Why can't you be with me?
Why is everybody still crying when they
know I am being well taken care of?

Christina Spaul

To Save The Children

I hurt when I hear of our children dying and being killed.
They didn't get a chance to live their life or have their dreams fulfilled.
To save the children is a dream I see.
To help them to be, all they can be, teach them about unity
and help spread love throughout the country
Where was the mother?
Why did the baby have to die?
Why was she so heartless and didn't listen to its cry?
She was to busy trying to impress
When the poor little baby was in distress.
She didn't care if the baby suffered
She was to busy cooking her new boyfriend's supper.
Her children eat hotdogs, while she fixes him steak.
She put him before her child, who died from a deadly fate.
Her children are running wild, feeling full of pain
The way she is rising them, is totally insane.
We must save the children, before it's too late
Their future is what's at stake.
Children are the future, this is why we live,
Why is love and affection so hard to give.

April Young

Faith

If the savagery of the heart tends towards bitterness
Then we must lend ourselves to God,
For in Him we find that despair of pain be diminished.
That we may look forward out of such darkness
To a morning of such surreptitious solitude.
To find strength in the newness of the infinite light of God.
Being the mere travelers by which the journey enfolds,
The light may seem dim and undistinguishable.
It is when this encroachment of darkness appears
That the soul must bring forth its memories of Son.
To enter not into the realm of this world,
Stands only not to become weakened,
The battle having been already fought,
The outcome since decided,
Let not the soul become weary.
Stand firm for the ground does not shift or move,
Tis only the wind that moves the limb but not the tree.

Licia Dailey

Flower

A lonely flower sits on the window sill,
the sun is its only friend.

The light gives it the strength to grow,
to bloom, to blossom, and show.

As the petals open so does its personality,
opening itself to the world,

The red color of its petals have opened,
springtime has come.

The sun light has helped it grow,
and become one.

Kathryn Watson

The Desert

A clean, smooth desert lay before me
A desert without sand
A desert of rolling meadows
A desert of supple hills
Rising to mighty peaks
A desert of caverns, crevices and valleys
Where the shimmering droplets of water collect
To form shallow pools
On the smooth, silky ground
A desert
Endless in sight
Rolling in curvaceous splendor
Long and lean
Smooth and silky
A desert teaming with life underneath
Tempting and accommodating to explore.

Ward J. Longolius

Hilo Hotel

Seated on the porch of the old Hilo Hotel
Comfortably rocking in highbacked chairs,
We were together, watching the rain.
At first, slow and mist-like, it was barely visible,
Then gradually increasing, it came pell-mell!
The wide eaves of the lanai protected us
As we silently rocked and watched.

Suddenly it was over and the sun came out,
In the distance we heard the pounding surf
And saw part of a rainbow.
The huge banyan tree and the chenille plants
Dripped diamonds on all who passed.

William E. Todd

Heading South

I'll make a list said he
of twenty friends who could help me
and after a brew or two
He could only think of a few.

I'll narrow my list down to ten
and he began again
I do know one little honey
Who wouldn't mind giving me money

I am heading down hill fast
I'm worse off than in times past
It looks much brighter the southern way
I must get underway

This bitter cold gives me such a chill
This really can't be God's will
I've tried every thing here and couldn't make it
This is my chance, I'll have to take it.

Goodbye friends and family too
When it's warmer I'll come to see you
I'll miss you all you can believe this
But I must really leave this - state of Maine

Gloria E. Sparrow

Modern Technology

Today God is saddened,
As He looks upon His world,
Because the men that He created,
Have created the miracle bomb.

Today god is grieving,
As he looks upon his world,
Because the Men who once worshiped him,
Now worship the almighty bomb.

Today god is crying,
As he looks upon his world,
Because the Voices that once sang his praise,
Now all praise the beautiful bomb.

Today god is weeping,
As he looks upon his world,
Because the men who once feared him,
Now fear the All Powerful Bomb.

Today god is mourning,
As he looks upon the ashes of his world,
Because all his children, that he loved,
Have been destroyed by the Miracle Bomb.

Drew Allen

A Thought For The World

Not many take the time out of their own lives to see
What life for some may truly be
As long as we are fortunate with our own self
It doesn't matter much, the life of someone else
Selfishness to the woman eating out of a trash can
Ignorance to what we call a bum, but in reality, he's a homeless man
Hatred to the man who doesn't have the same color skin
Jealously of the man who worked hard to earn the suit he's in
Frightened of the person suffering with HIV
Disappointed in the teen who's having a baby
Disgust for the one who shoots drugs into his veins
Questions of why it was the life of his own that person claimed
No concern for the one with the bottle constantly in his hand
Sorrow for the child who was beaten, yet for him we won't take a stand
Where does it stop and when does it end
Will there ever be a time when we treat all as friends?
Just a thought for today
But hopefully a change for tomorrow

Tracy Fogle

Change

It's as though lightning had touched the earth and started a fire among the trees. They started to burn, one by one. Soon they became engulfed in flames, and the whole area was burning. At first, they were bright red, then slowly, as their flames started to die, they turned yellow. When the fire had left, there hung the ashes like skeletal carcasses. Then, one by one, the ashes began falling to the ground. However, there is always one who with all its might tries to remain on top, but soon, from forces more powerful than its own, the ash loses its grip and starts to fall, helplessly, down, down, down.

From the beginning of this scenic but destructive event, until the very last ash has fallen to the ground, a whole cycle has taken place. When the last ash has fallen, alas! A new cycle has begun. The cold relentless snow falls among the darkened ashes below.

Matt Lissner

To A Grandpa

I remember the day so clear
To me you were so near
I grieve the thunderous stormy night
The telephone rang, I jumped
I jumped with fright

I heard my elders mumbling slow
For what they said I didn't know.
As the wind began to hover
Visions appeared, under my cover.

Then the wind came to a halt
I was come over by sudden jolts.
My skin was frozen to a chill
Even then, I lay there still.

I closed my eyes to go to sleep
Then the wind began to weep
I peered around the corner bend heard everything
I thought my life came to and end.

I stood by your box crying loud like a stormy thunder cloud.
Everyone watched as I paid my due and all I could think is
Grandpa, I will miss you.

Derek Barro

An Easy Man To Love

I have mountains of memories, most happy, a few sad;
But together over 50 years has only made me glad.

You knew him as a brother, I knew him as my love.
We went through life together, him soaring like a dove.

He awoke each new day with a smiley face;
Always upbeat and positive, a challenge to keep his pace.

He reached out to his fellow man seeing the good in all;
Loving life the way he did, and making it a ball.

I feel the strength he showered on me that I must carry on.
I must go forth with a half a heart because that is God's plan.

Oh, our little home's so quiet now without his robust laugh;
How hard it's going to be without my better half.

Guessing some times I envied him, so peaceful and so kind;
While I ramped and raved and worried, would almost lost my mind.

With all the time together, I've been so richly blessed;
There is a higher being, and I'm going through the "test."

Peace and quiet with him now and when I leave this earth behind,
no worries, cares, or sin;
I hope he'll open Heaven's Gate saying, "Welcomed love, come in."

Hilda Kehl

Life With My Wife!

Dedicated to Tabitha L. Carter

It would be more joyful to have known thee all of my life,
Oh, how happy am I to have thee for my dear precious wife.
Please my love; let me nurture thee under my wing, to have you as my friend, lover and wife to cling,
Like the beautiful Robins of the dew morning that cheerfully sing.
Our love is like the four seasons: Winter, autumn, fall and spring.
Upon my finger is a symbol of our marriage; a gold and diamond ring
Oh, with you, what a beautiful thing
Being with you makes me feel like a wealthy king.
You are like the honey that is in a tree;
and I am very much like the bumble bee.
You're the princess I've always wanted the world to see;
to my heart honey, you've got the key.
Oh, how much darling, do I love thee.
Much like the fish depends on the sea;
Like the sugar that goes in my coffee or tea;
Like the leaves that cling to the tree.
We shall live forever, together eternally.
On each earth for a while, happily then, to a greater place we shall go to be. Then I will forever be with thee.

Stephen W. Carter

Raining Love

It's raining outside.
To some, rain is sad, lonely, and depressing.
But rain is much more.

Rain is like love.
Sometimes it pours down;
Sometimes it falls lightly.

Thunder is like the heartbeat of someone in love;
It is loud and very moving.
Lightning is like the speed with which you lose love;
It can be powerful and destructive.

Rain causes floods;
Love can flood your heart.

Without rain we cannot live.
Without love we cannot live.
Let it rain all over the world;
Let love overflow your heart.

Benjamin Brown

Ode To The Creative Writer

Fantasy: What all is and could be;
Divine - the most insightful power
which yields to pain, the forgotten hour,
and whence is born immortal flower
to shadow stagnant reality.

Beauty: What comes of creativity;
Unto the silent heart be spoken
and from the vicious world be broken;
new lives, new places serve as token
to what wonder, what mystic the mind be.

Mastery: What awesome force to flee;
Beyond the dour stage to burn,
past all known that shift and turn,
while unseen magic is yet to learn
through feats of gifted artistry.

Katrina Keeney

Phoney World

This world is such a phoney place
Where no one can be themselves
Always putting on a false face
And leaving their true self on the shelf
Once their job is complete
And they've made a brand new friend
They change their face to bitter sweet
While they are out for more revenge
One day they'll wake up and realize
How miserable they really are
And wish they could change the days
When they were phoney and a bit bizarre
People want to know you for you
Not one of your acts to impress
So put away the ways you knew
And just be yourself at your best

Jean Ann Greider

Eye Of My Storm

Finger tips on lips, parted
impede the flow of arterial speech
which trickles down my hands
to lose its meaning

Embryonic ideas, longing to burst,
must first crawl through intestinal walls,
lined with sugar-coated spit

I'd grasp that sweetness with my last dying breath,
and run to white sandy beaches and hypodermic bliss,
preoccupy my mind, on fire, with a glaze of haze,
and burn it with a thousand soothing excuses

Do you see my sprouting, new born hairs-stunted by the hunt?
I wanted to nourish them with courage
from an armoured heart,
watch them poke their sharp ends through leather skin
strong and glorious...and fine

Though, in time, forgotten hunger rusts it shut
and follicles retreat into crevices once more...

afraid to be touched by blood

Sindy Lin

"The Last Gift"

"At first glance, it is but a mere necklace.
Neither elegant nor beautiful.
Made of purest silver,
Wrought in small hoops.
A small cross at its heart, held by a thin clasp.
At second glance, it is a gift of love.
Precious, but not to impress.
From torn soul to desire,
Given at the ending.
When came the night, to say the last goodbye.
At third glance, it is a heart.
Neither elegant nor beautiful.
But never having been worn, it lies in a drawer.
Dark and alone, its purpose unfulfilled.
Broken by your hand.
And at last glance, it is a memory.
Given to be with you always.
In the hope that you would remember.
A part of me to be near to your heart,
Even if I never would be."

Jonathan Ho

Norma Jean

When just a lad about thirteen
I had a friend name Norma Jean.
I carried her books home from school,
but I was just a bashful fool.
I carried her books up to her door
I'd get the courage I was sure,
but that chance I would surely miss
I only wanted one little kiss.
Now we're gone our separate ways
we're in our latter days.
Time's been good, and it's been mean,
but I'll never forget little Norma Jean.

Byed M. Jones

Hold Tightly My Love...

Hold tightly my love...
Hold tightly my hand as we walk together on this our road of life
Hold tightly my love...
Hold tightly as we climb the hill of joy, expectation, happiness and
dreams
Hold tightly my love...
Hold tightly as we walk through the valleys of despair, sorrow,
broken dreams and heartaches
Hold tightly my love...
Hold tightly as we walk together so full of dreams and hope
Hold tightly for there is another hand holding tightly, it's God's
hand
Hold tightly my love for God will give us the guidance through all
valleys
Hold tightly my love...
Hold tightly for today we are one, we are one in spirit with God
Hold tightly my love as we lean on each other through all times
Hold tightly, hold tightly we are but little children in the garden
of God searching for peace of mind, hold tightly my love...
Our rainbow will come and our star will light the way
Hold tightly my love, hold tightly...

Julian R. Plaster

Hold On

We've been apart, yet so near
Your voice always whispering in my ear
We once were and still are,
No matter how near or far.
We've seen love, yet none like ours,
What fools we'll be to let ours expire.
The burning passion that instills our hearts
shall never die, even when quenched.
We speak as though we have everyday
now tell me, what does this say.
A love like ours is hard to find,
An unspoken dream that lies inside,
our hearts where love is kept alive.

Ebonique Burns

Before I Goof It Up

I start each new day of the week with promise
Before I goof it up...
I try to think what did I miss?
As I sip my morning coffee from my cup;
To greet the day and many things
Run swiftly thru my mind.
When I meet my neighbor, help me to be kind.
Think of some small way to lift them up.
Be careful what I say.
Let my words be encouraging...
For a brand new brighter day.

Lou Cundiff

A Slow Death

The invasion of your soul-
You are nothing against this power.
You fight, but are weak.
"Help me!" You yell but no one hears.
You must fight this alone.
Using all your strength you are still nothing.
Your soul is trapped-
You weaken, less power, and now, nothing.
You surrender, quit the fight.
"The Force!" - A strong force -
You are pushed forward, further and further.
You see an end, well, no, a light, a bright light.
You are pushed into it.
But you are at ease, no longer have fear.
You pass through the gates. -
Gates of freedom which set you free;
Your soul is free -
released to soar, search, experience,
Then later, sent back,
to live life once again.

Heather Wilson-Baltazar

Easter Egg

The funeral's fire burns bright
in the stars which he so proudly
touched, flaunting every move while
dancing on the backs of the bruised.
If ever satisfied, it was never shown
by that thorough going miser. He caught
the disease when he was seven watching
the rotting, decaying society on the
electric box.
He was infatuated with that leafy green substance
flowing like time, never ending.
He would neglect everything to have it.
Always more dead than alive
the only thing he loved had killed him,
he drowned in it.
He died a rotten easter egg.
So pretty with paint on the out and
rotten with death on the in.

More have died from this
than any other disease.

Cyrus Brown

Crash Of The Wave

Crash of the ocean wave
spray of its gentle mist.
Call of the winged albatross
against tapestry of white and blue.
Sun rays illuminating vast views
of majesty beauty of blue green with white crests.
Life has its roar
through fragile beats it sings.
Whispers new hopes tomorrow
for its happiness and dreams
Ocean waves,
gentle mist,
winged albatross,
White fluff, and blue
Blue green with white crests.
I roar,
I sing, and
Tomorrow a new dream.

Gene Spraggins

Desert Song

Awesome vistas are a palette of loveliness
in muted purple, soft rust and palest turquoise.
Wind carved shapes stretch my imagination,
rock formations balanced seemingly on a buffalo nickel.
There is a quiet that stretches to foreverness,
a deep peace that stills my troubled soul.
I now understand the words L'Amour wrote
of "... loneliness that is never lonely..."
In the rush of a vagrant breeze,
I hear "...voices that speak only to me..."
In the mystical vastness,
I am at one with the world.
In this special place, this American Desert,
this woman feels the power of God.

Shirley Jean DuBois

Let's Go Fishing

Let's go fishing in our favorite spot
Makes not difference if it's cold or hot
Grab your hat and your pole
We'll go down to our favorite hole

Get a rock and sit right down
or if you chose, sit on the ground
Bait your hook and pitch it in
This is how your fun begins

If you're lucky you'll get a bite
The fish might take it out of sight
But just hang on and breathe a prayer
And hope, it's a fish hanging there

Could be a minnow or something worse
But still no reason for one to curse
If it's not a fish, just bait again
Sit back down and throw it in

You can't be sure how it will go
When your fishing in your favorite hole
If it goes wrong, don't give up
Just think of it, your luck was tough

Gladys Andrews

A Love Lost...

A love lost in a midnight storm
His tender touch swept away in the pouring rain
His voice lost in the thunderous roar
While my heart sinks in the depths of loneliness.
His image engraved in my mind
I reach out only to find
A love lost in a midnight storm;
As rain beats down on my lonely soul
He comes to me in my dreams, my thoughts
Tempting me with a mere stare,
Or a tender brush of his lips against mine.
When the rain drops fall,
I lay in bed thinking of
A love lost in a midnight storm.

Audrey Anastasia Bacchus

Ideas

Sometime between the blackest black of midnight
And the ruby crack of dawn,
  When your mind is an open door,
Ideas spark from the starry horizon like fireflies,
Filing themselves into your head
  like documents in a locked-up safe,
Then Mother undrapes the ink-spilled curtain
and the blue-glass sky is once again revealed.
  The ideas wander around in your mind
  Like shooting stars.

Rebecca Michele Elkin

Emotional Landscapes

The colors of the land, continuing the shades of the sky,
Have astonishing waves that ripple on by;
The significance grows important along its way,
Partaking in the silk of a fresh-sprung day.

While able to form the variants of red, yellow and blue;
Still defying the restraints that are all too few,
While able to shape seas of any hue.
As electric as a rainstorm, or
As magnetic as the earth's core,
Still caught in lightning's shadow, taking on any form.

The unrelenting consumption, devouring all
Like the free-lance liquid of a crashing waterfall;
Lying just beyond touch, but still not beyond sight,
Always fragile and delicate, quite as a child's might.

As if threads of lavender that are waiting to soar,
Or threatening and rapturous as April's mighty roar;
Indistinguished while lying in the wind,
But holding a steady glow above the earthen floor,
Laboriously drifting towards its next of kin.

Jennifer Rogers

Hazel Eyes

An individual
Strong and willed
Dreams of diamonds
Hazel eyed
Vision of careers
Being swept off your feet
Green pastures in tomorrow
All seen through your hazel eyes.

Maybe a doctor, a professional
But things got out of order.
Whirlwind romance, a wedding ring
Blinded.

Your family is now your life
Lost yourself in others
You work life and do not live it
Traditional views all held in your sights.

Those views gave me my life
You held me with your torchlight gaze.
Now I have your hazel eyes
And now your dreams will never die.

Ledys Julia Valle

Freedom

The jail held her
Well not the jail itself
But the people who put her there
The walls surrounded her
But all she could see
Was her enemies holding strong against her
She wanted to run
But the room wouldn't let her
She wanted to hide
But the room was empty

Falling in the darkness
The people laughed and cheered

Her crime was that of a servant
She devoted her life to those who hated her
She paved their paths and anointed their heads
They deviously forsake her
They took her love and taunted it
With their devious deeds of wickedness

The jail held her
Well not the jail itself...

Traci Stricklan

A Dreamer Dreams

A dreamer dreams. They love to
dream. They love the dream. Their love
affair with a dream is usually a short one.
They always have multiple affairs. The
dreams are glorious.
To the dreamer the dream is
everything. Even so they feel empty.
So they acquire more dreams. The void is
never filled. Yet they go on trying, never
fulfilling any of them and never feeling satisfied
So when they decide to chase a
dream, to fulfill a dream, can they do it
will they ever do it. What holds them from
asking for help? Maybe fear? Fear of rejection,
failure or are they afraid of the dream dying.
Maybe a part of their stigma is
they do not want to admit that they are
dreamers. That if they were to confront the
fact that they are dreamers they would
lose apart of themselves for ever. A Dreamer Dreams.

Leonard S. Newton

The Shadow Within

Some people are jealous of all that they see,
because I have lots of friends that hang out with me.
Little do those people know, what they see is just a show.
If I didn't act tough, wear dark make-up and baggy clothes,
I wouldn't be good enough. Being popular isn't all that it seems.
You cant be yourself, it's like a really bad dream.
when I'm with my family I can just be myself.
I can be nice, and wear whatever happens to be on my shelf.
But every morning I put me aside, for right now I have to abide.
By the rules of the game most people would call.
Life, the most precious gift of all.
But what I wouldn't give to let me show through,
to be nice, pretty and smart
Although I know my wish won't come true.
Because I have lived this double life.
My self esteem has been cut with a knife.
For no one I know would give a damn,
If they really knew - I am what I am.

Amanda M. Kirtley-Northrup

"When I Am Gone"

When I am gone you won't be alone
because I will be with you always.
When we can no longer touch, talk or
play you will grieve for knowing the fact
that you'd taken me for granted.

When you are alone with all of your thoughts
you will think about all the times you mistreated me.
You'll wish you were there when I needed you to be.

In your dreams at night you will think of me.
One day soon you'll be wishing
and wanting to be with only me.

Erica Yvette Patterson

"Tear"

In this world of great surprise
I see you, seeing nothing but lies.
Of all these premature truths untold,
The thought of love will never grow old.

In the gray and rain-clad sky,
These lies are known, as am I.
Thunder and lightning all around,
Everything hides and makes no sound.
Sad and alone, filled with fear,
Look for these—in my tear!

E. J. Kovach

Questions

So much to do, so little time
How many questions have come to mind

Where do I go, who do I turn to
Who do I find to regain that stability inside

It's hard, really hard to make it out there alone
But I've got to, if not for the sake of my own

Although it's hard to say good-bye
I've got too, I have too, I need to try

Now that I know what I must do
There's no question about it

I've got to make it to that high extravagant place in the sky
Where I can fly higher than high

To see the one and only person who I know to be true
My Savior Jesus Christ will see me through

He'll guide and keep me all the way
Until it is my dying day

At that point I will say to thee
I love you Lord, for what you have given me

Blessed be the one who has blessed me so
I will praise the Lord for he has given me love, this I know

Bonita Walker

"Deepest Fear"

In the late summer night as I began to sleep,
A feeling came over me, one I never felt so deep,
A feeling of helplessness and vulnerability,
Standing at the edge of my bed was a shadow watching over me,
The shadow came closer and my heart began to pound,
I froze in my bed to a quiet eerie sound,
Do I scream and hope that someone will hear,
The echoes of my voice with the deepest of fear,
Now standing over me with the sound of his breath,
I began to wonder if this was the fate of my death,
With a will to survive, I leaped out of bed
and faced the shadow who wanted me dead,
He came around and grabbed the top of my arm,
He threw me to the ground with no sense of harm,
He wrapped his hands around my neck
and I felt my body taking its last breath,
With the last hope of life that I loved so dear,
I opened my eyes with the deepest of fear,
The shadow was gone, I was lying in my bed,
Was he ever really there or was he only in my head.

Brandy D. Meyer

I Am An American

I am an American, of that I am proud.
And praises of my country, I will shout aloud.
From Europe, long ago, our pilgrim father's came,
Not for furs or fortune, or for fame,
But simple freedom was their only aim.
When they landed on these shores, away from England's moors,
Full of joy and thanking God,
They fell on their knees and kissed the sod.
Many years have passed since then,
Marked with the work of these great men,
Who tried to make Americans name, a symbol of freedom
greatness and fame.
From here we hear the cannons roar, of countries where
youth is taught war.
But glad am I as here I stand, to live and die in
this fair land.
I am an American of that I am proud and praises of my
country, I will shout aloud.

Ivora M. Burger

What Jesus Was Made

In the beginning, "The Word was God," so the scriptures say,
His pre-existence was before the bright early morning ray.

"He was made to be flesh," but not by the will of man,
He laid aside His heavenly role as part of God's own plan.

"He was made of woman," a virgin who lived upon this earth,
He came to fulfill the prophesy concerning His unusual birth.

"He was made under the law," His sovereignty would be just,
He came not to govern, His kingdom was not an earthly must.

"He was made a curse," and keyed to every mortal soul,
With love, mercy, and forgiveness, to save them was His goal.

"He was made to be sin," to pay the price for mortal man,
To create the redemption way, God's eternal salvation plan.

"He was made to die," upon a cross on Calvary's hill,
To complete His commitment by doing His Father's will.

"He was made to be alive," so His disciples would believe,
He came and ate with them, their instructions to receive.

"He was made to be a Saviour," so trust Him every day,
He told to all that He was the truth, the light, the way.

"He was made to be eternal," He coming back to earth again,
So be ready one and all, He is your God and eternal friend.

Harmon Aubuchon

Watching T.V.

Simba! Simba! Mufasa's dead!
"There's no place like home," is what Dorothy said.
Seattle rules, but Kurt Cobain is dead.
He took a gun and blew off his head.
Beavis and Butt-head—laughter is all they know.
Your Chia pet is the pottery that grows and grows.
And Marge Simpson's hair—what's the deal with that?
She can't even go out wearing a hat.
The Grinch Stole my presents, and took them far away.
But Tim Allen is Santa Claus, he brought them back
the next day.
I remember one time when Snoop Dogg was in jail.
He was there because his friend Dr. Dre forgot his bail.
Winnie the Pooh came in my house and ate all my honey.
But he just kept on goin' like the energizer bunny.
I ran yesterday, but I tripped on a bump.
I got up again and ran like Forrest Gump!!

Karen M. Fields

Strange And Psychotic

I am strange and psychotic
I wonder why they make lemon-scented Pine-Sol
I hear flying casts talking
I see a dead man under the couch
I want to get the dead man out of my living room
I am strange and psychotic

I pretend I know what's going on
I feel that flying cats are scary
I touch the dead man under the couch
I worry about the dead dog under the porch
I cry because the furry little cat few into
the window and died under the stairs
I am strange and psychotic

I understand that cats can't fly
I say lemon Pine-Sol should be called Lemon-Sol
I dream about snow and rain
I try to ignore everybody
I hope I get to move away
I am strange and psychotic

Soozee McVoy

Sweet Dreams

From your ebony hair to your sparkling
brown eyes
From your charming laugh to your
captivating personality
From your deep voice to the way you've
won my heart
From all of these things that remind
me of you to the memories I have
that makes everything just right
and all of these things that are
a part of you
You will all be a part of my dreams tonight.

Leondrea Clark

"Upon Waking"

"Out of the cave of transference, from the oblivion of before,
I crawl arachnid - like on coltish limbs."
"To sprawl in sweet release upon the littered forest floor,
a subject of my mother Nature's whims."

"I venture forth into the Wood, my tread a hesitant shamble,
the path before me lies both light and dark."
Then comrades flit out of to brush, to join in my initial
Gambol, through the gloom of this unsullied Park."

"Our trails diverge, I run alone and carom through some random
bends,
channeled now by Bramble, Bole or Thorn,"
my instinct tells me that, inexorably, the slope descends,
and suddenly I see where I am borne."

"The trees give way to Desert, a tractless burning waste, a broken
badlands filled with shifting Dune."
"Padding forward, Scorched and Weary, moving with a fevered pace,
seeking Succor from the Orb of Noon."

"Vision swimming, faint of heart, my gaze lights on a smudge of
Green, indecisive shadows cloak my brain."
"Could a lush Oasis lie beyond this obscure sheen?
Hope sets my feet upon the path again."

Gnuoy Lessur

A Little Angel

This is for a little angel I held in my arms, seemingly so long ago,
when she herself, was barely able to hold her own.

Though she is but a young girl today,
she has exerted the strength of one more than twice her age.

With always a winning smile upon her face,
you can't help but smile yourself, even on the worst of days.

One child that could never be forgotten,
and always remembered in our hearts,
for her beauty is upon us even in the dark.

And if you haven't guessed by now,
that little angel just so happens to be you.

To the little angel that stays within my heart.
I pledge this bronze eagle as your guardian angel, to watch over you.
As the eagle represents strength, and a quiet wisdom, so my child,
do you.

To try and match the strength in you, one so small,
may seem an easy task to do, but the eagle is the only one for you.

And no other could be so grand, as the infinite eagle,
to watch and protect you,
the one who has the strength to match your own.

You are an inspiration to us all.

Penny J. Neagos

The Little Girl

A little girl sits by the window,
her head hung in despair.
She listens to the raindrops tapping
And the hums of the wind

Her parents are no longer one,
but separated as a petty quarrel
divides them.

She's caught in the middle,
for which one to live with?
She does not want to hurt their feelings,
But what a hard decision!

So who to live with?
Only time will tell.

Jodi Brown

Only Human

Are you strong, are you weak?
When you walk, do your sneakers squeak?
Do you laugh, do you cry?
Do you like to eat blueberry pie?
Do you dance, do you sing?
Do you jump when the doorbells rings?
Do you like cars, do you like planes?
Do you like to make papers cranes?
Do you like bikes, do you like skates?
Do you ever use paper plates?
Do you like books, do you like to write?
Do you ever get in family fights?
Are you short, are you tall?
Do you like to pay baseball?
Do you swim, do you run?
Do you always like to have fun?
Do you like skirts, do you like pants?
Do you get mad when your parents say you can't?
Do you draw, do you paint?
When it's hot do you sometimes faint?

Katie Pridie

"Is It His Time, Lord?"

There he lay,
Struggling for air.
How much more can he bare?
We're praying for a recovery.
Lord, is it his time?
Is this his final step to climb?
With your hands, Lord
He has been blessed.
Will you heal him, will you touch his chest?
His biggest concern -
His wife and her well-being.
Wish he could stay among the living
But he belongs to you, Lord.
Are you calling one more home?
To us love, patience, and kindness he has shown.
Dear Lord, I'm gonna miss him.
But his home is with you.
Our memories are more than just a few,
Pop-pa, I love you!

Heather E. Turner

Grandpaw Is The Brightest Star

When I look up at the sky in the
night, what do I see?
I see the brightest star up there looking
down at me!
My Grandpaw is that brightest star, that I
see every night...
He's letting me know that everything's
alright!
When I close my eyes to sleep, I wonder
if I'll see that star again...
'Cause he was more than a grandpaw...
he was my best friend!
So all the memories, that I have, I'll
hold them so tight!...
And look for the brightest star in the
sky every night!

Juanita K. Hagerman

Memories Of Yesteryear

I remember: Lights on trees, sleigh rides,
caroling
I remember: The wreath on the door, shoes
on the floor, the sweet smell of gingerbread
I remember: Warmth by the fire, music playing,
presents all wrapped with bows
I remember: Candle light, silent night,
mistletoe toe
I remember: Grandmas smile, waiting awhile,
stories of St. Nicholas
I remember: Cookies and milk, a note to
St. Nick, saying my prayers
I remember: Climbing in bed, a kiss on the
head, visions of sugarplums
I remember: Church bells ringing, choirs
singing, Jesus is born!!!
I remember - do you?

Maryvonne DeSmyter

Storms

Storms are like people.
They can sprinkle you with soft sprays of water
like Mom with the garden hose,
dancing and laughing right along with you,
Yet some suddenly turn fierce, with burst of anger,
clouds puffed up like angry eyes.
Lightning, lashing and swinging their arms
then boom, the sound of thunder
as they knock you to the ground!

I'm sorry, I didn't mean to hurt you.

Bethany Hartwell

Friends

Friends are with you till the end.
Your heart can move in unpredictable ways and bend.
Friends are far or near.
Usually a friend will help you with your fear.
Once you've made your vow to be friends,
you know you've done your job to mend.
Two best friends without a clue.
Wondering and thinking what should they do?
Through good times and bad.
A friend of yours may be sad,
and when the problems is solved, you'll be glad.
Sometimes a friend has committed a crime.
But try to be their friend mostly all of the time.
Friends will always be there for you.
So try to be there for them too.

Pamela Wyman

A Walk Down The High Street

I was walking down the high street
With my mother yesterday
We were doing some window shopping.
As we walked by a I saw some
High school kids on their travels.

A little later we met them again,
As they passed one of them said;
"I think I am experiencing deja vu." And laughed

I wanted to say to her:
"Honey, you are only fifteen and
You have a lot of living to do yet
On your life's journey and you will
Learn many hard lessons before
You are through with life.

One of which is you need to show
And tell people in your life,
Your family and friends, that you love, care and respect them.
It is too late when they are not there anymore."

I wanted to, but I did not. She needs to learn this life lesson On
her own, I just hope is does not happen to her soon.

Anne-Marie Daly

Swimming Lessons

I spend my time like so many others;
swimming through the Sea's ever-churning waters.
At first, I just swim, without any reason;
just continue to look through impaired vision.
But, then I see the Shore with its smooth, warming beach.
It calls out my name, saying, "I'm not out of reach."
I begin to swim with strength toward the sand.
Nothing can hinder me; my goal is at hand.
As I get closer, the waves begin to roll.
It gets harder to swim, the Wave takes its toll.
My strength is diminished, I can't reach the Shore.
I get swept back to where I started before.
But when I again see my Shore, I will swim again.
The Wave... She just laughs... Waiting once again to begin.

The Sea of Life, and all it can be.
The Shore is Happiness, desired by many.
The Wave is my Love, who doesn't love me,
And I am myself... Swimming forever, endlessly.

David J. Peacock

This Is Our Life

It's easy to waste a lot of time on problems gone by,
It's easy to listen to our heads, even when they're full of lies.
It's easy to do what everyone else is doing,
While all the time inside, anger and hatred are brewing.
It's easy to feel sorry for ourselves when we don't get our way,
And if we dwell too long on these things then we go astray.
It's the giving of ourselves, and opening of hearts that's hard.
Sometimes when we look inside, we see that they are scarred.
From years of pain we've locked them up tight,
Not even letting in a small beacon of light
Turning on our defenses we learn how to fight,
Not even thinking of doing what's right.
But if we turned all our anger and hatred into love and doing good
Then maybe the world could live as it should.
And all the energy we use on a never-ending chase,
We could use to help save lives of the human race.
So let's stop feeling sorry for ourselves when we don't get our way,
We have been given a lot, so why not brighten someone else's day.
And let's be sure not to waste another minute,
This is our life, and it's time to be in it!

Julie Barksdale

Night's Promise

In the darkness of night - where light is unimaginable,
I feel myself reaching through the tender fog.
Wrapped in a shroud of blackness, my eyes see only stars
of longing for the warmth of tomorrow's light.

Though the night's darkness comforts my soul-
making its slumber a grateful gift, my
starry eyes wonder if ever they will open
to the reality of the suns morrow light.

Deep in dreams of unthinkable sights -
I must propel myself through that thickness
of doubt - if to escape the forever grasp
of dusks knarled pretense.

Oh daylight don't elude me now.
Creep slowly under my lids and erase nights dream horrors.
Hold my hands in your warm rays and
Caress my soul awake - alive - today.

Vicki Caraway

Another Miracle

The eyes of a child are honest and true.
So full of life and curiosity too.

The greatest blessing for husband and wife.
The center of their dreams, the miracle of life.

On a bright spring day. A symbol of love.
A wonderful gift sent from God up above.

It happens so often, many times every day.
But each time it's different in it's own special way.

And for someone we love, it will happen again.
So we wait with excitement for new life to begin.

The eyes of a child, a symbol of love.
A wonderful gift sent from God up above.

Another Miracle, God's blessing to you.
He'll always be there to see you through.

Jeff Gideon

A Child

Who's the father of my child? Do I know? Is he someone I loved?
Was it lust? Is he someone who will try to be with us always?
Is he someone who will only pay his debt for awhile?
Will he deny? Will he say that he has done nothing?
Is it his responsibility? Is it mine? Is it ours together?
Was the child made in an act of love?
Was the child made by mistake?
Will this child of Ours have both of us to parent him?
Or will he only have a mother to know and love?
Does anyone pay? I? You? The Child?
No, no one will if there is Love...

Becky Stafford

Making Dreams Reality

To make your dreams really come true,
First thing's first; you must believe in you.
Focus on the good; block out all the pains.
Forget about the past, and grab tight your future reins.

Take each new step with an easing stride,
Be humble as you go, therefore keeping your pride.
Keep fighting the battle till it's over, said, and done,
Coz if you gave it your best, you'll surely have won.

So now to put it in a clearer perspective,
Believe in yourself, and know your objective.
Always try your hardest in whatever you choose
And if you do that my friend, I know you can't lose.

Adam Anderson

Night Thoughts

The girl is laying on her back,
in her bed.

The tears soaking through her hair,
to her pillow.

She pulls the sheets over her naked body,
her sore body.

She can't believe what was done to her,
why it was done.

She needs somebody to listen to her,
to believe her.

She can't talk to her mother; she won't listen,
she won't believe.

She can't talk to her father; he won't listen,
he won't believe.

She can't talk to her sister; she won't listen,
she will believe.

Her sister knows the pain; she's lived it,
she caused it.

The girl slips gratefully into the blackness of sleep,
the forgetfulness of sleep.

Linda Quigley

I Imagine

I imagine myself an ocean, I imagine myself the waves,
my life just keeps on flowing with a never ending pain.

I imagine my heart an open door, that never closes or locks.
I welcome the hurt, I hide the truth, and the pain won't seem to stop.

I imagine myself as everything except the person I should be.
Sooner or later, I will be ready to imagine myself as me.

Pamela A. Garner

Thoughts Of Christmas

Christmas is my favorite time of the year
When families and friends all gather near.

Festivities and parties all being planned;
One big celebration that will be just grand!

Gifts to buy and cookies to bake,
Chocolate pies and ice-box fruit cake.

Hanging the holly, then trimming the tree —
This Christmas spirit is getting the best of me.

But wait, have I forgotten the reason
For this beautiful, wonderful Christmas season?

On that long ago night in Bethlehem town
When the wondrous light from the star shown down.

There were no cookies or pies to bake,
No trimming the tree or ice-box fruit cake.

No holly to be hung or parties to attend;
No gifts to buy for the family or a friend.

Only a stable that was filled with hay
Where God sent our Saviour on the first Christmas Day.

Sherri B. Anderson

On Arising

Lo, fainter than the light of dawn,
My heart beats ever so slowly —
Laboring, dying, trying, getting nowhere;
Lo, I must arise;
Push onward, upward,
Explode, create, energize,
Renewed by the sun, by the light
Calmly, I welcome the day,
Calmly, I walk into its embrace.
Calmly, I do.
Calmly, I'm renewed,
I'm refreshed,
Calmly, I live and rejoice!

Lucille Burns

This Morning

The sun rises gently
Over the hill outside my window,
Spilling its basket of radiance
And shedding the warmth that it wears.
The birds sing sweetly, pulling in tow
A green tractor that my daddy rides,
Ready for a day of summer haying.
The bees are buzzing in unified rhythm,
And the roosters audition for a par in Saturday,
A day that will be absolutely wonderful,
For it has begun with this morning!

Erin Hills

My God Has No Long Gray Beard

By God has no long
Gray beard, no snow-white hair,
Nor marks of countless ages
Pressing down,
My God is fresh each day, and He is there
In drops of morning dew
And pollen grains
That carry life around the endless fields.
His fresh, clear voice
Is heard in thunder rolling in
With summer rains,
And in the waves along the sandy beach.
My every breath
is new from Him, but He
Also is in the ancient stones,
The time-worn hills, and on the
Quiet face of death.

Fayne Sadler McElroy

Portfolios

Portfolios,
Portfolios,
Portfolios,
Performance task portfolios,
Simulation work portfolios,
Investigative dialogues go in portfolios,
And analytical observations all help create portfolios,
Those are just a few.
Student driven portfolios,
Balanced portfolios,
Simple rather than complicated portfolios,
Growth over time portfolios,
Picture portfolios too.
Collection,
Selection,
Don't forget reflection.
Last of all, best of all.
I like integrated authentic portfolios!

Mary Jo Olson

How Can It Be

How can it be; when did it happen?
That the area is hill tops and valleys.
See the sky light from one hill top to the next?
Hill and valleys, hill and valleys,
must like life.

How can it be, when did it happen?
Valleys must like the depressions of life.
Like troubles that flow on life's lows,
Low lands flowing between mountain hills.
— valley's like the gutter of life.

Hill and valleys, hill and valleys —
sloping down.
Valut — go half way up the mountain;
water, walk, praise and keep.
Hill and valleys, hills and valleys
remain steadfast ye faithful.

B. Benice Miles Jackson

Windows To Small Worlds

Open your windows. Let the love lights in.
Turn on your heart lights. Someone need a friend.
Children of the world smiling love on us.
Let the love lights in windows to small worlds.

Hear our children. Trusting voices moves faith.
Guide a child's world. Families value their fate.
See a small world through the eyes of love.
"Children need friends_____."

Gentle hearts touched, sharing language of love.
Friends to small worlds, caring angels of hope.
See a small world through the eyes of love.
"Lead them to peace_____."

Reach for rainbows. Dreams are changing our lives.
Every child holds promise rainbows of life.
See a small world through the eyes of love.
"Stand by their dreams_____."

Bless all small life. Love lights streaming the world.
Dress in God's love. Children gleaming with joy.
See a small world through the eyes of love.
"Open your hearts_____."

Gloria V. Russell

"Forget? After Fifty-Two Years Of Marriage!"

Ten long years ago today,
he quietly left his mortal home.
They said, "You'll forget after a while,
get used to sleeping alone."

Last night in my "too large" twin bed,
I dreamt as I sometimes do
that his body curled around mine
caressed me, warmed me, through and through.

So real was my dream, enhancing desire,
I whispered his name, reached out to embrace.
Fully awakened then, to cold reality,
my arms found only empty space.

Just nineteen and twenty when our marriage vows we spoke.
Matured together. Through times of the worst and the best.
How could anyone think I could ever forget,
the feel of his hands as they cupped my breasts!

Alice E. Rinker

Missing

As I start a new day,
I notice one thing goes unseen.

There is a woman I know,
But I have never met her.

I see and admire her,
But yet she is nowhere to be seen.

I feel her presence,
But I can not find her.

I hear her beautiful voice,
But from where it comes...I don't know.

I smell her sweet scent,
But it is only lingering and imaginary.

I think I see the love she feels for me,
But can she see the love I feel for her?

Guillermo Woolfolk

But I Hardly Knew Ya

We used to sing together
you and I and we knew that we were good.
They said we were and we believed.
Back then I hardly knew ya.

We went our way you and I,
not together very much.
Our paths went different ways.
They crossed sometimes as they are wont to do.
But still I hardly knew ya.

You've been taken now.
So sudden and so brutal
They've torn your flesh and
smashed your bones.
But then they hardly knew ya.

I'll cherish the thoughts
of the things we knew.
The clown that meant so much to us,
The songs yet left unsung
and I feel a tear drop from my eye.

But I never really knew ya.

Walter Pyle

Our Dog La Sheba

Our dog is so smart, I tell you no lie.
She maybe can't talk but, she surely does try.
So failing in human, communication.
She developed other means not requiring translation.
There are other ways to get, her messages across.
Like standing by the door, means 'Lets go Boss!'.
And there seems no end to, her word assimilation.
Over a dozen words have, the same definition.
So try to mask, 'I'm going to the park-you hear?'.
Ain't no matter the words used, she grins from ear to ear.
Try to fool her with a spray, one look and she's far far away.
Now people say that dogs, can't smile.
They should see our Dalmatian, with a smile as wide as the nation.
Cute little nibble bites too, to get a smile from you.
Tis a physical abnormality, the Vets like to say,
But why to explain anything, spontaneous and gay.
Just love them and pet them, and keep around.
They'll make your life richer, than anything you've found.

Jack E. Stewart

Dazzlin Diamond Duke

Dazzlin Diamond Duke's his name,
the hardest man there was to tame.
He traveled the world far and wide,
with many a women by his side.
No promises he kept, no vows he gave,
to the women he slept, nor his God that
would save.
He only hoped there'd be mercy for him,
and understanding from the women
he was in.
Then he met a young woman
who wasn't the same
as all of those others he'd forgotten by name.
Much closer in heart the two then became,
and Dazzlin Diamond Duke was beginning to tame.
First lovers they were
then a niece she became,
for he married her Aunt,
and finally was tame.

Carmela Ann LeBlanc

Chosen Family

As life choices guide my physical being
Further and further way from the home place of my youth,
I collect a "chosen" family.
Those rising from my daily acquaintance
Softly take on the color of my own heart...

I'm not sure what really happens, but I do know
Those rising expect no more or less than I expect from myself.
They are doubtless when I have doubt.
I never walk without their presence by my side;
And most important, I never have to ask...

My chosen family never feels an obligation
For we are a family of one heart not of one blood.
The bond that holds my chosen family close is that of selfless time,
Not that of responsibility or the expectations of others.
We are a family sharing the color of our own hearts...

Sheryl J. Kae

Scarecrow

You don't have to stand so close
If you ever want to knock me down
I'm just a scarecrow on a post
With my feet up off the ground
But there's something that you should know
Seasons come and seasons go
Night after night and day after day
They lay on the floor
'Till you sweep them away

Feeling the way I do
Nothing feels better than when you're true
And I want to hold you twice
But I touched you once, and I turned to ice
Then the feeling fades away
I can melt I'm made of hay

Well you can find me at the break of dawn
When the sun has set and the night is long
Just crying in the fields
When everything is wrong, nothing seems real
I'm just a scarecrow on a post

Jeffrey Ray Boyd

Here I Am, Again

Hey, here I am again; the little girl you once knew
The young child who followed your every command
And who I wanted to follow in your footsteps
The child who never spoke out of turn
Or never spared a thought of freedom

Here I am, before you. All grown up to what I am today
A rebel who goes against your words
A stubborn girl who won't follow you anywhere
And speaks her mind without a care
And thinks everything you do is unfair

Why would that girl leave, to places far away
Why aren't she here no more, who could of drove away
In replace is a lady, who does nothing that you say
And wants to go her own way
Cause I'm not that little girl no more.

Jennifer Aguilar

Some Lonely Night

Some lonely night you will remember,
This heart you broke, this love you stole.
Some lonely night you'll come back to me,
Begging me to see, what you now know.
Your cheating life will someday show you
That you were wrong to ever leave.
Your cheating life will catch up with you,
Break your heart in two, like you did me.
Your broken heart will remind you
Of all the loves you threw away.
Your broken heart will not let you be,
Will not set you free, from the hearts you break.
Your tearful eyes will finally see
All the loneliness that you have caused.
Your tearful eyes, they will finally know,
How you hurt me so, and all that I lost.
Those wasted days, are now memories,
Just reminding you of fallen tears.
Those wasted days, they will remind you
Of every love you knew, and be your worst fears.

Russell E. Hovden

If I Could Be A Color/Animal

If I could be a color...
I would be black as the night.
To be the darkness of one's nightmares.
To be the shadows in the bedroom corner.
To know one's thoughts be one's fears.

If I could be an animal...
I would be a fierce tiger.
To be warrior and defeator of
  many African tribes.
To have many villages surrender..
  unwittingly.
To take one swipe of my almighty paw.
To have whatever it is that
  I want, need, desire.

Julie L. Manthey

On Creativity

Creativity is a color,
Rather, it is the color spectrum,
Creativity is a sculpture,
Rather, it is the clay from which you mold.
Creativity is a language,
Rather, it is the use of words, be they soft spoken, or bold,
Creativity is a journey,
Rather, it is the unexplored entered into,
Creativity is all these things,
Rather, it is how big, and and how real, are you?

George Kosana

I Love You

Roses are red. Violets are blue.
Ami you're perfect the way God made you.
If I told you once, I've told you twice.
You're the only one for me, The Love Of My Life.
I love you Baby with all my heart.
Even if I didn't think so from the start.

As I look in your eyes and gaze at you girl
If find there's more value in you than a genuine pearl.
A face that's pretty and a mind to match.
Let's me know you're worth the catch.

So as I gaze in your eyes that shines like Diamonds
At the same time, I thank the Lord for me finding you.
As I count the ways to say I love you.
I still can't explain the ways I care for you.
I sum it up in one special way
And that's to tell you, I love you everyday.

Kevin Jerome Orange

The Musician

There he lay upon our bed,
the wooden instrument in his hand,
Plucking at the same few strings repeatedly,
searching for just the correct chord.

Time and again he plucked and tried
to find the rhythm of the song.
He even spoke a few words to me
and laughed as he went on.

I smiled in reply,
to encourage him to continue,
plucking, trying, listening.

Not a song was it,
just various notes
produced upon a wooden guitar.

But beautiful music it was to me
for it flowed from the gentle hand
of the man I love
lying upon our bed.

Cynthia M. Roush

Light Of The Darkness

The night comes like a dark blanket,
covering up the sun.

Bringing out the sinister creatures,
the ones people are afraid of.

But in this cold and lonely darkness,
there is a light.

A beacon for all the people,
who are afraid of the creatures of the night.

It brings happiness, joy, and warmth,
to all who can find it.

But to those who ignore it
and turn to the darkness,

Will only find fear torment and pain;
along with the terror that lies within.

Katie Glorieux

Cantos 14

My trust in illiterate passion
drives heavy upon the pin like stars,
their hotness, and their light.

In forms confined to liaison
it creeps about cracked craters,
however deep, and white.

It is the drop fallen wet,
watching me through the crystal glass.
Knowing I'll keep my eyes open.

Until, it stops to slap the face of the Earth.

A. H. Minor

Greed

The winds of promise dances 'round the heart and soul of these,
that think what they have become is just what they believe.
They race past life's chances for growth of soul and truth,
then look about with aging eyes still clutching at their youth.
No one reflects when death is the ending of their game.
All the parts that were their life continues just the same.
Who are we that walked this world and never left a mark,
except the one that stains our family's tattered hearts?
Perhaps it is all of us who run our miles in greed.
We should have stopped and given us to those who were in need.

Jimmie Malone Hennis

Beyond The Clouds

When I was a little girl
I liked to look up in the sky
And watch all the fluffy clouds
As they floated gently by
All shapes, big and small
My imagination ran free
Visions of animals and faces
Were looking down at me
I thought what fun it would be
If I were on one of those clouds
Relaxed and floating happily.

Years have passed; I'm growing old
And when I gaze up in the sky
I look beyond the clouds floating by
Oh, what a glorious sight to behold
Heavenly gates open to streets of pure gold
There is a mansion beside the crystal sea
That the Lord Jesus has prepared for me
I see loved ones who have gone before
Eagerly waiting on that beautiful shore.

Jeanne B. Whetzel

Kingdom

Intoxicated by urgency
Infinite sadness disconnecting us.
Reflections in the mirror return vacant stares.
We are a kingdom of fools.

Faded love destroys all hope.
Forever pretending.
Insecurity and insincerity reign as king and queen,
In the Kingdom of fools.

Madness and sadness smashing all Godliness.
Endless gloom and hidden impossibility drain
Our souls. All is in vain,
In the kingdom of fools.

Pain echoes through the streets.
Delusions bring horrible consequences.
Childhood dreams float to nowhere,
In the kingdom of fools.

Jamie Pease

My Heart Aches When

My heart aches when I see you; I'm longing for your touch
I've never wanted anyone or anything so much
I want to be with you, but know it can't be so
How I get by without you, that I do not know
When I see you with someone else and know it isn't me
It pains my heart because that's not how it should be
My love and devotion to you is unlimited and strong
Wrapped tightly in your arms is where I belong
My heart I poured out to you, you didn't even glance
She treated you so badly, don't I deserve a chance?
I guess I should wake up and realize what is true
Of all the things I want but cannot have,
The one I want most is you!

Brandy Harville

My Life Today

Today I see the flowers grow, and
watch the raindrops fall, today I see the
sunshine bright, and love in my heart
makes everything alright.

My yesterdays were not as bright,
filled with pain and a lot of strife.
But when you knew that I was sincere,
you can to me in my lonely room, and
showed me how to live again.

My life has changed, and so have I,
I want to live, no longer do I want to die.
Life has it ups and its downs, but with
God by my side, I no longer want to run and hide.
My eyes are wide open, and I can see,
I want to live, be happy and free.

Marietta E. Thurston

April Snow Years

The morning was white with the April snow
And when the sun came, we watched it go.
It vanished so quickly, left nothing to show
But the drink for the flowers. It made them grow
And that was the fruit of the April snow.

Our years melt as fast as the April snow.
We watch unbelieving. How quickly they go!
What is accomplished? Have we nothing to show?
The lessons we've learned, and we watch Love grow
That's fruit of the years gone like April Snow

Lois Allen Maag

My Special Lady

Oh how my eyes would gleen
for my special lady Marlene
all our years were so great
with so much love there was no room for hate
she made life heaven on earth
filled with love with each child's birth
but now my eyes no longer gleen
but instead are filled with tears
for the angels came and took my Marlene
oh how I shall miss my special lady thru the years

Kenneth R. Smith

Refractions Of Light

I am refractions of light
Bending, opening, cornering
Shining some
Dark some
When in sorrow
I am the shadow that escapes the refraction
I am the full bloom of daylight when at my best
When pensive I am reflective light
In hidden corners of thought
When vibrant I am shifting beams of shocking bright
When sensual
I am the galactic brilliance of being a women
There once was a switch out of my reach
But now in the splendid shimmer of self illumination
I have become choreographer and admirer
Of the dancing light within

Cheryl J. Long

"Our Mother"

Poems of mothers are not very many,
In fact I think there are too few,
So let us pause a while and think,
On a poem for all mothers, dear and true.

It seems to me as always,
In my mind I recall.
When an offspring gets in trouble,
Towards his mother's arms he'll fall.

A mothers love is tender, as well as very deep.
When as a child we were, she would tuck us in to sleep.

When as a child you'd play,
And get a bump or cut.
You would feel the pain is true,
But, your mother's heart you'd hurt.

We never liked to listen,
Or ever seemed to care,
And now we are to blame,
For the touch of silver in her hair.

A mother's love is beautiful, as well as sweet and great.
So give all your love today, and not wait until too late.

James Foley

Untitled

I once heard a bird sing, words of a song,
phone ringing, doorbell buzzing,
dogs barking,
and every single kind of sound.
One morning, waking up in a world of silence.

I see people talking their mouth moving,
but no sounds came out.
Everything's silent.
I look around for help,
trying to tell someone I can't hear.
But I can't.
Whatever I said, wasn't clear anymore.
It was like baby talk all over again.
It was like being born all over again.
Reborn into another world with same people.

Nothing has changed,
except I had been reborn and nobody knows it.
Except for me.
New world, new life, starting all over again,
in a world of silence.

Christina Costello

"We Are Of"

We are of sand and sea
Stepping from the sea
Evolving on the sand
We are of time and creation
Taking time to be created
Creating within time
We are of mind and spirit
Using our spirit to enhance our mind
Questioning our spirit with our mind
We are of air and water
Living by air
Being made of water
We are of question and understanding
Understanding the question
Questioning the understood
We are of machine and living
Living to be said to be machine
Proving yet we are living
We are of life and death
Being both but understanding neither

Michelle Minutello

"You And I"

I can read your eyes
You can read my mind
We are two of no other kind
A blind man learned to walk
on his own.
But you and I couldn't walk
without each others soul.
I dream of growing old and gray
Only with you would I ever stay
Our love is like a beautiful rose seed
Without it our hearts would only bleed
So together touching hand in hand
We'll just live life the best we can
I can read your eyes
You cannot my mind
And with that your love will
always shine.

Lorretta Lee Bennett

Mother Earth

Walk out upon earth's softness, dear,
and feel your cares flow away.
For we were taken out of her,
when made from Potter's clay.

We must get back to nature, dear,
way back to mother earth.
'Tis she who really cares for us.
and knows what we are worth.

Walk deep along our planet earth,
just feel your heart renew.
What nourishment you'll take from her,
let her so cherish you.

Sink deep your feet in adobe dust,
wiggling your toes in her loam.
You are, remember, an earthling man,
And mother is calling you home.

Phyllis D. Dunn

Elegy For My Father

You gave me life...
A heart that cries—
A mind that soars
and will not be still—
A thirst for the truth—
A will that will
not conform
to conformity—
A gift of suffering
that reveals mysteries
many fail to approach...

You gave me life...
And the courage to
thrust through life with valor,
Never accepting
the easy answer.

Linda McMillen

Silenced Passion

Ardent, this feeling
Intense yet, seemingly sufficient
A matrix to my soul...
companion integral?
Is this merely infatuation...
Or perhaps, a feeling which brings
life...re-birth to a once
perished dream
A warmth to the cold of love mislaid
Could this feeling promote healing?
Persuade my memory to bethink past days
when my love was betrayed
Would this feeling illuminate...
Glow true for an eternity?
Mine heart frozen...afright
And yet still hope driven...enticed
Unable to evade
how this feeling I ache
to try.

Michele Takeda

Untitled

The pain I feel, is the air I breath.
The same you do,
Though you don't know it.
The flame my candle burns
Is inevident to you.
My encougagable words go
Through you as if they were air.

Lisa April

Voice To Be Heard

Speak your mind.
No one listens.

Promote peace.
Hopeless cause.

Popularity conquers all.
Why even try?

It will pay in the end.
When is that?

Teenagers don't think.
What is this?

Leigha Senter

The Lonely Night

At night I dream
A dream of you
Your head upon my pillow
Your face is calm and beautiful
I can almost see your dreams
I long to smell and touch your hair
And feel your body next to mine
But when I reach out
To pull you near
There is only the lonely night

Ian Williams

"What Is Love"

Love is a misused word today
just let me explain to you;
we use it as only something to say,
when it should be the things we do.

So here is my prayer for each
lad and lass
As you enter your chosen field;
that everyone your life shall pass
will know you are willing to yield

And give to each one a part of
yourself - true
while you hurry along life's way;
that they may know love is something
you do.
And not just a word that you say.

Pearl J. Miller

Baby Blue

As I lay here in the dark,
I think through my heart.
I lay here and think of you,
You precious Baby Blue.
We lost you so long ago,
People said it was time we let you go.
Our parents and I know
That you watch us live and grow.
You watch over us in the Heavens,
With all the Rachel's and the Kevin's.
Over their families they will watch,
They will see their families thinking
Of them by chance.
But precious Baby Blue, just know,
I always think of you,
You precious Baby Blue.

Brandi D. Yarbrough

Supper Time In Heaven

When it's super time in Heaven
Where God's children are at rest,
They will gather 'round His table
Where there's nothing but the best.
The banquet table will be ready
Heavenly manna in vast supply
Where the tree of life is growing.
And living waters flowing by.
Everywhere there will be beauty
Gates of pearl and streets of gold.
They will view their lovely mansions
As God's heavenly plans unfold.
They will rest there from their labors
And forget Earth's toil and strife;
There they never more will hunger
For Jesus is the bread of life.

Elva Cudney

Untitled

She raised three boys
all on her own
Lived with a courage
not many have known

Though her life was filled
with so much pain
If you knew her
It was courage you'd gain

She always had a smile
along with a joke
Even when the hospital
was where she awoke

Many years passed and
she lived with dignity and pride
For as long as she could
the pain; she did hide

She's in a place where
she'll finally find peace
In God's arms
Her pain will now cease.

Mary Olivas

Our Love

As we walked hand-n-hand we
knew this was love.
The day you gave me flowers we
knew this was love.
The day you said "I love you"
we knew this was love
Then all of a sudden the
flowers stopped, the holding hands
stopped and saying "I love you"
stopped. We knew our love was gone.

Jamie Talbert

Very Early

When I wake up
in the early mist,
the sun has hardly
shown, and everything
is still asleep, and
I'm awake alone.
The stars are faint
and flickering.
The sun is new
and shy. And all
the world sleeps
quietly except the
sun and I.

Katrina Berova

If You Listen

If you listen you can hear
God's voice whisper in your ear
Telling you what you should do;
What is right and wrong for you.
Telling you which way to turn.
If you but listen you will learn
That He can fill your every need
and even help you to succeed
In everything you seek in life
He will ease your pain and strife.
So take some time all thought the day
To listen and He'll guide the way
and He'll be with you all the day long
He will never steer you wrong

Katherine R. Wilson

Wishing, Again

I am wishing, again
For the sunset,
To last longer
For the stars,
To be closer
For the moonlight,
To create a rainbow
A fall of snowflakes,
Without the cold weather
October's full moon,
For every Sunday
Cherry blossoms,
In December
For Peace,
To last forever
And for the sunshine
To dispel, my sadness
For just a day.

Martha Guardado

Always With Us

In a world that's ever-changing
With grief and pain and tears
God blesses us with loved ones
Though worn and wrinkled from the years
But if we stop to listen
And watch the lives they live
Our lives are so much richer
They have so much to give
And when their time has come
And God takes them away
Our hearts are filled with grief
Our skies are colored gray
But once again we stop
And memories start to flow
Instead of pain and sorrow
Tears of joy, our hearts aglow
Although we cannot hold them
We miss their gentle touch
They always will be with us
They've given us so much

Connie S. Applegate

Sad Soliloquy

Can time efface the memory
Of your presence by my side?
I watch obliteration
Refuse to coincide.

Can I forget the feelings
That are tearing up my heart?
Your absence proves how otiose
Our dreams while we're apart.

Our dreams have changed to my dreams
Now that you are gone,
And with only half the vigor
I have strength to carry on.

If somewhere in the distance
Our paths should cross again,
I hope that all the pieces
Are picked up and we'll be friends.

The silent tears have started
As they all too often do
When I realize how deeply
I am still in love with you.

Lisa A. Johnson

"Harder Than Words"

If I could just explain to you
If I could only tell you
If I only knew the words
To describe my feelings true
If I knew something better
than the easy, simple
"I love you."

Danielle Lynn Kirtley

Flashback

The clouds now cry for me,
And the leaves light my way,
And with a pocketful of sunshine
I will buy you the sky and its stars.

And every now and then I'll
Think back to our world
Where God's pools ruled and prevailed,
His foothills reached our highways,
And the days passed by like dreams
in the night.

While forever always the starlight
will shine in your eyes
and numb my heart.

Chad DeBoisbriand

The Spring Waltz

To Jean

The spring walked in,
When you came my way -
And fortune smiled
When we met that day.

For long I have treasured the memory -
Of all those sweet things
you said to me.

As fresh as dew,
on a summer's morn -
As fair as sunlight
that hails the dawn -
Much sweeter in voice,
than the nightingale's song -
That day when you came along.

Many years have passed
Since first we met
So nice to remember. Yes!
All the many things we used to do
And all those happy times
We had together.

Kenneth I. E. MacLeod

The Smile

Everywhere I go, people
want to know.
Why do I smile?
So I tell them, my smile
is nothing more than
a reflection of your own.
And thank you!
A smile is a gift.
Leave it, everywhere you go.

Robert Shepherd

A Wish That Came True

One night I wished,
Upon a falling star,
I wished for you,
And here you are.

I wished for happiness,
A wish that came true,
And it all started that night,
That I wished for you.

Who would have thought,
A wish so sincere,
That a star so far,
Could pull you so near,

Another falling star,
I wished upon again one night,
I wished for us to be together,
And please make things go right.

Coincidence you may call it,
Or you may even call it fate,
For all the time I have searched for,
You were well worth my wait.

Judy Thompson

Someday

You were a great friend,
A dream from a book.
But now I have to find another,
Where will I look?

I wish you didn't have to leave,
But God wanted you there.
I wish I could've gone too,
But life isn't fair.

When you left us,
I know you didn't fight.
Because you weren't afraid,
When you were embraced by the light.

I didn't cry long,
In my heart you'll always stay.
But I believe,
I'll see you again, someday.

Jody Eisenhauer

I Wonder

When will the sun shine no more?
When will the rain stop to pour?
When will someone walk on Mars?
Will we ever reach the stars?

I wonder...
Do babies really understand?
Is there a place with untouched land?
As an adult what will I be?
Will I outlive my family?

I wonder...
Is the end near on far?
Why wish upon a shooting star?
When will all the crime stop?
Who was first to see a raindrop?

I wonder...
What will I be like when I'm old?
Will I be rich with money and gold?
For who is this their last breath?
Is there really life after death?

I wonder

Marianne Lawson

New Mom

Little fingers poke my eye.
Tiny toe nails scratch my thigh.
Is it any wonder why
  as night progresses awake I lie?

Yet to sustain these proddings,
  I would gladly die.
But in sooth,
  I need not even try.

John O. Riordan

The Overcomer's Song

"Come up a little higher,"
My saviour calls to me.
"Each trial is a stepping stone
To give you victory."

"You need not fear the problems
You meet along the way -
Just turn them into blessings,"
I hear my saviour say.

A kitten does not run from mice.
That's not reality.
And neither does the child of God
Flee from adversity.

Christ is not tempted of evil;
Neither tempteth any man.
The enemy — He overcame —
Completing heavens plan.

That when we speak his name -
Declare his spoken word-
The devil cannot linger
For Christ was proven Lord!!

Betty J. Perreira

Nameless Memories

Wandering through, the air blows by
Nameless faces underneath,
Sleeping in, to their fate.
Names litter the walls above
Strings of rainbows at their heads
Floating like colorful halos
Tears float over
People say goodbye
To selfless men
Aboard a ship
Ever moving, souls go before
We give to you
Our love and respect
Thanks for all you did.
But you were still gone
Long before dawn.
The patriots of the Arizona.

Laurel Fox

Hate, Love

A war for hate, a war for peace,
a war for racism to increase.
A sign of hope a sign of love.
A sign of the dead all up above.
Different color, black or white.
Different reasons just to fight.
What's the point, there is no end.
All is hate, there is no friend.
It's time to smile, it's time to cry.
It's time to live. It's time to die.

Danielle Howe

Man On Bench
In Court House Lawn

Wayne, West Virginia

I asked him,
"Are you waiting for someone?"
"Nope."
"Maybe watching something?"
"Nope."
"Taking the sun?"
"Ain't been no sun to take."
A whole sentence, that!
"Do you report on what you see?"
"Nope."
I knew I was out of line,
Had been since the first question,
But curiosity prodded me
And, too, he seemed not offended,
Just miserly with words.
"Well, what are *you* doing?"
"Just sittin'."
"Why?"
"As compared to what?"

There he had me.

J. Thomas Justice

Daisy On A Hill

I sometimes feel
so small
like a daisy
on a hill.
It seems,
sometimes,
that what I am
is something less
than what I want to be.
Like a daisy on a hill I stand
standing strong-
but bending in the wind.
Small, simple,
and only
a little daisy
on a hill.

Darcy Kathryn Creviston

Bubbles

Spheres of transparent color
  drift
    mingle
      wander

Searching silently for
  nothing
    everything
      something

Allowing us briefly to
  drift
    mingle
      follow.

Tracy A. Woodward

Peace

Peace is as a dove flowing
Easily through the sky.
After the Sun sets, it gracefully
Comes to fill my heart with
Easyness.

Rebecca Pagano

To My Teacher

I will not be flagrant
in my love
For you
Judicially I shall measure its worth
Periodically I shall incorporate it
into my life
You who have tempered my soul
and healed my wounds
Measured my worth here
on this earth planet
Restored it to some
Semblance of being
When I
Distraught and filled with misgivings
Thought it better
Not to have a life at all.

To live again as you deem it
For others as well as for myself
As you taught me
I shall teach others.

Helen Titus

Sunset Of Life

As sunset falls upon one's life
Its golden rays reveal.

Qualities of faith, strength and love,
The years have made so real.

The sunset of life can be,
a most rewarding time

For those who find love and peace,
within oneself, and

Strength in the love of the creator,
up above.

Lucille M. Torres

Waiting For Tomorrow

Jesus wrap your arms around me
Tell me that the world is fair
Cleanse us from all thoughtless hurting
Teach us once again to care

Lead us Lord to love our brother
Open hearts for all to see
How You're living deep within us
Blessed by grace that set us free.

Craig Peters

A Paragon Love

She was put into my life,
On a summer afternoon.
Two people brought together,
By fate from a mother's womb.

That God could see such a destiny
He planned in days bygone,
Of a beautiful love so precious,
As to be a model hereon.

Like a star that sprinkles its light,
And our sun which bathes us in gold,
Our love will be a beacon of hope,
Until this world grows old.

Paul Anthony Linehan

Feathering The Nest

The kids are growing fast
and we are off,
for the first time alone.
To places we've gone
a hundred times before,
but now, alone...
The sounds of children
in their playground
rise above the music
in shrill waves of laughter
punctuated by shrieks
as swings reach high
and balls fly off bats well swung.

Vincent Scalese

Who's The Boss?

My husband thinks that he's the boss,
Somehow I don't agree.
The more I think about it.
I think the boss is me.

Of course I wouldn't tell him
Or never ever show it.
But my husband really is the boss.
As long as he don't know it!

Betty Jo Cole

Too Many Immigrants

Border Crossings mass migration
Sprawling cities fearful nation
Making inroads changing faces
Coming here from many places

Overcrowding high taxation
English only Legislation
Governmental Ivory tower
Give the people back the power

Changing language Undertaking
Educational remaking
Tighten up on immigration
Future problems We'll be facin'

Mainstream viewpoint sleeping giant
Long time residents defiant
Worldwide massive influxation
Threatening our self preservation

Voter backlash proposition
At the polls our ammunition
Stop this massive immigration
We want back our Sovereign nation

Darrell E. Ree

Psycho Sister Of The Famous Man

She walked
naked
across the crunchy white grass
goose bumps on dimpled flesh

Mucus dripped
from her hooked beak
plump fingers grasped
the cold metal gate

Pale puffy lips parted
a wide red tongue
planted
on the cold metal bar.

Kit Gearhart

Conflict, Conflict Resolved

Reason says be moderate
in all things that you do.
Then your peers will understands
and praise the temperate you.

Passion's louder voice demands
if it be fun, do all you can.
Now is the time to enjoy life.
Who knows how long, the span of man.

Passion never built a home,
Moderation never wrote a poem.
Age can with a careful blend
teach us on neither to depend.

The two must be united
like the cross hairs of a sight,
The one must blend with the other
like twilight merges into night.

Age, that kind old doctors
can put salve upon passions scars,
and remove the bounds from reasons
so that again we can see the stars.

Robert L. Laumeyer

Beyond The Gate

I've
dug my worms,
they're in my
pail.
I'm gitt'n ready to set
sail,
sail with those clouds 'way
up high.
Gitt'n some trout ready
to fry!
My pole's all fixed from an ol'
green stick,
my hat's all ready with flies,
hand-picked.
That grand-daddy trout will soon learn
his fate...
all I have to do is git,
Beyond the gate.

Colleen A. Barker

Untitled

Galloping wildly
manes streaming in the swift wind
they stop and linger
their eyes wildly pierce the sky
horses are the eighth wonder

Elizabeth Perrine

"My Father"

My Father is very special
One God sent for me
I never called him Dad
He's my stepdad you see
In his heart I know
This must have made him sad
For he loved me as his son
Though I never called him Dad
It's taken many years for
The boy in me to see
He's always been my Father

The Dad
God sent for me

Donald E. Minton

Eternity

When I die don't cry for me,
See you in Eternity.
Least that's where I hope to be.
So when you come look for me.

I believe there's after life,
Where there is no guile or strife,
Where God is and e'er has been,
Knows who's good and who has sinned.

Tried to live a Christian life,
E'er cherished my gentle wife.
Loved my children all the same,
Even if I mixed the name.

God has sure been good to me,
Trust one day His face I'll see.
Never thought death was the end.
Thought an Angel God would send.

'Til we meet I'll pray for you,
Knowing you will come here, too.
Help your Mother ride the storm,
Tell her Heaven's nice and warm.

Richard H. Lerch

"Everybody Have Their Prince"

You've been waiting for him
Ever since you were born,
Sitting there on the beach
All sad and alone.

That magnificent prince
Never came to take you away
To his beautiful castle,
In the land far away.

You've been dreaming of him,
Every night of your life;
Every second of day,
He was on your mind.

You've been wishing for him:
To come save you from hell,
And to take off with you,
With a sword in his hand.

Even thought you do know
That he doesn't exist,
You will still sit and wait
All alone on the beach!

Catherine Pevtsova

Among The Velvet

Stars
Like diamonds
Scattered across the black
Velvet sky
Sparkling, twinkling
Circling the Earth
As she circles the sun.
Mother Earth
Once young and strong
Now old
Her children carving great craters
Into her body
Her soul
Now dying
Among the Velvet
Another world dies
Another light goes out.

Cheri Johnson

Thinking Of You

If you're lonely
And need a friend,
Don't worry
Our friendship will never end.

Whatever you say
Or whatever you do,
I will always
Be thinking of you.

Whatever happens
Or what you'll do
You should know,
That I'm thinking of you.

If I get mad
And start to cry,
I beg you in pleas
Not to feel shy.

And if I had one wish
I'd want to wish for you,
Because you know
Our friendship is true.

Andrea Plsek

Breezes

In spring the breezes softly blow,
And flowers bloom so bright,
Kissed by gentle rains that fall
Durin' warm delightful nights.

Then nights become unbearable,
While roots search to stay alive
Thru long hot days of summer
Growin' deeper to survive.

Cooler breezes blow in autumn,
As plants bow their tired heads,
Blowin' seeds here and yonder
Renewin' our flower beds.

Winter arrives bitter and cold;
Its winds blow quite severe,
Whippin' snow in mount'nous drifts
Defyin' spring to appear.

Winter leaves and spring returns
With soft breezes at long last,
Kissed by gentle rains that fall
Heraldin' the year that's passed!

Karen S. Marshall

Dark Of Night

Dark of night,
why do we fear,
burn a candle,
and stay near the fire.

It is strange,
what humans do,
runaway and cry "boo-hoo",
when burnt by their own creation.

Why do we care about the night,
runaway and try to fight,
the natural cycles of the light,
stand back my child or it will get you.

It what,
what's it,
why must I stay
I have my wit,
and the moon to guide me.

Adam Seidl

Bonding Experience With Dad

My dad is so cool,
he never makes me sit on a stool.
Whenever I am blue
he will come to me right on cue.

He likes his girls so much,
he takes them out to lunch and such.
He lets me build things,
and he'll even buy me rings.

He's kind
and easy to find,
when I'm thirsty he gives me pop
and makes me feel right on top.

He gives me treats,
"hey" they're better than parakeets.
He gives me tons of ice cream
even though mom will scream.

Jessica Krogmann

My Old Rocking Chair

It's just a chair,
That's how it looks.
Kind of forlorn,
A little tattered and torn.

But it is really much more,
If it could just talk.
It's rocked babies to sleep,
And then watched them walk.

Children have grown,
And gone out on their own.
It's been moved here and there,
But it doesn't care.

It's been such a comfort,
A joy to behold.
It brings me much pleasure,
Now that I'm growing old.

So I think I'll just sit,
For a while reminisce,
What more can one ask,
Than bliss such as this.

Anna Read Williams

Sorrowful

In memory of my Great-Great Aunt Mildred Henry.

I never realized,
it would be this hard,
thinking about...
the good times we had together.

Now knowing,
we will never share,
those times again,
wishing I would have told you sooner,
that "I love you".

Now it's too late,
you're gone,
and you're never coming back.

Someday we will be together,
in heaven,
until then,
I will think of you,
Always.

Katherine Allison Haynes

"Love See No Color"

For I am black
But you are white
Still our souls
are destined to be
so don't let color
get in your way
of loving me

Crystal Moran

Forgive Us, Brothers

You went to serve your country
And when you came back home
Though you were back here with us
You seemed so all alone.

Why could we not hear your call
Your silence was so loud
You wouldn't come to us for help
You were much too proud.

Our hearts are heavy now
We know somehow we failed you
We won't get another chance
For what we did not do.

At times we are so busy
We don't hear that silent call
When our brothers need us
It makes us feel so small.

Dear brothers, listen to us
We have just one request
Won't you please forgive us
Then our hearts will be at rest.

Alice Pedersen

Escape

In times of loneliness
and despair
escaping into the world
of poetry
is the only way
to stay alive
and continue
Dreaming

Arnold Gonzales

Broken Promises

A paradise lost,
forever gone.
No one's fault
she is left alone;

The road is divided
and we can no longer hide it;

Love is never convenient
to those who seek
affection in the dark,
the light has blinded
both our hearts,
separated and ripped apart;

Farewell...adieu...good-bye,
I can no longer keep you
from hearing my cry.

Enjoli Meaux

Looking At Your Picture

You know me not
I know you so
I am not friend
I am not foe

I see you there
Yet you can't see me
You're the hottest guy
That I have seen

What once was long
Now is short
You won't be alone
I'll give my support

Your face is sweet
Your eyes are bright
I see you smile I feel your sight
I feel my heart is full of light

You show no fear
Your strength shows strong
This poem started short
But now ends long

Krystle Miller

Realities

'Tis the heart that
captures the truest
reality.

'Tis the mind that
allows those realities
to become true.

'Tis the soul that
keeps them real,
vibrant, solid.

P. K. Fraley

"Wishing"

The sun sets without you here,
as night falls around,
Wishing I could hear your voice,
but alas, there is no sound.

The stars appear in the sky,
as I look up above,
Wishing I was holding you near,
Wishing I had your love.

As day breaks on the horizon,
and things begin to rise,
I'm wishing I was waking up,
and looking in your eyes.

Another day, another journey
I'm missing you so much,
wishing I could be with you,
and feeling your tender touch.

So as the sun sets again,
and another night appears,
I'm wishing for the day... someday,
you'll be wiping away my tears.

Karen Eller

Blue

Blue is the color of the sky,
Blue feels like the ocean passing by,
Blue sounds like a bird in a tree,
Blue looks like cold iced tea.

Ashley Bolinger

Snow

Falling lightly
So that everywhere that it lays
There is peace
It is so beautiful untouched.
But is it not even more beautiful
When it is being touched by a child
Who is touching it for the first time?

Shawna L. Golasa

The Question

If this is the land of opportunity,
Why isn't everyone rich,
Or successful?
Or have a well-paying job?
Why are there homeless?
People starving?
People without jobs?
If this is the land of opportunities,
Where are the opportunities?

Dawn Roof

Untitled

Words of love
caring
sharing
holding hands
love is in the air
stars in the sky
the sand is cold and wet
beneath our feet
the breeze is warm
but chilled by the sea
we but only two in this
mixed up world of love

Kristina Marie Carlson

Ninth

It happened so sudden
Too fast for me
I didn't know what was happening.
My heart got broken,
My eyes got tears,
My words got messed up
Somehow, somewhere
The next day arrived
With my tears all dried
But my heart still trampled
Down deep inside.
My life grew sad,
Depressed but glad
When it has just hit me
I felt like I was dead.

Mindy Leake

Untitled

My son and I we
Went fishing,
But I know now
That he kept wishing
He wasn't there.
That bringing him
Wasn't fair.
He didn't like to fish -
Going home his only wish.
I shouldn't have pressed him
But rather blessed him for
Being the fine son that he is.

William S. Coates

Autopoema

from the meadow, to eleven,
within Ten limits only:
a pen can be tamed, but a thought
must be free.

science answers many questions,
all of them petty;
two thousand years, and the Three
is still ready.

from the right, having strayed
not far from home;
a catastrophe away
from a foreign throne.

the garage door interrupts
nightswimming
six strings fall silent.

Brad Gunton

Morning

Before the sun rises
In the early morn,
The horizon is streaked
With pink and lavender
clouds.
The birds are still
in slumber -
The sunlight has not yet
reached them -
Their songs of dawn
Have yet to be heard ...
And there is a stillness
Between the break of day
And the night that lingers,
That is as Serene
As our Master's Love.

Cynthia E. Gordon

Gone But Not Forgotten

It feels like only hours have slipped,
since your fingers grasped my hand.
Pulling it up to your lips,
making me physically understand.

Our love and passion intertwined,
it burned so hot and wild.
The embers glow from that fire,
deep to my soul inside.

Laughter echo's in my mind,
from stories you would tell.
They whisk me back in time,
to all the happiness I felt.

I allow myself to go to a place,
buried so deep inside.
Your touch left a trace,
of memories that will never die.

Cynthia Gunter

The Valley

The valley's outer beauty
can be seen while the sun's
everlasting rays shine down
upon it.
But as the sun sets
and the moon rises, inner
beauty is shown by the moonlights
sparkle.

Trisha Marie Long

Untitled

I, like
South America,
copy those before
me. With no image of my
own. We are one. We conform
to the already established
others. Yearning for
individuality; finding only
conformity. Uniqueness is
but a forgotten memory.
One which forever
alludes our fearful
graspings.
Conform!
Become!
There is no
escape for
the
blind.

Sara Herzel

Sunrise And Sunset

Sunsets are inspiring,
They are a beautiful sight;
They keep me inquiring,
They are there every night.

Yellow, purple, pink,
Every night a different shade.
It's amazing to think
Of the exquisiteness God made.

Sunrises are better because
It's the dawning of a new day.
It causes me to linger, to pause;
And as long as I see the sunrise
My day shall be okay.

Kamryn A. Cummings

Untitled

I hope one day you will find
This goal that you are seeking
I will be here to guide you
For to me you have a meaning

You've given me a friendship
No other one has known
And ever since your first letter
Stronger it has grown

I found someone who I can trust
Someone so promising and true
And whenever times are rough
"I will be here for you"

Although we may be far apart
I'm just a letter away
Just write down all your thoughts
And all you have to say

"I will be here for you"
Until the end of time
For I found something in you
That in another I could not find

Jesslyn Jardin

The Gypsy Lady

Each week she came to our doorstep
With a large basket on her arm,
And proceeded to sell her wares,
With all her gypsy charm.
I watched with fascination
In what treasures the basket held,
Violets and Primroses,
Or, carved pegs she made so well.
Mother, would sit her in our kitchen
And give a large hunk of cake,
And, with thought of the weather,
A large hot drink to take.
And now I am in America
I often think of her,
That tall, slim gypsy lady, who,
For a silver shilling
Would your future tell.

Doris Fiddyment Griffith

Of Love And Wind

I softly kissed my fingertips
and blew into the wind.
I whispered, please carry these
with all the love I have to send.

Be very careful with them.
Use the moon to light your way.
So he will have them when he wakes
to face another lonely day.

As you go by, please gently drop
My kisses, wet with tears
upon this man I love so much,
but hurry for daylight nears.

Could I ask you one more favor?
You can do anything it seems.
Tell him that he's my love, my life,
My happiness and dreams.

Debbie Baldesberger

Heartsongs

Eager tones betray his heartsong
when conversation frames her.
Uncloaked words spell more clues:
Her heart sings for him.
Intuitive mothering quivers:
Is she the *special* one?
Instant worry claiming:
Will they allow any
"words from the wise?" —
so much to consider
before embarking on
their lifelong sea.
Too soon I'm feeling excited —
perhaps it isn't her
I'm prematurely choosing.
Just can't help loving
whoever's loving him
and breathes his happiness.
We're sharing a mission —
filling his life with love.
I sing my heart for them.

Virginia Artho

We Have The Right

We have the right
the right to seek
the right to walk,
the right to teach,
the right to talk

It would be cruel behavior,
to deny us those rights
We would argue and oppose,
and not give up without a
good fight.

We have the right to be seen
as people,
not by the color of our face.
One could be judged by the
quality of heart, mind, body and soul,
not by the difference of race.

Listen to me for you must trust,
we are like you and you are like us.

Kristy Lord

Life Sentence

With every beat of my heart
I think of you
With every breath I take
I envision your smiling face
Food has sustained my body
Thoughts of you nourished my soul
Love has brought me joy and sadness
One is nothing without the other
Only when I have experienced sadness
Can I appreciate joy
When I am with you, I am alive
Without you, I only exist
Time is my prison
Without you I am but a captive
A prisoner of my desire
A sentence I gladly serve.

Patricia Jurgensen

Love On A Dead End Street

Sometime in everyone's life
when all things seem to go right
with the one you really love,
all the thoughts start fading
and you're anticipating
the time that it will end.

You stare so lonely
waiting for the moment
and your body starts on fire,
it was my fantasy
when you were next to me
two hearts turned into one.

But I left myself wide open
to love on a dead end street
you know nothing lasts forever.

Thomas Kistler

Making A Basket

Up goes the ball
Vicious it seems like
a big brown bear.
Wishing it goes in
X is the spot, right on
the dot.
Making a basket.

Jess Lippold

Travelogue

When first
we met I had to know
where ever you go
will you take me with you

When first
we became lovers
I had to know
where ever you go
will you take me with you

When first
you lay dying
I had to know
where ever you go
will you take me with you

Paul Miner

Solitude

The yearning spirit's wandering quest
finds this quiet place to rest;
Here silver notions help fulfill
the need of peace that pain instills;
Here feathery breezes prove a balm -
unwritten notes and yet a psalm,
and soothing waters help assuage
conflict that could turn to rage.

This
nomadic interlude
brings a sweet sweet
solitude.
Images are free
to glide
from mind to soul
and not divide.
Reason can be
clearly sought
in the silence
of a thought.

Bobbi Long Newman

A Summer's Night After A Fight

He hadn't been mad all day;
there had been things to do;
in the house, in the yard
- - - in the garden.
It was only while the two of them,
stuck in their ways like stone statues
that he had been mad.

Now, the stray bark of a lone dog,
and the murmuring of mosquitoes
outside the screen spoke the sounds
of the night.
He sat with a bowl in his lap
sliding peas from their smooth pods.
As the peas plopped against the bowl, a
slither of air sneaked in as his son
pushed opened the screen door.
Though this time, he smiled at his dad
and pulled up a chair to the table,
and he too shelled peas.

Danny Darnell Sexton

Our Sweet Dream Ends With Life

I know you've been saying
That your love for me is gone
That it was only a sweet dream
And a dream is always false.

You don't know how to lie
But even if you could
You shouldn't break my heart
With something that isn't true.

If you know you are always mine
If I know I'm always yours
Why don't you tell the whole truth
Our sweet dream ends with life.

Oriol Negron

"Crickets"

The stillness of the night
peaceful and calm
Suddenly crickets start
Singing a song.

The sun peeking up over
the hills
Makes the crickets
stop clicking their heels.

As they wait for the
day to end
They think of the music
they will play again.

Janice Kowemy

The Life Of A Sprinkling Can

The sprinkling can when
it was new,
Watered the garden where
all the plants grew.
Lettuce, carrots and tomatoes too,
All in straight rows
awaited its dew.

Now it is old and rusted
it seems,
As it leaks like a sieve
from all of the seams.
Still being useful,
although leaks and no shine,
The can's on the patio
planted with vines.

Dorothy B. Willhide

You Can Do It

For all who live in poverty,
For all who live in wealth,
Listen to the nursery,
Listen to yourself,
Many people try to help you,
Many people want you free,
Just think of it as sharing,
Don't think of it as charity,
Everyone is pulling for you,
Even if they don't know it,
Everyone wants you to succeed,
Even if they don't show it,
So try your hardest, do your best,
Go ahead...
Put your knowledge to the test.

Katie Kovach

I Will Build Upon My Own Foundation

I know much
I've travelled far
A vision I have
Been given
By God

This, I must do
Pulling from all I have
Every jot, every tittle
Must be original

It will come from me
It has been given
Only to me

I need help
Help, from the Creator
The Creator of me

This, I must build
Do it I will
Not upon what another has done
But upon
My knowledge, my skill, my wisdom

Gloria V. Lyles

Imagination

Just open your eyes and see
a magic to believe.
Sorcerers and wizards,
strange exotic lizards.
Where is this place.
With magic in the air?
It's neither here nor there,
It is everywhere!
It is your imagination,
wonders for you to see.
It is inside you,
as it is inside me.
So travel to the future,
Or wander through the past.
Maybe, make the Mayflower
have a broken mast!
This is your world,
so go ahead and deal!!
But please, please,
keep some things real!

Joshua Phelan

Precious Grandma

How are we supposed to act
Now that she's away
Is there a special way to feel
What are the words to say?
She would want us smiling
Our hearts full of love
Knowing she is at peace
In heaven, high above...
All the people she has lost
Now welcome her aboard
There is no pain or sorrow
But reuniting with the Lord
She taught us so much wisdom
Words will never measure
We'll greatly miss her presence
But memories we will treasure.

Jennifer Fuxa

Joy

Easter I received a
pretty cup full of candy
from a friend. That,
was a kind and loving
thing to do.

Soon there after my
cup was chipped. I felt
so sad, it was still new.
I didn't want to throw
it away, for then I would
only have a memory of
what it was.
I decided to keep my cup
and cherish the joy of
giving and receiving.

Donna L. Page

Why?

There lays his
body cold. I reach for
his hand to hold.
The sadness makes
me want to cry. Why
did he have to die?

The perished body on the bed.
Why is he the one
dead? Why did he have
to leave? Hopelessly, I
try to grieve.

Why did he have to go?
That is something I
will never know. As I
live on his memory
I keep. His life taken in his sleep.

Mandy Green

Many Days

Many days,
many years fly by without
even knowing who's there
for you. Then, suddenly
someone special walks
right into your life
and you are aware.
There your life changes
you and you grow, into
a beautiful, loving person.

Katherine Dietrich

"Merciful Soldier"

Death, the merciful soldier.
Reliever of pain, and heartache.

Tormented souls, maladjusted hearts.
Cleansed of burden, and of excess.

Silent and Uncaring.
Unbiased and Unforgiving.

Life is a disgusting timetable.

Punishment is living.
Pardon is death.

You know when you're dead.
Do you know when you're alive?

Now is the time for an awakening.
For everyone is pardoned.

William Saunders

Flowers

Violets are purple and yellow,
Daisies are yellow and white,
Lilacs are purple, while
Queens Ann's lace is white, and
Tulips are red, yellow and orange,
Lilies are orange and white,
And goldenrod is yellow and golden.
These are all very nice
Flowers, but there's nothing as
Nice as a rose, a rose
But there's nothing as nice as a rose.

Hillary Greene, Age 8

Broken

I feel as if I'm closing up,
anger and rage fill my thoughts.
I disappear in my pain,
my happiness floats away.
Depression comes my way,
I can't deny the hurt I feel inside,
Come and stand by my side.
Feel my hurt, see my pain,
watch my tears fall like rain.

Don't decide what's inside
by appearance alone.
Look deep and hard to see
the real one behind the guard.

Sarah Elizabeth Casto

Christmas

One night my friend and me
Went to pick out a Christmas tree.
Not too big,
Not too small,
Not too tiny,
Not too tall.
Decorate it so pretty.
Light it up so bright.
Decorate the house with glee.
Make it fun for you and me.
Go to sleep on Christmas night.
Wake up with your face so bright!

Caroline Elizabeth Burklin

The Luscious

So much forest,
Burned every day.
This is clearly,
Not the way.

The luscious forest,
Goes up in smoke.
And all the animals,
Can't breath and choke.

No more forest,
Just the ash.
And only for,
A little cash.

We grow the grass,
So cows can eat.
And then we use
The cows for meat.

We have to hurry,
Or we will find
The forests gone.
So use your mind.

Kelly Martin

The Glory Of God

Life is so beautiful
Full with the glory of God
The sky, the earth, all in between
Oh, just to magnify the Lord.

The wind that blows all around us
The calmness of the bright blue sea
The beautiful soft fluffy white clouds
Created for all the world to see.

God in all of His magnificent
Sharing so freely His wonderful love.
He is worthy and deserve to be praised
Because Love is what Love does!

Ethel Huffman Taylor

Grandmaw's Hymns

I remember those dear old hymns.
Grandmaw used to sing to me
Sweetly through the vanished years,
Come "Near My God To Thee".

To my memory I hear the Savior say,
Then as though her voice was near
I hear the words "Oh Happy Day".

Her presence always seems to linger
With the words "Come Angel Band".
And then I seem to hear
"All Other Ground Is Sinking Sand".

Those old familiar hymns
Have followed me where'er I roam.
And I'll ever remember them
Till I reach my Heavenly Home.

Mary V. Patterson

Eden

Last night I drifted dreamily,
Into sleep sublime
I found you in the Garden there.
You looked me in the eye.
I searched the soul I knew so well
To find that you had changed
Finally forgiven,
At last, you spoke my name.
Laughter lingered endlessly
Beneath the starlit skies
We reached across the timeless rift.
You led me through the night.
I reveled in redemption.
My peace had come to pass.
Enchanted, lost in Eden
I held heaven in my hands.

Shannon Terry

Approaching Death Soon

A man without faith
lives in fear
The end I feel
is drawing near
A man can tolerate
only so much pressure
He turns to fate
or something lesser
Alcohol, drugs, suicide
One of three he will have tried
If this is denied
he will have lied
I know.

Michial D. Vincent

In Loving Memory...1994

This time of year is here again...
Oh, how time slips away...
And though you're gone forever, Mom,
It's still a special day.

A day for sad remembering...
But happy memories, too...
Of all the years that we were blessed,
To have a mom like you.

You gave us each a life to live...
And showed us how to care...
For if we ever needed you,
We knew that you'd be there.

Your passing left as emptiness...
In many saddened hearts...
An emptiness that lingers still,
Though we've been years apart.

But the sadness of our losing you
Can never take away
The memories of the love you gave...
We feel it every day.

Elizabeth Zerbst

Untitled

Glass of champagne
Bubbled with happiness
Drained in a toast to forever
Put on a shelf
A treasured keepsake.

Moved to another shelf
More obscure
Misplaced in confusion
Accidentally discovered
Slipped from my hand.

Broken pieces
Shattered illusions
Of you, of me
Of us
Swept away.

Romayne Wilson

Cold And Lonely

Cold and lonely,
sick and addicted.
Cold fingers caress,
shivering flesh.
Screams aloud,
gone unnoticed.
Dirty nails,
chipped polish.
You question my thoughts,
I scream at your inquiries.
I rip your flesh,
and tear your clothes.
You sit back amused,
laughing,
blowing smoke in my face.
Cigarette burns and dark scars.
Now you are gone.
And once again I am,
cold and lonely,
sick and addicted.

Annie Flores

"O Life Of Mine"

Flow quickly on, O Life of Mine
Before the sun does fail to shine.
One life, one joy, one hurt, one death
O Life of Mine, please take a breath.

Enjoy the day before 'tis o'er.
Lest you find yourself ashore
Some distant land beyond the roar
Of a life that is no more.

Lana J. Wray

Sand Paper Tongues

They are cute and snugly with
sand paper tongues.

Their eyes sparkle and they have
sand paper tongues.

They come up to lick you with
sand paper tongues.

They purr and meow,
and chew your hair with
sand paper tongues.

They paw your face and lick you,
sometimes the sand paper hurts.

They are cute and cuddly,
with soft, soft fur.
Yes, they are kittens with
sand paper tongues.

Emily Laucks

Someone

Take me, my Lord,
Take me up into heaven.
There is nothing for me here,
No one who cares.
I want to be with you, Lord,
With someone who loves me.
If you don't take me now,
Take me soon.
If it's not my time, Lord,
Please send me someone who cares.
I need someone who loves me, Lord,
And I need someone to love.

Sarah S. Smith

Untitled

A tortured soul
amidst melancholy,
hath no control
escaping folly
of wandering thoughtful hours,
imprisoning one of lesser powers.
"Free thyself!"
I tell myself,
but the enemy never covers.

Kerry L. Briggs

If

If you want to see me come
over here with me. If you want
to hear me come here don't fear me.
If you want to talk to me take
your feet and walk to me.
If you want to smell me come
come over here and tell me.

Courtney Brown

Summer Fun

Summer is here, and
Out of school, just
living the life of Riley
Laying by the pool.

The pool is relaxing, and
fine it seems, but
still with all that
it didn't fulfill my dreams.

I took a vacation, and
Went to the beach,
A long-time dream
I was able to reach.

I took a walk in the sand, and
oh, what a beautiful sight, but
when I got in the ocean
I was filled with fright.

The tide had gone out, and
The waves were rolling in,
What a relaxing vacation
I want to go, again.

Lula Clevenger

Untitled

Together
we walk alone
on a path unmarked
Silently
our feet touch
ground with no direction
Lost
in our emotion
our hearts let go
Forever
we'll be searching
with our eyes closed
Wandering
in the darkness
of this foreign land.

Kira E. Rhodes

Treasured Whispers

Whatever became of the sunlight
That I saw in your eyes
Whatever happened to the smile
I dreamt about over many miles?

Did I cast a cloud
By any means
Or wrap the shroud
Over distant dreams?

I can feel your pain
Echoing through my heart;
I can see your hurt
Because of my part.

Today the wind was you
As I sat for hours,
Amid last memories
Amid dying flowers.

No more can I do
Weather good or bad —
No more can I cry
Over what I once had.

Barb Neeson

Mom

To my Mom - I Love You Very Much!
My Mom is nice,
Salt, sugar and spice.
She is fun,
Snow, rain and sun.
She is cool,
Snow, sprinkler and pool.
My Mom is sweet,
Snow, hail and sleet.
She is all mine,
Clouds, rain and sunshine.
I love her a lot,
Mind, brain and heart.
She is pretty,
Swan, flowers and kitty.
She never makes me feel bad,
Only special, happy and glad!

Jessica Bibee

Mystery Of The Sea Shell

She found a speckled shell today
A pink one yesterday
Colorful among the coral
Strewn along the way

She probed with curious fingers
The depths she could not see
To catch the roaring heard within
She knew to be the sea

With eager expectation
And then a startled stare
The fingers she withdrew were dry
No stain of water there

With puzzlement she came to me
The shell placed in my hand
To solve for her the mystery
Found in the golden sand

But how could I, though longing to
With understanding heart
Explain to her of tender years
God's wondrous work of art.

Jean M. Fox

The Storm

The clouds roll in
The day turns to dark
The street lights come on
As the storm makes its mark

The lightning starts striking
The wind starts to blow
The thunder is crashing
As the storm hits below

The trees are all swaying
The birds cannot fly
The rain starts to pour
As the storm passes by

The clouds start to leave
The dark turns o day
The street lights go off
As the storm moves away

The trees do not sway
The rain does not pour
The birds start to fly
As the storm is no more

Sandra Marie Miller

Earth's Final Wish

I find myself feeling pain,
and I sense a horrid sight,
Men hacking down tree and cane
on a moonless night.

The crystalline air has turned gray,
And the sun can't be seen,
All the animals seem to lay
as if they've never been.

The plants shrink and die,
The world has turned to nothing; gray.
There is no one there to sigh.
No night or day.

I wish I could open my eyes to see,
And maybe I could stop,
What things they are doing to me.
But my eyes are clouded by a tear drop.

Cristy Leann Bryant

Untitled

If I ever saw you in the sky,
I'd catch you,
when you try to fly.
If you were ever in a fire,
I'd come and save you,
and die for my desire
If you were ever broke,
and needed money,
I'd give you all of mine,
isn't that funny?
If you were ever in a play,
I'd come and see it,
every day.
If you start to love me,
I know I'd love you,
always a bit more.

Anna Anselm

Waiting

How long should a parent wait
To reach that destiny or fate
That with a child in harmony
Share privately, without parsimony?

How long must a parent wait
For honest union before too late
It is for them to share
Important thoughts, with none to spare?

How long can a parent wait
To with a child communicate
How long precisely can it be
For quarreling spirits to be free?

How long will a parent wait
For sincere love's wide open gate?
No one can foresee how long,
Only time can wait this song!

Earl C. Bateman, Jr.

"That Girl"

She walks into a crowded room,
That girl wears a frown.
She works all day and sleeps all night,
That girl feels down.
She scans the room and makes a scene,
But no one seems to stare.
That girl's invisible,
So she leaves without a care.

Pamela Makuta

Whisper

If I could be but just one thing
I would be a whisper
As quiet as a butterfly's wing
I would be a whisper

Loving words to a baby's ear
I would be a whisper
Secret things for a loved one to hear
I would be a whisper

Words of comfort when there's sorrow
I would be a whisper
Words of wisdom for tomorrow
I would be a whisper

And if you ever needed me,
All you have to do
Is talk as soft as can be
And I am your whisper

Aleshia Lynn White

"In Due Season"

Another year has slipped and gone
But my soul to God is won!
I miss with you, things to share
Yet, no more can my heart tear
I will resist that which is leaven
And my soul too! Shall go to Heaven
Yet, on earth awhile I wait
For God to open the pearly gate

Jacquelyn L. Seward

The Dove

Over the cliff a storm rises;
sapphire sea crashed up against
the rocky wall.

Wind was crying through the
bewildered air.

Tree branches and crimson
leaves whirled around like
kids at a circus.

My mind went wild thinking
of what could be happening.

Suddenly everything stopped.
The trees, water, wind, and my
racing thoughts.

As I saw a single white
dove flutter up from the mist.

Emily Mitchell

No More

No more harsh cries
Brought on by foolish lies.
No more cruel fights
Reconciled with passionate nights
No more false starts
Ending in broken hearts.
No more, No more.

No more drunken sorrow
Waiting for a loveless 'marrow.
No more lost time
Wishing you were mine.
No more regret
Hoping to forget.
No more, No more.

Dennis L. Colley

Congratulations Shelley Renee Garcia!

My Child;
You are the challenge
  of lives you touch.
A challenge to better understanding of
  our mosaic of cultures
Holding the beauty of
  an anglo in appearance,
But with a sensitive heart
  of your Pueblo heritage.
Holding the joyfulness of
  your Hispanic culture.
Somewhat assertive from
  that touch of Navajo in you.
Embrace all these cultures
  for that is what makes you
  a uniquely precious being.
Vision of dreams yet to
  be attained
For you are loved
  just as you are!

Vivian Wato

The Path

The path
I must travel it alone
No one to reach out a hand
The path's so dark
Shadows whispering my name
Trying to blind me from my destination
A cold wind blows
Chilling me and producing a shiver
I look around
The shadows are moving closer
Smothering me
I no longer breathe
The night grows darker still
Shadows press closer
All goes dark
I will never see again

Dawn Patterson

"America's Heritage - 1993"

Once upon a time
In the not so distant past,
Pen was put to paper
And now the "die" is cast.
While statesmen storm at taxes,
To hide life's darker deeds,
The blood of unborn children
To highest heaven pleads!
Talk not - "God" or "Mercy"
Talk not - "Liberty" or "Sin,"
America, America,
You are buried
From within!

Ruth A. Black

An Immortal Love

It's a weight upon your shoulders,
it's a tear inside your heart,
It's a feeling of lost hope,
when God wants two to part.

First comes shock, then disbelief,
then wishing one was here.
Until you finally realize,
the one you love is near.

Andrea Sagerman

amalgam me

i am
peeling off my sinister chrysalis
during the most hurricane thoughts
  twister confrontations
when before my hand was held
  [even loosely
  it felt secure]

i step out
grab the arcing moment
take the muzzle off my mind
  sublime
at first a tentative soul rhyme
to see who i am

wham!

fermata of the slick slip
fermata-singing mind sip

blanketed in watercolor song
blended diffused boundaries-non (but)
resolute
    there

naked oh naked my naked me
          bare

Sophy Shiahua Wong

Lost Is Not Absolute

I can't believe what I see
My thoughts, my dreams, my fantasies
All taken away from me

A flame burns deep inside
Emotions destroyed with lies
From the ashes I shall arise

Not knowing what to do
Not even the slightest clue
But one day I will come back for you

Harvey L. David Jr.

San Antonio 1996

Latinos laughed
And strutted the River Walk
As Lone Stars cried
Broken in old San Antoino.

The winding Rio
Flowed the tears
Of slaughtered souls
Lost foes in death.

Happiness floated
Barges of nameless eyes
Passing silent cypress
And Crockett's guarded stand.

Etched copper plaques
Names repeated
In a timeless chant
Uttered as unforgotten facts.

The Alamo proclaimed
For the Texan mass
A proclivity widely professed
Freedom hard won tames.

Johnny Lloyd Redd

Baby Boy

Ten little fingers
And ten little toes
Two blue eyes
And a little pug nose

A smile reflecting heaven,
A laugh like a seraph's song.
God grant our baby boy
May ne'er on earth go wrong.

We love our dimpled darling
And daily for him pray
Asking the Lord to lead him safely
Down life's broad highway.

Bonnie D. Phillips

Stop Look And Listen At The Cross Road

I did not listen
'Tho I have an ear.
I listened
But I did not hear,
I heard
But did not understand.
I understood
But did not give a damn.

I did not look
Although I have an eye.
I did not see
My brother die.
I saw
But did not understand.
I understood
But did not give a damn.

Everett B. Keating

Night Awakens

Night awakens -
Opening such twinkling eyes..
On her dreamy complexion
Soft with twilight lavender
And deepening steadily with its
rather cold advance -
Away have fled all the day's blush -
full pinks
And from her bright oval moon
she casts silver shimmer over
the now hushed and bespeckled,
great harbor.

(Night awakens to the flickering
harbor lights of the great
bay)

Paul Kogut

The First Night Flight

The room is vast, and empty,
The chairs are stately and still.
The hum from the escalator,
with no one on board.
The beat of the loud speaker.
Flight 1001 will be late,
Finally, the unlocking of the door,
And the roar of the incoming plane,
And people everywhere.

Joanna Ketcham

No End

It was beginning
No, again and again
the pain will not go away
It was the beginning
It'll never end
till I stop it

It's crumbling on top of me
eating me away not to see
the real thing inside of me.
It's beginning again
the pain, the suffering, the tears.
Everything pours down on me
just like a powerful waterfall
falling down on a river

It was ending
yes again
But soon enough
it will begin
because in my world
there is no such thing as the end

Arelly Saldana

The Angels Know

We were picture perfect
from the outside looking in
But I knew the secret
You took pleasure in your sin

You tried to keep me quiet
by striking with your words
Pray the screams were silent
That no one overhead

I made a peace inside myself
that you can never own
I don't feel the screaming now
that chilled me to the bone

If you ever get to heaven
and Peter stops you at the gate
Just calmly whisper in his ear
and he'll decide your fate

So make up a solid story
A good seller always tries
Hide behind your sweetest smile
because the angels know your lies

Tracy Callahan

"A Winter's Morn"

Frosted windowpane
snowflakes falling,
Crackling fire
hot cider's on.
Children bundled
rosy cheeks glowing,
Pulling sleds
to McCarthy's farm.
Mother's baking
thinking of loved ones,
Peaceful time
on a winter's morn.
Frosted windowpane
trees limbs laden,
Young deer frolicking
on this winter's morn.

Gary R. Ellenberger

The Whispering Wind

Dear Heavenly Father,
your whispering voice
I hear in the wind,

In the caressing breeze,
or the raging gale
that makes the mighty oak bend.

Your gentle voice I hear
in the stillness
of a warm summer night.

At the breaking of the misty dawn,
or the brightest
noonday light.

I behold your glory,
in the beautiful
rainbows ray,

Whether arched o'er a roaring city
or a deep
and silent bay.

I feel your glory in the setting sun,
at the close of day,
when my tasks are all alone.

Anna Holt Leak

Why?

A boy yells at another
and the other yells back.
The boys come to blows
and the cops are called.
The heat's turned up
and things get hot.
Weapons are pulled
and one is shot.
A knife hits pavement
and sparks.
One is bleeding.
He is now scarred for life.

Was it meant to happen
Or was it an evil accident?
Who knows how it came to blows.
Never knew it would go so far.
A fight between boys,
over a fifty cent baseball card.

Jennifer "Fot" Simmons

Best Friends

Life is not always fair
and sometimes not worth living
but you keep me going
and my spirits high

You are always there
whether I need you or not
you've stood by my side
through a hell of a lot

You are my best friend
and thank's are not enough
to express just how I feel
always remember I love you

Through it all you've put up with me
during the good and the bad
even though you don't have to
you are always there for me

For these reasons
I show gratitude
and hope that you're here
for quite a few more years!!

Holly Taylor

God's Love

God's love is full of grace; that
we must acknowledge he extends to
the human race.

God's love is full of compassion; that
we must understand he does not
withhold nor ration.

God's love is full of joy; that
we must believe is available to
every girl and boy.

God's love is unending; that
we must accept to the fullest with
our heart's singing.

God's love is all, for all.
God is love!

Isobel S. Gridley

Daughter, Daughter

You are mine.
strong of heart and
intriguing mind,
shell seeker, dreamer,
caring, loving and
kind...
So much to give, so
little time...
I'll cherish the day
someone will be thine...

Elinor Gallup

"6:00"

Resting on the front porch
My legs dangling from the swing
The sun is now descending
And softens everything
I gaze into pink horizon
I'm remembering my youth
Those days were kind and warm with me
Like that of sweet vermouth
Beneath the weeping willow
I use to sit with my books
Shaded by my poetry
The words that my life took
In parchment pages
I found elusive bliss
Like blue within an emerald
Or a lover's passionate kiss
How often I have forgotten
These days that I hold dear
To me they're now a memory
As I sit dying here.

Elizabeth Stow

Suppress

My frustration brings power
To the many powerless,
When there lives more of my pain
It creates more of their bliss.

The rosiest cheeks
Are washed up by tears,
The brightest of eyes
Are blinded by fears.

All of the beauty
Is dimly lit plain,
As I slowly close my eyes
To be hidden again.

Alexandra Joyce

Love Is

The tying bind that keeps us
together, though apart
The thread that holds together
two separated hearts
The hope that keeps us going
when skies seem dim and grey
The guiding light that shows our hearts
to a brighter day
The force that keeps us loyal
(a force time can't defeat)
The tingles you send down my spine
when our lips finally meet.
All these things, and many more,
are all gifts from above
One word couldn't describe them all,
but one comes close; it's love.

Eric Rodriguez

Why Oh Why?

Why oh why?
Can't little fishes fly,
Like a bluebird,
High in the sky?
Why Oh why?
Can't bluebirds swim,
In the water,
Like a fish?
Oh! But they can!
With a wish,
Half-inch of water,
In a dish!

Mary A. LaPlante

The Precious Hour

Time is so precious, but when gone
away, we wish there were more.
The sweet smell of the morning
Dew, the lovely sounds of singing
birds, the one you loved calls
you near. Where has time gone?
I wish it was always near. I
can recall my yesterdays, thoughts
of tomorrow escape me. Winter is here,
can't remember many things so precious,
time has taken away.

James P. Broy Sr.

Day Dreamer

Standing still staring
in wide eyed wonder
as dainty dogwoods dance
and distant dogs daring

can life be as simple as
smelling a rose in full bloom beauty
or watching winged wonders
building a nest

I find it so until
I hear with a clang
my mantle clocks call
from down the hall

Back to rêality I must go
to leave day dreams to others

Donald Holth

The Sunset Of The Year

Yellow red and orange
Are the colors of the leaves
That swirl around my feet
In the sunset of the year,
As I pick the last peppers-
Yellow red and orange-
Not a single green one left.
Soon the peppers are roasting
Over yellow red and orange flames,
And then a pretty palette on my plate.
As they warm me up inside,
I glance outside-
Yellow red and orange
Are the colors of the sky
At the sunset of this day
In the sunset of the year.
I try to hold them in my mind
For tomorrow everything will be white-
It is the beginning of the year's
Long cold night.

Keith C. Olsen

Rare Occasions

Thinking
Praying
Lost in thought

These are rare occasions

Ever so quickly they can come
Ever
so
gently
they
move
on!
So, make it a special goal
To take a moment of your time
To listen to your soul

Judy M. Breunig

Hearts

Two lonely hearts
standing in the rain,
trying desperately to see
through each other's pain.

Both heads down
while they walk apart,
neither knowing where to go
both with a broken heart.

They never see each other
through the blinding rain,
now two more hearts
slowly go insane.

Casey Lynn Hankins

Symmetry

The red wine, dressed deep in crimson,
savored on the palate,
runs to my head and
offers visions of God.

But too much wrongly sipped
brings Satan himself.
Respect it then as a gift from God,
and stay the demons.

Linda D. Clark

"Twinkle Of Love"

At night as I lay on the soft
green carpet of grass and gaze
into the dark black heavens above
with the beautiful twinkle of the
stars shining with love I think
of the universe so far away and yet
so near I wonder if the twinkle of
that star is the shedding of a tear
It's a tear of love for all those who
give of themselves for others love
for those who are kind and caring
who take time out from their own
daily lives to brighten the life
of another I hope as the years pass
so quickly away those twinkling
stars will continue to say Thank You
you'll always be loved it's sent to
you in the twinkle above.

Carol Ann Lankford

Rainstorm

As the rain comes down,
The thunder sounds,
With lightning again and again.

The wind was howling,
The coyotes scowling,
At the rain flooding their den.

Rain will leave,
And come again,
And make the weather unruly,
Sending the sun to hide,
And as you abide,
The clouds step aside,
And everything turns to sunny.

Nicole D'Arcy

The Decoy

I am but just a decoy
That drifts with shifting tides,
Tempting, trapping weary fowl,
With wings of wood and eyes of dye.

I watch with scorn as piercing shots
Halt freedom as it flies,
And woefully wounded brethren
Cascade through mourning skies.

Could I, I would one moment then
Cry out with warning calls,
To spare a life which freely flies
And then so limply falls.

Yet silently dwell inanimate shrieks
Within my splintered bill.
My wooden heart is filled with shame
But, helpless, drift I still.

Could I, would I just warn my kin
That they might fly so free.
Then here my weary wooden heart
Could drift in true tranquility.

Gerry Hughes

Link

Near some times, then far away
A strife is flowing like water's end
The blades of hatred forged in time...
No one's fault but mine.

John A. Wanczyk

A Tribute To Alfred

A man came this way
and he tarried awhile.
He brought with him love
and a warm hearted smile.

He knew about pain
and he knew about joy,
Yet somehow this man
Preserved the young boy!

A man came our way
and he touched us with grace,
For his love of life
Was etched in his face.

A father, a husband,
a brother, a friend.
This man who gave love,
was loved to the end.

A man came our way,
and he tarried a while,
He left us with love -
When you think of him, smile!

David L. Ackerman

Journey

Take away the lightning
And thunder will not roar
Every thought becomes forsaken
When reality comes thru the door

Every step begins a journey
Seek and you will find
That the path that leads to eternity
Is alive inside the mind

Take away the dreams of man
And watch the sky turn grey
Everything you see in this land
There was a dream to guide its way

Every storm brings on rainfall
A down pour from the eyes
Anger rips thru the walls
And sorrow says its goodbyes.

A. T. Dowler

Untitled

I am a person with feelings
I wonder what people think of me
I hear when people don't think I do
I see their expressions when they
look at me
I want them to like me
I am a person with feelings

I pretend that nothing bothers me
I feel as if life passes too quickly
I touch the surface of reality
I worry that I'll never do anything
with my life
I cry when I'm lonely
I am a person with feelings

I understand the humiliation brought
on by others
I say "See me for who I am,
not what I look like"
I dream that I'll find someone to love

Michelle L. Dodson

Freedom

To drift on the wind
Like a bird in flight
To be lifted up to
The uppermost heights

To feel freedom
Coursing through your veins
As you listen to the winds
Peaceful refrain

As you glide and dip
Your troubles fall away
And you find that you are
Looking at happier days

Leave your worries behind
And remain steadfast
Looking too your future
Overcoming your past

Cheryl Crichton Heilman

"The Love Of My Life"

The one I've waited for
Has arrived at last...
A spell on my heart
He has cast.

To that my eyes
Will see none other...
Than the beautiful face
Of my angel, my lover.

He is the love
I could never forget...
For in loving him
There could be no regret.

All of my dreams
He has fulfilled...
For he alone
Has my heart be stilled.

And so a lifetime
Could not be enough...
To share with him
This burning love.

Maria M. Jimenez

Someone I Once Knew

Someone I once knew
was always there, he always
helped me and he always cared.
And his eyes were like the
water blueish-green, and when
you looked at him you'd just
fall in a dream.
And you couldn't help
remembering his brilliant
smell, it was like cool
water in a brilliant sea shell.
And his skin was dark
and smooth like the
summer's sand, and I'd
be beside him cause
I was his biggest fan.
His hair was black with
a reddish touch, someone
I once knew is someone
I loved very much.

Joni Arnette

The Transformation

Oh how you were
fuzzy little worm
Happy in your world
With knowledge and faith unquestioning

Secure in days and nights
Lit up by the stars of others
Trusting and content
To be a worm

Then rain and cold
Settled hard on your soul
Sent you spinning yourself
Into that dark and lonely cocoon

Looking through the darkness
Rivers of time rolled on
From the questions and confusion
Come wings of joy

Now how beautiful you are
Happy little butterfly
Guided by the light
Inside yourself

Robert Wallace

The Beam

Around a corner
Down a stream
I see a spotlight
Like a beam

The beam is bright
It'll make you fight
For the power
Which is light

It's very strong
And never wrong
And its power lasts
Ever so long

Kristen Barnes

Dawn

Wind will blow, fire will burn
Waves crash in the sea
We all stand proud when it's our turn
But how disappointed we will be

Love and hate, hate and love
Tears flow as we cry
We all hear voices from above
Then we all must die

It's said that life is but a game
A game we all must play
Are we prepared for our shame
At dawn on judgement day

Derek J. Lambert

Say It Today

To me, it just isn't right
  to love someone
And never tell them so.
  Sometimes, it's a short road.
Sometimes, it's a long road
  As on this earthly journey we go.

On the short road of life,
  A word of love helps
remove every strife.
And if the road of life be long—
Love ever helps to make
  the weaker strong.

Josephine Moorefield

The Merry Muse

The retiring muse of poetry
Left a merry muse to run things
Giving her the chance she yearn for
To enjoy all kinds of fun things

First she threw in lots of giggles
Then some grins from ear to ear
Next some belly laughs for accent
To be use year after year

She stood back surveying proudly
What her verse ability had wrought
Knowing that the higher powers
Might well fire her on the spot

And indeed she was in trouble
They agreed they had to do it
So the merry muse was fired
And it looked as if she blew it

But when people kept demanding
All her giggles and guffaws
She was quickly reinstated
Amid thunderous applause

Doris Berry

Heartbroken

Night after night
I'm here alone
Hoping that you
Will call on the phone

Time goes by slowly
It seems to drag on
And I pray for the day
When the pain is gone

I can't stand another minute
Sitting here all alone
Hoping that soon
You find your way home

Memories haunt me
They won't let me be
Will you ever come home
And love only me

I hope that one day
My heartache will end
And you come back to me
And we try love again

Patti McMasters

To Caleb

I've painted for you
The most beautiful picture
Of pretty blues and pinks.
I've inlaid greens and golds
Because they are your favorite colors.
To this I've added a water fall
With streams of sparkling silver
And a bed of clouds
To rest your weary head upon.
I've given you the freedom to run
And trees to climb about.
And in the end I've given you
A river to quench your wildest thirst.
I drew a beautiful yellow sun
And warmed your soul with love.
But in return you gave to me
A pallet of black and grey.
And somehow through your darkened mist
I've found the courage to try again.
And I love you caleb

Brea A. McLeod

Do You

Do you know,
how I feel?
Do you know,
that it's very real?
Do you know, do you care?
That my life,
is full of despair.
Without you,
how do I live?
Don't you know
you have to give?
For my spirit,
is tumbling fast.
Do you even know,
of my dreaded past?
As I ask these questions,
through my tears.
I know that the person understands,
looking back at me,
through the mirror there.

Georgia M. Seeley

Eternally

Bitterest love: Sweetest hate
over my soul with coals, do rake
for can I love,
with broken heart
my fair world
torn far apart
ahh, to love
the goal of all
as eyelids close
and tears do fall
canst thou hear
my love professed
doth thou return it
with nothing less
for my love
exceeds the sky
my naive tongue
sheds not a lie
sweetest love: bitterest hate
I shall love thee; until far too late.

JoAnna L. Davis

Bubbles

I am in this encloser, this bubble.
It keeps me from finding myself.
I am here, I answer to my name,
but I do not know who I am.
I cannot express myself.
No one knows me.
I am alone, in this bubble.
It shelters me, but keeps me
From finding my real self.
I must escape, I must get out.
I must know the real me, and
others must know the real me.
I must break my self out, by myself,
for myself.
How, I do not know.
But soon I will be free.

Kimberly McKnight

Love

Love is patient and kind,
Love is there all the time.
Because our hearts might fall,
Jesus love makes up for it all.

He wrapped us in his loving flow.
To heal our broken souls.
To cleanse us through and through
So that God can see us, too.

He spilled out all that was in him.
He gave all that he could give.
Just so, we all could live.

To some this was foolish.
To some it was insane.
And some do not believe in his name.

But in the end
The some will see
The love that covers me!

Rita Bruce

Sh-h-h-h

Ah, Silence is a lovely thing
('Tis golden poets say)
And 'twould be fine if life would bring
A bit to us. But nay.

We must needs chatter endlessly
As o'er life's road we trod.
And talk we shall until (ah me)
We rest beneath the sod.

God gave us tongues to speak, and yet
'Twas a mistake, I fear.
When using them we oft forget
He gave us ears to hear.

Speech may be silver it is true
It helps the time to fill.
But take a hint from one who knows,
"For Goodness Sake, Keep Still!"

Frances Lebensorger

Life's Clippings

As we travel ancient highways
Mid the catastrophic splendor
Wander through these human cryways
Smiles in pride, the great pretender.

Though the multitude of reason
Sets the callous observation
Branded bare, in scarlet treason
Made their chartered reservation.

Inconsistent in the Measure
Passing through these traveled channels
Shapes these tender foils of pleasure
Stretched in bare pretentious panels.

Enter then the King of lightening,
Covered minds, in darkened corners,
Wash the serpents stain to whitening
Robe the new, in spotless garner.

Gleaning restorated clippings
From beginnings left entangled,
When life's often sordid slippings
Find the serpent, strangely strangled.

Helen Richards

Macho Man

Give me men of pride and hate,
Feed them fear no one has ate,
Kill the Pigs, Resist the State,
Macho Man is feeling great.

Endless lines of powdered slaves
Put the blocks to costly caves,
Common boys in common graves,
Macho Man begins to rave.

"Warning! Warning! Extreme danger!"
"What you mean 'we' Lone Ranger?"
Jesus Christ, stay in your manger,
Macho Man is getting stranger.

One and one and one make three,
I think I am therefore I be,
Napalm smells like victory,
Macho Man...anomaly.

Tom Gordon

The World Through Clouds

Perceive and yet see not,
Those things all around.

The smell of lost flavor,
Tell us we are there.

Who is or is not,
A sensation of status!

The touch of a breeze,
Or is it a thing unseen?

We are not divine,
But only divine through creation!

Without our soul inside,
Just another part of nature.

Just as 'Speak not
And be not heard.'

The lost of heavenly walks,
Have followed Eden.

Know yourself and be not afraid,
The sight of heaven all around.

William Mitchell

Phoenix

I am a phoenix
Fire in the sky
I'll live forever
But I always die.

Or am I a scorpion?
King of my world
Stinging all who comes to close
Death in my pocket.

Or am I just a lost child?
Searching for home
A freak in a world of freaks
Dying among psychos and fanatics.

Am I the hunter or the hinted?
Fire or ice?
Will I kill or be killed?
All I want is peace

Aaron Haganz

Untitled

A sunny day —
I'm running around the pond
searching
for frogs
and turtles;
trying not to be afraid.

There's a smile on William's face —
he got one!
He got them all.

Kirsten Kirousis Yanco

Crossing

Anything is everything,
True, if you have nothing.
The bridge is old.
People still cross.
They pray on the cross
Mark my words in permanent ink.
Words of wisdom from an ignorant mouth.
The old tire in the river beneath the
bridge...
Feels pain washed away, it fights,
But talks only to rocks.
Stones break windows and bones.
Hunger shows bones.
Dogs bury them, we lose them.
We lose our backbone, like a snake.
The boots on your feet were made of me.
Walk through the pasture with me.

Brian S. Siatkowski

Stand Up O Man

Stand up o man on your own two feet,
That God has given you,
Stand up tall and walk upright,
The way God planned you to.

Don't make your life a hell on earth,
And fall in Satan's hands,
But lift yourself out of the mire,
And raise up with God's plan.

Seek to know what's wrong and right,
And strive the best you can,
To help regain the paradise,
That God once gave to man.

If you would learn you've got to sow,
To reap the good you earn,
And also if you sow what's bad,
Then that's what your returned.

Stand up o man, and walk in light,
And help where ere you can,
And live in peace with love for all,
For this too is God's plan.

Arlene Windom

Spring Rain

Rumbling in the distance,
Little flashes in the sky,
Quietly announcing,
A thundershower nearby.

Smell of rain,
Stir of wind,
Gentle downpour,
Sun again!

Lynelle Gilman

You Are Not Alone

A touch
A smile
A listening ear
A helping hand
when you can no longer stand
You are not alone on your journey!
do not fear the unknown
for you will enter it in your own home
Surrounded by family and friends and
caregivers that really do Care
physical mental and spiritual aide
is what we provide
don't turn us away don't try to hide
open your door and let us in
we are Hospice

Linda Levens

Chocolate, Chocolate, I Love You!

Chocolate, chocolate I love you:
Melted or solid any kind will do!

You're rich and creamy
And oh so dreamy

People always say you're bad for me
But how you fill my heart with glee

Without you what ever would I do?
I could never live without you!

Chocolate, chocolate I love you!

Heather Nave

Transformation

Will power ever return
in this body caught in the
embrace of remembering only?
Sixty nine years of pain held in
every cell, the body giving way
in this moment of glorious freedom.
How does one hold life tenderly while
giving up those things loved?
Confined, held down, a whisper.
There is a way, a way to transcend,
to heal, to love, to create.
Refine the gold, mold it, make it
a thing of beauty. Then dance, dance,
dance as you danced in the dream, the
dream filled with numinosity, making
you whole, as you melt into the cosmos.

Phyllis Ward

Rapture

I started half full
You let me grow at my own pace.
Life distilled drop by drop,
Filled me to the brim.

You let me take my share
And I let you live in my soul.
Each day a new bridge,
Each night a new dream.

Our bodies together,
Discovered the ecstasy of creation
And the peace of silent affection.

Life continues to fill the void
Drop by drop.
Relentlessly.
At its own pace.

Percyvaldo F. Wendler

The Contest

I'm writing a poem
For a poetry contest
The judges will decide
Which poem they like best
If I may boast
Then I must confess
That this poem of mine
Is very much unlike the rest

I found this article
In Teen Beat magazine
Featuring Elizah,
Andrew, Devon, and J.T.T.
I read the advertisement
Mentioning the no entry fee
My eyes widened at
The possibility
Of having a poem
Published to be seen
Thank you
National Library of Poetry

L. A. Allen

"Life"

I'd hold you
  if my life told me not to
I'd pray for you
  if my religion was wrong
I'd stay with you all night
  if Dawn never came
I'd give you my life
  if yours had gone

Cari Jaenke

Carvings Of Love

Carvings of love wither deep;
as GOD! proclaims thy winning fleet.
As thou feel thy tears I cry,
thou wickedness is planted deep-
as if a throng is well rooted
beneath as scarlet seeps;
my crimson blood from thy heart;
pouring to an endless river from
which my heart still adorns.
As thou gallantly play thy role;
to pin thy heart upon thou scroll.
A lying tongue, at last! Will find;
a river of fire for thou to bind.
If thou will not accept, GOD! his law;
thou will proclaim thy winning flaw.

Sallie Murphy

Expressions Of Joy

Why do we let ourselves be angry?
Why don't we face life and begin
To know that our emotions
Have their origin within?

Doubt and hatred, envy and fear
Keep us shackled, though God is near.
We find Him in our quiet place.
There, life's problems we can face.

With each thought, we too create
and become masters of our fate.
By our acts we can express
God's love, through joy and happiness.

Harriet Keesler

Sea Of Cotton

As I drift along
In this silver ship
I sit and gaze in wonder
For sprawled out before me
Soft, white, and fluffy
Enhanced by sun
Appearing tranquil
Is a sea of cotton

And though beneath it
A storm may be brewing
Raw, dark, and savage
Driven by the wind
Carrying rain or snow
I still can't help but ponder
Whether it truly can be
That only angels can lie
On such a sea of cotton

Thomas Wisnowski

Sad Song

Poor me
Poor, blue me
Poor, poor, blue, blue me
Oh, who will come lamenting
Oh, who will sing my song
Who will cry a river
After I am gone?
Poor, poor, blue, blue me
Poor, blue me
Blue me.

Blue song
Blue, sad song
Blue, blue, sad, sad song
Dream a dream of sadness,
Tomorrow it will come.
Smile a smile of gladness.
Tomorrow brings the sun.
Smile, smile, glad, glad song
Sun, glad song
Glad me.

James Edward Morgan

"Travels"

My life is a rough road
Stretching straight ahead of me,
Trailing into the horizon
As far as I can see.

My dreams are my compass
Directing my straying feet
Instructing me where to go
When two roads meet.

My sorrow is my sail
That tosses me round about
When the foul wind blows
And causes my course to be doubt.

My joy is my anchor
On to which I hold
Without it the road is far to dangerous
For even the most bold.

The Lord is my captain
Guiding me along the way
Directing my path
During both night and day.

Christel Nash

"Peace"

Everybody if you can see,
treats everybody unequally.
If only if their eyes can
see, that they're just like
you and me...

If you treat someone equally,
you'll be treated respectfully.
If you be a peacemaker,
you'll be loved by people,
you'll see!!

Michelle Jacob

Vicious Cycle, Again

Loops through circles...
I'm trying to get somewhere.
Mind whats the matter...
How long does it take to get there?
Wanting Everything...
But not doing anything about it!
Haven't Figured it out yet.
I'm hurt! I'm Angry!
How do I get there from Here?
How do I start it?
How do I Finish it?

Shannon Baum

Eternity Of Love And Peace

Beauty seen throughout
the forgiveness of darkness
leaving us peace
through the world that it amounts
with the love of you
and many others
can bring peace
through the love of brothers
though in God's name we trust
will bring us life forever

Stephanie N. Ryan

"Forever Cry"

Forever cry
Is forever my soul has to,
Look forward to.

As fast as you were in my life,
My soul, my body, and my mind.
Just as fast as you were gone.

Forever cry,
Is all my body can do.

Why, why, why,
Why cry until I lose my mind.

Crying so deep, so lonely.
You never leave my mind, the feel.
For the first time I left so real.

Forever I knew,
That I was hooked on you.

So now I cry, because you're gone,
Knowing you will never be mine.

But I rather cry for you,
For life, forever, then to have never,
Ever, ever been filled up with you!!

Melisa L. Murphy

A Summer Day

There's a dear and precious memory
I think of from time to time.
It lingers only a little while,
Secured safely in my mind.
A thought of my old home place,
Where I lived as a child
Spending each day without a worry
Free as the wind blowing wild.
The memories lie not in the wood
the brick, stone, or tin,
They are of a child's rearing
Can you not go home again?
Back to the green grass shining
In the Summer sun,
To the beautiful pinks and purples
Casting shadows as the day is done.
As I stand and gaze out my window
And wander at the passing of years.
I can see home again

I see it through my tears.

Beth Harville Helms

To Be A Bird

I am a bird,
I can fly.
I am a human,
But when I die,
I am a bird.

I am a bird,
Free to roam.
Maybe, maybe not,
But I'm on my own,
When I'm a bird.

When I'm a bird
I'll fly high.
No 'crack' or 'coke',
Just me and the sky.
As a bird.

As a bird,
I'll fly around.
Only to eat and sleep,
Will I touch the ground.
To be a bird.

Jordan Ferguson

...the Federal Reserve is broke...

The federal reserve is broke
the F.S.L.I.C. Is up in smoke
the dow is down
the exchange is extinct
the economy is a ship
leveraged to sink

O' whatta we gonna do?
We cry out from our pew
what can pull us out?
Who can save our asses?

Came the cry
from today's generation
of huddled masses.

My collateral
is lateral
my finances are sum
and baby
you're the only one.

Michael S. Chernik

Nature's Contrast

If there was no sun,
Would it be fun?
If there was no rain,
There would be no grain

Had there been no seas
Where would go the seals?
Had there been no sky,
Where would the birds fly?

There must be music soft,
To soothe the coarse sounds,
Light heralds us aloft
Erasing dark scenes which lie aground.

There must be day.
Or else where would be life's ray?
The appearance of night
Blots out the potent, radiant light.

Vivian Anthony

Memories

The time has come my family
when mother will be away.
Keep the love between us
each and every day.

Love is so important
memories are the same.
Mother will always be with us
in the memory of her name.

Remember all the gatherings
that we had when she was here.
Keep them in your hearts
treasure them so dear.

Family is so important
Mother used to say.
Keep the love a'flowing
each and every day.

Look and you will see her
in the memories that we hold.
For Mother is still with us
in memories made of gold.

Carolyn Griffin

Free

Life after death,
Not being afraid to die,
No more pain,
No more suffering,
No more nothing.
Just to be set free is the
only wish for me. To have'd
the thrill to live life on
just before I died. Knowing
I tried my best and more
not to hurt another soul,
but it didn't turn out the
way I planed so now I'm
ending with this final
phrase, life after death; will
we be set free.

Annette Gordon

Alone

I tell you of my private cell
A fate worse than hell
Turned bitter by scorn and rejection
a prisoner of my fear and hate
I cannot bear this of late
Please God take me home

Scott T. Ripley

Waiting For A Wave

Once at the beach,
Out in the calm ocean,
On the perfect surfboard,
Far from shore,
And far from the crowds,
A young surfer,
With a feeling of adventure,
Waiting in the still sea,
For a great wave to come.

Erica Shipow

Another Fork In The Road

Look at all the endorphin freaks
running along the bridle path
casual power elites they are.
As the young men cross town
work out working - class
eke out their meager existence
choking their once innocent dreams
all these schemes that enslave
how does this seem to you?
That is your choice?
Run the heavenly path of freedom
or heave-ho the docks of burden.

Steven Mark Minichiello

New Home

God shines down on me and you
Every night and day
To try to find the right one
That he will send his way

I did not fear for where you went
When God put you to rest
Because I knew deep down inside
That he always picks the best

I really truly miss you
But you didn't go alone
A part of me went with you
When you went to your new home

Alisha N. Becker

As We Share The Same Cloud

As we share the same cloud
a million years from now
I will recall how sweet
and tolerant you were
in our instant on earth
me will pledged our love
for an eon
our love
that was born in that instant

Clifford Perkins Stowell

My Time

My time for loving
My time for giving
My time for sharing
My time for caring
My time for laughter
My time for joy
What's your time for?

Dorothy Champagne

A Little Boy's Dream

Fat Man's nuclear waist,
Silently threatening to break.
To release...
A bomb blast of blubber,
An earth shattering shudder,
And reverberating repercussions,
Of an overweight mistake.

Mike McGranahan

Love Is The Ticket Home

Here, life is good now,
more than enough to eat,
no death falls from above
or lurks within smoking ruins.

Yes, life is good now,
but not for everyone.
Unwelcome news sinks in,
is imploding her unveiled heart.

There, terrorism —
predatory, ugly,
twisted, sinister, dark —
last strike, Saudi Arabia.

Here, she meditates
to raise consciousness,
to heal rifts in her soul.
The only thing she can do.

Dorothea M. Rupprecht

Untitled

The falling rain sings
as it hits the ground,
making sweet music
for all those around.

Not many listen
but all do hear,
the drops of water
thrown far and near.

Soon the rain stops
and the sun breaks through,
starting the day
fresh and brand new.

Damyn Adams

Woman From York

There once was a woman from York,
Who used to eat nothing but stork.
The huge bird in question,
Gave her indigestion,
She's thinking of switching to pork!

Linda Johansen

She Walked With Snakes

She walked with snakes:
King snakes crawled beside her
Displaying friendship-yearning,
No harm done.

She swam with snakes:
Moccasins skimming peaceful waters
Displaying mutual respect,
No harm done.

She sat with snakes:
Rattlesnake coiled in tree-trunk roots
Displaying no fear, but
No harm done.

She walked with snakes:
They pursued conflicting ways
Displaying rejection, indifference,
Great harm done.

She walked on snake:
Garden snake on Father's lawn
Displaying great fear,
Some harm finally undone.

Jane Kilen

Inside A Moment

Explain a dream,
inside a moment.
Where life, is lost,
to an effortless scene.
Explain the emotion
compelled by a scream
felt piercing your moment,
inside your dream.

What opens you mind,
to fly so free.
Then draws you down,
into an electric salt water sea.

Are you aware
the endless space you roam.
The eerie sense of knowing
you haven't come here alone.

Have you discovered
as you enter despair

Inside this endless moment,
your dream became a nightmare.

Lura Taylor

God's Single Tear

God protects us with a single tear,
that will stay with us forever.
When the day comes,
when we join Him in peace.
We will live as He does.
With Him as one.

Jeanie E. Miller

Epoch

At present I lie in a bed of roses.
Now the stained petals array in poses.
At this very time,
Nothing lingers in my mind.
The thorns pierce, severing through.
Here I receive the immediate clue,
Knowing now the end is due.

Jennifer Leigh Curry

My Son

My son
Knows how,
Like the waves
Lapping the shore

To wipe the sorrow
From my life

He writes a smile
On my face
When we hold hands

My Son
There is only one
What life he has!

Wherever he goes
He leaves his exuberance
Within those he has met!

Carol Loftus Cahill

A Secret Place

Running through the grass so tall,
In my Secret Place I fall,

In the meadow far away,
I spend some time there every day,

A Secret Place I know and love,
A beautiful sky up above,

The open land and tall grass,
The wildflowers in a mass,

No trees, just the birds,
The silent birds that speak no words,

A Secret Place where I can think,
When my friends and I don't link,

I see the sun shine up above,
I also see a pretty dove,

My Secret Place I hate to leave,
This place is the best place I believe.

Molly Wessel

A Gift

From the moment we are born,
The rush to death begins
Life is a puzzle,
Not understandable and grim
Unless we have a proper
view of its end
This life is but a prelude
to a glorious existence
to come
Provided we have faith
in our father and his son
there is a gift
Freely given, available
to you and me,
in eternity.

Robert L. Pope

Peace

Peace is like a flower,
Just waiting to bloom.
Peace is like the moon,
Just waiting to rise.
Peace is like the ocean;
It has wrinkles in it.

Jessii Peck

Freedom

No one owes me
I owe no one
This is perfect freedom

No one owes me
Why should I judge people
I owe no one
Why accept people's judgement

What good is a philosophy
That doesn't make you happy
What good is anger
That doesn't manifest itself
Into something positive
What good is hate
If it only hurts yourself

What good is being right
If you're dead

Jeff Hinkle

My Daughter

She awakes only to smile,
a heart full of warmth.
A day filled with new adventure,
a night of blissful dreams.
Together is all we know,
from day to day we can't let go.
To share thoughts of happiness,
a life of love to come.
She is a rainbow of laughter,
a spring shower of delight.
A child at once she was,
an adult to be.
Only to leave my heart,
in total harmony.

Michele Zika

Untitled

"Drowning in a sea of books
What a way to go
I'd rather read myself
to death, than any other
way I know!

Ethelyn Lee

My Husband

He's talented, witty
And so full of fun.

His smile is like
A slice of the sun.

So why does he vex me?
I really can't tell.

Could it be all the mixes,
He mixes so well.

He likes quiet, sweet women
Who talk on and on

A wife, that's not busy,
But gets everything done.

The mate, that works not,
But gets paid every week.

And I know if I lost him
My life would be bleak.

Helen Lopez

Advice To My Daughter

To my daughter,
my only child;
don't be like your mama
don't be so wild.

Don't take chances
you can't take.
Don't purposely break hearts,
or your own will break.

Don't sit and analyze
what is in the past.
Listen to your mama,
mistakes don't last.

Don't forget to send
your prayers high above,
and never ever doubt
your mama's unfailing love.

Brandy Laurel

I Close My Eyes

Here it comes the midnight creeper
To drive the knife a little deeper.
I close my eyes
And see
The angels killing
But the cries are drowned out
But the preacher
Shouting "love thy neighbor"
I close my eyes
And see
A man atop the grave yard wall
Escaping from his grave
Or to it?
I close my eyes
And wonder
Am I lost
In the strange and hostile world
Of make - believe
Or am I lost in reality?

Amanda Lowe

A Rainbow

A rainbow is an ark of color
streaking across the sky
A rainbow is an everlasting love
that comes from a dove and no other
A rainbow is a Garnet Ring
embedded with ruby's all aglow
A rainbow is an angels path
across the shimmering lake
A rainbow is a circle of pearls
showered with emeralds and diamonds
A rainbow is a sign of promises
made from Jesus Christ to you
A rainbow is vein of gold
or so it seems to me
A rainbow is a special promise
like no other has been given

Stacey Collete Beall

The Factory

I listen and do not hear.
I sleep and do not shut my eyes.
I dream and do not wake.
Are these forty-eight moons to build
my path?
So far, the first twelve already have.

Anne Marie Ragland

My Special Friend

I have a special friend,
who fills my heart within.

He's made me laugh,
He's made me cry,
especially when we said good-bye.

I hope and pray,
that maybe someday,
that he'll be back to stay.

To see him again,
would bring joy within,
that I can hardly wait to begin.

I have a special friend,
who fills my heart within.

Laureen Copeland

Heavens Of Love..

The man we all loved
Is now gone.
He is now a white dove,
In the heavens of love.
We pray each night
That we will see the light.
Beyond the heaven of love,
When you see the angels above,
You know we are all loved.
Black or white,
It is all right
Because we will see the light
Beyond the heavens of love!
People will lie and people will cry,
But no matter what
As long as they believe
Up above they will see
A sky filled with love
Because he, the dove,
Will always make you feel loved.

Amanda J. Conner

"Realization"

Not a preoccupation
It's a realization -
Ribbons and buttons
And pieces of glass.

To most other people
Would look like trash,
But in my heart holds -
A special kinda class.

The future of these things
I hold uppermost in my heart,
Only the hand of death
Would part (me from these things)

That is why I worry
The hands these fall into,
My spirit wishes to keep
These treasures in view.

Wendy L. Lacy

Balloons

Big balloons, small balloons
All shapes and sizes
Lifting gently from the earth
Lightly floating to the sky.
Onward, upward they meander
Over rivers and rough terrain
Near to rocks and rugged valley
Safely returning home again.

Jane E. Hicks

Mundane Adventure

Come, walk with me.
Up, past, beyond meadows
Of flickering gold.
Feathery fennel fusses
With bountiful,
Bonnet bouncing butterflies,
And staccato bees.
Bronze faces, haloed,
By butter-bean white,
Surround a snafu
Of split rails
Ruefully riddled by rain,
The lullaby of time.
Hillsides gloat.
Jade sachets
Shifting in the breeze,
Emulate a sedative,
To my senses.

Jane L. Wiseman

Poor Blind Lady

Confused, worried, scared,
Walking across the street
Just stepping into her home,
Not knowing the people's faces,
Wondering what it would be like.
Not knowing if life needs me.
Pressured by what's around.
Not seeing, but imaging
What she thinks is there.
Thinking you stepped into a store,
But into an street,
Sleeping a hour,
But really four.
Seeing isn't believing.
Believing is seeing.

Amber Lee Montanio

The Colors of a Flame

As I look into the flame,
Wondering where,
For whence it came.
From the past,
Like a looking glass.
Or future toll,
Like a human soul.

It tosses and turns,
The colors burn,
As it reaches to the sky,
And glimmers there
In the human eye.

For hence it came,
That's what was told.
By stories both,
Bought and sold.
Of people past,
Present too.
This question I do ask of you.

Does the flame burn pure and true?

Stephen J. Donahue Jr.

Zia Pot

This one -
geode of the corn god
beseeched by ancestral prayers,
its geometric spin of sacred clay
auctioned into the 20th century.

Walter-Byrnell Figler

Just For You

You're scared of life
You're scared of death

So lay back your head
and take one deep breath

Think of all the people
who love you

Think of all the strange
Things above you

Then think of how you'd rather be
Dead with nothing or alive with me.

Jamie Paul Torres

My Prayer

Lord Jesus when I'm tempted
from you to turn away,
and follow paths of wickedness,
Lord Jesus, bid me stay:
Safely in the sacred shadow
Of the cross of Calvary;
always bring to my remembrance
that you hung there just for me.
Let me fix my eyes upon you
as the blood flows from your side;
let me hear you softly whisper-
"My Child, for you I will die."
Let me forever remember
your words, "Father forgive," and know
you will supply the strength
My life for you to live.
So, Jesus, when I'm tempted
Some evil deed to do,
remind me gently once again-
"My child, I died for you!"

Martha E. Morgan

An Arizona Storm

The roof is gone, the walls are down,
The cow was blown away.
The chickens never more will roost
It was a dreadful day!

A lake was born behind the barn,
The water was knee-high,
The river overflowed its banks,
The fields are still not dry.

Sing me a song of days gone wrong
And how it feels to be,
Free as a bird, but busted, in
This land of liberty.

Alberta Jean Spidell

Jay

I taught a little boy
by loving him.
I had nothing else to teach.
And he learned
by loving me
That nothing is out of reach.
And when he carries
his yesterdays
Into all of his tomorrows,
I will have given him
the tools he needs
To manage his joys and sorrows.

Colin Sterling

"Hollow Eyes"

The building is quiet with hollow eyes,
Passing rooms I hear low cries,
Chairs being wheeled from room to room,
Eyes big and hollow like doom,
Old woman staring, poor ole dear,
She seems so lonely, wants to talk,
With extended hand, I help her walk,
Tears running down the ole dears face,
Onto her dress and collar with lace,
Once she held her babies that cried,
Patted their hurts, oh how she tried,
She kissed their faces and loved them all,
Now her children won't even call,
A time to be born, grow up and get old,
Then you get sick, lonely and cold,
You're put in a home and how you fear,
Visits will be once or twice a year,
Hollow eyes in their room,
Help them out of their doom.

Gail Kuntzman

"Holy Spirit"

Holy Spirit Thou art mine.
Truly Holy Spirit divine.
Sent from the Father above.
Given through Jesus and His love.
Mine to know personally.
He'll intervene whenever I falter.
Through Him I can freely pray before the altar.
All I need do is call.
For He is here within me.
It's so wonderful to know.
That I'm never alone here below.

Beverly Daub

"I Miss You"

I can feel the pain of loneliness filling my soul
It's so dark and hollow inside
I often just sit and cry
I do love you, and that's no lie.

The days dreadfully drag by
And nights are even longer
It seems my love for you
is only growing stronger.

It's hard to go through this
for the both of us, I know
My thoughts in life now
is how far our love will go
Because no one
should ever feel all alone.

Wait, and I shall see
Just what life will bring me
But soon, I've got to have
your loving company.

Leslie Ann Lindstrom

The Ocean

The Ocean washes up upon the shore, a shore
Where birds can go and soar,
the sand is wet and very soft too,
when the ocean comes up behind, and
says to you Boo!!
Then the spray of the ocean lands on
your nose, and the soft, soft sand
tickles your toes.

Amanda Bloom

In The Wake Of Feeling

A leaf flutters softly to the ground,
Rustling gaily in the autumn air.
I stand alone.
The wind drives the clouds across the sky,
Driving but never reaching anywhere.
I stand alone.
With nothing on my mind,
With everything on my mind.
I stand alone.
Hands shoved deep within black holes,
Fists clenched.
I stand alone.
I stare at everything,
But my glaze falls short of seeing.
I stand alone.
With the worries of today,
The fears of tomorrow pressing against my brain.
I stand alone.
In the leaving of the day,
And the absence of night, alone I stand.

Megan Fitzpatrick

Always Love You

Such hell I went through-such
misery, I wanted to hold you
but you didn't want to see
me I said all I could to
keep you from leaving your
insulting comments were all I was
receiving finally you told me the way
you feel, my heart dropped, I
can't believe you feel no guilt —
you told me you loved me, and
I told you the same, all you
wanted was my body, I feel so
ashamed — I was more angry and hurt
than sad, we lost it that night,
the love that we had it's over
now, there's nothing I can do - it's
better this way but I'll always love you.

Julie Stutes

All Alone

When I lay down at night and close my eyes
I say my prayers quietly for there's no one around
And when dreams and nightmares wakes me up in the middle of
the night
There's no one there to wake me up
No one to share my fears, no one to hug me to reassure me it's
alright...

And in the morning, when I finally wake up
I thank the Lord that I've survived another night
And as I get up to meet the new day
I'm faced with a room full of silence for no one is there
It is unbearable that makes me want to go back to night

But then I remind myself that this is a new day
A new day of possibilities
I have to be strong and ready to see what this new day may bring
I have to fake it with sweet smiles
Walk elegantly with pride and continue to show the world
That I am happy and not only trying to survive...

Emelinda Punzalan-Mayuga

Love

Love is a look, a touch, shared between us.
A glance at a chance, to become one and enhance,
all of our feelings, hope and dreams.
That together we bring
into this new beginning.
Being supportive and honest,
with devotion undying.
Through times when we feel so uncompromising.
Learning to give and to take,
for love is at stake.
Forever growing together,
learning from our mistakes.
Entering into this union,
we are now more than just friends.
It's up to us whether it blossoms,
or whether it ends.
So please take GOD'S gift,
nourish it, cherish it and watch it grow.
So it can give you more happiness,
than you could ever know.

Cheryl L. Becker-Wiech

Our Love

The Ring you placed on my finger on our special day; is a symbol of our Love; The stems array carry the diamonds placing them with stride of beauty and grace.

As you and I strive with wonder and splendor for the proper direction in life, let us each Know our hearts beat as one; there is always added strength.

"My prayer for our life together is: May we always take time to listen; let us look for the sparkle in each other's eyes; when we touch or kiss is to feel and remember the depth of Our Love".

While Our Life stems with growth, may we always keep the trust and respect intact, as our love is to be free and flowing always.

(There is no Love such as Ours)

Regenia Bon

"Sweat Dreams"

In the beginning you took me by my hand and wouldn't let me go. You told everyone she's with me, she's mine. You slowly pushed your way into my heart, calling me your beautiful baby. You showered me with love and tenderness, asking "me" to be your wife. I let the wall down putting my heart and soul in your hands. I put my heart and soul in your hands believing in your heart. Over the years you have cheated on me and crushed my heart to pieces. Even after all you have done to hurt me, I look back to my "Sweat Dreams" of the beginning and find the strength to keep loving you. I know now what my Dad meant when he said, "Sweetie, one day you will know what true love really is." Look back to your "Sweet Dreams" and your bad days won't be so bad anymore. Your "Sweet Dreams"! Will mend your heart.

Connie Bates

Breaking Up

Why, oh why, did he leave me?
He said he loved me didn't he?
He swore it'd always be me and him forever,
but the next time we kiss will be closer to never.
He even said he was my very best friend,
right now I feel like my heart will never mend.
Constantly he dreamed of our future together,
now I guess believing it wasn't too clever.
Now I see his eyes look at me so cold,
He'll never again be mine to hold.
He said his love would never die,
but it did the night he tried to get high.
Now as I touch the necklace he gave me with the tiny cross charms,
I know I'll never forget the night he died in my arms.

Angela Binder

Reminiscing

In sleepy soothing solitude of solemn, sultry care,
A myriad of memories are waiting for you there.

The chilling bite of winter winds while sledding in the hills,
The moonlight on the mountain tops that eventide instills.

Feel the warming touch of springtime, flowering fragrance everywhere,
Daily, song birds sing serenely, nightly fireflies fill the air.

You've picked strawberries on a grassy hill, raspberries by a stream,
Blueberries near a sandy road, mulberries in between.

Then basked on sunny shimmering sands, in summers at the shore,
And took long walks at midnight that you'll cherish evermore.

In autumn all of August's heat gave way to cooler spans
While school bells brought a busier time to idle children's hands.

You dressed in costumes simply made of cotton, paper or lace,
To bid October fond farewell as seasons kept their pace.

November meals at Grandma's house before a cheery fire,
December's sweet surprises for any child's desire.

Daydreams of a future life may serve to take you far,
But its memories of the life you've had that make you what you are.

Edna Giddings Herring

Maybe

Maybe we are but sand, in the sight of sea gulls,
the turning of times, last winged witness, to face the sea.
Maybe we are but a froth, on an ocean's racing foam,
a spec of nothingness, on lime rock's, dissolving stone.
Maybe we are the imperceptible cutting edge,
of a lost horizon's, final creation,
the sheer balance of a pompous arrogance and the gift of existence.
Maybe we are but tiny ships' lights,
adrift in an early morning fog,
like wane and dying stars, a superimposed flicker,
of ancient fires started long ago.
Maybe we are but a swift arc of nothingness,
convoluted as the wind, yet soft, as the aroma,
of a pine tree's laden needles,
piled into slumbering perfumed heaps.
Maybe we are the grace and dignity,
of wide, white rivers, that surge,
and in a thunderous fountains fall.
Maybe we are, and maybe we are not at all.

Joseph J. Scott

He'll Never Know

He beat me everytime he would come home,
And, I knew one day I would have to make it on my own.

He would go out to parties and get drunk every night,
While I would lay there in my bed in a stage of fright.

This man I call "Dad" is a man I've grown to hate.
But, he took care of me, he put food on the plate.

Altho' I still must go,
It's strange that I still love him, but I guess
He'll never know!

Brent Wayne Bowers Jr.

Summer Wakening

Early robins and mockingbirds sang a perfect love song,
A pink tapestry of roses bloom their most enchanting,
And fragrant flowers yet of the year,
Bedroom covers had a sweet surrendering sweat,
That was share by two lovers of sixteen years,
Everything in the room delighted her senses,
She knew it was because she loved him,
More than life itself,
When quiet times came it was if church bells were,
Ringing peace for those who believe in miracles,
The benefits of the long lazy golden summer days with him,
Was a trill to her heart full of love,
The uncertainty of the future seem dim,
When he console and shower her sole with love,
The splendid mixture of their union,
Made her believe their summer blooms,
Would last throughout an early frost.

Jennifer Lee Morgan

Burning In Sense

Smoke rises from the incense
I am burning like ethereal ghosts
twisting in contortions of pain

Or frustration, because it's just smoke
an illustration of a breath of air
moving off the cold window

And dancing like I want to move
swift and slippery as an exhale;
spitefully graceful, ungraspable

Because I tried to touch it
twirling around my finger
and flying away on its silent breeze.

Bryan Davidson

The Mothering Kind

With every thought of you on my mind,
I've come to know you as the Mothering kind.
Out of my search and quest I finally find,
You're the one, yes, the Mothering kind.
The love you give, the tears you shed, they all intertwine,
The greatness of them all Madam Mothering kind.
Thanks for the friendship and adoration divine,
You irreplaceable Mothering kind.
All your worth and meaning He binds,
May God continue to bless and keep you as the Mothering kind.

Valerie Y. Butler

Endless Song

Sometimes I wonder who really cares, people have
so many hateful stares.
I sit and wonder why I'm me, I can't stop the pain I feel or see.
I wish I wasn't so alone, I need someone to love, to hold.
The thought of death is overcoming, I believe that's the
only way of escaping.
But suicide is beyond my reach, it's not considered one of my beliefs.
Death will come to me one day, and I will go willingly and say...
"Take me, I am no use here. No one loves me, no one cares.
Take me to a place of peace, I can leave and existence will cease.
Everything will be easier then, I will no longer be there when,
all life is full of sadness and grief."
Then, slowly, I will sadly fade away.
Who will care if I die anyway?
Life is like an endless song,
I shouldn't be here,
I don't belong.

Jahara Hojilla

Linda

The shadow casts across the stream,
And shade an everlasting dream.
The shadow dims the light of day,
And stands unyielding in the way.

The shadow remains from a former love,
And preys like a hawk upon a dove.
It strikes down lovers with an omnipotent force,
And leaves its victims in a strangling remorse.

You miss his love, you keep it alive,
And thus the shadow is allowed to thrive.

Mark M. Pittman

Whispers

Whispers webbing through my soul,
Into feelings that were dormant in silence.
Please be silent;
For your whispers...
As long as the Nile,
May bring life to a soul that is like a desert,
Arid and barren.

A resilient whisper, drawing me back to the past.
Foreseeing an understanding and love.
Unique to other hemispheres.

Whispers branching out to places.
Unknown to my being.
That only exist in my imaginary world.

Whispers:
  Non-conformant;
    Defiant;
      Strong;
        Vibrant;
          Crackling.
Shh... Shh...only whispers of lullabies are welcomed here.

Lucy Lewis-Eloi

Reflections

When I look into the mirror,
I don't see the man she sees.
I see a man that loved her deeply.
She sees a man that's obsessed.
I don't see the monster she does.
I see the real me.
I see the man that would love her forever.
She sees another obstacle in the search for Mr. Right.

Travis Prim

Flight To Freedom

Goodbye to one fond memory,
I'll leave before it sours.
I'm sure that someday I will miss
our happiest of hours.
Now restless voices call me from somewhere
I've yet to see.
I will fly out like a butterfly
who finally is set free.
My wings are bruised a little
from banging on this jar;
But now I leave this old security
and it will leave a scar.
Now I stretch forth my wings
against the warming sun.
With a little hesitation
my new journey has begun.
I'm a little frightened as I start to fly.
I have no certain destiny,
I just know I have to try.

Melodie Hawkins

Untitled

Serene, quiet, and placid, "a sober disposition" some would say.
Yet none know of the boiling black cauldron churning beneath this cool surface.
A tumultuous dark vessel, forever bubbling with
intense anger and insane fury.
Silently, quietly, this pot has
boiled through time with ever increasing passion and strength.
Never yet to overflow, never still to spill over from its fiery rage.

I fear this kettle to topple, so I clench tightly in a restraining, teeth grinding grasp,
"Fire Die!", yet I can command it only to sporadically simmer.
Alone sit we in the heat of the desert, forever embraced in this fierce, violent struggle,
Glad am I that should this pot prevail, scalded only will I be,
Yet it is this same solitude that aids this vigilant stewpot towards its flaming triumph.

Music. The stars. These are my sole companions in this considerable confrontation. Yet victory against this inflamed crucible, cannot
I claim with these alone.
Await I the one, in her angelic love to
forever stifle this blaze, to leave a shallow sooty saucepan,
Thereupon, will I at last be relieved from this eternal
exhausting conflict.

Amr Hassan

A Stranger

I look in the mirror and a stranger looks back
An old familiar friend all shrouded in black.
Where goodness once lingered there is no more
An undying selfishness fills each and every pore.
Unkind and unloving is what he's about
Full of mistrust and always of doubt.
With uncertainty prevailing when someone gets near
They all run away in uncontrolled fear.
Where giving once flourished
Greed now you will find.
Thinking only of himself
For others he is blind.
I look in the mirror and it's a stranger I see
But to look a little closer, I see the stranger is me.

Jennifer Stalcup

Every Night

Every night I drown in sad tears
as I sit in a dark corner of my room
I abuse myself with the passion I feel for you,
because I know I'll never have you
I picture my hands roaming through your blond hair,
and caressing your pink lips with mine
you tell me I am every thing you've ever wanted,
and I am able to believe you
I gaze into your hypnotic eyes,
never wanting to break the tranquillity
still the nights when I swear I can feel you
I will sink into a pit of despair
I will long for your touch
and crave your sweet smell
I desire your presence
and lacking it sinks me deeper and deeper
I understand you know nothing of my feelings
or of the loneliness that consumes me
But still every night I will blame you
for thrusting me further into depression

Nicole Gale Westfall

"Testimonies"

Testimonies can bring a smile to a frowning face....
They can make a dark room into a beautiful place....

Testimonies can bring together people who were once far apart....
They can be a mend to someone's broken heart....

Testimonies can give hope to someone who feels their at their end...
They can make two enemies the very best of friends..

Testimonies can bring joy to someone who is in doubt...
They can tell the whole world what being saved is all about...

Testimonies are acknowledgements of the things God can do....
What he did for me and what he
can do for you...

In order for a flower to grow
you must first plant a seed...
Testimonies can sometimes be
just what you need.

Testimonies are praises to God
for all he has done for you...
If you can hear this poem you
should praise him too.

Shawana Bulloch

What If!

What if red were the color of green;
Would that make sense to us then?
What if the number two were the number one instead,
Or six or eight or even ten.

What if to jump meant to sit down,
Would that confuse us in any way?
What if to sing meant to be quiet,
Or if January was really in May.

What if the earth was happy and peaceful,
And the air was healthy and clear.
What if we never worried about anything bad,
Would we ever think the end was near?

But what if instead of some peace, we had no peace at all,
And everyone hated everyone.
And we worried about being hurt or possibly killed.
Then no one would have any fun.

But why should we worry about all these things,
And I hope that you all get my drift.
Let's take each day one step at a time,
And not worry about saying "What If!"

Carrie Aschendorf

Sunshine Through Jalousies

As I walked past my bedroom door,
I saw a glimmer of light peeking through the slats of glass.
It stretched and tugged and squeezed between,
To touch all things within.

The sun in the sky, it tilted and shifted,
Until at last its arms of rays had stretched beyond
The slats of glass to point inside—
To touch, to find, to separate with a line.

It found the dresser half hidden in a niche
And illuminated with ever widening rays its find.
It shifted its rays to the drawer's face,
To slither down, to shades, to lace.

Rest it did on an orange plane.
It stretched and yawned enlarging its rays of light
And suddenly broke into tiny lights
To dance, to laugh, to shimmer, to glow
Until dusk defused the light.

Irene M. Gaza

Moments Of Trust

Time marches on,
Always over us or through us...
Hardly ever does it go around us.
At times, life may seem hopeless.
It's at moments such as these,
That we must hold our heads high...
and march on.
God brings people together at certain moments,
on certain days.
As we stumble along through life we should never fight,
nor question life's plans.
This is where one special value comes into play...
Trust
We have to trust that he knows where we are going.
And that each painful moment,
each moment of joy, as well as each test that we must face,
is just one of his ways of making us the kind of people,
that he believes we should be.

Tammy L. Walton

Southern Oasis

In the last cascading droplets of amber,
That illuminates these silent waters,
Of this Southern Oasis,
The warm breeze comforts me, tonight.
My heart warms in the glow,
Of the tree lights, and you at my side.
For I know, it is you, I wish to be with,
Forever, until the end of time.
If you will have and hold me, I will be there.
I can see in your eyes, how you adore me.
And in your arms, how you comfort me.
I can feel in my heart, how you love me.
Like no one else can.
Through my eyes I have shared with you,
What I have seen.
Through my heart, I have shared with you,
What I have felt.
On bended knee you knelt,
To give to me,
The only gift I need, love.

Lisa Lobeck

Sonny

Sonny and his sons went fishing in the keys one day
hoping for a productive, peaceful way.
They found a spot, moored the boat and parted.
Sonny chose waist deep water and speared a fish.
A nearby reef shark thought it was for him, for the
pickings had been slim.
Slowly the shark approached Sonny with the fish on his
spear. Sonny didn't see the shark because he took his
eyes out of the water and now it's too late to barter.
Sonny had removed the fish from the spear and
unfortunately his hand and right arm were near
The shark got the fish and Sonny's arm too.
Sonny and sons raced to a hospital to have his
bleeding arm repaired which the doctors did with no
time to spare. Sonny says in no way will this
incident leave him in a state of despair.

John L. Becker

Dear Precious Baby

So delicate and small, worth more than gold,
Now that you're hear, your life can unfold.

Until now you couldn't see them, but their words you could hear,
Loving sounds, gentle touching, told you Mom and Dad were near.

Mommies womb couldn't keep you from knowing the love,
That their Father and Master sent down from above.

The warmth and the comfort of your safe little place,
Has by a miracle been traded, for a smile on their face.

You'll be growing and learning, in your own special way,
Looking, listening and waiting to hear Mom and Dad say,

"We Love You"

So now little person, it's all up to you,
Take what they teach you and carry it through.

Don't ever turn away from their very special caring,
For you see, Little One, it's God's love that they're sharing.

May God bless you and keep you in his tender care,
Just show that you love Him and He'll always be there.

Donald Kiessling

Rage

Though we are black and beautiful
the world tries to make us feel uncertain
We are made to feel unclean,
at times this is unbearable.
The rage fills our blackness
and we often self-destruct.
We feel that we are in a glass bubble.
Our souls cannot ascend
to our potential greatest.
Hear us! Oh world.
lift the barrier from our lives.
Let us help make the
world a better place.
Help us too displace this impotent rage.
We can no longer be servant accept us as
equal friends. Help us from our destruction
take pity on our plight.
Understand our rage.

Ronald Killebrew

"First Love"

It was a winter night crisp and green,
We left the party and slipped the scene (behind the pines I mean).

She was dark haired babe, wild as hell,
The juices were flowing and we were under a false love spell.

Years ago during Lindon's era,
Before the "Hippy Queen" had her day.

The music was mellow and the magic was easy,
And I gave a ring to a high school honey.

I drank a beer, which was taught to be a crime,
Out of a trophy that wasn't worth a dime.

A high regard they called it but I knew better,
I won more glories from my high school sweater.

She showed me a scary side of life which I came to fear,
The realities that I never new were near.

She left in a fashion somewhat beguiled,
I guess she grew tired of the "American Pie" child.

Thomas J. Stilwell

Dying Love

There used to be a special guy, I thought I loved so well,
Now even when I think of him, so much it hurts to tell.
He always said he loved me, I guess I was naive,
He left me for another girl, it's still hard to believe.

He hurt me once right in my heart, he really hurt me bad.
I guess that it's the reason why my heart still feels so bad.
But it no longer bothers me and I want him to know,
I finally came to realize his love just had to go.

I know deep down within his heart he really tried to live,
But something deep inside his brain just wouldn't let him give.
I wish him many blessings, may his memory pass me by,
I look up into heaven, praise the Lord my love to die.

Christina Nichols

You Won't Hear A Sound

I guess I'll dry my eyes again
But what good will it be
When my heart's still trying to mend
When it's just breaking me.
I guess I have to say goodbye
to something I know couldn't be
And though you're gone, you'll still be here with me.
You're not anywhere around, yet in my prayers and poetry.
But you won't hear a sound.
I'm gonna say these words again.
The ones that I left out. I love you so. The rest you know.
The rest without a doubt.
I guess I'll dry my eyes again. You've made it very clear.
You won't be here, not anywhere around.
You're in my prayers and poetry but you won't hear a sound.
I'll tell you that I love you but you won't hear a sound.

Maria Theodora Kiapos

You Fly With The Eagles

You left this earthly plane not
to long ago. You are a free sprit
now. I know you are not far away.
You keep giving me little sign's.
Rest well my love. Enjoy you're heavenly slumber.

When I look above I can see you
flying on the wind currents.
You protect me during the day.
You are never far from my heart.

Burks Dockrey Jr.

Hi

Morning greets a man of twenty years of
age who cannot walk, run or play.
But he can see a world of beauty
and enjoys it every day.
"hi!" he says to the bus driver,
attendant, and friends.
As hiss wheel chair is loaded and
carefully strapped in.
"Hi!" he says to his teacher as she
greets him with a smile.
"Hi!" to us as we leave him for a while.
Afternoon arrives and the bus return for him.
"Hi!" he say happily as he's loaded once again
Excitement grips him as we near his
home and he sees his mother race down the driveway to greet him
with a smile upon her face.
"How was school?" she asks him as we get him off the bus
"Hi!" he says loudly as he gives her a big buss.
As we leave him for the day, I breath a great big sigh-
It seems a very happy life can be had with one word "Hi!"

Louise P. Wright

Service Not Connected

Veteran of war, whose name is in the Saga,
now that he is sick, linger around the plaza,
luckily that day, big crowd is on the area
for fund raising, for candidate of era.

Everybody, just looked and seem not to know
the weak veteran, dotage, ill and poor fellow.
To live in this world is struggle for a glow,
torment to the poor, paradise to well to do.

Tears that never drop at the bloodiest arena,
on that sad moment, can not hide the stigma,
but a Veteran who fought beyond cabala,
now standstill and wait for euthanasia.

"O Almighty God,-cried the Veteran of war,
is this the award for sacrifices done..?
Benefits were lost, securities had gone.
Has the government forgotten the call to arm...?

Why sickness declared as service not connected..?
Although suffered late, cause was from the battlefield.
If the veterans not properly awarded,
to serve the nation, likewise, to dig his own grave.

Porfirio A. Mariano

A Free Spirit

Some paddle idly in the shallow waters,
content to watch as life passes by,
Others venture out beyond the shelter,
stopping only when the waves get too high.
You swim among the open waters,
powerfully stroking through the pounding sea.
I catch my breath and smile in wonder
as you boldly frolic so far from me.
As the water crashes down around you,
you grin and shake the drops from your hair,
lean back your head and shout with laughter and
such enjoyment I wish I could share.
Back at shore they strain to see you,
enraptured by the joy upon your face.
And they wish that they too could jump and frolic
and cut loose the ties that bind them in place.

Kathy Barthell

A Lone Eagle

Somewhere along an empty beach
Beneath a pale June sky
My gaze was captured by the sight
Of a lone eagle flying by.

It didn't care, that I was there
Watching from the sand.
It circled once, above my head
With no intent to land.

Waves were crashing on the beach
A breeze was in the air.
Back it went, into the clouds
Where it didn't have a care.

I stood and watched this single bird
Till it was almost out of sight.
In my thoughts a silent wish was made,
That I could join up in its flight.

I wonder as it flew away,
Yet, no way could I have known.
What I found odd, you see, was unlike me
It seemed content to fly alone.

Russell S. Wigley

"A World At Peace"

A world at peace: It can't be here,
there's so much hatred and anger to fear.
A world at peace: It can't be here,
Blacks hating blacks, whites hating
whites and everybody, killing each other.
Oh please dear Lord, tell me there is another.
A world at peace: It can't be here,
Babies having babies and our teenage
Boys are going to Jail.
There is no choice, but heaven or hell.
A world at peace: It can't be here,
crack cocaine and rapist are taking
Our streets, even the music they
play has the wrong beat.

So let us stand straight and tall
on our feet. (Cause you see)
A world at peace: It can't be here,
Only with God there's nothing to fear.

Linda L. Scott

The Wise Maple Tree

Can this brazen creature be the quiet little maple tree
That stood so like a placid nun gently dozing in the sun?
All summers long I was aware of her mutely standing there
In a simple emerald gown, prim and chaste from toe to crown.
Now my heart is all but out, what can the creature be about
To flaunt such color in the air - to let each breeze play in her hair?
I plainly heard her sigh last night, she sighed and trembled with delight.
I peeped and saw her stark and bare, but she simply did not care!
The wind had stripped her left by leaf, her gown lay tarnished at her feet.
But, brave and tall she faced the night quite unmoved by her foolish plight.
And I heard her cry with a joyous shout, as her limbs lashed wildly all about.
"Let winter wolves, in hellish pack, strive and strain to break my back!
Let them bare their fangs, in fiendish glee, let them growl and complain, they can't hurt me.
With fingers of steel I'll cling to the sod,
And with a hundred arms, I'll hold to God."

Myrtle Watts

The Phone

I pick up the phone, not knowing what to say.
So I dial, as my mind starts to
think of all the wonderful things I want to say.
I hear the phone ring, and that voice I
yearned for so long to hear, says hello.
I freeze with no words, my mind goes blank, and I say hello.
There are just so many things I want to say to you,
like I love you. For my heart beats so
fast I can't say it.
I hear the voice so sweet and lovely speak
I tremble for I am so scared.
For the time will come when the phone isn't
there, and I will hold you in my arms saying
I love you, and showing you that I do.
But when you say good-bye, there will
be a tear in my eye. For I have to wait
just to say those lovely words like,
I love you

Steve Wences Wright

Aspen Tree

The slight tremors on the leaves of the aspen tree,
Are like a shimmering ripple soaring across an endless sea.
How they move and glisten; how they quiver and quake,
A soft, tender whisper is the sound they make.
Their pristine white bark guards them from the blazing sun,
As they guard us as we frolic and run,
They shelter us from harsh weather; lightning and rain,
The scars upon their skin bear our happiness; our pain.
The aspen is truly a miraculous tree,
Its glory and beauty shall live on for all eternity.

Jennifer Stoaks

Mothers Love

I brought you into this world, with love
in my heart, cuddling you close, hoping we
would never part.
The years have gone fast, the cuddling
has past.
You have made me laugh, you have made
me cry. I can't hold you no longer, no matter
how hard I try.
You have found a new life, as grown men
and grown women. I hope you will say, "It was
a good start were given".
Be good and be strong as you walk out
this door. For the cuddling and watchful eye,
I can give you no more.

Helen Lakatos

Summer Hummer

I saw in the heat of summer.....
that all is still.
I heard in the clove of honeysuckle...
that all is quiet.
Only the busy bees fly about
to each blossom, so tall and stout.
Then the bees leave and a bird floats in,
a beautiful hummingbird, light as a pin.
With rubies all glittering on his throat,
for on honeysuckle he seemed to dote.
I saw in the heat of summer....
that all is still, for he hovers away.
I heard in the clove of honeysuckle....
that all is quite, for only the busy bees fly about
to each blossom, so tall and stout.

Lana Sue Martin

War

Time...
Corroded through the sardonic chastised verse
In the traditional ceremony of paralyzed thought

Collaboration...
Through spills that fill her doorway
In the fatigued ripple of the evaporated night

Face down...
In the dirt of ancestral pride
Themis is now dead mortals

Decay... in myriads with mirages
Of virtual freedom and flight

Visions... of stabbing wounds
Test of time through the lifeless eyes of our beloved and stricken
Goddess

Exiled...
To a fair shore in the brilliant sunset of the dying shower of the
west
Repressive dominion reigns

Voracious and undaunted...
The dogs are on their trail; until divergent emblems reside

James Leckie

"Jonathon Taylor Thomas"

His face, so bright and cheerful,
His heart, filled with love,
He fits right in with
All the other stars way up above.

So cheerful, yet so serious,
So frightful, yet so brave,
Although he doesn't know it,
Joy and happiness he gave.

Beautiful in the inside,
Beautiful on the out,
I know he is the greatest guy.
There just is no doubt!

He's one terrific actor,
Now, how could you miss?
This bright, shiny, loving, cheerful, serious, frightful,
brave, beautiful, terrific actor is:
Jonathon Taylor Thomas!!!

Lisamarie Garino

Erosion

As the passing current slowly eats away at my soul
Piece by piece I am swept down stream
and rearranged into a form I cannot comprehend
as my walls begin to crumble I see no point in my ever-changing
state of mind.
Confused by what has broken off and floated away.
As this slow process begins to take effect, and the fear of being
exposed is relieved,
a new side is displayed to change opinions and rearrange
misconceptions.
Yet still pieces still break off and float away and are rearranged
into a form I cannot comprehend.

Joshua Clark

Beaty!

Best of all is a family having fun together.
Even with friends.
Any day is a day to be together.
The sight of love or care being together.
You can even be a part of it.

Kevin E. Beaty

Life Is Short

Leave your inhibitions, Grant no discrimination...
Expect nothing, Desire everything;

LOVE, GIVE, SHARE, BELIEVE

Endure these qualities, For life is short.
BELIEVE in freedom, make no mistake...
You are a teacher to those you wake.

SHARE your ideas, share each day...
You shan't live alone, you can choose a mate.

GIVE unto others, for you share their space...
Give them your heart, for it is your place.

LOVE is forever, memories are free...
Love is undying, as it should be.

To be ungrateful, to live in spite..
To cheat, lie, or steal, we know is not right.

We shall repent, We shall rescind,
All these negatives....Be gone with the wind!

LIFE IS TIME AND TIME IS LIFE...
EXPRESS YOURSELF IN A POSITIVE MIND...

for .... Life is short.

Matthew Webb Duthie

Snowing Love

As Love is like the Snow that Falls from Sky,
Just as from First Snow Fall, To First True Love.
The Feelings are Strong and Warm, like in a Glove,
Each Day is Cherished, Hoping It will Stay High.
The Moments together begin to Fly,
As the Birds beneath the Clouds above.
The Warmth of Love is like a Turtle Dove,
Just as Nights Sigh, the Days pass Us by.

The Love, then like Snow that Falls, is Cold,
Begins to Vanish, Melt and Fade away,
The Times Together seem to be No Swan.
As day by day the Feelings change, Grow old,
The Snow turns Gray and Melts just where It lays,
One moment It's there, the next It's gone.

Linda M. Mohney

"Best Friends Forever"

I need some advice!
So I asked you twice.
I think your special!
Do you think I'm nice?
I had to move someplace new,
I felt scared,
but before I knew it you were there.
I came to find out,
you were new too!
As a friend to you,
I'll always be true.
I like to share your company
when ever I can.
Spending time together is always the plan.
I like your hair,
and you like mine.
We laugh together all the time.
Someday we might live miles apart....
but you will always have a
special place in my heart!!!

Allison Wilson

Love, like friendship...

Love, like friendship,
appears in many shapes and ways.
It is not something you can limit,
not in amount, distance, or days.

Either can come from places unexpected,
places you would never think it could.
But when you realize it is there,
you know it can only be good.

But love can be one-sided,
and friendships misunderstood.
Everyone must live their life with heartache,
if I could make it easier I would.

Love or hate,
friend or foe.
If you never give either a chance,
you may never really know.

I thought I loved someone,
but I really do not know.
Be it love, or only friendship,
I want our relationship to grow.

Christine Wiegand

Sassy

streaming across the page
soaring with the sagacious midnight owl
shagging with the town's boppin' betsy
sleeping on a pillowcase of plush velvet
supine amidst layers of fluffy feather comforters
snitchety pink toes with tomato red polish all smiley-like
sassy
sassy is as sassy will
smooth as syrup laden southern iced tea
slowly coating a ledge of contentment
saucy in the throat
spurious assumptions slapped away like rejection
silly with intelligence
sneaky in clandestine cleverness
my sassy
slivers like a legless lizard
slimy and scaley
so so so

Susannah Sweigart

A History Lesson

Looking around me, all I see are faces.
Do they understand what he is saying?
Can they actually comprehend so much thought?
How can one sit and listen so intently
to something that can only interest so few.
Looking around me once again, I wonder:
Are they really listening?
What is this dead stare I see in their eyes?
It cannot be interest, curiosity maybe.
They seem as though they are looking straight through him.
Their eyes are as glassy as the spectacles on his face.
Yes, the man is extraordinary but he is from another time.
We have not lived his times so therefore we cannot understand it,
Just as he can never understand ours.
We become bored of the past and listen in disbelief,
realizing that the future is ours to change.

Tara Newman

Big Bertha

Big Bertha is round and solidly packed
Her breath is like none to compare
She pushes aside all who come into view
A terror to those who would stare;

Her breath is astounding, her spray unique
She pushes and tears up with ease
With wondrous eyes, all who behold
Remove from her path, if you please;

Nothing can bother Big Bertha you know
She's bent on destruction and pleasure
She'll break down and tear up and no one is safe
Her wide open strength, who can measure?

Big Bertha can churn up the wind as she passes
And no one with Bertha can gain
All turn at her presence and run from her sight
Big Bertha is some Hurricane!

Ruth A. Vogelsang

Under Dad's Care

Now listen here, my frightened child,
What grips your heart with fear?
Surely not the same old things,
Which you brought to me in prayer.
You thought I didn't hear you,
But I did and you were healed,
So what are you trying to find,
Trust in me and have peace of mind!
My will is that you learn from me,
That once my word goes forth,
It accomplishes the desired task,
Without any effort and without any force
When I desire to touch a life,
Transforming it as I go,
That's it my child the work is done, so get up and fret no more.
Don't look for skeletons in the closet,
That really don't exist,
Close that door once and for all, no matter how hard it is.
The purpose of this exercise it that you will be free,
Hold my banner high my child, rise up and follow me.

Jacqueline Gerasimidis

The Puzzle

I stand there, yet to reach the golden years.
My life lays like a puzzle at my feet.
Mixed up scrambled the broken pieces.
My emotions flying like leaves in the wind,
Ready to turn to ashes.
I say to myself as my life passes,
What can I do,
What will I do.
My caring soul tries to comfort me,
Touches me, reaches me.
I gently kneel down, take a few pieces
Put part of the pattern together.
Things come into focus,
Things come into pattern.
Suddenly everything that was shattered,
Turns out to be a picture
Of beauty of life, of happiness.
The true meaning of living
Opening my eyes I can again say,
I'm glad I'm alive today.

Louise Stuart

Before The Storm

You hear a faint whistle, and over the earth the wind starts to blow
a scary feeling runs through your body, what is coming, you don't know

The wind picks up and in the air there is a slight chill
you sit in confusion, helpless, as a hint of dust rolls over the hill

Around you everything is moving, as if the world is closing in on you; you ask yourself why
you look up for an answer and all you see is blue turn to gray sky

And then just like that, silence hovers over the ground
the wind stopped blowing and it seems like time stood still as you look around

The silence is so thick, you have to cut it with a knife
you have some time to think how short is your precious life

You gain courage when you dream about all the things you're going to do
but to accomplish these goals, you realize that it is all up to you

Sadness creeps in, as a tear runs down your cheek, alone you feel
but you look fear in the eye and say my dreams are real

Lightening strikes, thunder rolls, and the rain starts to fall
you stand there as if your back is against the wall

As fast as it started, the storm shortly passed through
anything can happen if you just believe in you

Your life starts the day you are born you ask yourself; when did I
realize the happiness life has to offer, and you remember it was
during the calm before the storm

Tony Duffer

Hush, Sista Miriam

Mother Miriam danced while the mad men said,
"Watch it, Mother Miriam or you'll be dead."
Now she fell into a trap and was full of dread.
"Watch your mouth, Big Sista, you'll be sorry what you said."
Gotta watch it, gotta watch it, ain't no place to go.
"We're gonna kick ya right out the door."
Gotta watch it, gotta watch it, or the warts will grow.
"Hush Sista Miriam, don't say no more."
"Gee Whiz, Lord, Where Shall I Go?"
To the cave, to the cave where Elijah lay,
A still small voice will come as you pray.
You'll dance in the middle of the night once again.
You'll dance in the middle of the day and sing.
"O Lord, But Where Shall I Dance Once Again?"
On the highway to heaven where Jesus sings,
On the highway to heaven where the tambourines ring.

Sharon Kimbrough Cooper

"What Do You Do?"

What do you do
When it doesn't seem like
Doing the right thing pays off?
When honesty doesn't seem to be
The best policy?
What do you do
When you try to go through
The system
And the system fails you?
What do you do
When friends oppose you for telling the truth?
Shake their heads and murmur, "You fool!"
Then turn their backs and walk away
Leaving you standing alone
With nothing but your conscience
And the satisfaction of knowing
You did the right thing.

Hattie Tyson

A Definition

"What is a poem?"
Students ask, as they sit down to write that first time.

"A paragraph!" "a fact..."
"A test?"
"I read one once—it was the best!"

What is a poem? Listen to me:
It's a picture with words, carefully chosen
and placed in certain spots
to give an idea and the sound
of something you felt or thought.
It has a rhythm, like a song
and it can be short—or very long
and it can rhyme (or not!)
and you can put commas where you want.

But...it flows like a river
or beats like a drum
or races around a fast track
and most of all, it's a special way
to create your own art out of something you say!

Sharon K. Preheim

Essence Of The Sea

These tiny drops of water from the ocean spray,
may pose upon the petals of a rose one day;
Or if attracted to a darker cloud of war,
Become engaged in battle on some distant shore!

Awakened by the sun, they start their odyssey.
They trek to heaven, then they trickle back to sea.
They fall to earth all equal in their purity,
Un-touched by time or tarnish of antiquity!

Meanwhile, the wind propels the cloud parade.
On sunny days the clown is seen in his charade.
On darker days the cymbal's struck and thunder warns
Of troops and tanks approaching for their cannonade!

The challenging of borders by the restless sea,
Is found inherent in our own hearts to be free.
She wraps her mother-arms of clouds around the globe
Protecting life to-day, and all that's yet to be.

Leland Embert Andrews

A Rainy Day

Good Morning, world. Where have you been?
The birds are singing in the glen.
The sky is grey with clouds, you say?
You don't wake early on a rainy day?

Well, let me tell you about the rain.
It's not really meant to be a pain.
It's mainly sent to strain the air.
To collect all the allergies floating there.

It washes the trees with a gentle bath
Or sometimes with a mighty blast.
How would kids know what puddles are?
Or why have wipers on our car?

Rooftops would have to just sit and chat
if they didn't have the song of the pitter-pat.
So see, dear world, you shouldn't moan
Because of the rain, your grass has grown.

Come on, Wake up! Be of good cheer,
You're much sweeter now, since the rain is here!

Evelyn Anne Condon

Thank You God

Thank you God, for everything.
For the trees, the flowers, the sun, and rain.
For the birds that fly so high
and for the stars that are in the sky.
For the rainbow after a storm
for the sun that keeps us warm.
For the children as they play
and for the right we have to pray.
When I am weak, you make me strong,
and give me strength to carry on.
When I stumble along the way
you lift me up, and help me pray
thank you God, for friends that're true
and for each day, I have with you
for the Bible and its words
for the answered prayers you've heard
thank you God for each day
and for your Son to lead the way
I know someday, your face I'll see
thank you God, for loving me.

Grace Sanders

The Dolphin

One day a small baby dolphin
Arises from her mother
The dolphin is small but helpless
After years the little baby is forced
To leave her mother
To enter the big vast sea
She went on morning for days
This was all new to her
She has no enemies
Her beautiful gray coat is starting to fade white
Seeking shrimp and food
Finding very little because of man she moves on
She is scared, she doesn't know what to do
She wonders the world
She mistakingly goes into a fishnet
The beautiful dolphin dies
Her life has come to the end
She has become one with the earth

Lizzie Orr

There Is No Up Anymore

Up and down, the maddening chaos;
Begins with life;
Ends with death. Or life. Why?
Up and down, the maddening chaos:
Face daily agitations;
That never stop. Why?
Up and down, the maddening chaos:
Work to make it;
An impossible effort. Why?
Up and down, the maddening chaos:
Stay alive:
In a diseased world. Why?
Up and down, the maddening chaos:
Grow old and alone;
No one cares. Why?
Up and down, the maddening chaos:
Why don't babies have a choice of life?
Down and down, the maddening chaos:
Is there no "up" any more?
Down, down, down, the maddening chaos. Why?

Glenda Picha

Silence

Silence.
The only thing heard is your footsteps,
Crunching through the fresh snow.
Your breath coming out in icy puffs,
Soars toward the icicles hanging above.
When at no warning, one breaks and falls to the floor.
Crash! The ice shatters into small fragments,
Breaking your dream-like silence
Like an off-key instrument in an orchestra.

Everything is white,
Like a curtain hanging over your eyes.
Then your love walks up next to you
And hands you a warm, steaming mug.
You sip the liquid and let the heat
Fill your whole body.
This is truly beautiful.
Let it fill you,
Don't break the trance it has.
Don't interrupt nature when
It is in its most beautiful state.

Scott Neilson

Tragedy

Just listen, hear the children die.
Just listen, hear the old-ones cry.
Time was, when we cared you see.
We taught them to live, to live free
We sent our youth, so young, so scared
Then taught them to die, like freedom, it's shared.

We grew tired and restless, in battles long
For the goal of freedom, had long seemed gone
Then came the peace, for battles end
We nursed our wounded, counted our dead.

For us it was over, for us it was through -
But we promised them arms to continue.
The arms that were promised, well they never came
When you're out of the battle, the story's the same.
The money was gone, the cupboards were bare,
And now when they die, we stand and we stare.

There were doves, there were hawks, labels galore,
Those who fought, those who ran, those who stayed home from the war.
But when the battles are over, and there's peace in their lands,
Pray God, we can wash their blood, from our hands.

Robert J. Backa

Eternity

Darkness and shadow come together
and the night trembles in anticipation.
From far below, the screams and curses
of the damned rise to roil with the fog.

Weaving in and out among the cylindrical shapes
of the lost and battered world.
Tasting, touching, smelling
things long forgotten.
Memories rise anew from the lost abyss;
Pained expressions cross demonic smiles.

Tugging, tugging at this darkness that never ends.
Pulling others down to rise to the top
of destruction and chaos,
Clawing, biting, kicking.

The damned are far behind.
For those they chase.
Those they seek,
Are memories that flee the mind.

Shelly R. Lyons

My Friend

Jesus I love you, Jesus I care
Even in my darkest hour of despair
I know that you are always there
You gave me the gift of love I share.

You didn't say that we wouldn't fall
But you did promise to answer, if we would call
So whenever I pray
I know you'll send your light to my night or day

I can face anything
With you at my side
Because you are my everything
And in you I abide.

My friend, my sweet sweet friend
The best that there is
On you, I can and will always depend
Because I am a child of His!

Ramona V. Barrios

The Sea

On that dark and stormy night - the seas were piling high,
The wind was howling coldly - a close and roiling sky,
Our course was North by East - we were pitching from crest to trough,
The gale force winds to our port- caused the waves to mist and froth,
The sea was wildly pounding - through hawse pipes to bridge it crashed,
The rolling was e'er so intense - the wheel was firmly lashed,
The lookout stared into the dark - his eyes were wide with fright,
The salty spray that stung his face - was to last through-out the night,
It was a time to remember - for panic was everywhere,
St. Elmo's light bright aglow - caused all hands to upward stare
At the dancing prancing fire - atop the mainsail mast,
Our Patron Saint was present - safety assured at last,
The waves were finally subsiding - and the dawn was soon to be,
The wind swung dead astern - ours now, a calming sea,
The arrival point was just ahead - our destination in sight,
And a glorious day a-dawning - after a raging stormy night,

Charles F. Sumner

Past, Present, Future

From the first evening I laid eyes on you,
I knew how special you were.
Your little brown eyes twinkled like the stars,
and your little smile lightened up my world.
I know then that with each day and each year
you would grow and no longer need me.
As hard as it was, I understood.
During those eighteen years, I hoped I have
comforted you, guided you, taught you,
and loved you with all my heart.
To be sure, I prayed.
I hoped you have gained as much knowledge as a scholar,
as much devotion as a lover, as much happiness as a comedian,
as much strength as a boxer, and as much grace as a ballerina.
Overall, I longed for your achievement.

Now the day has come, and all I want is for you to rejoice.
You have succeeded.
Please use your determination for future goals.
I wish you all the best of luck, for the next step is yours.

Congratulations Graduate!

Lori A. Fejko

The Dawn

The dawn so full of light.
It has the shine of a newborn.
All is new and full of hope.
It brings so many wonderful changes,
And the chance to correct our past mistakes.

Donna Price

"Rushing Water"

As I walk on the sandy beaches
Near the breezy Pacific Sea,
I hold the hand of the man I love
Who walks so soft and steadily next to me.

We stop and he looks deep into my eyes
And he says so lovingly,
"My heart flows with joy just seeing you,
like the rushing water that laps at our feet
so intensely."

As our lips slowly come closer
On a hot August day,
The salty water rushes around our feet
and grabs tightly a hold;
promising to stay.

Alyssa Kurth

Friends

To my friend who lets me be me,
And when I am troubled you help me see.
Who guided me through those stormy years,
And comforted me when you saw tears.
When I am down,
You were always around.
To help me up when I felt low,
And give me an answer when I don't know.
These are few things that you have done for me,
So maybe someday I could help you see.
Your friendship is very treasurable,
Cause it will grow so much until it's unmeasurable.
I know in my heart we can always stays friends.
We can stick it through until the end.

Stephanie Erin Littles

The Clock

The clock ticks like a bomb waiting to exhale
from its miseries of this world.
The clock tells us time so we can know
when we get out of class.
The clock moves as slow as a turtle
who is walking toward its meal.

The clock rings out like a crying bird
waiting for something to help it.
The clock sits as still as a
model at the end of the catwalk.
The clock smells as new as a
bag filled with potpourri.

The clock tastes the way that wood
should taste after sitting over the years.
The clock feels as smooth as a rose petal
after the morning dew has just fallen upon it.
The clock looks as old as someone doing
the butterfly in club boomerang.

The clock swings like a nightingale in flight.
The Clock Lives!!!

Quincy Hale

Brain

Brain, why brain don't you work,
all gooshy and gray,
Why can't I think?
My brain is going to fall to the ground!
Then a pile of mush sits beside me
saying,
"Why can't I work?"
tell me now, or I am nothing.

Karen Brodsky

Butterfly

Oh! You beautiful butterfly, lift up your wings and fly-fly-fly
You sit so softly on the petal of a rose as if you are praying in quiet repose
Tell me butterfly where do you go, when the snowflakes fall and the cold winds blow?
Do you sleep in winter and early spring until the flowers bloom again

You are oh-so-beautiful butterfly when you lift your wings to sun and sky
You are like a gentle summer breeze when you fly over the meadows and through the trees
What a wonderful way to spend the hours to watch you fly from f lower to flower.

When summer is over and winter is here will you please return again next year?
As you fly over the flowers and through the trees you are oh so beautiful and your beauty is free.
You bring such beauty to everything when you flutter those soft butterfly wings.

Now that summer is over and you fly away, we will miss you more than I can say
The flowers will miss you also I fear as we await your return next year
If I am here and I hope I shall be, I shall watch for your return to the flowers and trees.

Jean Furcolow

The "Promise"

Lightning paints its picture in the sky,
While a small, gentle stream rolls by.
Small raindrops kiss the dusty ground,
As thunder makes its boisterous sound.
Fleeing animals and swaying trees do bend,
As we question "Why God had rain to send."
The big picture now becomes ever so clear,
That somewhere a dry cry he hears...

The sun rose early the following day,
As the puddles gleamed and the animals play.
The Lord God almighty can do no wrong,
For he hears even the faintest song.
So if you have a need or just trying to stand,
Send up your prayers and he'll hold your hand!!!

Christopher B. Walls

"To Mend A Broken Heart"

Once your heart's been broken, the pain inside you burns,
you just have to mark it down as a lesson you have learned.
To mend a broken heart, you have to love again.
And once love comes around, you have to let it in.
I believe that I can mend your heart that's broken in two.
So I've written this little poem to tell you what I'll do.

First I'll find the pieces that are shattered on the floor.
And toss them over my shoulder for you won't need them anymore.
Those pieces are no good, no matter what you do.
But I've got the right replacements I've been saving just for you.
They've been on the shelf awhile, but they're just as good as new.
They're pieces of my own heart I gladly give to you.

I know they will serve you well, just give them a little time.
You'll never need to service them, and they won't cost you a dime.
Many people have tried to get what I've placed in front of you
But now you've got it and it's yours to keep
a heart that's made from two.

Walter Gordon

Listen To A Child

When your child speaks stop, give ear,
Lessons taught and thought not heard,
may come back at you like a haunting.
Listen to a child, he or she might be
warning you of things taunting body and mind.
Listen to child, go back in time, in your mind,
did you hear the warning signs?
There is much to be learned,
If we weren't so concerned with number one,
"Wait a minute, you said",
A minute late, is a minute to long
Didn't you hear a child's song?
Oh Lord, no!!!
It's to late a child gone.

Muriel McCoy

Expressions

Expressions of the mind -
kind, considerate and sweet

Expressions of the heart -
loving, wanting, needing and desiring

Expressions of the flesh -
warm, tingling, scrumptiously light
yet totally complete

To combine the expressions of the
"mind, heart and flesh" you will experience
the "most awesome" kind of "explosion"
that man will ever have the privilege to enjoy.

Anita Tyson

The Centurion

I, Centurion, stand in wonder, I have seen a wondrous scene.
There before me, bathed in glory, His words they echo on my soul.
Father, oh Father, they know not what they do. Forgive them,
forgive them, that my death be true. I'll love them, forgive them,
I'll do what I must do. My Father, my Father, let me come to You.

His name was Simon, and I pondered, on the scene that I had seen.
Christ's cross he carried, as he tarried, these words they echo
on his soul. Father, oh Father, they know not what they do.
Forgive them, forgive them, that my death be true. I'll love them,
forgive them, I'll do what I must do. My father, my father, let
me come to You.

And, one other, crucifixion, of a thief that's on the scene.
He is hanging, but he's smiling, these words they echo on his soul.
Father, oh Father, they know not what they do. Forgive them,
forgive them, that my death be true. I'll love them, forgive them,
I'll do what I must do. My Father, my Father, let me come to You.

I, Centurion, stand in wonder. I have seen a wondrous scene.
There before me, bathed in glory, His words still echo on my soul.
Father, on father, they know not what they do. Forgive them,
forgive them, that my death be true. I'll love them, forgive them,
I'll do what I must do. My Father, my Father, let me come to You.

Donald E. Reither

A Fever Dream

While Einstein scalpels the suspensions
occurring in the progress of time,
and the priests and holy men continue to
tithe the enlightenment
at the banquet of
passion,
position,
Salvation remains with Gale
lying in the twilight of a temple's stained glass,
dryads of sleep nuzzling her eyes.

Phil Chapman

Nature's Mirror

Dream of a world as true as a reflection..
Everything around you is suddenly tranquil and still.
Amorphous waterways holds everything in suspended animation,
As if time were forgotten...
A rippling river branch, a glimmering brook bank,
And a shimmering sun serpent generates all that is pure.

Look into a calm mirror.
Do you see a chickadee in a tree?
Do you see a breeze through the white birches leaves?
Or do you only see you?

Oh, mystical, watery eyes of nature...
Echo a rolling, tumbling, splashing wave upon a
Riffling, river water's gaze.
Reflect the shallow-
Reflect the deep-
Beholder of all that is near and far.

All that is water reflects-
Reflecting all that which is life.
Our star, the sun, is an orchestrator of photographic
Reflections illuminating all that is real and pure-nature.

J. William Anderson

As Time Passes

The desert has a beauty all its own,
The tall cacti blooming,
The rocks of different hues.
They could tell stories of old
When the earth was new and trails unforged.
Listen to the blooming wild flowers along the way
They bloom for a small part of nature,
They have no complaints—just keep growing.
Can't we do the same?
Living where we are planted and just keep growing
Into eternity.
Our hopes and dreams are all we can live on,
Our sunrise and sunsets are the same as anyone,
We are God's creatures of love,
And what we strive to do
Is guided by His hands.

Joie Curtis

Christmas Is Good

Christmas is good.
At Christmas you need a hood.

At Christmas you care and love.
You care and love just like a dove.

At Christmas you get that warm feeling,
when you think of the Wisemen kneeling.

Christmas is my favorite time of year.
It almost makes me shed a tear.

Christmas goes from when Jesus was born,
all the way to when His hands were torn.

Christmas is a happy time.
It is worth way more than a dime.

Christmas is very cold.
Anyway, that's what I'm told.

I'm here to tell you about Christmas.
It's a season I would not miss.

Allie Gill

That Face In The Mirror

I peered in to a mirror at a face I didn't know,
Wondering how did I let myself become this way.
I wasn't sure why I hurt from head to toe,
I just seemed to get more depressed with each passing day.
Everyone kept saying, that's just pregnancy it will pass one day,
It will be hard, but hang in there and show patience in some way.
I just didn't understand what it was they meant,
and all that talk it seemed, I grew to resent.
My mother said, when you lose some weight
the depression will subside.
But I fought more with my husband
and the depression became harder to hide.
Now I look back at my postpartum blues,
as a memory of a depression I had sunk in to.
A chemical imbalance and feeling over-weight,
That face in the mirror I had so grown to hate.
Summertime was good and gave me much needed rest,
and my mother's advice I found to be so true.
My family and friends had been nothing but the best,
because of that I lost twenty pounds and became much happier too.
I now feel ready to tackle another school year,
and I am so glad I've come again to know and be that face in the
mirror.

Debbie French

Special Delivery

Angels deliver, as they work through silence,
their thoughts form melodies, that over shadow all violence.

However all knowing, they may feel at the time,
always they are humbled, by Gods plan sublime.

Their essence glitter gold, white surrounding a "God send,"
and as foretold, they deliver to the hearts of all men.

When he who speaks to the heart of all troubled,
sends his angels, his blessings are doubled!

While angelic forces focus on completion of our true good intent,
we can rest assured, our troubles were well spent!

And for the glory to God in the heavens, do they all cooperate,
To make "man" concentrate on deliverances from God to emancipate!

Linda Bickers

Hurricane's Kharm

The trees sway to the wind's malevolent hymn
As the thunder torques my blood
Like a world between a tuning fork
That shudders once braced dust

Kharm abattoir of abaddon's infernous insides
Grate land with rasped teeth of stone
Ebulant fingers pluck demonic chords of life
Breaking strings I once had

Accumulating shadows stain flowers blight
Like mercury tainting hands
tainting hands once free and strong with life
Now pricked by acciculate light

A macabre opera preceding an execution
Of mass destruction
Nothing saved
Nothing gone
Only changed
All is lost
All is kharm

Deel Jacobson

Attitude

Attitude is a state of mind
which makes or breaks our day,
Will make a bright day dark
and control us along the way.

We are in charge of our destiny
in our hand we hold the key,
to be happy or sad
attitude right there will be.

Instead of that I don't care attitude
say, "I'm alive and well,"
the sun will shine bright for you
if on silly happenings you no longer dwell.

Attitude is a reaction
that can be good or bad,
unless you take charge and remember
we gain nothing when we're mad.

Make that smile last all day
fight your way through gloom and happy you'll be,
As I climb the ladder of life
my attitude—is most important to me.

Morris Duran

I Wonder Why?

Out my window nothing grows on concrete roads
Noise and stink fill the sky yet no one
seems to cry.
I wonder why?
The waters not safe to drink. Something
called pollution I think.
Even the air looks a funny pink.
I wonder why?
They took all the trees.
to make chopsticks for the Chinese.
I wonder why?
A black smoke pours out a stack.
I'm told they make oil to
light my lamp, so I can see
out my window at all this crap.
I wonder why?
We killed everything in sight
to be better than a bird in
flight. I the end we're nothing but
Fools who tried to rule. I wonder why?

Chad W. Ferrin

Winter

Winter is:
Soft snow swirling slowly downward
to greet gaunt ground,
Gradually covering the dreary deadness of
leaves and grass.
Silent, silver trunked trees standing still,
while whispering winds whisk wandering
whiteness into cold clouds.
Great, gnarled and twisted trees
flowering with frost by frozen waterfalls.
Bent, blown-down branches,
broken by blizzards.
Wild, wind whipped willows
and sudden, silent stillness —
tested tranquility.

E. Jane Whittinghill

Harmony

Harmony means to be happy - to be free
Harmony means that we have let go
Harmony means we are love - we can hug - we can fluff!
Harmony means we are balanced - we can laugh
Harmony means we can fluffy our aura and play!!
Harmony means we can swish -
because we have learned our lessons -
we have passed the test - and we can dance
Harmony means that we touch another with our love
Harmony means -
we take the sense of self from the heart center and
send it out!
Harmony means tip-toe - tip-toe - and say hello
Harmony is freedom - balance!
Harmony is development of our wings
Harmony is achievable by all - simply let go
That is how we learn lessons - we let go!

Farena

I Am Me!

As I stand upright, my body ever so straight, my feet are planted firmly, as I patiently wait. Some may hit me, or cut me, and then throw me to the ground, just to see me fall. I am me, and to my father, I will call. I stand on his promises, asking no reward. I live outside to keep my spirit free. I laugh at my sister, the sun, as she watches over me. I am me. I wave to my brother, the moon, as he watches me by night. He lights the skies, after dark, to let me know, things are alright. I worry, not to live outside, that how, I got to be me. My mother holds me ever so tight, this helps me, to be strong and grow up right. You see my brother after dark and my sister at early dawn. My mother, I depend on. She covers me, keeping me warm, I am me. But to know my father, you must be as I am, rooted in his commandments, and standing on his promises. I am me! You see, I am Me.!

Terry M. Jones

Remember To Remember

Memory is the beginning and ending
In all things of our daily life,
The good and beautiful abounding,
Not the ugly, evil or the strife.

Even the lowest has some beauty,
If we would remember to remember,
God's gifts are charity not duty
Or anything grave and somber.

For that which seems sorrowful,
Shattered or unpleasant this day,
In another day will be beautiful,
For peace of mind is this way.

To remember our own misdeeds
Gives us a silent embarrassment,
That we have left thorns or weeds
Instead of kind and loving sentiment.

Treat one kindly just for his good
And all his bad will fade away.
They will forget, knowing you understood.
Kind thoughts and deeds no words say.

Sylvia Griffith

Life

Life is like a spider's web
To succeed is to escape
To fail is to get captured
We are all flies trying to escape
But seem to be undecided
Our family is the spider
They come for the hunt
My lover is another fly
Trying to help me decide
I want to stay
But I want to leave
The spider will say and do
Anything to encourage you to come closer
Every fly needs its freedom
If it doesn't have freedom
It doesn't have life

Karen A. Evens

What Are You?

What are you?
Are you all that you have done,
or just what you are doing now?
Are you what you are wearing,
or all that you have worn?

Do you take things with you or leave them behind?
If you buy a jacket, are you a new jacket
or an old jacket with a new jacket?

If the Mighty Oak had an old jacket,
would there be acorn shells in its front pocket?

Pat Andrew Pagnotta

Keeper of My Garden

As the keeper of my garden,
You keep my furrows straight and clean,
You turned a place of rocks and weeds,
Into a lovely thing,

You clearly saw the rocks and weeds,
In this life so filled with sin,
And yet...Hid not your face from me,
But boldly asked me in,

You cast the rocks out one by one,
Reached down your holy hand,
And plucked the weeds up by the root,
To save this sinful man,

Yes...Through your grace and mercy Lord,
You've straightened every row,
And given me your holy word...
To eat...
That I....
Might grow.

Eddie L. Smith Sr.

Dreams

Dream maker, maker of dreams; shine down on me,
Thoughts so sweet, that I may hide from tomorrow
in thoughts and dreams beyond reality.

Tomorrow will call soon enough, and I will have
to rise again with humanity.

How good it feels to lie here now, in the abyss
of mind and soul. To garner dreams of fantasies,
hidden so in daylight hours, and bequeathed to me
only as darkness falls across the day, and the
mystic powers of the night take hold of my being.

Eli Richard Burdine

A Tormented Soul

Momma, the child cried out to me in my unconscious state of sleep.
Momma, wasn't I someone you thought you would ever need?
Momma, they gave you a choice, and you threw me away so to speak.
Momma, how could you do such a horrible thing to me?
Momma, I could have been the child you bounced on your knee.
Momma, it shouldn't be them there, it should be me.
Still in the middle of my sleep the tears streaming down my face.
The only answer I could give, it was an extraordinary case.
My child, I cried, I always think of you every moment of my life.
My child, what I did to you will always cut into my heart like a knife.
My child, you must understand, I was too young to take care of you.
My child, I beg of you to understand, there was nothing else that I could do.
My child, my child, there is really no excuse for what I did to you or me.
My child, I know there is no way I could ever make you see.
My child, I ask forgiveness, which I should have done long ago.
My child, I beg of you please, to finally let me go.
Momma, momma, I let you go every morning when you wake.
My child, my child, no you don't, everywhere I go, you I take.

Monica Smith

Best Friends

Best friends will never leave,
never come apart,
nor come undone.
They are there to support us all.
Through the falls,
and all the loves that have long been gone.
We shall never forget the kindness and fun we bring,
but there are the bad times that seem unbearable and yet unforgettable.
We help each other through everything now and to come,
but what is to come?
What is the future to be like?
Will we be apart?
Far apart?
Will we be friends,
or just memories in the mind?
Will we be what we once were?
I don't know, we will see,
Whether we will be best friends forever like we said,
or if it is just another bleak memory.

Krista Haifley

Untitled

I found a friend as sweet as can be
I have to come to grips she has HIV
I am crying inside I can not deny
Sometimes feeling low other times feeling high
She is lashing out from the pain inside
It's hard to hide fear has no disguise
Her hair is like sunshine her eyes like the sky
I look in those eyes and just wonder why?
I want to protect her and keep her from harm
Make her feel secure as I hold her in my arms
I know there has been pain others may have caused
But if she would just give me a chance
My mother lover would be put on pause
I have everything to offer and real love to gain
Will she give me the opportunity to ease her pain? Now, she is healthy happy, and sure and if I were wealthy I would find a cure
She has awakened something deep in my soul
Does she know I can't let go?
It will take its toll I won't deny
I ask myself as I look to the sky will there be a future for her and I?

Cat Cupit

Fog

I'm trav'ling through the fog today and strained are all my nerves
For it is very hard to see oncoming cars or curves
And while I, rather cautiously, proceed on this blind drive,
I cannot help but feel, that it's is almost true to life,
For here as there the next event lies hidden in the mist,
In either case one's forced to be a hapless fatalist.

Sure, careful planning helps a lot, tenaciousness and zeal
Occasionally makes our fate comply with our will,
Even as driving carefully, persistently, but slow
Will usually get us to where we intend to go,
But often, unexpectedly, abruptly turns the road,
Whether for better or for worse, it's far from what we thought.
With all our fellow travellers we're hunting luck and love,
Just as when we here kids and played the game of blind man's bluff.

We hope forever and we strive the future to secure,
We cannot stand uncertainty, we want to know for sure.
We sowed good seeds so we expect rich harvest in the fall
But wouldn't it be nice to own a perfect crystal ball?
...Except when trouble is about to enter our log,
When grief and sadness loom ahead...Thank God for life's sweet fog!

Henry P. Glass

A Child's Last Prayer

Dear Lord, I hope you're listening to what I have to say,
on this my last, my final, my very saddest day.
Dear Lord, my life has fallen apart right in my very hand,
my life has crumbled, blown away like a pile of lonely sand.
Dear Lord, I'd like to thank you, for all those whom I love,
and I'd like to ask you, to take care of me, as I venture up above.
Dear Lord, I'd like to apologize for everything I've done,
for all the things I did wrong, that weren't that much fun.
Dear Lord, I hope you're waiting, waiting to greet me,
as I go up above and become great, lovely, and free.
Dear Lord, I have one more thing to do,
I have to say goodbye, to my mom, my dad, and my sisters too.
Dear Lord, I thank you for all the things good in my life,
so I leave without fear, terror, or strife.
Dear Lord, I hope you listened to what I had to say,
for this is the last time I will ever pray.
Farewell.

Heather McAvoy

...'lay

With her chunky digit pointed fixedly and intensely at me,
she hollered "Titi, You — You stop bothering Mommy!"
A five word formula brewed beneath her auburn locks,
not to her pal Pooh - but to me she unhesitatingly mocks
with exactitude, crispness and rationalization,
revealing an oyster producing a gem sort of irritation.
Unafraid to talk back like her button-eyed stuffed bore,
I began moving closer to her like fish to a lure.
She'll find out this day who's a great deal smarter,
so I peered down glaring at the auburn-locked toddler
as the coal miners did the coal in my grandfathers day,
stood ready to respond there would be no delay.
Yet upon looking a bit harder at the auburn-locked toddler
was ensnared in the web of her quickly changed ardor,
saw her twinkling emerald eyes while merrily at play,
and withdrew myself from the matter of fact sort of way,
placed my hand on her chin where her oatmeal still lay,
crouched down low beside her and dotingly said "...'kay".

Antonia Lynch-Parham

Let's Leave The Real World Alone

Let's get together and leave the real world alone.
Let's have a cool drink and a chocolate ice cream cone.
Happiness is in, let's leave sadness alone.
Let's sing the songs of life as we talk with our kin on the phone.

Let's get together and leave the real world alone.
Let's stay home and never roam alone.
We watch Laurel and Hardy on our cable.
We live life and do what we are able.

Let's get together and see those silent films.
See Buster Keaton silents and the music sings about our times.
We sing together and drift off together.
We live together and communicate with each other forever.

Let's get together and leave the real world alone.
Let's get together and eat a caramel popcorn cone.
Happiness is in, let's leave the nonsense of world reality alone.
Let's drift off into our own reality, so leave us alone.

We sit at a table by candlelight and solve our problems with kindness.
We see Double Whoopee and Jean Harlow, laugh and develop our mental happiness.
Laurel and Hardy and Keaton make us cry and laugh and we leave the world alone.
We'll sit with candlelight and now the real world is alone.

Philip N. Glanz

Fall

Yes, the last flowers are faded now.
Jack frost is now nipping the air.
A change is made, but we don't quite know how.
The Master painter is busy, I do declare.

The colors of yellow, red, orange and gold,
Enjoy them quickly, as they soon fall to the ground.
Beautiful, yes, and a sight to behold,
As they fall down without making a sound.

We take long drives in the countryside,
Casting our vote on the prettiest sight.
With thee "oh's and ah's", come from far and wide.
Time to go home as it is almost night.

Another day will change the entire scene.
The Master's brush is still working you know.
There is only now a hint of shades of green,
But fall is truly a miracle show.

Lillian McAllister

Abundantly Exuberant

Nature in its existence
Man, the crowning glory of God's handiwork
Through him, man has the ability to stand firm
As the stars stand erect in the heavens.

The sun shineth its brilliance by day
The moon sheds light by night.
The clouds move harmoniously in peace
So should our deeds toward our fellowman.

Our faith in God should be lengthened
As the wind spreading its gentle breath through space.
Coherently in a frame of mind
Seeing only the good in others instead of the bad.

Our voice to others
Should be as kind and smooth
As an eagles wingspread
Gliding over the slopes of a mountain.

The togetherness of love as gentle snowflakes
Cover the ground on a wintry day.
The abundance of peace is ours
When man has the vitality to endure.

Willie M. Dismuke

I Remember

I remember the way our eyes met
the first day I noticed you
I remember the little call
and how nervous we was all
I remember now that first embrace
that kiss and the smile on your face
I remember all the wonderful times we had,
but I remember only one time best of all,
the time it had to end,
I remember how we said we'd remain friends
I hope I can remember us back together again.

Leah Robertson

Another World

Locked in a world where I do not belong,
waiting for the day I can go home.
Off in the distance I see where I should be,
where my friends and family are waiting for me.
Trapped on a planet, a planet unknown
where fear, anger and death does roam.
The laws of the land does not abide,
in this place I'm locked inside.
The walls are solid and very high,
surrounding us on each side.
The rooms are small and filled with gloom,
this must be the house of old man doom.
The trees are dead and the grass is brown,
the drift of evil is the only sound.
The march of power is the scene of all,
you have no chance if you're weak or small.
The strong is the only that does survive,
in this place where death is alive.

Dennis Hall

To My Beloved

A friend is friendship to the end.
Like windswept wheat, a friend must bend
And reach out with a helping hand.
And say, "My friend, I understand."

A friend to whom you bare your soul
And tho' the telling takes its toll,
If friend, he'll gently pat your hand
And say, "My friend, I understand."

I had a friend, a friend indeed.
I had a friend, one's all you need;
If you've a friend, grasp hold his hand
And keep it, 'cause you understand.

Celia D. Starkman

My Heavenly Home

Beautiful Heaven where my Jesus reigns.
Where there's no sorrow, no heart ache or pain.
I now lived with Jesus where joys never cease
From earth and its bondage I have been released.

There's much room in heaven, the city's four square.
The walls are of jasper and there's not a tear.
A stream clear as crystal flows right through
Not just for me friend, it can also be for you.

My friends and dear loved ones
Don't miss this sweet place.
There's one way to reach it through God's saving grace.
Oh come to the Savior, believe on His name.
He'll save the most wicked, the blind and the lame.

Rosa Cox

Unicorns

Horse that fly,
In the midnight sky.

The sky turns a different color,
As their wings flutter.

They glide across the sky with such grace,
It seems as if they are in one place.

With a shiny horn on top of their heads
The fly as we sleep in our beds.

Unicorns don't fly too far,
For you are a bright star.

Candace Gaskins

Old Men In The Sun

Old men sit quietly in the sun
Not dreaming of the glories of the past
But preparing themselves for the ultimate challenge
Approaching death.

But

One old man sat quietly in the sun
Dreaming of the triumphs and defeats
Of the past?

No!

But rather planning his attack
On the problems of the future.
Then

This old man tired of sitting quietly in the sun
Slowly got up
Pulled himself upright
And made his way out to meet the future.

Milton Tony Sherman

Untitled

Be sure to always study, the lines in your parent's face.
Always picture in your mind, the lines that are full of grace.

Hold their hands as much as you can, while they can feel,
For the hands that use to wipe away your tears, may all of a sudden be still.

Eyes that use to swell with love and pride, each time you entered a room,
May all of a sudden go blank, and stare back at you, filled with gloom.

Always tell them that you love them, each and everyday, for there may come a time
When they do not understand what you say.

Alzheimer's is a disease that can tear a body apart,
But one thing that it can not touch, is the love that is in your heart.

Nancy Owen Bell

"Little Child Believe In Yourself"

Little child believe in yourself.
Little child nobody is going to believe in you but you.
Little child never hold your head down.
Little child always hold your head up.
Little child the only reason to hold
your head up is to show them
you are somebody. You are somebody
little child little child. Believe
in yourself and always
show them you are somebody!

Brandy N. Hunley

Reaching For Life

When I reached beyond the stars.
Beyond all reason.
I have therefore reached for you.

As if the sun shone in dark places,
The wind blows in the depths of the soul.
Within I reached for you.

When life has become future.
The darkness no more.
The shadows dance within the soul no more.
I have reached for you.

When memory was worked in favor of another.
Fires of light burns within.
The soul has harkened.
To see the light beyond all comprehension.
The soul reached no more.

Within the flame designs are present.
The soul is formed into a vapor of life.
It has reached beyond its birth.
It was reaching for you.
The living light, the love of beloves.

Bethe Smith

I Opened My Eyes

As I lay here thinking of you, of
all the things you say, and do.
When I need a friend, on you I can depend.
we laugh, we talk, we share, we care.
mom, with all the things you have to do,
you still take time out for you know who.
when I need you, you are there,
always willing to show you care.
so as I lay here, I open my eyes,
The tears fall out, and I have to cry.
It's not you, mom, that takes time out
to show me what a mom's all about.
It was my dream mom yes indeed,
it was you Mrs. T.
You're my dream mom, and so special to me,
but most of all you're a true friend indeed.
If I could turn back time.
My dream mom would be mine all mine.
I love her so much, she's so dear to me.
no one compares to "Mrs. T."

Kathy L. Henley

Boy And Girl

Boy and girl,
Together their eyes were opened
to the sight that their love gave them,
the vision of life.
But now that love is faded,
like the light on a warm summer afternoon.
That's the saddest story of them all,
true love withered away by the friction,
and grind of living.
Maybe their love will be like a flower
broken in the wind never to grow again.
But maybe, if there is an ember in the
ashes the fire can burn again and
never ever dim.

Daniel S. Sitzes

To My Wife and A Starry, Starry Night

I. CHANCE

Dancing a dance of nothing, I feel her presence
But we know our hearts are not
Across the patterned wood floor My eyes meet yours
Our spirits awaken at the moment of One.

Violins are singing, they gently insist
Surely we dare not...resist? My hand touches your
Waist, my other takes yours together we waltz
'Neath ebbing lights, our eyes speaking silence
Still, yet flowing with newness unknown.

II. ADIEU

And now, dear one, where are the years when first
We met that fateful eve? And where is the
Passage of time that merges life into His eternal
Hand? I know not, sleeping dream, for nothing
More from life does desire bequest...Excepting..
Perhaps..One more gentle goodbye, my love, my
Wife, as they lay your loveliness to rest.

Robert Lin Mosey

White Beast

A dog, a white beast
The cotton takes shape as it flies through the air
Changing from a profile of a man
To the body of a great beast
I lay back and watch them dance in the wind
Uh-Oh
The white beast is now a dark gray
Shooting silver flames toward the earth
He lets out a booming roar
The tears from the man's profile pour onto the earth
As he waits to be devoured by the Beast.

Leslie A. Warner

Lost Love

The whole world turned a gray;
The day that you, forever, went away;

You're the one I love and adore,
But my love wasn't enough, you wanted more;

You once said you loved me with all your heart;
So why is it now that we're apart.

Jessica L. Farrow

Grandmother Willow

The wind through the willow calls to me,
Come sit beneath the weary old tree.
She stands all alone,
In a sea of green waves.
Her whips touch the ground,
Her earthly grave.
All days are spent weeping,
A tear and then two.
Never will she smile,
For me or for you.
Her sorrow I feel,
Deep inside it does burn.
Forever you love,
And forever you mourn.
Life is full of sad partings.
As we each spend a day,
Crying and weeping
for time passed away.

Debra A. Wayland

Be Careful What You Teach

A Poem To My Mother

My mother taught me to be independent
and was disappointed when I was
My mother taught me that I was born alone and needed no one else
and was disappointed when I didn't
My mother taught me to be independent of men
and was disappointed when I was
My mother taught me to be tough
and was disappointed when I insisted that she be tough
My mother taught me that an education was important and
was disappointed when I did not become a homemaker
My mother pushed me away
and was disappointed when I didn't need her
My mother taught me to be me
and was disappointed when I was.

E. Aracelis Francis

Slumber Land

Come Cassidy let me take your hand
And lead your into slumber land

Where fairies dance and flowers sing
Where rabbits hop and bluebells ring

Where spiders spin their magic webs
And cloves nod their sleepy heads

Where breeze soft whispers through the trees
The buzzing stops of all the bees

The big green frog is fast asleep.
He will not give another beep.

The butterflies have gone to rest
And all the bird are on their nest

How Cassidy you can go to sleep
You do not need to count the sheep
Far they will guard you while you sleep

But when you awake to a day brand new
There will be Mommie smiling at your

Pamela T. Alp

Untitled

Wedges of watermelon
 offered to Buddha
have lost their crispness...
 delight does not stay.
The price for one splash of color
 is many days of grayness.
 Occasional glimpses of love,
the memories and spirits of friends dance inside-
their music is my only relief
there is no hope of finding the sunlight today.
 When the isolation completely hollows-out
my insides, then there is some peace.
 I will wait...
and listen for the shepherd's flute.

Robert E. Young

I Believe

Angels are here for you and for me,
I often wonder, are they he or are they she.
It really doesn't matter
as long as their job gets done,
watching over and taking care of each and everyone!
I know someone's with me all day long,
I can only blame myself when I do something wrong.
If we keep our faith in the heaven's above,
what we'll get in return is an abundance of love.
Love from our family, neighbors and friends,
will keep us focused until our earthly time ends.

Norma Wood

Rip Tide

The flesh drags through the tides of the spirit.
A churn of hidden conflict within the surface.
Preparing ebulation.

The rip fighting its own flow.
Caught in its own boil.
Never considering the vastness of the sea.

A merger causing turmoil never united
never calm enough to realize its reflection.

A dangerous water.
An under toe pulling itself down.
Ripping from the inside out.

The yearn to be out to sea
a direction like a new morning, a sun rising.
Always stifled by the drag.

How small the strand that wrestles destiny.
The ambivalent lock closed to its conversion.

Always changing, always the same.
Not understanding the greatness of its strength
never fulfilling its desires by its own rebuke.
Its endless struggle its relentless clash till the ebb till the death.

Louie Wies

My Dream

I stood one day on a canyon rim
And stopped to look around
And suddenly felt, I don't known why,
That I stood on hallowed ground.

As I watched from my point of vantage
My thoughts sped back in time.
I thought of another hunter
Who watched with thoughts like mine.

I am sure in his primitive childlike faith
He must have been in awe
Of the magnificent beauty around him
And felt the hand of God.

As I turned to go, I saw it there
Like a jewel in a velvet bed
I reached to touch a part of my dream,
An Indian arrowhead!

Jack I. Pollock

Winter Flowers

Ours is a different season,
We are not as lilies of the field

Sewn deep into the earth
We must struggle through the hardened ground,

The struggle to come forth
for most would be a loss.

To stand alone and scattered
in the gray of winter.

Alas, not for loss, for we
will be seen completely,
joyously for those who look

Yes, we are winter flowers!

Mary Jane Sloan

"Longing"

Deep within my heart
hides an enduring secret
that you may never seek.

A yearning to kiss away the darkness,
the fears,
that lay deep in your sad eyes
From a world that no one cared to touch.

A chance our path's cross,
and touch.
Then and only then the secret will reveal.
And two souls will cling in ecstasy as one,
forever more.

Nora Nee

Lost Love

I have two children, I cannot see,
though my love is strong, as love can be.
Since a divorce, two went two ways,
one hides the children, to this very day.
No letter, no phone call, nor touch of their hand,
no picture, no hug or love shared with this man.
The children loved me, the last I took them home,
before mom moved again, to leave dad alone.
Their mom did move, then remarried too.
I am their father, usually alone and blue.
I'll wait for my children, in hopes that one day,
their love will return and come looking my way.
J.G.S. III are the initials of my only son,
for he is now eight, and a lovable one.
Then there is my daughter Jennifer Renee,
She's five and for her, my love grows each day.
If these two could return, change my one into three,
times could be tough, but I'd still be happy.

Jim Stewart

A Mother No More

A stranger appeared through the door
To take away what will be no more

To put to rest a mother's nourishing care
That has left a family in despair

He silence her cry so no one could hear
What she herself soon came to fear

A life without what she holds so dear
The loved ones who will soon disappear

A dagger struck once, then twice to the core
To silence the mother that will be no more

Her body limp and covered with blood
That left a family one less to love

A stranger with a dagger had taken away
The hopes and dreams of another day

He moved undetected through the light of day
To seek out his unsuspecting prey

And when the deed was done
He went back into the morning sun

There laid upon a blood stained floor
A mother who is no more

Linda Marie Tyler

Soul To Soul

He sweeps by in a breathless whisper,
Covered only by desolate shadows.
The sweet scent of his manness fills the air.
Passion envelopes her with maddening desire.
An overwhelming need to be embraced by his power fills her.
Turning slowly they glimpse one another with soft caresses.
A gentle smile of acknowledgment touches their lips.
They part holding the moment in their hearts,
As well as the unrelinquished desire they share,
To be forever bonded to one another,
Soul to soul.

Tracy L. Weidman

A Single Tear

The pain can be seen underneath her eyes.
As the sound fills the air with silent cries.
Her pain was unbearable with his memories they'll make,
And every single night she will lay awake.
Thinking of him and the times they had.
And she was honored and so glad.
They were together for the short period of time,
Together they were inseparable like lemon and lime.
The relationship wasn't as together as they thought,
Majority of the time they argue and fought.
One would go out, the other stays at home,
One has fun, the other sleeps alone.
They loved each other with heart and soul,
No longer remembering their main goal.
To love and cherish each time they had.
And never go to bed upset or mad.
They lied to each other that's why it didn't last,
Now they are bitter about the past.
They said their good-byes and they faced their fear,
No longer will she shed a single tear.

Andrea Wooten

There It Was

There it was, a single rose, born not of God's land but by
someone's hand,
Leaning against the granite stone as if there it belonged, there
was its home.
Its scarlet reflection on the polished gray tomb
Was a mirror of my broken heart with its mortal wound.
The rose, so perfect of face, up to heaven it gazed
To implore God's mercy here where my fallen love lay.
But who placed this rose on my beloved's grave? Not I.
And who knew his favorite flower, the rose? Only I.
Not so, not so, my anguished heart cried.
For there it was, the rose, another one's love, I couldn't deny.
And there it was, the rose, another one's grief mingling with mine.
Oh, Rose, who dared to deepen my wound and light the flame of
my ire?
But it stirred not with answers, for its heart was of silk and its
stem was of wire.
I knelt down beside it to tear out my pain
When suddenly behind me a voice, soft as the misting rain,
Said, "Hi, Mom," and a gentle kiss brushed my wet cheek.
"Isn't the rose beautiful? I made it for Dad," I heard my daughter
speak.
My face flamed with shame to think my love was that weak and so
quick to blame.
Remember not my angry thought, dear Rose, for now I know you
are his sentinel and messenger of love, dear Rose.

Eleonora M. Opatka

Wrinkled Remembrances In Black And White

Just a photograph of olden age
yet it seems like yesterday
that we romped in fields of thyme and sage
and wandered about to play

Never tiring, never stopping,
never pausing to complain
or worry about the days gone by
or what the years would bring

But the edges are frayed
the corners worn
and with them
have gone the years

Of happiness and innocence
transformed by fate
into a flowing gossamer mosaic
of laughter and tears.

Susan Mido

Black And White

There's a big problem in our
world today,
Between the black and white.
I'm not sure what to do or say,
To let people know what's right.
What is the only difference—
But the color of the skin!
I don't know what people think
this is,
But it's the world that we all
live in!
To me, it's just a coat of paint,
That will never ware away!
Whether you think it is or it ain't,
That's how I look at the world
today.
So, it doesn't matter what color you are,
We're the same; inside and out.
And if prejudice is the way you are,
Then you better figure out what this world is about!

Stacy Goodling

Judging Others

The sun reflects off our skin, and our appearance
It shadows over our inner soul.
But, the darkness reflects off our soul,
And it shadows our outer appearance.
We judge others by what we see in the light.
We judge them by the way they look.
And yet... we judge them too fast,
Too fast to see what they are really like.
I ask myself, "Why does this world suffer?"
"Is it because of the way I've judged a person?"
Sometimes, I look in the mirror, and I think...
Why have I judged a person, when I am no better than they?
Is it that I have not yet judged myself?
If I make fun of them,
Then I am the one who should be made fun of.
For my soul is much darker than theirs.
Yet... we look at the world, and we can only hope,
That someday, sometime, the world will come together,
And we will unite.... unite as humans
And, unite... as friends.

Stacy Crites

Our Strife In Life

While someone is laughing
Someone is crying.

While someone is resting
Someone is dying.

My poem gets worse,
and so does the curse the world beholds.

Someone is aching,
and another is breaking

The hurtling still abides,
and never dies.

I try to compel from it,
but then I feel that I have to yell!

While the evil are merry
our thoughts get scary.

Our minds are dirty with lusting,
and our mouths keep on cussing.

We all hurt and feel like dirt,
but we still go on our strife in life.

Melissa Errett

How Many Times

How many times can he break your heart?
Before it just gets too weak and falls apart?
How many times can he lie to your face?
Until you can just say goodbye to his unloving embrace?
How many times can you keep running back?
Before you realize his heart is empty and black?
How many times can he push you around?
Before in a pool of tears you will drown?
How many times can you take the beating?
Before you realize it's the devil you're meeting?
How many times do you sit and cry?
Listening to your tears as they roll by?
How many times did you want to leave?
Because you know it's only abuse you receive.
How many things can I say to you?
Before you realize this isn't the worst he'll do?

Angelina Mazzone

But Me

They said he wasn't like us, not like the rest; but me, I still called him brother.
They said he didn't belong, he's so different; but me, I still called him friend.
They said he left us, to be raised by one; but me I still called him father.
They said he was evil, that he was sick; but me, I still called him son.
They said it wasn't real, I was too young; but me, I still called it love.
They said he died when I was young, too young; but me, I still call him brother.
They said it looked bad, he's all wrong; but me, I still call him friend.
They said he denied us, he hasn't cared; but me, I still call him father.
They said he should be locked up, they took him away; but me I still call him son.
They said I deserved to be alone, I was too young; but to me; it's still called love.
They said at my funeral, that I was a tragedy; but me, I still hold my heart.
If they had thought my life was perfect, would I; I still lived my life.
They all watched me die with my brother, my friend, my father, my son, and my love; but to me, I still live in them.

Marcy Standish

Dad, When I Was

Dad,
When I was two and a half
months old you thought
I was the perfect baby to love
so you and mom decided to adopt me.
When I was one I was totally helpless and
I needed you for everything.
When I was two I was
just learning that you were
my daddy. When I was six
I was in need for help with
my homework and to learn
new things. When I was ten
I was in fifth grade and I needed
as much help in school as I do now.
I thought I was failing but I passed.
Now that I'm fourteen I act like I don't
need you for help with anything but I really
do - with my life and my choices.
I hope you have a great Father's Day!!

Maggie Price

Allegiance

No one asked, why send me, when they were sent across the sea,
our country to serve, to keep us free...
With allegiance they did serve.
Away from home many did go, and so quickly the young did grow,
into men, and into battles did flow...
Never a moment from duty swerve.

Salesmen, college boys, fathers were sent, fighting and dying
for freedom they went, stood their ground with bravery unbent...
Knowing well the task they had.
On foreign fields so many did fall, for God and country,
they gave all, that tyrants and madmen they forestall...
In a world seemingly gone mad.

Now our world is a much better place, because these refused
to turn their face, from duty and allegiance - did not disgrace...
To these we owe our eternal praise.
For all who fought in wars before, protecting ideals
from foreign foe, may we on them our gratitude bestow...
Yes, to all these - our glasses we raise.

Henry Newton Goldman

Nurses Blessings

Blessed are they who come to my floor
With a medical cart just outside my door.

Blessed are they who come in with a smile
Administer my medication and chat for awhile.

Blessed are they when I am in pain
Do all they can and never complain.

Blessed are they who fully understand
How weak are my knees and trembly my hands.

Blessed are they who never once say,
"You've told me that story twice today."

Blessed are they who give me I.V.'s
And diligently monitor them with such ease.

Blessed are they who bathe me with lotion
With talented hands full of healing devotion.

Blessed are they who make it well known
I'm respected and loved and not all alone

Blessed are they who ease my day
While at the nursing home I stay.

Faye B. Redding

Of Thy Love Do Thee Speak?

Of thy love do thee speak? With his eyes
like emeralds and have like burnt cinnamon.
Does thou love's touch make thee heart
flutter? Does thou love's gaze make thee
melt? The loveliest flower or sunset could
not ever compare to thy love's feathery
touch or voice like a cool summer
morning breeze. Of thy love do thee speak?

Brandi Spinn

Resignation

Oh dear my heart, if we must part
And each on a separate path must start,
If I could stay near and come if you call,
I would not mind at all, at all.

If I could ease your path through life,
Be there for you in sorrow or strife,
If I could only soften a fall,
I would not mind at all, at all.

And when you grow old, if you are alone,
As I shall always be, I own,
To be your comfort when all else doth pall,
I would not mind at all, at all.

And when in your grave you come to lie,
I will pray that I too might soon die.
And if we meet beyond death's wall,
I would not mind at all, at all.

Lorraine Margaret Coates

The World

The world plays fool to its own idiot sacrifice.
The world judges, but can't find the answers to its own.
The world pretends to be free, but each man has his own prison.
The world tries to be color blind,
but whites see blacks and blacks see whites.
Why can't we just see people.
The world says it loves life,
yet it takes it away from others.
The world says it understand.
What it doesn't understand it tries to hide.

The world wants change, but change for one man's domination.
Still the world is a beautiful place

Quentina Hamlett

Carousel

The lion so fierce when on the attack,
Welcomes the children on his furry back.
The horse with the pretty pink tail full of curls,
Is always a favorite of all little girls.
But if you should ask all the little boys,
They'll tell you the tiger is their favorite choice.
The very tall long-necked African giraffe,
Usually makes all the children laugh.
The graceful white swan is always the best,
For the elderly riders to take a brief rest.
The snarling brown bear is a fearsome sight,
For the more daring riders who can overcome their fright.
The rabbit's long ears and black beady eyes,
Give all the children a great big surprise.
The mystical unicorn with its long flowing mane,
Impressive as he passes again and again.
The unusual zebra is an awesome sight,
Resembling a horse, with stripes black and white.
Young and old love the carousel, with its musical sound,
And its wondrous animals, going round and round and round.....

Stephanie Sansone

The Aftermath

Bodies riddled with bullets
draped over razor wire
no longer flinch
until the wind moves
a hand dripping blood
for another crimson puddle to gather.

Fog steadily marches in
behind the tattered corpses
and cataclysm left by the Kaiser
covering the aftermath
like a coroner with a sheet
shrouding the horror
as vultures dine.

Who else would clean the messes men make?

Glen Kubasak

Unity

To gaze towards the heavens on a star lit night
And see the moon so shiny and bright
As it casts many shadows and I look down
I seem so small my feet on the ground
Yet with God all around in an awesome sense
I'm lifted and walk tall in confidence
That God in heaven and we on earth
Are one in unity with His Son and birth

Alma White Bates

Hot Off The Holy Spirit's Press!

"Live - it not Die-t"

I'm on God's live-it program, no diet for me.
I'm on the "live-it" program since He set me free,
I'm on the "live-it" program, Christ is my victory,
I'm on the "live-it" program today.

I'm eating from the banquet of the Lord,
I'm eating the "fruit of the Spirit" forevermore,
I'm eating love, peace and joy,
There is plenty for you and me,
I'm eating from the banquet of the Lord.

I'm on the "live-it" program, no deprivation for me,
I'm on the "live-it" program, no discouragement for me,
I'm on the "live-it" program, no depression in me,
I'm eating from the banquet of the Lord.

I'm on the "live-it" program, there is no fear and doubt,
I'm on the "live-it" program, I can stand and shout,
I'm on the "live-it" program, I want to be "fat" in God,
I'm on the "live-it" program, according to God's word.

Steven R. Chapman

Philosophy Of A Leaf

What is so free in this worlds of ours?
Strange it seems, as it floats for hours;
Only a leaf, a wondrous sight;
It's a belief, also a right,
Yes, it's a right to do as I wish;
Float day and night on wind with a swish.
Never a root to hold me strong,
Never a tie to keep me long.
Suddenly there and caught by a stone,
What a scare! Now it is gone;
Gone once again on the wind by a tree;
Never a stop until eternity.
Better that I keep on flying, too!
Better I don't sleep from nothing to do.
Just as the leaf would sit and decay,
So would I with no words to say.

Ina Bennett

Life's Path

Life's path is an endless ribbon of sepia hue.
Worn with time, it bears impressions of many a journey past.
Sunlight touches it with warm affection.
Snow, sleet and rain deteriorate its surface with a vengeance.
The ever changing sky and birds in flight glance down
at the passing scene.

The wind, depending on its whim, pushes clouds
in various direction, high overhead.

Sometimes, angry clouds, shrouded in dark shades
of grey-green move along with the clap of thunder
and the flash of lightening, thus marking their presence.

Zephyrs of wind and their sometimes turbulent gusts play
their interchanging rhythms, each to a different beat.

Only silence springs forth from this teller of tales.
Silent, yet depicting the joys and sorrows of all who
have walked here.

Young and old, rich and poor, sick and hale, the pious
and thief alike;

All have left a lasting imprint on Life's Path.

Lillian Copak

What Is A Hospital Without God

What is a road without a direction
Why give health care with no affection
What is life without some lovin'
What is cookie dough without an oven
Do we have a passion to heal the poor
Or do we throw them out the door
Do we let liquor drown family goals
Do we let cocaine evaporate souls
What is a brain without a mind
How can you think if your thoughts are blind
What is a hospital without God
Do we focus on the man in the chair
Or do we fiddle with the monitors there
Can we help a battered woman escape
Can we notice a victim of rape
Is a baby a what, an it, or a who
If a child is abused what will you do
If we do not take the time to care
When patients need out help-who will be there

Ashley Christine Willis

Untitled

I am a Gold Fish in a bowl
I wonder what it would be to be free
I hear the laughter, and people noises
I see the leaves outside blowing in the wind
I want to be free.

I am a Gold Fish in a bowl
I pretend to be a Bird, or Butterfly, or even a flea
I feel so lonely
I touch other Gold Fish in the bowl
I worry I'll never be free
I cry to feel the sunshine and the breeze

I am a Gold Fish in a bowl
I understand I am a pet to bring happiness to others
I say let me be free
I dream about the night stars, and moon above
I try to jump and jump out of my bowl
I hope I can be free

I am a Gold Fish in a Bowl!!!

Machelle Montgomery

As Only A Rose Can Give

Think of my love as a long-stemmed red rose
with beds of morning dew drops resting upon
its soft velvety-smooth petals
With the fragrant perfume as only a rose can give.

Look upon me as if I were a rose.
Delicate to touch, with velvety-smooth skin and my lips
as soft and red as the rose petals moistened by your sweet kisses,
With the fragrant aroma of my perfume for only you to inhale.
Caress me in you arms, as one caresses the beauty of a single
red rose with its soft, velvety-smooth petals and a fragrance
as only a rose can give.

I give you my love as one gives the gift of a single red rose
with the glistening beads of the morning dew.
May you capture and treasure its beauty as if it were a picture of me.
Inhale the sweetness of my perfume, as you would the fragrant
aroma of the rose.
My love for you is as the rose;
soft, aromatic, without thorns,
with love as only I can give.

Phyllis Dootoff

I Thank You

To a Dear Friend

Thank you for the Healing Card and prayers,
Which brought me to shed grateful tears.
Thank you for caring, sharing, and kindness,
In people today, these things are minus.
Thank you for listening, and being just you,
In the human race today, there are so few.
Thank you for being so thoughtful in what you say and do,
A dear friend you are, sincere and true.
Thank you for being the daughter I wished I had,
For some of my loved one's make me feel sad.
Thank you for the closeness, that illnesses had brought together.
With support for each other, we will learn to weather.,
Thank you dear friend for just being there,
To call and talk to and to compare.

Helen F. Brady

Family Secret

She holds her head down, won't look you in the eye.
I've always wondered why she became so shy.
She was once outgoing, but then she withdrew.
I never would have guessed that she'd been abused.

I felt rage. I felt anger. I felt pity.

My girlfriend came by and shared it with me.
Said the mother had told her of the abuse you see.
It was so hard to handle when she explained to me
that our girlfriend's daughter was abused by her step daddy.

I felt rage. I felt anger. I felt pity.

A year has gone by and you can see the whole family
sitting together in church as if they're so happy.
She hasn't told another soul, a counselor, preacher or psychiatrist.
The little girl is withering away. Oh God, would you tend to this?

I feel rage. I feel anger. I feel pity.

As I look in the shy girl's eyes, I see she's crying for help.
I've even thought to call the Welfare department. Report it myself.
But now the wife lives in denial, holding on to fantasies.
Besides, I'm not supposed to know.

It's a secret of the family.

Audrey Lee-Foster

Heaven

The open sky so wide and blue;
As you sit there and think
of the things you could do.
On an open field and the sun so yellow
Watching the cars go by with a young fellow
The trees sway as the wind blows
And you sit there and think.
No one knows;
Behind the trees
Beyond the clouds
Over the Rainbow
And with the breeze
There lies a spot that everyone loves
Cuz' that's where heaven starts;
The spot of Love

Krystle Downs

Papa Was A Grocer

Papa was a grocer
With seven hungry mouths to feed.
Mama called two or three times a day
To tell him what she'd need.

The cellar door would open, and,
With a tomato basket in his hand,
Papa'd take off his sawdust shoes,
Kiss Mama, and - my Land!

There'd be washboard cookies, ripe bananas,
Country butter - lots of stuff
To keep us happy - more than enough.

I've always wondered
And wished that I could ask it,
"Why were there never any tomatoes
In Papa's tomato basket?"

Anna G. Matthews

Don't Give Up

When life seems like a problem
and the answer's out of reach,
And all the minutes passing by
seem like an hour each;
When you just want to stay in bed
and never rise again,
Or crawl into a hole somewhere
and stay till "God knows when;"
Then just remember that these times
are only temporary;
Each day could bring the answer
to the burden that you carry.
For each new day brings with it
a whole new set of reasons,
And brand new promise that your life
can change just like the seasons.
Yes, just as winter yields to spring,
the same holds true for you;
If you have faith through all your trials
Your dreams can all come true!

Deona M. Johnson

Another Storyteller's Creed

Reality the mirror is a reflection of Dreams
It is what you make it, but not what it seems.
It's over the rainbow that no one can reach
Easy to understand; Impossible to teach.
It's the old notion that all Men and Real
that we believe what we see and discount what we feel.
The old tried and true is just one of our creations
So—reality is for those who lack imagination!

Sarah J. Finley

Jesus Take My Hand

My eyes are covered, I cannot see.
Oh, Lord Jesus take my hand and guide me.
For I cannot tell the days from the nights.
For I cannot see the light.
So help me Lord Jesus
That I may stand up straight.
I don't want to stumble or fall.
I just want to walk with Jesus,
Through the valley of darkness
And the shadow of death.
So I may see the golden gates
Of heaven some sweet day.
Lord Jesus take my hand
And guide me all the way.
So my eyes will open
In heaven some sweet day.

Goldie L. Patton

What Christmas Means To Me

A tree - a song - a candle bright -
A wreath - a gift - a star-lit night -
The shepherds - the wisemen - the cattle stall -
The Baby - the Mother - the Angels, all
Remind me that this is Christmas Day
As 'neath our tree my gifts I lay
And from my heart a Christmas song pours
And I light the candle outside the door.
The carollers stop and sing of the Babe;
They tell of the manger where He was laid;
And like the angels who long ago sang
They lead me to worship and praise a King.
I have no great treasures or wealth of great store
To bring to His feet like Wise Men of yore;
I bring Him myself: My love, my all,
I bow at His feet, I yield to His call.

Margaret L. Zahler

Shape Up America

Be thankful America
We are slipping in darkness,
Today seems like we are headed Bos-Ni-A.
The pilgrims were rich, because they saw God clearly.
Today we look up to man too sincerely.
We have lost our basic faith and trust.
We must turn to God. Turn back America. Shape up.
We are getting education, where is the rest?
Let us learn at home,
Stop pointing our finger at everyone.
Let us do our best.
Almighty God will take care of the rest.
Let us aid our children, they are tempted too.
Let us help and respect the old, they helped build stairways too.
Let us have compassion for the poor and the prisoners,
They are God's children too.
Men walking the moon, but come back to earth to rest.
Pollution, ozone, crime, bullets-flying, fires are burning.
Now! Here is the church. Here are our bodies.
Let us open the doors, and put out the fires

Charlene Nezart

In Love

My big sister is in love,
Her boyfriend's all she's thinking of,
She's on the phone both day and night,
She doesn't know if it's dark or light,
She always asks me what she should wear,
Then she says "do you like my hair?"
I'm sick and tired of hearing his name,
This boyfriend stuff is really lame.

Sarah Rall

Born Unequal

His eyes sunken deep into his head, his hair long and matted,
A broom in one roughened hand; his body, unprotected.

He was the servant of the house,
A young boy of nine, was he,
Employed at the house where his parents had left him,
Those whose faces he would never see.

Taught never to utter a word, taught only to obey,
Taught to keep within himself, whatever he needed to say.

Small was the world he saw through his eyes,
Limited were the opportunities before him,
His job was to serve and strain and scrub,
And to cater to his master's every whim.

What made him different from the rest of the world?
What did he do to deserve this?
He had never been shown love or affection,
His cheeks had never been caressed by a kiss.

Born unequal into this modern world,
Oppressed by the evils of caste,
Born unequal into a life of discrimination,
Haunted by the shadows of his empty past.

Natasha Thapar

Friends

Their pain is endless and it grows within
Their hearts reach out to their closest friend

I know their pain
And how their hearts cry
But why can't I reach them deep down inside?

Is it the shame they fear within?
Or is it fear that hinders them?

I wish I could mend their hearts of sorrow
And set their spirits free
But I'm merely a human being
It's God's love that they need

So help them God to understand
the power of love in your gentle hand
And when they need healing
Or a special friend
Tell them you're willing
To be with them to the end

Tamra Botts

"The Way Others Do"

You told me once
That you had been hurt
I wonder
Is that all you wanted me for
To hurt me
To break my heart
To make me cry
I don't know if I will ever be able
To trust anyone the way I trusted you
Is this the way
That girl hurt you?
I wouldn't want anyone
To feel the way
That you have made me feel
If this is what you wanted
I hope that you're happy
In time I won't be so angry or hate you so much
One day I might understand
Why you treated me
The way others have treated you.

Julie Lovett

Fragment

You remain - in my mind I see you still,
faded, yes, in ways and yet in others
fresh as yesterday.
One example - your voice
still tinkles clear as crystal in my ear.

You should know - I think you do
as memories grow more sweet in time, that now
as leaves begin to fall
I (we?) cannot help but know
that winter is approaching.

But as I go, to comfort me I've made
soft garments of my memories of you.
I wear them now and then to sleep
and in the deepest, darkest reaches of the night
you feel it too.

So now we are together as I choose
as near as near can be
without a word between us as we go.
Words we do not need and anyway,
what can I say, to me?

Samuel G. McKerall

Nursing Home

Sitting alone
In a nursing home. No one ever comes, no one ever cares.
Oh, the stories you could tell! What you've been through
Sick and well. So many stories good and bad. So many stories
Happy and sad. Oh, what you could say!
If only someone would listen. Sitting alone in a nursing home,
Suddenly, in your eyes, the tears glisten.
They glide smoothly down the dry, wrinkled cheeks.
You've not even the energy to frown.
You sit there for days, maybe even weeks.
You've waited and waited, for what seems like years.
Then suddenly come true your worst fears
No one wants you. They haven't for quite some time.
Sitting there, in your wheelchair,
You finally realize you've waited too long.
What's left to live for? Nothing, that's what.
Your time to go has come. As you gaze at the room, you sigh.
Through parched lips you whisper goodbye.
And slowly, on that rainy, dreary day
You and your stories pass away. Sitting alone in a nursing home.

Heather A. Osborn

On The Fourth

As I sit on the beach with my toes in the sand
You come to me, reach out and hold my hand
as we watch the fireworks in the sky
I look at you and your beauty catches my eye
As we watch the exploding multitude of colors
I can only think of you and no other
our days together have been a blessing
On me you have made an everlasting impression
As we watch the rockets burst in the air
It is you, my love, for whom I care
All my hopes and dreams with you I'll share

As I sit on the beach with my toes in the sand
You come and sit by me and I hold your hand
Our love is like the fourth with one exception
As the colors of light and sounds in the night
slowly fade away
This love we have is here to stay.

Jimmy Poor

Untitled

Inside me I see faces,
They were all different shapes, sizes, and colors,
They floated around not really knowing where to go,
I pointed out a light to them, but they didn't seem to want to go,
They were all smiling and laughing, but behind every smile there was much pain and sorrow,
If and since the pain and sorrow is there why do they continue to laugh?
Finally there was one little face staring back at me and I looked into the tiny reddened eyes and there were a ton of tears just wanting to come through,
I asked this tiny face, "Why do you smile when there is so much painbehind the smile?"
This faces answer was, "I didn't want for anyone else to be sad because I am."
So I looked around and all of the other faces were listening as I said, "Everyone has much sorrow behind their smiles and eventually everyone will turn and be like you in knowing that a smile can't last forever..."

Amanda Kotkin

pool Of fantasy

time triggers the fascination,
and i am...
released through a resplendent tunnel
of extreme inspiration.
tossed on the wave of a poisonous sea,
but secretly guided through the chasms
of stimulation.

a sudden flash of interest!

and i am...
arriving on the shore of reality.
conscious...
aware....
realizing the obvious difference.
remembering the thrill of deviation,
the pool of fantasy.

living, only to return.

David A. Rose

The Tall Ship/The City Man

The City Man, he hailed on board;
He came to the Bay to sail on the Maud.
This restless soul, his spirit throbbed;
As in a cage, freedom sobbed.
The Chesapeake beckoned—He went, vigorous of gait,
Like a buccaneer, to find his fate.

"Yorktown, by morning?" he queried the Mate.
"Might, Might." Scanned the Mate. "If the wind don't abate."
"Yorktown by morning, Captain?:
"Might, Might." Drawled the Captain. "If the tide ain't late."

Nobody hurried, nobody worried, no man a master,
Only the heavens dispelled disaster.

...And perched aloft, on the for'ard beam,
A friend aside to share a dream,
Encased in wondrous infinity.
Embraced by natures affinity.
Sailing thru rippling creation,
This, to me, was sheer elation...!

Harry Corsun

Love

Laughing and crying, love growing, love dying.
Love is making up and breaking up.
Whispering secrets in each others ear.
He's there for me, for him I'm here.
Being trusting and honest, loving and modest.
If you're in love you feel a sensation of flying high.
A feeling that you love for him will never die.
When you're in love he brings you chocolates and flowers,
You stay on the phone talking for hours.
And it really doesn't matter to you,
If your parents don't like him and you really do.
Loving someone is special and if you're lucky enough
To be in love,
Hold on to the feeling.

Sarah Horner

The Teacher

She comes to school and signs herself in;
She stops in the hall to chat with her friends;
The students never do what they are told;
They treat her like mice and they are the giant traps trying to catch her;
Although they love her they don't tell her so;
They see she's a teacher and that she should know.

Lori Kurts

The Everlasting Gift

This gift that I am giving you isn't something to be worn
It's a gift to you to celebrate the day that you were born
This gift that I am speaking of is filled with all my love
For it's a gift that's sent to me from someone up above

I owe so much for all you've done I don't know where to start
so I offer you a part of me a piece of my own heart
All the money and fancy jewelry can always be replaced
But if these words shall touch your heart it can never be erased

You deserve so much thanks it's not the kind I can repay
But all you have to do is ask and I'll give my best in every way
Everything I give to you is not as perfect as I'd like to show
But it's offered to you in the purest and most honest way I know

I wish I could make you see yourself the way that I can see
Then you would realize what you really mean to me
Sometimes I may not show it I'll be the first one to confess
But my feelings for you will never change you're far above the rest

For putting all your trust in me I thank you once again
For being someone special and an understanding friend
To a very special person a gift to you from me
I wish you a happy birthday the happiest it can be

Kevin K. Sakai

Dreams

Long ago forgotten dreams
live again, so it seems

In a field of daisies in full bloom
In the scent of lilacs in a room

In a rusted wagon not used today
seeming to smell of fresh cut hay

In a baby's laugh that fills the air
in an empty church that still holds prayer

In the steadfast love of man and wife
In the joys and sorrows of everyday life

If those who dreamed have passed away
Their dreams are alive and well today

Though life may change, dreams seldom fade
For dreams are the stuff, of which life is made

Delores Eller

You Can Cry

I'll never touch that gentle face, or hold that aging hand
I'll never hold that once feisty body that grew fragile-ever again.

They say a man shouldn't cry, or show their emotions-we don't know why
So the pain and tears I hold inside
To feel pain and sorrow and want to cry; is only human-don't question-why!

You're more of a man if you show how you feel, whether people think
you're tough and strong, or mild and weak, is not the question or
Part of the deal-it's about how you really feel.

So look at it this way — I'm human and I'm a man, what more can I say
Yes, I hurt and I'm gonna cry!
Here's one tear and here's another, it's because I love and miss you My Dear Grandmother!

Debby Colburn

Progress

I see trees; the trees being cut down for farmland and new housing complexes.
I see wildlife; the animal species being killed by poachers and sold at black markets.
I study the clouds; but they are being strangled and smothered by smog
I'd look at the sky, but it is being blocked by skyscrapers.
I try to listen to nature, but it's muffled by the passing of automobiles.
I'd walk in the woods, but crime makes it unsafe.
I would lay in the sun, but ozone depletion and UV rays might give me cancer.
God made the world simple, yet we made it difficult.
Man calls it Progress, but I call it destruction.

Brandy L. Reeves

Sunset

The sunset is like a lady with
ribbons in her hair, her dancing so
fair. I bring my hand to the sky, and feel
the wind like a spy. I close my eyes and
see her dancing, and close to her I see a horse
prancing. The ballet she dances, turns
people into trances because of its beauty.
She ends her dance when the sky is
black and color is no more in the sky.

Joanna E. Van Voorhis

Love One Another

Our Heavenly Father has voiced the command
That all His children throughout the land
Are to love one another without dissimulation.
If we would only obey, He would bless our nation!
So much turmoil, heartache, and strife
Could be removed from our sin-filled life
If we would embrace God's children as sisters and brothers,
While permitting our souls to freely love each other.
Each of us must make this choice
And declare our goal with unwavering voice;
That we will commit our hearts to God's command
Or be part of the problem that shrouds our land!

Betty B. Bush

"David's Locker"

Blue faced coffin stands on end waiting
for the lock to chant open.

Click, the lock unlatches the screeching
squealing encased tomb. Sun baked air
sucks in like a newly open can of pop.

The coffin's metal base is covered in
paper soldiers marching off to battle.
Hanging from a silver hook, a winter
shield dangles motionlessly frozen in
rigamortis. A lion's claw strikes out
grabbing the bag just before striking
the bottom floor.

A lonely shelf clasps three sides of
the tomb fearing to fall into the never
ending darkness.

On the plateau lies a calculator vigorously
snapping figures. Pens and pencils
gracefully hop into a ballet. A bag of marbles
stands at attention with the string drooping like a waterfall.

"Oh no, what's Happening?" Slam, silence, click.

James W. Hewitt

Innocence

Innocent people working hard,
and children playing in the yard.
This is how it was before
the bomb went off near the bottom floor.
The windows broke as the floor went down,
and people felt it all around the town.
Many had children whose lives were taken,
and everyone felt it as the world was shaken.
Families lost mothers and fathers,
sisters, brothers, children, and many others.
People were lost in the wreckage left,
and death left many people bereft.

Shoshanah Kauffman

Collaboration

A child sits waiting, waiting
Adults go on debating, debating

The solution is called Collaboration
A process of negotiation
Where decisions are made and problems are solved
And yes conflicts are resolved

This may not come easy
But valuable things in life seldom do
There is a need to try
There is a cause to satisfy

Until we find the tools we need
Can we begin to plant the seed
As a parent I want only one thing
The best for my child that love alone can't bring

Family - Professional collaboration
It sounds ideal I know
But if we work and work well together
Our minds will grow and grow
Ideas will flow and flow
Results will show and show

Judy Williams

These Hands

These were the hands that held my new born body to her breasts to suckle the nurturing milk that flowed from her nipples. These were the hands that bathed me in soothing warm water. These were the hands that gently held mine the first day of school when she walked me to my kindergarten class. These were the hands that opened the pages of story books often read to comfort me at bedtime. These were the hands that wiped away my tears.

These were the hands that held a quart of vodka to her mouth each day when I was growing up. As a child she told me the bottles contained special medicine. These were the hands raised to my face in anger when I threw away the bottles of special medicine. These were the hands that no longer wiped away my tears.

These were the hands that I gripped tightly when I found her lifeless cold body on the bedroom floor while desperately reaching for the phone to dial 911. As the speeding ambulance with sirens blasting raced to reach its hospital destination, I held her hands and refused to let go. Her fingers nails were freshly painted...they were frail and wrinkled. As I grasped her hands and refused to let go, a lifetime of memories appeared, etched and burned in the forefront of my mind—within seconds I had recalled every moment when her hands had presented life to me.

Could my hands give her life again?

Debra Pitta

Black Night Air

As I looked through the black night air,
I saw a little something as it moved swiftly by,
When I turned to look back it seemed not to be there,
So I went on and didn't bother to look again,
The next I knew there was a thump...then a
thud...and I didn't know what it was to be judged,
I kept a look out for a while, then seemed to get distracted,
Some odd minutes later, I had seemed to hear it again,
But only ignored it this time and went on doing
what it was I was doing,
Later that night I had woken up when there I
saw a sad-eyed puppy that was starving to death,
Within the next few days I seemed to have
rescued it from a terrible life,
Then came to realize I had done what so many
people had done for me.

Cassie Watkins

"My Mother's Son"

In the days when I was a child
A small boy sitting on the curb
Not knowing what the future holds
Could not see beyond this day
Only one among ten children
Six years old and not much more
Father's coming home for lunch
This is my joy, here he comes!
One shining moment in a life of uncertainty
The time is quick but life is slow
He is here today, tomorrow he will be gone
Death is certain, I'm all alone
I will never forget our very short time
Just a few memories my dad and me
Can't stop thinking, now I'm forty-three
Well, I rose up past that day!
Quite accomplished and self-taught
Life was hard but, I learned early
My boy and I sitting by the curb
The past is gone, the future is just beginning!!

Edward H. Faulkner

Little Lady

There once was a little lady,
had a family, too.
She raised them one by one,
taught them what to do.
They grew together as a family,
raised their vittles, too.
The little lady loved the flowers,
learned to raise them, too.
They came to take the place of children grown
and on their own.
Through the flowers the little lady,
was a friend to all.
She made them for the good times,
for the sad times, too
They said hello, they said goodbye,
what more could they do?
The little lady now is gone,
her flowers carry on.
They speak of love and birth and death,
but many remember the little lady best.

Sherry V. Alfonso

The Miracle Of A Tree

Within a tree there is quite a story.
They bloom and blossom and die in glory.

Their branches bud and bloom come spring,
The gathering place for birds to sing.

In summer the tree is at its best,
Beneath its boughs a man can rest.

Then suddenly the colors change, tis fall,
The most beautiful season of them all.

The orange leaves against the sky,
Burst into beauty before they die.

As the wind blown leaves fall and tumble,
They leave the trees looking oh so humble.

So tall, so bare, so sad, so bold,
The seasons are passing and the trees grow old.

The nights grow long and the nights grow cold,
As the mean hand of winter starts to unfold.

The trees stand shivering as the cold winds blow.
And soon their branches are burdened with snow.

But come next spring, when the worlds anew,
Those same old trees look new born too.

Jean Raftery Russell

Last Day

Piece by piece my life is taken. The tools
and wood I love are memories, a dream
of the days when I could climb stairs,
when I could walk to the kitchen and doze
at my table. I hate staying in bed.
Memory and dream mesh in my sleep.

My wife is talking long distance to our sons.
I sigh. She fears it's my last breath.
I wish I had the strength to talk, to comfort.
She holds my hand and loves them for me.
While drugs and death conspire to lull me,
pain tells me I'm alive, awake. She holds my hand
sharing her strength as world slowly fades.
I am ready to sleep. I am ready
to dream the long night by her side.

Tim Harkins

"Tribute To A Hero"

A name inscribed in cold, smooth stone
The lonely blare of a trumpet in tribute
The startling discharge of the serviceman's rifle,
jolting a broken heart to skip a beat
Stars and stripes presented in fold
A father's trembling hand and a mother's pool of tears
In it a reflection—
A tender infant in need
A child with wonder in his eyes
A proud young man devoted to his family and country and
ready to conquer all evil for the sake of peace and freedom
A shining smile of love and reassurance
A warm and eternal embrace
Arms outstretched with a hand waving goodbye and fading
in the distance
Another tear falls into the pool and the mirrored image
becomes distorted.
While a mothers lifetime of dreams shatter and die,
a new birth of hope and peace takes place restoring faith
and reviving the dream for a whole nation.

Sherry R. Demster

Through Your Fingers

I used to be able to feel your love
through your fingers, just by a slight touch on
the arm or pace or wherever you touched me,
I could feel the love flowing through your heart
traveling down your arms and cascading
into your fingers where as your love would
gently but with intense heat soar through
my pores into my heart I soul and burn
there forever more.
Once again...Please...Touch me baby
I need I want to feel your love flow through
your fingers into my every pore I being.
Love me with your fingers like you used to
one more time... please!
Forever more
Love me with your fingers
For...
Eternity

Corrine Fisher

Peace On Earth

Turn aside all anger and hate,
Return to God, it's not too late.
Love is the only healing power,
It is imperative, now is the hour.

Call to your I Am Presence each day,
To help you spread Love by God's way.
Not one thing is worth anything,
Unless it gives you everything.

Everything only comes to you,
When your love light comes shining thru.
So send your love to God each day,
And He will turn it back your way.

If each of us did this each day,
All hatred would be turned away,
Our cups would overflow with Joy,
And Peace on Earth would come to stay.

Mary Matthews

As I Pray

Sheltered in a mullioned glass pane
remote and perhaps
glazed with a tapestry of theory

Retch at the thought of a libertine in white
a perfect illusion of one so clogged with browned skeletons
he no longer knows
where to keep

A grin on the mask behind still another
Mayhem rules This-
an error of creation

Deeper he sucks into his seductive world
of flesh, of decay
drink his blood
let it run through
you are a slave of the will

Now open your eyes...
hold the Beads tight
and cease
to be a part of an illusory guise.

Joan D. Batara

I Am Dying Of Aids And You Don't Care

I am deformed, doomed and devious.
Desperate plagues have surfaces and dwelled,
over my head, alone, smashing my life.
You're bold, bountiful and merciless.
Granting wishes, my creep guardian.
The vengeance and rage has piled up.
Gnawing my brain and starting my death.
Startling dread has gone overboard.
I'm on a trip of self destruction.
Wonder lust has warped my mind quickly.
Quickened death by smoking non-filters.
My stronghold is board and broken too.
But are you mindless, vexed, critical?
Calamity is everywhere .... Right?
Yet, corruption is patient among me.

Robert E. Gittins Jr.

Demanding A Request From God...

I want my Brother back
with all my heart and soul.
I want my Brother back
Expressed in this wholesome poem.

He was a treasure just like all men should be,
I want my Brother back, because He belongs to me!

I was His older sister,
and known Him like my tall oak tree,
I want my Brother back, because He belongs to me!

When I was a few years old, our mother cried in pain
Giving birth to Him on Winter's coldest Day.

I want my Brother back
From wherever God placed Him to be,
From the deepest ground, or from the roughest sea
I want my brother back, because He belongs to me!

Now I put my pen away
and I warned just every one
If I don't get my Brother back,
I'll join Him "soon" one Day!!

Nina Kwiatkowski

Ripples Of Emotion

I watch as the pebble hits the water
spreading ripples across its once calm surface
how our lives are like that stone
the little things we do that affect others lives
a kind word here
words we wish we could take back there
all rippling out from us
imagine if we were never here
how much different this life would be
I would never have known you
and you would never have known me
how many lives have we touched
how many will we

Chuck Alkire

Like A River

We are like rivers;
Closely constricted by the banks;
Moving not on our own will, but how the current takes us.
Calm and placid on the surface,
Yet dangerous to penetrate.
We are shaken every time a stone is tossed at us.
The rippling disturbance remains long after the abuser is gone;
Around each bend is a new obstacle: Dams, bridges, waterfalls;
After each drought we are replenished by the rain;
We are like rivers.

Molly E. Figel

Saudi Is There: I Must Go

I must retreat from Love's defeat
And take flight for pity's sake-
And upon the sea, restore in me,
The will to find a mate.

On foreign lands I soon shall stand,
And leave my woes behind...
And renew my views from all the news,
In wild places I shall find.

From all I've found on Love's go round,
I've learned I can't depend-
On a women's mind - for Love is blind
In solitude I must now fend.

I dream a dream, some outlandish scheme,
To change the way things are
But it's far from me to change the key,
Of the song of Love thus far...

So in simple frets I sing regrets
For a Love that friends still ponder
And upon the face of the homeless earth,
My wretched soul shall wonder...

Herman W. Griggs

The Only Way

Some say a rainbow follows the rain
But all I've seen is a downpour of a pain
Everyone has left me alone
Sharp little razor blade has sliced me to the bone

The thought of death has crossed my mind
I thought they would miss me after time
When reality hit me, it really hurt
That's when I found out death was just a flirt

With the help from the voices from inside
I realized my thoughts had only lied
Death can not save neither me nor you
Cause the only way out is straight through

Erin Wells

Faith By Day

The splendor of daybreak mirrors the soul,
Happiness surrounds, life appears whole.

Like storm clouds that threaten, problems roll in,
Your kinship with God will let you begin

To see through the folly, add warmth to the day,
Envelop and hold you, chase fears away.

Mirrors, when broken, fall from their frame,
shards and splinters of glass to remain.

The answer we're seeking lie deep within,
They're there for the asking...let us begin.

Storm clouds will scatter, leave way to the sun
To shine down upon us, a victory we've won.

In silence and faith we tapped into love,
Hope for tomorrow...dreams from above

The sun is now setting in glorious hues
Golden and wondrous a message effused.

Patricia L. Sullivan

The Love of My Life

Although our pasts are so very different,
Love is what bonds our lives together.
Like a radiant sunset,
Every vibrant color reflects what I see in you:
Never-ending beauty.

Purple brings out the fun loving person you are;
Red reminds me of the passion that we share;
Orange resembles the warmth that your heart conveys.
Creation of a magical feeling.
Knowing that when I look into your eyes,
Every one of your inner beauties comes alive.
Together we will show the world,
That when our two hearts beat as one,
Everlasting love will prevail.

Kimberly A. Prockette

A Poet Writes

A poet sits by the desk, all day and all night.
Staring at the ceiling and into the light.
A poet sits and wonders what to write on the paper below
To make hearts feel warm and to make faces glow.
Like a story of love that two people share.
Who show how they feel and how much they care.
A story with hopes and dreams maybe a heartbreak or two.
The story can come true for anyone that believes, even you.
If you believe in dreams and want them to come true.
You have to make it happen, live your life in red not blue.
A poet will write about life and the things that go on.
Till the end of a long day beginning again at early dawn.

Bekki Souders

Listen My Child

Hush, Hush, my child for God is speaking
Be still, listen, no more weeping dry your
eyes, stand up firm, listen to what he wants
you to learn.

"Listen my child for I am here, I've never left
you I am near. Don't give up just have faith
for I am the father for goodness sake. I know
tomorrow, and all that you don't, so be happy,
don't give up, because I won't. I love you today,
tomorrow, and always. In your heart when
you hear me speaking, dry your eyes and stop
your weeping."

Renata Rhodes

My Father

Like a rock, My Father
Drives himself through the rainy days always looking to see
brighter sunnier days. Like a rock, my father, like a rock.

Understanding, My Father
One who looks at others mistakes and says learn from them,
and when you fall, always helping you back up. Understanding,
my father, understanding.

Caring, My Father
The one who shows concern about every person in his life, and
is there to help in every way he can. Caring, My Father, caring.

Strong, My Father
In his will, ways, as well as his opinions, never letting others
influence him in the wrong way. Strong, My Father, strong.

A father to everyone, My Father
Loving, scolding, and teaching every child that steers the
wrong way helping them become a better person. A Father to
everyone, My Father, a Father to everyone.

Running to win the race, My Father
always striving to do his best, always pushing for another mile
running to win the race, My Father, with God you will win the
race.

Jaynetta Smith

Accepting Life And Love

I was loved from the beginning, not knowing
Lost in a world of expectations on me.
Running from something I didn't understand
And was afraid to ask,
Loving everything in sight and receiving nothing.
Dying on the inside wanting to get out.
Realizing I was hiding from myself, hating the person
Inside not knowing what to do.
Recovery from the pain, learning to be me
And in the end.
Feeling deep down inside, I am loved from
Beginning to eternity's end...

Donna J. Henderson

Endless Aspirations

Time, please slow down
Do not hurry
for there is nothing to be wary
I guess there is...

Tomorrow is waiting
for us to go
and tell the stories untold
for us to reach
and warm the hearts so cold
for us to give
amidst the sufferings
for us to receive
our priceless blessings.

No wealth, no riches can buy the things
there are to learn
For the vision so splendid I will gladly succumb.
But, remember, Mother, someday I will return
For you to see what your child has become.

Ivy Marie A. Mendoza-Calitis

Sunsets

Giving birth to a fresh night
Saying goodbye to an old day
Orange flames and yellow streaks clashing
Until then, colors of the sun will play

A soft breeze blows
A peacefulness lingers in the twilight
Stars appear the sun slips away
This is the time when day greets night

The whispering winds
That know your name
They share secrets with the darkening sky
Come play the nocturnal game

Ashes to ashes
From dusk till dawn
The man in the moon is king
When the sun is gone

AmberLee Dawson

To Be A Marine

The sound of thousands of feet marching in perfect time.
A thousand voices shouting cadence, what a beautiful sign.
The wonderful music of the military band, so clear and loud.
Makes my heart flutter as we march along so lively and proud.

This is the time we have worked so long and so hard for.
Things planted in our minds that we will remember forever more.
A feeling that no where in this world, there is none better.
We have made it, we are number one, nothing else matters.

We can now go to better things to come in our future years.
And say it was worth it, all the worry, work, sweat, and tears.
All we needed was understanding, encouragement, and a little shove.
And all this came from the ones who cared, the ones we love.

As we march past the inspecting officers in the reviewing stand.
We know by now the situation is in the best of hands.
Let us never forget this part of our time in this life.
For now we are able to handle all of life's struggles and strifes.

But, right now we are so completely thrilled through and through.
To explain the feeling would be so very, very hard to do.
We could have been army, navy, airforce or some other extreme.
But we choose the best of them all, we are united states marines.

William Thomas Parker

Aching Hearts

My heart aches for someone,
But I can't say who,
All I know is that I like him,
And someone else does too.

So should I go for him,
Or should I stay behind,
And be what everyone wants me to be,
Friendly, nice, and kind.

But how can I,
When I've fallen for that someone,
What should I say to him?
What should be done?

Should I run away,
From what my heart tells me to do?
Or should I tell him,
That my love is true?

God help me out some how,
I don't know what to do,
Do I run away?
Or do I simply say "I've fallen for you?"

Jessica Talbot

When I Am Old

When I am old

I shall no longer tolerate
The injustices of my Youth
My pride, my strength, my faith
Will be the proof

I shall have mastered
The gift of faith
Mountains will move at my very will
At my command, miracles take place

When I am old I shall greet my mirror Self
Each morning
With thanksgiving and kind words

And remember that an artist's masterpiece
Does not reach its full value until it has
Stood the tests and trials of Time

These things shall I do when I am old.

But until then, I shall, effortlessly,
Lie down in pastures green
And bathe in the rays of
My Creator's wondrous blessing of Youth.

Roschelle L. Mears

Desolation

Desolation engulfs my life.
The howling winds ensue.
Entranced by the lonely sound.
My thoughts are fearful and few.
The thoughts are mainly mental strife.
I scan the broad horizon for any sign of life.
Solitary,
Stand I there.
Not a soul, anywhere near to care.

Anton Schmitz

Pins

Pins have been used from the earliest times
But, as yet, haven't gone out of style.
They've caused many a crime in centuries gone by,
At this you will probably smile!

Thorns from the bushes, hardened and sharp,
Our earliest ancestors used.
And then they grew useful in too many ways
And their neighbors they sorely abused.

Then a greater idea of pins was conceived
By a genius remarkably smart!
So from well dried out thorns to splinters of bone
Pins then had a wonderful start!

But the splinters of bone caused many a death
And in war they were made of great use.
So large and so strong were they rudely formed-
A wonderful means of abuse!

After hundreds of years the bronze age began,
But pins were fashioned by hand.
No machines had they - the process was slow,
And pins were high-priced o'er the land.

Now look at our pins! No daggers have we;
They're ever so useful and small.
Oh, what would we do without common pins -
Yet they're scarcely noticed at all!

Mary E. Drake

The One Year Anniversary

You were taken from our lives
It's been a whole year since we last laughed,
Cried and held each other.
There hasn't been one day where we haven't thought.
Visioned and missed your sincere smile.
May God keep you in his arms.
Until we meet again.
We love you and miss you always and forever.
The month of July comes with sad regrets
It brings the day I will never forget
No verse can say, no flowers can repay.
How much I lost on that sad day.
The pearly gates were open
A gently voice said come.
With no farewells.
You gently entered home.
So until we meet again my darling.
I will always miss you, and you will.
Always be in my heart.
May God keep you in his hands.

Evelyn Tallman

Untitled

As if in a dream, your face appears.
My heart begins to race. I feel the pounding vibrations
in my ears and against the confines of my chest.
I extend my thoughts to you and seek your response.
Sometimes I fear I feel too much. Too much too soon.
I am unsure where my feelings will lead, not sure where
I want them to lead.
I am captured in the pleasure of loving, the discomfort
of an undefined response.
My emotions are so strong, they bring bitter sweet tears.
Am I blessed to feel so deeply, so passionately, or cursed?
I wish I knew the answer.
I am afraid to lay open the extent of my feelings.
Afraid to mouth the words I Love You.
Afraid I will move toward you and you will move away.
There is so much I want to express, the terms and postures
scream to be released.
This is a love I have never felt before.
I am amazed, frightened, happy and sad.
Prepared to accept whatever path this love takes.

Catherine S. Roberts

"Sarah"

God smile upon her the day she was born. Her
road of life was laid out, as each day she
travelled her circle, of life, she radiated faith,
stability, peace and love. Sarah, was our rock,
she was our heart. As her circle was met he came
for her. The angels blew their horn to open the
gates, she smiled upon God's face as the angels
paved the way. Sarah plans were made from
heaven above, her special angel stayed to guide
us through this special day.

Ann Marie Shiflett

Enough

It carries lightly,
slung over my shoulder,
not carelessly, but firmly placed,
Time adjusted and comfortable
This bag of souvenirs and
memoirs of other years.
Take no offense that I refuse with thanks
The gift you offer to enlarge its content,
Fearing the ability of abundance.

Mildred F. McChesney

Sandcastle Dreams

Nothing more than water and sand,
Just a little piece of land.
Built with wishes, hopes, and dreams,
Love bursting from the seams,
The winds come and blow it away,
We can build another on some other day.

My life is built from sandcastle dreams,
Wishes destroyed by the suns precious beams.
Waiting for prince charming to come sweep you away?
In the sand is where you'll stay.
The winds come and blow it away,
We can build more dreams some other day.

Kimberly Elaine Wall

My Inner Shield

I carry an inner shield that no one can see unless I let them.
It's woven from time, a chameleon, a blazing sun, an angel and a
raccoon.
My chameleon loves to express his moods with his beautiful colors.
He is my protector, guarding me with camouflage.
But, he can not be my warmer.

My sun does that for me.
He loves shining brightly, keeping me warm with his blazing rays.
He loves to tower over the cold wind.
But, he can not be my generosity.

My angel does that for me.
He loves to give, and hates to receive he loves to help anything
in need.
But, he can not be my bravery.

My raccoon does that for me.
He loves to explore danger without fear and yet there's a sense of
politeness when he washes his tiny hands.
He also loves to provide a family.
But, he can not be me.

I carry an inner shield,
but without my chameleon, blazing sun, angel and my racoon I
am not me.
When it's time to leave humanity they will be remembered.

Brandon Burford

My Dying Love

My dying love I thought was so true,
You will never know how much I loved you.
The words you whispered so softly to me,
I thought you meant them for eternity.
And when you left you didn't say goodbye,
To this day I wonder why our love had to die.
As you live in heaven I live in hell,
When you spoke I did not tell.
You said to me words I did believe,
And now I don't understand why did you leave.
My love for you, you did take,
As you told me my heart would never break.
The moon, the stars, and the sun,
Will mean nothing to me until my days are done,
My love for you will last every day,
No matter how much your love for me slips away.
This heart will worship adore you,
My dieing love know these words I say are true.
So tell me my dieing love
Does that little bird mean anything to you, that little dove.

Deborah Gonzales

A Lifelong Companion

A rotting corpse.
Deadly alive.
Walking,
Walking into the distance.
Trying to find the reason,
The reason why he's not alive.
Searching,
Searching for a friend.
Someone to confide in.
It's hard because everyone's alive,
Except him.
The tears he cries are like acid,
Burning the last of his flesh.
He tries to call out because he's lonely,
But no sound escapes his lips.
He's cold, he sees someone in the distance.
The man is looking around.
Frantically searching,
Searching for a friend just like him.
He's no longer lonely.

Amy Luckett

You're A Special Kind Of Person

You're a special kind of person with a oneness of your own;
You're a musical expression with a sole distinctive tone;
There is not another like you in mind, spirit, flesh or bone;
You're a part of God's variety with a oneness of your own.

You're a special kind of person and created to be so;
Don't believe it cause I tell you, look around and you will know;
That when God began to mold us, not a one did choose their own;
For we're a part of God's variety with a oneness of our own.

You're a special kind of person, don't be sad and don't look blue;
Though others gifts are much applauded, and your's only get a few;
Just keep stirring up your talents, as yourself improve your own;
You're a part of God's variety with a oneness of your own.

Gary Brown

A Silent Passion

Take me away. Give me strength, hope and laughter. To far away places and peaceful morning afters.

Share with me always thought, word and deed.

Memories of long ago and thought planting seeds.

Bring to me visions of beautiful flowers, majestic mountains and joy by the hour.

Never release me from the love that unfolds. And keep me company when I grow old.

My love for you grows with each passing day.

Reading, a silent passion, forever with me stay.

Jera T. Shearer

Frightening Things

To hear a train's onrushing roar,
To feel an earthquake move the floor,
To see a person lie still and white,
To hear a noise, in the death of night—
frightens me!
To see lightning's sudden, blinding flash,
To hear thunders roaring, deafening crash,
To be without the soft look of Mother,
To lose either my sister or brother—
frightens me!

Karen Thompson

Imagine

Books take me away to a far away land
Where Horror Adventure and Fantasy stand.

Where castles reach way up to the sky
Where unicorns dragons and sorcerers fly by.

Where fruits can grow to an enormous size
Where aliens transform right before your eyes.

Where bugs will dance and plants will sing
There are so many extraordinary things.

There are no limits
There are no gimmicks.

Anything goes
Just wiggle your toes.

You're a fantasy child
Let your imagination run wild!

Danielle Lyn Schneider

The Willow Tree

I dreamt of you last night, I dreamt I saw you standing by a willow tree.
You were calling out to me telling me not to be afraid.
I came to you, you took me in your arms, and I felt safe.
You comforted me with your words, you told me of your thoughts and dreams.
I told you of my hopes and aspirations.
A gentle, but unsettling breeze blew across our faces.'
You then started to walk away. I tried to follow, but couldn't keep up.
You started to run, I called after you.
You turned and looked at me with a cold unfeeling face, then turned and continued on.
I stood there the hot, wet tears spilling down my face.
I sat by the willow tree, and wondered.
I wondered if,
you would ever come back.

Shannon Marie Stocker

Small

I wonder why,
I cry.
I feel so small, I want to die.
Even the tear,
I have in my eye.
Is so pathetic, I begin to sigh.

I am in pain,
I strain.
I grope for love, but only in vain.
Even the fear,
I have is a stain.
It won't wash away, in the driving rain.

I know the plan,
I can!
I am in pity, but there's gold in the pan!
Even in prayer,
I have faith in the Man.
I know my woes, are all in His hand.

Is it I who made me small?
Yes indeed, but there IS hope, after all.

Michael J. Donahue

Lies - Our Predator

The anger of a thousand years
who does it benefit?

Only those who gloat at the sight of a people tormented.
Suppress, regress, digress, why?
To soften the blows until tomorrow.
For "tomorrow is another day" sayeth Miss Scarlett
Speak the truth, it will set you free.
What if there is none that will hear it?
The twisted lies are great in might, and the people
feed on them like sweet ambrosia to the Gods.
Little squirming ants, we are but these.
Crawling along for another carcass on which to feed.
Attack!! Attack!! I must be the first in line for the feast.
But, alas I am also the first to realize that
I am now the ant entangled in the spider's web,
Now the carcass on which the spider feeds.

Laura Moody

Always And Forever

You have always been there for me,
Giving me a hug when I was upset,
Squeezing my hands to give me courage,
Listening patiently to all of my problems.
Bringing light into my dark life,
Peeling my layers to find what's really underneath.
Opening the door of my life, pulling me out into the open,
Closing the door of the past, gently wiping away my tears.
Opening my eyes when they have been closed,
Showing me the way to happiness.
Getting up at dawn just to be with me.
Laughing kindly at my silly mistakes,
Not minding when I laughed at yours.
The space in my heart that has been left unfilled calls out,
"Please, come back." I start to say "Thank You."
But just that is not enough for everything you have done for me.
So instead come the words which need not to be spoken
As I whisper, fighting to hold back tears,
"I love you"
And I will always and forever...

Jennifer Keenan

Roses And Pearls

A Daughter's Wish

Mommy sleeps on a bed made of roses
Her lips are pursed, just like always
Her once spiteful voice is now cold and dead
And on God's hand, she lies her head

The pearls she once wore around her delicate neck
Now control me, but I just want Mommy back
And no matter how much we hated each other
None can replace her — She was my Mother

Oh, Mommy, can you hear me, can you hear my wistful cries?
Oh, Mommy, do you love me, can you forgive me for the times?
The times I went, the times I left, I did it just to spite you
I thought, "That's what Mommy gets"

And I want to go to sleep, to sleep off my desolate woe
Without Mommy here, I don't think I'll never know
But I miss you, Mommy, I love you so much
And without you I know, I know I am not

And I'm sorry, Mommy, for all the pain I've caused you
I want you to know, Mommy, that I'll forever love you
And Mommy up in Heaven, if your omniscient ears can hear me
Please say "Hello" to my consummate Daddy for me

Dawn Sitarski

Mother Dreams

Momma, standing with her rose pink flowers,
Along the silvery sea in gown of white,
Along the golden sands she waits for hours,
To catch the setting sun's first amber light.

She watches flights of gulls across the sky,
And knows the taste of salt upon her face,
This acrid flight of salt in tatters fly,
Making a fretted-pattern of white lace.

She stands alone upon the beach and dreams,
Of things to come and those that have gone before,
Within her heart she feels the tough of wings,
That takes her back in time now gone, now O'er.

Mom, you'll always live upon this golden strand,
Of dancing waves and dreams' loving demands.

Lucille M. Kroner

Best Friends

Whenever it is we're always together
On shiny days and stormy weather
During the day and sometimes of night
Communication keeps our phone bills high.

We share secrets no one might care about
The important thing is: Our parents will never find out.
Only she knows what happened and how late
I came home from my first date.

In troubled or not
We're never apart
In happiness and sorrow
Each other we follow.

Can't wait 'till we graduate, 'till the school will be over
So we could sign each other's year book cover.
And after the High School ends
We're still be best friends.

We always were yelled at by teachers in class
Hey, we all have things we need to discuss
We'll never forget how we lied to our sub
We'll always remember the classes we cut.

Anastasia Shirinskaya

"The Garden Of Friendship"

The garden of friendship
resembles a giant patchwork quilt.
Lots of patches: Daffodils!
Bring to me of nature's best,
flowers so red are rosiest.
My best friend is Tiger Lilly...
She is so blessed.
Where she grows everything blends.
Long stem Roses are closest to heart,
not touching the thorns is sometimes hard!

Sunflowers so yellow, standing tall.
The word beautiful describes them all!

Every plant is sown right and growing.
The smell is so sweet,
happiness is showering.

This quilt has so many colors,
it's so lovely to see.
Every flower represents a person
God gave as a friend to me.

Joan J. Borman

Unconditional Love

Blessed are the mothers
They take the light of heaven
Use it in creation and form
It isn't only birth they give shape to
They influence us in their beauty and their love
In support they temper the fire
And say the world's not so bad
It will always get better
Weeping in sorrow when we weep
Laughing in joy when we have cause to laugh
The instruments of their boundless wonder
In sight of God, the universe, and everything that matters
Giving us reason for hope and fear
For despair and courage
Unconditional love casts no doubt
Chaos and order have a place among the stars
So too do mothers and fathers have a
place here on earth

Thanks for everything you've done for me.
I'll love you beyond eternity.

Mark Bowman

A Day Like No Other

I feel the cool breeze coming in after the rain
I see distant lights through fog and mist
A blanket of God laying across the woods
Caressing each tree, twig, and leaf
The trees glisten with water drops upon their fingers
Caught by the trees especially for me
I thank God for this day
For this life and glistening water
For holding the ground steady under my feet
For holding raindrops for me to eat
For giving me a day like no other
A day I feel the trees whisper and the rain sing
I feel lights glisten and water sparkle
A day like no other
For each day is a day like no other
For each day in its ending gives birth to many days
Untold days
And each day has its memory
Untold memories beyond compare
Caught by the trees especially for me

L. Terry Pynes

Untitled

There are ones who come into your life for a reason.
Bringing meaning and hope to your world,
as do the change of seasons.
Ones who may emerge at any given place or time,
holding answers to questions you have been searching to find.

They stay in the present, not the future or past.
Shedding light to your soul, making that feeling last.
Riches and fortunes are not made of gold,
the heart is alive, your self, your soul.

To those not touched, only a body is there,
but to those envisioned, a real soul cares.
Unique ways and a presence of energy,
cultivates a life, knowing just how to "be."

They visualize their life exactly how they want it to be,
manifesting their own destiny, yearning to be free.
Not everyone will cross the path of someone so rare,
living life to the fullest, never forgetting life is to share.

Susan A. Adams

They Say

She was a slim girl, says the Levi's 512 jeans
thrown across the chair;
a short girl too, says the petite size dress hanging in the closet;
and a clean, organized girl, says the neatly arranged shelves
and neatly made bed;
but not a girl for folding, says the clothes piled up on the desk.

A cat lived with her, says the catbox neatly scooped in the corner;
and she had a hamster, says the cage with bedding in it;
she was anorexic, says the half-eaten food in the trash
and the neatly hidden laxatives;
she got cold easily, says the heavy curtains and blankets;
she was lonely, says the diary hidden under the mattress.

Something went wrong, says the still and quiet room;
the food under the bed says she never ate at all;
the spilled pills say she was suicidal. And her?
Her tiny starved body lay on the floor
clutching the pill bottle, and a knife, life never to return.
Something went wrong, they say.

Kate Saurino

"Somewhere From Above"

I remember stepping outside
When I was sixteen
Into the cold Chicago December
Everything was as bad as it seemed

Walking along the railroad tracks
They guided my way
Because I didn't know which one to take in those days

I found myself in a graveyard
Looking around for awhile
I was thinking "Here's where it ends"
After all those miles

Then there came a moment
I looked up at the sky
The sun escaped through the clouds
That were flowing quickly by

I turned myself around
To return to the people I loved
And I felt a warmth inside
That came somewhere from above

Daniel Sweeney

Love Is...

Love is a thing that's hard to truly share,
No matter what happens you always seem to care.

Love is a warm feeling that you look so hard for,
The kind of love like you've never had before.

Love is something that can last forever and a day,
Love means more than words could ever say.

Love is harmful and can cause your heart to break,
Love put you to sleep to where you never awake.

Love is knowing that a person will always be there for you,
And will always be there no matter what you do.

Love is knowing that a person will never be gone.
They will always be there even when you do wrong.

Love is when a person stays through thick and thin,
And is there to stop the crying when you don't win.

Love is when you can look at a person and tell how they truly feel,
Only then can you tell if your love is real.

Kyna Robbins

The Green Man Speaks

"I, the laughing Lord of the Greenwood am most potent this season; I live for the Goddess' sexual pleasin'."

"The passion I feel for the Lady is real; before this ripe Mother I'm ready to kneel."

"This Spring I'll discover what she desires from her lovers. Now the Bel fires they burn; and my body doth yearn to sow my strong seed, for quickenings her need."

"From our mating shall burst forth life anew! Good Wiccan folk are you feeling lust too?"

Maria Cernuto

Lacking A Sense Of Shame And Guilt

Lacking a sense of shame and guilt
teen pregnancy is on the rise
a newborn peeks from the receiving blanket
blinking her starving eyes.
with dad's disappearance
teary-eyed mother needs help
social service (a dis-service)
because a single parenthood's kept.

Lacking a sense of shame and guilt
domestic violence is on the rise
a brutalized spouse peers through
the blacken and swollen eyes.
With the spouse's reassurance
it will never happen again
but over a time the cover-up starts
and the fear in her begins.

Jackie Mattison

Only In My Dreams

The lifeless wind surrounds me,
It hears my cries and screams.
A special place inside me
Holds comfort from my dreams
There I can be with you
And feel your loving touch.
Before, I never knew
Someone could love me so much.

I can feel the love within,
So deep and true.
Where have you been?
I wish I knew.
Slowly the stars wink and depart.
And you leave before the light of the day.
Yet I hope with all my heart
That someday you will stay.

Amanda Profitt

Mary Jane

Mary Jane, who is she?
Perhaps she is a weed, a weed, we know all too well.
She takes you to place, a place really green.
Here she grows near a pond
Where children come and play and laugh the day away.
Hey, who is that in those shadows over there?
Mary Jane is that you?
I have finally found where you grow.
Now I shall strike you down and cut your roots.
The roots that once helped you grow from the rich soil
Of this fertile place.
The place in which you used to thrive on the
Nutrient rich water from this small, secluded, green pond.
In this place that you call home.

Chris Russek

Ashamed

Sitting here at the age of forty four.
Ashamed not able to read like so many other adults.

Ashamed not able to read the bible.

Ashamed not able to read menu.

Ashamed not able to go higher on my job
because of reading problem.

Ashamed not able to help my children with
their homework when they were in school.

Ashamed not able to help my self understand
how important it is to read.

Ashamed for family, and friend to find out
that I couldn't read.

Ashamed of all the stupid mistake that
I have made because of not being able to read.

Ashamed no more doing something for myself.
Taking a reading class.
What a beautiful world it is in books.

Barbara McNeill

Walking In The Darkness

Two weavers weaving their futures through their gleaming needles
A girl walking
walking past houses to be lived in by many
but never by her.
The towns people whispering ignoring
as if she was as transparent as the musty air.
They have seen her before
but still she walks on in the darkness
Until someone takes her under their wing.
Engulfing her into a sea of hope.
But the thickening darkness surrounds her as she presses on.
Loneliness.

Susannah Plaster

Death

When I see you laying on the bed. I see fear come upon your face. Just knowing it is just matter of time.

That there is so much pain within. That sometime you wonder how you can stand the pain. You search and you search for answers, but nothing comes up.

But you know deep down that there is a much better place to go without the pain. So you go to sleep and you are gone.

Your soul have left your body behind. So you can go on, until next time. When you inner in the world with a new life.

F. Darlene Needham

The Ways In Life

There are many ways we can go in life,
but choosing the right ones
is sometimes pretty tough.
The right way is never the easy way to go,
but if you respect yourself you will do so.
Being honest with your heart
always pays off in life;
how? I cannot tell.
Even though the right
way is the hardest,
you will find rewards on the way.
Just follow your heart,
and you will never get lost
on the wrong pathway.

Anna Linevich

Mother Earth II

Oh, my children, what did you do?
Why must my sky be a faded blue?
Where are my clouds, and fresh spring rain?
Why do I feel such hurt, anguish, and pain?

Oh, my children, can you not see?
Where did you put my forests and trees?
Why do you inflict this pain upon me?
Can you not hear, my sorrowful pleas?

Oh, my children, where are you now?
Before rearranging, did you ever ask how?
How can I proudly display, my beauty for all?
When you've ravaged my surface, built all those walls?

Oh, my children, where did you go?
Can I have your support, in running the show?
Where are my creatures, that once roamed the land?
Why'd you destroy them, I don't understand?

Oh, my babies, what's happened here?
Why do you live in chaos and fear?
Where is the serenity, the peace in all things?
Will you not mend, my limp, broken wings?

Amy Diane Logsdon

Baseball

Baseball is a game played by nine men
Nine to each team, with reoccurrence again and again
To the plain eye the game may seem like a bore
But to those who play it is much, much more

It is a game, that is played 90% in one's mind
It is the only game of failure many do find
For hitting 40% makes one into a star
It is a game that is played in places near and far

On a baseball game the sun will never set
For across the world exists the next Ted Williams or George Brett
It is a game enjoyed by both sexes, the young and old
A game played in climates both warm and cold

A unique game where confidence overcomes fear
A game played with a glove, bat, and ball like sphere
The art of hitting, considered the toughest challenge alive
From the joy of a home run to catch made by a dive

Baseball is a love only found in the heart
The desire is what separates the greats from the rest apart
The tradition that exists, for nothing else is the same
The spirit can be found from sand lots to the hall of fame!

Michael Sullivan

Searching

In the shadows of a broken heart
I stand
Loneliness is a well known friend.
Searching through an old memory
Looking for some clue
If we are really through
There is too much for me to lose
Too much for me to say goodbye to.
Much hope is already gone
To be away from you this long
My heart feels an empty space
Because I'll never let anyone take your place
I wish there was a way
That I could of made you stay
I told you how I feel
And that my love was real
But inside a memory
From the past
Lives every love
That didn't last.

Stephanie Davis

Mother Nature (King?)

Men think are the ones who rule, but Mother Nature has shown them to be fools.

Mother Nature causes many disasters and all man can do is pick up debris and ashes.

Mother Nature comes through with a vengeance and all man can do is look upon it and he cringes.

Mother Nature makes volcanos rise and causes such terror man screams and he cries.

Mother Nature causes it to snow, makes everything come to a halt and nothing will go.

Mother Nature causes it to rain, causing so much damage that man loses much material gain and with it inflicting much pain.

Mother Nature caused lightening to strike and all man can do is get out of its sight.

Man thinks he is so macho but Mother Nature tells him this is my show.

Man can do most anything, but Mother Nature shows him she is King.

The power is in Mother Nature's hand hers is a no man's land.

Mother Nature is a delight as she brings out the most beautiful sights.

Mother Nature can be a raging but she can also be cool and calm.

Men why do you think you have it all, when Mother Nature is really the one making the calls.

Queen Shalom

Goodbye To My Gift From God

How do I say goodbye to a friend
When goodbye isn't the way I feel,
But I know I can't stay, he doesn't
Care, or so I'm afraid in my heart.

How do I say goodbye to the one who,
Very dear to my heart, holds me safe
And secure in his arms and says I
Make him feel manly when I trust him.

How do I say goodbye to a true
Gift from God? Who radiates His grace,
Goodness, and love, sent down from above
To me, to warm my cold troubled heart.

How can I say goodbye to him
Who has made me happy once again
And showed me the mark of a Christian:
Faith, hope, kindness, honesty, and love.

Why must I say goodbye even though
I don't want to? Thoughts of pain, or fear
Of love coming into my life and
Caution caused by a scar from the past.

Christina M. Hummel

What Makes A House A Home?

What makes a house a home?
Is it the annoyed parents, or the children that roam?
Is it the dirt, the messes, the stains on brand new dresses?
Is it the skinned knees, or bruising falls,
Is it the tiny handprints on the walls?
No, it's not the faults that you've counted,
It's the memories that you've mounted.
It's the love that's in effect,
And the ways that the people connect.
That's what makes a house a home.

Kelli Beitler

Down In Critter Country

Down in critter country, that's where I like to be,
Where the wild birds sing,
The Woodpeckers peck,
And the Canada Goose flies free.

The mirrored lake is a good, old place
To catch a look
At a Wood Duck's face
And a Crane looks back at me.

When I'm strolling from my cabin, camera in my hand,
There's a Bunting there,
A Towhee too,
And an Eagle high above land.

After I leave the valley, I long for the Pintail Drake,
The Warbler's song,
The Oriole,
And the Heron on the lake.

I'll come back to critter country, maybe in the fall,
Then I'll amble along
To the Field Sparrow's trill,
And the Shorebird's noisy call.

June Whitelock

Friends Forever Joanna

Friends forever we'll always be,
We had times together both fun and sad,
We would talk about happy things and we
would both smile,
We would talk about sad things and we would both cry,
God was in your life and I knew he was part of you,
Each day I could see a joy inside of you,
Each day I could count on you to make me smile,
But God took you home and you've gone away,
And each day I think of the memories,
Of a friendship that was and will always be true,
Of all the times I spent with you,
God had a plan for your life,
You followed him day by day and you were always a
great influence on me,
Now weeks have gone by and I really miss you,
But in my heart I know you are where you had always longed to be,
With God for all eternity,
You're up in Heaven by God's side looking down on me,
And I want you to always know, Friends Forever Joanna.

Jennifer M. Pratt

Ennui

Bones ache
Around the eyes that won't cry
Muscle flops
Relaxed but tense
Within the net of sagging skin
A lump of head
Droops
Curving the neck
Into a lopsided letter "C"
Behind lazy eyelids
Haze
Like a fog of stagnant cigarette smoke
Dulls reception
And I cease to see
I cease to hear
I cease to care
Anymore
And I only think
"Why?"

Jade Horning

Grandpap Ray

I lay awake in solitude
remembering of him.
I see the joy deep in his eyes.
A man so full of wit and whim.

His smile, enough to take away
the sorrows of this troubled world,
but I shall see it not again.
Into the darkness he's been hurled.

I weep now just remembering
the funny things he'd do and say,
for now I realize that he's gone.
"Lord, why'd you take this man away?"

On Heaven's door now lays his fist.
He gives it just a gentle tap,
and as he goes, before he's gone,
I say, "I love you pap!"

He turns and smiles and waves good-bye,
and then continues on.
A warm tear trickles down my face.
Grandpap Ray is gone...

Michael S. Solomon

Morning Sun

My love for you
is like the rising of the morning sun.
Nothing to stop the heat and passion
formed from within.
Little by little,
my love for you grows.
As the yellow-orange sun fills the sky
with its warm rays,
It fills my heart and soul
with loving thoughts of you.
As the rays pierce throughout the clouds,
your loving eyes pierces the depths of my soul.
In your arms
is where I want to be,
For I feel safe,
as the morning sun.

LaVerne Barrett

Of Memories

Pictures flash by of my childhood days
Reminding me of seasons' fickle ways.

Adolescents' mood swings both cheerful and sad
Like bright sunshine, and storms that are bad.

Then young adult so confident and sure
Sprouting new growth like spring sweet and pure.

Maturity steps in -life's fall has arrived.
Ripened wisdom - harvested and stored.

Then winters -long, lonely and cold
Leave times to remember - tales to be told.

God's gift of life not wasted, but used-
Memories kept safe while life is perused.

The cycle continues; the seasons go by -
Because of God's reasons we live, and we try.

Florence Fredericks

"Perfection"

My version of perfection may not be the same as yours, but through the eyes of a child perfection has many versions to it. My version of perfection goes like this, I beat up on my younger siblings, but I have to learn self-defence to be "perfect". I intend to be loud at times, but I have to learn how to speak above a crowd to be heard to be "perfect". I seem to be bossy every now and then, but I have to learn authority to be "perfect". I mess up in school but I have to learn from my mistake to be "perfect. My room is not exactly clean, but I have to learn to clean up after myself to be "perfect". I try to sleep in on school days, but I need my beauty sleep to be "perfect". I back talk when I disagree with your opinion, but I need to learn to express my own opinion to be "perfect". My version of perfection, nothing like yours, two versions of perfection reaching to one another, trying to make this world and every person in it "perfect."

Crystal M. Thompson

Thoughts Of You

Your love is like an ocean
My heart is like a shore
You wash Your love upon me
And I long for so much more

Your Holiness surrounds me
And fills me from the heart
And when I fall and sin again
You give a brand new start

I long to see and walk with you
Uplifted by Your hand
To walk in peace and love and joy
In this sin sick land

Now the time is very near
To bring this to an end
I long to tell the whole-wide world Of your love so pure and kind
I long to tell the whole-wide world of your love so pure and kind

Micheal J. Reynolds

Dalmatians

Dalmatians,
They're all over the nation.
They're cute, cuddly, and sweet,
Those black and white spotted dogs are absolutely neat.
Dalmatians are very playful,
And make you very cheerful.
Outside, they're full of energy,
Inside, they're very lazy.
They love to lay on your bed,
Sometimes, after they're fed.
I have a dalmatian at home,
And where I live is where she roams.

Kristin Joy Bojanowski

Poem To Ponder

Things that pertain to life:
To your divine nature and faith add virtue,
add knowledge, add self control,
add perseverance and Godliness,
add brotherly kindness, add love,
Be sure of your call and your will never stumble.

Heed the prophetic word, as a light that
shines in a dark place, until the day
dawns and the morning star rises in your heart.

B. Miles Jackson

L'Mage

A look in an look that transcends a smile
For one catch light to cast an idle dream

Secular highlight burnish light and form
A halftone rests in the flavor of tidings

A daguerreotype remains from eras by gone
Reflections vying for local recognition

Polarizing fashion strives to be heard
Tone recognizes black and white where none is

Solarization grabs the neg and turns eternity
A lens recreates from focal plane to infinity

A frame suffers antiquity from face no more
Light that fades timeless anticipation

Generations revolving in ancestral spheres
An annuity likened to forever memories

Herbert Leiman

Family Of Bears

In the deepest of the night,
there comes a little glowing light.
From underneath the closet door,
next to the clown on the floor.

There is a little table,
that has four tiny, little chairs.
Where the little family sits,
the family of the bears.

They are quiet, and are fun,
and a cheerful family too.
And if by chance you could catch one,
he might want to dance with you.

So in the deep of the night,
you ever think you hear a sound.
Don't be frightened and don't be scared,
it's just the bears you have found.

Michelle R. Melcher

Loving Golf

I love to play the game of golf,
love it in every way,
when hitting off that very first tee,
I'm thoughtful of where it will lay.

The fairway is so very green
the trees all spark with life,
the quietness and sereneness
releases the stress and strife.

And when I'm on the final green
and make that very last stroke,
and as the ball drops in the cup,
my dreams comes true, along with my hope.

So when you play the game of golf,
relax and enjoy each play,
And if you feel that you've played well,
it can really make your day.

Marilyn M. Golden

Sandpipers

A sandpiper is always a winner.
as he picks in the sand for lunch and dinner.
He doesn't have to stint and save.
And he always misses that next big wave.
He never utters so much as a peep!
One has to wonder, when does he sleep?

Millie M. Lee

Puzzle

The puzzle's beauty revealed at last,
As it sits on the table, complete
But when one tries to take it away
It becomes pieces at your feet.

You, I took for granted
A piece in my puzzle, you were
And someone tried to lift you
And my wholeness, I can't remember

There was so much I wish I had done
So much I wish I had said
When you were here I was oblivious
But without you, my soul feels so dead...

The wind carried you away
It scattered my thoughts with the breeze
It tries to take my memories,
Which are now my only needs.

The pieces of my life are shattered
And, in time, will be replaced;
But there will always be a piece missing—
The piece that holds your face.

Becky Mindock

Untitled

A crisp, mid-autumn afternoon
The air cool and clear
Smell the season
Slightly scented, dead, dry leaves
Eyes feast on vivid oranges, yellows
Reds, browns
Autumn and gingerbread cookies
Crispness
Spicy-sweet aromas
Leaves dance, shiver, prance down a path
Crunchily crumbling
Brittle and delicate
Like pages of ancient scrolls
Rustling leaves
Soft whispering winds
Sing me a lullaby

Melanie L. Campbell

"Book Of Life"

Have you ever turned your back on Heaven?
Have you ever walked away from Love?
Have you ever asked to be forgiven?
Just another note in the Book of Life.

Any life that's worth living, has a lot of up's and down's,
So if you can't answer the questions.
You'd better make a turn around.

You'd better hold on to heaven, and love him with all your might,
But first you got to ask to be forgiven.
That'll be a better note in the Book of Life.

If you're Lucky enough to be forgiven,
Don't ever turn your back on your heaven.
And love him with all of your might.
This'll close another chapter in the Book of Life.

So remember the basic questions, and the rest will come with ease.
Things won't seems so complicated, life will seem like a breeze.

So don't ever turn your back on heaven.
Don't ever walk away from Love,
Don't ever be afraid to ask to be forgiven,
And the Book of Life will be full of Love.

Anna Clark

Pain

Oh pain, I finally come to peace with you,
As you become an essential part of my life;
Now, there is no need to be blue,
Everything I have learned to take in stride.

Yesterday, today and tomorrow,
Are with you so beautifully linked;
This immense sorrow,
Ironically gives me the reason to live.

Oh source of every other emotion,
Now, I have nothing to fear;
This, in my life is a promotion,
And makes me to God more near.

So powerful is your impact,
It remains a permanent reminder;
Like a guiding stick, in fact
You make a perfect path finder.

Never want to leave me alone,
You are faithful and oh, so stable;
Because you constitute my flesh, blood and bone,
We are now inseparable.

Aparna Mirchandani

Dawn To Dusk

I sat and watched the sun come up with all its golden hue.
The glare falls on the grass that's wet with the morning dew.
The trees seem to open their branches and let the sun shine through.
The sun gleams through the window pane and such a light it sheds.
The flowers in the garden sighs and lifts their pretty heads,
one by one in the flower beds.

I watch the birds begin to flutter from their nest up in the trees,
they know it's time to fly about when they feel the morning breeze.
The butterflies and humming bees come by the hour, to taste the
nectar in the flowers.

The squirrels run and jump with glee as they leap from tree to tree.
It is now dusk and the sun is going down, all that's visible are
the shadows on the ground.
The birds all know it's time to find their nests, for soon it will
be dark and everything will rest.
The crickets make their chirping noise continually through the night.
The fireflies and their many friends make their mysterious flight,
until dawn is again in sight.

Barbara J. Williams

"The Mighty Blow"

Why hang the flags half mast this day?
Why does our nation kneel to pray?
What is this sorrow that we feel?
A sadness that we can't conceal.

A loss our country long will know,
To all of us a mighty blow
The president of our great land
Slain by some cowardly, unknown hand.

Shot down while on the grateful ride,
With his first lady by his side
His life blood now that flows away,
To stain her clothes this awful day.

First lady we extend our hand
And sympathy, throughout this land
Our hearts may ache, our heads are bowed,
But yet of you we're very proud.

This man, we grew to know and love:
"Dear Lord take him to you above
As for the one who took this toll,
Lord, please, have mercy on his soul"

Joe L. Murray

My Love Is For You!

My love is for you like pure gold
that lasts forever and always.
My love is for you like refined silver,
which is polished on all our days.

My love is for you like diamonds,
carefully cut to sparkle and shine.
My love is for you like precious stones,
with colors rich and fine.

My love is for you like fine pearls,
strung and knotted to stay together;
My love is for you like sweet fragrance,
poured out in exotic fervor.

Oh my love is for you alone,
my love...only for you;
My love is full of dreams together,
and my love is for you!

Linda M. Melton

Season's Contemplation

The blustery winds of March do blow
And beckon to my mind to slow
My pace, and here to pause awhile
To contemplate the Season's style.

Winter wears a robe of white
And lends a crispness to the night,
Which tends us more to indoor pleasure
Hearthside chats are Winter's treasure.

Spring, ah Spring... my favorite season
Perhaps of all, my only reason
For ever surviving life's daily mischances
For only in Spring my Soul heavenward dances.

But Summer has a joy of its own
All seeds have been planted and into plants grown.
The fruits of the garden have reached their full measure
All that remains is to enjoy them at leisure.

Autumn pursues Summer's languorous ease
Colors the leaves, stirs a chill in the breeze
Brisk is the step of the sylvan admirer
As Nature prepares to be Winter's survivor.

Elizabeth Skon Wangelin

No, Not Us!

Today, in thinking of the past,
  Of why our relationship did last-
We argue, yes, but never fight,
  For that would be impolite.
You never struck me, even once—
  For you are not a dunce!
No, you never did, the Lord forbid.
We had many controversial discussions,
  Which might have led to repercussions.
I am glad you realize
  That is it always well to compromise.
Well, no need to arbitrate,
  When we know our happy fate.
It is no sin to just give in,
  When it is no fun to win;
Admit that you were wrong,
  And just happily go along.
I'll take your hand, and I will understand.
You can't always be right, about the things we always fight.
P.S. Even a stopped clock on the wall is right twice a day!

Helen Pressman

To My Friend

The trail of life is long and rough
with many twists and turns.
To go down it one must be tough
to face scars, cuts, and burns.

Walking the trail hasn't been easy,
there have been mountains to scale,
And times it was extremely breezy,
Yes, a Herculean task was that trail.

But while walking down this trail
I must thank you my dear friend
Who is like a strong rail
that supports me to the end.

You help me swim when I almost drown
When I trip you help me stand,
You make me laugh when I had a frown,
Yes, you always lended me a helping hand.

The day shall come when we grow old.
The trail shall end and we shall die,
but when we walk on the streets of gold,
I shall thank you my friend, for standing by.

Timothy Womac

The Man In The White

Here I am in a room of Smokey white
I'm in my own Delusional State of mind.
These shoulder straps are tight as hell,
Any ways, what do they expect to find?

So I'm a little outta touch with reality
It is usually that way,
Cause when you cannot get that fix...
You tend to go a little insane!

Cocaine and crack they sure know my name, they call it everyday.
"Hey Mister, in the white, loosen me up
here, whatta ya say?"

The sweat on my face is drowning me, these
shakes are completely outta control.
Please call for the Man of Cloth,
For I need him to say my soul!

Cocained and crack have been my friends indeed,
They are the one's who will fill my needs when need be!

Unlike you, the damn man in the white!
For you are makin' me suffer night after nights,
Yea, I'm talkin' to you....
The Man In The White!

Terri S. Cockriel

She Came To Me

She came to me on Friday, and left the following day,
And how she left the scene was a most peculiar way.
She took her bags of clothing, and all her many dreams,
And burst out in a hurry, that's told the way it seems.

Her hair was full of luster, and she could really sing,
I guess that you could safely say it was her favorite thing.
She sat alone that evening, and sang a lovely tune,
That sounded like scarlet rose, beneath a rain in June.

She came to me for guidance, to tell her what to say,
Whenever her dad beat her, or when she kneeled to pray.
Would she say words of envy, or would they all be true.
"It's out of my hands," I told her, "this matter's up to you,"

She asked me could she stay, beneath my sheltered roof,
But I was kind of worried, I needn't tell the truth.
I told her, "Yes, it's fine with me," but I knew I was wrong,
For when I woke the following day, her bags and she were gone.

Terrence LeBrone Bostic

No Evidence Was Shown

The sound of footsteps in your house,
a burglar being quiet as a mouse.
With a large black bag carried in his hand,
the burglar will steal all that he can.
Sneaking around for jewelry of expense,
gold and silver worth more than 10 cents.
Fur coats and expensive men's suits,
maybe a tux with fitted black boots.
The burglar still searching and watching his back,
slips out the window not a sound nor a crack.
Down the sidewalk and down to a car,
breaking in with a large crow-bar.
Unlocking the door and getting inside,
throwing the bag that's large and wide.
No watch dog nor a guard at the door,
the burglar goes back, nevermore.
The burglary got away and so the days went on,
out of the country the burglar was gone.
The owners on vocation the house was alone,
the burglar took place but no evidence was shown.

Amanda Mitchell

Harvest In Oklahoma

June is the month for harvesting wheat
Sometimes it's tiring on the combine seat.
We're always thankful when the grain turns out well
With all kinds of weather, you never can tell.
Then comes hauling wheat to an elevator -
We'll know the weight and the average later.
Next comes disking or plowing the land
Each one lends a helping hand.
Meals are prepared and taken to the field -
The kind and amount depends on the yield.
Work goes on until late hours of the night -
Lights on the tractors make a beautiful sight.
Everyone is ready for a good night's rest
After many work hours, that seems the best.

Lavon Wiersig

Life's Rhyme

In another place in a past time, an infant child's cries are hushed by the sound of a rhyme. Who is this child? Who and what will she know? Who will she meet and where will she go? Nobody knows what life she'll lead. Her works and strives will soon be freed...

In this very place in the present time, a teenager gets a lecture and reads a rhyme. Who is this adolescent? Who and what does she know? Who does she meet and what places does she go? In her eyes everybody knows and yet nobody cares. She works and strives to be of importance in others lives...

In another place in a future time an old woman knits, as she rocks to the sound of a rhyme. Who is this woman? Who and what and did she know? Who has she met and what places did she go? Nobody knows what a life she has led, her works and strives long since put to bed...

What does this mean you ask? It means make everything count and good times last. "Dwell in the present, not in the future or past, live every moment to it's fullest as though it was your last."

Amanda Thomas

Starlight

Starlight, starbright keep glowing bright all night
Please guide me to the end of the trail
Starlight, starbright keep all the animals safe and sound
Starlight, starbright you make people's dreams come true
Starlight, starbright I look for you every night.

Tracy Aksamit

Lost Child

I know where I am going
yet I don't?
The path ahead is clear
But the further I walk
It becomes more and more faint
Less light, less air and finally
Total darkness

I panic, but no one seems to hear my
frantic cries of help
Until finally I get extremely tired
I dream of my warm house and comfortable bed
But when I awake
The horror starts all
Over
Again!!

Kamaka Martin

The Miracle

The miracle was me.
The miracle was there waiting to be released by me.
The miracle was self-development. The self-development provided inner thought control and peace within me.
The miracle was to learn and recognize who I am now.
The miracle was a self-discovery process.
The miracle unfolded and there I was a wonderful and powerful human being.
The miracle that was created in me was a gift from God.
I now know The Miracle that lies within me.

Rita Marks

My Cherokee Grandmother, Annie Rone

Her picture came today from my aunt in Kentucky.
And the old Indian women looks kinda plucky.
Standing proud and tall in a paleface dress.
Of her Indian blood you would never guess
Now I know where I got my high cheek bones.
From my Cherokee grandmother, Annie Rone.

Though my daddy knew, he never discussed it.
My uncle told us though he was told to hush it.
Now the secret's out and the cousins all love it.
We've got Cherokee blood, and we're damn proud of it.
But we're sad that very few facts are known.
Of our Cherokee grandmother, Annie Rone.

We don't know her clan and we wish we could ask her.
If bear, bird, wolf or panther was our ancestor.
It also might be deer, paint our wind.
From which of the seven clans did she descend?
What led her to her old Kentucky home?
My Cherokee grandmother Annie Rone.

Sue Raymer

Undreamed...

Take my hand the way you just did.
Take my hand and I'll tell you I love you.
Then you'll say you love me, too,
We'll walk hand in hand, on and on,
Day by day with love that will last
for an eternity to come.
Love is around us surrounding us
with peace. Love is touching us
caressing us with soft kisses.
Sending us into undreamed
heavens sensing only love.

Elizabeth Gonzalez

Reveal Yourself

I see people with a lot of masks and to carry it is a heavy task. See they try to act smooth and cool, but only themselves they fool. You see I have the tool that can get you in your own groove. Be yourself. Oh, it's good to have someone to look up to but, you still got to be yourself true. See this keeps you from turning blue and suppressing the energy that is you. All of us have that appeal that no one can steal; that something that keeps it on the real. It gives that unique feel that makes people know the deal. Even though the body is not a true representation just act right and it will be a true inflation. You see I spread my wings and fly knowing that I can never die. When I open the door I cause people to hit the floor and beg for more. It's the click of my heels that delivers that sensual feel. I have no frustration, so I with no hesitation giving a true charismatic sensation. I have no blunders, so when people see me they see thunder that makes them sit back, think, and wonder. I have power in my eyes that brings forth lightning from the skies to those I despise. My mind makes creations that gets the crowd's participating and a standing ovation. For it's the pleasure I bring that makes the crowd get up and sing ting-ga-ling-ga-ling-ling. I have that tingle that makes me single from all those I mingle. You want to control me you need much authority. Cause you see I need nothing to define my self worth for when you enter there you enter my turf. See when you act like yourself you're nobody's fool and that will always make you cool.

Kevin Adams

Lunch Break

It's snowing again.
Wouldn't mind if it wasn't so cold.
Wouldn't care if I was inside
where it is warm and full of
shiny people.
Instead, I'm outside
inside my little blue car.
No one to share my
neon orange peanut butter crackers with.
I can't stop chipping at the old polish on my nails
and thinking
"Gee, having a grand time,
  wish you were here..."
Wish you were here.
Wouldn't mind if it didn't snow so damn much.

Kristen Peterson

When

When the light in you dies,
  what is there left but darkness?
When the pleasure in you dies,
  what is there left but bitterness?
When the joy in you dies,
  what is there left but pain?
When the hope in you dies,
  what is there left but despair?
When the truth in you dies,
  what is there left but deception?
When the fire in you dies,
  what is there left but ashes?
When the strength in you dies,
  what is there left but frailty?
When the energy in you dies,
  what is there left but a lifeless body?
When the health is you dies,
  What is there left but disease?
When the life in you dies,
  what is there left?

Heather Skeba

For My True Love

With you I found a side of myself
that I never knew existed.
One reason I love you so much
is you always bring out the best in me
I have never felt this happy with anyone
and you are definitely something special
life without you would be death
and I would gladly give my life for you
You always make me feel wanted,
whenever I'm with you
You mean the world to me,
I don't ever want to let you go
I couldn't find enough ways
to show how much I care
I want to be with you forever
and I know we have a chance
Relationships without true love
is now a thing of the past
I just hope that since I have you now,
this true love we have will last.

Shannon Hathaway

Torn Apart

She was thirteen going on thirty
Long braids framed her tiny face
Eyes asked disturbing questions
And a heart being rendered asunder

When did it begin she wondered
This could never happen to me
No, it can't be. It must be a mistake
Mom! Dad! Wake me! A nightmare!

Mom turned her head, afraid to answer.
Dad walked passed with eyes downcast.
She looked around, the void engulfed her
Even the kitchen sink he plundered

She sat there, hugged herself tightly
It is true, it is true, she moaned softly
Hot tears tumbled down and overflowed
Her whole world crumbled around her

Embraced by Mom, together they found
Truth and honesty always overcome.
Shallow promises and false pretenses
Destroy stability and everlasting love

Nasmoon S. Creque

God Tell Her...

The silence I show outside
is only to hide what's deep inside
I never want to make her cry
because of that, I will always try
I wonder if her heart is ever sad
because if it is, that would be bad
I ask myself this question, only to find
it always lingers on my mind
Her happiness means more to me
as only You can see
There's not a day I start
without this wish for her in my heart
But God most of all tell her
Even though I can't say each day how much I care
My heart will always be there

Derek Melancon

Soldier-Mother's Sorrow

I sit alone,
beneath an open starlite sky.
The cool, crisp air touching my face
my eyes.

The gentle rolling hills
covered in a white blanket;
they seem to invite me to explore them,
calling to me...

The small foreign town lite up with street lamps,
the clock tower above all,
charming me...

Yet with even these riches all around me,
there is still emptiness...

He should be here -

He should be here with me -

He should be with me...

Chris Landry

Insanity

I feel the knob inside my brain
and turn it till it hits insane
all at once I feel no pain
as a horse runs by with snakes as mane.

I play with the demons in my head
as we dance around a bride in red
we laugh and sing to the walking dead
as they lay in their wood and satin beds.

With dead black flowers in our hair
we dance and sing to a witches lair
she casts her spells with grace and care
as her bright red eyes begin to flair.

I feel a deep innocent depression
and cry the demons my confession
the pain they promised they could lessen
has left an evil, cruel impression.

I swallow down a deadly pill
and get the sudden urge to kill
I lose the sense to think and feel
and know this world is very real.

Stacey Glebes

On Growing Old

The roses blooming in the bed
Outside her window, so she said,
Were planted by her love (now dead)
Some sixty years ago.

They built this house and she, a bride,
Cared for her home with loving pride
While he took care of things outside,
A garden—row on row.

And then her mind goes back in time
And on her face that look sublime
Tells me she's thinking thoughts that I'm
Not privileged to know.

It's sad to see her in her chair,
Her head haloed by silver hair;
The knitting laid aside with care,
Her fingers gnarled and slow.

But if I could grow old with grace
And have that peace upon my face
That seems to say, "You've won the race,"
Then years would be no foe.

Joy Taylor

When Angels Dance

Angels dance into our lives
And linger - for a moment, perhaps longer,
When we truly need them.

A glorious vision, a presence felt,
Soft words spoken, perhaps unspoken,
But somehow communicating their being,
Their comfort, their love,
Lifting us above the burden, the pain,
The anguish, the fear,
To a higher level of understanding and faith,
Of hope and peace and Joy,
When angels dance into our lives.

Beatrice B. Han

Colors Of The World

From the creator from above.
color is beauty within his soul.
For the creator who created the colors of the world.....
Never anticipated for his creation to hate.
For the creator who created the creation
Never seen vividly beautiful colors of such kind.
When his creation was done he gave colors
To every human, creature and
living things he wanted on his earth.
The creation he created... Was a statement he wanted to unfold.
He believe any color of a smiling face.. Has nothing to do with hate.
But the statement he wanted to make was not the colors of his
children's face.
But the heart he gave to every human creator and race.

Donna Pierre

Mother

I've said the prayers you taught me, Dear,
Each morning and each night.
I've prayed to Him who is Supreme:
"Please let me see her in a dream".

You've always said "Desire is prayer,"
That "Love is always everywhere".
'Twas like you, Mother, to be there,
To show once more how much you care.

You just stood there upon the stairs,
The only answer to my prayers.
As I looked across the room,
Your smile to me dispelled all gloom.

And when I looked into your eyes
Eternal Truth I realized.
From future grief I now am free,
I know you'll always be with me.

Marian J. Cobb

Pearls

If Dr. Luke, by chance, was in that crowd
at Peter's modest home in Galilee
and saw a man who made the blind to see,
the lame to walk, the woman who was bowed
with fever take up her duties, proud
to show again her hospitality,
would his much learning bring necessity
of proof before his mind belief allowed?

If we should share with friends how great the things
we've seen our sweet and gracious Jesus do,
would they rejoice at oral evidence,
or, trampling pearls - fine treasures fit for kings,
ask proof that what we said is really true,
demanding some recorded documents?

Contance R. Pollock

One Last Time (Epitaph)

Let me see that light blue sky,
or maybe hear an eagle cry.
I remember a place not touched by man,
I walked all day where clear streams ran.

The deer and the rabbit they did not fear,
I slept in the woods they lived that year.
I galloped green hills and saw buffalo run,
and knew my time on earth was nearly done.

Before I died I asked one thing,
I knew the place I wanted to lie and dream.
It was a place with my old friends,
all extinct animals who couldn't bend.

High on a summit where the air was thin,
to symbolize the way things for us had always been.
So they planted me in that good free earth,
and I saw my nourishment to seed give birth one last time.

C. J. Bohlin

Dreams...

All my dreams, all my dreams...
When I dream it seems so real,
Although I know it cannot be...
But what I see and what I feel...
Is way beyond fantasy.

To be the president of the United States,
Or even to become the mother of eight.
I can walk to the end of the world...
Swim the great big oceans,
And sore like an eagle, high above the clouds.

Bringing peace to the world, is one of my desires,
To destroy viruses, and killer diseases; by burning them, in fires.
Abolish poverty in our country, so no child goes hungry.
Soon, maybe, one day; hatred will go away.

And that the future that awaits us, be better than the past.
Only good health and happy occasions,
Be part of my family and friends.
And that as I awake from a long sleep,
My dreams will not come to an end.

Susan Oliver

Destination

Looking on ahead of me, the beautiful world.
The God gifted creation,
the classic life style.
I wished I could enjoy, all, within this world.
To wake up in the morning, maybe with a good men,
But circumstances has placed me there,
To face the bitter days.
Chilly nights, and sleepless
Hunger and thirsty and tattered clothes
To suffer this turmoil, and hardship of life
Do I envy this creation, God gifted world.
People around me, so happy with smiles
I cry within my soul, and wish a wishing star.
Lord, could I one day be there
and enjoy this gifted world.
Cruelty and hatred, is all that is stoned
No loving arms around me, no good good to taste.
Maybe a warm bed to sleep, or a lullaby song
I am an unfortunate person
with no destination of my life.

Diane Miller

Be My Desire

Why the game,
wondering from whence I came,

Be my desire,
this world is not for me either,
but my desire gives me a breather,

My desire is in my dreams,
I know not what it means,

Yet it takes me afar,
to a distant star,

A place where I am loved
without any query,
I get not weary,

The tears of being alone,
they're all gone,

The heart that was shattered,
pieced back together,

The silence of pain within it didn't take me where I've been,
This is my dream desire of trust within,
be my desire I'll keep this dream of where I've been,
My star, that took me afar.

Vivian Jlee McNeal

Working As A Home Health Aide

I give a helping hand to the elderly in need, which
  they do appreciate indeed.
Making home visits is my job, it doesn't feel like work,
  it makes my heart throb.
All day long I enjoy seeing the smiles of joy, sometimes
  even a tear in their eye. My duties involve personal
care, which includes showering, shaving and washing of hair.
  I listen to their stories, I give a pat and a hug, by
the time I'm ready to leave they are feeling and doing better.
  That's why I will love my job forever.

Joan Barker

Faithful Friend

Weeping willow, you know how I feel,
so keep on crying for me.
Hey best friend! A penny for your thoughts.
But I'll give you mine for free.
And look at this worry stone
I'm smoothing with my hands.
I have no doubt in my heart
that he really understands.
And you innocent child,
don't you ever grow old.
But if you do,
teach another what you've been told.
And when I fade away from here,
please don't let my friend be lonely,
because that tree is my best friend,
it's my one and only.

Amanda Schnitzius

I

Who am I? I am a happening nailed by gravity to a world
that is not of my choosing.
What am I? When looking into to a mirror I cannot see what
I am, for what I am is hiding within my soul.
Where am I? Am I at a crossroad shadowed by night? Must
I move further on and pray I do not fall into a chasm of nothing?
Why am I? If God would give me the answer, then I would
know if I am to deliver comfort, or a curse, or to condemn
the world and myself.

Freda Ackett

Peace

The flaming sun sets proudly in the west;
dusk spreads her mantle o'er the tranquil lea.
The plowman homeward plods his weary way
and leaves the world to darkness and to me.

The pine trees like church-organ pipes stand tall;
the mountain peaks with heavenly light are shod.
The cool wind whispers through the rustling leaves,
"Know ye, all men, there is a living God."

Night's blanket eases every woe and care;
the patterned lights of God form in the sky.
The peaceful bliss of calmed anxiety
is broken only by the night-bird's plaintive cry.

The message of God's will rings clear to me;
I know that I shall reap a treasure trove,
when I step through that last awaiting door
to be cradled in His arms of bounteous love.

Richard F. Hupp

The Shore Of The Molten Sun

The snow was laden upon the shore,
A glacier of forgotten memories of warmth past
The families that had bathed and glistened in the molten sun
Were now astray on the streets of winters lunge
Frozen icicles for drink
Meal yet to be found
Boxes and newspapers used for shelter
Only existing by the warmth of the once molten sun, now hidden
Prayer for the molten sun to show its warming rays again
Will they survive till spring?
To see the molten sun kiss the shore again
Will destiny end before it ever began?

Michelle Lynn Pifer

Debate of Life

The sun rises in the sky,
yet the flying bird does not see.
It is only concerned about how it will fly,
and what it will one day be.
The cat pounces upon the mouse,
but the mouse only makes fun.
For up on the hill there is a house,
where several more will run.
The truth of existence, many will say.
No one has substance,
so we all must pay.
Maybe it is fact,
maybe it is fiction.
Maybe it is an act,
maybe it is diction.
This I will never know,
I can only guess,
but I know we need to show
all of our success.

Angela Greenfield

That Not Spoken

Though it may be a faintly discernible space
Amidst apprehensions crowding
Still unfound throughout recognizable speech
Emaciated through stoic resolve
Clamoring beneath, behind, and just out of sight
Pervading within, refuting what's out
Perhaps obscured by time's endless evolution
Insufferably hidden for no moment longer
Apologies abound by my submission
For all that was said and that not spoken

Matthew Young

Until Love Is All That Remains

I'll remember the beauty of your soul, as I viewed
through the windows of your eyes.
I'll cherish the faint remembrance of your loving
caress on my bare skin
I shiver at the thought of your warm breath
tantalizing my senses as you whispered, "I love you,"
softly in my ear.
I'll hold dearly to the picture in my mind I
have of you as you looked deep into my eyes with
your own sultry brown eyes and spoke the words,
"I do", on the night you made my most precious
dream come true.
I'll never release the hope that our love will
endure, even this, and I'll wait for you, My Love,
until love is all that remains.

Micki Wilson

The War

There is a storm in the air — it sounds like thunder.

But it's guns and planes flying over there.
It looks like lighting in the sky.
But it's Skuds and Patriots, that make people die.
It's not like rain that falls to make our flowers grow.
It's chemicals falling, that kills — it kills our friends and foes.
This is called Desert Storm.
Dear God — This is so hard to understand,
How lives are lost because of one man.
Saddam Hussein - What is he? What does he stand for?
Why oh why does he want this war?
We have loved ones who are fighting in the sand.
How we look for them to come back to the USA Land -
We love and support our troops over there.
We want them to know we all care.
They have a job and it must be done.
Even though it comes from the sounds of guns.
We will keep our flags flying and ribbons on our doors —
Until the end of this horrible war!!

Sandra Reed

From You, To Me

Last night alone in the moonlight,
a soft breeze in the air.
I watched the clouds as they passed by.
I noticed a man in the sky picking up pieces
of a broken heart.
Gently placing each like a puzzle piece
in precisely the right place.
When he was done it was placed in his hand
where another did stand.
The two became one and were incased by
the stars that did shine in the night.
Then he held out his hand for
me to take hold.
As our hands took hold, the moonlight
reflected upon his face.
At that moment I realized that it was
you sending a message to me.
No matter where I go
You go with me in my heart.

Tammy Anson

Untitled

I stooped to smell a rose, one day
and it looked at me as if to say,
"I wish I were you and I could be
away from these thorns that imprison me."

But a different story it would be,
if the rose could see the thorns in me.

Karen Martin

My Father's Bible

Tucked neatly away in the library of my life is the word by which he lived.
My father, devout and faithful in all he did.

The stiff leather jacket cracked and faded, the corners gently
rounded from the years he cradled his Bible close in his arms.
Golden edges dulled as a sturdy thumb searched for a passage.
Once crisp linen parchment now limp from the warmth of his palm.

Pressed softly between the pages lies
the petals of a bloom,
preserved without record but not without a story.

The words you penned in the margins
echo your insight and the
promise of the light that you followed into eternity.
This is your legacy.

In that timeless place where you are,
you still speak to me.
My heart hears you sing with the angels.

Karen S. Ferdinandsen

Celebration

Looking for a poodle pup, we'll never forget the day,
It was 1981, the 25th of May.
There you were, a black ball of fur, with a white patch on your chest,
Our search was done, we'd found the one; no need to see the rest.

Memories now come flooding back, and we smile as they do
Seeing in our mind's eye, the beloved pet that is you:
Belly-scratching and ear-rubbing - pastimes welcome always,
Second only to fetching toys thrown down stairs and hallways!
You love oranges and ice cream, and something even more:
A laundry basket left unguarded on the kitchen floor!
And at the end of each day, as we wend our way,
Back to hearth and home,
We know you'll be there, ready to hear, about the battles we've won.
13 years of loving-joy every minute
Life sweeter, little boy, just because you're in it.
Thank you for simply being, precious little lamb,
And for giving us so many reasons to Celebrate Sam.

Marsha Daub

Country Pumpkin

If I was a pumpkin, I would be,
A country pumpkin, sitting in a beautiful
field out in the country. Watching everything
go by me. Letting the sun shine down
upon me. At night I get to watch the
twinkling stars in the midnight sky.
It's getting cooler now. It's getting
closer to halloween. Soon I will get a
face and a candle for light. "Yipee" I
get to sit on the porch so my owner can
watch me glow in the midnight stars,
"Hooray" he's coming to pick me it's halloween
Now I can sit on the porch and listen
to the children say "Trick-or-treat", halloween is
over I get to sit and watch over the country
scenes. That is what I would want to
be, a country pumpkin.

Lucrecia Nieves

Life/Death

Do not stand at my brave and weep
I'm not there I do not sleep.
I'm I winds that blind, I'm the
softly fallen snow. I'm gentle showers
of rain, in the fields of mining
grain. I'm not a morning hash,
I'm in a graceful rush. I'm the
beautiful blinds in air crafting flight.
I'm thee star shine of the night
I'm the flowers that gloom, I'm in
a quit room. I'm the birds that
sing. I'm in each lovely thing.
Do not stand at my brave and cry.
I'm not there I did not die.

Gina Barash

Sweet Dreams

I close my eyes in blissful sleep
and pray in beauty, dreams may keep
to see the calm, yet not awake
and banish nightly terrors sake
In golden rivers soft sweet sigh
as sleepily I float on by
to grasp the strands of passing dreams
the sleeping world's own strengthened beams

Past columns where nymphs congregate
to crystal arches of the gate
I calmly pass to grasp the seal
that broken will dreams reveal
the softest whispers, skin caressed
as silently my body rests
while merrily I drift away
in presence of sweet dreams, I stay.

Carrie Grasley

Break The Cycle

I didn't ask for the hurt and the shame,
But is it really wise to place blame?

Anger nearly destroyed me.
Forgiveness, that is the key.

Unlearn the anger, confusion and hate,
A better life will then await.

Forgive them Lord, as I must do,
Help me Lord, and I'll forgive you, too.

Peace and clam are with me still.
The pain won't return, it never will.

Those dark days, they serve me now.
The future is bright and I know how,

To choose what is good
and do as I should.

I count my blessings, large and small.
Now I walk proud and I stand tall.

Love, caring and laughter fill my days.
The past is there like a fuzzy haze.

Implications, they anger me still,
Abuse my kids? I never will.

Pamela K. Vorhees

Only The Best Will Come To You

Try your best to be your best; for your best is the most
that you can be.

Do your very best in all that you do; and only the very best will
come back to you.

Feel good about yourself; leave your worries and fears behind.

Forget about the pains and sorrows of the past
And look at what you're about to find.

Good things come to those who wait; and waiting is
sometimes so very hard to do.

Just believe in yourself and what you're feeling; and
only the best will come to you.

Joseph A. Kenner

Stronger

I am as strong as you, - in defeat and in victory.
No one else can catch me. - I soar through the skies.

Flying over white moons, - dancing on the twinkling stars.
I always win, - even when I lose.

Never again, you and me. - Touch me; grab me.
Ha! You will never. - Revolution and death.

Child of my birth, - dust in my mind's eye.
To be or not to be. - I will always be.

Green ears often destroy. - They make me.
Decaying tongues - lie on their tombs.

Black inventions, - and white too.
Mercy, I pray! - Compassion for you.

The other day
I asked for you.
You were not there.
I left.

Luis Armando Rodriguez

The Sky

Silently, he rolled in;
Then I felt his chilling breath.

And when I looked up, all I saw was his huge face,
Puffed with purple rage staring back down into mine.

His eyes flashed and his gusty breath whipped my hair
As I shrunk back with fear.

Anger mounted inside his clenched fists
And behind his rounded cheeks, as he crept closer.

Then as his fury exploded -
There was bolt after bolt, and roar after roar,
As I sat hugging my knees to my chest in shame.

Then his large bitter tears
Pounded the back of my drooping head
And I began to shiver.

After a time, the tears lost their sting,
And when I cautiously raised my head,
They caressed my face, and cleansed my soul.

And as the light filtered through,
And the shadows across his face faded away,
I saw the sunshine that had been hidden behind the storm.

Heather Terlecki

My Little Girl

To Madison, my daughter, on her first birthday

I knelt with an eager watch as a beautiful creation emerged me into
fatherhood into those little eyes I found the melting of my heart
with a peace of bewildered joy

I'll never forget in a room seemingly full to find a presence of
only three I'll never forget her first cry and my counting of her toes

I'll never forget the tears in her mother's eyes as she held the
life from within I'll never forget the turning of her head to the
words "Daddy's here"

I'll never forget walking her to the nursery with my feet not
touching the floor I'll never forget changing the first diaper, the
spit-ups, wet wipes, and more

I'll never forget watching her near the Christmas tree as I admired
God's precious gift I'll never forget late one night coaching her
and then to see her first rollover

I'll never forget saying at bed time to call if she needs Daddy and
every night she did I'll never forget racing home from work for my
hug and slobbery kisses

I'll never forget talking to her on the phone and hearing "Hi Daddy"
as tears filled my eyes I'll never forget her first awkward steps
and her many falls

I'll never forget each moment Mom and Dad share together
watching our little girl grow I'll never forget Mom being so excited
about her first birthday party

I'll never forget one moment, one memory, one laugh, no, not even
one small thing I'll never forget even in the years ahead that she's
my little girl

I still kneel with an eager watch admiring this beautiful creation
I'll forever call, my little girl

Tim Singleton

Never Never Land

In a cold sweat I wake in the middle of nite
There something wrong, something doesn't seem right.
I glance at the clock; it's the witching hour
And try to remember with all of my power
It all comes back to me in a sudden flood
Tears roll down my cheeks, tasting salty, like blood
I finally recall the dream I just had
But this is reality, and that makes me so sad.
Each nite my heart is heavy with sorrow
When I realize my dreams will be over tomorrow
But for a few hours my life can be fun
when I am together with that special someone
Just for a short while from dusk until dawn
But then in the morning, I know she'll be gone

Peter Baugh

Renewal

As the dew sparkles so invitingly,
And the sun shines brightly,
I sit and contemplate.

A rabbit is still, doesn't move-
We stare eye to eye,
And I wonder.

Two birds peck the ground, jumping 'round
Others sing and swoop-
I'm delighted and sigh.

People arouse, the traffic comes
Life awakens and my oasis shuts-
But I am fulfilled.

Francis Cole

The Truth

This life of ours happens to fast
We start to forget,
Those good times from the past

As we get older life slows down
Knowing that we will end up six feet under ground
Now you know that this is true
So why are you trying to hide the truth

The truth hurts as we all know
So why are you trying to play the roll
That roll might end very soon
So why are you letting it bother you

The roll is over and you are gone
Gone from this world were you belong
Now the worst has come and gone
Knowing that your memory will still live on.

Johnny Gallegos

Orange

Orange is like the leaves in the beginning of Autumn.
The leaves blow softly, early in the evening wind.
They're so beautiful, it reminds me of orange tulips at Easter.
Tulips blossom early in Spring,
and are as orange as the sun late in the afternoon.
The sun's bright rays warm me as I play baseball outside.
At night the sun goes down,
but never fear
it returns the next day.
I awake to a cool glass of juice, orange and sweet.
Fresh squeezed, if you please.
And there on the windowsill, as cool as can be,
is my soft and fluffy orange calico cat.
Right beside her is an orange ball of yarn.
Left over from the sweater my mom knitted
for my Great-Grandma when she was sick.
Worrying she'd not get better
and she never did.
Orange.....the color of beauty and worry.

Megan Casner

Life's Little Battle

Beneath the yellow moon afar
  The Galleon ships do bellow
Through clouds of white from yonder fight
  Arise a jolly fellow
A flash of glory, the cannons roar
  The sound of the battle's cry
Alas the victor true he stands
  And not afraid to die
So hoist the sail and set for sea
  Our journey is not yet done
Another ship now lays to rest
  Another battle's won
Yet, a pirate's gold is made for him
  Who seeks to please his own
But when the final battle's fought
  He'll find himself alone
For hell's great gates are open wide
  To take all those who fall
Seek not the fate for those who wait
  And don't receive their call

John M. Fletcher

The Good Old Days?

Have you ever heard people talk of the past?
They say, "I wish those good old days would have lasted."
Now to me the "Good Old Days," don't sound like much fun,
And I'm pretty glad that they're over and done.

Can you imagine no TV's with remotes?
And who can live without a stereo?
And they had no A.C. during the summer,
And they worked outside no matter what the weather.

Girls had to wear dresses, that was the rule,
Everyone walked uphill, both to and from school.
They started work young, but didn't get paid much.
They didn't have cell phones, computers, and such.

Maybe it's just the generation gap between the young and the old,
That make it sound bad...these stories they'd told.
Me? Well right here is where I am and where I'll stay.
Because I just can't see why they call them the "Good Old Days."

Michaela Kanger

A Tree

I wonder how my life would be,
If I could live it as a tree.
A stately sentinel, silently I stand
Stretching arms forth, out, across the land.
Sheltering those who come to me,
And doing so indiscriminately.
Feeding those who are in need,
From bark, and leaves, fruit and seed.
I would live my life without oppression,
Prejudice, racism, or repression.
Oblivious to emotion, immune to pain,
Not wanting prominence, nor seeking gain.
Innocent and truly free,
As a tree, I'd surely be.
But, alas, I'm not a tree.
I'm just a man, unfortunately.

John W. Peile Jr.

Untitled

There once was a man with a nagging wife
Who pestered him his entire life.
He vowed he'd get even with all womankind,
As he worked and worried with frenzied mind.
For devising torture he had a real knack,
He invented dresses with zippers in back.

Margarete F. Archer

"Predator"

Crouching low and lying still
Remaining poised for the kill
His prey has yet to know he's there
And there it stays so unaware
Danger lurks not far away
Anticipation for the stray
The master of this hunting game
Vicious without a face or name
For survival there is no longer chance
No way to escape the circumstance
With one slash he draws the blood
Pressing his victim into the mud
And the mud that accepts this lifeless corpse
Swallows it whole with no remorse
The killer triumphant with a cackling laugh
Hysterical and pleased in the aftermath
He is the predator always looking to feast
But tell me, is this man or beast?

Shannon Miller

Friends

I have always been there for you
You stood next to me when no one else would
in my times of need
Now you and I have grown apart
You do not want me near you and the sight of
you makes me ill
I was nothing but refined to you
I was the one who made you believe in yourself
I get paid back by having you make jokes about
me
What did I ever do to make you hate me?
Some say the people you want to be like, you are
mean to
Put them down, make them hurt so you felt
better than them
Why can't we just be friends instead!

Joanne McCain

Invitation

Come

There is a way to get anything you want
If you know how.

Come

Walk on this side of the tracks
Walk with us.

Come

We love it when another joins us
We want you.

Come

Just take one big bite little fish
And you will be hooked.

Danny Concha Jr.

Hubert's Pool Hall

After A Fight With The Wife

Only a hustler could understand
when I make the comparison
of the sounds of pool shots
to slow motion tap dance clicks.
But, every Joe who ever slid a stick
in his hand or ever blew the blue powder off a tip
knows what I mean when I say
every shot, every stroke, is
an attempt at redemption,
a glorious single second of
accomplishment as all your doubts
and failures roll off the felt into
the pitch black pocket of the past.

Roderick Vesper

Untitled

Thus your lips are wet and luscious
like a moist plum on a spring moment of trous;
your eyes are so gorgeous; looking
into I then find myself in a dream.
Your skin is like the sun glistening on a
newly fallen snow filled after a winter's blizzard;
(pail)
your hands are like clouds with no worries
in the world on a summer's day; soft and gentle
for now my love for you is like
a bush of white roses in fall;
long lasting, eternal.

Cristal Weinberg

Epitaph Of A Heart

Snow falling gently, and as each snowflake melts, when it hits the
earth; one heart, is breaking slowly.
She walks in the quiet scenery, thinking of how she has loved, and
been loved, but for some reason, something has always gone wrong.
Her beauty attracts many, but no one knows, how her smile hides
her pain, for smiles can hide the darkest secrets.
Why is life so difficult? Why must people hurt, and be hurt? Why
can't we trust, and be trusted? Ask the smile that hides the pain.
Time after time, she let people enter her soul, and each time, they
took it below, a level, where her heart cried out for mercy, but it
never came.
She walks alone now, thinking of how she never had that once in a
lifetime fulfilling dream, never gained respect, or achieved
success.
She will end this existence of misery, for she feels no one will
care. She floats off the bridge, into the icy water.

Phyllis Gibson

Poems

A short story. Imaginary. For real.
Thoughts. Visions. Craziness. Sanity.
A kaleidoscopic view of personal feelings
felt through out the inner man. Black,
white, pink, purple; couture; co-cheese;
More rhyming please! Aim high, go low. Be
something, a haiku perhaps. Maybe an epic. Long, short,
thin, fat, a poem is a poem and that's that!

Monica T. Ward

My Dream

To fly so far away from this,
without my troubles, problems, and bliss.
Leaving behind all my rages and fears,
no more worries and such painful tears.
All the times of drowning in my worries and so,
without all my worries, I can let myself go.
I'll travel to a place where everyone knows,
the biggest problem is the way the wind blows.
No cares, no hopes—as light as a feather,
perfect is everything, even the weather.
There is no other place with all this glory,
it's like a magical land in a child's story.
It's too bad this place is no more than a dream,
oh, so real did it seem.
As I wake-up and remember this place,
a smile forms across my face.
Then I think with delight,
this dream will come again tonight.

Katie Krueger

The Quest

With flaming sun and blooming moon,
And twinkling stars of twelve on crown,
She pales and pains to bring to life
The One, to ride on whitehorse bright.

The sleeping Spring, now, waves her wings,
While yawning Winter swan-song brings,
And the dimpled cheeks of golden dawn
Wears a magic touch of sweetness on.

Beyond those glossy grassy fields,
Beyond this dating land of biting lips,
In night's nipping silence, hard I spurred
In a perilous quest to meet my Lord.

Upon the carpet of the sylvan glen,
Near the silver lake of heavenly bliss,
With royal gaze, the rider stood
Claiming me to his lustrous race.

Elias Abraham

Diluted Memories

Miles and miles travelled Max Niles,
searching for a piece of the past
Memories from when he was a child, images that could never surpass.

Days and nights rolled on, yet soon he was there
Reaching his destination, which wept with certain despair.

Torn and stripped lay the motel, just the way he thought it to be
Nothing more could change this hell, as it stood down by the sea.

Across the rocks of the shore, under the glow of the moon
Beyond the stillness of the moor, to the safety of the lagoon.

Into the darkness of the deep, beyond the ocean's salty taste,
Went Max with anxious feet, wading out above his waist.

Caught between the rift of the tides, in a pool of color and light
Something great and wondrous hides,
quenching all of the pain and delight.

Inside Max a change took form, complex it was with its meaning
Easing a heart, tired and worn,
releasing the torment of the dreaming.

Deeper he walked into the sea, under the surf and the foam
Out of this world, from you and me
Back to a place he called home.

Jared Macary

I Am Strong

I may seem weak or skinny or just plain o'le fat,
but I am strong and I am black.

I may not speak your proper english, I probably
never will get the knack,
but I am strong and I am black.
Don't put me down because I can't read as well
as others, maybe it's because I lack.
But I am strong and I am black.
If I quite don't understand don't hold me back,
but I am strong and I am black.
Don't give me anything that I did not earn, don't
put me up on a rack.
For I am strong and I am black.
Don't take my silence and my calm demeanor as slack.
For I am strong and I am black.
I am willing to talk out problems but don't get
me wrong. I will fight back.
For I Am Strong And I Am Black.
I know now that knowledge is power and that's a fact.
For Am Strong And I Am Black...

Marcellus Dunbar

Do Not Weep For Me

Dedicated to the French Jews who perished in the Holocaust.

Do not weep for me my child.
I have lived a life that has brought happiness forth.
My words will be instilled in your life forever.
I do not have to leave you with artifacts that have been passed
Through the generations.
I do not have to leave you a will to testify my life.

Do not weep for me my child.
For I am old but young.
Inside I know that you will live the years I have been denied.
For you are my hope, love and time.

Do not weep for me my child.
At least I died a death that people will remember for generations.
At least I have not died alone.
I have died as one and as a thousand people united together.

Nava Cohen

Dear Sister, I Would Feel Honored

Dear Sister, I know your birthdays have been full of great pain;
Since it was the very day death took our Momma away.
I wish I could take the whys of yesterday and explain
But it exists within yourself to make the breakaway.

All of your pain and sadness will never totally cease.
To have and remember feelings is part of each of us.
Though loving thoughts of Momma can help bring an inner peace
Allow yourself to open up and feel all the sadness.

It was also Momma's birthday when Grandma left earth's life.
Conflicting feelings and emotions Momma knew firsthand.
But Momma seemed at peace and free of emotional strife
Anger; bitterness; jealousy had no hold or command.

Momma fought a dignified, ending battle with cancer;
Yet she remained loving, caring, kind, and appreciative.
Giving and being helpful and thankful was her answer
For remaining positive and not seeing negative.

I am so proud of Momma and who she turned out to be;
I never heard her curse anyone nor a mean word say;
I shall always love her as she lives in my memory;
And I would feel honored, had her last day been my birthday.

Linda Morrow

The Other Half Of Me

I keep those happy moments, stored within my soul
I've tried hard to forget them, but cannot let them go.
Those were the greatest moments, but quickly they went by
remembering the happiness, makes me want to cry.
What's happened to those days, we were so young and free
I was part of you and you were part of me.
Time can heal a wound, but also cause great pain
you always seem to lose, more than you seem to gain.
Time took you away, and now we're far apart
but I will always keep you, deep within my heart.
I've learned so much from living, not from what I'm told
I've learned that life can bring great change, and sometimes be
quite cold.
Our friendships not as close, as once it used to be
but remember that you'll always be, the other half of me.

Ryan Schuler

"There Is A Place"

Is there a place where the little ones go who never had the chance
to breathe their first breath?
Is there a place that they call home, where someone sees that they
are safely kept?
They are so young to die, yet too small to cry out for help in their
need
Yet they do not have a chance to let their cry out because we live
by what we believe
Never will they hear a lullaby song
Never will they see a room filled with toys or have a family in
which they belong
Never will Mommy or Daddy kiss them good-night
Never will they be hugged and held onto tight
Never will they wish on a star shining bright
Never will they have the chance to gain back their right
Where is the place that the little ones go who never had the chance
to breathe their first breath?
Where is the place that they call home, where someone sees that
they are safely kept?
Heaven is the place where the little ones go who never had the
chance to breathe their first breath
Heaven is the place that they call home where Jesus sees that they
are safely kept

Megan Hunsberger

Vacation

White clouds, floating in the blue
Green trees passing in review.

Trucks and cars swishing by
Planes and helicopters spot the sky.

We are on our way - a vacation.
All eyes and ears tuned in anticipation,

Of things to see - things to behold.
Wonderful sights - new and old.

Laughter and chatter will dominate,
As we travel from state to state.

Seeing America in all her beauty
Is our joy and our duty.

Laurie F. Wilson

Unanswered Question

I question their extinction
I wonder if it is true
I can not imagine the world without them
Yet I do
I've been misled
I've been destroyed
I've been laughed at just as much
Yet the question remains
Demands an answer
The one thing I just can't touch
My answer is not accurate nor politically correct
Yet I dwell upon this question
Will I get an answer yet

Meredith C. Roudebush

Dark Eyes

Dark eyes peer into the mirror in front of me,
Dark images is all that is reflected, I see.
Dark eyes; long ago void of any tears,
Dark smiles; a pretense, I fear.
Dark heart; dying from the starvation of its needs,
Dark soul; stained by lies and misguided deeds.
Dark thoughts; from what the eyes have seen,
Dark despair; the new master of the dreams.
Dark clouds; now gather in the mind,
Dark emotions; all that is left to find.
Dark is all that reflect back, you see,
Dark is the only thing there seems to be.

Gene Hintzel

Ode To Deer Hunting

At 5 am there was a knock on the door
Shelly yelled, "It's time - let your feet hit the floor!"
We grabbed some "hot seats to keep us real warm
And the "hunter orange" should keep us from harm.
The wind started blowing, I put my ear flaps down
who cares if I look like Bozo the clown.
We're all sitting here so warm and cozy
But where are the deer - am I just being nosy?
Laura has a rifle with a brand new scope
Will she get to use it - we can only hope.
Later, we'll return to this very same spot
We might get the big one or...we might not.
After our nap we came back to the woods
It wasn't as chilly - didn't need those darn hoods.
Suddenly there were noises and we got quite a thrill
Oh my gosh - there's a white tail on the hill!
We were all so excited - it was such a sensation
Then Shelly said disgustedly, "It's just a dalmatian."
Who would've known the day would end in sorrow
No deer today - but there's always tomorrow!

Sherry Lynn Dennison Moore

My Dear Friend

We've gotten into a lot of fights,
Many over stupid little things.
We may say things that aren't right.
So much stress and anger it brings.
Slowly we'll talk again.
Joy, pain, and laughter we'll share,
When we become friends.
Day after day, year after year.
I don't know what I'd do,
If we one day stopped talking.
I wouldn't have anyone to relate to.
But I guess I'd have to keep on walking.
Until I find another warm face.
I know I'd find out in the end,
That no other,
Can take the place,
Of my dear friend, my mother.

Erica Allard

True Love

True love is a feeling two people share. True love is a door to show someone you care. Your heart has away to tell if it's true, because a sign will show up above you. Don't ever let go or you will miss out that one true love that you dream about. You will know in an instant if you've found that special one. Your heart will tell you that this might be the one. So if you ever get that feeling that this might be it. Just go with your instinct and don't ever quit.

Renee Evans

Walk With The Lord

I walk with the Lord, I'm never alone
He shows me the way for it to be known
In the wisdom of his words I want to learn more
I feel the hunger and the thirst that I have been craving for
The peace that He brings within my heart
The Spirit of Love and Faith is where it all starts
I never knew that the Holy Spirit is within me
He guides my path to keep me free
I take each day to learn to be still
Just a quiet time to do the Lord's will
The miracles that He can do I want to cry out
Jesus loves me, He loves without a doubt
I thank you Lord for helping me so
Without you beside me I would be a lost soul
The sins of my life must have weighed a ton
You carried my worries until there were none
You gave your life for it to be known
To walk with the Lord I am never alone

Rae L. Belanger

Utopia

So much rage and terrible war.
Awful hunger and so many poor.
Crime on this planet is such a disgrace.
Take us to a Utopia place.
No evil, no violence, not even crime.
No people saying "Can you spare a dime?"
Earth is in danger of losing its mind,
It's all on the shoulders of mankind.
In Utopia, everyone's free,
Our political leaders must find the key.
In this place, sun will always shine,
And we can rejoice so things will be fine.

Adam Joshua Brandolph

Where Beauty Lies

The most beautiful thing I've ever seen?
One could as easily choose between hearing and sight.
For who can say has the more beauty -
God's sun by day so warm and bright -
Or His harvest moon on shocks of corn?
A soft spring day with birds and flowers all a bloom,
Or the quiet blanket of snow on a winter morn?

Is it the first rose of June, first light of day,
Or the cool silver rain after the heat of noon?
Could it be white sails of a ship on a sea of blue,
The earth from a plane in the sky above,
A mountain high, a babbling brook,
Or a garden wet with sparkling dew?

Is it the first sweet smile of a baby today
Or the aged face of a grandparent we love?
I think perhaps the most beautiful thing -
That which brings my heart to sing,
Is the light of love in another's eyes;
Or, is it God's light from His glorious skies -
Who can say where more beauty lies?

Catherine Collamore Gisel

Homeward Bound!

My broken heart doctors couldn't repair,
Remember our time together, but not despair!
My work on earth please put away,
For my pilot called me home today!

Soon my loved ones will be out of sight,
Be happy for me, I found God's light.

Please wipe away your heavy emotional pain,
Serving Jesus on earth gave me great gain!

Now let the sun quickly go down
Without forgiving one another, don't lose your crown!
Please try hard with all your might,
Ask his wisdom making your wrong turn out right!
Remember me as planes fly out of sight,
Jesus was my pilot with every flight.
One day He'll call you up above,
Come join me with my first love!

Dottie Whitcomb

False Self-Maintenance

So, you've decided to become a hang gliding instructor
a double negative—
one so careful frightening the tulips
with wings of serenity.
The height wasn't a problem—
invisible blood was always so exhilarating;
stealing air from alveoli
made it that much more stimulating.
Something about boundless conformity
blew you off the edge in an adrenaline whirlwind,
leaving toothpaste and warm milk behind
to find another master.
From above, a glance of heroism fading fast, eyes sweating,
the final loop is completed—a tilt here and there—
such a beauty, or so the Empress thought.
And you felt good, until the ground came too close.
Outwardly a sound mind and devastated body;
or was it a day's work done.
I thought you had a PhD, stocks and bonds, all the right moves.
Seems you've flown it all away.

Amanda Ivie

Lenny

There was a Salesman among the many
Who was known by the name of Lenny.
He was a born salesman you see
Who loved to sell things of the highest degree.
Governors, Lawyers, Scholars, were among his class of many
To those he would never sell who had but a penny.
Though a foolish man in his thinking was he
Who all for the love of money would sell his wife to be.
A woman of highest morals the kind you'd like to meet
Not a woman who you would find on the street.
A beautiful woman was she, the fairest in the land
What a pity, he couldn't see past the gold on his hand.
To sell his goods was his motivation and life
So he sold and sold until he lost his good wife.
Friends and years quickly passed him by
Until on his death bed did he lie.
The error of his ways did he finally see
If he could go back a better man would he be.
The moral of this story has one golden rule
To work and work for the love of money leaves you but a fool.

David Miller

Untitled

The vastness of it all.
Is man so small as not to be seen?
Are these the answers from which we glean
Knowledge, wisdom, and above all, truth?
The great is not too big
The small is not too little
There then is space for all to grasp.

Wise man: look into space.
Ignore the feeble indignation
Of our great omniscient race.
Who stops you from this pure and honest joy?
Neither sagely, but forgotten note
Upon which blind men fondly dote,
Nor ridiculing glance
From barbarians in advance.

Diana Mullman

Generations

A new generation has arrived; wipe the sweat off your brow
Time to dust off the rocking chair- you're grandparents now
A new name is added to the Christmas list, one more gift to wrap and
You'll find she fits just perfectly on her grandpa's lap.

Your chest sticks out a little further; your step has different pace.
You look a little different, it's that pride all over your face.
You've done your recollecting in the moments you've had alone
Of when your daughter was your little girl; now she has one of her own.

Where does time escape to- where in the world does it go?
One moment they are on your knee, and then before you know
They're in high school and dating, and you begin to let them go.
It's a natural phenomenon, but God it sure hurts so.

But that's why God makes grand babies to kinda' take their place.
You get to raise them all over again, a similar little face.
You get to tell them what their mother did when she was their age.
The book of life continues on- it just turned the page.

Ray Childers

Kathy Lynne

Five and fearless
riding bareback
on a large Chestnut
hair blowing in the wind —
she gallops, in ecstasy we suspect
The color has faded a bit
Later we learned Ectachrome did that but we had no idea then
her picture would fade the same way she has faded
away from us, on her ride through life. I suspect she is not so fearless now we don't know because her telephone was disconnected a year ago.
The woman who bought her business said "She's bought some acreage in Kern Country"
Exhausted detectives later, our hope is fading that we will again take a picture of her with our hungry eyes

Suzanne S. Camp

Oh How I Miss You

My Yorkshire Terrier Dog
You were so cuddly, so good,
Silky and always within reach.
When I returned home from work
Or elsewhere you met me at the door
Danced and jumped around with joy.
No one greets me now but I am sure
Mimi dog that you are happy in Doggie Heaven.

Charlotte A. Higgins

Promises

I cannot give you it, my love —
I cannot promise that a day will not be dismal,
Or that the walls will not collapse
Or all around become abysmal.
But I do affirmatively say
That, together, we can work it out each day!

Donna Hargrove

Our Own Ability

If there are deeds and duties,
One could see his own heart,
If there are objores and obligations,
One could see by being obliged,

Yet, oneself does not take this form.
Or sees where it leads,
Yet, oneself does know that there is
Or is a destiny for oneself.

Whether young or old, one possesses form.
Whether strong or weak, one sees power.
Whether smart or dumb, one knows itself.
This possession and power creates a humble heart!

If there are deeds and duties,
One can see its power
If there are objores and obligations
One can see its force.

Tomorrows power is today's duties.
Tomorrows form is today's deeds.
One's own mind, the commoner, we share.
But one's own ability, far by is the best.

S. J. O. Hoffman

Sister

Across the land, miles away
My sister will celebrate yet once again another birthday.
In 1941 she arrived, jet black hair and sky blue eyes,
Given talent lingering in her soul, a gifted spirit yet to unfold.
Her beauty lies so deep within, her creativity burst with fever to begin.
It's never too late no matter the year or date,
My sister once again will celebrate.
She amazes me the strength of her will,
Though I know she thinks I'm somewhat of a pill.
Her worst critic I'll probably always be
For I see my Sis and all her beauty
Love you oh yes I do, admire you that's a sure bet too.
Happy Birthday sister dear,
Oh how happy I'm glad you'll be so near.
You have strength only I can imagine
You are my sister and it's your day,
So may all your angels bring you a wish
And with this poem a great big kiss.

Dianne Ritz

Playful Puppyhood

As the puppies matured to become canine toddlers,
They began to wrestle with each other,
Growling playfully, patiently waiting to spring
Into an imaginary attack on an unsuspecting
Relative who would immediately retaliate
By pouncing on the wriggling littermate.
Many times this joust would procure the interest
Of near by kin who would do their best
To involve themselves in the sportive folly.
They continued to play until the game became less jolly
As the puppies began to tire with hunger felt.
Then they would seek their mother and melt
Against her to begin a rhythmic suckling to ease
Their craving for nourishment; nothing, then, could tease
The puppies away from a family gathering
As when they finished, they would nap when suckling
Ended.

Lee Ann Hanson

First Meeting

My world was a shamble,
I knew not what to do.
I was the epitome of lonesome,
Until I met you.

You radiate sunshine,
Understanding and love.
Your wisdom and patience,
A gift from above.

Just being around you,
The dark clouds lifted.
The wisdom you shared,
Was experienced and gifted.

A woman so wise, compassionate and gentle.
Reached out to my heart, with a force so mental.

That made me feel good, about myself within.
I knew without any doubt she was a special friend.

A friendship above all friendships,
With a friend above all friends.
I am so lucky to have the best,
The best for me, heaven sends.

Reo Hagood

Queen Of The Boardwalk

Though she lives in an alley under the pier, this is her castle, her home.
She rules with no malice toward anyone here, while dreaming of Paris and Rome.

She wakes in the morning to warm ocean breezes and sunlit dawns on the waves.
She digs in the garbage for her next meal while the gazes of others she braves.

She's the queen of the boardwalk; the beach is her kingdom; she knows all the sea gulls by name.
The ocean's her diamonds; the sands are her linens; but her head will not lower in shame.

She comes to the restaurant and smiles for a hand-out; the guests look away with disdain.
Their scraps they share with the sea gulls and pigeons, but for her, they only complain.

Kindness from others determines her wages; her treasure's another one's trash.
As life all around her continuously rages, her coals burn to but ash.

Hot summer days still have cold summer nights, especially down by the pier.
The glow from her fire is her only light as darkness envelopes her here.

Alone and forgotten, she cools with the embers, watching the surf pound the shore.
Tomorrow they'll find her, curled by the fire, hungry and cold nevermore.

She was the queen of the boardwalk; the beach was her kingdom; she knew all the sea gulls by name.
Now she's one of the diamonds set in the heavens—her spirit, an eternal flame.

Debbie Bremmon

Untitled

The night grows late and my vision bleary
My body aches and my soul is weary.
My mind is tired, and my thoughts they all cease,
So now I journey to that place of peace.

I close my eyes desiring only rest,
But ever on, my thoughts go ever on.
My thoughts of you can never be expressed.
So here inside, you haunt me till the dawn.

And when the morning awakens my heart,
Your visage rises up before my eyes.
I dread the day that we should ever part.
You are my sun you are my endless skies.
I love you more than you will ever know
Even so, my love for you doth grow.

Jennifer A. Dorsey

Remember Me, I'll Remember You

Remember the phone calls when we'd talk about
anything and everything,
Remember the days we would talk and hold hands,
Remember when we'd lay there and kiss,
Remember when we'd just party with our friends,
Remember me, I'll remember you.
I'll remember the feel of your skin, the way you'd
stare into my eyes, the way you'd touch me and hold me tight.
So please for my health remember me cause to find
out that you forgot me I'd never breathe again,
For even if you hate me, I'll never forget you,
To love you is to cry for not having you and to
forget you is to die,
So remember that I will always love you.

Heather Wirth

Because

And I am happy, so I dance to the songs in my head
Old as the stars, but young as the sunrise
And they tell me...
"You are graceful.
You should be a dancer when you grow up."

And I am thoughtful, so I write of the cascades of rainbows in my head. Varied as rainbow hues, yet universal as rainbows
And they tell me...
"You are poetic.
You should be a writer when you grow up."

And I'm lonely, so I play my guitar and sing of love
Fleeting as spring, yet lasting as time.
And they tell me...
"You are an artist,
You should be a singer when you grow up."

And they don't understand
that when I dance, or write, or sing,
I'm not thinking of future greatness.
I do it because
I must.

Laurel Halloran

A Brand New Day

The sky has opened from it's evening nap.
A new day has awakened.
Swirls of pink and white clouds say, "Good Morning".

The trees open their leaves and stretch in search
for the sun that gives them life, beauty, and strength.

The tiny animals begin to scurry about their daily
chores, as does man.

The flowers unfold their petals and burst open
to show their splendorous array of yellow, red, green
and blue, saying,
"Good mornir world, it's another beautiful,
brand new day.'

Mary D. Yost

Mom

You are very dear to my heart
And you always seem to do more than your part
Throughout the years we have had our ups and downs
But together we always found ways to rebound

I know I haven't been the easiest child
Although compared to some of my friends, I have been rather mild

Life has brought us together as mother and daughter
And if we had it our way, I would live closer to home
But for what ever reason, you know how I love to roam

Even though you are miles away
And we don't talk every day
Good and bad you are always there
And I know you genuinely care

As a child - ask me what I remember most
No, the answer isn't being called Jodi Podi or
eating cocoa and toast

My answer would have to be
Hearing daily how much you love me

Mom, you are very special and I just want to say
I love you and Happy Mother's Day!

Jodi Bennett

Unicorn Blue

It was blue, blue as the eve sky.
Its mane shimmered like the ocean so bold.
The horn all aglow like silvery moon beams.
Its name, Unicorn Blue.

Its bluest of blue coat was soft as an ocean breeze.
Its mane waved like high tide under an evening moon.
Its horn glittered like the skies brightest stars.
Its name, Unicorn Blue.

Its sleek blue body shimmering in the star-lit sky.
The explosion of sound was like thunder in the night.
Its muscular legs moved like lighting from a storm cloud.
Its name, Unicorn Blue.

Jolene Denman

If...You Love

If you talk together,
there is nothing you can't resolve.

If you walk together,
there will always be memories to recall.

If you listen to each other with your heart,
there will be happiness and contentment.

If you look deep into each others eyes and
read between the lines of your souls,
there you will know the true meaning of love.

If you give unconditionally one to the other
with respect, support and encouragement —
you will forever live and love each other.

J. B. Hausig

Laura's Basket

She visits me here in the Rest Home
With the Basket over her arm
And my eyes seen curiously roam
To the basket of goodies like a charm
Home made cookies, ham and cheese
Fruit of all kind, my taste buds to please
Thank you Sis, for letting me be able
To partake of food you share from your table

Esther Eickhoff

Why Don't Ya Talk To God?

How long do you talk to the Lord each day?
How many minutes do you stop and pray?
Have you ever thought about how he talks to you,
And all the things he's brought you through?

No one thanks him enough,
For all the things he's done,
You may not feel his presence,
But he was there when your life begun!

He's wondering when you'll stop and think,
That between he and thee there is a link,
He was your creator, he formed your life with his hand,
You are a very original creation, formed from only the sand.

The next time you find a spare moment,
Get down on your knees and pray,
You may think it no use,
But I bet you'll find plenty to say.

God's ears are always open,
And the clock is ticking fast,
Have a nice long conversation with the father,
And your life is sure to last!

Lorinda Ann Treat

I Am

I am cautious and revealing.
I wonder what places I will attend in the future.
I hear a peaceful breeze whistling through the calm waves of the water.
I see soft colors yet bright ones too.
I want to see my life ahead of me.
I am cautious and revealing.

I pretend to like when times are hostile.
I believe in myself to some extent.
I touch the positive figure of life that will learn to accept me.
I feel strength when my mind comprehends.
I worry when I'm not sure what to expect.
I cry when my feelings are in pain.
I am cautious and revealing.

I understand why there are so many questions and answers in life.
I say peace should always tried to be obtained.
I dream in color about the positive influences of life.
I hope for joy and success.
I am cautious and revealing.

Erin Costello

Alone

I stand alone,
In a massive room
Over canopied by looms of jade and oxlips
Yet grief is overcome by jealousy
Therefore I stand alone.

No human is here to mourn
Across my wanton corpse
It is too elusive to grasp in the claws of Attention
The magnificent is bountiful yet barren
And the cause is .... I Stand Alone

My murder has become a memory, forgotten, misplaced
Yet nobody is here to remember the rape of my life
That is why, I Stand Alone.

The cherubs that used to linger around me
Are now gone from the view of the naked eye
They are not here to comfort me cherish me,
So now, I Stand Alone

So now I rest my mind and body in a wondrous place
That no one else can see in a world filled with greed
and jealousy I Stand Alone

Gina Ground

The Light In The Dark

The men were gathered to plan a crusade,
To rob and ransack, murder and raid.

Their sign was a cross, burning so bright
A lighthouse it seemed; it lit up in the night.

The women were frightened, the children cried
While all the men charged with fury and pride.

Then a knife cut the dark, a shot blast rang out
And the men lay dead, there wasn't a doubt.

The steeds the Klan rode were like leaves on the ground
Their rules were unchanging; their rules wouldn't bend

Then one day it was over and done;
The Klan had lost, freedom had won

The words of our ancestors ring loud and true.
This country's promise is passed onto you.

All men are equal, we all have rights
Now stars are all light up the nights.

Toni Tagliarino

The Cure

It's not of my own choice,
Why I'm so all alone.
Not something I wish to voice,
I wish I could only dial the phone.

That one very special person to be there
For him my love I want deny.
That one person to really care.
Without him I begin to cry.

We seemed so perfect hand in hand,
I love him to smile at me so fine.
Could I be in a dreamin' land?
Or, is he really mine?

His kisses make me melt.
There's one thing always for sure.
These true thoughts I have felt,
For his true Love is definitely
The cure!

Jennifer Anne Burroughs

A Lady With Stars

You were so lovely, all in white,
With your stars and eagle shining bright.
A merry smile, twinkle in your eyes,
Never a frown or even sighs.
Loving, small and large alike, makes might.
Our life is an open book, we read from each day,
Never looking back to say, defeat overrode me... Nay!
Up and about, striving to be one great general on her way.
Serving your country is a job to do,
The eagle is a symbol of strength - of this America our Nation.
So is woman's duty wherever stationed,
Doors close, as others open along the way,
Just stand tall and say!
This America is every woman's land,
If she strives to learn all she can.
To love and understand.

Helen P. Russell

Daddy's Angel!

What is an angel, daddy?
A little girl did ask
Is she small, and is she pretty
Does she sometimes wear a mask
No, he slowly answered
She's none of the above
She's just a little person
Who I will always love
I have her picture, darling
That I carry close to my heart
So I will never be lonely
When we are far apart
Show me her picture daddy
Hold me up so I can see
Oh you must have the wrong picture daddy
That picture is of me

Clara Deas

A Thought

Just for today Lord
I would pray to feel my life in every way
To hear your voice and see your face
In all people...Every race
Just for today then...
I would find love, joy and peace of mind
And know within that all you have created is divine!!!

Gloria A. Stegall

Pretty Donna (The Cricket Song)

There is a silence dwelling
in this house of cards that is my heart.
An emptiness that moves from room to room,
scenting out the perfumed remains of you.
The sweet stink of you hangs in clouds
and breathes through my pillows and sheets.
The moon is large and cold
and I am haunted by these winged dreams.
And I hear the crickets crying my name.
The sun and the moon kiss like strangers
in the cold subways of my heart .
Days pass like sparrows in a storm
and I feel so hollow without your touch.
I have put myself into so many cocoons,
just trying to make this butterfly perfect.
I have dreamed the sun and the moon
and the wind into a wicked thing,
thinking of you. What can I do?

J. Gaither

Strive

Strive to flow with life's stream
Be not afraid of what the dawn will bring
Be not afraid of friend or foe
To the latter do not cling

Strive to have patience
The good fortune of clear thought
Seek wisdom - listen well
Be not angry or distraught

Strive to face life day by day
Reflecting bits of love
Like dew drops of sweet nectar
Pouring from above

Strive to waste not one
Precious moment of the day
Promise to live life to its fullest
Have fun along the way.

Dorothy Carver

Parents At A Children's Hospital

These are the eyes run dry of tears
Searching for hope
Closed in unmatched fervent prayer

They are the smiles soft and empathetic
Inadequate lips quivering as they try to comfort
Rejoicing- when "one" child goes home

These are the hands reaching forth
Through cold steel bed rails
Stroking an arm a hand or a head

These are the lives torn and scarred
Decluttered to but one priority
Frozen in time

These are those forced to study the foreign language "Medicine"
So as to understand and double check
Would be magicians, gladly lying down in their child's stead.

These are the parents at a children's hospital
Bound they are - to one another
For the sake of children

Sandra Lee Baker

I Loved You This Way

Today and tomorrow, forever and a day
We promised to love one another this way
Through sickness and health, through joy and pain
Through good times and bad times
Through sunshine and rain
I promised to love you with all my heart
I promised to love you till death do we part
Our lives are now joined, the path has been set
We'll walk it together in love till we get
To the end of the road where then we will stand
And watch the sun set, hand in hand
We'll look at the memories and then we can say
I did what I promised
I loved you this way

Deborah R. Nelson

A Good Homemaker

In order to be a good homemaker,
just start the day with a pray'r
Then cooking, cleaning, baking,
doing everything with care.
The children must be cared for,
with bathtub, toothbrush and bowl.
But whatever you do, dear mother,
please do not forget their soul.
Teach them about the Savior,
while they sit upon your knee
When they are older, they'll remember
that He died to set them free.
When they learn that the Heavenly Father
sent his Son to die on the cross
To pay for the sins of all mankind
they'll want to help with the cause.
The work on the cross was finished
by the suffering, sinless Lamb,
But we should point them to Jesus,
He was sent by the great "I am".

Violet I. Varud

What The World Has Become

In this world today, people are starting to fade away.
Kids are dying, while mothers are crying
and the society keeps on trying.
It's so hard to live in this kind of life,
whenever you walk down a street,
you have to worry whether a kid's carrying a knife.
Back in the days, people had lots of fun,
but now all kids think about are shooting guns.
I used to think that was cool, but now I realize I was a fool.
People that you choose for friends,
you think they'll be with you until the end.
Maybe the ones that are true,
but the ones in gangs, they'll come after you.
You'll always consider them as a friend,
but eventually it'll all come to an end.
You'll make one mistake and do something wrong.
After that, your life ain't going to be long,
and again you thought they were your friend, but all they
thought about you was just somebody else soon to be dead.

Gina Grant

Summer Exchange

Summer is a gift in June,
To be exchanged at Christmas time
A larger size is what's called for,
With bright warm colors to adore;
And, should the fit be ever so slight,
I'll take it back till they get it right.

Shirley J. Wozniak

"Contemporary Court"

Two all beef patties
and a clogged heart;
Dinner for two
but no wine to start.

The romantic date
lost its passion;
Two to tango
is now old fashion.

No knights in armor.
No chivalry.
No fancy dates.
No dreaming of me.

The sweet kiss good night,
now sleep over;
Flowers meant love,
not any longer.

Cinderella's lost
lacking her shoe,
and so she died
for what He didn't do.

Two sesame buns
and a stale soul;
Conversations
Weathered grey and old.

Women's lib took all
Now she goes dutch
Life's hard without
the "innocence" crutch.

No pure princesses.
No home-made meals.
No glass slippers.
No Avon on wheels.

Once a jacket worn
showed property;
All beds now shared
With no loyalty.

Prince Charming can't be
Without frog faith,
And so he died
'cause She made him wait.

Amanda Linton

Wayne's Fiftieth Birthday

Your hair has turned loose, your teeth have come out,
Your stomach has expanded it seems.
You still want to do the things you once did,
But they're a lot easier in dreams.

Some men despair when they lose their hair,
or get bent out of shape when it gray's.
You know you've grown old, you don't have to be told,
when what used to take minutes, takes days.

There's no need to cry, the years have flown by,
it could almost seem a bit tricky.
For when you went to bed last night, you were just 49;
but this morning old boy
You're 50!!!!!

J. Franklin Turner

I Lost A Love

You left me blowing in the wind. You left me there.
To whom it may concern, I laid and mourned for your touch, your care.
But you left me there.
What did I do? I can't feel my sorrows.
I can't touch you or feel your compassion and warmth.
You left me there, blowing in the wind, wild and free,
With no care or soul to confront.

Why? Just blowing in the wind, I couldn't understand the light that took my love.
You left me there to mourn my death and your new life.
I flew to a place of villagers and no faith.
What did I do?
Deathly drowning in my own fear
And so afraid to go after my dreams and to run to you.

Please, I beg you, set me free from these chambers of death upon all of us.
I want to blow in the wind, freely.
I am lost without you.
Please, just one touch that's all I ask from you.
Open your hand and I will fly, but I will come back to set you free.
You will not leave me here. I beg to differ.
I will blow in the wind free again and again.

Jenevieve A. Gardner

No Reason To Fear

I felt so confused inside; no place to run, no safe place to hide.
Your world is traveling so much faster than mine

At times our paths never seem to cross
There are days when I feel that
If I don't catch up I will be left behind.

My feelings are so hard to put into words
For they have grown from the very depths of my heart

At times I am very much afraid
That when the time comes for you to leave
Time, distance, and people will make all
The feelings you have for me depart.

When you left today I thanked God
For sending you my way
How did he know that you were the one I needed so?

In your arms I found my safe place to run
Through your gentle words I found my safe place to hide
Every tear I cried all the despair I felt inside
Disappeared when I saw the loving, understanding look in your eyes

Tears of sorrow now tears of joy
You knew just what to say to drive all my fears away

Nita E. Richardson

"Through The Eyes Of Love"

One night I was walking down the street.
I stumbled into a man with only blisters on his feet.

He had no coat, and only paper for a bed.
The night was so cold, his hands were frozen red.

I stood there for a moment as people walked by.
I could see a fear in him, as a tear filled my eye.

He just glanced at me without saying a word.
Then he closed his eyes, when from behind us footsteps we heard.

I gave him my last quarter and proceeded down the street.
In a faint distance I heard not two but four little feet.

I turned around and could see nothing through the fog.
I walked a little closer and saw it was a dog.

The man shook my hand and thanked me for the money.
With a tear in his eye he said, It will be just enough
to buy some food for my dog "Honey."

I will never forget that man in my dreams.
For now I've seen what love truly means.

Carrie A. Steffen

What Is Spring?

Spring is the lawn suddenly green,
And a boy out pushing the mowing machine.
Spring is Mom, with her packets of seeds,
And Dad, with his hoe, attacking the weeds.
Spring is the blue sky, and blowy white clouds,
Blustery rainstorms still in their shrouds.
Spring is the marbles that click in boys pockets,
And rings on girls chains, next to their lockets.
Spring is a girls shrill squeal of alarm
At worms squirming 'round, after a storm.
Spring is the breeze that carries a kite
Into the stratosphere, 'most out of sight.
Spring is out fishing in cool little brooks
Away from all papers and pencils and books.
Spring is the wiggly noise in a classroom,
With teacher impatiently low'ring the boom.

Mary Eileen Drake

My Family Tree

My Family Tree with numerous branches.
Many in finery while others in patches.

Centuries change the family lines,
Weaving around each other of exotic kinds.

Members leave for parts unknown,
Others lives are set in stone.

Finding one's roots is a full adventure,
Travels of freeman and those indenture.

Immersed in history the stories unfold,
Of members perhaps who were knights of old.

The common men who wished to pray.
Raised their families in God's just way.

What a splendid sight for me to see,
When I behold the tales of my family tree.

Margaret Anne Mosby

God And All

By the window, washing dishes
and contemplating wishes,
I looked out to behold
Three rays of sunlight, soft as gold.

They had come from heaven's dome
To grace this place I call home.
They sparkled through shadow of the trees
To light the doves taking ease.

As the doves loved in the sand
God came and hovered all around
I was caught up in the moment's awe-
To become one with God and all.

In that moment, so divine,
All of heaven had been mine.
As I reached for a dish they were done.
And the wishes—they were gone.

Evelyn Smith

Slowly Into The Night

The air is strange and eerie tonight.
The wind blows from the east
howling, screaming, piercing the dark night.
The day has been a mere feast.
All goes slowly creeping into the night.

The sky is no longer a shining jewel
it has been replaced by an ominous face.
The darkness is its only source of fuel
the shadows of the moon find their place.
All begins to slowly slip into the night.

The night warriors arrive under the guidance of the moonlight.
They look up and pray to the rising thunder,
while the rest of the world takes refuge in fright.
All fall slowly into the firm grasp of night.

The red blood of morning rolls over the tall peaks,
the reign of night hood slowly makes way for day.
The halo of stardust and moonlight begin to leak.
Nightfall, defeated, suggestively waits for the time when
daylight begins to stray.
Then all will slowly perish in the night.

Kendra Johnson

"Dad"

You would be proud, here or above, your life goes on.
Through children raised, you passed it on.
They in turn live your lessons, grandchildren,
now parents surviving the tensions.
Fulfilling the goals with their own expressions,
they carry the treasure and live the lessons.
Having within the memories and purpose,
the goals and desires march to the surface.
Cherish the moments, they may be too few,
as a new generation experience and do.
Your children are raised, you've passed on your love.
Oh you would be proud, from here or above.
Now there are great grandchildren learning and loving.
I feel with you pride of sharing and the knowledge of caring.
You and I are proud, here and above,
as all of the children are raised with our love.
Your life goes on, it's given away.
To the children who follow day after day.
You would be proud, from here or above, your life goes on.
Through children raised, you passed it on.

Judith E. Wilmington

The Voice

As I was walking alone on a wet sandy beach
I looked to the stars and cried,
"What have I done to deserve this pain!"
Then turned to the ocean and sighed.

A loud thunderous voice came from the waters and said these words to me
"You seem to be hurt and so full of sorrow,
and for that I will let you see."

The reflection of stars became visions of pain
as I saw your face appear.
I paused for a moment, then proceeded to ask,
as your eyes were filled with tears.

"Voice of the waters, this reflection I see, what does it truly mean?"
He said, "See with your heart and not your eyes.
For I assure you, this isn't a dream."

Silence approached and again it spoke. "Beware you are not deceived.
For this pain that you speak isn't delivered to you,
but from you and as she receives."

And when night turned to day as I was walking away,
I looked to the sky and cried,
"I promise, my love, that never again will I ever leave your side!"

George Temores

An Ocean Of Time

Your love echoes like an ocean's waves,
Never ending.
Turbulent at times,
calm and comforting others,
Sand an ocean craves,
Love your heart desires,
Your hearts beat together,
In a rhythm, a hymn of joy,
Like an ocean that has been there for years,
Your love has lasted for this,
For fifty good years,
Fifty years and two sons two daughters in law later,

You're still here,
Still in the silence, the waves,
A love shared by two,
You and he.

Alexandra Freiday Maiero

Untitled

The rain is not falling
I still have time
it's getting cloudy out
I can't decide
the first drop falls quickly...how will I choose?
The next one tries harder, going nowhere
it will never catch up
hard decision
how will it ever reach?
I have no hope
the first drop hits the ground
too much trauma
surrounded by many
time too rapid
it is getting confused
I am too slow
it will trickle away so out of reach
out somewhere new
I'm defeated

Elizabeth D. Andrzejewicz

Life

(Teenage)
Mom and Dad it's time to fear,
My teenage life is almost here!

Things will change on me everywhere,
Body piercings here and there.

Garbage for music and trash for clothes,
Black nail polish on my toes.

Funky hats and outrageous styles,
Hair that reaches a million miles.

See me bungee jump off a cliff,
I'll be on the ground in just a jiff.

Movies and concerts, stuff like this,
Will all be ended with a good-night kiss.

Teenage life will be lots of fun,
Teenage life will be #1!

Laura T. Smith

Breaking Peace

Tomorrow is another day, he thought, he prayed
As he sat there waiting for that day wanted

He survived another dark and terrifying night
He shivered at the thought of waiting to fight

Why was he there? Why should he kill?
He didn't know the dead man that lay there still

Sorrow for that man was what he felt, of course
Life should be simple, no ugly deaths or unburied corpses

He would be the next to perish, and why not?
His best friend died yesterday with a devastating shot

One shot it took, to the head, and it was over
Could it be that easy? Could his pain be over?

Just as daylight broke, so did the peace
The long awaited battle with the Vietnamese

The fighting lasted for about three hours
No man fighting there thought of "Flower Power"

One man's fate, like all the others
Was met that day, his life was over

Is that peace? Still the question remains
Who won this war?...ask these men

Jacqueline Ivy Jones

All Things In Time

The world is so very full of greed
Everyone wants more than they need

The harder you look, the less you find
But you must remember all things in time

You fall quickly in love and get carried away
But further down the road you must pay

In a hurry you want wealth and fame
But without happiness you end up feeling just the same

You take advantage of a friend that's on the ground
not realizing that you too, can be knocked down

Yet the fate of tomorrow is in man's mind
But you must remember all things in time.

Nadine Tiller

New In School

I wander down the halls,
and try to find my way.
I'm all new at school,
it's my very first day.
The other kids all walk in groups,
while I am by myself.
I open up my locker door
and put my books up on the shelf.
I walk slowly into the room
and quickly find my desk.
A boy is snickering from behind;
I can tell he'll be a pest.
The teacher steps up in front of the room,
I notice his very big ears.
He drones on about things I don't understand;
this will be a very long year.

Allison Kimball

Who Am I?

Who am I and why am I here?
What is my purpose? It just isn't clear.
Why do I feel so lost and alone,
With a husband, children, family, and a home?
What is this emptiness I feel inside,
This aching and longing that can't be denied?
What is this need that won't go away,
That keeps growing stronger with each passing day?
Why does each day bring such and dread,
When I should be enjoying life instead?
The answer is actually quite simple, you see.
I must come to know the real and true me.

Roseanna Becraft-Goforth

Wonder

When the wind blows and the flowers sneeze,
Are those that are living enjoy the breeze?
Do some stand back while others stare,
"What is happening over there?"
Are the hills ever angry, do flowers ever cry,
Why would they even try?
And if the sun sheds tears and the moon sheds rain,
What would happen to our world again?
So why does the crow cry and the raven cheer,
Do they do it all out of fear?
As the winter mourns and the sun hides away,
I wonder what is happening to our world today.
I will always wonder and might never know,
What the world holds for all to grow.

Katie Bronars

Lady Delight

A delightful night from the lady in white
Who crossed the stage and spoke the page
Written so long ago

She invited me in and it was then
I examined the verse of the Belle of Amherst

I sipped the cup of tea she offered to me
And mentally stored and recipe
For black cake
Absorbed in thought I caught myself in 1883
And glanced towards the garden's gate
And waited with her for master's form

Laughter and matter light-hearted like baby's breath and
Important as red and blue bird chorus
Jane set before us
A gift presented twice
Once from the fragile Belle of Amherst
Once more from the Thespian lady delight

Vicki McCleery

C.N.A.'s Heartache

I hear an elderly woman crying. I see her husband
standing by her side. The fear in their hearts
is all too clear, both afraid of how a life will
end. He takes hold of her hand, kneels down
and prays for God to help him linger on.
Somehow, some way, he knows his life
will never be the same. As a CNA I see
these things so every morning I pray
God give me strength so I can be strong,
give me patience so I can be kind and never
speak out of line. But most of all, help my
heart to heal when you decide to take
an angel home and give my heart the
faith it needs to carry on.

Patricia D. Gragg

One More Look

I see a little fade in the sky
that used to be the sun rise on a snowy morning.
Orange, pink, light blue and dark blue.
Think, think, just think how it would be,
Just nature and you.

Then it changes so you can barely see it.
The clouds of white come over the far away trees.

Then there are big cars and poisonous pollution,
and more and more people and big stores,
and huge malls and long roads
that used to be nice and quiet life
and wonderful nature and peace.

Just one more look
just one to say good bye.

Nick Roberge

Untitled

Listen to the wind, and whisper to me
the song of your heart, that sweet melody
let me in to share what you seek.
The rapture of the heart comes flowing forth
Listen to the wind, and whisper to me
the earth, the song and I are one.
We sing to you

Peace is our song

Donald Vernon Ward

Old Age, My Uncle

To sail the ocean at a tender age
In search of a life of things
unknown to the boyhood visions of the fatherland,
I knew my dreams had wings
And there were hills and fields and
High places of state and large domain
That I could put my heart and mind into,
and in time, attain.
From Ivy Halls to humble sheep where the
lonely prairie held a future fresh and new
The fields and homesteads yielded bounteous
hoards and a life with prominence and
Flourishing stately offices and country wide renown.
Now alone and clutching life's abundance,
Who is worth the sharing?
It is mine!

Signora Kamback

The Momma

It's that rancid, smell, sweetly that serves as the alarm clock.
It wafts around stump and trunk as a serpent encircling its prey.

Sunrise.

Like the caressing hand of a friend turned lover, the first golden
rays gently touch the shoulder of the Basin and she stirs, slowly,
but the touch is felt and life shudders through her body.

With a toss of the Spanish moss that serves as her tresses,
the Basin waits as the warning rays quicken her.

First the leaves respond, the trunks feels the caress and transmit
that delicious thrill to the roots. The water laps at the Cypress,
warning, warming.

Her friends awake, rubbing themselves from their nocturnal world
into the golden daylight.

They grunt, squawk, hiss and growl. They live as She lives.
Natural, alive.

The smell fills the nostrils. It's not death or decay, it's life in
its natural state.

Alive.

G. Gardener Garrison

Born Not Unto You

You didn't hear my heart
You didn't feel my touch
I wasn't felt within you
I didn't share your breath
But I have become a part of you
You have heard me cry and tried so hard to understand why
You have listened with love and
told me to believe in the power from above
Even though I was not born unto you
I give you praise
You are my mother in all ways

Deb Peters

O My Way Show-er

You showed me that getting older is not a sin
It's just complicated by the world we're in
Of course, life doesn't always work the way we want it to
and this in itself can take a toll on you
Yet, what's fascinating to me
is that you still continue to tote that barge and lift that bale
All the while pondering to what avail
So getting older is not a sin
It's just complicated by the world we're in

Lovetta Davis

Life Struggles

Lightning strikes across the sky,
Thunder returns and starts to cry.
I sit up in my bed,
Watch them and shake my head.
Afraid to move, afraid to speak,
Hearing the thunder as it begins to shriek.
Over and over,
Again and again,
When will they stop and see an end?
The pain it caused is my only friend.
They don't know what an impact it caused,
Listen - silence, finally they paused.
Now they have divorced and gone away,
To separate corners, I hope and pray.

Janie Moss

"Why"

"Many people drown in the world's stupidity, others just wallow in it."
Can there be a space
In your mind?
A space
reserved for a moment
in time
When the light
will shine through,
And you will have
Eternal Life.
Why can't you understand
This is for you
The one
Who threatens Humanity
each day?
From one soul
To another
Why?

Kathrine Geis

Art Show

There was no sound——
Yet, just a deep
And just as sweet
As Cello's notes
Or Violins'
Where those tones
of violet,
Of mauve,
And blue!

Or yellow-green
Like sunlight on new leaves...

Each blend of color
Was magic to my eyes, and filled my being
Just as chords of music can grip the soul,
And lift me to a world of beauty
Where hue on hue,
And tone on tone,
In many varied patterns
Create a stirring symphony!

Mildred J. Haynes

White Moon

Accustomed to the sunlit atmosphere,
and as delicate as the thin cloud
that skims the western horizon-
the moon in half-size
hangs against the calmness of
morning sky.
But why, oh moon, do you hang so
pale, yet at the same time, so stanch in
all your beauty, and apparently, so
unmindful of your diminished light?
In your brief daytime hour, are you
conserving energy for another moon,
or simply hesitant to share with the sun
the luxurious yellow grace, you give
so explicitly to the night?

Ruth Summers

Time

Time is ever fleeting, always running out
Expending it efficiently is not an easy route

Sixteen waking hours in every single day
Choosing how to use them is a game we all must play

No hard fast rules to follow, no study course to take
The sea of time engulfs us and we learn to navigate

Each one of us is different, our space in time unique
Squander it, or use it well, do your own critique

Each new days beginning gives us all the same amount
You're on the road to winning when you learn to make it count

Norma Cunningham

A Gambler's Prayer

Dear Lord - let me win with just one spin - as I pull the handle and wait for it to settle - those little ole "7's".
The payoff I'll fail to keep, just to show I am not cheap.

Oh Lord - I am as selfish as you can see, but - I am harming no one, only me.
With all the money in my bucket - I really could say that nasty word "yucket" and take the money and "tuck it."

But being human and not too bright, I will watch my winnings go out of sight.
Now I am a little uptight as each coin goes out of sight as I try to recoup with all my might - boy, am I uptight!

Now home and to bed, I bow down my head, as my prayers are said:
Now I lay me down to sleep, why in hell that money didn't I keep?
Then I start to weep; and damn it, I can't sleep.
I'll get even, you wait and see.
You think I am fooling?
Just watching me as I try again next week.
After all, I've got that gambler's streak!

Slot Machine Myrt

My Special Friend

I have this very special friend
He's always there for me when I need someone
If I'm feeling down I know he'll listen
He's even there when I need no one
When I think of him I smile and glisten
I talk to my special friend everyday
My friend even talks to me at times
Sometimes he helps me to dream of the beach and bay
When I'm feeling low he plays me chimes
My special friend's name is God.

Tonya Vaughan

Untitled

Sometimes I'm alone, and sometimes I'm not.
Other times I'm afraid, but not of the dark.
Right now I'm confused, from the loneliness and fear.
But later on I'll be consoled by friends who are near.
Tomorrow will make me better in ways I don't know.
Today is almost over and another almost gone, but not yet.
Tomorrow will be better so don't get upset.
Today is a trail of hardships and pain.
Tomorrow is victory of friendship I've gained.
Sometimes I'm alone, but mostly I'm not.
Other times I'm afraid but now I'm not.
Yesterday I was confused about what tomorrow might bring.
Today I'm consoled by being me.

Dennis R. Lizotte

Just Us

Precious memories guys,
that summer at the cabin-
our bleached ponytails tracing our trail on the river.
Hardly rowing,
just drifting, drifting —
stopping to marvel at an eagle's nest crowning a barren tree.

And the sun would slip behind the trees,
creating shivering charcoal motifs on the water,
only to shatter them with brilliant fire-colored fingers.

Meanwhile,
our giggles echo between the forest walls-
arguing back and forth, back and forth.
And when the bend in the river swept us to familiar water,
we pulled our experience to shore,
wrung it out,
and dried it over the warmth of a campfire.

Jennifer Busse

One For Dancing

Oh let me tell you love, of my desire,
to rescue you into my arms.
We've never had a chance,
to dance upon the blue glass.

My thoughts will slide on whispered winds,
to join inside your gentle head.
Your gentle, resting head,
I will never leave again.

I'll take you up on sighing waves,
we'll dance across their silenced graves,
into their stretching plains,
across the empty space,
through time,
when we arrive,
the night will shine.

(i've never been one for dancing
but i've always loved you,
near or far,
here
i'd take on the universe for you.)

Philip Boyd

Robert Browning

Just for a moment I tarried with Browning,
Felt the warm glow of his turbulent heart;
Laughed with his laughter, rejoiced in his power,
Knew that his fancy was ever apart;
Knew that his fancy would ever be wandering
Far from the tiresome burdens of life;
Fancy would fill him with symbols of glory,
Heedless of misery, worry, or strife.

Victor M. Earle Jr.

One Child Abused

An innocent child speaks his mind
A father approaches from behind
A slap across the soft sweet cheek
The child is helpless; too young, too weak.
No one to run to, no one at all
No place to hide, no mother to call

The father is sober as the next day's here
But the child still, is filled with fear
He hides in horror without making a sound
He awaits in the corner till the moment he's found
Not knowing what he's done, the child's confused
This is one situation for one child abused.

Tamara T. Perlin

Designed To Kill

The sapper with a rolling fertilizer bomb
Blasts away the silence of the morning calm
Frantic rescue workers, many a dad or a mom
Digging through rubble with a prayer or a psalm

From slavic sounding places after the cold war
Chemicals, nukes, the ability to slay more and more
The news media showcases the terror and the gore
From the streets to even the White House door.

Fired workers and angry souls now killing machines
Subway stations, schoolyards, other crowded urban scenes
Revenge on "the system" by any or all means
Is it learned behavior or carried in our genes?

Whether for political gain or a cheap thrill
Programmed by a society designed to kill
Cadavers cold and stiff, corpses lifeless and still
Anger to vent, headlines to make, blood to spill

William G. Ikerd Jr.

Alzheimers, The Thief In The Night

Alzheimers comes like a thief in the night
And preys on victims from all walks of life.
It may be a president, a movie star, a mom or a dad,
And the heartaches it causes are so very sad.
At first you don't notice that it has snuck in;
You think they're just forgetful every now and then.
As the symptoms get worse with each passing day
You just ask God to show you the way.
Sometimes you laugh at the things they say and do
Because if you didn't you'd cry the whole day through.
When you've done all you can to show you care,
You must seek help for the heavy burden you bear.
It seems so hard and cruel to leave them in a home,
Not knowing how much love and care they'll be shown.
Alzheimers effects everyone who gets in its wake,
And every year more lives it will take.
When the thief is done and God shows his hand,
He'll lead his children to the Promise Land.

Al Cade

Nostalgia

I close my eyes and see today
the Mohawk's lazy winding way
Thru rolling hills so richly green
And know their spring has come, unseen.
The road is so familiar there. My mind anew
recalls the clear sweet beauty of each view.
My childhood's eye still marks the far-off tree
against the sky-the same-thru all these years-to see.
Yet, could we but return a summer's day
Along the dusty old dirt road, our eager way,
Would we still find our world's scope, so,
The fairy-ribbon Mohawk far below?

Barbara Stoughton Carlisle

Transcendent Descendence

Crashing clouds,
Human crowds,
cacophony of car horns;

Ascend to heaven through a subterranean door.

Pigeons, planes and potholes
silent portraits for the imprisoned
in skyscraper jails;

Freedom begins at the bottom rung
of an unstable corporate ladder.

Bright, shining sun
Darkens our life
with ultra-violet penetrating rays;

The height of beauty is a perfect suntan.

Angelic guides descend trumpeting a message
drowned by the beat of clicking heels
rapidly going nowhere;

Infinity is vertical.

Patrick Scheidel

Flowers In The Meadow

My petals soft as a fine silk.
The roots of my soul deep in the ground.
I breath the fresh air.
Enjoy the view.
For I am the Mona Lisa of nature.
I dance smooth and slyly.
The wind is my music.
I smell of a sweet fragrance.
I symbolize an individual person.
I am original.
Different from any other flower.
And like people, I bud
I bloom
I wither
I die.
My body my roots rest in the ground.

Jessica L. Farley

My Lady My Lady

I must now believe, to nuture your soul is my destiny,
as my heart in the body is claimed for thee. Shall time
pass forever upon silver bells, cloaked within darkness,
amid winter swells, where the doves nest in snow,
their love in repose, atop cold crystal shells.

Please touch of these dreams, that I reserve for thee,
which I wrap and lie under the linen trees, there my breath
circles lightly embracing your flesh, over your bosom,
now naked in dress, with this love as my shield,
our humanity now mirrored, shall coddle in rest.

With your blood on fire, too match that in my veins,
compete in this union love whispers our name. Your scent on my
skin claims this heart in my hands, a spiritual bond,
of woman and man, filtered beyond meadows in green,
flowers within sensual streams, imprints unto eternal plan.

To nurture in love's dual sanity, a fledging form of eternity,
I draw strength from you through completion of we. I give you
this name with rings layed to hands. This child lays in waiting,
soon three souls shall stand. A miracle test of creation anew,
awakens my faith, this miracle bond, now cradled in you.

Barry Gene Bowser

We Wonder Why

We wonder what the reason is,
why we live and love and ponder.
And travel life's mysterious road,
Not knowing what comes after,

The road has many twists and turns,
And we seldom know the reason.
I like to think it is because,
Life also has its seasons.

From season to season the days are linked,
With hills and fields unfolding,
Where a rainbow bends to a peacocks whim,

And with a tranquil mind and a heart sublime,
We can perceive God's blending.

And we wonder why.

Joseph M. Marciante

I Wonder

I wonder when I sit and think,
I wonder where did it all begin,
I wonder how I got where I am,
I wonder why I'm the way I am,
I wonder just who am I,
I wonder if I'm the person I should be,
I wonder was man's hand the maker of me,
I wonder did they change God's plan for me,
I wonder what's in store for me,
I wonder so when I think,
I wonder, I wonder, I wonder.

Wendi June Medina

Dark And Light

Travelling through the forlorn tunnel
He stumbles in its darkness
Lost without a guide.

Born from the evils of the night
They shadowed his steps within the tunnel
Demons of his dark imagination.

Fright and terror filled his heart
As darkness seeped into his soul
Controlling his thoughts and emotions.

Suddenly light flooded onto his path
Chasing demons from his soul
Overpowering the evil of his way.

Embracing the virtuous light
He stepped from the depths of darkness
And followed the guiding light to the outside world.

Rebecca Henley

Moving Day

When you pack your household goods
as you move out today
you will leave something behind
that you can't take away...

And like a thief that steals in the night
you will pack away
something that belongs to us
for which you did not pay...

For all the lives that you touched
and the friendships that have grown
you will leave a lot of love behind
and ours will have a new home...

Ruth E. Guttromson

Run

The beast growls at my dark inner-self.
But I hear nothing but the wind howl.
I can't find myself.
I'm missing in a dark void.
Empty is the room.
Roaring is the beast.
There is an indecent glow.
But I'm afraid to run towards the light.
I'm afraid of what I don't know.
Help me.
I'm scared.
It's morning now, I'm tired.
I think I'm going to sleep forever.

Justin Lillie

"Grandma"

For almost a century I've walked this earth and each year I look back to the day of my birth learning to crawl and then to walk Soon after that I learned to talk.

As life progressed on I became a wife and a mother to know this feeling of joy there is no other I gave freely to my children and nurtured them all prepared them for life so they wouldn't stumble or fall.

To let each one go it was hard from the start cutting the strings still tugs at my heart I wanted to cry out wanting each one to stay But each had to go and make their own way.

As time marched on, a grandmother I became my children begat children to each child a name as grandchildren aged they bore young and time moved on my image in the mirror told me that my time was gone.

A simple prayer I prayed to God and just asked him why
Contentment filled my soul as I listened to his reply
You've had a good life as you lived here on earth
The one thing I promised on the day of your birth.

My heart now grows weary I've had a good past life has been good but good things don't last my time here has ended and I don't worry about things for today is the day my soul took on wings.

Charles Bell

The World Needs Love

Yesterday is dead and gone,
Today is filled with sorrow.
I pray to God for a better world,
If we should see tomorrow.

Death and destruction is at all time high.
It matters not who takes a life,
so wastefully we die.

Our homes are filled with T.V. talk shows,
gambling, sex and, doom.
If I could only fax to heaven,
I'd reserve myself a room.

The end of time is drawing nigh,
Oh Savior, please come soon.
Gabriel come blow your horn,
my ear awaits your tune.

If we could live at peace on earth
and love our fellow man,
I'd rather stick around this place
'Cause then life would be grand...

David A. Johnson

I Love A Certain Lady

Do I need to say that she
is someone who is beautiful
and wonderful to me? I love her
dainty manner and the color of her eyes.
I love the words she whispers
and what she says aloud.
And her charming company
for this I am forever proud.
She is my inspiration in
everything that I do and a
dream that comes true
I love a certain lady
if you want to know the truth

She is my loving wife!

Mary Perlow

A Sensual Thing... A Single Rose

It is pleasing to the eyes... forever.
Although it may not be as beautiful to the rose as the original,
its fragrance can always be remembered.
Listen carefully. The sound is quiet beauty, tender and sweet and
filled with the music of nature. It does not have to be audible
to be heard.
Feel how delicate it is.
One cannot taste a rose but one can imagine the delicate flavor.
A sensual thing... a beautiful lady.

Don Poole

If I Were Not Me

If I were not me, I'd want to be a tree,
For my uses to man always come free,

What can I do, just being a tree?
Then just read on and you shall see.

Sit in my shade and enjoy my flowers
For they may soon be fruit of many flavors.

My wood man must have, he makes much use of me.
From what would birds do, if there were no tree?

From my bark cures are made, and what of my sap?
Have you ever tasted syrup from a maple trees tap?

Some want to cut or burn me down,
But I would only return to the ground

To fill my role in God's great plan
To be of service to every man.

My secret is in giving, giving,
So that all else can go on living.

So now you ask
If I were not me, what would I be?
Why nothing else, but just a tree.

Inez Formby

Square Pegs

Our space, carved so round,
With so much room to grow;
We don't live tied and bound,
But we exist to cast a show.
 In giggles and grins we follow the past
 To the spot we'll try to make our part last.

Square pegs, in a circular world,
Where no one fits just right.
The perfect dimensions, never unfurled,
But we're always expected to put up a fight
 In dresses and suits we march to the place
 Where we'll lie, under flowers and grace.

John Walker

A Popular Death

I wished I lived in the 60's
Where love, peace and drugs, and happiness were their life.
Then that day came,
The day when tears fell from heaven and the sky above.
It was the day he could have been saved,
Instead no one tried when they heard the ear-piercing fire of the gun.
It was like a disease that hit the nation,
And even the news were shedding some tears.
It was when music was over forever,
And even God was more popular.
The earth cracked with anger,
And the oceans, streams, and lakes overflowed with burning tears,
Then the air was surrounded by heavy-hearted screams that rang.
That day and for days on,
The world was always carried up on your shoulders.
That was 15 years ago today on December 8, 1980,
When John Lennon died of a hail of bullets outside of his apartment.
It was in Central Park, New York a place he called home,
But in our hearts he will always stay,
So will his songs, and every little detail of life he's taught us.

Kelly Clute

Myself

Too long my eyes were closed
Too afraid to open my eyes - to the friendship - to the trust

I opened my eyes and there you were - standing before me - as always
Your arms opened wide - waiting for the time

You've always been there

Too long my heart was cold
Too afraid to trust - to love

You melted the ice and there you were - standing before me - as always
Your arms opened wide - waiting for the time

You've always been there

Too long I forgot - Too busy
Too concerned with others - no concern for myself

Standing before me - as always
Yours arms opened wide - waiting for the time

To open my eyes
To melt ice on my heart - To show me myself

To open me to all the possibilities
To show me the experiences - To show me the wonders

Of myself - The person you saw - hidden behind a mirror - the
 reflection of me

Who I really am - Who I've always been

Theresa McDonnell

Where The Eagles Fly

Mesmerizing reflections, upon snow capped horizons -
spellbound, in glowing orange - sunrises,
wild flora, splashing - basking green meadows,
in cradles of ancient mountains, abounding in singing forests,
so fragrant - with pine.

All - hailed, by fluted mountain warblers -
perched, echoing... against cascading slopes,
while heavenly sculpted steeds, climb afternoon thunderclouds,
breaking loose nectar, into encompassing - roaring streams,
winding - endlessly, in contented space.

Curious creatures, dart in and out of sacred sanctuaries,
flashed - by shadowed, soaring - feathered pilots,
creating intermingled thoughts, caught up in timeless memories,
bewitching fantasies, bathed by warm winds -
sinking my mind, deeper and deeper, into the hypnotic conjure,
of Rocky Mountain magic, in America, on a path into the sky.

Robert Warren Jaye

Logic

In golf, after age sixty, so it appears,
One loses ten yards each additional year.
Those two hundred yard drives that were so much fun,
Are down to one-ninety at age sixty-one.
At age sixty-five, forty more you have lost,
You're now at one-fifty and counting the cost.
At seventy years you're starting to worry,
A mere hundred yards is all you can carry.
Another ten years you'll think you've hit bottom,
You're down to zero but it's ad infinitum.

So what's to be done? Now don't rant and rave,
Use the old logic! The day can be saved.
Turn one-eighty, aim Away from the hole,
You'll drive Minus ten yards straight toward the pole.
As the years march by, don't look to the past,
Keep hitting backward you're Gaining ground fast.
And when at the century mark you arrive,
You'll again be hitting two hundred yard drives.
So don't be discouraged there's ever a way,
Logic is logic that's all I can say.

Allen J. Rubenkonig

A Friend

A friend is one who will be there,
who loves and cares for you.
Helps you when you are confused,
and don't know what to do.

Or is that what a friend is for,
sometimes I often ask.
These days, it's hard to find a friend,
It seems just like a task.

It's hard to find someone who seems
to want to be a friend.
It seems like they don't even want
to have a hand to lend.

I know I have a family,
who's always there for me.
They care for me and love me
when I'm in a time of need.

But there's no doubt of one true friend,
who I am thinking of.
We all should know of this true friend,
the mighty one above!

Eboni Monae Reavis

Like A Prayer

Your summer beauty believes in light
and the cities of lost gods and goddesses.

Ivy tears the wall with mercy.
There are too many roads.

Sitting in the dark we project ourselves as others
upon the white screen where we deserve mercy.

Somehow the destiny we refused to believe catches up with us.

Believe me when I say this crib was filled with corn
until the rats came and ate the fields.

The purple haze of spring night haunts me.
Somewhere there is the kiss of a toad man.

Soon we walk into the sea.
Gladiolus and string purses wait for us in the waves
all that has happened to the winter's tale and daughters.

Mia Pfost Lewis

The Olden Island

Oh sure, you wonder where old things go
when hardly seen anymore,
stuff like old fashion styles,
and films with blood and gore.

I'll tell you a secret, they're on an isle
that's kind of a Lost and Found,
it's where all old and neglected items
are known to be found.

Travolta was here, but we lost him last year,
'cause he became "retro." Dang!
Oh well, you know the saying on the isle,
"There's always the next old thing."

This isle don't exist, except in our hearts,
anywhere else? No!
But at least you've found out something,
where every old thing goes.

Adam Jessee

Question Mark (?)

Are we human,
or are we Stardust?
Star seeds to fill a Universe,
when we cherish each other
with a passion?
Does that passion explode
into new born stars,
that pierce the darkness
of the galaxy; giving birth to new worlds,
worlds that sing the song of love?
Do all our acts of love
seed the Universe with sparks of newborn life,
nestled in the bosom of the cosmos,
do we become infant stars
gleefully scattering our vibrant light
throughout the heavens, in that sleep called Death?
Is the intenseness of our passions, shooting stars,
lighting the way for others to follow?
If so - let the brilliant showers glow.

J. E. Dullea

All For My Lady Of Orange

For Mai

The very wallpaper of this house is all poetry.
Every palpitation of this heart is whole poetry.
This heart's walls, this home's auburning porch,
and its oaken floors, and its tan crawlspaces,
and its limegrass-lit cellar,
and its atticway branched with Eastern sun,
and the amber-windowed living room and parlor,
and the apricot cupboard and pantry,
and the peach-reflecting bathroom,
and the East bedroom window ablaze
with peach sun—
Everything of this heart's home is a soul battery,
of poetry, of prosodic energy, of spiritual lightning.
And every palpitation this one home of poetry creates,
every dynamism, every urge, is love and ardor incarnate
all for Vu Thi Mai,
All for You, Peach, My Darling Lady Of Orange.

William A. Watling

America Oh America

America oh america how beautiful you are even thou you won't take me far. Over the mountains through the wood I cross a stream with a beautiful gleam "but" it want be long to the day is gone and you and I will sing a lullaby as the wind blows.

As the night comes and the moon shines and the star twinkles in the night I wish upon the brightest star up in the sky. I close my eyes and made my wish and it come true. The wind whispered three words I love you. Believe in your dream it just might come true. America oh america soon the sun will rise again and I will grab my pen and write a special memo. At night I will get tucked in and wonder what the day will bring me tomorrow.

Letisha Nicole Montgomery

Waves

The Ocean's Symphony
I walk along such a peaceful path
Only to find I still can not grasp

This meaningful life I repeatedly see
Still only comes to me when I dream

The message would become quite apparent to me
Let go, cross over to the other side...

Of This Beautiful Sea
Watching, Waiting, Wondering Why?

My eyes suddenly open and the tranquility sets in
She has hypnotized me with her symphony once again!

Lillian Page Conner

Reaching Your Star

A dream is reaching that one star
in the sky filled with many others.

How you reach that one special
star is what really counts.

Do you cut the course,
or do you follow the track,
and even go the long way?

Is it the reward that matters to you,
or just the joy of winning?
The very best way to reach that star,
achieve that dream,
and obtain that goal,
is to try your best and give it your all,
and don't let anyone stand in your way!

Gina Marie Braswell

A Fathers Love

Many days and nights have passed,
Yet memories I see so clear,
So many things I see at last,
That forever I'll hold dear,
All the things that you have taught,
To help me throughout my life,
Each and everything you sought,
Through sacrifice and strife,
You've loved and made me who I am,
And who I'll always be,
From the time I was small, and now as a man,
You mean so much to me,
So as every minute passes on,
I just want you to know,
Every day from dusk til dawn,
From each and every one of us,
Dad we need you so.

Paula Medley

Colors

White, black, red, yellow, and brown
Are the colors to be found
Whats so different, why's one bad
Where'd you learn it, from your Dad
Separation, integration
Don't we all make up our nation
Hatred's taught and hatreds learned
How many more crosses will be burned
Equal rights, what's fair is fair
Tolerance, acceptance, are views I share
Who's to say which color's better
Read the constitution letter to letter
We've fought for what it stands for, for over 200 years
Isn't it time to put away your fears
I'll stand beside you or I'll help you up
I'll share my bread and I'll share my cup
We're in this together, one and all
What's it going to be, you make the call

Nick Pardy

I Am

I am a talkative girl who likes the Arts.
I wonder what it feels like to die.
I hear music in my head.
I see colors when I close my eyes.
I want to travel around the world.
I am a talkative girl who likes the Arts.

I pretend I live in the past.
I feel pressure to perform well.
I touch the clouds in the sky.
I worry about the world ending.
I cry when I see the environment being abused.
I am a talkative girl who likes the Arts.

I understand the unfairness of life.
I say you can accomplish anything if you try.
I dream about painting the perfect picture.
I try to keep a positive attitude.
I hope harassment will stop.
I am a talkative girl who likes the Arts.

Stefanie Marshall

My Mother, My Friend

Mother is gone now, and I miss her so
Though her thoughts were rambling, her steps so slow
Her hearing had weakened, not much could she do
Her eyesight was failing, her reasoning, too.

Devoted to family, taking care of her clan
Three busy children and one faithful man
Sisters and brothers, she loved each so much
She showed it gently, with prayers and through touch.

Her paintings she mastered, with skill and with art
A talent that truly came straight from the heart
Though she's not with us, I still feel her love
I sense that she's watching us all from above.

I loved this dear woman, such a part of my life
With whom I shared freely my joys and my strife
What a wonderful person this woman had been
A wife, a mother, a sister; my friend.

Emily Howard Reid

"You're You And I Am Me"

When I come to you with my problems, as I so often do
I come for understanding for what I'm going through.
Sometimes, I want you to just listen, for my burden you can't bear
It just helps to know you support me, and that you truly do care.
Please don't tell me, what you would, or would not do
If you were me, or if I were you.
We all go through problems sometimes in our life,
And we surely need others, during heartaches and strife.
So just let me talk, and get it all out.
For you have no idea, what my problem is all about.
So be you family, or friend, please try to understand...
Offer a shoulder to cry on, lend an ear, or maybe just hold my hand.
But please don't tell me, what would or would not be
If this were you or you were me.
We all go through ordeals differently, as you can see...
Because you are you and I am me.

Joyce Mattock Porter

Can You Hear?

God listen to your children's cries
Their lives are filled with hunger, pain and lies.
They go to sleep to the sounds of war
But dream of peace on a distant shore.
How can we tell them we fight in your name
Just because our religions aren't the same.
We teach them to see through hateful eyes
So we can justify our prejudice lies.
Why can't we teach them to love one another
Instead of hating because of race, religion or color.
Why must they live in these violent times
When they are innocent of our worldly crimes.
God lead them so they don't go astray
So tomorrow they can find a peaceful way.

Teresa James

My True Love

A year ago there was a party,
My sister suggested I should go.
She said her friend would bring her brother,
Someone I might like to get to know.

My sister explained he was just like me,
Shy and kind of quiet.
She said that we would have lots of fun,
I didn't know if I should buy it.

I went to the party and looked around,
I saw my sister waving hi.
Standing next to her was her friend,
And this really cute guy.

We hit it off and started dating,
And with a little help from above.
I think I did it, I finally found him,
My one and only, my true love.

Elizabeth Whittle

Dream

There's this dream I had one night
It didn't seem like it was right
It felt so real as if it was true
how I failed to hold on to you
In this dream I cried for you
you left me standing not knowing what to do
I'll dream and dream all through the night
to find a way to make things right
This dream I had which really burns
how much I wish I wouldn't return
And in this dream your love I lack
But when I wake I'll take you back.

Vincent C. Matagolai

Sonnet To Myself

Fair Self, virgin solitude becomes you,
But do not despair of posterity;
With none to claim nurturing love's value,
The soul may grow with thrice intensity.
Society dictates this ideal:
Sweet husband and child, three-person'd God;
Though the final purpose is renewal,
Reality proves the sentiment flawed.
Fragmentation will not lead to rebirth;
Integrity is needed to replace
The compromising of a woman's worth:
Wholeness is created by time and space.
The fruits of cultivated privacy
Will provide an abundant legacy.

Raja Stephenson

"Beauty, Through The Eyes Of The Beholder"

If you have ever seen the hours between dusk and dawn,
you would know what I mean when I say it's one of the most
beautiful things to see.
Between these hours one might see the most wondrous and
heavenly sights that one should be allowed to see,
and various others.

Between these hours one might notice that colors as we know
them may have simply disappeared with the sun. The world
becomes a world of blacks, whites, and grays. A wondrous world,
unknown by most. Between these hours one might do a lot of soul
searching, one might find out things about themselves never before
discovered, never searched for.
Between these hours one might wonder if they are still on earth,
or if they have crossed over into the beauty that is heaven.
A wondrous world. A beautiful place.

If you have ever seen the hours between dusk and dawn, you would
know what I mean when I say it's one of the most beautiful things
to see.

One of the most beautiful times to be.

Matthew O'Donnell

Work Ethic

The ceiling above my bed is white and rough
like the surface of the moon;
at 9 am on Monday morning,
with my quilt pulled snugly around me.

A sweet river of oxygen pours in through the window,
delicious air scented with pine and redwood,
sweeping into my nostrils and down my throat,
cooling, cleansing, healing,
connecting me to the acoustic fantasy of the inner forest;
Bird songs and hummingbird wings vibrate
on refracted laser beams of sunlit fog;
Illumination with perfect pitch,
except for the high grinding anxiety of a chainsaw
straining annoyedly,
sawing out slices of my brain.

Alex Wade

Cap'n Crunch

I look around and see the dreamers of the world.
But I awoke from my last dream screaming,
for you couldn't stay.

So I discarded hope on the way to work, faith over lunch
and prayed my last prayer for love to find me
while I fixed a bowl of cereal for dinner.

So live your life looking for love.
You let it go -
But I'm ok.

Kathryn J. Felitsky

Jealous Much

Seeing her next to him,
I begin to cringe.
Hearing her talk to him,
I feel sick to my stomach.
Knowing what could happen,
I want to butt in; right away.
Wondering what they are both thinking;
About each other.
I wish I were psychic.
Seeing, hearing, knowing, and wondering about them;
I wish I were her.

Amber Uttrich

Memories

The shadows of memories past
seem forever which to last,
for the nights and the days are that of the
unchanged.
And the bleak furniture
that fills the rooms of your mind
are never to be rearranged.

Arranged as to let light in
to show your untrue sin,
and cast away your dark shadows that hide in the weeds
Found in your own life's meadows;
planted by past memory done deeds.

Deeds of no fault of your own
While the heartache echoes on unspoken moan.
And sitting around a broken phone with a broken ring
and the happy blue birds of your head never do sing.

Sing the song of the forgave so ones life can crawl out of its own
cave. To see the light of life and let it shine down upon your face
to show all your beauty, and Godly grace.

Chris Blankership

Invitation To The Sea

The sand invites us to the sea,
It spreads its carpet wide and free.
as the sea meets the land,
it's gentled by the shifting sand.
As placid pools of captive tide,
and rippled furrows are scattered wide.
a masterpiece of sculpted pride.
So helpless on the waves they ride.
To gaze upon this endless scene,
a perfect sight so neat and clean,
no footsteps there, to mar the scene,
untouched, once more serene.
Only sand and sea and sky,
to feed the soul and please the eye.
So needed in a world gone wrong,
devoid of solitude, or beauty's song.

M. Anford Girard

Toni Sue

Toni Sue was my mother
All of her life she was a lover.
Now that she is gone she is an angel
In my life, she is at all angles.

She died of the painful disease cancer
I know that I am still her "little" dancer.
I know she is in the beautiful heaven
Where the bread is unleavened.

I know she is waiting for me
Because of Jesus, she was set free.
In my heart, she will always stay
My love for her keeps me going day by day.

Jo Repasky

The Secrets

Today I went along a path
That joggers use each day.
I didn't jog! I walked, and slow!
There were things to see along the way.

The snow was deep just over the hill
Below me in the wood
A bevy of quail nervously sought
Protection, where they could.

First one would rush shakily ahead.
The others would quickly follow.
Around tree trunks and bushes,
Thickly standing in the hollow.

The cars and trucks would thunder past.
I stood and gazed with smiles
Upon the "secrets" by the road
Where joggers run for miles.

L. Marjorie Cook

Best Friends

We dreamed of greatness,
He dreamed of being like his father,
I dreamed of being like mine.

Most people say we are twins,
if they only knew...

He gave me his dreams,
I gave hope and my promise,
That someday I would be as great as he.

He taught me to see color, but not in people.
He said, respect everyone,
but women more, 'cause
they make life worth living for.

He told me to live life to the fullest
because you never know what tomorrow will bring.
He gave me everything,
a childhood, dreams, and a future.

My father and I are best friends,
always have been and always will be.
We are two in the same, think alike,
Look alike—are a like.

Christopher C. Sieck

My Mother, My Center

Hub of wheel, support to turning circle,
Succor given, helpless offspring play the spindle part
In search for self they stretch to outer rim
Final lesson learned, we need each other

One by one, each succeeding year
We break away to leave an empty space
New direction, now employed to spawn new broad
On quest of modern hub, spindle, wheel and rim.

Hub now alone will shape and force separate way.
While spindles shape new branches, they synchronize with hub
And stories, hugs and kisses fill brief calls and visits
Like axle grease, lubrication provided, the squeak of emptiness erased

With heartfelt smiles spread on wrinkled face,
Hub still spins the wheel of love and dedication.
Each day becomes a trip to days gone by.
Of holiday gatherings and home made gifts for Mother's Day.

So still and silent, resting, no response
Hubs kisses smiles and laughter remain a memory
Flowers gather 'round, tears stain each face
Remembrances remain she gave us life for futures

Bertha Pobocik

The Price Of Love

In my life I've known of many,
Of how they've loved owning less than a penny.
And even though so much was sought,
They always knew love couldn't be bought.

Love was something on which they could rely,
It was certainly not something in which they could buy.
It would last forever and they knew it was nice,
To always know love had not a price.

When every bill and toll was exact,
They were still living on that precious fact.
It didn't matter if they had money or not,
Love had no price, it was always the thought.

No price, no tag, not even a bill,
This was all centered around how they feel.
If love was there and was exactly precise,
They would pay nothing for it, cause it had not a price.

Marsha Anne Hogue

"Victims Of Crime"

It can happen to you, me, our family.. the ultimate unfairness.
It happens to people everywhere in our society.. every minute or less.
An innocent person was robbed, beaten, raped, or killed.
Another victim of crime.. that got some criminals thrilled.
Nothing that happens later.. can make that fair, just, or right.
For the rest of their lives.. those victims will suffer day and night!
The justice system is quite a scuffle.
Sometimes.. victims do get lost in the shuffle.
The system guarantees the defendant.. a fair trial.
Just another criminal case.. another crime to file.
The judge, or jury.. doesn't understand the realism.
It doesn't guarantee.. any sort of fairness to the victim!
It begins within ourselves, family, friends.. and all our flaws.
We all need to do a better job.. of abiding and enforcing the laws.
So that nobody.. is deprived of life, liberty, and the pursuit of happiness..
Without guidance, discipline, and support.. people learn hate and ruthlessness.
From the justice system, to the victim.. all are a part of this efficacy.
Victims should be treated with respect.. as a matter of decency!
Public, open your eyes to see.. a message that's subliminal.
Victims of crime.. should have as many rights as criminals!

Derek T. Nardoni

Lost In The Clouds

A one and only, so pure and so divine, shade of blue
that can comfort only from inside.
Not a shade, but only it's own could ever compare,
to the magic we all own way up in the air.
Some days the clouds decide to go on ahead and roam on by.....
Soaring, soaring, soaring so high; like a bird, a plane,
or anything that flies.
Like a hawk or an eagle, with not a worry in sight.
Only freedom and joy as they glide their great flight.
As I gaze upon the divine softness of my heavens, a
heaven much beyond our sky, I can visualize myself choosing
the cloud I'd prefer to fly.
Fly away on my cloud, far away on my cloud. And off we
go, on a ride taking us so, so incredibly high.

-Lisa Lynn Camacho

Shower In Short

The water cleanses my face
Some shoot out like Native American spear heads
Poised and ready to separate flesh on contact
Roaring through space proclaiming
You deserve your sin-born torment
Missiles seeking to destroy a mass

Combined with these were caressing
Gentle tears like those one would expect to be
Wept from the loving seductive eyes of Mother Nature
They soothed the marks and scars left behind
By her yang
Bringing in momentary relief and sun light
Momentary because after she healed
The other scarred
Healed
Continuously
On and on
The battle ensued until
The metal was turned

Christopher Michael McLamb

Thank You

Thank you for making me,
Thank you for waking me,
Thank you for keeping me safe again.

Thank you for the sunshine
Thank you for the rain
Thank you for everything
That I stand to gain.

You are my life, you are my love
There is nothing that you can't
do from above.

Thank you for being there
When I've needed you most
Thank you for being there
When I was the host.

Without you I could not have made it thus far
Because you are who you are Christ, Lord, God
Mother and Father
My Saviour!
Thank you!

Jamie Moore Marina

Untitled

Light ship crystals spun about my brow,
twinkling downward in snowfall from the moon.

Was it me who was swimming
through the clouds just now?
Or did my mind think too fast
and born me akin to angels?

Just now the pavement is covered with dreams
falling in shimmering cascades from my hair.

It is cold, and the wind
lifts my arms again in flight.
Legs pumping, I skitter across
the frozen snow...

Unable to lift my depression.

And so I sit and dream of snow angels
watching the clouds drifting through the trees.

Here I am....
And I am here.

Craig Lamar Christophel

Gently The Meadow

While larks sailed slowly in sky so blue,
Gently the meadow sparkled with dew.
Morning broke brightly o'er hill and dale
And the sun came up, lifting the veil.

The grass swayed and ruffled in the breeze,
As flowers swayed with humming bees.
Gently the meadow rolled like ocean swells;
And cows grazed slowly in sweet grassy smells.

Gently the meadow held children at play,
So early in summer on a warm sunny day.
Swaying limbs on shady green trees.
Held each child swinging by his knees.

Gently the meadow came alive with joy,
As animals ate, watched by each girl and boy.
Young life was busy as nature flowed apace,
Beauty spread over meadow and smiling face.

As sun came overhead and grew very hot,
Children and cows found a cool shady spot.
Gently the meadow remained the same,
Still a place of beauty as when morning came.

Nina Wilder

Summer Loves

Summer loves they come and go
For the winter does not know
The story foretold, the spring time
shows, another summer love approaches

Your love for this is so grand,
and how your feet feel in the sand
as you hug your summer love,
you hear: Another summer love approaches.

Forget me not they say to you
I'll write you and I'll phone you too,
but you know that is not true,
So the nights turn cold, the days
grow short, but have no fear for
another summer love can appear.

Laura Manning

Time

It was always here,
And it always will be here,
Sometimes we adore it,
Sometimes we despise it,
There are endless amounts of it,
But it is too precious a thing to waste.
It runs out differently for every individual,
But every moment of it is yours to keep,
To hold onto, to love in your heart and in your soul forever.

Melinda Lee Romanko

Untitled

Given the greatest of basic needs
A life, a thought, the right to be

The world would be one's very own
If taken the path of honesty

Can't simplify complexities beyond control
But truth is light to guide the soul

In all of time it has been told
That truth prevails, and all else folds

The things of nature everywhere
Depict the finest, purest fare

From flowers to rocks and lightening, too
Mountains, oceans - Why not you?

Edith L. Charron

In Memory Of "Crackers"

There is a void, an empty spot in our home today,
Our beloved poodle, Crackers, has passed away.
Seems there's no way to stem the hurt, and the tears,
She was a member of our home, and family for sixteen years.
So much love, joy, and pleasure, she to us extended,
Doesn't seem possible, that her time with us is ended.
There was a lady like aire about her, we did respect,
Before she did anything, she'd stop and reflect.
How she loved to be nestled close in someone's lap.
Or just a hand stroking, or a loving hand pat.
She behaved well, not impish like some pet's, always good,
Loved by all who knew her, family, friends, the neighborhood.
She also enjoyed eating, fun, romping, and happy play,
When she'd had all of this, she wanted, just walked away.
Our loving memories, her pictures, will have to suffice,
As Crackers rests comfortably, peacefully, in "Dog Paradise."

Mary E. Horton

"Ocean And Love"

Silently it calls you by name.
Unaware you answer its call.
Suddenly you're waist deep;
Unsure how you got there,
Unknowing whether to go closer
or turn completely around.

Fascinated by its beauty
you take a few steps forward.
Terrified by its roar you cower with fear.
Soothing you with its caress
the world becomes oblivious.
Crushing you with its power you become its servant.

Myriad are the mysteries;
Inconclusive are the answers.
Continuous are the dreams;
Seldom are the joys.
Obvious are the beauties;
Blind are the terrors.
Inevitable are the innuendos;
Rarely are the pleasures.

Shannon Caldwell

Untitled

Complete rage in obsidian harmony
Boiled over a blue crimson flame
Unnerved calm as savage insanity
Shards of thought with fatal aim
Desirable need of the eternal solution
A festival follows the victories of war
Drain the blood from the body of delusion
Victorious in all, yet still, I want more
Long after the damaged are silenced
Opposing, no more, ability in still thought
No need will exist for metaphysical violence
Nor the need to weave the web for the caught

Jeffery Stone

"Shannon"

You brighten one's soul;
Your cheery ways are open for anyone to behold
Life brought you to us, to show us
how to live.
Death has taken you, but you've taught
us how to give.

In our hearts you will always be;
But let us have your soul go free.

Judy Beschoner

We Lie In Limbo
(On The Threshold Of The Great Decision)

We lie in limbo,
on the threshold of the great decision.
We stand between the sweeping tide of aggression,
and the tradewinds of co-existence.

We slow to a standstill,
between the ominous thunder of nuclear fission,
and the expanding power of peace.

We stand at midstream on a rock,
watching the flowing current run quickly
beneath our feet, an ear to either shore.

We gather 'round the launch pad
of human evolution to make our decision.
Will we explore the galaxy as the human race united?
Or paint the planet red with our blood
for the universe to witness our tragic failure.

We lie in limbo,
on the threshold of the great decision.

Gary Breton

Who Is My Enemy

Does my enemy want me to die?
Will my enemy destroy me by telling a lie?
Is my enemy a person or a thing?
Could it be a habit to which I cling?

Does jealousy cause my elan to rage?
Do worry and care accelerate my age?
Is my enemy a myth or a reality?
Or is it a life of banality?

Do I foolishly search for the enemy without?
While the one within gives out with a shout.
"Here I am, try to find me."
"Where?" say I cannot see."

Where is this elusive foe,
That makes me fret and worry so?
My spirit is pained by this jeering beast?
On my compassion and hope he is having a feast.

Dear God in heaven, I plead my case.
Look into my heart, myself I abase.
Exorcise this demon from mind and soul.
Replace it with love and, in life, a new goal.

Robert F. Bates

"Goodbye"

We have been walking along this road together.
The road that seemed straight forever.
When a curve came along,
we became one.
When there was a battle to be fought,
we always won.
When one stumbled along the way,
the one behind you swept you away.
Away from any danger and harm.
They kept you close beneath their arm.
But here is where the road divides,
now we have to begin living are lives.
There will be a path not taken,
always hoping a mistake not makin'.
Here is where we leave one another,
Tears falling,
one hugging the other.
Here is where we say goodbye,
every word worth making.
As we look down the road not taken.

Deanna Clark

Awkward Instance

Asphalt cracked and streaked remains in yellow painted
ghosts of hopscotch and four-square:

Gaping old day care ladies
thick-lensed and feeble
inclinations couldn't keep us
from him when he came,
forked with forgeries of custodies
and signatures... to shoulder
pasty waiting ladies free of blame
love finds no prerequisite in a name.

Fingers white in backseat windows,
cries like silent fishbowl faces
getting smaller...
eyes cracked like asphalt playgrounds
see the passing feet of children
grow weak of days remembered.

Mother said we wouldn't go
and shouldn't listen if he comes...
and months to follow searching...
But who remembers anyway... and what do children know?

Ian Cormican

Springtime

The day shines bright, the air smells fresh,
the cool wind blows the winter to its timely death.

The day is warm, the sun is bright,
the hint of summer sends people outdoors to enjoy the warm sunlight.

The birds sing their song, as the wind hums along in tune.
The flowers show their beauty when they are in full bloom.
They send their message on the wind where you can smell their perfume.

The warm weather is where people are out looking for love.
It is tangible in the warm springtime air.

Everything is fresh, in love, alive, and new; along with the love I send from me to you. With the warmth of the sun and the chill of the moon, mysteries are unraveled from beneath the morning dew.

Old friendships are renewed; problems are forgotten along with the wintertime blues. Memories that were drab suddenly become precious.

Live for today rather than tomorrow for then you will live tomorrow for yesterday, a day that will never come.

The spring is to be free like the blue bird above with his wings spread free to have the wind carry him to the beautiful clouds above.

Jan L. Scarber

My Favorite Teacher

I have never expressed the praise you deserve,
For taking part in all I have learned.
In life and love, each page that I've turned
You taught me life's best is that which is earned.

I have never mentioned that you were the one,
Who taught me self-worth and when you were done,
You made me feel I was second to none,
On top of the world, I sat with the Sun.

I have never told you the changes you've made;
I learned to be strong, when I was afraid;
I learned of love and the joy of giving;
I developed respect and a zest for living.

And now all these things are important to me;
I'm so very proud and lucky to be,
The daughter and student of one I adore,
My father, my favorite teacher, for sure.

Linda Battaglia

I Follow A Famous Father

I follow a famous father,
His honor is mine to wear;
He gave me a name that was free from shame,
A name he was proud to bear.

I follow a famous father,
And him I must keep in mind;
Though his form is gone, I must carry on
The name that he left behind.

Frances Worthington

Untitled

The darkness in my chest
grows stronger everyday.
It screams and cries,
it begs and pleads.
It asks God why life must be so hard,
why does it squeeze the tears
until all that's left
is the empty darkness of my soul.

How can He leave me at the bottom
with nothing there to hold,
but the whisper of His name.
And in this world, sorry does not suffice,
too often used in vain.
The things of which I dream
so quietly float away.
Please, please rescue me.

Mariah Mercer

The Truth

In every person there lies the truth.
The truth is with you wherever you are,
whether you are near or far.
The quality of an honorable person,
is to both realize and understand.
In order to realize, one must understand.
One must realize not to hate,
but understand how to tolerate.
The world has many varieties of people,
such as blacks, whites, yellows, and browns.
We all come from different countries, religions,
and backgrounds.
The valuable appearances on the outside,
are not as valuable as the appearances
on the inside.
That is the truth!

Rin Reth

July 4th

The sky is black with fireworks.
The waves are high, the tide is high.
July, July, July 4th the day we share.
We celebrate to the Lord,
For the people that died are sore.
They helped us split and paid the price.
For making the United States,
They had died.
We moan and groan for sorrow
has come upon these lonely forms.
Independence Day - We always celebrate
and thank the one's who helped us part.
Even though they died
their pride stayed alive.
And is in each and every one of us!

Ashley Faher

The Birds Are Chirping

While I sit outside,
I hear a subtle car driving by.
I listen to birds chirping,
making their beautiful music together.

And while the wind is blowing,
the birds are chirping,
cars are passing as I sit here:
Listening,
hearing,
a part of our great world.

Hearing the calm voices, quiet voices
of children, children talking,
discussing among themselves
questions that life has yet to answer.

Watching the clouds moving, moving away
as the vast spread of universe passes us by.

Kyle C. Rogers

Don't Be Afraid

Don't be afraid nor worried,
Sometimes you may think you're wrong,
But when you turn to Jesus,
You'll realize that you're really right.

The whole death thing happens,
And we all have to go through it,
And when it happens,
Just think he or she is looking down on you.

You may be mad at Jesus or God,
But it was his or her time to leave this planet,
And the truth is that Jesus is the first one to cry,
He knows what you're going through.

It's okay to cry and let your feelings out,
People do that too,
The person loves you,
And you love the person, too!!!

Rachel Leeper

"Light Of A Dream"

Last night I dreamed of barren
skies, open seas, and surging swells.
A stiffening breeze sailed by and by
my narrow skiff. As the sky had the seas,
And the sea had my small vessel, I was alone,
knocked aside by the wind. The icy mist down
my chin. I blinked away the prickling spray,
In time to see a wonder sight. A light.
No, an angel from above. Descending from high.
"Where have you been?
Where did you roam?
He is there,
And you are home."

Christine Nasrawin

Tree - The Giver

Uncertain of the destination,
it blew from the rustic roads,
clasped in the bosom of the winds,
not knowing where to board.
The journey completes, the soil absorbs,
nurses the seed till it crops.
Reborn is the life to repay its debts,
fruits to relish, shed to take rest.
Lesson to mankind, always it shows,
gives to everybody-never the head high it holds.

Manoj Bhatia

'Heed'

Caution your heart as well as your mind,
Before you know it your soul will be 'left behind,'
To wander aimlessly lost and alone
To chill your spirit so that it can never be
warmed by hearth or 'home.'

Caution your heart as well as your mind.
People look at you and laugh, you're 'left behind'
To wander aimlessly lost and alone
To call out to someone; anyone but no
one is 'home.'

Caution your heart as well as your mind.
Words of warning from people like me who
were 'left behind.'
To wander aimlessly lost and alone.
Please, caution your heart as well as your mind.

Diane Hallahan

The Day That You Were Born

Dedicated to my daughter, Dainelle

A diamond in the rough,
So lovely, so exquisite.
Could this treasure be mine?
This wrinkled, crying babe.

An emerald fit for royalty,
Priceless, sparkling jewel.
Flawlessly formed masterpiece,
By the loving hand of God.

Rubies blush with shame,
For their splendor is obscured.
By the squirming, red-skinned newborn,
Precious little star of India.

Pearls cannot do justice,
To the face that I gaze upon.
The wealth of nations matters little,
Compared to your richness and worth.

Gold is the what you shall have, the sun's bright rays forever.
Nuggets of love flow from me, yours without condition.

I hold this treasured moment in the palm of my greedy hand.
Years have passed but I remember, the day that you were born.

Bonnie Kirby

God's Nature

It's a rainy Spring morning, you can't mistake the sound.
The birds are searching for food that's all around. The
daffodils have bloomed, the buds are on the trees; nature has
fallen in love.
Oh, how I love Springtime. Everything is so fresh and new.
It seems like the whole world comes alive, and the grass
is covered with morning dew.
When the earth was first brand new, God created the sun;
the moon; the stars; the grass; the birds that chirp; and the
air we breathe. He created the water we drink, the cow
that makes our milk, and the flowers that bloom. No one knows how.
It's the things we take for granted, and things we just assume.
Sometimes, we don't appreciate the trouble he's gone
through to make this beautiful earth; all its creatures, and
every living cell under the heavens above.
For God is magnificent, and wonderful, and everything good
we can think of. There's not one thing he hasn't created that
we can think of. There are no words to express the meaning of
our Lord. Only to say that he is, and was, and always will be
God.......

Dawn Adele Disharoon

The Sleep Hangs Heavily

Sounds pierce through
muted shades of night
the distant call of a train moaning low
the grumbling guttural voice of an airplane
lofty in the clouds
the sleep hangs heavily
draped like dust
on the backs and necks and limbs
of the dreamers
the smooth deep rushing
of fast cars on knotted pavement
like rushing wind, they sound.
The night, the stillness, the dreams
hang heavily all around
as people breathe in warm cocoons
the laden earth turns swiftly
someone dies
someone is born.
The sleep hangs heavily.

Ruth Nesbitt

The Old Goat

There once was a licentious lecher of a lady,
Who at sundry times was unscrupulously shady.

Her utterances were impeccably uncontrollable;
At various intervals she tried to be amiable.

At other times her vernacular was as caustic venom;
Her discourse was unmitigatingly brutalizing and awesome.

Her litigation was as sharp as a two-edged sword;
Nothing could stop her fabricating abundant discord.

Immense pleasure was hers with every scandalous rumor,
No caller departed without lending to her jaded humor.

She was contentious, quarrelsome, and cantankerous,
She was unremitting, hot - tempered, and rancorous.

She was a licentious "old goat" of a lady,
Who at sundry times was unscrupulously shady.

Janet E. Chappell

There's A Place For Us

We walk in the shadow of love
What do we see
The blind holding hands
Saying follow me
Our pondering hearts has wonder astray
What can we do? What must we say
Know where to go, know where to play
Or find a true love that is here, here to stay
Is there a place for us?
Time is running out
We are drifting, drifting by the sea
As we stood there in a trance,
A current wave came by and absorbed me
The days, nights, months and years vanished always
May the memory of our love lasted forever
In the depths of our souls
As we bond in harmony

While we walk in the shadow of love.

Audrey Thomas

Faith

In my hour of choice,
you the hour!
Till death do us part,
His love of power.

Statuettes I'll give unto old soul,
my heart, my mind, my world takes its toll.
Trumpet sounds to the lost must confess,
wanting no memory I guess...

Understanding your fire within,
left outside my world of sin.
But I know an answer I fought,
Jesus Christ paid and bought...

Douglas Wayne Wells

"Prophesy"

Days are dim,
Lies too much.
My prophesy, I say in vain:
Dark shall fall
Day will die
Never to rise again.
The child shall rise in ghastly light,
Terror will be his name.
The hounds of hell shall be his friends,
Come join them in the game.
Death shall befall you
Earthly child,
Welcome to the night!!
Say good-bye to day
And join in demonic delight.
My prophesy, I say to you
The future it will be,
So enjoy your madness while you can
And speak of it not to me.

Andrea Kelley

Untitled

I'm sitting here, sitting here in utter boredom.
A kind of solitude in which all time is nonexistent.
Nobody speaks, no one breathes, all just simply sit there in an almost sickening silence
What are they doing, my patience is leaving.
Why do they sit and do nothing?
Frustration inside has built, sad disturbing frustration, due to them, over there sitting like that.
They sit so awkwardly. They are so awfully put together, not unique, not diverse, just mute.
Why- I ask why mute? Because it's all they know, all they've been taught.
Shame, all their pitiful little lives, no love, no dreams.
Not a small feeling of hope or faith inside.
All of it shattered into oblivion, never to get another chance.
Never to be able to open their eyes.
Their minds closed to any kind of change, any ideas.
Not an ambition in those dark blank minds.
And as I'm sitting I am witness to all of them, I feel sympathy for them.
It's not their fault, it is the ones with no remorse, no open minds.
They subjected them to words and paragraphs of unspeakable phrases and names.
They taught them to hate, to shut out all aspects of humanity and love.
Only to be left with no trust, no regret, just sorry little souls too scared to care.
Now, I ask, I ask that it all stops, please stop the hate.

Lindsey Richmond

The Unstyled

I do not behold that which is in vogue or a
matter of passing fancy. A tightly cinched
waist, my innards displaced to stylishly and
demurely enhance me.

I shall not give in to piercing my skin or
applying an artful tattoo. For pretty is, is
pretty be, not a laughing curiosity to be
pointed and snickered by you!

No stiletto high heels to feel six feet tall,
I suffer from vertigo and might take a fall.
No long cigarette holder to appear worldly and
wise, while coyly batting Bette Davis eyes. No
veil to cover the emotions on my face, who
cares if I am a public disgrace!

I do not care for the feminine mystique, that
a lady must be wane and weak, with simply
nothing in the world to do but focus my pea
sized brain on you!

Jane Welton

The Drifter

I was born to be a drifter
I was born to walk alone
I am most definitely not a righteous man
For many of my actions I can't condone

I am your worst nightmare
I'm your deep and darkest fear
No one shall escape my wrath
Around every corner I may appear

On Halloween I am your Jason
I'm the Kruger in your dreams
I'm the monster in the closet
I'm everywhere yet I'm nowhere or so it seems

The world has forsaken me
I have nowhere else to hide
There is no family to hold me
There are no friends to with whom I can confide

Nothing ever fazes me
My heart is made of stone
I was born to be a drifter
I was born to walk alone

Chris Dinger

This Child

In the headlines today
A three week old child was put away
Who is this child that lies bleeding
While his mother stands there weeping
A father whose big and bold
Made sure the world would never know
For he put a gun to this child's head
In a stand off with the law
The shots rang out
This child is dead
Now his mother will never hear him speak
To have and hold
For this nightmare is all has to keep
So please God save the children
Shield them from our destruction
And blind them of our rage
Help them to see past the corruption
Of our day and age
Preserve the innocence and beauty they possess
For once upon this Earth we are all just guests

Brenda Veney

Mother Had A Little Lamb...

She wept quite openly as they buried her daughter that day.
  Not fully understanding, why the Lord took her away.
Mother raised that girl from childhood.
  A loving family she would know.
And mother had that extra love that Sherri gave her soul.
  The lady buttoned up her coat as it began to rain.
She remembered many lonely days.
  When Sherri's face was filled with pain.
While clutching at her husband's hand she looked him in the eyes.
  Tears had filled his sullen face, revealing death's disguise.
The woman looked at all her children.
  Because Sherri was their guide.
Glancing at her oldest daughter and seeing all the tears she cried.
  As the priest began a final prayer some cars began to leave.
She was hoping it was all a dream.
  A game of make—believe.
Her husband hugged her tightly.
  Knowing her heart would never mend.
For lying deep within the ground.
  Was little Sherri....barely ten.

Martin A. Steepleton

A Paradise Poem

A butterfly that is flying
A people that will forget about dying
A fig tree that will be a persons minding
this is a paradise poem I am writing.

The smell of delicious food for everyone
The older one's will mount up with wings of eagle and run
The young ones being good, not having bad things they have done
Everyone will always have fun.

A quiet time in a park
A happy man that will dance like a lark
A person will never be eaten by a shark
To do God's will - that's the mark

When there will be sunshine not rain
when husbands will always love their dame
We will do the right thing and have no shame

Money will be thrown in the streets
many people will have many vegetables and choices of meats
As the greatest man Jesus was humble and
meek and washed one of his saints feet
come and enjoy the sunny heat.

Steven L. Hawkins

Untitled

You're standing on the beach at night,
And it's you above the sand,
That's below the waves crashing upon it,
With the sky that's above all.
On a clear night, look up at the sky.
At all the stars, at all the darkness,
At all the questions that can be
Asked with that picture.

Look at us.
At all the caring, at all the sharing,
At all the giving.
Look at all the questions that can be
Answered with this picture.
Picture perfect.

Anna Stankiewicz

The Real World

Too many things are left unnoticed, not enough
is ever said. Reality not yet realized. Things are missing
not materialized. Passion Great and deep, feelings
untouched. People we leave behind. We are running
out of time; burning bridges behind us, not to return.
Not a lot of trust. Noises from the distance and
yet they seem so close. Shadows from another dimension,
closing in on us. A trap set by man to catch his own hand.
Too many don't realize this is a promise land. Ties,
that bind us; don't always hold. There is so much left
for us too unfold.
Secrets in shadows, whispers in the dark, lies that shatter
our world apart.
Crying of an elder - soon to pass away. Getting ready
for our judgement day. Crying of a baby - coming in this
world. Giving us promise of a new pearl.
Close your eyes and think of me. Open your eyes and see
this is reality.
Powers from God, visions of trust, which way to go
in this forward thrust.

Melissa Roland

Moonlight And The Sea

By the seashore
The lonely tide embraces the welcome surf
As the white tossed waves kiss the shore
While moonbeams radiate their glow of turbulent
power tossing the gigantic waves toward the lonely shore
The silence of the night shadows over the sea
Breathing a whisper telling of a tale heard long ago
Of the magical moonlight and the wondrous sea
It was on a lonely night
A monstrous ship appeared out of nowhere
Heard tell of four crewmen sailed the torrid sea
When the full moon appeared tossing the ship high and low
In the distance a, foghorn was heard
Finally all was silent
The moon shown bright with luster
The clapping of the waves
Only they know the story of the moonlight and the sea

Genevieve J. Mello

A Robin Stopped By

A robin stopped by yesterday
  it's the end of April... almost May.
Had his brand new red vest on,
  a sign that spring is back in town.
Now spring-birds sing to greet the dawn
  and crocus blossom in the lawn.

In the dooryard tulips bloom,
  dogwood trees will blossom soon.
Daffodils nod in the breeze,
  a haze of green tints the trees.
Springtime softness fills the air,
  the earth is budding everywhere.

As nature blooms in resurrection,
  soul-deep we feel exaltation.
How blessed are we to be here
  to see God's springtime another year.
A robin stopped by yesterday
  it's the end of April... almost May.

Ray Owens

Humankind

It is said my name is Clovis.
Thousands of moons have come and gone;
The darkness and light of moons, come and gone.

It is said I have traveled
Thousands of miles from my first home;
Traveled the bitter trail from my first home.

But rather rose we up, together.
On five continents rose children of the light;
Children in all shades of brown, from dark to light.

We travel together out of the earth;
Travel the path together, from darkness toward the light;
Travel the path of eternity, from the dawn of Man to night.

Patricia Boyer

The Last Prayer

A little girl lay awake one night,
Alone in a hospital bed,
She closed her eyes and prayed to God,
And this is what she said;
"Don't let Daddy be too sad,
And don't let Mommy cry,
Help Annie not to be lonely,
And not to be so shy,
Give my dolls to the little girls,
Who need someone to hug,
And give my bear to the boy at school,
Who always sits alone on the rug,
Take the flowers beside my bed,
And give them to someone who needs,
A cheering up, or a brighter day,
Or has a yard all filled with weeds."
And as a single tear slid down her cheek,
And with the last breath she drew,
She said, "Oh, and God,"
"I want my wings to be blue."

Janet Potter

Without

Life would be meaningless,
without family and friends.
It makes you realize it,
when a friendship ends.
If life did not have any friends,
there would be no one to impress.
No one to love and care for,
and no one to caress.
There would be no babies to care for,
therefore life would end.
But who would really care,
without a friend.
There would be no one to care for you,
when you were sick or afraid.
There would be no one to cheer for you,
when you were in a parade.
So before you say something
you might live to regret,
read what I have written and don't forget.

Daina Michelle DeCamp

Innocence Robbed

If I don't look....maybe I won't see it.
If I try to smile...maybe I won't feel it.
If I hide....maybe I can deny it exists
And the hand clutches onto a dream that can never be
As the autumn trees forewarn us of a long cold winter
And so we wait
Like the last Autumn leaf
for the inevitable.

Cindy Field

We're All The Same

Why do you act as if they're different?
Can't you see we're all the same?
Look beyond their color,
Call them by their name.

Why do you act like they don't belong?
Can't you see they do?
God put us all together,
So he must love them too.

Why can't you put the anger behind you,
And learn to get along?
Can't you see that what you're doing
Is really very wrong?

Who cares about their color,
It's only their skin.
We should look much further,
To what they have within.

We're all in this together,
Can't you all be friends?
Isn't that the message
We should be trying to send?

Kristi Markley

Sea Worthy

Nothing on earth has the grace and majesty
As the giant mammals that call their home the sea
None as wonderful can walk on dry land
Their intelligence is thought to equal man
They die... we kill... for their precious oil
What chance would they have if they walked on soil?

The manatees... the dolphins... and the whales are here
Not for man's joy but for all of us to revere
Noah's flood could not take them... it could be hell
In oceans that grew as each raindrop fell
The oceans covered the earth... one could say
Giving the giants more room to play

The great manatee... not afraid of one thing
The giant humpbacks... with their ability to sing
Graceful dolphins... so willing to be friends
Never thought they would meet their untimely end
By the hand of 'friends' they are caught in nets
Not to be set free but to meet their deaths
They have done nothing to man... but grace the sea
And we have done everything to them that could be

Annette L. Caster

A Friend

A friend is someone
Who is always your friend.
Friends are anyone.
You care about your friends.
Friends do not pick favorites.
Friends are not on and off.
Some friends are better than others,
So they are considered your best friend.
Some people have more
Than one best friend.
Others have only one.
You will know who your friends are
When you find them!!!
Almost everyone has a friend.
Some people do not recognize their friends
Until they have what it takes to be a friend.
Then friendship happens.

Amy Zacek

Today, Yesterday's Tomorrow!

As another dawn awakens a new day
And the dew washes the night away

The sandman has long gone by now
Taking the sand that kissed my brow.

The dreams that come upon my sleep
No longer through my mind they creep.

And now reality engulfs a sleepy head
As I arise from my dream filled bed.

Back to earth comes my minds thought
To accomplish what in life I've sought.

The ladder of success I must assail
Or else in life, I'll inevitably fail.

With these thoughts congesting my brain
So today's problems I will just refrain.

Maybe tomorrow will be here for me
I guess I'll just wait and see

Because I always find with much sorrow
Today of course, is only yesterday's tomorrow.

Bob Overton

Falling Tears

In the still of the night when all is dark and quiet
Tears flow for those whose walk on earth has come to an end
With the darkness, our dreams are born and we are with them again
With the dawn we know it was only dreams and tears flow once more

In the morning light a bird sings and we hear their voices
A gentle breeze caresses us, and we remember their gentle touch
And in the smiles of their children we see their smiles

As the seasons change we welcome the rainbow colors of spring and summer
We see the visions of autumn's gold and red change to a wonderland of snow
We have countless memories of laughter and tears, smiles and embraces
And we realize they are not gone at all

We see the sparkle their eyes once held in the stars above
Their voices whisper in the wind
Their spirits soared with the eagle to rest in the arms of God
And they live forever among the stars and in our hearts

So when the tears flow, let them flow like rain upon the earth
When the rain falls we turn our faces to the sky, and feel its loving touch
And to those still on this earth we turn to give our loving touch
And in the love we give, their love lives

Diane J. Linn

Love In The Shadows

Moonlight filters through the window,
Light enough to outline his face,
Yet dark enough to deepen the room.
I stare quietly at him, watching him sleep.
He stirs and catches me gazing at him.
He pulls me close in darkened oneness.
We gently touch and stare; our hearts meld.
Not a word spoken, he draws me closer.
His hand follows my face as my eyes did his.
Soft, loving lips touch mine.
I want this moment to last forever.
Time never stands still.
We gaze at each other for a few fleeting moments.
Slumber envelops us and we close our eyes.
Love drifts back in the shadows,
Until awakened again.

Kathleen J. Hunter

Sunsets And Stars

Fiery burning hot in the sky above
Sparkle shiny diamonds of love
What a beautiful sight
Sunsets bright, stars take flight
They both take over the night.
Orange, red, yellow burning to flames
Stars of black skies have names
 Some big, some small
 Lighting up the sky
 Some wonder why?
They ask is it so lovely, colorful, and beautiful.

Heather Nichols

Peace

Peace
When I think of peace
I pause
I close my eyes
And listen to the stillness
I envision a dove in flight.
And I wish
If I could ever bestow a gift so free
It would be to bring peace, to all humanity,
And in the hearts of all mankind

If I could touch each person
With a gift so dear
And change this world, which needs a cure
I would touch each heart with a love so pure,'
And make this a world, a place we all adore
With no more crimes, or hate, or wars
But a whole lot of hope and faith to endure.

Christine Jn. Jacques

Friends

You stood by me through thick and thin,
when times got tough, you were a true friend.
You stood up for me when no one else would,
and you gave me a friendship that no one else could.
You gave me advice on many of my problems,
and violence wasn't the way you told me to solve them.

When I felt empty and sad, your smile and presence made me glad.
You let me know when trouble was near,
and you lent me a shoulder to shed a tear.

I want to thank you for being there,
for at times you were the only one that cared.
Thank you for having these qualities,
and for sharing them with me.
Thank you for being there to the end,
thank you for being a true friend.

Dionna Sterling

"Hidden Love"

As I talk with you everyday,
Nothing of my love for you comes out in what I say.
I will keep trying to tell you until I'm dead,
The words that keep going on unsaid.
With all this pain inside,
A smile will show for you on the outside.
At your side I will be kneeling,
Attempting to express my feelings.
If we stay as friends I will let it be,
In hopes you will never leave me.
The one thing I will hold always true,
Is that I will always love you.

Shane Moore

Death Of My Best Friend

Come sit with me and hold my hand
Have lost my best friend and my man
And the father of my child
A hug, a kiss will be enough
To help the skin hunger for a while
My best friend is gone
With him went the rainbow of my life
The brightest star in the sky has paled
The magnolia fragrance is not the same
Need a splint to carry my heart
So full and heavy in my breast
Please some one
Pierce a hole into the center of my heart
And let the grief seep out
Guardian angel make me whole again
In memory of Bobby

Diana Simmons-Martin

The Man At The Gate

I've met a man who has
talent and charm, but most of
all he keeps us from harm
Everyday he stands at
the gate; to keep out the
bad guys until very late
He loves his job, and I
can see why. He walks
to the car and always says "Hi".
We should appreciate someone
so kind
Protecting our future, and real
peace at mind,
And then you'll see him on a
cart at night. Riding and watching to be sure we're alright.
So I don't worry we're all ok
from early in the morning, until the end of the day.
So just take, it easy as long
as you can. The man at the gate is
"One heck of a man"

Bernice E. Sullivan

Tell You No Lies

Ask me no questions, I'll tell you no lies,
and you won't get no flies in your soup.
Stop telling me about that guy that was trying to get with you.
He ain't nothing but an old piece of shoe.
He's got time to grade and give first aid,
While you're out trying to make the lute, give him the boot, honey.
Tell him to go make his own money.
Which reminds me of this girl I knew.
She thinks cause it's the weekend it's time for freak'n.
She likes to make men tense but she ain't got a lick of sense.
She needs to rinse her reputation clean, and go live an
American Dream, instead of being a disgrace to the human race...
around the block and see how much that girl talks.
I throw rocks and bust her in her knot. She's got to get got.
Maybe I'll go get Drew and her crew, so we can do what we got to do.
Maybe she'll have a ring around her eye, maybe even die.
Ask me no questions I'll tell you no lies,
and you won't get no flies in you soup.
So baby don't cry, I love you bye bye!

Kendra Harvey

Sealed Fate

Nervously I wait, knowing what to come won't be great.
Sorrow fills my heart, because I know I'm not that smart.

Sweat will begin to form, as the room suddenly gets warm.
I know my face will grow pale.
He always yells with no avail.

He always starts out nice, but I know that I will soon pay the price.
Soon he will start to yell, and this time I won't be saved by the bell.

If I try to explain, it's as if I'm talking to rain.
He builds himself a wall, that way he can never fall.

My stomach will start to churn
And a chance for a new beginning is what I yearn.
But I've already sealed my fate, all I can do now is wait.

I wait by the mailbox everyday
Hoping that report card won't come my way.
But I know that is not my luck
Maybe I can bribe the mailman and give him a buck.

Finally the report card came
Unfortunately the grade was still the same.
There's nothing left for me to tell
Now it's time to face the music and hear him yell.

Ann Sbonik

"Chasing The Rainbow's End"

Simple times so far away
I long so hard for yesterday
I'm chasing the rainbow's end
I've been chasing it every day
Simple fates or determined dates
With relative similar times
I'm chasing the rainbow's end
And I feel I'm losing my mind
Destiny may play its simple role
Or you may have to go it alone
But never chase the rainbow's end
Cause you'll give up your life
And you'll lose your friends
Give up your rights and every thing you own
for fortune and fame and a pot of Gold
chasing the rainbow's end
chasing the rainbow's end

Gary Hudgins

Silence

Weaver of a silent spell
Release me from your hold...

The secrets you have bound inside of me
Have made my spirit cold...

The mind releases its pressure
As the mouth gives forth the truth...

You'll torture me no longer
Or consume me with your rage...

I am breaking these chains that bind my heart
And kept me in a cage...

a prison made of fear
A dungeon of doubt...

Release me from your silent spell
And let me out...

Marilyn West

The One I Want

When I look at you,
I see the world, a clear path all the way through
When I look elsewhere,
The path is rough, and no one else can do what you do.
As you can see,
Your the one and only
that can shine the light even when I'm blue.
People may say you're the worst person in the world.
But to me, you're the key to my destiny.
I may cry when life passes by,
and you're not there so I despair.
So listen to the words I have to say,
from deep down in my heart.
You're the one I want.

Stacey Sullivan

Green Beans

How well do your beans grow?
How well do they fair?
Are you giving them your tender loving care?

I see they are growing, a little each day.
You can tell, the little beans
are not far away.

You water, you toil,
the earth at their feet
and soon, have their destiny -
at your table, to eat.

Dawn Rose Johnson

It's Not Right!

Stopping a life whoever heard?
How could things come to be so absurd?
Leaving a baby with no choice,
Refusing to listen to its pleading voice!

Enough violence is doing the killing,
But I guess in our hearts we are not willing...
To let a baby breathe just one breath
Instead of making it be down right death.

If just one chance is all you can give,
Do it for your baby, and let it live.
Another choice? No, this one seems best,
It's better then putting a baby to rest.

Because killing a helpless baby is obviously not right,
hopefully later people will put up a fight.
If they do it will for the best,
in keeping your baby you will surely be blessed.

Is that what God said for all of us to do?
To make there be no me and you.
When God created this earth, he made it for us,
so let your baby live, 'cause life only comes once.

Amanda Ibarra

My Tree

When I lay in bed at night,
I hear scratch, scratch against my wall.
I am scared. Then I remember,
what I hear is just the tall tree
that shades me in summer,
the tree that I climb on in spring,
the tree that I remember in winter,
and the same tree that keeps its leaves in fall.
That is my tree,
my tree near my wall.

Katie Schwan

Shirley

The loveliest girl I ever saw
Came to Norfolk in the fall;
I met her by the swimming pool
Looking so young, refreshing, and cool.

As we talked at the J.C.C.,
I noticed her smile as warm as could be.
Fifteen years later, I married this girl,
And when I look at her, I still get a thrill.

She's always so kind
And loving towards me
And my feelings towards her
Are as true as can be.

This lovely, young lady
From Minnesota did come
To visit the South
On an adventurous run.

But as far as I'm concerned,
God sent her to be,
A loving, guardian angel,
To look over me.

Jack A. Feldman

Attitude

I met a man who had no shoes.
  If I were him I'd sing the blues.
It seemed so wrong when I chanced to meet,
  A man that smiled who had no feet.

Happy or sad we have to choose.
  Do I have more than no feet or shoes?
Can I smile with what I've got?
  The answer's yes, I've been blessed a lot.

Our attitude plays the starring role,
  Of those things beyond our control.
We simply choose how we feel,
  In our mind, our thoughts reveal.

Life is the game we all must play,
  It must be lived day by day.
No one knows what tomorrow may bring,
  That is why "Attitude Is Everything."

Duane Beaulieu

Lost In The Past

Lost in the past I can only wonder what awaits the future.
You came in and rescued me at the worst point of my life.
Then you walked out and ever since I've been lost inside.
Missing you so much I never thought I would make it through the day.
Everyone tells me your in the past and I should thank you and forget.
But no one truly understands.
You kept me from killing myself.
I thought no one cared, but you showed me you did, which made me think twice.
You were there when no one else was.
I could go to you when I could go to no one.
You found me a place to go when I had no place.
You showed me the way, when I thought everything was hopeless.
You risked your freedom and didn't really care as long as I was safe.
You were and always will be the best friend I've always dreamed of having.
And you'll always be my best friend.
I've had friends come and I've had friends go,
But you will never leave my heart and you'll never leave my thoughts.
I'll always respect you, and you'll always be with me no matter how far apart we are.
I'll never forget you or what you did for me, when no one else would.
I'll never forget, no matter what anyone says or does.

Jennifer Alford

The Old Tire Swing

Gone is the laughter that it once knew,
Gone are the little bare feet that once danced around it.
Gone are the tow-headed kids that once clung to it.
Gone is the enjoyment it once brought.
Nothing ages something more than lack of use.
Left are the fraying strands that suspend the tire.
Left is an eerie creaking of the rope against the bough.
Left is the lonely sentinel of a tree guarding its treasure.
Its sunny days of summertime pleasure are gone.
Its only use is as a reminder of a harder but yet a kinder, simpler time.

Gary Linderman

"I've Lost What Was Once Mine"

I went for one whole month not knowing what was inside.
Then, one month later, it finally stopped trying to hide,
the birth of a baby made by me and you.
The birth of Our child, that had props from the two;
of us that has bonded this little life inside.
The hopes of a baby, the joys, the pride.
But, on December 18, 1995, the pain was very great, the hurt, the cries.
For I didn't really know what would be my fate,
I was loosing our baby—the one I carried inside.
I was losing a life, a joy, a pride.
My baby is in heaven, from thence it came.
But, there will be another from his holy name.

Jessica Blandin

The Rocking

The old woman sat rocking, rocking, rocking,
While on the door there was a knocking, knocking, knocking.
But the aged did not stir, just stroked her black cat's fur.
Then the door opened and footsteps came a-walking, walking, walking.

Slow and silent steps down the hall,
A quiet tip-tapping on the wall.
The woman's muscles tense.
Of something spooky she has a sense.
Then a shadow falls across the floor, big and silent, ominous and tall.

A rough dark face, a mop of greasy hair,
Creeps closer to the rocking chair.
Evil yellow eyes stare straight ahead,
The woman's heart fills with dread.
A sharp silver glint slices through the air.

A bloodcurdling scream, a hiss, such gore!
The rocking, rocking, rocking stops forever more...

Laurel Gordon

Dream Of Me

Close your eyes and go to sleep
And don't you shed a tear
Cause I've got you close and I've got you tight
To let you know I'm here.
So dream my love of special times
Both times fact and fiction
For in both those worlds you will always see
My arms to give protection.
But when night surpasses and dawn has come
And my arms aren't there to hold you
Don't fear a bit just dream again and
I'll be there to hold you.

George Temores

A Quiet Time

Lord, give me a quiet time
A quiet time to seek Thee—to find Thee
A time to say how much I love Thee
A quiet time to pray.

Give me a quiet time to praise Thee
A quiet time to thank Thee
Time to whisper words of sorrow
for every sinful deed
And to pray that today and tomorrow
Thou wilt grant our earnest needs.

Give me a quiet time to listen
A quiet time to hear Thee
A quiet time to learn Thy Way
My time alone with Thee each day.

A quiet time— a time a special blessing
A gift unlike all other
When my God speaks to me.

Patricia Ann Pajaud

Remembering Her

You were here
But now you're gone
What I want you to know
Is that your memory lives on

I know you're in heaven
With angels on high
The one thing I wish
Is that I could have said good-bye

The times that I knew you
Those times were the best
The only thing I can hope for you
Is that your soul is at rest

You were loved by family and friends
We loved you till the end
Your memory will never die
To you our love we send

The best thing that I can hope for you now
Is that God has you in his hands
I know that you'll be watching over us
As the sun sets over the land

Nicole Lopes

Utopian Mind

My heart feels heavy;
My mind is light,
Thoughts flow deeper; twisting my sight.
My eyes can't focus;
My throat feels dry,
Tears swell harder; burning my eyes
Your eyes like starlight;
Your voice divine,
I wish to the heavens; wish you were mine.
My body is floating;
My mind in a haze,
Seeing the Garden of Eden, my heart's amazed.
Retracing my footsteps;
You on my mind,
Thoughts off the past; of when I was blind.
My mind once weary;
My fears left behind,
Thoughts grow clearer; my Utopian mind.

Jeffrey L. White

Remembering Resolution

Each step we take marks time spent thinking which way to go
The direction we proceed tells us how much we have learned
A bag carries our personal egos colored enchained with the spirit
Our hands wash the tides rolling in from the shore,
Tide's up!
Remember, how much it cost you to be here on earth
At the emerge of man's evolution
Separated from that great force, the Light of Peace
Remember, what we came here to put in order, our purpose in life
Please remember who died in order for you to live
Years coming will embrace you like cold dry ice molding in paper
No water to melt the white ashen skin burning through to the soul
A flash back in a mega second, separating your body from its soul
Jetting across a screaming pulse with no form or purpose
No remembrance of life before your earth walk
Grandfather pray for us, we are pitiful people
These writings speak not about the dark days of the earth
Only the time we have wasted and the spirit we have lost
Hurry your things and be safe in the womb of Mother Earth
Only take what will heal you and Remember your Resolutions

Carla R. Rivera

Life Can't Be Planned

Life can't be planned
It is simple, yet so difficult
To grow up, while staying young
Without complicating what has been granted

You may be reasonable
But unable to explain its complexities
How something can be taken
No warning, no reason

Much time may be exhausted
Many feelings encountered
Goals may be met, goals may be missed
But time is short and must be enjoyed

For when time does end
Life shall go on, sunrise to sunset
Showing no emotion
Not sharing its plan

Gary P. Dean

Clouds

Right above my head
Over the soft wisps of gold,
Beyond the roofs of buildings,
Higher than the waves of green,
Containing the clear blue color
Are the great white puffs:
Cottony softness of number nine.

They are the emotions of weather,
Bringing darkness over the sun,
Laying on the mountain tops,
Or moving on the rivers,
Sometimes blinding,
Sometimes moving, yet always shaping.

They cover the moon, depict the color of the sky,
Show the clearing of storms,
Move to the other worlds,
They are void or colorful,
Perhaps a lady or a train.
A blanket of fog, they are.
Lying right above us are the clouds.

Alexis Deitrich

The Pinch Saga

When the sextuplets, all girls,
cascaded from Cornucopia Pinch,
her society whispered of the gigantic genesis behind shocked lace
yet was envious of the glorious spectacle of a multi-debut in later years, while plump Peter Pinch,
after fifteen, flinching years of keeping his jacket three-buttoned,
now strutted, jacket ajar, like a Priapean cock.

But Cornucopia abed,
flat as a disempea'd pod,
wondered whether that one delicious cuckoldry
with Lawrence, the young rake
had turned on the power in her womb,
full blast.

Dr. Weeder, obstetrician,
smiled in the privacy of professional ethics
at stone sterile, plump Peter Pinch,
Improperly prolific Cornucopia Pinch,
and the unknown, omnipotent stud,
whom he fancied roaming,
a magnificent patch of public domain.

Saul L. Neidleman

Made For Each Other

With her wit and wisdom she peaks my curiosity and
sustains my interest

It's these and many other things that make her grow
more dear

The more I admire her and for the more that I
appreciate her she becomes endearing with every passing year

From that infectious laugh to the indescribable
way she can merely illuminate a room filled with strangers

With every loving gaze in which she lays upon my very
receptive countenance I am convinced, that is the
look that is for me and for me alone

A willowy, angelic touch tingles my skin and reverberates
through my soul, she is for me and I am for her

Together we share a bond that telepathically makes
us one being
This is truly a relationship that cannot be confined
to the inner layers of this life

Mark Atkins

Beginnings

At first light of day, a droplet from white mountain's mantle
Joins scurrying rivulets wending their way through
Fields of wild flowers nodding at passers-by.
A meadowlark trumpets the coming of the marchers.

Leaves pull away from restraining mothers
To float with the pristine parade.

Soft following breezes set the pace
And lift tentative wings of fledglings,
Then release them to glide ground ward
For a grandstand view as stream stumbles over stones
In its unalterable procession.

Soft showers fall in step with the swelling
Ranks to meet the rolling river.

Rainbow's end points seaward
Where Troops break rank and disperse
To become debriefed by mighty swelling wave
As it curls from blue ocean's mantle
And submerges into the surging darkness of night,

Awaiting sun's revitalizing rays
At first light of day.

Norma Horrocks

Untitled

Like a ghost's welcomed presence
you suddenly appeared
Your voice
a familiar calm that washed over me
healing the aged flaw
Awakening the small voice
that I thought I had silenced forever
reminding me of
what once was
what was never forgotten
After so many long years
could it be revived?

But just as the life
was breathed into it
the light slowly faded
the dusty lid closed
and the small voice curled up
against the aged flaw
and struggled for sleep.

Bobbie Peacock

It's Spring Fever

The north wind dances up the lane
and sets the robins flying
It has a message plain and sweet
for some folks hear it singing
O' hurry, gather daffodils,
there scattered all over the hills
The little buds unfold again
It's spring, It's spring, It's spring

The north wind races down the road
and sets the green grass flying
It wakes the bee's and the bears
and some folks here it yelling
O' hurry, fetch your bat and ball
put on your oldest shoes of all
It's turning warm and hot again-
It's spring, It's spring, It's spring

Christina Knotts

Summer Seasons

Summer, summer, summer!
What a wonderful word
it brings the lovely light into so many things.
People can go swimming,
we can have a long vacation from school.
We can relax during the wonderful summer.
Summer brings joy and happiness to everybody.
The one thing I love about summer
is you don't have to go back to school for a long time.

Crissie Brown

Standing At Night's Door

The sky's ablaze with fire's hue
As we bid a long day adieu
The sun slips into a pool of dark
Leaving behind its fading mark
And as the sun's flames diminish away
The moon and stars come out to play
The stars cast pictures way up high
While the moon changes faces in the sky
And during this nocturnal play
We lock our doors and sleep til day
With pillows soft we curl up tight
And with nodding eyes we call good night

Rochelle Shireman

If I Were So Lucky As To Have A Dream

If I were so lucky as to have a dream,
I could be most anything I wanted to be.
Limited only by bounds of my own,
The world would be mine to see.

I could be a pilot,
And fly through the air.
Or an archaeologist,
And make discoveries that are rare.

I could be a baker,
And make the sweetest pies in the land.
Or I could be an artist,
And draw my figures in the sand.

I could be a doctor,
And come up with a miracle cure,
Or live on the streets,
Because I was so poor.

But alas, a doctor, or baker or artist I am not,
And this is not as bad as it may seem.
You see, I have been so lucky,
So lucky as to have had a dream.

Michael Olesnevich

Remembering Him

For our sins he died
"Do not sin" we should have tried
Mother at the cross, father up above
All he asked is for peace and love
Praise and homage, not what he got
Hate and suffering is what we brought.
There if we were would we have praised?
Or would we be caught in the devil's daze?
What he received is betrayal and pain
But really who are we to gain?
Up above, open the gates did he
After we're dead for our souls to flee.

Michelle Aparicio

The Ocean

The ocean, as calm as a quiet spring morning
The ocean, as blue as the sky on a clear day
The ocean, as deadly as a gunshot
The ocean, as beautiful as life itself
The ocean, too vast in expanse for the eye to see

Amara Davenport

The Gun

The cold black steel handle
waiting in your palm.
You pull your safety lock
you hear the pop of your enemy's gun.

You pull trigger, your hand is shaking,
you hear, a click, a pop, then a bang.
You hear the shot scream through the air,
then you hear a scream of pain.

You drop your gun, in hopes no one saw,
you hear the crash of the gun hitting the floor,
Another shot screams through the air, your Hit.

The last sounds you hear is your own heart going,
thump-thump, for a minute it becomes louder,
then it fades away into silence, You're Dead.

All this because you had a cold still handle waiting in
your hand, and you couldn't wait to hear it go
Click, Pop, and Bang.

Alberta A. Alvarez

Life

Life is a great adventure
An exciting discovery
In living, loving and learning
And being the best that one can be.

Life is knowing when to change
It's taking time out to grow
Life is befriending a fellow man
When he's feeling very low.

Life is sometimes taking a risk
It's caring, sharing, giving
It's joy and pain, loss and gain
It's all about this thing called living.

Life is falling down and getting up
And struggling once again
It's dreaming the impossible
That comes true every now and then.

Life is stepping out on faith
Whether the task is easy or hard
It is head held high facing into the storm
And forever trusting in God.

Lillie M. Prioleau

Moribund

Damp and dusky defiled towers,
Far above the pimps and prowlers,
Lurking, smirking, in high moon's hours.
Notice my brow, bending, burning, waging war against the warning,
Puffed pink lip is being bit, by the vampires in a voluptuous fit.

Though my face facades a fasting from awakeness everlasting,
Every licentious lash lies lull,
Still the dreams will pull and pull.
Hidden well-it is a prison-and my chest is barely risen,
Inhaling all the pithy essence of my fatal concupiscence,
Darkening dreams of dormant dungeons, disclosed by a deceiving wall.
Walls of white and pinkening flowers, blooming up and rising tall.
Clusters of clouds beneath my head, aid my slumber, but instead
Of days with delightful dewy dawns,
There are gravestones on my lawns,
Telling tales of terrible terror
About the ones who made the error;
Trying to escape this ineffable horror,
But never making it past the dungeon door.

Rebecca E. Bredholt

"Thomas"

A fog rolls in
and settles inside the deaf man.
It only clouds his thoughts.
He only hears what he can see.
A faraway gaze
says a lot for a boy with no face.

An explosion -
a burst -
he is bitten by a bug;
sudden energy from a place we don't see.
His moves - uncontrolled -
disappear inside him,
without a trace.

No germs,
no partner,
no homework.

Alone, sifting sand through his fingers;
His choice is to play solitaire.
He needs no one
and doesn't care.

Tina Spaulding

Variances Of Sight

Quietly above the timberline
Where vivid colors run dry;
Crowded tones of brown survive.
Summer rain clouds waiting over peopled towns;
Watched by anxious feet...lingering on the mountain's edge.
Inhaling precious freedom; dropping prison walls then
Breaking shackles locked by ignorance causing
Descended paces to soar the valley below.
Determination - spreads the wings of change
Lifting up and away from isolation's point of inequity.

At snowflakes upward beginning,
Higher still than red rose's growth,
Moss coloring embraces the stone's peace -
Does everyone see the same
Shade of green?

Hatred's vile broth nourishes
Bigotry's strangle weed.
Close not your eyes to pretend,
Apathy feeds the wait.

Anne Gusler

Trust No One

I see something in the fog,
Something big, black, maybe unreal.
Is it?
Or is it alive?
Does it have blood running through its veins?
Does it have to breathe to live?

I go closer, closer still.
The fog surrounds me,
But I see nothing.
It must have been my silly imagination!
I turn just to be frightened by someone or
something.
At first I ask myself, who is it? What...is it?
Then I see,
It was a trick of light,
And my eyes fell for it!

Shannon Hansen

The Seagull

I see a seabird, away I see it fly,
How I envy that bird, so way up in the sky.

You seagull of the ocean, how awesome you are,
How I love to see you, so proud and up so far.

My seabird, so beautiful with grace,
Yes, my heartbeat races, as you soar in open space.

Oh seagull, I wish that I could be like you,
I long to be in the air, and carry myself through.

You seabird so high, alive without a worry,
Please take me up with you, as we fly up in a flurry.

Oh seagull, oh seabird, please take me to the sky,
Please give me some wings, so I can fly.

Yes, lift me far from the earth below,
And then let me feel the airy flow.

Fine feathered friend, I'll be away up high,
I'll spread my very wings, as I fly up with a sigh.

No more will I be, just waiting down here,
I'll be flying free, with the clouds so near!

Wendyl You

Brush Strokes

Test the canvas. Begin the scene.
With gentle dabs, erase the green.
The browns and greys all slowly fade
as each touch leaves a softer shade.
With sleight of hand go boundaries.
A loving sweep clothes naked trees
in flowing gowns of sparkling white.
This dreary world comes into light.
Fresh layers add - one thick; one thin,
and newborn contours now begin
to form and shape and blend anew.
The old scene swiftly fades from view.
As all the forms dissolve to one,
and shadows move in unison,
approach the palette for the last.
And, when the final brush stroke's cast,
before us lies a world pristine-
purged of all grey, brown, and green.
An artist's touch begins to show-
The world receives new-fallen snow.

Clinton Earl Hunt

"Assistance"

Giving your all when there's so little left to give
Reliving the worst when there's so much more to live
Open your eyes to the possibilities of truth
Open your hearts to God's children, the elderly and the youth

Why are some tested with tribulations and trials?
And others accepted with sugar-coated laughter or chocolate-covered smiles
Some roads possess sharp curves and steep grades galore
This is where we start to soul search and truly explore

Excavating your memories with blisters and sweat
To reach contentment, you must first embrace regret
Promises of painlessness were never spoken or heard
But the sense of His security was felt without saying a word

Hope was abandoned and replaced with self-pity
Pretending to disappear in the arms of an empty city
I'm working on my final test, all I have to do is try
When I beg for assistance, He's always heard my cry

Dominic J. Guimont

My Reason Why

You are the reason I have a sparkle in my eye.
You are the reason that I cry.
You are the reason my heart aches.
You are the reason my heart breaks.
You are the reason I listen to our song.
You are the reason I think all night long.
You are the reason I day dream.
You are the reason that I scream.
You are the reason I am so blue.
You are the reason my love remains so true.
You are the reason I stand and stare.
You are the reason that I care.
You are the reason I shed tears.
You are the reason I want to stay near.

Kristin Moon

"Falling Teardrops"

Teardrops, teardrops falling from my eyes you see,
So many times I cry with teardrops inside my eyes,
So many teardrops falling from me you see,
Teardrops, teardrops falling from me you see,
You ask me why so many teardrops you see,
I don't know why so many teardrops
are falling from my eyes you see,
Now no more "Teardrops" falling

Allen Coleman

On My Way To Heaven

The shadows from the above clouds remind me
of the shadows of my inner soul. My past sometimes
haunts me, however, I know expecting Jesus as my savior
keeps me walking forward, how great life really is to have
that choice. The stones I step on reminds me of my
life I once had and has been stored in my memory
for days to come, still I feel peace for never again will
I take that road of carelessness from once I came.
The trees remind me of tears, how I remember all
I had given to whom I've met within my lifetime,
fills my eye with tears of joy, for this road I follow
leads me home.
The grass so rich and full, fills me up with the
memory of the never ending battles of what was then,
what is now, and what is to come, I fear no more.
My time will never be over, but on this mountain
my time has stopped. My life has just begun.

Terrie Fasolo

A Law Officer's Wife

When she kisses her man goodbye
and watches him go out the door
she says "take care of yourself, God Bless you!"
Watches him go, always praying silently
God will bring him home safe.
She always cherishes little time together
he could be called out.
Shift work, don't despair, work around it, he'll be alright.
When he isn't home on time, she worries,
and curses at how it's possible
he is in more danger then criminals he's after.
When looking for friends she screens them carefully
then despairs when their child's friends are not
allowed to visit because of dangers.
When she speaks with friends she wonders
if she's said anything and if she's just killed her man.
Remember not to worry your man about your fears
he might hesitate.
Indeed she's special.
My man, I love him dearly.

Yolanda N. Doherty

There Must Be

There surely must be another life
Where each morning begins right,
And the day isn't ruled by strife,
Where there's always a smile in sight
And courtesy enough for all mankind,
Where valuables aren't of measure,
But the clouds with silver lined.
There must be this unique treasure -
A place where love is given by all to all.

Grace C. Allison

First Meeting

Awkward moments make for funny times
When we re-live those precious memories
forever engrafted in our minds

And many an awkward moment are derived
From such accidental meetings as yours and mine

So I take this time-out to pen you these lines
In hope that we'll laugh together... someday.
When we remember this precious moment, while
looking back in time.

Kenyatta Collins

Selection From Untitled Group Of Rambling Thoughts

I am sick of your house of lunacy
Where I sleep upon a cold hard concrete floor in my cage
watching the sunshine crawl across that brick wall over there
all day through the harsh rusty steel grating they use
to hold me in my place.
I am sick of your house of lunacy
where I play with my fifty cent nickel store harmonica
the tunes of insane madness which I have learned
over these last many few years.
I am sick of your house of lunacy
where my roommate is a big f***ing smelly ape
who sh*ts on himself cause he doesn't know any better
he's wearing a blindfold you know.
Why not escape if you are sick the ape asks me
who needs to, I am not sick really
besides I really do like the view in here
and I would miss the sunshine and the apesh*t.

Frederick Lee

Inspiration

I have exorcised my lover;
I am empty, unpossessed.

I need another demon,
one with a weakness for me;

A devil-eyed sex god
to loosen my joints and tighten my thighs,

A piece of hell
to keep me warm in bed,

A horned god to shed some blood,
a consort with smouldering eyes.

I need Lucifer to probe the dark,
teach me how to fall from grace.

I need a serpent to help me shed my skin,
sink his teeth into me,
give me the vision of venom.

I need Pluto to feed me the fruit of his vine
so I know where to find him when

I need a wicked f**k,
to plant the seed of power,
the pomegranate, the poem.

Jen E. Mueller

Until God Steps In

He grabbed me,
touched me,
under the belt.
Ouch!
His pouch,
between the knees,
whetting through me.
I cry in pain,
and shiver to pieces.
Blackness comes by
as I enter the land
of serenity.
This my only hope
for survival.
Now makes me grope.
Is there no end
to the madness of men.
I definitely doubt not.
Until God steps in.

Davette J. McCready

Untitled

As we lie here holding one another I can't help but remember
the way things were and wish they were that way again.
When you would make love to me, and look into my eyes, dead
in the eyes and say with absolutely no doubt in your mind,
that you loved me.
But right now you're thrusting your body against mine, but you're
not making love to me...there's no emotion involved.
As I look into your eyes...dead into your eyes, I see a longing,
a longing for her, and I see the story in your eyes, but you're not
making love to me anymore.
You stop the thrusting. Your body moves slower, you see her,
in your mind you see her, and it's her you're making love to.

Jillian Freeman

The Cliff

Aching and hurting
tearing me apart.
Everybody lies,
pisses on my heart.

I feel
broken down.
Edge of the cliff
jagged rocks on the ground...

Razor's edge so perfect below
singing to me, calling to me.
Jumping is ecstasy.
Nothing can stop me.

I'm falling now,
down farther and farther,
below any depth I've ever known.
And what I get for jumping,
for those few seconds
I could fly.

Tracy Vardy

Last Breath

The blood flows from the sockets that once contained eyes,
The subject crawls along the hard wood floor, searching for his last
breath.
Creeping around in his own pity - a puddle of regret upon the ground,
Soaking in with his own blood and sweat.
Now, of all times, he finally say's he sorry for what he has done,
But if one were to look any deeper into his soul,
He would see that he was not - he is not sorry now - and he was not
sorry then. As I try to catch my breath
The sick f**k on the floor is aching for his - I wonder if he will
get it. Maybe - maybe not. My only thoughts are that I am now
complete, I have given my pet what he deserves.
And, what he Well deserves awaits him, still...And, what he needs,
he will never see.

So, my friend beneath my feet - beneath my breath - beneath my
illuminating power, and with this afternoon's events - beneath all
upon this meaningless earth, I give you this bread - to weigh upon
your weightless soul, so that you may fall into your own dark,
pit of hell. A hell of your own.
In hell you will be injured, alone and without breath, forever.
Are you sorry now?

David P. Fisch

Untitled

There was a young girl from Wiscasset,
Who carried her boobs in a basket,
When asked why they fell,
She said, "Go to Hell,
When I want your opinion I'll ask it."

Frank B. Aycock III

Our Delusionary Life

Look about you right now!
nowhere... no where is to be found
Life... real living - going on
what is visible, isn't really
think, quietly... Outloud - if need be
how we accept everything so freely
frivolous creatures you see
Greedy indeed... passing time simply - we want to please us
Fool! How we long to wallow
a real imitator, in disregard of our nature
Jump back, turn inward - out, scream!!!
look; into, through, beyond the Eyes of a child
not yet tainted by Wisdom - ha! What a farce
but, it's not too late... yes... it Is
Pray - Hope... means to a better end?
or perhaps, another guise
what is real? what is not?
does anybody really care by now...

Michael F. Stacy

To My Love

You gave me Love and lit my heart
You gave me hope for a new start
Even tho' that day may never be
My dreams will keep you close to me.
You are the things that means so much
Your high ideals to your loving touch
You make me feel that I'm worthwhile
And puts on my lips a wondrous smile
So always know that to make my day
Just think of me and when you may
Give me a call and let me hear
Those four small words "I love you Dear"

Mary E. Kennedy

Love Is Our World

Love, the source all people need and hunger for.
Love, it is needed and wanted just that much more.
When taken advantage of it is said to become sour.
When used carefully, slow and by the hour, can blossom
into an everlasting flower.
Love, changes for people differently.
Also for different people like you and me.
Those that have love are very lovely people gentle and kind.
Those that despise love find it burdening on their mind.
Those that know nothing of love live each day in agony and strife.

Danielle Roche

Interpretation

With two eyes the blind man perceives
Two visions. One vivid, one complete.
The first is one of handicap,
beyond that even he can conceive.
The next displays a gentle man as he says
"A wise man relies on sight as an art.
Because he can still see.
Even if light no longer travels to the heart."
With two ears the deaf man hears two thoughts.
Pessimism proves strong in bursts.
But optimism prevents him from becoming cursed.
With two hands we can contribute to two deeds.
With two feet we can continue at two speeds.
How busy our tongues must be through and through!
For with but one, we accomplish as much as two.

Kris Isham

Untitled

An epitaph to death and a beginning to insanity.
False prophets preach the truth; prophets preach falsehoods.
Life in insanity is a mirror with a neon, flashing, vacancy sign on it.
The prophets preach the preaches learn.
Alter boys graduate onto milk cartons.
The prophets: 1..., preachers: 0...
Who are the preachers, prophets, and "Mother Theresas" of our time.
They are the ones who died trying to make everyone like them, then...
Boom?!
White light — an ode to silence and a prayer to infinity.
This is the invitation to The utopic wet dream.

Phil Tenfelde

The Overabundant Fluid

To find killing someone is a joy for all eternity.
Fill the bathtub with the blood of that someone.
Smell the aroma of freshly siphoned elixir of life.
Feel the blood running down your hand.
Taste the salt in it.
Wanting to paint your body with it.
Being attracted to the fluid is intoxicating.
Bathe in all in its red beauty.
Rub you whole body in the mixture.
Store the life water in bottles for a future occasion.
Have friends drink the bottles at social times.
Give friends a shot at picking blood types to drink.
Send some to the phone company and the post office.
Find out that the blood is really from dead friends.
Tell the police that they have been missing for days.
Start the process over again and again.
Before you are sought out and executed.
Then taste your blood instead.

Joe R. Flores III

Think About It

You used to call me, when she fell asleep.
and when she was out of town...
  we were in her bed.
She never got mad when you worked late hours
but she found out, I could have died...
  laughing

So we were together
  happy
  screwing
night after night.
Then after awhile
you had to go to bed early
and work late.
Then I met Her...

And She laughed

Kirsten Ann Brink

Cornbread Beans And Taters

My girl just left me, and now she's gone.
  I'm glad she's gone she was always telling me where I could go.
I was getting tired of eating cornbread, beans and taters every night
anyhow.
  And in my very own house her precious fruit was forbidden.
Why I will never know.
  But she did keep it well hidden.
Lord I did not hate her,
  But there's bot to be more to life than just cornbread, beans and
taters.

James H. Pinkston III

One Of Many

I am one of many
Tired of the endless fear
Addicts there are plenty
Drug demons always near

Willingness, open-mindedness and honesty
Have been the main key
Finding my lost spirituality
Has brought me my recovery

God's guidance keeps me wise
No longer do I despise
Me, myself and I
Thank you for helping me come home
Thank you, now I'm never alone

Free, finally free
to have peace of mind
I was blind, now I can see
Now I'm confident, strong and kind
to live life in recovery

Christie Harlow Lasnier

I Hear You Ole Fallen Comrade

As a child, I read about you,
As I grew older,
I visited some of the places
Where you had fallen.

It was at those times,
I began to feel your presence,
And hear the faintness of your voices.

As I step across the field,
In the blazing sun,
The woolen gray heats.
The roar of musketry gets louder.

The smoke blinds my vision,
But above the cannons,
The yells, and the bugles:
"I hear you ole fallen comrade."

Terry G. Gardner

Desire

Two hearts impassioned,
inflamed in love
engulfed in heart's fire,
Both fully fashion'd,
Soaring high above
Fused together with desire.

Parting, Never parting
Always intertwined
Wrapped together
Ending and starting
Tease the mind
Souls tethered

Spirits move as one
Part of the heart
Forever singing
Never shunned
Love is art
Immortal bringing.

Sarah Thomas

Shadow

I am not alone.
I can feel someone or
Something's presence.
I look around but
I see nothing,
Looking down
From the corner
Of my eye
I see a shadow.
I look up but
See nothing,
I hear a noise,
I turn only
To see a shadow.
I hurry to the
Spot but see
Nothing,
I look everywhere
But cannot
Find it.
All I see
is a shadow.

Rolanda Cowboy

The Old Car

The old car grumbles
Down the street
Complaining all the way.

The wheels are turned in
The bumper is sticking out
Like an old man's lip
It has a tan from the sun
Its shiny head sticks out in the sun
That makes it squeak and groan

As it passes others
It grumbles a welcome

The young makes fun of it
But it can not hear
It went deaf long, long ago

The old car does not
Like speed or loud music

It prefers quiet country nights
To the loud city lights

The old car is Old man walking
slowly Down the street

Jennifer V. Slough

A Touch Of Your Hand

A smile in your eyes,
And my heart is yours, to do with
as you like

Your lighthearted laugh caresses
my ears like a sigh,
It's my love for you; I can
no longer deny.

As you take my hand and
promise me forever, tears roll
down my cheeks and my lips tremble

As our love grows with each
passing day, I treasure the
memories we have made and
will continue to make.

Nicolle Burke

Hope

'Ere my life is spent
In vain lament
Of a silent tongue,
My tongue!
Which might have flung
A challenge...
Let not my courage die,
Before a truant cry
Wings back to find
The bleak
Lonely reaches of his mind,
And soul.

Margaret Zivanovich

Thoughts

Now and then
Past memories
Walk through my present thoughts
Awakening hidden feelings
Creating within me
Laughter
Tears
Warmth
and
Thoughtfulness
But never indifference

Patricia A. Bulko

Together

I'd always had a thing for you
I knew it from the start.
You wanted to be friends but then
You had a change of heart.
You approached me and you smiled
I was nervous too
You looked deep into my eyes
And I smiled at you.
Then you said the thing that I
Had wished that you would say
I said yes and now I know
Our love will grow each day.

Kristin Jacobsen

Nature's Creation

As I gaze upon a sweet
scented rose images
of her celestial features
enter my once empty thoughts;
The soft, red petals
return me to the gentle
kiss of her lips as I gaze
deep into her pure
cornflower eyes;
I inhale the sweet fragrance
of the transforming bud
and am reminded
of her long strands
of majestic hair
as I hold her near me;
And as I gaze once more
upon nature's beautiful creation
I believe that one rose
cannot fully match
her beauty.

Richmond N. Morse

Nobody Understands Me

Nobody understands me.
I don't know what to do.

I live in a society where
parents think they know it all,
Kids think so too.

I often call out "Help,"
Who knows what to do?

Parents are paranoid,
Over protective to boot.

Their favorite word is Homework.
They like saying "No Dating."

The alarm has sounded
"You're Grounded."

Make-up is a not,
I feel my life is shot.

It is weird but true,
Teenagers need freedom too!

Kelly J. Kazlauskas

"Should We Sign"

With one sweep
Of their quiller pen.
The white man says
That he is our friend.

When in his heart
And in his hand.
He wants not us
But all of our land

Gene Katze

Morning Tears

Giggles abound.
Nervous fingers ignite the torch
heralding hates
revelation

Open wounds,
exercised by anger's salve,
create the rubble of
morning tears

Joy's habitat,
host to praise's exodus,
now issues only an
ember's lisp

Family portrait,
gallery of a neighborhood,
where picnics serve dreams, wakes
to nightmares

A cross,
black visage in a phoenix-like stance.
smolders, building a pyre
of mercy.

Robert E. Baker

Grandma

Sitting in her chair,
Big glasses, her hands sewing.
My quilt flows with love.

Kate Spanos

Baby Talk

Long before you could crawl or walk
We used to have a talk
Long before you could speak or greet
We use to have a talk
You spoke with your eyes
You spoke as you cried
You spoke with your smile
You spoke of the Nile
You claimed me your friend
Your love until the very end
It's amazing the things you told me
Long before you could talk

Steven A. Lee

Untitled

Passers by yield the shade.
Balls of cotton form in the rays.
Grey and white give depths so clear.
Drifting masses in the distance appear.
Holding the light behind its gloom.
Casting shadows into my room.

Steven E. Williams

The Spirit Of The Eagle

Soaring through the sky
So graceful and high
The eagle spreads its wings
It is not afraid to die

Up against the wind
Passing through each cloud
Its spirit stays strong
And it remains proud

Now those clouds are brown
Pollution's all around
The eagle tries hard
Not to fall to the ground

As the symbol of our nation
Getting wiped out from creation
The eagle must be swift
To escape from innovation

I once saw an eagle fly
Over mountain and streams
This memory lives on
Through pictures and dreams

Richard Brust

Fleeting

It was so long since I saw you
so imposing, so eclectic, so vast.
I stood in your exciting embrace,
merging my present, future and past.

You seduced me with your glitter,
the fanfare felt so grand.
You beckoned me to your inner beauty,
sensitivity and love of the land.

Our relationship moved too quickly
your world seemed so surreal
Through the noise I began to know you
in the crowd I started to feel

Our existence together came and went
so fleeting went the time
The experience may fade with each day
but the memories will remain sublime.

Ileene-Marie L. Mooney

Confused

As I walked along this winding road,
I stumbled upon many stones.
I can't tell what they represent,
Or even if they're Heaven sent.
But what I do see,
Are pictures in my mind.
Glances of times to be remembered,
And others left behind.
I see a fork,
Which way do the paths lead?
Will I fail, or will I succeed?
Who's to know?
No one does!
We cannot tell,
And never will.
But in the end,
May we rest in peace,
On God's window sill.

P. J. Scanlon III

The Oklahoma Bombing

There's not a day that passes where
nothing goes wrong
But when a tragedy happens we
have to be strong.
I heard a bomb and got lots
of fears. When I found out what
happened I broke into tears.
Many people got hurt, many
people died, some people laughed
but many people cried.
What happened that day was
such a shame, the person that
did it had to be insane.
Families were crushed and friends
were, hurt, there was no warning
there was no alert.
It happened yesterday, it could
happen today, I never thought
the world would turn out this way...

Kelly Jung

Insomnia

If I were to count sheep
before sleep
would I count till the day that I die?

Would the sheep wear down
to the monotonous sound
of my voice in the bed that I lie?

If I count day and night
would only sheep be in sight?
With nothing else passing me by?

But what if I can't sleep
to the counting of sheep?
Another method I'll have to comply.

Rebecca Pawlak

Autumn

The crisp scent of turning leaves;
as the sun hangs lower in the sky
air that was once thick with moisture
has now claimed a slight chill
the fragrance of a perfect fire
sitting near, gathering its warmth
sharing the moment with another
sipping wine, enjoying the serenity

C. Heath Crumbacker

"What If"

Lost in tragic, deadness vails.
Lost in somber, mystic trails.
Look beneath the battered nails.
A window full of sisters shells.
I look beyond the window side
A lost sister, I cried.
Cluster of tears went down my cheeks
To show my depression
through the weeks.
Nobody else to be with.
To go on with my life,
What if.

Katherine Garcia

Unthought Words

Softly dropped, the words we hear
Around the grapevine, soon unclear
Secrets told without a thought
Words that we have not forgot

No regard for right or wrong
True or false, words hold us strong
Blinding us till we can't see
Blurring our reality

Spoken poisons change our mind
Leaving common sense behind
Hatred makes our hearts grow weak
From the first moment we speak

Kirsten Halter

For Those

For those who love
Time is eternity;
For those who care
Know they'll always be there;
For those who share
Life is beautiful;
For those who see the sky's
Have beautiful eyes;
For those who cry
Life is do or die;
For those who find happiness
Must confess;
That they have found
The beauty of love itself
In themselves.

Andrea Troutman

World Of Writing

A world of writing,
is a world of thoughts.
And a world of thoughts,
is worth adventures.

Across seas and bearing lands,
there is a world of writing.
And a world of writing is
worth a thousand words.

Words are what we use
to speak our minds, and to
open up a world inside.

The world inside is filled
with words that fill our mind.

Jennifer Vasquez

Our Stenciled Rocker

Our stenciled rocker,
Black lacquer thin,
Branded by four,
Sits in the corner,
Behind closed door.

My rockabye rocker,
Back bedroom put,
Lullaby wore,
Rests in the moonlight,
Needed no more.

Old stenciled rocker,
Boneyslat stallion,
Born again be,
Help saddle insomnia,
Gallop with me.

Old stallion,
My stallion,
Come ride with me,
Out to the pasture,
Contentedly.

Marilyn Pond Bonasia

"Reflections"

Crossed and snugged a knot is cast,
Another birth, another blast.
Lost or found, never around
The fear in your heart torments me.

Canned and bound as if I the prey.
I scream, nor screech of hearing sound
My ears are clear, but morbid now.
It curdled and stopped as it started

My veins burst with lust of joy,
To remain only fullest of fury
Substitution condemns those like me,
Yet a replacement cannot level the sea.

Why did I pressure and attend
My heart as it never did;
To drive more than pitiful water.
Finally my purpose didn't matter.

Shall it be those of the light,
I fear it not so because it's bright.
For me to move is to fight
Let not tonight, be my last night.

Charlie Jay O'Neal

Indian Summer

The thermometer read seventy-three
Last winter is read twenty-three.
The unbearable change is on
Why have the good days gone?

Long for the lost of fall
When you hear summer's last call.
High pressure air fills the sky
Shades of blue that make you cry.

Don't forget what I tell you now
The time to be outward bound.
Years will come and they will pass
So enjoy these days while they last.

These are the days that I love so
And I always try so hard to hold.
An eye blinks, it changes so fast
Because tomorrow will be the past.

Thomas G. Scoggins Jr.

Our Special Day

Our special day comes
But only once a year
It gives me a special feeling
Whenever it draws near

It's the day we made the decision
To live our lives together
And on that day I knew
You'd be with me forever

We've had many pleasant times
And some rough ones too
But even through our darkest hours
Our love always remained true

I knew you were the one for me
When you first came into my life
Now whenever I look at you
I know my choice was right

No matter what people think
No matter what they say
I know our future holds
Many more of our special days

Jeffrey Glenn Ayers

The Climb

Long ago I fell
I fell in a very deep and shadowy hole
I was really alone
I climbed out
I saw the sun
I gave a shout
I fell in the hole once again
I climbed out
I shouted louder
I grabbed a rope
I began to fall
I climbed up the rope
Touched a rainbow
And she smiled

Ray Yorba

We Will Miss You

We must each go on our way
As your soul sails on high.
Still memories will stay
To keep your spirit nigh.

There are days to remember
As we raised six children so dear.
Times we will remember
To keep your spirit near.

World War II was over
And life was looking bright
We felt we were in clover
As we hoped they were right.

Simple days of fishing
In raggy-tag clothes.
It wasn't just for wishing
Hard work kept us on our toes.

You are no longer here
To help us carry the load.
Still you will always be near
As my story has told.

Irene I. Woodring

Self

Love yourself
Every day
Love yourself
So others may.

Love the above
Not to excess
But love the above
Nevertheless.

Love is constant
Love is kind
Love is patience
A state of mind.

Love will keep you
Groomed and clean
Love will keep you
Mild, not mean.

Love yourself, and
You will find
You'll always be
A friend of mine.

Robert L. Marthey

My Brother

He wasn't my brother
It wouldn't hurt,
Or so I thought...
And then... he died.

They took him to this
final resting place,
The trumpet wailed
the farewell Taps,
The hurt creeped from deep
within my soul
And formed in crystal droplets
on my cheeks.
Then I knew...
He was my brother, too.

Madge F. Hans

"The Sound Of Your Laughter"

The sound of your laughter
Echoes in my heart -
And fills my life with magic,
Giving each morning a musical start.

Like a sweet melody
Playing in my ears
It brightens my darkest hour
And calms my deepest fears.

The sound of your laughter,
That's given away so free -
Is like an undying carousel...
That envelopes your love around me.

Your beautiful smile -
Your twinkling blue eyes -
Are like God's unending rainbow...
You're an angel in disguise!

Kay Jordan

Losses

I lost my dog but he came back.
I lost my watch; I'll buy another
I lost my child...
Every day for the rest of my life.

Mary Allen Wiggin

"Dependent"

A motherless child is like a
babe in the wild.
Set free not knowing where
or who to be.
You see, a child needs its
mother like no one other.
Not anyone can replace
that smile a mother puts on its face.
A mother is the one that
always gets things done.
Without a doubt no
child should be without... A mother.
I have to say with all honesty
not shame, without a mother
a child can truly never be tame.

Debbie Genraich

Kiss

The burning beach sand
beneath our bare feet
we run hand and hand
towards the glistening sea
the water
to the ankles
to the knees
to the thighs
the plunge
beneath the translucent waves
in the underwater silence
swimming towards each other
our faces wave
in the liquid light
when carried by love
we are lost
in a long kiss
on a wooden bench

Flaviu Cristian

Universe

Earth, the embryo
nourished by the Milky Way's
umbilical cord.

Sandra Louise Allen

A Child's Fears

A thunder crash, a lightning strike
Across the fierce sky.
A moon concealed by a cloud of gloom,
A frightened child's cry.

A mother's voice says "it's all right"
To calm her child's fears.
A kiss good night, and a soft cloth
To dry her child's tears.

The child sends a prayer to God,
"Please calm the storm I pray?"
He yawns and then he falls asleep,
Asleep to dream of play.

The morning comes and he awakes
To smell the morning dew.
A morning filled with happiness,
A day that's truly new.

Jamie Sanders

Astral Cognizance

Europe, Asia and Africa
Australia and Antartica alike
North and South America
None are veiled from their light

Witnessed creation in seven days
Hear seven petitions of The Prayer
Saw seven gifts of spirit
Looking down with twinkling stare

On all seven days
And over all seven seas
Give ear to seven notes
Aflame with gracious harmony

See seven metals obscurely
Abhor seven sins
Admire seven Wonders
Will you ever feel alone again?

Ever watching over
At dark hours of time
A magical kind of audience
Completeness beheld by their shine!

Timothy W. Harmon

My Lonely Heart

As I lay my head upon
Your pillow tonight.
My lonely heart cries
out for you tonight.
As I wonder of how
you sleep alone tonight.
From the distance of
our hearts tonight.
The sorrow that you
leave in my heart.
As it brings tears to my
eyes down upon your pillow.
My heart will await for
your love to arrive.
As I face the fear of
emptiness this lonely night.
For my lonely hearts cries
out to yours tonight.

Susan Ryant

"My Heavenly Haven"

There's a delightful place I treasure
By a pond outlined by trees,
Once again I feel God's presence,
In the soft and gentle breeze.

The birds and clouds above me
Sail silently thru the skies,
My thoughts all seem to join them
Erased are my tensions and sighs!

In the midst of God's might and wonder
How frail I must look to him.
Yet I feel His love within me,
And I know it will never end!

Carol Altman Carlsen

Creation

With your hands,
You can create many things.
But without your mind,
You can create nothing.
And without your soul,
It Is Nothing.

Sharon Morris

Our Little Angel

The newest star in heaven,
that we will see tonight.
Is that of little Taylor,
shining down on us so bright.
Although she's very tiny,
she is very strong.
She will be with us forever,
as the days and nights go on.
We really never knew her,
but love her with all our hearts.
As today is the beginning,
of her brand new start.
She's the newest little angel,
in the heavens way up high.
Looking down on all of us,
with sparkles in her eyes.
Although it's hard to say good-bye,
to someone that we love.
Just remember every night,
she's shining down from up above.

Kim Carson

Awaken

Oh little world
Of little faith.
You will never change.

Why revolutionize?
It only speeds up the inevitable.
Why stargaze with
Your eyes unopened?

Poor souls.
Proud individuals.
You have been loved
Without saying
Thank you,
And you will die
Not knowing
Why.

Judee G. Duncan

Eyes Of Nature

I Walk Through the Forest
Among the Trees,
I Look for Eyes I can not See
The Eyes of the Deer
The Bugs and the Bee
Eyes I do not see That see Me
The Eyes of a Squirrel,
a Mouse and the Bird in the Tree,
Eyes I look for but never see.
Eyes of Nature are always there,
They look at me
They sometimes stare,
These are the Eyes I do not see
The Eyes of Nature That See Me.

James Derr

My Flower

Mystical powers,
My own flower,
Blossom and flourish while there is still hours,
Orange and green,
Yellow and black,
Purple and red,
No matter what color,
Soon it will be the hour of power,
And the moment for my flower.

Lisa Gayle

Semantics

Then there was the word
Should
before want
in place of need
like a cracked bell ringing
incessantly
Should would have me sane
compliant
but after should comes the
Why?
Of a child caught between
wisdom and naivete
Let the world fly
crash about like Gods
their spoils a pitiful scattering
of feathers in a meadow
still not enough meat
What hell can be worse than this one?

Sarah Bramley

Walking Papers

It's time to give
you your
walking papers,
as a wise old
man once said.
For surely I do
not know which
way we shall be
lead. We may
reach a
mountain peak
with nowhere left to go,
or we find a river's stream
that will forever flow.
At any rate I sign my name
along the dotted line
and give to you a freedom
that may suit you
very fine.

Tina Novellino

The World Slips Away

I feel the world slipping away
The grass the dirt tugged from under me
I fall and fall
Grasping grabbing
All I find is air

Darkness falls
I stumble blindly I don't know where
Loneliness sets in
I cry and cry
Screaming for a friend
My hollow echo is the only reply

Trapped in this realm of darkness
I long to be free.

Brian Baldowski

The Reckoning

A clock is just a timepiece
It doesn't do much more
So why do people treat it
With authority galore?
It wasn't born a monarch
It will not die a king
But time's what makes the clock
And time's the reckoning

Marjorie A. Susens

"Colors"

Yes, if there were no colors,
Like the clear blue of the sky;
Or the snowy white of the clouds,
that float so softly by;
or the color of the trees so green,
it would surely make you cry;
And the yellow of a butterfly,
softly flapping its wings;
Or the beautiful red color,
of a red bird as it sings;
If there were no colors,
to brighten up our way;
we wouldn't be very happy,
this, or any other day;
Yes, if the colors, my love,
you could not see;
I could not see you,
and you could not see me;

Mildred Huddleston

The Grieving Process

There never seems to be a way
To show just how you feel
About a special someone
To prove those feelings are real

And when you finally find
A brand new way to care
You turn to show affection
And that someone isn't there

So you sit and cry
All alone at night
Never getting a bit of sleep
As you hold your pillow tight

When the day becomes the darkness
And the dawn becomes the light
Just let your loved one's spirit rise
And you'll begin to feel alright

And when you think of all the people
Who have come and gone
Just remember all the good times
And let their memories live on

Christina Margaret Larimore

Puffs

You've come a long way, baby -
your smoke blisters my eyes.
We trade chairs
but your smoke rings still
find their home.

Smokebreaks at dinner sustain you,
like rest stops on a journey
across the menu. You season
your steak with smoke;
for mine, I like pepper.

Your small daughter hid
the pack in the fire place.
You smile at the note
she snuck into the pack:
"Smoking is bad, Mom, bad for you."
But you puff.

Baby, you've come a long way
into the statistics of charred lungs;
I trade chairs with you -
but I'm still downwind.

Franz J. Leinweber

Ode To Nicole And Ron

The night was pale
The new moon grew
The air was sweet
...The babes slept through
And a dog barked in Brentwood

A friend came by
She'd asked him to
They said "hello"
...The babes slept through
And a dog barked in Brentwood

A figure dark
In black and blue
Destroyed two souls
...The babes slept through
And a dog barked in Brentwood

If we could know
What's really true
Would we understand
...Would the babes sleep through
Would a dog still bark in Brentwood

Patricia Lillie-Whelan

Colored Rags

Red and blue
used to symbolize the flag
But these days
They are colors of a rag
A car drives by...
The head lights out
They see a blue
And shots ring out
A blue is dead
Was shot in the head
Now all his friends
Are seeing red
I'll get my revenge
A blue rag said
As this on-going battle
Runs through his head
Lives that are wasted
Society dreads
This on-going battle
Between blues and reds

Cyndee McGuire

The Wayward Trip

Before Him now I do confess
My soul have sinned and I regret
Please help me mend the wrong I've made
And let again indulge His grace

My song is now a broken tune
And my flowers refuse to bloom
Look at the stars and at the moon
And trace the shadow of my gloom

Right with these knees all eyes aglow
Hearts do rejoice in words untrue
Shame, Oh man take all thee blow
My dreams it's shattered shall I for ego

There's only one to Him I run
He waits for me extend my arms
And when He lifts those loving hands
I see the prints of what I've done

Love known better this soul at last
My strength are ropes my pride are dust
That escapade that once I've trod
I know I've hurt the heart of God.

Mar B. Velasco

Your Touch

Your touch is what I long for,
your touch is what I need.
When all my days are cloudy
and I feel lonely and blue;
The one thing that I wish for,
is that special touch from you.
Your special touch will always last,
for a week or maybe two.
Until at last I'll need again,
that special touch from you.
Your special touch I'll always feel,
no matter where I'm at.
Your touch makes me so happy,
you can see because I'm never blue.
So remember if you ever doubt,
that all my smiles are true;
Believe your touch is all I need,
to make me smile at you!

Katie Nulty

Among...

Among the roses there are thorns.
Among the thorns there is despair.
Among despair there is pain.
Among pain there is sadness.
Among sadness there are tears.
Among tears there is blood.
Among blood there is life.
Among life there is a soul.
Among a soul there is emptiness.
Among emptiness, somewhere,
there is happiness.

Autumn R. Corcorran

The Robin

The robin, whose home was destroyed
in last summer's storm,
and whose babies were killed
by marauding raccoons,
has returned this year,
showing no signs of trauma.

He begins his joyful warbling
before the break of dawn
and, after the morning concert
busies himself with gathering
bits and pieces for his nest,
creating security for the future.

I'm impressed by his optimistic zeal,
but even more than that,
I am made humble
in the presence of his forgiveness.
No small creature this, but
a teacher of infinite proportions.

Carolyn Powers

Prime Time TV

Abandon
Abort

Desert
Divorce

Through away children,
husbands and wives,

Plastic families
and through away lives.

Arlene E. Valdes

When I Am Gone

When I am gone, cry not for me
my dearest; for I have loved
and had my love returned.

When I am gone, weep not for me
my daughter; for I have dreamed
and had my dreams fulfilled.

When I am gone, grieve not for me
my son; for I have often flown
to lands familiar and unknown.

When I am gone, shed not a tear
my grandchild; for I have lived
and watched as you life enjoyed.

When I am gone, mourn not for me
my friend; for we've experienced
the joys of kinship shared.

Rejoice, rejoice you well instead,
remembering I loved you all,
as I answer to my Father's call!

George S. Watson

Saddest Good-bye

I want to cry,
think to say good-bye.
I expect you one day,
call to say Hi.

I don't want you to go away,
but you are leaving any way.
My feeling is not enough,
this good-bye will be tough.

I am on the floor,
you are up in the sky.
A star will guide your way,
after you close the door.

Your ambition is more,
but I want you to know.
I will be here,
always waiting for you.

Evodio Hernandez Jeronimo

Believe

You have angels by your side
Walking down the winding roads
The angels feel your sighs
They know your pain
But your head is still held high
They picked you because you are strong
You love, you hate, you cry
And you still have pride
The angel is there by your side
Always and forever
Believe and you will see
The dreams you dream
Will come alive
Because you believe

Christy Varnell

Love's Expression

Eyes appraise and seduce—we embrace.
Touches ignite, your kisses fire me.
Passion consumes...
Fulfilling ecstasy,
Comfort, and peace.

Pamela R. Myers

If

There are some questions I have in
My mind, and I have had these
Questions for quite some time.
Question's like
If we died where would we go
If it was no heaven
If it were never so, things like
If the birds didn't sing, and the
Flowers didn't grow
If we had no earth
If it were never so
If the world was flat instead of
Round, would we fall of, would
We go down.
These things often make me wonder
Sometimes I just sit and plunder,
But
If love and God are always near
Then I know there's never anything
To fear.

Marcia Nicole Sonnier

Darkness Falls

Darkness falls across the land,
As day begins to die.
Doors are barred and windows latched,
As evening cloaks the sky.

Shadows loom in waning light,
And bleed a shrouded shade.
People hasten to their haunts,
As twilight's tears are made.

Moonlight veiled in blackened cloud,
Is drowning vision's plight.
Men adhere to cautious wonts,
Their world eaten by night.

Darkness falls across the land,
As day has gone and died.
Eyes peer into the abyss,
The universe made wide.

Kenneth Miller

A World Of Pain

Are we living in a world of glamour
and fame?

Or, are we living in a world of
flickering flames?

For we will never know for who's to blame.

But then again it's all a shame.

Are we going to continue to stain our
hearts with so much pain?

For who is to gain?

In this time and age, when will the
world ever change?

For in this haste, we're losing our pace.

Sherita Swinton

The Day The Tree Cried

Limbs were cut,
The tree cried,
No human heard,
Only other plants,
Heard the cry.

Scott Rios Caldwell

My Mom

You're cozy warm
You're nice and sweet
And you shine like a star
And when you go to work each day
I feel you're way too far.
You tuck me in
You say good-bye
You help me when I'm burning
And every time I make mistakes
You tell me that I'm learning.
You taught me everything I know
Like how to tie my shoe
And every time that you're not here,
I really, really miss you.

Lauren Paige Moore

Our American Flag

O Flag of a resolute nation,
O Flag of the brave and the free,
O Flag full of joy and color,
That we are proud to see.

The red shows blood,
That still is shed,
In other lands,
They now lay dead.

The white shows honor,
All spotless and clear,
A symbol of justice,
That is always kept dear.

The blue shows the sky,
So spacious up above,
How can we forget
Our God and His love.

The stars show sadness,
Because one day,
They were hung in windows,
For one who was away.

Rita D. Barr

What I Am Without God

I am a lost bird in a storm
Seeking a place that is warm
With no shelter among friends
This journey never ends
All I see are twists and bends
No mercy do they lend

Where is the shelter that I seek
In a tree by a creek
I find the branches there are weak
With no food for my beak

Off I fly again
With no peace or a friend
Until Jesus comes to mend
All my pain and then

He gives me a nest
A quiet place to rest
Safe from harm and distress
He is my friend the very best

Ethan Beaver

The Writing Of A Child's Poem

A story unfolds in a child's mind.
It starts as a fairy tale.
Then changes. Slowly forming a poem.
At first the words are jumbled.
They don't make any sense.
Then, like a lightning flash, it all
becomes clear.
Words flow onto the paper like the
sand in an hourglass.
The child writes quickly and
then corrects.
At last the poem is finished.

Danielle Moore

The Opening

Down its length the rifle barrel
is as dark as ebony keys on a piano.

At one end a cartridge waits in its
chamber to be struck by a hammer.

A spark of light flashes for
only a few seconds.

For a moment the rifle barrel
is not dark, it comes to life.

The bullet leaves through the
opening of the barrel.

As a robber steals money
The bullet steals life.

Kathy Bell

My Niece

You are my niece, my sister's child
Sometimes sweet, sometimes wild
Most dependable; a lot of fun
could be true friend or just a chum
Short, tall, fat or thin
In any contest you would win
my niece, my sister's child

Frances Frale

"Heart And Mind"

I never thought
there'll be a day
where you would be
so far away,
not in miles
nor in time
But in your heart
and in your mind
There may come a moment
in your life
Where you must part
to survive
But as you grow
you recognize
The time has come
to realize
that once again
you hope to find
what you have lost
in your heart and mind

Diana Delgado-Millington

Thanksgiving Prayer

Blessed Lord we give thanks and praise
to You; for all You have given us -
This table laden with Your blessings
We know is the Master's touch.

We pray You will bless those who
can't be here -
Our loved one's far and near;
But we will rejoice dear Lord -
this prayer we know you will hear.

Dear Lord help us to remember;
That You are the One who provides,
and if we will give You first place
in our hearts -
With us You will abide!
In Jesus Name Amen.

Patricia Summers

The Scented Rose

It is like a blooming rose,
The faint perfume I smell.
Reminding me of long ago,
A place we used to dwell.
In the meadow by the house
Where all the flowers grew,
I would pick a small bouquet,
And bring it back to you.
While placing them in water,
You would look at me and say,
"Please do not pick the roses,
For the scent will fade away."

A. M. Corbin

For Greg

follow the inside curve
of a tortoise shell night-
and the days in tidal flow
awaken cells-
warm to the movement of being

(two butterflies mate
in the air)

surprisingly he died-
leaving me behind,
missing him
as I do the lilacs-
remembering his scent.

earth rise-
hear the heartbeat
then whisper goodbye.

Michaele Stephens

Tar Cat Car

Two cats fighting in the road,
one run over,
the other one oh—!
Missed that truck, caught a car,
went to Kentucky which wasn't too far.
Came back home,
went out in the road,
Smash, went the tar
Ouch, went the cat
F-R-E-S-H C-A-T
F-R-E-S-H T-A-R
all over my new car!!!

Judy Delph

God Holds Tomorrow

I know who holds tomorrow
And I'm glad He's there for me
Because whatever happens
Beside me there He'll be

None other can accomplish
The things that He has done
He gave His saving grace
Through His one and only Son

No matter where I journey
In the things I do each day
He sent the Holy Spirit
To guide me on my way

The love He has for me
When I stumble or fall down
Is shown in His patience
From the one who wears the crown

He's waiting there for me
To grow and spread my wings
So I can tell to others
What His saving grace will bring

Jean Carter

Father

When I look into his eyes,
My heart it drips and melts,
Into a puddle of tears I cry,
The feelings I have felt.

The words he says breeze past my soul,
Like a feather in the wind,
And the laugh he can so tenderly sound,
Make all my troubles mend.

The way he moves so gracefully,
Makes my mind grow wide.
Is he a gift from heaven,
Or an angel from up high?

When he reaches out,
To take my hand in his,
Or to lightly stroke my arm,
I know that he is there for me,
To keep me from all harm.

For I have defined the word Father,
Both Earthly and Heavenly.
Is our Father here on Earth?
Or a Father we can't see?

Bobbie M. Williams

Secret Love!

Someone told you the secret that
I strongly kept.
Now that you know I've hardly slept.
Even though you know you seem
like you don't care.
This is a pain I just can't bear.
It seems to me my dream of
us will never come true.
If only you could see my tears
so blue.
You make my heart hurt oh
so much,
But you could heal it with the
slightest touch.
You know how to cure me,
But it's something you just won't do!
Even though you've hurt me my
love will always be true,

Kim Miskofski

Willing To Receive

O, Father, just to be with you
Gives me a hunger and a thirst
I know that when love began
Yours was given first.

You gave it to me freely
It was your special gift
All I had to be was willing
And give my arms a lift.

Your outstretched hands met me
And caressed a heart forlorn
My feet? They began to dance
I was a child reborn!

This gift is indeed the present
For I threw away my past
I now look forward to tomorrow
When I will meet my Lord at last.

Ruby Rager

Journey Of The Heart

My God has heard my cry for help
and you are His answer
you provide a place of refuge
where it is safe to explore

In this labyrinth of childhood
memories you gently lead the way
-opening my heart, mind, and
spirit to the truth

A healing balm for a wounded heart
A lullaby for the inner child
Rest for the mind
Hope for the spirit

This reawakening of inner wisdom,
born of hurt and tragedy, holds
the expectations of a new dawn
in this journey of the heart

Pamela J. Stegall

World Of Wonder

In a small white bath tub,
with nothing to do
sat a tiny boy wondering
with his chubby frog Lou.

Puerto Rico, or Belgium,
or under the sea,
yellow flowers and buzzing bee.
How fun it could be to visit them all,
to see new places, to look in a mall.

To eat new things,
to climb a tree,
to ride a horse
how fun it would be!

In a bath tub
that wish couldn't
come true,
it'll be just a hope
for the boy and Lou.

Nicole Jaspers

Who Am I?

I've sent you this poem
For only your eyes to see
I want you to guess
Who you think I could be
I wish I could talk to you
And tell you how I feel
When I look into your big brown eyes
All my words just disappear
My heart beats like crazy
Whenever you walk by
I wish I could say more
Then just a simple hi
I realize I don't see you much
Only once in a great while
But I know if I saw you more
I could always make you smile
So if you know who I am
And you feel the same way
Please stop by sometime
We'll make a date for someday

Andrea Wade

Two

I can't see in here.
I wonder what time it is,
Is it day or night?
Winter or Spring?
I wonder what color your eyes are
I can feel your arms and legs
And we talk for hours and hours.
By the way,
Are you black or white?

Gretchen Fahrenbacher

Where Did Yesterday Go?

When I was young
The years went slow.
Now I've grown old,
Where did yesterday go?

Where are old friends
I knew in the past?
Where is my first love
I thought would last?

Where are the dreams
I had of wealth?
Where is the radiance
And bloom of health?

New friends I have
And hold so dear.
No wealth have I
That much is clear

But peace I possess,
The best gift I know.
But still I wonder
Where did yesterday go?

Ann Boyles

The Fly

There was a horrible, awful, smelly fly
With nothing else to do but fly.
Decided to fly right into my eye
And buzzzzed my ear,
  and tickled my tie
So that is why I killed that fly
Who was a horrible,
  awful, smelly fly.

Brian Hostetter

Untitled

When you cry those silent tears
I hear the thunder inside of me

When you cry those silent tears
I hear the rain falling inside of me

When you cry those silent tears
I hear the ocean rising inside of me

When you cry those silent tears
I hear the clouds closing in on me

When you cry those silent tears
I hear the sadness inside of you.

Natonya Griffin

Let Me Fly Away

If I get too hyper
If I get too depressed
Unlock my chains and let me fly away.
If I get too tired
If I get too angry
Unlock my chains and let me fly away.
If my friends annoy me
If I get too jealous
Unlock my chains and let me fly away.
If I get too talkative
If I start to stutter
Unlock my chains and let me fly away.
If I start complaining
If I fall in love
Unlock my chains and let me fly away.
If I start not concentrating
If I start to work myself too hard.
Unlock my chains and let me fly away.

Erika Galica

Mary's Son

As I look upon a baby's face,
I put myself in Mary's place.
Gentle Mary, meek and mild,
Giving birth to Christ - the child.

I wonder how she must have felt,
As in the stable shepherds knelt
Paying homage to the one
She had birthed - Christ, the Son.

To know that at her breast she nursed
The very One who made the earth.
To rub his cheek, to hold the hand
Of this babe known as Son of Man.

How overwhelming it would be
To know that all eternity
Would forevermore be changed
By her Son with his Holy name.

She was the vessel God used to bring
To earth - Jesus Christ, our King.
But though she birthed the Holy One,
To her, he was still her son.

Kathy Edwards

Winter Blanket

Light downy snowflakes falling
  Falling from where,
Why from God's Heaven!
God's light downy symbol
  Of winter..... Calmly,
floating down to instill peace
  upon a cold world.

Linda J. Baughman

Blue Haze And Light Dark

A pale blue haze
A light in the dark
Not a sound in the world
Except the beat of our hearts
The stars shine bright
The moon is full
The scent of roses
Fill our souls
A soft low sigh
A deep dark moan
You hold me so tightly
That I can almost
Feel your bones
In your arms
I hope I will stay
Until we can see the first
Light of a new day

Melissa Chapman

Clueless

Short skirt, baby top
You never know where to stop
Pastel lipstick and nail color
Napkins make your bust look fuller
Nothing but the best for you
The latest layered "Friends" hair-doo
What are all the models wearin'
Calvin Klein, Guess, Donna Karan
Go out to the mall with friends
Follow all the latest trends
Oh my God! you've got a zit
Now you'll never get Brad Pitt
Wear your shirts very tight
Wash your hair every night
Don't forget your precious lipstick
You're a very "with-it" chick
People sometimes laugh at you
You're spoiled, dumb, and have no clue
All that matters is your look
I'd like to see you read a book.

Ana Sirabionian

Imaginary Love

My love comes to me
Out of calm summer breeze
His tender embrace
Takes my breath away
(His) eyes softly tell me
He'll never let go

Waves caress the sandy shore
A gentle breeze blows the sheer
Curtains of our moon lit room.

His kisses are passionate making
Me want more. Every touch and
Breath heightens my desires for him.
Making me want to stay forever.

He see's to it I have all
I'll ever need. I'll never leave.

Renee English

Mirror Of Creation

Mountain ranges, firm since time began;
Dwelling there, the lion and the lamb.

Rivers nurturing, trees and brush
Harboring creatures great and small.

Beautiful creation, all!

Charlotte J. Williard

His Child

As I sit here and wonder
How you left me as you did
I can't help but think
Will you ever want to see your kid

Now there's only thing in my life
Is your child I carry
It's not the best thing for me
We had plans to marry

As we drifted far apart
There's nothing left for us to share
Will you want to see your child
And be good enough to care

This is for him
And hope someday he will understand
That he has a child in this world
Waiting for him to hold his child's hand

Now he's gone
And his child is here
He looks like him
Now I have nothing to fear

Bonnie L. Perry

Oklahoma City Bombing

The loud roar in disbelief,
The bomb that hit to the
core of everyone.

Hear the sad song of the
dying,
The song that of which
was crying.

Many were unified,
In which died.

As the building fell,
It was like being at the
gates of hell;

In The Oklahoma City Bombing.

Ashley Metelmann

A Shadow In The Flame

Sitting huddled in black lace
an evil little smile
-innocent in every way
a spider
blood sucking
the widow of many
soon to be wife of another
temptress
twine the world in your alluring
web of desire
bate the trap
light the fire
drink the poison
and eat your meal
Savor it and truly love it
-that sweet smell of death
Soon it will be yours

Colleen Mills

A Love Burn

When love grows strong,
It shoots out like a wild fire,
That can't be controlled
and it will keep growing
unless it get's put out.

Alicia Tveit

The Wild Flower

I'm a wild flower
wilting indoors
I belong in meadows
and hills and rocks
I love the caress of the wind
and the kiss of the sun
I like to be admired
but not to be touched.
I was snapped from the field
and put in a fancy pot
down the hall, by the wall
and my delicate petals are falling
for lack of the wind and the sun
I'm a prisoner of love...

Lucia S. Maynard

Endurance

Endurance has been chosen
To be your special race
Get on your mark, get set to go
Keeping a prayerful pace

You need not run too fiercely
For one thing is for sure
The race is not for swiftness
But for those who will endure

Sometimes you may get tired
And long to rest a while
Don't give up and don't give in
But run an extra mile

For there will come a time
When your longing heart can rest
But only when you've endured
And done your very best

The Lord God knows your destiny
And just how far you've come
He's able to give you strength
Until your race is Won!

Lorrie Askew-Fleming

Halloween

Spooky things on Halloween
But Devil's Night is really mean.
People in costumes everywhere
Trick or treating here and there.
In every house there is some candy
Which on Halloween will come in handy.
People become scardycats
At all the ghosts, cats, and bats
Costumes are stacked at stores
Halloween is not one of those bores.
Bright colors are worn at night
So you can be seen in the dim light.

Jona Maloney

Son

Ethan James my little boy,
since you were born
my life has new joy!
Your smile, your laughter,
your beautiful blue eyes,
even your messy diapers
and your tired baby cries.
Is music to my ears and
makes my heart so glad,
I'm so truly happy that
I'm your Dad.

Jack Cunningham

To Be An Applegarth

I dream of regal horses
and damsels in distress.
I dream of flaming dragons
and fighting at my best.
I ride the country over
and carry banners high.
I guard the noble castle
and watch the colors fly.
I wear my shining armor
and challenge any man.
I surely will defeat him
and save this blessed land.
I own all the land around
and yet, the men are free.
I am their king and ruler
and they, my people be.
How proudly I display it,
my crest upon the hearth.
For nothing could be nobler,
than to be an Applegarth!

Andrew W. Applegarth

Technology And The Muse Or "Writ By Hand"

My computer has the best of me
With an attitude sadistic.
Yet I keep trying anyway—
I must be masochistic.
What I put in- I cannot save,
Its exit is mysterious.
The impact on my poetry
Is grossly deleterious.
Handwritten text I must employ,
(Which vastly lessens clarity),
The only way I can preserve
This poem for posterity!

Jim Spezzano

That's What They Say

Silence is golden.
That's what they say.
But, if words go unspoken,
Words go away.

Whispers are haunting.
They never end.
Filling a void.
Replacing a friend.

They hold no answers,
Those reflections on the past.
They just raise questions.
How much longer can you last?

We're all behind you.
That's what they say.
But, when you turn around,
They walk away.

Somewhere there's hope.
You'll find it someday.
Until then you'll cope.
At least, that's what they say.

Shawn Guiling

!In Sane?

There's a little man inside my head,
Who talks to me everyday;
The little man inside my head,
Knows what I hear and say.

People say that voices are bad,
But I know what to say,
Because the little man inside my head,
Helps me through problems everyday.

Stefany Harrison

Untitled

I see two stars in summer's night.
Hovering lost in blinding light.
Each so dull in heaven's net.
So each remains as yet un met.

But fortune moves on strangest ways.
It lengthens nights and shortens days,
may this night end and day begin
and bring two young people back again.

Melissa Brookman

The Seasons

Winter snows
Melt
Into the rains of Spring.
Spring blossoms
Into the flower of Summer.
Summer's heat
Caresses
The leaves of Fall.
Fall's harvest
Blesses
The cold of Winter
With Spring's promise
And Summer's warmth.

Patricia Oblon

Love Whispers In Silence

The quiet between us
comfortably powerful,
the silence building strength -
Take hold... embrace me,
engulf me.
I feel you breathing me in.

Silently, I tell you over
and over
The depth of my love
with my quiet
silent
embrace.

Shannon Gillespie

The Circular

It caught me in its spiral
The sweeping graceful lines
Of the staircase
And so deliciously invited me
To investigate.
As I gazed ahead before ascending
Lo and behold!
There she was
A gracefully clothed angel
Descending the airy, marble steps
Gliding down into my presence.
Ah! How lovely is the curve!

Marjorie Gilbert

Wild Man

Roses are red,
Violets are blue,
My love for you
Grows true and true.

I know I can't have you
all to myself,
But oh, don't fret wild man
Because, love you I can.

I long for your kisses,
hugs, and talks,
In hopes that you'll remember
our special walks.

So cherish our times,
As we commit our crimes.
And if it takes years
Don't fret or have fears,
For my love for you
is so very true.

I love you wild man!

Katrina Kashkin

"40 Years Old"

Oh Lordy you are 40
and still looking fine
Just like you did
when you were 39
you are sweet and pretty
and full of life
The very best mother
and a perfect wife
So there isn't much more
that I can say
But I love you
and
Happy Birthday.

Helen B. Phillips

Cloud Watching

I sit and watch the clouds go by
like great and portly ships on high,
Their sails unfurl with the wind,
and go the way its blowing send.

They roam the world in search of port,
but finding none of any sort,
continue onward with the breeze
like ships at sail, on endless seas.

Ann M. Garvey

Hopes And Dreams

Hopes may come true and
dreams too, so I think it's worth
while a wish.
Just stop by the well and drop
a penny down and see what happens next.
Will your wish come true
right away or will you have to
wait another day?

My wish come true, I can
now look up into the sky
and see all the places that my
imagination dreams of finally come
alive and clear to my own eyes.

Emily Aviles

Orthodontics

Ortho, ortho, ortho -
A lot about - I didn't know,
Until such time - I'd made up my mind,
To have my teeth realigned.

X-rays, plaster molds
wires too
Rubber bands and sticky stuff-
that tasted like glue.

Pliers that tightened wires
when they got too loose
Around one's neck -
would've felt like a noose.

After the pulling and tightening
It hurt to sneeze
And all I could eat
Was cottage cheese.

We've come to the end
and there were many frets
But after seeing my teeth,
I have no regrets

Fran Baird

Keep Your Chin Up

When troubles all upset you,
And it's hard to even smile,
And everything you try to do,
Seems scarely worth your while:

You ought to smile and take it,
And turn around and give
Your very best and all your wit,
If you should care to live.

You need to grit your teeth and grin
When others do you wrong.
You have to work to ever win,
And sing a carefree song.

You should act as does the clown,
Who is forever gay,
And keep your chin up when you're down,
Have faith in God and pray.

Bertha Gregg Cain

"Love"

It is a sentimental object
and one I hold very dear.
It is a priceless treasure
and I always keep it near.

It has a special melody
that echoes sweetly in my head.
It shines and twinkles in the light
and has a glow to shed.

It lives in peace and harmony
with the feelings all around.
And radiates its happiness
never being down.

It grows and grows continuously
much larger every day.
It always has a gift to give,
but never expects you to pay.

Its fire burns long and light
for all eternity
And the feeling keeps us together-
Forever you and me...it's love.

Melani Moore

You Thought

You thought,
they'd always be there.
You thought,
they'd always care.
But when one day,
their love was taken away.
You wish, you pray.
Hoping that some day
Your paths will meet again.

Nichole Lykam-Briggs

A Well Done From The King

Why are the innocent downtrodden
Why do they cry at night
Why does man behave so
It just isn't right
The Plight of the innocent
is a narrow road
to escape
the perils of sin
The sinful have a winding path
that will only end
In the End.
Do what you can for mankind
Aid if you can-
the helpless the homeless
the weak
Your reward is the Golden Crown
And a well done from the
King.

Sherry Lynn Rush

Loneliness And I

In the streets I wander
Though, I know not where I go
I find myself staring day after day

The nights just seem to fall
As soon as the sun shines
For when you are alone
There's nothing and no one behind

Now as the days follows
And the nights are all clear
I find myself crying
Wishing someone was near

I come abreast a stranger
One I have never known
Now we are two lovers
And I am not alone

Betty A. Washington

A Wonderful Morning

Sound a sleep
when morning arises
I am awakened
by Feathers surprises
he chirps and chirps
then I am there
and sits like a Flamingo
so I sit and stare
he is a love bird
with colors galore
he is so beautiful
oh my Lord
I thank you so much
for giving me Feathers
I love him a bunch.

Becky Youtsey

"A Mother's Touch"

You gave me life one
summer day,
And cared for me
in your gentle way.

You taught me it all,
from A to Z;
But most of all, you
believed in me.

You said I'm special,
one of a kind;
I seldom thanked you,
but you didn't mind.

You opened me up and
tore down my wall,
You're the one who
knew me best of all.

You've been there for me,
my whole life through;
So in my own special way,
I'm saying thank you.

Genai Walker

Bye Uncle Fred

I'm so sad and sorry
That you had to go, but
I'm here to let you know
Why you had to die —
So you could leave this crazy place
And be up in the heavenly sky
I miss you very very much
At the funeral we all took
It kind of rough
We all miss the great things
You use to do
But up in heaven
The LORD has some work for you
You are a one of a kind uncle
That's hard to find
You will always stay in my mind

Kamal Nigel Williams

I See Now

I thought we were real
lovers.
I thought we were true
friends.
But the way you ignore and
brush me off,
I see now where it ends.
There's no need to do explaining,
No need to return my calls.
With how very much I loved you,
I'm bouncing off the walls!

Don't tell me, you found another?
But no, that can not be.
How could you, with such a small
heart,
Find someone else to replace me?

I see now how it is,
No need to say a word.
I see now how it is,
Now my feelings are all stirred.

Kara Perry

One Me

Mind - why are you ever so restless?
Hurl pictures from long gone past -
Project fancy dreams of tomorrow
that never will be,
while at the precious present
you dwell on more chores and tasks.
Mind - can't you dwell, relax
and bring together
the ageless child,
mature me,
that has been,
is, and will be
and unite
just One me
in Harmony!

Sharon C. Krakusin

Siete

7 Seconds counting
7 seconds on the clock
Until my true love passing
To work to school or to the park
Oh I just don't care
7 seconds on the dot-
He's there!

Christopher Lee Manes

Untitled

Floating in purgatory
surrounded by constant thought
reflecting on a presence
and all that it had wrought

Up through a cloudy mist
was accompanied by a cocoon
the tension of its sinewy thread
shows the birth is soon

Elongated and crystalline white
the silk begins to tear
wings flexing up and outward
its brown eyes make me aware

You're the one who's finally free
from the tangents of the earth
tears flowing from my eyes
glorified by your rebirth.

John A. Nordstrom

Eternity

I look in your eyes
and all that I see
is the burning desire
you have for me
no words need to be
spoken
no feelings need to be
shared
every one can feel it
it's in the air
our love is undying
it will never go away
we'll still be together
when we're old and gray

Jennifer Bermel

Nirvana

Together in herds
Of thousands we
Cry out to the
Riff of his raging
Guitar; in a need
To belong, and in
A need to be heard.

Later in our existence
We will become unlistening
Adults and will be heard
By all, but will miss
The rage of his guitar
And the pain in his voice.

James Geeo

Iambling

What sings a song of sorrow
Or cries in deep despair?
What causes hidden laughter
Or brings a smile to bear?

What tells a tale of grandeur,
A history of fate,
And helps one to remember
A most important date?

How children may discover
This music minus notes
And learn the joy of tempo
Obtained without remotes?

From passion to compassion,
From cage to flying free
And with or without rhyming,
Salute to poetry!

Jean Gard

Sky

Oh sky, your face so bright.
You smile down on everyone,
from morning until night.
You heat each summer's day,
with your gleaming, yellow ray.
So cheerful all the time
as if unable to commit a crime.

Oh sky, we've spoken too soon.
Why do you fill the air with gloom?
You drench me with your tears
and scream about your fears.
Your face glows with fury,
as the people below you scurry.

Oh Sky so high why do you cry?
Oh, please won't you smile!
In your cheerful style, you shine
and make our lives worth while.

Rebecca Desjardins

Dark And Lovely

I love my color so dark and sweet
From the crown of my head
To the soles of my feet;
I do not care what people say
I'm telling you here this very day
Dark and lovely, yes siree
Dark and lovely, that's me!

H. Clark

My Father

A man with intelligence
Smart as a lashing whip,
A man that thinks
dumbness is not hip.

A man with faithfulness
to his wife,
To him, her and their children
are his life.

A man with patience
trying to fulfill his dream,
But he keeps trying
not giving up with a quiet scream.

A man with honor
never showing shame,
Upon his family because if
he did there wiLL be no one to blame.

A man with blessings
to have children and a wife who
loves only him.
Daddy, I love you.

Sherrita Saxton

What Age Is Best?

What age is best? Who can say
The age I am now is the best today.
Sixteen? Yes that was fine.
Eighteen and nineteen
are far behind.
Twenty to twenty-five were the
honeymoon years, full
of joys, and hopes, and tears.
Thirty was good, the children
were growing.
A few gray hairs and a
waist-line showing.
Thirty-five? I liked that too.
My husband still says,
"I love you true".
But forty is comfortable,
full and complete.
Forty's the age I'd like to repeat.

Katherine Andrews

Truly Blessed

I have been truly blessed
All I hold dear is at its best
My days are filled with joyous praise
For a God whose hand is forever raised
My God is the creator of all;
My savior that stands tall.
He is the protector of many
Through his eyes you'll see plenty
Love is with me...
Love is all around me
I live for my God
I sing about my God
For no one outshines
No one can ever find
Joyous celebration all around
Ssh, just listen to the sound!
Sweet harmony of peace
Embrace me. Never forsake me.
Yes... I have been blessed!

Allison Lockes

I'm Trying Hard To Understand

I'm trying hard to understand
that your time had come,
But why did you have to leave
with so much left undone?

I'm trying hard to understand
through all my pain and sorrow,
Through all the tears and memories
there won't be any tomorrow.

I'm trying hard to understand
why you had to go,
Couldn't God just understand
that we love and need you so?

I'm trying hard to understand
that you're where you wanted to be,
Reunited with your one true love
No more pain and misery.

I'm trying hard to understand
the things you'll never now see,
And maybe one day I'll realize
just why you had to leave me.

Maria Jones

Wilting Truth

When wilted flowers are thrown away,
And memories have faded.
Unknown are the gifts we gave,
Our happiness is shaded.

Behind a smile there lies a frown,
A sadness holding gloom.
Then the darkness comes around,
And sorrow fills the room.

Our feelings we cannot express,
Emotions kept inside.
Our heart no longer can digest,
Our mind becomes the guide.

Looming forward into the day,
Misery creeps inside our heart.
Within our conscience seems to say,
You have but left one lonely dart.

We have no longer any joy,
No one shall give us comfort.
Only silence fills the void,
Our life is growing short.

There seems no other timely escape,
When sadness opens the door.
We point the trigger at our face,
And rest forevermore.

Wendy Waugh

Eternal Love

I layed down gently on the
ocean shore, with somebody
lying next to me.
The water and sand caressing
my body also, with somebody's
love addressing me.
I slowly closed my eyes and
felt my thoughts drift away,
I woke up soon to the
next day.
I sat up like a sitting dove
and still the person lying
next to me is the one I love.

Kareen Duffy

The Great Duel

Alexander Hamilton vs Aaron Burr
He challenged
He accepted
He pointed to Hamilton
Hamilton pointed to the sky
The shot ran out
He fell
He fled

Melissa Kobelka

Untitled

You
I
Love!

Feel
Alive!

Life
Worth
Living!

Lyle Erickson

Beautiful Image

I seen true beauty once.
Walking past me gracefully
with a hint of mystique
in her endless dark eyes.

Presenting herself boldly, a
flawless sculpture made from
the hands of God himself.

A smile so angelic she looked
as if she belonged on the
colorful stain glass windows of
heavens church.

With a voluptuous fragrant
of morning frees magnolias
trailing not far behind her.

Yes that was beauty. Walking
in and out of my life as
quickly as lightening with
nothing more than a little eye contact.

Eric Harrison

Comforts Frighten Me

So smart looks the stereo-
set on the polished marble
top, the vase filled
with leafwhite lilies so
slender they could be the
stalks of Death. The fridge
crammed with bleak ice-thick
foods seems to say: 'Things
will always be this way' but
snowed petals know this can
never be. Across the torn
hedgesheets they moan:
'All comforts are lies. From
us they hide the sliming claws
clinging to our usual walls
scraping to break in. Comforts
lull like the blind blizzard that
makes black wings drink stones.'

Roy Joseph Cotton

Have Not

So tell me then, you Have Not,
Are you gonna eat today?
Of course I am dear Someone Sir,
Top Ramen's on the way.
And tell me please, you Have Not one,
How do you heat your house?
It's easy sir for me you see,
I wear an extra blouse.
But Have Not, Have Not, really now,
How are you gonna rent?
No problem sir, you see because,
I bought a brand new tent.
Just one more thing dear Have Not dear,
How do you get around?
I do it sir and keep my shape.
I walk without a frown.
One last question, Have Not please,
The kids, are they O.K.?
Concern yourself for naught, dear sir.
For them I always pray.

Linda Harding

Good-Bye

When the time has come upon us
in my heart, you will not know
Good-bye's will be unspoken
and I'll spread my wings to go.

When the time is finally here
the pain you will not feel;
Our parting will be sorrowful
and my sadness is real.

The time is now my friend
for my heart to say good-bye,
Our laughter may have stopped
but the memories will not die.

Janetann Hoffmann

"The Storm"

The rain beats down,
drenching me in sin,
draining away my will to resist.

Rivulets of water from the sky
mingle with tears from my eyes,
eroding a chasm in my soul
which only you can fill.

Damn you your desires.
Damn you for awakening mine.
Damn you for opening the flood gates
which carry my happiness downstream.

The storm in the heavens will pass
but the storm in my mind will not.
The lightning strikes,
and the thunder roars.

You stand atop a mountain,
your naked body silhouetted
in a silvery flash,
and you dominate my existence.

Jamie C. Tinker

Creation

Ideas form,
Words coalesce;
A story is born.
Readers now test
the mind shorn.

Kathleen Duval

The Silent Friend

As with time
the world goes by
people meet and join
travelling toward friendship together
But can they know
they are not alone
still another has come along
to bind them closest ever
They walk and talk
laugh and cry
giving praise to one another
and in these ways
they find that this silent friend
is wondrous love
to be with them forever!

Marvin R. Keener

Love

Love,
A word with many meanings,
A word with many feelings,
Your broken heart I will mend,
From now until the end,
Your love is like a red rose,
In the night it glows,
My spirit is high,
Like the clouds in the sky,
The symbol of our love,
Are the stars up above,
My love forever is yours,
Like a pearl in the deep blue ocean,
Pure and innocent.

Lulwa Al-Marzouq

Somebody's Teacher

I know a school teacher
Her name I won't say,
Whom I think is great
In every which way,
The years quickly pass
Most of them in school,
To teach the children
The "Golden Rule,"
If you are looking for her
She is easy to find,
Behind her desk
At the same old grind,
Listen my children
And you shall see,
That school can be a
symphony.

Helen A. Krawiec

My Endless Love

The day we met
I gave my heart,
Because I thought that
we would never part.

Since we did,
I'm in despair
and, all the things I worried about,
I just don't care.

All I want
Is for you to know
How much I love you so.

Crystal L. Turner

"Alone"

When you're alone
thinking you're hurt.
It's over he's gone for good.
Could I have
really loved such
a flower so beautiful as him?
Our love could have grown.
But he left me
with one petal of
affection of our love.
But, I hurt too much
when there was once
two, but now one.
Being with him was so much fun.
He's gone now it's
time to move on.
I have dropped
the rose of our love
to feel the hurt
which is alone.

Jessica R. DeCora

Dragons Myth

From heaven and earth
Of dark and light
Wings abound the dragons' flight
From ages gone past
To ones anew
Of legends and valor
The dragons flew
A breath of cinder to vanquish the land
An act of valor from swords own hand
Talons and scales
Their tails unfold
Hidden in peace
In lairs of gold
The dragons fear in one's own sight
To tales we tell of the dragons might
From the eldest heart
Of the youngest dreams
Of eternal myth
The dragon gleams

George B. Korosko

The Contestant

Wow!
48 thou,
I dream.

It should be enough
to inspire a rough
draft,
I think.

But what category,
religion, business,
or simple glory
attached
to words?

Maybe it's deeds,
the clearing of weeds
from the rosebed of doubt
I should talk about.

But there isn't time
to extract a rhyme
for any reason.
Maybe next season.

J. Paul Brennan

"I'll Be Watching"

When no one sees you
Death is looking

When no one's talking
Death is listening

When no one's there
Death is watching

When no one cares
Death takes your hand

When on one's crying
Death takes your breath

When you're laid to rest
I'll be watching

Lauren Williams

Natural Disasters

Voices break
through a glass silence.
Tears quench
anger and fears.
Life's wings pull me tight,
protecting me
from a world of hurt.
A world where
tears flood the earth,
pain quakes the ground,
heartache burns the soul,
and silence erupts hope.

Jennifer Broyles

Thinking

As I sit here thinking
Of myself, and me.
And of this world God created
The wonders, he made for us to see.

The hills, valleys, and plains,
The mountains, ocean and sea,
The growth of trees and flowers,
Birds singing in the tree.

That a world of beauty
We have all around.
God made them for our land
Greater love can not be found.

God gave us friends
Where ever we may go.
He leads our way onward,
For which we thank Him so.

So as life goes onward,
Always be helpful and true.
Let love be in your heart.
Lead you always your best to do.

Edna Lewien

The Lighthouse

Watching the sea
night after night
the light shining bright
protecting the boats
the boats that float
onto my rocks
the seagulls flock
up above
the light of
the Lighthouse up on the rocks.

Amy Doherty

Tomorrow

Today we live in,
A world that tomorrow dies,
Yesterday we were given,
The gift of eternal tries.

Yesterday they did lie,
We shall not forever survive,
Tomorrow everyone must die,
So today we'll be alive.

Today we'll have time,
To live, love, and lie,
To honor and drink wine,
For tomorrow we must die.

Die we must,
Tomorrow is the day,
We return to dust,
And live another way.

Philip J. Lentocha

Don't Give Up

Right now nothing but darkness
seems to surround you,
and the lights keep growing dimmer.

Don't give up hope, have faith.
For soon the time will come,
to be set free from this plight
which causes you anxiety.

Be calm, have patience, wait.
The glow of life has yet to reach you,
so you think, but I'm sure,
it is well on its way.
Coming closer, every day.

Smile, each morning when you wake.
Don't hesitate,
not even for a minute.
Then, look out of your window,
and see the world which awaits you.

The sun light will hit your face,
and the darkness will
have lifted.

Rita Yacubovich

Courageous Woman of the Dawn

Courageous Woman of the Dawn
Plant your feet, keep moving on
Love's ahead - just up beyond
Courageous Woman of the Dawn

Don't look behind, don't falter
Just let your steps be sure
Place your hand in His hand
This way you will endure

He'll help you with your children
He'll guard your home from harm
He'll make sure love is locked inside
So everyone is warm

One day He'll stand beside you
In a body you can see
He'll take you in his loving arms
And say "Come away with me

Let's have a life together
Off where the rainbow's glow
Courageous Woman of the Dawn
You're the one I want to know"

Donna C. Brown

Eye For An Eye

I greet Death
With my teeth bared.
A smile on my face,
A speech prepared:
"You will have me,
That I admit.
But here and now,
I won't permit."
I stand my stance,
Down on my knees.
I stare at Death,
And then it speaks:
"I can see
That you won't die
But you know what they say;
Eye for an eye."
I feel a loss,
I loose my breath.
My love has died,
And gone was Death.

Katie Scott

Untitled

The outs are out there
and here at my window
I stare...
is it a dream?
A bad dream?
Or is it real
Like a blooming flower...
Sometimes I wonder,
will it ever be the same...
A child of laughter
or
a child insane...

Susan Belmontez

Two Lovers Embrace The River

Starlight rays burn into my heart
As night-fall fills the sky.
All sounds remain on hold
Except the resonant whir
Of heat-tortured crickets.

Your touch, gentle and electrical,
Sears and caresses me.

My touch explores your
Iridescent play of colors,
As wave upon wave of cool water
Wash my sweating ground
And open our worlds of possibility.

Robert Garwood

The Path

Open the gates of heaven and hell
Unto this place I know not well

It is filled with fear and hate
With souls, waiting to meet their fate

Then the silence does draw near
I for see the path which is clear

There is a cross road which I do see
The path I take is unto me

But for which the path I do choose
The other one I, forever lose

Craig Martin

Silence

Silence is all I hear
The teardrops I now fear.
How can I stop these feelings
When will I start healing?
Not until I go back home
To the place I was born.
Silence is all I hear
The teardrops I now fear.
I have come form a far away land
To be here to hold your hand.
To take away your fear
And let you know that I am here.
But silence is all I hear
The teardrops I now fear.
Where are you?
I do not know.
But I realize you had to go.
What was this I feared?
It was silence all these years.

Sumbal Javed

I Am

I am an actor.
I am deep.
I am the cat that curiosity killed.
I am loyal.
I am strong.
I am the rays of the afternoon sun.
I am gentle.
I am loose.
I am the flower that sways in the wind.
I dream.
I hope.
I am one of a kind. I am me.

Drew Taylor

Untitled

This tragedy is tragic
No way to make it light
Not candle after candle can lift
the darkness of this night.

It's eerie that it happened
its unsuspectedness —
Came crashing in like thunder
in evil haunting dress.
It lifted us and swept us
away from here to there
Confused, bewildered, here we sit
but now I'm not sure where.

Take this darkness; bring us back
to where we used to be
To remember songs and birds
and blossoms on a tree.
But wiser now, we'll walk along
Not so quite... Naive.
Guided now, our steps will be
to walk and re-believe.

Elaine Lillie

Baseball

Batting and bunting,
All star game.
Stealing and sliding,
Energetic sport.
Bases are loaded,
Athletic ability.
Learning to be a pro.
League of your own!

Christopher M. Gillis

Some Day

Some day you'll love me.
Some day you'll care.
Some day you'll treasure the
moments we shared.
Some day you'll learn that love's not a
game.
Some day you'll find that I'm not
the same.
My heart won't be there,
My love will have died,
and you'll remember the tears that I
once cried.
Some day you'll know what it feels like
to die.
The day you realize I said goodbye.
Some day you'll hear a poem or a song
And say to yourself "I was wrong."
Some day you'll love me.
Some day you'll care.
Some day, my dear, I won't be there!!

Nicki Juneau

Colors

I've seen the orange glow,
as the sun sets in the west.

I've seen the green grass
as it sways in the wind.

I've seen red, red roses
how they delight any lover.

I've seen the blue sky
where birds love to fly.

I've seen the yellow dandelions
that children love to pick.

But, I never saw a rainbow
Until, I looked into your eyes.

Toni M. Berthold

Melanie

You are my child
and I love you.

I felt the pain
of the joy
you gave me.

In my yesterdays,
I cried the tears
of your tomorrows.

Acknowledging
in your presence,
the experiences
of my past.

And, in the absence
of my frustrations,
I am comforted.

For I see in you
a reflection of truth
which understanding alone
could not justify.

Jeannette Hailsham

Love To Be Seen

To love a person
Is to see a person.
To see a person
Is to feel a person.
And to feel a person.
Is to know a person.

Love is a thing that
can't be fooled
If it is then it
is to fall apart into
What it was at the start.

But, Always and Forever
love will find a way.
Through thick and thin
there has to be a way.

If a person is to fall in love
and see its future, then
It will last.
Not all things last forever but,
True Love does.

Shane Baeuerlen

Lament

Porpoise, sea-mouth turtle swim
Deep within him, deep within;
Colors across the water make
Road to the sunrise;
Wave's wake
Spills the glistening, glittering sea
In the all-but-empty shell of me.

Shell, husk, hollow and dry,
Under the sky here, under the sky;
Stuck in the sand, no way to walk
Road to the sunrise;
Sea-bird's talk
Shatters the glowing, distant free
In the all-but-empty shell of me.

Otter

Never True

Every child
dreams, hopes,
wishes, are
just of
a mother's
touch

Feeling, believing
the love she
gives...

....is true

It's sad to say,
not all wishes
come true.

Anthony Berzoza

Love In Sight

Love in sight,
A journey in the present,
Forever is the union.
In the mist of the morning breeze,
A dream were the hearts glitter
Prevails with intensity and promises,
The hope for the world,
A true essence of love.

Akbaralli Meghji

"It Could Never Be"

My heart is beating
With the stillness
In which water flows.

My knees so weak,
I can stand no longer.

My voice cracks,
with each breath I take.

I think of us embracing
one another.
Oh, how I wish you were here.

Then I awaken to reality
realizing it could never be.
For I am here and she is
there with you.
Baby I miss you.

Rhonda Lynn Shefra Singh

Our World

Open your eyes
And stop and see
All the beauty
As it's meant to be

The sky so brilliant
With colors so bright
That shines on our life
From morning till night

The flowers of every color
So dainty and small
The lush green trees
That grow so tall

The noise of the birds
As they flutter and fly
All around
In the bright blue sky

Enjoy this land
Its beauty to preserve
And all its resources
Please do conserve

Dianne M. Nadler

Joshua

My skin is wrinkled and thin
as tissue paper,
Yours is smooth and with
a rosy hue.
My hands caress you lovingly
yours pull at my heart.
I have gray hair
you have none.
We talk in words that
only we can understand.
I have lost all of my teeth
but it does not matter
because you have none.
I have lived a lifetime
but you have just begun.
When you sit on my knee
We are so near the
Source of Life,
Love. It has made us
Two of God's Children.

Geneva P. Brown

On A Winter Scene...

Snow falls,
Muting.
Lovely blanket
Trying to Create
a whole eternal white.
World are subdued
by this
blatant Parade of
Naive Virtue;
and prematurely,
All becomes Noble.
a dear Attempt,
but see!
This pretentious branch
one erratic, sober darkness
forcing truth...
in retrospect.

Mikela Boothe

What Loneliness Does

Up in my room.
Alone I am.
Crying I am.
Why?
I don't know.
Maybe a death,
Maybe just loneliness.
Maybe just the fact I feel stupid,
And having no one to be with.
Alone, Yes I am.
Crying, Yes I am.

Amber Elizabeth Long

Mom And Dad

Mom makes me feed a cat
Dad teaches me how to bat,
Sometimes they make me cry
Sometimes I ask why,
Then we have a little chat.

Mom and Dad are very nice
Just like two little mice,
They love me very much
They're always there in the clutch,
And they break the ice.

Jessica Limatola

"To My Darling Gay"

So many many times I've needed you,
A million times I've cried.
If my love could have saved you,
You never would have died,
It broke my heart to lose you,
You did not go alone,
A great big part of me went with you
The day God called you home.
He saw you getting tired
When cure was not to be,
He closed his arms around you
And whispered, "Come to me."
For all that you went through,
The day came when you needed rest,
God's garden must be beautiful,
For He only picks the best.

Clarence Darrough

"Butterfly"

I wish I were a butterfly
Free as the wind in the sky
Going from this flower to that
Just loving where I am at
Tasting the nectar of life
No struggles or strife
Surrounded by color and beauty
So simple and care free

I wish I were a butterfly
Do you have to ask why?
So fragile and so frail
A big wind or a bit of hail
Endangered by oh so much
Injured with the slightest touch
Yet no worry or no fear
Just the peace of being here

I wish I were a butterfly
Just fluttering by.

Deborah A. Clifton

Two Little Girls And A Bird

The little bird lay dying
Upon our carport floor;
Falling from its cozy nest
Above our kitchen door.

Two little girls stood watching
As it drew its last breath.
Their eyes were filled with sorrow
Knowing they witnessed death.

Two small girls knelt side by side,
With both hands clasped in prayer.
They prayed God would take the bird,
And keep it in His care.

Kim asked that Gram and Grampa
Attend the service there.
Then after strewing flowers,
They ended it with prayer.

A cross was made of rough sticks
And placed to mark the grave.
Now these two loving children
Were pleased their bird was safe.

Virginia E. Little

Our Trials

Sometimes our trials are many
And we may not know just why
Seems no one else has any
So we just break down and cry

Troubles are part of living
With them we learn to deal
It's good God is forgiving
When such bitterness we feel

There are people who don't care
At least, that's how it seems
But remember, God is there
To hear our prayers and dreams

He'll send new friends our way
To prove that someone cares
They help us through each day
And stop feelings of despair

Remember, sometimes it's trials
God uses just to teach us
That life's not always smiles
But His love can always reach us.

Rufus Curtis

Pippin

This little cat
all belled and safe
just had to go to you.
That guileless look,
the wond'ring eyes
must be Norwegian, too.
Just now and then
a soft small paw
will draw you close to her.
That haughty cat
lets down her guard
to snuggle up and purr.

Charlotte K. Wendel

To Victims Present And Past Rest

Our the flame of torches past
today is coming to lift our
lives toward our goals of
this day new to be or
stand and one to see
on this our place our
hour towl to be the best
and savor no rest
Towards or placed on tomorrow's stay
to be our hopes to see
this and to be our your
Autumn hour to sleep and be
Best and yet our toll be
paid pass and prey and come to see.

Edmund Walker Goddard

The Perfect Gift

Love,
It is the perfect gift,
You can give it,
You can receive it,
And it doesn't cost a thing.
It will never shrink in the wash,
It will never be too big,
Or too small,
It will always fit just right.
It will never wear out
And get too thin,
There can never be too much
It is something to last forever,
And will never end.
Love,
It is the perfect gift.

Chris Anderson

Faith Standing

Shades of brilliant crimson
set deep beneath the picture frame.
Walls hanging sounds
of vengeful hounds
which strengthen her darkened pain.

Distorted faces
hover over this tainted,
long awaited end.
Fading into mysterious advise,
from a distant non-existent friend.

Yet while in this brittle coldness,
Faith disrupts her still fear...
By surrounding the seeker,
and haunting the meeker
with forgiven wounds of yesteryear.

Donna Yount

Dreams

Count out your dreams
Like the stars at night,
And more will always appear
Each with a shining light.
Capture your dreams
With a butterfly net,
But don't display them on the wall
Because dreams won't set.
Make up new dreams
And let them come true,
Because only through dreams
Nothing's impossible for you.
Follow your dreams
And guide you they will,
They'll take you to lands
That magically become real.
Keep all of your dreams
Through each living year,
And even those you don't use
God will always hear.

Dana Morrison

Changes

Changes in life are never easy
but they are very necessary.
If a person doesn't experience
change he does not grow, if he
does not grow he does not learn.
All these emotions are part of
life. Happiness, sadness, tears,
hope, fear, hate, love, pain,
regret, and there are many
others. And as the Bible says
there is a time and place for
everything.

Diane Lane

Did Eye See ...

What I Was Looking... To Find?

I was looking for you
I saw me...There in You
I found Me...In You
I lost Me...in You
I lost You...in me
I lost me...

I Lost you
I found You...Gone
I Found...Me...Lost
The you...in me...is gone
The I in me...is found
I found Me...in my Mynd's...Eye
I...Am...Me...

Richard A. Porter

The Other World

In the other world
Any where you look
You see a green grass
The most beautiful blue sky
With the most beautiful flowers
Also the most friendly friends
With sweets that make you feel
Good inside!
I said to myself this
Is the "Perfect World"
Then I realized I was
already in the "Perfect World"

Beth Palmer

Nurtured Love

Love is like a flowering plant,
Impatiently waiting to bloom.
Nurture and tend to it,
And you will see results soon.

Care for it tenderly,
With loving, gentle hands.
Feeding will make it strong,
And its roots will with-stand.

From these sturdy roots,
Grow healthy leaves and stems.
Easily, they will do their job,
To hold these lavish gems!

Left, unattended,
These beautiful blooms will drop.
The leaves and stems will wither,
And lastly, the roots will rot.

Linda Ragsdale

The Basics Of Love

To all who came before me,
To all who fell behind,
Watch your step very carefully,
'Cause love will make you blind.
Never take a short cut,
Never run the mile,
Always stay in between,
The papers in love's file.
Keep your distance from the start,
And try to stay away from the end,
And watch out for the saying,
"I only want to be your friend."
For not all love is good,
And not all love is bad,
Just hope you'll never look back on,
That love you once had.

Ashley Finkbeiner

The Water Pipe

Rafting down a water way,
sometime on a summer day.
The water started getting faster,
stop this current mighty master.
I felt off and hit my head,
I'm so glad that I'm not dead.

Suckled up by a water pipe,
lined with seaweed stripe by stripe.
Help me, Help me, I am stuck
in a pipe filled with muck.

Stuck up in a water pipe,
I have to groan, I have to gripe.
Help me, help me, pull me out,
before I loose my mind
and start to shout.

Finally they turned it off,
boy oh boy I had to cough.
I went home and went to bed,
wondering why I hit my head.

Jennifer Carlson

Before Night

"The evening glow of sunset,
The after-glow of night,
The rising moon coming later,
Aw! - What a wonderful sight!"

Alfred D. LeJeune

Rose

In my garden is a rose bush
I watched as after every winter
it regained its leaves as a
baby would be born.
As it budded I could think
only of comparing it to a
preschooler learning to read and count.
When the flower bloomed,
it was like that child growing up
and finally the flower began to
wither and die I thought of
an elderly person getting ready
to make that journey to heaven.
Instead of rose it should be
called the flower of life.

Gwen Ribble

Friends

When you and I married
So many years ago,
We were the best of friends
How could you hurt me so.

I used to be number one
Our love would grow so strong
We laughed and cried together
How could anything go wrong.

Your friends come first with you now
They call and you stop the run,
Should I just throw in the towel
Where is my laughter and fun?

I wish I was your friend
Instead of just your wife,
Then you and I could be close
For the rest of our lives.

What can I do to make you mine again?
How can I let you know?
That you are in my heart
And I still love you so.

Shirley Cole

Change Of Seasons

Let the change of seasons
And the hands of time
Join the devil, make a legion
For now I see the sign.

Take me, give me the test
For I could never fail.
I've always given it my best
but no one could ever tell.

Silence my angry mouth
Bound my legs and hands.
No longer no angry sounds
Burnt offering look like sand.

No flowers, no prayers,
Let a lot of wine flow.
Dance with no guilt to bare
Tell all, for all is to know.

Nothing is left behind me
Especially loving memories.
There are no objects to be seen
And nothing to be deemed.

Deborah G. Case

Untitled

Could someone ever give an
excuse?
For the violence, the poverty,
and the abuse.
How long can our happiness go on;
when so much in our world is wrong?
People can be so unfair -
we hurt each other and say,
"Why should I care?"
But, if you look inside your soul;
you will see
the love you have deep within you -
and it will set you free.

Katherine Alanna O'Donniley

Mirror Image

I look in the mirror,
and what do I see?
I see someone.
Someone just like me.
Who is she?
She looks like me.
Moves like me.
Sees what I see.
Who is she?
I think I know her.
I know for sure I know her.
Who is she?
I think she is...
I know she is...
I swear she is...
I know who she is!!!
She's me!!!

Mokanna Lynelle Hampton

Somewhere

Where is somewhere?
Is somewhere home?
Or some place where,
You can roam?
Somewhere is where,
You can pray.
Somewhere is where,
Kids can play.
Somewhere is where,
You can call someone your own.
Somewhere is everywhere,
But also unknown.
Somewhere can be nowhere,
Cause nobody knows.
People are somewhere,
But never everywhere.
Somewhere is never too old.
Somewhere will never,
Be untold.

Jessica Brodala

Memories

Waiting in the room,
going down,
And waiting again;
And they remind me as I walk:
The sunshine, the sound, the scents.
All Memories
Wandering around as if they were free
and they control me.

Amy Rice

By Any Other Name

Closed as tight as a baby's fist
no promise to unfold.

Sherbet's lime shade enhanced,
licked by rouge splashed brilliance.
Entwined with fragrant layers
a deeper red unroll.

Never do I reveal my guard
of treasures by design.
When closely I am spied no
prickly tine.

Touch without a notion poised atop
my lengthy pedestal, endowed with
stickly needles fine.

Enchanting is my devotion
to beauty never flawed.
My velvety essence is the object
that enthralls.

Toni Miller

I Ain't Old I'm Antique

I ain't old I'm antique
my bones pop and squeak
Just part of my evaluation
Is what I like to believe
Still play the banjo
And sing a song
So what do I care
I maturity replaced with wisdom
One of these day you'll be able
To say it to
I ain't old I'm antique
Still got my hopes and dreams
Still got my ambitions and goal
Only my bones pop and squeak
I ain't old I'm antique
Hope to be able to say it at 100 and 3.
Still got friends what else do I need?

Timothy J. James

Spring Fever

Screeching kids
Bursting through doors.
Sometimes on all fours.

Lingering lovers
Lagging down corridors,
Having jealous quarrels.

Tired teachers
Turning pre-maturely gray,
Longing for summer play.

Lugubrious library books
Long overdue,
Buried in lockers so askew.

Crouching counselors
Scheduling fall classes.
Getting ready for the masses.

Summer's coming
With its cleansing sweep:
The janitors doing their upkeep.

Mary Jane L. Crawford

She Is

Based on my love for horses,
even though I don't have one.

Megan Early

The Fields I Love

The fields I love
Remind me of
The joyousness of youth
And far beyond
That childhood bond
Discovered is the truth.
Nostalgic dreams
Appear, it seems
Ever at the even
But visions warm
Of graceful form
Arrive as dark is leaving.
Such reverie
Can comfort me
But what can pass my muster
Yea, all, we know
Will come, then go
Sparkling with their luster.

Rita Lee Hoffman

Final Curtain

The stage is set,
The props are few
The only characters
are me and you.

The lines are plenty
emotions high.
Written so there's
no dry eye.

I knew my lines,
I took your cue,
I knew your heart
or thought I knew.

But suddenly, you forgot
your lines.
Forcing me to make up
mine.
And now the plot is
turned around
To the end,
Bring the curtain down.

Dyahanne Smith

Candlestick At Kim's

Candlestick with fingers empty
Setting on the table
Gives no light, gives no warmth
For it is not able
But it will if you will plant the seeds
With the candles that it needs
But it is up to you
If it is to be done

Candlestick with sockets empty
Fingers reaching toward the ceiling
Gives no light, gives no warmth
Does not have any feeling
Why do you sit and stare
As if there is something there
Can you admit that you care
For you can see the benefit
Of having it around

Frankie Dale Hines

Crossroads

You left,
Without saying goodbye.
You left.
Did you know that I'd cry?
Now you're up above,
Sending me your love.
Watching me grow,
(Making sure I do it right)
During the day
And all through the night.
I know you can't fax
Or even phone me
But I'll see you at the crossroads
So you won't be lonely.

Lorn Ratzow

Visions Of Love

The mist slowly fades away
And out of the shadows he appears.
Cautiously he reaches out for me.
We slowly melt together.

Gentle music fills the void
And our bodies and souls intertwine.
Love deeply reflects in his dark eyes.
A bond of trust seals us.

Quiet whispers fill my head
And sweet words tug at my racing heart.
Deep emotions stir and we move close.
Caresses leave me breathless.

Silently he slips away
And reality rushes forward.
The visions quietly fade to black.
Sadness washes over me.

Jana Stenklyft

A Tribute to Mothers

Without Mothers, where would we be?
Mothers are there to care for us
love us and listen to our problems.
Mothers give us that extra hug when we
are feeling hurt and lost.
Mothers wipe our tears away and
are always trying to make our lives
better than their own.
How can we ever repay them?
Money could not buy this love
that Mothers give to their children.
The only gift we, children, can give to
our Mothers, is love and affection
and pray the Lord will continue to
bless our Mothers.
Love to you Mother

Valerie McGeary

Fog

A hazy gray mist crawls in
Over mountains and settles in valleys
Hanging by fingernails
On towering peeks and cliffs
The gray ghosts rests in crevices
Making overflowing pools of haze
The mysterious fog is burdening
Blocking all senses
And leaving only guesswork
Stealthily the haze slides on
Without recognition

Chris Gray

Forever A Friend

Of all the times we've had to laugh
Or all the hours we've cried
The best ones now are yet to come
For our love is true and tried.
I feel as though you came right from
The bottom of my heart
Because your friendship in my life
Plays such a leading part.
You were my smile when dark times came,
A comfort for my need,
And I just want to tell you thanks
For the assurance of your lead.
Now as the years go flying by
And growing up gets tough,
I want you to know I'm there for you
Even if the path gets rough.
There's nothing that I wouldn't do
To make you laugh again;
You 'll always be so close to me
Because you are a friend.

Brooke Turner

The Power Of The Mind

Doc says it will stop
The depression and the pain
The imaginations loose
And the mind cannot be tamed
It's the power of the mind
Influenced by the brain
Imagination leads to... Insane

I loose my friends
I get depressed
And edgy thoughts then fill my head
Depression is a common thing
But does it drive most minds insane?

Wes O'Rear

Dad's Girl

She brightens my day
Is what I can say
She sleeps so pure
Her smile a cure
I'll do the rest
To make her life best
She's growing so fast
It's soon to be past
I've got a great deal
That's just how I feel

Today was a hike
Tomorrow a bike
A look in her eyes
To please me she tries
She jumps to my arms
I'll protect her from harms
A dad and his girl
Like an oyster and pearl
Our love so real
That's just how I feel

Edwar Thomas Kernick Jr.

Untitled

Kids are the ones that
Keep us going all the time
With out them we do not
Have anything that
Are helps today we need
Them a lot now.

David C. Polk Sr.

Bother

Why bother with complaints
that fall on deaf ears
in a world that ignores
what it wants not to hear?
it seems the more I speak
the more I am ignored
the more I try to help
the more I am abhorred
is happiness obtained
through telling ourselves lies?
it's easiest this way
for we can't see our own eyes.
why continue with my thoughts
like unwanted fodder?
if ignorance is our only bliss
than why do I bother?

Joey T.

Fire Of My Soul

The fire within my soul,
May seem dormant
At first glance.

The fire within my soul,
May be slow to start
At first touch.

The fire within my soul,
May be whipped into flames
When fanned,

The fire within my soul,
Will burn gently
With care and nurture.

The fire within my soul,
Will finally dwindle
To glowing embers.

The fire within my soul,
Too soon, will become
Cold, gray ash.

Miriam Giles

A Fraction of Time

In a fraction of time
I caught a glimpse of love.
But time past,
Years went,
Before I realized,
Or even knew,
That ache in my heart
Was real love.
All the while,
And at that moment,
I reflected to myself,
I almost let it pass,
In a fraction of time;
Love could have gone away.
In a fraction of time.

Cynthia W. Lunde

Dayz

Today is the day
that never Ends.

Tomorrow is the day
that never Comes.

Yesterday is the day
that never Was.

Harmonie Alger

Blind Justice

The judge sat alone
in the silent room.
His heart was filled
with doubt and gloom.

Was the verdict just?
Had he been fair?
He paced the floor
then returned to his chair.

He said, 'Dear Lord
I need to pray
ere I don this robe
of office today.

Please give me more
of your saving grace.
Help me to keep
my thoughts apace'.

The judge arose
with an open mind.
He thought, so often
Justice is blind.

Ruby F. Baker

"Love Refused"

What was I
but an innocent babe
longing for your nurturing breast.

What were you
save my entire world
and everything I had ever known.

What were we
but a natural pair
and meant to be with each other.

What were you
but a burden to me
a boy that I never wanted.

What was I
save a child myself
who wanted to live my own life.

What were we
but a Mother and son
who were never meant to be.

Daniel Vondenkamp

Vivian

With the lamplight gleaming softly
I the cloister far below
I had a lovely vision
Of a lady pure as snow.

The soft light shed its radiance
On her long and flowing hair
And reflected as a halo
While she knelt in silent prayer.

Her hair a cloud of sunlight
Her features chiseled fine
Be like a marble of Tuscany
Ideal of classic time.

Like topaz lamps of Ophir
From treasure ships of yore
Her eyes in golden glory
Shine on forevermore.

Such a matchless sacred beauty
No earthly power can know
In heaven only will I find her
Angel lady, pure as snow.

Charles Ross

Untitled

You are on my mind so heavy,
I don't know what to do,
Your absence makes me lonely,
When I am happy
I am blue.

It is so sad, for me to know,
Memories are all that is there,
I do not want to remember,
I want to feel your care.

My eyes so often tearing,
I try not to cry,
But when will I accept,
You did actually die?

Erica B. Samuels

Footprints Etched In Time

Dinosaurs once roamed this land.
Their footprints still remain.
And all who ever walk this earth
leave footprints just the same.

For all we are is what we touch
and what we leave behind.
And the only monuments we carve
are footprints etched in time.

As we walk along life's shores,
no matter where we go,
we leave impressions in the sand,
and yet, somehow I know

The tide must come,
the tide must go,
and carry out to sea
to touch the shores of other lands,

All that I am,
ever was,
or hope to be.

Bill Batten

Little Arms Of Love

The sweetest thing to me
This side of heaven's gate
Are those little arms of love
That's still too young to hate

They spur me on through life
As nothing else can do
They make the time pass easy
Outstretched when day is through

I can not help but feel
A touch of God's sweet hand
Who gave me such a treasure
Not found throughout the land

For nothing would I trade
To have to own and keep
For those little arms of love
When 'round my neck they creep

Please help me guide his steps
As through this life we stroll
For God, I love the little fellow
You have given me to hold

Louis H. Thompson

"Last Second Shot"

Five seconds left
with the ball in my hands,
As I pass midcourt,
I can only hope my shot lands.

Two seconds left
as I pull up at the arc,
I release,
with my shot on the mark.

I fall to the floor
with hope in my eyes
As I look up,
my shot flies.

It passes through the rim
nothing but net,
As soon as I let go,
I knew it was a sure bet.

The crowd jumps to their feet
They scream and they roar,
it's the greatest feeling ever,
if I could only do it once more.

Eric D. Garcia

Canyon De Chelly

Whispering winds and raging squalls
Etching ever-changing canyon walls
Creating finely sculpted faces
That nature lovingly embraces.

Centuries of time unfold
Summer heat and winter cold
Understanding finds rebirth
As fragments of the past unearth.

Endless wanderings of man
Imprinted in the timeless sand
Restless, changing as the scene
Tempered with interludes serene.

The distant past is mere conjecture
Mid evidence of enduring structure
That wind and weather rearrange -
The only certainty is change.

Marilyn D. Jackson

Time

It seems only yesterday
Fun times
Happy days
Sad times
Where has the time gone
Holiday times
Remembering faces
Faces lost in time
Time flies by
Time goes by
Can't stop it
Can't hold in to it
Can't capture time
Time, time is great
Time is worth living
Don't waste it
Talking of old times
Where did the time go
Where did it go?

Matt Hart

Giving

See that man standing all alone,
knowing no where to go.
Stop and talk with him awhile,
and afterwards he just might know.
That there are still some people,
who cares what he might do,
Someone to call a friend,
and that someone could be you.

The lonely face of a child,
when doubt and confusion are near.
Is like the sky before a storm,
showing a trace of fear.
Guide him in a way of truth,
so he can understand and respect.
Don't lie to make it easier,
or because of his youth.

Giving time and love
to someone who cannot call,
bringing happiness and a smile
is the most rewarding of all.

Blanche Logan

Time To Kill

A man had time to kill one day.
He did a deed and got away.
He used a chance to spew his hate
and sealed a jester's tragic fate.

A harmless prank weighed on his mind
and grew into the deadly kind.
Obsession fed his restless rage
while waiting for the setting stage.

For weeks the madman wished he had
the needed break to do the bad.
For him this feeling was a first;
he couldn't quench his gruesome thirst.

So when he finally took the life,
he did it quickly with a knife
and fled on foot when death had come.
He wasn't seen by anyone.

A private moment must exist
to murder without witnesses.
So if for me you have ill will
I hope you haven't time to kill!

Dan Forest

Washing Away

Pulling away
to be oneself
Scraping for acceptance
in those who don't know
Escaping to the world of fantasy
while clinging to security
Wanting to be different
yet the freedom enfolds
Drawing back to the web
by racing to the boundaries
Asking for absolution
yet not relinquishing the power
Burying the idealism
while realism produces destiny

Carrie Hodge

"A Matter Of Time"

On this great rocket called Earth
Traveling through the cosmos
on a measure we call time,
with the influence of the sun
we follow.

Where lies the journey's end
to this grand effort...

Ernest E. Seely

Nature

I look outside my window
I see dazzling pines
I see fairies playing in the leaves
The stars are twinkling
Mother Nature is sleeping
The sun is setting on the horizon
The moon is going to sleep
The beach is glistening
Life is waking like a newborn
My heart is beating gently
The fairies disappear one by one
The beach vanishes
All the beauty goes away
I feel a tapping on my shoulder
A musical voice wakes me up
It is my mother
I come out of my trance
My fantasy is over

Amanda Lynn Matta

One Moonlit Night

One night I stared at him.
While he sang I gazed at him.
As he gazed back at me,
I could only hope.
That one night he would talk to me.
Alone one moonlit night.

I sit up in my room
Wondering, wishing
That one night he will come
And talk to me.
Alone one moonlit night.

That night
I had dreamed would come
Never came.
So now I sit here waiting
Alone one moonlit night.

Ellena Studer

Friendship's End

Today I stumbled on a thought
and lingered awhile in reverie.
I wondered why this foe I fought
would hold fast to my treachery.
There was no need for argument,
now that moment's wasted, spent.

My tongue had stumbled earlier today
while speaking without thought,
on words it had not meant to say
and this was why we fought.
Truth was lost in what I said
which now lie heavy on my head.

Shall we not speak again my friend?
Is this where friendship comes to end?

Sheila Martel

Finger And Footprints

I washed some little fingerprints
from off my new front door,
I mopped some little footprints
from off my shiny floor;

But then I stopped and thought
as I never had before,
those little foot and fingerprints
were gone forever more;

I couldn't keep those little prints
Because they fade away,
The feet and hands that made them
Will all grow up someday;

But if I mopped and washed
throughout eternity,
Those little prints will always
be within my memory.

Wilma Wood

That Special Day

At the altar he stands
And waits for his bride

As down the isle she comes
With her father at her side

So beautiful she looks
On her wedding day

Like a bouquet of flowers
In a sun shine's ray

Her father presents her
And slowly steps away

The groom steps by her side
Forever to stay

To love, honor and cherish
Till death do they part

A total commitment
That comes from the heart

A commitment to know
Through life's joys and tears

They will have each other
So very near

Jean Hitchcock

Snowflakes

Snowflakes falling,
one on one.
Delicate, fragile,
silent and strong.
Uniting in snowbanks
with lacy might.

Snowflakes falling,
twirling in the wind.
Soundless, lightness,
power and cold.
Brushing up against the pine,
covering the fir.

Snowflakes falling,
all through the night.
Blanketing the sleeping world
to leave the winter bright.

Jean Hughes

The Oklahoma Tragedy

On a bright beautiful morning
of April of last year,
There was an awful tragedy
It brought about such fear.

The Oklahoma bombing
as reported by CNN.
Had occurred just a while ago
I wondered where I had been.

There were people with many injuries
All cut and scattered about,
But the children suffered the most,
That's without a doubt.

My heart will always remember
The fireman holding that child,
That picture is worth a million
To the mother that knows its smile.

I hope the one responsible
will recognize his mistake,
And ask for God's forgiveness
And live a new life without hate.

Linda Jenkins.

The Way

She walks above the lights of time
Above the earthly roar
And clasps in love
And joins the hands
Of the ones who've gone before
And lingers but a little while
Her fingers poised to wave
Before she enters through the door
That goes beyond the grave
Her memory stays
Where spirits fly
Her soul is ours to touch
To hold to hearts
That keep the bond
To the one we loved so much

Dolores Scharf

Weeping In Woods On A Snowy Evening

Whose woods these are I do not care;
If one owns land it isn't fair.
One cannot claim a piece of ground-
The Earth was made for men to share.

My horse makes a contented sound;
He's glad there's no one else around.
We watch the sugar-coated sky...
Somehow the silence is profound.

While sitting here I wonder why
(For life so quickly passes by)
Humans are always on the go.
My contemplation yields a sigh.

Within me peace begins to grow,
But now my tears fall with the snow.
And for humanity they flow.
And for humanity they flow.

Christina J. Powell

My Pride

What a horrible world
Which my family came
From slavery, but it's
Just that there's so much
Prejudice that no one
Will save from this horrible world

Stephanie Denice Wynn

Galilee Gathering

Fire of burning coals
sizzling fish and broken bread
breakfast by the shore

Sea of Galilee
Peter, John with Risen Lord
gathering of friends

Sharon M. Daley

Decisiveness Is Not Enough

Today is not enough to say
you mean it. People are to the
point to say they mean it, but
they don't mean it. Some say
they're right but they're not right!
Decisiveness is not enough for
me, tell me once and tell me again
I can't believe it enough to say
you're right, but maybe tomorrow
it may be better to be to the
point with me, because it may
not be good enough in my mind
to accept or to be at ease at
this particular time,
To be decisive is enough for
me, that's how I would like to be.

Robin L. Murray

Colors

Through the streets of blood
Flow rivers of tears
Baby's with guns
Children no fear
Shots going off
Screams rip the air
Another persons been murdered
For the colors they wear
Their hatred runs hot
Our fear runs cold
Tombstones are ready
They await deaths toll
Another mother sits crying
Her baby has died
For he's chosen a life
To let colors, rule his mind.

Darci Huth

Reindeer

Reindeer floating up so high,
Why do you float and not fly?
Is that your nose that's so red?
Why don't you hide it under your bed?

Oh, little girl on the ground,
Because I need to leap and bound,
With my nose I lead the sleigh,
I don't have a bed I sleep in hay.

Kristin Visbeck

Our Delusionary Life

Look about you right now!
nowhere... no where is to be found
Life... real living - going on
what is visible, isn't really
think, quietly... Outloud - if need be
how we accept everything so freely
frivolous creatures you see
Greedy indeed... passing time simply - we want to please us
Fool! How we long to wallow
a real imitator, in disregard of our nature
Jump back, turn inward - out, scream!!!
look; into, through, beyond the Eyes of a child
not yet tainted by Wisdom - ha! What a farce
but, it's not too late... yes... it Is
Pray - Hope... means to a better end?
or perhaps, another guise
what is real? what is not?
does anybody really care by now...

Michael F. Stacy

To My Love

You gave me Love and lit my heart
You gave me hope for a new start
Even tho' that day may never be
My dreams will keep you close to me.
You are the things that means so much
Your high ideals to your loving touch
You make me feel that I'm worthwhile
And puts on my lips a wondrous smile
So always know that to make my day
Just think of me and when you may
Give me a call and let me hear
Those four small words "I love you Dear"

Mary E. Kennedy

Love Is Our World

Love, the source all people need and hunger for.
Love, it is needed and wanted just that much more.
When taken advantage of it is said to become sour.
When used carefully, slow and by the hour, can blossom
into an everlasting flower.
Love, changes for people differently.
Also for different people like you and me.
Those that have love are very lovely people gentle and kind.
Those that despise love find it burdening on their mind.
Those that know nothing of love live each day in agony and strife.

Danielle Roche

Interpretation

With two eyes the blind man perceives
Two visions. One vivid, one complete.
The first is one of handicap,
beyond that even he can conceive.
The next displays a gentle man as he says
"A wise man relies on sight as an art.
Because he can still see.
Even if light no longer travels to the heart."
With two ears the deaf man hears two thoughts.
Pessimism proves strong in bursts.
But optimism prevents him from becoming cursed.
With two hands we can contribute to two deeds.
With two feet we can continue at two speeds.
How busy our tongues must be through and through!
For with but one, we accomplish as much as two.

Kris Isham

"Mother I'll Love You Forever"

When I was Just a baby boy
There was nothing I could do
I would always look up from my crib
And standing there would be you

You made me feel so warm inside
With your love and your care
And when the world seemed so strange to me
You would always be there

That's why mother I'll love you forever

As I get older everyday
I love you more and more
God knows I thank you for having me
Mother it's you I adore

That's why I'm telling you know
I want the world to know that I'm proud
You're sweeter than sweeter can be
Thank God you belong to me

That's why mother I'll love you forever

Lundgren Unwyn Peters

Capture The Moment

Ribbons and bows and pink teddy bears -
Tiny face scrunched, fresh from a world without cares.
White satin and lace, fingers tightly curled -
Eyes closed shut against the light of this new world.
Shades of lavender and pastels abound -
Whispering voices; barely a sound.
Wisps of brown hair ever so soft on a perfect head -
Hearts so filled with love, a tear is shed.
We capture the moment; this very special day...Today our little girl is Born!

Amidst a cloud of balloons, she stares wide-eyed -
Suddenly uncertain and a little afraid, we appear at her side.
A sea of smiling faces and so many voices calling her name -
A delicious cake with one lone candle and a single flame.
Hugs and kisses; she squeals with delight -
Inching closer, pointing curiously at the candlelight.
Party favors, bright balloons and a brand new toy -
A burst of song makes her laugh with joy.
The flash of a camera catches her eye and she smiles -
On toddler's legs she comes, collapsing into our arms as if she's walked a mile.
We capture the moment, this very special day...Today our little girl

is One!

Helen Ingrid Hill

A Valentine Of 30 Years Together

I know you don't like all that mush and stuff.
Don't screw up your face now, and go off in a huff!

I'm bound and determined to have my say —
"Pratt Street" or "Wheat Road", or come what may.

This little bear comes as "Teddy", you see-
Not a "Grizzly" (which often you turn out to be).

He holds in his paws his arrows and bow,
But the heart is my own, I'd like you to know!

It's older and wiser, tho' worn somewhat thin -
But still beats for you, whatever mood you are in.

'Cause I'm no saint either; I too, make life hard.
But I'm gonna keep tryin'. How 'bout you pard?

Rita Sasdelli

The Deceiver

I met a beautiful lady
She seemed so sweet
I thought she was an angel
I knelt down at her feet
When I looked up
To my surprise she was the devil, in disguise
Her face was all twisted, her eyes were a flame
My body trembled as she whispered my name
She reached for my hand
I drew away
I cried Lord please save this sinful man
I heard the devil laughing as she walked away
And a frightening voice saying "I'll be back another day."

Mardella Wilkinson

After The Storm

Darkening skies...showers ahead,
Close the windows of the old homestead.
The wind blows wild; the thunder roars,
Lightening brightens the distant shores.

A calm descends upon the grounds,
The storm has passed; fresh air abounds.
It carries a scent that tickles the noses,
An invigorating aroma of lilacs and roses.

A clean sweep has arrived from heaven above,
Our great Creator has showered down love.
He's made the grass greener and the crops grow tall,
Then wrapped the earth with sunshine...welcomed by all.

Jeanette L. Currier

Evening At The Beach

The tide rolls in like rich waves of caramel
The sun touches the ocean like my soul touches the sky
Seagulls glide smooth and swift
like the ocean liners cutting through the sea
deftly parting the water as though it were a comb
running down the center of my head
My body sinks as the sand
tries to cover me, gently like my bedding
and rolls off as smooth as rain
sliding down my back
The wind sends my hair swirling and snapping
Clouds gather in the sky like long separated relatives
swarming together like bees
The crisp cold scent of the ocean whispers of rain
as it rushes past me
Dried pieces of drift wood snap and pop
as flames jewel and frazzle, absorbing their essence,
releasing warmth that barely reaches my skin
before it is blown away by the chill wind
and it begins to rain softly

Amber Wanlass

Untitled

I am 85 years of age
I like to say something
when you get on in age you
think many things some good
some bad but most of the time good
which is good, people who
are happy will always be happy
now is the time to say adieu
some say it's naptime and
say my time to adieu
to you all I hope
that this will be good
for me too

Michae Terranoua

Look, Don't You See Him

Look, don't you see Him,
Standing by the door,
With His arms outstretched,
Saying, Welcome to the House of the Lord!

Look, don't you see Him,
Standing There,
With a smile on His face.
How He loves to see His children,
Gather in one place.

Look, don't you see Him,
With His face aglow,
Oh, how He loves us so.

So, come on in and stay a while,
For the presence of God is in this House.

And always remember, when we open our doors,
You're always Welcome,
In the House of the Lord!

Evelyn L. Collins

"Spring Shower"

The rhythm of the soul calls you,
echoing its voices in the hills.
All that is knowledgeable departs,
all that is old becomes young.
All that is peaceful blankets the earth,
and the world is reborn again.
The lion becomes the kitten,
and plays with his brother the man.
They all lay down in silence,
and the world has a moment to rest.
The branches of trees sway gently,
as they talk about times gone by.
And rain rolls down paths known by heart,
then suddenly silence again.

Everyone stops uncertainly,
and turns suddenly in dismay.
They think of the time they have lost,
and how much this delay will cost.
The rain and peace now just an illusion,
and the world goes back to its usual confusion.

-Michaela Basham

The Black Rose

The black rose, standing in a crystal-clear vase
It is stemmed naked with no leaves on it
It has no past, It has no present, It has no future

The barren mountains are looming in the background
Their rocks are radiating a high degree of heat
The sky is azure blue with no hope of rain in sight

As the man walks slowly toward the mountain range
He knows that his very existence is timeless
The blossoms of the cactus are stark white
Against the spiny-green sculpture

The crystal vase knows that it is beautiful
The black rose knows it will never wilt

The green sculpture that is placed against the mountain
Has been there for the past ten thousand years
And the white blossoms come every spring

As the man ascends the mountain, he knows that he stands tall and erect
He knows there is an inner sense of tallness that walks among kings

He knows a rightful place on top of the mountain is there waiting for him just as surely as the rose blooms
And the warm wind whispers against his face

Becky Lea Bowsher

"Friend"

I see him standing there in the fading light,
But I see him not, in the darkness of night;

I see him move with me in the brightness of day,
But when it grows cloudy, he will move away;

At times his closeness is that which you can touch,
and yet at others, that would be too much;

His presence is not so much that you can feel,
But you know in your Heart that He's there, and no-one can steal;

He can always be there for someone else to see,
For I call him my friend, He's my Shadow, Me.

Jack Edward Burton Sr.

Thinking Of You

Christmas time, it's here again,
Times of sharing, caring, and laughing on end.
Here, then gone again, that's the way it goes
No matter if it rains, sleets, shines or snows.
I can't explain it, for the touch is gone,
You are not here, but life must go on.
I miss you, I love you, that's all I can say,
While hoping and praying, I'll see you soon someday
"Merry Christmas to all, and to all a goodnight,"
That's what they say in the story books right?
Looking back to the days, when you were once here,
I remember your face shining so bright with cheer.
These memories will stay, always in my heart,
For again when we're together, we will never part.
Merry Christmas, and may the stars shine so bright,
For as you are now in heaven, I'm thinking of you tonight.

Jennifer C. Migneron

Dreaming

As I lay there listening one cool summer eve,
I thought I heard a small whisper coming from the light breeze.
I stayed silent for a moment,
Then I heard more distinctly - the sound of a mourner.
As the sound came nearer,
I was almost stricken with terror
But as I arose and looked about,
I saw a dim figure mount.

As the figure approached me, I could hardly believe,
That the thing I saw was a nice young gentleman; now I was relieved
He greeted me as if he had known me for a long time,
Oh, so gentle, so loving and kind.
The short time we were together was precious - every minute,
The things we learned about each other will always remain in my memory.
As it began to grow dusk, I lifted my eyes at his touch,
And smiled beyond at the windless breath of summer like gold of myrrh.

If was only a dream which never on earth
Shall come to life or rise to birth.
The star's shine on and the moon smiles too,
I'll always dream of that day - me and you.

Willa F. Moore

Futility

I saw the spider on the glass
running to and fro.

Is that me in my life
not knowing where I go?

Margo S. Barregarye

"The Real Me"

You look at me and see a girl,
who lives inside her own little world
don't believe that's all there is to see,
you'll never know the real me
I smile through a thousand tears
and adolescent fears, I dream of all
I can never be
don't say I take it all for granted,
I'm well aware of all I have.
Please understand...
it seems to me as though I've
always been someone outside lookin' in
here I am for all them bleed, but
they can't take my heart from me
and they can't make me drop to my knees!
Please understand...
you'll never know the real me...

Jeannie M. Street

Vicarious Lives

Behind a million burning windows
We lead our vicarious lives,
Suffering silently for doors we never opened
And others self-denied.
Embittered by the glimpse we caught
Of the life we should have led,
We had our dreams to choose from
But castrated them instead.

The fires flicker and dwindle
As the days turn to years;
Icy bewilderment,
Left alone with our fears.
Obsequiousness grants us no favor,
The waiting gains us no time.
Our unclaimed lives grow bored and disown us.
Freedom lies in tatters.

Brad Fabian

I See

I see a poor face with no where to go,
house burnt down, flooded, robbed.
Too proud to beg
Too proud to spend a cold night in a warm shelter,
but proud to freeze to death on a cold city street.

I see babies having babies,
14 year old girls, breast feeding with breasts
that have not matured yet.

I see a young body stealing food to survive,
spending two years in jail.

I see a drunken, white trash man,
and his black eyed, broken nose, and broken ribbed wife,
he'll see her again in only six months.

I see selfish, corrupt politicians taking weeks off,
because they're too stubborn to submit to a compromise.

I see a society taken over by greed, corruption, and materialism.

Kirsten Dooley

Hate

Hate
Burning like a deep dark sweaty fire
Misty pungent aroma
Bursting of a loud booming roar of rage
Leaving you feeling strong and powerful.

Sara O'Connor

What One Tear Could Bring

Silent tears of a nightingale, fall softly upon
your face. A face of any color, that belongs to
any race. Speak now, your beating heart sings,
softly now with ease. Sweeping over the ground,
and breezing though the trees. Your knees fall
quietly to this Rocky Mountain edge, crumbling
the stones away, to find exactly what you said.
With the meaning comes a fortune, that you alone
will grasp and touch. A fortune that is not
defined into a materialistic clutch. But however,
that of wisdom, that pities that of greed. The
wisdom becoming the one, that will go on to succeed.
This of what one tear has taught us, that our hearts
song was truly worth, was only the beginning of
a peaceful human birth.

Megan Renae Brooks

As Angels

As Angels we sing, as demons we cry,
as humans we stand silent as our souls slowly die
Now love fills our hearts, with hate in our souls
and this silence we feel, our minds it controls.
The difference of color, the hate and the war,
now history repeats all actions before.
We live and we learn and time passes on
and memories remain through the faces are gone.
The good and the evil which lies in us all,
the hope in our hearts and the dreams we recall.
As Angels our wings are tattered and bruised,
as demons we stand, lost and confused
As human we stand in the middle and mind
while silently searching for peace to find.
A hand full of hope, a promise, a wish
and the tears that we cry for all that we miss
So we hope and we pray and do all that we can,
Angels nor Demons, we're all merely Human.

Melissa Willis

Dust Devils

Dust Devils, restless spirits
that haunt the West
Desert mischief makers
that know no rest.

Are they souls of those who
perished from thirst and sun?
Condemned to wander the desert,
always on the run.

Twisting over hot desert sands,
searching for water and shade.
Uncovering bleached bones of unfortunate
travelers who lost their way.

They can appear without warning,
then their gone taking dust and debris,
spinning, soaring.

Dust Devils, according to science are
weather created and nothing more.
Is science right? Or could Dust Devils
be lost souls from back before?

Don Tracy

Journey

Left behind were well wishers;
Accompanying out were strangers;
In my heart were dreams;
Accomplished were scandals.

Purnima Gupta

Divine Intervention

Death came whispering in my ear
"Entreat me now, come near,
to a place, soft and dear
away from the race,
the plans of the year.
Look and see; have no fear."

Life cut through
with a brilliant sword,
standing there, seeming bored.

"You again!
with your darkness, gloom, and night.
I bring the word, the truth, the light!
And send you far into the future light.
Take your rightful place
now depart!"

With that,
the last enemy, smart,
took flight.

Julie Hatefi

Little White Cottage

O, little white cottage high on a hill
Your windows looking out to the sea.
You are heaven to me, and share a love
The memories of one who is far from me.

My dearly beloved, and only one
Laughed with me here and saw me last.
Stand at your threshold with tearful eyes
Wishing the war were done and past.

A war that is fought on distant shores.
In unknown jungles and under the water.
We give of our spirit and strength and men
We who were once Great Britain's daughters.

We give of our hearts and hopes and dream
Of fruitful days bearing love and peace.
When man have suffered enough to learn
That hate is a plague - then war will cease.

O, little white cottage, high on a hill
With your wind-tossed daisies and sun-kissed sea
Keep my spirit serene - my courage strong.
'till my lover returns again to me.

Gladys Buchanan Schucht

Grandmother

The spirit is separating from the flesh at last.
Her dim eyes are veiled by pain
or drugged by well-meaning doctors.
I finally understand that the body
is the prison of the soul.
Hers is like a chirping bird
exhausted from banging against the bars of its cage.
Her blood courses blue through bulging veins
wrapped like vines around her sharp brittle bones.
Her hands gesture helplessly to accent
the unflagging thoughts uttered hoarsely.
The delicate wisdom and gentle wit issue forth,
legacies of lost decades of despair.
Now tolerance, acceptance, even love of life
oh how crazy it all has been
lend grace and dignity to the lines.
Life falls into final perspective.
The battle rages in every corner of her body
as the enemy mercilessly destroys the fibers of her being.
But her spirit is serene.

Rebecca M. Pauly

Land Of Enchantment

Country flourishing with lush greenery and passionate humanity
where ancient ruins stand as relics of times past
how I long for you.
Mountainous and azure-skied,
how beauteous and enchanting you are.
Nation of the colorful Quetzal and legacy of the Maya,
where Spanish conquistadores discovered paradise,
Your mystery beckons my very soul.
Place of black Pacific sands and white Caribbean sands
I wish so much to see your countryside.
Flowing rivers penetrate the jungle
and lakes reflect the warming sun's rays.
What an astounding and fantastic creation God made.

Pablo R. Espada

Once Upon A Golden Dream

The darkness sets as dawn breaks,
frogs croak and the wind is serenading for me
I feel like a princess
When I kiss the frog it will turn into a prince,
A prince for only me
We shall live in a golden palace,
Oh, how giddy we shall be,
And when we grow old and weary,
we will settle in a beach house and watch the golden sea

Melinda Hecht

Remembering

The days and months go slowly by,
Your smile and touch begin to dim,
I see your face in my mind's eye,
And wish to see you once again.

I see my grand children run smiling and free,
And wonder what your thoughts would be,
To see these little boys laugh with glee,
At kites and birds and bumble bees.

My heart remembers your love of a child,
I know you are watching from up above,
Seeing them tumble and giggling wild,
Imagine you hugging and kissing with love.

When God called you to his heavenly hearth,
He left us to cope here on earth all alone,
You live forever deep in my heart,
And know you walk by my side, your hand in my own.

My father and brother have joined you up there,
Hand and hand forever under God's caring eye,
We remember you all and the love that was shared,
And pray you found peace in your home in the sky.

Lucinda Bosley

"A Bereavement Cope"

There are holidays and birthdays with
one card less, hurts in so many ways.

You are in our thoughts, vision and heart
and will never part.

Time does not heal all, ask any one that's
lost a son.

Cope is what we do as we go from seconds,
minutes, to hours and when at your grave we
lay the flowers.
The lump in our throats, the emptiness in our
stomachs, the heaviness in our hearts is a
big void that will never part.

Ellease Z. Odom

"The Cry Of Love"

My heart aches with a deepen sadness
Each time I see him, I falter
My heart cries out to him in the voices of a thousand souls
My body lust to be with him
Why, why can't I have him?
The pain - the anguish
Oh how, I wish my sorrow was done
I cry out to him, but he cannot come to me
I just need to be with him or I will burst
I need to tell the world
I love him!!
Oh sweet sorrow, leave me please
I cannot stand it!
This pain is too great for me to bare
My depression increases for I am dieing inside
My soul still weeps for him as my heart fails me
He couldn't come to me
And now my heart breaks into a thousand pieces
I die without seeing my one true love,
the sorrow of all my pain...

Luane M. Tatro

K.M.L.

In a corner
The speechless child sits
Debating love and love
Friendly love
And that which exists when one is in love
The difference
It's like black and white
But there's a fine line
And yet it's so hard to see
What happens
When a relationship
Contains aspects of each
Do you allow the mix of both kinds
Or keep your love to one type
Play it safe
Or take the chance
You think
In a corner
The speechless child sits
Debating, never to reach a safe answer

Justin Berdik

Senior Portrait

Senior portrait
frozen smiles locked in time
the innocence and wiles
behind the bright eyes and careful looks
thoughts about, "how do I look?"
Yet when a few years (or more)
have past and these memories
unbound are past
it might not matter how you look
much more, perhaps, the path you took
to live your life, -full of joy
or locked in steps of other's expectations.
It's dawning on you, it's time to choose
the life you'll lead, the type you'll lose.
Thus begins that all within the world could be yours
or will you 'settle'
smile frozen, eyes unblinking
thoughts hidden
Senior portrait.

Janice Spohn

Seeds Of Happiness

Little flower by my walk,
How I wish that you could talk.
Many are the things you could tell.
Story after story you would sell.

You would tell of smiles on the faces you meet,
Of sorrow, gloom, despair and defeat.
You would tell of families having fun
When their day's work is done.

Stories of youth that you met,
As upon the grace they sat.
Then of the aged as they hobbled by with a smile.
Life for them was but a little while.

Little flower, soon your life will pass.
And you'll fade and die at last.
A cluster of little seed you'll leave behind,
These to others will bring happiness and peace of mind.

When my life on earth is ore
And I cross to the other shore.
If it could be said of something I have said or done,
She brought happiness into the life of someone.

Vivian A. Baucom

God

Nothing is above the Law, and everything is me. I feed upon my self, I am life eternally.

Upon the cross at calvary, bound to the tree of life. I placed the truth for all to see, Christ, do not forsaken thee.

Take the fruit of the tree of life and eat plentifully, but don't take the knowledge tree for you shall awaken me.

I am as strong as my weakest link and that link is me, I fear the loneliness of my eternity!

Into my self I will go and eat my self from head to toe. When I am full then I rest, dream my dreams you're the last...

Vincent Hawkes

Never Ending Streams

Roses are red, violets are blue,
When my heart beats. It beats for you.
I love you so much. But you're out of my touch.
You have no clue. What I go through,
Day after day, and night after night.
Loving you is like trying to win an endless fight,
In which I will never give in.
When I don't have you to hold,
My life seems so cold.
You are all I think about.
Day in, and day out.
Although I can't love you, I do anyway,
Even though you are so far away,
I will love you, forever in my dreams.
As long as there are,
Never ending streams.

Jacklynn Rebecca Toy

My Boss

Why do you think I'm supposed to tremble in your presence?
Why is fear so important to you?

Can't you speak to me on your level instead of talking
down to me? Do you not feel I'm qualified to do my job?
Even though you hired me.

If you question my abilities, you should question your own
ability to choose the right person. You should look in the
mirror, are you happy with the person for which you are looking?

Melinda C. Walker-Burke

Just Me!

I once was a teacher a longtime ago.
I loved my students and they seemed to know.
I was only myself, which was the best way to learn-
That you are only You no matter which way you turn.

A Shakespearean fan can be an actor instead-
But I tend to be what is in my head.
I may be criticized for what I like and what I do-
But, I can only Me-
And-that is true.

I try my best to improve each day-
But sometimes it gets to be a chore in someway.
I will continue to try as hard as I can-
To be "normal" seems to be far from my span.

I do accept myself-
And hope others will.
To be impressive is not my deal!

Janis Barnes

Dear Daddy

If I could...
I would give you good health so you wouldn't feel pain or discomfort or dread the night, fearing you will never see daylight again.
If I could...
I would give you good health so your eyes wouldn't just stare, seemingly bare, but the mischief would be there as before.
If I could...
I would give you good health so you could tell your corny jokes and laugh and laugh and laugh...
If I could...
I would give you good health so you could walk outside and smell the air, sit in the front yard and wave at all that passes
If I could...
I would give you good health so you could travel... go to Hawaii and see the exotic sands, or to the hills of Kentucky and think of days past, or come to see me - where I live, where I work...
If I could...
I would give mom good health so you wouldn't worry about her...
If I could...
I would give you good health so you couldn't be with mom and me and *all* of your family that loves you so very much... forever
If I could...
You were always there when I needed you... and when I didn't.
You were (and are) my shining star and I love you daddy...

Reba Crutcher Qualls

Silent Tears Of Gold

My world stands still when I pause to pray,
And in the midst of thick darkness I find most to say.

Should your time to leave come before I go,
My greatest fear I want you to know.

For you order my world in a timeless passion,
And your dreams nurture mine in a most acceptable fashion.

Like silent tears of gold intermingled with fire,
My heart burns with joy as much as desire.

Each night when I lay me down to sleep,
'Tis your soul I pray my God to keep.

Each day I awake close next to you
I see my prayer answered and dreams come true.

And silent tears of gold from my spirit flow
In expressions of thanksgiving only a Spirit could know.

Russell L. Smith

A Lifetime Of Love

From Teddy Bears to Barbie Dolls,
Through G.I. Joe's and basketballs,
We spend our youth with happy hearts,
Endless energy and lightning starts.
Onto our teens puppy love pops.
Our challenge to parents - it never stops.
Then we leave home to seek life anew.
There's college and work and close friendships too.

A split second later we meet and we say,
"I do" and "I will" till my last earthly day.
We begin our lives with wind-filled sails.
Carving deep paths and blazing wide trails.
The children we raise make it hard to agree.
They grow, leave home and learn to be free.
Now a bit gray, we're old but together,
And we'll beat any storm, no matter the weather.

Randy L. Heibel

My Kite

There it is
up in the sky
Going back and forth

Red and white against the azure blue
What fun it is to make it fly

As long as I control it
With the string that's in my hand

It will dance as long as the wind doth blow
Even without a band

But if I let go of this piece of string
Or the wind should not blow

It will fly away and come to earth
And I will have
A broken kite

Donald F. Massey

From The Outside Looking In

Let not a night's flame consume a lover's soul
And let us rage to hold steadfast.
Why must we be so eager to let it go
It's not so hard to make it last.

It's with passion and love that we brew hate
But to love we turn a deaf ear.
I think it's not love that we want as of late
But rather it's love that we fear.

Sometimes love needs more than candy and flowers
Yet most times that's all that we give.
Sometimes love takes holding and talking for hours
It takes hearts willing to forgive.

We make love so complex, so complicated.
Love's just a seed planted at heart.
It's the time same love you found when you dated,
When you swore that you'd never part.

Remember that love is not a golden band,
Love is what brought you together.
It's the link between a woman and a man.
While rings fade, love lasts forever.

Travis Shaun Renfrow

Haiku

With each gust of wind
Seeds scatter, helter-skelter
Tassels wave goodbye

Yoshiyuki Otoshi

Cornell U.

Where das College is ben swingin'
On der hill, mit ivy clingin'
Mit der collitch songers singin'
High up from Cayuga's water
Meinself in bringin' smartish daughter.

Soon mit sneakers flippin floppin'
In ish luncher place is stoppin'
On der stool herself ben ploppin'
Mit der soup is slippin' sloppen.'

Next herself is havin' benders
In der sports cars mitout fenders
Burning dos candles on both enders
Til das collitch is suspenders.

Comes der card mut sayin' failin'
Comes der daughter weepin, wailin'
Comes der poppa mit hardish whalin' Mit das board mitout a nail in.
Den das poppa say "dumb brattin"
Meinself been thinkin 'dis mite happen
No more is daughter sittin' sattin',
Get un coat and get un hatten for mine mill make baseball batten.

Sadie E. Nannen

Death

As I walk through the gates of hell, my mind wonders,
Where is the light? Where are the angels? Why am I not
in the place I belong? The gatekeeper walks toward me, He speaks,
"Enter now through the gates 4 you shall burn for all eternity,"
"What did I do so wrong on earth?" What did I do?
He speaks again, "Enter now through the gates for you shall
burn for all eternity." My eyes widen, I scream, as I'm thrusted 4th
through the gates, I see fire burning, I see people burning,
their voices go through my body like nails, I feel their pain. A fire
sparks upon my feet, I scream, but no one hears, black opaque demons
circle me, their groans ring my ears. My eyes widen, I stare into
the fire that burns me, "ashes to ashes and dust to dust." He gazes
into my eyes, I kneel, I bow, he disappears into the darkness. A
fire burns my heart. It fills the room. My eyes widen as the demons
carry me off, and I realize, I'm not in heaven...

Valerie Pierce

My Best Friend... My Wife

From the first day that I met you, I knew you would be the "one";
No one before in my life has filled it with so much love and fun.
A beautiful face, soft brown hair, and a charming captivating smile,
Just a single simple thought of you can carry me easily a million miles.
Your support and understanding, in many tough times has helped me get through,
I want you to know and feel that I will forever always be there for you.
You truly mean so much more to me than all the words in the world could ever say;
I want to make you feel that special each and every day.
When I hold you in my arms, and close my eyes, I feel so much peace and love and care.
I want to truly and completely open and give my life to you,
and make it yours to share...
But it is so much more than sharing, because you are my love, my soul, my life...
All I want to do is grow old with you beside me as my best friend... my wife.

Robert Huerta

First Christmas

Long ago on a glorious morn
A babe in Bethlehem was born
He came not for himself you see
But to save sinners you and me

His life the sacrifice He gave
to save us from a fiery grave
So amid the parties and the fun
Remember why he had to come

To suffer and die on a cursed tree
So I could enter heavens glory
When we give our gifts remember his gift of love
For he left his glory up above

To pardon me and give me grace
To keep me from that awful place
So when Christmas comes remember Christ next time
He gave his life so he could save mine

It's not santas and trees and having a ball
But love the greatest gift of all

Ann Young

My Mother's Smile

My mother often wore a smile,
Upon her face it sat.
But when I really worried -
Was when I didn't know where it was at!

She knew that I was just a child
And I wouldn't do everything just right.
She prayed for my guidance and direction,
For God is love - just help her in her plight.

Serving God in this wicked world
May not seem to be the easiest choice.
But have courage and be strong -
Tell others and lift your voice!

For how could one not praise Him,
For what He did for us, on that cruel tree,
He bled, He died, and saved us from our sin,
What greater gift could God have given me?

So when I see my mother's smile
For all the world to see,
I know that God lives within her heart,
And because of her - He lives in me!

Vivian H. Perry

Gardens Of Life

If only a flower would swallow me whole, its petals
caressing my smitten cheek bone - nectar swimming in my soul.
I would flow through its stem reaching deep within the soil
Smelling sweet fragrances of the earth below.
A returning to the dust and ashes of whence I came.
I would rest in the arms of forever roots, in the metamorphosis
of dying leaves - bathing in its cleansing moisture.
Soon I would sprout through hardened layers of molten clay and
sticky mud!
The sun's beaming light beckons with rays of photosynthesis
and I rise from the safety of darkness!
I would break through the toil of growth, stretching into a
beautiful thing of petals, sweetness, a wondrous photosphere.
A colorful wonder, I would please the human eye, wash away a
moment of pain
Remind humanity of the beauty within, and that they also - can
rose from beneath it all...

Richard A. Lambert

Toast To A Traveler

Pour the red wine:
Remembering the good fruit on old vines
Here's to the cup turned down
To the heart who read mine and slept.
To the lip who drank and wept
For the troth that was not kept.

Pour the red wine and drain it dry
Remembering all earth and sky
Filled once our cups in youth
When together we measured truth
Where no cry would cancel debt.
No tears to cleanse the dye then set
Yours to ask; I, to give thee, yet.

Here's to the years that roll, endlessly
Bringing me again to thee
Here's to the bells that toll joyously
Announcing a safe return.

Helen H. White

The Destiny Of Man

"The destiny of man lie in his soul," so wrote Herodotus, the
ancient father of History many centuries ago.
How true is such philosophy thus recorded in history,
But we ignored the meaning, the vast significance
A message, timeless of importance.
If we but ponder what had been said about the human soul,
Perhaps we might attain the lofty goals,
The goals, to rid humanity of poverty of so many souls;
For unsolved problems which we now face,
Perplexing all of the human race,
No doubt solutions can be found,
If tending to the souls abound,
Not by a few in the universe
But by the vast majority,
By virtue of philosophy, and lessons of genuine history.

To cleanse us of our soul's defects forever, guiding our destiny,
Envisioned by Herodotus - the waywardness of man can end
But from the vices he must cease
And truth and virtue forever embrace, until the very end.

C. Antonio Provost

Brookside

As I sat and stared into the crystal-clear water, I saw the most
beautiful unique reflections.
Which nobody has ever seen before.
They reflected the light which showed all my favorite past times.
I wanted to catch them all and recapture the unbelievable feelings,
again, but I couldn't
I felt a feeling of happiness and joy again.
Just as I felt my whole life falling apart into tiny pieces,
It reappeared better than ever, right in front on my tiny face and
big brown eyes.
It looked like tiny little creatures were bringing my whole life
back together again.
Little creatures were hoping all around my body.
All of them were jumping into wonderful past times.
I soon drifted asleep and dreamed of my future.
I could see myself having the most wonderful times.
These tiny green creatures helped me come back into reality.
Soon it started to rain and rain drops were erasing my beautiful
reflections of my past time.
I woke up and left the little babbling brook, with a feeling hope
and joy in my life, again.
This is when I came to know my true self again.

Gina Iannaccone

A New Day

Chastise not the dawn for scattering
The shadows of the night,
For it brings a sweet renewal
Of all things living and bright,
With the first melody of birdsong
In the dew-drenched morn,
The sun rises full with promise
As a page of a new day turns,

Pause and reflect upon the gift
Of a new, unadventured day,
As we rise expectant, traveling
Upon life's well-journeyed way,
Bask in the vibrant, soothing warmth
Of the sun's life-giving caress,
As we brace ourselves to run
Once more this endless human race,

And remember we are here to give
Freely, joyously of ourselves,
For we are unfinished books of life
And our actions the stories it will tell.

Jonathan David Payne

Battle Cry

I used to sit right down and write whatever came to mind
And knew within this heart of mine that I would always find
The right word or right sentence to adequately express
The messages of love and hope, or maybe even stress,
That came to mind without travail, but also with true joy.
I thought I was a poet and that others would enjoy
The ditties and the foolish words that I so loved creating.
But now, my fountain has dried up and I am even hating
To put my talent to the test; to make it work once more.
What used to be enjoyment has become a bloody chore.

But yesterday I read the news: a contest is in place
For poets to display their gifts of using words with grace.
of painting with the lavish brush of rhythm, style and charm.
I thought I'd enter just this once. Could surely do no harm.
I know the competition's steep, that others have more skill
At putting words together. When one reads them, it's a thrill!
But my mind's made up to try, never did turn down a dare!
So here's my entry to the fray. May it earn a winner's share!

Lorraine A. Girard

A Bit Yellin' About My Ellen

In nineteen-hundred - and - eleven,
You came to earth, a gift from heaven.
Since nineteen - hundred - thirty - four,
You've been my cook, and much, much more.
You've made the bed, you've cleaned the house,
You've been a sweet and loving spouse!
Our kids can look to you as Mother,
The like of which, there ain't no other!
We lift our heads and hearts in love,
To GOd, our Father up above,
For all the gifts that we have got,
From Him, thru You; and that's a Lot!!

From Head - Hand - Heart of one called "Art",
Who's glad, of thee, to be a part.

Arthur Amt

The Last Goodbye

On that evening marked by a wasted sky,
The soft wind breathed through the grass.
I vanished somewhere between my life full of pipe dreams,
And my suitcase full of memories.

"Farewell," the sad wind grieved,
As I pulled out of that driveway for the last time.
There was always the sound.
And now I mourn a memory of that sound.

The open window let air engulf my hotel room to secretly make noise.
Aretha Franklin is keeping me company now;
Because I don't want to listen to the sorrow of the wind.

I tried so hard to carry myself high
Ever so high;
But even when I didn't believe that I had fallen...
I fell fast asleep.

Elizabeth Kathryn Bibb

Pirate Love

Waiting for me is she, like my burial
When the time comes.

The search, a system of trial and error;
Persistence remains in-between.

Knowing, knowing you exist beckons my digging;
Has left many scars on white beach sand.

The fables, the stories, beliefs and the map;
In my head, with uncertainty at each crossroad.

Another lead turns up but yet another
Empty hole where I wish to bury myself sometimes.

Frustration, for my treasure is not yet found;
Has another finished with my riches?

Weariness, foolish pride, sleepless nights I ride
As the path leads on.

Will I know? When the brightness of her shinning presence
Fills my eyes? What of her worth?

Foggy, unclear is the night gazing up above for answers
While I hold this shovel that has buried so many.

The shovel, a crutch perhaps? But what else is there?
To hold onto, yes, until she is finally found. Bury me!

William J. Lindfors

I've Been Thinking Of You

I've been thinking of you
You've been on my mind
You are the love I thought I'd never find
Although sometimes I may cry my love for you will never die.
The sound of your voice makes me happy
The day I spent without you
Made my heart blue
No one else could do what you do
To release the magic
The magic of love
The kind that bonds two lovers
Bonds them as one I've been thinking of you
You've given me a love I never knew
I could not bare to lose I love you
You are my missing link as I wonder and think
I see an image an image of you
Your eyes so brown your hair so smooth
And you sent a sweet one to which nothing can compare
I hope you will always be there as I think of you.

Akwasi Baah

"The Sweetest Word"

When your children are young and play outside
You watch them with love and so much pride
They play they are on some trips and far away
I'm sure these imaginary trips are changed each day.
They return from these trips and no more to roam
And come into the house and I hear those words "Mommie I'm home"
Now they grow up and out on a date.
Mother just feel concerned and set and wait
Then the door opens and coming near
Are the sweetest words a mother can hear
is "Mother I'm home"
As we grow old and our children go far away.
Now - if they are somewhere or out to play
Those sweet words a mother can hear - "Mother I'm home"
And now I'm old and alone in my room,
I hear the sound of my children coming home
And their footsteps I hear coming near and near
Are still the sweetest words a mother can hear
is "Mother I'm home" -

Velma L. Koch

Our Little Man

March 3, 1993 a son was born,
A 6 lb 6 oz bundle of joy.

Almost perfect in every way,
You are our little pride and joy...

You were born to us a gift of love,
And completed our family just right.

Although we may not know all there is to life,
We promise that we will influence your course in life.

We will watch you grow and become a man,
And teach you what we think is right.

We will love you, guide you, and grow with you,
As only a family can.

Through the years we hope you grow to be your own man,
And make your world as safe as you can.

Before long we will be old and gray,
And you will be a man away from home.

But remember my son, no matter where you are,
or, whatever you do,
We will forever love you,
and, you will always be our little man.

Ronald F. Dobiesz

The Little Low Bush

The little low bush yearned to be tall;
To be like the fir tree admired by all,
She knew that soon children would come
Select this fine tree and then take it home,
Adorn each branch with tinsel and gold:
'Twas the Yule season with special love to enfold.
What was her purpose there? She wept in dismay,
As that proud little fir was carried away.
Was she to stay quiet, humble as ever
To be always ignored, unnoticed forever?

Lo! In the dark of the night a spider sped down
Weaved her some lace for a magnificent gown.
The dew, in the dawn, covered each strand of that lace
And diamonds and sequins blazed forth in their place.
And all were amazed, struck with deep awe
At this transformed little shrub that they saw;
With her wondrous beauty she wondered no more,
She knew now exactly what she was there for
'Twas to show all that being lowly and small
Is as wonderful, as great, as something that's tall!

Virginia E. Wagner

My Dreaded, Daily Task

When the sun dips just below the tree tops in the distant grove,
My dreaded, daily task must begin.
Giving up the refuge of my lighted yard, confronting the darkening grove, I will pass through the wood to the garden where the light still holds. The grove challenges me as my cautious, determined foot falls alert the tessellated path to whip my ankles with clinging, briary vines. Like diamond-backed rattlers, newly-placed tree roots and fallen limbs promise stinging heels if I lock my gaze too long on the distant illumination from the garden.
Scurrying, susserating whispers and rancid wood-kill odors pervade me. In the midst of the guarded grove, the primordial wood scorn my raised hackles and shivery, prickling skin.
Masking on a brave face, yet wanting nothing more than to sprint like an olympian to the garden clearing ahead where I may shake off the enervating force, I school myself to walk.
If I run from the grove at twilight, the silvan sentry will never more permit my passing its portals to sustain the garden light.
I tread lightly, proudly, to the life-giving valve, watch the green foliage glisten from the proffered moisture and the light which has held for me before I face off once more with the dark grove.

JoAnn V. Dixon

Seed Of Peace

She shook her head; the doctor's confused; my husband's not dead; *nonononononono, oh please no;*

We'll look after you; it's the way it should be; it will be hard; you're vulnerable; not set rules to grieving; we'll take care of you;you're family; *i need room to breath*; we all need to grieve in our own way; do you mind if I take this as a keepsake; I'll understand if you say no; *how can i say no*; we miss him; go ahead and grieve; what do you mean you're selling your home; what do you mean your moving; what do you mean by giving his clothes away; why are you doing this; *i need to start over*; what about our grief; how can you do this; *i miss him too*; what do you mean time to yourself; we don't see your pain; we don't like the way you're handling things; but everyone grieves differently; do you mind if we take this; I know someone who really needs it; *they hurt too*; grieving will take a long time; go slowly; you can count on us; I set you up with a date; what do you mean you're not ready; get on with your life; *you're smothering me*; why are you mad; you're not grieving; grieve any way you can; *please you're pushing me away; i need space*; our family comes first now; you're lucky you can start over again; *i want my husband back*; you must eat; you must take care of yourself; let us help; *i must take care of myself*; you must not lose anymore weight; stop; you must not make any goals just yet; you must do what you feel is right; look you're causing family rifts; *stop*; why aren't you grieving; why aren't you dating; *stop*; call me, let's get together; make your own decisions; what do you mean you are leaving; how dare you; what about sharing and supporting; what about us; *No! Enough!*

Silence drifted, settling on her; *He would be proud of me; very proud.* Finally; a seed of peace.

Susan's husband was killed in a 1987 car crash caused by a drunk driver.

Susan L. Charlton

Cornbread Beans And Taters

My girl just left me, and now she's gone.
I'm glad she's gone she was always telling me where I could go.
I was getting tired of eating cornbread, beans and taters every night anyhow.
And in my very own house her precious fruit was forbidden.
Why I will never know.
But she did keep it well hidden.
Lord I did not hate her,
But there's bot to be more to life than just cornbread, beans and taters.

James H. Pinkston III

"Going Down Hill Fast"

My closet is packed with designer jeans
My medicine cabinet crammed with creams.
But now I find I'm "over the hill"!

I crack a smile — the denture slips
and try to ignore the bulge of my hips.
My bra straps are tightened up to my chin.
Yet Redhook says, "Relish the age group I'm in"

My posture is perfect with designer clothes galore.
But let's face it ladies — we now row with one oar!
So all you blue haired matrons
with the ruffles hiding fat
If you've passed the dreaded "60" mark
you'll never get to Bat.

Slow down on your wardrobe
Trade your creams for library books
The men want promiscuity
Not wrinkled, sultry looks!
So cancel Frederick's of Hollywood — get Penney's flannelette
But don't cast your silly dreams aside
'Cause that's all you're gonna get!

S. E. Neff-Rainey

Books

Everyday you overlook
A wonderful place full of books.
Take for instance Oliver Twist,
You can't imagine what you've missed,
Till you've cozied up with a book.
Next thing you know you'll be hooked.
Moby Dick, White Fang, Robinson Crusoe,
Some really good books written a long time ago.
Call of the Wild, Hardy Boys, Nancy Drew,
A Tale of Two Cities, Charles Dickens, too.
Fiction, myths, biography,
Go visit your local library.

Devin Chesbro

Neglected Eyes - As Seen By A Child Protective Service Worker

You knock on these doors
Like you have a million times before
Thinking, wondering, dreading
Hoping you don't find what you came to.

The doorknob slowly turns
As the door cracks open
You see no one until you look down
Beaming up at you are a set of eyes
Familiar eyes, neglected eyes
Saddened, dull, yet precious eyes.

The door swings open
As you see two more sets of eyes run toward you
Matched with their eyes you see a glimmer
Their smiles and the hope in their faces
Wanting, begging, so innocent
As they grab and hug your legs.

Sometimes it's not the wondering what you'll find
Behind those doors that is the hardest
It's knowing what you're leaving
As you close the door behind you.

Brenda Roetman

Life

What is life?
Life is emotions, achievements, and questions.
Friends, teachers, and role models have a part in influencing someone's life.

Emotions of happiness, joy, and sorrow.
Happiness, to have someone love you, to make your parents proud of you.
Joy, to see your relative who lives far away.
Sorrow, the most painful one of all,
you have lost a very good friend, or a loved one.

Achievements, goals, and awards
you achieve so much,
but yet gain so little.

So, is this life?
This is only a portion of life.
Life is a never-ending journey,
it is full of great memories.

Lorie Schneidt

We Always Wonder

We always wonder where they go
But one day we all will know
It's O.K. to shed a tear
But know their soul is very near
It's always close inside your heart
Even though you feel a million miles apart
Don't hold in your pain and sorrow
Go ahead and cry until tomorrow
We're God's little daisy patch
To him, he was a perfect match
He was the prettiest of them all
God picked him cause he stood so tall
He'll be O.K., he's not alone
Once again, you'll hear his golden tone
Yes, we all wonder where they go
But one day soon we all will know

Tiffany Seaver

The Colors I See

When it's raining only I can see,
the mirror of colors that reflects in me.
The rain brings colors that's subdued in
hues, and that's the way they look to me.

I've seen my colors growing all around,
in places in books that are all hard bound.
So when you walk by a flower that's
dancing in hues, remember the mirror
while remembering me, and than you shall
know all the colors I see.

Mary Katherine Nolan

Untitled

They quit looking into my eyes because
they know they will have to surrender to me.
They look into the air
As if the air would listen even if it could.
Sometimes I talk and I think I'm interesting too.
Then I realize I'm not looking into their eyes.
I try to be profound but of course I can't be.
Everything's already been said before.
I'm sick of talking and hearing talk.
I can hear the quiet now.
It's nice to hear.
Like a friend that has no mouth, just eyes.

Joni Camini

Kymala III

She thinks I don't see
all the little things
she's done for me

She thinks I don't know
that if she could
she'd give me her soul

So that our hearts would always be
the kind of love
written in the stars and in history

She often thinks she's just a shadow
in light of all that I've done
and that I will never understand her inner battle

To be a light of her own
for all the wonderful things she has done
and done alone

But what she doesn't see
is the shadow standing behind her
has always been and will forever be... me

Richard Drake Lewis

Missing

I stayed there with her until they came,
watching her hand wave above the current
then slip back again below the brush.
I stayed so that nothing would happen to her,
so everyone would know that this is where I found her.

They came with hats and dull brown boots,
tripping over the rocks, removing their hats
and shaking their heads. One held his nose
but I wasn't bothered by the smell that was
like breathing is someone else's breath.

It seemed hours while they cleared
the tangle of branches that covered her
and when they freed her naked body
I thought how she was now vulnerable
and liked it more when she was hidden.

I remember being afraid to look at her face,
but that it was not grotesque but quiet and normal.
The lids were closed, the lips together
as if formed in a way to show us that she was glad
to have finally been found.

Jennifer J. Jones

Thinking Of You

Running around in circles, not knowing what to do,
Bouncing into brick walls, thinking about you.
Doing something essential, but losing my track of thought,
Looking around for answers, not knowing where to start.
Crawling on the floor, looking for my pen.
Trying to get work done, but can't think to begin.
Sitting down to start my work, all I do is stare,
Want to make a phone call, but not knowing if you're there.
Trying to organize my work, but people are in the way,
Just wishing I could finish and try to end the day.
Finally the time has come, when I'm heading home,
Thinking about my bed, where I lie alone.
Nodding off to sleep, my last thought is of you,
Entering into a dream, wishing it was true.
Waking to my alarm that is ringing in my ear,
Another day has gone and another one is here.
Facing another day, doing the same old routine,
Can't wait again tonight, when I'll see you in my dream.

Christine Perreault

Chosen To Serve (The Circle Of Hope)

Over more than twenty years ago
I would not have known that I would be chosen to serve.
When abandoned, you came to my aid.
You lifted me.
You comforted me after the nightmares.
You dried the tears from my crying eyes.
You wiped my drippy little nose.
You taught me how to pray.
You disciplined me.
Three hundred and sixty degrees later...
When abandoned, I came to your aid.
I lifted you.
I comforted you after the nightmares.
I wiped your drippy little nose.
I recited with you God's Prayer.
I encouraged you through your fears.
At your bedside we sat and sang
Songs of Zion. Twin attention.
You are for me. I am for you.
God has chosen us to serve.

Keesha Marie Gibbons

Birds

You sit perched with splashes of color
throughout your feathers.
Puffing, pruning, looking.
Unaware your resting place is swaying
in the breeze.
You prepare yourself for the winged flight that
will launch you into your adventure for the day.
There are many kinds of you in many places.
To think not one of you falls to the ground
without my father knowing it.
I long to fly with you, my sweet friend
and see the world from your eyes.

Elizabeth A. Burge

Early Rising

When I wake, you are wrapped around me,
soft and warm as a blanket.
The sky is still black and the rain beats
a pulse against your cold windows.

As I watch and wait
the sky goes from black to indigo,
to silver, until all I see
is the mist of the winter rain and
endless clouds scuttling off to nowhere.

You stir and press your face
to the curve of my neck,
never even opening your eyes
as you smile.

You make my loneliness painful.

Shannon Hines

A Walk On The Beach

White sand stretching far beyond the eyes can see,
It's almost as if it is calling to me.
So soothing is the surf rolling onto shore,
But those pounding waves are what I adore.
Breathing in that salty seaweed smell,
Oh! I've found a beautiful cone seashell.
The air is getting chilly and the wind is starting to blow,
I guess it's time for me to go.
But I can't help but wonder what I will find,
When I take a walk on the beach, next time.

Tiana C. N. Dole

"Mother"

Sometimes late at night,
I think of you in the pale moonlight,
and have to fight back the tears in my eyes.
While setting in this pool of tears,
I drift back through the years,
back to a better place in time.

Every time I'd scratch my knee,
you'd fix it so tenderly,
with just a kiss and a gentle touch.
If I could talk to you today,
the only thing I think I'd say,
is mother, I miss you so much.

Mom I think you're so much more,
than I ever gave you credit for.
The light of love would shine with you near,
and I am a good young man,
raised up right by your gentle hand.
Mom it's not the same without you here.

Heath Depue

Every Man's Word

With every breath there is a sigh
With every truth there is a lie
With every laugh there is a cry
With every hello there is a goodbye
Deep within every man's soul
There is a pain the others don't know
A pain so great it can't be controlled
A pain you take with you as you grow old
So take this pain, for someday
You'll soar to the heavens above
But if you can not learn to live
You can not learn to love.

Erica Colson

Our Grand Daughter

You have brought more love and cheer
Into the lives of those so near
As we watch you grow each day
We'll see within you qualities bright and gay
Your beautiful face, and eyes so blue
Reminds us of life's truth.

Set your goals up high
As you study, reach for the skies
But always remember the love
That goes with you from above
And from your family and friends on earth
That has been with you from birth.

Helen C. Marcel

"Another Day"

Yesterday I looked up to see the sky,
As I turned my head I saw it pass by,
I looked for the reason why.

I looked for the answers everywhere,
All I found were signs telling me to beware,
I shouted into the air "Doesn't anyone else care".

I cry out to everyone the sky is gone,
But it is too late God has played his last pawn,
That is when I knew I had seen my last dawn.

I turned and started to walk away,
Then someone called out "Please stay".
That was why I knew there would be another day.

Andrew Braden

The Charge

The day is still the field grows green
Where once men with weapons were seen
Where red blood flowed in a rushing stream
To look at it now it seems a dream
But the markers are there for the men who fell
Would that their slayers be dammed in hell
Strong men, brave men that here did die
They gave their all
For you and I
Would you my friend if you were they
Charge and die
In the unmowed hay
Time will tell and
The chance may come
For you to finish
The work they'd begun
Then we will know
Both you and I
What it is like
To charge and die

Marshall P. Hall

Dreams

Have you ever wished on a star so bright
Only to realize your wish was so far out of sight.
Have you made a wish on a star so true,
only to realize this will never happen to you?
Have you ever thought of a time,
when young love was not a crime.
I dream my dreams everyday,
hoping you will come my way,
I think my thoughts all the time,
hoping one day you will be mine.

But until the day my dreams come true,
and my thoughts become one,
which will be the day I have you hun.
And until the day I can have you to hold,
I will continue to stand bold,
And love you for-ever
And ever.

Jessica Lee Ann Golwen

Untitled

Your eyes set my heart on fire,
and your smile stirs the ambers of my soul.
Your love would keep me alive
and immortal.
Give me your heart, I need it to survive,
to be immortal.
Love me as you have never loved before
and free my soul.
I need a love to last the test of time,
a love eternal.
Your love would make my dream a reality.
A miracle sought
and prayers answered.
Your love would keep me alive
and immortal.
Give me your heart, I need it to survive,
to be immortal.
To be forever comforted by your embrace,
a love to last the test of time,
a love eternal.

Eileen M. Maher

Day-After-Day

I sit across the room looking at his face.
His gin blossomed face.
I scream standing up to him,
I spit in his face!
I rage, trying to get his attention.
He doesn't hear me,
doesn't see me, doesn't love me!

He goes to his bar
complains about his horrible overwhelming day-after-day.
Staying till dawn at his familiar
comfortably drunken bar
drinking his usual poison.
Coming home, ignoring me, closing up tight
smelling sour with cigarette smoke
and that damn usual.

Codi Watt

Moon Gazers

Have you looked up at the lighted moon,
And thoughts of a love run through your mind?
Wondering where that love is.
What the love is doing.
Saying.
Thinking.
One thing about the moon, look at it.
Make a wish
And it shall come true.
If not in this world,
Then in your heart it shall stay.
And in a future life it shall be.
Good night...and dead keep.

Terry Jackson

My Palace

One day I sit here all alone,
upon the rock I call my throne.
I think, I read, I even play,
of what I want to become one day.
In my castle of course I'm queen,
upon my hand there lies a ring.
Of pearl, ruby, diamond, and gold,
I've had it for years, it never gets old.
Then I lie and go to sleep,
and nothing ever makes a peep.
And when it's time I have to go,
I say goodbye to the tree I know.

Jessica Melton

For My Dad — A Eulogy

His body took my daddy down,
December's betrayal of autumn.
I never thought of his body as wretched as Captain Bligh.
My heart had argued whimsically that the body was a
 tin roof under a New Orleans sky.
But his body grabbed this Russian immigrant,
 pushed him against the metal frame
 he could no longer rise to meet;
Until death stuffed its cancerous sock down his throat;
And left me alone with my broken oxen yoke shoulders
 that could no longer hug and kiss
 my Peter Pan, my friend, my dreams.

Paul Marcus

The First Man I Ever Loved

The first man I ever loved
was a kind and gentle man
He was the person whom
I could always trust and depend
The first man I ever loved
never cast a stone or looked down on me
He somehow always soothed the pain
that couldn't always be seen
The first man I ever loved
gave me my spirit and taught me grace
He gave me the strength and courage
that I would need for this world I would face
The first man I ever loved
will always be my life long guide
He will continue to watch me grow
and always be by my side
The first man I ever loved
is the best friend I ever will have
He will always be very special to me
for that man is my dad.

Terri L. Bruce

"Who Is This Person?"

Who is this person who means the world to me?
Sweet, soft, caring, and kind; her name must be Dee
How could anyone capture my heart like this?
She takes my breath away with each little kiss
Her beauty is that of an angel from above
She's perfect in every way and so full of love
Girls like her are rare and hard to find
I love her with my heart, there's no doubt in my mind
Beautiful like nothing I've ever seen before
Every time we're together I love her even more
Her playful attitude and sense of humor is what I like best
Loving, caring, compassionate as well, she stands out above the rest
And now I have her and she is mine
A treasure like this is truly divine
Her warm smile always brightens my day
Her soft, gentle touch takes my blues away
My love is strong and my heart beats true
There's no one I'd rather be with, only you
No one has ever had this much control over me
I've never felt this way about anyone; I Love You Dee

James Castro

My Child, His (God's) Child

My child, I am old, in my years of September;
So many things forgotten, yet some vividly remembered.
My child, I still remember special things like when you
first tried to stand;
Swaying to and fro, trustingly you reached for my hand.
Today, trying to stand swaying to and fro, I started to fall;
With trust I called and reached for you, then I remembered
you were not there, you didn't care at all.
I wept a mother's tears;
I cried "My child, where are you to reach out your hand
and take away my fears?
A gentle loving voice replied. "My child I am here."
"I am always near."
"Take my hand, I will never leave, my love is true."
"No more fears, no more tears, as now, My Hands have you"
As I looked into His Eyes. I saw a love I've never seen;
I felt such love, joy and bliss, on Him and His Hands
I can and will always lean.
My child, oh how I hurt all the times you were not there;
But, my child I will hurt no more, as I am His child in His care.

Ruby Keckley

The Beach

With all my friends standing upon the sand.
Searching for seashells near the clear sea shore.
We had walked spacious amounts of bare land.
But still we wanted to search more and more.
While walking, we came upon soda cans.
Some old sea shells and garbage - not too much.
But there's something lying beyond this land -
Something we could feel, but we could not touch.
The feeling in us was togetherness.
Something I had wished for beyond the years.
Spending time with each one brought happiness -
A pact that brought both happiness and tears.
Now, no matter what obstacles we reach,
We'll always think of the day at the beach.

Monica Mills

Y Not?

Does he remember when we spoke?
When so much was said without a sound

Like two children hiding from a scold
We found our closet from the curious eyes of passersby
With only volumes of rules as witness.

Without hesitation he pressed his body heavily against mine
and with strong arms pulled me tight, I lost my breath but found my
peace with the stranger I had come to know.

Intensity dripped from one flesh to the other
Our hands touched, groped, searched, mine begged for an answer
within the other:
Tomorrow Where Will We Go?

Our bodies swayed to the pounding within our chests
For a while time seemed to have stood still
"Let them have their moment" it must have said.

And for that moment he was mine
Stubbly beard against my cheek, kissing lips upon my neck
His morning cologne rubbed into my skin

I can close my eyes and forever we'll converse
But in my mind I wonder
Does he remember when we spoke?

Monica Pedalino

Christmas Blessings

How do I begin? What shall I say?
Just have a Blessed Christmas Day

May the Lord continue to look down,
as you serve His people in "Our Town."

I'm sure He is pleased at how He can see
you have helped your friends as well as me.

You have taken on a n'er ending task
and all we need to do is but ask.

Each person is special and has your attention;
no matter the problem, we've only to mention.

However, awkward, I still try to express
my sincerest wishes for your happiness.

Joy - like bells chiming in a church tower
bringing the news of a new found power!

Peace - to you and for all that it stands
for the whole world, each woman and man!

Love - like a filled balloon soaring higher and higher
flows from our hearts like the flames of a fire.

Linda M. Worden

"Will You See?"

What do you see when you look at me?
Do you only see the flesh out side?
Will you look at me through foolish pride?
Can you look deep enough to really see?

When you look at me do you see life's trials?
Will you look deep and sweetly smile?
Can you see the warmth that hides in there?
Do your eyes look and still care?

Can you look at me and kindness remember?
When you look at me, does your heart surrender?
If you look from your heart only with love,
Will you see what God see's from above?

Bobbie Thomas

My Life - My Wife

You're much more than a wife.
You're the one bright thread in my dull fabric of life.
You're my inspiration that never runs shy.
You're the stars of my heaven.
You're the blue of my sky.
You're the minutes, hours, and days of my time.
But most of all Darling,
You're Mine, Just Mine.

Nora M. Walker

Willie The Cat Once Again That Had Been

The adorable kitty cat that sits on our stoop we named Willie. He has the biggest blues eyes with such a soulful look that would melt any heart it is true and when he licks fingers with his little pink tongue and purrs he can even brighten the hearts that are blue.

He'd been a stray cat when we gave him a home, the look of a scrawny string bean, but since he's been fed everyday, filled out, he must be the cat once again he had been.

He's loved and adored such a warm little cuddle bug when he snuggles and purrs next to us. He gives us the comfort we need and we give him what he craves, our love and our trust.

We know Willie feels lucky he's found a good home by the way he continually purrs. He is fed well, loved and adored, so what more could a kitty cat ask for?

Willie seems happy and content to just lazily lay on our stoop in a carefree way. His furry white coat is now soft and shiny far from the dull matted mess it had been when we found him and took him in and as I say he must be the cat once again he had been.

Marolyn E. Baker

Untitled

On this quiet X-mas morning
As I drink my cup of tea
I'm reflecting on the night before
With all its joy's bestowed on me.

First of all I must say thanks
To our dearest God above
For answering all my prayers
And for all the wondrous love.

I prayed all day that he would see
All my children safely home to me.
The greatest gift that he could give
Is our love for one another
For Mother, Father, and Grandchild
And for a sister to a brother.

One more thing, I have to ask
Dear God, this X-mas day
Bring care and cherished loving thoughts
To those dear ones not here today.

Shirley J. Tarver

True Love

True love never ends
It's a love that lasts forever
It's a love that only you can mend
It's the love I feel when we're together

True love is what I feel
when I hold you in my arms
An eternal flame that always burns
and forever keeps me warm

True love is like a passionate kiss
You want it to last forever
A sensational thrill I never miss
when our lips are engaged together

True love is like sweet nothings
being whispered in your ears
Yet true love can be so painful
that I find myself in tears

I know true is the love I feel
It's the way for you I care
True love can only be the love
that you and I both share

Kimberly Schanken

"I Ran Away One Day"

I ran away one day.
  Leaving many precious things behind
  It was just me leaving
  To see what I could find.

To see if I could get away
  And just be me
  To live my life joyfully
  The way I want it to be.

It's really scary,
  When you have no one at all
  Just to touch your face
  And reassure you, that you won't fall.

Oh...How I long for
  Someone to really care,
  Someone with more than
  Five minutes to spare.

Someone to show me
  The things I need to know.
  Someone with a seed of Love
  Willing to let it grow.

Deandra Leith

Untitled

They gather in small rooms, anointed in silence
Solitude binds them, submission to ritual
Atmosphere of silver, tarnished, worn dull with age
Like faces that don't speak; thoughts without meaning
They don't see miasma of despair. A hope
fights the breeze, glances strangle the floorboards. What do
they see in the wisps, their faces the color of soap.
Can you gaze on wings of eternity? Can you
speak of the rhyme? I confuse you in my stately
stillness. Are you afraid I might rise, or converge?
The eternalness that speaks to you silently
Taking your share of life into mine; and we merge.
Look where my eyes have gone. Within, without body.
I am the chasm. In the eyes of love-see me.

Steve Eutzy

Today

Morning is dawning, the sun over the horizon is peaking.
Get up, see what today has in store for you.
This day, my friend is a gift to you, brand new.
The sun now glistens on the grass's adornment of dew,
Soon to be sparkled only by a few.
Get your spirit lifted from above.
Then you can welcome each new challenge with self assurance that you can tackle any problem that comes along, with a beautiful song.
Nothing is too great or too small,
You can handle them one and all.
Merrily along each new corridor we go;
Worrying about tomorrow, oh no;
But meeting it head on.
No, nothing is too great or too small;
We will take care of them all.
So, good morning today.
I welcome you, always.

Elsie Quattlebaum Welling

The Midnight Hour

In the midnight hour, there's a special power that sometimes brings people together love lasts forever, and lives in you and me. We're in love, can't you see? For we only met in time, before that twelve hour chime. We're here again, alone you and me under the sheets, playing with each others feet, remembering that night under the moonlight. A night just like tonight as we hold each other tight. Forever together never to part, yes my dear you're always in my heart. I will always remember yes I will, that midnight hour.

Ronique Bean

After Thoughts

Once upon a time in a far off place
Two lovers lie face to face.

Kissing and hugging
hoping and dreaming
both are waking and now are realizing.

For they both know this will never last
He wipes the tear drops from his eyes
and placed their love in the past.

Now the girl finds a boy
which is easily done,
And the boy feels empty
like a playground that contains no fun.

But this is where the story changes
And truth brings out more.
The boy was a man looking for love
But the girl;

Well she was just looking to score!

Jason Richardson

I Wish

I wish I'd had the courage to talk to you.
I wish I'd been able to tell you how much I loved you.
I wish I could have told you how much I would miss you.
I wish I could have told you good-bye.
Now I hope that you can hear my prayers.

Diane V. Metz

"Your Two Eyes"

A spark, a flare, no firefly
The brightest star, in dark shroud skies
No light compares, with your two eyes.

With power they pierce, so blue and bold
They offer ventures, all untold
My very soul, they do unfold

with each day, that I awake
I frequent think of steps I take
With each step, my heart does quake
With hope - to your eyes - a path I make

They give me hope, when I'm aggrieved
And lift me to goals unachieved
My souls shall ever, be relieved
For your two eyes, showed they believed.

Wilbur Robert Keesey II

Strength Of Granite Rock

Truth's turrets tower above castle of stone.
It rises from the ashes of dusty time and scorn,
To penetrate the mist of darkness forlorn.
Brilliantly shining from eternity's lighthouse always on.

The silent armor defends what illusion seeks to destroy,
To walk with the guard attired in battle-worn garb.
Where truth transcends myth and legend of lore,
Now stands unshaken awakening from love's open door.

David's giant was fallen by the truth of solid rock.
The earth can crumble in the thunder of fragments never caught.
But for those who watch from towers of stately stock,
They shine in the rainbow that only truth has brought.

Toni Baird

Out Of India

In a small village across the sea,
A young woman waits for her baby to be.
In America, a young couple mourns
A little girl who has just been born.

As God looks down and sees the tears
he gives them strength and quiets fears.
Her baby needs two parents, to guide her through life's quest,
and the mother knows within her heart, her decision is the best.

So the wheels are set in motion
and a lot of time goes by,
and her new family asks some questions...
such as why, why, why!

Her mom just wants to hold her
and her just wants her near,
her brother wants to care for her
and Memaw wants her here.

Make us ever grateful Lord, to the mother and her nation,
for this very special child who is part of God's creation.

Thank you God and thank you India-
she will always be loved.

Vel Edington

Loneliness Without Loneliness

Standing in the middle of the party,
Standing around all my friends.
Happy on the outside, but sad in the inside.
Why?
Because, while standing
around the many people,
alone I stand,
and worse off, alone inside.

Heidi Escalona

The Life Beyond

We live!
We laugh!
We love!

We can soar as the eagles above. We share good times with the bad, we are happy, and we are sad, from experiences we have or had. Now our lives may be destined, you see, but we decide how we want it to be. We learned life is not roses or cherries, for the load one is given, one carries. The weight on one's shoulders is like a fire that flickers and smolders. One has the chance to snuff it or let it flame, we all have the courage to do the same. So life must go on, it's evident, right or wrong, that this life is preparing us for the great one beyond!

Jimmy Dan Barthlein

A Longing

In these days how can something as simple
As a longing
Exist in such a hi-tech world?
Yet one blooms with lightness
On my heart
And shivers through my being.
It has no other name, nor a
Belonging, so
It waits there with no place to go.
Then I must go, and come back
Hopefully free
Of a simple longing, not meant to be.
Time is not always the enemy
For as the real dawn brings up
The sun
It shortens the shadows and kills
The song
And a simple longing is gone.

Patricia A. Hardin

Soaring Above You

You gave me my wings
So I can soar so heavenly high.
Flying, like an eagle,
against the pale blue sky,
watching over you with patience and time.
Protecting you from sin and crime.
Giving you love and laughter,
with guidance from my side.
Feeling your pain,
when all kidding's aside.
Soaring above you, always nearby,
always and forever, till the end of time.

Chrissy Lorusso

Blessing In Disguise

She was a blessing in disguise
And just as cute as in my eyes

As she grew, I sat and wondered
Was she mine or just a blunder

As years passed on my baby grew-up
From a little girl to a young adult

I should have known if my lady was true
To lead me on out of the blue

Then one day we had another
Splitting image she had a brother

Now I know deep in my heart
My lady was true, she had no other

George E. Sindik

Wonder

If I never see tomorrow,
Die today and leave you in sorrow,
Would you wonder why?

If you never again hear me talk,
Or never again see me walk,
Would you cry?

If you never again see my face,
Or meet me some place,
Would you come to my grave and say good-bye?

If memories of me enter your brain,
Will your heart fill with pain,
Would you let out a lonely sigh?

Could you remember how I was,
Feel sad what me leaving you does,
Would you wish I never died?

If I saw you on the other side,
Would you come to me and confide,
How many tears you cried.

Mo Javed

Don't Wait

Don't wait too long to make amends
And plant eternal seeds.

Tomorrow may not ever come
Our days aren't guaranteed.

God's love for us does far excel
All human loves we share.

Just tell God, you love Him too
He want's to know you care.

To wait too long, might be too late
And that's a tragedy.

To live one's life, and lose one's soul
— through all eternity.

"To err is only human, but to forgive — Divine"
And in God's heart - forgiveness, is precisely what we'll find.
So don't wait too long to come unto Him
And all your fences mend.
For we are blessed according to our faith
And our endurance to the end

Mildred Barnes

Old Woman And Baby On The Train To Matchiko

They were surely
Created by God as a flower arrangement
Would be created in another realm.

Framed against the varnished wooden window
They formed one entity, living though barely moving,
In the mostly still warm air of the country train.

Barely moving, yet there they were.
One bit of nature that captured
Some subtle twist of near opposition.

God, Woman, and Baby
Teased my mind with this
Display of selected nature.

Though I had myself practiced the art
of creating small worlds of chosen plants and stones,
Never had I so displayed in my miniature worlds
Such trace of my own might have been
That would have been lost entirely,
If not so unified for those few moments.

Elizabeth Lindley

Cherubic Night

Soft, heavenly eyes gaze into me
And all I see is you and no one else
I can not speak, no words to be found
As I am rendered still

We drift to another state of mind
Standing in the moonlit night
Walking hand in hand
Stars above giving off celestial light

We stopped and turned towards each other
Mesmerized by the love depicted in our eyes
The tender touch of you keeps me warm
As the wind blows through the mystical sky

You hold me close, your arms caress me
Your lips move towards mine
The gentle touch of your kiss goes through my body
And we are lost in time

Sarah DeRollo

Mr. Gray Hound

Mr. Gray Hound is a special dog;
His best friend is a frog.
Mr. Gray Hound is very great;
But he has never ate.
Mr. Gray Hound is so special,
because he's a wizard
that can change a horse into a lizard.
Mr. Gray Hound has two pups;
He never ever washes his cups.
Well, that's Mr. Gray Hound,
he really is great...
Maybe someday he'll find a mate.

Raina Verma

Why Not Be Friends With A Tree

Trees sometimes have leaves that are green
And trees are not at all mean
They sway with the wind cause they are not
pinned to the ground that lies below

Trees grow and grow even in snow
They're taller than you and I

So take my advice cause trees are quite nice
Why not be friends with a tree

Samantha Bluemke

Originals

I used to look in a mirror and see
Who was really looking back at me
I seemed to have a pretty good sense
Of myself, the real me, with no pretense

I knew who I was... But I became unsure...
So I looked outside to what others were

After a while, it seemed to me
I became all the things I was wanted to be
Instead of the things that I knew from the start
Of the way that I was in my own true heart

The should's and the oughts became my tools
I played their games and I played by their rules

We only fail when we play by the rules
Set up by others, we set up to lose
We all are originals, one of a kinds
With original hearts and original minds

Go back to your mirror, go back to the start
Trust your own judgement, live in your heart

Marcus D. McCoy

Imagination

Every now and then, I get a little bet lonely,
and I think about the day gone by.
Every now and then, my heart goes weak, and
I wonder what's going on. Tell me, is this
my imaginations?
Every now and then, I look for an answer, so
I look toward the talking skis. Every now and then.
I ask myself is this truly
What I want? Tell me, what's going on,
is this my imagination?
Every now and then I thank of my world,
and then I start to cry,
but then I smile, and say get a grip girl.
It's only your imagination.

Sonja Little Burns

A Child's Cry

With the rage that will never again disappear
Beside the mother's shattering heart
Beyond the charm of the orb
Under what we think is the truth
Above the promises that we break
Around the laughter that will never be
Through the graffiti that we paint
Along the blood that we shed
A child cries

Megan Alley

Untitled

I know I kept you awake at night
But that was to get you to hold me tight
When I opened my eyes and you looked at me
I'd lay my head down and go back to sleep
As time went by I had gotten to big
To be in your arms where I once fit
Now I'm a mother just like you
I had a great mother to see me through
You've taught me how a mother should be
And this mother's day I want you to see
Exactly how much you have meant to me

Pam Hunt

The First Rose

To my Mother, with loving memories

You remind me of the first rose
Of the summer
So tender and soft
Everyone always enjoys looking at
But like that first rose you disappeared
From here
But you're more then a memory
You're still my life
No one will forget you ever
Just like the rose you meant so much
To so many people
But like that first rose you disappeared
From here
But you're more then a memory
You're still my life
But now when I see that rose
It'll remind me of you
You sent this rose to me from heaven
You're the rose of my life

Scott Madden

"Worldwide"

How do you go on living
Without the least bit of hope?
Doesn't it matter that we all live
Within such a thin scope?

Living is hard enough
With love often being a mere jest,
It doesn't have to be that way, though
Any one can live with the best.

Nothing though, is free in life
It takes hard work and dedication,
Yes, we all posses it, held deep within
Yet, we give in so easily to frustration.

Having and believing in the hope
Will continually get you through,
It's just lying dormant, waiting to be beckoned
Just waiting, waiting for a call from you.

Stand and be counted for, stand tall and very strong,
Life is still filled with many hopes and many dreams,
Just waiting to come true for all of us
Yes!, succeed in life and promote "peace" stand tall and scream.

Edwina Joyce Gatton-Smith

Pip

The years have past by,
though I often ask why?

Why did you leave me the way you did?
I was so young, I was just a kid.

You meant so much to me,
you were the world, as far as I could see.

I had always been you and I together,
at my age, I thought it was forever.

You always taught me to be strong,
in my eyes, you could never be wrong.

You would discipline me when I was bad,
I guess you could say you were like my dad.

To this day I still ask why?
Why did they take you up to the sky?
The worse thing is, I never got to say goodbye.

I guess this is the only thing left to say,
that is I wish you could stay,
because there is nothing I wouldn't do to be with my Pepere
I love you!

Lisa McGuire

The Deadly Drive

Through the town, gliding along,
Oblivious to all as I roam,

I pass a house, another and another,
Focusing on the way home.

I see it dash. Not thinking, I go,
Awaiting the treacherous fight.

I feel the crash. I can't stand to look back,
But my eyes are drawn to the sight.

All I can see is a glimpse of the body,
Lying there still, all alone.
Is it dead or alive? I'm unsure. I don't know.

Quietly, timidly, I emerge from my car.
I tremble with fear as I go.

I walk into the street. I lower my head in silence.
And see it is truly...
DEAD!

Jennifer Mizell

Memories Of Time

In Memory of Ruth Caywood

When you go on a trip, there's always something to collect
Whatever you may take away, there's something you can never forget
It's something that if kept will have more worth than gold.
It's something that you can always keep, it never will grow old.

When you are alive you build up quite a collection of these
These treasure stories and people; these things called memories.
Although (someday) everyone must die, even the kind
One can live forever if they are kept in your mind.

Jenny Wildy

Poeilliteralization

Poetry says let the punishment fit the crime;
The government says that the world is on its time;
The Balkans are brimming with plutonium ash,
We kicked butt on Arabs to give our cars gas,
The Republicrats tell us all good things will last,
And the populace thinks all is fine.

Larry Monaghan

From Far Away

I come from far away,
my heart feels lonely.
Tears are covering my eyes,
but the wish of getting ahead
does not let me fall into sadness.

A very deep voice inside my soul
is whispering all the time: "go ahead,
fight, prove that you can do it,
you have the strength, you have the courage".

So it doesn't matter how lonely,
and difficult is the road.
Because at the end I will find sweetness,
and the reward will be great.
The loneliness will have vanished forever.
I will not be coming from far away any longer.

Isabella Bolanos

The Truth

Before you left you thought I was great,
But the things you do, turn me to hate.
You think you have changed my life,
But you haven't even busted my gate.

You made fun of my career,
And I won't even shed a tear;
That's what I want to do, I wish you'd learn to hear.

My life has taken a knew flight,
You probably don't even know my height.
Well I don't care, your attitude changes like day and night.

Things might change, but not now.
I'm not even looking to be your pal.
The sun does shine, so I won't throw in the towel.

For me the future holds a lot of hope.
Therefore, I won't let my grades slope,
But not for you, I want to grab that college rope.

I wish you would agree,
And go and flee.
I don't need you, you don't need me!

Holly Beach

The Touch

When you touch me, I feel the fire of love go through me,
It's unspeakable the love God put between you and I,
As your love flows over my whole entire being,
At this moment nothing could take the place of your love,

My heart beats so very fast, it beats your same beat,
The timing of each touch, the sweet words you whisper,
Only God could make such true love between two people,
Words could never explain all my love I have for you,

Each second, moment, years pass, God makes our love last,
The days are filled with all the trials passing us by,
God watching to see what trials that we survive,
To take you and I to one higher step, closer to God,

As we walk together in this life hand and hand,
Our hearts beat the very same beat like God said,
All in our love with mind, body and our souls,
Working hard each day to conquer all of God's joy.

Margie A. Schooley

Untitled

If life is a circle
(as it often proves to be...)
and we move around this circle
to create eternity...

Every hour through the ages - time moves on as if rehearsed.
Now consider what might happen, if direction was reversed.

If Up was Down and In was Out...
If Forward now was Back.
If I felt was Right and East was West...
Retreat was now Attack...

There'd be no way of knowing
who was coming - who was going.
There'd be no way to measure
any sorrow - any pleasure.

If growing Up meant nothing because Up was obsolete,
we'd finally all start growing and eventually complete...

Selene Ammaccapane

Today's Youth, Tomorrow's Leaders

Today is the future, though it may not seem,
the world is not an enemy, we are all a team.
If we live by this and show strength to all,
the next generation will be strong and not fall.
Loving each other is an example we set
to show a characteristic we won't regret.
Our opportunity to lead this earth
will someday come and take all we are worth.
We kids of today are the seeds of tomorrow -
if we don't work together, no one will follow.
So keep in mind what we will mean through the years
to everyone, everywhere as the future nears.

Teresa Lorenz

Friend

A friend is someone that you can talk to.
A friend is someone that you have fun with.
A friend is someone you hang out with.
But a true friend is the one who takes you by the hand
and leads you through the
dark times in your life as
well as the good times.
This is the kind of friend you
have when you have Jesus in
your life! Jesus is my best
friend and I pray he is yours!!

Margaret E. Green

No Mother's Love

The love that I needed when I was a child,
Just always seemed to be somewhere else for awhile;

I cried and I cried, I begged and I prayed,
That just maybe someone, would love me someday.

I had a home and food, and I had clothes to wear,
But the love that I needed was just never there.

I guess that my Mother did the best that she could,
But when it came to love, she just never understood.

A child needs love to flourish and grow,
Or they will always be lonely, even when they are old.

A Mother's love is so tender and sweet,
There is no other love, in this world can compete.

Now I am old and my hair has turned gray,
But the need for this love, just never went away.

My Mother is old and her life is growing dim,
But still I pray for her love in my heart. Amen.

Joyce Wooten

The Voice Of The Forest

From deep in the heart of the forest green
And borne on the wings of the mind
Comes a whispering voice that can not be gainsaid
With promise of joys you will find.

Come closer to my bosom, the voice seems to say,
I'll weave you a magical spell,
I'll string you a necklace with diamonds of dew,
Bring peace such as no man can tell.

Above you on high and at your command,
A fleet of great cloudships will sail,
While under your feet a live carpet of green
Will erase from your mind all travail.

The murmuring of the whispering pines
Will soothe like a loved one's cool hand,
While songs of the birds, full-throated and clear,
Add grace notes of harmony grand.

A master design beyond our poor ken
Has woven together and chorused
A rhapsody bright of earthly delight
And this is the Voice of the Forest.

Calrence C. Flora

The Last Resort

I remember that fatal phone call I got after school.
It was a girl. The first girl I ever kissed.
She said we weren't going anywhere
and that our relationship didn't have "that special thing" that it used to.
Thereupon, she hung up.

Every time I think back, my soul lets out a downhearted sigh,
expressing my pain and the love I had for her.
She was one of a kind, irreplaceable.
And my heart was shattered.

I sit on my bed, the sun's glow setting below the horizon.
With the gun in my hand from my dad's cabinet,
I know what is left for me.
The end of the gun goes into my mouth and pressure is applied to the trigger.
At that moment, a thought runs through my mind... Did I forget something?

Morgan Chen

White-Out

I lived when the Great Depression was,
but not as my husband did...and does.
Although the wolf lurked at the door,
though everyone around was poor,
poor proved harmless—just a word.
We youngsters found life green and good.

My husband grappled with the brute,
battled for sheer livelihood:
faced the fangs of hunger, cold,
weathered wounds that wore him old.

I lived, yes, when The Depression was,
but not as my husband did...and does.
Shielding me were Mother and Dad;
God was all my husband had.

Whenever now, with lowered head,
we thank the Lord for daily bread,
my husband, silently as snow,
stays a hushed white minute or so
with someone he can plainly see,
someone invisible to me.

Alta C. Thomas

My Love Forever

Lady of impetuous beauty, you hold my very soul,
For heaven and hell could not part us, as our lives blossom and unfold.

You are my one and only, for nothing could come close
Our hearts have joined together, as we make a lovely dose.

In this world of love and hate, hate thee I cannot
For I cannot feel this way, when I have you in my heart.

My eyes feast upon thee with much great delight,
As no other lady brings everlasting light.

Troubles I have none, for you bring me hope.
Together we make a knot, with a beautiful golden rope.

You are perfect in every way - mind, body, and soul
For you not want more; your qualities could fill a vast hole.

Death will not stop us, as our souls do fly,
Until we meet in the stars, in the great midnight sky.

Andres Escamilla

True Love

True love is given without the greed of personal gain.
Bestowing your devotion, no matter how difficult the pain.
True love endures when the circumstances are tough.
Survival is love's instinct in moments that are rough.

True love is steadfast and forever shared.
Especially emphasized when from tragedy one is spared.
True love views the inside of the heart and not what is out.
Restoring confidence in the case of any reasonable doubt.

True love is loyal no matter what situation arises.
Urgency forces lovers to attain reasonable compromises.
True love ultimately bears hope within the heart-
Particularly when the perfect life has fallen apart.

True love extends a helping hand when others retreat.
It's during these moments that love's aroma smells so sweet.
True love never fails our lover and friend-
It's the greatest gift that one could ever send.

Honesty and integrity are true love's ultimate goal.
While life's many battles attempt to destroy its soul.
Reach out to that special someone today;
Granting assurance that your love for them will forever stay.

Karen S. Hall

The Dark Sea

Many have tread in your waters
not knowing where they stand
Feeling only the currents of your soul
not knowing the depth of the man

Your body is vast and captivating
to be admired and revered
protecting the fragile that dwells within
To threaten you is to be feared

Who could know your power?
By appearance you're tranquil and still,
but beneath the darkness of your water
raging and passions you feel

Who dares to encroach upon your realm
One's safety is but a guess
Violators you swallow up,
but a rose pedal you caress

You my love, are the dark sea
I am but a wave of the ocean
We give life to those around us
Restoring, repairing, replenishing

Jennifer Sullivan

Spring In Washington D.C.

One of the prettiest sights that one will ever see
Is springtime in Washington, Washington, D.C.
Grass as green as emeralds, forsythia as yellow as gold
White majestic pear trees breathtaking to behold

Countless Japanese cherry trees blow in the wind
Providing a picturesque backdrop on the Tidal Basin
Pink and virgin white dogwoods grace manicured lawns
Lilies of the valley, so fragrant in the dawn

Tulips of beautiful colors seemingly having fun
Close and then open to the rays of the sun
Azaleas of pink and fuchsia blooming everywhere
All this wondrous beauty magic in the air

Tourists from 'round the world flock to this capital city
Exploring its many museums, photographing all its beauty
When their vacations are over, and they return to their own land
They remember the awe, the splendor, of this capital city so grand.

Pamela M. Ligon

Sonja

Two dark brown eyes are dancing with a mischief not concealed
I wonder what is going on that hasn't been revealed.
There is excitement in the air; a joy your spirit shows
A mystery that's self contained, a secret no one knows.

You chase a dozen butterflies through grasses wet with dew
And stoop to pick some flowers that seem to call to you.
A study that's in contrast, actions thoughtful; wild
I stand in awe and marvel at the sweetness of a child.

A face of sheer perfection, tan skin and long blonde hair
I gaze upon the wonder of this child that's in my care.
You make my life exciting, show me things I've long forgot;
A puff upon a dandelion, a wild forget-me-not.

I hold you close and steal a kiss, thinking as I go
Enjoy the moment while you can for time does not move slow.
In just a fleeting moment things will change and then,
My recollections will include, "I remember when..."

Much of the world around me, I've been missing I surmise.
It takes on new perspective when seen through children's eyes.
You're such a marvel God has made, I'm humbled when I see
Your loving, trusting, shining face, looking up at me.

Anna K. Shoemaker

Mysterious Beauty

Staring up at the stars
this beautiful dark night
I marvel at how peaceful a place can seem

Billions of stars form millions of constellations
Never breaking apart
or turning away

A comet skims across the sky
its tail of fire like a brilliant torch
The bright blue moon gives off a wonderful light
Only to be covered by clouds
again and again

I see the North Star bright in its light
never dulling until the dawn

An airplane flies across the sky
the gentle shush breaking the silence

The sun begins to light the horizon
The dawn is quickly approaching
I've lain here on the grass all night
Staring with amazement at
Mysterious beauty

Melissa Lancaster

Abortion

There's an ungodly type of destruction running rampant in the land;
Cold-blooded murder of the unborn that's aided by a doctor's hand.
It is a gruesome form of murder worse than Hitler's Holocaust;
And it wipes out generations for every unborn life that's lost.

Abortion is a heartless killer, and its victims have no choice;
Limb by limb they're torn asunder without a chance to lift their voice.
If they could speak from their surrounding, "Please let us live"
would be the cry;
It's not our fault that we're living; t'will be your fault if we
should die.

It's inhumane and immoral, controlled by satan's lustful game;
And its player's goal is pleasure with no remorse for sin and shame.
They satisfy evil desires lying in beds that are profane;
They don't respect God's Holy temple; their hearts are cold;
their lips are vain.

They take no thought for what will happen when to a clinic
one will go;
To destroy the fruit they're bearing, hoping no one else will know.
But God is watching, ever seeing all the evil that is done;
He will bring judgement on the wicked who've destroyed His
innocent ones.

Life is a precious gift from God given to all humanity.
To the unborn and the infant, young and old, bond or free.
Let them live; they have a right to choose in life what they will be;
Don't destroy God's gift of love, a precious, moral sanctity.

Leon Hardnett

All This Weight

Ten years ago I said goodbye to my precious mother.
Again, in nineteen ninety-five, to my only brother.
Pity parties, temper fits, and some moods I can't explain;
I wish, I should, why didn't I?, you know...regretted pain.

All along, within my heart, knowing pridefully I'm wrong;
I let bitterness take deep root and form a greet strong hold.
I've rebelled against you, Lord, and I guess I've blamed you, too.
Please forgive, and Jesus, help me cast all this weight on you

Mike Ray Hartman

Dreams

You may laugh at my dream,
Yet I am more that I seem.
I really know that I can,
'Cause I'm sure of what I am.
I'm hidden among all of these trees,
though my heart is not at its ease.
But I will rise above all the rest,
and fly freely from this sheltered nest.
All will see my grace and beauty,
as I go about on my duty.
Clip not my wings that I may not
fly, for how I flying high into the
sky. I will be good, and I will
be great, if you don't believe me
just wait!!

Crystal Berryman

No Luck At All

All the luck I have is bad,
which of course just makes me sad.
I try to hold my head up high,
but it's starting to drop and I know why.
This is tore - up,
This is broke down,
and this won't crank at all.
I feel depression is coming to call.
I just can't afford to take a fall.
I'm the mother of six,
I'm proud to say, so please,
won't you please send good luck my way!

Sandra Hayes

One

Our love is the first breaking
lights of the dawn;
it spills over luscious meadows
of happiness.

Our love breaks all definitions of the word.
It tramples, like wild stallions,
over any obstacle.

Our love is running water.
It goes on flowing for eternity,
never stopping.
Never ending.

Jeanette T. Hursey

Forever

Forever you said we'd be together
anything I wanted, you'd give to me.
I felt safe around you, loved you
So why did you have to hurt me
in such a way, no one can explain?
Was it the drugs and alcohol?
No, let me guess, it was the jealousy.
Did you think just because the outside
Scars have healed the inside ones
will heal just as fast?
What took just one second of rage
to do, is gonna take forever to get over.

Karri Janell Fisher

Pieces

People are like pieces of a puzzle.
Each edge creating a different characteristic
Making different edges the differences among all.
Just as each puzzle piece has its own spot,
Every person has his or her own spot
Where only a perfect match will fit.
Of course some people will have the same side
Which helps to make the world interesting.
But only one piece will fit the spot exactly,
One piece to complete the picture.
It is up to the individual to find the perfect spot
Only to be found by trial and error.
Once the spot is found, there is success.
There may be downfalls when the wrong piece tries to make a fit.
But when the pieces start to fall in,
Success only becomes greater.
The search is on.
Continue the search
The rewards are worth it!

Suzanne D. Enos

A Goodman

If ever one might wonder what it is that makes a man
I look at your dedication and to you I give a hand

For many men have falling, falling short by the side
misunderstood, forsaken many crushed in their pride

I hear them talk about you listen to the words they say
the constant criticism how it echoes everyday

But when the scales are measured and your deeds put to the test
I weighed your deeds so carefully your good out weighted the rest

A goodman when observant tends to see the things life needs
you wouldn't have to quote it, in his actions there achieved

A goodman knows within himself the roots from which he came
He know that educating himself if will help to ease his pain

Continue to build this nation you're the back bone of our race
continue to overcome your fears and meet life face to face

No, there is no doubt about it you're a goodman through and through
a mentor to society a leader and blessings to

Through all that life have out you through your manhood survived somehow
you stepped above the obstacles stand up and take a bow

I say to you my goodman from the rib of which I come
God created you a goodman that his work on earth be done.

Monique E. Forte

The House Next To The Tree

I wonder what it would feel like
to be a leaf falling from a tree
flying gracefully down to the ground with the wind
what if that were me

I wonder what it would feel like
in a pile on the ground
with orange, red and yellow leaves
swirling all around

I wonder how a leaf would feel
if one day it were me
all warm and bundled up inside
the house next to the tree

Amanda Lambert

Soul Mates

Lay down you sword
put away your shield
caress this grieving heart
forget to yield.

Reach beyond your dought
wipe away the tear that lies beneath your eye
shed light on my darkness
hold back your goodbye.

Succumb to your weakness
embrace this impatient soul that stands here
show me what I have not known
do not fear.

Breakdown the wall that blinds you
seek to feel what is there
clothe me with your endless treasures
have no despair.

Ease the thoughts that keep you distant
listen, if your destiny sings to me
follow the star that leads to my path
for soulmates we shall forever be.

Betsie True

The Storm Symphony

Dedicated to Jennifer E. Osborne

The sudden flash of silver caught my eye,
as the trumpets resounded in the Firmament.
Shadows of metallic flutes and polished clarinets
raced across the rolling grass upon the dunes.
The glint of forgotten saxophones, trombones,
and baritones filled the air with harmonies
that compelled my eyes to look toward the Heavens.
Great rumbles of timpani covered the sky
in a thick, heavy blanket of sound.
But then that song of an angry God fluttered away,
like a leaf floating from a tree.
Sweet, majestic sounds of French Horns
flooded the winds and brought them to an earthly calm.
A cool breeze momentarily greeted a wind chime.
Then silence...
I stood on the shore and listened.
My heart rose from my chest,
trembling like a captive bird in my hands.
For that single moment
I endured the symphony of a storm.

Meredith Arlene Dibler

Untitled

The valley was to see. The birds were singing
and the grass was such a pretty green and the
sky such a lovely blue.
As I gazed a the beauty all around me.
I saw her there, on a horse that was as white
as the first snow of winter.
A young lady with skin of a golden brown.
Her hair that shines like a summer's
sunset, with her eyes so blue they out
shine the stars at night. She is so
lovely to see but yet I could not touch
her because she was not really there
she was just a dream but so special
to me and if the only time I can be
with her is when I am dreaming
I won't mind for I am a dreamer
and my dreams are forever.

Thomas A. Maganzin

A Promise To Keep

A man and woman hand in hand
Place on one another a golden band
A sign of eternity - no beginning nor end
Vowing to be lovers and best of friends
Promising to trust and keep the love strong
Agreeing to forgive if the other is wrong
Let regrets be forgotten
But learn from mistakes
Take time for life's treasures
Children playing - falling snow flakes
Facing the unknown together
Till death do us part
Keeping love and God
Close within the heart

Christina Martinez

Ode To Aging

Out of the dark night
Comes my past to sit on my shoulder.

It whispers in my ear
Little nuances of ideas that used to be mine.

Blindly I reach for them
Not quiet recalling their importance.
Yet knowing that they were.
Once.

Faded thoughts, erstwhile youth,
Memories of grand plans no longer palpable.

Shrouded, hidden.
I sigh and with the dawn, dream anew.

Deanna Crockett

Two Lovers Of A Different Race

When they meet something inside
Them burns with passion
Something no one of their kind
would understand
Most certainly they are in love that's true
Everybody, everywhere seeks happiness it's true
But finding it and keeping it seems
difficult to do
They have become openly and boldly
In what love has buried in their hearts
Love embraces them in their thoughts
As time go on they are secured in their hearts
So they live by God's greatest and first
Commandment which is "Love"
Love when they hug
Love when they tug
Love when they snug
All this hugging, tugging and snugging
Is enough to know they're loving it.

Sylvia Fields Williams

Who Is God

He's the man who forgives our sins,
The one who lives within.
It was He who died on the cross,
Taking the sins from our hearts.
He's the one who calms the seas,
Opening a blind man's eyes, so he could see.
He's the one of solid love,
The one you see in a pure white dove.
It will be He who'll carry you away,
When you've lived your final day.

Tony L. Tollison

"Drifted Away"

I saw you laying there in bed,
Hopeless and full of dread.
My eyes begin to water
Knowing you were falling apart,
And while you were dying
You were taking every piece of my heart.
I watched you drift away
Then you suddenly said,
"We will meet again another day."
My eyes were full of tears
As I watched you die
But I knew we would meet
Again in the sky.
I pray every night
We will meet again
With happiness and joy
And we will never end.
Suddenly, I heard the death come to mind
And I knew it was over from the very first time.
And now there is only one thing to say,
"I loved you ever since the very first day."
And now I'm here, lonely and gray
And still wish you never "drifted away."

Celeste Silva

"Edifice Of Peace"

A worldwide "Edifice of Peace" we can build
for all of mankind who may enter as willed.
We're all created equal...every race, color and creed!
Diversity's a blessing enriching our needs.

It's so simple to build, if we all do our part.
Just look at His rules, our foundation and start.
Down through history we strayed from His path.
Look where it led us...to a world filled with wrath!

We're given a conscience and free will to choose.
If we all use them wisely...no one will lose!
This "Edifice of Peace" may we all say again
can be built for us all...we jut need to say...WHEN!

Patricia A. Wessel

"Let Go" To Live

Have you ever wondered what a seed goes through
to become a beautiful flower?
Or a caterpillar before he becomes a free spirited butterfly?
They must "Let go" of the old to experience their new life ahead.
The same is for you and I, nothing ever stays the same.
If we hang on to our past, we will only exist;
We need to embrace it, move on, then we too
will experience life anew.
Pain in loss is like a bottomless pit,
there's no place that feels safe.
Hollow empty space surrounds the ache in your heart;
You feel lost, hopeless in ridding yourself of the pain.
Your heart wants to latch onto something
to end the panic of survival,
yet the pain itself is the answer;
Embrace it, hold it, feel it, let it teach you.
It will become your friend and you will see
beauty and joy blossom out of your life,
Just as the flower has now become a friend to the butterfly.

Cindy Court

Rooks

Rooks circling overhead,
Cawing in craggy places.
I walk along forested pathways
and look at these rocks
and up into this sky.
They have remained unchanged
for so many, many lifetimes.
These cyclamen now thriving amongst the pine needles,
their delicate pale petals and heart-shaped leaves
will wither soon.
The corm of life will remain dormant
throughout the coming months,
the darkness of the soil all enveloping, suffocating.
But in the darkness, that spark of life will keep faith,
remembering other springtimes.
The circle of life and death
the rooks describe in the skies above
casts a shadow on my thoughts.
I look down at the beauty of the fragile flower
and remember other springtimes.

Valerie Michaelides

Life

Taking punches on life's big screen
Able to absorb, yet what does it mean
This might sound profound...
But I bet you this...
You never really duck, what you thought had miss

No mas', no mas'... a thing of the past
Catch up, catch up.. Am I moving too fast

Hard is the body, tough be the mind
You know what waits for no one...
That thing called time
That punch didn't hurt
But it pushed you to the ropes
Regaining your balance
Depends on your hopes
As long as your reach exceeds your grasp
There's really no telling, how long this thing will last

So here you are standing
Listening to the count
Just remember, on your horse
I hope to see you mount.

Joseph Baxter

The Tree Climber

I run into the nearby field of clover
Heading for my favorite stand of trees
Sturdy burly boughs seem to beckon me
Nature's ladder enticing me ever upward
Until the limbs become thin and bend
And refuse to support me any longer
My foot slips from the crooked cradle
My arms brush against the snagging bark
And feel its scaly skin scrape the flesh
I wince and pause to catch my breath
And try to calm my quaking heart
I must get down. I cannot stay
Amid this haven that is safe for little birds
But hostile to a climber such as I
My steps are labored, but with care
I free myself from this unfriendly host

Although the ease of going up
Was not the same as coming down
I had to prove it to myself
Over and over again — My youth demanded it

Marilyn Hayden

Brother Whose Soul Passed Beyond

And down the road march brother and sister,
His pals they were one time,
And tears drop slowly down the cheeks
At the empty space in line

Space that he once did fill,
To join them at their games.
Who once again will join that line;
But, not till judgment day.

Though days be filled with sadness,
And nights be filled with loneliness.
The time will come when we share our joy.
It's the day we meet up there.

Seasons come and go,
But memories linger yet;
Memories of our little brother,
Of the one we won't forget!
God bless each and every one of you!

Nadine Bancroft

For A Friend Is Shell

When the moon is full, friendship is allusive.
Acquaintance can be unkind,
when it comes to a true friend, she comes to mind.

She makes you smile,
likes you all the while.
Knowing your imperfections,
accepting its reflections.
Clouds come down, bring a frown,
but your friend shows her affections.

She is a friend, the sky is her domain.
Drops of rain,
filled with grief, she blankets with her charm,
comforts, relief.

To a life spent searching,
for a friend to tell,
it was found just in time,
for a friend is Shell.

Kal Michels Paviolo

"Stepdad"

I've always wondered what it would be like to have a son
I have to admit, he is a lot of fun

Sometimes I'm a little confused, but mainly amused
I look at him in amazement, never with abandonment

I look in his eyes and his stare and see they're so divine
Though a little sad that they're not mine

I'm honored to be a sort of replacement in his life
Because I have his mother as my wife

The thrill, the beauty, the love, the challenge made in heaven
But getting a little scared as he's approaching age seven

A lot of his little mischievous ways tend to get me a little mad
But he makes up for it when he introduces me as his "Stepdad"

Javier Mercado

"Best Friend"

My whole life I have had a best friend,
Who has always had a hand to lend.

He's always there when I needed someone
to talk to,
Because his love is always true.

My best friend knows when I am lying,
and could always tell when my heart is crying.

From my face he wipes my tears,
and simply takes away all my fears.

He's always there to comfort me,
And no matter what he will set my bondage free.

He keeps me out of worldly pleasures,
and lets me dig for deeper treasures.

Jesus always loves me no matter what I do,
you can have this Best Friend too.

Amber Ekedal

A True Faith

What is a true faith? People say it
comes from years past. That it was
passed down from generation to generation
with the hope that it would
be revered, with the same dignity and
respect it once maintained all these years.

Somehow though, it's always done
so with the best of intentions... but
it somehow gets lost along the way
or people don't give it what it deserves.
Young people pass it off as
"old folks" ramblings, myths, nonsense or superstitions.

So where does "true faith" originates?
I believe true faith is what you
make of it yourself, how much or little
importance you put makes no difference...
Faith comes from the peace you
make or have in your heart.
Trust in yourself to trust in God.

Halema F. Barnes

Time After Time

Mom and Dad you're so special to me.
Your eyes see things that mine can't see.
You lifted me up when I was down;
Put a smile on my face that was once a frown.
Your love has always been here time after time,
And I'm so glad you are mine.
I love you both very much
And appreciate your heavenly touch.
You've added spice to my life;
When I couldn't get past the strife.
When all I could see was nothing but pain,
You showed me I had everything to gain.
Thank you for always being there
And for all the ways you show you care.
I thank God everyday for parents like you
Who are so loving, caring, understanding, and true.
I know I am richly blessed
And in my heart is where you will rest.
Thanks for everything once again
To Mom and Dad, my dear friends.

Renee Reid

My Sis

I have a sister older than me,
  But she's as busy as can be.
She's up early in the morn to go for a walk,
  And while we walk, there's time for a talk.

A beautiful garden of roses she grows,
  And through giving to others her love freely flows.
She works in her garden and works in her yard
  But to her these services are never hard.
Not the least of her services go to her Lord,
  For she's served Him in love, deed, truth and word.

We go to see her, she feeds us well;
  If we ate it all we surely would swell.
We're both getting older; the snow has appeared,
  But it hasn't deterred us as much as we feared.

After an accident when she was hurt bad,
  "Tomorrow I'll feel better", to the doctor she said;
And the Lord, He was listening to what she had said,
  So he touched her and healed her from toe to her head.
Now she works for Him as she always did
  And holds up her vessel and holds open the lid.

Golda Marie Rock

Snow Falling Love

The winter is a cold time to most of us,
for me it warms me inside,
for my love falls with the coming snow.
Love comes and sees just like the snowflake and if it's cold enough
the love will burn stronger and stronger.
Hear the wind blowing, watch leaves fall from the trees and listen
to lovers across a room.
Leave not the season for they save them all to all enjoy
  the coming of love.
The color of white and the color of red,
how they collide with one another.
Blowing snow running through out the night brings lovers hearts
  closer and tight.
Her tears are snow falling,
just as her heart is golden,
watch for snow falling love for it just might cover you.

Kevin Propst

Faerie Tale

Divinity is a hard plateau to reach
How did you manage it in only a month?
You reflect silver
moonbeams dance on your naked arm
eyes of jade stare at me
sparks of love fly between me and the gaze
warm hands touch
shivers screech down my spine
a kiss of such magnitude
stars shrink back from its intensity
This is real
No cinderella here, only prince charming
can you feel it?
My heart is screaming, I love you
The words are an almost inaudible whisper
but what did it matter?
You knew anyway

Jennifer Cannon

Heat

Liquid silver road snake-twists and turns
'Round white bleached rock where gnarled trees
Stretch broiled arms to azure heavens beneath which burns
Gray, rocky asphalt seas.
Wind dragon breathing arid breath
Whispers its silver songs through parched lips.
Cloud sky beckons to ghost bird of death
Whose echoed screams crack across brittle trees like whips.
Scrubby bushes hiss in noonday's blinding sunlight,
Their spotty blooms faded colors from spring's last dance.
Dry river bed pleads for moonlit night
As the desert sizzles with the chatter of brief romance.
In and out the gray snake winds on its merry way
Over the vast emptiness of ancient days —
The noble guide — the ever faithful traveler binds
The souls of man and beast together in a fight for survival in many ways.
White bleached rock and gnarled trees now side by side
In sacred brotherhood stand mute with sad regrets,
Yearning deeply — reaching far — stripped of all pride
As in shadows, asphalt sea disappears, and garish sun without ceremony, sets.

Margaret L. Schroeder

Awaken

Should all mankind be sightless
would we know color or creed,
would bigotry and hatred abound
or would we feel great need

To trust a brother and sister alike
to love, nurture and cherish,
and hope for those helping hands
to keep us alive 'stead of perish

We breathe the same air - bask in the sun
enjoy the same fragrance of rose,
whether hearts be full or aching
tenderness everyone knows

Stand tall - hold thy head high
be thankful for every advantage,
differences aside - all humanity laughs
and cries in 'identical' language...

Evelyn M. Cole

Searching

As the wind blows back my hair, and blows it across my face.
I don't bother and I leave it there.
I feel at peace in this land. I like to feel my toes in the sand.
And play with the water as it licks my hand.

The air smells so sweet and I am home.
My heart is at peace at last.
All my life I have searched for my past,
And this is where it led me,
To the last place I would have looked.

This is my land where I will raise my children,
And they will learn to love it as I do.

Jacqueline Dunn

The Little Rose Bush

There's a little rose bush on the side of the house,
Each Spring as I walk by it, I am more determined
To rake the leaves around it and to weed and spray it;
But never do I take the rake and do it.

What a little raking, weeding and spraying can do
And some love and care would help it too.
What a beautiful full bush through Summer world grow
If I took the rake in hand and then the hoe.

Paula M. Libonati Schumann

Twilight Time

I stood in the woods at
Twilight time, and watched
The sun go down.
I heard the creek in its
Eloquent voice
Speak with ripples of
Bouncing joy
It seemed to speak
To the birds and trees
Perhaps, to the evening star.
But, it's hard to tell while
Under the spell of "The woods at twilight time"
Try it!

John R. Cronin

The Deceiver

The sun is setting, it's high tide
I walk along the beach terrified.
Everything inside me screams "no, no, no"
"Do not, Do not go!"
It may seem peaceful,
But the ocean's deceitful.
There is a disguise.
Behind those lovely blue eyes.
She reaches out and around my ankles go her hands!
I try to run, I try to hide
But, she is drawing me inside.
She tries to drag me out to sea
I twist, I turn, I try to flee.
But she is stronger,
She prevails
Everything I've tried has failed
She rips, rips me away, and out to sea
She's deceived another ... me.

Brandi Hardy

Love Hurts

The wind blew hard on that cold and stormy night.
That was the night you walked out on me.

You lost your love for me,
Now and forever.

Playing with my heart
Maybe, someday you will stop.

Your new flame walked out on you,
Like the way you walked out on me
She played with your heart,
Like the way you thought you would with me.

It's you getting hurt this time and not me.

Shanon Kimball

Dear Son

Dear son, the day has come when we have to part,
And I'm left alone with a broken heart.

But loneliness I have learned to bear,
And each night for you I say a prayer.

"May God keep you safe wherever you may be
And bring you home safely back to me."

But then I know I shall be very proud, dear son,
For one day you'll come back with victory won.

And that day I shall fully cry with joy,
For you have returned safely home, my soldier boy!

Mary Da Costa Nunes

Toes

"This little pig went to market."
Is my first memory of toes.
It seems I can faintly remember
When my toes could touch my nose.

But toes have aged with passing of time.
Now they have pains and an ache.
Is that a bunion or an ingrown nail?
'Tis something new each time I awake.

My toes are cramped in shoes
That used to fit so well.
I can't even walk awhile
Without resting just a spell.

Toes are great for getting in the way
When someone steps on me.
"Ouch!" and "Excuse me!" mar the day.
My toes just want to be free.

At night it's time to toss the shoes.
I plop down where I am.
The evening chore has started
When I clean out all toe jam.

Joan French

See The Truth

I'll never love another so much,
every time I felt your hand touch.
You went away another day,
now I think I should go my own way.
Although I think it will be hard,
I guess you never loved me so far.
So far to see the tears I cried,
everytime you said good-bye.
How bad you treated me when you were drugged,
or when you weren't and gave me a hug.
I guess you'll never see the truth,
how much I truly loved you.
I loved you more than you could know,
if you looked you could have seen me glow.
When ever I was with you.
I thought my dreams would come true.

Tracy Bender

Wild Onions

Unwanted and unintentionally we are born,
Rejected, we live in groups, yet we are forlorn.
We linger in our paths, convinced we don't belong anywhere,
With disdain, even the wind whips at our hair.
The sun which ought to help us grow,
Shines upon with a scornful glow.
We constantly wonder what is our purpose on this earth,
Celebrated is our death, dreaded our birth.
Our smell, considered intolerable makes us often avoided,
Without a second thought we are mercilessly destroyed.
When they come and tear us out of our home, the pain goes deeper than just the outside,
They can take our home, but they can't take our pride.
Although we are killed, we do not refuse to exist,
We continue to fight with a hidden fist.

Annie Pfeifer

Our Fifty Year Bond

We can count the years since our wedding vows,
But a calendar cannot measure
The vast increase that time endows,
When love invests its treasure.

Billie Davis

The Grinch That Resides At One Ten

As a girl I'd been frightened by them in bedtime stories,
but grownups assured me they were imaginary and really did not exist.
Until three years ago I believed that to be true.
Until three years ago...when I actually met a Grinch.

Drawn as small odd looking creatures, but that's just to deceive.
I can prove they move freely among us, appearing the same as you and me.
I say I know one of those we call grinches, this one a him,
residing in a house...and out front hangs the number One Ten.

Some neighbors told me there was a grinch that lurked nearby.
After listening politely I closed my door, laughing when I was inside.
I still recall the first occasion when, I saw his eyes glow red.
He seemed confused when I was not concerned to find...
that he was what they had said...but I'd come to be quite taken with
The Grinch That Resides At One Ten.

Lately for excitement I stand at the window, change my eyes to red,
then watch giggling at scared children scatter, as my roof slowly spins.
You see, I just learned how to do this, so they still think it's him...
The big grinch with whom I reside, at the house all know as One Ten.

If you believe nothing else I've told you, I hope you'll pay heed to this.
The truth is that within us all, there really does reside a grinch.

Consiwella R. Ray

God Bless

A good person had to leave
A good person had to leave from you and me
You ask the question why? We all inside will cry
We all inside will feel like we have just died.
She will always be loved
She is now being guided from the heavenly father above
Our memories of her are like two beautiful doves that is joined as one
Her memories are something so sweet that we all will keep
She was to people as heart of gold
She left to each and everyone of us a piece of her beloved soul.
She now doesn't have to worry about living in this world that is cold.
We all sometimes live in a sad day
But it's okay, just don't think your life is fading away
I know you're in pain, but the time has come
Don't be stuck in the rain, she will always be thought of
Never let your beliefs be weak because it's alright to weep
She is now living in peace
The time of a good person had come to an end
I want you to know that you will always have a friend that
is loved and that friend is the Heavenly Father Above

Stacey M. Dawson

All My Friends

All my friends have left me,
All my family's gone away
In this poem, I don't know what to say
'Cause all my friends have left me,
All my family's gone away
I feel so lonely right now, words can't explain
I have no one that's that close, except our creator
I love Him very dearly, He made our world
He knew what he was doing when he made us long ago
He made us who are and told us where to go
All my friends have left me,
All my family's gone away.
I feel so lonely right now, words can't explain.

Laurel Schabilion

Great Grandfather

With trembling hand he touched the hair
Of the little child warm and vibrant.
His tired eyes looked back...and he remembered
The dreams once nurtured that he shared,
Or those that failed...as some dreams do.

The setting sun reflected soft and golden
Strands of youthful hair...
And yet, embraced, perhaps no more
The thinning silver mane...
Or warmed the pale blue veins again.

Within his weary mind came
Thoughts of those long gone, who were his friends.
Yet to the child, would always strangers be,
And never know their comradeship!
How much to miss...and never know the loss.

He wondered briefly of future years that
Would no longer be a part of him.
But would unfold before this embryonic life,
And in his turn grow old or tired
Until the fading light should end.

John C. Wauchek

Voices

I hear the voices of yesteryear
In the house where I now live.
I hear the opening and closing of the door
The soft footsteps upon the floor
As those who have gone before
Come and beside me sit
To talk, as if with me to visit.

They speak of the other side
Where I too soon will reside
To rest awhile, out of reach
Of ignorance and fear,
Before coming again
To seek the universal plan
For the purpose of man
So speak the voices of yesteryear
To me in the house where I now live.

Norris O. Weathers

In The Nursing Home

She sits alone in her chair.
She waits, not knowing for sure for what,
But she sits and waits and sometimes she cries.
Cries for the beautiful young woman that once was her.
Cries for the handsome young man she wed at eighteen.
She cries for the babies that came from her womb,
That fed at her breast and slept in her arms.
Cries because her hands can no longer do for her.
Can no longer reach up and smooth her now white hair.
Her long auburn braids lay wrapped in a dresser drawer.
She cries because her legs can no longer support her.
Her feet are no longer able to carry her from room to room.
She no longer cooks, or bakes, nor does she sew and mend.
She can no longer kiss a skinned knee,
Nor does she kiss away her children's tears.
She no longer does the things that made her who she is.
Her children and grandchildren come to visit - then leave.
They do for her, because she can no longer do for them.
So she sits sadly alone in her chair - and waits
And sometimes she cries.

Alice Soden Girard

Morning Prayer

Dearest God in heav'n above, help me now to know thy love.
Be thou near me through this day and from thee, may I not stray.
As I'm faced with each new task, may I ever from thee ask,
Wisdom, strength and knowledge, too; which can only come from you.
Courage, too, to persevere even when things seem so drear.
When I'm loaded down with duty, may I not forget there's beauty;
And ne'er lose the quest of youth, always seeking after truth.
When I'm filled with doubt and fear, help me know that thou art near.
Midst the turmoil and the strife, help me live a God-like life.
Help me when I fall or stumble; keep me patient, keep me humble.
In the quiet of this hour, fill me with thy grace and power.
May I know the joy of living is in loving and in giving.
Dearest father, up above, fill me with thy perfect love.
Grant that others always see a reflection of just thee!

Norma H. Weinel

My Dad

My father sits in his easy chair.
A bag of pretzels and a bottle of beer
Accompany him as the Sonics blare.
His eyes are closed; he doesn't hear.

My mother reads the evening news
After the supper dishes are done.
She looks over and watches him snooze.
She rolls her eyes and clicks her tongue.

The atmosphere is getting tense.
She glares at him and shakes her head.
I want to rush to his defense
But I turn away from her eyes instead.

One day soon I will let her know
Everything about him is special to me.
He's good and kind and funny, although
My mother apparently fails to see.

Sometimes he's on another cloud;
Sometimes bad qualities are his.
But he's my dad and I am proud.
I love him exactly the way he is.

Cherie Nechvatal Linquist

White Clouds

The white clouds rolling by...
seemingly waving good bye...
To those who see their graceful movements...
forming many things the eye can see...
Some of us never see them for we...
look at the ground searching for life's worth...
But how sad, we miss their beauty...
and the riches around them because...
Life is like a cloud, floating one way then another...
the bumps are many, but then there's peace too...
Climb aboard a cloud, have your ups and downs...
enjoy the peacefulness, look around, and remember....
Clouds come, clouds go, enjoy them while they're here...
same with life, enjoy living because like a cloud...
Life floats away.....

Ann M. Barnes

Untitled

To the person, or person's who reported me dead,
nightly now, as you get into bed,
with your ear's in a drawer, your teeth in a cup,
your eye's on the table until you get up,
Awaken each morning and dust off your wits,
Reach for the paper and read the "Obits,"
If your name is missing, you know you're not dead,
So have a good breakfast and go back to bed.
But, as sure as shootin' the day will draw nigh,
When your toe's will curl up, and you too will die.

Helen Trantina Fritchman

Blessed From The Start

Angels are pure more pure than we know
Wherever you are, wherever you go, there fighting for you
So you can be happy and safe in all that you do
When times are rough and there seems to be no hope
No one to turn to no way to cope.
When you are all alone and feel sad and blue
And you're thinking the world has turned it's back on you
When you wake from your sleep from the sounds of the night
Deep in your vessel you're calm it's all right!
When you rise up in the morning and go through your day
Without a doubt or bad feeling, all is o.k.
It's God and it's Jesus that has made it so
Because you have decided to believe and let yourself go
All of this time we know in our heart
It's true we are blessed we are from the start.

Todd Wunderlich

Looking Back And Regretting

Wondering why everyone is seeing things one way,
and I'm seeing it another,
should I listen to my heart
or should I listen to my mother.
Looking back at all the times we spent
and realizing it wasn't worth the least bit
looking back and knowing that now I'm left with nothing (zip).
But all the words my kins preached never meant a damn thing,
but all he did was treat my heart like a toy he could fling.
Looking back now I realize
that every thing was true
that he was the infamous love of my life
that was way past due now I see that my kins were right
but now my heart is full of fright
cause I'm wondering if it's too late
what's left of me and who's gonna appreciate it
should I wait? Or should I move on?
Will Mr. Right come next? What if it's Mr. Wrong.
That's a question that's gonna have to be answered on a further view
so I guess all I can say right now is this poem is to be continued!

Sandhyia Gosine

Accidie

The fly making its tickling way across a face unchallenged
Is a fly becoming acquainted with either death or apathy.
For most of the living (it's safe to say)
It would be nothing more than a passing annoyance
And quickly brushed away.

It is also said a mighty angel was brushed off the face of God
Forsaking his wings he tumbled and reeled and hit rock bottom quite hard
Where, taking stock of the situation between rubs of his wounded pride
He saw he'd fallen into a vast, enviable lot—in short— nothing at all.

Truth is, he didn't care enough to populate the place, didn't plot or scheme or tempt
Instead he bided his endless time in the usual way forever and a day

And soon enough, he noted without surprise,
There were suddenly endless others who had also been brushed away.
Away from God, themselves, or from countless aching dreams
They fell away from the wherefore, gave up on the why
And settled down instead, like him, to all the more comfortably die.

What exists for we demons on earth, who believe ourselves so free
Is the wave of a hand executed in vain in a wave of accidie.

Cynthia Kazimir

My Sons

My sons were led by a line drawn in the sand,
They were told by some that it would make them men,
Everyone off into space, bombs bursting every morn,
Now my sons are in a new place called Desert Storm,
They say they will be home before too long.
Home is where they should be
The place called America,
They say that's where men are free.
People play hide and seek with their lives,
Now and then a Missile fires,
My sons, your sons, their sons, our sons and daughters are there.

Bobbie Jean Jackson

Untitled

Dedicated to my Father

Happy Father's Day from me to you
I hope you know that I will always love you.
I know that you are always there
And that you will always care.
Even though we are usually apart
We are always in each others heart.
I hope to see you more this summer
If I don't it will be a bummer
Even though you call me names
It would be nice to see you at one of my games,
I know you can't be there all the time.
When I was nine
some things were better,
But things change just like the weather.
But never
My love for you...

Oh yeah, I really don't care if you call me names
And don't feel like you have to come to all of my games,
I know you are busy.

Renee Marie Gammon

Lost Questions

Here lie the quandaries of all those civilizations before our own?
Have the heralds told of our torch's flames or the thorns of our failures?
Have the hours traipsed or toiled on in our absence?
Have the houses triumphed or toppled anytime since?
Have heroes of our time taken their glory or trailed in grandeur?
Have they heard the hoorahs of your galleries or taken retribution?
Has time held the hard truth of reality or taken it out of form?
Has the reverence that our knowledge required been passed on?
How then have they, outspoken teacher, opened the face of my world?
These are the quandaries of civilizations lost?

Jared Johnston

Tabby

The day was like a lazy golden tabby cat sprawled on the sun drenched porch.
I am apprehensive at the thought that tomorrow may not be as tranquil.
It is the pressures of time breaking us down, and the sun in our hearts renewing our inner strength, allowing the wanting desire within us to rise up again.
Oh, to have the magic-like faith of that assenting feline with no thought of the turmoil only moments before.
Yes, it is all worthwhile; the waiting, the striving for, the going on.
Let the rain that falls into our lives become the vagrant puddles of our yesterday.
We must look for the sunshine and chance of tomorrow that we too may have another day; just like the indolent, golden tabby.

Nanci Turner Wood

Our 25 Years

It seems just yesterday, you became my bride;
yet time rolls on, and the wrinkles I can't hide.
When we were young, and in our prime;
it seemed that there would always be plenty of time.
Through all the arguments, great and small:
Our love was always, the greatest of all.
Since time has passed, the children have left the nest;
The time we spend together is the very best.
As we get older and our hair turns gray;
our love is stronger, each and every day.
So my dear as we have to face a test,
The first 25 years, were the very best.
If time allows us 25 more;
it will still be you that I adore.
It is upon you so much, I depend;
you're not only my wife, you're my friend,
so as long as I live and survive
I will thank God, for each 25.

James C. Welch

The Girl I've Always Drowned Of

Horror! Horror! Must be a hundred jabbers in her purse
Finger-barrels got them attached too
'Sept smaller, more for anesthetizing
Same with them lip-and-eye shots
All sorts of mettle-colors hanging, like tribe stomp
Tickling the exact centers of liver and kidney
The Coral Casino's got erotic dancing
And the waves sound like bombs
Bombast closes slowly to mute
She sets up
Cotton, cooker skill-fingers
Girl-jamming and Lady-pumping the stuff
Tied off and eyeball pleasure
Christ! A millisecond's over already?
Please, just leave it hanging, I'll do the plunging now on,
Your jangle-colors cause untoward synergy (why's she shrinking?)
After a milli-minute and a hundred milli-stakes
Them jabs cease dispensing
Rifle called it tolerance
She used to read from a bed time baddy book

Robert Westermeyer

Untitled

A flame of gold. A flame
of red. Like a beautiful
jewel in a golden sunset.
A silver star. A moonlit night.
A sandy beach with a moonlit tide.
A forest of green.
A meadow of flowers
a lover to pass the hours.
Hand in hand thoughts
combined these are the
dreams of all mankind.
Hearts intertwined, bodies
unite, bring pleasure and
joy into the night.
Heartbeats together as time goes
by hour by hour breaths combined.
Bodies on fire as souls take flight.
Then love burning bright.
There love burning all through the night.

Anita Negrete

Seeing The New Old World

From here I see,
Everything that is,
Meshed into unnatural smallness
Cramped but not,
Beyond reach,
High above it watches,
With a face telling the wear of time.

The hazy blue,
The artificial mess as below,
A world I know,
But see like new,
It beckons me to my anger,
Like a nagging child
To return to that place which supports us all,
But to the singing bird which welcomes,
And the silence screaming my peace,
It is as difficult as waking,
From a walking sleep,
Which breeds dreams of wonder,
Down trails with new treasures at every angle, the eye can behold.

Joseph D. Landriscina

The Mole

Digging eating and breathing life
with the complete sensation of the breath of life
touching every part of its body
blind yet it can find its way through
the cold harsh soil
the twisting turning free movement in any and all directions
no segregation, no jim crow laws
no restricting laws
no binding forces can enchain it
the path it treads in distinguished
from all others
and people no matter
what origin, sex, or religion
notice its path and an follow its movement
often they try to mock it
by stepping on the continuous hill it made
they walk this hill
trying to find it capture it and kill it
because they don't appreciate the impression it left
behind

Megan Kulaski

Life

Some days I think like a rainbow,
Some days I think like a cloud,
Like all rainy days.
Like my friends, I play along,
But sometimes I need my own song,
To do what I want, and to be myself.
Some days it feels like
Everyone is against me.
And other days, I feel like part of the crowd.
Some days it looks like,
No one could hurt me,
But really I'm hurt,
Deep Down Inside.
I think that some days,
I made a fool or humiliated
Myself.
Other times, I think I'm
Perfect and grand.
But whatever the
Time, Day, Month, or Year,
To me, I am a Speciality!

Erin Kay Ladwig

A Mother Of Two

I don't know how she does it,
Takes care of them day and night,
Puts up with them and yells when they fight,
She attends baseball games here,
And baseball games there.
How does anyone keep track?

Two grown boys,
With all their girlfriends and toys,
One boy loving and caring,
The other boy loving and daring,
She loves them both equally,
For all eternity,
Each in different ways,
Within the heart of mom the memories will stay.

A mother of two boys and all their toys,
How does she do it,
She has honestly raised two of the most,
Loving, caring, and trusting boys I know.
Darlene you are one of the world's greatest Mothers.

Sarah Marlaena White

Sherbie

I have a little lovebird, who means
a lot to me
He's fun to have around and is a lot
of company
He's the color or sherbet, yellow
green and red
Sherbie is quiet a beautiful bird
what more can be said

He likes to bite my toes and he
likes to bite my ear
He does this when he's naughty but
I have no fear
I find his seeds scattered here
and there
They're on the floor, on the table
almost every where

Sherbie likes attention and he likes to play
He makes a lot of noise when he wants his way
He's full of mischief and spoiled as can be
He's my little pet and a lot of pleasure to me

Edie M. Granby

Field Of Hope

To snap on a helmet
To put on your pads.
To put on your cleats, and go wait on the stairs.
To have a coach come out, and say let's go,
It's like being pulled to death with a heavy rope.
Then I stretch and do drills, now I am ready to fight.
Then to clap proudly after agility drills, which are done right.
To swarm around a coach like hungry bees.
Then to kneel on one knee,
To look at our field of hopes,
Our field of dreams.
To let our emotions go, to feel fright.
Soon the war shall be over,
And only one will stand, stand up right.
As the other one falls, losing the fight,
My team has a victory.
Their team fell during that flight.
I don't know why I was so shook up,
Because it was only a practice game.
So neither one of us really won.

Michael Casanova

On Stormy Sea

Fierce waves break on distant shore;
Crashing through jagged rocks galore.

I, in my tiny ship; intensely tossed.
Doom and despair; all will be lost.

Mournful winds howl; as murmurs of death.
Lusty winds taking my despondent breath.

Fight and fight; I can fight no more.
Haunting sleep besets me; worn to the core.

Sea Gulls awaken me to magnificent morn:
With ravishing sunshine; the waves are adorned.

Anthony Leroy Mayberry

Struggle

Caged like animals, that's how they like us.
"Inferior," they leer as they laugh at us.
Sickening shrieks of surrender soak our dreams.
We drown in hopelessness day after day.
Death, hate, violence, that's all that we see.
Please, help us. Please...help. Please...

Uncomfortable, useless, unbearably cold.
"Befitting", they sneer as they snicker our way.
Forced to sit and listen and prove our mediocrity.
Voices, commands, forewarnings fly all around us.
Our thoughts are on fleeing, roaming the sky.
Stuck, entrapped, snared for all time.

Something new, original unimaginable.
"Impossible" they jeer as they joke of it.
The serenity, the stamina, the sacredness...so unreal.
It's freedom, it's strength, it's power and it's ours.
Authority to exploit and violate, as so many before.
Opportunity? Doom? Luck? Or damnation?

Kristie M. Fulkerson

A Portrait Of A Mother

I kneel to weep sorrows
for feeling almost dead
of a throttling impulse to love life
and so love you.

I broad over the reflection
of another lonely face
that became my own;
The coinage erected for society.

But I kept being you even when you changed.
Your desertion
has hammered a new me out of my loneliness.

To be lonely together
and we two would be one,
but now we are the mating caribou
fighting each other
to wed life.

Nicole Slaughter

Guardian Angel

I'm there when you're down
Even though you can't see me around
And if you wear a frown
I'll be the clown to turn it upside down
I'll look over your shoulder
As we both grow older
So, think of me first
When life is at its worst
I'll help you from your Tangel
For I'm your Guardian Angel

Susan Jones

Inside Of Me

There is a horse inside of me
With long hair like me.
Its galloping is a soft, assuring sound.
Its neighing is like a quiet whisper.
My heart is the home of the
galloping white horse.
The steady beat of my heart
is the horse's hooves when running.

I wish I could see it all the time
or maybe pet it once in awhile.
It makes me feel peaceful
Inside.
It's as white as the clouds on a
cheerful day.
Its galloping is swift, yet graceful.
I'm glad its here.

Christina Diaz

Sleep

As I close my eyes, I begin to fear, what new world will appear
I cannot sleep, I don't know why, death is near, that's no lie
I just now made it, I have fallen asleep, I saw the reaper as he
began to creep
He's coming near, I cannot go, I am stuck here for all I know
I try to run, it cannot be, my legs are stuck, indefinitely
He creeps nearer, and closer yet, the black robe has become a net
The robe is blinding, I cannot see, it doesn't seem like I am me
The reapers here, and ready to strike, I must admit, I do not like
As he wings the sickle fast, I can only pray to be the last
My head flies off, my soul escapes, and runs to a place of life in
drapes
I am here, but I'm not me, the reaper took my dignity
I float around in time and space, I look below and see the lace
I am bound, the rope is taut, my inner peace is in a knot
I try to break, but don't succeed, to my loved one, I begin to plead
She cannot hear me, I have no voice, that was all the reapers choice
I scream and yell, but still don't know, total darkness as the wind
does blow
Sleep is over, I have 'waken, my soul, really was taken

Mike Wengren

Good Friends

A good friend is a treasure, a big pot of gold
A good friend is like a new born baby (precious)
something every one wants to hold.
A lasting friend is like the world something
you think will never end,
A good friend knows your pain feel your fears
And stick by you with all his will

A good friend is a friend from beginning to end
A friend has no limits he's always there.
A good friend is like a flower cheerful
And free pleasant in every way as expected to be.

A good friend is a person that I'd like
to be to anyone who needs it regardless
of their feeling for me.

A good friend is a luxury a priceless thing
Something you cherish with all your heart
A many splendid thing.

Being a good friend is like being alive
It comes natural just open your eyes share
the love enjoy the times I'll be your friend if you'll be mine

Kory L. Lewis

His Throne

Open my eyes Lord, that I may see.
Open my ears that I may hear.
He surely has blessed me all these years.
He has given me the strength to pass His test,
and called me His child.
He has let me know the difference
between my will and His will.
I am able to except His choice for me.
When my time comes, my prayer is,
that I may stand boldly before the throne of God.
Be accepted and washed white as snow.
With all my sin's forgiven, known and unknown.
Amen

Evelyn M. Hunt

The Way Of Life

If you want love, my dears, first you must give it.
To receive full measure from life, you must live it.
You cannot master problems that come your way
Without first controlling yourself each and every day.

You cannot see beauty with vision narrow and dim.
Open wide your eyes, let your light shine from within.
Then this old world stretches before you, bright and clear,
A wealth of beauty surrounds you, bringing hope and cheer.

Each day will bring new meaning to the role that you play.
There will be love, truth and conviction in what you say.
Nothing will dismay you - not even pain and strife.
You will have found peace - the way of life.

Annora C. Brothers

Devoted

Too many days are left uncherished,
Too many blessings tend to perish.

Taking for granted the days together,
Ignoring the fact, that nothing's forever.

Waking each morn, with a schedule completed,
Relaxing, Comfort, already defeated.

Gazing endlessly, into loving eyes,
No talking or patience, only love that lies.

Companions, no question, we owe them our life,
For carefully carving our future with a passionate knife.

No matter the trouble or hardships we suffer,
We'll always be devoted to our Father and Mother.

Dannie Sue Mezei

The Perfect Friend

Today I found the perfect friend who knew everything I felt.
She knew my every weakness and the problems I have dealt.
She understood my wonders and listened to my dreams
She listened to how I felt about life and love and knew what it all
means.
Not once did she interrupt me, or tell me I was wrong.
She understood what I was going through and promised she'd stay
long.
I reached out to this friend,
To show her that I care.
To pull her close and let her know how much I need her there.
I went to touch her hand,
To pull her a bit nearer.
And realized that this perfect friend I found
Was nothing but a mirror.

Shannon Thorsgard, Age 13

Mom

There's a woman I love that no one knows
She's been there since my beginning and watched me grow.

Since the age of one she began teaching me the difference between wrong and right,
She taught me about people and how to live my life.

At times I was stubborn and didn't listen at all,
But when I get in trouble she'd be the one I'd call.

She kept my stomach full and clothes on my back,
So I dedicate this poem to her to say how much I appreciated that.

You would stay up with me as I watched all the late night games,
But when morning arrived you made sure I was awake for school by calling out my name.

Some nights you slept alone but didn't seem to mind at all,
Everyday after school you would take me outside and teach me how to play ball.

You told me things that at first I didn't understand,
But now I'm older and realize that it was to make me a better man.

We argued at times and always disagreed,
You warned me that when I have kids I would see how it would be.

I have none yet but know this for a fact,
The way my mom was is how I want the mother of mine to act.

You moved away cause it was something the family had to do,
How I miss the chances to say everyday, Mom I Love You.

Gregory L. Drewery

Trapped

The spider's web
catches his food
unable to escape, they struggle

Yet we all are caught
in webs of deadlines
priorities
and assignments

The spider is the person
who gave them to us
it ranges from the President
to a baby

We struggle to keep up
eventually it drives us crazy
like the spider's prey
about to be killed

But you should think
about this one question
who is really the killer
the spider or the web
maybe the spider is just caught in the web

Jason Haaga

Love So Deep

Myself,
i pledge an everlasting love
kindly excepting that from no other
engraved is this that i write

Caring for a love that may never be
after that feeling, so strongly weak
running from it all
behind your heart i have hid
one, to be so near, yet
never having been found
everything is harder when love is around.

Wendy Raye Brumback

I Need Thy Lord

My brother and sisters have a lot to bear.
I want them to know that someone cares.
There are some things Lord that I can do
but you know Lord it all depends on you.

I Need Your Mind Lord, for me to understand
the fears that plaque my fellow man,
that I might know what is on their mind
and with your thoughts an answer find.

I Need Your Mind Lord, that I might see the troubles on life's storm tossed seas. That I might see their most inner need and to their plea, my heart take heed.

I Need Your Lips Lord, that I might say the right words in just the right way to heal the ache and pain in their hearts, and your pure love to them impart.

I Need Your Hands Lord, to lend them aid for their troubles from his life are made by thoughtless words and unkind deeds, only through you Lord, can I tend their needs.

Lend Me Your Feet Lord, that I may not tarry and miss the chance for me to carry your love Lord, to my sisters and brothers.
Your way Lord, there can be no other.

Kathleen Hester

I'll Love You Forever

Just yesterday it seemed you were a little girl,
Running bare-footed through a field of golden sunflowers
Playing, care-free.

As you grew older, you loved me,
I loved you.

But today, you are gone.
But you, I will never forget.
Your smile, your touch, your laughter,
Are remembered by many.

You are gone-but not lost
You are always in my heart.

And someday, we will meet again
Among the clouds, so soft, so white,
But 'til then, I'll love you in my heart.

Tiffany Nelson

Like The Phoenix

I lay flat on the ground so no one will notice me,
But slowly the earth envelops me
And I sink into a suffocating despair
As I descend further and further the world I knew
forgets me,
And with my last breath I try to forget it
My limp frame slowly turns over and then I notice...
I'm still breathing and there's nothing around me
but the wide expanse of space and time
This is my world, but it's unfamiliar to me
Everywhere I look I see things for the first time
My vision is no longer clouded by ignorance and fear
Long ago I would have kept sinking, but like the Phoenix
I have consumed myself and my misguided past
in order to rise from the ashes and live again
I emerge from the haze and the obscurity and am free
to follow my insatiable desire to learn
...I soon discover the life I never knew I had

Damon Pettitt

Cards

Cards are like little notes,
Filling you with joy and quotes,
They can make you laugh and sing,
Even over the smallest little thing,
I love to see the pictures beautiful and bright,
Especially in the day light,
Before I go to sleep,
I like to take a little peek,
Of one of the picture sights,
Beautiful and bright.

Melissa Smith

Daniel

Daniel was the light of Babylon.
But from Israel he was born.
He learned to walk intimately with God,
His witness was true, always on guard.

To think of Daniel, it's with awe,
He was God's person as few people are.
This prophet, God chose was noble and good,
He gave us the future as only he could.

From him, final judgement was revealed,
And how our salvation is sealed.
Chosen by God to bring light to a dark age,
He was also destined for a lion's cage.

Daniel is a historical biblical man,
He got our attention as new prophesy began
His words comes from divine intervention,
We read to learn about our own redemption.

Omega B. Lewis

Racism

"My stereo is missing; it must have been a Mexican!"
"Though I didn't see who raped her, I know it was a "Nigger!""
The Pearl Harbor attack, though years ago in length,
Yet the blame still goes to the "Gooks" or the "Chinks."
From Italy, they moved here in masses;
The "Waps" they are called, by some classes.
And then there's the "dumb Pollacks",
Who always get the jokers knocks.
And of course, here in Flagstaff, driving behind anyone slow,
The one driving the car, can be no one but a "stupid Navajo!"
Is there no one safe from these racial slurs?
Does being a different color have to carry a curse?
Do the young of this world need this confusion?
If you or I were dying and needed a transfusion,
The red blood that runs through those precious veins
Would surely be good enough; regardless of skin or names!
Slanderous, racial remarks we hear everyday.
"Lord, we need change—start with Me, I pray!"

Judah Plett

Little Flower

Little flower, you're a lucky one
you soak in all the lovely sun
you stand and it all go by
and never once do but an eye
while others have to fight and strain
against the world and its every pain of living.

But you must, too, have wars to fight
the cold bleak darkness of every night
of a bigger vine who seeks to grow
and is able to stand the rain and snow
and yet you never let it show
on your prctty facc.

Linda Lan

"Purgatory"

Sacrifice purifies the soul.
The lands are barren and scorched.
Enemies plague your nightmares.
Perhaps someday you will wake,
Hence the nightmares may cease.
Everyday is a new realm we must explore.
Nowhere may peace be found.

Can you hear your own soul crying for
Remittance from beyond the
Angels embrace?
No. We thought not.
Even in your worst nightmare.

Robert C. Bowden III

Older Brother

When you were three and I was two
And we walked way down to the end of the block
To explore the mysteries of a vacant lot,
What was that chunk of stuff upon the ground,
all pink and blue?
You knew of course and told me,
And sensing the wisdom of your years
I knew you knew,
For I had seen those colors too
way up above.
That was long ago and years go by;
Yet I shall not forget -
When you were three and I was two
We found a piece of sky.

Richard Coan

Recovery

Day and night the memories go,
when will they stop only God knows.
You pray through the highs you pray through the lows
when will it stop nobody knows.
It seems to be another level you see,
of secrets untold, yet to be free.
They are hidden deep in recess of memory.
There are flashbacks of memories and secrets in there,
and a sign of warming to beware.
Beware, beware what does it mean
To confront the past is dangerous it seems.
Do you dare, to look and see, what's lurking beyond the new memory.
Everyone just wants to run, to just go out and have some fun.
How can I run? How can I be free,
When soon the memories overpower me.
It's not just the visions you see from the past
but the feeling and pain not knowing how long it will last
Sometimes it's just moments but most time it's days
and all you can do is pray and pray.
You pray, just to get through this day.

Jeanne B. Allen

Untitled

The silence in the house was frightening,
emphasizing the Loneliness of the grieving widow.

No volume from the television of Yankee baseball,
no forties music coming from the Radio beside his easy chair.

The aroma of the Old Spice she could still smell,
but never would feel that clean-shaven face.

Sadly, the Memories are the only thing she could
touch with her mind.

Grasping at these, the loneliness became overpowering.
and the Widow grieved evermore.

Judy Maxwell

Grandma Never Left Me

Somein bout grandma's words, so soft and comforting so; she always had a way of letting her love for me show.

The wisdom she did tell me, the instructions and guidance along the way; I now miss my grandma as she pasted along one day.

Sometimes I look in Mom's eyes, for an instance I do see; grandma's warm and gentle eyes staring back at me.

As I prepare for bed to lay my head to rest; I glance upon the starry sky and thank God that I'm blessed.

Grandma I do love you, way up in the sky; but I now know you're still with me when I glance in my mother's eyes.

I guess it's like God the father, who says with me he'll always be; grandma, ma, a little girl, grown up to be me.

I smell the chicken cookin, girl comb that nappy hair; my grandma'd say those word to me whist comin' down the stairs.

Sit yourself down and eat these grits and drink your milk to; I open my eyes and notice mom, it's not grandma...it's you.

So at night I'm thankful God, for sending me two; a grandma with such love for me and a mom that loves me to.

As I sit with my daughter and into my eyes she glazes; I wonder can she see my grandma, my mom...I ponder in a daze.

Kathy A. Hildreth

Black Fruit

Uppity Black folk for some strange fruit in my part of town.
Big beautiful Black fruit,
hanging sorrowfully by a thick,
knotted, brown branch.
Masa' said, "Try an' go an' I'm a turn you in."
But, he ain't listening to warnings.
I said, "Masa' caught em' an' turned him in..."
Lawd, I say, "Masa, caught em' an turned him in..."
Without a flinch, or any emotion on his hard, pale, white face.
Black fruit kept on swingin' in the hot summer sun.
Glistenin', like a shiny new penny.
Leavin' the world that ain't got love for fruit.
One day it's all gonna' stop.
Lawd, one day a change gonna' come.
No mo' Black fruit hanging sorrowfully from the trees..
swingin' in the breeze, till they're cut down...
down to they're knees.

Melissa Marie McGhie

Bones

There she is seemingly strong,
But crying inside, legs open wide;
Crying within, but not from her heart,
It's another heart that cries...
As it breaks,
And it's not just that heart that breaks,
It's also the fragile unborn bones,
They shatter like any other bones;
Like the bones of one running the Olympic sprints;
The bones that held up famous presidents;
Bones that stood behind the microscope;
While eyes held a vision that cured polio;
Bones that sat down on a school bus seat and wouldn't move;
Bones that ran across a field fighting for freedom;
The bones of men and women;
Who teach the masses, and help raise them from their ignorance;
Bones in hands that signed a sheet of paper;
Declaring all men free;
Declaring all men made of a divine creator;
Yet these same bones... break bones.

David K. Loeffel

Tears

Tears of joy
Tears of sorrow
Tears of laughter
Tears tomorrow
Tears with me
Tears for me
Thank you Lord for the prayers that sought me.

Debbie Lynn Eaton Wall

Grandma

You've touched my heart in so many ways,
To tell them all would take for days.
I love you so much-with all my heart,
I hope that we shall never part.
You've been a role model, an influence to us all,
Although you never stood too tall.
Sharing stories, giggles, too;
No one's touched me more than you.
You sang us songs, you loved us well,
You have made all our hearts swell.
Always being there, always caring,
You gave us all something worth sharing
Love is strong, and so are you,
There is nothing you can't do.
I hope the meaning of my words
Are expressed and fully heard;
For you have no idea, I'm sure,
How your loving nature lures.
Everyone loves you; you're a saint,
You coat the world with sunny paint.

Alana Pack

For My Father, Our Friend

Charles Thomas Benjamin 1921-1996

His greeting was warm, his interest sincere
He loved his family through the years
Christian and courageous and proud of this land
Always eager to lend a hand
His help and advice allowed us to grow
Such a hard working man was a pleasure to know.

The news of his passing in the middle of today
Suddenly devastated us in every way
We loved him for his genuine concern
How tragic it is that it was his turn
To say goodbye, to die and then
Leave us knowing he was the best of friends.

Marilyn B. Wassmann

Waiting

She sat on the dock that day
as she watched her love sail away

He said he would return in a day or two
The sails billowed as a light wind blew.

Three days passed and still she waits
Little did she know about his fate

She kept telling herself, he'll return soon,
It was now one week, and well past noon.

The days became weeks, the weeks became years
Every now and then she still sheds a tear.

Her life changed that day, as she watched her
her love sail away.

Little did he know what they had begun
for now she stands on the dock, with her son.

Steve Brown

God Has Control

The rising and setting of the sun.
The directions that the oceans run.
The changing of life from young to old.
These things we can't control.

God holds the sun in his hands.
And leads the oceans across the land.
He carries the secrets of age and time.
What causes a change in our heart and minds.

Trust in God with your heart and soul.
And his divine power will begin to unfold.
Don't worry about what tomorrow will bring.
God has control of everything...

Joyce A. Burnett

Spellbound

My life had been a crucible
of abandoned despairings
till my heart learned the deep songs
of your whispered secrets
the liberty of your passion
the wind caressing your hair
your love for me was blue-ribbon
your tenderness sweet ambrosia
your affection thoroughgoing and unfettered
your embraces and kisses eternal
spellbound forever
I felt the unrehearsed meter of life

Steven Todd Bryant

"Josephine Hester"

Winter's frost will not keep me
inside, for I am an active child!
The hair on my head is like a white,
fluffy, cloud.
My eyes like the dark night.
My forehead like the sun, bright, shiny.
The window to the world for me is my imagination.
I dream of sugar-plum fairies dancing
in my head, in a world of enchantment.
While angels of the Lord appear in white robes.
And when I wake up I see a
bluejay singing to a happy tune.
My voice is like a golden bell, just
like my mothers.
Sometimes I hear someone's voice on
the wind calling me a to dance.
I love to play the piano.

Josephine Marie Hester

Down The Street

As the golden leaves fall slowly to the ground,
The wind blows and the cold surrounds.
I walk alone down this long street,
Hoping that true love this way I'll meet.

The white flakes prance down to the floor,
The trees are bare, their branches tore.
Still I walk down this lonely way,
Praying for a women whose heart I'll sway.

The glistening rain flows to the earth,
The snow dost bow at life's rebirth.
Yet still I walk down this avenue,
Searching for a love that's bold and new.

The sun rises higher into the sky,
The flowers bloom the young birds fly.
But I am walking, still, down this empty street,
Still praying that true love, someday I'll meet.

Victor R. Norris Jr.

Untitled

During grief of death we see such sadness
so much pain to bear.
The soul being lifted,
God's divine creation seems removed
when indeed it is a new beginning.

This soul now relieved of life's bitter pain and strife,
now thrives and never, ever dies.
For they will forever live in our hearts and our soul,
only for us to carry on their hopes and fulfill their dreams
in our body and our minds and knowing they are never
forgotten.

Nina L. Roberts

"Freedom Of Choice"

So many times we wonder which way we should turn,
to God or other pleasures, of which we often yearn.
Although we don't acknowledge God, we are free to live our lives.
God gives us freedom to go each day on our merry way.
God's trust in us is strong enough that we will follow his way.
But satan pushes his way forth to try to make us stray, by
tempting us with all that glitter that soon will lose its shine.
When all the superficious gloss has turned so very dull,
we look around and soon we see that it isn't even a toss.
"Oh God!" is that first name we call when we are at a loss.
But if we use "Oh Satan!" instead, we'd all be in a stew.
God out shines all other idols. He gives us freedom of choice.

Barbara Helen Rowe

Always, Love

She takes a deep breath as he embraces her tight
It was he who brought her from the darkness to the light

They fought together against the storm
And he gave her a shelter inside love where it's warm

He will protect her against the bitter cold every winter chill
They cuddle closely as he sings to her about running to stand still

She touches him to cool him down from the summers burning sun
He will graciously return the favor, for it's his precious heart
she has won

His honesty and commitment she does so greatly admire
And for no other man she feels such passionate fire

Well known is how the power of freedom is nice
But in a faithful man's eyes she's found her paradise

He showed her God's grace and heaven's white rose
Like the willow that weeps, their love still grows

She views him as beauty and true without flaw
A bond of man and woman proves love is the higher law

She will give him true strength and kiss away his last tear
She tells him she loves him, always my dear

Tara M. Shuppon

Joy In Pain

A perfect rose in a garden of thorns.
A baby born 'mid the horrors of war.
A child's young heart denied the right to soar.
A peaceful dove injured by hatred's scorn.
A gentle word to a heart that is torn.
A treasure hidden behind a locked door.
An abused child that cries never no more.
A rainbow in the mist of a life's storm.

All of these are joys that waylay the pain,
Simple blessings that give the heart its soul.
The wind whispers the true message of hope.
The trees bend to the will of greed and gain.
Travelers on life's road must pay a toll.
The strong must carry on with life and cope.

Laura Moorman

Soccer

The tenderness of morning, the brightness of the sun,
The wind through your hair, upon the grass you run.
The ball upon the clean cool earth,
And you run and sprint for all your worth,
The smell of new cut grass,
And then you touch the ball at last.
You shoot, you score,
And you are alive again once more,
The game is won the game is lost,
And for you you'd pay any cost,
To smell the grass to touch that ball,
And that is life and that is all.....
Soccer

Lee Nevill

New York

Pigeons reign over unswept streets
and a manhole cover offers incense to the skyscraper sky
As the taxicab driver turns off my favorite song.
I linger among rusty swing sets
as bubblegum perfume and liquid rainbows wash broken glass from beaches of sticks and stone.
Washington's statue can no longer withstand the attack from above,
while sunshine and salsa flood my face on an early Sunday morning.
An old man teaches Tai-Chi to a crowd of pigeons
as a desperate ambulance lies paralyzed in gridlock.
On the fire escape the breeze shifts direction from pizza to chow mein, and a lawn chair and audience judges traffic on a scale of 1-10.
A sudden gust of wind sends yesterday's headline floating across the street, and an adult bookstore offers refuge from the Church bells.
Well- fed rats wait patiently for the downtown train, not noticing the echoes of empty shadows. A blind beggar checks his watch and retires to his cardboard mansion in the coruscating shadow of Trump Plaza. Having missed the last bus, fear keeps me company
As the moisture of the dark soaks my clothing.

Aaron Weiss

Summer Songs

Over parched fields I have wondered
Crushing the clods beneath my feet
I have come to sit among swaying rushes on sloping banks
to hear the sharp refrain of red-winged blackbirds
Echoing from mate to mate
I lift my head to catch my name carried in the breeze
and sing your back again

Mary John Spolsdoff Hazzard

A 'Somewhere' Love Is Linear

The Here-and-Now drifts aimlessly between my lines.
But you are Somewhere, 'ending' at a line
  that does not 'end.'

Perception fulgurates to points
  that must be joined;
Or released, they wander pointlessly .

Our points must come to linearity —
  'conceits' and not 'habituates'
  of random Time and Space.
Without a past, amorphously,
  they never can be integrate.
Without a future, 'purposes' cannot
  go beyond self-otherings.
Points go nowhere by themselves.
Only lines have 'endings'
  that go Somewhere.

And only You have hands that can hold tight
  to comet tails—the 'ends' of stars —
Until they fall in line

  Somewhere

C. R. Pitchell

Petimus Gratium - We Beg For Grace

They listen for the voice of God not alone in the agonies
of the past but in the hope of the future.
They look not outward but inward, and they search
not in the eyes of other men but in the
stillness and silence of their own souls.
The torch they raise is lit by their passion for life,
and is sustained by the essence of humanity: love.
The fear that grips them as they wait with outstretched arms
begging, "Eloi, Eloi, lama sabachtani -
My God, my God, why have you forsaken me?"
That fear will crumble and hope will overcome them as they kneel
and pray, "The Lord is my shepherd; I shall not want. He makes
me lie down beside green pastures and leads me beside still waters....
Though I walk through the valley of the shadow of death,
I shall fear no evil; for you are with me;
your rod and your staff they comfort me."
And the torch will be passed
and it will burn forever brightly.
And the voice of God will be heard,
and they will be awash in His love and His grace

Michelle Lee Chard

Desert Plain

A cold wind blows across the desert plain
While visions of warmth fill my head
A lonely bird flies over head looking for the way
I watch as he disappears from sight.

A rain starts to fall on the desert plain
While memories of sunny weather fill my head
A single flower tries to grow against all odds
I watch as it gives up its fight.

A gleam of sun begins to shine on the desert plain
While a thought of wonderment fills my head
A lonely bird returns to fly and a single flower
begins to grow
I watch and I envy their might.

A peaceful warmth envelopes the desert plain
While a thought of happiness fills my head
More birds begin to fly and more flowers
begin to grow
I watch as the desert plain changes before my sight.

Kellie D. King

A Sign Of The Seasons

Tall and proud I do stand
Not in the ocean but on the land.
My body is brown with a head that is round
And my toes stretch far under the ground.
In the spring, my head turns green
And birds and squirrels can be seen.
In the summer, animals escape the heat
By sitting in my shade; it can't be beat.
By early fall, the green on my head
Has started to turn orange, yellow and red.
It won't be long until the cold air
Leaves me standing alone and bare.

Karen E. Henry

My Goodness

Your voice is like morning dew on honey blossoms.
Your hair is like silk is the wind.
You eyes are like the ocean hitting the rocks.
Your lips are as sweet as honey dew melon.
Your body is lined with jewels
like a princess of the universe.
But who cares for I love you
and for you and always will

Dennis R. Rose

The Message

I've never found such a peace
  as I found upon that day,
I opened my mouth but kept silent
  so my Master could have His say.
Ofttimes as we travel life's road,
  it's I have, I am or I did!
When the light that needs to be shining,
  beneath our proud boasting is hid.
Oh, why can't I always remember
  how His precious Word says give no thought
To what to say, or whenever;
  His guidance just waits to be sought.
Now be still and listen so quietly,
  for I'm sure He's speaking to you,
It's a message I've heard so often —
  "Dear child, I really do love you!"

Raenel C. Hebert

In Loving Memory Of Patricia (Joseph) Smith

Mama, I'm really going to miss you; your strength helped me through.
I know I must continue in life and be strong; as I must assist the rest of the family in carrying on.

You will be missed as much as anyone can; just can't erase the memory of your helping hand.
You've cared for so many during your life; skipping no beats at being a devoted mother and wife.

I have realized that your leaving means you will suffer no more,
and though things will never be the same as they were before.
I will cherish the memories of the time we've shared,
and be able to travel life's road because I know you really cared.

I will raise your grandchildren by trying to keep them safe and sound;
by utilizing all the good teachings you've handed down.
I wish I had more time to help you acknowledge your true worth,
and to remember our blessed moments of your short time on Earth.

I will never forget the special relationship we had;
nor the number of times you changed my disposition from sorrow to glad.
To hold a conversation with you again would give me great pleasure,
unable to happen, old times I must treasure.

To hold your hand again or just see your face;
a wonderful touch, a beautiful site unable to replace;
I will miss you so much as we all will do.
You're at peace now Mama, and we all truly love you.

Arvella J. Swayne

If Only He Knew

He sits alone in the dark
with no one in site
he stands and stares
and sees no one in the cold dark night.

I sit next to him
but he can't see
if only he'd realize
that it's always been me

He stands in the light of day
I stand there and wait
he finally sees me
but now it's to late

As we stand apart but still together in the heart
He now sees
that his one true love
has always been me.

Angel Lynn Hendrickson

How Could It Be?

Sitting, wondering: How could it be?
Knowing one day in life my heart will be set free.

It's like a dream which seldom comes true.

Expressing your love towards peoples who are never there for you.

One day reality will strike a spark,
until then these people are destine to remain in the dark.

Darkness they acquire through love which is denied.

The light will only be brought fourth after the emotions dissipate and subside.

In the end joy shall overcome thee
until then:
Sitting, wondering...
How could it be?

Randy B. Donivan

A Weed In My Heart

What trembles in eyes when movement
is foreign and the weight velvet visceral;
a heaviness found in the shoulders lying
with night mixtures and stunned open sound
being all inclusive. Words leave in a death
march, a closed stride over dry hills returning
in the morning shadows wilted on kitchen tile.

An uncertainty appetite; to gamble all for loss,
inching up the weathered chord, an uneventful
task full of slip knots and rancor, my heart leans
heavily upon the dust, pulsing brain flowers
nestled among tumultuous cloud statues and star
dots where the slight careens off full eye globes
and moment is born and perishes. Curve, line
and angle, a glade of field grass splits
the mystery of itself, silent and replete.
Aspiring weed, when did you come to the event?

Scott Allen

Bad Love

The boy I met two summers ago
is not the man that I now know
He used to love, kiss, and hug me
cuddle up and call me honey
But now I feel the cold embrace
of hatred pounding at my face
He says he still loves me
but I do not know
it's hard to feel love through the pounding blows
He says if I leave him
he'll stab himself dead
I am so scared and afraid of him
So I guess if I don't
I'll be stuck in this hell
I cannot leave so this is farewell.

Tianna Rene Sheehan

Why

  Why does it seem that all my friends have a shoulder to lean on,
but when it comes to me, everyone is gone?
  Why did he break my heart and let me go,
right when I let my feelings show?
  Why does everyone tell me you're a pretty sight,
but if they looked past it all they would get a fright?
  Why when I look around this world of mine, all I see,
is people in love with everyone but me?
  Why did he say and promise too,
when his last words were "I Love You"?

Britni DeBusk

Good Bye Old Friend

What a friend you were,
a liquid friend, you wrapped your
whiskey arms around me.
You made me numb and free.
The warmth you gave me inside
was like the sun melting into
the concrete on a hot, cozy day.
I entrusted my life to you when it got tough,
but like the concrete,
you made it rough.
I presently thank my heavenly friend
whom I have today.
He showed me how to say goodbye
and never look back again.

Laurie Dove

War Of The Winning Run

The field has a sense of business about it,
And all of the employees have no doubt about it.
They come to their job wielding gloves,
Yet theirs is a job that not only they could love.

Mentors are they, ones of power and immortality;
Many of them are in true life and reality.
They are also warriors in their own special way,
Wooden bats their weapons of choice, to do battle to the end of the day.

Strikes are the main opponents in this war.
Yet the armies of nine have other things to watch for.
For if their battle plan is played out right,
A World Series Pennant can be won from the fight.

Eric Porter

And The Winner Is...

More than a conqueror
That's who you really are
Regardless of the battle you're facing
You must remember the victory isn't far

Don't become discouraged
With your head bent down low
Hold fast to His promises
So that your faith may grow

Remember your answers in the Word of God
And the Word is your victory
Satan is a defeated foe
And was disarmed way back at Calvary

You see, God doesn't start at the beginning
He begins at the end
The out come is already decided
And you have received... the win!

Verndolyn Caye Perry

A World Of Hate

Our world is filled with discrimination and hate.
Do you really expect to get anywhere at this rate?
We need to grow and understand.
There is only one race, and that is man.
Everything will be all right,
if we all get together and unite.
If all this fighting were to cease
we may be able to have world peace.
Just listen to what I'm saying here,
and there will be no more need for fear.
Because if we rid our world of hate,
we may be able to change our fate.

Paula Ibey

The Snow Hare

White in the gleaming moonlight,
White on white,
The snowshoe hare moves gently
Through the glistening snow of night.

Nose a' trembling, ears upright,
He's wary of the silence;
The pink eyes blink, he's on the brink
Of nature's raw-edge violence.

Rushing wing, the charging streak,
Grip of icy talon,
The awful shriek, as nature seeks
To hold herself in balance.

Reddened snow beneath the bough,
Hid from the gleaming moonbeam,
White birch shimmer, the landscape shivers,
And forgets what it has seen.

C. Worden Smith

Dreams

Eyes are closed to a mystic place,
All soon seen is an empty space.

Pictures start to run through the mind,
Memories soon are not left behind.

They start to travel at a steady stream,
To form what is called a dream.

These dreams will show what is in the heart,
The special things that cannot be torn apart.

Sometimes they are sad and make you cry,
Sometimes they understand the reasons for why.

The certain things that are held inside,
Know that when eyes close they need not hide.

Dreams show all that is ever real,
And the special things people can never steal.

Dreams keep life in a special kind of way,
How it was and what it is like today.

Kelly Peterson

For The Glory Of God And His Temple!

My Body, Reverence And Self Respect

Thus I shall Keep my Body Wholesomely Healthful, by Mastery of my Body's Needs:
Pure Air, Water, Nutrition, Exercise, Sunshine, Rest, Sleep and Diversion, Etc.
And to Shun All Impurities, Fear, Worry, Negative Emotions and All, Disharmony!
And also to Purge these Basic Crucial TOXIC CAUSES, of All Diseases... and Illness!

Also I shall Cause my Body to persevere Vital Life, and for keeping Refreshed,
For my Sagacious practical Lifestyle and all planned Achievements, at my Best.
By the Power of my Faith, Hope, Love and Truth, I shall live to keep me Free,
Free from Adversity! and to Praise all Good discerned, I Hear, Read and See!

My Light to Shine and Radiate my Unconditional Love, so to be Heard and Seen.
Our Creator's Endowed Mind Power to Choose, is no Greater Gift to Use I Deem.
To Strive my Best and Trust God's Immutable Cause and Effect Law to Reward me,
My Foremost Wealth is my Whole-Health; And that is my first Responsibility!

My Altruistic Objectives, I shall aspire to with my Faith every Lord's Day,
So to Cause all of my Deeds, to yield Benevolent Benefits, I humbly, Pray.
The Seeds I Sow and Grow, is for the Best Fruit I expect to Merit, and to Reap,
For my own needed Blessings; and to share all good, with humanity in Dire Need!

And I shall keep my Mind Renewed, for the Best Informed, that I, Can Be,
As God's Inspired, Holy Scriptures Revealed Profound and Sublime Truths, to me.
God's Divine Love and Grace I Revere each day and night! And closing, my eyes,
Now ready, to guide my Body, for innate time out, to Rest and Sleep in Paradise!

Matthew Karalius

A Fallen Star

The star starts slowly slipping from the sky
not noticeable at first, so no one wonders why.
This star that has always shone the brightest
has lost its anchor and, has now become the lightest.
This wonderful star that all the others hung around
has slipped and, is now falling to the ground.
The star that set an example of brightness and, stood for
all that is true, is now in question and wondering what to do.
Go away cried the other stars...your light no longer shines
So, out of their mist it goes leaving the others behind.
Falling into the darkness of the night, the star struggles
trying to hold on with all of its might.
Now upon looking into the sky all that can be seen is a flicker
of light...and everyone wonders...is that the star that use to
shine so bright?

Helen D. Woods

That Boy

He is the one
you dream about a ton
when you see him
your eyes light up bright
He comes around whenever
he decides you're this week's weather
you see him down the block
with the other girl he'd like to rock
he says he loves you
you're always wondering is it true
It's hard to tell
will he ever treat you well
will he call tonight
or did he catch a quick flight
you hate him so much
but, how he soothes you with his touch
you think he is so fine
then you wonder, is he all mine
He loves you, He loves you not
Its like picking flowers out of an endless pot.

Christy L. Juul

Today's Thoughts, Tomorrow's Memories

As it echoes through the woods
Disturbing the thoughts of human minds,
Its horrifying screech setting many moods,
You make yourself believe it was the sound
Of a child's fun,
But actually the shivering hand holding a
Firearm crosses your mind,
The repeated ring fills the quiet house,
A sorrowful voice talks as you listen,
The tears flow as if a nightmare has come
Alive,
The words too ironic to grasp,
The slow continuous steps of your child
Getting closer,
A sweet, innocent voice asking why you're
Sad,
The pain deepens as you embrace the
Situation,
The loud beating of your heart as you tell
Her about her dad.

Angie M. Holcombe

She Lives Alone

Do you know someone who lives alone?
Do you take the time to call her on the phone?
Or do you say "If I call she might be sleeping."?
When at the time she might be weeping.
Since her health and her eyesight have failed
She can't drive her car or even read her mail.
You think "She's o.k., her groceries are delivered to her door
And I told her to call if she needed anything more."
She could call "911" if she was injured or dizzy
But she couldn't call a friend — they might be busy.
Maybe you could take her for a ride in your car
She wouldn't want to go far.
"Just up the street to see that 'Brand New Store'"
(The one that's been there a year or more)
Perhaps you'd be surprised at the happiness you shared
By just letting someone know you cared.

Dora P. Rogers

To A Spring Chicken

What do you do when you're 75?
Why, you drop to your knees and thank God you're alive!
And well enough still to eat birthday cake.
(However it's processed, you still can partake.)

The fact of the matter, the down and the dirty,
Is some folks are dead when they're no more than thirty.
They're not six feet under; they're still breathing air,
But a check twixt their ears will reveal nothing's there.

The spunk you exhibit is well beyond equal
With this birthday over, you're planning its sequel
What will you do when you're seventy-six?
You'll be feisty as ever and up to new tricks!

Elizabeth R. Hoefer

"It's Time"

We began as Kings and Queens
We were grabbed hold of and knocked to our knees

This is how it was built
This is how it stands

The ground has been smoothed over much too long

Rumbles, shakes, never ending
Breaking, shaking, moving ground

Kings and Queens are uplifting
Emerging from the "Lost and found"

Moving the soil on which our hearts grew
Removing the prints of which our backs knew

Yes, our backs are strong, but we must stand straight
Making new prints for the souls that await

America — it's time
It's time to make the room

Kings and Queens uprising
A people — in full bloom

Winifred D. Billington

The Artist Answers Suicide

In the house of abandonment - I construct my dreams.
In the house of desolation - I renew my hope.
In the house of rejection - I build the fires of acceptance.
From the heart of the void - I create the house of the self;
  The beacon amidst the death and the darkness.
In the moment that exists between despair
  and the destruction of life;
I speak a name - The name of God - "I Am Who Am"
And once again; I choose "Life".

Cynthia L. Blaida

"Wishful Thinking"

Smell of spring - will you ever come?
Oh, birds that fly, so high and carefree
sometimes I wish that that could be me.

Summer's dew beneath my feet
warm breeze through my hair
my heart does ache, more than I
can bear - yes I want to let
go but do I really dare?

Beautiful leaves of red, gold, brown
does fall see through me? My
oh so sad frown?! The trees
laugh and call me a fool - foolish to
dwell, foolish to ponder, foolish to
build my world with hope and
dreams of a precious love with
no hurt or pain - nothing to gain -
just a love that gives and
never ceases.

Marcy A. McPheeters

Life

Look farther than the earth...
past heaven, the stars, the moon, and the sky.
How did we get here?
Was there really evolution?
Or is gravity pushing us down?
No one really knows.
You have to look farther than your mind.
Everyone is everything.
Think...
Brain power in common technology,
but energy.
No bodies.
Light.
Floating and wondering 'our' purpose
look farther than your conscience...
it may tell you what to do or is it
an angel speaking to you
look farther,
Life...

Christina Del Signore

Untitled

I awake one night wanting a midnight snack
as I laid there I made my plan of attack
I crept to the kitchen in my bare feet
and giggled at the thought of my stolen treat
left over pizza or luncheon meat
No! I think I may need something sweet!
Chocolate chip ice cream, that's what it will be
two giant scoops! Oh! Let's make it three!
Spoon in hand, I take a bite...
I notice my dog laying off to the right
Big sad eyes staring up at me,
I can't believe that I feel so guilty,
"Here you go pup, I'll share with you".
So much for my late night food rendezvous

Joy Abers

Abe Lincoln's Assassination Hat

The crowd listens to the great man's words in awe.
Suddenly, the sound of a gunshot goes through the air.
Some people in front gasp in horror.
The great man is dead.
Someone shouts with sorrow.
"Here is his hat!" says he.
This is all that is left of this gallant man.
This gleeful man who served thee.

Perry Collins

Childhood

I had a secret hiding place
Under a lavender lilac bush
It was a child's haven
A place to lie and dream undisturbed
Of the grown up time to come

This town where the lilacs grew was my security
It held the near, the dear and familiar
Family, friends, neighbors
The good things a child must have
To live in love and grow in maturity

Then the tragic war years came
The day a neighbor boy was killed
I felt old and strange and sad
My first inkling that people and things and life change
And childhood can only remain a memory

Rosemary T. McQueen

"The Journey"

Another day dawns as the sun arises,
A brand new day full of life supplied us.
A child is born, a journey has begun,
Out of the womb of death he began to run.

The sun is going down, darkness has fallen
The warmth of the light seems so foreign.
His life in darkness he began to walk,
Staggering and stumbling, his offence was the "rock".

For behind his offence the "rock", was shining;
The Light, the Truth, the Way, he longed for the finding.
For within the tomb was created a new Way.
Waiting to rise on that third day.

Another day dawns the "Son" arises;
A brand new day full of life supplied us.
A child of promise is born anew.
Out of the womb of death for me and you.

The chains of sin and death had no bonding.
To the God, made servant, Lord, then King.
He completed the journey for you and me.
His grace and glory that we might see!

Mark L. Lynch

The Memorable Christmas

The favorite memory that belongs to me,
Is the Christmas Eves spent near Grandma's tree.

Present filled the entire room,
With each kid hoping we could open them soon.

With the excitement building into the night,
There were 6 of us remember, it must have been a sight.

When the dishes were cleared and all naps were taken,
The time had come we'd all been awaitin'.

Paper was ripped and torn with glee,
Until there was absolutely nothing left under the tree.

There were clothes and toys and gifts galore,
Surely, she must have bought the whole store.

Now picture this room - 6 kids, their paper and toys,
Santa would surely find us, just by the noise.

The room was disastrous, as we'd all gone berserk,
To young to appreciate all Grandma's hard work.

Now as I look back, I can truly see,
Those Christmas memories are the best gift Grandma
could ever give me!

Thanks Grandma!!!

Dawn M. White

Love Is Like A Puzzle

Love is like a puzzle
you never find that missing piece
And when you fall in Love it seems your lover cease
You seem to want to follow him to let him know your
Love is true
But he fronts you like a dog and says he doesn't want you
you have to let him go and get on with your life.
Let him think you don't care even though you might
Love will have you thinking your man can do no wrong.
He's the sweetest thing and you place him on a throne
Love will have you as blind as a cow

He's messing around and you're wondering how
you seem to get mad over tiny things
But that's Love and that's what it seems.

Nytisha L. Sibley

Stay Strong

Stay strong through the night,
to thine own self be true.
Never do change, always remain you.
For God made you special,
and gave you something no one else can take away.
He does not want you to hide that gift,
it is to be used every day.
So stay standing when your legs feel weak,
when everything seems wrong,
when the world seems to beat you down,
grab your gift, leap up, and say I will stay strong.

John Murray

An Ode To Death

The mood that fills my heart to-day
Is one of sadness deep
It makes me feel is life worthwhile
'Twould better be one to sleep
That harbor of all our troubles
The oblivion of all dark cares
The abandon of thoughts, of battles fought
Of futile hopes and dares
That shadows of life to come some day
Of future all aglow
That lasting sleep, a draught so deep
My soul yearns for it so

Evelyn Swinburne Hildebrandt

Cold Winter's Day In July

It's a cold winter's day in July
My thoughts wander out
Beyond the horizon
Into the fields

The sky churns in progressive blackness
Boiling in poetic movement
Grace interwoven with primal force
a dichotomy of life

Rain sweetened air bearing many scents
Carrying the seeds of life
Awash in a clothing breeze
High upon a hill in my mind

Random movement in orchestrated majesty
The single with the multiple
Greens, browns and shades of lavender
A cascading, frothing, eternal spiral

But my visit here has ended
The absolute truth of change
It was a lovely visit
On a cold winters day in July

Gary Woodward

Untitled

Has the blind man seen
what the deaf man hears?
Tales told by infants
resemble greatly those forgotten
long ago, by the council of the wise
I, too, was made in the ancient forge
battered into being by the dreamer's hammer
brazen in the fires of the inferno
cured in the welcome rains
and blessed with a kiss by angels forgotten
I, too, have tasted ent-wine from the tarnished chalice
and swallowed draught of love from silver spoon
I have long since stripped myself eternal
for fear of falling - alone and eternal
but something together has brought us
to close the chasm betwixt life
and dreamscapes
where you dance to songs of love amongst the daisies
in your eyes I've found the other side

Kevin George

Crying

Crying.
Crying without a reason.
For a loss or a bit of bad luck?
No one knows.

Crying.
Crying without a reason.
For a friend, for a lost soul?
No one knows.

Crying.
Crying without a reason.
For something frightening or something unknown?
No one knows.

Crying.
I'm just crying without a reason.

Courtney Ehinger

Alone

Alone? Everyone does know
How to be alone
In the corner of a room
That no one dares to roam.

Without loved ones or peers
It is really hard to cope with those tears.
And those happiness no one to share
Thinking no one will try to stay and hear.

Alone? Someone would think is fun.
Others would like this word melt using the magic wand.
But for me alone will be a peace of mind
In this fragile world that I can find.

Susan Evangelista

The All Mighty Dollar

The all mighty dollar causes us pain and pleasure!
The all mighty dollar allows us to pay and to play!
The all mighty dollar helps us accept and deny!
The all mighty dollar contributes to our boredom or fun!
The all mighty dollar can create a sense of power or weakness!
The all mighty dollar has the ability to boost our self esteem or
crush our will!
The all mighty dollar brings us worry or can give us a sense of
comfort!
The all mighty dollar is overvalued!

Anthony M. Franchimone

The Crooked Tie

So piercing his eyes the face on the wall,
Sepia dark and inevitably old.
Her memory of crying down the hall,
The warmth of his voice and his smell of mold
Starched stiff and off white his surrounded neck,
Austere rules with no imminent reward.
His careful yelling then thoughts of neglect,
And already his swift tongue has gone sword.
Agony felt the humbling past gone by,
Tears grown within from the father before,
Who knows no lesson scorned by watchful eye.
Her saying not much but seeing much more.
I said life would be different with me,
But the crooked tie fits so easily.

Martin Moore

Jesus

C is for Christmas, for the loving and caring of the day Jesus was born
H is for the honor of Jesus.
R is for the reincarnation that Jesus brought to us three days after he died.
I is for the intitution God gave to our minds.
S is for our spirit, the part that God gave of himself to each of us.
T is for the things God left for us to follow as his words.

Kristen Nicole Dorman

Exterior Decoration

Today I saw a great array
of red and orange and gold;

With purple tints and evergreen,
what beauty to behold.

I rode along the countryside
to see fall's radiant hues.

The whole display will more than please,
man's most artistic views.

The greatest stylist of them all
has changed his color scheme.

Just overnight he did it all
while I was in a dream.

Mary Woolfolk

Me, Myself, And I

This poem is all about Me because
Me is all Me thinks about and sees.
Me's teenager now and Me thinks
about how Me's future will end and where it begins.

Myself is filled with confidence and pride.
Myself a bright woman with nothing to hide.
Myself is evidently kind and pure
Myself will be strong so me will endure.
Myself will never let Me let go
Myself will be strong so Me will know.

I is the one that tells Me and Myself to do believe
I is the one that longs to achieve
I is the one that will always excel
Because of I, Me and Myself will do well
Altogether we three will strive
We will remain on top - Me myself and I

Yaida Oni Ford

Mrs. Dalloway

Written after reading the novel by Virginia Woolf

Climbing the little tree-house in her mind,
pressed against ideas long-cherished, she thought for a while
Wondering whether sunlight sparkle could be turned in one's hand
Like a prism, reflecting, exploring, expanding on the actual experience
of life,
Waves of passion, fury, exaltation, contentment
Came, went
All refracted from their objective reality
And felt more powerfully
Once seen through the window of time

Particle and wave, all at one, this beating pulse of life...

Moments and impressions
Alike building up,
Beating on the shore of thought
Receding into the ephemeral foam of memory...

To plunge into pure existence...
the echo of the final desire,
instant of final brilliance
defining life,
the infinite memory stroking the shore one last and final time.

Huda Jaliluddin Khan

S.W.B. Jr.

Though the thoughts have been so many,
and the words have been so few.
Hence, I take this chance, this Father's Day,
to say that "I Love You."

Always there close by me,
never alone was I.
You made me laugh and made me smile,
and never made me cry.

The strongest words to guide me,
for reality that came too soon.
You began my journey, on your knee,
while singing me a tune.

"Golden Slippers" you would hum,
just to make me glad.
With homework first and then a car,
with you, I would get mad.

I could never repay, what you've done for me,
so I take this time to say.
You've been everything to me and more,
have a "Wonderful" Father's Day!

Bonnie Kaye Brockwell

Untitled

Once upon a time in the future ahead
Drugs, sex, and violence, innocent teens were dropping dead
Dolls, blocks and dress-ups, 8 year old Jessica played with for fun
Now 14 and Jessi lives life for her gang and depends on her gun
Trains, planes, and ball games,
Going to the movies, talking on the phone
Then Billy got Penny pregnant and they ran away from home
Jill started by stealing little things, with friends, just for fun
But she went too far, stole too much money, and now she is on the run
Classmates made fun of Amy, calling her a slut, a ho, and a tease
Now those kids aren't laughing at Amy's sexually transmitted disease
Ring around the rosey pocket full of posey
ashes, ashes, they all fell down

Cara Lindner

Betrayal

As the tears run down my face,
dew drops on leaves after a night of rain.
I feel the hurt within, but swallow all my feelings.
It is not safe to be living or to be dead.
After a longing moment of silence,
One feels betrayed.
All one wants is to be loved,
But why does love hurt thee so much?
As close to the touch,
one must feel betrayed.
Betrayed inside.
As the night goes by,
your feelings empty,
And no one can touch the real you.
Beneath the stars you hide,
A sleeping baby under a blanket.
Scared to come out
and face the real world.
Afraid, afraid inside that you have lied.

Vanessa Slater

The Girl Of His Dreams

Cowboy hat, boots, and a swagger;
So young - still a boy.
Long black hair, and shining eyes;
He found the girl of his dreams.

Cowboy hat, boots, and a determined stride;
Young-shouldering responsibility.
Long black hair, a child at her breast;
He found the girl of his dreams.

Cowboy hat, boots, and a stroll;
Still young - playing "ride the horsy."
Long black hair, a grandchild in her arms;
He found the girl of his dreams.

Cowboy hat, boots, and a cane;
Young at heart - "Papa play with me."
Black hair entwined with silver;
He found the girl of his dreams.

Carlena E. White

What Is It

What is it the child speaks of?
As she stands on the ocean cliff,
her blond streaking hair in the wind.

All the giant life around her ignores,
or does not understand her child language.
She wishes upon stars.

She stares at the rocks on the cliff,
her warm feet hurting in dismay.
She holds her helping hands to the sky.

But what can a child speak?
Wisdom.
The child speaks only wisdom.

Rebecca Kramer

"I Understand Your Loneliness"

I understand your loneliness, the heart-pain within.
Tell Jesus your problems, let his work begin.
Lean back in his arms, rest secure in his love.
You'll feel peace so gentle descend from above.
Yield to the "Potter", let him mold your clay.
You'll find you feel better with each passing day.
For he loves us and cares more than we'll ever know.
He's so anxious to bless us and precious gifts to bestow.
So learn to be patient, you'll save many a trial.
Overcome temptation and conquer with a smile!

Sarah Humes Anderson

"Decade Lost"

Ten years ago I knew my road.
Ten years ago I knew my load.
Ten years ago, then years ago.

But now today I went astray.
But now today I went.

The road grew long, the load too strong
Too long for me to stay.
Too long for me to pay.

The people say you make your way.
The people say, the people say.

Life goes on and you'll grow strong.
Life goes on and you'll be wronged.
But will I know the way.

Laura Litz

Nature

Time is like water, it's forever
Constant and always flowing

Water changes with the tide,
As time changes with the sun

Realityy is a state of mind,
As the unconscious is never known

What is life without death,
Is it the unknown we fear?

Why do we, as humans, question everything,
Is it really because we want to know
The truth? Or do we just want to hear
What we know to be the truth?

These are the questions we all
Seek the answers to...

Will we ever know, or will we
Just flow like the water and
Change with the tide.

Will time ever tell?

Jason M. Likas

To The One I Love

In the heat of July a child was born
In the dark of the night or early morn
To a fair maiden named Doris on a Haskell Country farm
The proud father was Albert, around Rule he farmed.

The cotton needs plowing and cows need feedin'
But God only knows what 2 brothers were needin'
The Hannsz family now numbered five in July 1943
The fair haired Lassie would their only daughter be.

She grew tall and beautiful with the passage of time
And many would be princes called on her so divine
Dad and big brothers ran them all away
Little did I know that in time I'd come her way.

Her beauty is so perfect and her charm is overflowing
I thank my lucky stars that it's her I came to knowing.
She's truly my lucky star and lifetime love
Every time she smiles at me I thank my God above.

For love you know is a priceless and precious gift
So when you're down Honey, I hope my little poem gives "u" a lift.

Rex Conner

A Walk With Mother Nature

As I walk along the desolate beach,
the only person I can see is Mother Nature.
The waves seem to say good-bye and hello
as they come go.
The shells left behind by the waves rough wake,
are the most precious things that God could ever make.
The birds fly above like busy bumblebees,
while busily working they call down to me.
For the finale of my long and wondrous day,
Mother Nature performs a show of beautiful rays.

Laura Graham

The Night Clouds

You watch the clouds flow.
You wish you were there, going slow with the flow.
No stars above, darkness is beyond.
Everything seems cloudy. You wish you were there.
Somewhere in the sky you notice the air.
Only now you think your a part of it.
You feel it in your heart. It's peaceful.
Wish life were that way.
"They're" taking you with them explaining the "life"
but you're confused. Somewhat abused in your thoughts,
someone is calling you. You don't listen.
You notice something glisten.
It's the stars, at least so you think,
but no, it's just your life passing by
sort of...like something that flies.
Wish you were there, but in a way you are.
Your soul is the flow in the clouds.
You finally realize that your just dreaming.

Nelda Alvarez

The Girl I Want To Be With

She is the tear that crawls down my face at night,
the one that reminds me I'm alone.
I realize how empty I am
Without her in my life.
I want to hold her in my arms,
the way the night holds me in its,
as I lay in bed at night,
wishing I wasn't alone.
The light of her golden hair
casts off the darkness,
driving away the shadows
like the Sun rising from the East.
The pale blue of the sky
reflected in her beautiful eyes,
And like I see the sky through my window,
I can see her heart through her eyes.
Her heart, as bit as the Earth,
With a wide open space
for me
inside.

Jeremy Wm. Farrington

The Petal And The Rose

As the petal of a rose blows softly in the wind,
the petal whispers words to me of you my best friend.
It tells me once a petal weeps and falls down to the
ground, that no other one can take its place in the soft
wind of sound. As it whispers words to me I understand
its phrase, and even though it starts to rain I can still
see it through the haze. It's telling me our friendship
is worth the price of gold, and to hold on to it like a
petal holds on to a rose.

Barbara Foster

Good Catch

When you asked me to call you when I got home, you threw me.
When you took my hand to cross the street, you threw me.
When flowers came "just because", I just about could breathe.
And the feeling I get just looking at you, sometimes I can't
believe that before I saw life as greys and hues that I mistook for true.
And now I see rainbows of color starting in your eyes of blue.
You threw me with so many things, how could it all be real? How
could the things I've prayed to find, so easily appear?
Just when I thought you'd thrown me for the very last time, you
threw me with a question that would make my spirit shine.
You asked me to share your life, your home and yes, your heart.
You said you hopes you didn't throw me to far to hear my reply,
I just had to pause and smile and hold back the tears in my eyes.
You may have throw me once again, but we truly are a match.
So my answer to your question is "yes"
Your throw is now a catch!

Gina Marie Innacelli

Dreaming Of Anchors

Outside was wet and when you fell
Down you dragged me with you
Laughing and crying you doffed your shoes and spread out among
the puddles
I cursed my life and I must confess, I cursed you Maggie
"Set sail, Maggie" I yelled and the crying stopped and there was
only laughter
For you thought me as drunk as you... I was not
"Set sail, set sail" I cried like a loon, as I ran in circles around
you faster and faster
Then you stopped laughing, didn't you Maggie?
You tried to pull yourself up, but your drunken body betrayed you
The circles had made me dizzy and sick and weak and I wanted to
Stop but the pull was far too strong...
When I collapsed, I dreamt of anchors
Cold, wet and gray
Spiraling down towards the ocean floor
Where I lay waiting
Among the clams
Arms outstretched in eager anticipation

Chris Stokas

Goodbye

So much to say
cannot form the words
cannot trust our voices
So much time
Still was not enough.
Our joy has turned to sorrow

We know what we want to tell each other
Explanations and apologies
Advice and praises
Feeble talk is all we can manage

Our eyes meet
Conveying our thoughts
The time draws nearer
As does the inevitable
Going our separate ways

Swallowing over the lump in my throat
Brushing a solitary tear from my cheek
Another still follows
Memories are all that remain

Goodbye

Jessy Seck

Stripped

The vase, it is broken
the car, it is stalling
the freedom, it is unprotected—why must things not be as we wished?

The vase, it is smashed to pieces
the car, it is vandalized without remorse
the freedom, it is stripped—why must we be punished so?

The vase, its shards lacerate the stripped feet
the car, its skeleton mocks the stripped car owner
the freedom, its absence leaves us stripped—why must the pain persist?

The broken vase, it is pieced together with glue
the stripped car, it is clothed with new parts
the freedom, it is replaced with oppression—WHY?

Why can broken vases and stripped cars be restored, while the
freedomless anguish in the fragments of their former freedom?

Timothy E. Bazzle

"No One Knows"

No one knows the secrets I've kept hidden all these years
When all alone I've tasted bittersweet tears
No one knows the me I've tried so hard to hide
When glancing in the mirror I've turned my eyes aside
No one knows the anger I've kept so well controlled
When raging in the night I've fought for breath and soul
No one knows the fear that keeps me locked in chains
When I shut myself away in the prison of his pain

Heather D. Amos

A Midnight Show

As the spotlight moon rises in the sky,
it douses the trees and the bushes in light
The stars resemble bright, sparkling eyes,
and a marvelous performance begins
tonight.

The trees and plants dance side to side,
swaying along as the bright yellow moon.
And its shafts of brilliant light
smoothly glide
through the shadows of the stages vast
open room.

It bounces its beams over green velvet floor,
until spotlight is off and show is done.
The midnight performance is over once more,
the performers can rest until next evening's come.

Paula Ann Dutko

Someone I'll Never Forget

Mom, you've been like a friend,
someone I can talk to.
You've helped me through the years
and for that I thank you.
Every mother should be jealous of you
because you are the best,
and in everything you do
you rise above the rest.
I know I can disappoint you,
but I promise I'm trying to please ya'll
and I thank you for loving me even when I do fall.
You have always been there for me, someone I can count on
and I know I'll always need you, even when I am gone.
Who's going to say if my clothes match?
Who's going to wake me up for class?
But no matter how far apart we are,
those memories will always be the best part of my past.
Thanks for everything you do and for just being there.
Thanks for loving me and showing that you care.

Jeremy Freeman (16 yrs. old)

Our World

Upon the wretched wings of death we fly,
through fields of bloodshed and a shattering cry.
The air is chilled and the sky ever bleak,
as the hurricane of violence reaches its highest peak.

We are yanked about, with war controlling the strings,
like helpless marionettes trying to dance but failing.
Children's laughter is no longer heard;
only profanity taking the place of a simple kind word.

Our poor world grows like this everyday.
Is this any place for our children to play?
Too many loving hearts are overtaken by pain.
Losing in life seems the only thing gained.

Somewhere the birds whistle a joyful tune,
and time is spent relishing the flowers of June.
The clean clear sky reflects a heavenly blue.
A grove of saplings wave as a gentle breeze blows through.

Bands-Aids will stop the bleeding and distress,
as tears dry up with a mere caress.
This is what the true world should hold;
Love, faith in God, and kindred hearts of gold.

Carrie Ellen Gustafson

To Sal

You got a letter in the mail one day.
It started with, "Greetings," and we all knew,
That you would pack your bags, and go away,
And we would spend two years praying for you.
Dressed in green, after six weeks of training,
Herded in a plane like so much cattle,
Off to Viet Nam, without complaining,
To a wasted world, to fight a battle,
Others said was wrong, and wouldn't bother,
To fight for unknown people and reasons.
You felt it your duty, like my father.
We, like you, endured the days, the seasons
The faded field jackets still keep you warm,
And remind me that God kept you from harm.

Barbara Van Cise Calderon

Love Of My Father, Emmons G

Not at all common as you can see, perhaps that is why they named him Emmons G. For common he is not by any sense of the word, because he is my father and this needs to be heard. Years ago he promised the Lord up above that if he were granted my mother's love, they would honor, and cherish each other. The years passed, a daughter was born. Next came a son, a second daughter and lastly to all another brother. We were taught as youths to speak the whole truth when asked by our mother and father. We were taught to be meek, to turn the other cheek, be true to yourself and never bring dishonor. The passing years of my life I have taken a wife raising four children, the same as my mother and father. The lessons they taught me to as a child ring true as I teach my own sons and daughter. Soon my time will come to pass from his world and the Lord will read my judgement letter. "Well done, my son", he will say unto me, "I will place you anywhere you would like to be." It matters not, Lord, as to where you place me, but promise me the same father; his name is Emmons G.

William C. Miller Sr.

Objection Expressed

When reading the works of another man
'Tis wrong to see an unwritten plan.
The words of his mind are different than yours,
To synthesize your thoughts into his, I deplore.

It's happened to me and I strongly objected,
At first was perplexed, then finally rejected
his thoughts - they weren't me.
They were his ideas, his life - it was he.

If you find the thoughts of another exciting,
Jot down your impression in your own writing.
Reconstruct your ideas as your own sensation
To be expressed in your own creation.

Norma Brody

Presence

Hungry yellow eyes
Shoulder blades of steel
Razor sharp teeth linger close and near

Slowly and calmly came a sad lonely cry
and soon the sky turned as black as night
The cry disappeared
and a roaring laughter appeared

His tail hit the air in a cracked whip flash
and I could feel his presence behind my back
The gnashing and gnarling of his teeth
soon enclosed around me like a wreath

I quickly turned, stumbled, fell
but the black wolf had already disappeared
He was seen never more
but you can still hear him cry out
His sad lonely roar

Laura Blennert

The First Snow Of Winter

As the first winter snow silently blankets the earth
Tenderly caressing every blade of grass and tree,
And in this brief encounter sharing an intimacy
Unparalleled in nature yet maintaining secrecy.

At first the cold, unfriendly land resents the
Intrusion into its private hibernation,
And ashamed to be seen in all its barren homeliness
Is melancholy in its humiliation.

Yet the gentleness and beauty of the pristine stranger
Arouses the interest of an indifferent earth
And realizing the chance to hide its frigid ugliness,
Allows the alien temporary berth.

In the quiet communion that follows
A bond is slowly perfected
Uniting strength and fragility
In a marriage neither expected.

But as the earth is smothered by the warmth of love
It struggles for independence and begins to fight for breath,
Not knowing that the outcome will certainly be
Its partner's slow, sad death.

Sarah Barrett Caruso

Me

A blank page, new times, and new beginnings.
I can be everything I am without hesitation.
I no longer have all that holds me back,
I am innocent again.
My mind thinks only of the simple.
I am no longer plagued by all that I thought I should think.
It is just me.

Makai Trujillo

Incarceration

You can't escape direction, supervision, and control.
You can't run from these walls or fly out of this hole.
Because it's all around you in front and in back.
It comes in the forms of government and in drugs like crack.

Whether in there or outside,
You still get that feeling —
Like you want to run and hide.

In a concrete jungle where everyone is tough
There's no need to stand tall, but you must stand up.
Like an animal in a zoo on display
You too can have visitors on certain days.
And no matter what you do or say,
Nothing can heal the pain today.

Whether you're locked up, locked in, or locked out
Whenever you feel like it, stand up and shout...
...Damn incarceration! I want emancipation!
From this terrible, terrible life of frustration.
So when you find euphoria grab it!
Because in this life, only once you will have it!

Domingo F. Lerma

Suicidal

I sit and wonder why
why it is I have to cry all the time

Looking at the stars above wishing my family
would show me some kind of love

Having thoughts of violence in my brain
smoking Marijuana to kill my pain

I only have but 3 or 4 true friends, and
even sometimes our relationships bend

I don't see no point of living,
thoughts of suicide is where I've driven

It's like the only time I'm happy is when I'm high
cause that's the only time I touch the sky

People tell me to cheer up and smile, but I don't
see that a plastic smile is worth while

It makes no sense to hide your feelings sometimes
I wish my life would end

People who don't know what I've been through
tell me to get over it, but until they walked at least
20 miles in my shoes I'm not trying to hear that sh*t
Maybe someday I'll see a brighter day but with all these clouds
in my head I don't ever see me being happy!

Jillian Winn

Untitled

She graces his branches with her delicate breath...
Blowing through his bows as they dance the waltz of love.
It is true he has felt the anger of the frost, dropped his leaves
and retreated deep within himself,
But now she blows the season of change across the tips of his
arms bringing with her the warmth of spring.
Their renaissance is upon them.
When the world comes to collect her or pollute her being-to
bottle her in some proverbial bottle, labels her and place her
upon a shelf-she finds sanctuary in his arms.
Released from her drifting ways.
Released from his hard wooded ways.
Together hand in hand they dance with flowing lace. The mystical
power of enchantment follow them into tomorrow, and tomorrow,
and tomorrow...

Clayne

The Love Note

I found an old love letter,
That was given to me a long time ago,
I could not remember from who, or from where,
I opened it up carefully,
To be sure it did not tear,
It took it out slowly,
The paper felt smooth and rare,
I unfolded it quietly,
As though someone else was there,
As I read it to myself,
It gave me a sudden chill,
Though I was not scared,
All it said was,
"Meet me here" from
I must of known at the time,
Who, what, where and why,
But now I can not recall,
What happened there or when,
All I have left from a broken memory,
Is this little old letter, and me.

Krista Nickell

I Begin To Be Clean

This time when barriers fall like rain,
It washes me away,
And I begin to be clean.

The moments when we touch,
Leave me shaking for days.
And I begin to be clean.

I can see the truth about me in your eyes,
I believe it's love,
And I begin to be clean.

Memories of darkness and pain
Fade into you
I'm clean.

Tina K. Caldwell

Still My Voice

I lost my voice some time ago
deep in the bucket of rattles and baby teething things
misfiled with my changing relationships
drowned out by the clatter of some miscellaneous working mother's resentment.

I looked in the closet next to dusty pumps
under a rack of outdated business garb,
it skittered just out of reach knowing it never belonged there.

Redefined priorities shined lights from different angels
bending through my lens of not feeling appreciated.

I looked and forgot to look for days.

Until with shirt untucked and blue eyes beaming,
Ben looked up from playing chop sticks one day
and in the sing song lilt of a five year old said, "I love you Mom."

Waves that had gently lapped at my feet, suddenly knocked me down,
and I heard it as it pushed through the rusted knob in my throat
to burst into the room like a bright light,
with a different texture now,
but still my voice.

Sally Jo Green

Going UP a DOWN Escalator?

Faced with having to go UP a DOWN escalator?
It can be done. It can be done by you.

Don't watch your feet, they know the task asked of them.
Keep your eyes on the top, look away and you lose sight of your goal.

Don not pause in your actions. You could lose footing, confidence,
and distance covered in reaching the top. One pause in striving for
the top and the escalator will not pause with you. Its sole purpose
is to keep moving; if not, it becomes stairs.

Keep your thoughts focused on the task at hand.
The escalator knows what it needs to do and does it well.

Support and assistance will be available but choose it wisely.
Handrails are moving but in the same direction as the steps, taking
you away from your goal.

Obstacles are a possibility. Others may not move from your path or
may even step directly in it. You are attempting to achieve a goal
others may not want you to achieve.

Faced with having to go UP a DOWN escalator? Take a deep breath,
keep your sights set on your goal, believe in yourself, and take a
step...just don't stop until you reach the top. It can be done. It
can be done by you.

Tammie Li Tourtellott

Memories Are Treasures

Memories are treasures, worth more than gold
Hidden deep, in the heart and can never be stole.
They're made in a fleeing moment, safely tucked away
And can bring much pleasure some other day.

One can store a lifetime in a small space.
So leave not any good one to lie there and waste.
Many of them are recorded by sadness and tears,
While others by happiness down through the years.

Some memories are collected early in life.
And others are added on by love and strife.
So fill up your pockets as you go on your way.
For they are for everyone and there's no pay.

Should you need guidance or get caught in a jam,
Call up some memories and your worries will scram.
I tell you, it's really a talent in each of us to use.
So lets save up a truck load, not just a few.

Isabel Robinson

If Your Hands Are For Another

I want for your hands to construct a nest with the
veins of my heart.

I want for your tenderness to run through me like
naked liquids, through my teeth, my throat, my
lungs, my ribs, until a warm spring is produced that
washes my insides with unexplainable delights.

I want your sleepless words to fly through my chest
hairs and suspend my anguish in a delicate air.

Fragile I want you. Strong I want you.
In droplets I want you. In rivers I want you.
Simply I want you.

If your hands are for another, and you tenderness
shall never be mine, and never will our words make
of the same dreams, I shall fall.

My heart shall become a red, hard, and absurd continent
that drifts beyond all sadness and becomes immobile.
My hands shall fall and all my words for you will
sleep and dying shall be the only simple thing
because forgetting you will take too much.

Gilberto Lucero

Can You

Can you see the bloom in my eyes?
Can you see the sorrows in my cries?
Can you see the happiness when you are around?
Can you see when the petals hit the ground?
Can you smell the fresh cut flowers?
Can you see those awful dark towers?
Can you see the smile shine bright on my face?
Can you see that very empty place?
Can you see what it is that I want you to do?
I want you to hold my hand and whisper "I love you"

Janine Ertel-Schneider

Day Care Center

New Direction Day Care Center
Is like a second home
For those who need attention
But cannot be left alone

They arrive in the morning
Where they spend a happy day
And meet with other people
That are happy and gay

They enjoy hourly activities
To keep them healthy and strong
Exercising is a special one
With that you cannot go wrong

When it's time to leave in the evening
And you must return home
You feel a little saddened
Because your choice is not your own

Hildred T. Brown

Love's Not

Love's not a gift
to have and hold,
Squeezed tight
until its warmth
gets cold.

A gem so rare,
to keep, enfold,
A dream
for young, and not
the old.

It is for all,
the meek, the bold.
Love is
to give; not bought
or sold.

Agnes Dorothy Bartok

A Lullaby For My Great-Grandson Cleveland

Go to sleep my little baby
My baby
Time to go beddie bye
When you wake up in the morning
And the sky is bright and blue
Even though the grass is wet with dew
You will see the Sun
Come shining through

W. B. Burwell

With Thoughts Of Beverly

Touch mine eyes such sweet refrain.
Let my heart with your symphony soar,
Flow, cleansing chill.. 'midst my spirit, so pure;
mountain stream, kiss your dreams of gold!

Winding paths of frail, autumn limbs,
shroud with tranquility the silent beauty of such untouched glory.
Innocence of blue, sprinkle with warmth our
winged brightness. Shower upon us!... down heaven's
stairways, to the castles we've yet to touch.

Sprinkle your whispers upon my heart... with wings of eagles, dare I
dream? Listen...closely...with pomp and ceremony, yes with joy!

Write your melodies upon the easel of my mind;
know the beauty of moments remembered...
moments untouched with trite contraire'.

Tip-toe upon polished stone...tingle with sheer delight!
Explore with ancient wonder each corner, each crevice...
with open arms, enrapture the taste of new-found laughter..of
child-like curiosity!

Snuggle delight... Close to your breast..
in the precious discovery of life.

Micheal Morris

Please God, Not Another Christmas!

It warms my heart this time of year, to hear a child's laughter... now brings a tear to see a twinkling star and have a happy memory, the only place now that happy be, is in a memory...for me. My heart capable still of getting warm, but cannot heal, irreversible harm! Through all the holiday seasons, to live, I realize there is no reason, for there was only one, which was my only son! But I'm still helpless, and nothing being, or has been done! So I must sit and sit, and cry and grieve, trying so hard 'to make it through the night' on this Christmas Eve with indescribable, unbearable pain in my heart, tearing my soul my mind apart! Then for a split second, a forced thought of new hope, a new year! But...then reality, I've thought that for the last three! Could someone save P.P.? If I would disappear? No longer in the way, no longer here? They say 'the broken parts of the heart grow stronger, which is true, but for mine, no longer. For a continual heartbreak continually cracks until it shatters, so a zillion strong pieces hardly matters. And all the king's horses and all the king's men can never put Patsy's heart together again, though will always thank you for all those years when you were my friend!

Patsy Pepper

Heaven

Have you ever wondered
just how heaven will be.
The place where we can go
to live throughout eternity.

The gates that are made of pearl,
streets of purest gold.
Walls made of jasper,
a place where we will never grow old.

To see our precious loved ones,
who have gone on before.
To worship our dear saviour
The one we will always adore.

As we gather around the crystal sea,
joyous we will forever be.
Singing those glorious songs of old,
Hearing the greatest stories ever told.

Perhaps it sounds just like a dream to live in mansions fair;
But you can have the blessed assurance, that heaven is really there.

Jesus has gone to prepare a place for those who are so true.
I hope to see you there my friend, for I plan to be there too.

Brenda Benton

Tainted Glass

No artist can perceive
or deceive what I have seen
And remain convinced
As to what true beauty means

A painted picture worth
A couple words at best
A thousand is what I've heard
I guess, worthless are those words

Tell me a tale so wonderful
That I need to sit up and listen
Tell me about a place so wonderful
I don't know what I'm missing

Tell me a riddle
Answered with a rhyme
Put the ending at the middle
And tell it one more time

Floating on mental feathers
Sleep walking with an hour glass
Twitching under pressure
Under a magnifying glass.

Andrew Tran

Time

Time...Oh, how it passes much too quickly.
To run and jump freely as I did in my youth.
The flowing meadows of wheat I use to run through.
The rainbow that had my pot of gold how magical my world was.
I saw life through a child's eyes for many years
So thankful I am to have seen such wonders.
Time...Oh, how it passes much too quickly.

Sandra Ann Serrano

Our Happy Home

This house is our home
for which we share,
In Friendship and Trust
Honor and Care.
Communication is the sky-
to making our lives
the best it can be.
To ask all the Questions
we have on our mind,
For all the Answers
we need to find.
As in living these words-
Our lives have grown
Only to make
Our Happy Home.

Peggy Dauzat Todd

Mom And I

Mom and I the best of friends
From the day of my birth
Until the very end
The love we had the things we shared
Nothing else in life could compare
The motherly love she gave to me
All through life into eternity

Isabel E. Berry

Holding

He stands behind me
somewhere between my soul and my consciousness
a shadow of someone else
his hands holding my memory
etching soft prints overlaid on ancient caves of regret.
I lay bare the touchstones of irrefutable longing.

Raw cravings held captive in the wishing well of yesterday
beg for attention. He binds old wounds open
yet I hold on too tightly to grief folding in on itself
a self portrait sketched with no vision
obsessive paintings on a canvas of wrong color.

He stands behind me
spirit walkers ride the easy cadence of his speech
catching omens in my mind like the dreamcatcher at night.

Salted mountains stand as monuments to worn out tears
a bruised and wounded heart lingers in a white washed house
awaiting sunrise, a stark contrast to alleys of despair.

He stands behind me
he pauses somewhere between his heart and my hands,
watching, as God's hands are folded over mine.

Peggy McMahon

"The Shaded Tree Only I Can See"

The shaded grass underneath the tree is a place that gives me peace of mind,
That one certain tree is one of a kind;
It's the answer to all my prayers and all my doubts,
It gives me those reassuring feelings that I know nothing about;
It reminds me of who I am and who I've become in a world like today,
It always has the patience to hear all I have to say;
For this tree cannot be seen from everyone's eyes,
It only remains in view to the one that has no disguise;
No fear can be found beneath this shaded tree,
Just the quiet sound of your heart beating for eternity:
For this is my place to keep and never to be lost or go away,
It is my sacred place and it is here to stay.

Alyson R. Murray

"Old Art"

He lived on a mountain where the trees were high,
On the tope of her peak, he could touch the sky.
He had an old log cabin with a broken stove,
With some cows and a garden in the west side grove.
He had a dog and a horse and some piglets, too;
A kind old man who was always true.
Once he had a girl, 'til they had a fight,
But leavin' his mountain just wouldn't be right.
I guess he was a loner late in his years,
Didn't like relationships, couldn't take tears.
Lived off the land 'cause that's all he knew,
Had a lot of sad feelings for what he'd been through.
He was born in the Blue Ridge, raised on the range,
Stayed in the country, didn't like change.
He had an old guitar that he got for a gun,
Played every day in the mornin' sun.
He passed away peacefully in his home,
Now on all frontiers he shall roam.
If you're ever on his mountain you will surely see,
It was a happy life as everyone's should be!

Don Arnold

This Mighty Oak Still Stands

I am this mighty oak that still stands
I cannot be hurt or harmed by any tricks or weapons made by man.
As a young seedling I was planted so I can grow,
So all the inhabitants could bask in my glow.
I am this might oak that still stands,
I was planted firmly into the ground by God's hands.
When the bad storms may come and blow off all my leaves,
I will sprout forth bigger, better and brighter leaves.
I am this might oak that still stands,
I am always in God's watchful eyes and protecting hands.
When hurricanes come and force me to lean to the side,
They just pass me over and I stand erect, upright and with my pride.
I am this mighty oak that still stands,
I am an important nourishing resource of this land.
When all these things happen to me,
I am this mighty oak that still stands erect and strong for all to see.

Durshon Louallen

Untitled

Desert breeze is lightly blowing
The secret of sage fills the air
Not a human soul is stirring
But some coyotes I can hear.

Moon has lifted clear the mountains
Gently balanced on the peaks
From the crescent pours the moonlight
Upon the rocks and sand it creeps.

Cactus rise up towards the heavens
Prayerful arms reach out to seek
Less of sunshine, more for moisture
To their creator they beseech.

In the distance comes a rumble
Low, like the growling of some great beast
And the darkness gives way to a brightness
No rain - just some lightening, dancing
on the peaks.

The desert is like the coyote
A trickster is its trade
Beware its ever changing moods and faces
For the desert can never be tamed!

Michael R. Carter

Del gratia

The eagle is so regal
as is the tiger and the buck.
But, somehow, not the cow
nor the chicken or the duck.

The giraffe that cannot laugh
or utter a sound - looks at the ground.
And, from above, sings like a dove
from within, where pangs of love abound.

The hippopotamus is, like a lot of us are
content to roll around in the muck
Looking for a mate and maybe propagate
believing not in love but luck.

We are all God's creatures with different features
sharing wealth from Mother earth
loving and living, living and loving
Life, for all it's worth.

George E. Lingenfelter

Nature

The clouds appear to be smiling when you gaily look upon them.
The flowers sway to and fro as you look at them with eloquence,
their aroma is taken by the forceful wind and spun around your
presence.
It's dancing, teasing your nose.
And then you begin to spin-your mind wanders and you let go —
You're faraway - in a dreamland perhaps -
but the powerful beauty dominates you and brings
you back into reality.
The colors are so ardent as you love to gaze distractedly
and mysteriously at their intricate design and structure.
The bee lands on the sweet, lavender lily and sucks on
its pollen - then leaves to enjoy its new findings.
Soon, a new day will come and take this statuesque beauty
away - bringing new loves and wonders to discover.

Sasha LeeAnn Lassley

"Saving Of A Soul"

My hair is long and wild.
Naked I stand facing the dark ocean.
My blue eyes glow with ancient secrets.
And I arch my back and throw my arms upward,
Praising the stars overhead.
"save me!" I cry,
"Save me!"
A start shoots across the sky,
And I plunge into the turbulent waters.
The cold burns my skin, cleansing me
I laugh crazily and swim parallel to the shore.
Suddenly, something lifts me up
A light of sorts
And places me in the sand.
The balmy night air blows back my tangled curls,
I feel calm and at peace.
I look up at the moon, and she winks at me.
Redemption, at last, is complete.

Erika M. Wright

The Farmer's Son

Soundless boots march in my sleep
Impatient chores await as if meeting someone
They haven't seen in years.

Fiercely looking to the heavens
Friend or Enemy?
The crops stand at attention.
Endless, aching, act of love; now in desperate need of
Liquid treasure.
The fields are his children.

Oaken stance, now gnarled and bent
Limbs bending, falling to the earth
He cannot see his shadow.
The one he served so faithfully
Now greedily reclaims him.

The boots placed last upon the pyre
Sacrificial legacy, like birds scatter
Their droppings
Cinders of unspoken love
The orange skies are weeping

Maria Garcia Stites

Biographies of Poets

ABBOTT, DORY
[b.] March 6, 1981, Brooklyn, NY; [p.] Jeanne and LeRoy Abbott; [ed.] P.S. 193 Huddle, Edward R. Murrow H.S.; [occ.] Student; [hon.] Sen. Donald Halperin Award 18th Senate District, world contest, Monitor Award, Attendance Award, Glee Club Award, Dance Award, Specda Award, Spanish Award, 3 Blue Honor Rolls, Arts and Crafts Award, Channel 13 Express Yourself Crafts Award, Athletic Blue Ribbon, Teachers Aide Award; [oth. writ.] I write my own stories about my Dad entitled, "My Mother and Me," "Peaceful Surrender," and "The Path of the Destroyer."; [pers.] Due to the illness and death of my father I needed to say so much and words seemed to be the way.; [a.] Brooklyn, NY

ABERS, JOY LYNNE
[b.] May 27, 1966, Farmington, NM; [p.] Linda S. Carter and Jay H. Rall; [ch.] Sarah 11, Jacob 7, and Draeque 2; [ed.] Mesa High School "85", Rio Salado Comm. College; [occ.] Bar Manager (tender); [oth. writ.] Nothing yet, but would like to write children's books...

ADACKUS, VIRGINIA
[pen.] VirAda; [b.] January 19, 1939, Chicago, IL; [p.] Mr. and Mrs. Benjamin Adackus; [ed.] Shields, Austin High School; [occ.] Factory (Machine Operator) Injection Mold Operator; [memb.] YWCA; [hon.] Merit award in elementary school for kindergarten monitor; [oth. writ.] Not published other poems, short stories as a hobby hopefully to become a reality.; [pers.] Don't like to lie about anything - believe in being truthful about everything even if it hurts me 'cause I will not consent to defamation of character which is my own.; [a.] Chicago, IL

ADAM, CHRISTOPHER
[b.] June 2, 1956, Wheeling, WV; [p.] Henry L. Sr. (Deceased) and Catherine E.; [ed.] Attended Stark H.S. in Orange, Texas, Graduated from Concord H.S. in Wilmington, DE. Attended Wilmington Music School and Wilmington College; [occ.] Musician, Songwriter, Recording Artist; [hon.] My first album with my music partner, David Buch, was played on large radio stations up and down the east coast. 2nd Record sold well in the States as well as parts of Europe and Australia. Currently working on what would be our 5th Record if we do decide to release it. Got large write-ups in several Philadelphia papers back in early eighties.; [oth. writ.] Have written at least 150 songs that I consider good enough to play for people in the record business. My partner and I have co-written quite a few as well. I've also written a play based on 18th century England and the plight a lot of Irish folks went through back in that time. (Convict Transportation to New South Wales, for instance); [pers.] Most of my songs are quite personal in nature. They have been inspired from real life situations as well as Dreams and often just things that occur to me on the spur of the moment. I try to write lyrics and music that will have some effect on the listener, even though they might not personally have been through the particular incident the song in question is about. I think a lot of sensitivity goes into my writing. It's natural for me. I can't write about what I'm not.; [a.] Wilmington, DE

ADAMS, GIOVANNI
[pen.] Giovanni Hakeem; [b.] October 26, 1982, Jackson, MS; [p.] Carolyn Adams, Larry Thomas; [ch.] Ryan Phillip; [ed.] APAC School of the Arts, Peoples Middle School; [occ.] Student; [memb.] Vice-president of School, Nation Junior Honors Society, Editor of Paper, Environmental Club Founder and President, Choir, Drama Club, etc.; [hon.] 9 place in school, Social Studies Award, Citizenship 3, etc.; [oth. writ.] Shame, Lover, Violence, Silence, Eyes, and so ends my Slumber, etc.; [pers.] This world is a cruel one in which we might be ashamed to live but also are a part of.; [a.] Jackson, MS

ADAMS, KEVIN G.
[pen.] Kevin Adams; [b.] March 10, 1982, Brewton, AL; [p.] Kenneth and Sharon Adams; [ed.] High school 9th grade; [memb.] National Honor Society; [pers.] Stay true to thineself and to thineself be true. Be in control in what you do to avoid things that would overthrow you. Believe and achieve, for whatever you put your mind to you do. There is a place and a time for everything and always strive to be better than what you have become.; [a.] Atmore, AL

ADSIT, SHEILA
[pen.] With husband it's Bobashela; [b.] January 16, 1940; [p.] Fred and Mary Peters; [m.] Robert Adsit, November 20, 1981; [ch.] Lisa, Joel, Amy Carrie, Chris; [ed.] St Ambrose College, Clarke College, IUPUI Indpls. University Purdue University of Indiana Liberal Arts degree Martin University; [occ.] Professional Mental Health Counsellor; [memb.] I am an associate of St. Frances with the Oldenburg Community.; [hon.] Service to 1986 Mankind Award from Greater Indpls. Sertoma Assoc. NESCO award. 3 T.V producer awards Vista award open window award from positive change Network Ind Consumer success story of the year award. Key consumer outstanding service award; [oth. writ.] Poetry Book "Blurred Genres" Behind Every Great God a new age. Handbook for the Hoi Polloi, "Blurred Genres" is in 27 book stores & 6 libraries; [pers.] Is that we are all made in the perfect image of God both male and female. I believe we are on this earth to learn love and to share our time talent and treasures to help build up God's realm. I believe that God is supreme unfathomable love with infinite mercy. I believe God's providential plan is still in place, thanks to the redemptions work of Jesus we also add to this redemptive good and can help heal I make whole mystical body of Christ. I believe that God wants fellowship that's why we were created with free will and that there is no limit to how much we can know. Love God and be engaged in all God's Divine Wonders and personality.; [a.] Indianapolis, IN

AGAJANIAN, SARA
[b.] January 16, 1983, Tarzana, CA; [p.] Harry Agajanian, Janis Agajanian; [ed.] In the 8th grade; [occ.] Student; [hon.] Honor Society, and D.A.R.E. Award; [pers.] Nothing really inspired me to write this poem. I was just writing what was on my mind.; [a.] Montebello, CA

AL-MARZOUQ, LULWA
[pen.] Lulwa Al-Marzouq; [b.] February 14, 1978, Kuwait; [p.] Mustafa Al-Marzouq, Salwa Al-Ghanim; [ed.] Al-Bayan School, American International School of Kuwait, University of South Florida; [occ.] Student; [hon.] Volleyball Award; [a.] Tampa, FL

ALATORRE, ROSALINDA
[b.] March 12, 1971, Brownsville, TX; [p.] Raul and Angelita Alatorre; [ed.] Hanna High School, Texas Southmost College, University of Texas - Brownsville; [occ.] Teacher - Albert T. Gonzalez Headstart; [memb.] Texas Headstart Association, National Headstart Association; [hon.] National Junior Honor Society, National Honor Society; [pers.] All of my writings come from the heart.; [a.] Brownsville, TX

ALBAN, GENEVIEVE
[pen.] Genevieve Alban; [b.] March 17, 1919, Youngstown, OH; [p.] Dr. and Mrs. Joseph Sofranec; [m.] Russell Alban, August 15, 1992; [ch.] Carolee Monroe, Gen Parm, John Novicky, Sally Anstrom, Marita Novicky, Mary Clark and Edward Novicky; [ed.] Ursulinh High School, Kent State University, Ohio, Reading Specialist; [occ.] Retired teacher, retired boardman Township Clerk - Treasurer; [memb.] Founder - Artists Guild of Anna Maria Island, Republican Women's President, Off Stage Ladies, St. Bernard's Guild; [hon.] "Freedom Foundation" Teacher's Medal, Honored at "Genevieve Novicky Day", Boardman, Ohio. Lifetime Membership in Boardman, OH, Women's Republican Club, excerpt from "History of Slovaks" included in congressional record, many awards for art, listed in "Who's Who in the South and Southwest"; [oth. writ.] Co Author "History of the Slovaks of Mahoming Valley" Ohio, 1976. Author of booklet "How To Help Children Learn" 1974.; [pers.] The beauty and tranquility of Anna Marie Island, Florida, inspires me to create works of art and poetry.

ALFORD, RICHARD L.
[pen.] My Lord and Me; [b.] September 2, 1950, Andalusia, AL; [p.] Richard Vincent Alford, Vera Lilian Alford; [ch.] Dell, Dana, Adrian, Noel, Mesha, Wendy; [ed.] Moultrie Senior High; [occ.] Evangelist Appliance Technician; [memb.] Christian Coalition Coolidge Church of God; [oth. writ.] Have written poems for churches, schools, and individuals.; [pers.] I know words worthy of remembrance ultimately come from above "from God to man from heart to hand," sent from Him to us in love.; [a.] Moultrie, GA

ALLYN, MICHELLE LOUISE
[b.] December 13, 1982, Lumberton, NC; [p.] Timothy Arnette, Dianne Arnette; [ed.] Orrum Middle School; [occ.] 8th grade student, Orrum Middle School; [oth. writ.] Poem published in Cobblestone Children's Nationwide Magazines also published in local newspaper; [pers.] I like writing poems because that is my way of expressing my feelings in my heart. I also enjoy reading poetry by Emily Dickenson.; [a.] Lumberton, NC

ALVES, ROUBINE B.
[pen.] Adrian Hunter; [b.] January 25, 1937, New Bedford, MA; [p.] Harry, Akrive Botseas; [m.] Charles Alves (Deceased), December 3, 1961; [ch.] Carolyn, Jennifer, Rebecca; [ed.] BS Ed., BA Eng. Lit., M. Ed. in Counseling; [occ.] Retired Teacher, Substitute K-8; [memb.] St. Spryidon Church Daughter's of Penelope, Philoptochos Society; [hon.] M. Ed. High Honors, BA Eng. Lit. - Phi Kappa Phi; [oth. writ.] This is Adrian's first; [pers.] Central Park is symbolic of any new experience in life (which may feel blissful at first) exam: Trying drugs, drinking, driving (any new found freedom). Adrian warns us especially teenagers to be cautious.; [a.] Portsmouth, RI

AMADEO, VINCENT S.
[b.] December 17, 1935, Port Chester, NY; [p.] Louis Amadeo, Nancy Amadeo; [m.] Audrey Joyce Amadeo, September 17, 1977; [ed.] West Chester Community College, University of Bridgeport; [occ.] Bio Medical Engineer; [memb.] New England Society of Clinical Engineering; [hon.] VA Connecticut Superior Performance Award; [pers.] My goal is to utilize Scientific knowledge in my writing. I am influenced by Biblical and American poetry.; [a.] Wallingford, CT

AMBURN, JO ANN
[b.] August 17, 1955, Austin, TX; [p.] Lee and Elva Copas; [ed.] Thomas Jefferson High School, Drury College, and (SMS) Southwest Missouri State University; [occ.] Pre-Law Student-Southwest Missouri State University (SMS); [memb.] Alpha Sigma Lambda - Alpha XI Chapter; [hon.] Graduation with Merit, Dean's List; [pers.] Life is like a beautiful rose: It propagates beauty and a lovely fragrance, but mingled with everlasting thorns.; [a.] Springfield, MO

ANAMTA, LAURETTA
[b.] Karachi, Pakistan; [p.] Christian H. Thompson, Gloria Thompson; [m.] Divorced; [ch.] Juanita, Amar, Sanam, Asad; [ed.] Bachelor of Arts; [occ.] Admin. Asst. BSC Program, LHR Univ. of Mgt. Sci-Lahore; [oth. writ.] Poems/A diary showing my return from almost insanity caused by a dreadful marriage, and the strength it took to be whole again. Diaries for each of my kids (begun a few hours before they were born): Amusing incidents, poems to them, and their touching thoughts.; [pers.] I believe that everyone can improve if they but focus on "One Step at a Time" - and never forgetting to give themselves a "Tap on the Back" instead of waiting for others to do it for them. There is goodness in each of us, though sometimes we have to strive a little bit harder to learn to trust ourselves.; [a.] Lahorg, Pakistan

ANDERSON, ESTELLE
[pen.] Redwood Wind; [b.] July 25, 1950, Los Angeles, CA; [p.] Langley and Helen Ward; [m.] Rusman Anderson, June 7, 1988; [ed.] University of Utah; [occ.] Wife, Freelance Artist; [memb.] Subud; [oth. writ.] Poetry Publ.: Ink Literary Review, Fall 1995; [pers.] I feel that all aspects of living should manifest a balance between substance and spirit, and as an artist, I seek to express one within the other.; [a.] Eureka, CA

ANDRZEJEWICZ, ELIZABETH D.
[b.] September 9, 1973, Long Island, NY; [p.] Pete and Donna Andrzejewicz; [m.] Edward A. Mills, October 26, 1996; [ed.] Niagara University - Communication Studies Morrisville College - Journalism; [occ.] Writer; [oth. writ.] Several articles published in a trade publication by McGraw Hill, photo journalism bylines and Public Relations Profiles for two major NYC Construction Management Firms; [a.] Arlington, VA

ANGEL, MARIE B.
[pen.] Mara; [b.] May 8, 1945, Irvine, KY; [p.] Samuel and Emma Brinegar; [ch.] (One son) Darrin Shane Angel; [ed.] 8 yrs. grade school, 4 yrs. High School: Fairborn Elementary School and Fairborn High School - Fairborn, Ohio; [occ.] Production Associate; [oth. writ.] Some poems published in job company paper "Mountaineer" at Firestone Ind. Prods., where I am employed. I am also a reporter for this paper; [pers.] I feel that God has blessed me with a gift of verse that reaches out to touch others and helps them to feel loved and understood. If I can help just one person then that is what should be.; [a.] Williamsburg, KY

ANKLEWICH, JENNIFER A.
[b.] July 23, 1985, Fairfax, VA; [p.] Tom and Jeanie Anklewich; [ed.] 6th grade; [occ.] Student International School of Dakar (I.S.D.) Senegal W. Africa; [oth. writ.] I Was So Embarrassed (short story), articles for school newspaper; [pers.] Writing may be considered work, but whether it is or not, it should be fun. Your writing will be better if you're happy with what you're doing.

ANSARI, SAEMA
[b.] June 8, 1978, Ije-bode, Nigeria; [p.] Shakeel Ansari, Arfa Ansari; [ed.] Student at Vassar College; [occ.] Student; [hon.] Who's Who Among American High School Students, Presidential Academic Award; [oth. writ.] None published but I have been writing since I was 8 or 9 yrs. old. It's for purely personal growth.; [pers.] Like frail footprints in sand that vanish too soon, time here is short; do good and make it worthwhile.; [a.] Brooklyn, NY

ANTHONY, WILFRED DEAN
[pen.] Wilfred Dean Anthony; [b.] May 17, 1940, Dallas, TX; [p.] Deceased; [ch.] Alicia Renee; [ed.] Bac Sci (Pharmacy), Texas Southern University, Houston, Texas, "Class of 74"; [occ.] Poet, Pharmacist; [memb.] Kappa Alpha PSI, Fraternity, Inc. National Pharmaceutical Association, Inc; [oth. writ.] Images (Book written in 1987) Poems published, Cosmopolitan Journal - 1987, Spotlight News - 1987; [pers.] When one among many shares his gift in writing it is a prized honor.; [a.] Dallas, TX

ANTINORI, TASHONN-ETIENNE
[pen.] Tashion Evangelista; [b.] April 3, 1958, Chicago, IL; [p.] John Francis-Antinori and Irene Evangelista-Antinori; [ed.] Chicago Vocational High, Grand Rapids Community College (AA), (AAS) Law Enforcement, Liberal Arts, Dean's List, Southern Illinois University at Carbondale Illinois Dean's List; [occ.] Model, Author, Artist, Actor; [memb.] United States Tennis Association, Western Michigan Horticultural Society, John Ball Park Zoological Society; [hon.] Dean's List, Illinois State Teachers Scholarship, Illinois State Grant (Educational); [oth. writ.] Novel! "Private Parts". "Body Watching the Collection of Tashonn-Etienne-Antinori, Etchings and Water Colors; [pers.] Making one proud of the essence of one's diversity. Humanism must succeed above everything else, it's the basis of the survival of mankind. I write for my generation, and for the one that follows; [a.] Kentwood, MI

APARICIO, MICHELLE
[b.] May 17, 1983, Northridge, CA; [p.] George Aparicio and Teresa Aparicio; [ed.] I'm presently attending St. John Baptist, De LaSalle School at Junior High Level; [hon.] I have been on the honor roll at my school since 1993.; [pers.] Writing poetry allows me to express my inner feelings, thoughts, and emotions. Life and all the beautiful things that the Lord has set upon us gives me inspiration to write my poems.; [a.] Granada Hills, CA

APPLEGATE, CONNIE
[b.] March 7, 1958, Galion, OH; [p.] Robert and Virginia Norman; [m.] Thomas Applegate, October 1, 1994; [ch.] Vanda, Aaron and Benji, step-daughter, Jessica Applegate, step-son Brent Applegate; [ed.] Crestline High School, Pioneer Joint Vocational School, North Central Technical College - Resident Activity Coordinator Courses; [occ.] Activities Director in Nursing home; [memb.] Church of God of Prophecy, Alzheimer Support Group; [hon.] Citizenship award, Pioneer Joint Vocational School 1976; [oth. writ.] None published several written for family and friends; [pers.] My poems are about life experiences through my eyes and the eyes of others. I learn a lot by really listening to people, especially the elderly. "Always with us" was inspired by the elderly people I worked with everyday that have passed away!; [a.] Crestline, OH

ARCHER, MARGARETE F.
[b.] October 28, 1914, New Albany, IN; [p.] Michael and Katie Fitzgerald; [m.] Dr. George F. Archer Jr., September 16, 1933; [ch.] David F., George F. III, Alan J.; [ed.] University of Louisville 1935, A.B. Degree in Economics, Louisville Girls High School 1931; [occ.] Retired; [memb.] Bethlehem United Church of Christ, J.B. Speed Museum and Alliance Historical Preservation; [hon.] National Honor Society; [oth. writ.] Religions Songs, Rhymed Poetry, Children's Songs and Games; [pers.] I like to put into poetic form, incidents that occur in everyone's life, painting anecdotal pictures with words.; [a.] Louisville, KY

ARNETTE, JONI
[b.] December 13, 1982, Lumberton, NC; [p.] Timothy Arnette, Dianne Arnette; [ed.] Orrum Middle School; [occ.] 8th grade student, Orrum Middle School; [oth. writ.] Poem published in Cobblestone Children's Nationwide Magazines also published in local newspaper; [pers.] I like writing poems because that is my way of expressing my feelings in my heart. I also enjoy reading poetry by Emily Dickenson.; [a.] Lumberton, NC

ARNOLD, DON
[pen.] Raymond Arthur; [b.] March 18, 1968, Dunedin, FL; [p.] Raymond and Betty Jo Arnold; [ch.] Joshua Arnold - 3; [ed.] Crystal River High School, Graduated 1986, Itt Technical Institute Tampa, FL (1 1/2 yrs.); [occ.] Technical Service Supervisor; [memb.] Florida Army National Guard (Inactive) 6 years active; [hon.] 1994 Technical Customer Service Person (Alltel Mobile) Military Awards; [oth. writ.] Other poems.; [pers.] I write about topics everyone can relate to, life's struggles and stories. Life is short and it would be a lasting legacy.; [a.] Gainsville, FL

ASHLEY, ELIZABETH
[b.] January 14, 1982, Wyoming, MN; [p.] Jill Christianson; [ed.] Chicago Lakes Area Schools; [occ.] Dairy Queen; [memb.] Shadow Creeks Stables Riding Club; [a.] Lindstrom, MN

AUBUCHON, HARMON
[pen.] Harmon Aubuchon; [b.] July 11, 1921, Kiefer, OK; [p.] William E. Aubuchon and Lena M. Aubuchon; [m.] Annabelle Aubuchon, April 14, 1946; [ch.] Richard Allen, Kenneth Lee, Charles Edwin; [ed.] Earlsboro High School, The David Ranken Jr. School Of Mechanical Trades, 8 Years, H.H. Robertson Computer Classes; [occ.] Retired from H.H. Robertson Co., Data Processing Engineering Supervisor; [memb.] Ordained Layman Maplewood Baptist Church; [hon.] Numerous Bowling and Softball Trophies, Greater St. Louis Bowling Association Double Championship 1973, Christian Recreation Ministry 1979, Layman's Emeritus Services 1965 to 1991; [oth. writ.] Prayers, Bible Verse and Thoughts, Inspiration Four Line Verse Poetry; [pers.] I try to reflect and glorify God in all of my writing. I am greatly appreciative of books writings of other great Christian writers.; [a.] Maplewood, MO

AXELL, TIMOTHY S.
[b.] March 18, 1971, Chicago, IL; [m.] Donna M. Axell; [ch.] Kayla Marie Axell; [pers.] My work is dedicated to Him "who alone possesses immortality and dwells in unapproachable light, whom no man has seen or can see. To Him be honor and eternal dominion! Amen." 1 Timothy 6:16 - The Bible; [a.] Springfield, IL

AYCOCK III, FRANK B.
[b.] September 25, 1938, Norfolk, VA; [p.] Frank and Nell Aycock; [m.] Helen "De" Aycock, June 6, 1970; [ed.] L.L.B. University of North Carolina, 1965; [occ.] Attorney at Law; [oth. writ.] Ode to Jack Mraz, Ode to Clyde Quick, Brief to United States Supreme Court in Graham V. Connor, 1989; [a.] Charlotte, NC

AYERS, JEFFREY GLENN
[b.] July 19, 1974, Pontiac, MI; [p.] Nancy Ayers and Lewis Ayers; [oth. writ.] Previously published in Of Sunshine and Daydreams, Memories of Tomorrow, and Whispers at Dusk.; [pers.] This poem is dedicated to everyone lucky enough to have found someone to have a "Special day" with.; [a.] Los Angeles, CA

BAEUERLEN, SHANE
[b.] April 17, 1981, Redding, CA; [p.] Sabrina Baeuerlen; [ed.] Rio Americano H.S., American River College; [occ.] Student at Rio Americano H.S.; [memb.] C.A.I.R. Capital Area Indian Resources, Pozar's Gymnastics; [oth. writ.] None published; [pers.] My poems are from my heart and are inspired by Yanni, a Greek musician. As a young poet, I go by what I know in life.; [a.] Sacramento, CA

BAIKER, MARY ELIZABETH
[pen.] Elizabeth; [b.] Briarcliff, NY; [p.] John and Anne Baiker; [m.] Divorced; [ed.] Croton Harmon High Westch. Com. College - AAS-Psychol Univ. of CA, San Diego, UCSD-BS-Psychol; [occ.] Executive Asst. Personal Admin., CH of BD.; [memb.] Co-Chairman - Rec Activities YW-YMCA Tarrytown, NY; [hon.] Eng. Literature, Photography, Figure Skating, Swimming and Dance (Semi-Pro.) 1961-1963; [oth. writ.] Poems, short stories, school newspaper; [pers.] I have been influenced by my parents - mother a singer, with a love for opera, father, a poet and musician ahead of their time. I dedicate this poem to my sis, Anita, who is one of the "Little Cherubs" on earth; [a.] Yonkers, NY

BAILEY, KATHRYN
[b.] March 14, 1937, Kentucky; [p.] Nila Blair - Shelt McQuinn; [m.] Lloyd Bailey (Deceased); [ch.] Rosemarie - Sharon Ann; [occ.] Retired - Hospital Worker; [hon.] Editors Choice Award 1995 and 1996 from the National Library of Poetry.; [oth. writ.] Various poems for friends and family.; [pers.] I thank God for giving me the words to express myself and I thank my aunt Hadie for believing in me.; [a.] Wellington, KY

BAIRD, FRANCES T.
[b.] March 21, 1941, Suffolk, VA; [p.] Joseph Taylor and Rosa A. Taylor; [m.] Brandford L. Baird, December 30, 1964; [ch.] Anthony L. Baird and Branden Allyne Baird; [ed.] East Suffolk High, VA State University; [occ.] Vocal Music Teacher, Tucson, Arizona; [memb.] Tucson Teachers Association, NEA, MENC, WIBC, AEA; [oth. writ.] A poem published in a medical journal.; [pers.] I write poems that are humorous and from my personal experiences. I hope that when others read them they will relate in some way and get a big "kick out of them".; [a.] Tucson, AZ

BAKER, ROBERT E.
[b.] November 22, 1951, Tripoli, Libya; [p.] H. T. and Virginia Baker; [m.] Anne W. Baker, July 13, 1991; [ed.] Associate of Religious Arts (ARA) Luther College, Teaneck, N.J.; [occ.] Pharmacy Clerk; [memb.] Bethel Evangelical Lutheran Church, Manassas, VA; [hon.] Summa Cum Laude, Luther College Staffer of the Month, Giant Food; [oth. writ.] Writings on various subjects for church newsletters, Public relations articles for FFA. Devotional writings published in the Home Altar; [pers.] Hopefully my writings will help define the beauty, grace and activity of the divine within a world which appears all too ugly.; [a.] Manassas, VA

BAKER, SANDRA LEE
[pen.] Sandra Lee Baker; [b.] September 2, 1959, Upper Darby, PA; [p.] Matthew Sharpless, Shirley Sharpless; [m.] David C. Baker, May 19, 1984; [ch.] Rachel, Joshua, Katie; [ed.] Sun Valley, H.S. graduate; [occ.] Home Schooling Mother owner of Christian Comforts Inc.; [memb.] Created In God's Image, Ketogenic Dirt Support Group, Home-Coach and Recipe Creator, the Family of God; [hon.] Honor Society SVHS; [oth. writ.] I have no other submitted or published writings this time.; [pers.] I write as God leads. It is an outpouring of an inward churning. I have lived this particular poem. Thanks to my Lord and Savior Jesus Christ I remain the mother of three children.; [a.] Mount Holly, NJ

BALASH, ANNA T.
[b.] May 9, 1960, NY; [p.] William Balash, Anna Masuk Balash; [m.] Yiannakis Ioannides; [ed.] John Bowne High School Agriculture College, CUNY (Majoring in english Literature and Secondary Ed.); [occ.] Primerica Financial Services Registered Representative; [memb.] Golden Key Honor Society, Dean's List, Women's Center, Two Coves Businessman's Committee; [hon.] The Silverstein-Peiser Award for Non-Fiction; [oth. writ.] "An Experiment in Teaching", "An Image in Walden and Leaves of Grass"; [pers.] The hope you instill in others and the joy you bring to another's life is reflective. Each brightens your own life in turn.; [a.] Astoria, NY

BALDESBERGER, DEBBIE
[b.] November 20, 1956, Grove City, PA; [p.] Patricia Flynn and the late John Flynn; [m.] Jerry Baldesberger, December 23, 1994; [ch.] Erin Lott, Dawn McKean and Melinda Baldesberger; [ed.] High School, Moniteau, West Sunbury, PA; [occ.] Cashier at Sheetz Store in Slippery Rock, PA; [oth. writ.] I had a poem, "Forever Love" accepted for publication in "Whispers" a literary Anthology by Iliad Press. George J. Howe Co. printed my poem, "Jerry's Life" in there company's newsletter. "Waiting, Still Waiting" will be published in an anthology by Sparrowgrass; [pers.] My husband, Jerry is my greatest inspiration. He is my "Special Love" and the joy of my life. Special Thanks to Jerry, my mother and my daughters, for I could not write about love, if they hadn't shown me what it was.; [a.] Slippery Rock, PA

BALIONI, DIANNA CLAIRE
[b.] March 5, 1982, New York City; [p.] Louis and Barbara Balioni; [ed.] Presently attending Bishop Kearney High School; [occ.] Student; [hon.] 6th Annual Children's Writing Contest, Brooklyn Reading Council, April 25, 1990, J. H. S. Honor student; [pers.] I write poetry so that other people know how I see things. Sometimes people don't hear my feelings. In my poems, they can feel my words.; [a.] Brooklyn, NY

BALL, APRIL JOHNSON
[pen.] April L. J. Ball; [b.] April 16, 1969, Akron, OH; [p.] Maurice and Linda Johnson; [m.] Stanley L. Ball Jr., November 20, 1994; [ch.] Alexis Victoria; [ed.] Firestone High School, Arlington Beauty Care Academy; [occ.] Cosmetologist, Susan Menick's Hair Designs; [memb.] Breast Cancer Association, Compassionate Friends, Reading Books Club; [hon.] In the top five graduating the Cosmetologist Academy.; [oth. writ.] Two articles in the local newspaper, several poems in the Compassionate Friends newsletters (Nationwide), also erotic writing; [pers.] Writing has always been natural to me. My style comes from my heart more than other authors. In my adult life, I've been greatly influenced by the death of our daughter.; [a.] Jacksonville, FL

BALLUCH, CHRISTOPHER A.
[b.] January 15, 1967, Sharon, PA; [p.] George Balluch Jr., Fay Myers Balluch; [ed.] Sharon High School, B.S. in Biology, Grove City College M.A. in Counseling, Slippery Rock University, Graduated Cum Laude; [occ.] Counselor, Catholic Charities, Sharon, PA; [hon.] Dean's List, Charles M. Bennett Memorial Scholarship, Outstanding Graduate Student Award; [oth. writ.] Poem published in American Collegiate Poets, Spring Concourse 1988; [pers.] "Know thyself", said Apollo. These words have given me direction, purpose, and a sense of peace in my writing and in my life.; [a.] Sharon, PA

BALY, TONY
[pen.] Tony Pereyra; [b.] September 2, 1921, Havana, Cuba; [occ.] I work always for an American Company. In Havana I did work for "Woolworth Co" and also for A Big Textiles Co. "Ariguanabo" and in United States for "The Garcia Corporation" a fishing Tackle Co., in Miami I work (almost 20 years) for Dade County Aviation Department at the Miami International Airport as an airport Clerk, From which I retired.; [memb.] S.A.S.S.E.M. France Composer Association - As a poet; [oth. writ.] I do have no less than 100 melodies with Spanish Lyric and few with English Lyric. I also have about 20 of my songs performed and recorded by several of the most famous Cuban and Puerto-Rican Singers. I do have at least 300 poems in Spanish and a good dozen in English. Now I have been lucky to have one of my poems be accepted and in a near future published by you!!!; [pers.] I think I was born a singer, poet and composer.

BANCROFT, NADINE
[pen.] Amanda Marie; [ch.] Two Birthchildren - 200 Foster and Day Care Children over several years.; [ed.] Practical Nurse Humanities Assoc. Degree Activities Director - Michigan; [occ.] Home Health Care Nurse; [hon.] Foster Parent of Michigan 1982, Michigan Senior Citizen of 1995; [oth. writ.] "Sunny" Book written by Amanda Marie; [pers.] Want my pen name of Amanda Marie used for my poems. I wrote "Brother Whose Soul Passed Beyond" in a book I am writing name "Dearest Darling" by Amanda Marie.; [a.] Clinton, MI

BANDY, PENNY
[b.] February 24, 1974, Rockwood, TN; [p.] Robert Bandy, Andrea Swice Good; [ed.] Lincoln Memorial University, B.A. in December 1996; [occ.] Student, Disc Jockey, Television Anchor, Assignment Editor; [memb.] The Endometriosis Association; [hon.] Dean's List, Who's Who Among American High School Students; [oth. writ.] Unpublished poetry, unpublished short story, unpublished memoir, news writing for radio and television, commercials for radio and television; [pers.] For me learning is the greatest of all achievements. Writing is a creative expression of an individual's version of that personal knowledge; [a.] Tazewell, TN

BARNARD, CHEYENNE
[b.] May 20, 1983, Collins, MS; [p.] Scott and Selina Barnard; [ed.] Student, Seminary High School; [occ.] Student; [memb.] Beta Club, 4-H Club; [hon.] I have always been a straight A student, and I was on the Superintendent's List for 6 years. I was chosen as the most helpful student and received awards in Science,

English, Math, Spelling, and Reading. I was also awarded in beauty pageants. [oth. writ.] If You Only Care, The Fisherman's Way, Spring, and Fall (which was published in The Anthology of Poetry by Young Americans; [pers.] Every poem I have written has been in honor of someone in my family. When I write I try to focus on something that person enjoys. Poetry is a talent and hobby I enjoy and hope to never give up. [a.] Sanford, MS.

BARNES, MILDRED
[b.] November 30, 1911, Salt Lake City, UT; [p.] Laura Anderson and Oscar Rhodes; [m.] Joseph Barnes (Deceased), June 22, 1936; [ch.] Carol Cutler, Valerie Johnson and Edie Murphy; [ed.] High School - one yr. Junior College; [occ.] Retired; [memb.] Daughters of Utah Pioneers, Delta Theta Chi Sorority; [hon.] Several Oil Painting Awards, One Poetry Award in a Church Literary contest; [oth. writ.] Mostly poetry hand-outs for lessons I give commemorating special-occasions Honoring special people.; [pers.] I've learned that nothing is more important than our attitude. I've learned that the more creative you are the more things you notice. I've learned to count all my blessings and would not change places with any one.; [a.] Newhall, CA

BARNETT, TERESA M.
[b.] February 5, 1959, Easton, PA; [p.] Stephen J. Tersak, Nancy J. Tersak, Henry Daniels; [m.] Robert J. Barnett Sr., December 8, 1983; [ch.] Bobbisu Ruth, Austen Benjamin, step-children Robert J. Jr., Thomas Daley, Megan Lynn; [ed.] Graduated from: Metuchen High School, Metuchen, New Jersey; [occ.] Self-employed, Taylor - business name "Teresa Sews"; [memb.] New Life Assembly of God Church, The Grampian Band-Ist Flute; [hon.] Leadership awards from the Women's Ministry Department of the Assembly of God's Churches; [oth. writ.] Short story published in a college circulatory magazine. Personal writings published for a family heirloom book. Many "Letters to the Editor" writings.; [pers.] NIV 1th 5:16-18; [a.] Lancaster, PA

BARON, JONATHAN REED
[b.] July 11, 1973, Brooklyn, NY; [p.] Bruce and Susan Baron; [ed.] Montclair State University, Marlbor High School, New Jersey; [occ.] Jack of many trades, master of none; [oth. writ.] "Orchid Unison", an unpublished collection of poems; [pers.] I try extremely hard not to date myself in my work. I never speak of televisions, stereos, or anything that is "man made." Instead, I look towards nature and emotions because they are timeless. My greatest literary Joy would be for a person from 1763 and a person from 2763 to sit down together and discuss my poetry, that is timeless!; [a.] Marlboro, NJ

BARR, RITA D.
[pen.] Rita Crowley Barr; [b.] October 20, 1929, Salem, OH; [p.] Raymond F. Crowley, Estelle M. Crowley; [m.] Richard G. Barr, March 20, 1955; [ch.] Karen, Carol, Gail, Dave, Gary, Brian and Shirley; [ed.] Ohio, Indiana, Kansas (elementary school), Ohio, 7th-11th (Columbus, Ohio), Jan. 1946 - 11th grade Livorno, Italy, Army Dependents School, 1947-1948 graduated Army Dependents High School Vienna, Austria; [occ.] Dairy Farmer Wife, Barr Farms Inc. Monroe, Wa.; [memb.] St. Mary of the Valley R. Catholic Ch. Monroe, Tualco Subordinate Grange #284, Monroe, Wa., East County Senior Center Monroe, Wa., Sky Valley Genealogy Society, Snohomish County Farm Bureau; [oth. writ.] Several articles published in local newspapers.; [pers.] I have wanted to be a free lance creative writer since I was 9 years old.; [a.] Monroe, WA

BARRIOS, RAMONA V.
[pen.] Mona Barrios; [b.] May 1, 1928, New Orleans, LA; [p.] Mr. and Mrs. Wilfred John Vincent; [m.] Eugene Allen Barrios Sr. (Deceased), June 2, 1951; [ch.] Allen, Michael, Robert, Larry, Anthony Barrios and Cindy B. Rossignol; [ed.] High School (John McDonough) 1 year Canan Bible College; [occ.] Retired - 40 years previously -PBX Switchboard and receptionist; [oth. writ.] I do have other poems, but I am planning on putting them into a book at a later time -; [pers.] I just have a deep faith in God and as a child of His, I have been inspired by Him. I have 6 wonderful grandchildren - Shane, Kim, Mike Jr., Chet, Kristen, and Louis IV, four step grandchildren, Heidi, David, Leonette and Stephen; [a.] Slidell, LA

BARTOW, DOROTHY
[b.] June 15, 1935, Flushing, NY; [p.] Dorothy and Edward Bartow; [m.] Divorced; [ch.] 2 boys, 2 girls, 8 grandchildren, 2 grt grands; [ed.] PS49 Whitestone NY, C.I.H.S. Central Islip, NY, Adelphi Business School, Bay Shore, NY; [occ.] Bus Driver (Van) for Suffolk Transportation; [oth. writ.] New Day, Blessings and others. Wrote for schools newspapers, poems published locally.; [pers.] See the beauty in life and everything around you.; [a.] Central Islip, NY

BATARA, JOAN D.
[b.] September 5, 1974, Manila, Philippines; [p.] Johnny U. Batara, Mercedes Dulay; [ed.] University of Santo Tomas, Philippines Institute of Children's Literature, CT; [memb.] Lunda Art Group, Federation of Philippine Photographers Foundation, UST Journalism Society; [hon.] Dean's List; [oth. writ.] Published news and featured articles in the Philippine Daily Inquirer and The Flame, UST-AB Journal; [pers.] Poetry is the language of the soul. Beautiful and strange perhaps but is true and enduring in more ways than one.; [a.] Jacksonville, FL

BATEMAN JR., EARL C.
[pen.] 'L Rae and true name; [b.] July 31, 1931, Roaring Spring, PA; [p.] Earl C. Bateman Sr., Ruby Ann See Bateman (Deceased); [m.] Mae Anna Bowers Bateman, August 10, 1951; [ch.] Earl C. Bateman III; [ed.] Hedgesville High School, University of Maryland, National Cryptologic School; [occ.] Retired, National Security Agency; [oth. writ.] NSA Cryptologic History Series, Baptist Convention of Maryland and Delaware promotional Literature, four volumes of verse for family and friends, family geneology; [pers.] I find the license of verse especially useful in chronicling special events in the lives of family and friends. Poetry makes a fine anthology of family history.; [a.] Laurel, MD

BATTEN, BILL
[b.] December 6, 1939, Oklahoma City, OK; [p.] Leland Batten, Vivian Batten; [m.] Carol Batten (1942-1996), July 29, 1961; [ch.] Tammy Szczerbacki, Debby Newell; [ed.] BS, Med, University of Central Oklahoma; [occ.] Chemist, Oklahoma Department of Environmental Quality; [pers.] Dedicated to the memory of my loving wife, Carol.; [a.] Oklahoma City, OK

BAUGH, PETER
[pen.] Duane; [b.] June 12, 1979, Hanover, PA; [p.] Perry and Stella Baugh; [occ.] Artist, Cashier at Wendy's of Danvers; [hon.] 2 poems previously published by the National Library of Poetry.

BAZAN, ANGELA
[b.] June 2, 1982, Dallas, TX; [p.] Kathy and Juan Bazan; [ed.] O'Banion Middle School; [hon.] I was in drill team for 2 yrs. and our team won 8 trophies and 2 plaques.; [pers.] I like to reflect my feelings by writing them down. I believe in being fair and try to be good to the people around me especially my family.; [a.] Garland, TX

BEAN, RONIQUE
[b.] September 30, 1980, Los Angeles; [p.] Jacqueline Williams and Ronnie Bean; [ed.] Chapman Elem., Peary Middle Sch., Gardena High School; [memb.] Girl Scouts of USA Gramercy-Van Ness, Troop 615; [pers.] I've started writing at a young age, this is my most valued. It's written in my hopes of what my first love would be.; [a.] Gardena, CA

BEATY, KEVIN
[b.] December 27, 1977, Channel View; [p.] Linda and Grady; [ed.] Northshore High, San Jacinto College; [occ.] Teacher Aide; [memb.] BMG Music Club; [pers.] Dear Reader, I hope you enjoyed my poem. Thank You.; [a.] Houston, TX

BEAVER, ETHAN JAMES
[pen.] Ethan Beaver; [b.] March 28, 1977, Sellersville, PA; [p.] Jim and Sandee Beaver; [ed.] Northeast High School Graduate, one year at St. Pete Junior College; [occ.] Data Entry; [memb.] Northside Baptist Church; [hon.] Honor Roll; [oth. writ.] I have written sixteen poems and nine short stories. None of them have been published.; [pers.] Jesus Christ is the center of my life. Without Him, my world would collapse and life might as well be terminated. I grew up in the church and knew all about Him. That was it, I just knew about Him. It was like hearing of a famous star or celebrity out of reach, until one day, when, I took a step back and looked at the entire scheme of things, I saw my life being wasted on things that did not really matter and that were destroying me, I then asked Jesus to free me from those things and He did. He placed meaning and purpose in the midst of a chaotic existence. He placed Love and joy in a hopeless, empty, and lonely soul. He continues to fill me every day as I draw closer to Him. I wish I could describe just how everyone needs Him. I will try to do it in my writing but you will never know Jesus until you meet Him.

BEEKS, KENNY
[b.] October 21, 1955, Abilene, TX; [p.] Lonell Beeks, Shirley Beeks; [m.] Divorced; [ch.] D'Ana Beeks, Crystal Beeks; [occ.] CNC Machinist, IRWIN Research and Development, Yakima, WA; [memb.] National Space Society; [a.] Yakima, WA

BELL, HEATHER ELIZABETH
[b.] June 1, 1977; [p.] James and Darlene Bell; [ed.] Illustration Major at Savannah College of Art and Design; [pers.] I would like to dedicate this, my first publication, to Mr. Robins of Maine for making me, "lose the morbid".; [a.] Savannah, GA

BELL, KANDACE
[b.] October 7, 1982, Stillwater, OK; [p.] Dexter and Edith Bell; [ed.] I'm an eight grade student at Alamo Heights Junior School; [occ.] Scholar; [memb.] Member of the Alamo Heights Orchestra, Texas Juniors Volleyball Club, Alamo Heights Baptist Church, Alamo Heights Junior School Choir; [hon.] Academic Recognition on TAAS test. Various Athletic awards. Honor roll student; [oth. writ.] Articles for school papers.; [pers.]

My thoughts, feelings, answers, and inspirations come from my heart and the higher power of my life, the Lord, two of my only guides.; [a.] San Antonio, TX

BELL, NANCY OWEN

[b.] January 17, 1946, Henderson, NC; [p.] Alexander L. Owen and Emma Johnson Owen; [m.] Joseph C. Bell Jr., November 9, 1963; [ch.] Sharon Denise, Catherine Ann, Joseph C. Bell III; [ed.] Henderson High School, Vance-Granville, Community College; [occ.] Clerk-Receptionist-Typist III at Vance County Health Department, Henderson, NC for 20 years; [oth. writ.] I have written a few articles and letters of interest for our local newspaper, but have not written anything on a professional level, with the exception of my poem which I submitted to you.; [pers.] As a child growing up, I always liked to imagine and dream of great things. It could be writing a book, to becoming a movie star. I often felt that I would never achieve the goals I had set for myself, after getting married at such an early age, but I have a great husband and loving family who support me and let me be myself. That's my inspiration.; [a.] Henderson, NC

BELZER, RALPH

[pen.] Ralph Lawrence Belzer; [b.] July 10, 1962, Elgin, IL; [p.] Ralph and Jeanette; [m.] Dalonda, February 27, 1982; [ch.] Sarah , Stephanie and Matthew; [ed.] Elgin High School; [occ.] Office Supply Sales, Phoenix, AZ; [memb.] First Free Will Baptist Church; [oth. writ.] Dozens of poems waiting to be published.; [pers.] The Lord had awakened me early one morning and bestowed upon me this gift, a desire I've never had before, that's how I know it's from Him; [a.] Phoenix, AZ

BENDER, TRACY

[b.] November 25, 1980, Hoffman Estates, IL; [p.] Dr. Mike Bender, Dawn Rohrssen; [ed.] Sophomore in High School; [occ.] Recall Sec./Lab Tech. for Dr. Bender's Office; [oth. writ.] Poems: All I Want, My Friend, There's More To Love, and more.

BENNETT, INA

[b.] June 8, 1915, Tahoka, TX; [m.] Samuel J. Bennett, October 1, 1940; [ch.] Claudia, Samuel J. III, 3 grandchildren; [ed.] Graduated from High School, 1932, Abilene, TX, completed 2 years at McMurry College; [occ.] Worked in an accounting office;

BENTON, BRENDA

[pen.] Brenda Benton; [b.] May 25, 1963, Freer, TX; [p.] Martin and Edith Ashley; [m.] Rick Benton, May 25, 1985; [ch.] David, Richard and Kevin Benton; [ed.] Nursing School - Achieved Degree for Licensed Vocational Nurse - 1982.; [occ.] Caretaker for Alzheimers; [memb.] Life Tabernacle United Pentecostal Church Ducanville Texas; [oth. writ.] Many unpublished poems about Jesus as well as my Mom and Dad, who have gone on to their reward.; [pers.] My desire is to promote the love and goodness of my precious Lord and Saviour — Jesus Christ. He is my reason for living. I owe thanks to Him for all my talents.; [a.] Waxahachie, TX

BENTON, PAUL

[pen.] Paul Mariano; [b.] August 2, 1981, Good Samaritan Hosp; [p.] Michael and Linda Benton; [ed.] I went to Our Lady of Lourdes for 9 years of my schooling and I am currently in my second year at St John the Baptist High School West Islip, NY; [occ.] Student and Play Piano for 11 yrs; [memb.] I am currently an associate member of the American museum of National History; [hon.] NYSSMA 3 award; [oth. writ.] None, this one is one of my first that ever entered in a contest; [pers.] Mountains are one of God's great creations and we all have to work very hard to save the mountains' vital woodlands, for the sake of our own existence, God bless and thank you; [a.] North Babylon, NY

BERDIK, JUSTIN

[b.] July 19, 1980, Pittsburgh, PA; [p.] Harry Berdik and Sandy Berdik; [ed.] Shaler High School; [pers.] I write how I feel. If I feel nothing I don't write. I mainly started to be like Jim Morrison Poet/Lyricist of The Doors. "In The Corner" was dedicated to a very special person. You know who you are! Much love. Guess who the boy is.; [a.] Pittsburgh, PA

BERG, KELLI

[b.] April 21, 1976, Pompton Lakes, NJ; [p.] Nancy Berg; [ed.] Pompton Lakes High School; [occ.] Management - Middle Atlantic Products, Inc. Riverdale, NJ; [memb.] Peta, ASPCA; [oth. writ.] Avid editorial writer for newspapers.

BEROVA, KATRINA

[pen.] Katie; [b.] July 13, 1984, Ukraine; [p.] Suetlana and Pavel Beroua; [ed.] Student in Pikesville Middle School; [occ.] Student; [hon.] Balto County Honor Roll, Certificate of Achievement in Tae Kwon Do, Certificate of Appreciation participating in D.A.R.E. Finished the John Casablanca's School of Modeling.; [oth. writ.] Short stories, poems entitled: Winter Sounds, at Night, Me, Music, etc.; [pers.] People should put their inner soul into their poems, so they seem mysterious.; [a.] Baltimore, MD

BERRY, ISABEL E.

[b.] August 4, 1941, Washington County, PA; [p.] Andrew and Mary Wounick; [m.] August E. Berry, November 28, 1959; [ch.] August Jr. and Isabel M.; [ed.] Grad. Jefferson - Morgan H.S. 2 years college Cal. U. PA; [occ.] Owner/Operator Isabel's Catering; [memb.] Carmichaels First Baptist Church RBA. Assn., Rices Landing American Legion Auxiliary Post 916; [hon.] Who's Who American Women; [a.] Rices Landing, PA

BERTRAND, SHARON

[b.] March 12, 1960, Lake Charles, LA; [p.] Jr. and Irene Blanchard; [m.] Roger Lynn Bertrand, December 13, 1980; [ch.] Matthew Joseph Bertrand; [ed.] Little Cypress Mauriceville High School and Lamar University; [occ.] Housewife/Auctioneer; [pers.] I use my poetry as a means of channeling my energy in a positive way. Due to continuous back and leg pain, writing has allowed me a means of escape, though momentary. My desire is that, thru my poems, my son will always feel a special closeness to me, even when I can't be near.; [a.] Orange, TX

BERZOZA, ANTHONY

[b.] February 9, 1981; [ed.] I attend Lincoln High School in Los Angeles. The subject I like is JROTC. At this movement I am C/Staff Sgt.; [hon.] I have awards from U.S.C. Med-Cor Program, the fourth ROTC Region of training and Editor's Choice Award from The National Library of Poetry; [oth. writ.] I had one of my other poems published in the National Library of Poetry's "Voice Within"; [pers.] I try to do the best of what I can do. The poems I write are just the feelings I have inside.; [a.] Los Angeles, CA

BESCHONER, JUDY

[pen.] Bridges, Jude; [b.] July 16, 1956, Northwest, AR; [p.] Hubert and Mary Beschoner; [occ.] Cleaning Service; [oth. writ.] "Karen", "Bern", "Kali Ma", "Life Journeys", "Hello, Mr. Jones", and others; [pers.] In writing down my thoughts, I hope to let those people in my life know how much better they have made life for others. The world is a better place because they cared.; [a.] AR

BETTS, LYDIA

[b.] June 8, 1966, West Covina; [p.] Jesus and Lily Betts; [ch.] Joseph Jesus, Amanda Amelia; [memb.] Catechist at Church Parish - teaching pre-school children; [oth. writ.] Several unpublished poems contained in personal journal.; [pers.] "Special" thanks to the late Frank R. Guzman, my inspiration, my Guardian Angel.; [a.] La Puente, CA

BIERI, KRISTEN

[b.] June 4, 1981, St. Louis, MO; [ed.] Shrewsbury High School Student; [occ.] Student; [oth. writ.] Over 150 poems - unpublished; [pers.] You are your own.; [a.] Shrewsbury, MA

BILDERBACK, SHERI L.

[b.] October 25, 1967, Illinois; [p.] Joyce and Roger Bilderback; [ed.] Masters in Business Administration, University of Missouri - St. Louis, B.A. in Communications, Legal Institutions, Economics and Government, Magna Cum Laude, The American University; [occ.] Staff Vice President for Governmental Affairs, Home Builders Association of Greater St. Louis; [hon.] Phi Kappa Phi, Pi Sigma Alpha, Dean's List; [a.] Saint Louis, MO

BILLINGTON, WINIFRED

[b.] December 22, 1961, Hartford, CT; [p.] Gertha Billington; [ed.] Weaver High School, Capital Community Technical College, Eastern Conn. State Univ.; [occ.] Administrative Assistant; [memb.] Staff Sergeant in the Air National Guard 14 1/2 years; [hon.] Dean's List; [oth. writ.] Several poems shared and given to friends and family. This is my first published poem. It was time to take the chance. Thank you!; [pers.] "Taking is easy, earning is an honor". My high school motto still holds true today.; [a.] Hartford, CT

BILOTTI, GINA

[b.] January 5, 1965, New Jersey; [p.] Frances and Jim; [ed.] BS Electrical Engineering, MS Engineering; [occ.] Corporate Engineer; [a.] Parlin, NJ

BINDER, ANGELA

[b.] February 28, 1982, Cincinnatti; [p.] Craig and Felicia Binder; [ed.] I am currently a high school student; [oth. writ.] I have many other writings, but none of which have been published; [pers.] Love every person on this earth, even those who have done you wrong; that is the first step to true divinity; [a.] Williamsburg, OH

BISHOP, COURTNEY ELIZABETH

[b.] July 21, 1976, Southampton, NY; [p.] Christopher and Jeannie Bishop; [ed.] Southampton Public Schools, College of William and Mary; [hon.] National Merit Scholarship Program - Commended Student, National Hispania Scholarship Program. Honorable Mention National Honor Society; [oth. writ.] A few poems have been published in Beginnings.; [pers.] I believe my writings reflect the inner turmoil and mental illness I live with - thanks to the love of family and friends. For Kevin, Thanks to Emily and Vincent.; [a.] Southampton, NY

BLAIR, VICKI

[b.] November 16, 1968, Denver, CO; [p.] Rodger and Joan Stewart; [m.] Harold F. Blair Jr., June 1, 1990; [ch.] Justin Connor Blair; [occ.] Banking; [hon.] Arts Awards for my Photography; [oth. writ.] Contained in Personal Journal.; [pers.] I have been influenced by the gothic Novels and poets, especially Edgar Allen Poe. Also personal experiences of love and pain, which I believe exist together throughout life.; [a.] Denver, CO

BLANTON, FAYE
[b.] February 27, 1957, Shelby, NC; [p.] Mr. and Mrs. William C. Hoyle; [m.] Divorced; [ch.] Two; [ed.] 9th GED; [occ.] Housewife; [oth. writ.] Always Like A Charm, Walls of Steel, Rose Petal; [pers.] I love drawing, poetry, collecting clowns, gardening, reading. I was influenced by my dear best friend Barbara Richard, this lady has helped me through some bad times, she was there when I needed someone the most and she still stands beside me no matter what.; [a.] Mooresville, NC

BOCCIA, APRIL S.
[pen.] Sunny; [b.] April 25, 1976, Brooklyn, NY; [p.] Myra and Marcello Boccia; [ed.] High School, 1st yr. of College of Brooklyn Colleges, transferred to Hostra University to complete degree; [occ.] Lifeguard and Swimming Instructor - full time student; [memb.] Lawrence High School Swimming Team Captain 1993-1994, Red Cross Club, Italian Honor Society; [hon.] Swimming - varsity in High School, Italian Honor Society Swimming Medals and Brooklyn College, Publication of another poem in Hofstra's Pont Magazine; [oth. writ.] Poems published in school newspapers and magazines from high school on to college, own personal collection of poems and original song lyrics.; [pers.] My poems and writings come straight from my heart, what I feel, what I see, what I've experienced in my past and what I'm yet to experience in my future, I have been greatly influenced by Douglas Wadekauper (my boyfriend who passed away on Dec. 26, 1995) I will love him forever; [a.] Hempstead, NY

BOGGS, LISA RENEE
[b.] July 31, 1958, Sylacauga, AL; [p.] James Boggs and Elizabeth Boggs; [ed.] Auburn University; [occ.] Social Worker State of Alabama - DHR; [hon.] Social Service Award for Excellence - 1994; [oth. writ.] I can currently working on several new poems. I would like to also write short stories in the future.; [pers.] My poetry is written because of my love for Jesus Christ. It is my hope that the readers of my poetry will fall in love with Him too.; [a.] Alexander City, AL

BOHLIN, CURTIS
[pen.] C. J. Bohlin; [b.] April 1, 1945, Michigan City, IN; [p.] John Bohlin, Irene Bohlin; [ed.] Purdue University, University of Las Vega (UNLV); [occ.] Host Caesars Palace, Las Vegas, NV; [a.] Las Vegas, NV

BOLTON, SACHA
[b.] March 10, 1972, Jamaica; [p.] Neville Bolton and Beverly Bolton; [ed.] I graduated from Cardinal Gibbons High School in 1989. I graduated from Palm Beach Community College in 1994. I have an associates degree in arts and accounting.; [oth. writ.] In addition to Dream Lover, I have written fifteen other poems that I hope will be published one day.; [pers.] I have always wanted to write poems and children's stories and my family has always supported any artistic endeavor I have chosen to undertake.; [a.] Coral Springs, FL

BORGER, GERALDINE
[b.] September 2, 1942, Clarence, PA; [p.] Mr. and Mrs. Frank J. Waxmunsky Sr.; [m.] Stanley W. Borger, September 19, 1964; [ch.] Vonda, Beth Ann, Doyle, LeAnn; [ed.] Graduate of Bald Eagle Area HS, Wingate, PA/ Attended Classes at Penn State Univ and Centre County Vo Tech School in Pleasant Gap, PA; [occ.] Housewife; [memb.] Mountain top Ambulance Club; [hon.] Cub Scout Den Mother Award, School Newspaper Editorial Award, School Library Award, Past Pres and V Pres of Snow Shoe PTA, Church School Teacher, Asst Pianist, Official Board Member of CMA Church in Snow Shoe, PA; [oth. writ.] Various poems to be published in hard back books for various publishers. Several Church bulletins and our local Church newsletter have contained my poems. Copies of some of poems were placed in Mt. Top Historical Bldg, one printed in a trucking mag.; [pers.] You will note the love of God and the beauty and joy of nature expressed through most of my writings and poetry. Parents, family and friends have been very influential in my writings.; [a.] Snow Shoe, PA

BOSLEY, LUCINDA J.
[pen.] Cindy; [b.] May 19, 1947, Caribou, ME; [p.] Dorothy and Raymond Barnes; [m.] Dennis L. Bosley Sr., March 17, 1973; [ch.] Lee - 27, Kristy - 26, Shannon - 21; [ed.] High School, Cosmetology School; [occ.] Homemaker; [oth. writ.] Wrote a joke poem for my brother's fortieth birthday, wrote poem that followed my great aunt's life for her eighty fifth birthday.; [a.] Washburn, ME

BOSTIC, TERRENCE LEBRONE
[pen.] Terrence Bastia; [b.] June 24, 1979, Chattanooga, TN; [p.] Jennifer Duckettt, N. Kenneth Bostic; [ed.] Elementary, Calvin Donaldson, Middle School, Alton Park, High School, H.S.A.T.; [occ.] Student; [memb.] V.I.C.A., National Poetry Society, F.B.L.A.; [hon.] Valentine Poetry, Contest, 1994-95, Numerous School Awards; [oth. writ.] Cata., she came to me., A special kind of Rose, and numerous others waiting to be published.; [pers.] Keep your head up even if the storm clouds get heavy. There's still a sun, even though it's not visible.; [a.] Chattanooga, TN

BOWDEN, ANGELA H.
[pen.] Angie; [b.] May 3, 1963, Baltimore, MD; [p.] Nellie H. Hicks; [m.] Terrence Bowden, June 22, 1991; [ch.] Tarilyn Denae and Terrence Jr.; [ed.] J.F. Webb High School, UNC - Greensboro, North Carolina Central University; [occ.] Second grade teacher, Butner - Stem, Elementary, Butner, N.C.; [memb.] NCAE; [hon.] Girl's State Nominee; [pers.] I love to stress the joy of inspiring students through my poems. I have written mostly poems which are school - related; [a.] Oxford, NC

BOYER, PATRICIA
[b.] October 12, 1925, Weaverville, NC; [p.] William Malcolm and Katherine Waters; [m.] Clyde Boyer, June 28, 1946; [ch.] John Gregory, Abigail, Judd Meredith and Clyde Merrill Boyer; [ed.] Life itself has been the best teacher.; [occ.] Poet, historian, flower gardener, grandmother; [oth. writ.] Various poems including "The Girl from Sacramento", "The Mountain Man", "The Lunchword", short stories including "Eulalie's Dinner", and a historical novel entitled "Kate and the end of the Modoc War".; [pers.] The relativity of all things is the basis from which I work and draw my inspiration.; [a.] Tulelake, CA

BOYLES, ANN
[b.] August 25, 1931, Clarksville, TN; [p.] Pat and Maggie William; [m.] Earl Boyles Sr. (Deceased); [ch.] Maggie Read and Earl Boylcs; [cd.] Central High School, 1 year Peabody College in Nashville, TN; [occ.] Credit Information Center - Nashville, TN; [oth. writ.] 1 Poem published in "Poetic Voices in America."; [a.] Nashville, TN

BRADBURY, MELISSA ALISON
[b.] January 13, 1983, Holland, PA; [p.] Edward A. and Margaret B. Bradbury; [ed.] Eighth grade student of Holland Junior High School; [occ.] 8th Grade student at Holland Junior High School; [memb.] Enhanced English Class at School, Wind Dance Acres Riding Club (horseback riding - I love to ride "Shahna, my small white Arabian mare"); [oth. writ.] I write many poems about people's feelings and my own especially when feeling lonely or sad. The style of my writing is brief and to the point but creates a lasting mental picture.; [pers.] My poetry focuses on how intense situations such as love or war make individuals feel isolated and alone. I love animals because they accept people as they are.; [a.] Holland, PA

BRADFORD, BELINDA
[b.] October 9, 1964, Sheffield, AL; [p.] Sam Wilkinson, Hazle Wilkinson; [m.] Delane Bradford, May 12, 1988; [ch.] Chasity, Kristin and Bradly; [ed.] Colbert County High; [occ.] Housewife and Mother; [a.] Town Creek, AL

BRADSHAW, DUSTIN P.
[b.] June 6, 1982, Fresno, CA; [p.] Gregory and Terri Bradshaw; [ed.] Am currently a "G.A.T.E." student at Hoover High School in Fresno, CA; [memb.] Drama Club at Hoover High School, Fresno, CA; [hon.] Presidential Academic Fitness Award, various School Commendations including Honor Roll; [oth. writ.] Working on a fantasy novel and possible sequels; [pers.] I really enjoy writing as a favorite past time. It is very simply, fun.; [a.] Fresno, CA

BRAMLEY, SARAH
[b.] 1963, England; [pers.] The only thing a woman can do married which she cannot do single is get a divorce.; [a.] Menlo Park, CA

BREITE, MRS. NORMA
[b.] New York; [p.] Mr. and Mrs. Harry Dodes; [ch.] Two; [ed.] B.A. from Queens College (NY) Phi Beta Kappa, Master of Arts in Teaching English - Harvard University (Mass.); [occ.] Teacher of English and Social Studies, Secondary School level; [hon.] Phi Beta Kappa many community awards; [oth. writ.] I love to write poetry and other written art forms, including book reviews.

BRENNAN, J. PAUL
[pen.] Thomas McDara, Ben Pullen; [b.] December 28, 1939, Brooklyn, NY; [p.] J. Paul Brennan and Frances Bailey; [m.] Patricia Brennan, December 20, 1973; [ch.] Ciaran Pol, Aedin Patricia; [ed.] Aquinas Institute, St. John Fisher College (A.B. 1974); [occ.] Clerk, Appellate Division 4th Dept., Rochester, NY; [memb.] Rochester Bibliophile Society, Radio Club, Cornette Owners Club; [pers.] The lyrical, often Ironic Imagery of Irish Poetry, appeals To me. Yeats, Kavanagh, Heaney and now, socially vocal female voices extend the range and power of poetical thinking.; [a.] Rochester, NY

BREWER, CYNTHIA HUX
[b.] November 2, 1964, Roanoke Rapids, NC; [p.] Rochella Hux, Percy Hux; [ch.] Angelica D. Perez; [ed.] Associate Degree in Nursing; [occ.] Registered Nurse at Dialysis Center; [memb.] Trinity Penecostal Holiness Church, Halifax Community College, Nurses Alumni Association; [hon.] Phi Theta Kappa. Received Nurse Scholars Scholarship from the State of N.C., Dean's List, President's List; [pers.] Influenced to write poem when performing Clinicals for nursing school in the nursery.

The pre-term cocaine addicted infant grabbed my heart and wouldn't let go. The poem is for her and others like her.; [a.] Roanoke Rapids, NC

BREWSTER, RONNIE R.
[pen.] Ronnie R. Brewster; [b.] January 24, 1966, Michigan; [p.] James and Maxine Brewster; [m.] Ellen Ann Pollard, February 24, 1996; [ed.] High School Graduate, Madison High, Some College, Church Specs Howard School of Broadcasting; [occ.] Engineer WXON - TV - 20; [oth. writ.] Not yet.; [pers.] Losing someone you love can have a devastating, heartbreaking effect on your life forever. I thank God for guiding and directing me in the path of inspiration and empowerment.; [a.] Madison Heights, MI

BRIGGS, KERRY LYNN
[b.] September 21, 1953, Tulsa, OK; [p.] Jimmie and Ruby War; [ch.] Charles Dale Briggs; [occ.] Avon, since May 1988; [pers.] I enjoy writing in a variety of styles and subjects, and praise God for the gift. The April 19, 1995, bombing of the Alfred P. Murrow Federal building, that killed 168 persons, left more than scars on our City, inspiring over a dozen poems of my own. I'll never view a skyline, yellow rental truck or photos of bombed buildings with the same perspective. I take pride in my community for reminding others how to grieve with grace. I humbly thank he world for responding to our need.; [a.] Midwest City, OK

BRITO, MA. AMABEL ANDAL
[b.] June 28, 1955, Philippines; [p.] Abelardo Andal, Amada Contreras; [m.] Pemco L. Brito, June 28, 1980; [ch.] Pemco James, Mark Darren, Robert Anthony, Lorraine Therese; [ed.] B.S. Foreign Service, University of the Philippines; [occ.] Full-time housewife; [memb.] Xi Omega Lambda Sorority, UPCM, Brotherhood of Christian Businessmen and Professionals; [pers.] Believe it or not, I see poetry everywhere, from the daintiest of roses, to the most obscure poses, there I go again...; [a.] Tamuning, GU

BROOKS, MEGAN R.
[b.] July 26, 1983, Mt. Pleasant, MI; [p.] Karen L. Brooks and Teddy L. Cochran; [pers.] Poems sing to a beat that is always inside of you. The beat of your heart. The same beat that makes you dream, gives you courage, lets you love, and gives you life.; [a.] Mount Pleasant, MI

BROOKS, WANDA
[b.] November 23, 1950, Roswell, NM; [p.] Walter and Rose Hogan (Porter); [m.] Donald Brooks, November 1, 1969; [ch.] Kimberly King, Regina Johnson; [ed.] Lake Arthur High, Lake Arthur New Mexico, ENMU - Roswell, New Mexico; [occ.] Housewife; [oth. writ.] Few articles written for Wolforth Newspaper in Wolforth, Texas, first time published for my poetry.; [pers.] I enjoy writing special poetry for my family and friends to help in the remembrance of joyful and sad occasions.; [a.] Roswell, NM

BROWN, CYRUS
[b.] January 27, 1981, Visalia, CA; [p.] Ian and Sue Brown; [ed.] Exeter Union High; [occ.] Student; [hon.] I have the honor of having wonderful friends and family; [pers.] I try to show people that being successful is not always the best thing to be. Respect the Earth.; [a.] Three Rivers, CA

BROWN, GENEVA P.
[b.] January 24, 1919, Honey Grove, TX; [p.] Dewey R. Camp, Norman L. Camp (Step Father); [m.] Clay C. Brown, November 16, 1940; [ch.] Paula Flyna, Susan Brown, Charles and Richard Brown; [ed.] Registered Nurse; [occ.] Retired; [oth. writ.] The Collected Works of Geneva Brown.; [pers.] I like to use words that will act upon an imagination to project a certain image that will reflect eternal beauty and wisdom.; [a.] Richardson, TX

BROWN, HELEN E.
[b.] January 24, 1919, Dighton, MA; [p.] Clarence and Clara Smith; [m.] Herbert N. Brown, June 11, 1942; [ch.] David, Janice, Fred, Peter, Ruth; [ed.] Business College Graduate: 1936 High Honors Taunton, MA; [occ.] Homemaker; [memb.] AARP, Cat lovers of America, United Church of Christ, Dover Cooperative Ministries Council; [hon.] Certificate of Merit from the National Education Association. (I did school volunteer work for several years); [oth. writ.] Several poems which I call poems of "Comfort and Encouragement." I share them with friends and others I meet who are troubled in one way or other, never published.; [pers.] My faith is the anchor of my life, and I try to communicate the Lord's love for each of us in my poems.; [a.] Dover, NH

BROWN, HILDRED
[pen.] Hildred Valena Naomi Tircuit Brown, "Gamma" [b.] July 6, 1898, Shreveport, LA; [p.] Rev. Joseph A. and Marie Tircuit; [m.] Leonard L. Brown, Sr. (deceased), November 22, 1932; [ch.] Leonard, Jr. (deceased), Lorraine Brown James; [ed.] B.A. Degree, Dillard University; [occ.] Retired Teacher, New Orleans Public Schools, New Orleans, LA; [memb.] Mount Zion United Methodist Church, Harmony Chapter #16 OES, Martha Grand Chapter, OES; [hon.] Sercie-Order of EAstern Star; [pers.] Live by The Ten Commandments; [a.] New Orleans, LA

BROWN, JAMIE
[pen.] J. S. Brown; [b.] May 10, 1974, Perkasie, PA; [p.] Roy and Sandra Brown; [m.] Ruth L. Brown, August 19, 1996; [ed.] Senior at Liberty Univ.; [occ.] Student; [oth. writ.] The Plow, Dying, My Garden, The Understanding, Sprinting From The Dark, Beneath The Tree, The Night Of The World Cafe; [pers.] My life has been greatly influenced by Plato, Ovid, Sophocles, Sappho and Rumi. The messages behind my poems discuss the blessed the damned and the quest of one to gain an understanding of the supernatural.; [a.] Lynchburg, VA

BROWN, LEON D.
[pen.] L. D. Brown; [b.] November 29, 1957, New Haven, CT; [p.] Jeanette and Charles Brown; [ed.] Wilbur Cross High School, New Haven Regional Training Academy; [occ.] Firefighter, EMT-D; [memb.] New Haven Firebird Society, I.A.B.P.F.F. Local 825, I.A.F.F; [hon.] Fire Emergency Rescue Unit Citations; [oth. writ.] This Heart, Touch Not, Autumn Breeze, Call, My Valentine; [a.] New Haven, CT

BROWN, SHEILA L.
[pen.] Sheila Brown; [b.] November 13, 1955, Oneida, NY; [p.] Donald R. Hull and C. Jeanne Felix Hull; [m.] Andrew James Brown, August 19, 1974; [ch.] Abram Jennings, Lesley Anne and Jordan Lee Ann; [ed.] Cazenovia Central School; [occ.] Window Clerk U.S. Postal Service; [memb.] A.P.W.U. and J.C.C.L.D.S.; [hon.] Regents Diploma; [oth. writ.] A collection of poems compiled from twenty years; [pers.] My writings are written from feelings that have become part of me.; [a.] Cazenovia, NY

BROWN, STEVE
[pen.] Steve Brown; [b.] May 25, 1951, Evansville, IN; [p.] Mr. and Mrs. Charles V. Brown (Father Deceased); [m.] Brenda Brown (Deceased), September 5, 1982; [ch.] Ashley Brown; [ed.] D. W. Daniel High, Central, SC, 1970; [occ.] Tele-Tech Ups Customer Service, Greenville, SC; [memb.] Past V.P. SC Vietnam Era Veterans Assoc., Past - Captain on Rescue Unit in Central, SC; [pers.] I like writing whatever thoughts come to my mind. I have been greatly inspired to write since meeting Girl Friend, Dien Smith, to whom I owe a lot. And by my daughter, Ashley, but I thank God for giving me the talent to write.; [a.] Greer, SC

BROY SR., JAMES
[pen.] James Pierre Broy; [b.] June 19, 1948, Balto, MD; [p.] Ida Cary; [ch.] J. J. Torrey, Raymond; [pers.] Time is too fast to allow it pass. Stop and see what life is to be; [a.] Reisterstown, MD

BRUCE, ROBERT F.
[b.] March 12, 1944, Milford, MA; [p.] John J. and Agnes A. Bruce; [m.] Marie A. Bruce, November 4, 1967; [ch.] Anne M. and Amanda J.; [ed.] Milford, MA H.S.; [occ.] Safety Mgr/Emt, PSC, Silver Spring Citrus, Howey-in-the-Hills, Fl; [a.] Mount Dora, FL

BRUCE, TERRI
[b.] June 14, 1969, Oklahoma City; [p.] Terry Bruce and Sue Bruce; [ed.] Carl Albert High School, East Central University, Oklahoma State University - OKC; [occ.] Administrative Assistant at Southwestern Bell Mobile Systems; [hon.] President's Scholarship, Provost's List of Distinguished Part-time Students, Who's Who Among American High School Students; [pers.] We often forget who we are and how we all began. I owe much to my parents and I love them with all of my heart. All children should be as lucky as I have been all of my life. Thank you.; [a.] Midwest City, OK

BRYANT, CRYSTAL
[pen.] Kera; [b.] September 7, 1971, Kettering, OH; [p.] Shirley and Jim (Deceased) Richardson; [m.] Rev. James Christopher Bryant, July 7, 1995; [memb.] Barnes Chapel UMC, Vacation Bible School Chair, Safe Children Foundation Volunteer; [hon.] American Poetry Assoc., Certificate of Merit, Silver Poet Award and Golden Poet Award; [oth. writ.] Childhood Memories published by the American Poetry Assoc.; [pers.] It is my desire to glorify Jesus by sharing feelings and experiences with others through my writings.; [a.] Owensboro, KY

BRYANT, HELEN M.
[b.] Washington, DC; [m.] Elton Lee Bryant; [ch.] Elton Lee, - John William; [ed.] Business High; [occ.] Retired - Dept. of Defense; [memb.] NARFE - AARP; [oth. writ.] poems about my family and friends at birthdays and at work.; [pers.] I strive to reflect the nice things to remember in life.; [a.] Temple Hills, MD

BUCHANAN, ELIZABETH
[pen.] Izzy; [b.] March 14, 1981, Parkersburg, WV; [p.] Beth and Dannie Cunningham; [ed.] 10th grade US yrs. old at Parkersburg Christian School; [hon.] Honor Roll at School; [oth. writ.] I have many poems that have not been submitted to be published.; [pers.] I want my poems to touch people's hearts. "For the love of a brother." Dedicated to: Matthew Buchanan.; [a.] Belleville, WV

BUGHER, SANDRA
[pen.] Sandi; [b.] June 9, 1968, Las Vegas, NV; [p.] Diana and Thomas Beeler; [m.] Robert Bugher, June 5,

1987; [ch.] Cody Bugher; [ed.] Rancho High School; [pers.] I feel that writing is really a relief from all the pressures of the world today and allows me to express my moods and feelings of things and people.; [a.] Las Vegas, NV

BUNCH, MARY FRANCES

[b.] August 7, 1969, Imboden, AR; [p.] Nannie Propes Gilliland, Gilbert; [m.] Widow; [ch.] Peggy Stroup, Francis Stroup, Susan Stroup, Becky Bunch, Bill Bunch; [ed.] Senatobia MS High, Drauchars Business College, some college; [occ.] Retired Jr. Accountant; [oth. writ.] Short stories; [pers.] Without our own personal and views, we cannot be true in our writings. I must truly feel what I write.; [a.] Yazoo City, MS

BURDINE, ELI RICHARD

[pers.] Our lives are governed by the day and the night. We are both body and soul. I hope through the power of writing to express that which cannot be seen.

BURGER, IVORA

[pen.] Ivora Burger; [b.] October 3, 1926, Waukegan, IL; [p.] Elmer and Blanche Evans; [m.] Helmuth Burger, October 15, 1945; [ch.] Sandra Waggoner Burger, Darrel Burger and Sheree Burger; [ed.] Grade School and High School; [occ.] Housewife, mother, Grandmother and great grandmother; [memb.] I am a member of God Lutheran Church - We were also members of Laborers for Christ Who built mission churches in the U.S.A. we were part of this for 10 years; [hon.] My rewards came from the love of Christian friends and doing for others - we have plaques from all of the churches where we helped build onto or added a new sanctuary and these are priceless to us.; [oth. writ.] My childhood story for my children and a family History of my husband's mother and father - poems written to go with gifts, a memory poem for my daughter in law whose mother died of cancer - several plays for our church.; [pers.] I feel that the Lord guides me and writing is a joy for me. I like to read a lot and this helps me grow, so I am able to discuss many subjects with high school education that my college graduates in my family can.; [a.] Paris, TX

BURKE, CHARLOTTE

[b.] January 25, 1924, Astoria, NY; [p.] Charlotte and Thomas Winkel; [m.] Jerome, June 28, 1947; [ch.] John, Robert, Paul, Michael, Thomas, Rosemary; [ed.] Bryant High School; [occ.] Retired; [memb.] Notre Dame Choir, Herrick's Theater Group; [hon.] New York University "Goodwife" Award; [oth. writ.] Several poems published in Susquehanna County transcript, previous volumes of National Library of Poetry and Sparrowgrass poetry forum.; [pers.] I am inspired by scenery and dreams in creating my poetry.; [a.] New Hyde Park, NY

BURKE, MELINDA WALKER

[b.] March 4, 1966, Birmingham, AL; [m.] Abraham V. Burke, October 17, 1988; [ch.] Gary, Tom, Richard, Christopher, Ebony; [ed.] Boys and Girls High School, Bklyn, NY; [occ.] Mis/Administrative Assistant for Non-profit Organization; [pers.] "The only change that can come in your life, is a change made by you".; [a.] Brooklyn, NY

BURNS, EBONIQUE

[b.] February 21, 1973, Louisville, KY:; [p.] Ms. Janice D. Dishman, Mr. Bernard Dishman; [m.] Charles L. Burns, May 27, 1994; [ch.] Charles III L. Burns; [ed.] Graduate of DuPont Manual Magnet High School in Math, Science and Technology, University of KY - Major: Arts Administration, Minor: Dance; [occ.] Jamken Management, Artist Manger (Title); [pers.] "For with the heart man believeth unto righteousness, and with the mouth confession is made unto salvation". (Romans 10:10) "And all things, whatsoever ye shall ask in prayer, believing, ye shall receive". (Matthew 21:22).; [a.] Cincinnati, OH

BURNS, LUCILLE

[b.] November 23, 1939, Yonkers, NY; [p.] Antoinette and Nicholas De Santis; [m.] Charles Francis Burns, August 14, 1965; [ch.] Francis Anthony, Joseph Michael, Marianne Elizabeth; [ed.] Hunter College of the City University of N.Y.; [occ.] Substitute Teacher; [a.] La Quinta, CA

BURRIS, LOIS

[b.] January 6, 1936, Blackwell, OK; [p.] Ethyl and Dale Cline; [m.] Floyd Burris, June 5, 1953; [ch.] Wayne and Dennis Burris, Tracey Blunk; [ed.] 11th grade; [occ.] Deceased; [memb.] Larry Jones "Feed The Children"; [pers.] Her inspiration came from God and her family.; [a.] Enid, OK

BURTON, COREY

[b.] September 27, 1985, Honolulu, HI; [p.] Richard and Margaret Burton; [ed.] 5th Grade Moraine Meadows Elementary; [memb.] Power Ranger Fan Club, Thrills and Chills "Goose Bumps"; [hon.] 4th grade honor roll, 5th grade graduation trophy; [pers.] My motto is "Never stop until your done."; [a.] Kettering, OH

BUTLER, CARL

[pen.] Karl Fötner; [b.] October 10, 1960, Junction City, KS; [p.] Anneliese Fötner; [ch.] Carl Jr., Tanisha, Marquieta, Calvin and Tamara; [occ.] Business Manager, Denver, Colorado; [oth. writ.] Songs, many poems of romance.; [pers.] I try to accomplish a sense of identify ability so others may relate to the words, with their own experience. Poems of love will surely live on.; [a.] Aurora, CO

BUTLER, VALERIE Y.

[pen.] Maui Flowers; [b.] October 29, 1966, Deland, FL; [p.] Pearl Wright; [m.] David A. Butler, December 3, 1995; [ch.] Adrienne J. 7 yrs. and Alexandria J. 8 months; [ed.] Wenonah High School (B'ham, AL), Pala Alto College (S.A., TX); [occ.] U.S. Air Force; [memb.] Carlos Coon PTA, Air Force Sergeant Association, American Red Cross (CRR); [hon.] Who's Who Among American High School Students; [oth. writ.] Several unpublished poems; [pers.] If it's meant to be, it is up to me!; [a.] San Antonio, TX

BUTTREY, DAVID SCOTT

[pen.] David P. Fisch; [b.] February 11, 1980, Franklin, TN; [p.] Roger and Elaine Buttrey; [ed.] Junior in High School; [occ.] Musician - Industrial Band called Filth (One Man Band); [oth. writ.] Author of book of poems Naked, Dazed, and Bleeding. In need of publication. Album (Industrial) New Wave Martyr Vol. 1-A Bullet for Jesus in need of label.; [pers.] I hope to show the world the brighter side of hatred and unpleasantness, for we have spent every moment we're allowed smiling at the world and its Christian morals. It's time we expressed our true feelings. The world is not wonderful.; [a.] Franklin, TN

CADE, AL

[b.] October 8, 1953, Louisiana; [p.] Charlie and Helen Cade; [m.] Paula, April 15, 1994; [ch.] Heather, Timothy, Nathan, Toby, Tammy; [ed.] High School; [occ.] Self Employed; [oth. writ.] Numerous other poems and songs, tributes to important people in my life; [pers.] My father passed away May 12, 1996 and until his death I had not written any poetry. I wrote the poem about Alzhiemers in memory of him and since that day the words just seem to spill out.; [a.] Conroe, TX

CALDWELL, SHANNON

[b.] April 1, 1979, Tallahassee, FL; [p.] Margie Hinson and Rex Caldwell; [ed.] Will graduate Mandarin High School, June 1997; [occ.] Full time student; [memb.] Deermeadows Baptist Church; [pers.] "Always be true to oneself."; [a.] Jacksonville, FL

CALITIS, IVY MARIE A. MENDOZA

[b.] January 24, 1972, Philippines; [p.] Lina Alcantara and Irineo Mendoza; [m.] Michael Calitis, May 2, 1996; [ed.] De La Salle University - Aguinaldo; [occ.] Registered Nurse; [hon.] Class 1992, Florence Nightingale Award, Leadership Award, Honorable Mention; [a.] Antioch, CA

CAMARA, PERLA D.

[pen.] Pearl Chambers; [b.] January 5, 1944, La Carlota City, Philippines; [p.] Melquiades Dioquino (Deceased), Loreto Decierto; [m.] Carmelo M. Camara Jr., April 20, 1995; [ed.] BSE Education, MA Education, LLB, High School - Holy Rosary Academy, Sipalan, Neg. Occ. University of Negros Occ. - Recoletos Bacolod City, Philippines, College - West Visayas State College - Ilo Ilo City Philippines University of Negros Occ. Recoletos, Bachelor of Science in Education; [occ.] Caregiver or Nursing Assistant; [memb.] American Heart Association, American Legion Auxiliary - Philippine Chapter - Unit 27, Boy Scouts of the Philippines; [hon.] High school scholar, third year college scholar, Philipino Editor, "The Normalite", College Organ WVSC - Ilo Ilo City, Philippines, Sole Contributor of Articles in Spanish to our College Organ (Mostly Poetry); [oth. writ.] Poems in native language - Filipino, English and Spanish were published in College Organs and in local newspaper.; [pers.] I want to touch the human heart and soul thru poetry. I was inspired to write poems by the great poets especially Shakespeare, John Milton, Omar Khayyam, Gibran and Dr. Jose Rizal, National Hero - Philippines; [a.] Los Angeles, CA

CAMERON, JOE

[pen.] Cam; [b.] September 13, 1926, Bronx, NY; [ch.] 2 and 3 grandchildren; [occ.] Artist; [oth. writ.] Many other short poems! Bird Brained, Treacle, Though, Fling, Night Women, Swing Me Dad, Night Crash, All In A Day's Work, Words A Bygone Ago, Imminence Postponed, For A Limited Time Only, Stood Up, State; [pers.] The Jangle of Jazz by Joe Cameron December 12, 1995 "We reach for sleeps high bar and swing a poems rhythm and reason hoping dreams activity will order our movements when we awaken to the Jangle."; [a.] Brookline, MA

CAMP, SUZANNE S.

[pen.] Suzy Camp; [b.] October 29, 1931, Detroit, MI; [p.] David and Mary Camp; [ch.] Jeffrey Scott, Kathy Lynne, Daniel Edward, Jonathan James; [ed.] Andrews School for Girls, (H.S), Wayne State University (B.S), Univ. of Illinois (M.S.W.); [occ.] Psychotherapist, private practical (Clinical Social Work); [memb.] NASW, Assoc. of Transpersonal Psychology, Unitarian - Universalist Fellowship of So. MD., Woodburn Hill Farm Community, IONS; [hon.] Tri-County Social Worker of the Year, 1982 (nominee for MD. Social Worker, of the year) Co-Founder Hospice of St. Mary's, Co founder, UUFSM (Unitarian Fellowship of So. MD.), Diplomate in Clinical Social Work.; [oth. writ.] Handbook for the Community Professional, Charles C. Thomas, 1972 (Co-Author, former name "Small"), poems etc., published in small private anthologies; [pers.] I am writing a creative non-fiction book about my personal and professional journey vis-a-vis modern cultural archetypes, especially the "False Memory" Debate. I plan to include my poetry in that book. I'm searching for "Truth of the End of Pen".; [a.] Mechanicsville, MD

CAMPBELL, BETTY JEAN
[b.] February 26, 1949, Brazos County; [p.] Mrs. Alberta Stauton; [m.] Bob James Campbell; [ch.] 5 boys: Anthony, Bob Jr., JJ, Bone, Sam, 3 girls: CC, Tina, Grace; [ed.] B. T. Washington Elementary, Neal Junior High, Bryan, Tex., Marion Anderson Elem. and High Sch. Madisonville, Tex., Computer Operating and Programming Competency Cert., from Blinn College, Graduate of Institute of Children and Teenagers Literature, Rhema Bible School. I wrote a play for Neal Junior High in 1961-62 entitled, "The Party." It was selected, cast, and staged.; [occ.] Wife, Mother, Student and Writer; [hon.] Several awards from New Jerusalem House of Prayer, Members, for religious work, Domestic and Custodian Supervisor Award, Editors Award from National Library of Poetry, two articles in the Bryan Daily Eagle on my religious work. A poem published in Forever and a Day, by National Library of Poetry.; [oth. writ.] Personal Property: I've written and composed 60 songs and 16 poems.; [pers.] Learning is very important to me, and through the containing words of great writers, I conquered fear and ignorance concerning a lot in my life. With compelling activeness I had a great animosity and very little tolerance for suffering and pain, on the contrary, neither vanished. In the quiet of my ignorance, and as a victim of needless suffering and pain, I learned an appreciation for both. For they had much to teach this seeker: Ignorance is a type of death also. Through my writings my much needed hope is: To share life the way I see it - with the seeker, while shedding some light on death's emissaries: Needless pain, suffering, and ignorance. For that which is not known can hurt. Thanks to all that supports: Be ignorance no more.; [a.] Bryan, TX

CAMPBELL, CHOU H.
[pen.] C. C. Persohn (French); [b.] April 12, 1967, Taiwan; [p.] Karl H. Parson Jr. and Happy Pierce; [m.] Jeff A. Campbell, October 20, 1990; [ed.] Belleville Township High School, East, Belleville Area College; [occ.] Server, Hooters, Union Station, St. Louis, MO; [memb.] First Christian Volley Ball Team; [hon.] Superior Merit Speaker Award, 4 years first place Chorus Award, Track Award, #1000 Scholarship to Hickey College from Junior Miss Pageant, Art Awards; [oth. writ.] I have several poems I have written but, never published; [pers.] I look for the goodness in people and always overlook the bad. Life is too short to look at the negativity in others. Life is what you make of it. So, make your own dreams come true.; [a.] Collinsville, IL

CAMPBELL, MELANIE L.
[b.] June 5, 1975, Cincinnati, OH; [p.] Deborah Wheeler, Herbert Wheeler; [m.] Jason R. Campbell, June 17, 1996; [ed.] Colerain High School; [occ.] Recovery Specialist, General Revenue Corporation, Cincinnati, OH; [oth. writ.] Several poems published in school publications and two poems in the McGuffey writer; [pers.] I try to fully express my personal feelings and experiences in my work. My goal is to have those who read my poetry actually feel what I have written.; [a.] Fairfield, OH

CAMPBELL, MR. MARK C.
[b.] June 27, 1958, Los Angeles; [p.] Wanda Campbell and William; [ch.] Ebony and Shalonda; [ed.] Fremont High School, Whitter College; [occ.] Transportation Engineer; [oth. writ.] A book of poems entitled, "Above The Volcano Are Music And Time"; [pers.] For my daughters I open a tiny window through which they may view their father's love with an open heart. And in each poem lies several unforgettable conversations, instances of revelation, laughing and not a few tears shed by all. I am from this world, still I live in a foreign ocean where a forest is the footpath to my front door.; [a.] Pasadena, CA

CAPE, LEROY
[b.] September 8, 1957, Bridgeport; [p.] Mazie Cape; [ed.] Bridgeport High School and Self Taught Artist; [occ.] Self Talk Artist; [memb.] Order of Eagles, Bridgeport, NE, West Nebraska Arts Center; [oth. writ.] Snow Covered Red Rose; [a.] Bridgeport, NE

CAPONE, MERRILLYN
[b.] January 26, 1938, Ballston Spa, NY; [p.] Myron and Permelia (Mundell) Weaver; [m.] Francis (Dicey) Capone, July 27, 1963; [ch.] Robert James Capone; [ed.] Ballston Spa Senior High; [occ.] Retired; [memb.] Mati Club Brookside Museum Tues and Thurs Bowling League; [oth. writ.] Several Poems published in local (weekly) newspaper: "Our 35th President", "Robert Kennedy", "Heart Full Of Sadness", "Wurster Boys", John John Kennedy", "My Family", "My Love For You".; [pers.] I only write what the Lord gives me the inspiration for.; [a.] Ballston Spa, NY

CAPPS, BARBARA MCCALL
[pen.] Barbara McCall Capps; [b.] July 20, 1954, Chapel Hill, NC; [p.] Clarence McCall, Louise Alexander; [m.] Jimmy Capps, July 28, 1979; [ch.] Brittainee Capps, Bryce Capps; [ed.] Orange High, Central Carolina Community College; [occ.] Attending School - Substance Abuse Counselor; [oth. writ.] I have an assortment of poems I have written. In the process of putting together a book.; [pers.] I started writing poems about 2 yrs. ago. I realized it was great therapy to put my feelings on paper. I express my deepest feelings in my poems. I write alot about my childhood.; [a.] Chapel Hill, NC

CAPPS, GLENDA
[pen.] Connor Glen; [b.] August 13, 1964, Ozona, TX; [ch.] Daughter - Morgan; [pers.] Influenced by: J. Morrison, T. Reznor, Poppy Z. Brite, Carmen and Necie.; [a.] Ozona, TX

CARDENAS, MELISSA
[pen.] Julio Cardenas; [b.] July 27, 1980, New York; [p.] Julio and Luz Cardenas; [ed.] Our Lady of Lourdes and Mother Cabrini High School; [occ.] I am a student and wanting to become a lawyer in the future.; [hon.] Student of the Month, Effort Awards, Achievement Awards.; [oth. writ.] I've never had my poem published, this is my first time.; [pers.] I've tried to express my emotions with love, honesty, and truth. I've been influenced by my teachers, parents, and friends.; [a.] New York, NY

CARLSON, KRISTINA MARIE
[b.] August 26, 1980, Renton, WA; [p.] Chris and Geraldine Carlson; [ed.] Attend Lindbergh High School going in to the 11th grade; [pers.] My writing is a reflection on my feelings, thoughts, and my point of view on every aspect of life.; [a.] Renton, WA

CARNES, OPAL REBECCA
[pen.] Becky; [b.] September 30, 1964, Groton, CT; [p.] Wilford E. Carnes; [ed.] Austin Town Fitch High, Youngstown State University, Institute of Children Literature; [occ.] CNA, Home Health Care Aid; [memb.] Calumet United Methodist Church; [hon.] Junior Achievement, 4 H Awards, Quilting; [oth. writ.] Short stories in my spare time.; [pers.] Have faith and believe in yourself and your dreams will come true.; [a.] Laurium, MI

CARPENTER, MARY
[b.] June 24, 1941, Mississippi; [pers.] Through my poems I wish to achieve an equal balance to my life.; [a.] Pilot Mountain, NC

CARPENTER, PAUL
[b.] July 1, 1969, Scranton, PA; [p.] Vaughn and Jane Carpenter; [ch.] Christopher; [ed.] 2 years Penn st. Univ., 2 years Study Marywood College (Finance, Business) did not complete, Scranton Central H.S. class of '87; [occ.] Firefighter Scranton Fire Dept.; [memb.] Local 669 IAFF, Everhart Museum Found.; [hon.] My new Girlfriend Kim and her son. Also my own son. They are my Honors. I am lucky to be around each of them often.; [oth. writ.] No others have been published. Many poems, songs and short stories. Also many paintings and drawings.; [pers.] My family and friends have kept my head in the right direction. Without them, life would be difficult. My writing influences have been many... (Poe, Tolkien, Vonnegut) etc.. Excluding my work submitted I have my own style.; [a.] Scranton, PA

CARROLL, DIANE
[b.] May 2, 1967, Oakland, CA; [p.] Valcour Carroll Jr., Mercedes Foote; [ch.] Demetris, Keith and Raina; [ed.] Received an Associate's Degree in Sociology in 1993. Currently I am working on my Bachelor of Science in the Biomedical field of study at Cal State Hayward. I also have a a certified Nurses Aide Degree and have completed courses like certified Med-Aide and career secretary.; [oth. writ.] Several poems that aren't published as of yet. The poetry is entitled "The Souls of My Pain".; [pers.] My poetry is a reflection of my life and all that has touched it. I write what I feel and what truths need to be told. I want people to think about their life and live it to their satisfaction. I write to touch all those who will listen.; [a.] Berkeley, CA

CARROLL, VICKIE
[b.] April 8, 1982, Midland, TX; [p.] James and Linda Carroll; [ed.] 8th grade student Greenwood Middle School, Midland, TX; [occ.] Middle School Student; [memb.] Member Midland County 4-H Club, Member Jesus Way Fellowship-Midland, TX; [oth. writ.] Several other poems which I have yet to share with the world.; [pers.] I love poetry because it is fun, it allows me to escape from the world around me, and I always find it exciting to feel real inspiration.; [a.] Midland, TX

CARRON, ROBERT JAMES
[b.] July 22, 1947, Long Beach, CA; [p.] Raymond Carron and Thelma Yvonne Noble Carron; [ed.] Corbett Grade School, Corbett, OR, Madison H.S., Portland, Reed College, Portland, B.A. 1969, Master of Arts in Teaching, 1970; [occ.] Artist (Landscape painter, photographer, poet/writer), Legal secretary office of the Attorney General of Calif; [memb.] Pacific Grove Art Center; [hon.] One-man Art Exhibits: First Unitarian Church, San Francisco, October 1990, The Pacific Grove Art Center, Sept Oct 1994. Cover for the Berkeley Art Center, 1993-94.; [oth. writ.] "The Mathematical and Scientific Proof of God"; [pers.] In the '70's I invented a

style of painting I call "Soft Edge". In the '80's and '90's I reinvented pointillism as a metaphysical painting style linking art and science in a unique way. Then I wrote "The Mathematical and Scientific Proof of God"; [a.] San Francisco, CA

CARSON, KIM
[b.] June 4, 1965, Dallas, TX; [p.] Bob and Shirley Palmer; [m.] Douglas Shawn Carson, March 27, 1991; [ch.] Heather Justine, Bobby Christopher and Brandon Samuel; [ed.] Mesquite High School, Graduate - 1983; [occ.] Transcription Typist, for Farmer's Insurance, Mesquite, Texas; [oth. writ.] I have written several other poems for friends and family, but never sent them off to anyone.; [pers.] My poems are the expressions of my emotions.; [a.] Mesquite, TX

CARTER, ANGIE
[pen.] Angie Freeman; [b.] March 20, 1970, Tyler, TX; [p.] Rose and James Freeman; [m.] Devlin Carter, September 15, 1995; [ed.] Robert E. Lee High School, Tyler Junior College; [occ.] Secretary for East Texas Medical Center, Tyler, TX; [pers.] Thanks Mom and Dad for teaching me to never settle for the moon when I can reach for the stars. To my husband Devlin, brother Bobby and Mom and Dad, I love you.; [a.] Tyler, TX

CARTER, GLORIA A.
[pen.] Cat; [b.] January 9, 1946, Roanoke, VA; [p.] Walters A. Carter Jr.; [ch.] Julia, Valerie, Kareem; [ed.] Carver High School, Jefferson Hospital (Nursing) Co.; [occ.] Clinical Research, Nurse Coordinator; [memb.] Research Nurse; [hon.] Golden Poet Award 1988 for Juanise, (World of Poetry); [oth. writ.] Juanise, To The Man In My Life, Beautiful Blackman, Sound Of A Voice, Thank You, Grandmother For A Mother's Dream, Memories Are Forever, Loving You; [pers.] Life is what you make of it. You are always in control of your happiness.; [a.] Charlottesville, VA

CARTER, MICHAEL R.
[pen.] "M.R." Carter; [b.] December 2, 1953, Los Angeles, CA; [p.] Richard E. and Sarah A. Carter; [ed.] Mt. Zion High, Mt. Zion, Illinois, Massey Jr. College, Atlanta, GA. Cypress College, Cypress, CA; [occ.] Artist of the West and Wildlife; [memb.] Founding 1000 "Western Music Assn." Tucson, AZ, Charter, Founding Member, "Gene Autry Western Heritage", "Museum", Los Angeles, CA - Charter, Founding Member "Roy Roger Riders Club" - "Roy Rogers and Dale Evans Museum"; [hon.] Art placement in permanent collection Roy Rogers - Dale Evans Museum (1986 and 1994), Listed in "Who's Who in the West", "Intnl. Dir. of Distinguished Leadership", "Who's Who in the World", "Personalities of America", 5th Ed., and Award for "Contribution to Preservation of Western Music" (1990); [oth. writ.] "It all Started With A Cowboy, "For" 30 "Thirty Years Together - A Tribute To Roy Rogers and Trigger", "My Old Sedena Home", "Silver Saddles", "A Cowboy's Lament"; [pers.] To preserve our heritage as Americans, as well as our Western heritage through sharing my poetry and artwork with everyone who will take the time to listen and learn this is my goal in life.; [a.] Temecula, CA

CARTER, STEPHEN WAYNE
[pen.] Steve; [b.] April 29, 1964, Dayton, OH; [p.] Clifford Allie and Freda Mae Carter; [m.] Tabitha Louise Carter, February 25, 1984; [ch.] Priscilla Shai (7), Sacha Rae (6), Brianna Kae (3); [ed.] Went to Valley View High School in Germantown, Ohio and Graduated in 1982 and moved here to FL; [occ.] General Maint. Tech. for Orange County Public Schools; [memb.] Blood Donor, Ministers License (United Christian Church and Ministerial Association), Americans Shoppers Travel Club, Parent Teachers Association, Grace St. Church of God Member; [hon.] Employee of the year 1995, having my poem published 1996, Central Fla Blood Bank Award received 1996 Spring Fling Award at Howard Middle Sch. Omnitrition International Inc. Bronze Supervisor Award; [oth. writ.] It Goes To Show You Never Know. I ran across and looking for poems, I looked in our cabinet where I keep love letters, poems, etc...that I have given to my wife ever since we met. I really didn't think I stood a chance of having the poem published that I wrote to my wife several years ago, it is an honor to me and has lifted my spirits and has made me feel proud.; [pers.] I am 32 years of age I have a beautiful wife who is 29 years of age. An 8 year old daughter in Heaven (Priscilla) a 7 year old named Priscilla, 6 year old named Sacha, and a 3 year old named Brianna, I am truly blessed. I've been married for 12 years, we get along great and I love her very much. My children are very good, well mannered, happy, they are so precious I am so thankful to be a husband and father. I want to be the best; [a.] Apopka, FL

CARTER-TAYLOR, LISA LU
[b.] June 26, 1966, Bloomington, IN; [p.] Fred O. Carter, Janet L. Carter; [ch.] Alisha Kaye, Angela Kirsten, Korey Lowell; [ed.] Eastern High, U.S. Army 764 Supply Training, Ft. Lee, VA; [memb.] Bloomington Baptist Church; [oth. writ.] Shadows, Special Lullaby, Perfect Times Two, Easter Celebration, What A Storm Is, A Tribute To Grandma, and various others; [pers.] "The Love She Made", was written about my grandmother - Mary Alice Barnes-Carter. I dedicate this poem to her memory. She inspired me with her everyday life, and the loving memories she made for all who knew her. I strive to keep those memories of her alive.; [a.] Bloomington, IN

CARUSO, SARAH
[pen.] Sarah Barrett; [b.] January 27, 1928, Saint Louis, MO; [p.] Leo and Anna Barrett; [m.] Sal N. Caruso, June 15, 1957; [ch.] 4 - Robert, Cathy, Jeanne, Patty; [ed.] Northside Catholic High School; [occ.] Housewife; [memb.] Coprus Christi Alumni Committee, St. Christopher Church Choir, Two Bridge Clubs; [oth. writ.] Write poems for invitations to various affairs - wrote special poem for birth of each grandchild - write poetry on various subjects - never submitted them for publication.; [pers.] I started writing poetry when the emptiness syndrome set in.; [a.] Saint Louis, MO

CARVER, DOROTHY
[b.] December 18, 1933; [p.] Thelma Baxter, Ross Baxter (Deceased); [m.] Arthur Carver, July 30, 1960; [ch.] 5 - Brian, Miles, Patricia, Karen and Eric; [ed.] Elementary School - New York, NY, High School - Stamford Conn., Stamford High, College - Indiana University Bloomington, IN; [occ.] Self employed artist; [memb.] African American Poetry Club, Honorary Member - Girl Scouts, Member of World Club Travelers; [hon.] U.S. Army Rifle, High School - weaving; [oth. writ.] Pondering - Memories, My Song - Tenderness, Birds - New York and others.; [pers.] Touch with gentle hands look with innocent eyes listen with a gentle ear, smile softly.; [a.] Cambria Heights, NY

CARVER, SARAH
[b.] October 12, 1920, Hampton, GA; [p.] Almon and Thelma Moore; [m.] Henry Carver (Deceased), August 26, 1939; [ch.] Linda, Eileen and Cathy; [ed.] Graduated 1937 from Russell High - attended Ogle Thorpe Univ. 2 years on a Scholarship; [occ.] Retired Federal Contract Specialist; [memb.] St. Andrews Presbyterian Church, National Honor Society, Quill and Scroll ABWA; [hon.] 10 years old valedictorian from GA Ave Elem. School, various work related Awards from general services admin.; [oth. writ.] Short stories and poems published in unknowns, parnassus, and broken streets; [pers.] Enjoy writing about personal faith, family and friends, and beauties of nature and human love and friendship.; [a.] Tucker, GA

CASE, DEBORAH G.
[b.] January 24, 1953, Tallahassee, FL; [p.] William N. and Virginia Goff; [m.] Russell Case, July 10, 1976; [ch.] 3 sons - Lucas, Bryan and Jeremy, 1 grandson - Casey; [ed.] Western Carolina Univ. (Math Education Major); [occ.] Accounts Reconciliation Specialist with Nations Bank; [memb.] United Way, I also support the battered and abused women's shelter; [pers.] The internal strife of mankind is reflected in my poetry. I hope it has an eye-opening effect on those who are blind to it.

CASE, E. R.
[pen.] I. M. Unon; [b.] November 3, 1921, Long Beach, CA; [m.] Verna M. (Deceased), August 9, 1941; [ch.] Sandra Kay and Thomas R.; [oth. writ.] Eight Seconds, In Memoriam, The Artist, The Brook, Civilization? I Believe, God Bless, Hello, Trouble, Nature's Voices, Dawn; [pers.] Live life to the fullest, enjoy, and do your best not to hurt anyone while passing through.; [a.] Warner Springs, CA

CASEY, CHARITY
[b.] October 30, 1981, St. Louis, MO; [p.] Allen and Pat Casey; [ed.] Murphy Elementary and North Jefferson Middle School; [occ.] Student; [pers.] The poem that I wrote called "Memory Poem was dedicated to my brother who died when I was 12 yrs. old.; [a.] Fenton, MO

CASSADY, SHIRLEY A.
[pen.] Shilley Anna Cassady; [b.] August 4, 1945, Freeburg, MO; [p.] Harold and Henrietta Cassady; [ed.] Parochial Schools, some college, various courses of interest; [occ.] Sales/Delivery; [oth. writ.] Poems, letters.; [pers.] I desire to teach as I learn, and learn as I teach. I care what happens to the spiritual, emotional and physical life of this universe.; [a.] Saint Louis, MO

CAUDILL, NANCY LEE
[b.] March 11, 1949, Vancouver, Canada; [p.] Robert E. Scruggs, Rose Scruggs; [ch.] Lee Eugene Caudill; [ed.] Forrest High; [occ.] Wrapper Operator, Uni Source Converting, Inc.; [memb.] Humane Society of the United States, World Wildlife, Doris Day Animal League, Disabled American Veterans; [hon.] Wrapper Operator of the Year (95); [pers.] Would love to see all animal and child abuse come to peace.; [a.] Jacksonville, FL

CAVALLARO, CHRISTI
[b.] March 9, 1970, Walnut Creek, CA; [p.] Cris Cavallaro, Elaine Brixen; [ed.] University of California, San Diego; [occ.] Actress/Singer/Musician/Songwriter; [memb.] American Federation of Musicians; [hon.] College department writing awards for fiction and non-fiction.; [oth. writ.] Songs, short stories, and literary critiques.; [pers.] I read to know that I'm not alone and I write, that others may not feel alone. I have been influenced by Hermann Hesse, Olive Schreiner and Lawrence Durrell among others.; [a.] San Diego, CA

CECCHINI, BABETTE
[b.] Warren, PA; [ch.] One son; [ed.] Business Administration, also studies in Philosophy and Literature; [occ.]

Property Owner and Management all fields of business; [pers.] I have always loved poetry; I have read and written it since a child. Thanks to my parents who introduced me to the world of literature.

CHAMPAGNE, DOROTHY

[b.] November 16, 1930, Worcester, MA; [m.] William Champagne, July 2, 1955; [ch.] Glenn M. Champagne; [occ.] Retired; [oth. writ.] One poem published in "Amidst The Splendor" for the National Library of Poetry.; [pers.] Time is precious. It should be used wisely. This I believe.

CHAPIN, SUZANNE

[pen.] Suzy; [b.] April 23, 1959, Minn; [p.] George and Maxine Chapin; [m.] Kevin Persons, September 28, 1991; [ch.] Christopher James Persons and Jennifer Persons; [ed.] Master of Science, Nursing Cal State University, Long Beach, Bachelor of Science at Mount St Mary's College, L.A.; [occ.] Nurse Practitioner; [memb.] Calvary Community Church, Westlake Village, National of Pediatric Nurse Practitioners and Associates, American Academy of Nurse Practitioners; [hon.] Sigma Theta Tau Graduate Honor Society; [oth. writ.] Contributor for Pediatric Emergency Assessment Modules, lyric writer, articles for previous professional positions.; [pers.] There are three things to do in my life .. find God, find His purpose for my life ... and Do It ... with love!; [a.] Agoura Hills, CA

CHAPMAN, STEVEN R.

[pen.] "Hot Off The Holy Spirit Press"; [b.] February 13, 1945, Brunswick, ME; [p.] Percy and Irene Chapman; [m.] Uldarica V. Chapman, September 1, 1973; [ch.] Floyd R. Chapman; [ed.] Biole Institute of N.E., St. Johnsbury, VT Missionary Ministerial - Graduate June, 1977; [occ.] Warehouse Clerical Support; [oth. writ.] The Living Word, Standing On The Threshold of Eternity, A Dancing Heart, I'm Drunk and I Don't Care, Come Party at the House of the Lord, The Finished Work, The Eye of the Needle, Noah's Theme Song; [pers.] I accepted Jesus Christ as my personal saviour when I was 7 yrs. old. He has been and continues to be the person who meets my personal needs.; [a.] Bedford, MA

CHAPPELL, JANET

[pen.] Janet Rudolph; [b.] December 13, 1959, Port Arthur, TX; [p.] Larry and Leora Holmes; [m.] John D. Chappell Sr., July 11, 1992; [ch.] Three boys, two girls; [ed.] 2 years local College and AMRA Correspondence; [occ.] Participant in Manufacturing Raw Steel Forgings.; [memb.] 2 years hospital volunteer, ISO 9002 Internal Auditor; [hon.] HOSA president, Dean's List, Cavalcade Princess; [oth. writ.] "The Old Goat", "The Gardener" published in College literary magazine in 1986; [pers.] The second greatest calling in all the land is one who provides others a living (bread for this life.) The first greatest calling is the one who provides bread for eternal life.; [a.] Nederland, TX

CHARD, MICHELLE LEE

[b.] March 6, 1972, Quincy, MA; [p.] Anthony and Margaret Chard; [ed.] Braintree High School Curry College; [occ.] Proofreader, Modern Graphics, Weymouth, MA; [memb.] South Shore coalition for Human Rights, Muscular Dystrophy Association, Trinity Episcopal Church; [hon.] Dean's List; [oth. writ.] Several articles for the Patriot Ledger, currently working on first novel - "Bohemian Paradise."; [pers.] Live life to the fullest, leave the regrets to the poets; [a.] Braintree, MA

CHARLTON, SUSAN

[b.] September 9, 1958, San Antonio, TX; [p.] Doug and Emaline Charlton; [m.] Widowed; [ed.] Mount Royal College, Denver University, University of Tenn.; [memb.] Volunteered M.A.D.D. and Victim's Assistance; [oth. writ.] Currently interested in writing children's stories.; [pers.] In writing the poem "Seed of Peace," it is my hope that my experience with grief, will be of benefit to anyone touched by sorrow.; [a.] Littleton, CO

CHEN, JONATHAN

[b.] August 25, 1974, Taipei, Taiwan; [p.] Jerome and Tammy Chen; [ed.] Poway High, University of San Diego; [occ.] Student; [memb.] Asian American Journalist Association; [hon.] Kappa Delta Pi, Dean's List; [oth. writ.] Several poems published in various publications. Section editor for the USD Newspaper, Vista.; [pers.] The most difficult part of writing poetry is not writing itself, but figuring out what poetry is.; [a.] San Diego, CA

CHIANESE, DOMINICK

[b.] February 21, 1981, Melbourne, FL; [p.] Janet and Dom Chianese; [ed.] Attending Southwest Jr. High, 9th grade; [hon.] Honor Roll at School; [oth. writ.] 108 other poems; [pers.] I am writing for Dominick as he is a semi-paralyzed 15 yr old. He cannot speak, swallow, or use his hands except for 1 finger that he types poems, school work and communication. This was due to encelphalitis at 11 yrs. old; [a.] Palm Bay, FL

CHITALE, ASHOK A.

[pen.] Ash; [b.] August 6, 1938, Sholapur, India; [p.] Anant and Indira; [m.] Anuradha, December 25, 1964; [ch.] Sons: Aniruddha and Niranjan; [ed.] M.D.; [occ.] General Practitioner; [oth. writ.] None published; [pers.] Strive hard for the best but be happy with what you get.; [a.] Wichita Falls, TX

CHRISTIANS, HOPE

[b.] September 12, Jamestown, ND; [p.] Douglas and Louise Christians; [ed.] I am currently attending Concordia College in Moorhead, MN., I will graduate the spring of 1999 with a dietetics major; [occ.] Student; [memb.] Concordia College Choir, our savior's Lutheran Church; [hon.] Dean's List, Who's Who in America.; [oth. writ.] Several poems, short stories.; [pers.] I write when I have a feeling about a particular subject. Writing with emotion is how I write best. I can't just sit down and write without emotion.; [a.] Chokio, MN

CIESLINSKI, HEATHER

[b.] October 27, 1977, Mount Vernon, NY; [p.] Robert Cieslinski, Francine S. Cieslinski; [ed.] Sacred Heart High School Class of '95, Marymount Manhattan College Class of '99; [occ.] Student; [memb.] Students Against Drunk Driving, Theatre Communications Group; [hon.] Dean's Scholarship, Competitive Merit Scholarship in Acting; [oth. writ.] This is my first published poem.; [pers.] Most of my writings are a reflection of a life experience. If you read my poems you may very well be reading a page out of my life.; [a.] Yonkers, NY

CLARK, ANNA D.

[b.] February 19, 1964, Sutton, WV; [p.] Vonda Slaughter and Ray Fisher; [ch.] John, Meaghan and Amy; [pers.] I really don't want my biographical data listed. But I would like to dedicate, my poem to my brother, Anthony Neil Clark, who was killed, August 27, 1993, in a car accident.; [a.] Zapata, TX

CLARK, JEANNE BAKEOVEN

[b.] June 22, 1947, Philadelphia, PA; [p.] John and Jeanette Bakeoven; [m.] Robert E. Clark, February 13, 1965; [ch.] Six sons Bobby Jr., John, Jim, Joe, Joshua, Jeffrey also 5 grandchildren Christopher Andrew, Shaynna, Alyssa and Jimmy; [ed.] Graduated from Bensalem, High School Bensalem, PA (1965) Graduated from NJ Central Bible Institute - Chesterfield NJ (1990); [occ.] Homemaker - enjoy music and presently taking accordian lessons.; [memb.] Attend Calvary Baptist Church Pemberton, NJ; [pers.] My favorite Bible verse is Galations 2:20 and my desire is to glorify Christ in all I say and do.

CLARK, JOSHUA

[b.] October 23, 1981, Rochville, CT; [p.] Susan and Mark Clark; [ed.] I'm a sophomore in High School; [occ.] Dishwasher/Busser at the Pizza Pub; [hon.] The Presidential Academic Fitness Award June 1992; [pers.] I am a sophomore in high school, and have been writing since 7th Grade. I don't know why I started but I did.; [a.] Twin Mount, NH

CLARK, RENEE

[b.] April 15, 1981, Warren, MI; [p.] Donald and Patricia Clark; [ed.] As of now I'm in 9th grade at Romeo Jr. High; [occ.] Babysitting; [hon.] In school, art, horseback riding, poetry, swimming and trying.; [oth. writ.] Happiness and Life; [a.] Romeo, MI

CLARK, STEVEN A.

[b.] March 15, 1966, Wichita, KS; [p.] Harold and Connie Clark; [m.] Julie Clark, June 26, 1993; [ch.] Breanna Clark; [ed.] Comeaux High School, Lafayette, LA; [occ.] U.S. Marine Corps

CLARKE, JAMES H.

[pen.] Jim Clarke; [b.] January 6, 1949, Cumberland, MD; [p.] Ross Clarke, Mary Eileen Clarke; [m.] Divorced; [ch.] Dawn, Christina, Misty, James, Eileen; [ed.] Allegany High, Greensburg Institute of Technology; [occ.] Electronics Technician, Boomtown Hotel/Casino; [oth. writ.] Song "Your Memory's Just A Heartbeat Away", "Out Of Sight/Out Of Mind", "I Can't Let Them Love Me", "I Believe In Me And You"; [pers.] The great writers of love stories and poets of the past expressed love in many ways. Some through inspiration, others through dreams. The greatest inspiration is love itself. Thank you "Linda Lussier, my inspiration.; [a.] Sun Valley, NV

CLAYNE

[pen.] Clayne; [b.] April 30, 1975, Tulsa, OK; [p.] Tom Layne, Laura Layne-Smith; [ed.] Farmington High, North West Arkansas Community College, University of Arkansas at Fayetteville; [occ.] Student/Artist/Writer/Poet; [memb.] Fellowship Bible Church Lowell AR; [hon.] Recipient of the Barrett Hamilton award in Art, Merit in English, grammer and literacy; [oth. writ.] Raised on Crow - the stories of a fallen home. A collection of the simplicity of life: An Angel An Elephant And A Conch; [pers.] The greatest things in my life have been: first God, grandparents, family, and the wondrous gift of thought. The praise is not for me but for Him - my father.; [a.] Garfield, AR

CLEVENGER, LULA B.

[b.] April 16, 1941, James Town, TN; [p.] Tip Carpenter and Katy Belle Carpenter; [m.] Stanley Clevenger, July 1, 1966; [ch.] Mary Lynette, Cynthia Denise; [ed.] Gibbs High, Cooper Institute; [occ.] Elementary Teacher, Corryton, TN., Elementary School and Supervisory/Dispatcher at Hallsdale-Powell Utility District; [memb.] V.M.C.A., Dry Gap Baptist Church Secretary and Treasury; [hon.] B.S. Degree in accounting, B.S. Degree in Business Management with Highest Honors; [oth. writ.] Several poems published in school papers, several un-published songs, started writing a book, but don't have it finished. I've written several cheers for School Cheer Leaders.; [pers.] I strive to reflect the beauties of life and the creation to mankind in my writings.; [a.] Corryton, TN

CLIFTON, DEBORAH
[pen.] "Debbie"; [b.] October 12, 1961, Yuba City, CA; [p.] Rich and Gwen Sacchetti; [m.] Roy Clifton, February 14, 1995; [ch.] Amber Mae, Mark Jay; [ed.] Quincy High, Yuba College; [occ.] Registered Nurse, ICU Rideout Hosp, Marysville, CA; [mem.] American Assoc. Critical Care Nurses, Peach Bowl Little League Board of Dir.; [hon.] Critical Care Registered Nurse; [oth. writ.] Many poems published in Appeal Democrat local newspaper, one published in hospital newsletter.; [pers.] My poems express emotions/feelings of people in comparison to nature.; [a.] Yuba City, CA

COATES, LORRAINE MARGARET
[b.] June 29, 1917, Chicago, IL; [p.] Hugh and Clara Cameron; [m.] William Coates, March 6, 1943; [ch.] Five; [ed.] Bowen High School; [a.] Benton Harbor, MI

COBB, MARIAN
[b.] October 20, 1915, East St. Louis, IL; [p.] Robert and Lonetta Jost; [m.] Cecil H. Cobb, July 2, 1933; [ch.] 3 Carol Dismukes, Barbara Hess, Dr. James R. Cobb; [ed.] Springfield High School 1932 graduate, post graduate studies; [occ.] Homemaker; [memb.] First United Methodist Church; [hon.] Piano, Fur Coat Contests; [pers.] I was thinking of my mother one day and the words of my poem started flowing from my pen where they came from, I don't know but I haven't changed a word. I do feel certain, one day I will be with her again.; [a.] Mayfield, KY

COCKRIEL, TERRI S.
[pen.] Dakota Sioux Rose; [b.] October 3, 1958, Levenworth, MO; [p.] Norman and Betty Cockriel; [ch.] Joseph Brian Smith, Patrick Andrew Smith; [occ.] Motel Deeds, self-employed by writing; [hon.] Hometown awards, out of state honors; [oth. writ.] Short stories, book, "Forbidden Love"; [pers.] I see poetry as an escape. I write on things that matter. AIDS, Battered Women, Homelessness, Gangs, Drugs Work, etc..., people should open their eyes more!; [a.] Lebanon, MO

COLBATH, ANGLEIA YONG
[pen.] Annie Yong Lee; [b.] April 18, 1978, Korea; [p.] Raymond and Signora Lee; [m.] Eddie Colbath Jr., February 24, 1995; [ch.] Desean Raymond M. Lee-Brown; [ed.] Copperas Cove High School, Lincoln Tech. Inst., Grand Prairie, TX; [occ.] Housewife

COLE, BETTY JO
[b.] November 9, 1937, Stigler, OK; [p.] Earl and Deola Few; [m.] Billy R. Cole, April 12, 1957; [ch.] Anthony Alan and Timothy Ray; [ed.] High School Graduate, Wasco High School, Wasco, CA; [occ.] Housewife; [pers.] I have written several poems, which have been only written for my family and friend's pleasures. I have never endeavored to have my poems published.; [a.] Wasco, CA

COLE, BRIAN
[b.] November 13, 1974, Malden; [p.] Cheryl Cole and James Cole; [ed.] Malden High School all 4 years; [occ.] UNICCO Security Services; [memb.] The Sci-fi Book Club. Star Wars - Fan Club, American Entertainment, The Sci-Fi Video Club; [oth. writ.] Poems - Giver of Life, When A Woman Cries, I Am, Zen, Forever Night, Absent Friend, For You, Before The Storm, Fallen Sky, Let Sadness Be Your Guide, Dreams Don't Come True, Deep In Thought and many more, short stories as well.; [pers.] Writing has always been something I like to do, but, I never suspected that I'd ever get into poetry. When I write it just all flows out of me, all on paper. I was never one to truly express myself, but now I've found away to do so, through my writings.; [a.] Malden, MA

COLE, EVELYN M.
[b.] January 18, 1924, Lincoln, NE; [p.] Floyd H. and Marie A. Zerbel; [m.] Orven S. Cole, April 9, 1944; [ed.] Havelock High (class of '41) Lincoln, NE; [occ.] Housewife; [hon.] I have been published by the National Library of Poetry in several anthologies in the past few years. (i.e.) River Of Dreams, East Of The Sunrise, The Path Not Taken, Best Poems Of '95 and '96, Through The Hourglass, The Best Poems Of The '90's and others.; [oth. writ.] Music (with lyrics) and much poetry - all types and subjects; [pers.] Our family moved to California in my Post-graduate year of '42. I had several occupations before I married. I had been the sole office help for my husband, a Htg and A/C Contractor for 50 yrs. (now retired) We celebrated our Golden Wedding Anniversary in '94. In an effort to learn to play the piano in '54 I began to writing poetry for my own pleasure and still do. The Lord has been very kind...; [a.] Los Angeles, CA

COLE, JACKY SEITZ
[pen.] White Feather; [b.] January 1, 1953, Delaware, OH; [p.] Carl and Jackie Cole; [m.] Divorced; [ch.] 2 sons - Anthony Steven Cimino II, LCPL Christopher J. Cimino USMC; [ed.] Olentangy High School - Delaware Ohio American High School - Chicago Illinois, Howard College - Big Spring, Texas Western Texas College Vocational Nursing, Snyder, TX; [occ.] Licensed Vocational Nurse, Nurse at a high school Campus RN student at the University of New York; [oth. writ.] This is my first published work.; [pers.] Whatever you feel, put it on paper, let the world see your inner heart, it will touch someone.; [a.] Sweetwater, TX

COLEMAN, ALLEN
[pen.] Allen Coleman; [b.] April 5, 1958, San Diego, CA; [p.] Deceased; [m.] Divorced; [ed.] 11th; [memb.] North Park Church; [a.] San Diego, CA

COLLIER, DAYNA
[b.] August 24, 1984, Arizona; [p.] John and Patricia Collier; [ed.] 7th grade student at Landmark Middle School in Glendale, Arizona; [hon.] I've been certified as an honor roll student, the last 4 years. Student of the month and citizen of the month; [oth. writ.] School assignment: half page poems, short and long stories; [pers.] I would like to write more poems and express my feelings.; [a.] Glendale, AZ

COLLINS, EVELYN L.
[b.] March 27, 1947, Charleston, WV; [p.] Leroy Dunham, Jaunita Dunham; [m.] William Collins, March 24, 1995; [ch.] Terrence, Kelvin, Tanya; [ed.] So. Charleston High School, Center College; [occ.] Claims Adjuster Casci Insurance Co. Chas., WV; [memb.] Vice-President of the Mount Zion Baptist Pastoral Choir; [oth. writ.] Have written several poems for friends and family members, for funerals and church anniversaries; [pers.] Through my poems I hope to uplift people and show them that God is the answer for all things and pray they will to come to know a God who loves us, and that through Him all things are possible; [a.] South Charleston, WV

COLLINS, JOE T.
[b.] December 23, 1946, Polk Co., NC; [p.] Henry and Thelma Collins; [m.] Jean, February 14, 1993; [ch.] Andy - Kami; [ed.] 12 yrs. East Henderson High; [occ.] Food Broker Rep.; [memb.] Fellowship Baptist Church; [hon.] Had one of my poems published in local newspaper Times News; [oth. writ.] Only about 15 other poems only 3 or 4 are what I think pretty good; [pers.] I write mostly about things or people who have touched my heart, when I have put the words from my heart on paper I get a great deal of satisfaction.; [a.] Hendersonville, NC

COLSON, ERICA
[b.] February 1, 1982, Houston, TX; [p.] Barrett and Rick Colson; [ed.] Currently a freshman at Sir Francis Drake High School in San Anselmo, CA; [occ.] Student; [oth. writ.] Poems and short stories.; [pers.] At 14, I don't have many life experiences so I try to write about the truth as I see it or whatever inspires me.; [a.] San Anselmo, CA

COMIA, GERALDINE
[b.] October 26, 1981, Chicago; [p.] Nestor and Dorcas Comia; [ed.] Our Lady of Lourdes Elementary School, Good Counsel High School; [occ.] Student; [pers.] For anyone to see anything clearly, they must look through someone else's eyes. And now I see.; [a.] Hanover Park, IL

CONDON, EVELYN ANNE
[pen.] E. Anne Smith, Evelyn Smith; [b.] July 5, 1933, Biloxi, MS; [p.] Elmer and Marguerite Smith; [m.] Deceased; [ch.] Walter E. Condon, Eileen M. McCann, Carol Anne Bachhuber, Lawrence, Condon, Janet M. Mulcair; [ed.] High School; [occ.] Retired Food Service Supervisor and Restaurant Manager; [memb.] Associate of Mercy, Local Church related and other local volunteer organizations.; [oth. writ.] Editor-in-Chief of High School Newspapers "The Rostrum," Columnist for Weekly "West Haven Town Crier," Editor and Publisher of "The New England Mercy Connection" a newsletter for Mercy Associate and Sisters of Mercy.; [pers.] Writing poetry brings me a great deal of joy and inner peace. It gives me a chance to give of myself to others.; [a.] Middletown, CT

CONLEY, THELMA B.
[pen.] Mickey; [b.] Brownsville, TN; [p.] Johnnie and Elene Bond; [m.] Divorced; [ch.] B. Harrison and E. Binelle Conley; [ed.] B.A. Spelman College M.S.W., Atlanta University; [occ.] Allied Health Admissions Counselor, Tennessee State Univ. Washville; [memb.] Delta Sigma Theta Sorority; [hon.] The Continual and unconditional love and respect of my offspring.; [oth. writ.] A study of the impact of the food stamp Program on the State of Tennessee, numerous unpublished poems and short stories, letter to the editor, Nashville, TN (1979).; [pers.] Meeting the needs of the immediate family has its own rewards and fosters a better society today and tomorrow.; [a.] Nashville, TN

CONNER, LILLIAN PAGE
[pen.] Lillian Page Conner; [b.] March 7, 1957, Springfield, MA; [p.] Shirley A. Mullis and James W. Page Sr.; [m.] Michael Gene Conner, April 1, 1988; [ch.] Daniel Christian and William Jon Fleming; [ed.] Technical High/

Horry-Georgetown High School - Spfld., Mass. with Honors Math Major/Arts Minor Horry/Tech. Conway, S.C. Medical Sec. Computer Analysis and Accounting I and II; [occ.] Field auditor throughout North and South Carolinas; [memb.] Wildlife Preservation, Humane Society, Arthritis Foundation, Save The Rain Forests, American Bald Eagle Preservation, Save the Earth, and Endangered Species Foundation; [oth. writ.] Other poems published in 1991 "Treasured Poems of America" and 2 poems to be published in "Whispers" anthology to be released in March 1997. Also, my eldest son, Daniel Christian, has had one of his poems published in "Perspectives" last year and received the Honorable Mention Award, as well as, the President's Award for his poem. I have also wrote several greeting card verses over the years since high school. My personal philosophy is to write about such things as peace, love, understanding, and harmony among all people on this earth and of "Mother Nature" herself.; [a.] Conway, SC

COOKS, CHARDE DEPRAY
[pen.] C.C.; [b.] August 5, 1985, Dallas; [p.] Lena L. Cooks, Otha Clark Jr.; [ed.] I am in 6B (the B stands for the Best) and I attend James Nelson Ervin Elementary Sch.; [occ.] Unemployed full time Student; [memb.] Active Member of JN Ervin Jaquretts Cheerleaders; [hon.] I have received several awards, Perfect Attendance, Cheerleaders Outstanding Performance, a honor roll for the entire school year. Teacher's Assist. Trophies A-Honor Roll and Talented and Gifted.; [oth. writ.] Title: Different Homes and Hats; [pers.] Jesus and Education success "I can do all things through Christ which strengthens me" Philippians 4:13; [a.] Dallas, TX

COONEY, MARK S.
[pen.] Tree; [b.] November 15, 1958, San Diego, CA; [p.] June Ann and Gary Cooney; [m.] Renate T. Cooney, January 9, 1987, Vojeas, Denmark; [ch.] Stefan 17 yrs.; [ed.] Lake Park H.S., Class of "77", 9 yrs. with US Army; [occ.] Full time student and Mobile DJ; [memb.] Member of Schweinfurt Germany, Gammers Guild; [pers.] I reside in Germany after leaving the Army I settled down and stayed in Europe and loving it. Life is just as well swinging nice and swell crazy seems I thought wake up now this I ought dream me on Mr. Sandman Wake feet often now! Me ran; [a.] Schweinfurt, Germany

COPELAND, LAUREEN
[b.] February 7, 1959, Ravenna, OH; [p.] Clarence and Laura Moore; [m.] James Julius Copeland, July 25, 1981; [ch.] Jamie Nicole Copeland; [ed.] Crestwood High School - Mantua, OH, High School Diploma, Bob Jones University - Greenville, SC, Bachelors of Science; [occ.] Grocery Store Bakery Dept. Manager; [memb.] WIBC - Bowling Conference Greenville Civic Band - Flute Furman University Summer Ban Flute/Piccolo; [pers.] Along life's path you meet some pretty special people, some of whom you will always admire and care for deeply. These are life's cherished treasures.; [a.] Greenville, SC

CORBIN, ANNA M.
[pen.] Anah Layton; [b.] May 2, 1948, West Virginia; [ch.] Two; [oth. writ.] The Book of Truth, Promise of Life

CORNELISSE, TRUDY
[b.] January 4, 1923, Grand Rapids, MI; [p.] Charles and Martha Feenstra; [m.] Verne Cornelisse, November 9, 1945; [ch.] Kenneth, Marilyn, James, Charles; [ed.] Grand Rapids Christian High; [occ.] Executive Secretary; [memb.] Professional Secretaries International, Bradenton (FL) Christian Reformed Church; [hon.] Diploma from The Institute of Children's Literature for completion of Writing for Children and Teenagers Course, Secretary of the year from local chapter of PSI; [oth. writ.] Family history stories, book of poems (in process of being published); [pers.] I strive to offer high moral standards for the improvement of society; [a.] Sarasota, FL

CORSUN, HARRY
[b.] August 13, 1921, Brooklyn, NY; [m.] April 6, 1975; [ed.] High school; [occ.] Retired; [oth. writ.] High school newspaper; [pers.] This reflection was written many years ago, soon after graduation (high school). The 'Maud' has, long ago, departed the Cheasapeake.; [a.] Jamaica, NY

COSTELLO, ERIN
[b.] January 7, 1979, Mt. Kisco, NY; [p.] James Costello, Bridget Costello; [ed.] I am a student at Yorktown High School I am going into my senior year, I hope to attend college in the fall of 1997.; [occ.] High school student and babysitter.; [memb.] Member of the Student Senate, going to hopefully be a member of key club or yearbook, member of the women's I across team, basketball team and was a football manager.; [hon.] Honor roll, awards for I across and basketball awards for being on active senate member and committee member.; [oth. writ.] I had a poem published for Illiad Press; [pers.] I write with my heart and deep emotion and I hope it reflects the mood of every generation.; [a.] Yorktown Heights, NY

COTHRAN, CATHERINE
[b.] April 22, 1939, Huntsville, AL; [p.] William Patton, Ruby Patton; [m.] Ralph H. Cothran, August 20, 1960; [ch.] Stephen, Raoul, Cyzanne Yvette, David Yohande; [ed.] Howard High School, Little Rock Vocational School Covenant College; [occ.] Retired Licensed Practical Nurse; [memb.] Orchard Knob, Missionary Baptist Church, Church Women United of Chattanooga, National Association of Negro, Business and Professional Women, Chattanooga Club; [hon.] Admitted to the Institute of Children's Literature, writing for children and teenagers course; [oth. writ.] One poem published by a local newspaper and several others by the National Library of Poetry and the World of Poetry.; [pers.] I am inspired to write from the deepest emotions of my life and also the wonder of nature and current events of my environment.; [a.] Chattanooga, TN

COTTON, ROY JOSEPH
[b.] September 11, 1953, Cape Town, South Africa; [p.] Hymie and Sheila Cotton; [ed.] University of Cape Town; [occ.] Died March 10, 1985; [oth. writ.] Ag, Man (Upstream Publications, Cape Town, 1986). My Coveyerquick Eagles (Firfield Pamphlet Press, Cape Town, 1995) Senior Poetry Anthology (MacMillan, London, 1983).; [pers.] Most of his poems reflects a consuming anxiety which drove him to search for peace through books, music, writing and religion. His untimely death at the age of 31 cut short his promising career as a poet.; [a.] Denver, CO

COURT, CINDY
[pen.] Cyd; [b.] November 17, 1952, Eugene, OR; [p.] Both dead; [m.] Divorced; [ch.] Angela 24, Amy 19, Grandson Juron 2; [ed.] Two years in College in Business Management; [occ.] Textile Control Manager at American Linen, Eugene, OR; [memb.] "The Golden Bytes Club", I'm a "Rookie" at computers; [oth. writ.] Nothing published but a few read publicly. One was at my mother's memorial.; [pers.] My poetry reflects experiences we face in life. I hope the reader can identify in such away that will encourage, comfort, or simply understood.; [a.] Springfield, OR

COWART, ROBERT
[b.] October 15, 1975, Houston, TX; [p.] Linda and Mario Arriaga and Wallace and Regina Cowart; [ed.] Currently a Junior at Texas A&M University; [occ.] Student; [memb.] Corps of Cadets at Texas A&M University; [pers.] Every person you meet knows something you don't learn from them. Pay attention to details. Never waste an opportunity to tell someone you love them. I try to incorporate these, ideas in my daily life.; [a.] Spring, TX

COX, TRAVIS ALLEN
[pen.] Allen Bradshaw; [b.] January 12, 1935, Waldo, Lamertine, AR; [p.] Nathan Oel and Hazel Bradshaw Cox; [m.] May 1964; [ch.] Leah J., Rebekah C., Michael Allen, Deborah L.; [ed.] Master of Music (Violin) 1963, BA (History) 1991, Post Grad. Work (Music); [occ.] Professional Violinist Ark, Symphony Orchestra and Violin Teacher; [memb.] Previously taught music on Univ. level for 20 years also played Oboe in U.S. Navy Band memberships-Phi Alpha Theta (Hist.) Frat., Phi Mu Alpha Sinfonia played Violin in several symphonies (30 years); [hon.] Fellowship for doctoral work North Tex. State Univ. in music Composition; [oth. writ.] Poems (dealing with love of nature and its preservation) and religion and moralistic poems misc. articles for newspaper (biog., memoriams, and moralistic) eg. "God's Sacred Handiwork (ded. to Okla. City Bombing Victims); [pers.] My hope is that through writing and music and Christian influence to bring more solidarity of character to our society and preservation of our rapidly diminishing natural blessings (from Ark. the natural state to far reaches of planet.); [a.] Searcy, AR

CRAWFORD, MARY JANE L.
[b.] August 12, 1921, Bryant, SD; [p.] Rejna Jane Corey, Bert N. Corey; [m.] Orville A. Crawford, November 24, 1943; [ch.] Jerome Michael, Judith Ann, Janice Rae; [ed.] Gr. 1-8 Country Sch., Hamlin Co. So. Dak. 1935, Hi sch Wash. Hi Sch, Sioux Falls, So. Dak 1939, Eastern State Normal, Madison, S.D. (2 yrs) 1939-1941, Seattle Pacific, Seattle - 1 summer 1963, Pacific Luth un. Tacoma, Wa BA 1966, Un of Wash. MA in Lib Sciences 1970, Un of Wash - poetry and short story courses for 5th yr in Education while being a Sch. Librarian 1963-1970; [occ.] 1980 Retired Sch. Librarian - was grade sch. librarian at Bremerton, Wa., Jr. Hi Lib at Enumclaw, WA 1970-1985; [memb.] NEA and local Ed groups, DAR - Daughters of Amer. Rev., Lutheran Church member; [hon.] 2nd in Hamlin Co. in gr 8, Bryant So. Dak. In upper 40 in class of 600 at hi sch. Sioux Falls, SD at graduation.; [oth. writ.] Interested in music. Piano lesson in hi sch and Eastern State Normal. Cello - hi sch orchestra. Have sang alto in college and church choirs. Taught piano in each parish where my husband was Lutheran pastor.; [pers.] Poetry intrigues me - like to tell of an incident in my life in short, descriptive terms. My jr. hi library experience led me to write Spring Fever - told it like it was.; [a.] Enumclaw, WA

CROFF, HAROLD NELSON
[pen.] Croff, Harold or "Cookie"; [b.] July 5, 1944, Manchester, Depot, VT; [p.] Marjorie P. McEckron; [m.] Divorced; [ch.] Anthony Har-nel Croff; [ed.] Burr and Burton Seminary, Central Texas Junior College; [occ.] Professional Chef; [memb.] Life Member - VFW Post #9192; [hon.] Elected to Boys State, Lions Club Schol-

arship and Muellar Cable TV Scholarship; [oth. writ.] Several poems published in the Manchester Journal; [pers.] People ought to express what's in their heart and not what's on their mind. When the two become one - you have genuine love!; [a.] Houston, TX

CROSS, JASON R.
[b.] September 7, 1979, Thomasville, NC; [p.] Rondal and Judy Cross; [ed.] Silver Valley Elementary, South Davidson Middle, South Davidson High; [occ.] Student; [memb.] Cid United Methodist Church UMYF - President, Lexington Cotillion Club, (School Clubs: Beta Club, Student Council-Rep, Band, FCA - President, Quiz Bowl, Cross Country - Captain, Track); [hon.] Silver Valley Civitan, School Citizen of the Year (1991), Benard H. Thomas Leadership Aca.; [oth. writ.] A short story "Village In The Valley" and other poems published.; [a.] Lexington, NC

CRUDUP, MARILYN HAYNES
[b.] November 2, 1948, Quitman, MS; [p.] Mary D. Adams of H'burg; [ch.] Nick and Kelvin Haynes; [ed.] High School grad. and college 2 yrs.; [occ.] Mother; [memb.] St. Matthew Baptist Church; [hon.] Children Youth Services and HIV Co.; [pers.] This poem is dedicated to my sons Kelvin and Nick Haynes for whom I will always love.; [a.] Montgomery, TX

CRUMBACKER, HEATH
[pen.] C. H. Crumbacker; [b.] March 11, 1971, Hagerstown, MD; [p.] Art and Sondra Crumbacker; [ed.] Hagerstown Junior College, Shepherd College; [occ.] Network Administrator First Data, Hagerstown, MD; [pers.] When in doubt, seek God.; [a.] Williamsport, MD

CUA, JAMES E.
[pen.] James Bower, Seth Chandler; [p.] Lowell Bower and Susan Bower; [m.] Laura Cua, April 24, 1996; [ed.] Dover High School, UNLV, Community College of the Air Force; [occ.] Aerospace Propulsion Specialist - United States Air Force; [memb.] American Red Cross Association; [oth. writ.] Currently Working on First Novel; [pers.] I believe self expression is the greatest release a person can achieve. As for influences, I do not limit myself to any one style. I can always learn something new from any form of writing.; [a.] Las Vegas, NV

CUELLAR, LENORA
[b.] December 12, 1975, Plainview, TX; [p.] Gloria and Ambrosio Cuellar; [ed.] Graduated at Plainview High and took a year off college and hopefully go to college; [occ.] Assistant Manager; [memb.] Rodeo's Clubs; [hon.] Stockshows and Rodeos; [oth. writ.] Poetry, stories and etc.; [pers.] Small minds talk about other people. Medium mind talk about problems. Big minds talk about ideas.; [a.] Plainview, TX

CULLING, JOHN
[b.] November 10, 1923, Kansas City, MO; [p.] Dorothy Townsend and Ruben Culling; [m.] Gale Culling, August 12, 1971; [ch.] Diane, Laurie, Carissa, Drusilla and Christine; [ed.] Webster Groves High School, Purdue University; [occ.] Research, The Carondelet Corporation; [oth. writ.] Presently writing a book of short essays.; [pers.] By receiving, honoring, adding what we can to the wonderful gifts we have received from others and then passing them along I believe we achieve a form of immortality.; [a.] Saint Louis, MO

CUNNINGHAM, E. J.
[pen.] E. J. Cunningham; [b.] July 18, 1934, Philadelphia, PA; [p.] Patrick J. and Kathleen C. Cunningham; [m.] Dolores M. Cunningham, October 16, 1969; [ed.] University of Scranton, BS english, Drew University, Land. M. Litt; [occ.] Retired Teacher of English; [memb.] Board Member And Treasure Of The Foundation For Judaed - Christian Studies Seton Hall University; [oth. writ.] Poems and short stories published in school literary magazines.; [a.] Maplewood, NJ

CUNNINGHAM, NORMA
[b.] November 5, 1929, Jackson, MI; [p.] Walter and Ellen Van Camp; [m.] Philip J. Cunningham, October 19, 1952; [ch.] Brian and Mark; [ed.] Jackson High and Jackson Community College; [occ.] Phone-Receptionist, for Cunningham - General and Mechanical Contracting; [memb.] (Husband's Business) Son Mark also works here.; [hon.] National Forensic Awards for Dramatic Declaration and Debate; [oth. writ.] Can anyone remember, patches, fame, good thinking and - many not yet offered for publication; [pers.] I try to choose subject matter that is of interest to everyone, my love for the animal world shows up now and then.; [a.] Jackson, MI

CUNNINGHAM, PATRICIA PEOPLES
[b.] October 2, 1948, Dothan, AL; [p.] David and Olar Peoples; [m.] Kenneth E. Cunningham, August 23, 1986; [ch.] David Byron and Mort Sheldon; [ed.] High School - John F. Kennedy Cuyahoga Community College both in Cleveland, OH; [oth. writ.] Other poems include, "Part Of The Picture", and "How Do You Know".; [pers.] Through "God" all good and loving things are possible!; [a.] Laurel, MD

CURRIE, JOSHUA R.
[pen.] Joshua R. Currie; [b.] February 14, 1980, Swickley, PA; [p.] Thomas and Lynn Currie; [ed.] East Palestine High School; [occ.] Student and Lifeguard; [oth. writ.] Currently in the process of writing a novel and a book on Ancient Norse Mythology.; [pers.] Being the first poem I've published I would like to thank one of my greatest teachers Ms. Lorie Magee who taught me to "only connect", I am greatly influenced by Early Celtic writings.; [a.] Unity, OH

CUTSHAW, SHIRLEY
[b.] May 26, 1952, Haywood County, NC; [p.] D. E. Smith, Lucy Erwin Smith; [m.] Ronald Dean Cutshaw, May 26, 1970; [ch.] Stacy Cutshaw Moore, Amber Cutshaw; [ed.] Pisgah High School; [occ.] Teaching Assistant Hazelwood Elementary, Waynesville NC; [memb.] Finchers Chapel United Methodist Church, Laureat Nu, Beta Sigma Phi, Haywood County Teaching Assistants Association; [oth. writ.] I have written several poems for personal satisfaction, special occasions and church use. I have never attempted to have any of my writings published before.; [pers.] My writings are a reflection of my feelings, emotions, memories and a love of God.; [a.] Waynesville, NC

DALE, TOMMARI
[b.] May 23, 1955, Richfield, UT; [p.] Thomas R. Dale and Mary Lee Taylor; [ch.] Misty Young, Lacie Mecham, 4 grandchildren; [ed.] Richfield High, Salt Lake Community College, College of Eastern Utah; [occ.] Disabled due to a seizure order; [hon.] Dean's List, Employee of the Week, Outstanding Work Performance on my Performance Evaluation; [oth. writ.] Essay for Daughters of the Utah Pioneers, several Country & Western Songs; [pers.] A lot of my writing has been based on years of abuse. I hope some of my writing can reach out to other victims of abuse and help them in some way. Writing poetry and reading poetry have been my means of escape. [a.] Huntington, UT.

DANIELS, LANCE M.
[pen.] Lance Morrison Daniels; [b.] May 31, 1962, East Orange, NJ; [p.] Margaret M. Daniels and Clifford R. Daniels (Deceased); [ed.] Graduate Elizabeth High School College Prep.; [occ.] Freelance writer; [memb.] None at present; [oth. writ.] Several other poems and songs too numerous to mention; [pers.] After living several years of torment and depression, I have finally found inner peace within myself, my only goal is to share my knowledge and wisdom with others in hope of making a positive difference in the world.; [a.] Elizabeth, NJ

DARDEN, MICHAEL WAYMAN
[pen.] Mike; [b.] October 18, 1970, Guntersville, AL; [p.] Mike and Ann Darden; [ch.] Kelby; [ed.] Jefferson State College, Pinson Valley High School; [occ.] Norfolk Souther Railway; [memb.] New Covenant Fellowship; [oth. writ.] "A Beginning Of And End"; [pers.] If is those who know the Lord that possess the secret of life. This is why my poetry must reflect the beauty of God's world.; [a.] Pinson, AL

DAUB, BEVERLY IRIS
[pen.] Dawn Elaine; [b.] October 29, 1936, Lancaster, PA; [p.] Harold Larainne and Charlotte Scott; [m.] Nedin E. Daub, February 17, 1957; [ch.] Daniel and Marcia Dawn (Deceased), Scott; [ed.] 12th grade; [occ.] Retired Floral Manager; [memb.] Choir, Garden Club, Bible Study; [hon.] Work Radio - 1984 (The Happy Three); [oth. writ.] Florida Gardener "Poor Fluffy Duffy" 1978, Garden Club Orange Pork "Prayer" 1976 - 1977 - 1978; [pers.] My poem was inspired in a precept Bible Study from John.; [a.] Orange Park, FL

DAVID JR., HARVEY L.
[b.] May 5, 1970, Fort Smith, AR; [p.] Harvey David and Janie David; [ch.] (Trey) Harvey L. David III; [ed.] Northside High School, Westark College; [occ.] CNC Operator at Baldor; [pers.] I believe that if you can touch the mind, heart, or even the soul. Then you have created a unique emotional feeling that is unexplainable to describe in words.; [a.] Barling, AR

DAVIDSON, BRYAN
[b.] August 26, 1976, Hartford, CT; [p.] Christine and Paul; [ed.] Suffield Academy, Suffield, CT, Syracuse University, Syracuse, NY; [occ.] Student; [memb.] Hendricks Chapel Choir; [hon.] Emmett Kent Public Speaking Prize, Dean's List, Dean's Scholar, Golden Key, National Honors Society; [oth. writ.] Lots, but all unpublished.; [pers.] The past is past, the future, unknown. Live for the moment and appreciate everything before it fades to memory.; [a.] Suffield, CT

DAVIS, ANNABELLE
[b.] July 16, 1965, Provo, UT; [p.] Ted and Ramona Davis; [ed.] George Washington High, Denver, Co. Brigham Young University, Provo, UT. - BS. Degree, Early Childhood Education - Certification, special Education (severe/profound); [occ.] Special Education Teacher, Oakridge School, Provo, UT; [memb.] PEA, UEA, NEA, (Provo, Utah, and National Education Associations); [hon.] Varsity Letter Girls Volleyball. Most dedicated player - Volleyball. International Thespian Society - G.W.H.S. Chapter; [oth. writ.] Informal publications in the Oakridge School Newspaper and Year Book; [pers.] Writing poetry became a hobby when I lost a very dear friend. The things I write about are things with special meaning to me. Hopefully, through my poetry, I can share some of my feelings with others.; [a.] Provo, UT

DAVIS, BILLIE
[b.] April 18, 1923, Grants Pass, OR; [m.] George H. Davis, May 22, 1945; [ch.] Gloria; [ed.] Ed.D. University of Miami Coral Gables, Florida; [occ.] Professor Emeritus, Evangel College Springfield, MO, Writer; [memb.] Delta Kappa Gamma, Phi Delta Kappa, Central Assembly Church; [hon.] Distinguished Alumnus, U. of Miami School of Education. Distinguished Alumnus, Drury College, Springfield, MO; [oth. writ.] Books and articles Gospel Publishing House Springfield, MO, articles - Sat. Eve. Post, Reader's Digest, many educational and religious publications; [pers.] The best thing you can do for yourself is learn. The best thing you can do for another is teach.; [a.] Springfield, MO

DAVIS, ELISABETH A.
[pen.] E. A. Davis; [b.] December 5, 1963, Innsbruck, Austria; [p.] Christian and Erika Achhorner; [m.] Tim Davis, June 11, 1989; [ed.] Hauptschule High School, Kufstein Austria, Frauenfachschule - 3 year Degree, De Anza College - AA Degree, San Jose State University, BA; [occ.] CFO - Print Network, Inc.; [a.] San Jose, CA

DAVIS, JULIA L.
[pen.] Smurf ETT; [b.] February 12, 1980, Hampton, VA; [p.] James and Mary Whitten; [ed.] In 3rd year of high school, intend on going to college in Colorado for Ph.D.; [occ.] Restaurant Crew Member; [memb.] German Club; [hon.] 9th grade honor roll, 10th grade high honor roll; [oth. writ.] 24 more that are my own writings.; [pers.] Life is only what you make of it.; [a.] Bellevue, NE

DAVIS, LOVETTA
[pen.] Love; [p.] Robert Paul Bisbee III, February 14, 1995; [ed.] The Catholic University of America, B.A. 1995, Magna Cum Laude; [occ.] Graduate Student; [memb.] Alpha Sigma Lambda; [hon.] Charter Member, Alpha Sigma Lambda, May 11, 1995; [pers.] I am thankful that I am blessed with a gift that allows me to transmit my ideas, thoughts, feelings, perceptions, emotions, and dreams into words, and am honored that others recognize this.; [a.] Washington, DC

DAVIS, M. CATHY
[b.] May 2 1946, Newton, AL; [ch.] Donna and Dionne; [occ.] President of MCD Transportration, Inc; [memb.] Professional Organizations related to Transportations Industry and National Association of Women Business Owners, Institute of Poetic Science; [hon.] Certified Transportation Broken, 1994 Women Business Owner of the Year, Middle Tennessee, Industrial Category, 1995 Transportation person of the Year, Middle Tennessee; [oth. writ.] Self-published - 3 volumes of poetry, magazine articles in several publications.; [pers.] Poetry is creative self therapy and a level of self-confidence must be reached before poetry can be shared with others. To read a poet's work is ot be really introduced to that person.; [a.] Smyrna, TN

DAWSON, STACEY MARIE
[b.] September 30, 1979, Baltimore, MD; [p.] Michael Dawson and Michele Dawson; [ed.] Senior at Edmondson - Westside Senior High School, Balto., MD; [occ.] Dining Services Assistant, Charlestown Retirement Community, Balto., MD; [memb.] American Red Cross; [hon.] Dramatic Reading Contest Award, Girls Softball Award; [oth. writ.] Several other poems written, but not published.; [pers.] "God Bless" was written especially for Ericka Jefferson a former classmate who was murdered. And I have to give thanks to God for blessing me with a loving brother Dennis Dawson and loving friends Tammie Simmons.; [a.] Arbutus, MD

DE LEON, ROSA JEANETTE
[b.] May 20, 1982, San Antonio, TX; [p.] Roberto De Leon and Maria De Leon; [ed.] James Madison Elementary, Horace Mann Middle School, and presently attending Business Careers High School (9th grade); [memb.] Interact Club, P.A.W.S. (Students with a purpose), Future Teachers of America; [hon.] University Interscholastic League Competition - Ready Writing - 2 yrs. - 1st place, TAAS Writing/Writing Composition Score "4", The American Legion School Award, President's Award for Educational Excellence; [oth. writ.] Poem "Take Me To Your World" published in Anthology of Poetry by Young Americans (1995). "My Sister" published in 1996 edition.; [pers.] My dreams never fade and I always try, even though I may not win. I have been influenced greatly by my parents who have strived all their lives through hardships in order to give me the best straight from their hearts.; [a.] San Antonio, TX

DE VASIER, LUKE
[pen.] Topaz; [b.] July 26, 1980, Union City, TN; [p.] Patty and Gary Moore/Rick and Karen De Vasier; [ed.] 9th grade (completed) and still going; [occ.] Unemployed; [memb.] RPGA Network; [oth. writ.] Several poems for school; [pers.] I have been influenced by Edgar Allen Poe.; [a.] Paducah, KY

DEBUSK, BRITNI NICOLE
[b.] March 9, 1983, Brownfield, TX; [p.] Dr. and Mrs. Ronald E. DeBusk; [ed.] Presently enrolled in 8th grade; [occ.] Student; [hon.] Outstanding 7th Grade, Girl #One; [a.] Brownfield, TX

DECORA, JESSICA
[pen.] Giggles; [b.] July 4, 1982, Sioux City, IA; [p.] Colleen Pipes and Mark Pipes/Leonard DeCora; [ed.] I'm in 9th grade, at Ponca Public School in Ponca NE.; [occ.] Student; [pers.] My mom she found it and told me it was good to send it in the two people who inspired me the most was Jason Yahola who broke up w/me. I wrote it because I love him so much and he made me feel so alone when he broke up w/me; [pers.] When I write I'm in my own world. I owe it all to Jason Yahola and Colleen Pipes.; [a.] Ponca, NE

DEITRICH, ALEXIS JUNE
[b.] May 19, 1977, Ft. Summer, NM; [p.] Robert and Catherine Deitrich; [ed.] College Freshman Majoring in Criminal Justice at Marshall University; [hon.] West Virginia Governor Honors Academy (1995) Academic Awards, Woodmen of the World Life Insurance Award for American History; [oth. writ.] "Parable of the Rose", "The Little Girl", "My Surrender", "Healing Peace" and others.; [pers.] I have discovered that the best attitudes of, life are those of optimism and faith.; [a.] Huntington, WV

DEJONG, MELANIE
[b.] February 7, 1972, Grand Rapids, MI; [p.] Michael and Linda DeJong; [ed.] Kent City High School, Central Michigan University; [occ.] Receptionist, MCA Mortgage Corporation; [hon.] National Honor Society, Girl Scout Gold Leadership Award, Girl Scout Gold Award; [oth. writ.] "The Class Of '90" published in 1990 Kentonian Year Book; [pers.] I've been writing poetry since Jr. High and hope to someday be a songwriter.; [a.] Wyoming, MI

DELLAQUILA JR., JOSEPH
[b.] January 14, 1971, New Haven, CT; [ed.] Penn State; [occ.] Writer and Artist; [oth. writ.] Caged Life (A work in progress).; [pers.] I write from an emotional center point that conveys strength and determination and also that all things can be accomplished by looking inward for the strength to overcome all obstacles.; [a.] Cheshire, CT

DEPEW, KIMBERLY
[pen.] Kimberly Depew; [b.] April 5, 1971, Lawton, OK; [p.] Stephen Rice, Victoria Rice; [m.] Robert Depew, May 30, 1991; [ch.] Brandon Kyle; [ed.] Burkburnett High School, Vernon Regional Junior College; [occ.] Homemaker; [oth. writ.] 'El Gato', 'Sunshine Morn', 'I Like Kitties'; [pers.] You can use poetry as an expression of your thoughts and emotions.; [a.] Gainesville, TX

DEPUE, HEATH
[pen.] Heath Depue; [b.] June 20, 1966, Lakeview, MI; [p.] Fred W. and Viola L. Depue; [m.] Mary Fury, July 23, 1988; [ed.] Mancelona High School, Mancelona MI; [pers.] For me poetry makes me write. I'll think of something and then at night the words come while I'm asleep. So I think they touch people at heart because our truest and purest thought comes while we're sleeping.; [a.] Alden, MI

DESHERLIA, LISA
[b.] June 29, 1960, Saint Louis, MO; [m.] John DeSherlia, May 15, 1993; [ed.] Variety of special and public and a few Parochial Schools, St. Louis Community College - Meramec, University of Missouri - St. Louis; [occ.] Student; [memb.] Prison Fellowship Ministries; [hon.] Dean's List, A winner of a Disabled Student Award at College; [oth. writ.] Two letters to the editor published in local newspaper, pieces published in college newsletters, poem and two pieces published in church newsletters. [pers.] In my writing and actions, I earnestly seek to reflect God's deep love for every individual. I tell people that Christ willing died and rose again for all of us. My gratitude for his goodness has profoundly affected my life and my writing.; [a.] Saint Louis, MO

DESJARDINS, REBECCA LEE
[b.] May 24, Norwich, CT; [p.] Robert and Karen Desjardins; [ed.] Saint John's Catholic School (Grades K-5), Plainfield Central School (Grades 6-8), Killingly High School (Grade 9, presently grade 10); [occ.] Student; [memb.] FFA; [hon.] Honor Roll for School, Star Greenhand (FFA), 1996 J.V. Coaches Award, (Killingly Redgals Softball); [oth. writ.] Numerous poems and other writings - none yet published.; [pers.] Inside of everyone, there is a poet because the best poetry comes from the heart.; [a.] Plainfield, CT

DETTRO, HEATHER
[pen.] Heather Dettro; [b.] November 20, 1983, Decatur, IL; [p.] Mark Dettro and Nancy Hughes; [occ.] Student; [hon.] Honor Classes; [oth. writ.] This is the first of my poems to be published.; [pers.] I would life to dedicate my poem to 3 friends, Patricia Ardnt, Sarah Estes, and Rachel Eastin.; [a.] Evans, GA

DIDAK, LISA JEAN
[b.] May 20, 1986, Santa Monica, CA; [p.] Mark and Anna Didak; [occ.] Student; [a.] Los Angeles, CA

DISHAROON, DAWN ADELE
[b.] August 21, 1959, Philadelphia, PA; [p.] DeAlton P. Disharoon and Norma M. Disharoon; [ch.] Myles Christian Rigby; [ed.] Woodrow Wilson High School, Bucks County Community College, Barbizon School of Modeling; [occ.] Bindery Technician, Delaware Valley, Bindery, West Trenton, NJ; [memb.] LPRA, PTO; [hon.]

Editor's Choice Award, National Library of Poetry, 1996; [oth. writ.] Poems published in The National Library of Poetry's Anthologies, Where Dawn Lingers, The Best of the 90's, and Into The Unknown. Other writings: Copyrights on four poem, Books, Dusk To Dawn, The Dawn's Early Light, After The Dawn, And When The Dawn Comes. Also, a multitude of poems, songs, and four children's books unpublished.; [pers.] Dream, for unconsciously your subconscious holds old memories, and new thoughts of life's dreams. Dad.; [a.] Levittown, PA

DODSON, MICHELLE
[b.] March 10, 1977, Independence, MO; [p.] Joey and Peggy Dodson; [ed.] William Chrisman High School; [oth. writ.] I have been writing stories since the 10th grade, 3 years ago, made up songs when I was nine and recently I submitted two poems to a book called "Famous Poems of the Twentieth Century"; [pers.] For me, poems are one way I can let out the emotions that sometimes build up.; [a.] Kansas City, MO

DONAHUE JR., STEPHEN J.
[b.] February 18, 1978, Weymouth, MA; [p.] Stephen and Christine Donahue; [ch.] Andrews, Amie, Steven; [ed.] South Shore Vocational Regional Technical High School Johnson and Wales University; [memb.] Vocation Industrial Clubs of America (VICA); [hon.] National Honor Society Boy's State '95, 3rd place medalist in State VICA Bakery and Pastry Arts Competition Marlborough, MA '96

DOOTSON, CHAD M.
[b.] Minnesota; [occ.] Drawing on free time.

DORMAN, KRISTEN
[b.] December 30, 1984, San Jose, CA; [p.] Edward A. and Beverly Dorman; [oth. writ.] 1. The Light, 2. Secret Window, 3. The Man In The Window 4. The Friend Within Me; [pers.] I dedicate my poems to my dad who now lives in heaven and in inside my heart I love you dad.

DOVE, LAURIE
[b.] March 21, 1964, Pittsburgh, PA; [p.] James and Patricia Maguire; [ch.] Travis Dove; [ed.] Currently Attending College of the Southwest; [occ.] College Student seeking a Degree in Elementary Ed.; [memb.] First Presbyterian Church; [pers.] I strive to write about my personal experiences with life. "Goodbye Old Friend" was written for an imaginative writing class at New Mexico State University in Carlsbad.; [a.] Carlsbad, NM

DOWNS, KRYSTLE JO
[b.] May 8, 1986, Big Rapids, MI; [p.] Kim and Russell Downs; [ed.] Kindergarten - 5th grade; [memb.] Orchestra, Choir, Girl Scouts, DARE (Drug Abuse Resistance Education); [hon.] Perfect Attendance, Honor Roll, Spelling Bees; [oth. writ.] Personal writings for own interest.; [a.] Sears, MI

DRAPER, CORENE LUEDECKE
[b.] July 5, 1924, Eldorado, TX; [p.] John and Lizzie Luedecke; [m.] George Wilford Draper Sr., December 12, 1942; [ch.] George W. Draper Jr., Mary Ann Draper Elliott Candi Draper Homer; [ed.] High School Graduate Lots of Self Education; [occ.] Homemaker; [memb.] First Presbyterian Church, Hospital Auxiliary; [hon.] Previously published poetry author; [oth. writ.] Poems and short stories shared with family and friends.; [pers.] Peace and harmony among family and friends has been a life long goal. My real "treasures" in life have always been my children, grandchildren and great grandchildren.; [a.] Eldorado, TX

DREWERY, GREGORY LAWRENCE
[b.] April 5, 1970, Detroit, MI; [p.] Alonzo Wilson, Emma J. Drewery, Joseph Drewery; [m.] Sharon D. Drewery, June 15, 1991; [ed.] Charles D'Amico High School, Albion, NY; [occ.] High Voltage Probe Tester for Electrostatic Volt Meters; [memb.] Pace Softball Club, 1988 Member of VICA, YMCA Member; [oth. writ.] Several poems written for friends, relatives and co-workers.; [pers.] In all of my poems I strive to bring a sense of joy or happiness to those who read them in a world filled with stress and confusion.; [a.] Albion, NY

DUFFY, KAREEN
[b.] July 21, 1976; [p.] Raymond Duffy, Elizabeth Duffy; [ed.] James Madison H.S., New York City Technical College; [pers.] I strive for people in the American Society to love and not to hate people. Hate is very powerful and destructive. That is why I chose to write a love poem instead, Eternal Love.; [a.] Brooklyn, NY

DUISBERG, ANNABELLE
[b.] July 31, 1912, Danube, MN; [p.] Alvina and John F. Kottke; [m.] Dr. Peter C. Duisberg, December 18, 1946; [ch.] Twins: Jerry and Larry; [ed.] High school, St. Cloud Teachers College, Univ. of Minn. (College of Education), 1 semester in Univ. of Pennsylvania which led to a Quaker wedding with Dr. Peter C. Duisberg; [occ.] Housewife, Librarian and research for S.W. FL Coalition for Peace Education; [memb.] Englewood Community Presbyterian Church, S.W. Florida Coalition for Peace Educ, Democratic Executive Committee of Sarasota Co. Englewood Democratic Party; [hon.] Valedictorian, high school, Hutchinson, Minn. honors, St Cloud Teachers College, St. Cloud, Minn BSc Cum Laude, Univ of Minn., Post grad scholarship from Mpls. Women's Club in recognition of my establishing first Int'l Students (and Interracial) rooming house for U of M leadership at Westley Edu. where I sang in the choir, I was a discussion leader of their Sun. evening sessions; [oth. writ.] Comedy skits for annual Talent Nite at Presbyterian Church, for 3 successive years, Letters to the Editor and to Congress and Pres. Clinton re social justice issues resulting from group decisions in both Englewood Democratic Party, and the S.W. FL Coalition for Peace Educ.; [pers.] An eloquent Methodist minister moved me in my youth to commit myself to economic and social justice, which I've implemented via study and action groups with information from Quaker periodicals, and others that accept no corporation advertising. I'm a Ralph Nader fan. I taught free classes in Int'l folk dancing as a way to influence youths in intercultural appreciation and friendship, wherever my husband had his Int'l Conservation of Natural Resources works. The last 12 yrs we're on Costa Rica where I got the Univ. of Costa Rica to add Int'l Folk Dancing to their Phys Ed. curriculum for full credits.; [a.] Englewood, FL

DULLE, BARBARA
[pen.] Barb Dulle; [b.] July 30, 1944, Saint Louis, MO; [p.] Lee Schmid and Dorothy Schmid (Both Deceased); [m.] Philip J. Dulle (Deceased, November 9, 1990), June 22, 1968; [ch.] Cheryl Lea, Kurt Henry; [ed.] Rittenout High School; [occ.] Floral Designer; [oth. writ.] I have many poems but I have never tried to publish them. My friend talked me into doing this. Thank you Heather Bright.; [pers.] I write for my own personal satisfaction. It seems to help me release my sadness, instead of keeping it inside me. When something affects me, I write about it.; [a.] Breese, IL

DULLEA, JOANNE EDNA
[pen.] J. E. Dullea; [b.] December 7, 1932, Riverside, NJ; [p.] Elliott (Del) Dullea (F) Dsc.; [ch.] Five living, one deceased; [ed.] MVTHS. (Phila, PA) University of Del, Lakeland Bus. College; [occ.] Secretary Specialist/ Dept. of Labor; [memb.] Arts/on/the park - Lakeland; [hon.] Arts in park poetry - art awards - a/i/p/ - Philadelphia Art Museum etc; [oth. writ.] Childrens stories jody bear creation - new letter articles - poems in newspapers; [pers.] After being an accountant, business owner, locksmith - am settling back into painting, astrology and writing. "The only way the world owes you a living - is to put more into it than you can get out of it in one lifetime.; [a.] Lareland, FL

DUNCAN, JUDEE G.
[pen.] Judee G. Duncan; [b.] December 3, 1947, Bell, CA; [p.] Reuben and Doris Zeller; [m.] Divorced; [ch.] Sean, Todd, and Marc Duncan; [ed.] Lowell High and Arapahoe Community College; [occ.] Asst. Mgr. for a Mexican Restaurant; [memb.] Board of Director for Homeowners Asso.; [hon.] Graduated High Honors, student body vice president; [oth. writ.] Written numerous poems over a period of 10 years and have written eulogies for deceased friends and family.; [pers.] The power of the pen and spoken words can move the human spirit. Let it dance and sing and lift you to greater heights of knowledge.; [a.] Mesa, AZ

DUNLAP, CASSIA META
[b.] August 10, 1974, La Jolla, CA; [p.] David and Kathern Dunlap; [ed.] Konawaena High, University of Hawaii, U. of Colorado, U. of Utah, Institute of Children's Literature; [occ.] Dept. of Ed. Elementary enrichment Program Instructor; [oth. writ.] Children's Works Pending.; [pers.] As an educator, I live the responsibility of assisting, molding, and encouraging todays children for the near future. As each day passes I face the laughter, realities and the worries and see them through the eyes of a child. Their lives become mine, relived.; [a.] Kailua-Kona, HI

DURAN, KIMBERLY R.
[pen.] Kim Renee; [b.] March 8, 1963, Santa Fe Springs; [p.] Angela Hatcher; [ch.] Shaun and Christopher Duran; [ed.] Chaffey College; [occ.] Supervisor; [memb.] PTA and Football Boosters; [hon.] Citizenship Award from President Carter; [oth. writ.] I have written many special poems for different people related to various life situations.; [pers.] I believe people should do their very best to create optimum success.; [a.] Las Vegas, NV

DUTHIE, MATTHEW WEBB
[pen.] Matt-Man; [b.] February 27, 1958, Durango; [p.] Robert C. and Mary E. Duthie; [ed.] Durango H.S., Western State College, Emicy Griffith Opportunity School; [occ.] Real Estate Broker/Owner-Recycle Realty and Development; [memb.] Original Aurora Renewal, Rangeview Optimist Club, Cherry Creek Jaycees, Aurora Sales Professionals International, Delta Sigma Pi Alumni, Colorado Leadership Forum; [hon.] 'I Dare You' award in Citizenship, who's who in High School American, District Golf Champion, Booster Award's, AETT and SPI; [oth. writ.] (Song about Life and Love) compiled in Matt Duthie's 12 string Cobalt Blues...; [pers.] Five life to love and love life to live. There is no need to shorten our lives with negative energy. Encourage-Support-Five long and proper.; [a.] Aurora, CO

DWIGHT-RIFFLE, LINDA
[b.] September 20, 1954, Pecos, TX; [occ.] Artist; [oth. writ.] "Me", "Girl In A Prism Cell (Part 1 and 2)", "Win-

ter", "A Gift Of Christmas For Her"; [pers.] Writing has always been a method of self expression for me. I have worked through many problems in my life by writing and consider my poems to be my best friends.; [a.] Newberg, OR

EAGLE, ASHLEY
[b.] January 6, 1978, Richmond, VA; [p.] John and JoAnn Scarpa; [occ.] Part time Auditor but plan to go to radiology school.; [memb.] DECA Club; [hon.] Won third place in a Science Fair, Captain of Cheerleading Squad for two years; [pers.] I just wanted to say thank you to my mother for all that she has done for me and for helping me through the rough times in my life, so I dedicate this poem to my dear mother, I love you Mom.; [a.] Richmond, VA

EARLE JR., VICTOR
[pen.] Elare; [b.] August 23, 1966, New York, NY; [p.] Victor Earle, Elizabeth Ohnan; [m.] Esther Hiloreth (Deceased), August 12, 1982; [ed.] Thru 2 years at Princeton University, one year Phemeo's Business School NY City, NY; [occ.] Retired; [oth. writ.] First Effort; [pers.] Working on Tremise untitled "One God-One Religion"; [a.] Cary, NC

EARLEY, LUZ E.
[b.] March 20, 1970, Bronx, NY; [p.] Mr. Julio Pinero and Mrs. Luz Esther Pinero; [m.] Clarence Earley, Februrary 27, 1990; [ed.] Sunset High, studied at the University of Texas at Arlington; [occ.] At home artist, painter, computer art; [pers.] Because I feel indeed blessed by the Lord, my words are an attempt to speak for those who find themselves speechless perhaps they will find a little of themselves in my thoughts.; [a.] Famersville, TX

ECHARD, DIANNA L.
[b.] October 3, Lenoir, NC; [p.] Gaither and Joan Echard; [ed.] BA degree from Greensboro College; [occ.] Correctional Sergeant - Dept. of Corrections/Business Owner; [memb.] Reserve Officers Association Poetry Society of America; [pers.] What you are is a gift from God, what you become is your gift to God. Build on what you can be, not what you could have been. (Disgard Mediocracy).; [a.] Raleigh, NC

ECKERT, ROBERT
[pen.] Kid; [b.] November 20, 1964, Pottsville, PA; [p.] Robert and Mary Eckert; [m.] Void; [ch.] Kayla Quercia; [ed.] Graduated 1983 (recently applied to I.C.S.) '83; [occ.] Carpentry; [memb.] Before my current predicament I belong to USWA for 6 years; [hon.] In High School I took flying lessons for 2 years and have always felt gloomy for giving it up, so recently I took my ground school test and passed with flying colors.; [oth. writ.] A year or 2 ago you people printed a poem of mine in I believe it was "Under The Harvest Moon"; [pers.] I strongly believe for every action there is an equal opposite reaction of which the people who lied under oath at my trial for the 1st time the law ever heard of my name, are getting their just reward. An avid reader psychology, self-help books I exude enthusiasm. Looking to start new friendships.; [a.] Pottsville, PA

EDDY, VICKI RAE
[pen.] Vicki Rae; [b.] October 13, 1954, Hot Springs, SD; [p.] Bruce W. and Edna Y. Glover; [ch.] Jeffrey Scott, Jesse Ambre and Heather Amber; [ed.] High School Graduate, Tractor, Trailer Driver; [occ.] Mother; [memb.] Harvest Christian Center, El Paso, Texas; [oth. writ.] I've written close to one hundred poems. This is my first one published.; [pers.] I believe that faith is the foundation of life. I believe it is the one thing that strengthens the human spirit and lasts.; [a.] El Paso, TX

ELLENBERGER, GARY R.
[pen.] G.R.E.; [b.] April 1, 1955, Warren, OH; [oth. writ.] A wide variety of poems, Country Songs, Children's Story Poetry and Newspaper Articles.; [pers.] While emotional highs and lows are often the writer's friend, sometimes simplicity is inspiration enough. My poems "A Winter's Morn" in this publication, was written over break-fast at a cracker Barrel Restaurant while looking out a frosted windowpane, reflecting on my youth.; [a.] Colorado Springs, CO

ELLER, KAREN
[b.] March 14, 1965, Midwest City, OK; [p.] Albert and Dolores Gisi; [ed.] Midwest City High School; [occ.] U.S. Postal Worker, Oklahoma City, OK; [memb.] American Cancer Society, First Christian Church member since early childhood, president of library committee (Jr. High); [hon.] College Scholastic award for Geography, several talent show awards, nominated best actress in Drama (Jr. High) several idea proposal awards from USPS; [oth. writ.] I'm written many poems and songs since my childhood. None ever published; [pers.] I find that poetry is a wonderful way of putting feelings into words; [a.] Oklahoma City, OK

ELSEN, JEANNE M.
[b.] September 25, 1950, South Bend, IN; [p.] Richard Elsen, Mary Theresa Elsen; [m.] David W. Civetti, May 4, 1996; [ch.] Robert M. and David M. Stephens; [ed.] Sandia High School - Burroughs College, Albuquerque Community College; [occ.] Licensed Massage Therapist and Registered Instructor; [memb.] American Massage Therapy Association - Director of the Retreat Committee for first church of Religious Science; [hon.] Volunteer of the Month, April 1993, First Church of Religions Science; [oth. writ.] Three different Booklets on specialized Neuromuscular Techniques created for further study for massage therapists - currently working on a book about the muscular system of the body; [pers.] I am committed with my studies of the human body and I strive for excellence as a therapist to help heal through the power of touch.; [a.] Albuquerque, NM

EMERSON, FRANCES L.
[b.] May 20, 1952, Kansas City, MO; [p.] Frank and Barbara Sanders; [m.] Calvin Emerson, July 25, 1981; [ed.] Currently Enrolled at University of Oklahoma's College of Continuing Education - Bachelor of Liberal Studies Program. Associate - Computer Sci. TJC; [occ.] Programmer Analyst; [memb.] Rogers County Wireless Assoc. (An Amateur Radio Club) - current Sec./Treas.; [oth. writ.] Other than High School Creative writing, only recent poetry of various types - Patriotic, Spiritual; [pers.] I wish to dedicate this poem to both my father and his mother. I find a poem will often appear, almost in full, out of the blue. This one took very little editing once put to paper.; [a.] Claremore, OK

ENGLISH, KATHRYN
[pen.] Katyah; [b.] June 6, 1948, Kansas; [p.] Gail and Angie Reif; [ch.] Karah English; [ed.] Woodbury University Los Angeles, Calif. and the School of Hard Knocks; [occ.] Travel Agent; [pers.] Thank you and Halleluyah!; [a.] Honolulu, HI

ESTES, JOHN
[b.] October 7, 1958, St. Louis, MO; [p.] Mr. and Mrs. Bruce H. Estes; [m.] Alice Estes, February 14, 1995; [ed.] Assoc. of Arts Degree in Fine Arts Brevard Comm. College, Cocoa, FL 1987 Massage Therapy Grad. Twin Lakes College, Santa Cruz, CA 1983; [occ.] Lic. Massage Therapist/Performing Artist in local Community Theatre Productions; [oth. writ.] Environmental Political Articles for the Missouri Earth Advocate, in 1976-77. Editorials and poetry in the Cornelian College Newspaper, 1978-79. I have also been a songwriter and musician for many years; [pers.] My personal ambition is to become a successful freelance writer. Writing is an art that frees the mind and feeds the soul.; [a.] Merritt Island, FL

ESZ, DEANNA
[b.] July 23, 1945, New York City; [p.] Ethel and Richard Esz; [ch.] Jill Burgess, Christina McGuirk; [ed.] Fairleigh Dickinson University BA-Psychology; [occ.] Community Services Case Manager; [memb.] Marin Child Abuse Prevention Council, Novato Youth Coalition; [oth. writ.] Articles on child abuse for area newspapers. Currently writing autobiographical short stories.; [pers.] I strive to write about what I see and see in order to write.; [a.] Novato, CA

EUTZY, STEVEN W.
[b.] October 2, 1961, Omaha, NE; [p.] Ann Williams and Bill Eutzy; [ch.] Michael, Tara, Amanda and Katrina; [ed.] 3 years completed on a Pre-Med degree; [occ.] Concrete Finisher; [hon.] Dean's List 3.92 GPA; [oth. writ.] Several poems and short stories for college; [pers.] Poetry is a reflection of the spirit. The spirit shines strongly in everyone. Learning to express ourselves is the most important thing we will ever learn. To thyself be kind.; [a.] Sioux Falls, SD

EVANS, AIMEE
[pen.] A. Rose Evans; [b.] August 19, 1983, Athens; [p.] Julie Frank, James Evans; [ed.] Continuing; [occ.] Student; [memb.] American Birding Association; [hon.] Finalist in School Belles/Incarnate Word Spelling tournament; [oth. writ.] Book reports, diary, several unpublished poems.; [pers.] "Always try to be happy. If everyone did this, the world would be a much better place."; [a.] Cleveland, OH

EVANS, AMBER
[b.] May 7, 1982, Millington, TN; [p.] Tammie and Scott Evans; [ed.] At Hillard High School; [occ.] Student; [hon.] Honor Student Sport's Award's; [a.] Hilliard, OH

FABIAN, BRAD
[b.] July 30, 1966, Los Angeles, CA; [p.] Ralph Howe, Cynthia Howe; [ed.] Homefield School, England; [occ.] Rat Race; [oth. writ.] Unpublished short stories.; [pers.] Reluctant Existentialist, Passionate Agnostic. I hope one day to unravel my faith through writing.; [a.] Key West, FL

FABIANO, RITA DELORES
[pen.] Rita Delores Fabiano; [b.] July 25, 1942, Philadelphia, PA; [p.] Adeline Cecilia Fabiano, Peter; [m.] Divorced; [ch.] Adeline Lena Cecilia; [pers.] My poem is dedicated to my Mother who is always by my side guiding, inspiring, and encouraging me to write. I also want to thank my friend Flora Jane Wirt for believing in my "talent."; [a.] Philadelphia, PA

FARLEY, JESSICA LYNN
[b.] July 4, 1982, Baltimore, MD; [p.] Beverley and Brian Farley; [ed.] High School Student; [hon.] Jr. Varsity Soccer; [pers.] I enjoy writing on subjects of nature, animals and human sensitivities.; [a.] Sykesville, MD

FARMER, RANDY W.
[b.] July 7, 1958, Wichita, KS; [p.] Kenneth and Jean Farmer; [ch.] Kristopher, Kocy, Kiley; [ed.] Caribou High School, Caribou Maine; [occ.] Manufacture Engineer for Boeing Aircraft, Wichita KS; [pers.] I dedicate this poem to my grandfather: Jack Farmer and Claire Rucker and especially to my Dad Kenneth Farmer. This is for all the stories that kept us spellbound. Stories of your youth, adventures and how mystical life was through your eyes.; [a.] Wichita, KS

FARRINGTON, JEREMY WM.
[b.] October 4, 1976, Rye, NY; [p.] Ard Farrington, Vicki Farrington; [ed.] Rye High School, Siena College; [occ.] Student; [oth. writ.] Published in High School magazine called Spectrum; [pers.] I'd like to thank my family for everything and all the unrequited love that has made my poetry possible. My influences include Yeats, Frost, and Morrisey.; [a.] Rye, NY

FASCI, GRACE E.
[pen.] Kitty; [b.] December 16, 1929, Bristol, CT; [p.] Frank Burgar and Blanche Burgar; [m.] Joseph H. Fasci, July 18, 1954; [ch.] Melony, Sally, Tina, Laura and Geri; [ed.] Bristol High School; [memb.] Youth Fellowship; [hon.] Top honor swimming instructor, Mother of the Year, proficiency of merit in typing; [oth. writ.] "I Wonder", "Close To My Heart" etc.; [a.] Plantsville, CT

FASOLO, THERESA M.
[pen.] Terri M. Fasolo; [b.] October 3, 1950, Syracuse, NJ; [p.] Joseph J. Fasolo and Daisy Frankino; [ed.] GED and 1 1/2 year Vocational College - Ivy Tech Vocational College Lawrenceburg, Indiana 47001; [occ.] Disability; [memb.] Hogan Hill Baptist Church, North Hogan Hill Rd, Milan, Indiana; [pers.] Devoted Christian. I write whatever I'm led to write, and whatever I write I share it with church members. I write songs also, someday maybe someone will need to hear the kind words of a stranger.

FATHIE, KAZEN
[b.] November 11, 1929, Tehran, Iran; [m.] Birgitta Holmstrand, June 15, 1958; [ch.] Arman, Arezo, Ramin; [ed.] Medical College, Tehran, Iran with much additional medical training in U.S. and Sweden; [occ.] Neurosurgeon, President - Neurological-Neurosurgical Inst. of Las Vegas; [memb.] Clark Co. Med. Soc. (Treas) Fellow, Amer. Coll. of Surg., Vice Pres., Int. College of Surg. Ch. Board of Dir., Amer. Academy of Neurological and Orthopaedic Surg.; [hon.] Rotary Int. Paul Harris Club, Humanitarian Award 17 times. 1994 Physician of the Year - Cl. Co. Med. Soc. 1995 Distinguished Phys. Award NV State Medical Assoc.; [oth. writ.] Books published: "Desire - Book of Poetry", "Another Poetry Book", "Payam-E-Arman"; [pers.] My religion is humanity and the way fellow humans are treated. I do not want to be called Iranian, American, Persian or Italian, but called human.; [a.] Las Vegas, NV

FAUCETTE, NATHALIE
[pen.] Cornelia Fancette; [b.] June 14, 1951, Germany; [p.] Mr. and Mrs. W. J. Fancette; [ed.] B.A. from UNC - Chapel Hill NC, M. A. from Duke; [occ.] Currently working or computer degree; [memb.] Toast Masters; [hon.] German Exchange Student (Deutche Acadmishe, Austanch Student); [oth. writ.] Masters Thesis

FAULKNER, EDWARD H.
[pen.] E. Henry Thomas; [b.] March 16, 1953, Cinti., OH; [p.] Richard and Frances (Deceased); [m.] Tammy Lynn Faulkner, May 28, 1995; [ch.] Ryan 12, Jenna 11; [ed.] 10 yrs. GED Linn-Benton Community College Advanced Mathematics; [occ.] Engineer Design Technician; [memb.] JC's 1992, Elks 1993; [hon.] Presidential Merit Award presented by the Oregon J.C.'s for Outstanding Service; [oth. writ.] Presently working on a personal bio describing my life as well as my travels. The book will include poems depicting the roads I travelled to get where, I am today.; [pers.] A person once asked if I was bitter because of my life's hardship. And I replied, to be bitten, I would have to go backwards. It is better to go forward and gain strength from your past!; [a.] West Chester, OH

FERDINANDSEN, KAREN S.
[b.] May 3, 1959, Cleveland, OH; [p.] William and June Stephenson; [m.] Michael D. Ferdinandsen, October 9, 1982; [ed.] Huron High School, Ohio State University, Bowling Green State University; [occ.] Elementary Computer Teacher, Ontario School, Sandusky, OH; [pers.] My passion for writing is influenced by the power of the written word. Great writing demands respect for the potential a poem, story or book has on reaching the heart of human emotions.; [a.] Sandusky, OH

FICHTER, ROSS ALAN
[b.] November 30, 1965, Dover, NJ; [p.] Lanson and Carol Fichter; [m.] Carolyn Taylor Fichter, December 22, 1990; [ch.] Bethany Grace (4), Kirsten Elizabeth (30), Jessica Brianne (1); [ed.] BS. Elementary Ed/Special Ed. from Bob Jones University, Greenville, SC in 1989, Parsippany Christian School, Parsippany, NJ 1984 (High School); [occ.] Completed 7 years as special Ed. Teacher at Hidden Treasure Christian School, Greenville, SC., currently employed as Painter - Landmark Painting and wall paper, Montague, MI; [oth. writ.] No published works. 2 plays performed by school students - "Even A Child" and "One Gift Of Love", also have written several poems and short prose pieces for use in classroom.; [pers.] My writings stem mostly from personal experiences and emotions. I am a romantic at heart but practical in life. My favorite authors are Mark Twain and Charles Dickens. I also enjoy poetry of Christian Rosetti. I am a Christian whose main goal in life is to serve my Lord.; [a.] Mears, MI

FIDLER, DENISE MARIE
[b.] November 9, 1959, Peoria, IL; [p.] Richard B. Fidler and Jane L. Fidler; [ch.] 15 years old cat, Sugar; [ed.] Kokomo H.S. and Ivy Tech. Kokomo, IN; [occ.] Hotel Desk Clerk; [hon.] Phi Beta Kappa; [oth. writ.] Poems and Greeting Cards.; [pers.] The love of a true friend is powerful will.; [a.] Thousand Oaks, CA

FIELD, CYNTHIA R.
[b.] April 2, 1951, Detroit, MI; [p.] Joe and Angeline Habdas; [m.] Jeffrey Field, October 23, 1993; [ed.] Wayne State University; [occ.] Occupational Therapist

FIGLER, BYRNELL WALTER
[pen.] Walter-Byrnell Figler; [b.] May 9, 1927, St. Louis, MO; [p.] Benjamin Figler and Cora (Schmeider) Figler; [ed.] St. Louis County Public Schools, St. Louis Institute of Music BM MM, Fulbright Grant - study in Munich 1953, post graduate study - U. of Illinois; [occ.] Retired Professor of Music - Ft. Hays State U.; [memb.] Life Member the Nature Conservancy, Sierra Club, also member, Nat'l Trust for Historic Preservation, member music fraternities, Phi Mu Alpha, Pi Kappa Lambda; [hon.] Recording (piano) for Capstone Records - name of album is "View from the Keyboard". Fulbright Grant Germany - Bavarian State Music Academy (1953); [oth. writ.] Between Friends and Concerts article on a semester in Europe playing concerts and visiting friends published in Grand Cru - A Wine Magazine from Chicago (now defunct).; [a.] Hays, KS

FIGLIOLA, ANTHONY
[b.] November 9, 1980, Saint Charles; [p.] Steven and Anna Iasimone; [ed.] Currently attending Rocky Point High School in long island New York; [occ.] I am in 10th grade, and I bus tables at a local restaurant; [memb.] I am a member of The Rocky Point Cross Country, Winter Track and Spring Track; [hon.] I was student of the month. Numerous awards for cross country and track.; [oth. writ.] I have been writing poems for years. I have entered a few school contests but never won.; [pers.] This poem was from the heart, to a special person in my life who has made me believe in love at first sight.; [a.] Sound Beach, NY

FINLEY, SARAH J.
[b.] February 18, 1972, Muncie, IN; [p.] John and Patricia Finley; [ed.] B.S. Ball State University, Muncie, IN, 1994, MS Akron University, Akron, Ohio; [occ.] Graduate Assistant, Akron University Geology Dept.; [memb.] Society of Economic Paleontologists and Mineralogists, Ohio Academy of Science; [hon.] U.S.G.S. Intership, Reston, Va (1994), State of Indiana Vocabulary (1989), Scholarship from College Bowl (1990) Delta H.S., Geology Student of the Year, Ball State University (1994), J. David Love Foundation Grant (1996); [oth. writ.] Published abstracts for geochemistry and micropaleontology used for conference booklets.; [pers.] As I write, I hope to capture the poetry of my science with the poetry of my words. The trick is to juggle Albert Einstein with T. S. Eliot.; [a.] Akron, OH

FIX, JO ZEITZ
[b.] October 27, 1953, Lancaster, CA; [p.] Joe and Cecelia Zeitz; [m.] Al M. Fix, April 17, 1974; [ch.] Brandon - 21, Jehremiah - 19, Harmony - 15; [ed.] B.A. (U of MT) in Education, Masters in Whole Learning in progress (Regis U. - Denver, CO); [memb.] Montana Education Ass., National Education Ass., International Wildlife Film Festival; [oth. writ.] Up Lolo Way - Mississippi Poetry Ass., Hop-Along-Harmony-Poetry Guild, NY; [pers.] My Mom's love of language and Pop's adventurous spirit, shared through Sunday desert outings, were very impressible on my writing. I love to explore my surroundings, be outdoors, and look to nature for a simplistic expression of daily living. It is important to listen of your own voice and draw from your own rich experiences.; [a.] Missoula, MT

FLINT, REACHEL REBECCA
[pen.] Lew, RRF Aka Becky Flint; [b.] November 19, 1952, Columbus, OH; [p.] Harry Dean and Mable Mae Broadus; [m.] Darryl Flint Sr., February 14, 1970; [ch.] 4 Children, 6 Grandchildren; [ed.] H.S. graduate, Medical Assistant; [occ.] Homemaker; [memb.] VFW Auviliary Columbus, Ohio Church of Christ Of Apostolic Faith 1200 Brentnell Ave Columbus, Ohio 43219; [hon.] Certified Phybodimist, Medical Assistant, Coordinator for Senior Citizens of Church of Christ of Apostolic Faith, National Library of Poetry, Wife, Mother; [oth. writ.] I am trying to get other poems copy written I am now trying to puting together a book of little encouraging words LEW/RRF, Current Writings for different programs, Graduations, obituaries, Speeches, Birthdays, Obituaries, Speeches, Birthdays, Inspirating writing, Sermons, I would like to have a card business.; [pers.] I love writing poetry to uplift others whom seems to have different trials in life my poetry is a God given gift if I can bring a little encouraging words along with a smile,

I feel this is truly worth while I was encouraged by my Biological Parents and a senior citizen (mom) Mrs. Sarah V. Smith.; [a.] Columbus, OH

FLOEN, COLIN
[b.] March 16, 1963, Red Wing, MN; [p.] Robert and Marlis Floen; [m.] Elizabeth Floen, July 1, 1984; [ch.] Ashley; [ed.] AA University of Phoenix, BS Sociology NY State University; [occ.] Purchasing Manager Sheraton Hotel, Warwick, RI; [hon.] Various medals throughout naval career including Navy Commendation medal and Kuwaiti Liberation medal; [pers.] A sense of humor and hard work makes our time on this planet most tolerable.; [a.] Fall River, MA

FLORES, ANNIE
[b.] June 5, 1981, Santa Clara; [p.] Laurita A. Llorens; [ed.] Sophomore at Lincoln High School; [occ.] Student; [pers.] Trisha this poem is for you. Here's my 15 minutes of Fame. Finally someone had the guts to publish some of my work.; [a.] Stockton, CA

FLOWERS, MARGARET
[b.] January 13, 1947, Sioux City, IA; [p.] Mr. and Mrs. R. E. Hartnett; [ch.] Michele Flowers; [ed.] Grand Prairie High and Cosmetology and Asten School of Therapeutics; [occ.] Massage Therapist; [memb.] Aquarian Foundation; [oth. writ.] Several, but none published; [pers.] Great importance exist in knowing ourself and mirroring God's expression; [a.] Dallas, TX

FLOYD, BRIAN
[pen.] Tiny Flody; [b.] October 26, 1970, Tullahoma, TN; [p.] Lewis and Shirley Floyd; [occ.] Salesman, Auto Audio, Tullahoma, TN; [pers.] Don't ever judge somebody by the way they look. Get to know them before you make a judgement!; [a.] Tullahoma, TN

FOLEY, JAMES J.
[pen.] James J. Foley; [b.] February 23, 1919, Glasgow, Scotland; [p.] James Matthew and Jean Agusta Foley; [ed.] 8 years of school; [occ.] Retired; [memb.] VFW, Brotherhood or Railroad Fireman; [hon.] Medical School WW II; [oth. writ.] Many short poems.; [pers.] Dedicate poem to mother Jean Foley and loyal friend of 35 years Leona M. Post.; [a.] Coraopolis, PA

FOLLETTE, KATHLEEN
[b.] Monroe, WA; [p.] Robert E. Casey and Verle (Mosier Casey); [m.] Walter L. Follette, December 27, 1951; [ch.] David Bruce, Robert Alan and Barbara Elaine (Thomas married name) six grandchildren; [ed.] Sultan Union High School, Everett Junior College, General Hospital of Everett School of Nursing; [occ.] Homemaker and Pianist; [memb.] Dr. C. H. Hofrichter Guild, Children's Hospital - Seattle; [oth. writ.] Have written some poems and limericks in the past - none published.; [pers.] I am influenced in my writings by my beautiful surroundings, my family, and my travels. I love humor and wrote "A Toast" for my late father and his fettle attempt to conquer the errant mole.; [a.] Snohomish, WA

FORD, CASEY MARIE
[pen.] Mary, Casey; [b.] July 1, 1978, Brockpockport; [p.] Michael Ford, Lorie Ford; [ed.] Graduated from Brockport High; [occ.] College Student; [a.] Hamlin, NY

FORD, YAIDA ONI
[b.] June 5, 1980, San Juan, PR; [p.] Earl and Linda Ford; [ed.] Evergreen High School Junior (96-97); [occ.] Student'; [memb.] Optimist Club, Evergreen High School's Chamber Choir, Multi-Cultural Group, and Associate Student Body Leadership; [hon.] 1995 and 1996 Optimist Club Oratorical Contest 2nd place winner. District Contest 1st place Winner, Dr. Martin Luther King Jr. Writing Competition Award.; [pers.] Individuality is an incredible thing. When I'm writing I try to include that as much as possible, and when I'm finished I can look down at my creation say that's me...that's Yaida.; [a.] Vancouver, WA

FORSTER, N. AILEEN
[pen.] N. Aileen Forster; [b.] April 10, 1926, Frosthurg, MD; [p.] Thomas and Alma Brode McCormick; [m.] John R. ("Jack") Forster, April 8, 1944; [ch.] Three daughter; [ed.] High School, Business College, and some University Studies; [occ.] Retired Secretary; [memb.] University Christian, Church of Normal, IL. (Disciples of Christ) denomination. Am not a "joiner" but support most liberal/moderate causes!!; [hon.] Honorable mention of poem entitled "Hands" during an Illinois Wesleyan University (Bloomington, IL) Amateur Writers conference - about 1977-78 or 79.; [oth. writ.] Wrote poems, prose and essays for my congregations, weekly newsletters for over 5 years - University Christian church of Normal, IL. (Disciples of Christ) and under the heading of "The Night Writer."; [pers.] I have always enjoyed writing, especially meaningful prices dealing with nation/worth concerns. Enjoy humor and satire. My philosophy can be summed up in 3 words: Love, tolerance and pence.; [a.] Normal, IL

FRANK, COURTNEY MICHELE
[b.] June 4, 1981, Saint Joseph, MO; [p.] Dr. and Mrs. Richard Craig, Mr. and Mrs. Mike Frank; [ed.] Mount St. Scholastica Academy; [occ.] Student; [memb.] Tennis - Varsity, Drill Team, Pep Club, Cheerleader - Co-Captain, Residence Hall Advisory Board, Secretary/Treasure of Sirch Club (Students in Response to Community Happenings); [hon.] President's Honor Roll, Math Award, Music Award; [pers.] I try to reflect current events in my writing. They are sometimes easier to understand if we can relate to them.; [a.] Saint Joseph, MO

FRANKLIN, JYM L.
[pen.] Jymi; [b.] April 24, 1962, Post, TX; [p.] Jenola Franklin; [ch.] Brandon; [ed.] B.S. Computer Science, Univ. of TX. at S.A.; [hon.] U.S. Army Award for Valor; [oth. writ.] Several other poems not published, (A Blessing, Forever, Sisterhood) just to name a few.; [pers.] My friend is dedicated to a true friend and a person I will always love Bellet A. Reed; [a.] San Antonio, TX

FREEMAN, LISA A.
[pen.] Lisa Browning, Freeman; [b.] February 8, 1967, Bearea, OH; [p.] Carlos and Ellen Browning; [m.] Dwayne J. Freeman, October 9, 1985; [ch.] Aaron J. Freeman, Tiffany A. Freeman and Ethan G. Freeman :; [ed.] Independent Baptist Academy, Barberton, OH; [occ.] Homemaker/mother of three; [memb.] Truth Baptist Church West Salem, OH; [hon.] High School homecoming Queen; [oth. writ.] This poem is one of several I have been writing, such as Independence Day, Suffer Not The Children, Baby of Mine, Through Dying Eyes, Victory Garden, Victorian Dreams, and others to friends and family; [pers.] My writings come from God. There are always circumstances we cannot control but God can. He gives me the words and I write. Poetry is an escape for me to express what sometimes lies heavy in my heart, I call them works of heart. One of my inspirations is Helen Steiner Rice.; [a.] Burbank, OH

FREEMAN JR., ORLAND E.
[b.] March 22, 1924, Bisbee, AZ; [p.] Orland and Occa Freeman; [m.] Jo Ann Day Freeman, September 22, 1946; [ch.] Constance, Candus, John and Scott; [ed.] Graduate, University of Arizona, New Agents Class - Federal Bureau of Investigation (FBI) FBI National Academy; [occ.] Retired Special Agent, FBI; [memb.] Society of Former Special Agents, FBI, American Legion; [oth. writ.] Just completed novel entitled "Chestnut" based on past FBI experiences.; [pers.] To be a simple honeymaker in the beehive of life is my aspiration. Hopefully my poetry will provide a glow of sunshine in the darkest corner, stability to the unsteady, and a rainbow on a dreary day.; [a.] Paradise Valley, AZ

FREIH, RENEE L.
[b.] August 21, 1963, Long Beach, CA; [p.] Calvin and Jean Freih; [ed.] As in Paralegal Administration from Morrison College, as in Criminal Justice from Truckee Meadows C.C., BS in Management University of Maryland; [occ.] President, JRF Consultants; [memb.] American Diabetes Association, National Geographic Society, Thomas Kinkade Collectors Society, World Wildlife Foundation, San Diego Zoological Society; [hon.] School Honor Roll and Dean's List, Recognition Award from Phi Beta Lambda.; [oth. writ.] Published poems in school Saibblings - a publication of stories, poems and verses.; [pers.] I want my writing to make my audience more aware of our environment and do motivate then to make positive efforts to preserve and protect our land and its wildlife inhabitants. I'm influenced by the naturalist and the believes of the native Americans.; [a.] Dana Point, CA

FRENCH, DEBBIE
[b.] April 8, 1962, Eads, CO; [p.] Frank and Jean Lobach; [m.] David French, July 9, 1988; [ch.] Cassidy James and Kodiak Franklin; [ed.] Sheridan High School, Sheridan College, Black Hills State University and classes through Univ. of Wyoming.; [occ.] K-12 Music Teacher at Cottonwood Elem. and Wright Jr./Sr. High in Wright Wyoming.; [memb.] Founder-Director-Member of Wright Community Choir. Member of Saint Francis Church in Wright. Member of Numerous Committe's of Campbell Co. School Dist. in my 11 yrs. of teaching; [hon.] Numerous Awards and Certificates from the school dist. for my help will children. Nomination from my elem. Principal for U.S. West Teacher of the year, 1989. Who's Who Among Jr. Colleges from Sheridan College and Who's Who among Colleges and Univ's. from Black Hills State; [oth. writ.] Only songs I've written that started out as poems - but none published; [pers.] Nothing is more important to me than my family and friends who inspire me to be the best I can be, and to touch lives as an educator is precious treasure to me.; [a.] Wright, WY

FRIEDEL, ARTHUR W.
[b.] November 14, 1937, Pittsburgh, PA; [p.] Anthony and Elizabeth Friedel; [ed.] B.S., M.Ed. University of Pittsburgh Ph.D. The Ohio State University; [occ.] Professor of Chemistry Indiana University Purdue University Fort Wayne; [memb.] American Chemical Society National Science Teachers Assoc. Phi Delta Kappa; [hon.] Friends of IPFW Outstanding Teacher Award, Indiana University Facet Award; [oth. writ.] Journal Articles on Research in Chemical Education This is the first poem I ever wrote; [pers.] I enjoy watching students learn and show insight into science problems.; [a.] Fort Wayne, IN

FUSARO, RITA
[b.] June 6, 1937, Endicott, NY; [p.] Winfield and Mary Kjelgaard; [m.] Attorney John - Deceased (May 30, 1994), February 22, 1963; [ch.] Josephine, John, Michael, Rebecca; [ed.] Catherine LaBoure School of Nsg. Dorchester, Mass., (Boston), Sacred Hurt High School - Weymouth, Mass. Elem. School - Weymouth, Mass. Elementary School from Maine to MD; [occ.] On disability - former Nsg. Supervisor - RN. Staff - Pem. Director of Alzheimers Unit; [memb.] Past A.N.A., Ct. Nsg. Assoc., Natl. Trust for Historic Preservation; [oth. writ.] First time I ever submitted anything. I am a niece of Jim Kjelgaard, Author: Big Red etc. and Betty Kjelgaard, Short story Author - Red book, etc.; [pers.] Recently widowed, on disability, many financial and legal problems. Still in probate - more than broke and I wanted to know if I had any talent or way to earning power while ill.; [a.] Stamford, CT

GALLIEN, KIRA
[b.] May 12, 1982, Houston, TX; [p.] Gardean Delma, Ron Tharling; [ed.] Cimmaron Elementary, North Share Middle School, North Shore High School; [occ.] Student; [memb.] North Shore Sound of Tunder Band; [hon.] 2 Bronze Band Metals in North Shore Middle School Band, 1st Place Science Fair Award in North Shore Middle.; [oth. writ.] Young Love, Your Memory Surrounds Me, (Do you know any thing about the Lillad Press in Sterling Heights Michigan); [pers.] How I got inspired to write "Jot Wanted" is my real mother dropped me off on my grandma and now she wanted me back so one knight I got mad at her and wrote that poem it got such a great response from my family I sent it in.; [a.] Houston, TX

GAMMON, RENEE M.
[b.] February 23, 1983, CMCM in Lewiston, ME; [p.] Pamela Gammon and Butch Gammon; [ed.] 8th grade but I was in the 7th grade when written Buckfield Jr. High School; [occ.] Student; [memb.] Buckfield Jr. High School Student Council, Band, and Chorus, Sports; [a.] East Summer, ME

GARCIA, KATHERINE
[pen.] Kat; [b.] January 12, 1983, Houston; [p.] Frank T. and Francisca Garcia; [ed.] Lamar Jr. High School; [occ.] Student - 8th grade; [memb.] San Jacinto Girl Scouts, YMCA, Brenda's Spinning Sports - Dance - Jazz Gymnastics Team, Lamar Jr. High Cheerleader; [hon.] Girl Scouts Silver Awards, 2nd place, I love dance, 6th place, show stoppers dance, cheer leading safety award trophy; [a.] Richmond, TX

GARCIA, MARC
[pen.] Adrian Green; [b.] September 5, 1973, TX; [ed.] Thomas Jefferson High School for Science and Technology; [occ.] General Construction; [oth. writ.] "Ignorance Lost" is being edited at this time.; [pers.] `Discipline's Offspring' was written for myself and others who question our own artistic abilities, from time to time.; [a.] Reston, VA

GARDNER, CHRISTOPHER
[pen.] CK Gardner; [b.] February 12, 1967, Dallas, TX; [p.] Ann and Ted Gardner; [m.] Marju Lehmijoki, August 2, 1997; [ed.] Honors BA - Southern Methodist Univ., MLIII - Univ. of Edinburgh MA - Yale Univ.; [occ.] Ph.D Candidate at Johns Hopkins Univ. (History); [oth. writ.] Book reviews in the periodical history, A series of collected poems personally published; [pers.] I enjoy poetry that takes quotidian moments or words, highlights them, then impact the riches and library of possible meanliness contained (in appreciated) within the seemingly mundane; [a.] Baltimore, MD

GARDNER, TERRY G.
[b.] January 15, 1945, Lancaster, SC; [p.] Everette and Vivian Gardner; [m.] Divorced; [ch.] Jonathan Gardner; [ed.] Lancaster High School Clemson University B.A., Clemson University M. Ed., Post Graduate - Winthrop and USC; [occ.] Director, Lancaster Adult Education; [memb.] South Carolina Adult Education, Director, S.C. Assoc. for Adult and continuing Education, S.C. School Administrators, Assoc. Civil War society and US Historical Preservation; [hon.] South Carolina Adult Education Director of The Year - 1995 Outstanding Civil War Re-enactor 43 N.C. - 1987; [oth. writ.] "I Hear You Follen Warrior", "The Long Gray Line", "Oh God, Forgive Me", other assorted war between the states poems and short stories; [pers.] I write about my fallen ancestor. Some entered considerate service at 12 and 14 years of age. When I think of my troubles today, then I think of what my ancestors faced. Task of clothes, food and fighting an army 3 times their size.; [a.] Lancaster, SC

GARINO, LISAMARIE
[b.] September 29, 1985, Englewood Hospital; [p.] Jerry and Judith Garino; [ed.] 6th grade; [hon.] I have a lot of cheerleading trophies and medals. I won a beauty contest; [pers.] I do love J.T.T.; [a.] Bergenfield, NJ

GARNER, PAMELA A.
[b.] October 31, 1972, Amsterdam, NY; [p.] Mrs. Joan Garner, The Late Richard L. Garner; [ed.] Currently pursuing degree in Social Work.; [occ.] Student; [hon.] Dean's List; [oth. writ.] Several poems published in local newspaper, written in memory of my father.; [pers.] This poem is dedicated to my late father my inspiration. "I miss you Dad."; [a.] Altamonte Springs, FL

GARNETT, LARRY
[b.] October 31, 1948, Madison, VA; [p.] Aaron and Ruth Garnett; [ed.] Madison County High School; [occ.] Builder; [pers.] Poetry has always allowed me to express the best side of me.; [a.] Madison, VA

GARVEY, ANN MARIE
[b.] March 16, 1949, Dubuque, IA; [ch.] Thomas Daniel Polson; [ed.] St. Joseph Academy; [occ.] Special Education working with the mentally and physically handicapped; [pers.] I shall never cease standing in awe of my Lord Jesus Christ, and am forever greatful for what He has given me - Salvation.; [a.] Des Moines, IA

GARY JR., MARTIN ROBERT
[pen.] Marty; [b.] December 29, 1976, Johnstown, PA; [p.] Shirley and Martin Gary Sr.; [ed.] High School Grad. with 2 years Airforces ROTC Training.; [occ.] Currently working cook; [memb.] Recently acquitted a community symph. band, Franklin Mint, US Mint Antique buyers club; [hon.] Several ribbons in AFJ, ROTC including: Recognized Leadership in Academics, The Publication of my Poetry!; [oth. writ.] Have written numerous poems but never thought of contest possibilities. Most written for friends and family.; [pers.] I used poems as away to express my true feelings having not to involve any other in conversation. Having suffered some medical problems writing lets me relive stress and emotion thus keeping me happy and far from depression. "A poem worth writing are worth sharing".; [a.] Elizabeth City, NC

GATTI, JENNA LYNN
[pen.] Jenna Lynn Gatti; [b.] May 18, 1986, Flushing, NY; [p.] Ellen and Nicholas Gatti; [ed.] Student presently enrolled at P.S. 133 Queens NY; [occ.] Student; [memb.] Girl Scouts U.S.A. for 5 years; [hon.] Scholastic Excellence from grades 1, 2, 3, and 4; [oth. writ.] Unpublished poem titled "Girl Scouts"; [pers.] I am ten years old, I enjoy rollerblading, swimming, biking, reading, and writing. I have been playing the piano for five years. I am also a member of the church choir. I have a dog named Beethoven, two cats named Oreo and Chipper, two gerbils named Earl and Simba, and lots of fish.; [a.] Bellerose, NY

GAUVIN, DANIELLE
[b.] May 22, 1985, Tucson, AZ; [p.] Michael and Janet Gauvin; [ed.] Henry Elementary School; [memb.] Girl Scouts of America Sahuaro, Bobby Sax, Ice Skating Institute of America; [hon.] Academic Achievement Award (Henry Elementary), TUSD Elementary Honor Orchestra; [pers.] I dedicate this poem to my brother Jeffery.; [a.] Tucson, AZ

GAZA, IRENE M.
[b.] Honolulu, HI; [p.] Mosho Gaza and Hatsumi Gaza; [ch.] Deborah Tasato, Allyson Tasato, Keith Tasato, Dayle Tasato; [ed.] Our Lady of Loretto High, Los Angels, CA, University of Hawaii-West Oahu Campus, Pearl City, Hawaii; [occ.] Administrative Assistant to the Securities Principal; [memb.] Honolulu Academy of Arts; [oth. writ.] Prose: Myself-My World, Cans Of Money. Poetry: My Son, Dayle, A Dawn To Purpose, A Broken Toy, Miss-understanding, The Puppet, and others.; [pers.] The "quality of life" is very important to me. It enervates, illuminates and enlighten to higher and better things.; [a.] Honolulu, HI

GIBBONS, KEESHA MARIE
[b.] August 4, 1964, Washington, DC; [ed.] Northwestern High, NVCC, and University of Virginia; [occ.] Information Management Officer, U.S. Gov't; [memb.] S.O.M.E. Volunteer, B.I.G. Washington, DC - Region XI Maryland Writers Association; [hon.] Honorable Mention - "Never" March 31, 1992; [oth. writ.] "The Change" American Poetry Anthology, Vol IV, #3-1985, "Focus" Best New Poets of 1986 (Edited by John Frost), and "Never", World of Poetry 1992; [pers.] This poem is dedicated to my Great-grandma who offered her kindness unto me and for whom God allowed me to provide the same until her death on October 31, 1995 at age 102 yrs.; [a.] Oxon Hill, MD

GIBSON, FRANK H.
[pen.] Frank H. Gibson; [b.] November 9, 1907, Des Moines, IL; [p.] Charles and Julia Gibson; [m.] Wanda Gibson, September 18, 1993; [ch.] By first wife (3), 6 grandchildren, 3 great grandchildren; [ed.] B.A. San Jose State, M.A. Stanford Univ.; [occ.] Retired; [memb.] Roosmore Lions Club, Riverside Co, Magnolia Rotary Center Club; [hon.] 6 golf trophies and other awards, post president of Mutual 22, Roosmoor Walnut Creek; [oth. writ.] Narrative poems, and poems for my grandchildren; [pers.] Write just for fun and for my grandchildren.; [a.] Walnut Creek, CA

GIDEON, JEFF
[pen.] Jeff Gideon; [b.] July 29, 1963, Tyler, TX; [p.] Hoyt W. and Betty Gideon; [ed.] BBA Mgmt Texas A and M Univ 1986, BBA Finance Texas A and M Univ 1986; [occ.] Asset Manager with AMC Real Estate Inc Irving TX; [memb.] Texas A and M Association of Former Students; [hon.] Eagle Scout; [oth. writ.] Poem published in the Ft Worth Star Telegram; [pers.] Inspiration is essential for quality writing!; [a.] Bedford, TX

GILMORE, ARVILLE
[b.] September 10, 1922, Entiat, WA; [p.] Ralph, Faye Whitehall (Dec.); [m.] Louis Gilmore, September 8, 1966; [ch.] F. Annette - Faye A. -Ralph D. - Darrell A.- Willette C.; [ed.] Graduate of Rentow, WA. High School - College Chabot, Jr. College, Hayward, CA.; [occ.] Retired from Business Office Work.; [memb.] Rebekah Lodge, Elks-does. League Bowling; [oth. writ.] Wrote for School paper, in High School - won an Award for Writing - have several poems in current Anthologies wrote many poems for private collectors.; [pers.] My poetry reflects natural beauty and human nature. The inspirations come from the experience of life.; [a.] Winter Springs, FL

GILMORE, TOMIKO
[pen.] Q, Miko, Smiley, and Smiles; [b.] August 20, 1974; [p.] Gregory Gilmore, Amy Gilmore; [ed.] Kiddey College, Burns and Pattengal Elementary, Murphy Middle School, Cooley High and Breithaupt Vocational Technical Center; [occ.] Burger King employee; [memb.] VICA ar Breithaupt; [oth. writ.] None that have been published but some I have written daily as a hobbie such as: What they say about my generation, my people say, why I love sex, and a man without love.; [pers.] My poems focus on reality the question of our lives and being not fantasy nor fiction. I am a realist, I pride myself on being that a realist cannot be either right or wrong but open to every possibility and that's why my poems are real.; [a.] Detroit, MI

GIORDANO, JOSEPHINE
[b.] October 21, 1963, Queens, NY; [p.] Cosmo and Joanne Di Bella; [m.] Joseph Giordano, July 17, 1994; [ch.] Thomas, Nicholas and Marina; [ed.] Sacred Heart Academy, Hofstra University - B.B.A., Adelphia University M.B.A.; [occ.] Certified Public Accountant and Owner -GIO Music Creations; [hon.] Beta Xi Chapter Honor Society; [oth. writ.] I have written several poems and songs.; [pers.] My poetry and songwriting is based on my hopes and prayers for the salvation of the world and the future of our children. I have been greatly inspired by the values instilled by my parents, the love of my husband and children and by the treasured memory of my uncle George.; [a.] Massapequa, NY

GIRARD, ALICE SODEN
[pen.] Alice Soden Girard; [b.] January 20, 1933, Durand, WI; [p.] George and Hazel Soden; [m.] Jim Girard, November 8, 1991; [ch.] Two; [ed.] High School; [occ.] Retired; [memb.] United Methodist Church, U.M. Women, Moose Lodge; [oth. writ.] "Months", "First Born", "Words from the Wise", "Grandmothers and Grand Daughters", "Melon Time", "The Old Steps", "Aging? Not Me" and many others.; [pers.] My husband Jim and I are trained lay chaplins for hospitals and nursing homes. Photography, writing poetry and crafts are my hobbies. Pictures and articles published country extra; [a.] Durand, WI

GIROVARD II, ANDREW T.
[b.] June 27, 1980, Joplin, MO; [p.] Harvey and Sharol Stein; [ed.] Joplin High School 11th Grade; [occ.] Wal-Mart Associate; [memb.] National Forensic League (N.F.L.); [a.] Joplin, MO

GODDARD, EDMUND WALKER
[pen.] Edmund Walker; [b.] October 13, 1954, Griffin, GA; [p.] John H. and Loula W. Goddard Jr.; [ed.] Darlington School, Rome, GA, Phi Delta Theta Fraternity Mercer University Macon, GA; [memb.] Pen and Quill Society, Phi Delta Theta Fraternity (Mercer University), Georgia Gamma Chapter Macon, GA; [hon.] Pen and Quill Society Member, Since 1973; [pers.] Poetry is loves way to tell time.; [a.] Griffin, GA

GOINS, ANTHONY L.
[b.] October 2, 1951, Charlotte, NC; [p.] Walter and Bertha Goins; [m.] Catherine Massey, January 1, 1970; [ch.] Anthony Jr., Kimberly, Roger, Charlene; [ed.] East Lincoln High; [occ.] Raschel Lace Textile Mechanic; [memb.] The In Fisherman, Buckmasters, Bass Angers Sportsman Society, National Rifle Association, Life Member-North American Fishing Club; [hon.] Contribute to other wildlife funds and agencies; [oth. writ.] Wrote poetry to High School Sweetheart; [pers.] I love to be out enjoying nature which influenced me to write this poem; [a.] Maiden, NC

GOLDMAN, HENRY N.
[pen.] Henry Newton Goldman; [b.] December 3, 1925, Augusta, GA; [p.] Martha T. and Henry N. Sr.; [m.] Catherine Ann, August 14, 1948; [ch.] James Byron and Judith Linda; [ed.] Richmond Academy (HS) Chicago Technical College; [occ.] Retired Projects Mgr.; [memb.] A.A.R.P. Westminster Presbyterian Ch. Green Meadows Country Club The International Society of Poets; [hon.] Editor's Award for Poem "Make Of Me A Tree" Anthology, "Tomorrow's Dream"; [oth. writ.] Poems "Allegiance" In anthology "Into the Unknown" "Our Flag" in Anthology a delicate balance. Poem "Make Of Me A Tree" In Anthology "Tomorrows Dream" Poem "The Golden Thread" in anthology "Best Poems of 90's" Poem "Peace" Next publication of "Poets Corner" Some 30 other poems unpublished. Poem "Scourge of God" Unpublished as of to date; [pers.] To share my deepest thoughts in rhyme, find comfort in these words sublime, inspire uplift, exhort in kind, all others who in like do find. If we share nothing, we receive nothing.; [a.] Augusta, GA

GONZALEZ, KRYSTIAN D.
[pen.] Krystian D. Gonzalez; [b.] June 3, 1982, Victoria, TX; [p.] Santiago and Evelyn Gonzalez; [ed.] Student, Victoria High School; [memb.] High School Drama Club; [hon.] Various Performing Awards (Reciting Prose, Poetry, Performing Duet Acts and Group Acts); [oth. writ.] Poems and short stories (not published).; [pers.] "Peace begins in one man's mind, but in another man's heart".; [a.] Victoria, TX

GORDON, ANNETTE
[pen.] Annette Gordon; [b.] March 30, 1981, Redmen Organ; [p.] Karon and Myles Gordon; [ed.] I'm in the 9th grade, at Amanda Clear Creek, J.H.; [occ.] Student; [hon.] Art Award; [oth. writ.] I have other poems that I've wrote.; [pers.] I've always wanted to be a writer, so I started writing about how I feel.; [a.] Lancaster, OH

GORDON, CYNTHIA ELEISE
[b.] December 17, 1953, Washington, DC; [p.] Flora W. Gordon, William H. Gordon; [ed.] Prince Georges Community College, MD, The American University, Washington, DC, B.A., Degree in Communications, 1977; [occ.] Correspondence Specialist, Equal Employment Opportunity Commission, Washington, DC; [memb.] Metropolitan Museum of Art, Associate Member; [oth. writ.] Poem titled "Grey" published in an anthology titled Pegasus, 1975, The National Poetry Press, Los Angeles, CA; [pers.] I am greatly inspired by the beauty of Nature, which I try to incorporate into my poetry. Haiku is my favorite form of poetry.; [a.] Capitol Heights, MD

GORDON, FLORA W.
[b.] September 9, 1924, Lynchburg, VA; [p.] Jacob J. Henderson, Bertha C. Henderson; [m.] William H. Gordon, February 3, 1951; [ch.] Cynthia E. Gordon; [ed.] Cardoza High (now called Central High); [occ.] (Retired) Homemaker; [oth. writ.] Poem titled "En Masse" regarding the meaning of a union and its membership. Not published, but used at a union meeting. Many unpublished poems.; [pers.] Almost everything inspires me to write poetry, - people, places, nature - a God-given ability to express my thoughts in writing.; [a.] Capitol Heights, MD

GORDON, LAUREL E.
[pen.] Laurel E. Gordon; [b.] October 3, 1982, Palo Alto, CA; [p.] Jim and Marcia Gordon; [ed.] 7th grader in Northshore Junior High School - Public school; [occ.] Student; [pers.] I write to express feelings that I don't feel quite comfortable with anywhere else.

GORREZ, EDDIE
[b.] August 4, 1928, Philippines; [p.] Proculo Rodriguez and Eleuteria Rodriguez; [m.] Frank Gorrez, March 17, 1956; [ch.] Amelia, Jo Ann, Francis, Luisa; [ed.] Silliman High, Silliman University, Philippines, Travels and Residence in the Solomon Islands, Nepal, Belize; [occ.] Homemaker, grandmother; [oth. writ.] Unpublished letters to my children and a few poems; [pers.] I feel that I must share my glimpses of this wonderful, beautiful world!; [a.] Arlington, VA

GOULET, GEORGE C.
[b.] August 30, 1948, Detroit, MI; [p.] Cletus Goulet, Gwendolyn Goulet; [m.] Divorced; [ch.] George Jason Goulet; [ed.] Robichaud High School, Dearborn Heights Mich.; [occ.] Truck Driver, Wilson Carriers, Taylor, Mich.; [oth. writ.] Personal poems to wife and friends; [pers.] All my poems come from within my heart and how I feel at the moment. This poem was given to my fiance Kaye Smith who lives in Clarksville, TN.; [a.] Inksten, MI

GRANDON, ALICIA
[pen.] Mary Ann; [b.] September 26, 1983, Ft. Smith, AR; [p.] Toni and Terry Grandon; [ed.] 8th grade Coleman Junior High School; [occ.] Student; [pers.] I've been influenced by myself and my English teacher Mrs. Schriver and the poems that I've read.; [a.] Alma, AR

GRANT, GINA
[pen.] Slinky; [b.] March 31, 1981, Bridgeport, CT; [p.] Judy Grant, Donald Grant; [ed.] Currently student 10th grade Platt Regional Vocational Technical School; [occ.] Studying to be a licensed hairdresser; [hon.] An Award for most books read for summer program - 3rd grade won 1st place in DARE poster contest - 5th grade. I was third chosen out of 28 kids to draw a mural on my elementary school wall; [oth. writ.] Other poems I have written. "A Wounded Heart", "My Given Love", Unforgotten Fear", "Breakup".; [a.] Stratford, CT

GRAUMANN, RYAN
[b.] January 15, 1985, Palo Alto, CA; [p.] Tim Graumann, Clare Lindsay; [ed.] Gateway School, Merit Enrichment; [occ.] Student; [memb.] Wolf Haven; [hon.] Fourth Place at the Soquel Art and Cookie Festival; [pers.] I like to write poems about nature because I have always loved the great outdoors.; [a.] Soquel, CA

GREEAR, CHERYL K.
[b.] September 25, 1964, Saint Petersburg, FL; [p.] Edward Greear, Virginia Greear; [ed.] Northside Christian High School, St. Petersbug, Junior College and further

continued education; [memb.] (PETA) People for the Ethical Treatment of Animals (NWF) National Wildlife Federation (WWF) World wildlife fund; [oth. writ.] A poem and a story on animal rights which I am presently working on. These works are for the respect of all living creatures that I hope this world will someday see as necessary.; [pers.] My work is created by passion and compassion and driven by the inner most part of me to reflect none other than my soul, and to be expressed by none other than my heart.; [a.] Saint Petersburg, FL

GREEN, MANDY
[pen.] Mandy Green; [b.] December 4, 1981, New Orleans, LA; [p.] Keith Green, Kimberly Gook; [ed.] I am now a sophomore at Slidell High School; [hon.] A-B Honor Roll and NEDT; [oth. writ.] Several poems for people I know and for my private journal; [pers.] I speak from heart and put myself into the poems I write.; [a.] Slidell, LA

GREEN, MARGARET E.
[pen.] Meg; [b.] November 11, 1960, Texas; [p.] Janyee Thompson and Percy Kruse; [m.] Kevin R. Green, February 1, 1995; [ch.] Frank, Tabitha and Esther; [ed.] I am currently attending DeVry Institute of Technology. I will receive a BS Degree in February 1998; [occ.] I own a business along with my Husband; [memb.] I am President of the DeVry Christian Students Assoc., Editor of the Phi Beta Lambda Newsletter and I also am on the board of the Chess Club; [pers.] All my writing is dedicated to my children.; [a.] Phoenix, AZ

GREEN, MERICA ANN
[b.] June 7, 1977, Charleston, SC; [p.] Ret. SFC Arthur Lee Green Jr., Leola Blie-Green; [ed.] 1995 Graduate, St. Andrew High School; [occ.] US Army Petroleum Supply Technician Bonsia; [memb.] St. Phillip A.M.E. Church, Young People's Department, Youth Choir; [hon.] Edisto District YPD, Edisto District Missionary Society, St. Andrews High School Band, St. Andrews Gospel Choir; [pers.] I would like my poems and life living to be helpful to someone. My poems express my true feeling.; [a.] Charleston, SC

GREENE, AYANA
[b.] January 12, 1977, New York, NY; [p.] Louise and Daniel Greene; [ed.] Howard University, Marketing BBA; [occ.] Staff Manager; [memb.] Gamma Iota Sigma Jack and Jill of America, Student Liasons WYNEX, inroads Networking Ass'n Inroads; [hon.] Attendance award, Center for Professional Development, Scholarship Dean's List; [pers.] You have the power to decide your own future. Create your own destiny. Decide your future before your future decides you.; [a.] New York, NY

GREGORY, GARRY
[pen.] Garry Gregory; [b.] November 6, 1946, Juneau, AK; [p.] Gerrett and Helen Gregory; [m.] Joan Gregory; [ch.] Scott and Christopher Gregory; [ed.] B.A. from Redlands University Physician Assistant Degree from U.C. Davis; [occ.] Practicing Physician Assistant; [memb.] AAPA, CAPA; [hon.] Student of the year UC Davis PA/FNP School, Senate Resolution for time as CHP officer medals from Vietnam conflict; [oth. writ.] Three other poems, one published by veterans voices spring '96; [pers.] I currently write poetry reflecting my feelings and personal experiences from my two tours in the infantry in the Vietnam conflict. Also showing the emotional and physical conflict arising from those tours.; [a.] Carmichael, CA

GRESHAM, SONJA HENRY
[b.] October 24, 1953, Chicago, IL; [p.] Milton and Shirley M. Henry; [m.] Kevin Gresham, May 16, 1979; [ch.] Three; [ed.] 1 yr. College, Olive Harvey Community Coll.; [occ.] Collector in the Banking Industry; [oth. writ.] The Root Of All Evil (A Musical Drama); [pers.] Unless we become in tune with ours souls, we will lose the most important asset we own.; [a.] Hanover Park, IL

GRIBBLE, LISA K.
[b.] October 22, 1971, MO; [p.] Joe and Virgie Cantrell; [m.] Dennis Gribble, June 3, 1989; [ch.] Kendria, Kendrick, Dennis II; [ed.] Portageville High School; [occ.] Darling Store Fixtures, Piggott, AR; [memb.] Member of the Hayward Baptist Church; [oth. writ.] Several other poems in school, paper and cards to friends and family.; [pers.] This poem was brought to me through the Lord, In Memories of my Father who die with cancer. June 6, 1996.; [a.] Gideon, MO

GRIEP, DOROTHY JEAN
[pen.] Dorothy Jean; [b.] April 1, 1936, Delano, MN; [p.] Herbert and Catherine Bauman; [m.] Gerald Griep, October 12, 1957; [ch.] 11 children, 22 grandchildren, ages 37-16; [ed.] High School Honor Student, 2 yrs. College, Med. Tech. and X-Ray Tech.; [occ.] Homemaker Director of Religion (DRE); [memb.] St. Stephens Catholic Church Altar Rosery Society; [oth. writ.] None published, mostly for friends and family High School and college newspapers and year books.; [pers.] If you trust in God he will help you. And if you look for him. He is present in so many ways. Especially through children.; [a.] Marathon, NY

GRIFFIN, NATONYA NANETTE
[pen.] Nanette Griffin; [b.] February 19, 1975, Huntsville, AL; [p.] John L. Herndon III and Tommie Griffin Herndon; [ed.] Lee High School Graduate 1994; [occ.] I am a Junior at Jacksonville State University. I am studying Computer Information Systems.; [memb.] First Baptist Church, NAACP, Future Achievement Student Tech. (FAST), African American Association; [hon.] Ed White Middle School winner of $100.00 and to be in a book. At Lee High School, I got to be in a poetry book called Expressions. I was in it all four years.; [pers.] I know the wind will blowout the stars in these people's eyes: Nathaniel G. Griffin Sr., Tommie G. Herndon, Mrs. B. Gulley, Mrs. Bonnie Roberts; [a.] Huntsville, AL

GRIFFIS, IDA
[pen.] Ida Griffis; [b.] September 15, 1943, Fredericksburg, VA; [p.] Ralph Chaffee, Lois House; [m.] Linwood Griffis, June 28, 1961; [ch.] Juanita Ann, Paul Linwood, Jim Lee; [ed.] Stafford High, Northern Virginia Community College; [occ.] Supply Technician, Civil Service, MCB, Quantico, VA; [memb.] Calvary Pentecostal Church; [hon.] Federal Length of Service Award (30 yrs.); [oth. writ.] A collection of poems written since 1985; [pers.] My writings are inspirational, a God given talent. God's love is revealed to mankind through these writings are encouragement, comfort and even a sense of humor. I shall be faithful to share His sovereignty, and forgiveness within my writings.; [a.] Stafford, VA

GRIFFITH, MRS. DORIS FIDDYMENT
[pen.] D. Fiddymenter or 'Miss Finny'; [b.] July 30, 1909, Shepperton, England; [p.] Mr. and Mrs. George and Caroline Fiddyment; [m.] Harry Frederick Griffith, April 4, 1946; [ch.] Only stepchildren (3); [ed.] Boarding school short time at Oxford - (College of Nursing, Nursing Exams) War Time Nurse, at Ramsgate Hospital and Brompton Hospital, London and Private Nursing the Aristocrates; [occ.] I am 87 years old and retired now (needless to say!); [memb.] University Women's Club, AAR Persons - Church Clubs Episcopal (Being British Born) I did do volunteer work at 'Bok Tower' Lake Wales and Pink Lady; [hon.] Nursing awards, we do not boast about those. The countess Montbatten and Mr. Churchill honoured me. By a dinner at Simpson's in the strand (with others) London, 46 years ago.; [oth. writ.] I have a book of poems not published, I have never shown anybody (hand written); [pers.] I do not pretend to be an author just somebody who scribbles an occasional thought I trust a good one!; [a.] Lake Wales, FL

GRIGGS, HERMAN W.
[b.] August 16, 1957, Ellijay, GA; [p.] Harold Maynard Griggs Sr., Erna Lee Sanford; [m.] Judy Vick Hatchett Griggs, August 10, 1986; [ch.] Step-ch. - Scott, Robert, Daniel, Joe, Mary, ch- Heather, Hillary; [ed.] Gilmer County High School, Spartan School of Aeronautics 3 yrs Army Aviation, J.B. Hunt Transportation; [occ.] President- CED - Griggs MFG, Inc. Ellijay, GA (custom interior shutters); [memb.] National Federation Independent Businesses. United States Chamber of Commerce. Board of Directors, Griggs MFG, Inc.; [oth. writ.] Over 200 songs written and performed on the guitar in my own unique style. Plus numerous other poems on various subjects.; [pers.] My search for truth and economic stability makes me wonder what we could best do to make the world a littler closer; [a.] Ellijay, GA

GRIMES, CLARA
[b.] May 1, 1941, Banks, AL; [p.] Harvey and Lena Newman; [m.] Terry L. Grimes, July 25, 1992; [ed.] Central High School currently enrolled at Chattahoochee Valley Community College Phoenix City, AL (Major-Elementary Ed.; [occ.] Computer Lab Coordinator, Phoenix City, AL School System (Susie E. Allen Elem. School); [memb.] Lakewood Baptist, Order of the Eastern Star, Alabama Education Association, National Education Association; [oth. writ.] "The Day The Ghost Turned Orange-Vantage Press, 1996; [pers.] I work with Kindergarten and First Grade students in an inner city school. I strive to make a positive difference in the life of at least one child.; [a.] Phoenix City, AL

GRIMSLEY, NICOLE
[b.] June 7, 1981, Glasgow, KY; [p.] Carlotta and Jimmy Grimsley; [ed.] Celina High School; [memb.] Junior Beta Club, American Heart Association; [oth. writ.] Wrote a number of poems dedicated to boyfriend, first one published.; [pers.] I have been influenced by great poets such as Edgar Allan Poe and I hope to marry my boyfriend Justin Trull soon in the future.; [a.] Tompkinsville, KY

GRINSTEAD, ELIZABETH
[b.] April 6, 1946, Chicago, IL; [p.] Anna and Edgar Proue; [m.] Richard D. Grinstead, November 13, 1965; [ch.] Richard J. Grinstead; [ed.] St. Louis Academy grade school Christian Fenger High School Chicago IL.; [occ.] Homemaker; [oth. writ.] Christmas Reflections The Small Summer Cottage "My Tootsie, My Cat"; [pers.] The poems that I have wrote have been through my own personal experiences. It is truly an honor to have my poem published in this book.; [a.] Chicago, IL

GRIVSKY, ALEXANDRA
[b.] November 29, 1977, Brussels, Belgium; [p.] Michael and Sophia Grivsky; [ed.] Sophomore at George Mason University studying as a communications major.; [occ.] Student at George Mason University; [memb.] Member of the National Author's Registry.; [oth. writ.] Published

the poem again in the National Library of Poetry's Anthology Beneath The Harvest Moon in 1996.; [a.] McLean, VA

GRUBBS, JULIE C.
[pen.] Diemond; [b.] December 15, 1969, Goldsboro, NC; [p.] Lowell Nelson Crawford, Rachel Woody; [ch.] Jerame Shane Crawford Grubbs; [ed.] Heritage High School; [occ.] United States Post Office; [oth. writ.] I have wrote a book of unpublished poems.; [pers.] Freedom of thought envisions our mind, the more we look the more we find.

GUARDADO, MARTHA
[b.] August 16, 1945, El Salvador; [p.] Andres Leonor and Leonor Merino; [m.] Luis Guardado, October 24, 1970; [ch.] Katherine; [ed.] 11 Years; [occ.] Office Clerk; [oth. writ.] Poems; [pers.] My verses, the beautiful blossoms of sadness.; [a.] San Francisco, CA

GUILING, SHAWN
[b.] November 15, 1975, Sikeston, MO; [p.] Forrest and Gail Guiling; [ed.] Thomas W. Kelly High School, Southeast Missouri State University (current), Certified Nurse's Assistant (CNA); [occ.] Staff Writer at Capaha Arrow, campus newspaper, full-time college student (junior); [memb.] First Assembly of God Church Psychology Club - Treasurer, Psi Chi, Volunteer at Southeast Missouri Hospital; [hon.] Phi Eta Sigma, Psi Chi, Alpha Mu Gamma, National Dean's List; [oth. writ.] Several poems published in Journey, Southeast Missouri State's Literary Magazine, several articles published in Capala Arrow, Southeast's Campus newspaper.; [pers.] In some of my poems it is my intent to portray features of my life in rural Missouri. In all of my poems, it is my intent to slow that, with God and family, there is hope to be found somewhere even when life seems dim.; [a.] Charleston, MO

GUIMONT, DOMINIC JASON
[b.] February 11, 1964, Los Angeles, CA; [p.] Darrell J. Guimont Sr., Jean M. Moret; [ch.] Dalon Avery Guimont, Angelina Nicole Jones; [ed.] Holy Family Catholic School, Orange High School, University of Maryland, Community College of the Air Force; [occ.] Microcomputer Services Coordinator, Deloitte and Touche LLP; [memb.] International French - Creole Cultural Society, Parents United; [hon.] Air Force Commendation Medal, Air Force Achievement Medal, Air Force Good Conduct Medal, U.S. National Defense Service Medal; [pers.] Life's most difficult challenge is survival. "Assistance" is dedicated to Angelia Nicole Jones - A survivor.; [a.] Silver Spring, MD

GUNTON, BRAD
[pen.] Leroy Stipe; [b.] March 20, 1978, Cleveland, OH; [ed.] Clover Hill High; [occ.] Student; [pers.] "If they give you ruled paper, write the other way," Juan Ramon Jimenez.; [a.] Midlothian, VA

GUPTA, PURNIMA
[pen.] Purnima Gupta; [b.] August 13, 1946, Allahabad, India; [p.] Dr. and Mrs. K. V. Mital; [m.] (Divorced) December 1989, February 28, 1968; [ch.] Daughters - A. Mini Gupta and Suvarna Gupta; [ed.] M. Arch. - University of Illinois 1970, B. Arch. - Univ. of Roorkee 1968; [occ.] Insurance Representative; [memb.] Founder Secretary and past President of "Roorkee University Alumni Assn-North America" including various local chapters; [hon.] "Outstanding New Citizen of 1977-78 for achieving success in architecture, my chosen field and for remarkable success in fostering community spirit in Chicago as proclaimed by the President of the US. First prize - National Design Competition, India 1946.; [oth. writ.] Have been publishing stories and poems in "Hindi" since 1980 in Delhi Press Publications.; [pers.] Coming from Indian Society where a woman is not allowed to make her own mistakes and keep going, I have come to a point where living my own life my way is a struggle at worst and an accomplishment at best at the cost of losing friends and relations along the way including a loveless marriage.; [a.] Raleigh, NC

GUSS, ERIN C.
[b.] March 1, 1979, Saint Charles, IL; [p.] Carolyn and Ted Guss; [ed.] Beginning my final year at South High School, then I'm on to college, (not sure where); [occ.] Student and part time secretarial work for a real estate broker; [memb.] National Honor Society, Spanish N'tl Honor Society, Mentoring, Student Council; [hon.] Honor Roll for 3 years; [oth. writ.] This is my first time getting published, so most of my poetry is still under cover.; [a.] Crystal Lake, IL

HAAGA, JASON
[b.] January 24, 1985, Hartford, CT; [p.] Eric Haaga and June Haaga; [ed.] Currently in 6th grade at Vernon Middle School, Vernon, CT; [pers.] Poem was written as part of a 5th grade project for the seek (gifted) program at Meridian Middle School, Buffalo Grove, IL; [a.] Vernon, CT

HAGEMAN, WARREN
[b.] January 6, 1943, MN; [p.] Evan and Emma Hageman; [m.] Gabriela Hageman, December 5, 1987; [ed.] B.S., Business Admin., Mankato State U.; [occ.] U.S. Civil Service; [a.] Arlington, VA

HAGERMAN, JUANITA KAY
[b.] July 15, 1968, Welch, WV; [p.] Burley and Mary Muncy; [m.] Jonathan Ray Hagerman, September 12, 1988; [ch.] Scotty Ray Hagerman (1 child); [ed.] I only completed the 8th grade in school, I was also a writer in school; [occ.] House wife and Mother, a writer, and I spend my time with the elderly and help when I can; [hon.] Golden poet award, silver poet award, poet of the year award, honorable mention; [oth. writ.] I also like to write short kid's stories, stories on my families past and poems on my life, my friends and the people I love and care about! Oh, yea, one of my favorites is song writing!; [pers.] I would love to keep writing on all the beauty of the past and seek out the mew in the future. And loved ones whom I'll never see here again, hopefully to share with the world all the beauty it really has! Juanita Kay Hagerman; [a.] Warriormine, WV

HAILSHAM, JEANNETTE POPE
[b.] September 15, 1961, Pittsburgh, PA; [p.] Titchmon Pope and Marjorie Pope; [m.] Larry Hailsham, April 22, 1986; [ch.] Melanie, Amanda, Larry Hailsham; [ed.] Carrick High School, Allegheny Community College, University of Pittsburgh; [hon.] The National Dean's List, Who's Who Among Students in American Junior Colleges, Citation for Outstanding Service to the Pennsylvania House of Representatives; [pers.] It is just as difficult to do what's right as it is to do what's necessary.; [a.] Pittsburgh, PA

HALL, KAREN S.
[b.] March 17, 1960, Brevard, NC; [p.] Mark and Evalina Sanders; [m.] Phillip L. Hall, December 27, 1986; [ch.] Tyler Earl Hall (Ty); [ed.] Rosman High School, Tennessee Temple University; [occ.] Homemaker and Mother, Former Teacher; [memb.] Alpha Delta Kappa, Secretary; [hon.] Alpha Delta Kappa; [pers.] My desire is to use the talents and abilities that God has given me to their greatest potential to bring honor and glory to Him.; [a.] Rock Hill, SC

HAMILTON, EDGAR ALLEN
[b.] March 28, 1947, Richmond, VA; [p.] Donald L. and Vernon D. Hamilton; [m.] Pamela B. Hamilton; [ch.] Dina Annette, Barry Allen, Kristy Marie; [ed.] Powhatan Public School Huguenot Academy - Graduated University of Richmond - Past Year; [occ.] Factory worker; [hon.] National Honor Society Quality Leadership Award from E.I. DuPont Co. - Spruance Plant Honorable Discharge - U.S. Army Vietnam Vet.; [a.] Richmond, VA

HAMLETT, QUENTINA Y. A. D.
[b.] July 11, 1972, Wash., DC; [p.] Eva P. Hamlett, Fredrick L. Young; [ed.] Washington Dix Street Academy Sophomore at The University of The District of Columbia; [occ.] Student; [pers.] I'd like to dedicate this poem and it's publication to my grandmother Elsie V. Hamlett and to the rest of my family. Thank you for your love and support.; [a.] Washington, DC

HANES, JEREMY
[b.] November 23, 1976, IL; [p.] Ko and Linda Hanes; [ed.] T.F. South, Calumet College of St. Joseph; [occ.] Assistant Manager, Cook at Aurelia's Pizza; [oth. writ.] Some poems I put in school newspapers; [pers.] Be yourself! Don't change for anyone. Be the best you, you can be. Thank you, to my Mom, Dad, sister, grandma and family I love you guys.; [a.] Lansing, IL

HANNA, DORETHA PRIOLEAU
[b.] March 11, 1948, Fairfield Co; [p.] Sara D. Prioleau and The late James Prioleau; [m.] Alphonza Louis Hanna Jr.; [ch.] Alphonza L. Hanna III and Celeasha A. Hanna; [ed.] Fairfield High School, Allen University, Univ. of South Carolina, Winthrop University; [occ.] Pre-School Teacher; [memb.] Elder - Lebanon Presby Church, Girl Scouts Organization, P.T.A., School Improvement Council, National Educ. Association, Community Economic Committee, Precinct Member; [hon.] Masonic Appreciation, P.T.A., S.C. Foster Parent Association Award, Youth Club Appreciation Award, Geiger Elem. Teacher of the Year, Who's who Among America's Teachers, Church's - Mother of the Year; [pers.] As we approach the next millennium, we need to search our soul to discover 'Self' and to find out where we go from here. Sometimes, in order to make a difference, we have to make a change within ourselves. Especially, if we are to make an astounding difference to mankind or to follow your dream.; [a.] Ridgeway, SC

HANNA, MARY ANN PASALICH
[pen.] Nugett, Angel Eyes; [b.] January 10, 1936, Cumberland, MD; [p.] Hazel May and Chas W. Miller; [m.] George W. Miller, April 15, 1980; [ch.] Chas W. Hanna; [ed.] Allegheny High Trenton's Business School; [occ.] Music Teacher (Piano) 37 yrs.; [memb.] MTNA "Music Teachers National Assoc. Member #722157; [hon.] Outstanding Performance Piano Competition, Good Standing Plaques from Teachers Association; [oth. writ.] Time, Snow, A Child in Need of Love; [pers.] "Without love forgiveness humbleness we have nothing."; [a.] San Diego, CA

HANSON, LEE ANN
[b.] March 7, 1952, Boulder; [p.] Edwin W. Lowrey, Virginia Lee Such Lowrey; [m.] Divorced, June 16, 1973; [ch.] Jason, Tallis, Erik; [ed.] I received an Associates Degree from Arapahoe Community College in 7

quarters before I began working as a medical laboratory technician at Swedish Medical Center. Shortly after my college graduation, I was married; [occ.] Home maker Canine Obedience Instructor; [memb.] Eastern Star (Fraternal Organization) Columbine Norwegian Elkhoud Association where I served as show chairman in 1994; [oth. writ.] Several unpublished poems, several unpublished short stories including a pseudo autobiography concerning medical technology work; [pers.] As all people are, I am an unique individual having diversified traits and talents. I try to use those categorized qualities to their extreme best based on my limited perceptions; [a.] Thornton, CO

HARDNETT, LEON

[p.] Ernest Hardnett Sr., Sarah Hardnett; [m.] Anna M. Hardnett, January 9, 1979; [ch.] Theron J., Aaron T., Joel L.; [ed.] West High, BSET Southern University, Baton Rouge, LA; [occ.] Material Service Coordinator; [memb.] Promise Keepers, Church Point Ministries; [oth. writ.] I've written about 15 poems one of which was published in the Southern University Digest. Co-written several musical dramas depicting the lives and problems Teen agers face in Inner City America; [pers.] I try to focus on God's love for humanity in my compositions. To give life is an expressions. To give life is an expression of God's love, preserving it an expression of mercy, but to destroy it is an expression of judgement which is a choice that should be reserved only for God.; [a.] Baton Rouge, LA

HARP, CHERYL E.

[b.] December 6, 1951, Paducah, KY; [p.] Mr. and Mrs. Carl Cousins; [m.] Nathaniel Harp, May 22, 1976; [ed.] High School Diploma, Clerical Occupations Beauty School Graduate; [occ.] Telemarker for Preferred Community Services; [hon.] Beauty College Awards, Perfect Attendance, Most Cooperative Student, Soaring Heights Awards; [oth. writ.] "Rhonda Lynn Denise Johnson", "Gerald Allan Harper; [pers.] Using my mind for something constructive helps get my mind off so many others idol problems.; [a.] Indianapolis, IN

HARRIS, RYAN MATTHEW

[b.] January 7, 1973, Salt Lake City, UT; [p.] Larry and Janet Harris; [ed.] Pleasant Grove, High School Utah Valley Community College; [hon.] Honor Student - Pleasant Grove High School, Dean's List, Utah Valley State College, Student Government, Tennis Team, Radio Disc Jockey, Entertainer, Comic; [oth. writ.] Many short stories poetry - working on novel.; [pers.] Ryan died December 21, 1992, at 19 years of age. It was Ryan's dream to be an author or writer but his life was cut short by a tragic death after a 6 month battle with Leukemia He wrote this poem while he was sick.; [a.] Pleasant Grove, UT

HARRISON, ERIC

[pen.] Eric Harrison; [b.] May 25, 1979, Texas; [p.] Sharon and Gail Lee; [ed.] Currently a Junior at Prescott High School; [pers.] I have to give thanks to my sister and mom, for helping me pick out this poem.; [a.] Prescott, AZ

HARRISON, JEAN

[b.] September 29, 1922, Sedalia, MO; [p.] Rufus and Margaret Smallwood; [ch.] 5 boys, 1 girl, 9 grandchildren, 2 great grandchildren; [ed.] Smith-Cotton High and Central Business College, Sedalia, Missouri. Various college courses U. of MO., at Rolla. Drury, SMS, Springfield, MO; [occ.] Retired Civil Service Secretary, Engineering Technician and Construction Inspector; [memb.] Catholic Church, various Church Organizations, Lebanon Garden Club, Nat. Assoc. of Women in Construction, Lebanon Garden Club, Ozark Penmasters' Guild, Cedars of Lebanon Prayer Group; [hon.] District and Diocesan awards for Community and International Commissions. Blue ribbons and awards for horticulture and arrangements, runner-up for Senior Citizen of the year; [oth. writ.] Several poems published in the local paper. Was Ft. Leonard Wood Reporter for Omaha District Newsletter. Article "The Role The Corps Plays at Ft. Leonard Wood", published in Omaha Dist. news, also in Waynesville and Lebanon, MO, papers. Several travel articles published in local and Diocesan papers. Have written some unpublished books.; [pers.] My philosophy is to keep on going through all odds, never give up. With inner strength you can overcome anything.; [a.] Lebanon, MI

HARRISON, STEFANY EILEEN

[b.] October 30, 1981, N. Hollywood, CA; [p.] R. Michael Harrison, Robin Harrison; [occ.] Student at Valley alternative Magnet School Van Nuys, CA.; [hon.] Many spelling, Math, awards. And I was an honor student my freshman year of high School at Highland High in Palmdale, CA.; [pers.] I've always enjoyed writing poems, I never thought I'd actually get one published!; [a.] Lake Elizabeth, CA

HART, LOMA SUSAN

[b.] June 22, 1921, Pemberton, WV; [p.] William David and Vessa P. Jones; [m.] Paul G. Hart, April 27, 1943; [ch.] Paula Susan Baldwin-Richard P. Hart; [ed.] Woodrow Wilson High-Beckley College, Retired Banker, Adult Sunday School Teacher Calloway Heights Baptist Church, Amateur Artist; [occ.] Retired; [memb.] Beckley Art Group - National Association of Bank Women-Calloway Heights Baptist Church; [oth. writ.] Several poems published, 6 golden poetry awards. Two Editor Choice awards.; [pers.] I strive to reflect Christianity, home, children, family and the beauty of our great universe I have always love poetry and I am greatly influenced by poetry of all kinds especially Helen Steiner Rice.; [a.] Cool Ridge, WV

HART, T. SHARON

[pen.] Sharown; [b.] January 31, 1974, Charlotte, NC; [p.] Alma Hart; [ed.] Lincoln University, PA Bachelor of Science Degree in Elementary Education; [occ.] Graduate student; [memb.] Hebrew-Israelite Community (Yahudee), Education Club, Volunteer and Mentor Groups; [hon.] Dean's List, Who's Among students in American Colleges and Universities; [pers.] Everyone is blessed with a talent. I thank E(y)aw Hooshua for my talent, and use it for his praise.; [a.] Matthews, NC

HARTMAN I, MIKE RAY

[b.] April 2, 1952, Fort Worth, TX; [p.] Fred C. and Ruth M. Hartman; [m.] Judy Kaye Hartman, May 11, 1975; [ch.] Michael II and Angel; [ed.] 1970 Graduate of Green B., Trimble Technical High School; [occ.] Auto Parts Stock Handler and Power Truck Operator; [oth. writ.] Three songs I wrote were under contract back in 1982. Unfortunately, nothing happened.; [pers.] I dedicate this poem to all of us who have lost loved ones. Please, trust in Jesus.; [a.] Joshua, TX

HARVEY, BERYL

[pen.] Lady Dynamite; [b.] July 27, 1938, Trinidad and Tobago; [p.] Nathaniel Clarke, mother deceased; [m.] Divorced; [ch.] Shanida and Sharon (Twins); [ed.] MAS Emanuel Private School Trinidad, Nelson St Girl's RC School Trinidad, St Theresa's Convent Trinidad, Hackney Hospital England; [occ.] Nursing Instructor/Dir of Human Resources; [hon.] Nurse of the Year 1962; [oth. writ.] Newsletter editor and founder, Cruising with Lady Dynamite, editor and founder Battered Woman Exclusive; [pers.] Poetry is an expression of my feeling from the heart, and I see in and around me. I wish my mother was alive to read my writing, she read poetry to me as a child.; [a.] Silver Spring, MD

HARVEY, KENDRA CAPRI

[b.] September 26, 1981, Heidelberg, Germany; [p.] Kennith and Angela Harvey; [ed.] Hayfield Secondary High School; [occ.] Student; [pers.] I express my feelings in my poems. I really didn't think I could do it, but I did!; [a.] Lorton, VA

HASSETT, DOUGLAS D.

[b.] December 19, 1952, Kansas City, MO; [m.] Cindy Hassett, May 12, 1990; [ch.] B.S. 1982 Northern Arizona University; [ed.] Self Employed, Lighting Manufacturing/Sales; [occ.] Alpha Tau Omega Fraternity; [pers.] Pursue your dreams and use your God given talents.; [a.] La Quinta, CA

HAWKINS, STEVEN

[pen.] Steven Lee Hawkins; [b.] November 19, 1978, Greenville, SC; [p.] Tommy and Janice Hawkins; [ed.] Wade Hampton High School, currently pursuing a Bachelor of Science degree in Electrical Engineering at Greenville Tech.; [occ.] College Student; [memb.] Watchtower Bible and Tract Society Jehovah's Witnesses; [hon.] 2 Ratings of superior at the South Carolina High School Orchestra Festival. NAACP Act So Award.; [oth. writ.] "It is Fall" published in The Greenville News-Piedmont. It received special mention in newspaper contest. "All former things" published in Whispers at Dusk, a National Library of Poetry Publication.; [pers.] I strive to write about how God and the Bible will solve the problems mankind faces and how God's Kingdom will bring paradise on earth.; [a.] Greenville, SC

HAY, BRENDAN

[b.] February 19, 1979, Long Island, NY; [p.] John Hay and Maureen Hay; [ed.] As of now, Carle Place High School (Senior); [occ.] High School Student; [memb.] National Honor Society, Spanish National Honor Society, Tri-M Music Honor Society, Drama and Musical Company, Ensemble Singer; [hon.] New England Young Writer's Conference (Finalist), Gold Medal Columbia University High School Literary Magazines, (Member of Staff of Helios); [oth. writ.] Several poems published in the School literary magazine, Columnist for school newspaper.; [pers.] Thank you to my parents, girl friend, and English teacher Mrs. Ziminski and Mr. Morris for encouraging me to write. Hopefully, this is the beginning of a long career.; [a.] Carle Place, NY

HAYES, SANDRA

[b.] September 29, 1959, Greenville, SC; [p.] James and Betty Redmon; [ch.] Six - Tiffany Jessica, Troy, Trae, Kristopher and Jennifer; [ed.] Graduated high school at age 16 on May 31, 1976; [occ.] Mother and all that employees; [memb.] Heart Council, Cancer Society, North Shore Animal League, Columbia House; [pers.] Live each and every day to the fullest, give to others, teach the children well for they are the future of the world, and thank the Lord every day for being alive.; [a.] Gainesville, GA

HAYNES, KATHERINE ALLISON

[b.] April 25, 1980, Portland, OR; [p.] Fred and Carolyn

Haynes; [ed.] Wapakoneta High School Ohio, Sam Barlow High School, Gresham, OR; [occ.] Junior at Barlow HS; [oth. writ.] I have written several other poems but this is the only one that is published; [pers.] I wrote this poem in memory of my great-great aunt Mildred Henry died June 4, 1996. Thank you mother for encouraging me to enter the contest.; [a.] Gresham, OR

HAZZARD, MARY JOHN SPOLSDOFF
[pen.] Mary John Spolsdoff Hazzard; [b.] December 3, 1951, Fresno, CA; [p.] Johna, Verall Spolsdoff; [m.] Gordon Wayne Hazzard, January 13, 1990; [ed.] Central Union High Fresno (CSU), California State University Fresno BA (Continued Ed La Verne University) have not completed MA though.; [occ.] Elementary Teacher; [memb.] Honor Societies, Kappa Delta Phi, Phi Delta Kappa, Delta Kappa Gamma; [hon.] Magna Cum Laude (CSUF) 1996 Teacher of the Year for Rosedale North School Past, Matron Order of the Eastern Star; [oth. writ.] None are published yet; [pers.] When all else fails I try to follow Philippians 4:8. The joy of the spoken or written word is not the belief that someone will under stand you through it but that they do.; [a.] Bakersfield, CA

HEALEY JR., THOMAS M.
[b.] June 23, 1962, Methuen, MA; [p.] Thomas M. Sr., Rusty Dees; [m.] Frances M. Faford, February 14, 1982; [ch.] Matthew David 13, Shauna-Marie 1; [ed.] Greater Lawrence Regional Vocational Technical H.S. class of '80 (Gr. Law. Reg. Voch. Tech. H.S.); [occ.] Welder/ Steel Fabricator; [memb.] N.R.A. (Not Current Unfortunately); [oth. writ.] Much written nothing published; [pers.] An American poet once read: There are things known, and unknown and in between, there are doors. If that be so personal/expression thru poetry is one of the greatest to open, don't wait for personal triumph or tragedy to inspire your words keep the door open always for what is on the other side is truly inspirational; [a.] Fort McCoy, FL

HECKER, J. R.
[b.] May 9, 1976, Kettering, OH; [p.] Steve Hecker and Jo Hecker; [ed.] Graduate of Centerville High School, currently 3rd year Sophomore at Ohio University in Athens, OH; [occ.] Student; [oth. writ.] Independent songwriter for local bands in Athens; [pers.] "Live your life, not their life."; [a.] Athens, OH

HEISMAN, AMANDA
[b.] October 22, 1981, Columbus, OH; [p.] John Heisman, Elaine Heisman; [ed.] Currently a freshman student at Toledo Christian Schools; [occ.] Student; [memb.] Soccer, basketball, cross-county and track teams; [hon.] Honor roll student, Girl Scout Silver Award, U.S.N.M.A. Math Award, GTTCM Math Award, Athletic Awards; [pers.] Never give up! Be determined to do your best in all situations.

HEIST, SCOTT M.
[b.] June 18, 1980, San Diego, CA; [p.] Elisabeth Wright, Donald Heist; [ed.] Junior, Fork Union Military Academy, Fork Union VA, 22205; [memb.] St. Joseph's Church, Palmyra VA; [pers.] I spend most of my time at the beach, surfing. Surfing is my main hobby, writing poems is something I do to pass time away.; [a.] Churchton, MD

HELDMAN, TINA J.
[b.] August 8, 1979, Bluffton; [p.] Ralph Heldman and Doris Heldman; [ed.] Cory - Rawson High, I plan to go to college at ATI in Wooster Ohio to study cattle and sheep production.; [occ.] Work on my family farm; [memb.] Future Farmers of America (FFA) 4-H Club; [hon.] Star Greenhand Award in (FFA); [a.] Rawson, OH

HEMPHILL, WALTER H.
[b.] May 15, 1924, Marion, NC; [p.] Hicks Hemphill - Nelle Early Hemphill; [m.] Rena Wilson, June 27, 1947; [ch.] Ronald W. Hemphill; [ed.] High school - some college; [occ.] Vice Pres. Mfg, Shaw Industries, Inc Dalton, GA (Retired); [memb.] Lions International; [hon.] Melvin Jones Fellow - Lions International Distinguished Service Award, Jayees, 1959 Lifetime Honorary Member, GA Sheriffs Assoc. Veteran WWII - US Navy; [pers.] I was greatly influenced by growing up on my grandfather's farm during the years of The Great Depression when life values took on greater meaning.; [a.] Dalton, GA

HENDERSON, VONSHA RENEA
[b.] November 21, 1970, Ferriday, LA; [p.] Dorothy Hutton, Alberta and Wilbert Henderson; [ed.] Ferriday High, Northeast Louisiana University; [occ.] Teaching Graduate Assistant, Northeast Louisiana University, Monroe, LA; [pers.] My life is mine, and I am making it better.; [a.] West Monroe, LA

HENDRICKS, E. MARLENE
[b.] July 24, 1931, Oakland, CA; [p.] Arthur L. Peppard, Jeanetta Redmond; [m.] Divorced; [ch.] Three; [ed.] High School (Sequoia Union High) various College Studies, various Universities - no degree Student of Pact Rich Ives; [occ.] Retired Apt. House Operator; [memb.] Trinity Episcopal Church, Phi Theta Kappa Honor Society; [hon.] Just one MRS.; [oth. writ.] Newspaper articles, fiction and creative non-fiction poetry.; [pers.] Poetry waiting is an explanation of sound and emotion and memories, a very personal pilgrimage.; [a.] Everett, WA

HENNING, JOHN WILLIAM
[b.] March 21, 1985, Freehold, NJ; [p.] Brian and Linda Henning; [ed.] Student of Trinity Christian Academy 6th grade; [occ.] Student; [memb.] World Tae Kwon Do Federation; [hon.] D.A.R. Award Black Belt - Tae Kwon Do; [pers.] The principle of my life is my poem, "Who is Christ in life."; [a.] Plano, TX

HENNIS, JIMMIE MALONE
[b.] July 5, 1952, Houston, TX; [m.] Ronnie, June 21, 1968; [ch.] Four sons, three granddaughters and one grandson; [ed.] Self Educated Texas G.E.D. 1981, I was born with an addiction to the printed word.; [occ.] Ranch Management Consultant, Ratites, Exotic Hoof Stock, Common Live Stock; [memb.] I do not join clubs. Board of Directors, 1974-1986, Cleveland Youth Baseball Assoc. Cleveland, Texas Vol. Teacher, Cook 1989-1992, Camp Wood Head Start, Camp Wood, Texas; [hon.] Community Service, Tarkington I.S.D. - 1971, 73, 74, 75, 76, 78, C.Y.B.A. - 1981, 82, 85, 86, Camp Wood Head Start 1991, 92; [oth. writ.] Commissioned Historical Research Hardin- Simmons University, Live Oak Ranch Shippers Stevedoring, Port of Houston Private Family Histories Sports Journalism, Cleveland Advocate unsubmitted Children's Books, Short Stories Poetry; [pers.] We are mankind each responsible for the results of our own actions. Love, Hope, Peace.; [a.] Merkel, TX

HENRY, JANET R.
[b.] March 23, 1955, San Mateo, CA; [p.] John and Naomi Silva; [m.] Robert A. Henry, September 1, 1990; [ch.] Matthew Robert, Jennifer Nicole; [ed.] Scottsdale High School, Scottsdale Community College, Arizona State University; [occ.] Homemaker; [memb.] Associate Member of the International Society of Poets; [hon.] Editor's Choice Awards for "Parents Remembered" in The Rainbow's End and "Thank You, Guardian Angel" in Carvings in Stone - both published by the National Library of Poetry; [oth. writ.] Various poems, children's rhymes/short stories. Other publications by The National Library of Poetry include "Seed Of Faith" in Recollection of Yesterday and "Parallel Lesson" in Best poems of the 90's.; [a.] Scottsdale, AZ

HENRY, KAREN E.
[b.] October 2, 1962, Mechanicsburg, PA; [p.] Pauline Weary, Gary Burd; [m.] Richard T. Henry, September 21, 1985; [ch.] Joshua T., Zachary P., Alexis E.; [ed.] Cumberland Valley High School Bloomsburg Univ. of PA - B.S. Shippensburg Univ. of PA - M.Ed.; [a.] Lewisberry, PA

HERNANDEZ, CARMEN
[b.] June 11, 1947, El Paso, TX; [p.] Jose and Anita Acosta; [m.] Roberto M. Hernandez (Deceased), July 22, 1966; [ch.] Sandra, Robere, Brian, Elain; [ed.] El Paso High School; [occ.] Housewife and mother very important job; [memb.] Holy Trinity Catholic Church; [oth. writ.] I write poems on impulse from the heart; [pers.] In all of us there is good, we just have to look for it.; [a.] El Paso, TX

HESTER, JOSEPHINE MARIE
[pen.] Josie Hester; [b.] June 7, 1982, Chicago, IL; [p.] Theresa and Leonard Hester; [ed.] Completed the fifth grade at St. Alphonsus School before her tragic death; [occ.] "Angel" writer in Heaven; [memb.] Girl Scout of America 1990-1992, St. Alphonsus Altar Server 1991-1993 (Served a funeral mass the morning of her death); [hon.] Often received a straight A report card consistently being on the honor roll. Highest Girls Scout Cookie Seller - 1992, Altar Girls Server Award for 1992-1993, 1993 Building Runner-up (second place) for St. Alphonsus School in Chicago Tribune Spelling Bee; [oth. writ.] Josie's essay on George Washington (1993) was selected as the recipient of "The Mount Vernon Ladies Association of the Union Award" (prestigious national honor); [pers.] "I think Dr. Martin Luther King Jr. is one of the top three heroes to this world, (Mom, Jesus, Dr. king)." My daughter, Josie, was one of the kindest, most sensitive, funniest, most intelligent people I've ever known. She already was an angel on earth and now is one in heaven.; [a.] Chicago, IL

HESTER, KATHLEEN A.
[pen.] Kitty Ann; [b.] April 5, 1996, Milwaukee, WI; [p.] Deceased; [m.] Wayne Hester Ejcop, July 2, 1973; [ch.] 3 - 8 Grandchildren, 6 great grand children; [ed.] High School; [occ.] Retired; [memb.] American Legion, Emmanuel Baptist Church, US Marine Corps.; [oth. writ.] Poems - short stories, nothing published.; [pers.] I want to praise the Lord in my work. I write children's short stories.; [a.] Lake Charles, LA

HEWITT, ROBERTA
[b.] June 25, 1967, Portsmouth, VA; [p.] Lois DiPietro, John Hewitt; [m.] William Holmes; [ch.] Melanie, July 23, 1992; [ed.] Revere High School; [occ.] Administrative Assistant and Lockheed Sanders; [pers.] This poem is dedicated to my brother, Butch. His body is gone, but his spirit lives on.; [a.] Nashua, NH

HICKS, ARTIS
[b.] December 11, 1980, Washington, DC; [p.] Mr. and Mrs. Matthew Hicks; [ed.] Saint Ignatius Elementary,

Junior High School, Bishop McNamara High School; [occ.] Student; [memb.] Church Choir - Fort Foote Baptist Church "The Vessels Of Praise", Acting - The Fort Foote Players, School Newspaper "The Stang"; [hon.] Honor Roll, President's Education Award, Archdiocesan Music Program Award, Prince George's County Safety Patrol Award, Who's Who Among American High School Students, and Outstanding Average in Science/ Biology Award; [oth. writ.] Little Evey The Girl With The Water Can, Glasshours, "Little Evey The Girl With The Water Can" was published in anthology of poetry by Young Americans 1995 Edition.; [pers.] When all fails try, try again, but with the initiative that you will do the best.; [a.] Fort Washington, MD

HICKS, JANE E.
[b.] April 4, 1956, Croydon, England; [p.] Gordon and Mary Strutt; [m.] Byron C. Hicks, December 2, 1995; [ed.] St. Hilary's School, Alderley Edge, Cheshire, Lancashire College of Agriculture; [occ.] Dairy Technologist; [memb.] Suffolk Wildlife Trust, Lee Abbey Christian Outreach, Church Mission Society, Reese Air Force Base Volunteer; [hon.] Trustee of Mildenhall Archeological Society; [pers.] I am inspired by the interesting things I see and the people I meet. My motto is 'Live, love and laugh through life!'; [a.] Lubbock, TX

HIDALGO, EMILIO
[pen.] Emilio Hidalgo-N; [b.] April 7, 1920, Havana, Cuba; [p.] Ernesto Hidalgo and Emilia N. Hidalgo; [m.] Moraima Hidalgo, April 16, 1977; [ed.] Bachelor in Arts (Havana College) Law School (Havana University) both in Cuba. Liberal Arts (Xavier University-New Orleans, L.A.); [occ.] Retired; [memb.] Inst. Cubano-American de Cultura (New Yorks/Miami), Ass. for Puerto Rican-Hispanic Culture, Inc., (New York)-Asoc. Pro-Cuba (Elizabeth, N.J.); [hon.] From Spanish Newspapers in New York for declaiming Spanish Poetry in Carnegie Hall, Town Hall and Licoln Center and previewly performed in Mexico, Puerto Rico, Venezuela and Dominican Republic.; [oth. writ.] Several poems and short stories in both English and Spanish. "S.O.S. for Mankind" - (An unpublished non-fiction novel co-written with Mario Torres Barrahi.); [pers.] I strive to project equality among all men in my writing. My philosophical conceivability arise from Jose Marti's and Abraham Lincoln's ideologies; [a.] Bronx, NY

HIEL, CORINA
[b.] February 26, 1938, Las Cruces, NM; [p.] Celso and Magdalena Castillo; [m.] Gunter Hiel, February 16, 1980; [ch.] JoAnn, Cathy, Helen, Joe, (Grandchildren) Jonathan Felipe, Ann Marie, Stephanie, Joe Krislynn, Emily, Victoria, Danny, Eddie, (Great grandchildren) Jonathan, Vanessa; [ed.] St. Aloysuis Catholic School, Tulare High School, Franklin High School in Los Angeles; [occ.] Collector; [memb.] Bushnell PTA, Camp Eire Leader, Den Mother, Foster Mother, St. Ignatius Youth Teen Leader; [hon.] Marian Award as a Campfire Leader, 10 of my girls received the Catholic Marian Award; [pers.] My poems are about love, the hurt, loneliness, betrayal, but we may feel alone, we are not, God is by our side, to give us courage to love and trust again.; [a.] Covina, CA

HIGGINBOTHAM, WILLIAM L.
[pen.] Bill Higginbotham; [b.] June 17, 1922, Alba, TX; [p.] Langley and Emily Higginbotham; [m.] Murlen Higginbotham, January 17, 1948; [ch.] Danny, Steven and Joe; [ed.] Graduate Carlisle High, Two years at University of Houston; [occ.] Consultant - B&M Machine works; [oth. writ.] An Assortment of short stories and poems.; [pers.] My goal in writing is to leave to those who follow, a few faint foot prints scattered at random across a land that was once mine; [a.] Houston, TX

HILDRETH, KATHY A.
[pers.] I am thankful that the Lord is always with me so, even through the hard times I find peace and joy and strive to share my joy and the peace of God with others.

HILLIARD, JOHN THOMAS
[b.] August 5, 1973, Clearfield, PA; [p.] John Q. and Karen A. (Tobias) Hilliard; [ed.] Harmony Area High School, The Pennsylvania State University, and Mount Aloysius College; [occ.] College Student, Mount Aloysius College, Cresson, PA; [memb.] National Honor Society (Harmony Chapter); [hon.] Who's Who Among American High School Students and The Presidential Academic Fitness Award; [pers.] This poem was written in memory of my uncle, Bruce Edwin Tobias (b.) Nov. 25, 1949, departed this life July 19, 1996. It symbolizes the pain that his brothers and sisters felt during his battle with illness.; [a.] La Jose, PA

HOCHREITER, MARGARET V.
[b.] August 23, 1919, Buffalo, NY; [m.] Deceased; [ch.] Mary C., E. Joseph, Robert J.; [ed.] High School. E.J. Meyer Memorial Hosp., School-Nursing; [occ.] Retired - R.N.; [pers.] This poem is an original work of art - permission is granted to publish.; [a.] Englishtown, NJ

HOCKEN, PATRICIA
[pen.] Pat Hocken; [b.] November 20, 1941, Newark, NJ; [p.] Dorothy and Barney Coll; [m.] Lee Hocken, June 10, 1994; [ch.] Bonnie Lynn; [ed.] St. Mary's Wharton, NJ and Dover High in Dover, NJ; [occ.] Owner of Walk -N- Comfort Shoe Store and 30 years as Professional Artist in Lancaster, PA; [pers.] I look deep into my inner self and strive to reflect what's in my heart.; [a.] Prescott, AZ

HODGE, CARRIE
[b.] July 15, 1970, Cape Girardeau, MO; [ed.] BS in Elementary Education; [hon.] Dean's List, Phi Kappa, Phi Honor Society; [pers.] I strive to express everyone's truest emotions in my poetry.; [a.] Arvada, CO

HOFFMAN, BURTON S.
[pen.] Burt Hoffman; [b.] Baltimore, MD; [m.] Rita Lee Hoffman; [ed.] Forest Park High School, University of Maryland University of Baltimore, Mt. Vernon School of Law; [occ.] Appeals Officer; [memb.] Federal Bar Assoc. MD. Soc. of Accountants, B'nai B'rith JFK Lodge, Bethesda Place Community Council, Jewish Community Center, B'nai Israel Congregation; [hon.] Richard Newman Memorial Award, Beta Alpha Honorary Scholarship Society, Certificate of Editorial Excellence, Regional and National Performance, Awards, Excellence in Quality Award; [oth. writ.] "Will You Die This Christmas?", Feature articles, and guest column for the "Sphinx" in "The Baloo", also articles for the BPCC Newsletter, Government publications and reports; [pers.] Words are the wings of the eagles of thought, soaring through the heavens of expression and meaning.; [a.] Bethesda, MD

HOFFMAN, LAUREL EILEEN
[b.] September 10, 1970, Thousand Oaks, CA; [p.] Rita and Robert Hoffman; [ed.] Some High School and junior College; [occ.] Singer/Keyboardist for Majority Dog, Secretary for an architect, Barista for Starbucks; [memb.] Majority Dog - Rock Band, Zelig - acoustic duo; [oth. writ.] Self-published poetry books, some lyrics for Majority Dog (rock band) and Zelig (acoustic duo); [pers.] Find a goal and be productive, love the symbiotic people, do things for yourself.; [a.] Newbury Park, CA

HOFFMAN, RITA LEE
[b.] Washington, DC; [m.] Burton S. Hoffman; [ed.] Coolidge High School, American University; [occ.] Retired; [memb.] B'nai Israel Congregation Board of Governor's and Sisterhood; [hon.] BSH Excellence Award, Performance Awards; [oth. writ.] Invitations and acknowledgements; [pers.] Words are gems that respond to the crafter's skill, lovingly polished, sparkling and shining. They thus illuminate the darkest corners of understanding.; [a.] Bethesda, MD

HOJILLA, JAHARA
[b.] March 22, 1982, Yokota, Japan; [p.] Ed and Marchita Hojilla; [ed.] West Carteret High School (Freshman), Morehead City, North Carolina; [memb.] Naomi #70 Rainbow Girls; [a.] Newport, NC

HOLCOMBE, ANGELA MICHELLE
[pen.] Angie; [b.] April 12, 1979, Decatur, GA; [p.] Thomas and Diana Holcombe; [ed.] Faith Academy; [oth. writ.] I have written other poems but I have never anything published.; [a.] Lawrenceville, GA

HOLT, GINGER
[b.] October 18, 1968, Fort Worth, TX; [p.] Carl Hopkins and Marie Maxfield; [m.] Dough Holt, February 9, 1985; [ch.] Brad Holt and Serra Holt; [pers.] This poem is dedicated to Mr. Frank L. Baker in memory of Mrs. Nancy Sue Baker.; [a.] Azle, TX

HOLTH, DONALD
[pen.] Don; [b.] March 6, 1961, Arlington Heights, IL; [p.] Carter and Selma Holth; [m.] Debbie Holth, September 16, 1989; [a.] Saint Louis, MO

HORROCKS, NORMA
[b.] February 14, 1928, Louisville, KY; [p.] Lou and Paul Rasner; [ed.] University of Calif Long Beach, Univ. of Calif at Irvine Fellow-Writing Project 1984; [occ.] Sub teacher - Lake Elsinore School Dist.; [memb.] Canyon Lake Women's Club, Canyon Lake Travel Club, Canyon Lake Assoc. of Women, California Retired Teacher's Assoc., Zoological Society of San Diego; [hon.] Phi Alpha Chi Honorary Teachers Society, Canyon Lake Woman of Year 1987; [oth. writ.] Newspaper writings - four years - children's book "Early Bird-Late Bird- Ghost writing; [pers.] Mutual respect toward all living things, tenderness and empathy are necessary for the peaceful survival of our earth.; [a.] Canyon Lake, CA

HOUSTON, JACKIE
[b.] May 6, 1970, Sherman, TX; [p.] Billy Jack and Thelma Houston; [ed.] Bachelor of Science in Elementary Education; [occ.] Fourth grade teacher; [memb.] National Education Association, Association of Texas Professional Educators; [pers.] My writing is an expression of myself. I write about what is important to me and my innermost thoughts. Putting feelings on paper is much easier to me than expressing myself vocally.; [a.] Louisville, TX

HOWARD, ARCHIBALD M.
[b.] July 8, 1966, Monrovia, Liberia; [p.] Moses and Alice Howard; [ed.] Currently pursuing a Masters degree in Telecommunications Management; [oth. writ.] "C'est La Vie", "Where is Our Love", "Why I care", "Just Thinking of You"; [pers.] I am blessed to have a beautiful and wise mother, lovely sisters, and a father who truly appreciates and honors women. Because of

them I've learned to make our world a better place by honouring and treasuring the values of a woman.; [a.] Gaithersburg, MD

HUFF, CARMEN
[b.] December 27, 1956, Pennington Gap, VA; [p.] John and Lorene Humbert; [m.] Ken Huff, July 28, 1978; [ch.] Kenny; [ed.] High School Graduate; [occ.] Homemaker; [memb.] Boy Scouts of America, Asst., Scoutmaster, Springboro Missionary Baptist Chapel, Carlisle High School Band Boosters; [a.] Franklin, OH

HUFFSTUTLER, KATHY
[b.] December 1, 1958, Fresno, CA; [p.] Joseph and Kathleen Vogel; [m.] Brian Huffstutler, February 19, 1986; [ch.] Nicole and Kyle Huffstutler; [ed.] Fowler High - grad, 1976; [pers.] As a survivor of physical and emotional abuse, I write to express our hidden pains. The "unabused" part of society needs to be exposed to the unspoken results of this tragic experience.; [a.] Clovis, CA

HUNLEY, BRANDY
[b.] February 4, 1982, Anniston, AL; [p.] James and Lillie Glover, James Hunley Jr.; [ed.] At present attending Anniston High School, 9th grade, Honor Student.

HUNTER, HELEN
[b.] January 24, 1953; [p.] Both from Czechoslovakia; [m.] Paul Drexel, January 5, 1985; [ed.] Degree in Interpreting and Translating from Edinburgh, Scotland, Graduate studies in Business and Theology; [occ.] Professional Speaker and Director of the Mission Connection, Creating and Supporting Missionaries; [memb.] Toastmasters International; [hon.] Winner of the British Trades Alphabet Writing Competition; [oth. writ.] 3 books: "Let The Dead Bury Their Dead", "The Naked Warrior", "Betrayal In The Parsonage"; [pers.] My personal goal is to see the world and recruit 6,000 people into missionary service. In my writings, which span several continents, I portray the drama of human emotion.; [a.] San Antonio, TX

HURSEY, JEANETTE THERESA
[pen.] Jenn; [b.] August 17, 1977, Ohio; [p.] David and Joan Hursey; [ed.] Graduated from Northville High School in Spring of 1995, going to Central Michigan University; [occ.] Full time student; [memb.] PETA (People for the Ethical Treatment of Animals); [hon.] Graduated from High School with honors-National Honor Society. Going to Central Michigan University with an academic scholarship. Majoring in Human Resource Management.; [oth. writ.] Kept in a personal journal, very few people have read them.; [pers.] Life is a long discovery, Carpe Diem.; [a.] Northville, MI

HURST, RISA M.
[b.] February 10, 1984, Lakeland, FL; [p.] Marilyn J. Hurst; [ed.] 7 years - Jefferson Elem., Clem Churchwell Elem., Oak Hills Terrance, Zachry Middle School; [occ.] Student; [memb.] Northwest Little League - Softball; [hon.] Writing Rewards - 2nd grade 1st place McKinley County School District Gallup, NM Honors, English - Zachry Middle School; [oth. writ.] Wrote Stories for School Anthology.; [pers.] I hope I win. It'll be the only thing I've won my whole life!; [a.] San Antonio, TX

HUTCHINSON, LYLE W.
[b.] November 9, 1976, Sioux Falls, SD; [p.] Marianne Hoefert, Frank Hutchinson; [ed.] High School - Washington High; [occ.] Hutchinson Technology - No relation; [pers.] I live my life simply, and I enjoy every minute of it!; [a.] Sioux Fall, SD

IBEY, PAULA A.
[b.] January 4, 1979, Washington, DC; [p.] Francis Ibey, Janet Ibey; [ed.] Oxon Hill High School Class of 1997; [occ.] Student; [hon.] Who's Who Among American High School Students (94-95, 95-96), Honorable Mention in Maryland Distinguished Scholars Program; [oth. writ.] Several poems on the State of our Nation and World.; [pers.] My goal in life is to help in making the world a better place.; [a.] Clinton, MD

INNACELLI, GINA MARIE
[pen.] G. Marie; [b.] February 20, 1969, Long Branch, NJ; [p.] Joseph Innacelli, Jeanne Innacelli; [ed.] Shore Regional High School The William Paterson College of NJ; [occ.] International Export Traffic Manger, Old Bridge, NJ; [hon.] Delta Phi Epsilon Founding Sister, Greek Senate Public Relations chair, founder and Editor of Greek Newsletter; [oth. writ.] Poem published in Greek Newsletter; [pers.] I try to capture a feeling as accurately as possible in my writing. If am happy or sad when writing, I hope the reader can feel what I felt.; [a.] Old Bridge, NJ

INTERIANO, ANGELA MARIA
[b.] September 29, 1975, Honduras, CA; [p.] Yodan Guillermo, Alma Pineda; [ed.] Evander Childs H.S., Baruch College; [hon.] Arista Honor HS program; [oth. writ.] Some poems published in the HS newspaper; [pers.] When I write I try to express my feelings and ideas the best way possible getting the inspiration or knowledge in my experiences. I also try to include the reality combined with the dreams knowing always in my mind that we have a future where we can make our dreams come true, I smile and try to be happy.; [a.] Bronx, NY

JACKLIN, BOB
[b.] January 18, 1945, Elizabeth, NJ; [p.] Robert and Miriam Jacklin; [m.] Sharyn Jacklin, August 22, 1992; [ed.] Abraham Clank High School, Roselle, N.J., 2 years Union College Cranford, N.J. - 3 years U.S. Army - 389th Army Band, (Drummer) July 64-67; [occ.] Self employed. Fly Fishing Guide and Outfitter; [memb.] American Legion, Federation of Fly Fisherman, Trout Unlimited; [pers.] Lee Wulff was one of the Worlds best known Fisherman and Writers. He invented the Wulff Series of Flies for Trout and Salmon in 1929. As a boy Lee was my Hero. It has been my great privilege in life to have known and be a friend of Mr Wulff. On April 1st 1993 while thinking of Lee who had just passed away I was inspired to write this poem. The World of Sport Fishing owes a lot to Lee Wulff. This poem is my Tribute to the Late Lee Wulff.; [a.] West Yellowstone, MT

JACKSON, BARBARA BENICE MILES
[pen.] B. Miles Jackson; [b.] June 24, 1948, Forth Worth; [p.] C. B. Miles and Maybelle Dugan Miles; [m.] Divorced; [ch.] Tracy Danyell Jackson; [ed.] I. M. Terrell - Class of 1966; [occ.] Head Start - Day Care Association of Forth Worth and Tarrant County; [memb.] Carter Metropolitan C.M.E. Church; [hon.] State Employee of the Year 1990, Usher of the Year for Carter Metropolitan Church; [oth. writ.] Poems: How Can It Be?, The Whole Truth, Turn, Atmospheric Condition, Renewal, Go Your Way, Ancient of Days, Silent Voices, Void of Time, Be Sure, Keep, Changing Times, House on Southcrest, House on Southecrest, Listen And See; [pers.] In great times of sorry and sadness look up and know.; [a.] Forth Worth, TX

JACKSON, JON NICHOLAS
[pen.] Nick Jackson; [b.] July 25, 1977, Ironton, OH; [p.] Roger and Barbara Jackson; [ed.] Ironton High School, Ohio University; [oth. writ.] Several poems written weekly.; [pers.] The mind is the most powerful force in the universe, and to live life to the fullest: you must experiment with all it's facets. My influences are Jack Kerouc, Bob Dylan, Samuel Taylor Coleridge, and Syd Barrexx; [a.] Ironton, OH

JACKSON, MICHELLE
[b.] July 22, 1979, Atlanta; [p.] Annie Lee Madison and Dexter Easley; [ed.] Junior in High School at Henry Grady High School; [occ.] Cashier at Kragers and full time High School student; [memb.] Key Club, African Alliance Club; [hon.] Purple Heart in JROTC, Outstanding Cadet, JROTC, Cash Award in Brown Marel Brown Poetry contest, Outstanding Volunteer in Key Club; [oth. writ.] "Why should I feel ashamed", "What's is the real definition of a Sista."; [pers.] "Careless what other people think on care and believe what you think."; [a.] Atlanta, GA

JACKSON, MS. TERRY ANN
[b.] October 12, 1966, Marion, VA; [p.] John and Shirley Jackson; [ed.] Graduated high school; [occ.] Full time poet; [pers.] Poem inspired by the undertaker of the world wrestling federation.; [a.] Marion, VA

JACOBSON, DEEL
[b.] February 18, 1981, Fairbanks, AK; [p.] Nora Jacobson; [ed.] Currently 10th grade home school student; [occ.] Flamenco Guitarist; [memb.] Cibola Arts Council; [hon.] Numerous school awards for academics and track and field; [oth. writ.] News article published in Lake Tahoe local paper at approx. age twelve; [pers.] Carpe Diem (Seize the day).; [a.] Grants, NM

JAENKE, CARI L.
[pen.] Brooklyn; [b.] June 12, 1976, Eau Claire, WI; [p.] Vicki Jaenke; [ed.] Chippewa Falls Senior High, 1 year completed at UW Stout-Menomonie, WI; [occ.] Security Guard; [hon.] Gamma Sigma Sigma - National Service Sorority, George Wendt Memorial Softball Ability Award; [oth. writ.] A couple poems wrote for and published in the High School Yearbook. Hundreds of others poems wrote for mine and others concerns.; [pers.] Be your own person and don't let anyone get in the way of accomplishing your dream. It may take time, but it will happen.; [a.] Chippewa Falls, WI

JAMES, CYNTHIA LYNNETTE
[pen.] Lynn; [b.] February 16, 1972, Savannah, GA; [p.] Robert M. and Joyce J. James; [ed.] Elementary: Sacred Heart Interparochial School (Savannah, GA), High school: St. Vincent's Academy (Savannah, GA), College: Ga. Southern University '90-91, (Satesboro, GA.) GA State University '91-96 (Atlanta, GA); [occ.] Assistant Director w/a summer camp/tutorial program: Grace Academy of Social Development; [memb.] St. Benedict the Moor Catholic Church (Savannah, GA); [hon.] Graduated from GA. State Univ. w/a BA in Psychology and a minor in African-American Studies.; [oth. writ.] Have written several poems most recently about life as an African-American, also occasional poems (ex. weddings, funerals, etc.); [pers.] The best motto for life that I've ever heard is: "keep it simple" if you keep a balance spiritually, mentally and physically (mind, body, and soul), then all else will fall in place naturally.; [a.] Savannah, GA

JANKE, JEFFREY T.
[b.] September 9, 1971, Oxnard, CA; [p.] Tom and Joanie Janke; [ed.] Futures in Education High School; [occ.] Office Manager; [memb.] Church of Christ Member

League Bowler Membership; [hon.] Second place trophy for Taekwondo Karate Tournament, High School G.E.D. Diploma, Employee of the month at Wendy's; [oth. writ.] "The Symbol Of Love Is The Diamond", Three articles published in newspaper for times advocate. Other poems published for church Bulletin; [pers.] My favorite writer in Edgar Allen Poe, and favorite poem is "Elderado" by Edgar Allen Poe. I usually get ideas for my poem's from the bible but not all my poem's were Biblically influenced.; [a.] Escondido, CA

JEAN, WESLY
[pen.] Wesly Tean; [b.] August 8, 1970, Haiti; [p.] Piere Moise Tean; [ed.] Evasmus Hall High School and currently attending New York Technical College; [occ.] Clerical; [pers.] In life I see no goods or bad, but a preparation of the future.; [a.] Brooklyn, NY

JENKINS, LINDA
[b.] September 24, 1958, Heidelberg, MS; [p.] Vermell Merrell, Late Arthur Merrell; [m.] Martin Jenkins, September 28, 1979; [ch.] Ashley Lynn, Alison Jaclyn; [ed.] Quitman High School, Quitman, MS, Meridian Community College Meridian, MS; [occ.] Registered Nurse, South Central Regional Med. Center Laurel, MS; [memb.] Shubuta Baptist Church Shubuta, MS, Emergency Nurses Association; [a.] Shubuta, MS

JENRETTE, KENDALL W.
[b.] August 29, 1979, Atlanta, GA; [p.] Isaac and Vernyce Jenrette; [ed.] Senior in High School at Woodward Academy; [occ.] Student; [memb.] Spanish Club, Junior Civitian Varsity Wrestling Team, Jack and Jills Friendship Baptist Church (usher); [hon.] 1995-96 2nd in Area and 6th in the State. National Merit Semifinalist; [oth. writ.] Poems published in School Literary Magazine, Duke Univ. Young Writers Magazine, Local Newspaper; [pers.] My poetry is a way for me to express my thoughts and feelings. The readers are left to interpret my works. Only after completely submerging themselves in my verse.; [a.] Atlanta, GA

JESCHONEK, BRANDY L.
[pen.] Brandy Laurel; [b.] September 2, 1975, Johnstown, PA; [p.] James and Janet Jeschonek; [ch.] Brianna L. Jeschonek; [ed.] Ferndale Area High School, Indiana University of PA; [occ.] Student; [pers.] Poetry is a beautiful language. I urge more people to learn it.

JESSEE, ADAM W.
[b.] October 23, 1984, Vancouver, WA; [p.] Steven and Holly Jessee; [ed.] 5th grade Northport Elem, Northport, WA; [occ.] Student

JIMENEZ, ESTRELLITA S.
[pen.] Relly; [b.] May 10, 1945, Manila, Philippines; [p.] Florencia Jimenez (Mother); [ed.] Bachelor of Science in Nursing, Philippine Union College, Master of Nursing, University of the Philippines; [occ.] Registered Nurse; [memb.] Seventh-Day Adventist Church; [hon.] Class President, Nursing '67, Phil. Nominee to 3M-ICN Nurses Fellowship 1977; [oth. writ.] Few poems and short articles in Manila, published also in the Academy of Nursing of the Phils (ANPHI) papers.; [pers.] My love for skating has been inspired by my Mother and by Brian Boitano whom I admire for being the greatest figure skater because of his classic, perfect technique, elegant artistry, and lovable personality.; [a.] Sonoma, CA

JIMENEZ, JUANA
[b.] July 9, 1981, New Haven, CT; [p.] Maria and Anibal Jimenez; [ed.] Cooperative Arts and Humanities High School - Educational Center for the Arts (ECA); [occ.] Student (at the above schools); [memb.] St. Rose of Lima Church Youth Group.; [hon.] 1st place Drug Abuse poetry contest 1991; [pers.] I try to write things that I'm scared to confront it's what most people find interesting. My motto, open the doors to the center of your mind, you'll find many secrets hidden.; [a.] New Haven, CT

JOHANSEN, LINDA
[b.] July 14, 1959, Maryland; [p.] Heinz and Barbara Isern; [m.] Kenneth Johansen, September 4, 1992; [ch.] April, Leslie, Stephanie, Sarah, Rachel, Zachary and Katie; [ed.] High School Diploma; [occ.] Supervisor, Friendly Ice Cream; [hon.] Professional Duckpin Bowler 7 game Women's World record holder Hall of Fame; [pers.] I wrote this limerick when in the third grade and it never left me. I loved it and decided to enter it in the contest.; [a.] Baltimore, MD

JOHNSON, BERTHA MAE
[b.] September 30, 1945, Washington, DC; [p.] Mr. and Mrs. Ethel and John Curley; [ch.] Two Laurence Greene, Donnell Greene; [ed.] Roosevelt High School District of Columbia; [occ.] Food Clerk and part-time piano player; [memb.] Greater Tried Stone Baptist Church; [hon.] Certificate of Award 2D Specialty Training Program a Rep. in "Music" June 1982; [oth. writ.] The Love of My Dad, Looking for Love, Happy Birthday Song, God's Divine Peace, "Time" Jesus Is Well Please", Golden City; [pers.] My first love is music. And I am a singer.

JOHNSON, CHERI
[b.] August 9, 1962, Earth; [p.] Lois and Charles Johnson; [occ.] Photographer; [a.] Friendswood, TX

JOHNSON, DEONA MAE
[b.] October 15, 1959, Manistee, MI; [p.] Harry Jeruzal, Eva Jeruzal; [ch.] Nicole Koren, Rochelle Dee; [ed.] Manistee Catholic Central High School, West Shore Community College; [occ.] Area Clerk for Well Tech. Eastern, Inc.; [memb.] Saint Joseph Parish, Phi Theta Kappa National Honor Society; [hon.] National Dean's List, Phi Theta Kappa Honor Society; [oth. writ.] Inspirational Poetry; [pers.] The most valuable thing you have is the one thing that cannot be taken from you - your faith.; [a.] Onekama, MI

JOHNSON, MEGAN
[pen.] Valerie Vandiver; [b.] September 25, 1981, New Orleans, LA; [p.] Connie Johnson, Ed Johnson; [ed.] Currently in high school at Greeley Central High School; [hon.] Presidential Academic Fitness Award; [oth. writ.] Nothing published yet.; [pers.] I like to write poems because that's how I express my feelings.; [a.] Greeley, CO

JOHNSON, MONICA
[b.] July 3, 1923, Saint Albans, VT; [p.] Joseph and Mary Wersebe; [m.] John P. Johnson, May 12, 1957; [ch.] Robert McGowan, Patricia Welch and Susan Johnson; [ed.] High School - Nursing School; [occ.] Retired

JOHNSON, OLAF
[b.] March 2, 1977, Guyana, SA; [p.] Wilbur Johnson, Desiree Johnson; [ed.] South Shore High, Bklyn, NY, Staten Island College (cwwy); [occ.] Student and Youth Lead Instructor, Outward Bound NY.; [memb.] Outward Bound NYC, Pre -Med Society, Fashion Club, National Georaphic Society.; [hon.] Creative Writing Award Alpine and Mountaineering Award. (Colorado), Canoe and Portage Award (Canada), Music achievement award.; [oth. writ.] None published; [pers.] I'm nothing like anything else, yet everything completes my being.; [a.] Brooklyn, NY

JOHNSTON, ANNETTE P.
[b.] May 18, 1906, Cincinnati, OH; [p.] William and Ida Prickett; [m.] Hugh M. Johnston, December 23, 1933; [ch.] Nancy and Alan; [ed.] One yr. Teacher's College, Oxford, Ohio-3 yrs. at Ohio State Univ. Columbus, Ohio; [occ.] Retired, live happily at presby, Retirement Center, active at 90 yrs.; [memb.] Fairfax Presby. Church, Weta, Planned Parenthood; [oth. writ.] I have written poetry for many yrs. - Collection of 28 is a prized possession, but none published; [pers.] I strive to show my love of family and my appreciation of the beautiful world God has given us.

JOHNSTON, JO ANNE
[pen.] J.J.; [b.] October 5, 1941, Highland Pk., MI; [p.] Mr. and Mrs. Carl Rogers; [m.] Widowed, April 8, 1961; [ch.] Four; [ed.] 2 years of college; [oth. writ.] Many they haven't been see; [pers.] Does it really matter what we say? When what is said to be fact today: Could become fiction tomorrow. Its better to be still. From the quite comes noise.; [a.] Plymouth, MI

JOHNSTON, KENNETH JARED
[pen.] Jared Johnston; [b.] June 2, 1980, Mobile, AL; [p.] Wayne and Wanda Johnston; [ed.] Currently 11th grade - Washington County High School; [occ.] Student, Washington County High School; [hon.] Jr. Women's Club Poetry Contest, 1st prize; [a.] Tibbie, AL

JONES, BERYL O.
[pen.] Bo John; [b.] May 24, 1930, Jamaica, WI; [p.] John Simmonds and Albertine Simmonds; [m.] Errol Jones (Just Deceased), July 4, 1959; [ch.] Errol Dane Marlene, Zena, Harold, Donald, Valton, Juliet, Sean, Alicia; [ed.] Kingston Technical, Milo Teachers College, Fordham University NY, Kan Jamaica WI; [occ.] Teacher-General Ed. Math and Science Specialist; [memb.] Church Council St. Thomas Aquinas - Catholic; [hon.] Work Related; [pers.] It is my desire to inculcate positive attitude in my children, and in my students or within anyone whose life I touch. If my writing can give a ray of hope to any one them I shall continue to write.; [a.] Bronx, NY

JONES, BETTY TAYLOR
[pen.] Betty T. Jones; [b.] January 7, 1953, Somerset, KY; [p.] Alvis Bray, Ellen Bray; [m.] Divorced; [ch.] Christi D. Taylor; [ed.] Shopville High, Florida Comm. College Jax. (FCCJ); [occ.] EMT/Paramedic, R. N. Student; [memb.] American Heart Assoc. Jax. Fire Rescue Volunteer Fire Fighter; [hon.] Miss Go Give Award, which is one of the highest honors achieved in Mary Kay Cos. Inc. President of Volunteer fire fighter x 1 yr.; [oth. writ.] Other poems for committee's and activity papers or projects in community.; [pers.] Words written sometimes say more than words spoken and with greater feelings.; [a.] Jacksonville, FL

JONES, BYRD MERRITT
[b.] January 18, 1935, North Carolina; [p.] Arthur Eugene Jones, Grace Myrtle; [m.] Norma Jean Edney Jones, June 16, 1996; [ch.] Lisa Marie Jones 23; [ed.] Seventh grade; [occ.] Semi-retired Glazer, fourty five years; [memb.] Henderson County Genealogical and Historical Society; [hon.] Poem: "Abuse" now hangs in Henderson County Sheriff's office. Poem: "Our Uncle Elbert" writer December, 1985 published in The Times News.; [oth. writ.] "Mama's Knees" 1996, "Love Returned" - 1993, "Beauty In Reverse" - 1995 "This Ring" 1995, "Morning Awakening" 1995, "Great Pyramid" 1992 "Tennessee Plowboy" 1993 "Love's Embrace" 1995; [pers.] Norma Jean was my sisters childhood play-

mate and girlfriend, and I was just the tag along. Norma Jean and I was separated about fourthy five years. We were married June 16, 1996. I write from feelings of inspirations.; [a.] Mountain Home, NC

JONES, CYNTHIA A.
[b.] September 5, 1947, Texarkana, AR; [p.] Sheila M. Clark and Max S. Jones; [ed.] BA, Trinity College, Washington, DC, MSW, School of Social Work, Univ. of North Carolina, Chapel Hill, NC; [occ.] Director, Lawyer Assistance Program, State Bar of Georgia, Atlanta, Georgia, Licenses: Licensed Clinical Social Worker Certified Employee Assistance Professional.; [memb.] Outstanding Young Woman of America, 1979, Who's Who Among Human Service Professionals, 1988; [pers.] I am a gentle spirit searching for answers to life's challenges.; [a.] Marietta, GA

JONES, LATONYA L.
[pen.] Pumpkin; [b.] August 19, Longview, TX; [p.] Linda and Wilton K. Jones Sr.; [ed.] Jodie McClure Elementary 3-5 Foster Jr High, 6-8, Longview High School 11th grader; [pers.] All praise and honor goes to God. My parents and my older brother, Wilton Jr. have stood behind me 100 percent.; [a.] Longview, TX

JONES, MURDIC H.
[b.] August 25, 1950, Chas., SC; [p.] Mr. and Mrs. O. M. Jones; [m.] Separated; [ch.] Bridget, Gary and Wilson; [ed.] A.S. in Mech. Eng. Tech., 72 Credits toward Physics; [occ.] Retired from CNSYD, starting writing career; [memb.] Writer's Journal Club, Member of 1st Baptist Church of Bonneau, SC; [hon.] 1st Honor Graduate from Murray Voc. High School (May 1969); [oth. writ.] Poem: When Love Dies, being published in your "Morning Song", Doing final Revisions of my 1st Novel: "Surviving Base Closure" for Agent Representation; [pers.] In High School I won a local citizenship Essay. My English teacher told me that I should be a writer. My parents told me to get a job, which I did. Now that I am retired. It is time for me to follow my dream.; [a.] Bonneau, SC

JONES, SUSAN L.
[b.] October 8, 1965, Winston-Salem, NC; [p.] Leo and Lois Scofield; [m.] Mitch Jones, July 21, 1984; [ch.] Michael C. and Joanna L.; [ed.] Graduated in 1983 from Middleburg High School; [occ.] Administrative Assistant; [pers.] My inspiration was a cousin of mine named Guy David Roberts is a very special person and I wrote this for him to let him know I would always be there if he needed me.; [a.] Orange Park, FL

JONES, TERRY M.
[b.] August 15, 1958, Charlottesville, VA; [m.] John J. Jones, September 13, 1986; [ed.] Louisa Country High School; [occ.] Admission Counselor University of Virginia Hospital Charlottesville, VA; [memb.] First Baptist Church Louisa, VA; [hon.] United States Army National Guard; [oth. writ.] Other writings not yet published personal inspiration, to friends and love ones.; [pers.] Special thanks to my spiritual sister, Mrs. Carson Lewis of Louisa, VA, fro allowing her personal inspiration to be shared with the world.

JORDAN, KAY
[pen.] Skooter; [b.] April 28, 1953, Tenn; [p.] George - Wanda Bouldon; [m.] Don Bona; [ch.] Bobby, David, April; [pers.] I wish to thank my family for their loving and continous support of all my endeavors throughout my life, and my fiancee, for giving me "the sound of his laughter". He is my rock and inspiration. I love you all!; [a.] Grand Junction, CO

JULEY, RACHEL
[b.] March 24, 1977, Green Bay, WI; [p.] Dean and Mary Jo Juley; [ed.] Sophomore at the University of Wisconsin - Stevens Point; [occ.] A communications major with a journalism emphasis at university of Wisconsin - Stevens Point; [hon.] Dean's List, was inducted into Phi Eta Sigma National Freshman Honor Society; [oth. writ.] I have written many other poems, but none of the others have been published.; [pers.] I write poetry to get my thoughts out on paper. It helps me deal with what's going on in my head sometimes. I never really thought that writing would get me anywhere until now.; [a.] Green Bay, WI

JULIO, ELIZABETH
[b.] Hancock, MI; [p.] Lawrence and Elizabeth Julio; [ch.] Nichole, Elizabeth, Kathryn, Gregory, and Maria Saunders; [ed.] Hancock Central High, Suomi College; [occ.] Student, Accounting; [hon.] Dean's List, Suomi Bowling Hall of Fame 1996; [pers.] I'm a survivor of domestic violence; [a.] Hancock, MI

JUMP II, GARY
[b.] January 21, 1967, Bay City, MI; [p.] Gary Jump I, Sharon Jump; [ed.] Bay City Central High School, Bay Arenac Skill Center, Bay Area Adult Ed. Apprentice Training; [occ.] Production Worker for General Motors Corp.; [memb.] Saint John's Catholic Church Ushers Club; [oth. writ.] Several other of my poems were published local newspapers several years ago.; [pers.] I write to honor the True Beauty in women which many men are blind to now a days. Also I write to honor my mother and father and most of all God for without whom I would not be here today.; [a.] Bay City, MI

JUSTICE, JAMES T.
[pen.] J. Thomas Justice; [b.] December 14, 1931, Huntington, WV; [p.] Brady Justice and Elizabeth Dickerson Justice; [m.] Susan Gretkowski, June 17, 1992; [ch.] Hilary K. F. Justice; [ed.] Wayne County (WV) High School, Marshall College (now II), Temple University, Ohio University, J.D., Cum Laude, Suffolk Law School; [occ.] Attorney; [memb.] Massachussets and Federal Bars, Manchester Yahct Club, Manchester Harbor Boat Club; [hon.] Best Brief, first yr. Law School, Phi Delta Phi (Hon. Legal Society); [oth. writ.] Roads And Rest Stops, an unpublished collection of Poetry, Side Roads, Back Roads And Detours, an unpublished collection of short stories and flash fiction, anonymous poem published in local newspaper.; [pers.] A man without vice is in danger of making vices of his virtues. T. Wilder.; [a.] Manchester, MA

KAIRYS, KRISTINA
[b.] January 4, 1982, Pgh, PA; [p.] Angella Kairys; [ed.] Baldwin High School; [occ.] Student; [memb.] F.B.L.A., Future Business Leaders of America, attended at Gulf Middle School; [hon.] Achievement, student of the month, citizenship honor roll; [pers.] I am dedicating this poem to Mr. Richard Ardizzone, for his support, friendship, and for his sense of humor. I am also very proud for my accomplishments.; [a.] Pittsburgh, PA

KAWASAKI, DAISUKE
[b.] January 6, 1976, Nigata, Japan; [p.] Tomizo Kawasaki and Fumie Kawasaki; [ed.] Hannan High, Osaka; [occ.] Student at Kansai Gaidai Hawaii College; [pers.] I try to open my mind as wide as I can when I write so that I can enter my mind and find out something I like.; [a.] Honolulu, HI

KAZEMBE, JAMAL
[pen.] Jamal Kazembe; [b.] March 25, 1982, New York, NY; [p.] Philaysha and Darrell Davidson; [ed.] Seventh - grader at JHS 142 in NY; [occ.] Student; [memb.] Morning Star Full Gospel Assembly A.B.Y.P.U.

KEENER, MARVIN R.
[pen.] Max D. Damian; [b.] January 25, 1943, Schaefferstown, PA; [p.] Raymond and Grace (Klick) Keener; [ed.] Grad. 1962 - Heidle Burg Twp., Eastern Lebanon Co, PA, some Formal Bus. Ed.; [occ.] Semi-Ret.; [memb.] Phi Theta Pi Frat.; [oth. writ.] "Shalom," "Blessings" and other poems still to be published; [pers.] I pray for world peace and harmony among people, however, I am cautious of "The Hand Reaching from the Gutter, it may only want company."; [a.] Lebanon, PA

KEESLER, HARRIET L.
[b.] September 3, 1907, Devil's Lake, ND; [ch.] Bill, Martha, Bob; [ed.] BA degree from University of Illinois; [memb.] Alpha Xi Delta Sorority St. Andrews Episcopal Church; [oth. writ.] Many other poems. Lyrics for 60 original songs. I like to create - whether it be in music, poetry or art; [pers.] I am 89 yrs. old at age 72 I started organ lessons and in 5 years had written 60 songs both lyrics and music. Some were copyrighted - none published. At age 79 started art lessons. In 7 years I had painted 120 paintings.; [a.] Jacksonville, FL

KEFALAS, TERRY
[b.] July 18, 1955, Washington, DC; [p.] Chris and Helen Kefalas; [m.] Cherri Ferrara-Kefalas, May 20, 1989; [ch.] Katie; [ed.] Wakefield High, NVCC; [occ.] Director of Distribution, Music Sound Exchange; [oth. writ.] Several songs (Lyrics Only) - nothing published.; [pers.] I write about things that are somewhat personal and have meaning to me. I hope my writing has some meaning to others and that some folks can relate to some of it first hand.; [a.] Centereach, NY

KEHOE, TESS WOLKOFF
[b.] March 21, 1983, Lafayette, IN; [p.] Regina L. Wolkoff; [ed.] Hanover Elementary School, University High at LSU, and Nitschmann Middle School; [occ.] Student; [hon.] All-Parish Choir, Junior Beta; [pers.] Dreams don't just come true, you have to make them happen.; [a.] Bethlehem, PA

KELLEY, ANDREA
[pen.] Shandi Dracos; [b.] July 23, 1978, Greenville, MS; [p.] Richard E. Kelley I and Donna A. Kelley; [ed.] Graduated in May 1996 from St. Joseph School, Greenville, MS. Currently a freshman at Mississippi Delta Community College in Moorhead, MS; [occ.] Full-time student at MDCC; [memb.] National Honors Society; [hon.] Highest Senior Average in Physical Science, Principal's List; [oth. writ.] Sparrowgrass Poetry Forum-Summer 1996, Fall 1996, Spring 1997. National library of Poetry - Fall 1996. Famous poems of the twentieth Century - Fall 1996.; [pers.] My poetry springs from my peers' total acceptance of drugs, alcohol, and violence, as well as the outcome of these deadly "past times".'; [a.] Leland, MS

KEMPKE, GERALD
[pen.] Gerald Kempke; [b.] March 3, 1956, Joliet, IN; [p.] Alfred and Genieve Kempke; [m.] Denise, October 11, 1986; [ch.] Liz, Joshua, Dallas; [ed.] Received my G.E.D. in 1992 at the age of 36; [occ.] Over the road Truck Driver; [oth. writ.] I have also written many songs. I've played guitar since the age of 8, I also have 52 other poems. Such as "Oklahoma City" "96 Olympic", "Flood

of 93"; [pers.] I feel all mankind should never forget the events that happen in this world, my poem help them to remember, I would like to hear from the public and if their hearts were touched.; [a.] Gillespie, IL

KENDRICK, BETTY L.
[b.] October 25, 1943, Handshoe, KY; [p.] Lonzo and Minnie Owsley; [m.] John Kendrick, November 24, 1960; [ch.] Kimberly, John E., Karen and Anthony; [memb.] Church of Christ; [oth. writ.] Biography of Bird Owsley published in the Knott County History book.; [pers.] We can usually overcome obstacles in our lives if we set our mind and hands to it.; [a.] Kendallville, IN

KENELY III, CHARLES
[b.] April 13, 1947, Washington, DC; [p.] Charles Kenely Jr. and Eula C. Kenely; [ch.] Charles Joseph Kenely and Anthony Edward Kenely; [ed.] Spingarn Sr. High School, 2 years attendance at Howard Univ.; [occ.] Electronics Technician, Quality Dept at E. Systems, Inc.; [hon.] My parents. My children. My sister, Dr. Marian Elizabeth Bobo, a special someone.; [pers.] Through my writings, I attempt to put a handle on fleeting thoughts from the mind and heart.; [a.] Garland, TX

KENNEDY, JULIE
[b.] November 28, 1979, Fairfax, VA; [p.] William and Frances Kennedy; [ed.] Thomas Jefferson High School for Science and Technology (1997); [occ.] Student, Thomas Jefferson High School for Science and Technology; [pers.] Grandpa would be proud. I hope that we can all preserve life and not fear death in this ever changing world. My advice has always been to have fun, make the best of the time you have.; [a.] Fairfax, VA

KERLEY, OLIVER D.
[b.] February 11, 1966, Baxter Springs, KS; [p.] Sandra Rosser; [m.] Necoma Kerley; [ch.] Amanda, Daniel, Zakk; [ed.] Riverton High; [pers.] To my children: Life is full of ups and downs. It's better to try and fail than to stand on the side and watch.; [a.] Tulsa, OK

KESSLER, MARINA BRIANNE
[b.] October 27, 1979, San Diego, CA; [p.] John P. and Beverly A. Kessler; [ed.] Currently a Junior at South Bend, High School; [occ.] Student; [memb.] High School Debate Team, High School Volley Ball Team. H.S. Drama Club - Pacific Kids, Critters and Crafts 4-H Club; [hon.] Many honors and awards through 4-H who's who in American High School Students; [a.] South Bend, WA

KIESSLING, DONALD
[b.] December 2, 1939, Benton Harbor, MI; [p.] Dorothy Hanes; [m.] Alice Kiessling, July 7, 1984; [ch.] Kim Owen, Tonya Franklin, Chris Wages; [ed.] Benton Harbor, High School; [occ.] Self Employed, Musician, Sound Operator; [memb.] Hospice, Crystal Springs Church of God; [oth. writ.] Several poems, religious hymns, various newspaper articles; [pers.] I feel that if you have been given a talent in form you have an obligation to share it with all others. We are all able to influence someone, whether we see the results or not.; [a.] Benton Harbor, MI

KINGSLIEN, BRIDGETT
[b.] March 9, 1977, Medford, OR; [m.] Terry Kingslien, July 1, 1995; [occ.] Supervisor, Goodwill Industries, Corvallis, OR; [memb.] Church of the Nazarene, Corvallis, OR; [pers.] Nothing is impossible with God.; [a.] Corvallis, OR

KINMAN, AMY
[b.] September 14, 1983, Phoenix, AZ; [p.] K.C. and Elizabeth Wright; [ed.] Presently 7th grade student at Heritage Middle School, Chino Valley, AZ; [occ.] Full time student; [hon.] President-Student Council at Coyote Springs Elem. School, Prescott Valley, AZ. As 6th grade student. I strive to make Honor Roll grades; [oth. writ.] Poem: The Girl And The War, Book: Anthology of Poetry by Young Americans. Publ: Anthology of Poetry, Inc., 1996 Edition; [pers.] Family, including younger brother and sister, recently relocated - now living on a working cattle ranch, CV Ranch, Paulden, Arizona. Dad is Ranch Manager - Foreman.; [a.] Prescott, AZ

KIRSCH, JAMES H.
[b.] March 12, 1943, Chicago, IL; [p.] Howard and Dorothea Kirsch; [ed.] 4 yrs. High School; [occ.] Janitorial work; [oth. writ.] Meaning Of Christmas, Freedom, Being Thank-ful, What Easter Means To Me, Where Is Spring?; [pers.] I have written tributes to people I know for Anniversaries, weddings, birthdays, Mother's Day, Father's Day, and Death's.; [a.] Three Lakes, WI

KIRSCHNER, ABIGAIL JOY
[b.] July 21, 1978, Alpena, MI; [p.] Arnie and Loleta Kirschner; [ed.] High School Senior; [occ.] Student; [hon.] The August Derleth Young Writers Project in 1987. I wrote a poem that won me the award; [oth. writ.] I have a small collection of about 50 poems.; [pers.] I have a love for poetry and I hope that someday someone might read one of my poems and be truly touched. Each one of my poems comes straight from my heart and my sole inspiration is Jesus Christ. I write simply to bring God praise, I dedicate to Him each phrase.; [a.] Alpena, MI

KISTLER, THOMAS
[pen.] TK; [b.] June 26, Paterson, NJ; [ed.] Glassboro State College; [occ.] Singer/Songwriter; [memb.] ASCAP, The songwriters Guild of America, Sigma Phi Epsilon, The Nutley Jaycees; [hon.] Special Performance Award ASCAP 1995-1996; [oth. writ.] It's the Little Things, Lisa, Lisa, With Every Christmas Wish, Something Real.; [pers.] Learn not everything, just a lot about a lot. TK; [a.] Park Ridge, NJ

KLAY, NATHAN
[b.] January 5, 1980, Holland, MI; [p.] Dr. Robin Klay, Timothy Klay; [ed.] Holland Christian High; [occ.] Student; [memb.] Reformed Church of America; [oth. writ.] Poems published in local literary magazines; [pers.] In writing poetry, I find myself uncovering more questions than answers. I most enjoy the poetry of William Carlos Williams, Carl Sandburg, and other early 20th Century poets.; [a.] Holland, MI

KLEPADLO, LARISSA
[b.] May 12, 1981, Scranton, PA; [p.] David Klepadlo, Linda Klepadlo; [ed.] Scranton Preparatory School; [occ.] Student; [hon.] 1. Academic High Honors, 2. Ignatian Scholar Award, 3. Magna Cum Laude in the National Latin Exam, 4. Bishop's Award for Religious Education/Youth Ministry; [pers.] Every writing is a signal to the soul of someone. Therefore, never stop giving until there is no one.; [a.] Clarks Summit, PA

KLESSE, AMY BETH
[pen.] "Mary Jane"; [b.] June 15, 1980, Livingston, NJ; [p.] Sue Klesse and Richard Klesse; [ed.] Junior at Somerville, High School on Somerville, NJ; [occ.] Student; [memb.] Thespian Troupe #659, People to People Student Ambassador Program, North Branch Reformed Church Youth Group; [hon.] High Honor Roll French Award, Citizenship Awards; [oth. writ.] I have had many poems published in my schools literary magazine "Confusion", "Distractions", "Daybreak".; [pers.] Poetry should always be written directly from one's heart. In my writing, I try to symbolically reflect my deepest thoughts and feelings.; [a.] Branchburg, NJ

KOCH, VELMA L.
[b.] December 29, 1901, Broken Bow, NE; [p.] Doll and Jack Coleman; [m.] Dead, January 30, 1943; [ch.] Three children; [ed.] 7th grade; [occ.] Retired; [memb.] Violet Rebekah Lodge #42 First Christian Church; [oth. writ.] None published just poems for friends birthday etc. and I keep a diary for many years. Publish chairperson for my lodge; [pers.] When I was born in 1901. Nebraska did not issue birth certificates until 1904; [a.] Salinas, CA

KOFMAN, ALEXANDER
[b.] October 17, 1966, Rostov-on-Don, USSR; [p.] Naum Kofman, Mara Kofman; [ed.] State University of New York at Stony Brook; [occ.] Student; [hon.] Dean's List; [pers.] My goal is to awaken the part of the human mind which is responsible for understanding the truth and its value.; [a.] New York, NY

KOROSKO, GEORGE B.
[b.] February 11, 1961, New Brunswick, NJ; [p.] Robert and Margret Korosko; [m.] Patricia Korosko, August 30, 1992; [ch.] Kelsey and Kimberly; [ed.] Monroe Twp High School Jamesburg, NJ; [occ.] Water Treatment Operator; [memb.] American Legion S.A.L., Post 177 Old Bridge NJ; [oth. writ.] I've written around 15 other poems - 3 children's books, 2 songs. I've never pursued publication, this is my first piece published.; [a.] South Amboy, NJ

KRAMER, D. M. PIERSON
[b.] December 22, 1936, Indianapolis, IN; [p.] S. and M. Guthrie; [ch.] Four - one deceased; [ed.] H.S. grad. - Southport H.S. - Indpls. and some evening courses; [occ.] Retired Office Mgr. - Bookkeeper; [memb.] Presbyterian Church - Retirement Community Aux. MBR, M.A.D.D. (Mothers Against Drunk Driving), Mbshp #001774861 Charter Mbr. Nat. Museum of the American Indian Smithsonian Institution.; [oth. writ.] Many - yet unsubmitted/unpublished. Presently outlining a potential book which will contain images of life, from my perspective of both wonderful, religious and tragic experience. Some reflections, some poetry etc. - both serious and funny. Also several poems.; [pers.] Living nearly 60 years now - life, has taught me much! Happiness - sorrow - extreme grief - how to keep going on, or trying! I wish to reach out to others who are experiencing some of the same or similar - to give hope, when it seems unreachable.; [a.] IN

KRAMER, REBECCA KRANE
[b.] May 12, 1985, Hartford Hospital; [p.] Rita and Jeffrey Kramer; [ed.] I am a middle school student in 6th grade. My goal is someday be a doctor; [occ.] I am a student; [hon.] I have won many Piano Awards. Two are 1995 and 1996 CSMTA Piano trophies for Outstanding performance. I got grand prize in my D.A.R.E. graduation with my poster; [oth. writ.] I like to compose and once one of my songs got published. It's name is "Mist Over The Cathedral" published in 1995. I also enjoy writing essays, stories, and poems.; [pers.] In addition to my writing, I like to dance ballet and have participated in many recitals. I love to participate in the arts which allows me to be creative in developing activities.; [a.] Storrs, CT

KROGMANN, JESSICA KAY

[b.] December 18, 1986, Lake Preston, SD; [p.] Arlyn and Jana Krogmann; [ed.] I am in the 5th grade, 10 years old. I go to Sioux Valley School.; [pers.] I love to write poetry it can be a great past time and a challenge.; [a.] Brookings, SD

KULASKI, MEGAN MARIE

[b.] April 11, 1977, Chicago, IL; [p.] Richard Walter and Carol Jean Marie Kulaski; [ed.] St. Henry's School, Father Ryan High School, University of Evansville; [occ.] ESR at Sun Trust Bank; [memb.] World Wildlife Fund, Newman Center, St. Henry's Catholic Parish; [hon.] Jack Long Award, Service Award, Dean's List; [oth. writ.] This is my first publication.; [pers.] My writings reflect my observations. My observation reflect the simplicity through which God works. Thank you, Dr. Longmire.; [a.] Nashville, TN

KWIATKOWSKI, NELLY

[b.] March 7, 1963, New Jersey; [occ.] Free Lance Writer; [pers.] William Wordsworth was my inspiration to write, mother Nina - Writer Father Roman - Architect; [a.] Wayne, NJ

KWIATKOWSKI, NINA

[p.] Father, Army Captain - Mother, Teacher; [m.] Architect; [occ.] Accountant; [oth. writ.] Short stories; [pers.] My hurtful soul "got the spiritual" healing from reading master of poetry: Robert Frost, also Polish Master of Poetry, Adam Mickiewicz.; [a.] Wayne, NJ

LAIYEMO, MD. ADEYINKA

[pen.] Adeyinka Laiyemo; [b.] October 5, 1967, Nigeria; [p.] Mr. and Mrs. Laiyemo; [m.] Rashidat Laiyemo, December 1, 1993; [ch.] Maryam; [ed.] Luba Comprehensive High, I Jeby-ode, Nigeria, University of Lagos, Lagos, Nigeria; [occ.] U.S. Army; [hon.] Best School Certificate Result, I Jeby Education Zone 1984. Principal's Prize for Overall Best Stud. 1984. Proprietor Prize for Academic Proficiency 1984. 1st prize, National Competition for Young Scientists, I Jeby Educational Zone 1984; [oth. writ.] Features writer for daily champion, a national daily newspaper in Nigeria 1990-1993.; [pers.] Let there be peace in the world.; [a.] Brooklyn, NY

LAKE, MATTHEW

[b.] May 8, 1978, Toccoa, GA; [ed.] High School; [occ.] Student; [oth. writ.] Raving of MAD Teenager (a unpublished work) that contains poems, essays, short stories that reflect the soul of a troubled teenager.; [pers.] All my works rather art, poetry or music reflect the over coming of a not so perfect life. And the hope of a better.; [a.] Toccoa, GA

LAMBERT, DEREK J.

[pen.] Derek J. Lambert; [b.] August 21, 1974, Battle Creek, MI; [p.] Gary W. Lambert, Marianne Guthrie; [ed.] Battle Creek Central H.S., Michigan Tech University, Michigan State, University, Monterey Peninsula College, Defense Language Institute Foreign Language Center; [occ.] Airman First Class, United States Air Force; [hon.] National Honor Society, Dean's List, Congressional Scholar, Who's Who of American High School Students, Airman Of The Month, Outstanding Student Of The Month, Special Tribute - State of Michigan; [pers.] I believe there is a poet in everyone, it's just most are afraid to try. You must stand proud and believe, for the only regret is that of not knowing what could've been.; [a.] Battle Creek, MI

LAMPINEN, JOSH

[pen.] Josh Lampinen; [b.] April 7, 1980, Lakeland, FL; [p.] Barbara and Robert Lampinen; [m.] Divorced; [ed.] Started my Junior year this August '96; [occ.] Work at Bi-Lo; [memb.] Boy Scouts of America; [hon.] Who's who Among American High School Students; [pers.] You must have fun. Don't take things too seriously.; [a.] Maryville, TN

LANCASTER, MELISSA

[b.] July 17, 1975, Cape Girardeau, MO; [p.] Lesley and Karen Lancaster; [ed.] Sullivan High School in Sullivan, MO; [memb.] The Free Willy Foundation; [oth. writ.] Numerous unpublished poems and short stories.; [pers.] A dream is a spark buried deep inside your heart. With love and hard work, that spark can turn into a flame. Writing is my spark. It is now becoming my flame.; [a.] Bloomfield, MO

LANDRISCINA, JOSEPH

[b.] September 17, 1977, Oakland, CA; [p.] Dave and Carol Landriscina; [ed.] Sophomore year at University of California, Riverside, Creative Writing Major; [occ.] Carrier for the Californian Newspaper; [oth. writ.] The Unanswered: A collection of short stories (to be published in a year).; [pers.] I feel that poetry comes from a great conflict or frustration within, or from the simplest tricks our own physical nature plays upon us. A lack of this in anyone's life breeds a lack of thought.; [a.] Murrieta, CA

LAPLANTE, MARY A.

[pen.] Meri and Lucky LaPlante; [b.] November 10, 1926, Sanford, ME; [p.] Paul V. and Anna Adams; [m.] Arthur J. LaPlante (DOD February 21, 1981), March 21, 1956 (Passed away one month before our 25th Anniversary); [ch.] Carol Ann (December 21, 1962); [ed.] Sanford H.S. (.44), UNA Summer and Nasson College (ME, '52-'53),; [occ.] Retired '91-present, I've been the "driving Miss Daisy" with working friend (living, seeing the U.S.A from MA-NM-CA-IL-MA-FL-NJ-FL-MA-NJ-FL-Cal in the same car, just drove across big TX Fr. FL-CA). (Grand total = 126,000 MI, including my commuting times in MA!); [memb.] Past member: BPW (Bus. and Prof. Women's Club (NH), presently: N. Shore Animal League, Natn'l Children's Cancer Assoc., Easter Seals, PVA (Paralyzed Vets.). Nat'l Parks, past member: NASCOE (Nat'l Assoc. County Off. Employ), also NH St. Office, Goodall-Sanford Inc., Chorale, Perf. at Hosp's. etc. (Home of Palm Beach Sit Material), Sanford, ME; [hon.] Top 10 (H.S.), Dean's List (College Nasson). 1st girl and 1 boy to climb up and over 10 walls in H.S. obstacles course. 1st Girl (and 1 boy twice) to get 100% in Science Course, H.S.), the only person Acctg. Prof (at Masson College) to ever given an A+ grade in final 3-hr. exam. I award myself to never give up or my husband's recovering from an almost fatal accident in 1955 (took 7 yrs.) and never giving up for him to beat cancer, but he lost the battle but without one complaint, what an honor to witness such a thing, because he had so much to give to poetry, music, art, he was also gifted as a 6th grade teacher who taught, changed, and inspired, (and inspired me too). I feel honored that you have chosen one of my "Why Oh Why" poems. I am thrilled and grateful, and I feel I can perhaps make a few people smile and make a few people smile and chuckle a little. In 1969 I had a stroke (or virus that "chewed up" my sensory nerve roots on my left side). But I trampled the streets of Boston to work with no pain in my foot, arm, or hand (I felt like Frankenstein with my plop, plop left foot). But also concurrently while working myself, I was lucky to be able to be strong to carry on while my husband was recouperating twice-once with an almost fatal (1955) Freak, but simple, skidding-in-snow accident in NH, and then cancer (Boy! That took courage to never give up.) (DOD 1981). In 1960 I was lucky to be able to get the bank to loan. Then in 1963, I was able to add on a Pine Grove drive-in in me (about 25 miles from Durham, NH) where we prepared and served fresh seafood and meat. Then in 1962 we were very fortunate to be able to have Carol; [oth. writ.] Have other poems and tributes I've written and sent to people. Hope to write and publish and "Add-On" poetry book (as I write more poems of things I've seen and experienced), some I've written primarily the tributes or birthdays poems, are more than 20 lines, and I have a hard time writing short letters.; [pers.] I love to write, and recite, short live, learn, and laugh poems for kids, young and old, and all, big, fat, skinny, small, short or tall. I like one-liners too (either my own, or others) and my Husbands, "Live while you're living", "Thoughts are things," and my daughter's adopted Grammy's" if it isn't one thing, it's 2", and Mary will pour", and my mother-in-laws: Oh Him! He wouldn't pay a nickel to see an earthquake," and "Love, love, you funny thing, look what you did to me. One of mine = make God a friend you visit it every day.; [a.] Sacramento, CA

LAPRADE, JULIA

[pen.] Julia Laprade; [b.] January 18, 1922, Franklin Co, VA; [p.] Ira and Nannie Laprade; [ed.] B.S. degree Radford College; [occ.] Retired - taught public school 40 years; [memb.] Antioch Church of the Brethren; [pers.] I believe in the one true God and his son Jesus. I believe Love is a strong force in our world.; [a.] Callaway, VA

LARIMORE, CHRISTINA

[b.] May 17, 1981, Detroit, MI; [p.] Thomas Larimore, Carol Larimore; [occ.] Student; [hon.] Several vocal music awards certificates, several academic certificates 9 creative writing award certificates, 1 honor roll trophy, 1 academic medal recognition by The Midwest Talent Search; [pers.] Always say what you feel. Whether it be in poetry or music or even just by talking to someone. People may not always agree with your opinion but it's better than keeping it all bottled up inside.; [a.] Detroit, MI

LAUMEYER, ROBERT L.

[b.] August 31, 1932, Wolf Point, MT; [p.] Rose and Joe Laumeyer; [m.] Kathleen McGlynn Laumeyer, August 31, 1953; [ch.] Robert A. Laumeyer - Jean O'Leary, Barbara Miner - Mary Runkel; [ed.] H. S. Nashua Mt. Colleges attended Northern Montana College, University of Montana - Arizona State University; [occ.] Retired; [oth. writ.] Poems in New voices in American Poetry 1980 and 1987. National Library of Poetry - walk through paradise - at Waters Edge - Beyond the Stars; [pers.] Some of the past, we would undo. Life's much easier when its not so new.; [a.] Boulder, MT

LAWALL, BETH ANN

[pen.] Beth Lawall; [b.] September 13, 1976, Fairfax, VA; [p.] Robert Lawall, Janet Trimmer; [ed.] Fairfax High, Northern VA. Community College, will be transferring to George Mason University.; [occ.] Waitress at the Olive Garden in Fairfax, VA; [pers.] Never give up on anyone or anything, and remember to smile it makes the world go round.; [a.] Fairfax, VA

LEAK, ANNA MAXINE HOLT

[b.] February 28, 1928, Jefferson Co., IN; [p.] Allen L. Holt and Leah V. Barber Holt; [m.] Ralph Bauer Leak,

June 9, 1968; [ch.] 3 step-daughters; [ed.] High school (N. Madison HS Indiana), 1 year Business school Indpls IN; [occ.] 43 1/2 years Retired Exec. Sec. Legal Nath Hq. the American Legion; [memb.] American Legion Auxiliary Victory Memorial U.M. Church, Choir Director - Christian Builders, SS Class Teacher - Vice Pres. U.M.W. (United Methodist Women); [hon.] Many awards for my work; [oth. writ.] Through the years I have written hundreds of poems for different people and written citations for the American Legion - they published one - ("The Pilgrims Thanksgiving"); [pers.] I am a dedicated Christian - I try to treat all people with love.

LEAVITT, JENNIFER C.
[b.] September 18, 1985, Oxnard, CA; [p.] Leti Perez and Ben Leavitt; [ed.] 6th grade gifted and talented education (G.A.T.E.) student; [occ.] Student; [hon.] Student of the Month, Student of the Year, Track Award and Citizenship Award; [pers.] Animals have been my guidance counselors for as long as I can remember. Now I want the world to see them as I do, as the perfect equals for man kind.; [a.] Oxnard, CA

LEBLANC, CARMELA ANN
[pen.] Carmie; [b.] July 19, 1959, Crookston, MN; [p.] Mary Ann and Richard (Mickey) LeBlanc; [ch.] 3 children, John age 14, Jade 13, Luke 9 mo.; [occ.] Mother; [memb.] Church of Jesus Christ of Latter Day Saints; [oth. writ.] All poems - Dealin' With Duke, Hillbilly Cat, Waitin' on Willie, Billy's Makin' Hillbilly Rock, Mary Had A Little Lamb - new version Luke Chapter 2 verses 42-51 story about, Experimenting with Eddie; [pers.] I met Duke at Dick Tracey's Bar in July of 1986 at Mpls. MN. I wanted him to meet my Aunt then. Today is August 26, 1996 and they still haven't met. I dream often they meet and really think that this time it's real but have awakened to find it's not. Duke will be 43 yrs old. My Aunt Debbie will be 42 yrs old. I'll be 38 yrs old. They have both lived in Minnesota all this time.; [a.] Invergrove Heights, MN

LECKBEE, CHRISTINE
[b.] June 14, 1950, Houston, TX; [p.] Marshall Love, Lou Love; [m.] Charles A. Leckbee, May 3, 1969; [ch.] Jodi, Charles M., Theresa, Beth, Christina, Mary, Angela, Stephen; [ed.] Permian High School Graduate; [occ.] Caregiver/Teacher Kids in Care Daycare; [memb.] Odessa Cultural Council, Permian Playhouse Community Theater, Stagehands, Guild, Band Boosters; [oth. writ.] What Are Left Over? Spoken Spectrum; [pers.] Twenty-seven years of marriage and eight children - I feel compelled to write about it, I feel lucky that I want to, I am happy to let others read it.; [a.] Odessa, TX

LEDFORD, SHERRY
[b.] February 28, 1959, Knoxville, TN; [p.] Frank and Ella Mae Miller; [m.] Kenny, October 27, 1988; [ch.] Brittany 7 years old; [ed.] High school - Tucker High, 1 year at DeKalb College; [occ.] Customer Service Mgr. at Jackson National Life Ins.; [oth. writ.] Years of poetry writing but nothing ever printed; [pers.] This is in honor of my father - Frank Miller.; [a.] Marietta, GA

LEE, BEVERLY ANN
[b.] May 15, 1956, San Bernardino, CA; [p.] Ernestine Walton and Floyd Bishop; [m.] Brian Avery Lee, December 18, 1982; [ch.] Belita Lee, Shalonda Wilson, Sontae Wilson, Tomorris Mangum; [ed.] Bachelor of Science (Sculpture), Master of Science (Education Administration); [occ.] General Education Instructor (GED); [memb.] Stockton's Teacher Association; [oth. writ.] Several non-published poems inspired by my daily environment and journey through life; [pers.] Since word's can be so powerful and long-lasting, I choose to use them to bring comfort, joy, and healing.; [a.] Lodi, CA

LEE, JENNIFER
[b.] June 17, 1984, Bronx, NY; [p.] Jung Hee Lee and Jong-Whan Lee; [ed.] I.S. 259 McKinley Junior High School (Brooklyn, NY); [occ.] Student; [memb.] National Junior Honor Society; [hon.] Stop World Hunger! Essay Contest Honorable Mention May 23, 1996, Letters About Literature Essay Contest, Honorable Mention March 1996, Scholastic Tab's September Student Writing Contest Runner Up September 1995 - Association of Assistant Principals Special Merit June 21, 1995, Award for Excellence in Mathematics June 21, 1995, Certificate of Achievement in Art June 21, 1995; [pers.] I may only be twelve years old at the moment, but I definitely know that writing is a gift that everyone possesses but doesn't know about it. Just remember: "Feel the fear, and go for it, just take it one day at a time!" Anything is possible.; [a.] Brooklyn, NY

LEFFLER, JACOB DANTE
[b.] January 18, 1976, Toms River, NJ; [p.] Alan F. Leffler and Karen E. Leffler; [m.] Janae Leffler, June 21, 1997; [ed.] Cedar City High School, University of Utah; [occ.] Full Time Student/Computer Science Major; [hon.] National Dean's List, Dean's Honor Award Scholarship, University of Utah, Industrial Education Sterling Scholar, Exchange Club Student of the year, Cedar City, UT; [oth.writ.] Poetry "Envious Traits", "Rain", "Wedding", "Trust"; [pers.] I refuse to let social injustice rob me of the Utopia in my mind.; [a.] Cedar City, UT

LEFLER, AMY
[pen.] Aim; [b.] September 16, 1981, Davenport, IA; [p.] Nancy and Al Lefler; [ed.] I am in 9th grade at North High School Pre-school and John F. Kennedy; [occ.] Student; [hon.] President's Education Award; [pers.] I try to write my poems based on the mood I am in or how I am feeling; [a.] Davenport, IA

LEGG, BETTY L.
[b.] September 8, 1939, Sutton, WV; [p.] Woodrow and Sylvia Parsons; [m.] Frank A. Legg, June 28, 1956; [ch.] 1 son - Michael A. Legg; [ed.] Richwood High School, Raleigh County Vo-Tec (L.P.N. Training); [occ.] Homemaker; [memb.] Past Member of Oak Hill Civic League, Contact Program and American Nurses Association, Fayette Art League and current member of Jones Ave. Church of God; [hon.] Awards in Acrylic Painting; [pers.] To keep my life centered in the will of God. To strive to inspire others through my poetry.; [a.] Oak Hill, WV

LEIMAN, HERBERT
[pen.] Herbert LeMan; [b.] February 12, 1932, Brooklyn, NY; [m.] Ruth Leiman, September 19, 1959; [ed.] B.A. Penn. State Courses in Creative writing at Florida International University being taken presently; [occ.] Professional Photographer; [oth. writ.] Novel - "Legacy Of Time" Novel - "Whisper To Me Gently" Screenplay - "Body Brokers" Screenplay - "So Shall The Crow Fly" Short Story - "Silent Discretion" Short story - "The Assassin" 4 - poems; [a.] Hallandale, FL

LEMIEUX, GAIL
[b.] May 13, 1960, Portland, ME; [p.] Robert and Alice Paquette; [m.] Mark W. Lemieux, May 8, 1981; [ch.] Derek Adam, Dale Michael, Brad William; [ed.] Biddeford High School Graduate - Class of 1978; [occ.] Domestic Engineer; [oth. writ.] I have written many other poems, none of which I have ever submitted for publication.; [pers.] My technique seems to surface from the sensitivity and awareness within me.; [a.] Biddeford, ME

LEMONS, DONNA JEAN
[b.] April 17, 1976, Aurora, MO; [p.] Larry and Linda Lemons; [hon.] Through School won a music contest playing the saxophone in which I received a 1, I was awarded student of the month and was again a nominee, later on after a few years; [oth. writ.] I write stories but their not published; [pers.] God has given me a talent that I can take and share with others; [a.] Crane, MO

LENZ, DEBORAH
[pen.] Deborah Haines; [ch.] Joseph Nolan; [ed.] Founder of Soulmate International a very ancient company teaching, Enlightenment; [occ.] Writer, Enlightened Teacher, America's Leading Cult Deprogramer; [hon.] I have been honored by all who have allowed me to share in their journeys, by all of the hundreds of thousands I have rescued and will continue to do so; [oth. writ.] My special book "Those In The Light, Those In The Dark"; [pers.] I come to all in the light, where truly the poet lies, and even speak of darkness, so long it has cried. In all, I honor, sending it back to the light, where even darkness has forgotten its flight; [a.] Santa Fe, NM

LERMA, DOMINGO F.
[b.] December 10, 1975, San Antonio, TX; [p.] David and Judy Lerma; [pers.] I like to express my true feelings in my writings, sometimes my poems are dark and disturbing. Sometimes they're peaceful and pleasant.; [a.] San Antonio, TX

LEVENS, LINDA
[pen.] Linda Levens; [m.] John Levens, July 20, 1968; [ch.] Melissa, Andrea, Matthew, Jessica and Cynthia; [occ.] Homemaker Hospice Volunteer; [pers.] I strive to see the inner goodness of everyone I meet. My poem was greatly influenced by my work as a Hospice Volunteer.; [a.] Mission Viejo, CA

LEVETT, TRINA
[pen.] Trina Stroud; [b.] November 12, 1966; [p.] Horace and Barbara Stroud; [m.] George Levett Jr., May 25, 1993; [ch.] Kevin Hogan II, Jordan and William Levett; [ed.] Grambling State Univ. 1984-1988, BA-Mathematics; [pers.] I write to release, unlock all the emotions that were caged during the course of my life. I write from experience, but most of all from my heart. That's all I know!; [a.] Conyers, GA

LEWIEN, EDNA
[pen.] Edd; [b.] April 13, 1898, Scotia, NE; [p.] George and Anne Sautter; [m.] Rev. Charles Lewien, August 10, 1921; [ch.] LaVerna Lewien Bonacci; [ed.] Scotia High School; [occ.] Retired, prior to retiring I was a minister's wife, seamstress, and salesperson; [memb.] United Methodist Church, United Methodist Women; [pers.] I enjoy bringing inspiration to my family and friends by writing a poem especially for them on their birthdays and anniversaries. Reading poetry and books is a favorite hobby.; [a.] Omaha, NE

LEWIS, STEPHANIE
[pen.] Dawn; [b.] September 2, 1964, Jacksonville, FL; [oth. writ.] I have written other poems for my church's newsletter.; [pers.] My desire is to bring hope to a dying world of a loving savior. My writings are by inspiration of God's presence.; [a.] Jacksonville, FL

LEWIS-ELOI, LUZ
[pen.] Lucy Lewis-Eloi; [b.] April 14, 1958, New York; [p.] Angelita and William Lewis; [m.] Fenel Eloi, July 14, 1979; [ch] Antoine Eloi and Janelle Eloi; [ed.] M. Ed. minor in Theology and Spanish; [occ.] 1st Grade Teacher; [memb.] NEA and Leominster Assembly of God; [hon.] Nominated for teacher of the year in Fitchburg, MA; [oth. writ.] I have never written before, so the poem Whispers was part of my first anthology.; [pers.] All my poems reflect emotions and thoughts that are caused by past or present situations or experiences. Poetry is a therapeutic tool to me.; [a.] Leominster, MA

LIKAS, JASON M.
[b.] February 16, 1973, Greenville, SC; [p.] Phil and Debbie Likas; [ed.] Mauldin High School, Clemson University, B.S. Architecture; [memb.] Mauldin United Methodist Church, Pi Kappa Alpha Fraternity; [pers.] Thoughts are silent in ones mind, but loud when written.; [a.] Mauldin, SC

LILLIE, ELAINE
[b.] September 1, 1945, Barre, VT; [pers.] My appreciation and thanks to Howard Ely and all on the selection committee.

LIMATOLA, JESSICA
[pen.] J. J.; [b.] August 22, 1986, New Jersey; [p.] LouAnn and Michael Limatola; [ed.] Eisenhower Elementary School K-4th, St. Stanislaus School 5th grade; [occ.] Full Time student, Morgan-Parlin Panther cheerleader (Captain); [hon.] Trophies for cheerleading, Dancing School, Soccer. Certificates: (2) Student of the Month; [oth. writ.] Poetry and reports for school; [pers.] I write poems because I love it. And it helps me express myself.; [a.] Parlin, NJ

LINDERMAN, GARY
[b.] February 16, 1967, Moulton, AL; [p.] Don and Dorothy Linderman; [m.] Johnnia Linderman, June 16, 1990; [ed.] BSED Athens State College; [occ.] Math Teacher, Softball, Football Coach, Farmer; [memb.] Cotaco Methodist church, NEA; [hon.] Who's Who Among American Teacher, Cum Laude, Dean's List; [pers.] It is by the Grace of God that I have been blessed and by His grace I will continue.; [a.] Somerville, AL

LINDNER, BILL
[pen.] W. A. Lindner; [b.] March 2, 1950, Torrance, CA; [p.] Bill and Ann Lindner; [ed.] BSEET - Devry Inst. Pomona, CA; [occ.] Field Service Eng.; [oth. writ.] Unpublished - Rhymes or reasons of love, fantasies of love; [pers.] Pain of the heart is a terrible thing to endure. Some people can, and are better for it. Others can't and are destroyed. God, grant me that strength to endure and grow.; [a.] Azusa, CA

LINDSTROM, LISA MICHELE
[b.] August 8, 1961, Minneapolis, MN; [p.] Ward Engebrit and M. J. Engebrit; [m.] Jeff, July 25, 1992; [ed.] Hopkins Lindbergh Sr. High School - 1 year U. of Minn - Literature Insurance Schooling including legal; [occ.] Poet, Publisher, Insurance Consultant, jack of all trades; [memb.] National Book Dealer's Exchange, All American Eagle Race Team, Distinguished Member of the International Society of Poets - Poems Across America; [hon.] 2 Poet of Merit Awards, 15 Editor's Choice Awards and a lot of self satisfaction; [oth. writ.] My own book was published "Adequate Justice-Beginning Healing Through Poetry". I am ready with a second book and near beginning my third book. I just need marketing help as I am solo.; [pers.] I enjoy art, specifically Impressionistic art. My goal is to describe these paintings as I feel that is what Lord Byron and all of the Artists wanted us poets of the future to do to bring back both of the most magnificent forms of art on earth.; [a.] Yorba Linda, CA

LINEHAR, MARK
[b.] March 1, 1966, Salem, MA; [occ.] Computer Repair Tech.; [pers.] Journey with me past the sweet blooms and rolling fields, where the things we appreciate leave us. Come now into the unknown, and all too familiar.; [a.] Salem, MA

LIZOTTE, DENNIS R.
[b.] January 8, 1949, Fall River, MA; [p.] Irene A. and Roger J. Lizotte; [m.] Debra Kay, August 23, 1980; [ch.] Child died in May, 14 yrs. old; [ed.] H.S., 3 yrs. of College, 2 yrs. Trade Schools, 26 Service Schools; [occ.] Maintenance Superior at John Randolph Hospital; [memb.] Lincoln Continental Ownership Club, Tri City Crusers; [hon.] Numerous, mostly service oriented but several for car shows; [oth. writ.] Various poetry and prose. Working on Publication Presently.; [pers.] Every day is a new beginning and all personal efforts lead to a satisfying goal.; [a.] Prince George, VA

LLOYD, ANNE
[b.] November 4, 1921, Muskegon, MI; [p.] Burrell Ladd, Josephine Ladd; [m.] Harve C. Lloyd, May 29, 1946; [ch.] Deborah Degner, Kevin Lloyd; [ed.] St. Mary High School, Creative Writing Class at Muskegon Community College; [occ.] Retired Homemaker; [memb.] Prince of Peace, Catholic Pioneers, Lincoln Golf Club, Top-of-World Ladies League Golf Assoc.; [hon.] 2nd Place Winner Seniors Council on Ageing, Muskegon 1996 County, Winner of Writers Club of Muskegon, 1995; [oth. writ.] Years of publication in local Muskegon Chronical, amateur cards, published poem in creative writing anthology, many articles in local newspapers, both MI and FL; [pers.] I feel my poetry writing is a gift — one that must not be wasted. My dear mother who died when I was four has grown more dear and closer in my poetry about her — which are many. [a.] Muskegon, MI.

LOBECK, LISA
[b.] July 3, 1970, Minneapolis; [ed.] Washburn H.S., Music Tech, Dakota County, Technical College; [occ.] Truck Driver; [hon.] Editor's Choice, Poet of Merit, Honorable Mention, Presidents List; [oth. writ.] Reflections In The Streets Of Emotion; [pers.] This poem is written for my husband, Mike. I love you.; [a.] Minneapolis, MN

LOCKES, ALLISON M.
[b.] September 12, 1980, GBMC; [p.] Stanley and Lila Lockes; [ed.] Edgewood High; [occ.] Still in high school, beginning eleventh grade; [memb.] Art Club, Jazz Band, Marching Band, Future Business Leaders of America, Forensics, Gospel Choir, Cross Country and Track Team; [hon.] 2 time winner in Martin Luther King Jr. Oratorical Contest, 3 times winner in Afro-American Speech, Silver Medalist in Act-So NAACP Olympics, Track and Basketball Awards/Medals; [oth. writ.] Several unpublished poems along with books that I personally illustrate and write, a handful of speeches.; [pers.] A true essence of infinite beauty...an expressive and overwhelming outpour of words creating beautiful harmony to relay what I feel in my heart...that is what I strive to capture.; [a.] Edgewood, MD

LOCKLEAR, BONNIE
[b.] November 14, 1935, Harrison, AR; [p.] Floyd Hihath-Erma Hihath; [m.] Roy N. Locklear, September 20, 1965; [ed.] Meridian High, BSU College; [occ.] Production Specialist Department of Education Boise; [memb.] Pastoral Care Group, Attend: Four Square Living Faith Church; [pers.] I enjoy reading poetry and delight in the flow of the poem as it brings forth its message.; [a.] Boise, ID

LOGSDON, AMY D.
[b.] October 13, 1965, Elmer, NJ; [p.] Terese Pagliarini and Craig Powell; [m.] Jeffrey B. Logsdon, February 4, 1994; [ch.] Brandon, Brooke and Brittany; [ed.] Graduate of Greenway High School, Phoenix, AZ, Graduate of ICS in Forestry Wildlife conservation; [occ.] Permit Coordinator at Cox Cable of Phoenix; [hon.] Quality Clug at Cox Communications (Cox Cable) and various other safety and productivity awards at work.; [oth. writ.] I have approximately 300 and poems in two 3 ring binders as of yet unpublished, one poem written for my sister Missy's Wedding and printed on the invitations.; [pers.] I am deeply grateful to spirit for this special gift of writing poetry. And I want to share a heart thank you to all of those at the National Library of Poetry for this wonderful opportunity.; [a.] Phoenix, AZ

LONG, CHERYL
[b.] June 27, 1962, Florida; [p.] Albert and Jeannie Le Duc; [m.] Deceased; [ch.] Daniel Long; [ed.] American School Chicago; [occ.] Homemaker; [oth. writ.] Written many poems to published in the future. Working on novel.; [pers.] I have been inspired by Phyllis A. Whitney to write and by my sister Becky to live. I miss you Mom. I dedicate this to you.; [a.] Clayton, GA

LONGAUER, EILEEN SULLIVAN
[pen.] Eileen Sullivan Longauer; [b.] November 30, 1943, Washington, DC; [p.] Dr. and Mrs. John B. Sullivan; [m.] Earl J. Longauer D.D.S.; [ch.] Brian Joseph, Shannon Kerry; [ed.] Bishop O'Connell High, Mary Mount University, University of Penn. School of Oral Hygiene; [occ.] Office Manager, Dental Hygienist; [memb.] American Dental Hygienist Asso.; [oth. writ.] This is my 1st time published.; [pers.] I strive to reflect basic feelings and emotions in my writings and to make people think.; [a.] Arlington, VA

LOPEZ, HELEN HOPE
[b.] November 24, 1942, Worland, WY; [p.] Reuben Mary Chavez; [m.] Sam Lopez, September 2, 1961; [ch.] Sam Jr, Timothy, Marcy, Sara, Josie; [ed.] Early Education Worland Wyo Jr High School Sunnyside, WA Junior College Sunny Side, WA; [occ.] JC Penny Clerk Children's Dept; [memb.] Member of Assembly of God Church, former childrens teacher in christian education; [oth. writ.] One poem in colors; [pers.] My poetry reflects solutions that come to me after years of thought and reflection. Every day things that puzzle me suddenly become clear; [a.] South Yakima, WA

LOPEZ JR., RICARDO AARON
[pen.] Rick Lopez; [b.] November 13, 1982, Harlingen, TX; [p.] Ricardo A. Lopez Sr., Sabrina S. Laiuppa; [ed.] Honors Eighth Grade Student, Memorial Jr. High School - Harlingen; [occ.] Student - Gifted and Talented Program; [memb.] National Junior Honor Society, Boy Scouts of America; [hon.] Duke University Talent Search, State Honors, Odyssey of the Mind (1st Place), UIL - Best Actor (1st Place), Creative Drama (1st); [oth. writ.] Barnett Shoals School Anthology (published poems), numerous short stories.; [pers.] I view my own soul and that of others and seek to reflects the world around me in a perspective for all readers.; [a.] Harlingen, TX

LORENZ, TERESA
[b.] March 5, 1981, Oil City, PA; [p.] Linda and Dennis Lorenz; [ed.] St. Stephen School, Venango Christian High School; [occ.] Student; [memb.] Drama Club, Local 4-H Club; [hon.] Outstanding Achievement in Spanish I, Excellence in Biology, Willa Cather Award for Written Expression/Freshman English, American Citizenship Award. My poem, "Today's Youth, Tomorrow's Leaders" won 1st place in the Catholic Daughter's of America contest in 1995-1996/local chapter and 2nd place Statewide; [pers.] I try to express how I feel through my poems.; [a.] Oil City, PA

LOUALLEN, DURSHON DONTA
[b.] November 2, 1976, Washington, DC; [p.] Arthur and Marilyn Louallen; [ed.] Paul Laurence Dunbar SHS and Virginia Union University; [occ.] Student; [memb.] Scripture Cathedral Church, Howard University Upward Bound Program and NAACP; [hon.] National Honor Society, Virginia Union University Dean's List; [pers.] I like to write poems so others can relate to the topic that is in my poems.; [a.] Washington, DC

LOVE, EBONY
[b.] August 18, 1976, Denver, CO; [p.] Brenda Love; [ed.] Columbia University, School of Engineering and Applied Science; [occ.] Student; [memb.] National Society of Black Engineers, Society of Women Engineers; [oth. writ.] Plenty of unpublished poetry!; [pers.] Inspiration is an ephemeral miracle, awakened as a lazy sleeping beast, stretching its gaping maw to spew out funky jazzy funk.; [a.] New York, NY

LOW, ART
[pen.] Art Low Sr.; [b.] September 18, 1956, Martinez, CA; [p.] Mildred Cook and Al Low; [m.] Divorced; [ch.] Art Low II and Qiana Marie Low; [ed.] Riverbank High, American River College; [occ.] Locksmith; [oth. writ.] Several poems and thoughts in an unpublished book, "Words From The Heart", Which is a joint effort with my son, Art Low II; [pers.] I have been inspired by the many walks of life I have experienced, my friends, family and everyday occuranced, which help me express my true self, and the way I perceive the world.; [a.] El Segundo, CA

LUCKEY, TAMMARA
[pen.] Vaybird, Tamy; [b.] November 3, 1960, Fort Myers, FL; [p.] Geraldine (Wans) and Vay Luckey; [m.] Nancy Carroll-Luckey, December 12, 1992; [ch.] Gizmo (my dog); [ed.] Okeechobee High School graduate 1978, Real Estate School - Local 630 Union Plumber; [occ.] Plaster 13 yrs. Know all stages of Plastering; [memb.] Manager of 5-8 yrs. olds Softball (coach) have to pass course to get certified; [hon.] Walton High School Awards, MVP - Volleyball - 1976-77; [oth. writ.] None published; [pers.] That people should not judge others because of sexual orientation, color, and sex. That all people deserve respect, no matter what their lifestyles may be. To look out for our youth and help guide them.; [a.] Lake Worth, FL

LUNDE, CYNTHIA
[pen.] Cynthia Wyatt; [b.] November 18, 1956, Bessemer, AL; [p.] The Late John Wyatt, Ressie Gore Wyatt; [ch.] Jeremy Garner, Michelle Thorton; [ed.] Stanhope Elmore High; [occ.] Quality Assurance, John Knov Manor Nursing home; [hon.] Blue Ribbon at the Elmore County Farr; [pers.] Writing is like my companion, one I could also share and give as a gift to others. A gift from God is my writing and it allows me to express the real me. I have talked to paper, the way I long to walk to people.; [a.] Montgomery, AL

LYLES, REV. GLORIA V.
[pen.] "Ecclesiastes" and "SOJ"; [b.] September 4, 1944, Damascus, MD; [p.] The late Nepier and Grace Lyles; [ch.] 3 adult children; [ed.] B.S. American University (1977), Georgetown Law School, Oral Roberts Univ. Masters of Divinity, Howard University (92), Ph.D. Candidate, Fuller Theological Seminary (1994-Present); [occ.] Ordained Minister and Professional Student; [memb.] Evangelistic Board and Board of Elders, (GMCHC) Washington, DC, Ordination Committee, Full Gospel Church of the Lord's Missions Intl., Inc., Washington, DC, Board of Advisors, Comanche Christian Center, Tulsa, OK; [pers.] If one applies Philippians 4:13 to their life achievements are limitless. "I can do All Things through Christ which strengtheneth me." (KJV); [a.] Silver Spring, MD

MAAG, LOIS MAY
[pen.] Lois Maag; [b.] August 7, 1939, Jasper, MO; [p.] Louis B. and May Allen; [m.] Allen Lee Maag, September 4, 1955; [ch.] Allen Leon Maag, Karen Maag Gibbs; [ed.] Savannah High School, Savannah, MO., Missouri Western State College, Hillyard Vocational and Technical School; [occ.] Little Angels Daycare, Music Teacher, Story Teller, Worker; [memb.] Faith United Church of Christ; [hon.] Missouri State, Camper Awards for several years, Toast Master International, 1994 1st place Humorous Speech Contest, St. Joseph Toasmasters and 1994 1st place Speech Contest Area MI Fall; [oth. writ.] Poetry Published Landhandler Magazine, Kitchen Klatter - Articles in Copper's Weekly and Message Magazine I am editing a book of poetry, "String Of Pearls", at present for possible publication.; [pers.] I walk each minute of every day in the awesome presence of my living Lord, Jesus. His Sweet Holy Spirit is my Comforter and Guide - May he receive all the praise and Glory!; [a.] Saint Joseph, MO

MACK, CATHERINE
[b.] October 24, 1984, Columbia, SC; [p.] Frank Mack, Nina Mack; [ed.] Hammond School (1-7 grade); [occ.] Student; [hon.] Continental Math Medal 2nd grade 5th grade; [pers.] I am grateful to my English teacher, Mrs. Ellen Turner for encouraging me in my writing; [a.] Columbia, SC

MACK, MADERIA GLARICE
[pen.] Maderia; [b.] October 28, 1952, Chicago, IL; [p.] Leroy and Bessie Moreland; [m.] At present separated, Davor D. Mack Sr., July 9, 1971; [ch.] Davor David Mack Jr.; [ed.] St. Francis de Paula (Elementary Loretta Academy and Emil G. Hirsch (High) 1. Semester Loop Junior - College Forget Name) Nursing 1 1/2 Sem. Calif.; [memb.] Tabernacle Baptist Ch. Chg. (PE.L) National Epilepsy Foundation National Multiple Sclerosis Society Bend an Ear Society; [hon.] Honored By Boy Scout's and Brownies as Den Mother and Brownie Leader Camp Pendleton CA., year 1983 in San Diego CA; [pers.] I have always felt that I was put here up earth for a reason. I now know why! For my words to be heard or read, and if they are at least I feel one someone can carry their own.; [a.] Chicago, IL

MACKENZIE, ROBERT W.
[pen.] R. W. MacKenzie; [b.] July 13, 1943, Delano, CA; [p.] Deceased; [m.] Divorced; [ed.] B.A. Eng. Lit. SF State 1969, Cont. Student Eng. Lit. 1969-75, BE Educ. SF State, 1977, with Educ. Cred. Elem.; [occ.] Taxi driver; [memb.] Golden Gate National Parks Association, National Trust for Historic Preservation; [oth. writ.] Poetry, short stories, narratives-nothing published.; [pers.] Basic civilities are lacking in many people who inhabit this planet today. Many individuals lack the common countries of please and thank you. I believe strong and binding relationships with people of both sexes builds integrity, wit and character in people; [a.] Oakland, CA

MACLEOD, DR. KENNETH I. E.
[b.] Scotland, UK; [p.] Kenneth MacLeod and Christina (Gaelic Poet); [m.] Deceased Jean P. Wilson (Pianist), April 25, 1935; [ch.] Deirdre, Sandra, Fiona, Iain; [ed.] 1930 Fortrose Academy (Father Rector), 1935 Edinburgh Med. Sch. MD., 1950 Univ of Michigan M.P.H.; [occ.] Retired; [memb.] Rotary, Mass Med. Soc., Science Assoc Advancement; [hon.] 40 years acknowledgment of Fellowship in the American P.H. Assoc. Some minor awards e.g. school prizes, music, art etc.; [oth. writ.] 1. "Castle Braham" novel, 2. "The Ranker", 3. A Victim of Fate, 4. "The Crisis in Authority", Music (a) "Ceolradh Chridhe" 1943, (b) "Music from the Heart" 1971 jointly with my mother and my wife; [pers.] Liberal - believe all men descended from a black "Eve" who lived in Africa 2 millions of years ago. Believe that Religions divide more than race, that Love and Care conquers all.; [a.] Ocala, FL

MAHON, JONELLE L.
[pen.] Jonelle Bridenbaker; [b.] March 4, 1962, Riverside, CA; [p.] Jon Jerry and Patricia Bridenbaker; [m.] Mark A. Mahon, September 1, 1995; [ch.] Stepson, Bobby Ray Mahon; [ed.] Rancho High School; [occ.] District Attorney's Office, Supervisor of Data Input; [a.] Las Vegas, NV

MAKUTA, PAMELA
[pen.] Pamela Makuta; [b.] November 25, 1979, Pittsburgh, PA; [p.] Daniel Makuta, Kathryn Makuta; [ed.] Junior, Deer Lakes Jr., Sr. High School; [occ.] Cashier; [hon.] Penn State University, Essay Contest Winner, Deer Lakes High School Science Fair, Who's Who Among American High School Students, Alle-Kiski Historical Society History Fair - Honorable Mention; [pers.] Modern life is rubbish.; [a.] Cheswick, PA

MALLOY, ELLEN M.
[b.] Chicago, IL; [p.] George I. Malloy and Mary (Minnie) Malloy; [occ.] Retired; [pers.] Life is such a precious gift. A wonderful family, relatives and friends are all so very special. To share with others, to help and serve are promises we can make. In this way we show appreciation for what God has given us.; [a.] Burbank, IL

MALONEY, JONA
[b.] August 9, 1984, Derby, CT; [p.] Lisa and Mike Maloney; [ed.] 6th grade completed; [occ.] Student; [hon.] Creative Writing Award - High Honors since 3rd grade - Music Award (4th Flutiest) - Won Kangaroo Glue Art Contest for State of CT (not grand price - I received 100.00 worth of glue products) 1994; [oth. writ.] No Where To Go - Traces of "T" - Quack Quack - I'm so Confused - Ode To Mom - Hoping all will be published some day.; [pers.] My writing heads toward Life and Nature, it all comes from the heart!; [a.] New Britain, CT

MANN, CAROL ANN
[b.] December 16, 1944, Alexandria, VA; [p.] Don and Elsie Watts; [m.] Divorced; [ch.] Jeffrey, Donald, Nancy Lee; [ed.] Life 101; [occ.] Food Service; [hon.] Horsemanship, Dancing and Archery; [oth. writ.] A few unpublished poems.; [pers.] Rod McKuen's book "Lonesome Cities" is an inspiration. I would love to meet Steven Patrick Morrissey. Song writer, singer, and a very

sensitive man (A warm hug and deep empathy to those whose love is lost or denied).; [a.] Westminster, CA

MANNING, LAURA
[b.] January 18, 1982, Part. General; [p.] William and Amy Manning; [m.] April 15, 1978; [ch.] Two; [ed.] Court Street Academy, EW. Chittum, and Nansemand Suffolk Academy; [memb.] Soccer Association, Peer Club, Drama Clud, (EYC) Episcopal young Churchmen; [hon.] Poetry Contest, Citizenship Award (2), Track and field (1st Place), soccer trophies, best singer award; [oth. writ.] Rain Drop, Noool, I am alone, I miss you, Trashy; [pers.] Don't take things for granted.; [a.] Portsmouth, VA

MANOLAS, ALEXANDRA
[pen.] Alexandra Manolas; [b.] October 20, 1959, Chicago; [p.] Harry and Angeline Karales; [m.] John L. Manolas, April 29, 1995; [ed.] MacCormac Jr. College, Elmhurst, Il, Elmhurst College, Elmhurst, Ill.; [occ.] Legal Secretary at Brinks Hofer et al. Chicago (Intellectual Property); [oth. writ.] Who Cares? published in 1976, miscellaneous poems to honor friends and family on lifetime milestones; [pers.] I try to live each day to the fullest as each day of life with my family and friends is to be treasured. I am blessed with good health and a loving family and I try to reflect strong compassion for others in my writings.; [a.] Glenview, IL

MARCEL, HELEN C.
[b.] July 29, 1922, LA; [p.] Allen and Neolla B. Cantrelle; [m.] Gilbert P. Marcel, August 20, 1945; [ch.] Allen Marcel/Sharon Frye/Evelyn Helm; [ed.] B.A. from Southeasten Louisana University in Hammond - 1945; [occ.] Retired (9 years) School Teacher in New Orleans Schools; [memb.] First United Methodist Church in Covington AARP, LA Arthritis Assoc.; [oth. writ.] Many poems and diaries nothing published (This poem was written our granddaughter was born - Rebecca Marcel Helm; [pers.] It's the little things in our daily life that make life meaningful and worthwhile. Family and friends are most important.; [a.] Covington, LA

MARCIANTE, JOSEPH M.
[b.] March 14, 1940, St. Louis, MO; [ed.] G.E.D., Basic Institute of Technology (Drafting); [occ.] Retired - Baker-Art Teacher and Drafting Teacher Metro Christian School; [memb.] Life Christian Center; [hon.] Several murals published in local newspapers - murals in schools and church's. Award for mural in St. Louis Senior Center; [oth. writ.] A Picture Paints a Thousand Words; [pers.] I have been drawing and painting for over thirty years without formal education in the field. I greatly appreciate the poetic flow of the psalms and endeavor to reflect them in art.; [a.] Saint Louis, MO

MARCUS, PAUL
[b.] December 27, 1949, Greenport, NY; [p.] Virginia and Samuel Marcus; [m.] Nancy Marcus, May 19, 1984; [ch.] Jonathan Paul Marcus; [ed.] B.A. English - University of Massachusetts, 1971, 1985 - Licensed New York Massage Therapist; [occ.] Connective Tissue Therapist; [oth. writ.] Clustered together: Poems from the Pavilion - an Anthology - 1986. Sports Medicine Articles Published for Chelo Publications 1990-1996.; [pers.] I work and write to renounce suffering and a global commitment to dying. I write to elucidate the joyful wholeness of being alive.; [a.] Bernardsville, NJ

MARIANO, PORFIRIO A.
[b.] March 27, 1922, San Mateo, Rizal, Philippines; [p.] Lorenzo and Apolonia A. Mariano; [m.] Eugenia B. Mariano, June 30, 1947; [ch.] Nini, Evelyn and Arthur Mariano; [ed.] 2nd yr. College of Philosophy and letter, Course - Journalism, School - University of Sto. Thomas, Place - Manila, Philippines; [occ.] Retired Gov't Records Officer, Republic of the Philippines; [memb.] Philippine Veteran Association, Philippine Records Management Association, Inc.; [hon.] Service Award Certificate with a silver Long Service Pin for having completed 30 years of continuous and satisfactory service in the Government of the Republic of the Philippines.; [oth. writ.] As a Filipino Vernacular writer Short Stories and Novels published on the following magazines at Manila, Philippines: Sinagtala, Ilang ilang, Bulaklak, Tagumpay, Radio Script Writer - DZBB Manila, Philippines Programs - Drama Musical, Radio Script Writer - Director, DZEC. Q. City Program, Juvenile Deliquency; [pers.] Writing is the best tool to settle disorderliness, rather than to use power, violence and impulsiveness.; [a.] Kilauea, Kauai, HI

MARKS, RITA
[b.] May 31, 1953, San Mateo, CA; [p.] Joseph and Sarah Marks; [ch.] Lazet Howard and Tanesha Howard; [ed.] Canada College, Redwood City, CA AA Degree, College of Notre Dame, Belmont, CA expect Computer Science degree in 1998.; [occ.] Sr. Admin., Asst. Purchasing Agent at Sun Microsystems, Inc., in Mountain View, CA; [memb.] Member of Fremont Bible Fellowship Church in Fremont, CA; [hon.] Dean's List - twice, American Business Women's Scholarship three times, Redwood City Citizen's Scholarship, Canada College Scholarship, Bay Area Urban League Scholarship.; [oth. writ.] Self, Rare Bird, Who Was That? The Love, Life, I want you, Education. Unpublished poems: Slow Down, The Joy You Bring and various others; [pers.] All the honor, praises, thankfulness, glory, and my blessings go to God for providing me with the talent to write poetry and to share with others to enjoy. I thank my daughters for their love.; [a.] East Palo Alto, CA

MARLEY, GENEVA I.
[b.] August 8, Hoisington, KS; [p.] Mary C. Shaw and Arley R. McEvers; [m.] Robert J. Marley; [ch.] Robert A. Jolene - Danny Ray; [ed.] High School Cosmetologist College; [occ.] Retired Cosmetologist; [memb.] Ladies Auxiliary V.F.W.

MARSHALL, JERRY
[b.] March 11, 1959, Blytheville, AR; [p.] Harold Marshall, Sue Giuliani; [m.] Kay Rudisell Marshall, June 18, 1996; [ch.] Jerry Neal, Christopher Allen; [ed.] Smithville High School, U.S. Air Force; [oth. writ.] "Ignorance" was my first attempt at poetry.; [pers.] I dedicate this to my wife, Kay. Thanks for your love, support, and encouragement. I love you.; [a.] Smithville, MS

MARTIN, CRAIG
[b.] January 30, 1975, Shelbyville; [p.] Doug and Brenda Martin; [m.] Kelly J. Martin, September 21, 1996; [ch.] 1 girl; [ed.] Shelbyville High School; [a.] Shelbyville, IL

MARTINEZ, CHRISTINA MARIE
[b.] November 2, 1973, New Rochelle, NY; [p.] Francis and Judith Vitolo; [m.] Vincent Martinez, May 6, 1995; [ch.] Philip and Anthony Martinez; [ed.] Brinckerhoff Elementary School, John Jay High School; [pers.] When you want something in life reach out and take it. It's the only way you can make your life a success. If you hide behind a closed door, who will know what you're capable of?; [a.] Bronx, NY

MARTINEZ, SUSANA MATOS
[b.] May 25, 1914, Toa Baja, PR; [p.] Maria Matos and Nicolas Matos; [m.] Carlos Martinez, February 27, 1950; [ch.] Maria and Eva Martinez; [ed.] B.A. Bilingual Education (Lehman College); [occ.] Housewife - Retired - Widow; [memb.] Puerto Rican Institute and (ECHA) Estabon Cultural Hispano Americano; [hon.] For Outstanding contribution to the East Harlem Council 1993 - Hispanic Community for Poetry writing 1993, Municipal Administration of Catano, PP in 1988 - Show Ramon Pena 1995 - Cultural values of Catano 1988; [oth. writ.] Books-poetry in Spanish (Cristal and Petalos - fiction book: Under the Apple Tree - published the three books.) Unpublished poetry and Spanish novel: Daughter's Destiny (Las Hijas del Destino); [pers.] In my writings I try to reflect justice, judgment and equity. Nature is a very strong influence when I write.; [a.] New York, NY

MASIAS, DANIEL H.
[b.] January 4, 1965, Oakland, CA; [p.] Daniel and Constance Masias; [m.] Susan Masias, November 18, 1995; [ed.] 11th grade (GED acquired); [occ.] Custom Home builder; [oth. writ.] All other work unpublished and unseen. Hope to publish in the future, example Childrens stories, and fairy tales and a hard won autobiography in the making; [pers.] I am a man that has spent a lot of time doing things against what God has planned for us, I intend to trust the rest of my life to the land and do what I can to see that this is a better place for the children in the future.; [a.] Hayward, CA

MASSEY, BEATRIX
[b.] February 12, 1951, Giessen, Germany; [p.] Delmar Pitts and Ursula Schmidt; [m.] Frank Massey, May 19, 1992; [ch.] Naomi Lyvonne, Kevin Kareem; [ed.] Professional Training School for Girls; [occ.] Restaurant-Worker; [memb.] Jehovah Witness; [hon.] Award of Merit Certificate for Poem "Separation"; [oth. writ.] Entered poetry-contest with poem "Separation" in 1989; [pers.] I write about the hard truth about human life today and that only our heavenly father can give us hope for a better future.; [a.] Dawson, GA

MATHIS, AMEENA
[pen.] Ameena Goggins-Mathis; [b.] October 13, 1967, Buffalo, NY; [p.] Janet Harbin-Mack and Jerry Goggins; [m.] Divorced; [ch.] Asha Mathis and Amani Mathis; [ed.] Riverside H.S., Empire State College; [occ.] Commercial Cus. Serv. Rep. M and T Bank; [memb.] Zion Dominion C.O.G.I.C.; [oth. writ.] Several poems, plays, short stories (unpublished); [pers.] I give all honor to God and Lord and savior Jesus Christ for blessing me with the poem "The Face of Good Friday" the Lord revealed this poem to me when I was at prayer on good Friday. It is my prayer that when people read it, they are reminded of how Jesus died so we could have the victory over the devil; [a.] Buffalo, NY

MATTA, AMANDA LYNN
[b.] August 18, 1985, Pittsburgh, PA; [p.] John and Denise Matta; [ed.] St Theresa School; [occ.] 6th Grade Student; [memb.] Choir; [hon.] Allegheny County Federation of Women's Clubs for 1996 Festival of Arts, and Munhall Woman's Club Literature Contest 1996; [pers.] I enjoy reading Charles Dicken's and Edgar Allen Poe and spending time with my brother John. My favorite book is "Great Expectations".; [a.] Munhall, PA

MATTHEWS, ANNA G.
[b.] March 15, 1915, Massillon, OH; [p.] Harry and Florence Ress; [m.] Howard Arthur Matthews, June 22, 1940; [ch.] Jane Woodring, Margaret Kettler, William

Matthews, 12 grandchildren, 5 great grandchildren; [ed.] St. Mary School, Mass. OH, Washington High School '32, Kent State Univ. '34, Art - Marc Moon 1 Session and Margaret Stiles 20 yrs., Bob Hazlett 1 Session; [occ.] Housewife, Elementary teacher grades 4, 5, 6, 7, 8, 10 yrs. plus tutoring also; [memb.] St. Mary's Church, Massillon Woman's Club (50 yrs.), SSS Sorority; [hon.] Smile Girl at Kent State; [oth. writ.] "The Pumpkin on Grandpa's Farm" (Poem), " A Trip To Wilderness Center" (story), (in Wilmot, OH), this was published in our local paper, "The Independent"; [pers.] My life has been filled with love of children, family, friends and nature, and my creative works seem to have been influenced greatly from these sources. Thank you.; [a.] Massillon, OH

MATTINGLY, CLARK H.
[b.] June 25, 1940, Grand Island, NE; [p.] Robert H. Mattingly and Ardis M. Marshall; [m.] Barbara J. (Rethmeier) Mattingly, May 20, 1962; [ch.] Son, David L. Mattingly; [ed.] High School, Neligh, NE - Graduated, Graduated Electronic Computer Programming Institute Doane College, BA in Business BAI School of Banking, Univ. of Wisconsin; [occ.] Information Systems Auditor; [memb.] Denver Chapter, Information Sys. Audit and Control Denver Chapter, Certified Fraud Examiners Ancient, Free and Accepted Masons (A.F. and A.M.) Scottish Rite of Freemasonry, S.J. USA Sesostris Temple, A.A.D.N.M.S. of Lincoln, NE; [hon.] The Alumni Senior Award, The Doane College Alumni Association Membership in Pinnacle, The National Honorary for Adult and other Non-traditional Students; [oth. writ.] Non published; [pers.] I feel an obligation to strive for self improvement that I might someday glorify the name of my Lord Jesus Christ.; [a.] Colorado Springs, CO

MAUM, COURTNEY
[b.] September 4, 1978, Stanford, CT; [p.] Linda and Robert; [ed.] Student at Greenwich Academy; [hon.] Published in "Apprentice Writer" and "Connecticut Student Writers" won first place for non fiction at Stanford Arts Festival in 1994.; [a.] Greenwich, CT

MAYLAS, JANEL P.
[b.] April 8, 1983, San Diego; [p.] Joseph and Jesusa Maylas; [ed.] 8th Grade C, Challenger Middle School; [memb.] Challenger M/S Band, Flutist, Mira Mesa Girl Softball (San Diego); [hon.] Good Citizenship Award (Mason Elem. San Diego); [oth. writ.] "I Dream" is my first ever poem.; [pers.] I thank God, my Mom and Dad for the inspiration.; [a.] San Diego, CA

MCALLISTER, LILLIAN
[b.] January 22, 1922, Valley City, IL; [p.] Lewis and Charlotte Edmonston; [m.] Richard McAllister, February 22, 1941; [ch.] Bryan, Phil, Charlene; [ed.] High School Seminars and Workshops in various areas throughout my life. One led to Caterer of weddings and parties for 15 yrs.; [occ.] Retired - A regular volunteer; [memb.] United Methodist Church IL, HCE, UMW, Red Cross Board Cancer Board, Church Women United, and Local Social Clubs; [hon.] Several reading Club Honors - 50 yrs. member in extension (now HCE) Home-Community Education. 28 yrs. -4H Leader a Heap O'Living along life's Highway - Byeagara guest and the Best Loved poems of the American People-Selected by Hazel Felleman 2 of my favorite books.; [oth. writ.] I write for local newspaper - over 40 yrs. a short story - "Coping With Als" was published in "Sunshine and Shadow" in 1985. My husband had Als. Wrote poems for local use like Clubs - exension - newspaper and for my own pleasure - helped research material for a hard back book that was published last year 500 copies were sold more on order. It was pike Co.; [pers.] One and 2 room schools. My love for poetry began in high school and in the 50's did some more. Have a long one written on a bus trip to Alaska. Tour guide ask a group of 55 people to write a poem. I was the only one.; [a.] Pittsfield, IL

MCCANN JR., CARA JAMES
[pen.] James McCann; [b.] July 30, 1966, Newark, NJ; [p.] Cara J. McCann Sr., Betty R. McCann; [m.] Elineth McCann, December 23, 1989; [ed.] University High School, West Side High School, U.S.A.F., S.C. Criminal Justice Academy; [occ.] Law Enforcement Officer Greenville County Sheriff's Office; [memb.] Refuge Temple, Leader and Founder of "Clear The Air" Program for High School Students, Palmetto Law Enforcement Officers, Association; [hon.] Gifted and Talented Program Interpersonal Skills Award; [oth. writ.] Jesus is Your One Stop Shopping Place for All Your Needs, The Title of Mother, We'll Have The Victory, God is With You From Jan. To Dec., Reaching For A Dream; [pers.] My poems and writings are religious in nature. I write to inspire, to teach and encourage mankind. My talent is truly a gift from God, our Lord and Savior Jesus Christ.; [a.] Greenville, SC

MCCARTHY, FREDRICK H.
[b.] September 6, 1929, New York City; [m.] Sheila P. McCarthy, November 26, 1956; [ch.] Fred Jr., John G., McCarthy J.; [ed.] Wagner Evening College SD NY; [occ.] Retired Consolidated Edison Co. NY; [oth. writ.] None, never took the time to do something I always thought go could do week.; [a.] Staten Island, NY

MCCAULEY, JENNA
[b.] August 10, 1984, Danbury Hospital; [p.] James D. and Lisa McCauley; [ed.] Nursery School-Bright Beginnings, K-5 Hill and Plain - New Milford, CT, 6 and 7 Schaghticoke Middle School; [occ.] Student; [hon.] Gymnastics, Swimming, Basketball, and Foul Shooting Awards Honor Roll in Schaghticoke Middle School in New Milford; [oth. writ.] Personal collection of poems written in school and independently; [pers.] I like to write poetry because it stimulates my feelings and thoughts, and takes me to places I've never been before.; [a.] New Milford, CT

MCCHESNEY, MILDRED F.
[b.] July 31, 1904, New York; [p.] Walter and Carinno; [ed.] High School - M.A. degree, AB College, Advanced Courses; [occ.] Retired, Former teacher at Social Studies and, lates Chief of the Bureau of Social Studies for NY States Education New York); [memb.] Church, Historical Societies, Library Associates, Civic Gyms; [hon.] Member of National first of woman chip of a bureau of the NY Education Dept. State and local history, in education church, writing for publication.; [pers.] The life one lives and one's inheritance influence interest in one's desire for expression in the written words. Commissions of Lutheran Church of America.; [a.] Troy, NY

MCCLEERY, VICTORIA R.
[pen.] Vicki McCleery; [b.] April 7, 1947, Detroit, MI; [p.] Anthony S. Bliznik, Victoria S. Bliznik; [m.] William A. McCleery, June 14, 1986; [ch.] Michelle Lynette Peters, Heather Lynn (Rothenberger); [ed.] Lamar University, Beaumont, Texas Bachelor of Applied Arts and Sciences; [occ.] Office Service Assistant at Texas A and M University Research Station-Beaumont; [hon.] First prize in the Carlton Cards Creative Poetry Writing Contest-Dallas, TX; [oth. writ.] Award winning poetry for the Creative Department at Carlton Cards- Dallas; [pers.] Poetry for me is like a snap shot, a reflecting pool. Poetry is a diary without a lock.; [a.] Beaumont, TX

MCCORMICK, KATEY
[b.] February 26, 1979, Bluemont, VA; [p.] Cecilia Galloway, Patrick McCormick; [ed.] Currently Senior in High School (James Madison); [occ.] Receptionist in family Law Firm; [hon.] 3 publications, honor roll for 3.8 GPA 2 years. Semi-finalist in Iliad Press Poetry Contest.; [oth. writ.] School Literary Magazine, Iliad Press Annual Collection of Poems; [pers.] The only way I have ever found inner peace is when I reflect my emotions through the words in my poetry.; [a.] Vienna, VA

MCCOY, MARCUS D.
[pen.] MMC; [b.] October 20, 1950, Detroit, MI; [p.] Dr. R. C. McCoy and D. Jean McCoy; [m.] Mari B. McCoy, June 9, 1990; [ch.] Joey, McCoy; [ed.] B.S. Michigan State Univ., Speech; [occ.] Industrial Video Products

MCCOY, MURIEL
[b.] March 4, 1944, Newburgh, NY; [p.] Mitchell and Henriett Elliott; [m.] Alfonso McCoy, August 29, 1964; [ch.] Darbin, Relma, Alfonso Jr.; [ed.] 12th grade; [occ.] Homemaker, Poet, Lyrist, Singer, and Creator of small crafts and ideas; [hon.] I have a few, the greatest honor to me, is to be a chosen one of anything positive.; [oth. writ.] "Brother" - in "After The Storm" grandbaby - first born - in "Rainbow End", "Lifes Keys - Marriage," "Steal Away" - in-spirit of the Age, "It's Time To Say Goodbye to Mother", Beneath the Harvest Moon," "Hunger" - Best poems of the 90's; [pers.] I've never strove to be famous, all through as a child I was, I just want to be good at what ever I do, I hold no "College degrees" My degree is living loving, giving to others, also accepting others for whom ever they might be, and not as I would have them be.; [a.] Phoenix, AZ

MCCULLOUGH, DANNY RAY
[b.] November 24, 1953, California; [p.] Charlie and Verna McCullough; [m.] Linda McCullough, March 5, 1983; [ch.] Two; [ed.] John C. Fremont High School, L.A., CA., El Camino College, Torrance, CA, Life Bible College, Azusa, CA, Providence Theological Seminary, L.A., CA; [occ.] Senior Pastor, Elottim Family Worship Church, Pomona, CA; [memb.] United Way, End Time, Ministries International; [hon.] Dean's List, Original Oratory, Outstanding Pastorial Award; [oth. writ.] In the process of writing a book to be published at the end of the year.; [pers.] In everyone's life there are reasons or obstacles that render and stop us from realizing our dreams. These obstacles are called "Walls of Opposition". Whatever you are desiring is usually found on the other side of your wall - therefore "What happens to you is based upon what happens in your first."; [a.] Rancho Cucamonga, CA

MCDANIEL, BRENDA JANE
[b.] October 16, 1952, California; [p.] Bruce and Elise Pickens; [m.] Riley Dale McDaniel Jr., August 28, 1992; [ch.] Sharon Elise Harris; [oth. writ.] Many unpublished poems. Fictional novel in progress. Currently in submission - short story.; [pers.] Inspirational messages.; [a.] Downey, CA

MCELLHENNEY, KAREN
[b.] February 21, 1965, Lancaster, PA; [p.] Roy and Brenda Hess; [m.] Keith R. McEllhenney, August 27, 1994; [ed.] Lancaster Mennonite High; [occ.] Asst. Prop-

erty Mngr.; [memb.] Manor Brethren In Christ Church; [pers.] True-loves are few, yet they endure through the ages of time to eternity. Blessed are the truly loved.; [a.] Shrewsbury, PA

MCELROY, FAYNE SADLER
[b.] May 13, 1915, Cross County, AR; [p.] Joe Hannie McElroy, Bessie McElroy (Nee Sadler); [m.] Alice Catherine (Nee Edwards), June 7, 1942; [ch.] Marc Currell McElroy (Deceased), Keith Alan McElroy; [ed.] Wynne, Arkansas High School, Arizona State College (Now Ariz. State University); [occ.] Retired; [memb.] No pertinent memberships; [hon.] None pertaining to literature or any writings - began writing poetry seriously in my 81st year.; [oth. writ.] Various poems (being assembled for possible publication in book - some prose - no significant publication.; [pers.] I try to make meaningful statements about the state of the earth, our society, and about life and experiences in general. I try to emphasize clarity, brevity, and when possible, humor.; [a.] Oxnard, CA

MCELYEA, ADDIE R.
[b.] July 3, 1950, Dothan, AL; [p.] Mose and Nancy Brown; [ed.] Ashford High School - George C. Wallace Junior College; [occ.] RN - Southeast Alabama Medical Center (SAMC) Dothan AL; [memb.] Alabama Nurses Association, American Association of Critical Care Nurses (AACN), American Heart Association; [hon.] American Honor Society Phi Theta Kappa, Dean's List; [oth. writ.] Several poems published college newspaper, College Yearbook, College Poetry Review - Spring 1979, Treasured Poems of America Summer 1996, Poetic Voices of America Spring 1994; [a.] Ashford, AL

MCFARLAND, CONSTANCE V.
[b.] June 12, 1935, Madison, WI; [p.] Harvey and Gwendolyn McFarland; [ed.] Wisconsin School for The Visually Handicapped, Milton College (Bachelor of Music Education with minor in English); [occ.] Retired Medical Transcriptionist; [memb.] St. Paul Episcopal Church, Fond du Lac Oratorio Chorus, Midwest Association for the Blind, Fond du Lac Women's Chorus, Fond du Lac Writers' Club; [hon.] C.A.R.O.L. award for leadership from Fond du Lac Jaycees; [oth. writ.] Assorted poetry published in Fond du Lac reporter; [pers.] I have been totally blind all of my life. It has it's frustrations, but aren't we all frustrated at times. You don't have to see in the physical sense in order to have vision.; [a.] Fond du Lac, WI

MCGOUGH, ANN
[pen.] Arean Markey; [ed.] Columbia Univ. New York M.A.; [occ.] Free Lance Writing (Retired Classroom Teacher of Latin - 45 years); [hon.] Pi Lamda Theta - Columbia Univ., 1938 National Swimming Record Breast Stroke - 100 yd.; [oth. writ.] Various Haphazard; [pers.] All God's children should have the blessing and happiness of writing.; [a.] West Haven, CT

MCIVER, JIMMIE
[pers.] I would like to dedicate this poem to whom it was originally written, Laura Hines. I love you, Laura, and the flower's still growing strong.

MCKINNIE, TIMOTHY MICHAEL
[b.] August 6, 1976, Detroit, MI; [p.] Juanita McKinnie, Miles McKinnie; [ed.] Wayne Memorial High, Eastern Michigan University, Sophomore; [occ.] College Student; [oth. writ.] I have had one poem published in the youth in Action newsletter published by the church of God in Christ districk Churches.; [pers.] Inspired by a good influential upbringing, I feel that my unique writing style causes the reader to think, while at the same time the reader can enjoying and appreciate the artistry and imagery of my work.; [a.] Wayne, MI

MCLAMB, CHRISTOPHER MICHAEL
[pen.] Soma Irot; [b.] July 25, 1979, Harrisburg, PA; [p.] Bonnie Ann McLamb; [ed.] Harrisburg High School John Harris Campus and Harrisburg Arts Magnet School; [occ.] Musician and Student; [memb.] Bi-GLYAH, Harrisburg Men's Chorus, National Forensic League, Tri-M; [hon.] State Champion and National Qualifier in Oral Interpretation of Poetry, 1996.; [oth. writ.] A poem published in professional essay concerning Martin Luther King, Jr.; [pers.] When life dumps shit on you, use it as material.; [a.] Harrisburg, PA

MCMAHOM, PEGGY
[b.] September 17, 1949, Chelan, WA; [p.] Nile Lambert and Eva Lambert; [m.] Brian McMahon, June 12, 1971; [ch.] Sean and Catherine; [ed.] Chelan High, U. of Washington, BSN; [occ.] Nurse Practitioner, Instructor Community Health Aides, Alaska Native Medical Center, Anchorage, AK; [memb.] ANA (American Nurses Association) Association for the Advancement of Health Education, National Association of Pediatric Nurse Associates and Practitioners, First Christian Church; [oth. writ.] Contributing Author for Community Health Aide/Practitioner Manual, two articles on mental health issues for local newspaper, my only published poem in Alaska Fisherman's Journal.; [pers.] In my writing I give a voice to my own personal struggle with depression and strive to help break the isolation felt by those living with mental health problems.; [a.] Anchorage, AK

MCMAHON, ELLEN
[pen.] Ellen Easley; [b.] September 6, 1968, Bentonville, AR; [p.] Jack and Minnie Easley; [m.] Joe McMahon, October 14, 1989; [ch.] Patrick 5, Jason 4; [ed.] Valedictorian of Spray High School in 1986 (Spray, Oregon); [occ.] Housewife, Disabled in Auto-Accident May 1995; [hon.] Class of '86' Valedictorian, '86' Who's Who Among American High School Students - Honors and Merit Roll through High School - top 100 finalist in the Miss America Cold Pageant for Oregon in '86'; [oth. writ.] Have only been seen in a small company newsletter. Many more poems and short stories. Just waiting for their time in the spotlight!; [pers.] I only write to help myself and others see and feel more around us. Writing is a vacation for me! Maybe someday my own book!?!?; [a.] Garfield, AR

MCMAHON, STEPHANIE
[b.] March 6, 1986, Newton; [p.] Peter and Cathy McMahon; [ed.] Presently in the 5th grade at Benjamin Franklin Classical Charter School, Franklin MA; [occ.] Student; [memb.] Franklin School of the Performing Arts - Drama, Franklin Dance Workshop; [hon.] President's Physical Fitness Award, Dance Achievements Awards; [oth. writ.] Many stories and poems; [pers.] My love for animals inspires me and I care for the earth and try to make it a better place and save the animals!; [a.] Franklin, MA

MCMILLAN, ANTHONY C.
[b.] November 7, 1972, Owosso, MI; [p.] Sherry Chapko, Allen McMillan; [ch.] Seth David; [ed.] Owosse High, G.R.J.C., G.R.C.C.; [pers.] Let justice be true, and let those who would mock its intention receive our darkest corners.; [a.] Corunna, MI

MCMILLEN, LINDA
[b.] November 19, 1940, Dighton, KS; [p.] Grant Hyames Jr., Marie Lind; [ch.] Michelle, Korinna, Lisa, Devin; [ed.] Master of Divinity - Phillips Graduate Seminary, Ph.D. Candidate - Iliff School of Theology; [occ.] Ph.D. Student, Ordained Pastor; [memb.] P.E.O.; [hon.] Alpha Beta Gamma, Summa Cum Laude - Phillips; [oth. writ.] Articles in several newspapers, illustrated children's stories for my grandchildren, reams of papers for masters and Ph.D. Degrees.; [pers.] I believe life is a journey of transformation, both personally and socially, and that poetry is the truest mirror of that journey.; [a.] Denver, CO

MCPHERSON, GLEN ALLEN
[b.] September 6, 1964, Philadelphia, PA; [p.] Glen and Beatrice McPherson; [m.] Kimberly Kay McPherson, October 21, 1995; [ch.] Chelsea and Jeanine; [ed.] Bayside High School graduate; [occ.] Fiberglass Repair - Busch Gardens; [oth. writ.] Poem written called "Grandmom"; [pers.] I have to thank my parents, and my Grandmother who passed away last year. "May the angels fly beside you in the morning and lay you down at night to watch you sleep".; [a.] Virginia Beach, VA

MCTAGGART, KAREN
[b.] June 24, 1962, Westfield, MA; [p.] Gerald and Helen (Barnes) Sikes; [m.] Robert J. McTaggart, August 8, 1987; [ch.] Robert P. McTaggart; [ed.] 1980 graduate Gateway, Regional High School, attended Westfield State College, (80-83) presently attending the Elms College Chicopee, MA, as a non-traditional student; [occ.] U.S. Postal Service (Distribution Clerk); [memb.] American Postal Worker's Union; [hon.] National Honor Society (Gateway); [oth. writ.] Article - Union Newspaper (The Rifle) Personal Journal; [pers.] I've always enjoyed writing. It wasn't until recently that the reality of writing about what I know and have experienced, positively influenced my writing.; [a.] Agawan, MA

MEAD, CHARLOTTE A.
[b.] August 9, 1954, Baltimore, MD; [p.] Charles Kolh and June Kolh; [m.] Richard Mead, October 15, 1976; [ch.] Raegan Kimberly and Richard Rollin; [pers.] I feel poetry is a way to express a feeling of the moment - personal to you, yet meaningful to others.; [a.] Gaithersburg, MD

MEARS, ROSCHELLE L.
[b.] February 8, 1969; [p.] Sheila E. Fernanders; [m.] Richard Mears III, June 5, 1991; [ch.] Richard Kallai; [ed.] BA Washington and Lee University (Journalism/Spanish) M.S. Univ. of Tennessee, Knoxville (Curriculum and Instruction); [occ.] Counselor, Cleveland State Comm. College; [memb.] FLTA.; [hon.] Honors graduate; [oth. writ.] Several poems published in "Discovery" 1987 literary annual of Chopticon High School articles for the "Tide" News paper in MD; [pers.] Poems and writings that reflect women in the various stages and phases of life and living are what I like to focus on most.; [a.] Cleveland, TN

MEAUX, ENJOLI
[pen.] E. Millie; [b.] December 3, 1978, Alexandria, LA; [p.] Barbara Meaux; [ed.] Holy Saviour Menard Central High School; [occ.] Student; [hon.] Music Awards for Piano; [pers.] Broken Promises is dedicated to Evie Gremillion. The motive in my writing is to express all aspects of love and the misgivings of life.; [a.] Alexandria, LA

MEDLEY, PAULA DIAN
[b.] June 9, 1968, Lexington, KY; [p.] John and Dian Jager; [m.] Steven Medley, June 18, 1993; [ch.] Allie D. Jager; [ed.] Aurora High School; [occ.] Pre-school teacher; [oth. writ.] I write poems all the time none that have been published until (now); [pers.] (Life Is Always Worth Living), I wrote this poem for my husband, for his dads birthday, he had a stroke and felt he wasn't worthy of life anymore! We proved him wrong, and gave him a reason to go on.; [a.] Republic, MO

MEGHJI, AKBARALLI
[b.] October 9, 1956, Ishaka, Uganda; [p.] Mahomedali Meghji, Shirinkhatun Meghji; [ch.] Rahim Meghji, Mary Meghji; [ed.] Ben Franklin High School, Rochester, NY, UCLA - Los Angeles, CA; [memb.] UCLA Alumni Association; [hon.] Deans List (Spring 1978); [pers.] Guidance from the bible, desire for higher education. Hopes and wishes for a brighter and peaceful tomorrow for all.; [a.] Reseda, CA

MELLO, GENEVIEVE
To whom it concerns - Poem in Tracker

MELLONAS, CHRISTOPHER
[pen.] C. N. Mellonas; [b.] December 24, 1958, Fitchburg, MA; [p.] Gloria Lessard and Ray Lessard; [m.] Kathryn Bartlett-Mellonas, October 18, 1991; [ch.] Charles Bartlett/Kassie Cope; [ed.] Winthrop High School, Winthrop Mass.; [occ.] Chef; [oth. writ.] Several other unpublished poems, - The Promise, Innocence Lost, Life's Prayer; [pers.] Seeing our problems with clarity is the first step toward changing our future.; [a.] Cottonwood, AZ

MELTON, LINDA M.
[b.] November 15, 1958, Huntington Park, CA; [p.] Henry Kelbert, Elsa Kelbert; [m.] Arthur E. Melton, November; [ch.] Pamela Cheri, Amanda Rose, Alisha Marie; [occ.] Word Processor Moss Adams, Bellingham, WA; [pers.] Writing poetry helps me become focused on a deep feeling, pleasurable experience, enjoyable moment or times of spiritual uplifting. Satisfaction with a prose is evident when the poetry fully elicits the precise point of expression and virtually causes me to recapture and share the sentiment.; [a.] Lynden, WA

MEO, KIM S.
[b.] July 15, 1965, St. Clair, MI; [m.] Joseph A. Meo, February 15, 1991; [ch.] Emily K. Meo; [ed.] BSW Wayne State University; [memb.] National Association of Social Workers; [hon.] Golden Key National HOnor Society; [oth. writ.] A Trilogy of Poems published by S.E.M.A.R.N. and displayed in Trapper's Alley, Detroit MI; [pers.] I hope my achievements in life shall be these - that I will have fought for what was right and fair, that I will have risked for that which mattered, that I will have given help to those in need... that I will have left the earth a better place for what I've done and who I've been. (C. Hoppe); [a.] Clawson, MI

METZ, DIANE V.
[b.] July 9, 1977, West Allis, WI; [p.] Joseph H. and Aldonna M. Metz; [ed.] Catholic Memorial High School, Silver Lake College (present); [occ.] Student Major - Special Education, LD; [memb.] Campus Ministry Student Wisconsin Education Assoc. (S.W.E.A.), Student Council for Exceptional Children (S.C.E.C.); [hon.] Glenn Davis Award 1995, Silver Lake College Religious Service Award 1995, 1996; [oth. writ.] A couple of poems in H.S. literary magazine and a monolog for the Senior Class play.; [pers.] To make this a better place to live, reach out and touch a child's hand.; [a.] New Berlin, WI

MICHAEL, JOSEPH STEPHEN
[b.] November 8, 1985, Honolulu, HI; [p.] Scott and Mary Michael; [ed.] Pershing Elementary School (MO), Flat Shoals Elem. School (GA), Memorial Middle School (GA); [occ.] 8th grade student; [a.] Conyers, GA

MICHAELIDES, VALERIE
[b.] March 8, 1954, Gloulestershire, England; [p.] Nicos Michaelides, October 27, 1973; [ch.] 2 boys, Alex and Steph; [occ.] Studying for a B.A (Hons) Degree in English Literature and looking after the family; [hon.] Diplomas in interpreting and translating and European humanities; [oth. writ.] Poems and short stories about village life in the Mediterranean; [pers.] I discover my identity and my place in the world through my poems. In poetry I can be myself.; [a.] Cyprus

MILLER, DIANE
[b.] May 18, 1957, Karachi, Pakistan; [p.] C. E. Coleman; [m.] Divorced, February 12, 1979; [ch.] One daughter 16 yrs old now; [ed.] Pakistan Studies and American Correspondence High School Chi. Ill.; [occ.] Visitor in U.S.A.; [hon.] For my performance in compositions and composing in the education fields of Cambridge schools, in the music dept.; [oth. writ.] Stories, poems, and songs (a hobby for my self); [pers.] Have great desires of working thru my instincts of visualizing things and penning it down. A great challenge for me.; [a.] Spring Field, MO

MILLER, KATHLEEN
[pen.] B. K. Gilson; [b.] November 8, 1951, Marshalltown, IA; [p.] Barbara Kathleen Gilson; [m.] Dennis Sherman Miller, November 2, 1991; [ch.] Hayley Debra Shannon Richard, Carrah Anne, Stephanie, Aurora, Jonathan, Sherman, Olivialin, Andrea; [ed.] Marshalltown High, Semco High; [occ.] Homemaker; [oth. writ.] Personal collection of creative writings and poetry.; [pers.] In my poetry and other writings I draw from my own personal relationships and friendship. The people and places I write about are real.; [a.] Abilene, TX

MILLER, KATHLEEN M.
[b.] December 19, 1962, Long Island, NY; [p.] Mary Walsh and George Blanchard; [m.] Christopher R. Miller DDS, October 19, 1991; [occ.] Dentistry

MILLER, KENNETH
[b.] July 25, 1970, New York, NY; [p.] Kenneth and Mary Miller; [ed.] Moon Valley, High School, Glendale Community College, Arizona State University; [occ.] Author; [memb.] National Rifle Association, ASU Alumni Assoc.; [hon.] Gamma Beta Phi, Phi Theta Kappa, Dean's List; [oth. writ.] Novel - "To Be Damned" published by Commonwealth Publications.; [pers.] I tend to rage against modernism in my writings, as I find it bland and unfulfilling. I long for a return to the lush description of Romanticism, and find solace in the works of Hawthorne, Melville, and Poe.; [a.] Glendale, AZ

MILLER, SUSAN J.
[pen.] Suscha; [b.] December 7, 1945, Bronx, NY; [p.] The Late Esther and Abraham Miller; [occ.] Auditor; [pers.] "Within the word life is the word if, is this just a coincidence?" Suscha; [a.] Huntington Beach, CA

MILLIGAN, SHEENA
[b.] November 26, 1984, Jacksonville, FL; [p.] Daniel and Angela Milligan; [ed.] 6th grade, Coronado, Middle School Coronado, CA; [occ.] Student; [hon.] 3rd grade Student Council Representative, 4th grade Student Council, Vice President, "Just Say No" Club, 5th grade Student Council President, Dare Club, Cheerleader and Conflict Manager; [oth. writ.] Several short stories and poems printed in school paper.

MINTON II, DONALD E.
[b.] February 19, 1956, Plainfield, IN; [p.] Donald E. Minton (Deceased) and Eleanor Hardin Minton Green; [ch.] Misty, Donnie, Erica, Kevin; [pers.] Inspired by God for my stepfather for father's day 1995 Albert D. Green who my mother married when I was 13. Have 4 sisters Donna, Barbara, Debby, Deanna Minton, 1 Brother Al Green III.; [a.] Garden City, SC

MINUTELLO, MICHELLE
[b.] September 15, 1981, Saint Petersburg, FL; [p.] Louis Minutello Jr. and Suzane M. Minutello; [ed.] Currently a High School Freshman as of 1996; [memb.] Key Club International, FBLA, Y Club, Saint Paul's Catholic Church; [hon.] Second Place in Oratoricale Contest 2 years in a row; [oth. writ.] Currently in the process of writing a book; [pers.] Always be a leader, never a follower.; [a.] Cleveland, GA

MIRANDA, YNIRIDA
[b.] July 31, 1976, Downey; [p.] Eulogio Miranda, Evangelina Miranda; [ed.] John Glenn H. S.; [occ.] Kaiser Permanente Hospital, Appt. Clerk; [pers.] This poem was written for Dave Navarro. He is a respectable Guitarist and someone who I greatly admire.; [a.] La Mirada, CA

MIRCHANDANI, APARNA
[b.] August 4, 1969, Bombay, India; [p.] Mr. Ajit J. Mirchandani and Mrs. Indira A. Mirchandani; [ed.] Bachelor in Business, Bombay University (India). Am currently pursuing a Bachelor's Degree in Computer Science.; [occ.] Student; [memb.] Alpha Gamma Sigma Honor Society; [hon.] The National Dean's List Award; [pers.] Dedication is the key to success.; [a.] Fremont, CA

MITCHELL, AMANDA RAE
[b.] August 21, 1978, Montgomery, AL; [p.] Phillip Mitchell, Linda Mitchell; [ed.] Lake Region High School; [memb.] I am a member of the Lake Region High School Band and the Historian for the band, also I am secretary of the Lake Region High School Interact/Thunderact Club; [hon.] Junior Civitan Faithful Service Award; [pers.] I have always enjoyed writing poetry. My favorite poem that I wrote would have to be the "Chocolate Rose". My favorite published poem is "Nothing Gold Can Stay", by Robert Frost.; [a.] Winter Haven, FL

MITCHELL, TAMI L.
[b.] July 9, 1964, Indianapolis, IN; [p.] Tom and Pat Kirk; [m.] Mark Mitchell, October 24, 1987; [ch.] Just in Spirit; [ed.] Carmel Clay District VU University, House of James Beautity College; [occ.] Secretary for In-Line Torque Converter; [memb.] Our Lady of Mount Carmel Church, Jazzersize; [hon.] When I was in High School 13 years ago I was in the Central Southern State Contest and I was the 1st place vocalist.; [oth. writ.] I wrote to other poetry contest. Searching, What Are Friends, Our Christmas Poem; [pers.] I want to touch and to inspire peoples hearts when they read my poems.; [a.] Westfield, IN

MOCK, LYNDA
[b.] June 4, 1962, Bedford, England; [p.] Pamela and George Dance; [m.] Robert William Mock, March 12, 1983; [ed.] John Bunyan Upper School, Bedford, England; [occ.] Housewife; [pers.] I had started writing poems a few years ago. Dedicating them for my family

and friends. I find it very enjoyable just to sit down and write a knew poem. Knowing in that some way it has touched someone else life.; [a.] Tucson, AZ

MOLNAR, EDITH B.
[b.] November 4, 1939, Hungary; [p.] Valerie and Eugene Molnar; [m.] Widow, May 1957; [ch.] Laszlo T. Beres; [ed.] BA Degree from Teachers College Pecs, Hungary, MA-Director (Regisseur) in Film-making, Budapest MAFILM; [occ.] Freelance-writer; [memb.] SAWCA/Writer group in San Antonio; [hon.] In teaching (Hungary, Budapest) - several; [oth. writ.] Self-published Bouquet of wild flowers (1996) in English and Hungarian (Selected poems) Poetry, Essays, Articles, Working on non-fiction life-story, (Translations for film script from Russian - to German in the 60's) working on translation from English to Hungarian, in "Committed" by Duke Embs; [pers.] "I must leave the mark, that, I had been stationed here, to give hope for the less unfortunate" (Arts Poetica) Motto: I need to speak, and learn by teaching.; [a.] San Antonio, TX

MONAGHAN, LARRY
[pen.] LEM, Dr. Hemp; [b.] April 16, 1949, Baltimore, MD; [p.] John and Betty Monaghan; [m.] Peggy Monaghan, June 24, 1972; [ch.] Jeni, Sean, Candi, Ian, Josh, Mary; [ed.] Glen Elg High School, H. Sam Houston Academy of Health Sciences, Pittsburgh State University, KS State College; [occ.] Senior in Communication, Broadcasting, PSU; [memb.] Nat'l Press Photographers Ass., KS Assn of Broadcasters, KSC Normal, KS Libertarian Party and KS Freedom Fighters; [hon.] Decorated Veteran - Vietnam, Outstanding Sports Broadcaster - 1995 PSU Comm. Dept. Dean's list; [oth. writ.] Articles and poem in high times magazine, Editorials for the Collegio, Morning Sun and Baltimore Sun, several unpublished short stories; [pers.] If you have trouble remembering redneck jokes, you might be a redneck. People with no addictions have no aspirations. They're just cattle.; [a.] Arcadia, KS

MONTGOMERY, HELEN M.
[m.] William Ray Montgomery Sr. (Deceased); [ch.] James Darrell, Raymond Scott; [ed.] Topeka High (KS), Grand Canyon University (Phx, AZ), IBM Processing School (AZ), Moody Bible Institute (IL); [occ.] Retired School Teacher - Speaker and Writer on Early American History; [memb.] Topeka High Historical Society Senior Coalition, Pueblo Grande Women's Club, Ridgeview Baptist Church Senior, Adults and ABW Women's committees, Richard Nixon Presidential Library; [hon.] Two awards from Business and Professional Clubs; [oth. writ.] Several articles printed in the "Freedom's Com-Cor" newsletter. Articles in local newspapers and political newsletters.; [pers.] Find out what you can do, and do that little well. No one knows what is great and what is small. Helping others you will find joy, and you will not have time to think of self.; [a.] Danville, IL

MONTGOMERY, LENORA
[b.] November 12, 1947, Martinsburg, WV; [p.] Rose DuPuis - Gladston Clark; [m.] Monty Montgomery, February 25; [ch.] Angie, Tammy, Tracy, Joseph; [ed.] Queline Berkeley Springs High Sch. WV, New York Regents College, California State Univ. Pomona; [occ.] Nursing Instructor Long Beach, CA; [hon.] Teacher of the year 1995; [oth. writ.] Reflections, The Face In The Window, readings for my grandchildren, Abagael, Carrah, Sammi, Tessa, Cozette Berlyn, Shyene Autuma, Shane and Derrick!!; [pers.] Sacred are the Aged, my our great Spirit in Sky watch over them.; [a.] Norwalk, CA

MONTGOMERY, LETISHA NICOLE
[pen.] Letisha; [b.] June 1, 1986, Jackson, MS; [p.] Perry and Vicky Montgomery; [ed.] 5th Grade Carver Elementary School, Raymond MS 39154, Dr. Edward Wiggens, Principal, Bill Elkins, Assistant Principal; [occ.] Student; [memb.] Spring Hill M.B. Church, Raymond, MS; [hon.] Citizenship Award, Perfect Attendance; [pers.] If you have a problem always try to find a way to solve it. Always try to find in your heart a way to help others.; [a.] Raymond, MS

MOONEY, ILEENE-MARIE
[b.] February 21, 1955, Chicago, IL; [p.] Morton Lowy, Bernadine Self Lowy; [m.] William R. Mooney III, May 28, 1989; [ch.] William IV, Melissa, Patrick; [ed.] Marywood HS, Good Counsel HS., DePaul U.; [occ.] News Monitor; [oth. writ.] Non-fiction and fiction novels pending publication, freelance articles, several poems.; [pers.] I've been inspired to go beyond my self made limitations. That Freedom to soar will remain within my spirit forever like a beautiful song.; [a.] Chicago, IL

MOORE, GAIL ALICE
[b.] August 17, 1962, Montgomery, AL; [p.] Hubert Otto Moore and Lettie Steineck Moore; [m.] Roger Lynn Moore, November 10, 1990; [ch.] Rachael Lynn, Nicholas Alan; [ed.] Jefferson Davis High School, Troy State University at Montgomery; [occ.] Secretary with the State Department of Conversation; [hon.] 1980-81 Jeff Davis Poet Laureate, Dean's List; [a.] Montgomery, AL

MOORE, SANDWANDA
[b.] September 9, 1967, Baltimore, MD; [p.] Frances Patterson; [m.] David Moore, September 30, 1995; [ch.] Shameera, Vincent, Chrissy and David Jr.; [ed.] Carver Voc. - Tech. High, PTC Career Institute (For Nursing Assistant); [occ.] Nail Technician/Custodian; [memb.] Education Ministry Committee; [hon.] 2 Citation Awards Given By Mary Pat Clarke, 3rd Place Award for Dramatic Reading; [oth. writ.] I have many other poems which are unpublished as well as this one. My dream is to publish a book of my poems to be sold in many book stores.; [pers.] My poems are my life, if you've read them then you know without even meeting me personally.; [a.] Baltimore, MD

MOORE, SHANE
[b.] October 18, 1977, Phoenix, AZ; [p.] Fred and Karen Moore; [ed.] Centennial High, College of The Air Force; [occ.] Member of the U.S. Air Force; [memb.] Member of Combined Federal Campaign; [pers.] I am able to write my poems thanks to the inspiration my life long friend and soulmate, Molly Campbell provides for me everyday.; [a.] Peoria, AZ

MOORE, SHERRY
[pen.] Sherry Lynn Dennison Moore; [b.] May 21, 1960, Tacoma, WA; [p.] Gerald D. Dennison, Sandra Sybert; [ch.] Chad Delano, Derek Lorenzo; [ed.] Warren Co. R-3 High School; [occ.] Manager - Dairy Queen Restaurant, Warrenton, MO /bookkeeper - Gary's Welding, Truxton, MO; [memb.] Friedens United Church of Christ, YMCA; [pers.] Live, laugh, love. There is a bright side to any situation! Gary W. Handlang has taught me to enjoy the earth and all its creatures.; [a.] Truxton, MO

MOORE, WILLA F.
[b.] March 22, 1934, Tallapoosa Co, AL; [p.] Mr. and Mrs. Herbert L. Fuller Sr.; [m.] Ivan B. Moore, April 5, 1953; [ch.] Angela, Ricky and Lee, five grandchildren; [ed.] Graduated from High School, training for practical nurse - worked in hospitals, did private duty nursing and worked for New Surgeon in Montgomery, AL, as a nurse/receipt for almost 20 yrs.; [occ.] Disabled - Read a lot and watch some game shows; [memb.] Member of Daughter's of Am. Rev. Beta Club, member of High Pine Baptist Church, Roanoke, AL; [hon.] I was selected as class poet, most studious girl in high school, received 2nd prize in an essay contest - past program director of W.M.U. I have talked Bible Schools and past Secretary and Treasurers of my church where I was reared; [oth. writ.] Over the years I have written numerous poems and other articles of interest I love to read poetry; [a.] Roanoke, AL

MOORMAN, LAURA
[b.] May 9, 1980, Dublin, GA; [p.] Thomas Van and Judy Moorman; [ed.] Currently a Junior at East Laurens High School; [memb.] Art Club, Literary Club and Beta Club; [hon.] 1994 Presidential Academic Fitness Award, 92-93 daughters of the American Revolution Essay Winner, Certificate of Merit for the talent search of mathematically and verbally gifted students (7th grades) given by Duke; [pers.] How a man plays the game shows something of his character, how he loses shows all of it (unknown).; [a.] Dublin, GA

MORGAN, JAMES EDWARD
[b.] September 3, 1919, Sedalia, MO; [p.] George E. Morgan and Mathilde Morgan; [ed.] BFA and MA (plus); [occ.] Artist (Retired Professor); [memb.] Honolulu Watercolor Society; [oth. writ.] Poetry and Short Stories (None published); [pers.] This is a magnificient universe, and one's mind is one's sole individual resource. Use it with the full knowledge that there are no return trips.; [a.] Kailua-Kona, HI

MORGAN, JENNIFER LEE
[pen.] J. Lee; [b.] December 29, 1952, Brownsville; [p.] Sara B. Leal and Late Wally Leal; [ch.] Marcos L. Martinez, Jessica L. Martinez, Lesley A. Morgan and Scott L. Morgan; [ed.] Bachelor Degree in Elementary - General and Bachelor Degree in Elementary Art; [occ.] B.I.S.D. Teacher; [memb.] National Historic Preservation; [oth. writ.] Various songs and poems from 1972 - today.; [pers.] A song, a poem, an art piece, to me is like the breath of new life, expressing it's emotions by the artist. I try to express my love for my family and the world through my art works. My greatest influences are my family, best friend John and my late Art Professor George Truan.; [a.] Brownsville, TX

MORGAN, MARLON
[b.] September 26, 1965, Denver, CO; [p.] James and Johnetta Morgan; [m.] Rochelle Morgan, May 28, 1995; [ch.] Charmaine, Marlon and Randy Morgan; [ed.] Flint Academy High School, Michigan State University; [occ.] Sports Writer, The Florida Times - Union, Jacksonville, FL; [hon.] Outstanding Contributions to the Media Award from the Fort Wayne (Ind.), Urban League and the Office of Multicultural Services at Indiana - Purdue University at Fort Wayne; [pers.] This poem was written for my wedding to reflect my views on the sanctity of marriage.; [a.] Jacksonville, FL

MORRIS, SHARON
[b.] June 5, 1976, Iowa City, IA; [p.] Kristina and Michael Dundee; [m.] Gary Morris, January 1, 1995; [ch.] Chase Emmanuel Morris; [ed.] Sherrard Junior Senior High School; [occ.] Cashier; [hon.] Dean's List, Nominee for Illinois State Representative, Who's Who Among American High School Student; [pers.] I am deeply gratified to be selected. I could not have done it without the encouragement from my husband city and

my best friend Dana and the inspiration from God above. Thank You.; [a.] Green Rock, IL

MORROW, LINDA

[b.] March 22, 1953, Burlington, CO; [p.] Harvey Runge and Ella Runge; [m.] Bob Morrow, March 2, 1974; [ed.] Burlington High School, Colorado State University, University of Northern Colorado; [occ.] Elementary Fifth Grade Teacher, Eyestone Elementary, Wellington, Colorado; [memb.] Fort Collins Reading Association, National Science Teachers Association; [hon.] Rural Electric Youth Tour (1970) Winner, Dean's List; [oth. writ.] Rural Electric Youth Tour Essay, poetry for important people in my life.; [pers.] I strive to impart emotional strength and support in the poetry I write for others.; [a.] Bellvue, CO

MORSE, RICHMOND N.

[pen.] Race Oliver; [b.] August 23, 1976, Weisbaden, Germany; [p.] Rick and Cheryl Morse; [ed.] East High, Larimie County Community College; [memb.] Dead Poet's Society; [oth. writ.] One poem called "A Small, Frozen Pond" in LCCC Literary Magazine the High Plains Register; [pers.] If you believe in something enough, anything is possible. Peace, love, and friendship are the answers to making things happen. Thank you, Tracy for your inspiration.; [a.] Cheyenne, WY

MORTON, CHARLES W.

[b.] August 6, 1916, Knoxville, TN; [p.] William P. Morton and Jennie Morton; [m.] Norma L. Morton, January 19, 1946; [ch.] Nancy Ann Vest; [ed.] BA University of Tennessee, MBA Indiana University; [occ.] Lt. Col. USAF (Ret.) and retired Industrial Development Coordinator; [memb.] Military Order of World War; [hon.] Numerous Military Awards; [oth. writ.] Two presentations at the national level on "Managing A Value Engineering Program" one is in the Library of Congress. Four (4) poems in the Library of Congress. Wrote the "Minuteman Project Officers Manual" on the Minute man Missile; [pers.] Poetry through ear appeal is more communication than conventional verbage or writings. Ear appeal improves retention as President Lincoln's famous words "Four Score and sever years ago".; [a.] San Bernardino, CA

MOSER, LINDA W.

[b.] September 20, 1952, Frederick, MD; [p.] Harry Wood, Elsie Wood; [m.] Dwight Moser, September 2, 1972; [ch.] Kevin Wesley Moser (Deceased); [ed.] Brunswick High School; [occ.] Customer Service Assistant Biowhittaker, Walkersville, MD; [memb.] Bethany Lutheran Fellowship Comm./Sarah Group Women's Group, Newsletter, Com-passionate Friends, Leesburg, VA; [hon.] National Honor Society; [pers.] Live each day as though it may be your last.; [a.] Jefferson, MD

MOURTOS, CONSTANTINA I.

[pen.] Legend; [b.] September 2, 1979, Michigan; [p.] Dawn Steinbrink, Wayne Steinbrink; [ed.] Cousino High School; [occ.] Student; [hon.] Black Belt in Tang Soo Doo Karate, Rated number one in the Michigan Karate circuit, 1991; [oth. writ.] The Watcher, The Nome, Me; [pers.] I am immortal, I have inside me blood of kings. Thanks to my favorite English teacher Debbie Schlater. Your the best.; [a.] Sterling Heights, MI

MURPHY, SALLIE ANN

[pen.] Sallie Ann Murphy; [b.] July 4, 1962, Philadelphia, PA; [p.] James Murphy, Nina Lee Shelton; [m.] Patrick William Murphy, May 10, 1986; [ch.] Sean Murphy; [ed.] Barna College Health Science grad 1992 Fla Institute of Muscle Therapy goal 1992; [oth. writ.] Vultures and victims will be published in 1997. Inspirational poetic verses especially written in dedication of my son, who was taken from me, also dedicated to all the victims in the world; [pers.] Henry Wadsworth Longfellow was my great, great grandmothers cousin and who much aspired me in the wisdom of writing. The breath of writing is for us all to learn, to love, and to share sorrows.; [a.] Pompano Beach, FL

MURRAY, ALYSON RENEE

[b.] July 4, 1971, Massillon, OH; [p.] Mr. and Mrs. Alistair Murray; [ed.] Perry High School graduate (1989); [occ.] Self-employed; [oth. writ.] "Book of Verse" was my very first poem book published for family numbers; [pers.] I enjoy writing poetry as it relaxes my inner thoughts. Every poem has my personality in it and shows great value of the person I am.; [a.] Massillon, OH

MURRAY, JOE L.

[pen.] Ransom Gold; [b.] September 3, 1946, Steubenville, OH; [p.] Joe and Louise Murray; [m.] Martha J. Murray, September 22, 1980; [ch.] Joe, Michell, Kenya, Jacqulen; [ed.] East Liverpool High; [occ.] Welder; [memb.] Bethelhem Baptist Church; [pers.] To live life to it's fullest, and treat others as you would like to be treated; [a.] Atlanta, GA

MURRAY, JOHN

[b.] July 31, 1981, Springfield, MD; [p.] Deborah Murray, Ian Murray; [ed.] Sophomore attending Villa Maria Academy; [memb.] Student Council Peer Leadership. Show Choir Peer Counselling Varsity Golf and Basketball; [hon.] First place in Regional Daughters of American Essay Contest, Presidential Academic Fitness Award, American Legion Scholarship Award; [pers.] Life at times can be very hard. I hope that you will be able to strive and overcome your adversities. When you do you will have piece of mind and a wisdom of life you didn't have before.; [a.] Girard, PA

MURRAY, NORMA SUSAN

[b.] September 25, 1956, Los Angeles; [p.] Angela and Ralph Montellano; [m.] Keith M. Murray, July 4, 1986; [ch.] Jeanine Sarah Kaltenbach, Sarah Melissa Murray; [ed.] Sacred Heart of Jesus Elementary, Sacred Heart of Jesus High School, East Lost Angeles College, Southland College of Legal Careers, Continuing Education through various seminars; [occ.] Legal Secretary, Secretarial Coordinator, Notary Public; [memb.] San Gabriel Valley Legal, Secretaries Association, National Notary Association; [hon.] Published poetry, writings, etc.; [oth. writ.] Editor of major law firm (Skadden, Arps, Slate, Meagher and Flom); [pers.] The soul is the window to life. Whatever you projected you attract.; [a.] Los Angeles, CA

MURRAY, ROBIN

[pen.] Buttons or Princess; [b.] January 8, 1966, Georgia; [p.] Mr. Harold Gilmoro and Mrs. Vandalee White; [ch.] Adrienne, Amher, April; [ed.] Neptune Senior High Rotc, Diploma Awarded; [occ.] None now but, I'm attending school now; [pers.] I would like to write poetry and be kind of recognized.

MYERS, CHRISTINE ANNES

[pen.] Cammy; [b.] March 26, 1965, Tacoma, WA; [p.] Dr. Ron L. Myers, Kay Annes Myers; [ed.] Graduated High School also graduated Cosmetology School... still attending the school of life; [occ.] Nail Technician, Specializing in Acrylic Nails and Hand Painted Nail Art; [oth. writ.] I have never submitted any of my other writing for publication. I was encouraged to send you this one by a co-worker. When I write, it comes from the very depths of my soul - and from the heart.; [pers.] I believe that we are all here to learn all we can. Teach what we know, and to love... with all our hearts. With that, you really can't go wrong.; [a.] Annapolis, MD

MYERS, PAMELA R.

[b.] May 28, 1950, London, Ontario, Canada; [ed.] B.A. University of Guelph, 1977, B.S. Columbia College, 1995; [occ.] Computer and Internet Trainor; [pers.] The Internet is the future and the future is now!; [a.] Columbia, MO

MYLES, LESSIE

[b.] February 13, 1952, Cordele, GA; [p.] Benjamin and Essie Myles; [m.] Divorced; [ch.] Lateef Myles; [ed.] A.S. Clark High School Cordele, GA 1969, Adelphi Business School 1971, 1985 Hofstra University - Word Processing Course; [occ.] Poetry Writer, Word Processor; [hon.] World Displayed at Community Fairs, Festival and Workshops. Poetry Sold at "Treasure Cache", Levittown, NY; [oth. writ.] "Oh Lord Hear My Cry", "The Void", "Praise", "My Child, A Gift From Above", "Tunnel of Life", "Mother" and others.; [pers.] My poems are a direct reflection of my personal relationship with our creator and his son Jesus Christ and my hope is that others may see the need to acknowledge God in their own lives.

NASRAWIN, CHRISTINE

[b.] May 12, 1983, Karak, Jordan; [p.] Fred and Tammy Nasrawin; [ed.] Stockdale Christian Jr. High, Ridgeview High School; [occ.] Student; [oth. writ.] Many of writing are kept to myself. This is my first publication.; [pers.] When I write I try to give my readers a lesson to learn or just something that interests them all of my writing is from my heart.; [a.] Bakersfield, CA

NAVIA, ROWENA C.

[b.] March 20, 1967, Manila, Philippines; [p.] Robert and Angelita Navia; [ed.] B.A. Political Science, University of California, Irvine, JD from University of California, Hastings College of Law, San Francisco; [occ.] Attorney at Law, San Francisco, CA; [memb.] California Bar; [oth. writ.] Short stories and poetry published in local papers, academic paper, publication pending.; [pers.] One grows only through experience and as sting so eloquently said, "Let Your Soul Be Your Pilot".; [a.] San Francisco, CA

NEAGOS, PENNY J.

[b.] May 22, 1963, Detroit, MI; [p.] Jim and Sharon Highlund; [m.] Ronald A. Neagos (Ron), July 23, 1994; [ch.] Brittany and Mandy Zedde; [ed.] Graduate of Denby High; [occ.] Customer Service Rep. at Quality Quick Print in Troy; [pers.] A little angel was inspired by and for Dana, a 6 yr old who went thru brain surgery to remove a tumor. My poems help me express my feelings to those special people now before one day it may be too late.

NEEDHAM, FRANCES DARLENE

[b.] January 28, 1954, Bishop, CA; [ch.] Michael Douglas Layne; [ed.] West high school, one year of college for cooking went back to Adult School for my GED for finish high school; [occ.] I am a cook for twenty years; [hon.] Just my GED for high school; [oth. writ.] I am writing my life. Also poems.; [pers.] I am in the study of astrology and metaphysics.; [a.] Bakersfield, CA

NEESE, NICOLE L.
[b.] May 20, 1980, Winston-Salem; [p.] Timothy Neese and Ruth Hughes; [ed.] Southwest Guilford High School; [hon.] Honor Roll Writing Awards; [pers.] Poetry is the thoughts and dreams of the soul.; [a.] High Point, NC

NEESE, RICK
[pen.] R. L. Neese and Leon Rixx; [b.] June 24, 1961, Selbyville, TN; [p.] Joan Crowell (Unionville, TN), Ray Neese (Nashville); [ch.] Kristoffer Zachary, Adam Richard; [ed.] Shelbyville Central High, Masters Institute!; [occ.] Musician, Drummer, Writer, Lyricist, Vocalist, (Pest Control Tech To Pay Bills)!; [oth. writ.] 112 Lyrics (all forms), collection of poems, 1/2 book written...all unpublished material; [pers.] "As wise a man it takes to gain value in his elusive affair for physical status and attributes, seems for the most to be an utter fool when it concerns the nature of his soul. Wisdom is found in one's heart...not one's mind; [a.] San Jose, CA

NEGRON, ORIOL
[b.] March 23, 1927, San Juan, PR; [p.] Rosa and Thomas Negron; [m.] Carmen Badillo Negron, October 25, 1947; [ch.] Oriol Jr., Joseph, Spencer, Priscilla, Tommy, Magally, Eric, O'Dean.; [ed.] Academic AD Degree in Psychology. Also a Doctorate degree from Los Angeles University of Metaphysics; [occ.] Retired but navigating in the vast world of computer.; [memb.] AARP of Metaphysical Church; [oth. writ.] Besides several unpublished poems, a thesis in Metalegia. A rough description with flaws discovered after years of new discoveries.; [pers.] The world hasn't found out the missing link of it's roots because it's people are terrified to be called "Superstitious" when facing the task of discovering the truth.; [a.] Las Vegas, NV

NELSEN, NORMAN R.
[b.] December 13, 1936, Staten Island, NY; [p.] Bernhard and Gladys Nelsen; [m.] Divorced; [ch.] Ronald Keith Nelsen (Deceased), Katherine Elizabeth Nelsen; [ed.] Princeton University AB 1958, Woodrow Wilson School of Public and International Affairs; [occ.] Retired International Marketing Executive/Consultant; [memb.] The Presbyterian Church, Basking Ridge, NJ, Scholarship Committee, The International Society of Poets; [hon.] Phi Beta Kappa; [oth. writ.] "Revival in Sea Of Treasures, "Critters Who Aren't Quitters" in Spirit Of The Age, "On Castle Rock Road" in Where Dawn Lingers, "Risky Mission" in Across The Universe, "Loonacy" in Best Poems of The 90's, "The Tree Tao" in Portraits of Life, "Water And Wind: The word and Spirit" in The Colors Of Thought, "Mass Murder A Cathedral Town" in Day Break On the Land, "Poetic Justice" in of Moonlight And Wishes.; [pers.] Often I write of the unity and diversity in what God has created and continues to create.; [a.] Basking Ridge, NJ

NELSON, CHRISTINA M.
[b.] February 11, 1949, Baunach, Germany; [p.] Ekstrand, Margaretha; [ch.] Shawn J. Nelson, Melissa M. Sharpling; [ed.] Grade School and Business College in Germany, High School, Business College, EP Community College, El Paso, TX; [occ.] Accountant; [memb.] International Graphoanalysis Society; [hon.] American Business Womens Assoc. - Women of the Year 1986, held several offices in both Am. Bus., Women's Assoc. as well as Nat'l Assoc. for Women in Construction; [oth. writ.] Have written several poems hoping to get published. Will enter other contests.; [pers.] I write my thoughts at the moment. I wish to write about hope, faith and encouragement even on a rough day. Everyday life inspires my writing, with Gods help.; [a.] El Paso, TX

NESBITT, RUTH RENEE
[b.] August 10, 1979, Japan; [p.] Roger and Judy Nesbitt; [ed.] Kentridge High School; [occ.] Student; [memb.] International Thespian Society; [oth. writ.] This is my first publication; [pers.] You only have understanding when you realize that there are some things you can never understand.; [a.] Kent, WA

NEW, JEFFREY W.
[b.] January 5, 1964, Knoxville, TN; [p.] William and Mary Beth New; [ed.] Central High, Univ. of Tennessee (No Degree Earned); [occ.] Lighting Director, Technician Bandit Lites Inc.; [oth. writ.] Personal Journal; [pers.] Nature is beauty evoke my imagination beyond my own dreams. I am a avid reader of Langston hughes poetry.; [a.] Knoxville, TN

NEWMAN, BARBARA
[pen.] Bobbie Newman; [b.] September 22, 1940, Butler Co, MO; [p.] Byford and Vera Long; [m.] Roy F. Newman III, August 1, 1959; [ch.] Charles Jeffrey, Terra Newman, Devine and Brian Daniel Newman, seven Grandchildren, Melissa, Megan, Alex, Kevin, Ben, Brian and Brandon; [ed.] American Dependents School Narimaser, Tokyo, Japan, Howard Community College Columbia, Ma Univ. of MO for easy Division; [occ.] Retired College, Howard Community College, Counselor, Columbia, MD; [memb.] Howard Community College Alumna Association - past membership in many civic organizations. Currently a very dating grandmother.; [hon.] Dean's List; [oth. writ.] Poetry, short stories, articles, children's fiction; [pers.] I strive "to give something of lasting beauty to mankind through the written word". Always a lover of poetry and literature, my private education his been exceptionally broad as herself.; [a.] Clarksville, MO

NEWTON, MICHAEL A.
[pen.] Terrae Filius; [b.] June 15, 1947, Las Vegas, NM; [p.] Adopted Henrietta Armstrong and Oscar White; [m.] Glynda Newton, March 1995; [ed.] GED, U.S. Military and Life; [occ.] Jewelry Designer; [oth. writ.] A variety of poetry and short stories based on my life experiences; [pers.] UT Prosim! (That I may do good); [a.] Austin, TX

NICHOLAS, SCOTT D.
[pen.] Scott D. Nicholas; [b.] February 21, 1961, Tacoma, WA; [p.] Ben Nicholas, Frances Nicholas; [ed.] B.S. Computer Science, California State university, Sacramento June, 1991; [occ.] Systems Analyst, State of California; [memb.] Local Spiritual Assembly of the Baha'is of Rancho Cordova, CA, Past Volunteer Big Brothers/Big Sisters of the Greater Sacramento Area; [hon.] Dean's List (several times) during my undergraduate work at California State University Sacramento.; [oth. writ.] Other than articles for my high school newspaper, this will be my first published work.; [pers.] I wrote "Through The Eyes Of A Four-Year-Old" in a high school poetry class when I was 16. It was my second choice of poems to submit. My first choice a poem entitled "Goal", is 37 lines long and could not be edited to the necessary 20 lines format.; [a.] Sacramento, CA

NICKELL, KRISTA
[b.] August 3, 1983, Sacramento, CA; [p.] Rick Nickell and Darlene Normandin; [ed.] 8th grade. Went to Capital Christian Center, Elk Grove Elementary and Joseph Kerr Middle School; [memb.] Elk Grove Teen Center (Christian Youth Group) Club Live (Act Against Drugs), Renaissance Group and Silver K Club; [hon.] Academic Talent and Search, University of California, Sacramento, July of 1996. Honor Roll 3.71 G.P.A. (Grade Point Average); [oth. writ.] Poems - The Stone Wall, The Storm. (Not published), Books - The Stalker, Dream Keeper. (Also not published); [pers.] Quotes - "Shoot for the moon, even if you, miss you'll land upon the stars". Meaning: You must strive for what you believe in, and though you may not get what you want, you'll get something.; [a.] Elk Grove, CA

NIGHTENGALE, KELLY DON
[b.] October 11, 1957, Leadville, CO; [p.] Vernon Nightengale, Lorraine Nightengale; [ed.] A.A. Electronics, Butte College, CA I'm currently a Senior at Chico State Univ. Calif. majoring in English (reentry student).; [occ.] Full time student; [hon.] Dean's List; [oth. writ.] "A Mourning..." is my first published work.; [pers.] If you should grow tired of chasing the almighty dollar, try chasing the muse instead.; [a.] Durham, CA

NIKKEL, LOUISE ANNETTE
[b.] October 30, 1950, Houston, TX; [p.] Gene and Nell Davis; [ch.] Rob Nikkel, Geoffrey Nikkel; [ed.] Robert E. Lee High School - Texas, Bakersfield College, Calif.; [occ.] Registered Nurse Geriatrics, Med-Surgical and back up for the emergency room; [memb.] Kern R.N. Society, Country Oaks Baptist Church; [hon.] Dean's List; [oth. writ.] Unpublished poem written 1979 in Hawaii; [pers.] Today and Tomorrow was written for both my sons. A transition for leaving high school and entering college - to give thought to their direction.; [a.] Tehachapi, CA

NISTLER JR., GARY R.
[b.] March 25, 1967, Oklahoma; [p.] Gary and Charlotte Nistler; [ed.] Bachelor of Arts in English and Bachelor of Arts in Psychology from August College, Augusta, GA (now Augusta State University); [occ.] Taekwando Instructor; [memb.] United States Taekwando Alliance, Southeastern Psychological Association, International Fantasy Gaming Society; [hon.] USTA top ten awards, Dean's List, Cadre of Cycle (US Army Infanym), Army Achievement Award; [oth. writ.] Sports articles for local running club, and as most hopeful writers, many short stories/children's stories in search of publishers.; [pers.] Two statements which guide my life, "Truth Conquers All", and "Use Your Head, But Follow Your Heart" with these two in mind life is, as Michelle and Keith would tell me, "No Problem"; [a.] Martinez, GA

NORDSTROM, JOHN A.
[b.] February 6, 1965, St. Paul, MN; [m.] Sharon, June 1996; [occ.] Engineer, U.S. Navy; [oth. writ.] Several other poems to my wife Sharon.; [pers.] Live for today and catch up on sleep when you dead!; [a.] Great Lakes, IL

NORMAN, TAMEKA
[b.] July 24, 1980, Frankford, Germany; [p.] Ava Norman, Charles Norman; [ed.] Bok Tech High; [occ.] High School Student Studying Food Service, Phila, PA; [oth. writ.] 9 Months of Pain, Hearts are Easily Broken, (but none of them has been published yet); [pers.] I try to keep my poems similar to life. My poems are based on other people's experience; [a.] Philadelphia, PA

NORRIS JR., VICTOR R.
[pen.] The Loving Fool If; [b.] October 3, 1978, Twentynine Palms, CA; [p.] Laurie and Victor Norris Sr.; [ed.] High School Graduate, currently a Freshman at Azusa Pacific University; [occ.] Student (Full-Time); [memb.] Young Authors Conference Lenwood Commu-

nity Church Air Force ROTC Detachment; [hon.] USAF ROTC Scholarship up to $55,000.00. Dean's I Scholarship Azusa Pacific University, National Merit Scholarship, Semi Finalist; [oth. writ.] Several poems published in school newspaper articles also published in school paper.; [pers.] All I can do is write how I feel.; [a.] Barstow, CA

NUNES, MARY DA COSTA
[b.] June 25, 1925, Fairview, NJ; [p.] Sarah Supino (90 yrs. Old) Father Deceased; [m.] Manuel da Costa Nunes, March 3, 1945; [ch.] Ralph-48 yrs. old (C.E.O. Home for the Homeless in NY, Lydia Hofmann 47 yrs old; [ed.] High School; [occ.] Retired - Great Grandma at present taking a course in writing; [memb.] Marilynn Hickey Min. and Kenneth Copeland Min., took a General Bible Course - Liberty Home Bible Institute - Lynchburg, VA; [oth. writ.] Stories for children. (Institute of Children's Literature in Connecticut.); [pers.] I have such a desire to write (in poetry or story form) about the Lord to the young children. I feel that the Lord will have me do this yet in this lifetime.; [a.] Lancaster, PA

O'DONNELL, CHRISTINA
[pen.] Christina O'Donnell; [b.] April 14, 1983, Lubbock, TX; [p.] Charles and Janet O'Donnell; [ed.] Middle School (student, 8th); [memb.] Aurora Chapter of the National Junior Honor Society; [hon.] Perfect Attendance, Honor Roll, (A'S), Science Project, Secretary of the student council for Ora Dee Clark Middle School; [oth. writ.] None others published, yet!; [pers.] Achieve your dreams, believe in yourself, and most of all, free yourself; [a.] Anchorage, AK

O'DONNELL, MATTHEW JAMES
[b.] December 27, 1979, Saint Paul, MN; [p.] Robert O'Donnell, Judy O'Donnell; [ed.] Henry Sibley High; [occ.] Lifeguard, Student; [oth. writ.] "Sunrise", "Sunrise, Through The Eyes Of The Blind", "Eternity", "Sarah", "Love", and "Def. of Luv", none published; [pers.] Anything that was ever written, was meant to be read.; [a.] West Saint Paul, MN

O'NEAL, CHARLIE JAY
[b.] August 4, 1978, Memphis, TN; [p.] Beth Wismiller and Barry O'Neal; [ed.] G.E.D; [occ.] Student; [hon.] Honors Biology Credit, and Scholars: United States History; [oth. writ.] None published, several poems and a few short-stories. All written as a hobby.; [pers.] To Jennifer Friend and Deana Whitehead for life, love, and liberty.; [a.] Memphis, TN

OBERSHAW, CHRIS
[b.] July 10, 1980, Valentine; [p.] David and Julie Obershaw; [pers.] Happiness is found few and far between, what I mean is my inspiration rest completely in my loved.; [a.] Alliance, NE

OGENE, CHUMA P. C.
[pen.] Paolo; [b.] December 25, 1969, Washington, DC; [p.] Dr. and Dr. (Mrs.) Obi S. Ogene; [ed.] Applegrove Elem. Oxon Hill, MD, Ekuln Primary School Enugu Nigeria. Diploma in Graphics, I.M.T. Enugu Nigeria. NDFA in Fine Arts (painting) I.M.T. Enugu Nigeria; [occ.] Artist, Designer, Writer, Sales Associate (Marketing); [memb.] Smithsonian Institution, Nat. Assoc. of Nigerian Artist, Museum of Modem at New York; [hon.] Awards and Certificates for sports and Art Competitions Listed in the International Directory of Creative Artist "L'art African Contemporain" Published in France; [oth. writ.] Several narrative poems and short stories. Creative forward for exhibition catalogues. Diploma and college degree theses on art methods and materials.; [pers.] I am deeply inspired by God, nature and mythology and this affects my paintings in a poetic way, and my poetry in a painterly way. I look forward to a deeper understanding of mankind thro poetry.; [a.] Washington, DC

OGILVIE, DAVID J.
[b.] November 13, 1964, Long Island, NY; [p.] Robert Ogilvie, Karen Gomes; [m.] Susan F. Ogilvie; [ch.] Robert Alcantara; [ed.] Sachem High School, Military; [oth. writ.] Several poems unpublished; [pers.] This poem was written for my wife when we were dating.

OGLE, DONEA FAY
[b.] August 10, 1946, San Angelo, TX; [p.] John T. and Virginia Smith; [m.] Richard Ogle (1944-1988), June 5, 1965; [ch.] Robert, Edward, Kitrina; [ed.] Alamogord High School, Central Texas College, Angelo State University; [occ.] Office Manager, Bookkeeper; [a.] San Angelo, TX

OHMART, BEN
[b.] September 20, 1970, Albany, GA; [p.] John Franceschina, Vickie Ohmart; [ed.] Monroe High, Catholic University; [occ.] Writer; [oth. writ.] Plays published by Scars Publications, stories and poems in x-ray magazine, feh! Interbang, The Unknown Writer, The Rutgers Review, continues to write screenplays and lyrics.; [pers.] I owe everything I am to my parents and grandparents. This book is dedicated, with love, to them.; [a.] Syracuse, NY

OLSEN, KEITH C.
[b.] July 9, 1956, Porterville, CA; [p.] Philip C. Olsen and Florene H. Olsen; [ed.] Balboa High School, Panama Canal Zone, University of California at Santa Barbara, Monterey Institute of International Studies, Sonoma State University; [occ.] Teacher: English, Spanish, Social Studies, Elementary School General Curriculum; [memb.] Board of Directors, Alliance Medical Clinic, California Teachers Association, Phi Beta Kapta, Healdsburg Historical Society, St. Paul's Episcopal Church, U.C. Alumni Association; [oth. writ.] "Nuestra Comunidad" Spanish news column in the Napa Valley Times, 1985-1987; [pers.] I grew up speaking Spanish in Panama and learned Portuguese when I lived in Brazil for two years. I believe the universal truths are expressed by being true to our inner selves.; [a.] Healdsburg, CA

OLSON, MARY JO
[b.] December 24, 1951, Harvard, IL; [p.] Maynard and Jeannette McCullough; [m.] Richard Ralph Olson, June 19, 1976; [ch.] Erica Jo, Trevor Richard, Annica Jo; [ed.] BS in Education - Northern Illinois University, MA in Leadership and Education - Saint Xaviers University; [occ.] First Grade Teacher, Clark Elementary School - South Beloit, IL.; [memb.] Prince of Peace Church, American Legion Auxiliary, National Education Association, Township Clerks Association for the State of Illinois, Committee Member for B.S.A. Troop 602, Clark School P.T.O. and Inservice Team; [hon.] Former American Field Service Student to Belgium, 4-H Club Congress Winner for Illinois State; [pers.] As am educator, I take the children where their at and strive to help them reach for the stars. Writing daily with children helps to show the true purpose of communication whether it be letters, notes, grocery lists, or poetry.; [a.] Roscoe, IL

OLSZEWSKI, ANTHONY ERICK
[pen.] "Ski"; [b.] August 20, 1970, Texas City, TX; [p.] Ana-Maria Campos and Oscar W. Olszewski; [ed.] J. Frank Dobie High, San Jacinto College - Central; [occ.] Assistant, Dreamworks SKG, Universal City, CA; [oth. writ.] Songs and Lyrics for my own orignal music.; [pers.] I feel we are all brothers and sisters of this planet, we need to sustain the life of our planet before our "Energy" returns to the origin!; [a.] Los Angeles, CA

OPPENHEIMER, NICOLE
[b.] June 26, 1980, Lakewood; [p.] Maureen and John Oppenheimer; [ed.] Manchester Twp. High School, Manchester, NJ; [pers.] I owe many of my accomplishments to my parents who taught me to reach for the moon because I might just hit a star.; [a.] Whiting, NJ

ORBIN, SALLY A.
[b.] February 16, 1952, Sewickley, PA; [p.] Joseph Orbin, Mary Orbin; [ed.] Allegany High School, Frostburg State University; [occ.] Programmer/Analyst, Sacred Heart Hospital, Cumberland, MD; [memb.] North American Riding for the Handicapped Assoc. (NARHA), Hooves for Happiness Board of Directors, St. Ambrose Catholic Church Newsletter Committee, Sacred Heart Hospital Employees Sharing Fund (Treasurer); [hon.] Cum Laude Graduate FSU, numerous horse show awards; [pers.] I love animals and nature, and I volunteer as a riding instructor in a therapeutic riding program for disabled individuals.; [a.] Cumberland, MD

ORELLANA, YANIRA MARGARITA
[pen.] Sharon Lee; [b.] June 28, 1976, El Salvador; [p.] Salvador A. Orellana, Sofia Orellana; [ed.] 2nd year at Los Angeles Harbor College, Wilmington Jr. High, Pheneas Banning High School; [occ.] Student at LA Harbor College; [hon.] Principal's Honor Roll, 1 certificate for poetry in class for the same poem. Graduated w/ honors in Jr. High; [pers.] Poetry is a master piece. A valuable writing that was created to give people or reader hope and to make them dream. I read poems and I drift into another world, one that is a world of beautiful literature and new kinds of feelings while reading and making a poem I can dream.; [a.] Wilmington, CA

ORR, LIZZIE
[b.] October 13, 1982, Manhasset, NY; [p.] Debbie, and Les Orr; [ed.] Ashland Middle School; [occ.] Babysitter; [memb.] Girl Scouts, Swim Team, Speech and Debate; [hon.] Honor Roll; [oth. writ.] Many different poems stories and articles for the AMS Bear Facts Newspaper.; [pers.] I enjoy writing about Dolphins. I hope that someday I will get to swim with these graceful creatures.; [a.] Ashland, OR

OSENI, OLADIPO
[pen.] Amy Styles, James Ineso; [b.] May 13, 1977, Lagos, Nigeria; [p.] Taofia Oseni and Helen Oseni; [ed.] St. Gregory College (High), Northeastern University; [occ.] Student; [memb.] African Organization Committee, American Society of Mechanical Engineers; [hon.] Math Achievement Award; [oth. writ.] Essay published in local newspaper.; [pers.] As a romantic, I search for beauty in our souls. As a writer, I describe that which I have beheld.; [a.] Lynn, MA

OWENS, KIM
[b.] March 21, 1974, San Antonio, TX; [p.] Valerie Owens; [ed.] Sam Houston High School (San Antonio, Texas) (1988-1992) Southern Methodist University (Dallas, TX) (1992-1996); [occ.] First year Law Student at Columbia University School of Law; [memb.]

Phi Alpha Theta; [hon.] S.M.U. Memorial Scholarship, S.M.U. Stanton Sharp Award for Outstanding Service and Academic Achievement, National Black Law Students Association's Nelson Mandela Scholarship; [pers.] I give all the glory and credit to my Lord and Savior Jesus Christ. My mother is a strong and beautiful person because she raised me by herself. Poetry reflects the heart.; [a.] San Antonio, TX

PABST, PATRICIA ANNE
[pen.] Pat Pabst; [b.] July 24, 1938, Hermosa Beach, CA; [p.] Jerome McElroy, Florence McElroy; [m.] David Brest, June 20, 1987; [ch.] Gayle, Shelley, Fred; [ed.] High School Drop-out California State University, Dominguez Hills Magna Cum Laude, Interdisciplinary Studies, BA CSUDH, MA English 1993; [occ.] Graduation Evaluator, CSUDH currently on disability leave-hepatitis "C"; [memb.] Past Member American Field Serv. Cal State U. Dominquez Hills Alumni Assoc. Academy of American Poets; [hon.] National Honor Soc. PHI Kappa Phl. selected to read at the 1984 "Poetry Alive Festival" by the intellectual life committee at CSUDH. (The Professional Readers Were Ann Stanford, Barry Spacks, Garrett Hongo and Thom Gunn).; [oth. writ.] Had my poem "Special Delivery" published in "Menya" 1988 Journal of Literature and art Cal State Univ. Dominguez Hills 14 short stories (submitted - 4 got rejected) 51 poems (submitted- about 10 rej's) "Till There Was You"; [pers.] "God's Grandeur" by Gerard Manley Hopkins and "The Second Coming" By William Butler Years are my two favorite poems. Rough Beast or dearest freshness? I write in an attempt to reconcile.; [a.] San Pedro, CA

PACILLI, JASON
[b.] March 22, 1958, Brooklyn, NY; [p.] Sara and Richard Pacilli; [ed.] Bachelor of Fine Arts, School of Varid Arts, other schools, Master Fine Arts, National Academy of Fine Arts, Cooper Unit; [occ.] Consultant, Sales; [hon.] Dean Honor List for Master Eagle Graphic Award. Certified Instructor Lead I, II, III, many service and leadership awards; [oth. writ.] First time published.; [pers.] In honor of a special time, we call it life. If I touched one person I've touched everyone.; [a.] Brooklyn, NY

PAGE, DONNA L.
[b.] August 17, 1936, Los Angeles, CA; [p.] Bruce and Loretta Page; [m.] Michael Moberg, 1957; [ch.] Eric, Cynthia and Barbara; [ed.] High School graduate, 2 years college, San Mateo, CA, Long-term Care Nursing Certificate - Olympia, WA, Private Pilot Certificate - 1976; [occ.] Nursing Assistant; [hon.] First Women in U.S. History To Place 2nd in a 250 mile motorcycle endurance race on a Suzuki 200 Motorcycle for The American Federation Of Motorcycles.; [oth. writ.] Columnist for Press Publications, Oakland, CA 1970-71 "Lay-it-On The Line by Donna Page.; [pers.] Discover your innerself, share it with those you love and the universe extend your hand and smile to those you meet daily.; [a.] Rainier, WA

PALMER, DAVID L.
[pen.] Davin; [b.] November 14, 1963; [p.] Joe and Pat Palmer; [ed.] Kalani High School, Windward Community College; [oth. writ.] None as yet published.; [pers.] Inspired and written for Anita Cary. May we all find happiness with our selves. (With a blink of my eye), happiness always...; [a.] San Francisco, CA

PARK, KANDICE
[b.] July 2, 1954, Casper, WY; [p.] Mr. and Mrs. William A. Kimsey; [ch.] Jim Bill and Tiffany; [ed.] Associates Degree Nursing; [occ.] Pharmaceutical Sales; [memb.] South Cobb Poetry Club; [hon.] Who's who in High Schools 1972, National Honor Society, Polk County High School Benton, TN; [oth. writ.] "White Sails" and "Jumble of Words" waiting to be published; [pers.] I strive to put emotions and feelings into my poetry. I strive to make a picture of emotions both sad and joyous we all share.; [a.] Mableton, GA

PARKER, CHRISTOPHER
[b.] October 22, 1974, Clovis, NM; [p.] Lafoy and Sammie Parker; [m.] Jennifer Parker, May 1, 1995; [ed.] Associate of Art, Garland County Community College; [occ.] Waiter; [memb.] First Assembly of God, Thespian Society; [hon.] Dean's List; [pers.] I wish that every person who I cross paths with in life sees in me a reflection of Christ's passion for others.; [a.] Hot Springs, AR

PARKER, PATRICIA LUCILLE
[b.] December 29, 1949, Des Moines, IA; [ed.] University of Iowa, B.F.A., Drake University, educational graduate work; [oth. writ.] Editorial writing and editing. Editor of a newsletter. One book of poetry is looking for a publisher.; [pers.] Truth is central to my poems. I look for different points of view and fresh ways of speaking age - old wisdom. I use lines from my poems in my visual art works.; [a.] Des Moines, IA

PATORA, DEBORAH
[b.] November 14, 1957, Brooklyn, NY; [p.] Virginia Marino, Saverio Marino; [ch.] Jake; [ed.] State University of New York at New Paltz; [occ.] Equipment Sales Manager, Metropolitan Concessions; [memb.] National Wildlife Federation, ASPCA, Humane Society of the U.S.; [hon.] Dean's List, Magna Cum Laude; [oth. writ.] Selected sonnets and poems, musical compositions: Trio for Oboe Clarinet and Bassoon, 12 tone compositions for voice and piano; [pers.] Love life without compromising your spirituality.; [a.] La Habra, CA

PATTERSON, VIVIAN
[b.] August 1, 1934, Biddeford, ME; [hon.] I have a doll house that my husband (Deceased) built and myself. My mom-in-law made most of the furniture and decor. It is displayed at the Margaret Strong Museum in Rochester, NY (11 rooms in and in scale); [oth. writ.] Poetry transports me to places I've dreamed, I've written poems for our home journal, for our church newsletter.; [pers.] Whenever depression sets in a poem will perk me right up and the people who read them are instantly energized.; [a.] Old Orchard Beach, ME

PAULY, REBECCA M.
[b.] August 30, 1942, Ashland, OH; [p.] Robert Mehl and Virginia Scott Mehl; [m.] Glenn Bentley, March 5, 1985; [ch.] Jeffrey Thomas Pauly; [ed.] B.A., Smith College, Cum Laude, 1963, M.A., UC Berkeley, French 1966, Doctor of Modern Languages, French and Italian, Middlebury College, 1984; [occ.] Professor, French and Italian, West Chester University; [memb.] American Association of Teachers of French, Amer. Assoc. of Teachers of Italian, Literature Film Association, American Society for 18th Century Studies; [hon.] GKA National Italian, Honor Society; [oth. writ.] Books: Lee Berceau et la Bibliotheque: The Transparent Illusion. Documentary Video and CD-ROM: A Month in France. Numerous articles in professional journals.; [pers.] Life long interest in culture and anthropology, in relationship between self and language, between memory, imagination and identity, and in the balance between the lyric and the rational.; [a.] West Grove, PA

PAVIOLO, KAL MICHELS
[b.] August 20, 1958, Arcadia, CA; [p.] Gary Frost, Jan Frost; [m.] Daniel Paviolo, June 3, 1989; [ed.] Accounting Certificate (32 units), Associate of Arts - Economics (Cerritos College), Bachelor of Science - Organization Mgmt. (University of La Verne); [occ.] Manager; [hon.] Departmental Honors ULV; [oth. writ.] Children Stories, currently in edit.; [pers.] I was inspired in my early years, by the works of Shakespeare. I performed extensively from the age of 13-28. Music is a big part of my life, and now inspires my writing.; [a.] Brea, CA

PAWLAK, REBECCA
[pen.] Rebecca Pawlak; [b.] May 11, 1977, St. Louis; [p.] Michael and Kathy Pawlak; [ed.] Northwest House, Springs High School, one year at the University of MO at St. Louis; [occ.] United States Air Force; [pers.] Living life is easy. Living a full life is a simple task by no means.; [a.] House Springs, MO

PAYNE, JEANNETTE HUNTER
[b.] September 23, 1908, Montezuma, IA; [p.] Mary A. and Stephen A. Hunter; [m.] Alonzo Payne (Deceased 1971), August 23, 1933; [ch.] 1 child Mary Carolee; [ed.] Junior College AA degree 1983 have always enjoyed reading or writing poetry, for my own pleasure. Have had about 20 or 30 published in local news media in Nev. Montana and CA.; [memb.] Military Widows #13. Gold Star Wives and Order of Eastern Star, have been doing Volunteer work for 50 years. Still doing it one day a week; [hon.] Poem of the Month Award Las Vegas Review Journal for May 1963; [oth. writ.] Have traveled extensively since my husband died and have written reports of the trips for family and friends who are 'Arm Chair Travelers'. No longer able to go themselves. Nothing ever copywrited or sold.; [pers.] I love people and like to see and do things for them if possible.

PEDALINO, MONICA
[pen.] Assunta; [b.] August 9, 1971, New York, NY; [ed.] New York University, Hofstra University; [occ.] Pursuing a law degree; [hon.] Hofstra Original Poetry Contest, several poems published in local newspapers; [pers.] I write to immortalize the memories that keep me alive. I have been influenced by the great works of Edgar Allen Poe.; [a.] Whitestone, NY

PEDERSEN, ALICE
[b.] November 26, 1941, Little Falls, MN; [p.] Frank and Rose Pekarek; [m.] Earl W. Pedersen, December 8, 1962; [ch.] Sheryl Leigh, Kathleen Alice, Mitchell Patrick; [ed.] Correspondence Course General High School Equivalent; [occ.] Administrative Secretary; [oth. writ.] Unpublished song/poem collection; [pers.] I hope to develop my songwriting ventures.; [a.] West Saint Paul, MN

PEILE JR., JOHN W.
[b.] August 21, 1956, Misawa, Japan; [p.] John W. and Reiko Araseki Peile; [m.] Lorreta Leigh (Holmes) Peile, December 8, 1979; [ch.] Trisha Leigh Peile; [ed.] Victor Valley High School, San Bernardino Valley College, Skadron College, Cal State - San Bernardino, Long Ridge Writers Group; [occ.] Cost Accountant; [pers.] Each of us has the ability to touch the lives of others. How we do so, is the decision. Choose well.; [a.] Las Cruces, NM

PELHAM, JENNIFER
[b.] January 20, 1982, Sierra District Hospital, Porterville, CA; [p.] Mike and Cindy Pelham; [ed.] Steve Garvey Jr. High in Lindsay, CA., Linden High School in Linden; [occ.] High School Student (Freshman), writ-

ing songs; [oth. writ.] This is my first 'wanted' poem, but I have been writing a song with my uncle, and writing reports for School. I also write poems just for fun.; [pers.] I have been influenced by today's singers (N.K.O.T.B., R. Kelly, Boys II men, LL Cool J., Mariah Carey, etc.) I hope to one day become as admired as they are. My friends and family are by me all the way. They're the best.; [a.] Linden, CA

PELLERIN, LINDA RONDEAU

[pen.] Linda Rondeau Pellerin; [b.] September 22, 1949, North Adams, MA; [p.] Wilfred G. Rondeau, Jeannette Foote Rondeau; [m.] William F. Pellerin, August 22, 1970; [ch.] Aimee Pellerin Phillips, Laura Marie; [ed.] BA in Liberal Studies, Belmont Abbey College, Belmont, NC; [occ.] Prospect Researcher, Belmont Abbey College Belmont, NC; [memb.] APRA (American Prospect Researchers, Assoc.), CAPRA (Carolinas Area Prospect Researchers Assoc.), Woman's Club of Gastonia, Chair of Communications at St. Michael's Catholic Church, Delta Epsilon Sigma National Scholastic Honor Society; [hon.] G. Richard Shaft Broadcasting Achievement in Women's Programming, SC UPI Individual Reporting Award, Society of Professional Journalists Sigma Delta Chi Byliner Award (honorable mention), Tennessee Associated Press In-depth Reporting, East Tenn. Soc. for Professional Journalist non-deadline; [oth. writ.] Co-author of "50 Most Eligible Men in Columbia", various short stories and poems in Agora (literary magazine, of Belmont Abbey College), Stories and features for Catholic News and Herald, Charlotte, NC.; [pers.] Life is more interesting them fiction, use it to learn and teach.; [a.] Gastonia, NC

PEMBERTON, RENEE

[b.] September 25, 1956, Ft. Thomas, KY; [m.] Dave Pemberton, April 14, 1984; [ch.] Tara Lynn, Taylor Anne; [ed.] Bellevue High; [occ.] Housewife and Writer; [oth. writ.] I've written poem books and other books; [pers.] I thank God for a talent to write. I hope my writings encourage others; [a.] Elsmere, KY

PEPPER, PATSY

[b.] November 12, 1951, Jackson, MS; [p.] Dr. and Mrs. Louie F. Wilkins; [m.] Tommy Joe Pepper, July 4, 1975; [ch.] Patrick Louis Pepper; [ed.] Brookhaven High School, Ole Miss, El Centro College, JRP Professional Models School, Braniff Intn'l Hostess College; [memb.] BHS Band, MS Dixie Darlings Percussion Twirling Corp, Kappa Delta, University Dancers, PHI TAU Lil Sister, Drama Club, Intn'l Models, Russian Ballet American Tour, Buster Cooper Dancers, Labrowski World Renown Singers, S.E.G., Entertainers Union, Cul. Union; [hon.] Miss MS's American Teen, U.S.M. Bathing Beauty Queen, Miss MS's Tri-County Talent Queen, LA's Miss Cinderella Sunshine, MS's Miss Hospitality, 1st Alt. Miss Brookhaven, MS's Jr. Miss, MS's Lions Club State Swimsuit Beauty, Glamour Magazine's Ten Most Beautiful Co-ed, Top Five Beauty Ole Miss, Most Beautiful Warrant Officer's Woman Waiting out the War, 'The Girl from Coca Cola,' Intn'l Rolls Royce Model, Mrs. So. NV '76, 1st Female Door Girl of Las Vegas; [oth. writ.] 1st book of poems written for daddy in the 3rd grade; written hundreds of poems and songs, never submitted to be published; [pers.] My poems come when I am consumed with deep, passionate emotions that completely overwhelm and control my mind and come out in poems.

PERKINS, CHRISTOPHER ROBIN

[pen.] Donncadh; [b.] January 24, 1973, Harvard, MA; [p.] Carlos and Kathleen Perkins; [ed.] Graduated '92 after many different schools across USA and West Germany. College for short time and "Never Going Back" (Song lyric); [occ.] Laborer/Ind. Sales; [memb.] MFNA, (Mech. Force North America); [hon.] Who's Who Among American High School Students; [oth. writ.] Found most extensively in Genie's New Age Round Table Category 2 Topic 8; [pers.] My poems reflect a person who was raised Christian's struggle to reconile its intolerance of the modern world with it's profession of goodness "There are more things in heaven and earth than are included in your philosophy".; [a.] Falmouth, VA

PERREAULT, CHRISTINE D.

[b.] June 27, 1964, Salida, CO; [p.] Walter Virgil Stauffer, Margaret Ann Hoffman; [m.] Stephen K. Perreault, March 4, 1985; [ch.] Silas Stephen, Chad Walter, Terence Lake and Nash Evan (4 boys); [ed.] Buena Vista High School, North Central Michigan College; [occ.] Housewife and College Nursing Student; [memb.] Holy Childhood Catholic Church, St. Annes Altar Society; [hon.] Phi Theta Kappa, Honor Society; [pers.] I would like to dedicate my poem, "Thinking Of You" to my husband of whom I truly love.; [a.] Harbor Springs, MI

PERRYMAN, JON RAY

[pen.] Ima Aggie; [b.] October 29, 1938, Bryan, TX; [p.] Blair and Ray Perryman; [m.] Divorced; [ch.] Staci Lyn Perryman; [ed.] Texas A and M University (Class of '60), (2 Degrees); [occ.] Retired Teacher (30 years); [memb.] American Numismatic Association, Presbyterian Church; [hon.] 1) Honored as a Golden Poet in 1991 by World of Poetry, 2) Service Award from Brazosport Independent School District - 1962-1990 in Freeport, Texas; [oth. writ.] Poem - "The Carrousel Of Life" published in 1991 in book Listen With Your Heart (Quill Books); [pers.] My motto: "Lord, help me to live for others, that I may live like thee!"; [a.] College Station, TX

PETERSON, KELLY

[b.] July 22, 1978, Crown Point, IN; [p.] Wendy Peterson; [ed.] Currently a Senior at Lake Central High School, St. John Indiana, graduating end of January; [pers.] I have been writing for almost four years now. My dad inspired me. My first poem was to my dad. He read it before he died and he cried. I write how I feel inside. I dedicate my poems to my friends Aimee, Amanda Kristy, Karen and Joanne. They helped me through it all. My dad inspired me and my friends helped guide me.; [a.] Dyer, TN

PETERSON, KRISTEN

[b.] January 2, 1972, Lynn, MA; [p.] Kenneth Peterson and Loraine Armstrong; [ed.] Bachelor of Arts, Salem State College - major English; [occ.] Councillor, Working with Mentally Challenged Adults.; [memb.] Massachusetts Wildlife Association, Salem State Wind Ensemble; [hon.] "Voice of Democracy" Scholarship awarded for essay. Dean's List; [oth. writ.] Newsletter, "Houston Avenue Highlights." Monthly editions. Greater Lynn Mental health and Retardation Association.; [pers.] In life we are given many gifts. The ability to convey an emotion using only a pen and words is the most amazing gift of all. Someday's I believe I can write as well as Anne Sexton, my favorite Poet, other days I believe I'll build a fire!; [a.] Lynn, MA

PETERSON, MS. J. T.

[b.] Brooklyn, NY; [p.] Mrs. Marion Finn, Joe Pietro; [m.] Peter, July 23, 1960; [ch.] 1 - Patricia Ann; [ed.] New School for Social Research - NYC, Dramatic Workshop (NYC), (Irenia Piscotor); [occ.] Legal Sec'y; [memb.] New York State Motors, Public Association; [hon.] English Medal, Art Medal, P.S. 132 Brooklyn New York (Letters routinely published in Daily News "Voice of the People"); [oth. writ.] Poem based on: "The Khamsin" - novel set in the middle east circa 1944 - (USAFIME), United States Armed Forces In The Middle East - unpublished; [pers.] Stanistofsky said it best: In short - "Experience is the best teacher", whether you like it or not (sic).; [a.] Riverdale, Bronx, NY

PEVTSOVA, CATHERINE

[b.] May 18, 1981, Saint Petersbugh, Russia; [p.] Elena Pevtsova, Alexei Pevtsova; [ed.] Kailua Elementary, Kailua Intermediate; [occ.] 9th grade student in Bozeman High School; [memb.] National Junior Honor Society, Girl Scouts; [hon.] President's Award, Honor Roll, Silver Award in GS; [pers.] I enjoy writing poems because, I can express my feelings and thoughts through them!; [a.] Bozeman, MT

PHILLIPS, HELEN B.

[pen.] HBP; [b.] December 3, 1901, Pine Bluff, AR; [p.] Helen Knox Badford; [m.] William W. Phillips, February 20, 1922; [ch.] Five; [ed.] High School and one year at Linden Wood College in St. Charles, MO; [occ.] Retired - "95 years old"; [hon.] Mostly a normal life Jr. League of Pine Bluff, Life Member of Salvation Army, Life Member of Jefferson Hospital, Life Member of Methodist Church and so many more.; [oth. writ.] Many little poems started at about 12 yrs. old. This is the first poem - I have ever sent - I write poems, because I enjoy it.

PHILLIPS, MARGARET B.

[pen.] Maggie B' Phillips; [b.] December 6, 1927, Sumrall, MS; [p.] Irene and Alton Lee; [m.] William W. Gragg, January 1946, widowed 1986, Lucien G. Phillips, July 1993; [ch.] Donald E. Gragg, Sandra M., Timothy W., William A.; [ed.] High School class of 1945. Lower Columbia College 1976-1977 Longview, WA. ECKANKAR Writers Group in Vancouver, Wa. 1980's ECKANKAR Writers Seminar June 1996, Montreal Quebec, Canada; [occ.] Retired - Artist, Writer; [memb.] ECKANKAR, Lifetime Volunteer, currently serving as Secretary of Hospice of Kitsap County, Board member, Spiritual Advisory Council. Past community activities in Longview, Wa. Red Cross, Blood-Program Chairperson, Portland Oregon Blood Program Board, Health Drives and other.; [hon.] Listed in American Artist of Renown, 1981-1982 edition, Maggie B' Gragg. Cartoon sketchbook of Mt. St. Helens.; [oth. writ.] Unpublished; [pers.] Member of ECKANKAR, Religion of the Light and Sound of God. Share experiences with other Eckist at seminars and attend ECK artist groups and writing groups when available. Art and writing grows through spiritual experiences; [a.] Bremerton, WA

PIERCE, VALERIE M. J.

[b.] December 30, 1981, NJ; [p.] Timothy and Kathy Rose; [ed.] 9th grade and still going; [hon.] Honor Student

PIERRE, DONNA

[pen.] Donna Pierre; [b.] December 23, 1976, Grenada, WI; [p.] Theresa Pierre and Cref Cosmos; [ed.] "College Student", Miami Dade Community College; [memb.] United State Tennis Association; [hon.] Most Valuable Tennis Player, Honor Roll; [pers.] I vigorously write about "Life and Reality". The generalization of my poems is based on statements, and the prospectiveness of life. Therefore I try making others and individuals like yourself think, all my poem is based just on that life reality means.; [a.] Opas-Locka, FL

PIFER, MICHELLE

[pen.] Michelle Lynn Pifer; [b.] February 26, 1976, Shelby, OH; [p.] Mr. and Mrs. Fred Pifer; [ed.] Crestview High School, Pioneer Joint Vocational School; [occ.] Chemical Operations Specialist in U.S. Army; [hon.] Honor graduate at Crestview H.S. 1994; [oth. writ.] None published; [pers.] I discuss some of the difficulties in life in my poems in a descriptive manner. This poem in question The Shore Of The Molten Sun asks if mankind will see the light of day again.; [a.] Mansfield, OH

PINKSTON III, JAMES H.

[b.] January 10, 1955, Wichita, KS; [ch.] Campus High School 1969 - 1973; [ed.] Koch Industries Michita, KS; [occ.] Pratt Fire Light, Camping Club, Pratt Kansas; [oth. writ.] Out With the Darkness and In With The Light, Pie in the Sky, Only in Your Dreams, Night Shift Blues, Grandfather and the Butterfly, Just Like a Kansas Storm; [pers.] About eighty poems wrote many not yet published. Just as many poems not yet wrote.; [a.] Valley Center, KS

PITCHELL, CONSTANCE R.

[ed.] BA Bryn Mawr College, MA Radcliffe College; [occ.] Philosophy Editor; [hon.] BA, Magna Cum Laude, with Honors; [oth. writ.] Five vols. of poems, annotated - unpublished including an appreciation of Paul Weiss, poems and essays.; [pers.] My purpose is to express the truths of metaphysics (abstract philosophy) using the language techniques of poetry - emphasis on Time and Space.; [a.] Chevy Chase, MD

PLETT, JUDAH JOY

[b.] October 7, 1978, Neepawa, Manitoba, Canada; [p.] Reginald and Charlene Plett; [ed.] Thomas Elementary - Flagstaff, AZ, Mt. Elden Middle School - Flagstaff AZ, Coconino High School - Flagstaff, AZ; [occ.] Student and Bookkeeper; [memb.] Flagstaff Tabernacle Church, Chambers Choir at Coconino High, Varsity Club at Coconino High; [hon.] Honor Roll, Honor Choir; [oth. writ.] "A Mother's Love" 1995 (short story). Article on Drug Abuse for D.A.R.E. program.; [pers.] My greatest accomplishment would be to be as great a writer as my mother to whom I owe my deepest gratitude.; [a.] Flagstaff, AZ

PLETT, REGGIE BEN-DAVID

[b.] March 24, 1981, Visalia, CA; [p.] Reginald and Charlene Plett; [ed.] Thomas Elementary - Flagstaff AZ, Mt. Elden Middle School - Flagstaff, AZ, Coconino High - Flagstaff, AZ; [occ.] Student; [memb.] Flagstaff Tabernacle Church, Chambers Choir - Coconino High, Flagstaff Soccer Club; [hon.] Honor Roll, Honor Choir 1996; [oth. writ.] Several short stories, several poems published in Northland Portfolio - May 1994; [pers.] I enjoy writing just how I feel inside - inspired by my Mom and two of my elementary teachers, Mrs. Pat Flick and Mrs. Kanan.; [a.] Flagstaff, AZ

POBOCIK, BERTHA J.

[pen.] Bertha Pobocik; [b.] October 1, 1940, Flint, MI; [p.] Austin and Bertha Huber; [m.] Albert Pobocik, July 20, 1990; [ch.] Julie Ouimet, Jennifer Harris, Scott Jackman, Theol Jackman II, Brian Jackman; [ed.] High School graduate of Davison High School, 1 year Secretarial Training at Baker College, 1 years Business Management at Cleary College; [occ.] On RIF Lay off at present; [hon.] Customer Service Award Michigan Jobs Commission, Rehabilitation Services, 1995; [oth. writ.] I have just started to submit my writings for publication. This is a first.; [pers.] To me writing is like the mirror of my soul, where the written word becomes an artistic masterpiece coloring each page with a lingering image of what went on inside my heart.; [a.] Swartz Creek, MI

PONDS, JAMES

[pen.] J. Ponds; [b.] March 29, 1962, Amory, MS; [p.] J. D. Ponds, Linda K. Hughes; [m.] Priscilla A. (Mullins) Ponds, May 3, 1986; [ch.] Kayla LeAnne, James A. M. Ponds; [ed.] Hatley High, Big Bend Community College; [occ.] Cooper Tire and Rubber Company Associate; [memb.] B.A.S.S., FAA Credit Union; [hon.] Honorary Discharged U.S. Army MP Corps., Army Achievement Medal (2), Good Conduct Medal; [oth. writ.] Personal Poetry Unpublished.; [pers.] I strongly believe in helping those in need because personal satisfaction is a richness that no monetary value can be assess to. My poetry may not change the world but the message is clear.; [a.] Nettleton, MS

POOLE, DON

[b.] March 3, 1947, Oakland, CA; [p.] William Poole, Joan (Jody) Poole; [ch.] Dawn Louise, Crystal LaRean, Rocky Matthew; [ed.] Redwood High School, College of Marin, Santa Monica City College; [occ.] Insurance agent Insurance Co. planning - New York Life Insurance Co.; [memb.] Soldotna (Alaska) Rotary Club, Alaska Bowhunters Association, Pope and Young Club.; [oth. writ.] "A Special Friend" and "Twas the Bowhunt Before Christmas" - a bowhunter's poem similar to Clement C. Moore's "The Night Before Christmas".; [pers.] Poetry is an emotional experience, a release of inner thoughts and desires.; [a.] Soldotna, AK

POOR, JIMMY D.

[b.] November 7, 1956, Houston, TX; [p.] Roger Poor, Mary Poor; [m.] Iris, June 18, 1976; [ch.] Jim Caleb, Amber Grace, Beau Anthony; [ed.] Searry High; [occ.] Maintenance Tech.; [memb.] Letona Missionary Baptist Church, Letona Vol. Fire Dept.; [pers.] God provides the beauty of art and poetry which comes only from the heart and soul.; [a.] Letona, AR

POPOVICH, ELIZABETH

[b.] July 16, 1982, Saint Louis; [p.] Richard and Susan Popovich; [ed.] Entering 8th grade attends, Parkway Northeast Middle School; [occ.] Student; [memb.] Singer in a Band, belongs to several Basketball teams; [hon.] Two time "Presidential physical - fitness Award" winner.; [oth. writ.] Another poems "Summer Days" was first published in '92 in "The Gates" - A Parkway School District, publication.; [pers.] I've found that I am influenced by spirituality and life's little lessons others have learned.; [a.] Saint Louis, MO

POPOVICH, MARC D.

[b.] June 19, 1971, Washington, DC; [p.] Roddy and Elizabeth Popovich; [ed.] English Educ. BA University of Maryland; [occ.] Technical Writer and Craftsman; [memb.] National Council of Teachers of English, Modern Language Association, Dean's List; [hon.] Sigma Tau Delta, Kappa Delta Phi, Eagle Scout; [pers.] I have drawn much inspiration from the romantic writers. My writing tries to celebrate the dignity of the quiet life, the joys, struggles, and passions we all know.; [a.] Gaithersburg, MD

PORTER, ERIC

[b.] December 22, 1981, Butler, PA; [p.] Barry Porter, Karen Porter; [ed.] Butler Intermediate High School, Butler Catholic School, St. Wendelin's School; [occ.] Student; [memb.] St. Peter's Parish Family, American Taekwondo Association, Pennsylvania Junior Academy of Science, Butler High Environmental Club, East Butler Hunting and Fishing Club; [hon.] Daughter of the American Revolution Historical Flag Contest First Place in Local, State, and Regional Divisions, Honorable Mention in National Division, Daughters of the American Revolution Award for Outstanding work in American History, President's Award for Outstanding Academic Excellence; [a.] Fenelton, PA

PORTER, MARIE

[b.] December 6, 1979, New York; [p.] Robert Jr. and Louise McCann; [ed.] Currently 11th grade at Hardee Senior High School, Wachula, FL; [occ.] Crew Member at Little Caesars Pizza; [memb.] 9th grade - Blue Star, Brigade Flag Corps, 10th grade Blue Star Birgade Indoor Guar II, Chorus - 9th and 10th grade; [hon.] Age three Little Miss Broad Acress, 1996 entry in district competition Guard II Jan 2, 1995, Marched in Gov. Chiles Inaugural Parade, Tallahassee, FL, with Blue Star Brigade; [oth. writ.] Personal collection of poems and stories.; [pers.] I write what is in my heart to write. In writing, one can be at any place, at anytime. If you are not afraid to be yourself, you can understand that some things can not be understood.; [a.] Wauchula, FL

PORTER, ZEBULON THURMAN

[pen.] Thurman Hoppis; [b.] May 25, 1977, Japan; [p.] Susan and Randy Porter; [m.] Fiancee: Eryn Atwood; [ed.] Barstow High School, Starting Barstow Community College; [occ.] Student and Line Cook; [memb.] Grace Bible Church in Helendale, California; [hon.] Awarded in Tennis and Football; [oth. writ.] None published; [pers.] I thought I world hated me. I was wrong, for I went to Indiana and there she was. Eryn is the world to me and she loves me.; [a.] Helendale, CA

POTTER, EDWARD

[pen.] Ed Potter; [b.] February 5, 1921, Plattsburgh, NY; [p.] Carl Potter, Maud Potter; [m.] Alice Scott Potter, October 15, 1978; [ed.] Plattsburgh High School, Hamilton College 1942; [occ.] Retired; [memb.] Emerson Literary Society; [oth. writ.] The Game (dramatic monologue in blank verse), many sonnets and other poems, promotional literature for Aetna Life Insurance Company, editor of the Lantern (a newsletter); [pers.] Knowing that one's deeds and words - like echoing ripples on a pool of still water - reach out forever to touch other hearts and minds, in creating poetry we must carve with care for eternity - as we do in sculpting marble. Hobby sculpting in marble.; [a.] Pleasant Valley, CT

POTTER, JANET

[b.] December 22, 1982, Decatur, IN; [p.] Neil and Connie Potter; [ed.] South Adams Schools; [occ.] Student; [memb.] First Missionary Church Youth Group; [oth. writ.] Personalized poetry written specifically for family and friends. "The Last Prayer" is dedicated to my best friend, Christy Conrado.; [pers.] The football players tried to take the field, the Marohing Band refused to yield.; [a.] Berne, IN

POTTS, CINDY BRENINGER

[b.] December 20, 1970; [p.] Dave and Linda Breninger; [m.] Michael Potts, May 20, 1995; [memb.] Children International, KVMR; [pers.] Dedicated in memory of my mother Judith Lynn Breninger - I will always cherish my memories! To Michael - I love you.; [a.] Sacramento, CA

POULEMANOS, ADAM
[b.] December 25, 1983, Hamilton, OH; [p.] Steve and Linda Poulemanos; [ed.] Fillmore Elementary School; [occ.] Student - 7th grade; [hon.] Five time 1st-4th place placements in yearly Cultural Arts Contest, various other writing awards; [oth. writ.] Several poems published in local School poetry book; [pers.] To me, writing is a metamorphosis of both the imagination and the real.; [a.] Hamilton, OH

PRICE, MAGGIE
[b.] August 30, 1981, Cincinnati, OH; [p.] Terry Price, Nicola Price; [ed.] Currently a freshman at Loveland High School; [occ.] Student; [memb.] Loveland Presbyterian Church Youth Group, Volunteered at Camp Stepping Stones (Handicapped Camp), Student Venture, Drama Club; [hon.] 2nd grade, 1st place award for writing, 4th grade, 1st place for a painting that I painted.; [a.] Loveland, OH

PRIESTLEY, LORETTA S.
[b.] April 30, 1952, Princeton, NJ; [p.] Sylvia and Harley; [m.] William A. Priestley, December 20, 1986; [occ.] Housewife; [memb.] First Baptist Church of White Springs; [oth. writ.] I have 20 more poems, unpublished; [pers.] I want to help people with my poems. Give them hope. Let them know that somebody is there to help. Give than a light at the end of the tunnel!; [a.] Lake City, FL

PRINCE, JOHN ELTON
[pen.] John E. Prince; [b.] June 21, 1935, Woodland, AL; [p.] Gillis Elton Prince and Mattie Lee Heard; [m.] Frieda Englmaier, February 24, 1962; [ed.] B.C.S. 1967, University of Nebraska, at Omaha; [occ.] Retired, USAF; [memb.] Church of Christ; [hon.] Made Career in USAF, attained grade of CMSGT, writes poetry as a hobby; [oth. writ.] Several poems and song poems, this third national poetry anthology to be published.; [pers.] When people are free to choose, truth will brighter Shine.; [a.] Fort Walton Beach, FL

PRITCHARD, SABRINA L.
[b.] September 18, 1980, Elizabeth City, NC; [p.] William and Gwen S. Pritchard; [ed.] Sophomore at Northeastern High School; [hon.] Athletic Awards; [pers.] I wrote this poem and dedicated it to my boyfriend, Ryan W. Bell.; [a.] Elizabeth City, NC

PROPST, KEVIN A.
[pen.] Kevin Propst; [b.] April 1, 1969, Detroit, MI; [p.] Charles Propst and Barb Kilsore; [ch.] 1 Boy, Steven A. Propst; [ed.] High School Grad.; [occ.] Landscaping Waterville, OH; [memb.] Eagles, Bowling Green, OH; [oth. writ.] I have two books that I have completed, all on my own. I never published any of my works.; [pers.] I love music it's my best friend, the doors are my favorite band, if not for Jim Morrison of the doors I wouldn't be writing poetry. I love to write poetry, it makes me feel like I need too!; [a.] Haskins, OH

PRUITT, BETHE SMITH
[pen.] Bethe Smith; [b.] April 10, 1960, Hamilton County, TX; [p.] Billy Smith and Alma Downey; [m.] Jim Pruitt, October 1, 1988; [ch.] Amanda Ruth, Gianetta U., Samuel J., Jamie K.; [ed.] GED, McKenzie College, TN - Wes. College; [occ.] Homemaker; [hon.] McKenzie College, Dean's List; [oth. writ.] I have many poems and have written some songs.; [pers.] I have been writing poems since I was seven years old. Poetry is my life, each thing I have written is a part of myself. Each line is a part of my life's blood.; [a.] Chattanooga, TN

PULA, VICTOR
[b.] January 18, 1966, Baltimore; [p.] Robert and Irene Pula; [m.] Marcella DiMarco; [ch.] Chelsea, Nick and Terrica; [ed.] High School, a few semester of college; [occ.] Roofer; [pers.] For years, I tried to write poems and songs wasn't always hated them. It wasn't until I learned to be honest that I started coming up with material that I was satisfied with.; [a.] Baltimore, MD

QUALLS, REBA CRUTCHER
[b.] April 4, 1951, Hopkins County, KY; [p.] Charles and Frances Crutcher; [m.] James Ben Qualls, October 6, 1972; [ch.] Jessica Bree Qualls, March 22, 1977; [ed.] Graduate - University of Kentucky; [occ.] RN, Manager of Quality, Bon Secours Healthcare System; [memb.] National Association of Healthcare Quality, Florida Association of Healthcare Quality, Sigma Theta Tau; [a.] Nokomis, FL

QUINTANILLA, JULIE MARIE
[pen.] Banana Girl; [b.] November 16, 1978, Bremerton, WA; [p.] Juan Quintanilla and Dolores Guzman; [ed.] Oceanview High School, Agent, Guam (Class of 1996); [occ.] J C Penney Associate; [memb.] Drug Free Club, Year Book Club; [hon.] 1993-1994 - Certificate of Achievement - 58 hrs. of reading - Oceanview December 23, 1994, Certificate of Appreciation (poem recital - Living with Aids) - World Aids Day Committee, June 10, 1996 - Certificate of Appreciation for Outstanding Performance on "Poetry Alive" - Oceanview High School; [oth. writ.] Voice of an Unborn Child, A Love Letter, Hard To Say Good Bye..., I'm Giving You Up for A Friend - published at Oceanview's school newspaper. Living with Aids - written especially for World Aids Day ceremony - Guam 1994.; [pers.] I was inspired by a teenage romance in which led me to poetry to express all the pain that I was going through. And up to this present day, I feel the pain and rely on my poetry to get me through the day. I found that poetry is the perfect solution to stress.; [a.] Aurora, CO

RAGER, RUBY
[pen.] Ruby Rager; [b.] September 25, 1954, Greenville, KY; [p.] Howard and Rosalie Ward; [m.] Steve Rager, November 22, 1974; [ch.] Stephen Nathan Rager; [ed.] Central City High School, Western Kentucky University; [occ.] Middle Grades Teacher; [memb.] Phi Theta Kappa; [hon.] President's List, Dean's List, Magna Cum Laude 1995 WKU; [oth. writ.] Several spiritual poems and stories, psalms; [pers.] I love the Lord with all my heart I want my writings to glorify him and inspire and encourage those who do not know him to experience his love through my writings.; [a.] Central City, KY

RAGLAND, JANICE A. KOSROG
[pen.] Jann; [b.] September 19, 1944; [p.] The late Mrs. Ruth Lee Batten Kosrog McIntosh, Mr. Albert Ludwig Kosrog; [m.] Donald Eugene Ragland (Rags), June 14, 1969 at St. Mary's Catholic Church, Pensacola Escambia Florida; [ch.] Don Robert Ragland, January 18, 1971, Dolly Elizabeth Ragland, March 12, 1972 grandchildren - Robert "Jake" Ragland September 15, 1994; [ed.] Ferry Pass Elementary, W.A. Blount Jr. HI., Pensacola Technical Hi. School; [occ.] Wayne Dalton Corp. Ellyison Industrial Park Pensacola, Florida; [memb.] Olive Baptist Church, Pensacola, Florida "His Followers" Bible Study Class Mrs. Russell (Sandra) Crosby, Teacher; [hon.] Thanksgiving of 1995 I visited Cairo, Egypt, Ammon, Jordan, and Jerusalem, Israel for 12 days with Judy my twin sister. What an awesome experience. I hope someday to have the honor of doing a return trip.; [oth. writ.] I wrote a valentine poem for my husband in 1992.; [pers.] I did a study on the word "love" for our ladies Bible study class devotion. Olive Baptist Church where I attend has a banner ministry and out of my poem "love" a banner was created in November 1995. I am delighted my poem was chosen to be published.

RAHIER, KAREN L.
[b.] April 19, 1975, Overton, TX; [p.] John E. and Late Donna J. Green; [m.] Bobby Shane Rahier, May 30, 1993; [ch.] Michael Madelene and Zachary Eldon; [ed.] Carthage School, Carthage, Texas; [occ.] Housewife and Mother; [pers.] I would like to dedicate this poem to my mom who passed on Dec. 1993 and thank to my husband shane for his support.; [a.] Effie, MN

RAINES, JESSE G.
[pen.] Jesse; [b.] March 29, 1933, Johnston County; [p.] Riley W. and Eunice S. Raines; [ch.] Five; [ed.] Mebane High and Attended Elon College; [occ.] Retired; [memb.] Life member of "The Telephone Pioneers of America." Member of Hebron Methodist Church.; [pers.] To help mankind in his earthly journey and reflect the Glory of God.; [a.] Mebane, NC

RALL, SARAH JOY LYNNE
[b.] May 23, 1985, Mesa, AZ; [p.] Joy Lynne Abers; [ed.] 6th grader attending Jefferson Elementary; [occ.] Student; [memb.] Girl Scouts; [hon.] Honor Roll 95-96, 5th grade

RAMANN, KIMBERLY
[b.] June 7, 1982, Long Island, NY; [p.] Timothy and Frances Ramann; [hon.] Eagle Society, Honor Roll, Presidential Academic Fitness Award, Band Honors Award; [a.] Wilmington, NC

RAMOS, CYNTHIA A. N.
[b.] January 18, 1946, Honolulu, HI; [p.] Natural or Real Parents: Joseph Demicola, Eleanor Demicola, Adoptive Parents: Alexander Burgess, Edith Burgess; [m.] Joseph P. Y. Ramos, March 12, 1962 (Divorced January 3, 1989); [ch.] Jennie J. Joseph Jr. and Alexander J.

RAMOS, ERICA ANNE
[b.] September 18, 1970, Alice, TX; [p.] Richard and Janie Ramos; [ed.] UT - Pan American; [occ.] Theatre Arts Teacher; [hon.] Who's Who Among Students in American Universities and Colleges 1993, The National Dean's List; [pers.] When the muse sings I listen. It is impossible to write about something I do not feel inside my soul.; [a.] Brownsville, TX

RAMOUTAR, NISHANNA
[b.] May 21, 1982, Brooklyn, NY; [p.] Ann Kalman; [ed.] Public School 104 K to 8th Grade Freshman Student in Fort Hamilton H.S.; [occ.] Full time student, Summer Camp Counselor; [memb.] Brooklyn Central YMCA and The YMCA of the Greater New York.; [hon.] Principal's List, Honor Roll, various subject accomplishment awards. 1st place prize in another poetry contest.; [pers.] If you think education is expensive, try ignorance. Thank you Mrs. Cohn and Mrs. Romano.; [a.] Brooklyn, NY

RASBAND, TIFFANY
[b.] December 31, 1979, Ogden, UT; [p.] Robert Rasband, Saundra Rasband; [ed.] I am currently a Junior at Ben Lomond High School. I will graduate in 1998; [memb.] I am an officer of Ben Lomond's drill team, Bonnie Lassiers. I also take private lessons from the dance establishment; [hon.] For elementary in the 5th grade. I received Hope of America Award and later, in

8th grade, received Freedom of Leadership Award. I have been a 4.0 student for five years and as a result, I won the President Award; [oth. writ.] I am very fond of writing stories. Whether it's short stories or 250 page novels, I'm always up for the challenge. I've also written other poems which have placed 1st place.; [pers.] I just want to let all ambitious young writers know that their dreams can come true. I am 16 and for my whole life, I've been deaf. Yes, I am handicapped, but does that stop me? No go for it, this maybe your only chance.; [a.] Ogden, UT

RAUDONIS, RENEE
[b.] January 7, 1981, Phoenix, AZ; [p.] Robert and Rosie Raudonis; [ed.] Eisenhower High School (10th grade); [occ.] High School Student; [memb.] Color Guard with Marching Band, German Club; [hon.] "A" average award for 9th grade. San Ramon Valley School District Author Ribbon Award; [oth. writ.] Doopey, The Wings, and The Magical End Of The Milkbone (written in 5th grade), and several short stories and poems; [pers.] Your mind is the key to opening up a whole new world, use it.; [a.] Shelby Township, MI

RAYMOND, GLORIA
[b.] June 17, 1944, Burlington, UT; [p.] Alexander and Ida Beaupre; [m.] Francis LaFountain, October 15, 1962; [ch.] Tina, Chrisihaura; [ed.] Cathedral Grammar, Burl-High School, Essex Teck School; [oth. writ.] I have 3 loose - leaf books based n my feelings and altho many people think they are good, I have never had one published.; [pers.] I like putting my feelings about different subjects on paper. Most I write poems about children, love, dreams and hope. I can express myself and how I feel.; [a.] Burlington, UT

RAYMOND, NONA J.
[b.] April 1, 1967, Concord, NH; [p.] Sharelle E. Allin and Rainey S. Allin; [ch.] John Rainey Raymond; [ed.] North Stratford High, NHIC of Claremont; [hon.] Dean's List; [a.] Claremont, NH

REDD, JOHNNY LLOYD
[b.] July 12, 1946, Harrisburg, AR; [p.] Henry Lewis Redd Jr.; [m.] Marshia Smith Redd; [ch.] Jonna Lynn Rowlett; [ed.] Treadwell HS Memphis, BA English Arkansas State Univ., MA English Arkansas State Univ.; [occ.] Asst. Prof. of English; [oth. writ.] The Cosmic Quad c. 1996, Resurrection Mary, short stories and poems.

REED, DONALD A.
[b.] November 5, 1919, Hampton, NE; [p.] Earl and Mildred (Anderson) Reed; [m.] Verla (Mortensen) Reed, December 7, 1939; [ch.] Arthur Royal, David Roland; [ed.] High School - (Trade School Swallow Airoplane), Civil Service Exam Prep. - Franklin Institute - Rochester, NY; [occ.] Retired Union Pacific R.R. Conductor (MA and PA-Salesman Welding supplies); [memb.] Unions Pacific Old timers, AARP, (UT United Transportation Union); [hon.] Union Pacific R.R. Acknowledges with Sincere Appreciation, the Outstanding Dedication and Devoted Service of Donald A. Reed, to the Union Pacific Railwood 36 years conductor - Brokeman no Demerits; [oth. writ.] poems to my wife Verla (the most important person in the world to me). On mother day birthday, anniversary and special occasions.; [pers.] Motto do your best and be kind. A good wife doubles a man's pleasures and divides his cares. Confront improper conduct not by retaliation, but by a example.; [a.] Cheyenne, WY

REESE, MARY ANN
[b.] July 18, 1954, Weirton, WV; [p.] John Zumer and Mary (Strunak) Zumer; [m.] Donald Reese, April 24, 1976; [ch.] Matthew David; [ed.] Oak Glen High School, W.V. Northern Community College (WUNCC), Bethany College (soon to complete a BSW in Social Work); [occ.] Professional Artist. Pets and Wildlife in Oils - own Business; [memb.] Unarius Academy of Science Catholic Church, Humane Society World Wildlife Fund, Alzheimers Support Group; [hon.] Rotary Scholarship Dean's Award, Renner Scholarship a best of show and two 1st place in art shows.; [oth. writ.] First poem submitted have written editorials for local newspapers; [pers.] I devotedly search for truth about life. Our souls and all of nature as does spiritual love endues through time and are immortal. Adversity is opportunity to know thyself and gain wisdom in the school of life.; [a.] Weirton, WV

REEVES, RUBY JOSEPHINER
[pen.] Ruby Reeves; [b.] January 6, 1936, Bronx, NY; [p.] Timothy and Josephine George; [m.] Richard D. Reeves, October 6, 1956; [ch.] Darryl, Richard and Derek; [ed.] Touro College, B.A. Cum Laude 1982, Fordham M.S. Education 1985, New York Theological Seminary Ministry Certificate 1988; [occ.] Teacher, College Professor; [memb.] Eastern Stars - Recording Secty. 1995, Afro Arts Cultural Centre Inc. Literary Chairman 1990, Lou Lutour Evangelistic Ass. Inc. 1979, World Poets Resource Centre Inc. 1977, Tapping Seniors 1996; [hon.] Phyllis Wheatly Award 1994, Honorary Doctorate 1987, Who's Who in Colleges and University 1980, Crowned Poet Laureaute 1979, (World Congress of Poets), Distinguished Americans 1978, (Community Services); [oth. writ.] "The Journey" - published Crisis Magazine 1984, "The Graduate" Touro College Manuel 1982-1987; [pers.] I can scarcely contain myself, when the likes of me, in other men I see. And yet, what is a man, but the rock upon which he stands.; [a.] New York, NY

REID, ELEANOR PINNELL
[b.] October 24, 1937, Gauley Bridge, WV; [p.] Lois McDonald Pinnell and William Perry Pinnell Sr.; [m.] October 24, 1963 (28 yrs.); [ch.] Maria Murphy, Fred Reid, Donna Moore, 6 grandchildren; [ed.] Buckhannon Upshur HS., WV Wesleyan College (1 yr.), Glenville State College (2 yrs.), Fleet Business School (1 yr.); [occ.] Retired Secretary; [memb.] Heart to Heart Women's Fellowship, Mt Zion United Methodist Church Lothian, MD, Church Worship Committee, DAR; [oth. writ.] Have written twenty-six poems since March of 1995 - gift from God.; [pers.] The gift of poetry was given to me in March of 1995 by God and I strive to reflect the love of God as I have experienced his love through personal trials in my life and my faith. Enjoy reading and handcrafts. Dedication: To Heart To Heart Women's Fellowship at Mt. Zion United Methodist Church in Lothian, MD.; [a.] Lothian, MD

REISIG, JOSHUA
[pen.] JC; [b.] February 12, 1981, Baltimore, MD; [p.] Debra Perseghin, Wayne Reisig; [ed.] Archbishop Curley High School - Sophomore

REITHER, DONALD EUGENE
[b.] March 28, 1954, Grove City, PA; [p.] Edwin Phillip and Charlene Reither; [m.] Barbara Anne Reither, October 15, 1994; [ch.] Travis James and Ashley Nicole Reither; [occ.] Corrections Officer; [memb.] First Baptist Church, Grove City, PA; [oth. writ.] Personal poetry and short compositions; [pers.] I feel that one's soul, spirit, and emotion should be transferred into the created composition. In effect, placing one's being into the writing.; [a.] Mercer, PA

RENFROW, TRAVIS
[b.] May 28, 1978, Dundee, KY; [p.] Doris and Jerry Renfrow; [ed.] Graduated from Ohio County High School in Kentucky. Plan to attend Western Kentucky University in the fall of 1997; [memb.] Beaver Dam Church of Christ, Fellowship of Christian Athletes, Varsity Letterman in Football.; [hon.] Co-designer of the Ohio County school System Logo; [oth. writ.] Have one poem on the hopeless Romantics page on the internet.; [pers.] I feel like the only thing that I limits us as people is the phrase: "Good Enough". Set goals, and when you achieve them, take pride, then set higher ones.; [a.] Dundee, KY

REPASKY, JO
[b.] March 4, 1982, Wyandotte, MI; [p.] Toni Sue (Deceased); [ed.] Dawney Christian School; [occ.] 9th Grade Student; [memb.] Precious Moments Club, National Geographic Society; [hon.] Disney's Dreamer and Doer Award, Confirmation; [pers.] Philippians 4:13 - I can do all things through Christ who strengthens. This is my life verse.; [a.] Oviedo, FL

RETENSKI, ANTHONY J.
[b.] August 13, 1979, Long Island Jewish Hospital; [p.] Stacey Ann and Anthony Retenski; [ch.] Anthony J. Retenski Jr.; [ed.] Longwood Senior High School; [hon.] Honor Roll, Business in Accounting Award Prejudice Hurts Essay Award; [pers.] I believe all people must unite to create peace and for each of us to achieve our individual dream; [a.] Shirley, NY

RETZINGER JR., LEO P.
[pen.] Peter Retzinger; [b.] August 18, 1925, Northbrook, IL; [p.] Leo P. Retzinger Sr., Ann Retzinger; [m.] Virginia Schutzen Retzinger, November 30, 1946; [ch.] Six boys, five girls; [ed.] Wilmot High School, Wilmot, Wis., University of Wisconsin, BS in Electrical Engineering, 1950, Masters in Electrical Engineering, 1951; [occ.] Business Consultant Student of Archaeology, Philosophy, History; [memb.] Tau Beta Pi and Eta Kappa Nu, Honorary Engineering Societies, Graduated with high honors, U of W, Graduated #1 in USMC Airborne, Electronics School, 1944; [hon.] BS/EE with honors, MS/EE with high honors, Four US Patents issued in computer electronics Technology; [oth. writ.] Philosophical Essays, Poetry-not published; [pers.] I am a freelance seeker of truth and believe one should strive to seek knowledge, and wisdom, showing love, understanding tolerance and compassion for all.; [a.] Reseda, CA

REX, STEPHANIE
[b.] March 19, 1979, Newport, WA; [p.] Kelly and Margaret Rex; [pers.] This is dedicated to my dad and also to Dustin. Both in my heart forever.; [a.] Deer Park, WA

REYNEN, BRIAN J. J.
[pen.] B. J. J. R.; [b.] October 19, 1966, Chicago; [p.] John Reynen and Fran Reynen; [ed.] Glenbrook North H.S./DeVry; [occ.] Programmer; [memb.] American Cancer Society, Baal Tinne Security; [oth. writ.] The Phoenix, Solitude, Cailin, When I Met You, Caliburnus, I Am, For You...; [pers.] Poetry is the written reflection of your heart and soul.; [a.] Northbrook, IL

REYNOLDS, MICHAEL J.
[b.] November 4, 1949, Boise, ID; [p.] John and Grace Reynolds; [ed.] Columbia College Dropout, Boise State

University; [occ.] Housekeeper; [memb.] Community Christian Center; [pers.] My poems come to me as I worship and adore the word Jesus Christ.; [a.] Boise, ID

RICCIARDI, SUSANNA MARIA
[b.] July 21, 1975, Glen Cove, NY; [p.] Anna and Joseph Ricciardi; [ed.] Glen Cove High School, University at Stony Brook; [occ.] College Student; [oth. writ.] "Loneliness", "Wanting You", "Loving The Person Inside", "The Terrible Crush", "Life Is Too Short", "Tesoro", "True Friendship", "Forbidden Love", "Solitude", "Desire As A Sin", "You Rock My World", "Judgement Day", "Letting Go", "My Teacher, My Friend"; [pers.] Not many people know about my love for writing, and only a few have read my work. My writings express exactly what my soul is feeling. People can get to know me just by reading my work. I can express myself better on paper, I guess I feel safer that way. The world can be cruel.; [a.] Glen Cove, NY

RICE, AMY
[b.] March 8, 1981, Vineland, NJ; [p.] David Rice, Diane Rice; [ed.] The Pilgrim Academy (High School); [hon.] "Who's Who Among America's High School Students"; [oth. writ.] Poem in school poetry books.; [pers.] Time takes everything and everything takes time.; [a.] Hammonton, NJ

RICHARDS, MARY V.
[pen.] Windrian Afwe; [b.] May 17, 1960, Lynwood, CA; [p.] Leonard and Kim Hampton; [m.] Leo (Buddy) Richards; [ch.] Michael James and Kyle Nolan; [oth. writ.] "Bright Reflections", Elemental Greetings - Fire, Elemental Greetings - Water, Elemental Greetings - Earth; [pers.] My desire is to bring the beauty and power of nature to all who hear my poems. I have found peace within myself through nature and wish to share the experience.; [a.] Fontana, CA

RICHARDSON, FRANCIS M.
[pen.] Francis M. Richardson; [b.] December 19, 1917, Indianapolis, IN; [p.] Francis and Florence; [m.] Bonnie, May 30, 1941; [ch.] Karen Sue; [ed.] High School - Arsenal Technical Schools - Ind'pls, IN, Trade School at Tech as Millwright for Ford Motor Co.; [occ.] Retired and a just writing poetry for fun; [memb.] V.F.W. in Beech Grove Indiana; [hon.] I am the oldest person to ever graduate from an Industrial Millwright Course; [oth. writ.] About 200 poems which I would like to get published in my own book form. Most of which are of about the same quality.; [pers.] I would like hearing from some of my friends.; [a.] Apache Junction, AZ

RIDENHOUR, JUDY C.
[b.] April 23, 1939, Man, NYC; [p.] Charles and Willie Mae Foster; [m.] Divorced, August 1958; [ch.] Carlton, Lisa, Eric Ridenhour; [ed.] Adelphi U. 1988, M.S.W., C.S.W., New York State B.S., C.W. Post 1984; [occ.] Certified Social Worker (Psychiatric Rehabilitation); [memb.] N.A.A.C.P., Nassau N.O.W. Assoc., Black Social Workers, St. Thomas (Soup Kitchen Homeless and Sunday School Teacher and Choir Mem) Episcopal Church, Malverne, LI, NY, Artistic Director/Founder of Roosevelt, Community Theatre, L.I., N.Y., Radio Talk Show Host Wkjy, Garden City, L.I., N.Y. "All Talking Drum"; [hon.] Dean's List (2 yrs.), Cum Laude 1984 (C.W. Post - L.I.U.) Queens Dist. Attorney Crime Prevention Program 2 yrs 1970-1971; [oth. writ.] Song "I Feel A Hurt Comin' On"; [pers.] I try to teach all those who can to help themselves and lend a hand to those who can't. And remember we are all members of the human family so listen intently because every soul has something to say.; [a.] Brooklyn, NY

RIORDAN, JOHN OVERTON
[b.] November 14, 1956, Chicago, IL; [p.] Clifford T., Naomi Ruth Riordan; [m.] Mary Beth Riordan, July 28, 1990; [ch.] 2 Kathleen Erin, James Overton; [ed.] De Paul University, Northwestern University, Morraine Valley Community College; [occ.] Owner: Riordan Artistry, Inc. (Customized Art); [memb.] The Cousteau Society, Green Peace, National Arbor Day Foundation, The Wilderness Society, Environmental Defense Fund; [hon.] Mayor Daley Youth Foundation Scholarship, Illinois State Scholar, graduate Magna Cum Laude - Morraine Valley, graduate honors - De Paul University Midwestern and National Karate Champion from Northwestern University; [oth. writ.] Many software engineering specifications! ...and other small poems.; [pers.] Nothing is forever, all, fortunately and unfortunately will pass.; [a.] Villa Park, IL

RIOS, PATRICIA
[b.] December 18, 1980, Manhassett, NY; [p.] Julio Rios and Norma Serrano; [ed.] I am in tenth grade in Saint Mary's High School; [occ.] Student; [oth. writ.] I've had other poems published by the National Library of Poetry and in the Poet's corner magazine.; [pers.] My poems are writing from my soul.; [a.] Roslyn Heights, NY

RIVERA, CARLA R.
[pen.] Tekawitha; [b.] October 10, 1954, Washington, DC; [p.] Juan Rivera, Bernice Rivera; [ch.] Daymieon, Ratiea; [ed.] Spingarn High School, Montgomery College Rockville; [occ.] Principal Administrative Aide Montgomery County Division of Transportation; [memb.] ICOG Church of God; [oth. writ.] Several other poems: Sweet Honey Stone Mountain and Just in Time; [pers.] I believe if you draw near to God, then God will draw near to you.

RIVETT, SUSAN
[b.] February 25, 1979, Redlands, CA; [p.] Kirk and Cathie Sennett; [ed.] High School 12th year, Palmdale High School; [occ.] Pep Boys, Sales Rep.; [pers.] My writing expresses my thoughts and feelings. I like to entertain my readers and let them absorb other aspects on life and looking at things in a different perspective.; [a.] Palmdale, CA

ROBINSON, AMY
[b.] April 24, 1984, Pittsburgh; [p.] George Robinson, Kathy Robinson; [ed.] Currently in Seventh grade at West Mifflin Middle School; [oth. writ.] This is my first published poem.; [pers.] I try to see beauty in everything. Geodes are my inspiration.; [a.] West Mifflin, PA

ROBISON, CRAIG TODD
[b.] December 11, 1963, Whittier, CA; [ed.] Long Beach State University B.S. Finance; [occ.] Fashion Model, Actor; [pers.] I consider myself a student of life functioning in a society that imreatens to conform me to the suppression of the daily grind. A place considered secure by most, yet void of dreams and the mystery which makes life worthy living; [a.] Brentwood, CA

RODRIGUEZ, ZUSANA SANCHEZ
[b.] August 19, 1974, Los Angles, CA; [p.] Ms. Ceferina Sanchez; [ed.] Grad from Montgomery High Sch. in 1992, went to Southwestern College for 2 years, non-grad. Self-Educated myself, and now work in an attorney's office.; [occ.] Personal Secretary at an Attorney's office; [oth. writ.] I have lots of poems, but I never thought about sending in any of them. I use to write poems for other friends and fam. and use to sell them, so I could pay for my education, books and supplies. I am thankful for this opportunity.; [pers.] This poem was written for my unborn son. Maybe one day, I touch my other children with this poem.; [a.] Watsonville, CA

ROGER, ROSALIND S.
[b.] May 2, 1956, New York, NY; [p.] Joseph V. Roger, Sofia E. Roger; [ch.] Sara E. Roger; [ed.] Cathedral H.S. NY, Kennesaw College, GA; [occ.] U.S. Army - Staff Sergeant Signal Support Systems NCOIC; [memb.] Association of the United States Army New York Road Runners Club (Lifetime); [hon.] "General of the Army Omar Bradley Award", Army Commendation Medal (20/c); [pers.] I am very grateful and fortunate to share this poem inspired by my late mother. Her faith and spirit in giving has profoundly impacted my life to share the same.; [a.] El Paso, TX

ROGERS, JASON
[b.] September 13, 1974, Thomasville, NC; [p.] Freddie and Judy Rogers; [ed.] Thomasville High; [occ.] Carwash Manager; [memb.] Pleasant View, Baptist Church, American Bowling Congress; [pers.] I strive to use the special talent God has given me, to touch and warm hearts of many readers, through the beauty of my poetry.; [a.] Thomasville, NC

ROGERS, JENNIFER
[b.] July 20, 1974, Peoria, IL; [p.] Wayne and Judy Rogers; [ed.] Central High School, University of South Florida; [occ.] Student; [hon.] Phi Theta Kappa; [pers.] "Emotional Landscapes" is dedicated to my mother Judy Rogers, whose support and persuasion led me to write, and my father Wayne Rogers, who will always be in my thoughts and prayers.; [a.] Port Richey, FL

ROMAN, ANTONIA C.
[pen.] Princess, Tonae; [b.] September 27, 1965, Brooklyn, NY; [p.] Andrea Carrion, Ismael Roman; [ed.] Wheatley High School, Queens College; [occ.] Book Keeper, Real Estate Investor; [hon.] Music and Citizenship Eve Jerome Award, Tireless Effort and Dedication Nene Music Productions; [oth. writ.] Written songs used for recording; [pers.] This poem is dedicated to the love of my life, Felipe Andrade. I will always love you.; [a.] Ridgewood, NY

ROMILLIE, EULALEE
[b.] Jamaica, WI; [p.] Mr. and Mrs. Felicia Thomas; [m.] January 8, 1976; [ch.] Savin Romillie; [ed.] St. Andrew Technical High Sch. Durham College of Commerce (Secretary), Institute of Esthetics (Massage and SPA the Therapy) University of the West Indies (Psychology); [occ.] Cosmetologist; [pers.] I was influenced by the National Library of Poetry, which inspired me to explored my inner ability to become a poet.; [a.] Queens, NY

RONSONET, WILLIAM
[b.] December 3, 1948, New Orleans, LA; [p.] Willis and Albertine Ronsonet; [m.] Rosemary Ronsonet, March 3, 1973; [ch.] Seth Anthony and Sadie Marie; [ed.] New Iberia Senior High, Art Scholarship (Drawings), U.S. Navy Mess Management School "C", New Iberia Votec - Electrical, Carpenter; [occ.] Inventory Control - Voorhies Supply Co., Inc. - New Iberia, LA; [memb.] United Blood Services, VFW Post 1982 - New Iberia, LA; [hon.] Military Awards in Cooking Life Saving Award; [oth. writ.] Poem: Andriane, To A Friend - What Is Love?, What Is A Sweetheart?, What Is A Friend?, What Is A Mother?, What Is A Dad?, What Is A Wife?, What Is A Brother/Sister?; [pers.] Being well gifted in art drawing and somewhat in writing. Hoping that someday one or most of my art drawings will be seen nationwide.; [a.] New Iberia, LA

ROSE, BENITA A.
[pen.] Benita Rose; [b.] February 14, 1958, Willimantic, CT; [p.] Raymond and Zigrida Rose; [m.] Eduard Anthony Gibbs, July 24, 1993; [ed.] Bachelor of Music degree in piano performance from University of Connecticut. Currently attending graduate school at the Hartt school of Music; [occ.] Concert Pianist, Piano Teacher; [memb.] Music Teachers National Association, International Society of Poets; [hon.] Francis Parker Scholarship Award, Evelyn Bonar Storrs Scholarship Award, 1974 CSMTA State Piano Competition, 1977 University of Connecticut Concert Competition; [oth. writ.] Approximately 30 poems accepted for publication by various literary publishers including Night Roses, Cader publishing, the Iliad Press, and sparrow grass poetry forum Inc. and poet's guild; [pers.] Live by following your heart!; [a.] Willimantic, CT

ROSS, CHARLES DORAN
[b.] June 13, 1926, San Francisco, CA; [p.] Charles Edwin and Louise Doran Ross; [m.] Maria Ester Ross, March 3, 1956; [ch.] Constance, Mary, Anne; [ed.] Piedmont H.S., Piedmont, CA, U. of San Francisco, San Francisco, CA, General Secondary Teaching Cred. Education, San Diego State U. of Redlands; [occ.] Retired; [oth. writ.] Poem - Lady MacBeth, short stories - Maggie, Ell Nora, Lazy-L, Snake Ranch, Vashti Sangamor all four are tales of the supernatural; [pers.] I try to portray the beauty of the world around us. I am influenced by the art and British poets: Scott, Lord Byron, Tennyson and Matthew Arnold.; [a.] Downey, CA

ROSS, MIKE D.
[b.] April 25, 1969 - August 13, 1995 (Deceased), Princeton, IN; [p.] Dean and Sandy Ross; [ed.] University of Southern Indiana, Indiana Section of Advanced Water Treatment; [occ.] Princeton, Indiana Water Department; [oth. writ.] Many other poems starting at age nine until his death at age 26.; [pers.] Mike's Aficionado of music was a real inspiration for writing. His philosophy was "do your own thing" and accept others which was reflected in his poetry.; [a.] Princeton, IN

ROUNTREE, THELMA T.
[b.] November 3, 1942, Howard Co., IN; [p.] Albert and Ica G. Tucker; [m.] Richard E. Rountree, May 24, 1969; [ch.] Kip, Kimberly (Dirk and Terr from former marriages); [ed.] Pittsboro High School 1961, TCC-AA 5-1-87 (Tallahassee Community College), FSU - Bach Arts 4-27-91; [occ.] Homemaker, Freelance Writer; [memb.] BSF Bible believers Fellowship Ch; [hon.] 1st place in Fiction 1986-87 Fla Com College Press Assoc. The Eyrie Award for Artistic or Literary Excellence 1986-87; [oth. writ.] TCC Jr. Coll, the Eyrie FSU; [pers.] The external world and my internal spirit arise together in the poems. Impact statements are to thorn on awakening in your hearts.; [a.] Tallahassee, FL

ROUTZHAN, BRADLEY GALEN
[pen.] Brad; [b.] September 13, 1955, St. Joseph, MO; [p.] Mr. and Mrs. Sandra K. Evans; [m.] Divorced, December 28, 1989; [ed.] Millersburg Area Art Assoc. Watercolorist York Academy of Arts - York, PA 3 yr. Professional Diploma - Illustration: Major graduated (1976) 3.0 average, continuing education Bradley Academy for the Visual Arts York PA. Computer Graphics; [occ.] Free-lance Artist "Original Concept Designs" Housekeeper Harrisburg Hospital 7 1/2 yrs.; [memb.] Millersburg - Art Association, Doshi - Gallery for Contemporary Art Hbg. PA 17109; [hon.] 2nd Place - photographic award - Millersburg Area Art Association Christmas Awards Program for Members at (local) Community Banks (Mbg.), Citizen Commendation Award (1986) - Received from Mayor Stephen Reed (Hbg.) for finding $28,000.00 in U.S. savings bonds and returning them to their rightful owner.; [oth. writ.] Titled: "Home Is Where the Heart Is" (Book of Poetry), 26 poems, and have continued to do other writings as well.; [pers.] My creative writings exist and are inspired from life itself, my personal walk with Christ, and my love for the simplicity and beauty of nature that is around me. My artistic endeavors and achievements diverse in approach are based on design elements, photographic memory and visual concepts.; [a.] Millersburg, PA

ROWE, BARBARA H.
[b.] March 12, 1940, Swedesboro, NJ; [p.] Rev. B. Franklin Money, Beatrice W. Money; [m.] Robert E. Rowe, June 11, 1994; [ch.] Todd Murray, Michael Murray, Steven Murray (Deceased); [ed.] Swedesboro High School - Swedesboro, NJ, Gloucester County College - Sewell, NJ, General Communications Inc. Rockville, MD; [occ.] Receptionist - CPA Firm; [memb.] Shiloh Baptist Church Landover, MD; [hon.] Dean's List - General Communications, Inc. Rockville, MD; [oth. writ.] I have many other writings, but none have published at this time.; [pers.] I have a positive attitude towards life. I hope that my positivity will reflect in all aspects of my life I hope through my poetry that others will read and see the spiritual and positive side of life.; [a.] Lanham, MD

RUANO, INGEBORG ALICE
[pen.] Inge; [b.] April 15, 1975, San Francisco; [pers.] Look up to yourself, no others. Be content with who you are and proud of what you do in life.

RUE, TAMMY
[b.] June 17, 1962, Charlotte, NC; [p.] Mary Theis and Buddy Winecoff; [m.] Michael Rue, January 3, 1982; [ch.] Jennifer, Tabitha, Christopher, Rue; [ed.] Garringer High School, Albemarle Road Jr. High, Statesville Road Elementary School; [occ.] Ericsson Stadium Cleaning Services; [memb.] PTA; [oth. writ.] I've written other things but never been published until now.; [pers.] I write on how I feel about life at that moment.; [a.] Charlotte, NC

RUPPEL, APRIL
[b.] December 26, 1980, Burbank, CA; [p.] David W. Ruppel and Rebecca A. Ruppel; [ed.] North Hollywood High School; [occ.] Student 10th grade; [memb.] Foursquare Youth Group at Chatsworth Foursquare Church; [hon.] My poem; [oth. writ.] My other poems, Religion, A Friend etc.; [pers.] My statement would be live each day as if it were your last; [a.] North Hollywood, CA

RUPPRECHT, DOROTHEA M.
[b.] July 8, 1933, Braunschweig, Germany; [p.] Heinrich and Betty Kamrad; [m.] Donald K. Rupprecht, December 8, 1966; [ch.] Katja, Melody and Michele; [ed.] Graduated with Honors Anna Vorwerk Schule, Germany (Equivalent - AA Degree); [occ.] Homemaker, Writer; [memb.] Birchwood Community Council, South Central Alaska Museum of Natural History, Citizens Advisory Council, Alaska Railroad Lord; [hon.] Certificates of Appreciation from above Organizations; [oth. writ.] "Dimensions of the Heart" Collection of Poetry (Unpublished), "Parallels", novels (Unpublished) currently editing it.; [pers.] Each one of us can make a difference in the evolving family of man - writing is my way.; [a.] Eagle River, AK

RUSSELL, GLORIA V.
[pen.] Gloria V. Russell; [b.] May 10, 1931, Washington, DC; [p.] Mildred and Julian Gala; [m.] Joe D. Russell, December 26, 1959; [ch.] Maria N. Russell; [ed.] Catholic High School Girl's Academy, Washington, DC., Private Music Lessons, Washington, DC, Piano Lessons, San Diego, CA, Music Theory, Community College, El Paso, TX; [occ.] Home maker; [mem.] Gospel Music Association, Choctaw Bay Music Club, Member of the National and Florida Federation of Music Clubs; [hon.] "The Ballerina Waltz" presented in the "Choreography Showcase" Fort Walton Beach Ballet Co. FL June 13 and 14, 1980 "Prelude to Love" featured in Parade of American Music. Choctaw Bay Music Club, FL "Christmas Memories, When I saw the real Santa Clause." Published in the Las Vegas Sun. December 24, 1989. "Sea of Love" played on the Zoe Riley Radio Show, Fort Walton Beach, FL; [oth. writ.] Several hymns performed in Churches. Musical setting for "Alice in Wonderland", "Lady of Lourdes" (Opera in 3 Acts.), "Prelude to Love" (recorded by George Liberance) songs performed by Maria Russell, daughter and professional pianist in Las Vegas, NV.; [pers.] Spiritually inspired throughout my life, I expressed myself with words words and music. The translation of songs and poems into ideas, action and acts of love is my ultimate goal.; [a.] Las Vegas, NV

RUSSELL, JEAN RAFTERY
[b.] April 26, 1937, Ipswich, MA; [p.] James and Dorothy Raftery; [m.] Thomas Allan Russell, August 29, 1971; [ch.] Jim Edwards/Jan Perret; [ed.] Graduated from High School 1955, College...only three semisters in Creative Writing; [occ.] Photographer at Calder Race Course (horse racing) in Miami, Fla.; [oth. writ.] Short stories and lyrics; [pers.] I enjoy writing, humorous pieces are my favorite, perhaps they'll brighten someone's day; [a.] Fort Lauderdale, FL

SABOL, DOROTHY
[pen.] Cricket; [b.] March 10, 1966, Youngstown; [p.] Earl Smith, Helen Smith; [m.] Vinee Sabol; [ch.] Jason, David, Sarah; [occ.] Wife, Mother, Newspaper Carrier; [memb.] Gospel Baptist Church; [hon.] I have none other then during my school days for various activities of sort. Unless we can include my poem summer morning which is recently published in this book into the unknown. But most everything I do I receive honor in my heart.; [oth. writ.] I have no other writings at this time, only ideas that come to me frequently, on a variety of basis, my desire is to write these ideas of variety in given time to accomplish a completeness.; [pers.] We are all given the same amount of time, 12 hours a day, 12 hours a night. It is how we choose to use our time that matters. Just because one may not have a spouse or no children, does not necessarily mean they have more time then another. I write this for it's in my heart to let others know be careful not to assume about another time. How are you using your time?; [a.] North Lima, OH

SAENZ, ALEJANDRO
[pen.] Sadder but Wiser; [b.] August 31, 1974, Bryan, TX; [p.] Alma Saenz; [occ.] Student at San Houston State University; [hon.] Sacrosanct Honor in American Fictional Transcendentalism (S.H.A.F.T.); [oth. writ.] Shadows in the Dark, Lying on the Couch, Roses, In Memory of Her.; [pers.] "No one can feel love or hate with as much passion as a madman, I am insane and love is my insanity." Any, and all of my talent has been inspired by the light in her eyes. She gives me the spark that unleashes a blazing inferno.; [a.] Huntsville, TX

SAMPSON, ESTELLA MAY
[pen.] Stell Sampson; [b.] June 16, 1950, Philadelphia, PA; [p.] George and Florence Malin; [m.] June 24, 1971; [ch.] Edward Neil, Thomas Elwood, Stephen Roland, Elwood Jackson; [ed.] Sun Valley High, Aston PA; [occ.] Dietary Cook, Gunnison Valley Hospital, Gunnison, CO; [hon.] Recognition from peer's for poetry and painting accomplishments; [oth. writ.] Many poems written for the enjoyment for family, friends and myself.; [pers.] Dreams today could be tomorrows... Patience... Perspective... Persistence, Hard work... ability to believe in oneself, dreams... reality life; [a.] Gunnison, CO

SAMUELS, ERICA B.
[b.] October 23, 1967, Kingston, Jamaica; [p.] Hazel Baker; [ed.] A.A.S. from Community College of Philadelphia, in Finance. Graduate of Olney High School Graduated from PA Advancement Middle School; [occ.] Police Correctional Officer; [hon.] Awarded Sportsmanship and Citizenship from High School and Middle School; [oth. writ.] I have many unpublished poems, that I share with family and friends.; [pers.] I say to all people "Dare To Be You" life is about chance. Don't be afraid to try.; [a.] Philadelphia, PA

SANDERFER, J. DAVID
[b.] October 12, 1955, Dayton, TX; [m.] Elizabeth, October 12, 1974; [occ.] Mechanic; [pers.] I believe in freedom - with discipline thanks to Gail Mangham. E-Mail is jdave at flash net.; [a.] Houston, TX

SANDERS, ANTONIO
[pen.] Tonto; [b.] June 16, 1956, Omaha, NE; [p.] O. D. and Delores Collier; [m.] Deborah Sanders; [ch.] Tesha, Jr., Micheal, Rashad, Mario, Tiffaney and Brittiney, Chalio; [ed.] Trimble Tech High, Ft. Worth, Killeen Jr. College; [occ.] Warehouseman and carpenter; [memb.] Better influence Assoc. National Children's Cancer Society, Inc.; [hon.] Several hometown poetry contest. Military awards, Awards for tailoring and design. Greatest honor is fatherhood; [oth. writ.] Over 150 poems which include "One Day At A Time" and "Always Lonely"; [pers.] God had blessed me in many outlets. But his greatest Gift to me are all my children.; [a.] Wichita Falls, TX

SANDERS, BENJAMIN
[pen.] Benjamin Sanders; [b.] February 13, 1971, Phoenix, AZ; [p.] Edward Sanders and Patricia Sanders; [ed.] Currently attending Phoenix College; [hon.] Member of the National Honor Society; [pers.] I write from a personal perspective. I hope that my writings about love, nature, and humanity find a universal theme in content, to all who read them.; [a.] Phoenix, AZ

SANDERSON, KATHLEEN L. A.
[pen.] Kat; [b.] November 10, 1949, Long Beach, CA; [p.] Harold B. Anderson, Virginia Anderson; [m.] William Donnie Sanderson, May 2, 1981; [ch.] Flynt William, Noelle Tiana; [ed.] Brigham Young University B.A., Lewis and Clark College M. Ed; [occ.] Reading Specialist Holdaway Elementary, Thayne, WY; [pers.] Writing helps me try and look at things as they really are or should be, and not only as they seem to be; [a.] Freedom, WY

SANDIFER, ROGER
[pen.] William Short; [b.] June 11, 1943, Ged, LA; [p.] G. C. and Annie Sandifer; [m.] Priscilla; [ch.] Tom, Mike, Elaine, Danny, Laura; [ed.] Vinton High - Cheniers Business; [occ.] Self Employed; [oth. writ.] Have written much poetry, and a book called "Chance". Up until now my writings have been for my own pleasure.; [pers.] I become William and escape into the realm of the pen. He is my alter ego, my window to mans existence, my past and my future.; [a.] Lake Charles, LA

SANDRIDGE, MARIE E.
[b.] November 11, 1944, Quincy, MA; [p.] Clifton W. Hayes Sr., Marie C. Hayes; [ch.] Anitamarie (Evangelista) Person, Carmine Evangelista Marie Kathleen Sandridge, Sunshine E. Sandridge, Lucy F. Sandridge, Christopher W. Sandridge; [ed.] Lourdesmont Catholic H.S./Scranton, PA, Immaculate Jr. College, (Wash. DC), Univ of PA, (Phila, PA), University of Montana (Missoula, MT); [occ.] Sales/Insurance; [hon.] Literary Award, Music Award (Piano); [oth. writ.] Children short stories and various other poems (Currently writing novel); [pers.] Have 6 children of my own, I realize what a precious gift from God a child is, and try to portray in my poems and short stories, how things may seem through a child's perspective. As we grow older and mature, and have more accountability, we gain wisdom, from opinions, and our lives seem so complex. Along the way, we lose the childhood innocence, naivete, unwavering trust and faith. Work and family responsibilities cannot afford us the time to let our imaginations be anyone, anywhere, anytime we want. But, even if only for a brief moment, I can bring those cherished memories of childhood delights to life once more, then I will have achieved my purpose that we should all not only allow ourselves to let go and be "children" once in a while-but that we need to do so-so that we, our children, and our grandchildren, will not lost sight of the true meaning of the "gift of life"!; [a.] Laurel, MD

SAPP, DONNA PARROTT
[b.] November 25, 1974, Stone Mountain, GA; [p.] Richard and Bernice Parrott; [m.] Brian Christopher Sapp, December 17, 1994; [ch.] Logan Christopher Sapp; [ed.] Brookwood High School, State University of West Georgia; [memb.] Alpha Lambda Delta, Delta Zeta Sorority; [hon.] Dean's List, Alpha Delta Kappa Scholarship Recipient; [pers.] I just want my parents, husband, and beautiful baby boy to know that I love and appreciate them with all my heart.; [a.] Carrollton, GA

SCANLON III, P. J.
[b.] February 2, 1974, Maryland; [p.] Patrick and Patricia Scanlon; [ed.] 2nd year Penn State University, Sacred Heart H.S., Carbondale, PA; [occ.] Student; [hon.] Who's Who in America H.S. Students '92, Dean's List '95; [pers.] May tomorrow grant all the wishes of yesterday, and ponder the ones of today.; [a.] Carbondale, PA

SCHELLER, DEBRA L.
[pen.] Debbi Prosperi; [b.] November 14, 1959, PA; [p.] Tony and Jane; [ed.] Barber Child Care, Rest' Manager - Bar Tender, Tech. and Community 4 1/2 yrs.; [occ.] Child Care; [memb.] Book Club in my town.; [hon.] This. It's a honor Just knowing that my personal thoughts might be read, and respected by people that I don't even know.; [oth. writ.] Too many to write them all down.; [pers.] I mostly write about God, and life. Isn't that what it's all about? otherwise... who knows?; [a.] Caraopolis, PA

SCHETTLER, TRYN R.
[b.] December 31, 1923, The Netherlands; [p.] Eppe and Henderika Koning; [m.] Edward J. Schettler, April 30, 1980; [ch.] Rita VanderPoorte, Pam Coda and Greg Schettler; [ed.] European Schooling; [occ.] Retired; [memb.] Christian Reformed Church, Myasthenia Gravis Foundation; [oth. writ.] Collection of unpublished poems; [pers.] I try to express my frustrations and dilemmas in my writings.; [a.] Grand Rapids, MI

SCHILD, HOLLY
[b.] November 28, 1984, Chattanooga, TN; [p.] Jerry W. and Cheryl H. Schild; [ed.] Student at Sewanee Elementary School - Sewanee, TN; [memb.] Honor Choir, Morton Memorial Methodist Church, Choir, Abba Babba Club (honor students) National Wildlife Assoc.; [hon.] 1995 - Honorable mention in The Federal Junior Duck Stamp Design Contest of Tennessee - 1996 - 1st place in 4th thru 6th grade Federal Junior Duck Duck Stamp Design Contest of Tennessee; [pers.] My favorite poet is Edgar Allan Poe. I like to write poems that intrigue and mystify the reader. I also like to write about my innermost feelings.; [a.] Monteagle, TN

SCHNEIDER, JANINE
[pen.] Janine Ertel-Schneider; [b.] November 3, 1963, Encino, CA; [p.] Ronald Ertel and Sharon Ertel; [m.] James Schneider, March 21, 1987; [ed.] Saint Bonaventure High, Ventura Junior College; [occ.] Office Mgr. "Ertel Cabinets and Millwork, Inc."; [memb.] US Navy Ombudsman Assoc.; [oth. writ.] This is my first publication. I have been writing poem's for years, but purely for personal enjoyment.; [pers.] I enjoy writing from my heart. Whether it is love, happiness or one of life's many disappointments.; [a.] Oxnard, CA

SCHOELLER, DEIRDRE MCCARTHY
[b.] May 2, 1934, Kildare, Ireland; [p.] Delia and Arthur McCarthy; [m.] James Schoeller, July 1, 1959; [ch.] Patrick, Dorothy, Jacqueline, Wendy; [ed.] National School, Kilcullen, Ireland, St. Leo's College, Carlow, Ireland, University College, Dublin, Ireland; [occ.] Real Estate Broker former Model and Pan Am Stewardess; [memb.] Suncoast Assoc., of Realtors Florida and National Assoc. of Realtors, St. Pete Beach Chamber of Commerce, Finance Committee and Women's Retreat, Committee of St. John's Catholic Church, Treasure Island Yacht and Tennis Club; [hon.] 4 year Scholastic Scholarship to St. Leo's College, Carlow and University College, Dublin, Ireland, Winner of Miss Ireland Competition and Cover Girl Contest for Women's Own Magazine, London, England; [pers.] I seek and find joy in the beauty of nature, that to me, reflects the presence of God and thus enhances my spirituality.; [a.] South Pasadena, FL

SCHOOLEY, MARGIE
[b.] September 28, 1946, Zanesville; [p.] Mildred and Elva Talbert; [m.] Paul Schooley, December 26, 1987; [ch.] My birth children - my step children and many foster children; [ed.] I am doing home school to get my diploma I finished the 10th grade; [occ.] State Foster Parent of Five Children; [hon.] Poem - Fountain Of Tears, poem -Every thing; [oth. writ.] I am writing a book of poem's of my own I am now on my 30th poem I pray I can get it published in the near future; [pers.] I would not be able to write poetry, if I didn't have Jesus in my life Jesus is my life, I devote my life to Jesus and to many, many of God's children, also I love my husband Paul, I pray that my poem's can help other people: That many lives will be touched and souls saved for Jesus: I dedicate my poems to my Lord, Jesus and my husband Paul, all my children.; [a.] Zanesville, OH

SCHULER, RYAN
[b.] March 5, 1979, New Albany; [p.] Marc and Doris Schuler; [ed.] Senior High School; [occ.] Student; [memb.] German Club President; [oth. writ.] Various other poems including: "The Darkness Is My Friend", "The Dolphin And The Whale", "Tapper Of The Coffin", and "Black Rose".; [pers.] My poems are mainly influenced by personal experience and my darkest inner

fears. I have been influenced by Edgar Allan Poe, Emily Dickinson, and the poetry of Jim Morrison of the Doors.; [a.] New Albany, IN

SCHWARTZ, ILENE STEPHANIE
[pen.] Ilene Schwartz; [b.] October 15, 1982, Princeton, NJ; [p.] Warren and Rachel Kae Schwartz; [ed.] Presently attending Leesville Road Middle School, Leesville Road, Raleigh, NC 27613; [occ.] Student 8th grade

SCHWIETERS, KYLE
[b.] June 11, 1974, Duluth, MN; [pers.] Dedicated to and perhaps inspired by Jennie Janota. In case the book doesn't come, maybe this will do.

SCIACCA, LAUREN ANN-VERONICA
[b.] September 18, 1979, Wakefield, MA; [p.] Vincent Sciacca, Maryann Sciacca; [ed.] I am currently entering my senior year at Wakefield High School and plan to attend college in Massachusetts, also.; [memb.] I have been extremely active in the WHS Drama Club for three years going on four.; [hon.] I won an acting award this year for the Best Secondary Actress in the play, You Can't Take It With You. I usually make the Honor Role. I have also received many nominations for my performances.; [oth. writ.] Some of my poems have been in various magazines as well as short stories.; [pers.] I love writing about human emotions. I try to create poems that express the dramatic, kind, and romantic sides of the mind. I often find myself drawing or painting pictures to illustrate my poems. I just adore being creative everyday.; [a.] Wakefield, MA

SECK, JESSY
[pen.] J. C.; [b.] December 18, 1980, Warren, MI; [p.] Rev. Ronald A. Seck and Jeannie Larson Seck; [ed.] Chippewa Valley High School; [occ.] 10th grader at Chippewa Valley High School in Clinton Twp., Mich.; [memb.] Young Rivers Youth Ministries, Leader in church youth group; [hon.] Championship Michigan Bible Quizzer or years several Presidential Academic and Physical Fitness Awards, High Honors District Academic Achievement Awards; [oth. writ.] Have written for school and church newspapers and bulletins as well as for enjoyment, do my own comic as a hobby; [pers.] God has given me this talent, and I want to use it for him.; [a.] Clinton Township, MI

SEMPLE, M. FAY
[pen.] Fay; [b.] October 19, 1933, Boston, MA; [p.] William and Marjorie; [m.] 1954-1982; [ch.] 2 sons - 2 daughters; [ed.] Brookline High School, Vt. Junior College (1 year); [occ.] Retired; [memb.] SMC Investment Club, First United Church of Norwood, AARP, MADD; [hon.] Former President of New England Assisted Housing Mgmt. Assn. - former President Management Company; [oth. writ.] For 18 years I have written personal poems for friends, business associates, family or any subject appropriate for an occasion.; [pers.] I have always found pleasure in writing personal poetry to express my innermost feelings. I find great satisfaction in recapping events in poetry form to the delight of the recipients.; [a.] Norwood, MA

SENIOR, KATHRYN E.
[b.] October 9, 1982, Anaheim, CA; [p.] Cliff and Jenny Senior; [ed.] Fullerton: Nicolas Jr. High, I'm in High School (Freshman); [occ.] Don't have one; [hon.] Just school awards for: Choir accomplishments, students of the month, perfect attendance, and a Jr. High Diploma; [oth. writ.] Just poems that sit in a notebook pad, that no one but my friends have read.; [pers.] I never really wanted to be a poet. I just wrote down my feelings. I didn't think it would be this good. I mostly sing, dance, act and am artistic; [a.] Fullerton, CA

SENTER, EDIE A.
[pen.] Edie A. Senter; [b.] June 21, 1963, Culver City, CA; [p.] Josephine Sandoval and Edward Sandoval; [ch.] Katherine E. Senter; [ed.] Trinidad, Colorado, Onshore Computer College; [occ.] Sales Manager, Truitt Bros., Inc., Salem, Oregon; [oth. writ.] Several poems published.; [pers.] I always try and give a part of myself in everything I write and hope that the joy, the sadness, and the experiences somehow touches someone else.; [a.] Salem, OR

SERRANO, SANDRA
[pen.] Sandra Stone; [b.] May 7, 1957, Wakegun, IL; [p.] Tim and Betty Serrano; [ed.] North Hollywood High, Pierce Jr. College (then went to work); [occ.] Secretary/ Actress; [memb.] S.A.G. (Unions) and A.F.T.R.A.-Wildlife Way Station, CBWA-Caring for Babies w/ Aids; [hon.] Championships - L.A. Figure Skating 69 and Pacific Coast Figure Skating 70 - runner up Miss Burbank and now this.; [oth. writ.] Several poems from Spiritual, Erotic, Holiday all sorts. None ever published.; [pers.] I want people to read my work and feel the emotion that moved my hand in the first place.; [a.] Marina del Rey, CA

SERVERDIJA, SYLVIA G.
[pen.] Sylvia Godoy; [b.] September 2, 1936, Elsauce, Nicaragua; [p.] Hermogenes Godoy, Soledad Benedit; [m.] Nikola C. Severdija, September 19, 1959; [ch.] Niek Martin, Dean Anthony; [ed.] Santa Rosa - Silviano Matamoros School of Business Micarogua; [occ.] University of Miami Information Technology - Scheduler; [oth. writ.] Non published several poems written in Spanish and English. This poems is my first publication.; [pers.] As humans, recognizing the given gift of knowing right and wrong, we must work for perfection and not to excuse ourselves by saying "I am human".; [a.] Miami, FL

SEVILLA, EMERITA N.
[pen.] Narra; [b.] December 7, 1926, Manila, Philippines; [p.] Perfecto and Dolores Nepomuceno; [m.] Victor J. Sevilla, December 10, 1949; [ch.] Victoria, Victor Jr., Enid, Vincent, Vidal, Virgil, Valentin, Vinci, Elaine; [ed.] College of the Holy Spirit - Elem., Maryknoll College - High School, University of Santo Tomas - Bachelor of Literature in Journalism; [occ.] Writer; [memb.] Phi Lambda Sigma, Perpetual Rosary Association, Perpetual Eucharistic Adoration, Cactus and Succulent Society (Phils.), Sunset Succulent Society (West Los Angeles); [hon.] Philamlife Presidential Awards, Provident Insurance Awards; [oth. writ.] I - Published Works: Springs Of Joy - Bookmark, Inc. 1992, Silver And Gold - Salesiana Publishers, Inc. 1995, Treasures From Heaven - Bookmark, Inc. 1996, II - Various articles and poems in magazines and newspapers over the years; [pers.] Life on earth is a pilgrimage to our true home in heaven. If any of my poems or written work can help a soul attain that goal for which it was created in love by God, then the raison d'etre of my work will have been fully realized.; [a.] West Los Angeles, CA

SHALOM, QUEEN
[p.] Margaret De Graffenreid; [ch.] Bernice, Mary-Avon; [ed.] Wilkes-Barre Business College and University of Pittsburgh; [occ.] Home Educator; [memb.] Writers Center; [hon.] Dean's List; [oth. writ.] Nonpublished works; [pers.] Never give up! Persist even in the face of adversity!; [a.] Washington, DC

SHARP, JO ANNE
[pen.] Jo Anne Sharp; [b.] April 17, 1945, Ripley, TN; [p.] Grant and Frances Russell; [m.] Henry Lee Sharp, November 20, 1961; [ch.] 3 sons; [ed.] High School 12 yrs.; [occ.] Industrial Work, Sewings; [memb.] Pilgrim Rest Baptist Church 802 West Garfield Elk IN 46516 I Foster Parent, Eastern Star Member; [hon.] I have the honor to be a member of the O.E.S Brotton Whitted Chapter. Means order of the Eastern Star; [oth. writ.] I wrote a poem for the Sunday Church Programs OH Grace and Mercy.; [pers.] It's a joy for me to write poetry it goes deep down in the soul, I am a Christian and love it. I go to Pilgrim Rest Church 802 West Garfield Ave Elk, IN; [a.] Elkhart, IN

SHELBY, RYAN
[pen.] Jon Amstred; [b.] April 19, 1981, Dallas, TX; [p.] Jan and Arnold Shelby; [ed.] Plano High; [occ.] Student; [memb.] BBYO - Bnai Brith Youth Organization, Stand; [hon.] Honors student, National Honors Society had a scholarship year; [oth. writ.] Stories published in school publications.; [pers.] To be born is to die and to die is to be born.; [a.] Plano, TX

SHENBERGER, SHANNON
[b.] July 24, 1983, Mannheim, PA; [p.] John Shenberger, Donna Shenberger; [ed.] Eight grade student at Warwick Middle School for the 1996-97 school year.; [hon.] High Honor Roll, February 1992, Principal's Honor Roll, April 1992, Warmick Scholar, June 1994, Presidential Academic Fitness Awards Program, 1994, President's Education Awards Program, 1995 First Honor Roll all year 1996; [a.] Lititz, PA

SHERMAN, CAROL Y.
[b.] August 6, 1956, North Carolina; [p.] Mary and Lee Gray; [m.] Calvin Sherman, March 24, 1973; [ch.] Terrell and Erica; [ed.] High School B.S. in Theology; [occ.] Certified Nursing Asst. and Home Health Aide also an Associate Minister.; [memb.] Member of the Community Baptist Church, formly in the United State Army Reserves 1976-1974; [oth. writ.] Children's Nursery Rhyme Book (not published) Selection of poems entitled African Violet (not published); [pers.] It gives me such pleasure to write poetry. I hope that others can see the beauty of God's gifts through my writing.; [a.] New Haven, CT

SHERMAN, MILTON TONY
[pen.] M. Tony Sherman; [b.] December 3, 1910, Atlantic City, NJ; [p.] Joseph Sherman - Mollie; [m.] Phyllis Sherman (Deceased), 1937, re-marriage Lois Hont Alley, 1990; [ch.] Elza 1940, Suzan 1943; [ed.] Office of V. B. Smith 1926-1933, Univ. Penn. B. Arch, 1993, NY Univ. Crad. Design, 33-37 student instructor industrial college of the armed forces 55-56; [occ.] Architect Consultant, Painter, Aircraft Pilot, Writer; [memb.] Certificate Beaux Arts Institute of Design 1933-34, Registered Architect NY 1936, FL 1948 National Council Architectural Boards 1956, Aircraft's Owners and Pilots Association, US Coast Guard Aux and Power Squadron; [hon.] Castaways -Sunny Isles FL, Tropicana Resort Las Vegas Nevada, Fontaine Bleau Hotel New Orleans LA, Zero Food Process and Storage N. Miami FL, Yankee Clipper Hotel Ft. Lauder FL; [oth. writ.] Published to Design A Better Kitchen Florida Contractor and Builder Dec. 1966, Newsletter of the Palm Beach American Institute of Architects 1989, Palm Beach users Group, 1992-93 Autobiography "Confessions of An Architect" 1990.; [pers.] So much to learn! So little time "When you are about to fall pick your direction put one foot in front of the other and continue" Bon Voyage!; [a.] Royal Palm Beach, FL

SHERRELL, JOHN A.
[b.] October 9, 1936, Jackson, GA; [p.] George and Mary Sherrell; [m.] Margaret Rawls Sherrell, July 20, 1964; [ch.] Jackie Rooks, Dennis Rooks, Bonnie Richardson, Becky Cardell; [ed.] High School and Cincinnati College of Embalming, Graduating courses in Real Estates and Emergency Medical Technician at Griffin Tech., Griffinga.; [occ.] Funeral Director - Embalmer; [memb.] Second Baptist Church of Jackson, GA, Jackson Kiwanis Club, Indian Spring Lodge 307 F and Am, Scottish Rite of Freemasonry Royal Arch Chapter #54 Georgia Knights Temper of Georgia Veteran of the US Army; [oth. writ.] A book of poems written by John A. Sherrell entitled I Can Feel Your Heart, in the process of writing a novel to be completed in January of 1997.; [pers.] Some of the greatest blessings of my life have been seeing the enjoyment of people reading my poems.; [a.] Jackson, GA

SHINE, BAMBI JOY
[b.] September 28, 1960, Burlington, VT; [p.] Douglas Beede, Norilla Tisei; [m.] Todd D. Shine, April 16, 1988; [ch.] Shawna Lynn, Sommer Jo, Kristal Brook; [ed.] South Burlington High Essex Junction Vocational; [occ.] Owner of: Bambi Dear Enterprises; [memb.] Children's International Village United Methodist Church Junior Chamber of Commerce; [hon.] Numerous Awards from Junior Chamber of Commerce, Write-up Competition awards, diabetes research awards, state book writing competition, champion; [oth. writ.] Poem published in "A Muse to Follow". Several poems and stories in personal library; [pers.] My writings come from the heart. My children are my inspiration. My husband is supportive and continually encourages me to write. I couldn't do it without him: Todd, I love you, and thank you love always!; [a.] Pompano Beach, FL

SHNAYDER, JULIA
[b.] February 12, 1982, Passaic, NJ; [p.] Jacob and Inna Shnayder; [a.] Wayne, NJ

SHOCK, GEORGE F.
[b.] January 14, 1960, Flora, IL; [p.] Lester R. Shock, Patsy R. Shock; [m.] Divorced; [ch.] Hayli Dawn Shock (6); [ed.] West Richland High School, Community College of the Air Force; [occ.] Warehouse Technician for Sherwin Williams; [memb.] Indiana Air National Guard "Recycling Works" Committee, Effingham, Ill.; [hon.] U.S. Air Force Commendation Medal; [pers.] My writings are my attempt to convey in words the emotions that are in my heat. "Sunshine" was written for DeAnn.; [a.] Newton, IL

SHUPPON, TARA M.
[b.] July 18, 1973, Newton, NJ; [p.] John and Toni Shuppon; [ed.] Wallkill Valley Regional High School; [occ.] Managing Assistant for Showcase Masters; [oth. writ.] Poems and stories published in the independent publication "Modern Muse".; [pers.] I try to capture lifes smiles and tears in my writing. I feel there is truth in what comes from the heart.; [a.] Franklin, NJ

SIATKOWSKI, BRIAN S.
[b.] May 5, 1972, Baltimore, MD; [p.] Charlene Wingate and Jerome Siatkowski; [ed.] Graduated High School 1990, Ranklin Sr. High - Reisterstown, MD, Graduated Cabrini College, May 1994, PA; [hon.] Wrestling Champion State of MD 1990 for Franklin High, (Balto. Co.); [oth. writ.] Several poems published while attending Gardner-Webb University in boiling Springs, NC; [pers.] I strive to reflect the human side of life in my writings that sometimes are not discussed, that all people will find peace in their hearts.; [a.] Reisterstown, MD

SILVIOUS, ELAINE
[b.] April 19, 1985, Gaithersburg, MD; [p.] Stephen Silvious and Janet Silvious; [occ.] Student at New Market Middle School; [oth. writ.] Have written several poems, one published in local paper.; [a.] Mount Airy, MD

SIMCO, JACK D.
[b.] January 22, 1923, Mt. Burg, AR; [p.] Thomas F. and Iva (Peters) Simco; [m.] Wanda Faye (Birchfield) Simco, August 14, 1946; [ch.] One son (John); [ed.] Eleventh Grade "High School Mountainburg Public Schools; [occ.] Retired Builder Contractor Current Occupation, Working on my 150 A. Farm; [memb.] Pigeon Creek Freewell Baptist Church. Ordained Decon for 28 years; [oth. writ.] Proses and songs poems that tell a story had one song published in California titled "My Little Train" (no Hit) I've written over 500 poems and proses and song words. Its one of my hobbies; [pers.] (January 22/23) Mountainburg, Arkansas I have no special education I'm self taught. I strive to write form Heart, I write nature and and things I imagine out in the forest and what I dream and see and things that come to me when I'm hicking, I makes notes; [a.] Mountainburg, AR

SIMMERS, WONZA
[b.] February 6, 1921, Arkansas; [p.] W. D. Meeker, Elinore Smith Meeker; [m.] E. F. Simmers (Deceased), December 6, 1937; [ch.] David, Robert, Michael, Daniel, Timothy and Patrick; [ed.] GED in my forties Dundalk Community College, an honor student, student activities, won an essay contest writing Martin Luther King $100.00; [memb.] Democratic member and R.L.D.S. Church where I was women's leader, historian church school teacher and supervisor. I was honor student Dundalk College, editor, reporter, manager of college newspaper and also Chimera's, college poetry magazine; [hon.] 1. Developed a weekly column for local paper called "Simmering" (play on name and events occurring in area. 2. Who's Who in Junior Colleges. 3. "Best in the Region" National Challenge exhibiting "sensational" professionalism for Dundalk College's "The Lion" for story contest, news emphasis, Photo contest and originality for 1985; [oth. writ.] Wrote and edited college newspaper and managed the Business Office, sold advertisement to the local merchants; [pers.] In my youth, many persons taught me the way not to go! This included my relatives, especially my parents and sisters. Therefore I took the road less traveled. It was a lonely road...I wasn't lonely. It was quieter way but I saw and I heard a lot. Especially I learned to read, to write and to raise 6 sons of whom I was very proud - four went to college.; [a.] Baltimore, MD

SIMMONS, HEIDI
[b.] April 19, 1980, Walla Walla; [p.] Tami Olmstead, Greg Simmons; [ed.] Is currently attending high school; [occ.] Student; [memb.] Member of 1st Assembly of God; [hon.] Several good citizenship awards from school. Today's Little Dream Girl Pageant was Wash. State winner of Miss Congeniality; [oth. writ.] Has written various poems, none of which have been published.; [pers.] Would like to see people more accepting of other's differences to be able to recognize your weaknesses and try to learn from them.; [a.] Walla Walla, WA

SINDIK, GEORGE
[b.] August 14, 1959, Mobile, AL; [p.] Emmett and Shirley B. Sindik; [ed.] Abramson High School Delgado Community College New Orleans, LA; [occ.] Import/Export Business; [pers.] If you put your mind to it, and put your right foot in front of the other, you'll walk a straight line.

SINGLETON, ERIC I.
[b.] August 12, 1967, Tacoma, WA; [occ.] Restaurant Manager; [pers.] I have nothing to say, although my pen does.; [a.] Washougal, WA

SINGLETON, JENNIFER
[pen.] Jayle Ess; [b.] June 6, 1955, CA; [p.] Francis and Dorothea Haynes; [m.] John C. Singleton; [ch.] Amanda, Amberly, Travis; [ed.] Fashion Design/Merchandising Marketing/Sales; [occ.] Director of Operations Starlight Theatres; [oth. writ.] Several poems, motivational works, educational materials; [pers.] Since all of life's answers are within, in order to learn the wisdom of the ages, all you have to do is stop long enough in order to listen.; [a.] Reading, CA

SINGLETON, TIM
[b.] February 3, 1958, Montgomery, AL; [p.] Bill and Carolyn Singleton; [m.] Connie, February 2, 1991; [ch.] Madison 4, Jake 2; [ed.] BA - Math and Psychology Huntingdon College, Commercial Banking University of Oklahoma; [occ.] President, CEO, Singleton and Associates, Development Group; [memb.] Frazer Memorial United Methodist Church; [hon.] 1. High School Student of the year - Montgomery City Schools, 2. American Business Women's Boss of the Year; [pers.] "The words that travel from my heart merely reflect only a small portion of the life of blessings given to me by my Lord."; [a.] Montgomery, AL

SIRIANNI, JENNY L.
[b.] June 18, 1971, Redondo Beach; [p.] James and Judy A. Sirianni; [ed.] Graduate of Carpintertia High School Class of 1989. Attended and graduated from Santa Barbara Business College; [memb.] Member of church Bell Choir and Sanctuary Choir; [hon.] Muses "Best Towsperson Award". Spirit Award from Santa Barbara County Board of Education; [oth. writ.] "Black and White, The Game of Life, He is the Wall, Way Did They Have to Die? Children; [pers.] My poems speak about life and my personal experiences. I speak from the heart through the beautiful language of poetry; [a.] Carpinteria, CA

SISK, EILEEN
[pen.] Eileen Adams, Eileen Tetreault; [b.] November 8, 1952, Henderson, NV; [p.] Hugh Sisk and Susan Shellenbarger; [m.] Samuel R. Mellar, April 15, 1995; [ch.] Jeffrey Hugh Tetreault and Douglas Gerard Tetreault; [ed.] BA, Communications - January 1979, California State University Fullerton; [occ.] Freelance Journalist; [memb.] Society of Professional Journalists, Society of Newspaper Design, Northern Virginia Country-Western Dance Association, Court House Players.; [hon.] Subject of Biographical Record, Who's Who in the South and Southwest 1995-'96. Four Awards of Excellence, Society of Newspaper Design, 1990 and 1992. Four Merit of Awards Long Beach, CA, Pro Photography Show, 1978; [oth. writ.] NF book - Honky-Tonks, Guide to Country Dancin' and Romancin' (Harper Collins West, 1995) articles, in Nevada Magazine, The Washington Post, Los Angeles Times, Denver Post, Las Vegas Review - Journal, St. Helen Star and Daily Calistogan.; [pers.] The key to this poem lies in the last three words.; [a.] Hayes, VA

SKAGGS, JAMIE
[b.] March 12, 1971, New York, NY; [p.] Jim Skaggs, Carol Skaggs; [ed.] Northport High, Binghamton University, New York Chiropractic College; [occ.] Chiropractor; [memb.] American Chiropractic Assoc.; [hon.] Graduated Chiropractic College Cum Laude; [oth. writ.]

This is my 1st publication.; [pers.] I haven't been influenced by anyone particular author or style. I instead write about the feelings I have about people or places. "God's Gracious Gift" is the literal translation of the name. `Jane', the person who inspired this work.; [a.] Northport, NY

SLOAN, MARY
[b.] November 21, 1954, Greenville, SC; [p.] Bailey and Bernice Brown; [ch.] Jami, Lori; [ed.] Pickens High, Greenville Technical College; [occ.] Manager, Bell Alantic Nynex Greenville, SC; [memb.] Liberty Ministries Church, Cultural Change Co-Chairperson; [hon.] Honor Student, Successful Single Parent of Two Beautiful Girls, Employee of the Month, Children's Church Leader; [oth. writ.] "I Am, I Said", "Where Are You Now", "A Gambling Man", "They Are Looking", "You Alone"; [pers.] I write is from my soul, all I express is from deep within. Truly it is into the unknown.; [a.] Easley, SC

SMEGAL, SHANNON
[b.] February 23, 1981, Camden, NJ; [p.] Kimberlee Smegal and Brian Smegal; [ed.] Maple Shade High School; [oth. writ.] I've been writing all types of poetry since I was very young, however this was the first time I've ever done anything with it.; [pers.] I believe that poetry is away of letting your feelings out, which is very important I write what ever comes to my mind, sometimes something will pop into my mind out of the blue. So I write it down and work with it later. I basically write about love. So naturally I like Shakespeare.; [a.] Maple Shade, NJ

SMITH, EVELYN
[pen.] Evelyn Smith; [b.] Mineral Wells, TX; [ch.] Sue, Newman, Shirley, Allen; [occ.] Retired Sales Person; [oth. writ.] Book Headed for summer, a book of love and hope for widows other poems.; [pers.] I believe in the owner of God and all life. We are one in love and life.; [a.] Arlington, TX

SMITH, KENYON
[b.] June 24, 1973, Mizpah, NJ; [p.] Janice Smith; [ed.] Oak Crest High (89-92); [occ.] Maintenance J.C. Penneys'; [hon.] Melvin Newton Scholarship Award Oak Crest. Poetry and Writing Award; [oth. writ.] Poems: "Cleopatra Black Egyptian Queen", "Sweet Nautica From Me Too You".; [a.] Mizpah, NJ

SMITH, NANCY S.
[pen.] N. Smith; [b.] September 20, 1955, Valparaiso, IN; [p.] William Ludington and Evelyn Spiroff; [m.] David L. Smith, November 6, 1972; [ch.] Michelle A. and David II; [ed.] Valparaiso High School; [occ.] Food Service at Flint Lake Elementary; [oth. writ.] A few poems that have never been published.; [pers.] Friends and Family can be a wonderful inspiration in anything, anyone can do.; [a.] Valparaiso, IN

SMITH, WINIFRED
[b.] August 16, 1931, Boston, MA; [p.] Herbert L. Robertson, Mary L. Robertson; [m.] James A. Smith, November 30, 1957; [ch.] Mary Ann, Theresa Diane, James Henry, Karen Loraine; [ed.] Manual Arts High, L.A., CA; [oth. writ.] One poem published in Famous Poets Anthology of Hollywood, CA; [pers.] Writing poetry has been a creative hobby of mine for a number of years. My reward is that people will enjoy reading my poetry. [a.] Los Angeles, CA

SMITH III, ALFRED
[pen.] Gordon, Gord; [b.] September 13, 1983, Toms River, NJ; [p.] Alfred "Bud" Smith and Deborah; [ed.] Presently seventh grader in Pinelands Reg M.S.; [occ.] Student; [memb.] Pop Warner Football Pinelands Regioal Soccer Team - Science Club; [hon.] "Good Citizenship", "Perfect Attendance in School for 8 years", "Poetry Contest", "Art Contest"; [pers.] I have three brothers Drew, Matt David - I like to sit and think a lot - then I write what I think about. My imagination can take me many places, I am influenced to write by my Pop-Pop.; [a.] Tuckerton, NJ

SNADER, JULIE M.
[pen.] Julia Sheridan; [b.] July 21, 1976, Ann Arbor, MI; [p.] Benjamin Krautblatt, Sandra Johnson; [m.] Chad Snader, December 30, 1994; [ed.] CMR High; [occ.] Legal Secretary; [a.] Newark, DE

SNYDER, EMILY M.
[b.] December 6, 1917, Pittsburgh, PA; [p.] Edward C. and Emily K. Miller (Deceased); [m.] John E. Snyder, December 28, 1957; [ch.] Stepchildren: Johnnie Ray Snyder - Sally Nudo; [ed.] AB-Lake Eric College, also 5th year plays Ed., MA - University of Pittsburgh; [occ.] Retired; [oth. writ.] Have been returned; [pers.] Winters - as retirees abide in Florida.

SOLOVIEU, ANNA
[b.] August 2, 1981, Tbilisi, Republic of Georgia; [p.] Micheal Solovieu, Manana Razmadze; [ed.] Honolulu Waldorf School, (freshman); [occ.] High School Student; [hon.] Semi-finalist in Illiad Press. 1996; [oth. writ.] Wind, Variations, To You, Easter Night, Choice, Unrelated Souls, Changes, For my Father; [pers.] ...I wonder if we can get the sense, to open all wisdom of life and death....; [a.] Honolulu, HI

SONNIER, MARCIA NICOLE
[b.] August 17, 1983, San Francisco, CA; [p.] Nina Everette, Robert Sonnier; [ed.] 8th Grade Student; [hon.] 4 quarters Honor roll student through sixth grade; [oth. writ.] Several poems not yet published and short story books.; [pers.] When writing my poems I write from my heart in hopes to capture the reader's emotions. I have been greatly influenced by my mother Nina Everette and grandmother Phyllis Whitfield.; [a.] El Sobrante, CA

SOUED, CALI MAURICIO
[b.] November 24, 1956, Caracas, Venezuela; [p.] Youssef Soued and Maria Soued; [m.] Ana Esther Soued, May 19, 1984; [ch.] Jennifer and Jessica Soued; [ed.] Boston University Florida International University; [occ.] President IL Argento Corporation; [memb.] Jewish Community Center and Temple Reth-el, Charlotte North Carolina; [hon.] FMA Honor Society of the Financial Management Association; [oth. writ.] Articles on Venezuelan newspapers on finance, politics and economics; [pers.] I try to reflect my feelings and inner thoughts in my writing; [a.] Charlotte, NC

SPANOS, KATE
[b.] October 13, 1982, Washington, DC; [p.] Ann Kennedy and George Spanos; [ed.] St. Agnes School, Bishop Denis J. O'Connell High School (9th grader); [occ.] Student; [memb.] O'Neill James School of Irish Dancing; [hon.] Presidential Academic Award, 1st Place in School Science Fair; [oth. writ.] "Freedom", "Ireland-ahhhhhh!"; [pers.] I would like to thank my grandmother, Ann Caldwell Kennedy, who has encouraged me to write. I also want to thank my parents and my teachers and my friends.; [a.] Arlington, VA

SPARROW, GLORIA E.
[b.] September 14, 1932, Pittston, ME; [p.] Ara and Marion MacInnes; [m.] Divorced; [ch.] Kathleen Pelley, Patrick Quinn, G. Dawn Pallis, Robert Quinn, Timothy Quinn, and Elizabeth Robertson, 18 grandchildren; [ed.] Litchfield Academy, plus Gray: Bus.; [occ.] Retired; [memb.] Litchfield Grange, Health Club; [hon.] Dairy Queen of the Grange in 49 and Salututorian of my graduation class in 51; [oth. writ.] I have never entered any competition before.; [a.] Litchfield, ME

SPAUL, CHRISTINA
[pen.] Christy; [b.] February 21, 1975, Junction City, KS; [p.] James Spaul, Ruby Spaul; [ed.] Perryville High School, went through 11th grade; [occ.] I work at a store Double D Gro. Roland AR.; [hon.] Who's Who in 1992; [oth. writ.] None others have ever been submitted to anyone; [pers.] Most of the time my poems come from my feelings.; [a.] Perry, AR

SPEARS, DEBORAH
[b.] September 30, 1971, Modesto, CA; [p.] William Vernon Spears, Marie Spears; [ed.] Hughson High School, Modesto Junior College; [occ.] Nanny/Student; [memb.] Humane Society of the United States, American Heart Association; [oth. writ.] Poems published in local Stanislaus County Anthology programs, articles for schools newspapers; [pers.] I believe my writing gives others an insight into emotions not often spoken about, as well as, giving some a glimpse of the things I dream possible.; [a.] Modesto, CA

SPROUSE, BRIAN
[b.] January 4, 1981, Hearne, TX; [p.] Marsha and Kevin McCarthy; [ed.] Sophomore at High School; [memb.] Creative Arts and Sciences Enterprise; [hon.] Superior ratings in School Band 4.0 grade average in school; [pers.] A lot of my influence comes from the music I listen to. Especially a band named Type O Negative.; [a.] Hohenfels, Germany

SPURLING, DONNA
[b.] December 4, 1959, Madera, CA; [p.] William and Charlene Haddock; [m.] Henry Spurling, February 6, 1976; [ch.] Sarah, Mike, Randy and John; [ed.] Madera High in Madera, CA.; [occ.] Self employed through Excel Telecommunications; [memb.] Volunteer EMT/Ambulance in Clark Fork, Idaho. Search and Rescue for Bonner County, ID.; [hon.] I guess this is my first.; [oth. writ.] Nothing published, "Mom's" was the first poem I ever submitted. I've written many others, but gave most of them away.; [pers.] I like to write about my true life, so I thank my children for inspiring this poem, I lived all of it, plus a lot more. God bless all moms.; [a.] Sand Point, ID

STACY, MICHAEL F.
[pen.] Dean; [b.] August 21, 1960, Taipei, Taiwan; [p.] John and Anna Stacy; [ed.] Montgomery High, University of California, San Diego, Point Loma Nazarene College; [occ.] Teacher, Marguerite McBride School, Ventura, CA; [pers.] Be happy in your mind and soul - all else is irrelevant for life is short.; [a.] Ventura, CA

STADLER, STEVEN P.
[pen.] Steve; [b.] December 3, 1959, Scranton; [p.] Nicholas and Margaret Stadler; [m.] Deborah L. Stadler, February 14, 1992; [ch.] Keith Robert and Jonathan Craig; [ed.] Scranton Technical H.S. 1977, Pennsylvania State University, Grad. in 1991 Mass Communications Major; [occ.] Certified Nurse Aide; [hon.] Editor's Choice for "Astral Projection" in 1989, your `Of Dia-

monds and Rust'; [oth. writ.] Several poems published in American Poetry Anthologies in 1989, the poem entitled 'Astral Projection' in 'Of Diamonds And Rust' in 1989; [pers.] I love the works of Baudelaire, Rimbaud, and of Blake. I am greatly influenced by many horror fiction writers, such as Stephen King and Clive Barker, to name just a few.; [a.] Scranton, PA

STAFFORD, BECKY
[b.] May 10, 1964, Coronado, CA; [p.] Tom and Joan Diaz also step-mother Carol Diaz; [ch.] Michelle Workman; [ed.] Bladensburg High School, Daytoma Beach Comm. College, Anne Atunder Comm. College, Quarter Master School Ft. Lee VA; [occ.] Faro Blanco Marine Resort (Reservationist) prior occupation - Property Management; [memb.] Chamber of Commerce in Annapolis MD; [hon.] Completed Quartermaster School in Ft. Lee Va, 8 yrs in Army RAMC - Sgt., Proper Mgnt. Level 3; [oth. writ.] Title "A Black Rose", "The Love Alphabet", Note: I have written over 200 poems, 30 songs, short stories, quotes; [pers.] "Procrastination" only leads to lack of "Destination"... Today are the tomorrows we thought about yesterday...; [a.] Marathon, FL

STALCUP, JENNIFER
[b.] September 3, 1974, Dallas, TX; [p.] Russell Stalcup and Suzanne Stalcup; [ed.] South Garland High School, Eastfield Community College; [occ.] Retail Sales Manager; [pers.] I always try to write what I know. I am greatly influenced by the people closest to me, and because of this, I not only write for myself, but I also write for them, thank you.; [a.] Garland, TX

STALLMAN, LEEANN
[b.] April 1, 1982, Kankakee, IL; [p.] Richard Stallman, Sue Beemer; [ed.] Current Freshman at Bradley - Bourbonnais Community High School; [memb.] Student Council, French Club, Church Youth Group; [hon.] Academic Achievement Awards at Bourbonnais Upper Grade Center; [pers.] Poetry is to me a reflection of freedom; [a.] Bourbonnais, IL

STANDLEY, SERENA
[b.] June 3, 1985, Walnut Creek; [p.] Patricia and Russell; [ed.] Edna Hill Middle School; [occ.] Student; [hon.] I have had straight A's my whole life!; [oth. writ.] This is my first poem. I am so happy that I'm in this anthology! May be someday I'll write more poems! (I would like really to); [pers.] I thank you all so much for making this possible! I hope that you enjoyed my poem. I have never been in a real book before! Thank you!; [a.] Brentwood, CA

STARKMAN, CELIA D.
[pen.] Celia D. Starkman; [b.] December 15, 1903, New York City; [p.] Louis J. and Flora Levy (Deceased); [m.] Harold B. Starkman (Deceased), August 18, 1927; [ch.] Susan Robins, James Starkman; [ed.] Hunter College 1925, Honor Society 1st Fecepient of Science Scholarship during Jr. year; [occ.] Retired Teacher of Science; [hon.] 1st recipient of Science Scholarship during Junior year at Hunter College in 1924 - sent to Woodshole Biological Center in Woods Hole, MA to study Marine Biology.; [oth. writ.] First time entry for National publication, entry of poem during 1977 3 month cruise of the QEII.; [pers.] Nature and Human relationships inspire me to put down my thoughts on paper.; [a.] New York, NY

STEGALL, GLORIA A.
[pen.] Victory; [b.] June 13, 1943, Detroit, MI; [p.] Luteria and Melvin McConico; [ch.] Terlyn L. Nowell; [oth. writ.] Mood, In the Michigan Chronicle; [pers.] The writings, I have been blessed to share are a gift from a still small voice inside of my heart.; [a.] Detroit, MI

STEINBOCK, DUSTIE
[b.] February 19, 1984, Larimer County, CO; [p.] Carol Steinbock, Bryan Steinbock; [ed.] Currently in 7th grade Jr. High School; [occ.] Student; [memb.] I enjoy riding my horse in rodeos, placing softball at school, going to school, and race car events.; [hon.] I have a little sister named Ashley and a stepsister Lisa and stepbrother Richard. I plan on attending yet school and becoming a large animal veterinarian.; [oth. writ.] I have written other things for school projects. I enjoy writing poetry and short stories.; [pers.] Everyone has the ability to achieve. Achievement starts with believing in yourself. I try to do the best I can in all my life events.; [a.] Fort Collins, CO

STEMPLE, KELLY
[b.] May 15, 1971, Westwood, NJ; [p.] Robert and Christine Stemple; [ed.] Park Ridge High School; [occ.] Warehouse Employee; [a.] Park Ridge, NJ

STENSON, GARY
[b.] June 15, 1966, Bellflower, CA; [p.] Frank and Patricia Stenson; [m.] Lena, May 30, 1991; [ed.] Old Dominion University Norfolk Va.; [occ.] USN; [memb.] Golden Key National Honor Society, World Affairs Council Greater Hampton Roads, Fraternal Order of United States Navy Seals; [pers.] My writings reflect the fact that human kind is only an insignificant part in the perfect system of nature's checks and balances. Yet, we concentrate all our efforts to try and dominate this system rather than harmonize with it. Each day we bring our species closer to the end of its life cycle.; [a.] Virginia Beach, VA

STEPHENS, MICHAEL D.
[b.] June 29, 1948, Canon City, CO; [p.] Judith L. Morgan; [pers.] I've been writing for a very long time. It is the land I live in.; [a.] Bellingham, WA

STERNBACH, IKE
[pen.] Ike Sternbach; [b.] October 31, 1926, New York City, NY; [p.] Harry S. and Sophie Sternbach; [m.] Elizabeth Sternbach, December 21, 1947; [ch.] Richard and Elyse; [ed.] Charles Sumner JHS. School of Industrial Arts H.S. City College Univ.; [occ.] Retired; [memb.] Wellington 'E' Assoc. Tenrus colony Ellenville Seniors, Spring Glen Congregation, Jewish War Veterans; [hon.] Presidential Citation, Asiatic - Pacific Campaign, Philippine Liberation, World War II Victory, Army of occupation with Japan Clasp Good Conduct Medal; [oth. writ.] Several poems published in local newspapers - and a "Tribute to the 32nd infantry division" printed in the U.C.O. Reporter - West Palm Beach, FL; [pers.] Speak your truth quietly and clearly, and listen to others, even the dull and ignorant, they too have their story.; [a.] West Palm Beach, FL

STEVENS, LEONARD
[b.] November 1, 1934, Sussex, England; [p.] John and Beatrice Stevens; [ed.] Bexhill Grammar School, England Sussex, College of Marin CA, USA, Sonoma State University, CA USA, BA Art, BA Theater, MA Psychology; [occ.] Lighting Designer; [memb.] NZA Operatic Society Auckland/New Zealand, various New Zealand and American theater groups, including one year with the American Conservatory Theatre Traing Program; [hon.] Communications Award - Royal Air Force - London, Prof. bronze silver dance medals - ISTD London, Pres. Royal Overseas League - Auckland, New Zealand, three successive, Alpha, Gamma, Sigma Awards, C.O.M. CA USA; [oth. writ.] 'Gudakesha' Warrior of the Heart (101 poems about love and life), 'Dammit I love You' (a book in process), the creative use of daily upsets to improve relationships, uncover unconditional love; [pers.] Working with drug addicts and schizophrenics, I was confronted with a new definition for love. Three years studying with enlightened teachers in America and India, gave me an eastern perspective on the same subject. As the connections between the two become apparent, my writing progress from personal discovery and relationships to socio-political conflicts and their resolutions fueling my work are many 'almost magical' experiences. I feel we all possess unconditional love, and are able to see the world through fresh eyes, but very few of us actually uncover this part of life.; [a.] Greenbrae, CA

STEWART, JACK E.
[b.] May 9, 1919, Seattle, WA; [p.] Mother deceased; [m.] Lila A. Stewart, March 16, 1973; [ch.] 5 prior marriage; [ed.] High school and no formal course - various college 10 hours; [occ.] Retired Coast Guard CDR (1965); [memb.] None kept up, Ex-Propeller Club - Ex. Naval Institute, Ex Nat'l Geographic; [hon.] Various service medal over 28 years; [oth. writ.] None printed about half a hundred poems various lengths (on 5 page bio); [pers.] Never really thought the poems I was writing over the past 25 yrs. were of any merit - they were too easy to write!

STEWART JR., JAMES GORDON
[pen.] J. Stewart Jr.; [b.] December 9, 1956, Camp Lejeune, NC; [p.] J. G. Stewart Sr. and Mary C.; [m.] Divorced; [ch.] James G. III, Jennifer Renee; [ed.] G.E.D., 126 credits toward B.S. and DeVry; [occ.] Disabled (Broke back in 1986); [memb.] St. Michael and all Angels Episcopal Church; [hon.] National Defense Medal (1974 USN) and Dean's List at DeVry; [oth. writ.] A couple in small town paper.; [pers.] My poetic endeavors are generally inspired by portions of my life, both positive and negative.; [a.] Phoenix, AZ

STILWELL, THOMAS J.
[pen.] James Still; [b.] March 16, 1949, Thomasville, NC; [p.] Mary Kathryn Dixon, T. B. Stilwell; [m.] Marlene A. Stilwell, November 8, 1980; [ch.] Katie Lane Stillwell; [ed.] Masters, Public Administration Bachelors, Biology; [occ.] Sales Associate, Furniture Industry (Major Ret./USAF); [memb.] Aldersgate United Methodist Church, TROA (The Retired Officer's Assoc.; [hon.] Three Meritorious Service Medals, Three Air Medals, Citizen Award from Thomasville Senior High School; [oth. writ.] Several poems, none published.; [pers.] Greatly influenced by the works of Thomas Wolf, Rudyard Kipling, Robert Frost, and Henry Wadsworth Longfellow.; [a.] Sumter, SC

STOAKS, JENNIFER ANNE
[pen.] "Jen"; [b.] January 22, 1981, Denver, CO; [p.] Grant Stoaks and Shari Potter; [ed.] I am currently a devoted student attending Desert Mountain High School; [memb.] None yet. I'm young and still discovering my true identity; [hon.] I have won several awards for horseback riding and also for my exceptional grades.; [oth. writ.] I write many poems, mostly about love and heartache, but "Aspen Tree" was a heartfelt and truly inspirational poem to me, and those who have read it.; [pers.] I think of poetry as a "cleansing process" for the soul. You true feelings and personality really come forth through this beautiful experiences.; [a.] Scottsdale, AZ

STONE, JEFFERY
[b.] August 3, 1970, Nelson County, KY; [p.] Richard and Patricia Stone; [m.] Laura Glastetter-Stone, September 29, 1994; [ed.] BS Mass Comm. Murray State Univ., MS Corporate Comm. Lindenwood College; [occ.] Admissions/Financial Aid Advisor, Adjust Faculty; [memb.] Juko-Kai Martial Arts Assn., JLE, Ltd. Media Group; [oth. writ.] Unpublished works from poetry to short story's to film scripts.; [pers.] I give to the world the secret to limitless thought, you need but take up the pen.; [a.] Maysville, KY

STONESTREET, ELMER E.
[b.] January 20, 1937, Cumberland, MD; [p.] Eston and Kathleen Stonestreet; [m.] Mildred Jean Stonestreet, August 19, 1972; [ch.] Richard Alan, Tracy Lynn, Duane Richard, Daniel Warren; [ed.] Shaw High School, Cleveland, OH; [occ.] Sign Production; [oth. writ.] None - only "Warm and Gentle Thoughts" Unpublished - Copyright 1977; [pers.] Introductory thought... Leave Something Behind Forever; [a.] Richmond, VA

STRAND, CINDY
[pen.] Mrs. C. Lee White; [b.] May 12, 1953, Salt Lake City, UT; [p.] Mr. and Mrs. Albert Eric Strand; [m.] Mr. Richard Michael White, October 13, 1973 - Divorced 1979; [ed.] University of Utah, Graduate Bellevue, Community College, Bellevue, Washington; [occ.] Computer Info. Systems; [memb.] International Society of Poets; [hon.] Poet of Merit Award, Presidential Honor Roll, Dean's Honor Roll, Bellevue Community College; [oth. writ.] "One Last Goodbye", "He Strengthens Us To Stand", "If I Were A Tree", "Froggies and Lilly Ponds", "Embrace Of Nite", "Enchanted Love"; [pers.] Poetry and literature enrich the human mind.; [a.] Seattle, WA

STREETS, CAROLYN LOUISE
[pen.] FTP; [b.] March 28, 1974, Yale, New Haven; [p.] Frederick and Annette Streets; [ed.] B. A. English, Ottawa University 1996; [occ.] Church of Christ in Yale Chaplain's Office; [hon.] Awarded Scholarship by the International Studies Association, Studied Shakespeare and Contemporary Theatre, Middlesex University, London, England; [oth. writ.] Millions of poems, but never submitted.

STRONG, DEANNE
[b.] October 9, 1962, Bozeman, MT; [p.] Charles Kraft and Rev. Edith Tieman; [m.] Jeff Strong, July 18, 1987; [ch.] Brandon - 3, Chelsea - 7; [ed.] Bozeman Sr. High, Graduated 5/81 Davenport College, Grand Rapids, MI Bachelors of Business Administration; [occ.] Office Manager; [memb.] Director for Nursery at First Presbyterian church Mentor for Prevent Child Abuse; [oth. writ.] Poems and children's stories (none that have been published); [pers.] I enjoy writing about real-life experiences. My loving husband and precious children are my greatest inspiration for writing.; [a.] Bozeman, MT

STUART, HENRYETTE MAXWELL
[b.] September 15, 1904, Stanton, TN; [p.] William H. and Albertine McMahon Maxwell; [m.] Clifton H. Stuart, May 5, 1927; [ch.] Sara Neal Stuart Venters, William Maxwell Stuart and Louis Phillip Stuart; [ed.] McFerrin School, Martin, TN, Logan College, Russellville, KY, George Peabody College for Teachers, Nashville, TN; [occ.] Homemaker; [memb.] United Methodist Church of Stanton, TN, Stanton Preservation Trust, Stanton Garden and Historical Society; [oth. writ.] Two genealogy books, sections of Haywood County, TN, history book.; [pers.] I have written poetry most of my '92 years of life for personal pleasure and for family and friends.; [a.] Stanton, TN

STUEVE, CHRISTY
[b.] February 22, 1950, Corvallis, OR; [p.] Gordon and Helen Cleveland; [m.] Charles Stueve, March 9, 1968; [ch.] Heather Kessi and Shane Stueve; [ed.] Philomath High School; [occ.] Homemaker; [memb.] Blodgett Community Church; [pers.] I try to show a personal walk with a personal Lord. I'm expressing a deep love towards him and a sincere desire to know him and serve him more. I praise him for his personal involvement in my life as I humbly bow before him.; [a.] Philomath, OR

SULLIVAN, PATRICIA
[b.] October 14, 1943, Marlborough, MA; [p.] Albert Jolie, Flora Jolie; [m.] Richard Sullivan, March 5, 1961; [ch.] Rochelle Ann Graham, Jeffrey Patrick, Eric Christopher; [ed.] Ste. Anne Academy; [occ.] Executive Assistant, Marriott Lodging, Regional Office Woburn, MA; [oth. writ.] This is my first effort.; [pers.] I would like my work to reflect my sincere belief that with faith in a Higher Power, and belief in yourself that you can achieve wonderful things. I have been greatly influenced by my deep faith in God, the ministry of Robert Schuller, as well as the writings of Wayne Dyer and Bernie Seigal; [a.] Marlborough, MA

SULLIVAN, RICHARD
[b.] January 27, 1938, Syracuse, NY; [p.] William and Genevieve; [m.] Gail Davis Sullivan, July 18, 1982; [ch.] Chris and Kyra; [ed.] Syracuse, Univ. B.A. - 1960, Christian Brothers Academy - 1956; [occ.] Retired Elementary School Teacher Soquel Elementary School District, Santa Cruz, CA; [pers.] Poetry speaks to me in the language of the heart.; [a.] Santa Cruz, CA

SUMMERS, PATRICIA J.
[b.] April 12, 1930, Omaha, NE; [p.] Merlin-Alice Broadstone; [m.] Deceased; [ed.] All grade school, all high school - Geriatric Aide both basic and advanced courses; [occ.] In Social Services (Care Giver); [memb.] The Seventh Day Adventist Church; [oth. writ.] "The Old Book", "My Lord"; [pers.] On Nov. 22, '78, my sister knowing she wasn't going to live much longer - asked me to request of the Lord "A Prayer" pertaining to the coming of Thanksgiving and that is what I wrote down in "Thanksgiving Prayer".; [a.] Grand Island, NE

SUPENBECK, HATTIE
[b.] July 11, 1914, St. Louis; [p.] Oliver and Lulu Supenbeck; [ch.] Harry Portwood; [ed.] Elementary, High School, Key Training Service, Caregiver American Heart Assoc.; [occ.] Retired; [memb.] First Christian Church of Florissant; [hon.] Of the Visitor at Catholic Church, St. Macaikys-poem "A Good Gift" published; [oth. writ.] "Remembering," "A Piece of Verse," etc. (none yet published); [pers.] Poetry is a releasement of the soul - the very inner thoughts that are so private. [a.] Northwoods, MO.

SWEARINGEN, CAROL V. B.
[b.] December 16, 1928, Brainerd, MN; [p.] Frank and Lillian Brandt; [m.] William Swearingen, June 30, 1950; [ch.] Richard, John, Lois and Frank; [ed.] Brainerd Mn School System, Illinois Central College Psychology; [occ.] Housewife, Sculpture of heads and masks; [memb.] Gone through the church scene from Lutheran to Bible to Baptist Missionary, National Children's Cancer Society; [hon.] Not silver, not gold but now that I'm old my secret award is my Life in the Lord.; [oth. writ.] "Beginning to End in Clay Sculpture", "The Big Picture", "How to Carve in Soap", unpublished short stories and poems plus a journal of personal events relating to the Lord. Also children's music for Christian Camps.; [pers.] I have spent a life time in the objective study of the inner man, his promised likenesses of Christ, his evaluating influence in my life and his relationship to God, our Father. I have written it all down as the only legacy for my eight granddaughters.; [a.] Washington, IL

SWEENEY, DANIEL MARTIN
[b.] July 17, 1970, Chicago, IL; [ed.] Graduate Morgan Park H.S. 1989, Chicago; [pers.] I grew up around a lot of graveyards so that's something I know about.

SWEENEY, STEPHANIE
[b.] November 9, 1946, Philadelphia, PA; [p.] John Schaefer and Rita Schaefer; [m.] John Sweeney, November 12, 1984; [ch.] Leandra Ashman; [occ.] Administrative Director, Hematology Oncology Associates of San Antonio; [pers.] My awareness to the suffering of the homeless has grown through the years and I desire to make their plight known to all.; [a.] San Antonio, TX

SYTNER, ROCHELLE LYN
[b.] March 30, 1980, Brooklyn, NY; [p.] Barry and Sharon Sytner; [occ.] 10th Grade Student; [hon.] Graduated Elementary School as Valedictorian; [a.] Beverly Hills, CA

SZUMANSKI, MARK
[b.] April 19, 1978, Maywood, IL; [p.] Al and Kathy; [occ.] Student; [oth. writ.] "Beginnings"

TAFEL, DAVID H.
[pen.] "Hamilton"; [b.] January 29, 1971, Pittsburgh, PA; [p.] Ted and Sallie Tafel; [ed.] High School G.E.D., U.S. Navy; [occ.] Carpenter and Writer; [hon.] Received Liberation of Kuwait Medal and other awards.; [oth. writ.] Mainly about day to day life, love, hardships, etc.; [pers.] "There is always something to learn from an ear that listens".; [a.] Fort Myers, FL

TAGLIARINO, TONI
[b.] December 16, 1980, Houston, TX; [p.] Jeri Tagliarino, Sam Tagliarino; [ed.] Pasadena High School, 10th grade; [hon.] President's Education Awards Program 4th and 10th gr., Duke University Talent Search Program 8th gr., Pentathlon Team 8th gr., Friends of the Pasadena Library Poetry Contest 1st place 8th gr., State Recognition for S.A.T.'s 7th gr.; [pers.] Writing is a world which you create. Imagination is the key to open the door.; [a.] Pasadena, TX

TALLMAN, EVELYN
[b.] November 13, 1922, South Westerlo, NY; [p.] Mrs. Hazel F. Mabie; [m.] Deceased, January 23, 1940; [ch.] One; [ed.] Greenville Central High School, National Baking School, Chicago, Illinois; [occ.] Retired, writes poetry; [memb.] Social Service with Albany Co., Social Security Benefits; [oth. writ.] World of Poetry, Sacramento, California

TAMAS, SUSAN JULIANNA
[b.] November 6, 1975, New Jersey; [p.] Maria and Karoly Tamas; [ed.] San Marino High Brooks College; [occ.] Legal Secretary; [a.] Pasadena, CA

TAPIA, JOHN M.
[b.] May 21, 1948, Long Beach; [p.] Felix S. Tapia, Mary Montizor; [m.] Carina Amante Tapia, November 7, 1987; [ed.] A graduate Art (February 3, 1967) major at Banning High School in Wilmington, California. A graduate of Culinary Arts Cooks Apprentice Program Kapiolani College Honolulu, Hawaii (May 8, 1974);

[occ.] Chef; [memb.] I remember when I was a little kid and frighten I ask God help me and the golden being appears late.; [hon.] I was rated Number One Chef August 12, 1988 by the Long Beach Press-Telegram newspaper Long Beach California; [pers.] I have been greatly influenced by a golden being of light that eminent golden rings of light. I have seen this vision since I was a baby, but did not know the golden being name until manhood.; [a.] Menifee, CA

TAYLOR, ETHEL HUFFMAN
[pen.] Sweetie; [b.] July 22, 1951, Montgomery, AL; [p.] B. J. and Odessa Huffman; [ch.] Jonathan Wayne; [occ.] Retired Air Force, Licensed and Ordained Evangelist; [hon.] Golden Poet Award Highest honor, Black History Poet Award, Honor for Spiritual Advisor of The "Singing Sons of God" (a Gospel group group) Several "Merit of Awards"; [oth. writ.] Several poems published in different books. Written songs and had music order for them.; [pers.] My main goal is to reach souls and lead them to Christ through my poems. I have been inspired by the Holy Spirit as I strive to have a book of poetry published in the very near future.; [a.] Montgomery, AL

TAYLOR, LURA D.
[b.] February 15, 1961, Redding, CA; [p.] Lynn M., Bruce S. English; [m.] Gregory Lee Taylor, November 20, 1993; [ch.] Sabrina Lynn, Marissa Tee, Joliet, Buckeye, Rother, Nova, Joliet, Art, Choir; [ed.] (Pops, Madriqas) English and Psychology (it wasn't assigned I just sat in); [occ.] Mom, wife, store clerk and generally happy always; [memb.] ("68") Old's 442 Club a few football rools (woman against men that think I didn't know the game); [hon.] A second place singing contest. Life with all its craftiness.; [oth. writ.] Finished, Prison, Open into One, In Our Moments, A Tear, Human Race, Endless, Sweet Princess, Laugh with the Moon, Talk to Yourself...; [pers.] Learn from all you touch and cherish, the gift we can all become to a higher tomorrow, maybe if we return it will be a better world! Love to Mrs. Hudleston, Mr. Markham, Mr. Hollahan, Mr. Capes, (es. Gramy, Mom) extras, Skeeter Dan and Doug - my husband most of all.

TAYLOR, MARANDA
[b.] October 18, 1980, Duluth, GA; [p.] Dwight and Vickie Taylor; [a.] Sugar Hill, GA

TAYLOR, TAMARA
[b.] June 18, 1968, Bethesda, MD; [p.] Judith Demont; [ch.] Jennifer Taylor; [ed.] Junior at the University of Md (currently) graduated in 1989 (with honors) from computer learning center; [occ.] Substitute Teacher at Kentlands Children Center; [hon.] Honors Graduated from Computer Learning Center (1989); [pers.] The objective of my poetry is to envoke emotion in readers who have had experiences and situations similar to my own. If they begin a healing, then I have achieved my purpose; [a.] Gaithersburg, MD

TAYLOR, THOMAS E.
[pen.] Poe or Chief; [b.] April 9, 1975, Montgomery, AL; [p.] Raymond and Lynda Taylor; [ed.] Greenville Christian School, Charles Henderson High, Troy State University; [occ.] Alabama Air National Guard; [memb.] 1st Presbyterian Church of Troy, Beta Club, National Honor Society; [hon.] All "A" average during high school, honor graduate of air force tech. school.; [oth. writ.] Several other poems never published.; [pers.] I strive to use my gifts according to God's perfect design. I also want to thank Kim Fuller for showing me the article. Stay cool and God bless!; [a.] Troy, AL

TEMORES, GEORGE
[pen.] George Temores; [b.] April 19, 1970, Merced, CA; [p.] Isidro and Benita Temores; [m.] Kerri Lynn Temores, April 6, 1996; [pers.] I dedicate this poem to my wife Kerri. For without her encouragement and belief in me, my poems would not be possible.; [a.] Casa Grande, AR

TEMORES, GEORGE
[pen.] George Temores; [b.] April 19, 1970, Merced, CA; [p.] Ysidro and Benita Temores; [m.] Kerri Lynn Temores, April 6, 1996; [pers.] Strive to know God Jehovah and He will make Himself known to you.; [a.] Casa Grande, AZ

THOMAS, ALTA
[pers.] I live at the base of The Olympic Mountain on The Olympic Peninsula. My greatest joys are: Family, high country, and the choice of a poem's acceptance every now and then.; [a.] Sequim, WA

THOMAS, AUDREY
[pen.] Audra Teena Thomas; [b.] August 1, 1949, Baltimore, MD; [p.] John Smith and Mamie Smith; [ed.] Paul Lawrence Dunbar High Sch., Ohio State University, U.S. Army Reserves; [occ.] Entertainer and Sole Proprietor of Audio - Visuals tapes and poetry; [memb.] The columbus challengers, fraternity order of police, believers in Christ Ministry Building Fund, The Department of Mental Health; [hon.] "Tigers" of McCollough club, U.S. Arm's reserves, runners - up the top 100 "E" Class the highest financial contribution in (HIV. OP) Convocation Spurt Track Teams - Relate Broad Jump; [oth. writ.] One poem published in Local Newspaper, articles for the Le Respite Home, Inc. up coming events, one poems published in the McCollough Magazine 1 united house of prayer for all purple.; [pers.] I strive to reflect, how to make your child a star, to bring a spark of light in the hearts of children and adults and give them hope for tomorrow and joy for today thur my spiritual songs and poems I have been greatly influenced.; [a.] Columbus, OH

THOMAS, FRANCES M.
[pen.] Frances M. Thomas; [b.] February 12, 1923, Indiana, PA; [p.] John S. and Anna E. Moore; [m.] Marshall E. Thomas, May 5, 1951; [ch.] Rodney, Randy, Curtis J.; [ed.] Indiana High School; [occ.] Retired; [memb.] Trinity United Methodist, UCT #598, AARP #2581, Happy Home Makers; [pers.] Poetry lover and admirer of Helen Steiner Rice.; [a.] Indiana, PA

THOMPSON, JENNY
[pen.] Jen-e, Nicole; [b.] June 16, 1980, Galveston; [p.] Bruce and Lupe Thompson; [ed.] Sweeny High School; [memb.] Art Club, HOSA, Sweeny Scholar, Honor Ball; [hon.] Honor Roll; [oth. writ.] A poem published in the book, anthology of poetry by young Americans.; [pers.] Even though you go through many struggles in life, your dreams can still come true!; [a.] Brazoria, TX

THOMPSON, KAREN
[b.] February 4, 1947, Rochester, NY; [p.] Rob and Dorothy Clark; [ch.] Four Tammy, Gene, Michael and Paul; [ed.] AA in Psychology, Miami-Dade Community College; [pers.] I recently have become spiritually aware of myself and my surroundings and began my thoughts on paper. Poetry is a way to express one's emotions freely - without judgment.; [a.] Gallatin, TN

THOMPSON, MICHELLE
[pen.] Michelle Rene; [b.] May 8, 1961, Covina, CA; [p.] Jean Boiselle and Sharron Allen; [m.] Charles Thompson, October 28, 1978; [ch.] Charles Jr., Christopher Corey and Chase; [ed.] High School Graduate, Carson High School; [occ.] Homemaker; [memb.] Volunteer year round for the Central Lyon County Youth Coalition; [oth. writ.] Published one poem in High School book "Verbatum", I have written about 100 poems since I began writing at 13 yrs. old; [pers.] I wake up in the middle of the night with two or three sentences in my head and I have to get up and start writing.; [a.] Dayton, NY

THOMPSON, SCOTT
[b.] November 6, 1983, Portland, ME; [p.] James and Sylvia Thompson; [ed.] Is now attending Noble Junior High School Berwick, Maine; [memb.] Boy Scouts; [hon.] Presidents Award for Educational Excellence High Honors all 4 terms 5 of 6th grade, 1995 Spelling Bee Runner-up; [oth. writ.] An entry in Ralph Fletchers how to make a writer's notebook to be published this fall.; [pers.] My goals in writing are to publish one of my own stories and to keep writing, writing writing.; [a.] North Berwick, ME

THRESS, CHARITY
[b.] September 6, 1982, Medina Hospital, Medina, OH; [p.] Terry and Sally Thress; [ed.] Cloverleaf Jr. High School 8th grader; [occ.] Student, Band Member; [a.] Lodi, OH

THURSTON, MARIETTA E.
[b.] July 8, 1942, Washington, DC

TILLER, NADINE
[b.] October 22, 1951, Trenton, NJ; [m.] James Tiller; [ch.] Jonathan, Tiffany; [occ.] Nurse - Helen Field Hosp. Trenton, NJ; [memb.] Friends of Friends Social Club, Macederian Baptist Church; [oth. writ.] Many other poems in my own personal collection.

TINCHER, KATIE
[b.] August 25, 1981, MV; [p.] Randy and Trina Tincher; [ed.] El Toro High School; [hon.] Many Soccer Awards 4.0 GPA in 8th grade, Freshman Rep, for Pepclub, V.I.P. Club, and PAL.; [pers.] Always have a smile on your face, which will brighten up your day.; [a.] Lake Forest, CA

TINKER, JAMIE C.
[b.] October 14, 1968, Sacramento, CA; [p.] James Tinker, Martha Tinker; [ed.] California State University, Sacramento BA in Psychology, Chapman University MA in Special Education; [occ.] Language Arts, Social Studies, Drama and Choir Teacher, Huachuca City School, AZ; [hon.] Scabbard and Blade Honor Society; [pers.] With my poetry, as with my teaching, I feel that I am an artist - I paint pictures with words and my canvas is the human mind.; [a.] Sierra Vista, AZ

TITUS, HELEN
[pen.] Helen Titus; [b.] October 20, 1921, Candor, NY; [p.] John and Tekla Lubinec; [m.] Widow, May 29, 1939 and November 9, 1951; [ch.] Two daughters (each marriage); [ed.] High School Grad and Private Drama School in New York City; [occ.] Retired Nurse's Aid Self-Employed Writer; [memb.] Screen actor's Guild American Federation or Radio Artists, American Federation of Radio and Television Artists during the 1940's; [oth. writ.] Epic poems written for and sent to Pres. John F. Kennedy, never published same nor did I give the late pres. to publish same without my permission proverbs written by me and sent to the above; [a.] Torrance, CA

TODD, GEORGE
[b.] March 5, 1963, Manchester, TN; [p.] Donald and Brenda Todd; [ch.] Hailies Halies (Foster Child); [ed.] GED, Paralegal, Computer Operations Specialist; [occ.] Computer Programmer; [memb.] Alcoholics Anonymous, Global Church of God; [oth. writ.] A Child's World; [pers.] If the mind can conceive it and the heart can believe it you can achieve it.; [a.] Manchester, TN

TODD, PEGGY DAUZAT
[pen.] Sunshine; [b.] November 19, 1958, New Orleans, LA; [p.] Percy and Theresa Dauzat; [ch.] Jay and Johnathan; [ed.] College background in writing and legal work.; [oth. writ.] Children's short stories; [pers.] It has taken years for such an accomplishment, but it could have never existed without the love and support of all of my family. I hope that each person follows their dreams, as well as what lies in their hearts and in their lives.

TOLLISON, BOBBY J.
[b.] March 3, 1956, Fountain Inn, SC; [p.] James Q. and Frances M. Tollison; [ed.] 12th (GED); [occ.] Top Helper, G.M. Mech.; [memb.] Aaron Tippin Fan Club; [hon.] Honorable Discharge (U.S. Army) 1974-1977; [oth. writ.] 7 songs with a publishing company in Nashville; [a.] Greenville, SC

TOLLIVER, GERALDINE
[pen.] Gerry Saunders Tolliver; [b.] March 25, 1948, Crown City, OH; [p.] James B. Saunders; [m.] Margie Sturgeon Saunders, July 21, 1967; [ch.] Shelly and Jennifer Tolliver; [ed.] Graduated from Hannan High School, Frazier's Bottom, WV; [occ.] Housewife; [oth. writ.] I have written other poems, but have never had any published.; [pers.] I feel that in writing poetry, it releases one's enter beauty, no matter what style of poetry.; [a.] Ashton, WV

TOLSON, FRANCES E.
[b.] September 15, 1913, Licking Co., OH; [p.] H. H. and Mary Hoover; [m.] Melvin L. Tolson (Deceased January 18, 1994), November 8, 1953; [ch.] 1 stepdaughter deceased, 4 grandchildren, 4 great grandchildren; [ed.] Newark High School, Bachelor's - Ohio State Un., Master's Art Education and Kent State Un.; [occ.] Retired Art, Teacher; [memb.] State Retired Teachers, Carroll County Retired Teachers, Carroll County Commission for the Advancement of the Arts; [hon.] Who's Who in American Education, Who's Who in the Arts (1971-1972); [oth. writ.] Christian Life Letters, The Lookout, Free Press Standard, World of Poetry, Christian Evangelist; [pers.] I try to express my feelings so the readers get a picture and a feeling from them.; [a.] Carrollton, OH

TORRELLAS, REBECCA E.
[b.] April 29, 1976, Ponce, PR; [p.] Hernan and Marianela Torrellas; [ed.] St. Joseph High School Texas A and M University; [occ.] Junior in College; [memb.] Treasurer of Hispanic Journalists Association.

TORRES, ADELE M.
[pen.] Adele; [b.] April 28, 1975, Austin, TX; [p.] Frank and Sylvia Torres; [ed.] High School Graduate Attending College; [occ.] Cashier at parents restaurant; [hon.] UIL one act play "Best Actress" several awards from poetry interpretation (U.I.L.), and several art awards; [oth. writ.] Have collection of poetry ranging from topics on love to personal hardships.; [pers.] Expression in any form has meaning to individuals who internalize. Acceptance towards the expression is true human nature.; [a.] Alice, TX

TORRES, LUCILLE M.
[pen.] Lucille M. Torres; [b.] February 17, 1947, Espanola, NM; [p.] Julian R. Torres; [ch.] Robert, Lucille and Delilah; [occ.] Musician; [oth. writ.] Compose music I am joy walk with my dog and spending time with my two grand daughters.; [pers.] I enjoy playing guitar, and a singing. I compose most of my songs and writing poems.; [a.] Albuquerque, NM

TORSKE, LOWELL G.
[b.] September 9, 1953, Redlake Falls, MN; [m.] X'd; [ch.] Shaun W. Torske; [ed.] R.L. Turner High, Brookhaven Jr. College, Richland Jr. College; [occ.] Mfg. Supervisor; [memb.] American Motorcycle Assoc., Texas Motorcycle Roadriders Assoc.; [pers.] We are all artists searching for that medium which best expresses our spiritual self.; [a.] Dallas, TX

TRAN, ANDREW
[pen.] Winterglass, Alan; [b.] January 1, 1970, South Vietnam; [p.] Richard and Lauraine Tran; [ed.] University of San Diego, Western State University of Law; [occ.] Law Student at Western State University of Law; [memb.] Asian Club Officer, Red-Cross, Literary Corp, LAVAS; [hon.] Dean's List, President List, Outstanding Community Service Recognition; [oth. writ.] Reader's digest, local newspapers, and personal collections of poems and short stories.; [pers.] Words are the windows through my soul.; [a.] Anaheim, CA

TRAVIS, DEBRA J.
[pen.] Debrat; [b.] January 1, 1957, Saint Lucie, CO; [ch.] Two; [occ.] City of Fort Pierce Housing Authority Resident Services Aide (2 years); [memb.] Fort Pierce Housing Authority Resident Council Inc.'s 1st Vice President; [pers.] I began writing poetry in 1995 and I had no idea that I would ever enter any into a contest. Thank you for giving me the incentive to with my initial ideas.; [a.] Fort Pierce, FL

TRAYLOR, AMANDA
[b.] March 2, 1983, Hondo, TX; [p.] Cynthia and Dennis Traylor; [ed.] Student; [pers.] Thank you, God.; [a.] Pearsall, TX

TREAT, LORINDA ANN
[b.] March 14, 1969, Tulsa; [p.] William J. Walker and Linda and Henry Thompson; [m.] Claude S. Treat, March 20, 1987; [ch.] Maranda Ann and Katy Lorraine; [ed.] East Central High School, Barbizon Modeling School; [occ.] Mother and Housewife; [memb.] Berryhill Southern Baptist Church; [pers.] I have my parents to thank for my Christian up bringing and encouraging me in everything I've done. I thank God for my gift of writing.; [a.] Sand Springs, OK

TREMAYNE, ASHLEE MICHELLE
[b.] February 21, 1986, Santa Rosa, CA; [p.] Joseph and Allene Tremayne; [occ.] Student; [memb.] Santa Rosa Soccer League; [hon.] Student of the Month, perfect attendance for 1 year, skipped 4th grade to 5th grade; [pers.] My Uncle Albert Vierra inspired my writing as he has written songs.; [a.] Santa Rosa, CA

TROCHE, AMANDA
[pen.] Mandy; [b.] September 19, 1980, Georgia; [p.] Gail and Tony Troche; [ed.] Cimarron Memorial High; [occ.] Student; [memb.] Future Homemakers of America for 2 years; [hon.] Honor Roll in School; [oth. writ.] This is the first poem of mine that has been published. All of my other poems have been kept in a notebook.; [pers.] In my poems I try to say the words that people would say if their hearts spoke and not their mouths.; [a.] Las Vegas, NV

TROTTER, MELODY
[b.] May 10, 1965, Marion, IN; [p.] Vera Fallis; [m.] Robert E. Trotter; [ch.] Dawn Spencer, Jeremy Spencer; [ed.] G.E.D.; [oth. writ.] Influences: Ozzy Osbourne, Patsy Cline; [pers.] I am a person with multiple personality Disorder, and would like people to know that it is possible for MPD's to live normal lives.; [a.] Broken Bow, OK

TROUTMAN, ANDREA
[pen.] "Ullrich"; [b.] September 28, 1964, Gerolzhofen, Germany; [p.] Christa Marie Ullrich, Robert and Elizabeth Troutman; [ed.] Payson High School, North Seattle Community College; [occ.] School Bus Driver, Seattle WA, Counselor - Fircrest School; [memb.] Wheel, NAACP, Center for Missing and Exploited Children, Domestic Abuse Womens Network, Angeline's Day Center for Women; [oth. writ.] Several other poems, none of them published, currently working on an autobiography, and have also written fantasy short stories.; [pers.] I write realities of life, love, freedom, suffrage, violence, torment, sacrifices, happiness, and peace. I strive to be a loving free spirit, for myself, my world, my brothers and sisters. Togetherness in a nation of diversity.; [a.] Seattle, WA

TROUTTE, JENNIFER
[b.] February 28, 1983, North Little Rock, AR; [p.] Phillip and Rachel Troutte; [ed.] 8th Grade; [occ.] Student; [hon.] Outstanding Artist Award, Band Scholarship, most Improved Musician, I have received several trophies in softball also. Some of my poems have been printed in the local paper the Benton Courier.; [oth. writ.] "The Sound Of Silence", "The Purple Flowers", "I Walked Upon A Dream", "The Wolf's Hunt", "The Wolf's - "Hibernation".; [pers.] When others can feel your words as well as hear and see them, you know you are truly gifted.; [a.] Benton, AR

TRUE, BETSIE LYNN
[pen.] Betsie; [b.] June 5, 1971, Maryland; [p.] Deloras True, Steven True; [ch.] Charity True, Kayla True; [ed.] High school diploma, Certificate of Arbor, cooking school, in addition passed Children's Literature Test; [hon.] "Most Creative Story" written for my line of work Eastern Communications Incorporation.; [oth. writ.] Submitted story "My Favorite Season" to Children's Literature Institute of Connecticut.; [pers.] I would like to thank my Mom, Deloras, for being my biggest inspiration. Mom, I'm picking up where you left off. I love you!; [a.] Baltimore, MD

TUCKER, JO
[pen.] J. D. Stoddard; [b.] September 28, 1941, Dallas, TX; [p.] Joseph and Robbye Doucet; [ch.] Timothy K., Jesse A., Cody E.; [ed.] University of Texas at Arlington; [occ.] Admin-Assistant, Genesis Center, Manchester, CT; [memb.] AARP, WWF; [hon.] Ordained Preacher; [oth. writ.] Several poems published, have written many songs and stories.; [a.] Manchester, CT

TULL, TAMARA SUZANNE
[pen.] Tamara Tull; [b.] December 9, 1970, Los Alamos, CA; [p.] Marcia, Roy Christie; [ed.] AA Child Ed. currently working on masters degree.; [occ.] Student CSUN; [memb.] Hillel at CSUN; [hon.] Prestige award at Hillel, honors at AVC; [pers.] I try to make my poetry moving to all to read. If I strick an emotional cord then I've done my job.; [a.] Lancaster, CA

TURLEY, THOMAS
[b.] November 26, 1952, New Haven, CT; [p.] Joseph Turley, Dorothy Turley; [m.] Sandra Turley, September 2, 1975; [ch.] Lacey Lynn, Shane; [ed.] Maloney High School, Meriden, CT, graduated 1971; [occ.] Self-employed, Retired from US Army October 1995; [memb.] Assembly of God Church, Meriden, CT; [oth. writ.] Songs: The Execution, Give Me The Words; [pers.] My goal in life is to continually prove that my God is a God of the impossible. I am living proof.; [a.] Springfield, MO

TURNER, BROOKE
[b.] April 6, 1980, Minneapolis, MN; [p.] Rex and Sharon Turner; [ed.] Durango High School (11th); [occ.] Student; [memb.] "Nat'l Thespian Society"; [hon.] "Who's Who '96", "Honor Roll"; [pers.] "I thank God daily for the friendships I am able to share with the people that I truly love"; [a.] Durango, CO

TURNER, CAROL
[pen.] Carol Turner; [b.] May 10, 1943, Cincinnati, OH; [p.] James and Margaret Henninger; [m.] Timothy M. Turner, June 17, 1982; [ch.] Cynthia, Bryce, Bryan and Brady; [ed.] Withrow High; [occ.] Secretary, Defense Investigative Service, Alex., VA; [oth. writ.] I write poems for fellow employees who are either retiring or changing place of employment. Also a new poem at Christmas for my family; [pers.] I find poetry as a way to express my inner feelings.

TURNER, CRYSTAL LYNN
[b.] December 3, 1978, Marion, OH; [p.] Wayne E. Turner Sr., Ellen M. Turner; [ed.] Senior in High School. Attending Tri River Voc. School will graduate in June 1997 from Harding High Mrn. Ohio; [occ.] Food Service Micheal's Rest; [memb.] DCHO Tri Rivers; [pers.] I just write poems from my broken heart. Writing poems help heal the hurt, you feel in side after breaking up with boyfriends; [a.] Marion, OH

TUTUNGIAN, MICHELLE
[b.] March 7, 1982, Milford, MA; [p.] John and Donna Tutungian; [ed.] Freshman at Bishop Feehan High School; [occ.] Student; [memb.] Franklin Dance Company American Heart Association St. Mary's Youth Service Corps; [pers.] I thank my mom and dad for urging me to enter this contest. I enjoy writing about real life issues such as racism, the topic of my poems, I hope by the age of 16 I will have my own book.; [a.] Franklin, MA

TYLER, LINDA MARIE
[b.] June 20, 1960, New Orleans; [p.] Herman and Julia Tyler; [ed.] Academy of the Holy Angels and meadows Draughton Business College; [occ.] Self-employed Accountant; [pers.] I am currently embarking on a career as a children's story writer.; [a.] New Orleans, LA

TYSON, ANITA
[b.] October 17, 1958, Kinston, NC; [p.] Eleazar Tyson Sr., and Martha Tyson; [m.] Peter D. St. Louis, October 3, 1987; [ch.] LaToya N. S. Tyson McCoy and Willie L. B. Tyson McCoy; [occ.] Owner of "The Honey Bunches Inn for Tots" Home Day Care; [oth. writ.] "Missing You", "Why Me", "The Wind", "Romance", Intimacies", "Caring", "The Heart", "Forever You, Forever Me", "Love (Te Amo)", "Feelings", and last but now least my favorite "Butterflies/Variety (Spice of Life)".; [pers.] I have never been published before and if I am this time I will be greatly honored. Thanks for the opportunity. Raquane - this one's for you.; [a.] Kinston, NC

TYSON, HATTIE M.
[pen.] Hat Tyson; [b.] March 13, 1958, Robersonville, NC; [p.] Arthur Cromwell Jr., Hattie P. Cromwell; [m.] Stacey Tyler (Fiance), February 14, 1997 (Engaged); [ch.] Tia Camille; [ed.] Roanoke High, NC Central University; [occ.] Minister, Oasis Ministries, Durham, NC; [memb.] Oasis Christian Center, BMI, Small Business Association; [hon.] French Award; [oth. writ.] "Love Song For Matt" Hill Top Records, Hollywood, CA; [pers.] You must take responsibility for your own destiny, trust God, believe in yourself and never give up.; [a.] Durham, NC

UHOUSE JR., DAVID C.
[b.] June 11, 1965, Elmira, NY; [p.] David C. Uhouse Sr., Charlotte Ann Otten Uhouse; [m.] Mary Ann Uhouse, June 28, 1995; [pers.] Imagination belongs to everyone, although to some it can be forgotten or misplaced over time, it only takes a moment of tranquility to reclaim.; [a.] Le Raysville, PA

UNCHESTER, SALLY
[b.] April 14, 1980, JFK Hospital; [p.] John and Dorothy Unchester; [occ.] High School Student; [memb.] Sunday Nite Live - a youth group in New Providence, NJ at the Presbyterian Church known as SNL in my mem.; [pers.] I would like to thank my creative writing teacher Mr. Shall Cross and my close friend Brooke Reilly for influencing me to write this poem.; [a.] Mountainside, NJ

USHER, CAROLE LEE
[b.] March 20, 1965, Monticello, GA; [p.] Charile and Nellie Hunter; [m.] Robin Usher, May 28, 1988; [ch.] Riva Shantell Usher, Robin De Nelson Usher; [ed.] Jackson High School graduate 1983, Certified Nursing Assistant at a nursing home. Who's Who Among High School Students; [occ.] Certified Nursing Assistant at a nursing home; [memb.] PTA at children's school; [hon.] Most outstanding CNA at nursing home in '95. Perfect attendance certificates from job.; [oth. writ.] I have a number of things that I hope will someday be discovered; [pers.] When you think your family and friends are against you. You should pull the strength deep from within your soul and remember that God is with you always.; [a.] Griffin, GA

VALDES, ARLENE E.
[b.] January 10, 1933, Blanding, UT; [p.] Montez Rowley Black, David Potten Black; [m.] Divorced; [ch.] David, DeAnn, LeNan; [ed.] BS Psychology, Social Work, Brigham Young University; [occ.] Retired; [memb.] Church of Jesus Christ of Latter-day Saints; [hon.] Phi Kapa Phi; [oth. writ.] Some poetry for personal enjoyment and for use in teaching Sunday School. Some Reader's Theatres.; [pers.] The best investment you can make is to carefully maintain what you have. And in the case of education, to always work at increasing what you have.; [a.] Murray, UT

VALLE, LEDYS JULIA
[b.] April 19, 1973, Weehawken, NJ; [p.] Pedro and Carmen Valle; [ed.] Currently attending Howard University College of Medicine; [memb.] Phi Eta Sigma Freshman National Honor Society, Golden Key National Honor Society; [hon.] All-American Scholar Award, National Collegiate Education Award, Pennsylvania State Conference Scholar Athlete Award, Dean's List; [a.] Abingdon, MD

VARNELL, CHRISTY JEANETTE
[b.] February 11, 1981, Arkansas; [p.] Carla Varnell and Jerry Varnell; [a.] Stafford, VA

VERMETTE, DEBBIE
[b.] June 14, 1981, Dover-Fox Croft; [p.] Wendy Vermette; [ed.] Eward Little High School; [occ.] Babysitting; [memb.] Air Force Jr. ROTC; [pers.] No matter what your troubles are, always look to the future and keep your head held high.; [a.] Auburn, ME

VERRILL, MRS. CHARLES
[b.] April 7, 1932, Nashua, NH; [p.] Mr. and Mrs. Wilber Anderson; [m.] Charles H. Verrill, January 9, 1959; [ch.] Charles E. Verrill, Todd H. Verrill, Scott A. Verrill; [ed.] Wetherbee Elementary, Essex High School Lawrence General Hospital, Interior Designers Guild; [occ.] Interior Designer; [memb.] California Council For Interior Design Certification; [hon.] High School Valedictorian, Bauer Award (high school), English Award (high school); [oth. writ.] Poems for family and friends only.; [pers.] My poems have been an effort to bring a little laughter or comfort to friends, to help relieve the stress in todays world.

VIANDS, ROSEMARY K.
[pen.] Scorpian; [b.] October 26, 1959, N. Towanda, PA; [p.] Russell E. Morrison Sr., Wanda; [m.] David F. Viands Jr., February 28, 1992; [ch.] Ginger B. Pratt; [ed.] I have a G.E.D. Diploma from Marywood College, Scranlon, PA; [pers.] I would like to dedicated this poem to my father who passed away July 20, 1996. And to my mother Wanda Morrison, Russell Jr. Pam, Mike, David F. Viands Jr., and my 16 yrs old daughter Ginger.; [a.] Scranton, PA

VIERRA, N. LYDIA
[pen.] N. Lydia Bueso, N. Lydia DeVierra; [b.] August 20, 1966, Carmel, NY; [p.] Anthony Perez and Norma Bueso; [m.] Dwayne Vierra, December 31, 1992; [ed.] Escuela Las Morochas (Venezuela), Clear Lake High (Houston, TX), Alvin Community College (Alvin, TX): A.A. Television Comm.; [occ.] Flight Attendant, United Airlines; [memb.] Prior Employment/Internships, Kriv-TV, Ch. 26, Fox News, (Houston, TX), KSSR-Radio, 98 Rock, Promo (Houston, TX), KACC-Radio, 91 FM, Newscaster, Writer (Alvin, TX), Model/Actress ADR Agency (Honolulu, HI); [hon.] Finalist in several art logo contests, O.J. Simpson Collage ("General Public's Revenge") featured in "Folio 94" August 96 issue (P.S. no comp. used); [oth. writ.] There's more where this came from — unpublished!; [pers.] Inspired to draw, paint, write by the ways of the world. Influenced by MTV (alter. music), poets (Emily Dickinson and Bronte), Artists (pop, contempo.), and most importantly our Bible. Traditionalist, Against "Computer-created" Artwork! Pro Paper, Pencil and Paintbrush!; [a.] Honolulu, HI

VINCENT, MICHIAL D.
[pen.] Michial D. Vincent; [b.] July 23, 1953, Mayfield, KY; [p.] Milford G. and Gussie B. Vincent; [ch.] Ivy Michial Vincent; [ed.] Grade School-Carr Elementary, High School-Fulton City H.S., College-University of TN at Martin; [occ.] Plant Mgr. Town Talks Golf Headwear, Inc.; [memb.] Am. Lung Assoc., Am. Hart Assoc., Buechel United Methodist Church (Past) Twin City Youth V.P., sustaining Member Boy Scouts of AM.; [hon.] Personal-Highly over-rated, misleading, Deceiving, popularity, family influenced.; [oth. writ.] Time Capped Closed, short story influenced by personal life.; [pers.] Late bloomers do blossom. Ridicule only offends thy spokesman. Believe in God, honor they family, cher-

ish true friendship, work hard, play hard, and you will have accomplished.; [a.] Lou, KY

VISCIA, BREE
[b.] October 16, 1987, Napa, CA; [m.] Kelley and Steve Viscia; [ed.] 4th grade; [occ.] Student; [memb.] Special Friends Wheel Chair Club at Vichy Elementary; [hon.] Special Friends Wheel Chair; [pers.] While riding my bike one day, ideas seemed to fill my mind, so I jumped off my bike and began to write my first poem.; [a.] Napa, CA

VOGELSANG, RUTH A.
[pen.] Ruth A. Vogelsang; [b.] September 24, 1938, Miami, FL; [p.] James and Florence H. McRae; [m.] Richard O. Vogelsang, December 27, 1972; [ch.] 2 daughters, 1 step-daughter, 2 step-sons; [ed.] 12th grade, graduated from Miami Senior High School; [occ.] Housewife; [memb.] North Anderson Baptist Church; [oth. writ.] I've had a few short articles, published in an Opalocka, FL. Police newspaper before we moved to South Carolina.; [pers.] Moved from Florida in 1984 to South Carolina. I have been writing poems for my own pleasure since I was a teenager. This is the first time I've had any of my poems published; [a.] Anderson, SC

VONDENKAMP, DANIEL
[b.] March 10, 1972, Rock Springs, WY; [p.] Arnold and JoAnn Vondenkamp; [m.] Tonya M. Vondenkamp, July 1, 1995; [ch.] Christian and MyKael Vondenkamp; [ed.] Rock Springs High School; [occ.] Drive/Warehouseman; [oth. writ.] This is my first published work; [a.] Rock Springs, WY

VORHEES, PAMELA K.
[b.] August 20, 1953, Joplin, MO; [ch.] Michele, Johnny, Scotty; [ed.] Bachelor of Science in Ed., Masters of Science in Psychology; [occ.] Special Education Teacher; [pers.] Dealing with problems and working through hurtful memories is the only way to truly put them behind you and have a better quality of life. Hopefully I've passed this knowledge onto my children.; [a.] Joplin, MO

VORIES, JOSHUA D.
[b.] March 8, 1984, Columbia, MO; [p.] Kim and Dawn Vories; [ed.] 6th grade Christian Liberty Academy; [hon.] 1st place Edwardsville Christmas Art Contest, 1st place R and D Forum for Song "I'm an Irishman" Johnson Cry, KS; [pers.] I wanted to share my faith in Jesus Christ and inspire people to care for others who are hurting.; [a.] Edwardsville, IL

WALL, DEBBIE LYNN EATON
[b.] November 12, 1961, Forsyth County; [p.] Herbert Junior Eaton, Harriet Sereptsia Hartman Eaton; [m.] Bruce Allen Wall, September 11, 1993; [ed.] 1-12, plus 4 years of college, 1 year Bob Jones University, 3 years Forsyth Technical Community College; [occ.] Child Care Provider, Wedding Coordinator and Silk Floral Wedding Arrangements; [memb.] Anthropology Museum, Shakespeare Festival Theatre, Gospel Light Baptist Church, National Time Gardening Club, American Heart Association, American Diabetics Association; [hon.] Rep Club Award at school, Volunteer Ladies Auxiliary at Talley's Crossing Fire Department, Dean's List; [oth. writ.] Mother, Father, my Husband, Life, Friends, Church; [pers.] I have always loved and appreciated poetry. It is a big part of my life and my feelings. I have been blessed by the writing from Fanny Crosby and Helen Steiner Rice. I have been greatly blessed by their writing as well as others.; [a.] Kernersville, NC

WALL, KIMBERLY ELAINE
[b.] June 9, 1981, El Paso, TX; [p.] Jack Edward Wall and Barbara Elaine Wall; [ed.] Socorro High School; [occ.] High School Student; [memb.] Health occupations Students America, Socorro High Top Shelf Choir, Socorro High Speech and Debate Team; [oth. writ.] Two poems published in Socorro Independent School District Literary Anthology (1995-1996) 2nd and 3rd place; [pers.] Through my writing I try to explain to myself and others my thoughts on life situations.; [a.] El Paso, TX

WALLS, CHRISTOPHER BRIAN
[pen.] Chris Walls; [b.] December 12, 1977, Bryson City, NC; [p.] Buddy and Ann Walls; [ed.] Swain County High School; [occ.] Irrigation Technician; [memb.] FCA, CFC, FTA, Beta Club, Student Council, Church Youth Group; [hon.] Who's Who Among America's High School Students, A Honor Roll; [oth. writ.] The Ballad of Swain High Lost Love Graduation; [a.] Bryson City, NC

WALTON, TAMMY L.
[b.] April 3, 1973, Saginaw, MI; [p.] Gilbert and Mary Walton; [ed.] Arthur Hill High School, Saginaw, MI 1991 Graduate; [occ.] Storage Accounting/Billing Clerk, Stevens Worldwide Van Lines, Inc.; [memb.] National Honor Society Bone Marrow Donor Program; [oth. writ.] I have received acknowledgement from George Bush, (then Vice President) for a poem that was forwarded to him. I have also wrote short stories.; [pers.] When I write I try to reflect what I am feeling in my soul. With my writing I hope to show people that it is okay to show their hopes, dreams and even their fears. I find that with my writing I try to encourage the whole human race to live without fear of what is ahead.; [a.] Saginaw, MI

WASCOM, RENEE'
[b.] May 28, 1934, Bayou Barbary, LA; [p.] Odess M. Willie and Wallace Willie (Deceased); [m.] Elbert Deonald Wascom, November 20, 1965; [ch.] (Step children) David Wascom, Charlotte Lewis; [ed.] French Settlement High School, Southeastern College, Hammon B.A. (1957), Louisiana State University (B.R.), Retired M.E. 1963 State of LA; [occ.] Retired Elementary School Teacher; [memb.] AARP Member, Colyell Pentecostal Church, Missionary Pen Pal for 18 Missionaries Per Month (They send letters back thanking us for poems); [hon.] Senses of Easter in Church Bulletins poem The Creek - Poetic Voices of america - Spring 1996, poems Dinner on the Ground "The Old House", "Senses of Easter" in Echoes from Heaven of Austin, NV thru 1995 and 1996.; [oth. writ.] Name poems and others for friends, family and missionaries in Mexico, Texas, Oklahoma, Florida, Tennessee and LA also poems for some friends in California.; [pers.] The poem was written about life on a farm when our main monetary crop was strawberries. It was a happy time. Poems inspired by God.; [a.] Livingston, LA

WASHINGTON, AVA M.
[b.] January 15, 1955, Lakewood, NJ; [p.] Ervin V. and Donna M. Brown; [m.] Marcus A. Washington, September 18, 1993; [ch.] Marcus A. Washington Jr. and Marsellius C. Washington; [ed.] BA Sociology from Georgian Court College Lakewood, NJ, May, 1979; [occ.] Housewife; [oth. writ.] "Father Who Are You" - A tribute to Patricia White - unpublished and I have no Malice, a semi-biography (not finished); [pers.] Dedicated to my "miracles, Marcus A. Washington Jr. and Marsellius C. Washington" and to my husband Marcus who "dared" to believe in the power of God.; [a.] Stone Mountain, GA

WASHINGTON, KAREN
[pen.] K. K. Cranshaw; [b.] May 29, 1961, Cleveland, OH; [ch.] Irving Cranshaw; [ed.] East High - Tri C Community College; [oth. writ.] Writing poetry is one of my hobbies; [pers.] My writing let's me explore my mentality as well as expressing my personality.; [a.] Cleveland, OH

WASSMANN, MARILYN B.
[b.] February 29, 1948, Willimantic, CT; [p.] Charles Thomas Benjamin, Evelyn Hitchcock Benjamin; [m.] Paul Anthony Wassmann, April 9, 1988; [ed.] B.A. Drew University 1971, M.L.S. - Pratt Institute, 1973, M.A. The George Washington University, 1979, University of Maryland University College, 1992; [occ.] Cataloyer, Librarian, Arts and Sciences Division, Library of Congress Washington, DC; [memb.] DC - MD - VA Chapter of ARLIS/NA, (Art Libraries Society of North America); [pers.] My grandmother and father wrote poems for their families and friends to capture memorable occasions. I continue this tradition by writing poems for significant events, and the desire to write poems may be genetic and inherited because my niece has started to write poems and short stories for her generation.; [a.] Hyattsville, MD

WATERS, JENNIFER K.
[b.] October 5, 1971, Aiken, SC; [p.] Robert and Lois Key; [m.] Donald Waters, November 4, 1989; [ch.] Justin Robert and Jordan Andrew; [ed.] Silver Bluff High School, Aiken Technical College; [occ.] Homemaker/CNA; [oth. writ.] Several children's poems that I hope to publish someday in children's books.; [a.] Beech Island, SC

WATKINS, CASSIE
[b.] April 5, 1983, Ohio; [p.] Dianna Watkins; [ed.] Currently attending Woodstock Middle School; [memb.] Was in Band in 7th E is a member of Drama Club at Woodstock Elementary.; [hon.] I won 1st place for the Young Authors Fair Poetry Contest, while a attending Chapman Elementary, in fourth grade.; [oth. writ.] Book of Poetry; [a.] Woodstock, GA

WATKINS, GARRETT H.
[b.] September 10, 1935, Cranston, RI; [p.] Perry and Naomi Watkins; [m.] Joanne (Deceased), August 12, 1978; [ch.] Tonya and Gina; [ed.] RPA-Real Property Administrator, Building Owners and Managers Institute International, attended USAF Air University, and USAF Leadership School; [occ.] Writer, USAF retiree; [hon.] Nominated for the Outstanding Airman of the Year Award (twice) and one of America's Ten Outstanding Young Men (TOYM) Award, Recipient of the Air Force Commendation Medal (three times); [oth. writ.] As a People; [pers.] The brotherhood of man continues to elude all of mankind.; [a.] Clinton, MD

WATLING, WILLIAM A.
[pen.] Tinh Hong Ki, Wm. A. H. Watling; [b.] August 13, 1951, Joliet, IL; [p.] W. H. Watling Sr., Ann Marie Ganster; [m.] Mai Thi Watling, April 22, 1994; [ch.] One (deceased); [ed.] Symerton Village School, Wilmington High School, Joliet Community College (Honors), Eastern Il. Univ. (Honors) Graduated JCC 1974, Graduate EIU '76.; [occ.] Machine Operator, Sponge-Cushion, in Morris Inc. we had '94-'96 contract to do carpet pad of U.S. House of Reps. and Pentagon, and typically for 1st-class hotels, resorts.; [memb.] First United Methodist Church, resigned from NRA US Army Intelligence Corps. Vietnam '70-'71 North region; [hon.] Honors Grad./Dean's List, Who's Who in American Community College '74. Feature Journalism Award '74.

10 years Security Efficiency Award, Dec. '91. Employee of the Month, Oct. 1995, at Sponge-Cushion, Inc.; [oth. writ.] Book: Driving To the Big Surreal, c Wm. A. Watling unpublished, all poems. Poems published in Joliet, Wilmington Newspapers, and in college (Joliet) yearbook, many feature stories in (Joliet) college '72-'74 newspaper, poems printed by National Poetry Press (3 books) and in 2 other anthologies. Note: All rights mine and in Vietnam Hai Ngoa Magazine.; [pers.] Zen! Christian. Came to agree with RFK course on Vietnam, as does my Vietnamese wife! Democrat. Anti-crime activities to support sheriffs Dept.'s support equality for minorities and women in hiring, promotion, pay. Pro-choice. "Popular" poem linked (Fall, '91) Attitude that caused Viet atrocities to that of Clarenoe Thomas.; [a.] Morris, IL

WATSON, AMANDA
[b.] January 17, 1981, Elmhurst, IL; [p.] Thomas and Robin Watson; [ed.] Sophomore in Port Charlotte High School, Port Charlotte Florida; [occ.] Student; [memb.] Drama Club, Interact (Service Club), First Christian Church (Youth Group); [hon.] "Rookie" reporter freshman year; [oth. writ.] Column-student section "Charlotte Sun Herald "Port Charlotte, FL; [pers.] I know that with faith in God, I can overcome hardships in life - and have a fulfilling life. Dreams can become reality.

WATSON, KATHRYN
[b.] January 29, 1979, Concord, MA; [p.] Nancy and James Watson; [ed.] Souhegan High School; [occ.] High School Student/Athlete; [hon.] National Honors Society, Student Council, 3 Varsity Sports, Field Hockey, Basketball, Tennis; [pers.] I feel that life is a constant struggle the uphill climb is the toughest, traveling and maneuvering over constant is one of peace and reflection after you go down you must go up.; [a.] Pepperell, MA

WATTS, MYRTLE C.
[pen.] Myrtle Creach Watts; [b.] November 7, 1915, Dorchester, SC; [p.] Anna Jane Way, Edgar W. Creach; [m.] Thomas Kirkland Watts, March 13, 1935; [ch.] Five; [ed.] Berkley Business School, Winthrop College, SC; [occ.] Housewife; [memb.] Bethune Woman's Club, Former Member, Poetry Society of South Carolina, Bethune Methodist Church; [hon.] First Place Award General Federation of Women's Clubs and Shell Oil Company April, 1966; [oth. writ.] Songs and poems; [pers.] I am an optimist, "What the use in yelling when you can't find your socks, What use in telling the world about your knocks, What's the use sighing, when you have lost a fight, Why not forget yourself awhile, Put on a big broad grin teach someone how to smile, and you will learn how to sing", my favorite author is Emily Dickenson and Joyce Gilmore.; [a.] Bethune, SC

WEINEL, NORMA H.
[b.] September 15, 1930, Chicago, IL; [p.] Isbrand Harder and Dorothy Harder; [m.] Clair L. Weinel, June 11, 1948; [ch.] Clair L. III, Gary Wayne, Norma Kim; [ed.] Hinsdale Township High School, Inter-American University of Puerto Rico; [occ.] Homemaker, Care Giver; [memb.] Order of Eastern Star, Daughters of the King - St. Nathaniel's Episcopal church; [pers.] We should never allow what we can not do to keep us from doing what we can. Wherever we are or whatever our circumstances we can choose to live a life that will benefit and enrich other lives.; [a.] North Port, FL

WELDON, DAVID M.
[pen.] David M. Weldon; [b.] September 16, 1955, Superior, NE; [p.] James and Charlotte; [m.] Linda, August 16, 1975; [ch.] Jeramey, Sarah; [ed.] College, Law Enforcement, Psychology, Writing; [occ.] Police Officer; [memb.] International Society of Poets, Distinguished Member, Tread Gahtlu, MT, Wildlife Federation, Rocky Mtn. Elk Foundation, N.A.H.C.; [hon.] Community, Activity, Youth Programs; [oth. writ.] Poetry, monographs; [pers.] I enjoy writing about life experiences, people, family and humor.; [a.] Sutherlin, OR

WELFORD, STEPHEN
[b.] September 17, 1972, Mobile, AL; [p.] Mr. Alvin and Mrs. Janet Welford; [ed.] Theodore High School - Theodore, Alabama, BA, The University of Alabama-Tuscaloosa, AL; [occ.] Graduate student, Political Science, Vanderbilt University - Nashville, TN; [memb.] National Trust for Historic Preservation; [hon.] Valedictorian (THS), Magna Cum Laude (UA), Phi Kappa Phi, Golden Key, Who's Who Among Students in American Colleges and Universities; [oth. writ.] Poems published in Treasured Poems of America, Maxwell's Crossing, articles published in The Harbinger, The Crimson White, and the Tillman's Corner News, the SOMOHA newsletter '94-95; [pers.] Through the lenses I mold called poems I search for peace, peace with my observations, with my circumstances, with my experiences, and, most of all, with myself.; [a.] Nashville, TN

WELLS, DOUGLAS WAYNE
[pen.] Doug; [b.] August 30, 1957, Washington, DC; [p.] Eula Mae Wells, Jimmy Willingham Wells; [m.] Divorced, December 17, 1993; [ed.] G.E.D.; [occ.] Cook; [memb.] Church - Embry Hills Methodist; [hon.] Bowling, Band, Trumpet Soloist; [pers.] Made touch with unknown by a visit from them. Mother inspired me write this poem from a subconscious idea silent roses!; [a.] Chamblee, GA

WENDLER, PERCY
[b.] October 12, 1937, Curitiba, Brazil; [p.] Creusa Wendler, Albano Wendler; [ed.] Med. School, University of Parana, Brazil, Fellowship: N.Y.U. (NYC), Columbia Presbyterian (NYC); [occ.] Retired; [memb.] NYS Medical Society; [hon.] A.M.A. Recognition Award; [oth. writ.] The Waters of the Old Well; [a.] Marco Island, FL

WENZ, KIMBERLY STARR
[pen.] Kim Wenz; [b.] October 9, 1968, Haleyville, AL; [p.] Tammy Townsend and Robert Wenz; [ed.] Pinson Valley High School; [oth. writ.] None published; [pers.] Life is not perfect. But, there are moments of perfection scattered in between the disappointments and regrets.; [a.] Concord, CA

WESSEL, MOLLY
[b.] June 4, 1985, Davenport, IA; [p.] Jon and Linda Wessel; [ed.] Going into 6th grade at John F. Kennedy Catholic School; [occ.] Student; [memb.] O.L.V. Church, Girl Scouts Gymnastics, Spectrum, Band, and Volleyball, Cheerleading; [hon.] City and State Pageant finalist, perfect attendance for 5 years of school; [pers.] It is a way to get away from everyday life and to put my feelings on paper.; [a.] Davenport, IA

WEST, CATHARINE R.
[b.] October 18, 1957, Springfield, OH; [p.] Frank Cornwell and Dee Cornwell; [ed.] Eastwood High, El Paso TX Angelo State, TX., B.S. Chemistry 1980, Oklahoma State Univ., Graduate Student; [occ.] Instructor, Vocational Chemistry, Tulsa Technology Center; [memb.] Texas Archaeological Society, Oklahoma Anthropological Society, Vocational Industrial Clubs of America, American Vocational Association; [hon.] Alpha Lambda Delta Gamma Sigma Epsilon Cum Laude B.S. 1980; [oth. writ.] Poem in quarterly magazine "Lucidity", trade journal article in AVA Journal.; [pers.] My heroes are Austen, Dickinson, McCaffrey and Sayers. What incredible talents!; [a.] Tulsa, OK

WESTERMEGER, ROBERT
[pen.] Vaughn W. Wernli Jr.; [b.] December 31, 1961, Santa Barbara, CA; [p.] Vaughn Westermeger M.D., Renee Westermeger; [m.] Monica M. Westermeger, June 13, 1987; [ch.] Michael (6), Timothy (3) and Madeline (6 months); [ed.] BA, SDSU, MA and Ph.D., California School of professional Psychology; [occ.] Licensed Clinical Psychologist; [memb.] American Psychological Assoc., San Diego Psychological Assoc., Assoc. For Advancement of Behaviour Therapy; [hon.] Phi Beta Kappa, (1987), Phi Kappa Phi (1987); [oth. writ.] Habit Smart: A practical approach to changing addictive behaviour ISBN-1-56072-328-9, pending Publication first Novel "Objects And Their Fields."

WHIPPERMAN, MINDY
[b.] October 28, 1982, Harrisburg, PA; [p.] Diane Cline and Lonnie Whipperman; [ed.] New Cumberland Middle School; [memb.] New Cumberland Youth Football Association (Midget Cheerleader), Builder's Club; [hon.] General Excellence Award (3 years), Presidential Academic Award, Distinguished Honor Roll (2 years), Science Fair - "PH of Water" (1st place - school Division), (2nd place - District Division); [oth. writ.] "Pride" poem (1st place); [pers.] I dedicate this poem to the memory of my grandfather, Anthony Pinti, who passed away on October 13, 1995. His kindness will be remembered always. My goals is to be the best I can be and make everyone I love proud of me.; [a.] New Cumberland, PA

WHITE, DAVID LEE
[b.] April 30, 1963, Santa Rosa, CA; [p.] Mr. and Mrs. Warren and Gloria White; [m.] Lisa Kay White, October 10, 1992; [ch.] Kyle Lee White; [ed.] Elementary Pinner - Olivet K-8, Santa Rosa High, United State Army 1986-1995; [occ.] Security Officer; [memb.] Boy Scout's of America; [hon.] Editor Choice Award, Honorable Discharge United State Army, Army conducted Ribbon, State Active Duty Ribbon, Army Achievement Metal, Markmen and Share Shooter Metal. Attendance Ribbon, etc.; [oth. writ.] Too Baby Heart, other writings, that unpublished at this time, but with hope see publish late dates.; [pers.] In memory of Lillian Marie White, as she began her passing, as to birth of my son during the same time as he stands to be her twenty-fifth great grandson, enter her life of joy, should remain as his guarding angel in world of above.; [a.] Grand Island, NE

WHITELOVE, MINISTER
[pers.] The spirit mind that is the creator in me, which makes all I do creative.; [a.] Chicago, IL

WHITTINGTON, AMANDA
[b.] May 19, 1981, Hollywood, FL; [p.] Rev. Timothy and Linda Whittington; [ed.] A 9th grader at Hibriten High School in Lenoir, North Carolina; [memb.] Key Club, Chorus, Band private piano, and the Fellowship of Christian Athletes (FCA); [hon.] I won 2 awards. I won a "superior" at a solo flute contest, I won another "superior" at a band festival; [oth. writ.] I write other poems and stories.; [pers.] All of my work comes from my heart. When I'm happy, sad, angry or excited. I take

those feelings and turn them into something wonderful.; [a.] Lenoir, NC

WHITTLE, ELIZABETH
[b.] September 2, 1975, Jax, FL; [p.] William and Selma Whittle; [ed.] Southern Baptist Academy (High School), Florida Community College of Jacksonville; [occ.] Child Care; [hon.] President's List (2 semesters), Eagle Award (Best Female Athlete in school); [oth. writ.] Won school and Regional contest with poem from high school. Wrote articles for school newspaper and year book.; [pers.] I have always enjoyed reading poems and hope to please others with my writings.; [a.] Jacksonville, FL

WILDER, NINA
[pen.] Vye Crawford; [b.] December 28, 1924, Bogota, TX; [p.] Tinnie Crawford Dunn (Deceased), John Wesley Dunn; [m.] Vash Robert Wilder (Deceased), August 13, 1941; [ch.] Three daughters (and 1 son Deceased); [ed.] Abac College Credits in Bookkeeping and Tax (12); [occ.] Retired; [memb.] Kingwood - CCYP; [hon.] SS Honaraky Cert. and Authors Award by International Harvester - Teacher's SS Award; [oth. writ.] Faith of LaChita Preacher Tom. Short stories - Gently the Meadow, Book of poetry.; [pers.] The remedy for loneliness is to call or visit someone, especially a shut-in.; [a.] Moultrie, GA

WILGER, MARIE
[b.] July 4, 1984, Trenton, MI; [p.] Duane and Margaret Wilger; [ed.] The seventh (7th) grade, in St. Joseph's Elementary School of Trenton MI; [hon.] Principals List at St. Joseph's Elementary School in Trenton; [a.] Trenton, MI

WILLHIDE, MRS. DOROTHY B.
[pen.] Dorothy B. Willhide; [b.] December 22, 1928, Fountaindale, PA; [p.] J. Edward and Lucy S. Boncing; [m.] Charles A. Willhide, October 26, 1957; [ch.] Four boys and two girls; [ed.] Graduated 1946, Waynesboro Sr High Attended Waynesboro, Business College; [occ.] Retired; [memb.] St. Andrew Catholic Church AARP, YMCA, Waynesboro, Hospital Auxiliary

WILLIAMS, BOBBIE
[b.] October 25, 1981, Portsmouth, OH; [p.] Debbie and Jim Bob Williams; [ed.] Lewis County Junior High School 9th; [pers.] I wrote my first poem in 4th grade and haven't stopped writing since. A word to the wise: If you have a talent, don't waist it.; [a.] Tollesboro, KY

WILLIAMS, ERIC D.
[pen.] Will; [b.] January 27, 1975, Wilmington, NC; [p.] Valerie S. Williams; [m.] Crystal Lane (Fiance); [ed.] John T. Hoggard High School, Cape Fear Community College; [oth. writ.] Although Mirror Images will be my first published poem, they are many more to come. (Culminating The Dream and Almost Perfect); [pers.] I know my poetry will not change the world, but I hope, it will have a positive effect on the people who live in it.; [a.] Wilmington, NC

WILLIAMS, GLENDA THOMAS
[b.] June 5, 1950, Asheville, NC; [p.] P. James R. Thomas, Mafra P. Thomas (Both Deceased); [m.] Thomas S. Williams, November 10, 1967; [ch.] Ava Marie, Susan Irene; [ed.] A.C. Reynolds H.S.; [occ.] Homemaker; [pers.] I am lead to write what will inspire the heart and uplift humanity.; [a.] Asheville, NC

WILLIAMS, JUDY
[pen.] Grace Miles; [b.] October 28, 1964, Trinidad; [p.] Modestus and Omelia Monsegue; [m.] Pete Williams, June 9, 1984; [ch.] Patrick, Jasmine; [ed.] Tranquility High (trinidad), Kingsborough Community College, The Health Science Center at Brooklyn; [occ.] Occupational Therapist; [memb.] American Occupational Therapy Association, Advocate for children with special needs; [hon.] Dean's List; [oth. writ.] Cherished few; [pers.] Life may hold challenging situations that cannot be changed but may be accepted and viewed in a light that will awaken the strengths, goodness and talents that lie deep within us.; [a.] Brooklyn, NY

WILLIAMS, STEVEN E.
[b.] July 6, 1968; [p.] Thames and Rita Williams; [ed.] Montville High, Three Rivers Community Technical College; [hon.] Dean's List; [pers.] This is my published piece of work and I would like to thank Dr. Posner for her guidance and inspiration.; [a.] Oakdale, CT

WILLIAMS, SYLVIA F.
[pen.] Sylvia Fields; [b.] January 16, 1961, Hudson County, NJ; [p.] The Late Clarence Fields and Mrs. Theta C. Fields; [m.] Separated; [ed.] High School Ternell's Bay High, Six months Webster Career College Los Angeles, CA, Marion County Tech. Nurse - Aide Training and Certification Training for Certified Nurse Aide; [occ.] Certified Nurse Aide, of the state of South Carolina; [memb.] Member of Door of Hope Holiness Church of Marion South Carolina. Pastors Elder Michael and Malinda Blue; [hon.] Awarded a trophy from she Webster Career College Student Activity Coordinator and Perfect Attendance, High Merit Score for file clerk without typing, from Merit system of Columbia SC; [pers.] Since I began to realize civilization, or may I say, was old enough to realize civilization, I've noticed how people don't seem to accept mixed - relationships - people of different rules falling in love.; [a.] Rains, SC

WILLIAMS SR., KAMAL NIGEL
[pen.] Trash Mah; [b.] May 29, 1973, Boston, MS; [p.] Anita Williams Burke and David Burke; [ch.] Kamal Jr., Khari and Kashe; [ed.] Raphael Hernandez, St. Patricks School; [occ.] Used Car Dealer

WILLIARD, CHARLOTTE J.
[pen.] B. A. Stillwater; [b.] January 4, 1937, Cleveland, OH; [p.] Charles William and Pearl S. Kennedy; [m.] Walter F. Williard (Deceased), December 31, 1958; [ch.] Pamela Ann and Robert Chas.; [ed.] Graduated Mentor High School, Mentor, Ohio '55; [occ.] Manager, Motel and Apts. Seaside, Oregon; [memb.] Actively involved with Chamber of Commerce, Lodging Assoc., Convention Center Rd.; [hon.] 2nd place in Photography Contest - Scottsdale, AZ; [oth. writ.] Many, many, unseen as yet, poems, stories, thoughts. Ecology to erotica - heights to depths.; [pers.] Love inspired me and set my heart open to expression. Be it pain or joy - we need to work it out and the arts give us freedom.; [a.] Seaside, OR

WILLS, ISABEL
[b.] August 6, 1917, Pittsburgh, PA; [p.] Deceased; [ch.] Bambi Wills Elliott; [ed.] BS/Psy-UPgh, MS/Psy-UM, MSed-UM; [occ.] Retired School Psychologist; [memb.] APA, NASP, NSPCB, FASP, SFCNWA, ISCHWA; [hon.] Poems: "Song of Lament", Nat'l Lib. of Poetry's Days of Future, 1989. "Deep Well", Amherst Soc. American Poetry Annual, 1989. "Yellow Brick Road", Writing for Children, Annual Report, Highlights Workshop-Chautauqua, 1993. "Can I Stop A Flying Fish?", Hob-Nob, Winter 1994-5. "Friend and Lover", Lavender Life, 1995. "A Tree Is To Hug", Quill Books "Echoes from the Silence, 1995. "Rainbows Everywhere", Iliad Press' Voices, 1995 (Honorable Mention).; [oth. writ.] Poetry, articles printed in Innerself Mag. '92-3. Prof. educ. writing 1978-90, Academic Therapy Pub., Thomas Pub.; [pers.] I have always felt need/desire to share what I am learning about the universe. It comes out best in poetry.; [a.] Miami, FL

WILSON, CORIANNE
[b.] April 16, 1981, Caliente, NE; [p.] Clifton, Christine Wilson; [occ.] Student in 10th grade at Delta High School; [memb.] L.D.S. Church, School Orchestra; [oth. writ.] I have written many poems, short stories and am now working on a novel. This is my first entry in competition.; [a.] Delta, UT

WILSON, NICOLE GRACE
[b.] May 20, 1983, Denver, CO; [p.] Edgar and Karon Wilson; [ed.] 8th grade, Hill Middle School, John Amesse Elementary School; [occ.] Student Hill Middle School; [memb.] Usher Board and Junior Choir Member, Peaceful Rest Baptist Church, Blue Angel Cheerleaders Squad; [hon.] Several Awards Earned by Blue Angel Squad in competition against other cheer leading groups.; [pers.] I wanted to talk about the African American Male by saying something positive about the male today.; [a.] Denver, CO

WINERT, DARREL
[b.] October 28, 1967, San Diego, CA; [p.] Charles E. Winert Jr., Betty Winert; [m.] Angela R. Winert, August 31, 1988 (Divorced December 5, 1994); [ch.] Gene A. Winert; [ed.] Tippecanoe High School, Upper Valley Joint Vocational School (Adult Education); [occ.] Steel Worker; [a.] Tipp City, OH

WINTER, JENNIFER
[b.] August 26, 1983, Vancouver, British Columbia, Canada; [p.] Ted and Shirley Winter; [ed.] Ben Franklin Middle School (8th Grade); [occ.] Student; [memb.] National League of Junior Cotillion Dance Unlimited Dance Academy, Drama Club; [hon.] "The Flower Child", "The Rose", "In The World Of Make Believe", "The Woodlands Studio for Actors, Write on Hoosiers, National League of Junior Cotillion; [oth. writ.] The write on Hoosiers Magazine; [pers.] I hope my writing influences people as much as Bob Dylan and Jim Morrison influenced me. My Grandparents live on Wolfe Island.; [a.] Valparaiso, IN

WISBY, LETHA J.
[b.] May 8, 1913, Hot Springs, AR; [p.] Deceased; [m.] Divorced, April 6, 1938; [ch.] One son; [ed.] High School Night School - Writing Booking English, College of Marin Co. some Law Classes. Insurance Classes Home Making - Private School 1st through 4th grade; [occ.] None - pat office mgr. of insurance office 24 year; [memb.] I have been to busy with writing - I learned the computer as soon as they were available. Now I am writing song word for wedding internet Franlin, Franlin have to my songs to date.; [hon.] Honor for public speaking class. I have been asked to write the story of a doctor. His life story he is recording I will go with that at 83 that's a big chore. I have sold art in oils I was voted in art class as the best color coordinator in the class. Landscapes an still life; [oth. writ.] Crackers and in publishers now - to work in October. My life story finished in editors office now. Lots of writing nothing published the man on the path, also being edited.; [pers.] My brother taught me to read and write, at age 4, my father, carrel poems I wrote about my time with him teacher school, had a hard time teaching me, that is why father put me in a private school.; [a.] San Marcos, CA

WISEMAN, JANE L.
[pen.] Jo Margaret McKenzie; [b.] March 27, 1944, Athens, OH; [p.] Margaret and George Parsons; [m.] David J. Wiseman, May 28, 1961; [ch.] Jana Renee, Evan, David Owen Earl; [ed.] Attended Ohio University, Ohio State, Eleven years music instruction. Graduate of Rutland High School. Homemaker, piano teacher, girl scout leader; [memb.] Girl Scout of America National Poetry Society; [hon.] Music Awards, various writing awards; [oth.writ.] Childrens stories, poetry, children's stories, children's puppet productions.; [pers] The soul is a "Trunk" unlocked by words. May my word be a key that stirs the emotions of my readers, reaching their souls.; [a.] Rutland, OH

WISNOWSKI, THOMAS
[b.] October 1, 1956, North Tonawanda, NY; [p.] Julian and Jane Wisnowski; [ed.] AAS Degree at Erie Community College and B.S. Degree at York College of C.U.N.Y.; [occ.] Occupational Therapist; [pers.] Nature makes poetry writing effortless because it provides so much poetic beauty, if we all just take the time to notice.; [a.] Seneca Falls, NY

WITT, HOLLY A.
[b.] Madera, CA; [p.] Tex Adams and Melda McHaffie; [ch.] Tonya Witt, Jenette Witt; [ed.] Leggett Valley High school, West Hills College, California Polytechnic State University, San Luis Obispo, University of California, Santa Barbara - Extension; [occ.] Legal Assistant-Law Office, Aregory C. Jacobson; [hon.] Dean's List, all star softball league; [pers.] Family is very Important and are a wonderful influence in my life. I'm a firm believer in Karma, so I treat everybody as I want to be treated with kindness and a sense of humor.; [a.] San Luis Obispo, CA

WOLF, NATASHA AMBER
[pen.] Amber Wolf; [b.] April 26, 1980, Fort Stewart, GA; [p.] Joe and Jackie Crowder; [ed.] Conner High School; [occ.] Student; [oth. writ.] Summer Time, Interview With The Noon That's High, Cemetery, One Day, etc. (None are published but someday they will.); [pers.] There's a long road ahead of us and some may walk to the end of it and some may not. If you're willing to try it go for it, but if not, turn around and walk away and don't look back.; [a.] Burlington, KY

WOMAC, TIMOTHY
[b.] September 16, 1981, Athens, TN; [p.] Sterling Womac, Juanita Womac; [ed.] K- 8th Calhoun Elementary School, Freshman McMinn County High School; [memb.] FFA; [hon.] Citizenship Award, Presidential Award, Reading Award, Math Award, Social Studies Awards; [oth. writ.] Many poems, but haven't been published.; [pers.] I try to find the good in mankind in Bible Stories, history, and from my own experiences.; [a.] Calhoun, TN

WOOD, NANCI TURNER
[b.] September 14, 1942, Fulton, NY; [p.] Herbert and Velma Turner; [m.] Gerald Lewis Wood, Disney Fairytale Wedding, New Year Eve - 35 years after our Jr. Prom; [ch.] Nancy Diana, Douglas Anthony, Ashleigh Paige; [ed.] APW High School, CCBI Syracuse NY, Licensed Real Estate Broker, Licensed Insurance Agent; [occ.] Pres. Medical Book Ends, Instructor Southwest Florida College; [memb.] Sigma Mu Beta; [hon.] Dean's List, Rookie of the Year, Salesman of the Year, Million Dollar Round Table; [oth. writ.] The Mole And The Chirpie Bird (Co-author), Mr. Moon, Have You Seen My Lovely; [pers.] My desire in writing is to bring joy, motivation and sunshine to my readers.; [a.] Fort Myers, FL

WOODRAL, VALENTEEN
[pen.] Valli Woodral; [b.] November 2, 1982, S.L.C., Utah; [p.] Mary and Ronald Woodral; [ed.] Junior High in Thermopolis City Middle School; [occ.] Student; [hon.] Honor Roll, Music Awards/Band and Choir; [pers.] I hope my poem will inspire many other people to try to find any of their talents. I believe that everyone has hidden talents that they can find; [a.] Thermopolis, WY

WOODSON, ROBBIE WHITE
[b.] January 28, 1954, South Boston, VA; [p.] Phoebe Platt and Charles White Sr.; [ch.] H. Rodney Woodson; [ed.] Wester High School Class of 72, Coppin State College Class of 1976; [occ.] Relay Operator; [memb.] Bethel AME Church; [hon.] Cum Laude, Coppin State College Class of 76, Dean's List; [oth. writ.] In the winter of 1996 two of my poems will be published. One by Owing Mills Poetic Society and the other by the Poetry Guild.; [pers.] Once again I woke up. And because of it, the world is mine.; [a.] Baltimore, MD

WOODWARD, GARY L.
[pen.] Gary Woodward; [b.] August 9, 1953, Swindon, England; [p.] Whitney W. Woodward and Dorothy A. Russell; [m.] Alfreda Woodward, August 28, 1988; [ch.] Tulsa Doonkeen, Tulesa Doonkeen; [ed.] Deans Honor Roll, University of Central Okla., Southeastern Okla. State University; [occ.] Field Investigative Review and Evaluation, State of OK; [memb.] Phi Sigma Epsilon, U.S. 82nd Airborne Div., joint special operation command, Pope AFB, N.C.; [hon.] Dean's List, U.C.O., Army Commendation Medal with Oak Leaf Cluster; [oth. writ.] Appeared in "Rise and Walk" the Dennis Byrd story, over 300 songs and 200 poems numerous musical compositions on guitar and piano.; [pers.] To grasp the clouds, or a moment thought forever seized abreast as what once was said to thy own self be true if to live must be said again!; [a.] Oklahoma City, OK

WOOLFOLK, GUILLERMO
[pen.] Bishop Hayes; [b.] September 14, 1980; [p.] Gill Woolfolk and Ursula Woolfolk; [ed.] Attending Weaver High School; [occ.] Full time student; [memb.] National Lung Association; [hon.] National English Merit Award; [pers.] If you can't rely on talent, always count on effort; [a.] Weaver, AL

WOOTEN, ANDREA
[pen.] Lenga Marie; [b.] November 24, 1977, Cincinnati, OH; [p.] Loretta and Tommy Wooten; [oth. writ.] In the Palm of Your Hand, Compassion, One Good Night, Swingin, Angel, Serious Love, Alone, Won't Happen Again, Always Strong, My Life, I Love You, Dominic, Love, Wondering, Decisions, In My Heart, I Close My Eyes I Dream of You.

WORDEN, LINDA M.
[b.] February 12, 1936, Gouverneur, NY; [p.] Delbert and Melva Huckle; [m.] Harland G. Worden (Deceased), June 2, 1962; [ch.] Lisa Jean, Doddie Ellen, Terri Lynn, David H. Worden; [ed.] Gouverneur High School, Rochester Business Institute (Associate's Degree Medical Sec.); [occ.] Secretary, Syracuse City Schools, Special Education Department, Syr., NY; [memb.] Deacon in the Elmwood Presbyterian Church, Member of Church Choir; [oth. writ.] "Happy Birthday, Doddie"; [pers.] Whatever talent or gifts I possess, I owe to my Heavenly Father. He has been my inspiration and help all through my life. Praise His name.; [a.] Syracuse, NY

WORKMAN, DOROTHY DEE
[b.] June 9, 1927, Brookings, SD; [p.] Esther and Andrew Allison; [m.] David L. Workman, June 18, 1949; [ch.] Margaret, Kris, Allen, Eileen; [ed.] BA Chemistry, MA Counseling, MA Clinical Psychology; [occ.] Mental Health Counselor; [pers.] Aging brings its own pleasures, pains, fruits - as does any other stage of life.; [a.] Vancouver, WA

WORTHY, CAROL Y.
[pen.] Carol Y. Worthy; [b.] February 20, 1969, Ashville, NC; [p.] Izinia and Bruce Thorrington; [ch.] Micheal Alexander, Nikiyah James, Devin Lee; [ed.] North Miami High School North Buncombe High School Blue Ridge Comm. College Majoring in Business Admin. in Nursing; [occ.] Student at Blue Ridge Comm. College. H'ville, N.C.; [pers.] I try to write my poems to make you think. I would like to thank Mr. Winters at North Miami High School a wonderful teacher and man, I probably wouldn't be published if not for him; [a.] Hendersonville, NC

WOZNIAK, SHIRLEY
[b.] September 16, 1937, Toledo, OH; [m.] Jerome Wozniak, August 22, 1959; [ch.] Bonnie Poticny, Sandi O'Brien and Bob Wozniak; [ed.] Davis Junior College and University of Toledo; [occ.] Assistant to the Chairman of Pharmacology Department of the Medical College of Ohio; [memb.] Valleywood Golf Club, Women's Auxiliary of Toledo Association of Home Bldrs., Women's Guild of Miami Children's Home, Alpha Iota Sorority, The Toledo Club; [oth. writ.] Wrote monthly column several years ago for Medical College of Ohio publication "On the Record" regarding Health Science Bldg. news items. Published poetry in local newspaper.; [a.] Toledo, OH

WRAY, LANA
[pen.] Rae Harris; [b.] March 8, 1944, Cleburne, TX; [p.] Joe (Deceased) and Helen Harris; [m.] Divorced; [ch.] Scott and Steven Wray; [ed.] Grad. High School-1962 from Cleburne High School, Bachelor of Arts - Tarleton State Univ. 1987, MA from FSU-1996; [occ.] History Teacher at Cleburne High School; [memb.] Phi Alpha Theta UEA (United Educators Association), TCSS - (Texas Council for The Social Studies); [hon.] Dean's List (1 sem. only) at TSU, Graduated Summa Cum Laude (TSU, 1987); [oth. writ.] Several other poems - none published before; [pers.] Having gone through some difficult times (emotional and physical) in my life, I seem to be able to handle difficult times through my writing. Sometimes the poems just flow through my mind until I write them down on paper.; [a.] Cleburne, TX

WRIGHT, MARY
[b.] October 15, 1935, Newbern, TN; [p.] Jessie Shaw, Lota Shaw; [m.] J. B. Wright, November 26, 1952; [ed.] GED Dyer County High School; [occ.] Housewife; [memb.] The Church of Jesus Christ; [oth. writ.] "One Way To Heaven", "If You Want To Be One Of God's Children", "I'm Ready To Go Home", "The Hallelujah Choir", "I Need To Walk and Talk With My Lord", "When I Receive My Robe And Crown"; [a.] Newbern, TN

WRIGHT, SUSAN
[ed.] BA - Journalism - Communications Indiana University, Bloomington, Indiana: MA - Theatre/Arts/ Northwestern University, Evanston, Illinois; [occ.] Writer - Talk Show Host; [memb.] Pi Beta Phi Alumni; [oth. writ.] Publisher/Editor of "The Quechee Times", Quechee, Vermont contributing editor for "The Hub" Bowling Breen, KY; [a.] Raleigh, NC

WYMAN, PAMELA
[pen.] Pamey; [b.] December 8, 1983, Saratoga; [p.] Maria and Patrick Wyman; [ed.] Going in Seventh (7th) grade; [occ.] School; [memb.] Troll Book Club, D.A.R.E.; [hon.] Special Recognition, Special Achievement; [oth. writ.] Write daily in a journal, but never submitted anything to be published; [pers.] I've read many books. I plan on making my career in writing. That would be my wish come true.; [a.] Corinth, NY

WYNN, STEPHANIE DENICE
[b.] March 12, 1985, Petersburg; [p.] Mary and Jasper Wynn; [ed.] 6 grade Student at Vernon Johns School; [occ.] Student; [hon.] Honor Roll Award Young Author's Award; [a.] Petersburg, VA

YAPP, JEAN FLORENCE
[b.] March 26, 1983, Cleveland, OH; [p.] Linda Jean Yapp (Deceased), George Nucomb Yapp II; [ed.] 8th Grade; [occ.] Student; [pers.] Dedication, I dedicate my heart to my home boys, I dedicate my soul to my home girls, I dedicate my life to my family, I dedicate this poem to you.; [a.] Broadview Heights, OH

YATES, JAMES
[b.] June 7, 1947, Louisiana; [p.] James and Helen Yates; [m.] Delores Yates; [occ.] Welder; [pers.] When God saved me. He gave me the words to write to him I give thanks.; [a.] Longview, TX

YORK, KATINA MICHELLE
[b.] March 17, 1973, Chicago, IL; [p.] James York and Clementine York; [ed.] St. Martin De Porres Academy (High School), University of Illinois at Chicago College; [occ.] Pharmacy Technician; [hon.] American National Honor Society, Dean's List; [oth. writ.] Poetry published for The World Of Poetry Inc., Quill Books; [pers.] I express my emotions through writing poetry. In conjunction with my other endeavors, I strive to achieve excellence in writing.; [a.] Chicago, IL

YOU, WENDYL G.
[b.] October 13, 1947, Honolulu, HI; [m.] Regina M. You, September 5, 1987; [ed.] Roosevelt High, Self-taught Artist and Poet; [occ.] Minister, Artist; [oth. writ.] Writing as a hobby-for music and reading enjoyment; [pers.] Many of my poems deal with human relationship, lessons to be learned in nature, and spiritual values. My spiritual beliefs, love for art and music, and my wife has been an inspiration to me.; [a.] Honolulu, HI

YOUNG, ROBERT E.
[b.] September 2, 1943, Boonville, MO; [p.] Kay and Virgil Young; [ed.] BA - studio art and psychology Maryville University, St. Louis Grateful for my Benedictine roots and as a child and as an adult.; [occ.] Chemical Dependency Counselor; [oth. writ.] Have spent a number of year in the monastery, 3 years in the Army and in the last 20 years involved in care-taking of the physical and mentally ill.; [pers.] Journalling letter writing to editors, poetry have been instrumental in helping me focus my own thoughts and feelings and also seem to help others affirm and share their own feelings in turn.; [a.] Saint Louis, MO

YOUNG, RUSSELL R.
[pen.] Gnuoy Lessur; [b.] January 2, 1968, Lehighton, PA; [p.] Marion and Russell Young; [ed.] Lehighton Area High School; [occ.] Nurse; [memb.] Lehighton Lodge - Free and Accepted Masons #621, Boy Scouts of America; [hon.] Past Master, Eagle Scout; [oth. writ.] Lodge Educational Lectures, Cartoon Strip in School Newspaper; [pers.] As I have been inspired by the early fantasy writers ... so, I pray, may others find the initiative to keep Rhetoric, chivalry and Romance alive.; [a.] Lehighton, PA

YUJUICO, QUEENIE
[b.] November 15, 1975, Seria, Brunei; [p.] Juanito V. Yujuico Jr., Rosita B. Yujuico; [ed.] St. Scholastica's Academy, Pampanga, Philippines, University of Santo Tomas, Manila, Philippines; [occ.] Artist/Painter, Ron Lee's World of Clowns Inc., Henderson, Nevada; [hon.] 2nd place winner, interschool painting contest '90, 4th place, Interschool painting contest '91; [oth. writ.] A number of unpublished poems like piece of the puzzle, against the hands of time, as star footprints etc.; [pers.] My passion is the very medium to my art. And my art the mirror of romance.; [a.] Las Vegas, NV

ZAMAL, ANDREW
[b.] December 11, 1949, Guyana, South Africa; [p.] Donald and Khairul; [m.] Patricia Bernadette Zamal, October 14, 1972; [ch.] Elizabeth Ann Zamal, Diane Angela Zamal (Deceased at 7 years and 9 months); [ed.] Primary School, High School, Government Technical Institute, University (All Institutions in Guyana); [occ.] Foreign Service Executive Officer; [oth. writ.] I went to the Old Country Chapel: Reflections on Easter, 'O' Twinkling Star of Bethlehem; [pers.] As a traveler in the transient journey of life, I have experienced many tragedies and have always felt the loving kindness of God in those times. In many poems, I strive to promote His Glory.; [a.] Washington, DC

ZIMMERMAN, JESSICA
[pen.] Jess Roberts; [b.] April 30, 1979, Mt. Holly, NJ; [p.] Vicky Stabilito, Dwight Roberts; [ed.] Delran High School; [occ.] Student; [oth. writ.] Poem "Weeping Willow" published on the National Poetry Society's Compilation Collections.; [pers.] Doubt not all that you read, for much of it may be true if you read with your head. I have been inspired mostly by Nature, deep dreams and even deeper thinking.; [a.] Delran, NJ

ZIMMERMANN, BRANDI
[b.] August 27, 1982, Marshalltown, IA; [p.] Randy Zimmermann and Connie Zimmermann; [ed.] Currently a Freshman in High School; [occ.] Student; [a.] Tama, IA

Index of Poets

Index

A

B

C

D

N

Y

Z